THE HOWLING STORM

Conflicting Worlds

New Dimensions of the American Civil War

T. Michael Parrish, Series Editor

Kenneth W. Noe

THE HOWLING STORM

Weather, Climate, and the American Civil War

Louisiana State University Press

Baton Rouge

Published by Louisiana State University Press
www.lsupress.org

Printed in the United States of America
First printing

Designer: Laura Roubique Gleason
Typeface: Whitman
Printer and binder: Sheridan Books

Jacket illustration: *Winter Campaigning: The Army of the Potomac on the Move, 1863*, by
    Alfred R. Waud. Courtesy Library of Congress.
Maps created by Hal Jespersen.

Library of Congress Cataloging-in-Publication Data

Names: Noe, Kenneth W., 1957– author.
Title: The howling storm : climate, weather, and the American Civil War / Kenneth W. Noe.
Other titles: Climate, weather, and the American Civil War
Description: Baton Rouge : Louisiana State University Press, [2020] | Series: Conflicting
    worlds: new dimensions of the American Civil War | Includes bibliographical references
    and index.
Identifiers: LCCN 2019058460 (print) | LCCN 2019058461 (ebook) | ISBN 978-0-8071-
    7320-6 (cloth) | ISBN 978-0-8071-7419-7 (pdf) | ISBN 978-0-8071-7420-3 (epub)
Subjects: LCSH: United States—History—Civil War, 1861–1865—Environmental aspects.
    | Nature—Effect of human beings on—United States—History—19th century. | United
    States—Environmental conditions—History—19th century.
Classification: LCC E468.9 .N64 2020 (print) | LCC E468.9 (ebook) | DDC 973.7/1—dc23
LC record available at https://lccn.loc.gov/2019058460
LC ebook record available at https://lccn.loc.gov/2019058461

For Nancy

Contents

Maps

Acknowledgments

As a baby boomer, I grew up watching too much television. I still enjoy the "origin stories" that explain how the characters first met or the mystery began. This book has two origin stories. The first one takes me back to the late 1990s, when Kent Brown and Nancy Grayson first encouraged me to write about the Battle of Perryville. I quickly realized that the summer drought of 1862 would be a major character. In time, comments about droughts and floods seeped into my Civil War classroom, until I began repeating "someone should write a book about Civil War weather."

I suspect that the real origin story goes much further back, however. My grandparents, Jesse and Thelma Noe, owned a farm in Southwest Virginia. As bad at farming as I was, I grew up in gardens, put up tons of hay, fed and watered animals, chased them when they jumped the fences, and once plowed a field with a horse because my grandfather though it was a vital skill. One summer I planted a field of corn and watched it die in a drought. In the background of those memories, I hear the weather forecasts on the local news in Roanoke. My grandparents had little interest in current events and ignored sports, expect when my grandmother's Dodgers were doing well, but when the weather came on, I had to be quiet. One of my first lessons was that weather mattered, at least when you are trying to farm the steep side of a place appropriately named Poor Mountain.

In between those origin stories and this book, so many people helped make it a reality. I am much indebted to the archivists who assisted me, especially including my student and friend Tommy Brown of Auburn University; Ellen Keith of the Chicago History Museum; Hillary Dorsch Wong of Cornell University; Kathy Shoemaker of Emory University; Samantha Norling and Nicole Poletika of the Indiana Historical Society; Debbie Hamm of the Abraham Lincoln Presidential Library; Ed Busch of Michigan State University; Dennis Northcott of the Missouri History Museum; Tutti Jackson of the Ohio Historical Society; Alan Thompson of the Prairie Grove State Battlefield Park; Rosie Springs of the State Historical Society of Iowa; John F. Bradbury, Anne Cox, Elizabeth Engel, and Laura Jolley of the State Historical Society of Missouri's archives in Columbia and Rolla; Michael Anne Lynn of the Stonewall Jackson House; Charles Nelson of the Tennessee State Library and Archives; Desiree Butterfield-Nagy of the University of Maine; Tom Buffenbarger, Rodney Foytik, Chuck Moody, and the marvelous and much-missed Richard Sommers at the US Army Military History Institute; George Carnahan of the Vermont Historical Society; and Meghan Bryant of the College of William and Mary. Gloria Frazier and Mark Strohbeck granted me permission to quote from their ancestor's online papers. Auburn University's Interlibrary Loan staff found nearly all of the obscure volumes I sought.

A work of this kind also requires talking to smart people who know a lot about certain topics. Cary Mock corrected my clumsy grasp of wartime weather more than once and shared material from his monumental research on historical climatology. Kevin Law offered additional help in regard to West Virginia. Tony Lupo corresponded with me about his research on La Niña and Wilson's Creek. Josh Johnson, the chief meteorologist at WSFA-TV, enthusiastically read the entire manuscript and made vital suggestions and corrections that included double-checking additional sources. At Auburn, John Beasley and Joey Shaw kindly answered numerous inquiries about soil.

I am immensely grateful to my Civil War colleagues who took time out of their own work to read and correct chapters of this book. Many thanks to Keith Bohannan, Steve Engle, Lorien Foote, Will Greene, Earl Hess, Chris Kolakowski, John Marszalek, Brian McKnight, Jen Murray, Barton Myers, Megan Kate Nelson, William Garrett Piston, George Rable, Anne Sarah Rubin, Stuart Sanders, Kathryn Shively, Matt Vogeler, Lee White, and Brian Wills. Carol Reardon volunteered to read three chapters and earns a special prize. Bob Claxton emailed me about weather history, and Eric Wittenberg shared forthcoming work with me. I also learned much from Aaron Astor, Jim Day, Mark Franklin, Rick McCaslin, and Peter Thomas. Any remaining errors, of course, are mine alone.

Over the last few years, many of my students have expressed interest in the "weather book," and all get a "War Eagle." The Draughon family's decision to create and fund the Draughon Chair in Southern History made my research happen. And I celebrate my Auburn colleagues. Keith Hébert and I have been talking about the Civil War for a long time. Chris Ferguson shared my interest in mud, Charles Israel advised me to read sermons, and Rupali Mishra pointed me toward Mike Davis's work. Kelly Kennington encouraged me to use "red goo" as much as possible. And thanks too Jenny Brooks, David Carter, Ruth Crocker, Ralph Kingston, Matt Malczycki, Eden McLean, Alan Meyer, and Tiffany Sippial.

Questions and comments from several groups made this a better book. Thanks to Rev. George Mathieson at Auburn United Methodist Church; the Auburn University Nineteenth Century Study Group; Ben Severance and the Southern Studies Conference at Auburn University Montgomery; Aaron MacKinnon at Georgia College; Brian McKnight, Jen Murray, and colleagues at the University of Virginia at Wise; Paul Quigley and Bud Robertson at Virginia Tech's Center for Civil War Studies (Go Hokies); and Cassy Ivey, Barton Myers, and Lucy Wilkins at Washington and Lee University. Special thanks go to Daryl Black and Pete Miele at Gettysburg's Seminary Ridge Museum, who spent weeks after my talk driving around looking for red clay in Adams County. Several editors also published articles from my research while also offering good suggestions. Thanks Andrew Bledsoe, Doug Fornberg, Lorien Foote, Terry Johnston, Earl Hess, Andrew Lang, David Loiterstein, and Aaron Sheehan-Dean.

It has been a pleasure working with LSU Press. My special thanks to series editor Michael Parrish and to Rand Dotson. An anonymous reader offered spot-on suggestions that helped the final product immensely. Kevin Brock was a marvelous and meticulous copy editor. As for the excellent maps, I have long admired Hal Jespersen's cartography, and I am most pleased to have his work featured here.

A few paragraphs back, I described my grandparents, and I am sorry that they are not around anymore to see me writing about weather. My father and my siblings are, and I thank them for decades of love and grace. My son, Jesse, is in Japan and had nothing much to do with this book, but I wanted to mention him anyway. My wife, Nancy, however, played a major part, more than she realizes. Just the dinner conversations about mud alone would earn her the dedication, but there was a lot more to it than that. She is my sunshine on the darkest days.

THE
HOWLING
STORM

Introduction

> The howling of the storm, the cry of the wounded and groans of the dying, the glare of the torch upon the faces of the dead or into the shining eyes of the speechless wounded, looking up in hope of relief, the ground slippery with a mixture of mud and blood, all in the dark, hopeless, starless night; surely it was a gruesome picture of war at its most horrid shape.
>
> —Henry Kyd Douglas, *I Rode with Stonewall*

The American Civil War was fought outdoors, in slippery red mud as well as blood, and sometimes in the howling storm. Yet for generations, too many of the war's students have behaved otherwise. Judged from our air-conditioned offices, classrooms, or comfortable recliners, it has been far too easy to pretend that the playing field was always level and dry. Moving troops through deep mud, heavy snow, or extreme heat is difficult for modern armies equipped with Humvees and helicopters. Yet students of the Civil War still too readily jump to tired conclusions that a mid-nineteenth-century general's inability to move an army twenty miles a day through muck and mire must have grown out of his ineptitude or petulance.

This book is based on the counterpremise that a full understanding of the war requires regrounding it in the physical environment in ways that the farm boys who donned blue or gray understood to the point of taking it for granted. It takes the Civil War back out in the weather and renarrates its military history, from Fort Sumter to the end, by including summertime heat, winter cold, snow and ice, dust, rain, and the deep red mud that characterized the southern climate and especially the war's unusual weather. Instead of the classic binary struggle between "the Blue and the Gray," *The Howling Storm* follows modern environmental historians in assigning agency to the environment and treating climate and weather as a sort of third army, sometimes a perceived ally but often an antagonist.[1] As Mark Fiege observes, "the terrain is never neutral. . . . [T]o engage and defeat its enemy . . . an army had to mobilize against that enemy and also against weather, terrain, disease, and other natural conditions."[2] Psychologist Ben Shalit likewise notes, "combat does not have to take place between men alone, it is often described as occurring between man and his environment—fighting the forces of nature or even blind fate." Soldiers "can respond, avoid, or adapt, but can never affect and shape" those forces in the same way that they can defeat human enemies.[3] Civil War soldiers took advantage of good conditions, avoided bad weather when they could, and adapted everything—from their tactics to their shelter and dress—as the war went along. Their leaders, meanwhile, constantly reassessed whether "the forces of nature" were unbeatable foes or inferior powers subject to their will. The book's chronological approach is designed to demonstrate learning curves over time.

Thinking of the war as fought by the Blue, the Gray, and the Weather forces us to confront its familiar narrative in new ways, both on the battlefield and on the home front. But *The Howling Storm* is not encyclopedic. Its length aside, there still is much that it does not interrogate in depth, such as politics, the relationships between weather and race and gender, the outdoor setting of emancipation, the lives of civilians and prisoners, and the harsh existence of military animals. All of these topics are vital and beg for new analysis through the lens of climate, weather, and environment. Here, however, the focus is on muddy boots on the ground. Yet even then, some issues, such as the naval war, the storm-tossed garrisons of the Atlantic coast, and the partisan war, go wanting due to space considerations.[4] Hopefully, this volume at least primes those pumps. And finally, this book is written by a historian, not a geographer or meteorologist, with the particular perspective that entails.

Some basic definitions are required up front. *Climate* and *weather* are not the same. Mark Twain once summed up the difference nicely when he quoted a child who wrote that "climate lasts all the time and weather only a few days."[5] Over a century later, the modern National Oceanic and Atmospheric Administration (NOAA) put it only a little differently, stating that "climate is what you expect, weather is what you get." Daily temperatures, precipitation, cloudiness, wind speeds and directions, barometric pressure, and other measurements record the specifics of a particular day. Climate, in contrast, "is the average of that weather" over a long period of time. Sometimes daily weather challenges climatic averages with unusual conditions, record highs, or unusual lows.[6] For example, Aprils in western Alabama's *climate* tend to be warm and muggy. But on April 12, 1861, as shots rang out at Fort Sumter, it was specifically 58 degrees Fahrenheit and cloudy at 7 A.M. in Greensboro, Alabama. That was Greensboro's *weather* that fateful morning. Throughout the war that followed, soldiers, generals, and civilians made assumptions based on what they knew about climate in the proverbial "Sunny South" only to be delighted or dismayed by the fickle daily weather they actually encountered.[7]

This is not the first book to consider the Civil War's climate and weather, but it is one of only a few. Early discussions reflected a different intellectual world. Anecdotal and systematic wartime observations, the rudimentary state of meteorology, religion, folk beliefs, mystery, and postwar agendas shaped what people believed. As M. Wynn Thomas later wrote, "what we blithely call 'the weather' is in fact a complex socio-scientific construct, and both the science of weather and the sociology of weather have changed radically since the mid-nineteenth century."[8]

Consider, for example, Edward Powers. Six years after Appomattox, the Chicago engineer wrote *War and the Weather,* the first and still the most notorious book on the topic. During the war, enough rain fell after battles to convince soldiers that cannonades produced storms. Powers sets out to prove this, convinced that artillery fire—or else explosive devices attached to hot-air balloons—could produce rain during droughts or in the dry West by tapping into an airborne "river of air." Ranging back to the war with Mexico and forward to the Franco-Prussian conflict, Powers lists 130 Civil War engagements that he asserts had been followed by precipitation. In a later edition, he developed elaborate explanations for all those other battles that did not produce rain, took on his critics, and petitioned the government for three hundred field pieces (or else two hundred siege guns) to prove his case. Although his ideas seem fanciful today, he attracted remarkable supporters at the time, including generals such as Joshua Lawrence Chamberlain, John Schofield, and William Tecumseh Sherman as well as soldier-presidents James A. Garfield and Rutherford Hayes. Powers finally got his federal appropriation in 1890. His experiments, conducted with former Confederate brigadier general Daniel Ruggles—who had patented his own airborne weather bomb—failed. Yet the rainmaker and his surplus howitzer remained a fixture in the West into the Great Depression, and the myth of artillery causing storms lives on.[9]

By the 1930s, meteorology had become a science based on hard information, not old soldiers' tales. Yet there are Civil War connections to that story as well. In 1814, the US Army directed surgeons to record weather data. With better equipment and standardization, the Civil War army gathered data at stationary posts and temporary observatories such as one near the Wilderness in 1864. Surgeons at forts took regular measurements of temperature, wind, precipitation, and barometric pressure. Meanwhile, an extensive national civilian system of "synoptic meteorology" emerged. At the beginning of the 1840s, a fierce debate roiled among scientists about what caused storms. Searching for data, James Pollard Espy established a nationwide network of local weather observers who submitted regular reports. Espy not only was among the first to theorize the role of vertical convection in storms and polar fronts but also suspected that massive battles caused rain. It says much about the state of the science that in 1843 "the Storm King" became the army's first full-time meteorologist. Five years later, after a brief stint with the US Navy, he moved to the Smithsonian Institute. Working there with Smithsonian secretary Joseph Henry, Espy built a network of more than 500 volunteers by 1861. In return for monthly reports, they received modern instruments, forms, and detailed instructions. The war largely killed the system down south—attempts to create a parallel Confederate organization came to nothing—but a few fascinating southerners did continue to collect data for the Smithsonian. Observations, meanwhile, went on without cessation in the North, including in the streets of Gettysburg in July 1863. Weather observers were a tenacious lot.[10]

After the war, in 1870, Congress created the Weather Bureau out of the army and Smithsonian systems. The Signal Corps administered it for twenty years until it passed to the Department of Agriculture in 1891. The bureau's charge was to use accumulated data to forecast the future for the benefit of farmers and businessmen. By 1900, it administered nearly 200 local stations and supervised over 3,000 volunteers. University-trained scientists from around the world worked with the bureau while establishing training programs at American universities. The bureau strove to establish a common taxonomy. Weather forecasts and maps became a common feature of American newspapers. New discoveries increasingly made those forecasts useful. Notably, in 1922, Norwegian meteorologist Jacob Bjerknes and his colleagues revived Espy's theory of worldwide polar and tropical weather fronts that interfaced to produce changing weather conditions. While the Weather Bureau initially resisted the new ideas coming out of Norway, by the 1940s, meteorologists and ordinary people routinely chatted about warm and cold fronts, barometric pressure, tornado and hurricane warnings, and many of the other features Americans today take for granted on the six o'clock news. That knowledge became especially vital during World War II, especially on D-Day and in the Battle of the Bulge.[11]

Modern meteorology in the twentieth century had little effect on Civil War studies, however. Even as the field otherwise evolved after World War II, weather remained background scenery. Studies of the soldier experience going back to Bell Wiley's classic scholarship sometimes described how combatants marched in bad weather, stood guard in the rain, or survived cold Virginia winters. With varying interest, the authors of battle narratives usually noted weather conditions before getting to the drums and trumpets. Civil War popular culture acknowledged the effect of weather on the war, if only in the daily question for the living historian, "aren't those wool uniforms hot?"[12] Overall, however, wartime weather seemed too trivial to study in depth. Even the most basic information remained unknown. A month before his death in 1953, the noted biographer Douglas Southall Freeman pleaded in his last public address for rudimentary weather data from the war. "There are a great many days when we know nothing about the weather," he said, "we have no report of the temperature; we do not know whether the dust was rising or the mud was covering the men; we do not know to what extent the weary soldier was burdened by sand, or to what extent his advance was facilitated by a hard-surfaced road." Freeman estimated that with a national effort of five years' duration, "we can double what we know in the way of meteorology of the War."[13]

Another fifty years passed, not five, before someone partially granted Freeman's wish. Military historians raced ahead of the Civil War community in integrating weather into their work. Harold Winters's essays in the seminal volume *Battling the Elements* notably point out paths Civil War students could follow. A collaborative work incubated at West Point, the book seeks to explain "how seemingly evident factors such as weather, climate, terrain, soil, and vegetation are important, cogent, and sometimes decisive in combat." In one essay, Winters expertly compares the effect of mud in World War I to Ambrose Burnside's ill-fated "Mud March."[14]

Finally, Robert K. Krick responded to Freeman. His *Civil War Weather in Virginia,* an annotated day-by-day almanac based largely on the records of one Smithsonian observer in the District of Columbia, immediately became a vital reference. Krick, to be sure, does not look beyond the terrain trod by Robert E. Lee's (and Freeman's) army. As later chapters of this book will make clear, such information still can be frustratingly difficult to come by for the war's western theater and harder still for the Trans-Mississippi.

Yet, in attempting to delineate the weather that the armies in Virginia faced, Krick not only reawakened interest in the topic but also introduced the National Archives's collection of military and Smithsonian reports to Civil War scholars.[15]

Other historians, in the meantime, approached Civil War weather from the perspective of environmental history. Nearly two decades ago, Jack Temple Kirby lamented how Civil War scholars and environmental historians routinely ignored each other. He noted six areas in which the war directly affected the environment: the life and death of animals, the spread of disease, the death of men and the resulting effects on the land, the destruction of cities and towns, ravaged farms, and ruined forests. Kirby asked scholars to work collaboratively in order to better understand the war's ignored environmental consequences.[16]

Again, it took time for scholars to respond, as Christopher Morris noted of southern history more generally a decade ago, but the last years have produced crucial works. Mark Fiege and Ted Steinburg broke the ground. Andrew McIlwaine Bell, Lisa Brady, Katheryn Shively Meier, Megan Kate Nelson, and G. Terry Sharrer successfully reoriented historians toward the Civil War's denuded forests, abandoned fields, malarial swamps, mountains, microbes, and ravaged cities. All of them gave the environment—and sometimes its weather—agency. Brady and Nelson also joined historians Richard P. Tucker and Mark Smith in reimagining the late Union war effort as a conscious assault on the southern environment, especially the agricultural and urban "improvements" that nineteenth-century Americans took for "civilization." Bell and Meier sought to understand how soldiers survived or succumbed in often-hostile disease environments. Judkin Browning and Timothy Silver considered how the Peninsula's environment, including its weather, helped wreck George McClellan's hopes in 1862. While my conclusions in a later chapter differ somewhat from theirs, what matters here is that there now exists any debate at all in a world that routinely stereotypes "Little Mac" as a timorous slacker. The first-ever conference bringing together Civil War and environmental scholars took place in 2011, and many of the papers presented there later appeared in a well-received volume edited by Brian Allen Drake.[17]

Civil War environmental history as it has emerged demands both interdisciplinary and intradisciplinary conversations. Historians need to know something about geography, geology, and meteorology to tell the full story. Mike Davis's *Late Victorian Holocausts* provides a crucial if controversial model. Davis uses U. S. Grant's world tour of 1877–79 as a starting point for grasping three of the worst famines of the nineteenth century. Alternating drought and massive flooding meant that, between 1877 and 1902, from 30 million to 50 million people starved to death in Africa, Asia, and South America. Those disasters, and clumsy or cruel imperial responses, set the stage for the triumph of Western expansion against weakened peoples. Davis calls it "the secret history of the nineteenth century."[18]

Civil War weather did not kill millions, but it was out of the ordinary, in part for the same root causes that Davis examines. The famines of the era derived in some manner from the effects of the El Niño–Southern Oscillation (ENSO) phenomenon, which closed the heavens in some parts of the world and brought monsoons and floods to others. El Niño today is a regular feature of weather forecasts—and even the occasional subject of late-night comedians—but it only entered public consciousness in the 1980s. Scientists, however, first confirmed its existence in the 1920s after a period of observation and theorizing that stretched back into the 1790s.

The basics are simple enough. In Davis's words, El Niño and La Niña ride "a vast see-saw of air mass and ocean temperature" in the Pacific and Indian Oceans. Off the western coasts of Ecuador and Peru, the ocean is quite cold. But in some years, for reasons that defy easy explanation, the northeast trade winds slacken or stop, currents shift, and the "conveyor belt" breaks down. Summer subsurface waters off Peru warm up, currents and trade winds churn warmer water to the surface, and west winds transport the warmth toward land. The jet stream shifts. Across much of the world, weather patterns slip out of joint in December—hence "El Niño," or "Christ Child," as fishermen first called the phenomenon. The results are dramatic. Indonesia and northern Australia see drought, but heavier-than-usual rain falls across much of Asia, western Europe, Latin America, and South Africa. Precipitation increases in parts of the United States too, especially in California, the Great Basin, and—most crucially for this study—the Gulf Coast. Southern winters grow colder. Some years, in contrast, bring the other end of the seesaw, the less understood La Niña—the name means "little girl"—phenomenon, which climatologist Richard Grove described as "extreme normal." During La Niña years, heavier-than-usual rain falls in parts of Australia, Indonesia, northern South America, and the Pacific Northwest. But both California and the American South grow dry, and the Northeast experiences unusual cold.[19]

Some scientists and authors invariably began to wonder how much

ENSO affected the distant past. Brian Fagan and Richard Grove both found hints of El Niño–related droughts going as far back as around 3500 BCE in North Africa and the Fertile Crescent. Using archeological, paleoarcheological, and scientific evidence, Fagan suggests that ENSO-related drought regularly struck ancient Egypt. Grove theorizes that the biblical drought that affected Joseph in Egypt, the declines of the Mycenaean culture and Troy, Europe's Dark Ages, and the collapse of the Mayans all fit ENSO's pattern. Fagan includes the similar decline of the Ancestral Pueblo people of the American Southwest. In 1812, El Niño helped destroy Napoleon's hopes in Russia, and ENSO was active during the "Little Ice Age," a period that brought a cooler climate to Europe and the Americas from around 1350 into the nineteenth century.[20]

And the Civil War? Meteorologists have described a severe "great Civil War drought" that extended across the American West from 1856 through 1865. In 2006, a team led by Celine Herweijer attributed that drought to "moderate yet persistent La Niña–like conditions."[21] Drought beginning in 1845—and apparently ENSO—combined with the Civil War drought and overhunting to weaken the powerful Comanche Empire and other Plains nations at the worst possible moment.[22] Meteorologists Tony Lupo and Mike Madden, meanwhile, have hypothesized that La Niña in 1861 brought extreme heat to wartime Missouri. Most recently, Judkin Browning and Tim Silver cited Herweijer to posit an extended La Niña through the Civil War. Grove and Adamson, on the other hand, have suggested that El Niño was the real culprit, identifying a "weak" El Niño in 1861–62, a "moderate" event for 1863–64, and a stronger El Niño at the end of 1865.[23]

Complicating matters is the fact that ENSO is hardly the only factor that shapes American weather. A connected, more complicated, and less understood phenomenon operates in the Atlantic. The metaphorical conveyor belt of the North Atlantic Oscillation (NAO) runs from a low-pressure system near Iceland and Greenland to a high near the Azores. Higher pressure there and lower pressures in Iceland (NAO+) translate into strong westerly winds across the North Atlantic that bring cool summers and milder winters to northern Europe and drier conditions to southern Europe. The American Northeast experiences milder winters but warmer summers. When differences between the two pressures become less pronounced (NAO-), arctic winds dump heavy snow on western Europe and bring colder winters to the American East Coast and South. Some authors link an NAO- to the extreme cold of Victorian England, shivering soldiers in the trenches of World War I, and Adolf Hitler's failures in Russia and the Ardennes. Recent research also calculated a negative NAO during the winters of 1862, 1864, and 1865. If an NAO- overlapped with El Niño, the Civil War's odd weather suddenly makes more sense.[24]

The debate over ENSO's and the NAO's activity and role in history will continue in the coming years before definite conclusions emerge. But this much is certain: Civil War weather was not "normal" as we have assumed. Fifty years ago, historian Paul Gates first signaled the importance of weather to the war and pointed to strange weather that, he argued, doomed the Confederacy. Gates described heavy spring rains followed by droughts in 1862, 1863, and in Virginia again in 1864. Extreme cold weather during the winter of 1863–64 plagued man and beast. Aside from Mark Fiege and Armistead Robinson, however, few historians noticed.[25] A fierce debate about the failure of the Confederacy raged without its most basic foundation. The food shortages, inflation, taxation, and other hardships "plain folk" there suffered—and the disillusionment and loss of will that followed—make up the entire litany of historians' "internalist" interpretation of Confederate implosion. Yet one can trace all of it back to the unusually wet winters and summer droughts that caused the food shortages. The early 1860s, it turns out, was a terrible meteorological moment to launch an agricultural republic in wartime.[26]

The Union also suffered losses due to unusually bad weather, Gates noted. Standard texts mentioned the triumph of King Wheat over King Cotton thanks to sweeping midwestern mechanization. But as Gates knew, northern states saw disaster too. At the end of August 1863, "an early and severe frost" ruined crops across the Midwest. Early in September, a heatwave brought drought, and on September 18 an even more crippling frost followed. Snows occurred as early as October 22 from the Rockies to the Ohio River. The end results were significant crop losses in the Union states. Although historians widely ignored Gates's conclusions, he was exactly right.[27]

And what about the battlefield? Countering "internalist" historians of the war are "externalists," who described a war that was won and lost by the armies, not on the home front. As The Howling Storm demonstrates, weather shaped every campaign, often more decisively than we have fathomed. Ultimately, we cannot understand the battles unless we include that third player, the metaphorical "Army of Weather," be it the heavy rain before the Battle of Cheat Mountain, the snow that tortured Stonewall Jackson's men at Bath and Romney, the sleet at Fort Donelson, or the stifling heat that smothered Jubal Early's Confederates at Washington. Affected by ENSO and the NAO, climate and uncommon weather shaped the Civil War from its genesis to its conclusion and ultimately aided a Union cause that materially was more equipped to handle it. Yet at crucial moments, such as on the Peninsula or after Gettysburg, weather allied with the Confederates long enough to drag out the war and make emancipation possible. To paraphrase Mike Davis, this is a secret history of the Civil War.

The Howling Storm is based on quantitative and qualitative sources. US Army and Smithsonian reports provide extensive data for the eastern theater, more-scattered information for the West, and sadly little for the Trans-Mississippi. Ships logs from the US Navy provide additional information despite a regrettable habit in the "Brown Water Navy" to flaunt regulations and ignore recording temperature readings. At times, I had to refer to more distant sites and comparisons in hopes of least approximating the weather. I also consulted letters, diaries, memoirs, regimental histories, and the *Official Records*. My initial task was to identify the best of such sources without bogging down in another lifetime of research. To do that, I read my way through the war using secondary accounts and made note of the people, sources, and collections that scholars relied upon most often for weather information. I then added a few more sources in an attempt to fill obvious holes. Ultimately I read everything I could find from 470 participants in the war—420 soldiers and 50 civilians. As in previous books, I identify them by name, when possible, in hopes of not adding to the oblivion that so many of them feared. Many readers surely will wonder how I missed their favorite soldier, but I am confident that my sample represents the war generation's relationship with the weather.[28]

There are always difficulties with such sources, especially postwar recollections. Virginia is overrepresented, while voices from west of the Mississippi are too faint. Soldiers no doubt were as likely to exaggerate about the weather as anyone else. In this volume, readers will often encounter soldiers' broad assertions of the worst weather ever, as inevitably verified by the oldest local citizens. Recollections of wartime weather also fit into wider questions of Civil War memory. How did aging men and women remember the war—including its weather—as they grew older? Did the snow get deeper, the nights colder, and the mud thicker? Did old foes bond over their suffering and emphasize it as a result? Did those who refused to forgive and forget remember bad weather as one of the injustices forced upon them in their youth? Do humorous or stoic depictions of harsh weather mask trauma? We have few answers. M. Wynn Thomas has argued that for poet and wartime nurse Walt Whitman, weather was a "mnemonic device" and a "fixative of memory" that would help his audience remember the rest.[29] After a decade of research, I am convinced that Whitman was not alone. Contemporary descriptions of weather actually match up well. The details may vary, but soldiers agreed to a surprising degree when it came to what they endured. Weather made an indelible impression on a generation more rooted to the soil than ours. They expected us to understand.[30]

Chapter 1

The Darkest Clouds

Fort Sumter to Manassas, Spring and Summer 1861

At 4:30 A.M. on April 12, 1861, a ten-inch mortar shell arced through the starry night sky and exploded almost directly overhead Fort Sumter in a shower of light. It was the signal for all the Confederate batteries in Charleston harbor to commence their bombardment. Samuel Wylie Crawford, Fort Sumter's surgeon and a soon-to-be ad hoc battery commander, remembered a beautiful predawn sky that morning. "The sea was calm," he added, "and the night was still under the bright star light."[1] But the weather soon began to change. The wind shifted noticeably as a powerful nor'easter moved in from the sea, bringing low, gray clouds that morning and frequent rain squalls in the afternoon. It grew warmer too. Spring came late to Charleston in 1861, but by early afternoon, the high temperature reached 70 degrees for the first time in ten days, a full 10 degrees higher than the previous day.

All day the shore batteries pounded the fort. During the night, both sides largely rested their wet and weary gun crews. After midnight, only Confederate mortars kept firing, at slow fifteen-minute intervals. While saving ammunition and providing repose to exhausted gunners were the primary reasons for the slower pace, the worsening weather played a significant role. Long gone was the bright starry sky of the last evening of peace. A powerful storm finally hit Charleston head on just after dark, lashing both the fort and the shore batteries with high winds, crashing waves, and hard showers.[2] At Fort Moultrie, it was "the pelting rain" that convinced the post's commander to restrict his fire through the night and keep his men dry.[3]

The nor'easter raged on intermittently into early morning. A particularly strong squall at 7 A.M. stopped the bombardment for an hour before the clouds blew away. The new day grew bright and warm, conditions that a Charleston minister later attributed to divine providence. By early after-noon, redoubled shore fire had reduced the fort to a chaotic wreck of fire, smoke, and rubble. Post commander Col. Robert Anderson was low on ammunition, and spreading blazes threatened to ignite what powder was left in reserve. Just after 2 P.M., with the temperature rising to a high of 74 degrees—it the warmest day of the young year in Charleston—Anderson agreed to a truce. Deafening sound gave way to silence. The weather re-mained clear and warm as the garrison officially surrendered the next day. As the Federals saluted and lowered their flag, an abbreviated barrage ex-ploded one of the fort's guns and killed the first soldier to die in the war. The garrison then sailed away for New York City on the steamer *Baltic*. As if an omen, the storm pressed on before them, like a pillar of smoke and fire out of the Old Testament.[4]

Floodwaters lay off to the *Baltic*'s port side as it sailed up the coast, as a se-ries of earlier tempests already had inundated the country. From the Caroli-nas to New York, and as far inland as Chicago and Saint Louis, the weather in the first half of April had been metaphorically as unsettled and stormy as the fate of the nation.[5]

American Aprils are characterized by rain and what historian and me-teorologist David M. Ludlum calls "fickleness." The growing absence of the major weather depressions that shape winter weather—increasingly stark variations between polar and midlatitude temperatures and baromet-ric pressures in the Northern Hemisphere, the warming southern latitudes, and the significant seasonal difference between warming land and cooler ocean temperatures—all combine to produce rising masses of warm air laden with moisture. Localized storms and showers routinely follow as the air masses reach high enough to cool and condense. The end results vary in timing and intensity, but "April showers" are real.[6]

All along the Atlantic coast in 1861, April showers became more than a poetic device. From the Potomac River south to Richmond, flooding from a series of storms had overtopped banks, denuded bottomlands, and swept away bridges. News of the bombardment in South Carolina first arrived in Richmond late in the day on April 12. It was the warmest day of the month there too, with an afternoon high of 64 degrees. After 4 P.M., a late-afternoon thunderstorm flashed and rumbled through the city. "The commotion of the elements above" were not enough to distract attention from what the novelist, editor, and would-be Confederate bureaucrat John Beauchamp Jones called "the tempest of excitement agitating the human breast." By morning, two more inches of rain had fallen, inundating streets and raising the James River.[7]

Elsewhere in Virginia, war news and storms similarly confronted people in equal measure. Continuing rain dampened an expected secession debate in Rappahannock County. A correspondent from Loudon County noted that rainy weather there—some of the worst in his lifetime, he said—had held up the mail for ten days. North of Richmond, fourteen-year-old student Benny Fleet complained that the flooded Mattaponi River had stopped the mails. On April 16, when the news from Fort Sumter finally arrived at his family's plantation, he ranked its significance equally with the glad tidings that the river finally had fallen.[8] North of the Fleet plantation, the Rappahannock River flooded to levels not seen in Fredericksburg since a legendary flood of 1814, causing damage to homes, riverside mills, and the bridges connecting the city to Falmouth on the east bank. Out to the west, in Southwest Virginia's Great Valley, it had been raining intermittently for almost a week. It was "ugly weather," according to surgeon's apprentice John Apperson, who also complained of "a great deal of rain, mud &c." When Apperson and the local militia mustered on April 13 in response to anticipation of news from South Carolina, it was "upon a prominent hill and the wind blew very furious and cool." It rained on April 15, and the sixteenth proved to be a "very bad day—raining snowing and blowing." Memories of Fort Sumter would forever mingle with recollections of nature's storms.[9]

Tensions and water both also ran high north of the Potomac. In Washington, "the great Easterly storm," as attorney and Patent Office examiner Horatio Nelson Taft called it, approached the city with drizzle on April 7. Harder rain wet mustering militiamen, outnumbered regulars, and milling crowds of anxious civilians almost every day after that through the sixteenth. Sopping-wet Washingtonians agonized about armed threats from Virginia even as heavy rains and Potomac flooding tore apart bridges and practically isolated the city.[10] "How it does rain!" declared *The Times* of London correspondent William Howard Russell on April 8. "Last night there were torrents of water in the streets literally a foot deep," he continued. "It still runs in muddy whirling streams through the channels, and the rain is falling incessantly from a dull leaden sky. The air is warm and clammy." On April 12, with rumors of Sumter reaching the flooding capital, Russell headed for Baltimore, where he again discovered flooded streets.[11]

Back in Washington, Pres. Abraham Lincoln officially responded to Sumter's surrender on April 15 with his momentous call for 75,000 volunteers to subdue the rebellion. Taft noted, "it has rained some today, and it [is] threatening a storm tonight." The next day was just as wet and gloomy, but a welcome change in the weather finally brought a dry day on April 17. Those were anxious times in Washington, with rumors of imminent invasion and uprisings in Maryland, capped by the Pratt Street Riot in Baltimore on April 19. Aided by the drier skies, Maryland secessionists severed telegraph wires and burned bridges, cutting off Washington from the North. As Taft waited for deliverance, he also took note of the better weather. It turned hot on April 23, reaching into the eighties as US Marines finally arrived to bolster the city's defenses.[12]

~~~

Across a divided America during the initial weeks following the attack on Fort Sumter, armies were born. While militia musters like Apperson's in Southwest Virginia marked the opening days of the war, both sides soon gravitated to the Mexican War practice of creating new state volunteer units from scratch. Men of local prominence enlisted companies, units of roughly a hundred men each. Would-be soldiers rushed forward for a variety of reasons that historians still debate. With colorful names and elected officers, freshly minted companies left home to speeches, cheers, and tears. They migrated to centrally located camps of instruction to be combined, ten at a time, into regiments. There they began to learn the business of soldiering, with a heavy emphasis on drilling in formation. Conditions were primitive, unhygienic, unhealthy, and overall a rude awakening to the young men who had rallied to fight.[13]

Camps also were muddy. While rain and mud are uncomfortable inconveniences today, in the nineteenth century, they portended more to brandnew soldiers. Historian Kathryn Shively Meier reminds us that the Civil War generation assumed a firm link between rainy weather and sickness. Ague, dysentery, malaria, rheumatism, and typhoid were sure to follow, soldiers counseled, once the rain started. Simply trying to march in soggy fields with shoes encased in mud induced exhaustion. Rain also depressed the men, leaving them more susceptible to disease. No recruit could brush off bad weather, especially as others grew ill. Not surprisingly, they regularly described rain and mud in their letters and diaries as a signal features of camp life.[14]

Long-term climatic norms as well as seasonal change shaped soldiers' experiences as they went into the first camps of instruction that spring. The location of those camps mattered greatly. Modern climatologists divide the United States into discreet climate zones, each with distinctive characteristics. The US Department of Energy currently recognizes seven distinct regions. The "Marine" zone, confined to the Pacific coast, with rare exception remains beyond the bounds of this study. Two others, the "Hot-Dry" and "Mixed-Dry" zones, touch upon it periodically. Both arc south on the map like a bicolored rainbow from central California into New Mexico, the Texas Panhandle, and southeastern Colorado. With some overlap in Arizona and the California desert, the "Hot-Dry" zone usually runs to the south of the "Mixed-Dry" band. On average, this area receives less than twenty inches of rain per year, while the average temperature remains above 45 degrees all year. The "Mixed-Dry" zone is just as dry but cooler on average, with average temperatures dipping below 45 degrees in the winter months.

The "Hot-Humid" zone, in contrast, encompassed much of the new Confederacy in 1861. More or less recognizable as the Deep South, it ran from the Gulf of Mexico north into the geological Black Belt. Today it runs irregularly east along the Gulf Coast from East Texas through southern Georgia before it huddles the coast up into North Carolina. Unlike the dry zones, this section is wet, receiving more than twenty inches of rain per year. It also is a warm area that either tops 66 degrees for at least 3,000 hours during the warmest six months of the year or reaches 73 degrees or more for 1,500 hours during the warmest six months.[15]

In the "Hot-Humid" zone, spring already had arrived in April 1861. Aprils generally are warm and showery there, with spring building toward hot and muggy summers. Unlike in the cooler North, where farmers were just beginning to stir, southern crops already were in the fields. Expecting to be cut off from the northern foodstuffs the planters typically imported, many farmers already had altered their crop strategies. "Much more corn and much less cotton has planted than usual," a Georgia farmer explained. "Farmers are all determined to fill their corn-cribs and smokehouses at home and not be longer dependent on the north-west."[16]

Thanks to abundant sun and rain, the signs were promising. The *Augusta Chronicle* predicted remarkable corn, oat, and wheat crops in Georgia despite fears of late frosts that might damage cotton and fruits. The editor of the newspaper in Columbus, Georgia, claimed that he had never seen more promising fields. Clearly, he observed, God favored southern agriculture. Reports from Mobile similarly indicated good planting weather in Alabama after a dry 1860. In Baton Rouge, one observer predicted record corn and sugarcane crops as well as bountiful vegetable gardens. A Nashville correspondent anticipated a record wheat crop. The *Charleston Mercury* reported burgeoning corn and cotton crops from Florida to Texas, despite delays in some areas, such as Black Belt Alabama, where too much rain had fallen. A letter from Texas predicted that recent rains would rejuvenate dry wheat and corn fields.[17]

By May, observers everywhere boasted about Confederate agriculture. There were regional variations, of course. In Texas, cool May weather made for an easy winter-wheat harvest.[18] In northern Louisiana, a wet winter and spring gave way to "a poet's dream of May," in plantation daughter Kate Stone's words. Her mother's vegetable and flower gardens were "in a flourishing state. . . . Mama is having quantities of peas, potatoes, and all things eatable planted, as our only chance for anything from this time until the close of the war will be to raise it ourselves."[19] A Baton Rouge editor described the most promising corn crop he had ever seen.[20]

Another correspondent described the first Confederate capital, Montgomery, Alabama, as "exceedingly sultry" and compared it to a "'bake oven.'"[21] One journalist reported bountiful wheat and corn there, predicted a large wheat harvest, and added that enough rain in June would yield bumper crops of corn and cotton.[22] At the end of May, an Alabama farmer praised the local wheat and oat crops but added that the "corn is very small" and the cotton "very sorry."[23]

Conditions, while still good generally, were less remarkable farther east. The Florida Panhandle around Union-held Fort Pickens was a trouble spot. A localized drought there left cisterns empty, and people worried about water. An Augusta, Georgia, editor reported hotter weather in late May along with thriving cotton but less developed corn. A cold snap arrived two days later; hot weather returned only at the end of May. The wheat harvest that followed across Georgia and into Alabama was remarkable, according to one Georgia correspondent, producing twice the usual crop.

Corn excelled as well, he added, although cotton lagged. Doubting that the anything-but-ideal weather could allow harvested wheat fields to now produce corn, a Georgia editor urged his readers to plant peas instead of fall wheat—few apparently heeded the advice—and to buy and denude useless pine forests in order to plant more peas and hay.[24]

The *Charleston Mercury*, meanwhile, sounded warnings about cotton, which lagged due to cool temperatures and then late May's cold. Good weather, a writer opined, would produce only an average crop across the Confederacy. The end of the month saw renewed 90-degree temperatures and drought conditions spreading northward as far as the Savannah River and beyond into South Carolina by late June. Drought hit middle Georgia especially hard before rain returned at the end of the month. Vegetable gardens and grains suffered there. "The weather Monday was again intolerably hot," a *Mercury* editor wrote, "and the thermometer kept up far in the nineties during the day. Juleps and punches and cobblers are in great request at present."[25]

Yet all told, good spring weather and bountiful crops boosted Confederate morale, and the early summer drought in scattered places did little to diminish it. "Does it not seem that Divine Providence is pouring out His choicest blessings on our favored people," a South Carolinian wrote at the end of May, "filling their garners simultaneously, with the withdrawal of provisions on the western rivers? Does God not say in this, 'Be of good cheer, for I am with you?'"[26] Ministers preaching on June 13, the Confederacy's first official Fast Day, pointed to ample rain, fertile fields, and full storehouses as clear signs of God's support. A Georgian boasted, "there is no danger of starving if Lincoln send[s] five hundred ships to blockade our ports."[27] Even the heat and disease would help, the *Mercury* predicted. "Go ahead, brave Zouaves of New York, whom we were apt to spit upon," the editor wrote, paraphrasing Horace Greeley. "Don't mind yellow fever; don't mind black vomit, don't mind bilious fever, or cholera, or measles, or small pox, or hot weather, or hard living, or cold steel, and hot shot! Go ahead!"[28]

Spring also came to blossoming military camps of instruction in the "Hot-Humid" zone. Most recruits had been farmers, but they now experienced spring differently. The first days in camp were challenging. Scottish-born

William Watson, a sergeant in Baton Rouge's Pelican Rifles, provides one example. He mustered into Confederate service at Camp Walker, formerly New Orleans's popular Metairie Race Course. The grounds were marshy and surrounded by mosquito-ridden swamps and noxious sewage ditches. The men initially arriving at Camp Walker also had to deal with heavy rain and depths of muck caused by "unusual weather for New Orleans at this season of the year." Marched to their company campground on April 30, Watson and his comrades stacked arms in "drenching rain" and stood in "black soft soil with mud and pools of water here and there." Wagons arrived carrying boards that "were thrown down to lay on the floor of the tents to keep the men off the wet ground. . . . The rain still continuing, it was evident that the first night in camp was likely to be rather cheerless." Mercifully, the rain stopped the next day, and the ground began to dry out. Different weather shaped the next two weeks at Camp Walker: "broiling heat, bad water, and mosquitoes," with temperatures occasionally reaching 90 degrees.[29] The editor of the *New Orleans Daily True Delta* noted how the beginning of "a genuine southern summer" on May 6 left many people unprepared for the heat.[30]

Other recruits told similar stories but noted cooler temperatures. The "Mixed-Humid" climate zone is as rainy and humid as the "Hot-Humid" zone just to the south, but this region is colder in the winters, averaging below 45 degrees. The northern extent of the "Mixed-Humid" zone in 1861 encompassed almost all of the rest of the Confederacy and the Union borderlands. Over a year, this region also experiences no more than 5,400 "heating degree days," a modern measurement that records the cumulative difference between mean average temperatures and a base temperature of 65 degrees over a twenty-four-hour period.[31]

As they did farther south, some newspaper editors in the "Mixed-Humid" zone observed good weather for farming and promising fields of wheat after rain-delayed planting. On April 22, for example, the editor of the *St. Louis Daily Missouri Republican* noted that hot weather had arrived at last after a cool spring. But elsewhere there were problems. Rain and cooler weather across the trans-Appalachian expanse of the "Mixed-Humid" zone played havoc with farms. On April 27, the editor of the *Arkansas State Gazette* in Little Rock complained of two weeks of "rain, rain, rain; and the consequence is mud, mud, mud—not a little mud, but a profusion of that article." Rain delayed planting in central Arkansas, although by mid-June an immense wheat crop neared harvest.[32] At the beginning of June, a Missouri editor reported that recent cold weather had endangered the local fruit crop and threatened wheat yields. Another added that "exceedingly moist . . . showers and sunshine" reminded him of "the smiles and tears over the countenance of a two-year old baby." The season, he concluded a few days later, was "very unlike summer." Yet crops grew well, "never looking better," according to an editor in central Missouri. Abundant wheat fields stretched as far west as Kansas.[33]

Spring in the "Mixed-Humid" zone, marked by cooler temperatures and an unusual abundance of rain, surprised soldiers from the Deep South. A correspondent for the *Charleston Mercury* wrote that Virginia in mid-May was "shocking cold" for men without tents.[34] Then a brief heatwave arrived toward month's end. Heavy winds on May 27 blew clouds of dust through hot Richmond, the day's high reaching 93 degrees. Men coped with rain as well. In Arkansas, Cpl. William E. Bevens of the Jackson Guards found himself in the western half of the "Mixed-Humid" zone in the spring of 1861. The spring seemed unusually rainy. May 7, when Bevens's company left Little Rock, was a "gloomy day. The rain poured down in torrents." Trying to ignore the weather, the recruits marched to a church for a flag presentation. "Every living soul in town was there," he continued, "streets, yard and church overflowed with people, notwithstanding the rain."[35] Bad weather inconvenienced Union recruits too. On May 6, Capt. Robert McAllister of the 1st New Jersey marched his company through the wet streets of Trenton and complained that the hard rains made a "bad time for parading."[36] A month later, an Illinois recruit rejoiced in sunshine on June 4 "after wading in ankle deep mud for a week."[37]

Two final climate zones encompass the rest of the continental United States, including New England, most of New York and Pennsylvania, and the upper Midwest. At the northern fringe of the Union, in northern Maine and westward from Michigan's Upper Peninsula and across the northern counties of Wisconsin into Minnesota and modern North Dakota, the "Very Cold" zone rests atop a map of the nation like icicles on a roof. ("Very Cold" areas also exist as frigid islands high in the Rocky Mountains of modern Colorado and Wyoming.) This region records at least 9,000 heating-degree days during the year, a measurement that translates into long, brutal winters and short summers. The massive "Cold" zone extends across the great bulk of what was Lincoln's Union, westward across the Great Plains and Rocky Mountains almost to the Pacific coast, and south to the "Mixed-Humid" zone. It reports between 5,400 and 9,000 cumulative heating degrees in a given year. Longer winters there bring a host of consequences. Historian Ted Steinberg, for example, theorized that long cold winters had retarded the development of regional horsemanship, helping lead to the warmer Confederacy's early edge in cavalry.

Temperature was the key difference between Union and Confederate weather in April 1861. Much to their chagrin, recruits in the "Cold" zone reported just as much rain that spring as men to the south. Indeed, spring was just arriving in most of the Union as the war began. May nights still were cool enough to disturb exhausted rookie soldiers' sleep after long days of drill. It was rainy too. Regiments in Pittsburgh frequently cancelled drill because of the damp conditions. Sgt. Luther C. Furst of the 39th Pennsylvania described heavy rain, adding that it seemed to rain every Sunday, washing out the preacher. Heavy showers also disrupted the regiments' first significant march, an eight-mile hike that left the men "as wet as if we had swam the river."[38]

As June approached, however, days in the "Cold" and "Mixed-Humid" zones became wonderfully pleasant and even occasionally "sultry."[39] Some soldiers could hardly contain their enthusiasm. Civilian chaplain Augustus Woodbury described the 1st Rhode Island's mid-June expedition from Washington to Frederick, Maryland, as a pleasure excursion.[40] Confederates in camp noted the approach of summer as well. Pvt. Franklin Lafayette Riley of the 16th Mississippi, stationed near Corinth, wrote that the "nights are cool, but by noon it's hot. Fortunately, before Dress Parade, it usually rains."[41] Summer came last to the highlands. On June 18, Col. Robert Hatton of the 7th Tennessee complained that "the air is really cold—so cold, that I hastened out of my cot, at daylight, to go to a log-fire in the rear of my tent."[42]

Lt. John Newton Lyle of the 4th Virginia, camped near the Potomac under the command of the former professor Thomas J. Jackson, likewise noted lovely June weather in the Shenandoah. "We had no tents and didn't need any," he explained, "so balmy was the June weather in the valley of Virginia." No one enjoyed the conditions more, he added, than his brigade commander. Brigadier General Jackson "spurned sleeping indoors," Lyle explained, "spreads his blankets in the yard and rested on the bosom of mother earth, with the sky as his roof. To a suggestion from our Captain

White that the exposure might injure his health, Jackson replied that he liked to sleep with the air blowing all over him, and that he thought that it was doing him good."[43]

~~~

By late spring, the new regiments were drilled to a point of functionality. Spurred on by ambitious generals, anxious politicians, and civilians eager for victory, troops moved into the field. In retrospect, the confusion that followed was unremarkable. Inexperience and chaos—but also the first real effects of climate and weather—characterized the war's first engagements.

The first land battle of the war came at an unlikely place. On May 26, Union troops crossed the Ohio River into western Virginia, hoping to seize control of the vital Baltimore and Ohio Railroad, Washington's main connector to the Midwest. The movement also was designed to aid opponents of secession in that part of the state. Outnumbered Confederates retreated in haste from the railroad. A week later, on June 3, a small column of roughly 3,000 Federal troops, under the overall command of Maj. Gen. George B. McClellan, caught up with them fifteen miles south at Philippi. The Confederate commander, Col. George A. Porterfield, and about 800 troops defended a critical bridge there. On the night of June 2, Brig. Gen. Thomas Morris, leading the pursuit, decided to advance in two columns, stage a double envelopment, and bag Porterfield at dawn.[44]

Unfortunately for Morris, an unanticipated if typical mountain storm, the first of many that season, blew up during the night. As his men marched fifteen miles toward the town, the road became a quagmire. The north-central counties of modern West Virginia, where Philippi lays, rest in an extension of the "Cold" climatic zone that pokes southward into the Appalachians, which shield the region from the atmospheric effects of the Atlantic. The most mountainous counties in the northern and eastern part of the current state thus remain five to ten degrees cooler than the rest of West Virginia, with freezes common as late as mid-May. (Earlier in May 1861, a foot of snow had fallen in western Maryland.) In summer, patterns shift. Rain systems and thunderstorms sweep northeastward into the region from the Gulf of Mexico, making clouds, humidity, and wet weather common. In summer, the north-central region becomes the rainiest part of the state, averaging close to fifty inches of precipitation annually. Thun-

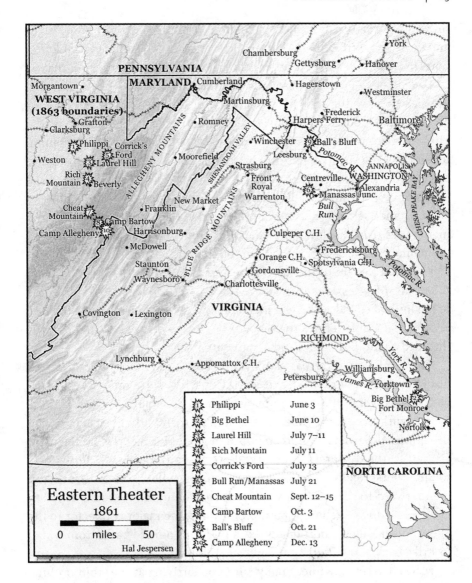

Eastern Theater
1861

0   miles   50

Hal Jespersen

	Philippi	June 3
	Big Bethel	June 10
	Laurel Hill	July 7–11
	Rich Mountain	July 11
	Corrick's Ford	July 13
	Bull Run/Manassas	July 21
	Cheat Mountain	Sept. 12–15
	Camp Bartow	Oct. 3
	Ball's Bluff	Oct. 21
	Camp Allegheny	Dec. 13

derstorm activity peaks in June and July, often bringing violent storms and flash floods.[45]

Conditions for raw troops—the men had been in uniform five weeks—were thus miserable and exhausting. Lightning flashed and thunder rumbled. "Many men fainted, and were left by the road," Morris later reported. Most, nonetheless, were on hand and ready to fight at sunup. The assault initially went smoothly as the first column surprised sleeping Confederates and drove them from town. Porterfield had casually dismissed civilian reports that the Yankees were approaching, assuring his subordinates that no one would be out on such a squally night. He put out no pickets, allowing his men to sleep in their dry tents. Disaster followed. Unfortunately for Morris, once aroused, the Rebels were able to keep going. Slowed by the rain and mud, and confused by the darkness, the second attacking column took the wrong road and left the back door open. "The failure to capture the entire rebel force," Morris explained, "can only be attributed to the storm during the night. This unforeseen occurrence served to call forth an endurance seldom exhibited, and I feel that the heroism of officers and men was as truly displayed in a march of fifteen miles in pitchy darkness, drenching rain, and over a mountainous country as in the irresistible attack and hot pursuit of the discomfited enemy." The storm did not dictate the result; Morris's advantages were several. Yet bad weather contributed to the initial Federal surprise—men dozing instead of on guard—and then allowed the Confederates to escape south as the delayed second column thrashed about in the mud and wet underbrush.[46]

The Confederate retreat, derisively called "the Philippi Races," lasted until Porterfield's army fell out at Huttonsville, forty miles south. Disgusted, the overall theater commander, Gen. Robert E. Lee, replaced the colonel with Brig. Gen. Robert S. Garnett. As the weather began to warm, Lee funneled Garnett reinforcements in hopes of losing no more territory. Garnett fortified Laurel Hill, on the Beverly–Fairmont Road, with 4,000 soldiers while sending Lt. Col. John Pegram's smaller force of about 1,300 men forward to the western slope of Rich Mountain. There he hoped to hold the vital Parkersburg–Staunton turnpike, the major connector to the Shenandoah Valley. Additionally, both positions offered bases from which to strike back at the Baltimore and Ohio Railroad.[47]

McClellan, meanwhile, finally left Ohio, arriving at the front on June 23. Leaving Morris at Philippi to pin down Garnett, he assembled three brigades at Clarksburg. Brig. Gen. William S. Rosecrans advanced from there with his brigade to Buckhannon, where McClellan and the two other brigades joined him on July 2. Heavy rain and cold weather slowed McClellan's careful preparations; he complained to his wife that he had to sleep under two horse blankets to keep warm. Finally, on July 7, the Federals set out for Rich Mountain, arriving three days later. Learning of a path up the mountain from a local Unionist, Rosecrans and McClellan hastily developed a plan to march into Pegram's rear and turn the Confederate flank.[48]

Rosecrans was on the move before dawn on July 11. He discovered that the promised path barely existed. The topography was brutal, marked by steep climbs, deep ravines, and heavy underbrush. Mountain laurel and wild grapevines created natural abatis. The march would have been difficult in perfect weather, but two hours after Rosecrans started, heavy showers set in and lasted through the morning.[49] "Every upward step, every moss-covered rock and water-soaked log was a potential falling place," historian Jack Zinn later wrote.[50] Pegram could hear enough to know an attack was coming, but in the confusing terrain, he guessed incorrectly about its direction and massed his men in the wrong place. According to later accounts, the young commander also was absent from the field when the Federal assault began near the mountaintop in a cold, driving rain. After a stand-up fight of some three hours, a final charge broke the exhausted Confederates. Bayed by Federal pursuers, Pegram surrendered the next day.

Garnett made haste for Beverly until erroneous reports came in that the way was blocked. He then shifted course toward Cheat Mountain.[51] Morris pursued. "Owing to the heavy rain," he reported, "the roads were rendered very difficult for the men and the few wagons of ammunition and provisions. By 11 o'clock the rain became a drenching storm, and continued for several hours, the roads in the mountains becoming nearly impassable."[52] On July 13, he caught up with the Confederates at Corrick's Ford and routed them; Garnett fell mortally wounded. The consequences were enormous. Northwestern Virginia was lost to the Confederacy, and the "Young Napoleon" McClellan emerged in the press as the Union's man of the hour. The seeming moral was that numbers and superior leadership in the end could outweigh both the rain and bad roads. But western Virginia had more lessons to teach before 1861 was over.[53]

Diagonally across the state to the southeast on the peninsula formed by the James and York Rivers, another small but seemingly crucial engagement roared up on June 10 at an old church called Big Bethel. There the Confederates had better luck. The first part of June had been warm but cloudy down on the Virginia Peninsula, with some rain and a notably hard shower on the night of June 5 that left an inch of precipitation. June 9 was the first fair day of the month. That night a Federal force of seven regiments took advantage of drying roads to advance inland eight miles from Fort Monroe, still in Union hands at the southern tip of the Peninsula. Their assignment was to eliminate the enemy's forward positions and shove them back into their works at Yorktown. A heavy predawn fog as well as inexperience and a lack of standardized uniform colors contributed to a tragic friendly fire incident on the march that all but derailed the subsequent assault. When the fight finally happened, it was under a remarkably bright, clear sky, with temperatures nearly in the eighties. Shielded by earthworks and equipped with artillery, a thousand outnumbered Confederates easily drove away the battered attackers.[54] Maj. Gen. Benjamin Butler, the Massachusetts politician who commanded Fort Monroe, made many excuses for the failure, including that "the length of the road and the heat of the weather had caused great fatigue."[55] Butler's second in command agreed, reporting that "some difficulty was experienced in keeping the men in proper order during the retreat, the men being so exhausted by thirst as to rush out of the ranks wherever water was to be had."[56] Both argued, in short, that the hot weather had benefited stationary Confederates by wearing out the Union men in motion.

To anxious Confederates, Big Bethel seemed a stupendous victory, more than a counterweight to Philippi. The men who fought it basked in both glory and the hot sun. Tidewater Virginia is routinely the hottest part of the state and is, by far, its most humid region. The day after the battle marked the beginning of an unusually hot and humid summer in the state, with increasing temperatures that climbed into the nineties five days later. The heatwave was widespread. To the north in Hagerstown, Maryland, a soldier reported temperatures of 105 degrees on June 15. Charleston and Augusta papers reported similar readings ten days later.[57]

~~~

Philippi and Big Bethel seized attention north and south for a moment, but in retrospect, they were small affairs, soon to be forgotten. Across the Union, citizens argued about the next steps. Official Washington chose to believe that secessionists were in a minority and that southern Unionism would return to the fore with a little encouragement. In Washington, Maj. Gen. Winfield Scott, the army's aging general in chief, developed an overall strategy to end the conflict based on that hope as well as the corollary of inflicting the least amount of damage possible. Scott desired a rapid reunion once the shooting stopped. His unfortunate experiences in the war with Mexico had suggested lessons about the limits of poorly disciplined volunteer troops. Scott's plan focused on creating an effective naval blockade of the southern coast while primarily using regulars to secure control of the Mississippi River valley through joint army-navy operations. Surrounded and cut and two, the Confederacy would implode in time, with relatively little bloodshed or bitterness. Northern public opinion wanted nothing to do with the Virginia-born Scott or his "Anaconda Plan," however. Treason had to be punished, and time was of the essence. The ninety-day volunteers Lincoln had called out after Sumter would see their enlistments run out in July. The Confederates then seemed to offer up a golden opportunity when their government moved its capital from Montgomery to Richmond after Virginia's secession. "Forward to Richmond!," Horace Greeley demanded in his *New York Tribune* on June 26, with a subheadline reading, "The Rebel Congress Must Not be Allowed to Meet There on the 20th of July." Many northerners agreed, as did their president. Even had he not, Lincoln was too smart a politician not to weigh the political pressure back home. And so it was "on to Richmond."[58]

Maj. Gen. Irvin McDowell, commanding the Union host gathering in and around Washington, objected. He needed more time; his men were not properly trained. Lincoln dismissed his concerns. The plan that followed had much to recommend it. McDowell had about 35,000 men under his immediate command. He would march them from the city and attack the smaller Confederate force of 20,000 soldiers under Gen. P. G. T. Beauregard, the hero of Fort Sumter, at Manassas Junction. The road to Richmond would be open. The one caveat was that the Confederates had also placed about 11,000 men under Gen. Joseph E. Johnston in the northern Shenandoah Valley to block any incursion coming south that way. Were Johnston somehow to get his men to Manassas first, McDowell's favorable odds would disappear. To avoid that possibility, Maj. Gen. Robert Patterson at Harpers Ferry had to occupy Johnston.[59]

Forced to go on the offensive, McDowell at least wanted to do it quickly, before the Confederates could respond and the summer deepen. His target date was July 8, but delays in organization and problems in securing transportation cost him a week. While he waited, an apparent omen suddenly appeared as a previously unknown comet rose in the northern sky at the end of June. Having first appeared in the Southern Hemisphere, the Great

Comet of 1861 blazed forth in splendor in the North American sky during the early days of July. Its massive head was nearly the size of the moon, while its tail forked upward across the northern half of the sky. Observing it, people reflected upon everything from the book of Revelation to the end of superstition in a modern age. Southern editors delighted in pointing out how it hid the North Star. Mary Chesnut remembered how young men in Richmond cleverly used it to entice young women outside for "philandering." According to one observer, even Lincoln was transfixed, brooding about a prophecy regarding the death of his sons. Most Americans, however, had trouble seeing a massive phenomenon in the northern sky as anything but a war omen. The *New York Herald* named it the "War Comet of 1861." Adding to the heavenly wonders, a meteor streaked across the sky directly from north to south on July 4 of all nights.[60]

Northern Virginia's climate, however, most troubled McDowell. Intense heat and frequent violent thunderstorms characterize Julys in the state, with the hottest week of the entire year usually around the summer equinox. A La Niña event that summer would have meant even hotter than usual conditions. The area from Washington east to Manassas lies in the same hot-temperature zone along the Chesapeake Bay that contains the lower Peninsula. Summer temperature readings are especially high there, with an average mean high of 88 degrees in July. While a brief cool spell coincided with the comet, the overall trend was hot and wet.[61]

Federal troops arriving in Washington sometimes succumbed to the heat. From Fairfax Court House on July 1, Pvt. Dick Simpson of the 3rd South Carolina complained about his regiment's rainy march, "every one wet, and the road muddy and slick," only to camp "in a clover patch, or I should say a mud hole."[62] When the weather turned hot again, it produced stifling days as far north as Boston on July 7; Chaplain Alonzo Quint of the 2nd Massachusetts remembered parading through that city on "an intensely hot day, never surpassed in any campaigns in Virginia or Georgia."[63] The dog days had arrived with their proverbial heat. At the front, it was brutal for men in wool uniforms. Washington endured 90 degrees on July 7 and returned to that level every day through July 10 before a brief cooling trend dropped highs to 74 degrees by the fourteenth.[64] The *Richmond Whig* on July 9 reported temperatures "high up in the nineties" as "perspiration trickled freely down the cheeks of obese people."[65]

The summer heat also brought afternoon and evening rain and thunderstorms to northern Virginia, the lower (northern) Shenandoah Valley, and

Washington every night between July 6 and July 13, with July 12 the one exception. Furious storms on July 9 and July 10 were heavy enough to disrupt McDowell's preparations.[66] From her home west of Manassas, Amanda Virginia Edmonds quietly compared the weather to the Confederacy's political situation. "Our country is so enveloped in the darkest clouds," she wrote.[67] Weather across the Blue Ridge Mountains in the Shenandoah was almost as hot and just as rainy. It poured there on July 6 before turning hot again. For new soldiers such as Pvt. John Apperson, soldiering in such heat was tough. "Our march to-day was a truly hot one," he wrote the next day on the road to Winchester, "many of our men became too sick to walk and we had no way of transporting them except the ammunition wagon." Then rain, probably part of the same system that drenched Rosecrans's and Pegram's men at Rich Mountain, settled in on the tenth.[68]

By then, rumors swirled that the weather had grown so oppressive that there could be no Federal movement that summer. They were wrong. On July 16 McDowell's army finally was ready to move on Manassas, albeit ten days off schedule. By later war standards, it marched incredibly slowly, requiring three days to cover the distance. Several factors slowed the pace. Training and discipline were painfully lacking. Felled trees in the road stopped columns, as did fears of ambushes. Heavily laden with gear, the men gobbled down their rations to the degree that McDowell had to stop his advance on July 19 and send back for more food.[69]

But the climate took its toll as well. For days, heat and rain pummeled the new recruits. Most Federals were without tents per McDowell's marching orders. Cpl. Elisha Hunt Rhodes of the 2nd Rhode Island thought himself fortunate to have a waterproof rubber blanket to sleep upon. Made of vulcanized rubber and often cut to do double duty as a poncho, such blankets were not yet standard issue, despite a quarter century of study in the War Department.

Skies were clear and dry on the first stifling day out of Washington, July 16. Temperatures rose into the eighties. Men and horses moved slowly, stopped frequently, and suffered thirst. The next day was hotter still, 86 degrees back in Washington. Clouds of choking dust rose all along the column. It grew hotter still on the third day, July 18, reaching 90 degrees as the two armies made first contact at Blackburn's Ford on Bull Run. Cattle driven with the army to provide fresh meat to the ranks faltered in the heat.[70] "The day was hot," Pvt. William B. Westervelt of the 27th New York wrote, "and the men but little used to marching, so it came very hard to us."

His regiment halted at Centreville, three miles from the enemy lines. Lacking tents, the New Yorkers cut down vegetation and "built bough houses to protect us from the dew and sun."[71] While the next day was somewhat cooler, with a high of only 82 degrees, a torrential storm overnight soaked the army as McDowell finalized his plans. July 20 then reached 90 degrees. Soldiers again crafted shelters from pine and cedar boughs to escape the sun.[72]

Confederates were on the move as well during those hot July days. Beauregard's advance elements at Fairfax Court House initially fell back in the wake of McDowell's approach. South Carolinian Dick Simpson, marching with that column, remembered July 17 as brutal. "The day was excessively hot and the road hilly and rocky," he wrote. Worse, they were "double-quicked for two hours . . . having all their baggage to carry." Some men "fainted in their tracks, while others fell from their horses. Some dropped on the road side with scarcely breath enough to keep them alive, but only one man died, he from the effects of sun stroke."[73]

Hesitant and confused, Major General Patterson did little to accomplish his mission in the Valley. On July 18, General Johnston began sending men from Winchester to the railroad depot at Piedmont, intending to use railcars to shuttle his men to Manassas. The line was small, cars were few, and expertise was in short supply. It ate time. Heat and rising dust clouds made the march hard, then near sunset on July 19, it began to rain. The first elements of Johnston's army, under Brigadier General Jackson, began arriving in Manassas late in the afternoon, with more following the next day. Together, Beauregard and Johnston finalized their plans. They would stack troops on their right flank and attack the enemy's left at dawn. A few miles away, fellow West Pointer McDowell finished up almost exactly the same attack plan and began positioning his men in the moonlight.[74] As historian E. B. Long later wrote, the two similar battle plans "could have resulted in both armies going in a circle."[75] But McDowell moved first, with the hot previous days in mind. "The divisions were ordered to march at 2.30 o'clock A.M.," he later explained, "so as to arrive on the ground early in the day, and thus avoid the heat which is to be expected at this season."[76] He opened the attack a little after five in the morning; the sun was already up. It was "a beautiful morning," according to Pvt. Henry Kyd Douglas of the 2nd Virginia, and "clear and bright," in the words of Pvt. John O. Casler.[77] Taking advantage of both surprise and superior numbers, the attack hit the Confederate left and drove it across the Warrenton Pike onto the higher ground beyond.

By midmorning, Confederate units began to break and run near a house on a slight eminence. Home to the bedridden widow Judith Henry, it stood tucked into the southwestern angle formed by the turnpike and the Manassas–Sudley Springs Road. There the Federal advance bogged down. Several reasons account for the loss of momentum. Lack of sleep, exhaustion, incomplete training, confusion due to similar flags and nonstandardized uniforms, and especially the determination of Jackson's unbloodied Virginia brigade all were part of the answer. But Virginia's climate and the weather that day also played a major role. Simply stated, it was already beastly hot by midmorning at Bull Run, so much so that excited rookie soldiers in wool quickly became exhausted. July 21, in fact, was the second-hottest day of the year so far, with the mercury reaching 94 degrees in Washington at 2 P.M. Dehydrated soldiers grew thirsty quickly. McDowell and others noted men slowing down and even halting for water, particularly at the ford at Sudley's Mill.[78] Sgt. Elnathan B. Tyler and his comrades of the 3rd Connecticut joined the battle already covered in dust, with "perspiration streaming down our faces"[79] The Federal attack started to slow down even before Jackson came up.

To be sure, Confederates were hardly immune to the heat. McHenry Howard's 1st Maryland was among the last of Johnston's units to arrive on July 21, rushing from the depot straight into action. He described how "some of the men eagerly lapped the muddy water which stood in the fresh deep prints of horses' feet in the road."[80] On Henry House Hill, according to Lt. John Newton Lyle of Jackson's 4th Virginia, "the blistering rays of a July sun came down from a cloudless sky. The water in our canteens was hot and nauseous."[81]

Blinding, suffocating dust mixed with smoke was a related factor. As historian Mark M. Smith has pointed out, it distorted vision, perception, and even color.[82] "The dust was most distressing," Howard wrote, "so thick at times that it was impossible to see more than a few feet ahead of one, and floating high above the tree tops, so that, as is well known, the enemy were able to trace the march of our column and mark its process—as we did theirs."[83] William E. Bevens remembered "the red dust stirred up by our running" that "made us look like red men. We hardly knew the features of our file leader."[84] At one point, Johnston saw "a heavy cloud of dust such as the marching of an army might make" and feared it was Patterson's troops.[85]

Well into the afternoon, the two armies—dust covered, overheated, parched, increasingly exhausted, and surely dehydrated—fought. Wounded men suffered tremendously from "heat and thirst."[86] Horses did too. Confederate colonel John Lay reported that "two [horses] died from heat and exhaustion; others are permanently injured, I fear."[87] Unit cohesion disappeared. Federal soldiers began breaking off contact, falling back to the rear. In contrast, Johnston's still-arriving regiments kept entering the battle. At 4 P.M., Beauregard launched a massive counterattack. Screaming the "Rebel Yell," his Confederates hit the wavering Union line and drove it back toward Bull Run. Retreating in order at first, the retrograde soon disintegrated into collapse as men ran for the fords and bridges. Pres. Jefferson Davis, who had just arrived from Richmond, desperately called for a vigorous pursuit. Beauregard and Johnston demurred, citing their troops' own disorder and exhaustion. McDowell's defeated army and a second army of demoralized civilian sightseers streamed back toward Washington.[88]

Along with factors usually discussed, heat played a significant role in the outcome of the First Battle of Manassas. Weather likewise shaped the retreat of McDowell's defeated army and the decision not to pursue them. The retreat itself that night would never be forgotten by those who experienced it. Exhaustion and defeat gave it a bitter taste, but so did the fickle weather. It started to rain hard, with almost an inch and a half falling before the storm ended on July 23. "It was a weary, painful night," Chaplain Woodbury affirmed, "the road seemed to stretch on and on. . . . Still we pressed on, and soon after the dawn, which broke cloudy, rainy, and uncomfortable, the waters of the Potomac and the city of Washington appeared."[89] For some, the retreat was almost too much to bear. "Many times I sat down in the mud determined to go no further," Corporal Rhodes admitted, "and willing to die to end my misery."[90] Businessman Charles Lewis Francis watched the broken army enter the city, afraid "that the existence of the nation was in its greatest peril. To render it worse, that direful day was dark and gloomy, and it rained in torrents."[91]

Back at Manassas, "hard rain" awakened jubilant but bone-tired Confederates. Creek beds flooded and roads grew impassable with mud. Beauregard insisted that any pursuit was now impossible due to "the unusually heavy and unintermitting fall of rain [that] intervened to obstruct our advance."[92] A "slow but steady drizzle" lasted well into the next night. Temperatures declined steadily. Soldiers simply sought shelter. The 1st Virginia made makeshift tents from their blankets. McHenry Howard described taking refuge "under some flat bush shelters" made of tree branches. "Dripping with rain," they proved "worse than no shelter at all."[93] Others turned to another duty. "It didn't just rain it poured all day long the 22nd," John Newton Lyle explained. "Captain White and I went with a detail and buried the killed of the College Company. . . . They were laid side by side in a trench and, as Captain White prayed, the tears streamed down his and our cheeks, swelling the tide of raindrops that beat in our faces."[94]

Rain cleared off on July 23, two days after the battle, but it left deep mud everywhere. Lyle complained that "the rain that fell on the 22nd had wet everything and the place smelled funky."[95] The Confederates cautiously pushed forward to Centreville, close enough to Washington to see the city from picket posts. Northern Virginia remained typically hot and humid, with highs in the eighties or occasionally even the low nineties. Heavy rain set in once again on July 28. August was cloudier and rainier—it rained seventeen out of thirty-one days—but at least slightly cooler, with the last 90-degree high on August 10. Col. William C. Oates of the newly arrived 15th Alabama related the "ludicrous" scene of one of his captains "marching at the head of his company with a great umbrella stretched over him. It had a most unmilitary appearance, but the captain was large and corpulent, a lawyer by profession, unused to the sun, fifty-two years old, and therefore excusable."[96]

Mud was everywhere. Franklin Riley complained of "ankle top goo." Cpl. Napier Bartlett of the 3rd Company, Washington Artillery claimed that "it began to be said that one had to take a good wallow in the mud to make himself respectable."[97] A lack of adequate shelter and raingear became painfully apparent. On the "cold, wet, windy" night of August 23, with temperatures falling into the upper sixties, Riley explained, "outside we wore blankets to keep out the rain. Inside we snuggled under the same blankets to try to keep warm. We desperately need oilcloths," he added, referring to the poor cousin of the rubber blanket, a cotton or linen blanket painted with boiled linseed oil, the best Confederates could hope to obtain from their own quartermasters. "If this is Aug.," he pondered, "what will it be in Dec?"[98]

Much of this suffering was lost on civilians. In the aftermath of the battle, President Davis had declared a day of national thanksgiving. Ministers again pointed to God's favor in providing clear weather for the battle. In South Carolina and Virginia, Presbyterian divines suggested that God's blessing on secession had made for perfect farming weather.[99] For the Confederates in northern Virginia, however, summer weather took a physical and emotional toll.

Dick Simpson wrote a long letter during mid-August's chilly spell, lamenting both the bad weather and the army's failure to manage it effectively. The strain was growing. "For the last four days it has been raining constantly," he complained, "sometimes coming down hard and then dropping off to thick mist. It is such a rain as gives one the blues so bad now that I can scarcely live. Everything seems sad and dreary." As he wrote, Simpson grew angry. "What would you think if Harry for instance had been out in the rain all day and got soaking wet and was to lay down at night out in the yard with nothing but an oil cloth and then sleep all night? Well just such have I done. In the morning I would wake up almost frozen but sound [and] well." Simpson expressed pride, "but there is no constitution that can stand up under such."[100]

Conditions were just as bad for the Federals. Heat felled many. From Georgetown Heights, Luther Furst claimed that two entire companies of the 39th Pennsylvania were down with sunstroke.[101] Cpl. Edwin Birley of the 1st Regiment, Dan Sickle's Brigade (later the 70th New York) described his regiment's march across the Potomac on August 8 "right in the heat of the day the hottest of the citizens of Washington say they can remember for yrs." It was 95 degrees. Thanks to the heat as well as their heavy equipment, Birley added, "there was about 2 or 3 hundred of our men had to fall out several got sun struck and 2 or 3 died from the effects of it."[102] Noting that "it is raining now every day," Captain McAllister added, "we have two hundred men sick from chills and fever." Bad weather and illness had "nearly ruined our Regiment."[103]

But change was in the offing. On sunny and hot July 27, George McClellan took command of the new Military Division of the Potomac.[104] As historian Ethan Rafuse has related, McClellan moved quickly to reshape and rebuild the force he renamed the Army of the Potomac with a combination of ability, discipline, and military paternalism. The major general reorganized the army, reinstituted drill, and began obtaining standardized uniforms and weapons. He also began to deal with managing the weather through providing proper shelter. A new season arrived.[105]

Chapter 2

The Elements Are Hard to Conquer

Missouri and West Virginia, Summer 1861–Winter 1862

Geographically, Missouri is a continental state, far from the oceans and generally free from the coastal effects that shaped the early war in Virginia. In terms of climate, all but the northernmost counties of Missouri are in the "Mixed-Humid" zone. Human geography further divided the state as war approached. Initially settled by southerners, Missouri in 1819 instigated a national crisis over the western expansion of slavery. Along the Missouri River west to Kansas, planters and farmers produced tobacco and hemp using slave labor. In 1861, most of them defied Washington. By then, however, the state also had attracted scores of northerners from bordering states, as well a sizable contingent of German and Irish émigrés. The pro-Union German community was especially strong in Saint Louis. In the Ozark Mountains to the south, another, more localized Unionism held sway. Politics likewise reflected Missouri's fault lines. Gov. Claiborne Fox Jackson was an ardent proslavery Democrat. The state's most influential congressman, Francis P. Blair Jr., was the brother of Lincoln's new postmaster general and son of a Republican powerbroker. Thanks to the Blairs, the new commander of US troops at the Saint Louis arsenal was a volatile Free-Soiler, Capt. Nathaniel Lyon.[1]

After Fort Sumter, Jackson refused Lincoln's request for troops, mobilized the state militia, and asked Jefferson Davis for weapons. Davis sent four field guns, which found their way to the militia's Camp Jackson in the Saint Louis suburbs. With support from Blair, Lyon mobilized a Unionist militia, the Home Guard, and waited to be attacked. On the night of May 9, heavy rain finally convinced Lyon that the militia would not come out. The next day, as skies cleared, Lyon marched to Camp Jackson to arrest the militia and seize the guns. Mobs attacked his men on the way back, resulting in the deaths of twenty-eight civilians and two soldiers. Jackson used the incident to drum up support for secession while creating the new Missouri State Guard to defend the state. For leadership, he turned to Sterling Price, a prominent Democratic politician, former governor, Mexican War general, and enemy of the Blairs. When a fragile truce collapsed, Jackson and Price fled and called for State Guard volunteers to rendezvous at Boonville, a town on the Missouri River in the heart of prosecessionist Missouri. Lyon followed, using steamboats to get his Home Guard to Jefferson City. He routed an element of Price's command at Boonville on June 17, then halted to gather supplies and wait for reinforcements. With another Federal column approaching from Fort Leavenworth under Maj. Samuel D. Sturgis, Price and the State Guard turned to the southwest, hoping to recruit while securing help from Confederates in Arkansas.[2]

The summer of 1861, meanwhile, grew ferocious. Temperatures in the nineties and afternoon thunderstorms—two reliable hallmarks of summer in Missouri—developed. Measurements from Boonville are lacking, but in Saint Louis, the period between June 19 and June 21 saw temperatures rise into the nineties, as did June 25. Soldier recollections confirm torridity. Sgt. Daniel Matson of the 1st Iowa described the weather as "intensely hot." His column halted during the warmest hours. Heavy rainstorms as well as heat bedeviled Sturgis's approaching Kansas column, at times miring it down on the wet prairie. A third Federal column left Saint Louis on railroad cars headed for Rolla, in the southern part of the state. From there it marched to Springfield, led by troops under Col. Franz Sigel. Soaked in a summer storm, Sigel and his men entered Springfield on June 24.[3]

On July 3, Lyon was finally ready to go after Price, although the roads were thick with mud from recent storms. It was 81 degrees in Saint Louis that day and would rise to 90 degrees by July 6. Certainly, the march felt hot. "The oppressive hot weather continued," Matson remembered, "and water was scarce. The regulars had made the boast that they would show the volunteers how to march," he added, but "in the intense heat many threw away their extra clothing and some their blankets."[4] On July 7, Lyon reached Clinton and Sturgis's command. Two days later, Lyon heard the bad news that a larger force of Missourians under Governor Jackson had defeated Sigel four days earlier at Carthage, west of Springfield, on bright and hot July 5. In part, Sigel blamed the defeat on the heat, as well as his troops' inability to eat or drink during the battle. Despite the rising temperatures, Lyon ordered a forced march to relive Sigel. Leaving behind their baggage, his men pushed hard through the July heat, halting to rest dur-

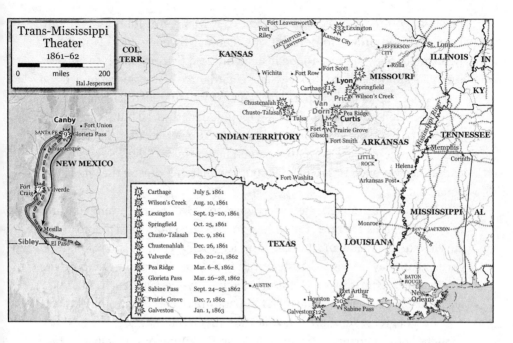

ing the day only infrequently. The regulars and most of the Iowans were dressed in wool, while the others wore flannel shirts over their regular clothing as a sort of uniform. Straggling on a massive scale followed. Intense heat, physical exertion, and heavy uniforms also led to heat exhaustion, with symptoms including dizziness, fainting, fatigue, headaches, and nausea.[5] Pvt. Ralph D. Zublin of the 1st Iowa seemingly described this condition when he wrote that because of the "oppressive" heat and dust, "along the road side were strewed by scores the regulars. . . . Out of our company of 97 men, only 27 marched into camp and stacked arms. Other companies were completely broke up. Of the Iowa City company in our regiment eight men came in."[6]

Lyon arrived in Springfield on July 13. His sick and exhausted regiments staggered in over the next several days. Heat and thunderstorms continued unabated as the new brigadier general plotted his next move. Most of the state was now under Federal control. But because of an overly ambitious operational plan and Sigel's defeat at Carthage, the Missouri State Guard not only had escaped but also in a direction that allowed Jackson and Price to recruit sympathetic Missouri secessionists closer to Arkansas. Heat and hard marching, meanwhile, had left his army exhausted. Lyon too received little support from his superiors in Saint Louis, especially the newly appointed department commander, Maj. Gen. John C. Frémont. Lyon received orders to detach Capt. Thomas Sweeny and his regulars. Refusing to obey, on July 19, he instead ordered Sweeny south to Forsyth, ostensibly in order to confront a State Guard force of considerable size and seize a rumored supply depot. The captain's twisting march of nearly fifty miles, through July heat, storms, and mountain defiles, all but shattered the 1,200-man expedition in forty-eight hours. Hunger, heatstroke, and mud reached epidemic levels. Matson remembered this as "the severest test of endurance yet encountered, in fact but few marches during the whole war equaled it."[7]

The greatest problem was the intense heat. In Missouri, temperatures over 100 degrees are rare. Yet on July 20, Matson claimed to record "Mercury 110 in the shade, most of the distance an open prairie, no water. Men gave out and lay utterly exhausted by the roadside. When the camping site was reached, companies did not average twenty-five men each, in ranks." He probably exaggerated; the high temperature in Saint Louis that day was only 82.5 degrees. Yet there is no question that it felt that hot. The next day brought "rain pouring in torrents."[8] Franc P. Willkie of the *Dubuque Herald* wrote, "sometimes it was so hot that the men fell out the ranks melted by the savage heat; an hour later a terrific thunder storm went howling through the mountains, and apparently so very near to us that one could, as it were, thrust out his arm and grasp the hot thunder-bolts which clove the air like a million enormous and eccentric rockets."[9] Sweeny finally reached Forsyth and routed a few dozen State Guardsmen. Discovering the town abandoned by its residents, demoralized soldiers plundered as their officers lost control.[10]

The real enemy waited to the west. Confederates and prosecession Missourians, not yet united under one flag, concentrated in the far southwestern corner of Missouri. The State Guard camped three miles north of the Arkansas line and three miles east of the Indian Territory at Cowskin Prairie. Brig. Gen. Ben McCulloch's Arkansans, Louisianans, and a handful of Texans were just to the south in Arkansas.[11] Like Lyon's men, McCulloch's had suffered greatly. Rain and flooding on the Red River held up Capt. Elkanah Greer's Texans in the Indian Territory for days. Sgt. William Watson of the 3rd Louisiana, who had complained in New Orleans weeks earlier, noted that the guiding rule now was "to get the march accomplished before the intense heat of the day set." Heat, dehydration, and rugged terrain quickly told. On the second day out, "the sun was intensely hot. Canteens were soon empty.... As the sun grew hotter some of the men began to drop out." The next day brought them high into the Boston Mountains. "The sun was intensely hot," Watson wrote, "and the road was very bad."[12]

On July 28, Lyon learned that Price and McCulloch were united and marching into Missouri, toward Cassville and the main road to Springfield. He decided to meet them head on despite the exhausted condition of his own army. "This would be a major error," historians William G. Piston and Richard Hatcher conclude. "The Federal army was in wretched physical condition, food was scarce, and morale was fragile in many units."[13] Lyon's new campaign also coincided with a brutal heatwave across Missouri. After a brief cooling trend, temperatures topped 90 degrees in Saint Louis every day save one from July 27 through August 7, rising to 100 degrees on August 1 and a blistering 103 degrees on August 4. The temperature two days later was 100 degrees—105 degrees according to a newspaper report—and fifteen people in the city had died due to heat.[14]

On that torrid August 1, Lyon's hungry and road-weary men stumbled west. The Army of the West covered ten miles before camping for the night in the hills along Wilson Creek. Seven miles to the west, the Confederates and Missourians rested as their commanders discovered Lyon's approach. The day that followed, August 2, tested both armies as never before. After "a bright beautiful morning," the weather grew blistering hot.[15] Temperatures hit 110 degrees according to Matson, a reading that would near all-time recorded highs in Missouri if accurate. Half rations, diarrhea, and dehydration added to the discomfort. Heat exhaustion and its more dangerous corollary, heatstroke, appeared in the column, the latter bringing with it confusion and life-threatening stress to the heart and brain.[16]

Lyon's army finally came unglued in the heat. Thomas Knox of the *New York Herald* explained what happened: "The day of the march to Dug Spring was one I shall never forget.... [I]n a vain search for water, I fell behind the column as it marched slowly along. As I moved again to the front, I passed scores of men who had fallen from utter exhaustion. Many were delirious, and begged piteously for water in ever so small a quantity. Several died from excessive heat, and others were for a long time unfit for duty." At length, Knox found the spring along a shady road. In an effort to drink, desperate soldiers tore the springhouse from its foundations and threw it aside. When the main body came up, "the men caught sight of the crowd at the spring, [and] the lines were instantly broken. At the spring, officers and men were mingled without regard to rank, all struggling for the same object. A few of the former, who had been fortunate in commencing the day with full canteens, attempted to bring order out of chaos, but found the effort useless." The 1st and 2nd US Infantry Regiments attracted special notice. Some soldiers desperately turned to a hog trough and then a "scum-covered pool . . . where cattle and hogs were allowed to run." Human feet turned that pool to mud, but men continued to drink. "An officer tendered a five-dollar gold piece for the contents of [a] canteen, and found his offer indignantly refused. To such a frenzy were men driven by thirst that they tore up handfuls of moist earth, and swallowed the few drops of water that could be pressed out."[17]

Little more than a mile away, the advanced elements of both armies collided. Parched scouts from the Missouri State Guard had ridden all morning "against the burning rays of a hot sun," according to Guardsman Peter D. Lane. Many had lost their hats "and now came riding up with handkerchiefs tied around their heads to shelter them from the burning rays of the sun." Thirsty and already worn out at 10 A.M., "almost melting in the hot and sultry sun," the secessionists attacked, hoping to seize the spring. They failed. Lane lamented that he had to "forego the pleasure of a cool drink of water from those springs, and [we were] compelled, like the lion in the combat with the mastiffs, to save ourselves by flight. This we did, and returned toward the main forces some ten miles south. . . . We now began to suffer from the want of water," he continued, still "almost melting in the hot and sultry sun. I chewed several bullets until they crumbled in my mouth, but still I perspired almost in streams."[18]

At the end of the day, the Federals controlled the water, but the encounter shook Lyon's confidence. His little army was on the verge of collapse. After initially pushing on, he decided to retreat to Springfield, reversing his course on August 4 as temperatures climbed to their pinnacle. Mc-Culloch, in overall command of the southern army, pursued. The next day, the mercury again reportedly rose to 110 degrees as the Federals stumbled back toward Springfield in clouds of road dust. McCulloch followed as far as Wilson Creek, content to control the water supply. Price reported that the heat and dust had left his men unable to walk.[19]

Well watered and shaded, soldiers tried to recover while McCulloch and Price argued. On August 9, McCulloch finally agreed to attack Lyon at Springfield before the Yankees could slip away to Rolla. He called for a night march to begin at 9 P.M. "Just before nine," William Watson remembered, "the sky had become clouded, and a few drops of rain were falling."

Another thunderstorm seemed to be brewing. This brought sudden indecision at headquarters. Many of McCulloch's men lacked cartridge boxes and carried their ammunition in cloth haversacks or even their pockets. Others were equipped with flintlocks, prone to misfire in wet weather. Never enthusiastic about the attack, McCulloch claimed that he would arrive at the field with powder too wet to ignite. He delayed the assault.[20] It soon became obvious that the Texan had overreacted. Light rain continued for another two hours and then stopped. William Watson wrote that "the night became fine, [but] nothing was said about marching."[21] There would be much second guessing later. "If it had not rained on the evening of August 9 and stopped us," Bugler Douglas Cater of the 3rd Texas Cavalry complained, "we would have made a night's march and attacked the enemy as Springfield at daylight August 10th."[22]

But as it was, the southern army tossed and turned on its arms while Lyon seized the initiative. To be sure, the command situation in Springfield was equally dicey. Unwilling to march away without a fight, Lyon had lingered in Springfield, trying to decide what to do next while his troops rested. When he learned of McCulloch's position, he planned a night attack of his own for the wee hours of August 7. But when his advance units moved too slowly, he fell back to Springfield, afraid of losing the element of surprise. John Schofield alleged that Lyon was on the edge of mental collapse and had canceled the attack due to premonitions. If so, on August 8, he saw a new vision, for he boldly disregarded the counsel of almost all of his officers and refused their advice to fall back to Rolla. Instead, he drew up plans to move against McCulloch after dark on August 9—ironically, the same night that McCulloch had planned to attack Lyon. His battle plan came from Sigel, who would lead 1,200 men into the Confederate rear while Lyon and the rest of the army marched down the Wire Road before turning south into the enemy camp. McCulloch would find himself within the Army of the West's pincers. With the regulars in the van, Lyon's column marched at 6 P.M. into a setting sun and clouds of dust. They remained dry as rain pelted their foes in the distance. The night was dark, illuminated only by a crescent moon. At about 1 A.M., the Federals saw the firelights of the southern camp.[23]

"With glittering bayonets flashing in the morning sun," Lyon attacked at first light and achieved a complete surprise.[24] His troops seized the dominant high ground and pushed the enemy down the opposite slope. McCulloch and Price were discombobulated at first and further confused by the phenomenon of acoustic shadow, or sound refraction. Usually caused by some combination of ground absorption, wind direction, wind shear, temperature inversion, and rolling terrain, acoustic shadow can deaden sound on parts of a field and amplify it elsewhere by refracting sound waves either into the upper atmosphere or toward the ground. The southern commanders struggled to mount a response. But timely Confederate artillery fire fixed Lyon on the high ground—known ever after as Oak Hill, or Bloody Hill—and Price mounted the first in a series of three counterattacks between 6:30 and 7 A.M. At about 9:30 A.M., Lyon fell. McCulloch, meanwhile, directed some of his men to assist Price while leading others against Sigel, who had attacked the southerners' rear on schedule, driven aside limited opposition, and was pushing hard toward the main fight in column. McCulloch's counterattack was devastating. The tired Federal brigade disintegrated and fled in disarray, its commander included.[25] "The sun was now out bright and hot," Watson wrote, "and the dust and smoke were stifling. Our men, parched with thirst, drank and filled their canteens." His men briefly rested, McCulloch now moved on Bloody Hill. "The sun was now intensely hot," Watson continued, "and the men were considerably fatigued, but they pressed on."[26] On the hill, ammunition was low, canteens were empty, and the day grew hotter. Sturgis, commanding the army after Lyon's death, fought off one last attack and then, just before noon, decided to withdraw to Springfield. The Battle of Wilson's Creek was over.[27]

The Confederates helped bury the dead, a repugnant process in the heat. "By the early part of the forenoon" of August 19, Watson wrote, "the sun got intensely hot, and some of the bodies began to show signs of decomposition, and the flies became intolerable, and the men could stand it no longer."[28] Desperate to deal with the smell, soldiers dumped bodies in sinkholes or simply left them for wild animals. In Springfield, Sturgis handed command to Sigel, who retreated to Rolla. McCulloch and Price paroled their prisoners to save food and parted, McCulloch marching back into Arkansas and Price heading toward Kansas. Eventually, on September 20, he captured Lexington, Missouri, after a week-long siege.[29] The weather remained "excessively warm," according to cavalryman Pvt. Ephraim Anderson of the State Guard. Pursuing "Jayhawkers" on September 2, he remembered that "we were very thirsty, and drank water, with a relish, so muddy that our horses would scarcely touch it." Thunderstorms left the roads "in a miserable condition, obstructing the progress of our train very much." Reaching Lexington, however, Anderson noted a change: "It was now the middle of September—the summer was gone—the rich green foliage of the forest was putting on the mellow tint of autumn."[30]

~~~

Climate and weather, meanwhile, determined quite a different campaign back east. McClellan's departure for higher command did not stall the war in the future West Virginia. In Wheeling, Unionist leaders established a "restored" loyal Virginia state government in July. The new legislature subsequently passed a new-state ordinance and called for popular ratification in October. Any chance of successfully creating a new state required holding on to the occupied northwestern counties while extending Federal occupation farther south. The signs were hopeful. After Rich Mountain, McClellan's replacement, Brig. Gen. William Rosecrans, controlled the Monongahela River valley and had extended his lines south to sprawling Cheat Mountain in Pocahontas County. There Col. Joseph J. Reynolds commanded a brigade protecting the main road into the Shenandoah. The countryside was rough, hilly, and forested. Rain typically was frequent.

In July, Brig. Gen. Jacob Dolson Cox opened a second front, driving his wing of the Federal army up the Kanawha River from the Ohio to Charleston. He moved on to Gauley Bridge, an imposing natural fortification where the New and Gauley Rivers form the Kanawha. Retreating steadily from Cox, Brig. Gen. Henry A. Wise, a former Virginia governor, and his poorly equipped Confederates fell back to beyond Sewell Mountain in Greenbrier County. Wise spent most of his time arguing with another former Virginia governor, the even more inept Brig. Gen. John B. Floyd. Like Wise, Floyd commanded a small Confederate army, his positioned recklessly forward across the Gauley. He blamed Wise for the lack of cooperation that would have given the combined Confederates a numerical advantage against Cox.[31]

Saving western Virginia for the Confederacy required taming the prima donna generals, uniting Confederate forces, and stopping Cox and Rosecrans before reversing their advances. Jefferson Davis turned to Gen. Robert E. Lee. The president hoped that Lee could coordinate the two ex-governors in a combined movement against Cox while checking Rosecrans. Geographically, Lee's new command encompassed a line of rugged mountain posts arcing from Wise's base at Sewell Mountain north to near Cheat Mountain. It shielded the Shenandoah Valley to the east and the vital Virginia and Tennessee Railroad to the south. Cognizant of recent losses, Richmond diverted several thousand reinforcements from Virginia and Tennessee to Lee's command. Most ended up going to Brig. Gen. William Wing Loring, who had replaced Garnett, at Huntersville.[32]

The reinforcements encountered steep roads that wore them down and incessant, almost daily rain that commenced during the last week in July. Cheat Mountain, in the words of historian Hunter Lesser, was "legendary" for its rainfall and cool summer weather. Rain, mud, and extreme temperatures would define the next stage of the war there for the next three months. As noted earlier, summers in "Cold" zone West Virginia are usually wet, with heavy rains and flooding not uncommon. Lee's new arrivals discovered that once churned into mud, the region's loamy limestone soil made for difficult marching. Worse, once the earth had absorbed all it could, rain and mud simply ran along the surface or oozed up in tents.[33] "Mountain[s] are very pretty things when you wind along between them on a railroad," Pvt. Richard Waldrop of the 21st Virginia wrote home on July 23, "or even when riding slowly over them on horseback, but to have to walk over 3 of them in one day, through mud & water, detracts very much from their beauty."[34]

The two Confederate commanders on the Cheat Mountain front reacted differently to the added regiments as they arrived. Pvt. John H. Worsham of the 21st Virginia remembered Loring complaining that "they were a fine looking body of men, but not soldiers." What made men real soldiers, Loring boomed, was the ability to endure bad weather in the field.[35] In contrast, Lee knew how to win their affections. Unable to persuade Loring to act, Lee left him at Huntersville on August 6 and rode ahead twenty-eight miles to Valley Mountain, the obvious staging area for any movement against Cheat Mountain. There his concern and willingness to share their burdens, including the rain and mud, impressed the men. Worsham remembered a guard who "took a seat on a log, thinking he could protect himself and his gun from the rain better in that position." Caught and accused of sleeping at his post, the private faced execution until Lee counseled leniency. After all, he said, any one of them might have done the same under the circumstances.[36]

Worsham interpreted the soldier's story as an example of Lee's Christian kindness, but the general's letters suggest that Lee was simply being honest. From the outset, he regarded the campaign as a "forlorn hope expedition." Nothing he saw in the depressingly rainy mountains subsequently did much to change his troubled mind. His men were hungry, poorly clad, and often sick. As August passed by, the general grew sick of the constant storms. "There surely is no lack of moisture at this time," he lamented to his wife on August 9. "It has rained, I believe, some portion of every day since I left Staunton. Now it is pouring, and the wind, having veered around to every point on the compass, has settled down to the northeast."[37]

Conditions were much the same nearby. "The rains had set in and seemed almost incessant," Pvt. Thomas Head of the 16th Tennessee remembered. "The ground on which the regiment encamped was marshy and damp, and the men, weary of the long and arduous march just completed, began to fall sick, and many of them died. The weather became damp and cold, and it rained continually. . . . [M]any of the men died of malarial and typhoid fevers."[38] Col. Robert Hatton of the 7th Tennessee blamed "excessive, continued rains, flooding our camp, wetting the men and every thing in their tents," for rampant illness. High water ran through his own tent several times, "once, to the depth of six inches." The shelters began to mildew and rot.[39]

On August 14, the rain finally stopped, only to be followed by the first of several unexpected cold snaps. Early autumns are the norm in West Virginia, but below-freezing temperatures usually commence in late September, if not October.[40] Yet in 1861, temperatures fell to below freezing on August 14 as ice formed all around Valley Mountain. "We have Winter on us, this morning," Hatton wrote incredulously. "The rain has ceased, at least, temporarily, and the wind is blowing as cold as is usual in Tennessee in November. Have not known a more sudden change in temperature. Yesterday, it was raining and warm. In the evening, growing cold, but continuing to rain; by midnight, it was so cold that I got up and piled on top of my cot, all my coats and pants, to keep from getting cold." August 18 brought a warming trend but also more rain. "To-day, has been exceedingly wet again," Hatton moaned. It "has rained all day, making the roads worse and worse. It is a hard case on us, indeed. . . . It blocks our enterprise terribly. Men, we *can* overrun and overcome. The elements are hard to conquer."[41]

At least one Confederate, a soldier in the 6th North Carolina, drowned in the flooding that followed.[42] By August 23, the 7th Tennessee's campsite was so flooded that Hatton rode high into the mountains looking for another spot. "A Tennessee hog pen would scarcely be more uncomfortable, as a location," he observed. "We will move, this evening, if it will but stop raining long enough. For the last three weeks, we have had only three days without rain. It is raining now—has been since daylight. When it will cease, there is no calculating. Our men—officers and all—are blue at the balk in our enterprise, occasioned by the rain."[43]

Federal soldiers, no less than the Confederates, found themselves "blue" and worse due to the incessant rain and cold. On August 13, snow amazingly fell on top on Cheat Mountain. For Col. John Beatty and the men of his 3rd Ohio, the weather could have been deadly. On the "quiet, orderly little" Elk River near Rich Mountain, the Ohioans not only had camped near its bank but also "allowed it to circle our sick and wounded" on an island midstream. All was well until around noon on August 19, the second day of rain after the brief dry spell. The river began to rise rapidly, roughly a foot an hour. At 4 P.M., branches, logs, and trees raced downstream. Two hours later, high water almost reached the regimental hospital tent on the island. "Thirty or more boys stripped, swam to the island, and removed the hospital to higher ground" nearby, Beatty remembered, but they could not bring the sick and wounded back across the water. Within an hour, the new site was nearly inundated, while "logs, brush, green trees, and all matter of drift went sweeping by at tremendous speed." Beatty sent wagons across the river, using a launching point upstream to account for the violent current; chained the wagons together; staked them to the ground; and then placed his sick and wounded on top of them. One team of horses drowned in the effort. The colonel climbed a tree. "It was now quite dark," he continued. "Not more than four feet square of dry land remained of all our beautiful island; and the river was still rising. We watched the water with much anxiety. At ten o'clock it reached the wagon hubs, and covered every foot of ground; but soon after we were pleased to see that it began to go down a little."[44]

A break in the weather finally came on August 24. Confederate commanders began to hope that the roads would dry out enough for a movement "before the snow catches us," as Hatton explained. The pace of activity picked up. Officers held inspections, and scouts pushed forward to Union lines.[45] But the rain was not over after all; on August 27, it started up yet again.[46] The next day, the 16th Tennessee moved forward "through torrents of rain, through mud and through branches of water" to Big Spring.[47] "You may be surprised, hot as it is with you, at my talking of winter quarters," Lt. Ham Chamberlayne of the 21st Virginia wrote to his family, "but it is fall weather with us & the roads are almost impassable now. The rains have been, I may say, incessant & heavy wagons travel the roads perpetu- ally."[48]

On August 29, a deeply melancholy Lee lamented that "it rains here all the time, literally. There has not been sunshine enough since my arrival to dry my clothes. . . . It is raining now, has been all day, last night, day before, and day before that, etc. etc. . . . It is quite cool too. I have on all my winter clothes and am writing in my overcoat. All the clouds seem to concentrate over this ridge of mountains, and by whatever wind they are driven, give us rain." When he wrote his wife again on September 1, the weather still consumed him. "It must be quite cold there now, judging from the temper- atures here," he observed, "and has been raining in these mountains since July 24th. . . . The constant cold rains, with no shelter but tents, have ag- gravated [the measles]. All these drawbacks, with impassable roads, have paralysed our efforts."[49]

The last consideration was the most paramount. Rain was more than a depressing annoyance. Bad roads and undelivered supplies prevented Lee from attacking the outnumbered Federals at Cheat Mountain. Supply wag- ons sank up to their axles and could not move. Flooded fords were impass- able. John Worsham described teamsters who asserted that "it was hard for them to haul from Millboro (sixty miles away) any more than it took to feed their teams back and forth. I saw dead mules lying in the road with nothing but their ears showing above the mud." Because of the rain and the bad roads, Lee could not clothe and feed his men, who had to forage the inundated countryside for blackberries, chickens, and occasionally corn.[50]

As a new month began, the rain finally seemed to stop for good, except for occasional storm. "Here the fall begins to come in earnest," Chamber- layne wrote. "We have had such cool fair weather as greatly to benefit the sick, dry the roads and many ways expedite some movement."[51] Yet as late as September 9, the roads remained bad. Lee worried that "the weather is still unfavorable to us. The roads, or rather tracks of mud, are almost im- passable and the number of sick large."[52] Nonetheless, he believed that he could wait no more. On the previous day, September 8, he had ordered his six brigades, about 5,000 men in all, to draw ammunition and prepare to march to Cheat Mountain. His complicated plan involved five separate bri- gade movements and three coordinated attacking columns moving against Reynolds's brigade, which was divided between the fort on the summit and the Elk River valley camps. Because of the distances and assignments

involved, as well as the terrain and the state of the roads, the first Confederate column marched on September 9, but others were not to leave camp
until the next day or even as late as the eleventh.[53] With all five brigades in
position, the surprise attack would commence at dawn on September 12.

At first, the weather cooperated. "Something getting out of order with
the clouds," a member of the 16th Tennessee wrote, "it did not rain on us
that night, to the astonishment of all."[54] The morning of September 10
was "bright and beautiful," according to Thomas Head. "The valley was
wrapped in a dense fog," he went on, "which extended to a certain uniform
height, presenting to the view of the beholder the appearance of a vast lake
or sea, out of which the different hill tops emerged at irregular intervals as
islands."[55] But nature remained as much Lee's nemesis as the Union army.
After eleven straight dry days, torrential rains returned on the morning
of the eleventh, the worst possible time. Rain bedeviled the Confederate
march all day, as men stumbled up and down slick mountain paths or silently followed local guides through wet thickets and deep mud holes. Col.
Albert Rust's lead attack column lurched through the wet darkness toward
the jump-off point, with soldiers holding on to the jacket or belt of the next
man in front in hopes of not falling. Men and mules slipped anyway and
plowed down hillsides. When night fell, darkness overwhelmed the attackers as they tried to sleep on wet and even flooded ground. A Tennessean
wrote that "the windows of the heavens were wide open, and rain in torrents fell as it never fell before since the flood." To cap the scene, an angry
bear wandered into camp seeking shelter.[56]

September 12 dawned cold and exceedingly foggy. The men of the 16th
Tennessee, "having flint-lock muskets, which had been loaded the evening
before," woke up to discover that "the loads had become wet" and had to
be extracted from the barrels. A few fired their weapons to clear them,
which would have ruined the surprise had the Federal garrison heard them
across the deep, wet woods.[57] Other weather-related problems quickly developed. Rust was to launch the attack at dawn, the other Confederate
columns responding to the sound of his gunfire with their own advances
to the summit. But as Lee approached with the main column, skirmishing
broke out in the thick fog at a critical crossroads. The Confederates drove
in the pickets but, in so doing, alerted the Union force. Inside the rude fort,
infantrymen, gunners, musicians, teamsters, and sutlers grabbed weapons
and took up positions. In contrast, Rust took until long after sunup to get
his wet and weary men in line, "notwithstanding the rain." Skirmishing his

way to the fort with depleted numbers—many men had thrown down their equipment and fled after first encountering the enemy—the colonel judged it too heavily defended. Hearing tall tales from prisoners that depicted the summit as a veritable Sebastopol, Rust retreated without informing Lee. Around 10 A.M., with still no signal from the attackers, Lee realized that something had gone awry and ordered a withdrawal. A spoiling attack from the fort reinforced the confusion. The third Rebel column never moved at all. So ended the Battle of Cheat Mountain.[58]

Unwilling to give up, Lee fell back a few miles but hovered nearby until September 17, still searching for a way to turn the position. Skirmishing continued. Conditions remained the same.[59] With a reference to the book of Exodus, Sgt. Walter Clark of the 1st Georgia wryly wrote that "night comes in cold and drizzly and starless. No fire is allowed by the officer of the guard. Standing alone on an outpost in Egyptian darkness and numbed with cold, while the muffled patter of raindrops on the fallen leaves continually suggests the stealthy footfall of an approaching foe, I reach the conclusion that it subjects a man to some inconvenience to die for his country."[60]

The Federals on Cheat Mountain assumed that the campaign would continue on into the winter and foraged accordingly. Instead, Lee retreated to Valley Mountain on September 18. A week later, he headed south to join Floyd and Wise, leaving only a token rear guard. The Confederate war effort had gone equally bad in the muddy southern counties and required immediate attention. August had been just as rainy, and Wise in particular had complained about incessant rain and the illness that seemed to follow. Equally concerned about what he viewed as Floyd's incompetence, he had refused to heed that general's calls to join him at a point where they would have to fight with a wide river at their backs. On September 10, just as Lee's army moved into position at Cheat Mountain, Cox launched a series of assaults against Floyd's muddy entrenchments at Carnifex Ferry. Floyd retreated across the river that night, blaming Wise. The two generals promptly launched an ugly new phase of finger-pointing that dragged in both President Davis and the man now disparaged in Richmond as "Granny Lee."[61]

The weather remained rainy. On September 22, Maj. Rutherford Hayes of the 23rd Ohio described a "cold, drizzly, suicidal morning." While he was "healthy and independent of weather," his men were weary of living on "wet ground, under wet tents."[62] Then a Category 1 hurricane known as the "Equinoctial Storm" swept northward from Florida, hit North Carolina on September 27, and plowed up the coast to New York City and Boston.[63] Heavy rain associated with the approaching system struck on the twenty-sixth after a brief dry spell. Men without tents "or shelter of any kind," according to Thomas Head, "groped their way in the darkness to the barns and outhouses of the neighborhood and sheltered till morning."[64] On that same day, Lee wrote that "it is raining heavily. The men are all exposed on the mountain, with the enemy opposite us. We are without tents, and for two nights I have lain buttoned up in my overcoat."[65] Unwilling to remain without shelter, Col. John Savage of the 16th Tennessee housed his men in a nearby barn and burned the farmer's fence rails for warmth.[66]

The Federals suffered worse. Writing from his tent on September 27, Major Hayes described "a very cold rain-storm. . . . Rain for fifteen hours; getting colder and colder, and still raining. In leaky tents, with worn-out blankets, insufficient socks and shoes, many without overcoats. This is no joke."[67] Things were little better at Cheat Mountain, where Colonel Beatty reported "tents . . . waist high in water, and where others stood this morning the water is ten feet deep. Two men in the Sixth Ohio are reported drowned. . . . The river seems to stretch from the base of one mountain to the other, and the whole valley is one wild scene of excitement."[68] J. T. Pool of the 14th Indiana observed that "it seemed as though the storm-king had become angry with the puny efforts of the contending hosts and was about to settle the disputes in the wilds of Western Virginia by annihilating both parties."[69]

At Sewell Mountain, Lee expected the Federals to renew the offensive and was surprised when they withdrew on October 6 to build winter quarters. "The mud and floods have pretty much ended this campaign," Hayes wrote while serving on Rosecrans's staff.[70] Lee tried to pursue but could not. Not only were his men worn out but a new storm also wrecked the roads.[71] "The weather is almost as bad here as in the mountains we left," he observed.[72] "Winter was rapidly approaching," Head agreed. "The roads were bad. . . . The weather was becoming quite cold, and having a limited amount of clothing, and that badly worn out, the men suffered severely and began to fall sick rapidly."[73] Richard Waldrop observed, "I dont see how it is possible for us to stay here" on an overcast October 26, "for even now it is quite cold & our tents afford us very insufficient protection. . . . I dont see what can prevent us from freezing and starving."[74]

In the end, one man did not stay. At the end of October, convinced that the coming winter made further operations impossible, a humbled and graying General Lee shunted command off to Brigadier General Floyd and began the journey back to Richmond. His military career for the moment seemed ruined.[75] Much had gone wrong at Cheat Mountain to threaten Lee's reputation. Leadership failures, hunger, rampant illness, old and inadequate equipment, and terrain all played significant roles. Confederate morale was low, and men fought without zeal. Some critics pointed the finger at Lee's byzantine planning. Outnumbered Federal defenders, in contrast, had fought with the same skill and zeal as they had throughout the West Virginia fighting. Yet most of the participants were adamant that they could pinpoint the major problem elsewhere. "The failure was owing more to mud than anything else," Worsham concluded. "In all my experience of the war I never saw so much mud."[76] Writing his wife, Lee sadly agreed. The "Ruler of the Universe" had "sent a storm to disconcert a well-laid plan, and to destroy my hopes."[77]

As 1861 drew to a close, harsh mountain weather still had one more significant role to play in western Virginia. The Bath-Romney Campaign of January 1862, as Robert K. Krick asserted, was "one of the war's military operations most affected by weather."[78]

During the autumn and early winter of 1861, Maj. Gen. Stonewall Jackson's men camped in the northern Shenandoah Valley, headquartered at Winchester. Their commander had little intention of simply riding out the winter there, however. Jackson took command of the district on November 4 as the weather turned cold and exceedingly windy. Immediately, he sought permission to make a forward thrust west into the Alleghany Mountains, culminating in a quick assault on the 10,000-man Federal garrison at Romney, forty-three miles away. An important hub in the regional road system on the south branch of the Potomac River, Romney was the key to the western approaches to Winchester. Recapturing it, Jackson maintained, would safeguard the lower Valley and his flank as well as disrupt growing regional Unionism. He needed reinforcements, however, and begged Richmond to order Loring's weary troops to him. Secretary of War Judah P. Benjamin left it up to Loring, who finally agreed but with the same diffidence and lethargy that bedeviled Lee around Cheat Mountain. One brigade arrived in December, but the rest remained in place. Jackson grew impatient. In mid-December, he launched a largely unsuccessful raid against the Chesapeake and Ohio Canal.[79] According to one biographer, "a combination of balmy weather, a wish to provide his green troops with more military experience, and a desire to occupy his mind with something else" produced this expedition.[80] His men remembered it less fondly. Henry Kyd Douglas described spending "the nights as well as the days in the open air. One morning our heads were so white by the heavy frost, that like Marie Antoinette such one appearance to have gone grey during a single night."[81] Another soldier wrote that "the frosts here are like snows, and already the ice has frozen in our tents half an inch thick."[82]

Jackson returned to Winchester surprised to find that the balance of Loring's command still had not arrived. Muddy and rainy November had given way to a warmer and surprisingly lovely December in the Valley. To be sure, somewhat colder mountain temperatures, snow-covered mountains, and occasional snow and wind below made for challenging conditions. Still, December proved remarkably congenial overall, a sort of third Indian summer.[83] John Apperson confided in his diary that "the weather has been remarkable good and I hope it will continue so during the winter."[84] Richard Waldrop similarly wrote his mother that "we have had the most remarkable spell of weather for this season of the year I ever saw. . . . [E]xcept for one or two days has been as mild almost as Spring."[85]

That unseasonable weather—possibly shaped in some manner by a newborn El Niño of 1861–62—seduced Jackson. Loring now had most of his force up. Encouraged nonetheless by the favorable weather and convinced that God blessed the expedition, Jackson set January 1, 1862, for the movement west toward Romney. Marching later than planned that day, the column left on an unusually warm and sunny morning. At nearby Cumberland, Maryland, where an observer recorded the temperature every day at 7 A.M., it was already 55 degrees. Sgt. Walter A. Clark of the 1st Georgia remembered "a touch of spring in the air."[86] Many Confederates threw their blankets and overcoats into their units' wagons.

They soon regretted it. The sun disappeared in the afternoon. Around dark, a cutting wind struck from the northwest. Temperatures dropped precipitously through the cold, clear, moonlit night. A massive cold-weather system blew down from Pennsylvania, one that locals later would call the worst in memory. Camped in a hollow near Pughtown, the Confederates watched the wind blow out their fires as they shivered. The weather worsened the next day, with a high of only 27 degrees at 7 A.M. Rain and light snow now added to the men's cold miseries. The steep road grew icy as Jackson's army marched to Unger's Store. The train, carrying cold-weather baggage and food, fell behind. The next day, January 3, was 18 degrees at 7 A.M. Nevertheless, Jackson drove his men hard to surprise a Union position on the Virginia side of the Potomac at the resort town of Bath. Disagreements with both Loring and Brig. Gen. Richard B. Garnett, who had taken command of Jackson's celebrated Manassas brigade—by now called the Stonewall Brigade—followed. Neither man moved quickly or ruthlessly enough for Jackson's tastes. Aside from skirmishing, the day ended inconclusively. That night, snow fell before turning to rain and hail. Two inches lay on the ground in the morning. Lacking tents, the men cut down pine boughs and made rude pens. Soldiers in the 4th Virginia simply built fires and arranged their beds around them. Most slept poorly, if at all. Those who did slumber awoke covered with snow. The 7 A.M. temperature that day was 24 degrees.

Jackson's command problems continued on January 4. Frustrated with his lieutenants, he took personal charge in the afternoon. He led the men over bad roads and through four inches of snow to Bath. When militia failed to close the escape route, the Federal garrison fled safely across the river to Maryland. Jackson's lead elements pursued them to the Potomac, while the rest of the Army of the Valley plundered Bath for overcoats, tents, and shoes. The men in town slept out of the weather that evening, but Loring's regiments spent another night in the field in their pine-bough huts, braced against the wind and burning fence rails for warmth.[87]

For the next two days, Jackson's artillery pounded the Federals across the river while his cavalry burned bridges and tore up Baltimore and Ohio Railroad track. The shot and shells stirred up icy, packed snow into sharp-edged clouds. The weather remained cold, with a morning low of 8 degrees on January 5 and a slightly warmer 20 degrees the next day. Worse, it snowed and hailed again the night of the fifth, leaving the armies mired in six inches of snow, ice, and mud. On the Potomac, the ice erased Jackson's last hopes of crossing into Maryland. Worried about Federal reinforcements as well, he turned away from the river and headed south.

For the men in his command, the march back to Romney was a two-part creeping horror show, divided by a frigid four-day respite in the cold rain at Unger's Store. It began in a blizzard; historian James I. Robertson has called January 7 the worst day of the campaign. John Newton Lyle compared it Napoleon's retreat across Russia. The morning temperature was 26 degrees. Ice and sleet matted beards and exposed hair; sometimes it covered men completely. Some soldiers were barefoot.[88] Steep mountain roads were "as slick as glass," according to Walter Clark. In an effort to keep the train moving, teamsters rough-shod their horses and "rough-locked" the wheels with chains. It did little good. Frozen and frequent creeks running across the road presented agonizingly cold barriers. Horses fell constantly, and riders eventually dismounted. Wagons and teams slid off the road. Soldiers sometimes measured daily progress in yards. Men slipped and broke bones. Others deserted. At night, lacking axes, Loring's command could not even build fires. Jackson's popularity plummeted. Asked where the army was going, Loring allegedly quipped, "the North Pole." Frostbite and pneumonia became widespread; historian Robert Tanner estimates that Jackson lost 2,000 men to illness before he left Unger's Store.[89]

For even the healthy, the march would be remembered as hell frozen over. "The road had become one sheet of ice from frequent marching over it," Worsham remembered, "and the men would march in the side ditches and in the woods where it was practicable. Guns were constantly being fired by men falling, and many accidents were occasioned thereby. In some instances the horses had to be taken from the cannon and wagons, which were pulled by men with chains and ropes."[90] Apperson, meanwhile, described Jackson, "Jehu-like," pushing a wagon. It snowed and sleeted on January 9, although the temperature had risen slightly to 34 degrees. Apperson noted that by the next day, the weather had warmed up just enough to produce mud. The sun even shined briefly at Unger's Store. But it soon started raining again, and the rain turned to snow on cold January 13 (21 degrees at 7 A.M.) as the army resumed its march to Romney. Worsham's comrades discovered that they slept more warmly when they simply placed their oilcloths on top of the snow rather than clearing it away, as it offered some insulation. The next day, sleet fell on North Mountain as Jackson entered the town with the Stonewall Brigade. Over the next several days, the other units straggled in piecemeal. The town was empty; the Federals had burned everything and fled on the tenth.[91]

Flirting briefly with the idea of marching into Maryland, Jackson finally gave in to reality. He ordered the men into winter quarters at strategic points and directed that they build log huts. The general returned to Winchester and soon called his Stonewall Brigade back to the town's relative comfort as well. Only Loring remained to hold Romney. Jackson probably wanted to allow those brigades to rest while the stronger Stonewall Brigade undertook another march, but Loring's unlucky men screamed bloody murder. It sleeted and rained constantly in Romney, and the town's streets resembled open sewers. Waldrop complained of continuing rain, hail, sleet, and snow as well as mud "ankle to shin deep." He sarcastically boasted of his "room with no glass in the windows." Those soldiers not as lucky as him had no alternative but their tents. Some tried to build log huts, but the lack of axes hindered their efforts. A war of words, meanwhile, erupted between Jackson and Loring. Richmond took Loring's side and ordered Romney abandoned. Jackson responded with his resignation, which General Johnston suppressed.

The army in and around Winchester watched as first snow and then torrential rains began to fall almost daily, well into February. Loring's angry men soon joined them, although the general himself left Virginia behind. In the end, the campaign came to nothing.[92] "Many men were frozen to death; others were frozen so badly that they never recovered," according to Worsham, while "many of the men were incapacitated for service, and large numbers, having burned their shoes while trying to warm their feet at the fires, were barefooted."[93]

In the aftermath of the campaign, and especially after Jackson's death in 1863, the general's supporters blamed Richmond and Loring for its failure. Had Loring marched quickly, they reasoned, his men would have missed the worst of the winter while much would have been gained for the cause. This approach, first spelled out by Jackson himself, failed to acknowledge the privations Loring's men had encountered that autumn on the Cheat or to admit that Loring could not foresee the change in weather any more than Jackson. Robert Tanner, in contrast, points to Jackson. Operationally sound, his plan fell apart tactically in the face of a harsh winter. Nor could he work with other officers. Finally, Stonewall asked too much of his men and failed to give them encouragement when the march became tough. Yet, as events in other theaters proved that winter, he was hardly alone. The winter of 1861–62 would see more such campaigns, undertaken by generals convinced that will and discipline could overcome the elements.[94]

Chapter 3

Mud Is Triumphant

On the Potomac, Summer 1861–Winter 1862

"This has been a fine cool day but bright," Horatio Taft wrote from Washington on August 21, "with a feeling of Autumn in the air."[1] For the Bull Run veterans stationed along the Potomac, as well as the new recruits pouring into theater every day, the last days of August and the first weeks of the new month brought transitions in weather as well as in leadership. September is usually a month of pleasant weather in Virginia, and 1861 was no exception. Gone were the gloomy skies, the unseasonable chill, and the frequent rain of previous weeks. Major General McClellan seemingly had brought sunshine with him to brighten the defeated army's gloom. Confederates, meanwhile, thanked God for clear skies and beautiful weather. If anything, it was too hot; high temperatures in the first half of September rose regularly into the eighties, several degrees above the norm in Washington. The fifteenth was hot enough for Col. William Oates of the 15th Alabama to again complain about his captain's unmanly umbrella.

But the heat did not last, as is also the norm in September. The last ten days of the month witnessed another transition. Autumn arrived almost on schedule. Highs fell to the seventies while the leaves began to turn color. Mornings were dewy and nights turned cool, with temperatures dropping into the low fifties by month's end, well below the norm. Men now found sleeping uncomfortable. A soldier of the 20th Georgia wrote his local newspaper that the regiment was using ten cords of firewood per day.[2]

The drizzle and rain of mid-August largely gave way as well. Three days out of four were dry until the dark and gusty arrival of the Equinoctial Storm that inundated Cheat Mountain. Significant rainfall occurred only on the night of September 4 and into the next day, all day on stormy and windy September 17, and during the night of the twenty-second, at least according to Pvt. Franklin Riley of the 16th Mississippi, a meticulous weather observer. Not for the last time, soldier records differed from what Smithsonian weather observer C. B. Mackee recorded in Georgetown. Mackee noted rain on September 5 and again beginning in the evening of September 21 rather than the next day. The differences suggest spotty local showers popping up. Lt. Oliver Wendell Homes Jr. of the 20th Massachusetts complained of marching through drizzle and brief rain on September 18, a day Mackee described as clear. Still, the monthly trend was reasonably good weather. Even the hurricane turned out to be easier on the lower Potomac, although it blew down tents, flooded camps, and left deep mud. Col. Regis de Trobriand of the 55th New York later described wind-blown sheets of rain in theatrical detail but focused on the travails of a surgeon trying to keep his tent from blowing away.[3] Taft dismissed the day as simply rainy and the night as "very windy."[4]

The hurricane aside, September was lovely. "The weather was sublime during this period," Pvt. Edmund R. Brown of the 27th Indiana concluded, "that mild, smoky, dreamy fall weather, known as Indian summer."[5] Most likely an "anticyclone," a large weather system rotating in a clockwise manner and perhaps part of the Atlantic's Azores-Bermuda high, had stalled over Virginia. Indian summers follow when descending warm air creates a temperature inversion of warm air over cold, which works much like a lid on a pan, holding in unseasonable warmth for several days.[6] This first, premature Indian summer of 1861 did not last long, however. October, often the driest month of the year, came in wet and gloomy. It rained seven times that month. More than two inches of precipitation fell in Georgetown during a violent thunderstorm on the night of the seventh, the eve of one of McClellan's grand reviews.[7] Two weeks after the hurricane, Lt. Charles Minor Blackford of the 2nd Virginia Cavalry called the October 7 event "the most violent storm of wind and rain I have ever seen in camp."[8] Union soldiers agreed. Brig. Gen. Alpheus Williams wrote, "I never saw it rain harder, and the wind blew a tempest."[9] The 5th Connecticut completely fell apart. Stragglers on the march tore down fence rails to burn for fires, got drunk, and began shooting. Sgt. Rufus Mead Jr. wrote home with shame that the men had killed about forty hogs, two mules, two horses, nearly killed a teamster, and "insulted & abused the inhabitants all the way." One drunk shot two comrades, killing one.[10]

But October soon dried out. The total amount of rain that fell all month in Georgetown (3.5 inches) actually was typical. Richmond was drier still, with only 1.25 inches, although skies remained dreary enough for the editor of the *Richmond Whig* to describe "cut-throat weather."[11] Nights grew increasingly cold, with temperatures more or less steadily declining until they reached the forties and occasionally fell near freezing. The morning of October 14 brought heavy white frost. "The suffering of the sick men was intolerable," according to Colonel Oates.[12]

Facing the prospect of a cold winter, soldiers began casting about for ways to stay warm. Spooning comrades for their warmth grew commonplace. From Centreville on the Confederate defensive line, Col. William Nelson Pendleton described another expedient, writing home that "these nights are very sharp in an open tent." The initial solution was "to have a large fire before the tent and to leave the front open all night." But soldiers also needed blankets, he added. Officers and newspaper editors had sought them as far back as July in anticipation of winter, often circumventing disappointing official channels. The former priest now appealed to his fellow Episcopalians. "How much suffering must result from this exposure!" Pendleton exclaimed. "How many valuable lives must be sacrificed!" Men with only one blanket would not survive the winter, he asserted. "Give to the cause all the blankets you can spare." He cautioned donors not to send carpets or quilts, however, as they were too heavy to carry and too hard to dry.[13]

Writing home for blankets became a common expedient on both sides. "Blankets are the most needed of anything else," the 1st New Jersey's Capt. Robert McAllister explained to his wife, asking for all the home folks could spare. "One blanket is all the Government allows a soldier. How they're supposed to keep warm is a mystery to me."[14] Other soldiers proved to be more inventive. Adding makeshift fireplaces and chimneys to tents was another common early expedient.[15] Federal soldiers could be more creative still. Capt. Newton Curtis of the 16th New York remembered orders from his colonel not only to add fireplaces but also to get men off the cold ground. "The company tents were raised on logs or frame work," he explained, "two or three feet from the ground, banked or plastered with clay, a floor was laid and a fire-place built in each, so that were comfortable to a degree little suspected by our friends at home."[16]

Lt. Edgar M. Newcomb of the 19th Massachusetts, camped in Maryland, described another common alternative. The storm of October 7 convinced him that he needed to find a way to sleep off the cold ground. That meant building a "double bed." "Two tent-poles, resting on rocks till they were raised 18 inches from the ground, formed the sides," he explained, "several boards (begged, bought or stolen, according to the necessities of the case) formed the slats, and one huge log the pillow. Two ticks filled with straw, and confined within their proper limits by stakes driven alongside the bed, are our feathers." To his chagrin, the bed was so comfortable that he could not sleep in it—he had grown too used to the hard ground.[17]

Other responses were more novel. "We have just finished our so-called California oven to warm our tent," Cpl. Elisha Hunt Rhodes wrote, describing a heating method possibly brought to gold-rush California by Chinese immigrants. "It is a large hole in the centre of the tent covered over with stone with one canal, or passage, to carry off the smoke and another to let in a draft of air. The passage ways are under ground, and we left off the top stone of the oven to put in wood. It works well and keeps us very warm."[18]

By mid-October, soldiers on both sides assumed that they would go into winter quarters and began acting accordingly. General Johnston agreed, but he was unwilling to make the decision without permission from his superiors. He prodded Richmond on that stormy October 7. With cold weather approaching, the authorities needed to decide whether his army should winter in tents or wooden huts. Concerned about the local timber supply, Johnston endorsed a suggestion from General Beauregard to have the War Department furnish lumber from elsewhere. Secretary of War Benjamin read Johnston's dispatch with "deep regret." He had hoped that the general would remain active in the field and find "the roofs to shelter the troops during the approaching winter . . . on the other side of the Potomac." Reluctantly conceding that Johnston did not have the arms or men to invade Maryland before winter set in, Benjamin forwarded a pet plan he had developed with the assistance of two friends of the secretary of state, both government contractors. Once he received the go-ahead from Johnston, Benjamin would dispatch ten portable sawmills. The construction of wooden huts could commence as early as October 21 and be completed no later than December 10, he maintained. As Johnston's biographer suggested, the subsequent meeting between the general and the contractors produced only confusion. Johnston believed that one of them had agreed to provide the lumber as well the mills "and otherwise aid in the construction of huts for winter quarters." The contractors, thanks to a confusing conversation with Beauregard, left convinced that Johnston had decided to have his men build log huts instead. And so nothing happened in the way of shelter.[19]

Johnston's foes also derailed his expectations of a quiet winter. Major General McClellan was not done at all with campaigning. According to his chief medical advisor, "it was the general understanding that the army was not to go into winter quarters" at all. McClellan hoped to move against Manassas in November, before winter set in, if Lincoln would give him the reinforcements from the West that he wanted.[20] When it eventually began, however, that movement was tentative and disastrous. Johnston had left Col. Nathan "Shanks" Evans's brigade upriver at Leesburg to watch the Potomac crossings north of Washington. Across the river near Poolesville, Brig. Gen. Charles P. Stone's Corps of Observation functioned similarly for the Federals; Maj. Gen. Nathaniel P. Banks's division stood on guard downriver. As autumn advanced, McClellan began to consider seizing the fords and ferries, perhaps even capturing Leesburg on the Virginia side. Historian Ethan Rafuse suggests that Little Mac mostly wanted to placate an inpatient northern public with action while demonstrating leadership as his struggle with Major General Scott for control of the army came to a head. Whatever the reasons, on foggy October 19, McClellan ordered a division to Dranesville as a reconnaissance in force. Hopefully, a bold bluff would stimulate a Confederate pullback without much cost. When Stone sent erroneous reports the next day that it had worked, McClellan ordered him to launch "a slight demonstration" to make sure.[21]

In fact, Evans had only fallen back to a stronger defensive position. Worse, Stone misunderstood his orders. He not only launched two demonstrations but also pushed scouts across the river at precipitous Ball's Bluff. Confused in the darkness, the nervous scouting party failed miserably, reporting back that they had found a small enemy camp. In fact, they had seen nothing more than a line of distant trees. Misinformed, Stone took the initiative. Around midnight, with temperatures falling into the low fifties and his chilled men devoid of coats, five companies of the 15th Massachusetts crossed the Potomac. They discovered no Rebel camp. Instead of simply pulling his men back, Stone sent the rest of the regiment across the river to reconnoiter. In the morning, Confederate pickets saw the intruders and opened fire.

Col. Edward Baker, President Lincoln's old Illinois friend and still a senator from Oregon, commanded Stone's right wing. Hearing the skirmish, he hurried reinforcements to Ball's Bluff, using a handful boats to ferry men over. Baker then crossed the river himself and took command. A debacle followed. That afternoon, Evans attacked in force. The Confederates killed Baker, decimated the Union regiments crowded at the top of the steep bluff, and at dark drove the panicked bluecoats into the river. Because of the lack of boats as well as panic, many Federals drowned.[22]

In the cacophony of condemnation that followed Ball's Bluff, Lincoln wept for his friend, Stone blamed Baker, the northern public blamed Stone, and congressional Republicans used the defeat to begin trying to seize control of the Union war effort. According to most historians, Ball's Bluff convinced McClellan not to launch another offensive movement until his army was better prepared. But a more basic factor also was at work. The weather grew miserable on the night of the battle and stayed bad for days. October 21 had been clear, with a high of 60 degrees, perfect fighting weather, but drizzle began at dark. A "driving rain" followed as the temperature dropped.[23] For some soldiers, especially those who had fought at Bull Run, the reason for the change suddenly seemed obvious. "The reverberations of the artillery . . . brought gloomy clouds," Pvt. Randolph Shotwell of the 8th Virginia remembered, "and almost as the last musket shot flashed through the dusky twilight, a drenching rain descended on victors and vanquished alike."[24]

Shotwell pitied the pickets "throughout the whole miserable night and without supper or any sort of shelter from the storm. . . . Oh! chilly, stormy, despiriting day that followed!" Thanks to the "customary cannon-called rainstorm," the Potomac was at "freshet height" and ran "like a mill-sluce." The current washed dead men toward Washington and made the extraction of wounded and dead from the bluff all the more difficult. Burial details accomplished their work in rain and mud.[25] That night, the rain stopped, but then the weather turned "bitter cold."[26] Highs fell into the forties, with high winds that both accentuated the chill and made crossing boats from Maryland to the bluff difficult.[27] Lacking tents, soldiers "made themselves shelter by leaning rails up against something and covering them with straw."[28] William Howard Russell of the Times assured his readers that Washington was safe, as the muddy roads gave "promise of Balaklavian difficulties."[29] The weather continued cold for days, with a morning temperature of 39 degrees and a "heavy white frost" on October 25.[30] In Centreville, Confederates experienced "a heavy frost and some ice. . . . I never slept as cold in my life," Dick Simpson of the 3rd South Carolina exclaimed. "I had three blankets and an overcoat, but I was awake from twelve oclock so cold I could not sleep. I don't know what I will do this winter."[31]

~

But winter had not come yet. In the Northeast, observers marveled at a "remarkable" and unprecedented growing season that witnessed an October without frost as far north as Vermont. A relative lack of rain, meanwhile, dried up wells and springs in New York and throughout New England.[32] In Virginia, temperatures briefly rose back into the sixties at the end of October, although frost returned at night. Horatio Taft called those days "delightful," a word shared by many.

Then another cyclone struck. A mammoth joint army-navy expedition, the largest in American history, was gathering at Fort Monroe to seize Port Royal, South Carolina, when a fierce nor'easter struck on October 28. Four days later, the expedition's seventy-seven vessels were at sea when they encountered heavy gales. The "Expedition Hurricane"—apparently only an extratropical storm by the time it made landfall—had started in the Gulf, crossed Florida, and come up the Atlantic coast, dumping 3.4 inches of rain on Charleston on November 1. It skirted coastal North Carolina early the next morning as the ill-starred Federal invasion fleet sailed into its teeth at the Carolina Capes. Two ships sank, and the eponymous expedition stalled for days. On shore, the fort guarding Hatteras Inlet disappeared for hours beneath the waves. Four Indiana soldiers drowned. The storm surged on northward, flooding the coast from New Jersey to Maine with near-record high tides that destroyed homes, battered shipping, and played havoc with regional transportation and communication networks. In New York, the harbor reached depths not seen since 1833 while the city flooded.[33]

Soldiers stationed around Washington endured heavy rainfall on November 1 as well. Two inches fell that night and the next day.[34] The 50th New York Engineers woke up that night in the middle of a mudslide. "The whole ground on which our tents stood suddenly started for the Anacostia River. We brought up about halfway down the hill," Col. Wesley Brainerd remembered, "and the water rolled over us a foot deep."[35] McClellan described "pitch dark and pouring rain" as he escorted the ousted Winfield Scott to the railroad depot before dawn on the second.[36]

Confederates suffered too. "On the night of November 1 we experienced one of the most terrific storms of wind, rain, and hail that we had to contend with during the war," wrote Pvt. Edgar Warfield of the 17th Virginia. "The storm continued throughout the night. Every tent in the camp except two was thrown down and the contents scattered. The storm did not cease until the afternoon of the 2nd, and during that time the men were without shelter, thoroughly drenched, and unable to cook their meals."[37]

Local showers continued for days. While hardly unusual for Novembers along the Atlantic coast, they still sometimes eluded Mackee's often-cited reports. On November 6, for example, rain fell in Georgetown, but snow fell at Centreville. It snowed again between November 8 and 10.[38] Things were no better in Maryland, where Alpheus Williams complained of "the devil's own weather." On November 5, he described his brigade's forced march to Muddy Branch on the Potomac "in a cold rain and deep clay mud. . . . Arriving at the ferry, we had a doleful position on the muddy banks, crowded with the arriving troops, cold rain, and high winds." Subsequent weather was so windy that, aside from "one or two boats," the troops could not cross the swollen river. Those who had already done so "lay in the mud day and night without shelter and badly provisioned," he added. On the ninth, Williams wrote, "we have had two violent easterly gales with rain followed by high northeasterly winds, very cold and disagreeable."[39]

As if to say a final farewell, a brief warm spell occurred on the tenth. Autumn often produces two or more Indian summers, with at least one coming late in October or early November. Some rain fell, and daytime highs rose into the sixties. Bugler Oliver Norton of the 83rd Pennsylvania found this brief, second "Indian Summer. . . . uncomfortably warm" and the rainy days "every way unfavorable."[40] No one expected it to last. On November 15, the Rev. Henry H. Tucker warned the Georgia legislature that soldiers would die at the front because of harsh winter weather and a lack of provisions. The next day, as if on cue, the *Alexandria Local News* reported an icy gale arriving in Virginia from the northwest.[41]

The weather turned clear and cold again, much to the discomfort of the men. "My fingers are so still and cold that I can't write well," Charles Brewster explained, "it is a regular blustering windy November day and although the sun shines as brightly as in July still there is no warmth in it and wind cuts right through a fellow." With no sense of irony, Brigadier General Williams noted, "we seemed to be just in that point where a constant strife is going on between the north and south winds."[42] On November 24, it began to snow, with a sharp wind out of the north.[43] In Maryland, Sergeant

Mead measured about an inch accumulation. Farther south in Centreville, Franklin Riley measured six to eight inches, followed on November 27 by sleet. The snowstorm ushered in a prolonged round of bad, if inconsistent, weather that lasted until December 3.[44]

~

Charles Brewster noted that "the prospect now is that we shall winter here. The Col has given permission to the men to put stoves in their tents which he refused before."[45] But more than cold weather, it was the bad roads born of the rain, snow, and sleet, repeatedly frozen and unfrozen into goo, that shaped multiple decisions to enter winter quarters.

Environmental historian Ted Steinberg identifies mud as the Confederates' "secret weapon" and the Federals' "public enemy number one."[46] But it was not just any mud. Soils are complicated concoctions of organic and geologic materials shaped over long periods of time by chemistry, geology, and living organisms. Similar looking soils can be quite different than those just a few miles away, leading to an extensive and complex taxonomy. At the starkest, most basic level of that taxonomy—the rudimentary level followed in this book—the modern US Department of Agriculture classifies a dozen basic "soil orders" in the nation. The soil of northern Virginia is predominantly a red clay called "Ultisol," which makes for an especially gooey and deep mud that caused northerners to marvel. With notable exceptions high in the Appalachians, down the Mississippi Valley, in Florida, and at scattered enclaves elsewhere along the Atlantic coast, various varieties of Ultisols are the dominant soils of the entirety of what was the Confederacy west into Texas. They are extensive in humid areas worldwide, have weathered dramatically over time, are acidic to a notable degree, and are relatively low in fertility at any depth. It is the relatively high iron oxide content in that clay that makes southern soil classically reddish or orange in color. In contrast, it is relatively low in humus content. Ultisols also drain poorly, do not solidify well, and get even muddier as one digs deeper.[47]

Union soldiers loathed the South's "bottomless" red clay. When it rained, they just kept sinking, instead of encountering a solid stratum as most would have found back home. With the exceptions of Delaware and eastern Maryland, much of New Jersey, and isolated sections of Pennsylvania (into Gettysburg) and in southern Ohio, Ultisols are absent in the states that composed Lincoln's Union. So-called Spodosols dominate most of New England, upstate New York, and the extreme upper Midwest. They tend to be ashen gray near the surface but are a sandy brown below. They contain little clay and, depending upon location, can be sandy or loamy. Alfisols and Mollisols characterize most of the Midwest. Alfisols, typical to northern hardwood forests and the Mississippi River valley, vary in color from region to region, from black to brown to reddish. While they contain more clay that many soils, they also contain more minerals and less aluminum than Ultisols. Overall, they are fertile. Mollisols, most prominent in prairie lands from Illinois and Iowa to the west, are rich and dark, almost black near the surface.[48]

Ultisols, in short, helped define the Confederacy. They were its true "sacred soil," differentiating it from the North almost as much as did climate, culture, politics, and slavery. And to some men in blue, red-clay southern soil was immoral as well. Historian Adam Wesley Dean observes that northerners as far back as the Missouri Crisis linked southern slavery to wasteful corruption of the soil. By the 1850s, antislavery Republicans were almost obsessed with regional soil comparisons. They regularly, if unscientifically, criticized the South's allegedly inferior land as the end result of backward, slave-based farm practices. To Federals in northern Virginia at the end of 1861—young men who had grown up amid the rhetoric of degraded soil and southern barbarism—the deep, red, sticky mud and bottomless roads confirmed what they were already primed to believe about southern backwardness and barbarity.[49]

Confederates, too, complained about the mud, if without the moral judgments. A *Charleston Mercury* correspondent explained that "in some places, where the 'bottom of the road' has suddenly 'fallen out' . . . some enterprising teamster, with a vigorous 'heighho!' has passed to the right or the left, into some field where fence rails are missing, and taken advantage of more solid ground. In this way, it not unfrequently happens that in a few weeks the turnpike acquires a wonderful breadth." One place in particular, "two or three hundred feet in width, and quadruple that in length, is now all road, and in this weather quite moist."[50]

In Centreville, Johnston had wanted to abandon campaigning and go into winter quarters for almost a month, since before Ball's Bluff. He also had reached his wit's end with Richmond. On November 2, he wrote Benjamin complaining that he had had no contact since mid-October with the War Department contractor whom he still believed was supplying lumber for shelters.[51] Nine days later, Johnston wrote a fellow officer: "I am embarrassed on the subject of winter quarters. I made arrangements a month ago for the beginning of preparations, but was disappointed by the supposed contractor, who gave up the undertaking without giving me notice. I suppose that, on occasion, your troops could make themselves log huts in a few days. Here we can't find the logs where the huts will be wanted."[52]

Benjamin replied with frustration and astonishment, stating categorically that there was no deal between the War Department and the sawmill operator. Indeed, the contractor had informed Richmond that Johnston had "declined his services." Blaming Beauregard, Benjamin had not sent the portable sawmills he had promised because Johnston had never bothered to tell him where he wanted them delivered. Now it was impossible to obtain mills or even milled boards, except perhaps some for roofing. Johnston's men were on their own.[53]

Victims of a blame game, most of the Confederates only started moving into winter quarters around the time of the November 24 snowstorm. Private Shotwell described the central encampment in late November "white with tents" on marshy, red-clay earth, looking for all the world like "a gigantic ant-hill." Shivering in his tent, the bare ground wet enough to emit water when he planted his tent pole, he longed for a warm cabin. But those came slowly.[54] Improving weather, Johnston's occasional hopes for a renewed movement, and rumors of relocations, however, left some camps incomplete well into December. A soldier in the 2nd Georgia wrote home on Christmas Day that Brig. Gen. Robert Toombs's brigade still had no orders to build winter shelters despite the return of cold weather.[55]

To heat those shelters, many still relied on nothing more than big fires outside their open doors. Woodlots and civilians' fences suffered accordingly. William Oates remembered nothing about that winter so much as "the almost intolerable smoke that the oak wood of Virginia, strongly impregnated with alkali, makes at a camp fire." Desperate to warm up, soldiers "could neither read, write-nor converse—you could do nothing but cry and curse or pray, and I am of the opinion that very little of the latter was done."[56] Others installed fireplaces and chimneys made of sticks and daub, stones, or even bricks. Staff officer W. W. Blackford proclaimed nothing so warm as a tent equipped with a fireplace and chimney. There were hazards to such practices, of course. A soldier in the 11th Georgia wrote that several tents already had burned down.[57]

The majority of Confederates eventually built log huts. The hodgepodge of structures that followed reflected their grassroots architectural origins. Describing the "shanties" the 4th Texas built, for example, Pvt. Val Giles concluded that "the style of their architecture would have puzzled an expert. Some were on the hill, some under the hill, some above ground, some underground. A few were large, but mostly they were small." Individual messes pooled their labor and resources to construct a cabin, which sometimes left unpopular soldiers such as Shotwell literally out in the cold. "Mess Number 2 had a high house," Giles continued, "while Mess Number 5 had a low house. Number 3 had his chimney inside, while Number 7 had his on the outside. As for doors (when there were any), they were liable to be anywhere." One mess of "foreigners" dug into a hillside and erected a pine-log front and "clapboard door."[58]

In stark contrast, the generally well-to-do men of the 3rd Company, Washington Artillery constructed elaborate shingled barracks of notched logs that housed twelve men each. They also boasted "a rough puncheon floor, window sash, brought in by parties on horseback from some remote abandoned house and a door."[59] A soldier in the 6th North Carolina wrote home that the enlisted men in his regiment lived in pine cabins, but the officers had cabins made of poplar.[60] Capt. C. J. Cochran of the 23rd North Carolina lamented as late as January 26, 1862, that Confederate cabins were "not good," but bad weather and a lack of lumber made anything better than these impossible.[61]

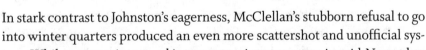

In stark contrast to Johnston's eagerness, McClellan's stubborn refusal to go into winter quarters produced an even more scattershot and unofficial system. While some units moved into ersatz winter quarters in mid-November 1861, others remained out in the cold into December and beyond. McClellan initially remained committed to a winter campaign. By December, however, he had started thinking about operationally transferring his army by water to the lower Chesapeake instead of going overland. While that pushed operations back to spring, as did the need to wait on Maj. Gen. Don Carlos Buell and Maj. Gen. Henry Halleck to make complementary marches in the West, McClellan remained anxious to keep his men sharp. Then there was the growing pressure from the White House, the new Joint Committee of the Conduct of the War, and the northern public as a whole. Accordingly, McClellan refused to declare a public end of campaigning.[62] The men would make-do in their tents, ready in theory to move at a moment's notice. Individual division and brigade commanders were willing from the start to allow the men to make realistic accommodations for cold weather, however. The results were de facto winter quarters, accomplished in piecemeal over an extended period of time and largely consisting of modified tents. It was only in mid-January 1862 that Dr. Charles S. Tripler, McClellan's medical director, finally convinced his superiors that the army's health required at least *unofficial* winter quarters.[63]

Several factors went into a unit preparing more substantial camps once allowed. Choosing the right location was the first priority. While much of that was out of the soldiers' hands, ideal winter campsites were in the woods and sheltered from the wind. Alpheus Williams, for example, boasted that his brigade's camp was located in "evergreen woods, . . . very comfortable located and much less exposed than the regiments of other brigades, encamped on high table lands open to all the high winds of the season." Such sites had to be cleared, however, with the scrub often reused as an additional windbreak. Williams's men "cut out the small scrub pines and grubbed up the roots," leaving "a square completely hedged in, in which they pitch their tents, and on the edge of the square piled up the bushes so as to completely cut off the cold winds." Units might also use pine and cedar boughs, or even transplanted trees, as decoration. Following regulations, officers usually required some semblance of streets and order.[64]

Heating shelters resulted in several approaches. Like the Confederates, some Federals built fireplaces and chimneys. Adj. Mat Richards of the 96th Pennsylvania wrote from Fairfax County, Virginia, that his regiment had traded "tobacco, schnapps, 2 decks of cards & 6 pies" to a group of "Dutch" soldiers camped in a local kiln in exchange for 35,000 bricks to build fireplaces and chimneys.[65] A popular alternative means of heating were small, cone-shaped, sheet-iron stoves purchased from sutlers. The Hainsworth stove, built in Newport, Kentucky, was the most popular. Charles Brewster relished the heat his stove provided so much that he resisted leaving his tent for a log cabin. Bugler Oliver Norton happily noted that the stove in his large, conical Sibley tent not only warmed the premises but also came with two griddles for cooking. One drawback was that the stoves required an opening in the top of the tent for a pipe chimney. That was doable in the wall tents of officers or in small, four-man wedge tents, but not in Sibleys, whose relatively flat roofs admitted accumulated rain though any chimney hole.

Another popular heating adaptation was the "Crimean Pit." This involved placing a stove into a cellar two or three feet deep beneath a tent's wooden floor and then venting it through the top of the tent via a stovepipe. A variation involved placing the stove on the earth inside a tent, then venting the stovepipe down into the ground and horizontally outside to a vertical chimney pipe.[66] Such an exhaust system did not even require a stove. Brigadier General Williams noted a technique in his brigade in which soldiers dug "deep cellars and build regular fire-places, carrying the chimney through the ground under the wall of the tent to some distance away and use the barrel for a chimney."[67] The 2nd Rhode Island modified this technique so that a second trench brought air into the furnace; they even boasted about it in a how-to-do-it story printed in a Providence newspaper that was soon reprinted north and south. Pvt. Wyman S. White of the 2nd US Sharpshooters, however, complained that the smoke did not always go outside, presenting the men in his tent the option of "being made bacon or of staying outside."[68]

As Elisha Hunt Rhodes had done in October, other soldiers turned to variations of California ovens. Increasingly, the high command recommended that system as the best option. In mid-November, Surg. Daniel McRuer of Brig. Gen. John Sedgwick's brigade had first demonstrated a California setup. Dr. Tripler liked the results so much that, with support from division commander Brig. Gen. Samuel Heintzelman, he wrote McClellan's chief of staff (and father-in-law) Randolph B. Marcy, imploring headquarters to endorse the practice. Acknowledging McClellan's unwillingness to construct "extensive huts" that would "give the appearance of going into winter quarters," Tripler enthusiastically advocated the California system as the healthiest means of heating tents. He went on to quote McRuer:

> A trench 1 foot wide and 20 inches deep to be dug through the center and length of each tent, to be continued for 3 or 4 feet farther, terminating at once end in a covered over fire-place and at the other in a chimney. By this arrangement the fire-place and chimney are both on the outside of the tent; the fire-place is made about 2 feet wide and

arching; its area gradually lessening until it terminates in a throat at the commencement of the straight trench. This part is covered with brick or stone, laid in mortar or cement; the long trench to be covered with sheet-iron in the same manner. The opposite end to the fire-place terminates in a chimney 6 or 8 feet high; the front of the fire-place to be fitted with a tight movable sheet-iron cover, in which an opening is to be made, with a sliding cover to act as a blower. By this contrivance a perfect draught may be obtained, and no more cold air admitted within the furnace than just sufficient to consume the wood and generate the amount of heat required, which not only radiates from the exposed surface of the iron plates, but is conducted throughout the ground floor of the tent so as to keep it both warm and dry, making a board floor entirely unnecessary, thereby avoiding the dampness and filth, which unavoidably accumulates in such places.[69]

Tripler soon had McRuer build a demonstration model for every division. Some men embraced it, but a few years later, a proponent sadly admitted that it somehow never completely caught on in the Army of the Potomac, despite its obvious warmth and fuel savings.[70]

As was becoming typical, soldiers could not help but add their own flourishes. Some of Williams's men followed McRuer's advice and placed the fireplace outside the tent. "Most every tent has its fire," the general explained, "which is built in the mouth of a trench in the front. The trench is carried through the tent covered over with flat stones and earth and terminating behind in a turf chimney surmounted by a barrel to increase the draft. In this way the fire is carried under the tent; the stones, once heated, keep up the warmth a long time, and a tent is made very comfortable."[71] Lt. Edgar Newcomb described a similar "California" technology he used that placed the fireplace inside the tent.[72]

True to the popular song, most Union soldiers largely tented on the old campground, but not all. From his vantage point above the Potomac, Texan Val Giles remembered, "the low range of hills on the Maryland side opposite were covered with white tents and log cabins."[73] A minority of Federal units built log structures, despite headquarters' insistence that the army remained on campaign. There was no uniformity; officers often left the men to their own devices, depending on how closely the regimental colonel wanted to hew to regulations. Pvt. John D. Billings termed this attitude "go-as-you-please."[74] "My regiments have very bad tents," Brigadier General

Williams lamented, "but they are making all sorts of huts and warm shelters for winter. . . . It is quite a curiosity to go through the camps and see the various devices to keep warm."[75]

Lacking prescriptions or often even positive orders to build, the floorplans of Federal cabins ended up as diverse and idiosyncratic as their Confederate counterparts. At one end were the ubiquitous hybrid tent-cabin "huts," which Billings described as "stockaded."[76] Late in November and again in December, Dr. Tripler recommended this scheme to headquarters as preferable to simply erecting tents over pits dug into the ground, a common practice he condemned as unhealthy due to the potential for moisture, poor ventilation, and dirt accumulation. "I suggested enclosures of rails or palisades some three feet high," he reported, "to be roofed over with the tents." Combined with California ovens, stockaded tents offered the best alternative to the cabins of formal winter quarters.[77] Some men combined the two schemes, however, including Wilbur Fisk and his comrades. They dug a "basement" two feet deep and then, "in regular Tippecanoe style," added a horizontal log wall to a height of another two feet, "over the whole placing our cloth tent. The basement protects us securely from the wind," Fisk explained, "is quite warm, and affords us a chance to stand erect anywhere within our circumscribed limits."[78]

As Billings noted, the "basements" were optional but made for warmer tents. The walls, in practice, could be anywhere from two to five feet high. Soldiers used mud to fill in the chinks between logs. Again, there were many variations. Men built fireplaces of brick, stone, or wood, depending on availability, or added stoves and attached an outdoor chimney "after the southern fashion," unless bricks were available. "When built of wood," Billings explained, "the chimneys were lined with a very thick coating of mud. They were generally continued above the fireplace with split wood built cob-fashion, which was filled in between and lined with the red clayey soil of Virginia; but stones were used when abundant." Empty barrels became chimneys. Cabins might also include rafters and gables stuffed with tents, rubber blankets, or ponchos.[79]

At the other end of the housing spectrum were elaborate barracks such as those of the 27th Indiana. Relocated to near Frederick in early December, the Hoosiers built 120 barracks, which Edmund Brown asserted were "the wonder and admiration of all of Banks' division." They even became a tourist attraction. Modeled "in a general way" on "the log cabins of the pioneers of Indiana," the ten-by-eighteen-foot structures featured round-log walls chinked with mud and roofs made from split clapboards placed atop stringers. Interior log walls divided each cabin into "seven apartments to a company, all in one row, under one roof." Each "apartment" contained a fireplace "built as our fathers built theirs. There was a frame work of wood, lined inside with stone, laid in mortar and surmounted with a chimney composed of sticks, plastered inside." Most also had glass windows and other features foraged from abandoned local homes. Officers, meanwhile, adjourned to "one-room log houses," some with gable roofs and most boasting plank floors. The regiment's colonel praised the camp, colloquially called Hoosier City, as "a perfect city." Brown later remembered his two months there as "the halcyon days of our soldiering."[80]

In between the examples of the 2nd Vermont and the 27th Indiana, all sorts of other styles appeared. The 10th Massachusetts felled a nearby grove of yellow pines in order to build their own "barracks," sixteen feet by twenty-four feet in size, each large enough to hold forty-eight men, or half a company. Every company had its own favorite plan on how to construct the structures, however, which finally resulted in a hodgepodge of architectural diversity.[81] The men of the 55th New York built low cabins with six-by-six-foot interiors that Colonel de Trobriand described with fascination. They were "log cabins, square huts made of round logs, generally split in two and plastered with mud, which closed the cracks. Upon these walls, three or four feet high, the tent was placed for a roof. A door made of boards, or a rubber blanket, opened to the interior." Crowded with homemade furniture, the men heated the structures with a "California fireplace." The regiment also boasted an officer's mess of fancier design, "which they bought ready-made in Washington." It was "perfectly constructed, furnished with doors and windows, and capable of being easily put together and taken apart."[82]

Despite the labor that went into their construction, the lifespans of many winter camps could be measured in weeks. Again, the Army of the Potomac was not officially in winter quarters. Williams's brigade, for example, finished their log huts and heated tents in mid-November only to be ordered to a new position near Frederick on December 4. Taking advantage of a cold snap that froze the muddy roads hard, they moved only to suffer from "snowing, sleeting, raining, freezing" weather when they arrived. The troops summarily refused to begin constructing new quarters until they were sure they would have time to live in them. Notably, deciding when to build anew was the men's decision; Williams was little more than an observer.[83]

Some units also had additional housing needs to meet. Artillery and cavalry had to create shelters for horses and mules, such as the "good board sheds" of the Artillery Reserve Corps. Not all served well; one report indicates that cavalry units lost two to three horses to the cold every day.[84] Pickets invariably were left to their own devices. Some simply disobeyed orders and stoked fires, sometimes with their officers looking the other way. Adjutant Richards noted that when they could, Federal pickets occupied "deserted country houses" that comrades already had stripped for items useful for their tents and cabins. Although "dilapidated and torn to pieces," with work they became "pretty comfortable quarters." Some men decorated each house with a saucy name, such as "'Continental' 'Death to Confederates' 'Hotel de Whiskey' 'Hotel de Schapps' 'Hotel de Rum.'" At the front, pickets constructed "sheds made of rails, covered with evergreens—Some have put up small very strong blockhouses with musket holes to fire through."[85] Randolph Shotwell remembered pole-and-brush lean-tos from the battle at Manassas swarming with lice. William E. Bevens of the 1st Arkansas sought shelter in a structure made of cornstalks.[86]

December arrived with a vengeance, as a winter storm swept south from Canada. "Snow, sleet, and rain seemed to vie with each other in rendering our situation dreary in the extreme," Shotwell wrote. "Our thin tents afforded scarcely any protection from the elements; but flapped and shook in dismal accord with the surroundings. Few or none of the men had overcoats, most of us had the thinnest of summer clothing without even warm underclothing, while the nature of the soil kept our blankets damp day and night."[87]

Decembers in Virginia can be mercurial and often surprisingly temperate. The apparent advent of the 1861–62 El Niño brought an added element of abnormality. In Georgetown, Mackee recorded high temperatures that ranged from 35 degrees on December 3 up to 70 degrees on the ninth, but overall, half of December days reached into the fifties, including the final three. By way of comparison, Washington's mean average December high temperature is only 46 degrees. Rain and snow likewise held off until three days before Christmas, and precipitation was light even then. Combined with colder temperatures, dry weather made roads rough but solid enough for supplies to arrive, including much-needed blankets and clothing in Union camps. In the Shenandoah, as noted in the previous chapter, the mild weather tempted Stonewall Jackson to move on Romney. In the Federal army around Washington, formal reviews, parades, and sham battles were common at midmonth, commanders taking advantage of firm ground and clear skies. Real blood spilled too, as McClellan launched minor probing operations and skirmishes that Confederates interpreted as preliminaries to real campaigning. While cold nights and morning frosts remained the norm—Charles Brewster noted water freezing in pails after "three or four hours"—soldiers generally described the weather as pleasant, "charming," or "spring-like."[88] Brewster himself thought the weather as "warm as September."[89]

Virginia civilians, meanwhile, expressed delight at what they knew to be unusual conditions. "Did you ever feel such weather?" Susan Blackford wrote to her husband on December 9. "Your mother has roses blooming in her arbors now. I never knew that before in December." Her husband responded: "The weather is the most remarkable I have ever known. It has been perfectly clear for a month and no colder than the average September."[90] In Washington, Horatio Taft dispensed with his overcoat and extinguished the fires in his house. The tenth was "too warm . . . for comfort. The Sun was quite oppressive in the middle of the day."[91]

Unusual temperatures soon regressed to seasonable averages. Rain, sleet, and snow fell on December 22, the day after the winter solstice, with strong winds from the northwest. Although the snow did not stick, it continued into the next day. Bitterly cold weather followed. General Williams lamented the negative effect the sudden weather change had on his still-partially sheltered men and especially the horses and mules, which were fully exposed to the elements. "There will be hundreds of horses and mules dead tomorrow morning," he observed, blaming the government for not furnishing him with enough lumber to construct barns.[92]

At Centreville, ice covered Confederate shelters. On windy Christmas Eve, temperatures only reached 36 degrees at midday. Although the next day was a little warmer, snow remained on the ground, making for a white Christmas in northern Virginia. Giles described "heavy laden clouds" over the Potomac that "hung low over forest and river. The world was wrapped in a white mantle of snow. . . . The snow was gently and silently falling, deepening on the hills and valleys, melting as it struck the cold bosom of the dark river."[93] Shotwell described "a deep mantle of snow . . . over shoe-tops" and sleet.[94] Eighteen inches lay at the picket camp of the 1st Arkansas. Snow fell again at the end of the war's first year.[95]

In Washington, bad weather and the resulting lack of an advance depressed spirits. "The old year goes out today, bright and dry," Taft wrote in his diary, adding that "the boys have a Dark lantern to exhibit. The President looked in at the boys show. Gen McClellan is sick abed. A fight is expected over the River now anytime. The Army seems to be getting ready."[96] Yet aside from Jackson's Bath-Romney Campaign, there was little action in the new year. January 1862 came in windy, warm, and lovely, just as Jackson experienced in Winchester. Men went about in shirtsleeves. The army otherwise stood idle as McClellan's typhoid fever prostrated him. The general's illness worried Lincoln enough that he began to bypass him and issued a flurry of orders to other generals, especially in Kentucky and Missouri. He also fired his corrupt secretary of war, party hack Simon Cameron, and replaced him with War Democrat Edwin M. Stanton. As historian Ethan Rafuse points out, bad financial news, the *Trent* affair and its threat of war with Great Britain, a restless Congress, and Republican displeasure with McClellan put increasing pressure on the president to do something somewhere.

Virginia remained uppermost in importance, however. McClellan's apparent refusal to march assumed increasingly large proportions as Radical Republicans and others, blithely unaware of the realities of logistics and moving men and supplies in winter, sniped at him for everything from arrogance to cowardice.[97]

Many real factors, in fact, prevented McClellan from marching south in January, but weather was central. While January is a cold month in the Upper South, typically the last week of December is the coldest of the year in Virginia. But the first week of January 1862 easily surpassed its immediate predecessor. Just as Jackson discovered in the Shenandoah, extreme cold and snow blanketed the Virginia front.

On January 3, the weather turned bitterly cold in and around Washington. Temperatures dropped into the teens by the morning of the fifth. The Potomac nearly froze over. Both men and animals struggled to stay warm. Lacking boards to build stables, Charles Wainwright's artillerymen hiked two miles each way to cut down evergreens for windscreens. The only measurable sleet and snow in Georgetown and Washington fell on that frigid night and into the following morning, leaving about an inch of accumulation that lingered for days. A few miles away at Manassas, the weather was even worse. Snow, sleet, and cold bedeviled the Confederates for five long days, from January 3 through January 7, before high temperatures finally climbed out of the twenties. Franklin Riley measured two additional inches of snow.[98]

Again, the fickle weather shifted. Meteorologists have long noticed a tendency for a few days of warmer weather to occur in Virginia, starting around January 7. Temperatures in 1862 indeed rose steadily after the first week of the year. Highs reached into the forties on January 9 and hit a remarkable 66 degrees in Georgetown on the damp twelfth. Wainwright likened it to a spring day, and frozen roads became mire. Such thaws rarely last long; that of 1862 was no exception. At midmonth, the mercury plummeted yet again along the East Coast, tumbling back into the forties at midday. Temperatures as a whole remained a tad cooler than the norm. At Cape Hatteras, Oliver Coolidge described heavy gales. His comrades spent days on board ships, unable to disembark, as the winds dragged the vessels along the bottom and began destroying them. In Washington, Taft noted that the streets were covered in ice on the morning of January 16.

Rain and snow followed periodically for the next several weeks. February in Virginia is typically the snowiest month of the year. That held true in spades along the Potomac in 1862, thanks to an apparent series of low-pressure systems crossing the state. In Washington, snow fell four times in February—on the third, eleventh, fifteenth, and seventeenth. Temperatures, while typical on average, fluctuated as well, from a low of 17 degrees on the morning of February 10 to a daytime high of 64 on the thirteenth. Overall, every day save one had a high temperature above freezing, but eleven days began below freezing. Cycles of freeze and thaw rendered chewed-up roads almost impassable. Pickets struggled to remain warm and dry at night, while other men spent their days holed up in their tents. The editor of the Alexandria newspaper described the weather as extraordinarily unusual.

The most tangible result of the constant freezing and thawing were the oceans of churned red-clay mud. Horses fell constantly, wagons mired down, and firewood and food grew scarce. In the capital, mud ran through the streets like rivers; outside of Alexandria, it was axle deep. Bootblacks turned to washing boots for pay. It was worse in the country, where team-sters hauled half loads to avoid bogging down. In an effort to save his horses, Brig. Gen. Joseph Hooker ordered his teamsters to stop delivering supplies entirely while infantrymen "corduroyed" an eight-mile stretch of road with felled trees.[99]

Soldiers searched for new nouns and adjectives to describe the mud. Lieutenant Newcomb likened the area around his tent to a "mortar-bed," while another described it as "treacle."[100] Elisha Hunt Rhodes joked that he was "thinking of starting a steamboat line to run on Penn. Avenue between our office and the Capitol."[101] Jokes abounded about the "Sacred Soil" of Virginia. One of the fullest discussions came from Mat Richards, the ad-jutant of the 96th Pennsylvania. "It is a soil that readily becomes mud," he explained. "The water is not absorbed nor does it even seem to run off—there is no limit to the depth of Virginia mud—it is difficult to find a hard place. . . . The ground is best described by comparing it to a sponge." The end result was that the army simply could not move, whatever the stay-at-homes thought. "Men can't march far," Richards explained, "when they have to fight for their boots." Impatient civilians in Washington who re-fused to understand why the army had not yet advanced, he concluded, deserved "a *muddy* grave."[102]

His targets were clear enough. On January 27, Lincoln ordered a gen-eral movement against the enemy on Washington's Birthday. McClellan responded that moving as the president wanted was both dangerous and unlikely to achieve real results. He instead proposed what eventually be-came the Peninsula Campaign. The general would place most of the troops on boats, transport them to the Rappahannock River, and place his army between Johnston and Richmond. Johnston would have to follow, which safeguarded Washington. Lincoln, distracted by his son Willie's illness, re-luctantly agreed on February 27.[103]

In camp, bad weather continued. Cold temperatures, rain, mud, and dark skies left soldiers and civilians alike gloomy. Oliver Norton lamented: "'All quiet along the Potomac' has become a by-word, it is used so often. Nothing is stirring. Mud is triumphant."[104]

Chapter 4

Blood on Ice

The Trans-Mississippi, Winter–Spring 1862

The Confederacy's founding fathers dreamed of western expansion. Historian Donald Frazier maintains that building a western empire for slavery was "a basic goal of Southern independence, not an afterthought." Southern Democrats had long supported Manifest Destiny and championed filibuster invasions in the Spanish-speaking south. Secession added new urgency. The Confederate constitution included provisions for the formation of new states out of territories. Texas, in particular, became "the instrument of Confederate imperialism." In 1861, Confederates struck out to expand their new nation's western boundaries. As it would turn out, the West's winter weather decisively shaped all three campaigns to follow.[1]

One thrust involved the expanse just north of the Lone Star State, the Indian Territory, formed in 1834 as part of the federal effort to resettle Indians forced out of the Southeast in the 1820s and 1830s. Its strategic location between Texas and Kansas, valuable resources, and manpower potential led both sides to court the so-called Five Civilized Tribes living there. As historian Mary Jane Warde explains, the Confederates tried harder and initially reaped bigger rewards. Family and cultural ties to ancestral homelands now in the Confederacy, as well as a legacy of slaveholding, led many legislatures in the territory to lean southward. Texans further offered to protect the frontier from Plains nations after the US Army pulled out of the region. In contrast, the Lincoln administration's relative lack of interest, coupled with Secretary of State William Henry Seward's blundering statements about the region's white future, caused friction.[2]

But not everyone approved. The general mood was apprehensive. The "Civil War Drought" had hit the territory hard. Sparse rain after September 1859 meant failed crops, inflation, and hunger. War would bring additional miseries. Many older residents, remembering the trauma of removal, just wanted peace. In the Cherokee, Creek, and Seminole nations, old divisions going back to removal further complicated the situation. As for the Creeks, more properly called the Muscogees, the aging political and military hero Opothle Yahola emerged as a leading Unionist who argued forcefully for rejecting Confederate overtures. He attracted other Unionists, including dissident Cherokees and Muscogees as well as representatives of smaller western tribes. Enslaved African Americans fled Cherokee and Creek masters to join him. Having vainly written Lincoln seeking help, in November, Opothle Yahola ordered a hasty concentration of his Loyal Indians at the confluence of the Arkansas and Cimarron Rivers on the northwestern frontier of the Five Nations' settlements, near modern Tulsa. Warde estimates that about 9,000 people complied, including about 2,000 fighting men, up to 300 escaped slaves, almost half of the Muscogee nation, and Seminole veterans of the wars in Florida.[3]

Confederate authorities viewed the Loyalists with alarm. On November 2, Brig. Gen. Ben McCulloch ordered troops into Kansas, telling them to live off the land and operate until the weather turned cold. On November 15, a detachment of Texas cavalry, joined by about 1,400 Confederate Choctaws, Chickasaws, Muscogees, and Seminoles, went after Opothle Yahola's group. Under Col. Douglas Cooper, they caught the slower Loyal column at the Cimarron River near dark on the nineteenth. In the Battle of Round Mountain, the Loyal Indians bloodied the attackers and then set the drought-dry prairie grass on fire before retreating to the northwest. Lacking forage and concerned about reports of a Federal advance into Arkansas, Cooper retreated. The Loyalists kept moving, sometimes through snow and sleet. Some sought shelter in caves, while at least one party dug into the ground for shelter. Early in December, after both sides had time to rest and replenish, Cooper tried again. On December 9, the two sides collided and fought at Chusto-Talasah. It was a vicious and often hand-to-hand affair. Cooper claimed victory but again retreated to regroup. Opothle Yahola headed north to the protection of the Federal army in Kansas (see map 2).[4]

By that time, winter had descended on the plains, with a "howling" north wind and snow.[5] Cooper and Lt. Col. Chilly McIntosh, a West Pointer and son of a leading proremoval Muscogee family, designed a two-pronged operation to trap the dissidents. On a bitterly cold Christmas night, McIntosh found the Loyalist camps. The next day broke cold. McIntosh attacked at noon, captured hundreds, and sent the balance (mostly women and children) reeling northward in small, scattered parties, bereft of their supplies

and horses. The suffering that followed the Battle of Chustenahlah was horrific. First sleet, then a blizzard followed. The survivors trudged through
wind and snow to Kansas, poorly clad and often shoeless. Pursuing Confederates killed and captured some of them, until dwindling forage and ice
turned them back south; one man froze to death. More Loyal Indians died
from exposure, their bodies scavenged by hungry wolves. Once in Kansas,
their agonies continued. Federal authorities at Fort Row were unprepared
for the waves of starving survivors from Indian Territory. Weeks passed
before supplies arrived in hastily laid-out refugee camps that often lacked
tents, food, clothing, blankets, and even axes to cut firewood. Hundreds
more died. Many refugees who had survived the infamous Trail of Tears
in the 1830s described what they had just endured as a second such night-
mare, "the Trail of Blood on Ice."[6]

Confederate Texans' main enterprise, however, involved the New Mexico
Territory. A lightly inhabited realm of rugged mountains and treeless de-
serts, New Mexico extended from Texas west to California. It was the key
geopolitical missing piece in the Confederacy's dreams of western expansion. Southern leaders pointed to the region's great mineral wealth. Without New Mexico, creating a Confederate California and a railroad to the
Pacific were impossible. Worse, Republicans would hem in slavery from
the west and keep it on what Lincoln had called the "course of ultimate
extinction." With secession in Texas, events initially seemed to go the ex-
pansionists' way. Aging US general David E. Twiggs, a pro-Confederate
Georgian, surrendered the army installations in Texas in February 1861
and ordered his troops to march away. Twiggs's actions, damned as treason
in Washington, emptied the frontier forts of West Texas. Moreover, the US
Army decamped just as two years of severe drought forced the area's hungry
Apaches and Comanches to step up their attacks on frontier settlements.[7]

Texas Confederates, along with companies of the proslavery Knights of
the Golden Circle, slowly filtered west to fill the void. They occupied Fort
Bliss, near El Paso, in late June. Troops under the command of the bold but
erratic Col. John R. Baylor then struck north across the New Mexico border and captured Fort Fillmore, built near Las Cruces in the prosecession
Mesilla Valley. On the hottest day of the summer so far, with highs topping
100 degrees, Baylor ran down the fleeing garrison in the Chihuahuan de-

sert. The bluecoats suffered sunstroke, and some even lost their minds in the relentless sun. Flushed with success, Baylor proclaimed the creation of the provisional Confederate Territory of Arizona, stretching from the Mexican border north to the 34th parallel and west to California, with himself as military governor.

Two remaining stumbling blocks to securing firm control over Confederate Arizona remained. The Apaches were a nonaligned third player in a burgeoning tripartite regional war that occasionally spilled over into Mexico. Meanwhile, about one hundred miles north up the Rio Grande, Fort Craig stood south of the northern boundary of Baylor's Arizona, protecting the main road to Albuquerque, Santa Fe, and the massive Union supply base at Fort Union on the Santa Fe Trail. Its commander was Col. Edward R. S. Canby, a veteran officer who most recently had forced the Navajo into a peace settlement. Canby had assumed command in March after William Loring's resignation from the old army. He was determined to hold the fort at all hazards. His patrols regularly skirmished against Confederate horsemen as well as Apaches.[8]

In Richmond, another soldier had his eyes set on New Mexico. Brig. Gen. Henry Hopkins Sibley was best known in 1861 as the inventor of the ubiquitous conical Sibley tent, which he had modeled on Comanche teepees, and the Sibley tent stove, which would keep many a soldier warm that winter. While still in blue, he had plotted unsuccessfully to deliver Fort Bliss to the Confederacy. In a meeting with Jefferson Davis in June, Sibley spun a tale of easily seizing pro-Confederate New Mexico with a minimum of blood and money. He argued that the majority of the rank and file—and indeed most Anglo and Hispano New Mexicans and Californians—supported secession and would join him. From Fort Union, living off the land, a mere brigade could seize the Colorado gold fields, pass through Mormon Utah while recruiting additional soldiers, and take control of California. Willing to take a risk given the relatively low cost, Davis authorized Sibley to raise a brigade of mounted Texans. By late October, three regiments encamped outside of San Antonio in periodically rainy weather.[9]

On October 21, Sibley began marching west on the Overland Stage Road from San Antonio to Fort Bliss, seven hundred miles away. Bureaucratic delays had cost time, food, and fodder. It already was too late in the season for crossing West Texas. Then, there was the question of water. As a rule, the "Hot-Dry" zone of the American Southwest typically receives less than twenty inches of rain per year. In West Texas, however, normal annual

precipitation decreases steadily as one moves westward into higher elevations, from well over twenty inches in San Antonio to fewer than ten in El
Paso. The highest monthly precipitation, moreover, falls in the summer as
afternoon thunderstorms. The years immediately before the war saw even
less precipitation due to the extended drought. Prairie grasslands thus soon
gave way to the dry, sandy Aridisols of the Desert Southwest. Much of the
campaign would consist of slow, dusty marches from waterhole to waterhole until Sibley reached the Rio Grande Valley.[10]

Three days out, as Sgt. William Lott Davidson of the 5th Texas Cavalry
described it, "a blue blizzard of a norther struck us." Prevalent in West
Texas, blue northers are cold fronts that rapidly move south, with strong
winds and plummeting temperatures, as well as a peculiarly dark blue sky.
Reaching Uvalde on the Nueces River, "chill November's surly blast" caught
the Confederates again on the open prairie. "There is no timber to shield
us," Davidson continued, "and the wind has fair sweep at us." Increasingly,
men walked rather than ride in hopes of staying warm through circulation.
Soldiers sickened from exposure as well as disease. Sibley's brigade increasingly went hungry, as did their animals. Apaches stole horses and mules.
Thin air challenged bodies. The first groups arrived at Fort Bliss on December 13. "And now we have marched 700 miles," Davidson wrote, "facing the
north wind in the middle of winter."[11]

Sibley pushed on into the Mesilla Valley to join Baylor. Alarms sounded
as far north as modern Wyoming. Unionist pioneers hastily formed state
companies and regiments, both for home defense and to safeguard the vital
trails back east. One of those new units was Company E of the 1st Colorado, originally recruited to serve in Kansas but now held in place. In mid-
September at Fort Laramie, Pvt. Ovando Hollister described the arrival
of "sober Autumn" in the Rockies, "with his nipping frosts and withered
leaves dancing down to burial, while the wild wind moans their requiem
through the bare branches." Three inches of snow fell on the night of October 9 as the regiment prepared to march for New Mexico, but a delightful
Indian summer followed.[12]

At Fort Garland, along the Colorado border with New Mexico, another
raw unit faced autumn in the mountains. Company A of the 2nd Colorado
left home without overcoats, expecting to be supplied by the army. Disappointed, they had exactly one old gray coat, regularly allocated to the
soldier standing guard at a particularly cold and drafty corner of the fort.
This led to laughable confusion at first, as the officer commanding the fort

demanded to know why the same man was always on guard. His question led to a bit of playful doggerel that imagined nightmares about the coat and the officer's wish that "some pitying soul would take, That coat and burn it for my sake, Or cast its shreds to the winds of heaven."[13]

The dearth of proper equipment soon quit being funny. Desperate to hold Fort Craig, Canby consolidated his far-flung command and called for reinforcements from as far away as California. In Colorado, the new "Pike's Peak" units began to hurry to Santa Fe's relief, but only Company B of the 2nd Colorado reached Canby before Sibley attacked. Weather and climate led to that delay. On February 4, Company A followed its brother unit, taking the shortest road by San Antonio Mountain to save time. Winter struck them there with full force. Ellen Williams, who made the march with her bugler-husband and two small children, wrote that "each day was giving us more difficult roads and deeper snows and intensely cold weather. The frost was severe," she continued; "it broke the king-bolt of one of the heavy freight wagons like it was a pipe-stem—a bolt of iron as large as one's wrist." The column stopped at the foot of the mountain for repairs. "A pail of water brought from the stream and placed in our tent," Williams went on, "in an hour had frozen so much you could not dip a small cup in the centre."[14]

The situation worsened when scouts reported that the pass over the mountains was "already blocked with forty feet of snow." Company A retraced its steps to the Rio Grande, turned into the Taos Valley, and made for Raton Pass, 7,500 feet above sea level. Snow continued to fall, burying tents, wagons, and finally the road itself. On some days, the column could only trudge two miles. "Squads of soldiers would march ahead to break the track," Williams remembered, "alternately changing to rest each other, while others with shovels went ahead of the teams to clear the way for the poor jaded animals." She herself walked the entire way, afraid to ride on her wagon lest it slide down the steep mountainside with her children. When the Coloradoans again encountered deep snow, they remained stuck for a week. Mule teams finally reached them from Santa Fe and dragged the column on to Fort Union.[15]

By that time, the first battle of the New Mexico Campaign had been fought. Aside from Company B's Coloradoans, Canby's regulars and about 3,800 New Mexico militiamen and volunteers had composed the defensive force of Fort Craig. Many of them were of Mexican descent and hated Texans, despite Sibley's recruiting fantasies. On February 7, with conditions turning colder, Sibley put his restyled Army of New Mexico of about 2,500 men into motion for Fort Craig. Skies were clear as the column marched into the cooler "Mixed-Dry" climate zone. Afternoon high temperatures were in the fifties, near normal for the region, but nighttime temperatures ominously plummeted into the teens and on down, reaching 8 degrees at 7 A.M. on February 9 and February 10. Three days later, as the Confederates approached the fort from the south, a storm struck from the west, apparently part of the same general system that waylaid Company A in the mountains. Light snow and sleet fell the next two nights before morning temperatures rose back to the freezing mark and afternoon highs reached into the sixties. Sibley's men were completely unprepared. Few had coats or blankets, many were barefoot, and half rations ran low, in part due to continuing Apache raids. Hunger led to unauthorized foraging. Smallpox thinned ranks. Sibley himself was almost prostrate with a recurrence of kidney disease, which he self-medicated with whiskey. The men lacked enough wood to build fires, forcing them to rely on cow chips.[16]

When Sibley took one look at Fort Craig, he realized that it was too strong to storm. For three days, amid recurring dust storms, his forces tried to lure Canby out. Unwilling to trust his raw volunteers, the Union commander ignored the bait. Sibley then marched his men across the icy Rio Grande and north to a ford astride the Federal supply line near Valverde. Canby now had no choice but to fight. On the cold morning of February 21, with a temperature of 30 degrees at 7 A.M. and snow blowing, the battle opened. It remained cold all day as Sibley's little army thrashed the Federals tactically. But thoroughly exhausted and dehydrated—Canby controlled the river all day—the Texans allowed the Federals to escape back into the fort. The Confederates then stopped to comb the field and loot a store for blankets and overcoats.[17] The wounded suffered terribly. Davidson remembered "hundreds of their wounded . . . floundering in the river and [they] would have drowned without assistance. . . . [T]hey were wet, cold and freezing, and our boys built big fires along the bank to keep them warm."[18]

His supply line now cut, rations running dangerously low, and morale sinking, Sibley pressed on. Wind, cold, and occasional snow dogged the Texans. The column took Albuquerque on March 2 only to find that the Union garrison had removed all the supplies they could carry and burned the rest. Sibley had to feed his men off the civilian population, embittering the residents. The same was true in pro-Union Santa Fe, which fell a few days later. Camped east of Albuquerque in chilly mountains and valleys that marked both the southern expanse of the "Cold" climate zone and the northern edge of New Mexico's Central Highlands, worn-out Confederates grazed their horses but complained bitterly of winter weather. A sandstorm blew through on March 8. Another blue norther followed. Snow fell on March 12 and the next day.[19]

After the cold system passed, Sibley's final attempt at Fort Union began. An advance force of cavalry under Maj. Charles L. Pyron rode out to seize seven-mile-long Glorieta Pass, located at the southern end of the Sangre de Christo Mountains on the Santa Fe Trail. On March 25, Pyron reached Apache Canyon, at the western end of the pass. Snow still covered part of the ground.[20] The next day warmed up, however, and by noon, many Confederates were asleep in the sun. "A volley of musketry fired into our camp," Davidson wrote, announced that a force of Coloradoans and regulars under abolitionist minister Maj. John Chivington had struck. Spearheading a movement from Fort Union, Chivington routed the outnumbered Confederates before both commands backed away and awaited reinforcements.[21]

March 27 remained cold and quiet as soldiers dug graves and rifle pits. The rest of Col. John P. Slough's Federal force came up to rejoin Chivington, while Lt. Col. William Read Scurry's weary Confederates arrived at Pyron's camp at Johnson's Ranch. There they built big fires, having left their own camp without blankets. Only the following noon did the Texans' wagons come up. The next morning, Slough sent Chivington on a flanking movement to Apache Canyon and then moved the rest of his command down the pass. Scurry, meanwhile, sent his men into the narrow canyon, spoiling Slough's plan to catch the Confederates in camp. The two forces collided before noon. The Texans eventually drove off the Federals, but it was a Pyrrhic victory. Discovering the lightly guarded Confederate train in the rear, Chivington had pillaged and burned the wagons.[22] It was a bleak night for the hungry Rebels, as a foot of snow fell on their smoldering supplies. "Several of our wounded froze to death," according to Sergeant Davidson. "We took off our coats and piled them upon them, we built the best fires we could build for them, we rubbed their limbs and bodies but all to no avail, they died in spite of all we could do."[23]

Both sides claimed victory after Glorieta Pass and promptly fell back, the Confederates to Santa Fe and the Federals to Fort Union. Local women in Santa Fe, including Canby's wife, Louisa, took pity on the hungry and cold Confederates and revealed where the Federals had hidden blankets and supplies. Louisa Canby also set up hospitals to get the wounded out of the cold. Sibley planned to hold the town and brought up reinforcements.

But when Colonel Canby marched on Albuquerque, Sibley abandoned his wounded, Santa Fe, and Albuquerque too. On April 15, Canby attacked a portion of the retreating Confederate army near Peralta. A raging dust storm allowed the Rebels to get away.[24] Ovando Hollister remembered how "the wind blew tremendously all day and the air was moving sand."[25]

Sibley now received more bad news. The long-awaited pro-Union Californians were finally arriving. Beginning in December 1861 and continuing through January 1862, a series of massive Pacific storms had produced forty-five days of rain and what remains to date the worst flooding in the recorded history of California. So inundated were the Sacramento and San Joaquin Valleys that thousands died, the economy crashed, and the state government fled to high ground in San Francisco. Floodwaters extended as far north as British Columbia and as far east as Utah. In the Sierra Nevadas, up to fifteen feet of snow fell. Modern meteorologists describe the event as a megaflood, a once-in-a-thousand-years storm.[26]

As far as the war was concerned, the major byproduct of the megaflood was that it delayed the departure of the "California Column" until April. When it finally appeared on the western horizon, Sibley already was limping home, though initially having turned west into the mountains to avoid Fort Craig. Once again, the Confederates lurched from waterhole to waterhole as they stumbled back to Mesilla and then El Paso. Blocked by the mountains' "shadow effect," little rain from the western deluge ever reached the desert. Temperatures rose steadily through the month, with 80-degree days increasingly common, a high of 92 degrees by April 13, and an afternoon reading of 104 degrees at Fort Craig at the end of April. Late in May, with temperatures now routinely in the nineties or above, the brigade began the final retreat to San Antonio. The Confederates again moved one regiment at a time to maximize available water supplies. Once again, they encountered extreme heat, dust, and especially thirst on the march, as the Apaches and Comanches poisoned the few available wells with dead animals. Extreme heat, dwindling water, and constant Indian raids tormented the rear guard.[27]

Sibley's grand venture failed miserably, and Confederate hopes of a western empire died. Historians assert that while Canby's Federals fought well, logistics determined the outcome. One must add climate to that equation. Sibley's unrealistic hopes of living off the land withered away in the drought-ravaged western desert, then in the cold and snow. His only consolation was that, without the megaflood and the tardy arrival of the Californians, he might have not escaped at all.[28]

~~~

In Missouri, Maj. Gen. Sterling Price occupied Springfield and set out up the Kansas-Missouri border. On September 20, around the time of his successful siege of Lexington, east of Kansas City, cooler weather suddenly appeared. Facing the approach of Major General Frémont's slow-moving Federal force—the column that made Colonel Cooper back away from Round Mountain—Price retreated. The Federals reoccupied Springfield and made it their base for distributing supplies, including cold-weather gear such as flannel shirts, overcoats, and blankets. Men suffered for shelter as the weather turned cold, but the Confederates had it worst. Price's army hemorrhaged two-thirds of its disillusioned troops before arriving on October 20 at Neosho, a few miles from both Arkansas and the Indian Territory. Mornings were frosty, many were barefoot, and the weather grew colder. Meager clothing, rain, and colder temperatures contributed greatly to widespread illness and continuing morale problems.[29]

November brought crisp conditions, sharp winds, and occasional snow. Price retreated to Pineville in the hills along the Arkansas border before again marching north when the Federals abandoned Springfield under orders from Lincoln. Increasingly suspicious of the Missourian's military judgment, Brig. Gen. Ben McCulloch refused to join him. Instead, he put his men into winter quarters in Arkansas. Alone, Price led his forces to Osceola, near the Kansas border and sixty miles north of Springfield. Ephraim Anderson of the Missouri State Guard remembered "large fires" at Osceola that were "kept at night, as the weather was cold, and few of the men had more than one blanket."[30] The Federals shivered too, as evinced by the *St. Louis Daily Missouri Democrat*'s call for socks and mittens. "Handling guns in winter weather, with naked fingers, is pretty tough work," the editor observed.[31]

At the end of November (just as back east in Virginia) heavy rains and snow appeared. Light snow fell in southwestern Missouri on November 29. This was followed by a snowstorm in Saint Louis that began during the day on November 30 and continued through the night, leaving a mantle of three inches that lasted until December 6. Locals pronounced it the biggest snow in many years. Three inches also fell in the state capital. The weather otherwise remained cold, with occasional squalls.[32] Writing to McClellan, Halleck complained that "the cold here is very severe, and our troops, in miserable tents and poorly clothed, suffer very much, and the sick list is enormous."[33]

Farther west, on the northwestern rim of the Ozarks, Price faced a crucial manpower crisis. His men's enlistments were running out. Meanwhile, a rump convention at Neosho had formally announced the state's secession and entrance into the Confederacy. Price not only had to convince his remaining men to reenlist but also had to get them to join new Confederate units that he could lead beyond the state's borders. As his biographer indicates, most of the men still wanted to fight, but with winter coming, they wanted to go home first, secure warm clothing, and see about their families. Left with little choice, Price acquiesced while begging Missourians for more volunteers.[34]

Again as in Virginia, the weather turned oddly warm across Missouri. In a story headlined "Return of Summer," the editor of the *Hannibal Messenger* proclaimed that "such mild balmy weather, as the last few days this time of year, was never known before in this latitude by the oldest inhabitants."[35] Except for a cold snap at midmonth, it remained unseasonably pleasant, if sometimes rainy, until snow fell on December 21. Price retreated again, south to Springfield, in hopes of shortening his supply line. The same winter storm system that slammed into the combatants before Chustenahlah now struck the Missourians. "The snow continued to fall during the night," Ephraim Anderson wrote, "and the next morning was lying on the ground five or six inches deep, rendering it disagreeable under foot, especially to the men whose shoes were not good, and those constituted a large number." Christmas was cold and rainy. At Springfield, Price's army erected log huts and settled in for winter.[36]

Federal soldiers, too, faced a cold winter. In mid-December, Pvt. Alexander Downing's 11th Iowa started west from Saint Louis to Jefferson City. On December 22, the weather turned cold, and "it snowed all day" in the state capitol, "the snow falling in large flakes." By nightfall, it was so "intensely cold" that the men "were compelled to build fires." Lacking firewood, they burned forty or fifty canoes stacked at the rail station. The next morning, as a "cold northwest wind" blew through, the soldiers "made all the 'secesh' skedaddle, and commandeered vacant homes and stores in the town of California." Downing's company trod on to Lookout Station, took over a vacant store, built bunks, fired up stoves, and settled in snuggly to garrison that town.[37]

Missouri's growing guerrilla war prevented some unlucky regiments from enjoying their winter in front of pot-bellied store stoves. The 81st Ohio was one. Stationed along the Northern Missouri Railroad between Saint Louis and Centralia, its men marched out after guerrillas on December 20. At night, Cpl. Charles Wright remembered that the weather grew "so cold that the water froze in our canteens." A few days later, he again complained of the cold, explaining, "we could get but little fuel of any kind, and the wind blew so hard that the flames would not mount upward, but blazed along the ground, giving out but little heat." Sleet and ice followed. Icicles hung from coats. Wright found himself "anxiously awaiting the command to 'fall in,' when we knew that we could warm ourselves by hard marching."[38]

Guerrillas eventually would constitute the main Confederate threat in Missouri, but at the end of 1861, Price's army remained the major concern. On Christmas Day, Halleck created the Military District of Southwest Missouri and awarded its command to Brig. Gen. Samuel R. Curtis, a West Pointer, civil engineer, and more recently a Republican congressman from Iowa. Halleck told him to launch a campaign as soon as he could, drive Price's army into Arkansas, and destroy it. Curtis promptly left for Rolla, where he organized the Army of the Southwest out of the three divisions stationed in the area. There remained one sticky problem. Lincoln had stipulated that Halleck had to get McClellan's approval before he unleashed Curtis, and an ill McClellan was slow to respond. Halleck craftily spun Price's retreat to Springfield, which he initially misunderstood, to argue that Curtis had to strike before Price and McCulloch could reunite. On January 13, 1862, Halleck received new reports that Confederate cavalry was moving north. He now could wait no more and ordered Curtis to march on Springfield.[39]

Neither general had any illusions about what a winter campaign in the Ozarks would entail. Even in good weather, the main highway from Rolla south into Arkansas, called the Telegraph Road, was a rugged, narrow dirt lane that evinced little modern engineering. Farms and barns in the highlands were relatively few, and the Confederates already had stripped most everything of value, so supplies would be sparse. Curtis could rely only on what little his wagons could carry. But as historians William Shea and Earl Hess note, at some point along the way on the Springfield Plateau, "the [supply] line would become so long the teams and teamsters would consume the contents of the wagons before they reached their destination. When that happened, . . . the Army of the Southwest would reach the end of its tether and advance no more." In an effort to maximize his range to its limit, Curtis ordered his men to travel as lightly as possible, with the most basic necessities on their backs or else in a mere handful of wagons. He could not control the seasons, however. Winter in the Ozarks is routinely bitterly cold, with frequent snow, sleet, and ice. Occasional warm spells only bring thaws that reduce frozen Ultisols to muck. In Rolla, Curtis and his newly appointed quartermaster, Capt. Philip Sheridan, had their work cut out for them as they surveyed the barren, snow-covered road to the southwest.[40]

On January 3, Curtis reported the same bad conditions that all but immobilized armies across the South. "The weather turned very bad yesterday evening," he wrote, "with rain and sleet—such weather as none but a soldier would be out in."[41] By chance, Anthony Trollope, the celebrated English travel writer, arrived in Rolla from Saint Louis just then. He described a landscape of snow and ice, "with an occasional half-frozen stream across it." The mud was so thick that his companion got stuck. The next day, they traveled to Curtis's camps. "There had been a hard frost for some nights," Trollope wrote, "but though the cold was very great there was always heat enough in the middle of the day to turn the surface of the ground into glutinous mud. . . . The mud stuck like paste and encompassed everything."[42]

Bad weather continued. On January 8, a Saint Louis war correspondent reported rain, snow, and sleet the previous day, plus enough ice to coat everything exposed to the elements. Streams flooded. Curtis's column, nonetheless, moved out on January 14, a cold but sunny day. The initial destination was Lebanon, a town halfway to Springfield on the eastern edge of the Ozark Plateau. Noting the sunny skies and a change in the wind, Curtis hoped for better weather and optimistically expected to cross the roughly fifty miles quickly. He was soon disappointed. The column advanced only five miles the first day out before pitching camp, as supply wagons bogged down in clay mud and slush. A hellish mixture of red clay and water froze at night and required men with axes to free the wagons the next morning. Curtis made another fifteen miles before stopping at an abandoned campground still littered with boards previously put to use as sleeping platforms. January 16 brought "moderated" weather, but, according to Cpl. L. G. Bennett of the 36th Illinois, the "frost and snow gave way to mud, thin, sticky,

Missouri mud, through which the men splashed and plunged, as jovial as ducks in a thunder shower." Reaching the Big Piney River, Curtis discovered the water too high to cross. The troops waited four days before the Big Piney and Gasconade Rivers fell enough so they could cross "a bridge of army wagons."[43]

Curtis pushed on hard despite the conditions. His army of about 12,000 men arrived in Lebanon without their train on January 24, having covered about sixty miles.[44] The general reported four inches of snow on the ground a week later. "The crust will not form hard enough to hold the teams," he reported, "while it forms a terrible resistance to wheeling." Worse, his men's "miserable" shoes had worn out in a mere week on the road. Writing to Brig. Gen. Franz Sigel back in Rolla, he added that "the roads are indeed very bad, but they are far worse for the enemy than for us if he attempts to retreat." The hard freeze had solidified the roads enough that Sigel should expect an easier time if he approached Lebanon. High water remained a threat, and "we must . . . soon expect another thaw, and constant bad roads will be the rule and a change for the better a rare exception."[45] Corporal Bennett complained that "the weather was as variable as the capricious temper of a lunatic, from heat to cold, rain to snow, but always with more or less mud."[46]

When Price discovered that Curtis was in Lebanon, he called upon Confederate forces in Arkansas to send help. Unconvinced that the Yankees would be crazy enough to launch a winter campaign through the Ozarks, McCulloch hesitated. More snow fell, eight inches at Fayetteville on January 29 and more periodically over the next several days. Curtis rested his men until February 10 and then marched for Springfield, relying on the cold and roads "frozen quite solid." "You have moved through the coldest and most stormy period of a winter," a staff officers proclaimed, "and so far you have brought your trains and equipments through snow, mud, floods, and frosts without his hearing of a murmur and without the loss of property or men. But the success of this winter campaign now requires a further draught on the patience and the fortitude of this army. We must strip for a forced march and final conflict."[47]

The new march required every ounce of fortitude. "By then rain, snow, and rising temperature had done their work on the roads thoroughly," according to Bennett. The "deep cut roads became quagmires through which artillery and wagon trains were with difficulty dragged." Without their wagons, cold men slept without blankets or tents, as the ground was too hard to drive tent stakes into it. Instead, they either used rocks and wood to hold down the corners or huddled under their overcoats on beds of fence rails and old cornstalks elevated from the mud. Shoes again wore out. More snow fell on February 13 as the army arrived at Springfield.[48]

The Federals discovered to their delight that the enemy had fled. That meant that while Curtis possessed Springfield's shelter and supplies just as another winter storm hit, Price's exposed men on the road had to fend for themselves. Many were shoeless and poorly clad. Missouri artilleryman Samuel John McDaniel sounded what would become a standard soldier's lament: it always happens to us. "The weather had been pleasant in Springfield, but the night we commenced the retreat it began to change, to bad," he complained. "The rain set in about midnight, a slow drizzle from the Northeast. Towards daylight it changed to snow and sleet." Price marched on all day and through the night of the thirteenth "through drizzle and snow. . . . The snow and sleet still falling. . . . All day, in the downpour, we crept on. The storm increased with the decline of the day." McDaniel continued: "The wind rose to almost a gale. . . . Towards midnight the wind changed to the Northeast, and the cold increased in severity in our drenched hides." Finally giving out—he had contracted measles—the artillerist crawled into a wagon and slept. When he awoke, "I felt like I was dying, I was so chilled. The snow was all over us, and our clothes frozen on our bodies." Rain and sleet froze to wagons and caissons and weighed down the trees along the road.[49]

Price's army trudged on through ice and rain down the Telegraph Road, jettisoning gear, abandoning wagons, and leaving hundreds of exhausted soldiers along the roadside. Winter weather continued unabated. Ephraim Anderson described on February 13 "thin fine snow, almost ice." The prairie environment meant that there was little firewood and thus few fires when they stopped. That night, it was so cold that men pulled down their tents and used them as bedcovers. Some died from exposure. Boldly, Curtis divided his pursuing army and followed, hoping to snag "Old Pap" in his pincers where the roads rejoined. Alert to the pursuit, Price drove his men to the Arkansas border, although the hard pace meant abandoning part of his train. It also meant that more men slipped away. Steadily, Curtis closed the gap. The Federal pursuers fared better on the cold, icy road. According to Nathan Harwood, roads were both "dryer and harder." Good news from Tennessee—Grant's triumph at cold and sleety Fort Donelson (see chapter

5)—also heartened the men, who concluded that the enemy were cowards who would not fight.[50]

They were wrong. A mile from the border, the secessionist rear guard stopped to fight Curtis's cavalry before turning south into Arkansas. The weather remained bad. McCulloch's Confederates were forced to give up their winter camp at Cross Hollow, which boasted extensive cabins with brick chimneys. Curtis later described them as better than what his men had lived in at Benton Barracks. Sgt. William Ruyle of the Confederate 5th Missouri remembered the march south as "one of the coldest I ever saw, sleeting and snowing."[51] Curtis followed, but gingerly. At Little Sugar Creek, he encountered fresh troops on February 17: McCulloch's displaced men had joined the fight. The two secessionist forces reunited at Fayetteville before continuing south seventeen miles more into the Boston Mountains. They stopped at Cove Creek on February 21. Price behaved badly. Barely speaking to McCulloch, he told his State Guardsmen to either enlist in Confederate service once and for all or walk back to Missouri. Hundreds promptly took him up on his offer and set off for home; Price's army almost imploded. What saved it from doing so was Curtis's decision to halt in far northwestern Arkansas. His supply line was wire taut, his army needed additional men and horses, and now he faced McCulloch as well as Price. The Union commander spread his units out around Little Sugar Creek to avoid overtaxing one area's resources while keeping the enemy off balance with occasional jabs. Curtis's men cheered his decision to halt and rest.[52]

They would not have much time to recuperate, however. March 1 was unseasonably warm, but the weather turned cold again in the wake of a thunderstorm before midnight. The next day was drizzly and cold when Maj. Gen. Earl Van Dorn, the Confederacy's new overall commander in the Trans-Mississippi, arrived at Price's headquarters under orders from Richmond. He took command of both secessionist forces—Price's Missourians and McCulloch's Confederates—uniting them as the two divisions of his Army of the West. Learning that Curtis had halted, Van Dorn impulsively decided to counterattack. Two days later, a diversionary brigade moved back up the Telegraph Road toward Fayetteville while the main force headed for Bentonville. The men traveled light, with three days' rations stuffed in their pockets; Van Dorn expected his army to "conquer or starve." The weather remained miserably cold.[53] "The snow and sleet were blinding," Sgt. William Watson added on March 4, "and the roads in an awful condition. We halted for the night, but of course anything like sleep was out of the question." The Federals, assuming that their enemies would stay put until the storm passed, called in their patrols. The next two days were sunnier, but Watson woke up on March 5 covered in more snow. Union soldiers reported icy roads and a punishing north wind. Reaching Bentonville the next day, the Confederates took the town only to find a rear guard having just left. Curtis was pulling back, burning what he could not carry. It was sunny but still below freezing and bitterly cold.[54]

On the evening of March 6, thoroughly confused about Curtis's intentions, Van Dorn decided to stage a night march to the north, envelop the enemy, and cut off Telegraph Road in the Union rear. The night was again cold and snowy. Tired men shivered in place or fell out as wrecked bridges and felled trees slowed their march considerably. By morning on the seventh, with the sky overcast and temperatures again below freezing, the army was well behind its timetable. When the head of the column reached Telegraph Road, Van Dorn gambled. He ordered the army to divide and use two different roads around Pea Ridge in order to make up lost time. The two divisions would reunite near Elkhorn Tavern and from there attack the Yankees. Unfortunately, Curtis was ready for them. The two armies fought a divided battle from midmorning until night on hard, frozen ground. Price's men achieved some success to the east near Elkhorn Tavern, but the other Confederate contingent fared poorly. McCulloch died in the fighting to the west.[55]

The night that followed the first day of the Battle of Pea Ridge was agonizing, especially for the wounded. A north wind blew hard. Both sides initially did without fires. The Federals tried to sleep, but many lacked blankets.[56] The Confederates had it worse. William Watson lamented that someone in the Confederate rear had stolen his regiment's blankets and overcoats. "We then insisted on making fires," he continued, "as better to be killed by the enemy than be frozen to death."[57] Early the next morning, Curtis attacked near Elkhorn Tavern. According to Harwood, "a mist" of fog, mixed with the previous day's atmospherically trapped gunsmoke, "slowly lifted and received our magnificent line of battle, the stars and stripes floating boldly out from right to left. . . . By eight o'clock the smoke and mists had lifted, revealing clearly the enemy's position."[58] As the infantry hugged the cold earth, Federal artillery pounded the Confederates. "We rose up with joints stiffened with cold and fatigue and in no great condition or inclination to renew the fighting," Watson admitted.[59] Federal gunners disabled several guns before Sigel launched a parade-ground attack. Exhausted, hungry, and cold, Van Dorn's troops broke for the rear, in an orderly manner at first but then scattering.[60] They kept going until they reached the safety of the Arkansas River, beyond the Boston Mountains.[61]

March typically marks the beginning of the rainy season in northwestern Arkansas, and 1862 was no exception. The week-long retreat south brought new weather-related agony: cold nights, high wind, near-constant sheets of rain, sleet, and snow. Roads became bogs. Swollen rivers and streams required frequent wading. Many men had no coats, blankets, or tents, and some lacked shoes. They built shelter as best they could out of fence rails and wet straw. Food was scarce, and soldiers begged or stole from the isolated farms along the way. Fires were hard to start due to wet or ice-coated wood.[62] "We suffered almost death," Ruyle concluded. "Many were doubtless brought down to their graves soon by the hardships they endured on this retreat."[63]

Van Dorn's army came apart on the road to Van Buren. Near the end, a thunderstorm struck. Many exhausted men slept through it, but those of the 3rd Louisiana did not. These men tripped over sleeping soldiers as they raced to high ground, afraid of drowning in a rising creek. In the morning, the water was too high to cross, and they were without food. "There was only the remnant or the wreck of the 2nd brigade here," Watson continued, "but who was in command of it, or whether it had any commander, we did not know, every regiment seeming to act for itself, and every company to act for itself." His comrades felled a tree, crossed the swollen creek, and made for Van Buren.[64] "The army arrived in Van Buren in straggling squads," Sgt. W. H. Tunnard of the 3rd Louisiana remembered, "tired, hatless, barefooted, hungry, dirty and ragged. They had been in rain-storms, climbed steep mountains along narrow and rugged foot-paths, waded deep and cold mountain streams, starved, slept without tents or blankets on the wet and frosty ground; in fact endured untold hardships and horrors. The retreat was more disastrous than a dozen battles."[65]

Seeking to understand Federal success at Pea Ridge, Shea and Hess correctly point to several factors. Halleck had developed a viable operational strategy that Curtis executed with skill. Both excelled logistically. Curtis also led solid subordinates. In contrast, Confederate leadership was poor. Van Dorn ignored logistical realities and, as a battlefield leader, made one bad decision after another. Nor did his lieutenants shine. But again, one must consider climate and weather. In the end, like Sibley, Van Dorn and

Price asked too much of their men. Marching and fighting in winter was always hard, but it was better to serve in an army that provided enough food, clothing, blankets, and tents. Missouri thus remained firmly in Federal hands for the rest of the war, and the northern half of Arkansas soon would fall under Union control as well. Van Dorn granted his men little respite after their harrowing retreat. Two weeks after Pea Ridge, he marched his men to the Mississippi. Initially aiming at reinforcing New Madrid and Island No. 10, he instead marched his army for Corinth. Meanwhile, on the Tennessee River, three other armies had learned lessons of their own about fighting in winter.

Chapter 5

Noah's Day

The West, Winter 1861–62

While the nation foundered in the stormy spring of 1861, Kentucky looked for a life raft. A leading slave state, it was home to many Unionists. Trade and affections ran north and south on the modern transportation systems that exemplified Henry Clay's vision of a nation knit together economically. By 1860, Kentucky was both northern and southern in character. The secession crisis thus tore at its entrails. In November, a plurality of voters rejected both Lincoln and the other Kentuckian in the race, Southern Democrat John C. Breckinridge. They gave a majority to John Bell's vague promises of preserving the Union. In Washington, Sen. John J. Crittenden failed to forestall disunion. Fort Sumter paralyzed the state government until May 1861, when it embraced armed neutrality and vowed to defend itself against either army. Few actually wanted neutrality, however. Competing state armies drilled. Men slipped away to join companies in Tennessee or across the Ohio. Lincoln accepted neutrality for the time being but quietly shipped guns to Unionists and blockaded goods transiting through Kentucky for the Confederacy. He also sent Lt. William "Bull" Nelson of the US Navy, a Kentucky native, to recruit. To lose Kentucky, Lincoln suggested, could mean losing the war. As summer lengthened, Unionists won crucial elections. Southern Rightists now simply hoped to block Kentucky's full embrace of the Union.[1]

Kentucky's fragile neutrality and geopolitical position shaped both sides' military deployments. The Union army and navy massed forces at the confluence of the Ohio and Mississippi Rivers at Cairo, Illinois. As the crow flies, it was not fifty miles from Cairo across Kentucky to Tennessee, where Confederates inched up to the border and fortified the major rivers. While both sides focused on the Mississippi, the Confederates constructed Fort Henry on the flood-prone banks of the Tennessee River. A few miles away they built Fort Donelson on the Cumberland River. Both were badly located; in winter both rivers tended to flood. Richmond hoped that winter's impassable roads would buy time before any Yankee advance in the spring.[2]

Neutrality collapsed in early September. Hapless Maj. Gen. Leonidas Polk sent a force under Brig. Gen. Gideon Pillow to occupy Columbus, located along both the Mississippi and the Mobile and Ohio Railroad. Major General Frémont responded by dispatching Brig. Gen. Ulysses S. Grant to seize Paducah. Gov. Beriah Magoffin was prosouthern but blamed both sides. The legislature demanded that the Confederates leave. With neutrality dead, both armies grabbed space. The Confederates constructed a line of posts stretching east from Columbus, through Forts Henry and Donelson, and on to Bowling Green. Extensive entrenchments at the last commanded the Barren River and the crucial Louisville and Nashville Railroad. Extending on eastward, the line continued through Brig. Gen. Felix Zollicoffer's camps in southeastern Kentucky to Cumberland Gap. Zollicoffer hoped that rainy fall weather and bad mountain roads would offset his paucity of men and artillery and help keep Federal forces at bay. He moved up the Wilderness Road, skirmishing, garrisoning towns, and pushing the front away from the gap.[3]

On October 21, a small Union force commanded by Col. Albin Schoepf

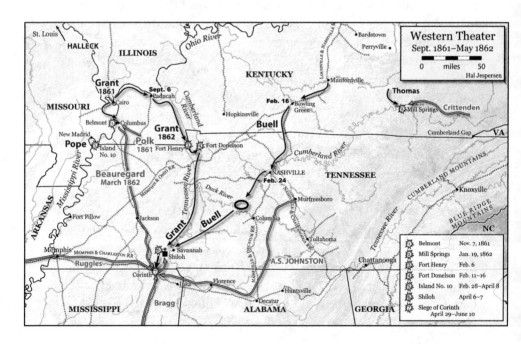

stopped Zollicoffer in the Rockcastle Hills. Zollicoffer fell back, confident that winter weather would soon make the roads impassable for his enemies. Schoepf advanced to Somerset, while Brig. Gen. George Thomas marched his men to Crab Orchard. Midwestern regiments, meanwhile, hurried across the Ohio to occupy Louisville and then fan out south to the Green River. The first departmental commander, Brig. Gen. Robert Anderson of Fort Sumter fame, grew ill and gave way to Brig. Gen. William Tecumseh Sherman. Zollicoffer by then had advanced to Mill Springs, fifteen miles from Schoepf on the south bank of the Cumberland. There he began erecting winter quarters, planning to strike into the heart of Kentucky when the weather allowed. Three inches of rain and an inch of snow fell in nearby Danville over three days as the Confederates arrived at Mill Springs.[4]

In Washington, rumors swirled about Sherman's sanity. Maj. Gen. Don Carlos Buell took command in Kentucky. Never charismatic, Buell brought stability and badly needed administrative and logistical skills to the theater. But he also faced a dilemma. The Lincoln administration pressured him to launch a campaign into East Tennessee, where resurgent Unionism was giving Confederate authorities fits. Buell resisted. He argued that Bowling Green and Nashville, not Knoxville, were the proper military targets. With bad roads and meager supplies, East Tennessee could not support an army logistically during the winter. Then there was the worsening weather. In Louisville, rain fell ten out of thirty days in November. Precipitation was average for the month—3.68 inches—but closer to the front in Danville, almost 8 inches fell in November, more than double the norm. It was cold too. After November 22, high temperatures never rose above the forties. Two inches of snow fell on December 2. Unwilling to mimic Curtis in Missouri, Buell did nothing except send Thomas to wet and foggy Lebanon. When Thomas sent two regiments to reinforce Schoepf, Buell overruled him and recalled one of them.[5]

Yet Thomas was right to worry; Zollicoffer had decided to advance. On December 5, with temperatures approaching 60 degrees, the Confederate general crossed the river to Beech Grove, located in a three-sided topographic horseshoe created by a bend in the river and a nearby creek. There were two flaws in his plans. His force was weak, outnumbered, and poorly armed. Then there was the river. Confident that he could recross if necessary, Zollicoffer had his garrison of about 4,000 men build boats, row across, dig in, and cut a field of fire across the horseshoe's open side.[6]

On slight high ground contained within the horseshoe, the soldiers built "miniature log cabins, chinked and plastered, clapboard roofs, and wooden chimneys."[7] Zollicoffer blithely ignored the fact that the Cumberland was prone to winter flooding. Perhaps the dry weather fooled him. It only rained four days to that point, while the monthly precipitation total was about half the norm. The river fell steadily.

When his commander, Senator Crittenden's Rebel son George, learned that Zollicoffer had placed his little army in a trap, he immediately ordered him back across the Cumberland. It was too late. Zollicoffer replied that the river was rising, and they could not get back safely. All Crittenden could do was send for reinforcements and then go to Beech Grove himself to take command. When he arrived on January 3, 1862, falling back was impossible due to heavy rain and occasional snow that fell the night before he arrived. It rained all the next day too, dropping over an inch of precipitation. The river kept rising. Highs collapsed from 61 degrees on New Year's Day to only 36 degrees on January 3. As everywhere else on the war front, winter had arrived, leaving chilled Confederates with a rising river and steep muddy banks at their backs.[8]

Worse still, as Crittenden rightly feared, the Federals were coming. On cold December 29, 1861, Buell finally had reacted to Zollicoffer's aggression. Concerned about his flank when he moved on Bowling Green, and under pressure from Washington to do something, Buell ordered Thomas to drive the Confederates off the Cumberland. He added that the Federals should stop at the river rather than push on into East Tennessee. Schoepf tested Zollicoffer's defenses almost immediately while Thomas left Lebanon with six infantry regiments, a regiment of cavalry, a battery, and six hundred wagons, exactly the sort of sizable train that Curtis had refused to take through Missouri.[9] At first, the weather cooperated. Lt. Jeremiah Donahower of the 2nd Minnesota was nonetheless hesitant, for they marched in "a country where rain and mud usually dominated in weather and roads." Lebanon lies roughly at the southern edge of the midwestern Alfisol soil range that stretches south from the Great Lakes into the Kentucky Bluegrass. From Lebanon south, the column passed briefly through a crazy quilt of Alfisols, Udept Inceptisols on the erodible slopes of the Appalachians, and red-clay Ultisols. About halfway from Lebanon to Campbellsville, they then entered the vast expanse of the southern red clay that extended to the Gulf. At the same time, the post–New Year's Day weather system that bedeviled Virginia and Missouri hit southeastern Kentucky with similar vengeance. It rained heavily for the next two and a half weeks, except on January 5, when it snowed. Almost 8.5 inches of rain and 6 inches of snow fell that month in Danville. "The result," Donahower continued, "was mud and roads that soon became a succession of deeply cut mud holes, and the roadside and the fields mud quagmires."[10]

As the column approached Columbia, rain fell harder. "On January 8th, 1862," Pvt. James Birney Shaw of the 10th Indiana remembered, "we left Campbellsville in a rain—in fact it rained all the time we were there. The pike from there on to Columbia was shoe-mouth deep in limestone mortar." Roads worsened. Beyond town, the turnpike ended and only red-clay roads existed. Cold winter rain swirled the clay into goo. "All will agree that the worst roads on the face of the earth at that time were between Columbia and Logan's Cross Roads," Shaw added. "The mules sank to their bellies, the wagons to their axles, details were made to help the teams along, but our progress was very slow." In three days, they covered eighteen miles.[11]

The rain briefly halted after January 5 in Danville and Louisville, but Thomas's men described continuing precipitation. Sharply contrasting temperatures as well suggest that Thomas's strike force straddled a stalled cold front.[12] "On the tenth," Donahower wrote, "the regiment marched and after floundering through nine miles of miry roads and under rain we went into camp. . . . On the twelfth the bad roads made it necessary to halt after marching seven miles, as our wagons were reported fast in the mud." Road conditions had deteriorated to the point that his company was detailed to keep the wagon train moving, "which was done by prying and by corduroying the miry spots with poles and brush. Wading in mud almost knee deep and cold and persuading obstinate mules to get up and pull hard and pull together proved a disagreeable work." Over an inch of rain and another of snow fell between January 12 and January 15. Red-clay mud, wet clothing, backbreaking labor, and frustrating stop-and-go efforts ate away at morale. So did half rations, occasioned by the wretched state of wagon transportation. Blankets never dried. Finding dry wood to burn was difficult.[13]

January 17 was again rainy, but at least temperatures rose into the sixties. Thomas reached Logan's Cross Roads, ten miles north of Beech Grove, with three infantry regiments and an artillery battery. The rest of his force and his train remained bogged down back up the road, so he sent for three of Schoepf's regiments and two of his batteries.[14] Snow fell the next day, followed by the heaviest single day's rainfall of the month.[15] One man remembered "the darkest night and the coldest and most pitiless and persistent rain we ever knew."[16]

When Thomas halted, Crittenden decided to seize the initiative and attack through the ongoing downpour, wrongly informed that flooded Fishing Creek had kept Schoepf at bay. Massing his troops, Crittenden marched at midnight with 4,000 badly clad and inexperienced Confederates. They moved up the sloppy road to Logan's Cross Roads, with sheets of rain, wind, and sleet blowing in their faces. Artillery foundered. In terms of weather, it was the worst night of the campaign. The plan was to follow the road straight into the Yankee camp at the crossroads, deploy, and attack in force. Because of the mud and darkness, however, it took six hours to cover ten miles. At daylight on January 19, with temperatures in the fifties and the mud in the road a foot deep, Crittenden's already exhausted advance encountered Federal cavalry three miles from camp. They drove the horsemen off and pushed up the road into the Union picket line. The 10th Indiana and 1st Kentucky Cavalry bore the brunt of the early onslaught. Drizzle and a dense morning fog merged with smoke to create an almost impenetrable dark veil that no wind pushed aside. Within a few minutes, men could not effectively distinguish friend from foe. An hour passed, with intense firing but little movement. As the Confederates extended their flanks, however, the Union defenders withdrew up the road through a ravine. They halted at a stout split-rail fence that ran along an intersecting country road. This fence line soon became the vortex of battle, drawing in an increasing number of troops. Drizzle and black fog still smothered the ground.

While rain affected both armies, it especially hindered the Confederates. Many—like McCulloch's men in Missouri—carried flintlocks that refused to fire due to exposed pans and wet powder. Historian Stuart Sanders estimates that the rain rendered one in ten Confederate muskets useless. Some soldiers later claimed that as many as half were inoperable. Crittenden's men also stopped frequently to wipe off their guns, leading to a fits-and-starts advance.[17]

Meanwhile, Schoepf's force across Fishing Creek attempted to aid their comrades. "The roads were almost impassable," according to Capt. F. W. Keil of the 35th Ohio, "and as was the general remark, 'the bottom had fallen out.' It can not be said positively that this was true," he added, "only that the legs of the men were not long enough to reach the bottom, if 'still there.'"[18]

Reaching the creek, Capt. J. H. Putnam of the 31st Ohio "found it very much swollen from the recent heavy rains and running rapidly, so much that we were compelled to stretch a large hawser across for the men to support themselves by, to enable them to keep their footing, . . . each man carrying his cartridge-box and gun on his head to protect them from water." Their battery faced a dilemma, as "nearly all of the teams stalled. . . . [T]he water was so cold that the horses soon became so chilled that they could not pull, and many of the guns were pulled out by hand. . . . All safely reached the shore except one or two horses and mules that were drowned."[19]

Three hours after the battle began, the Confederates remained stymied, trapped in the smoke-filled ravine in front of the fence. Unable to locate his regiments to the right, the nearsighted Zollicoffer rode off to find them. In the sooty darkness, he stumbled directly into the Federal 4th Kentucky. For a moment, his blue uniform, Federal-issue cap, and white raincoat—either made of rubber or oil cloth, depending upon the account—protected the general from discovery. When a Confederate staff officer entered the scene, however, several Federals simultaneously fired. Zollicoffer pitched from his horse, shot three times. The Federals dragged his body out of the road, placed it on a board to keep it out of the mud, and began taking souvenirs.

With his second in command dead, Crittenden mounted another assault. Thomas ordered two more regiments to the fence as the rain began to slow.[20] Donahower reported, "nine companies of the Second Minnesota Infantry, carrying 605 muskets on their shoulders, . . . plowing through the mud and the dripping rain at a dog's trot toward the junction of the Mill Springs Road."[21] Soaked to the skin, they went into action, with only the fence between them and the enemy. According to Drummer William Bircher, "the smoke hung so close to the ground on account of the rain that it was impossible to see each other at times."[22] After a half hour, the Confederates fell back through a flooded plowed field. At first, the retreat was orderly, but when elated bluecoats attacked with bayonets, Crittenden's men broke; some did not stop until they reached Beech Grove. Thomas followed them slowly in line of battle. Schoepf's men arrived and joined the creeping chase.

That evening more rain fell. The Federals halted near the entrenchments, anticipating a morning attack. But low on rations and convinced that his men could not hold the works, Crittenden spent the night ferrying his men across the Cumberland. In his haste, he abandoned most of his artillery, ammunition, supplies, horses, and wounded as well as many healthy men. Some soldiers drowned trying to swim against the swift current. Once across, Crittenden burned his boats. What was left of his little army—wet, exhausted, and defeated—all but disintegrated during an eighty-mile retreat. Men threw away their weapons and headed home.[23]

Historian Stuart Sanders concludes that several factors defeated the Confederates in this battle, normally called either Mill Springs or Logan's Cross Roads. As elsewhere that winter, Federal leadership was superior. Terrain emboldened soldiers fighting on the defense. But the weather was decisive. It slowed the army on the march, delayed deployments, limited visibility, rendered Confederate arms inoperable, and made sustained attacks impossible. Weather at Mill Springs helped placed Kentucky firmly in Union hands.

Only Buell's orders to stop at the Cumberland prevented a full-fledged Union invasion of East Tennessee early in 1862. But as historian Earl Hess points out, Buell's concerns were justified. Thomas agreed that the bad roads and a paucity of supplies would have made such a march difficult. Instead, after two dark and wet days sleeping in the Confederates' snug cabins, Thomas's regiments began retracing their steps.[24] The 2nd Minnesota crossed Fishing Creek while "still at flood tide and very cold." Temperatures hung in the forties during the day but sometimes fell to near freezing at night. More rain fell. Many men by then were sick with measles, typhoid, and diarrhea. "The exposure to rain and cold," Donahower explained, "and the wearing of wet clothing almost continuously since leaving Columbia was showing its effect upon many, and much sickness and one or two deaths occurred." On February 1, deep mud left the Gophers "creeping along by holding to the fence on the road side." On the night of the tenth, it snowed.[25]

Others suffered too. Shaw wrote that "on the 19th we arrived in Lebanon and no one ever saw it rain harder. No wind, but the water simply came down in streams about the size of a wheat straw. We marched in sections at carry arms, and the muskets carried with the hammer down on the tube filled the gun barrels half full of water."[26] The sun only came out the day before they arrived, February 5. According to Bircher, "as we marched and the hot sun poured down upon our damp clothes, it caused a steam to arise from the regiment as if they were cooking." They had little time to rest. Two battles had been fought during their retreat, and soon they would be on boats steaming south in more rain.[27]

Union victory at Logan's Cross Roads elated Unionists north and south, but Buell's eyes remained fixed on Gen. Albert Sidney Johnston's Confederates at Bowling Green. There the Confederates had endured a winter marked by illness, poor supply, and the same bad weather that bedeviled comrades elsewhere. In nearby Clarksville, Tennessee, the closest Smithsonian weather observer, Prof. William M. Stewart, remained active despite Tennessee's secession. Stewart recorded five inches of precipitation in rainy November, nearly two additional inches in drier December, and five-plus inches in January. Skies were uniformly gray. Temperatures varied, but as elsewhere, a relatively mild mid-December gave way to a colder January.[28]

Safeguarding the railroad to Nashville sometimes necessitated venturing out into that winter weather in order to blunt rumored Federal advances. Pvt. Johnny Green of the Confederate 9th Kentucky complained that those excursions inevitably took place in rain. On one march late in December, "the rain was coming down in a bleak steady down pour. . . . [T]he road was very muddy & crossed by frequent little streams flooded to their fullest. As we would wade into the ice cold water, so deep as to come much above our k[n]ees, we would sing, 'Cheer boys Cheer we march away to battle.'" On December 20, they marched to the appropriately named Dripping Springs and braced for the enemy. "The weather was terrible," he continued, "rain & sleet all day & when halted we were drenched to the skin. It turned very cold & soon our clothes were frozen still on us." Instead of fighting, they fell back toward the main army, sleeping on fence rails during a sleet storm. "We had tents at this time," he explained, "but the weather was very cold with snow on the ground. We had not learned to build chimneys to our tents & spent a very cold Christmas."[29] Capt. George Dawson of the Confederate 1st Missouri lamented the weather—"my feet are almost frozen," he wrote—and damned the lack of decent shelter. "This is an immense army to winter this way & many a fond mother will mourn the loss of their brave sons, and many a dear wife perhaps will weep for their lost husbands—for death must be frequent with men living this way."[30]

Many of the Federals stationed nearby on the Green River would have agreed with Dawson's dim assessment. By the end of January 1862, Bowling Green was "one vast mud hole."[31] The riverbanks consisted of Inceptisols, but Alfisols otherwise extended south past the town. Marching feet and wagon wheels quickly penetrated to the clay in the substratum. Col. Benjamin Scribner of the 38th Indiana remembered "roads almost impassable, in places knee-deep with mud, or rather thin clay mortar. After returning, . . . the men would wade into the ponds, peculiar to this locality, to wash the mud from their garments, after which they would stand before the camp fires to dry, or turn in together in their tents with their wet clothes on."[32]

After Mill Springs, Anthony Trollope traveled to Bowling Green. He described "muddy" Federal camps with the soldiers "all in tents" and the generals in log shanties. The situation was much worse back in Cairo, "the most desolate" town in America, according to Trollope. Its gray ramshackle dreariness, sickly population, filthy lodgings, and especially its deep mud repelled him. He called it "thick, moist, glutinous dirt" and added, "who were the founders of Cairo I have never ascertained. They are probably buried fathoms deep in the mud, and their names will no doubt remain a mystery to the latest ages." The greatest disappointment was that he had come to see the gathering Union host only to find nearly all of it gone. The flotilla had left the day before, February 2. "There were only a thousand soldiers at Cairo. . . . Very many were drunk, and all were mud-clogged up to their shoulders and very caps.[33]

A day late, Trollope missed the initial culmination of months of thought and debate about what to do with the Confederate river forts on the Kentucky-Tennessee border. Buell still favored reducing Bowling Green and moving on to Nashville, but his rival Halleck remained focused on the Mississippi. Back east, McClellan leaned toward Buell but was too sick and preoccupied with Virginia to force a decision. Finally, he had Halleck send Grant into western Kentucky to threaten Columbus and prevent Polk from sending reinforcements to Bowling Green. Thanks to fog and Cairo's incredible mud, Grant's two columns got started a day late, on January 10. At least the soil of western Kentucky largely was firmer and more forgiving Alfisol. Yet they encountered the same weather system that tortured Thomas on the way to Logan's Cross Roads.[34] "The weather was very bad," Grant wrote, "snow and rain fell; the roads, never good in that section, were intolerable. We were out more than a week, splashing through the mud, snow, and rain, the men suffering very much." A few died.

Grant, nonetheless, returned satisfied. He had checked Polk and strengthened his working relationship with Flag Officer Andrew Foote. The general also had learned hard but vital lessons about the limits of campaigning in winter weather, something he had not acquired during November's sunny excursion to Belmont, Missouri. Above all, he came back with good intelligence. Lightly armed Fort Heiman, still under construction opposite Fort Henry on the higher bank of the Tennessee, was reported vulnerable to capture. That, Grant asserted, "confirmed views I had previously held, that the true line of operations for us was up the Tennessee and Cumberland rivers."[35] To his disappointment, Halleck dismissed his ideas until the end of January, when rumors of Beauregard heading to Kentucky from Manassas, along with his rival Buell's triumph at Mill Springs, finally led him to unleash Grant and Foote against Fort Henry.[36]

Grant moved quickly, despite a snowstorm, to assemble his men and supplies. With roads inundated with high water and mud, river transport was crucial. The assault force boarded transports and left Cairo on February 2, leaving behind most of their cavalry and wagons. With only thirteen such vessels available, Foote shuttled Grant's three divisions down the Tennessee in stages. They arrived near Fort Henry to find that persistent and massive rain had taken its toll there too. At the fort, poorly situated in a floodplain and vulnerable from several points of high ground, the river ran thirty feet above normal, high enough to make torpedoes anchored in the channel useless. Parts of the fort itself were two feet under water, while floodwaters inundated some of the lower batteries as well as the countryside for hundreds of yards in the rear. And the river was still rising. During the two previous weeks, over four inches of rain had fallen nearby in Clarksville, and more was coming. Rainfall actually worsened as Grant's strike force arrived, with 1.1 inches accumulating on February 3 and an additional 1.4 inches on the sixth as a low-pressure system moved through, followed by an anticyclone. At least it was growing warmer thanks to wind from the southwest. After several days in the thirties, the temperature reached 56 degrees on the day of the battle.[37]

Grant planned to launch an attack on Fort Henry using his ground troops and Foote's gunboats. When the hour came, the rain had stopped and the sky was clear, but Grant's infantry found the movement slow going due to the high water behind the fort. With the river so high, Foote's four ironclads and three wooden gunboats steamed boldly up to the wall of the fort, firing as they came in. Only a token force responded. Trusting that the mud and flooding would slow Grant's soldiers for a time, but equally concerned that the waters had left only one avenue of escape, Brig. Gen. Lloyd Tilghman already had abandoned Fort Heiman as indefensible and sent most of Fort Henry's 2,500 men off to Fort Donelson before the attack even began, keeping only a skeleton crew to cover the escape. After little more than an hour, Tilghman surrendered.[38]

Grant and Foote took Fort Henry quite literally at the flood. Suddenly, the swollen Tennessee River and its valley was wide open to Union forces. Unimpeded by Confederate defenses, some of Foote's gunboats kept steaming all the way to Florence, Alabama, and the Muscle Shoals. They returned with a captured enemy gunboat, having destroyed other boats, supplies, and a vital railroad bridge. In hindsight, the Confederacy never recovered from losing Fort Henry and the territory it was supposed to protect. Grant did not follow up immediately, however. Fort Donelson still blocked the Cumberland and represented a threat in his rear. He informed Halleck that he planned to march the twelve miles from Henry to that fort and conquer it as well. With confidence in his abilities and only contempt for Fort Donelson's commanders—politicians-turned-generals John B. Floyd and Gideon Pillow—Grant thought it would take no more than forty-eight hours to capture.[39]

That was wildly optimistic. Part of the subsequent delay was self-inflicted. Grant wanted reinforcements. Foote had to repair his battered flotilla and steam back to Cairo, a necessary backtracking in order to go down the flooded Cumberland.[40] But as Grant admitted, weather played a major role, too, writing, "the rain continued to fall so heavily that the roads became impassable for artillery and wagon trains."[41] Red-clay mud in some places was ankle deep. Too, thanks to a cold front out of the west, temperatures crashed after the capture of Fort Henry. Between February 7 and February 10, afternoon highs barely reached into the thirties and dropped below freezing after dark.

Grant was only ready to move on February 11. He sent six regiments ahead by gunboat and then marched east with the balance of his 15,000-man force the next day. Optimism and unseasonable warmth were in the air. The sky was clear, and the afternoon high rose to 68 degrees thirty miles east in Clarksville, the warmest day of the month. The day was so pleasant that many Federals threw away their blankets and overcoats, assuming that they would not need them again. Grant himself left their tents behind. The column stopped that evening two miles from the fort. The next morning, the temperature was a comfortable 54 degrees at 7 A.M. in Clarksville, rising to 57 degrees in the afternoon. While Curtis in Missouri took Springfield that day, Grant encircled Fort Donelson as the gunboat *Carondelet* shelled it.

Then a massive arctic cold front moved in from the west. Temperatures plunged into the thirties on the night of the thirteenth and kept falling, reaching into the teens by morning. It started raining again around dark, lightly at first but then heavily. Sleet, two inches of snow, and a strong north wind lashed the soldiers during the night. Lacking their tents and often their overcoats and forbidden to build fires that might give away their positions, men huddled under blankets while soaked uniforms froze. It was no better inside the fort that night, where men lacked tents and blankets and woke up covered by snow. Other defenders were unable to lie down at all, as rifle pits filled with water that froze. Many men suffered frostbite. Some stayed warm by trying to improve their frozen breastworks and entrenchments.[42]

February 14 dawned "cold and cheerless," in Union division commander Brig. Gen. John A. McClernand's words.[43] Brigade commander Col. Richard J. Oglesby described his men as "nearly torpid from the intense cold of the night."[44] Locals averred that they had rarely seen a worst blast of winter. In Clarksville, it was 11 degrees. In the cold, Grant extended his lines nearly to the river. As historian Benjamin Cooling points out, the wind was so stiff and the ground so snowy and icy that Grant called off major army operations. He left this day's action largely to Foote, hoping for another Fort Henry miracle. Instead, the flotilla ineffectually pounded the earthen fortification in the afternoon from a safe distance, as the high temperature rose to only 16 degrees. Almost a half inch of freezing rain doused the troops, and that night nearly three inches of new snow fell.[45]

As Grant later admitted, his men endured the arctic snap without adequate shelter or often even fires.[46] Surg. John H. Rerick of the 44th Indiana wrote that "the day had been one of the coldest for that part of the country. . . . A snow-storm blew up during the night, and when the morning light dawned the waking heroes could be seen in all directions creeping out of grave-like hillocks of snow that covered the ground."[47]

Inside Fort Donelson was chaos. The Confederate commanders debated whether to surrender, try to hold the fort until help arrived, or attempt a breakthrough. At dawn on the fifteenth, with the temperature at a brutal 10 degrees but skies clear, their assault surprised the Union right. Although the crackling snow and laden brush were serious impediments, they caught the enemy unwares. Driving away two Federal brigades, the Confederates opened two roads. Grant, who had left the field to confer with Foote, never heard the fighting; high winds blew the sound away from him. Once informed, he returned quickly, determined to stop the enemy breakout. The Confederates stopped themselves instead: Floyd and Pillow lost their nerve and retreated.[48]

The major fighting at Fort Donelson took place on one of the coldest days of the winter, the fields covered with snow. The high that day reached only 23 degrees; that night it was 21 degrees at 9 P.M., then 18 degrees the next morning.[49] Men fought and died in the cold, mud, and snowy slush, "in which the unfortunate pedestrian floundered and rolled like a rudderless boat in a gale." Their daytime exertions kept some of them warm enough—Iowan Daniel Matson remembered the afternoon as warm—but at night the men and the mud froze.[50] For the wounded, the frigid night was agonizing. Franc Wilkie of the *Dubuque Herald* wrote: "The streams were frozen and a light snow began to fall toward morning. There were no tents or fires, and the troops suffered intensely; if the uninjured found the cold unendurable, what must have been the condition of the wounded? Hundreds of them lay out all this dreary night, without shelter, food, water, or medical assistance. Many died who, amid other surroundings, would have recovered. It was horrible beyond comprehension, and yet without remedy."[51]

Floyd and Pillow, as well as a disgusted Col. Nathan Bedford Forrest and his men, took advantage of the darkness to escape into the windy night. The senior generals left Brig. Gen. Simon Bolivar Buckner to surrender the fort and remaining garrison the next morning. Buckner hoped for favorable terms—Grant was an old friend—but the Union commander offered nothing except an "unconditional and immediate surrender." Buckner had no choice but to accept. Many factors led to that conclusion. From the initial siting of the forts until the final ignominious moments inside them, Confederate leaders performed poorly. Grant, in contrast, usually acted skillfully, led good subordinates, and had the stronger battalions. Foote's cooperation helped immeasurably. One again cannot overlook the significant role of weather, however. Soldiers in both armies endured a bitter cold and wintry precipitation. Wounded men died of exposure, sometimes frozen to the ground by their blood. Operationally, flooding negated Fort Henry's already limited effectiveness and set events in motion that elevated Grant to prominence. Fully one-third of Confederates in the theater, nearly 15,000 men, became prisoners. Buckner soon found himself imprisoned in cold Boston. Refusing to bow to bad weather, Grant and Foote ripped a gaping hole in the Confederacy's western line that never healed.[52]

~

After the falls of the river forts, Sidney Johnston abandoned Bowling Green and retreated on bad roads to Nashville. His forces arrived on Valentine's Day, the same day of the heaviest fighting at Fort Donelson. Reports reached him there about the fort's capture. With the city's own river defenses inadequate, Johnston concluded that Nashville could not be held either. He decided to save his army, surrendering the city's vital industries and laden warehouses. On February 16, the Confederates again retreated, this time to Murfreesboro. The weather turned cold again and brought a new round of sleet, snow, and high winds. Waterways flooded, and bridges washed out.

Once in Murfreesboro, Johnston gave up on holding the rest of Middle Tennessee. He issued new orders for the troops all along the broken Confederate line, from Columbus into East Tennessee, to retreat and rendezvous below the Tennessee River. Influenced by General Beauregard, lately exiled west by President Davis to serve as Sidney Johnston's second in command, that rallying point became the vital railroad junction at Corinth, Mississippi. The Confederate high command began shifting all available troops in the region there, stripping posts on the Gulf Coast to replace the men lost at Mill Springs and the river forts.[53] Meanwhile, the weather worsened. In Decatur, Alabama, Capt. John W. Caldwell of the 9th Kentucky described the deteriorating conditions: It began "sleeting, raining and [the wind] blowing very hard and in a few seconds the most terrible storm I ever witnessed was upon us. The sleet & rain and large hail fell in torrents. . . . Every tent in our camp was leveled with the ground. Camp kettles were blown through the air, wagons upset and trees blown down."[54]

Union troops moved quickly to exploit the opportunity the fall of the forts created. Grant wanted to keep moving up the Cumberland to Nashville but halted at Clarksville, lacking enough transportation and overwhelmed by his prisoners. Besides, he reasoned, Buell was on the way to Nashville anyway. Having pulled his army out of their scattered posts along the way from Louisville after Fort Henry, Buell's Army of the Ohio was indeed moving south, by foot, rail, and riverboat. Along the way, his soldiers experienced the same cold, sleet, and mud that Grant's men endured in Tennessee, including the violent cold snap of February 13. The weather moderated as they reached Bowling Green but turned rainy and cold again on the night of the eighteenth. Snow fell the next day. On February 20, yet another cold day, flash flooding raised the Barren River fifteen feet above normal. Buell's men nevertheless forged on the Nashville, sleeping in "houses, barns, and straw piles," before reaching the city on February 25. Cold weather and rain characterized the entire advance.[55] The column arrived in chaotic Nashville to find the Cumberland still flooded. Pvt. Levi Wagner of the 1st Ohio remembered, "we found the river at flood tide, the bottom lands all flooded, and the rain was still pouring down." The road was above high water, but since the Rebels had destroyed the main bridge, "we could not cross and were compelled to stand there in the rain for several hours, waiting for a ferry boat to come and take us over." Once the men were across, the weather deteriorated, as "the air had become much cooler, and the rain had turned to sleet." At least the next morning was bright and clear.[56]

Dampening spirits further was the fact that they could not claim the honor of taking the city. Bull Nelson, a brigadier general of army volunteers since September, had a division already there. Sent ahead on steamers to Fort Henry, Grant had sent the troops down the Cumberland. Nelson officially occupied the city on February 25 and raised the Stars and Stripes over the state capital just ahead of the Army of the Ohio's lead division. Buell was annoyed. Grant and his entourage visited three days later without finding the department commander, which made matters worse. Buell claimed both the city and Grant's theater of operations as his own. He complained to Halleck, who searched for any excuse to deflate Grant's growing reputation. Citing insubordination as well as an alleged inability to control his men—and new rumors about his drinking—Halleck essentially fired Grant on March 4 upon his return to Fort Henry. Halleck then ordered Maj. Gen. C. F. Smith to move the army down the Tennessee to Savannah, near the Mississippi border. Only on March 13 did Grant resume command—Halleck had overreached—and arrived in Savannah to find that Smith had divided the army between that town on the east bank of the river and Crump's Landing and Pittsburgh Landing on the west side. Grant quickly ordered the army to reunite at Pittsburgh Landing while he waited in Savannah for Buell. Situated high above the river, the landing seemed safe from flooding. From there, the Union armies would move jointly against Johnston. Grant later confessed that he had no thought that the enemy might strike first.[57]

Meanwhile, it kept raining. In Clarksville, across the state, it rained half of March's thirty-one days. The region around Savannah typically is wetter than Clarksville and about two degrees warmer. The writings of soldiers at Pittsburgh Landing and at Corinth certainly suggest a great deal of rain. One Confederate wrote on March 23 that he had not seen such foul weather in years, citing incessant rain, sleet, and snow. Pvt. Alexander Downing of the 11th Iowa, which arrived on March 17, described "nothing but a jelly of mud." A belt of Ultisols runs along the Tennessee all the way into the Deep South, so at Pittsburgh Landing, the Iowans found the same red clays that simultaneously tortured Union soldiers from Arkansas to Virginia. Two days later, Downing complained that "there has been so much rain that water stands on the surface" of their campsite. "We cut brush and place it on the ground in our tents to lie on at night." It was cold as well until a dry warming trend began on March 26. Cpl. Leander Stillwell of the 61st Illinois wrote, "we had just left the bleak, frozen North, where all was cold and cheerless, and we found ourselves in a clime where the air was as soft and warm as it was in Illinois in the latter part of May." It did not last. Precipitation returned on April 2, followed by more rain as well as hail two days later. "By night," Downing added, "it got very warm." Another front entered the Tennessee Valley.[58]

Grant waited along the Tennessee for the arrival of Buell, who was behind schedule. Reinforcements were still coming in to the army at Nashville, including many of the regiments that had fought at Logan's Cross Roads. To save time, most of them diverted to Louisville in order to board river transports. Captain Keil of the 35th Ohio described the roads from Lebanon to Louisville as "horrid. . . . [T]he teams stuck in the mud, and the teamsters were whipping, hollowing and 'cussing.'" When the wagons mired down, they "were lifted out by placing levers under them, and with main force literally 'boosted' out the 'chuck holes.'" Keil believed that the worst day, February 19, would "be remembered by the men as the most disagreeable one of the many disagreeable days during our term of service. The rain fell in torrents all day, and the men were drenched to the skin." On February 27, they boarded steamers in Louisville for Nashville.[59]

The counterclockwise riverboat trip down the Ohio and Cumberland Rivers took soldiers through an otherworldly landscape. Five inches of precipitation in February and an additional ten inches in March meant flooded rivers. Not since the 1840s had the Tennessee been so high. Soldiers described destructive flooding on an enormous scale. The 31st Ohio, for example, boarded a transport on February 25, bound for Nashville. The Ohio River was as swollen as its tributaries. "The river had overflowed its banks," Captain Putnam observed, "and the scenery was anything but beautiful. Submerged fields, with stunted timber protruding above the water, floating fences and haystacks, and houses with water running in at the second story windows, were the principal scenes which met the eye. The water god appeared to reign 'supreme.'" Drummer Bircher of the 2nd Minnesota reported seeing a barn floating down the river, with chickens on the roof, which his hungry comrades vainly tried to catch. Floating debris also made the river dangerous. The first evening out, one man drowned while walking across a plank to another boat. "The river being so high, and running so swift," Putnam lamented, "it was deemed useless to undertake a search for the body."[60]

On March 1, Putnam's boat turned into the Cumberland. The flooding there was worse. "The scene on both sides of the river was complete desolation," he continued. "The river was never seen in such a state by the oldest inhabitant. Usually a modest stream, the Cumberland had spread out for miles, submerging field and forest. Little villages along its banks were depopulated, the water in many instances running over the roofs of the houses. Everything moveable had been swept away. . . . [I]t appeared that a second flood had devastated the earth." He particularly remembered a transport that had wrecked when it "got into the woods."[61] As Keil noted, transport captains took "short cuts across country; the main channel was avoided, so as to keep out of the sweep of the current."[62] Col. William Grose of the 36th Indiana remembered a shortcut that passed "over farms, and by houses with the first story filled with water and the family in the upper, with their boats cabled to the building."[63]

The massive flooding played a second major role in delaying Buell's overland march. The general sent out two divisions, one to seize Cumberland Gap and the other to cut the Memphis and Charleston Railroad in northern Alabama. He got his cavalry moving on March 15 but dispatched his other infantry divisions piecemeal over the next two weeks, not leaving Nashville himself until March 25. The weather was good at first—a sunny and warming stretch began on March 16—but heavy rain, snow, and the resulting bad roads, mud, and high water, soon returned. At Clarksville, it rained for six straight days beginning on March 19. Daily highs fell to the low forties, while nighttime lows hovered just above freezing. Buell's columns inched along until they bottlenecked some forty miles down the pike at Columbia, along the flooded Duck River. The river was running forty feet deep and extended two hundred yards into the surrounding bottomlands. Buell decided to build a proper frame bridge across the Duck to replace one burned by the retreating Confederates. He estimated this would take no more than five days and ordered his engineers to assemble a pontoon bridge also, even though he had already sent his pontoons ahead to Savannah. The Army of the Ohio did not begin crossing the Duck until March 29. By then, the rain had stopped and the river was fordable, as impatient Bull Nelson proved when his troops stripped down to their underwear and waded in. Once across, he pushed his division hard despite the return of the rains and the end of the macadamized pike. Buell's army followed in their churned-up wake.[64]

Buell's march to the Tennessee River, however plodding, caused great concern at Confederate headquarters in Corinth. Any hope of regaining Tennessee meant defeating Grant before Buell could reinforce him. Johnston waited as long as possible, hoping to increase both the size and training level of his army. On April 2, as reports filtered in from the north, he decided it was now or never. His forces began moving north the next morning, intending to attack on April 4. Time-killing confusion marred the movement almost immediately. Beauregard's complicated marching orders, based on Napoleon's Waterloo orders and a single map, would have challenged even seasoned veterans. A traffic jam in Corinth delayed movement. The roads north were narrow, spongy from the recent rains, and dotted with swampy expanses and sharp ravines. Creeks were swollen to their brims.[65] Edmond Livaudais of the Orleans Guards wrote that during the night, "the rain increased twofold. . . . [I]t was only the beginning of our miseries."[66]

Rain fell all that night and into the next day as the Confederates floundered north in red-clay mud. Units took the wrong roads or marched in the wrong order. Traffic jammed up again and again. Infantrymen had to pull artillery from mud holes. By evening, most of the army was strung out along the road. Johnston delayed his attack until the next morning. The weather turned cold after dark, and around midnight a hailstorm began, followed by more rain.[67]

This heavy predawn rain did more than cause sleeplessness and discomfort. Flooding streams and rendering roads nearly impassable, it ultimately forced Maj. Gen. William J. Hardee to delay the initial attack yet again. He finally moved forward at dawn. By 10 A.M. he had stopped again, in need of reinforcements to complete his line of battle, which took more time. It was 2 P.M. before the army was prepared to strike. By that time, some of Johnston's generals wanted to cancel the assault entirely. As they argued, the men were worn out and nearly out of rations. Beauregard also recommended retreat, citing both the men's exhaustion and what he assumed was the loss of surprise, due both to minor skirmishing and a rolling panic that involved Confederates firing their rain-soaked guns to see if they still worked. Johnston would have none of it. He would attack at dawn. That night, in the wet darkness, chilled but forbidden to build fires, the Confederates listened to the sounds of the nearby Federal camps and waited for morning.[68]

Sunrise was gorgeous. Sunday, April 6, dawned with the promise of a better day. Hoosier John Rerick remembered that it "opened as lovely and beautiful as any sung of by the poets," with "balmy air" and singing birds. It was a Sabbath morning that needed no priest or minister "to direct the mind upward from nature to nature's God."[69] Looking at the same sunny, cloudless sky, Leander Stillwell happily thought of home until he saw the reflected sun on approaching gun barrels and bayonets. Confederates poured from the woods into two unprepared Federal divisions. Grant had committed the same error that he had made at Fort Donelson, assuming that a bayed enemy would not strike first. Federal officers had ordered no entrenchments, laid out camps haphazardly, and dismissed early warnings of the enemy's approach as mere nervousness. Near disaster followed. Throughout the day, the Confederates pounded the Federals back, past little Shiloh Church and toward the river. Many ran, but others fought stubbornly.

Hobbling from a fall from his horse, Grant arrived from Savannah at midmorning and constructed a last-ditch line near the river. Buell joined the defenders early that afternoon, so shocked by the thousands of broken shirkers along the river that he told his staff to "draw your swords and trample these —— into the mud!" Grant refused to consider retreat. Buell sent for his army, starting with Nelson's division. Meanwhile, the Confederates wasted valuable hours attacking a "Hornet's Nest" of Federal troops they could have easily bypassed on its flanks. They lost more momentum when Johnston fell mortally wounded. That night, Beauregard halted the attack two miles from where it began. Concerned about the army's disorganization but confident, he planned to drive the Yankees into the river if they did not flee first.[70]

The night grew cloudy. Rain started up again around 10 P.M., with lightning, thunder, and hail toward morning. Many Confederates slept in captured Federal tents. Others lay outdoors, sometimes in water two or three inches deep. Prisoner Daniel Matson of the 14th Iowa woke up in a cornfield nearly underwater. Grant escaped into a hospital tent only to have the gore and agony drive him back out into the rain. The storm soaked and chilled sleepless Federals, as a legion of reporting officers later made clear. The next morning was wet but warmer, with afternoon temperatures approaching 70 degrees. Buell and Grant counterattacked in the rain. Wet artillery powder silenced Beauregard's big guns. Steadily, Buell and Grant fought the Confederates back before Beauregard ordered a full retreat. Grant let them go.[71]

The weather was no better as the Confederates made their way back to Corinth, and the roads were worse for wear. In some places, mud was knee deep. "The night of the 7th the heavens were opened & the rains descended as they did in Noah's day," Pvt. Johnny Green complained, "but we were so exhausted that we laid down in the mud & got what sleep we could. I remember that I had dropped off to sleep when such a flood was running down the side of the hill I was attempting to sleep on that it got in my nose & almost strangled me before I woke."[72] The nights turned cold; on April 9, the high was 38 degrees in Clarksville. Many men made good use of the blankets, overcoats, oilcloths, and uniforms plundered from the Federal camps.[73]

The battlefield around Shiloh remained "a wilderness of mud."[74] Lt. Col. Wilbur Hinman of the 65th Ohio remembered a "long, long night. . . . A cold rain fell continually. Every thread of out clothing was saturated, and we were chilled to the very marrow. Our teeth chattered, and every muscle quivered as with a Maumee ague. Blankets and overcoats—our own had been left back the previous day—were gathered from the field. They were stripped from the dead, who needed them no longer, to cover and warm the living."[75] The wounded suffered immensely in such conditions, but at least some reaped one odd benefit. Soldiers began to report that some men's wounds glowed with a faint but eerie blue light they called "angel's glow." Odder still, those men later seemed to survive their wounds at a higher rate. Recent research suggests that the cold weather and lower body temperatures that followed allowed luminescent bacteria called *Photorhabdus luminescens*, living within parasitic nematodes in Shiloh's churned mud, to enter wounds and destroy deadly bacteria. The glow occurred when the nematodes vomited the bacteria.[76]

"April 8th dawned gloomy after a night of rain," wrote Chaplain John J. Hight of the just-arriving 58th Indiana. "The sky was overcast by clouds and these were sifting a misting shower. . . . The little bottom and the hillsides was a sea of mud, deep and almost impassable."[77] William Bircher described the scene as "horrible. . . . [D]ead men were lying in the mud, mixed up with sacks of grain and government stores, some lying in the water and others trampled entirely out of sight in the deep mud."[78]

After Shiloh, Grant launched a half-hearted pursuit through the rain. His army and Buell's then sat for a week in rain and mud before finally starting out in the direction of Corinth. The weather was mixed along the way, increasingly warm, sometimes sunny, but often rainy enough to keep the roads in bad shape. Wagons and guns once again sank up to their hubs. Some of Buell's regiments lacked tents and dry clothing; their supply wagons were mired in roads back to Savannah. Hinman complained that he wore wet clothing for ten days after the battle. Around April 16, the rain slackened, the roads began to dry out, and trains began to arrive. Yet overall conditions remained wet, muddy, and hard for both the pursuers and the pursued. Roads remained all but impassable.[79] The historians of the 58th Indiana wrote that "during the remainder of April we had some pretty tough experiences in soldiering. The country was the most desolate and forsaken we had ever seen; the rains continued and the mud was very deep and very nasty. Sickness increased and many deaths occurred."[80]

In the meantime, Halleck arrived. He assumed command of the combined armies and called for reinforcements from Maj. Gen. John Pope's Army of the Mississippi. On April 8, just as the smoke at Shiloh had cleared, Confederate forces at Island No. 10 had surrendered to Pope after nearly a month of campaigning in the same cold, wet weather. That cold rain decisively shaped Pope's campaign, in fact, by raising the river to levels not seen since 1858. High water flooded Confederate river batteries at New Madrid, Missouri, and on the island itself, making the rapid construction of an artificial channel on the west bank feasible. As historian Lisa Brady notes, Pope's massive and successful construction project became the model for later attempts at reengineering the Mississippi and for turning nature to the Union's advantage more generally. The high water also was a godsend for Flag Officer Foote's ironclads and transports and prevented the island's Confederate defenders from escaping through the swamps along the bank.

While he waited for Pope, Halleck attacked Buell and Grant. He was not alone. Public criticism of Grant's "surprise" would have driven him from the army had Lincoln not intervened. By the end of April, Grant was removed from real command by becoming second in command to Halleck. At Corinth, meanwhile, Beauregard and his battered Confederates waited for the 100,000-man Federal juggernaut. Reinforcements arrived in the form of Van Dorn's Pea Ridge army, about 14,000 men. Their trek from northwestern Arkansas to Mississippi had involved muddy roads and crossing the swollen, sometimes foggy, and treacherous Mississippi. Beauregard, nonetheless, remained seriously outnumbered, with perhaps 70,000 men all told. Many were sick with environmentally borne diseases, such as dysentery and typhoid, that infested the town's rancid water supply. The rain, runoff, and butchering of animals near flooded creeks, with men dumping the offal in the water, made the situation worse.[81] Confederates expected the rain and resulting mud to hold off Halleck. As one wrote on April 30, "our friend, the weather, retards his progress."[82]

Back at Pittsburg Landing, the weather alternated between clear and cloudy. Mornings were largely cloudy. Rain fell in the afternoon of April 25. On clear and warm May 2, Halleck began his slow descent upon Corinth. Unwilling to be surprised like Grant, he moved carefully, entrenching regularly. Contrary to accepted wisdom, it was not just caution that turned Halleck's march into a crawl—bad weather and roads had much to do with it. The historians of the 41st Ohio described the region as "an excellent place for corduroy roads. A week or more was occupied with short marches of two to four miles, as the roads permitted, for sometimes the repairs of the day were washed out by rain of the following night."[83]

Inside Corinth, Confederate soldiers dealt with the same challenging conditions. Pvt. Ephraim Anderson remembered how comrades drilled in the morning and evening but sought shade at midday. Beauregard twice tried to line up a superior force against one of Halleck's advancing columns only to be stymied by both Van Dorn's tardiness and heavy rain. The fresh-water situation inside the city worsened, and the army got sicker. Historian Thomas Connolly observes that by late May, 20,000 Confederates were ill. Increasingly pessimistic about his chances of holding Corinth, Beauregard decided to save his army. He abandoned the crossroads town and fell back along the Mobile and Ohio Railroad, aided by dry weather and solid roads until another three-day rainy spell began on June 1. The need for good water drove him to Tupelo, where he constructed a strong defensive line. Then, on June 14, he telegrammed the War Department that he was sick and was leaving Gen. Braxton Bragg in charge temporarily while he went to a spa in Alabama. Davis reacted angrily and fired him on June 20. The department was now Bragg's.[84]

Halleck, meanwhile, took Corinth and stopped in his tracks. As Earl Hess maintains, his decision made sense. The Union rear remained a no-man's land crisscrossed by guerrillas. Halleck needed reinforcements to control it. Bad roads and less useful rivers made for logistical bottlenecks. He also was unwilling to risk his army's health by pursuing Beauregard farther south into the feverish swamps of a fabled central Mississippi sum-mer. He instead decided to send a division back to Curtis in Arkansas, dis-patch Buell to liberate East Tennessee, and disperse the rest of his army to healthy cantonments. They would guard their supply lines and wait for autumn.

As for Vicksburg, the Confederacy's great bastion on the Mississippi, Halleck decided to let the navy worry about it. Having taken New Orleans at the end of April, Rear Adm. David Farragut's fleet reached Baton Rouge on May 9 and Vicksburg on May 18. The ships remained there until May 26 before steaming back downriver. Inflated estimates of the small garri-son and concerns that the river might fall to levels dangerous to his deep-keeled blue-water ships compelled his retreat. But Farragut later returned, fought his way past the city's guns on June 28, and made contact with the Federal Western Flotilla. Five thousand troops began building a canal, hop-ing to reroute the Mississippi at DeSoto's Point to bypass Vicksburg. Rising heat and the falling river stymied their efforts, as did the garrison and the Confederate ironclad *Arkansas*. Early in August, Washington recalled the disease-plagued expedition. Vicksburg remained in Confederate hands.[85]

Away from Vicksburg, the summer of 1862 was bucolic for Federal soldiers. J. H. Putnam, camped at Boonville, Mississippi, wrote that some Federals "constructed perfect gems of rural villages, with broad streets and willow mansions, with arched door-ways, latticed windows and evergreen arbors. In walking among these miniature cities, a person could not easily dispel a thought of Fairy Land."[86] Confederate camps, perhaps less fey, also featured natural or constructed shade along with other measures designed to beat the heat. Ephraim Anderson wrote, "our tents were raised a couple of feet from the ground to allow for a free circulation of air, and to make room, at a sufficient height, for sleeping berths, which we were in the habit of constructing when it was likely the command would not move for several days." The berths "were generally erected by driving forks in the ground and laying small poles across; they were rather hard, but to us not uncomfortable, and kept our blankets in good condition."[87]

Such measures were necessary because of a dramatic change in the weather. In mid-June, soldiers in both armies began to write accounts of intense heat, infrequent rain, thunderstorms, rising dust clouds, thirst, sunstroke, and growing sickness.[88] The great rainy period that shaped the first five months of 1862 had ended, replaced by a developing drought.

Chapter 6

A Perfect Bog

The Peninsula, Spring 1862

Winter refused to yield on the Potomac in February 1862. Charles Brewster described one storm, noting that the wind toppled a chestnut tree into his tent, blew down every tent in the 2nd Rhode Island's camp, and collapsed a cabin belonging to the 36th New York, killing a sergeant inside.[1] Confederates complained bitterly too, but at least their reddish soil was a familiar problem. Dick Simpson wrote that he had been "stuck fast up to my knees. I could not budge a foot, for every time I tried to take up my foot, my shoe would slip off." Plenty of other men in the "mudscape" had pants the color of red clay from the knees down.[2]

After the war, Joe Johnston argued that such conditions made offensive operations all but impossible in northern Virginia early in 1862. Federal activity along the Potomac required a defensive response, however. Johnston believed that McClellan was preparing to strike. He could not know that his opponent's goals were simply to secure the Baltimore and Ohio Railroad and—under pressure from Lincoln and Congress—drive off the Confederate's Potomac River batteries. Although he had yet to bring along the president, McClellan's eyes remained firmly fixed on a turning movement through the Chesapeake Bay. Given the information available to him, Johnston reacted understandably. On February 19, three days before Jefferson Davis's inauguration as the Confederacy's elected president, Johnston arrived in Richmond. It was rainy, with a high of 43 degrees. The general met with Davis and his cabinet for seven long hours. All agreed that, at some point, his outnumbered army would need to abandon Centreville, and perhaps cross the Rappahannock River, before the roads dried out and McClellan came south. Johnston left convinced that he had the president's permission to pull back as soon as the weather improved. Davis, in contrast, believed that Johnston's plan was to hold in place as long as possible. Such needless confusion was indicative of the two men's souring relationship.[3]

Three days later, on a rainy Washington's Birthday—the same day that Lincoln vainly had designated for an all-out movement against the Confederacy—Davis spoke beneath a massive equestrian statue of the revolutionary hero and an umbrella. He refused to move the inauguration indoors. In a driving rain, with temperatures in the upper forties, a sizable crowd listened to Davis and the pattering rain beneath their own umbrellas, ankle deep in red Richmond mud. It rained all day and poured during the evening reception.[4] North of Richmond, Benny Fleet described "a dreadful day, it commenced raining this morning soon after day, & has been raining hard all day. I sincerely hope it will not be an omen for his presidential term."[5]

After the inauguration, conditions trended drier and warmer, with highs rising on some days into the fifties. March came in like a lion, with stiff winds and high temperatures cascading into the midthirties. Another inch of snow fell along the Potomac on March 2, followed by two days of rain. According to Adj. Mat Richards of the 96th Pennsylvania, the roads constantly froze, thawed, and refroze into irregular jigsaws before thawing for good into mud "in its original glory and profundity."[6] Yet all signs pointed to a Federal movement south as soon as the roads dried out. One indication was that quartermasters began to issue new tents, sometimes called "shelter halves" or *tente d'abri* after a French model that McClellan had admired during the Crimean War. The Union commander intended shelter tents to replace large, cumbersome, and expensive wall tents and teepee-like Sibleys that required precious wagon space and decent roads for transportation. Soldiers could now carry their shelter on their backs. Every individual in the initial regiments received a "half shelter," which he buttoned to a comrade's half and erected on a light wooden framework. Fence rails, saplings, or occasionally bayoneted weapons eventually replaced lost or broken government-issued frames. These new tents, cramped and stuffy, were immediately unpopular.[7] Capt. Newton Curtis of the 16th New York complained that "the ridge pole was so near the ground that the occupants could neither sit nor stand upright."[8] Soldiers soon nicknamed them "dog tents," for as Pvt. John Billings wrote, "when one is pitched it would only comfortably accommodate a dog."[9]

March 5 dawned with temperatures around freezing, just like the last few mornings. The rain had ended in the night, but the roads remained bad. Bugler Oliver Norton of the 83rd Pennsylvania related how the previous night's "torrents" had washed "great gullies in the streets" that had frozen "as hard as stone" as the temperature dropped.[10] McClellan's army, nonetheless, began to stir. Troops moved to seize the river batteries, and engineers tried to erect a bridge across the Potomac using canal boats as pontoons, so that Major General Banks's corps could march against Stonewall Jackson's forces at Winchester. The plan failed miserably when the canal boats turned out to be too wide to get through the appropriate lock on the Chesapeake and Ohio. Johnston, however, assumed that the sudden activity meant that a big enemy push had begun. He hastily issued orders for a retreat, abandoning many of the river guns and one million pounds of rations. On March 7, his artillery and supply train quietly withdrew from the Manassas front. Laden with items from supply depots and leaving the rest in bonfires that smelled of sizzling bacon, the infantry followed the next day. Johnston was determined to cross the Rappahannock to safety.[11]

The retreat was hard, if relatively short. The temperatures—24 degrees at 7 A.M. but 40 degrees by 2 P.M.—continued the cycle of freezing and thawing roads. Worse, the wagons tore them up even more for the foot soldiers who trailed behind. Brig. Gen. Richard Taylor described the road as "tough and heavy, and crossed by frequent streams, affluents of the neighboring Potomac. These furnished occupation and instruction to a small body of pioneers, recently organized, while the difficulties of the road drew heavily on the marching capacity—or rather incapacity—of the men."[12] On March 11, the army crossed the Rappahannock. It had covered forty miles in four days over some of the worst roads imaginable, sometimes in rain and sleet that went unrecorded in Georgetown. After sedentary months in camp, men were in no shape physically for such a hard slog. The effort killed horses and mules too, by the hundreds. Cpl. Napier Bartlett of the 3rd Company, Washington Artillery later remembered, "we could have walked all day upon the prostrate bodies of the horses which fell by the wayside."[13]

Two days after crossing the river, Johnston informed Davis of the move. Incredulous, he appointed Robert E. Lee to an advisory role. Pushing Johnston down the chain of command, Lee received the authority to issue orders directly to that general's subordinates, including Jackson in the Valley.[14]

In Washington, a similar power struggle continued. Recent Union victories in the West, the fruits of so many winter campaigns, made McClellan's inaction politically unbearable for Lincoln and Republicans. The fiasco involving the narrow canal lock was the last straw. McClellan, in turn, was frustrated with Lincoln's refusal to sign off on his turning movement, and he was livid when the president seemingly questioned his patriotism. McClellan finally suggested that they bring together the Army of the Potomac's division commanders to weigh in on his plan. Eight of twelve supported their commander. The next day, March 9, Lincoln bowed to the professionals. The army would change its base from Washington to the Chesapeake no later than March 18. But, still pessimistic, Lincoln appointed three of the four "no" voters—Irvin McDowell, Edwin "Bull" Sumner, and Samuel Heintzelman—to corps command. He also mandated that McClellan leave behind sufficient troops to defend the capital and clear the Potomac of the enemy batteries.

After the meeting, reports came in that Johnston was retreating. McClellan hastily pushed his army toward Manassas despite the raw weather. It was a hard march for his men too, so out of condition after the long winter. Arriving at Johnston's abandoned works and camps on sunny March 11—just a day behind the Rebels—McClellan and his lieutenants deemed the muddy roads too wretched for further pursuit. Yet spirits were high. The mud precluded drill, occasional sunshine was refreshing, and the flight of the enemy seemed miraculous.[15] "'We expect to be in Richmond in a fortnight,'" Maj. Thomas W. Hyde of the 7th Maine wrote home.[16]

Federals explored the Confederates' cabins with a mixture of envy and disgust. Maj. Charles Wainwright was unimpressed, writing that "most of the men . . . lived in hovels built in the ravines, which are numerous, with a roof of logs covered with dirt. They were wretched things and awfully dirty."[17] Yet a few days later, Mat Richards could not hide his pique over the "excellent log huts" he found at Manassas. The "blooded frozen chivalry," he wrote, "have passed a very comfortable winter." Still, he was unable to resist taking a swing at southern indolence and soil. "This is a beautiful country," he observed, "and although the soil around this vicinity (red shale) looks impoverished and worn, I have no doubt that our Pennsylvania farmers with their subsoil plows and manuring would convert it in short time into a perfect garden."[18]

Johnston's retreat cleared the Potomac of artillery, but it created consternation in other ways. Newspapers blasted McClellan when they discovered that the southerner had equipped his works with logs painted black. They assumed—incorrectly—that the "Quaker guns" had fooled Little Mac. In a March 11 cabinet meeting, dissatisfaction with McClellan came to an ugly head. After Secretary of War Stanton hammered McClellan's generalship, Lincoln announced that he was relieving the general of everything except command of the Army of the Potomac.[19]

McClellan learned of his demotion when reading about it in a newspaper. Insulted, he also began having second thoughts about his Chesapeake plan. For one, Johnston's retreat placed him between Urbanna and Richmond. Then there was the Confederate ironclad CSS *Virginia*, popularly known on both sides by the ship's original name, the *Merrimack*. Bad weather prevented a planned Confederate sortie on March 7, but the next morning was sunny and calm. As Lincoln met with McClellan's division commanders in the capital, the *Virginia* steamed into Hampton Roads, sank two US Navy vessels, and ran a third aground. The weather delay proved crucial. The next day, with the sun again bright and clear on calm water, the *Virginia* returned to find the Federal ironclad *Monitor,* which had arrived after almost sinking in gale-force winds and high seas the previous day. All that day, the two ironclads fought before *Virginia* withdrew up the James River.[20]

Notwithstanding the "gunboat panic" that followed in Washington, the real problem for McClellan was the threat the Rebel ironclad posed to his fleet of transports. Cut off from Washington by sea, the army could find itself isolated on its beachhead. Unwilling to undo months of work and persuasion—or give in to the White House either—he improvised. The turning movement would proceed, only farther south at Fort Monroe, still in Union hands at the tip of the peninsula formed by the York and the James Rivers (known as the Virginia Peninsula, or the Peninsula). His army would advance on Richmond from there. The *Monitor* still would have to deal with the Confederate ironclad, which denied the James River to McClellan, but the navy expressed optimism. Both his new corps commanders and Lincoln approved the change in plans on March 13, as afternoon drizzle fell on the capital. McClellan immediately finalized preparations to move most of his forces to the Peninsula. Transports assembled at Annapolis for the Urbanna landing steamed hastily for Alexandria, opposite Washington. The army retraced its steps to the Potomac.

For newer soldiers who had spent their careers in camp, the march was grueling, and the weather made it worse. Over 1.5 inches of rain fell on the

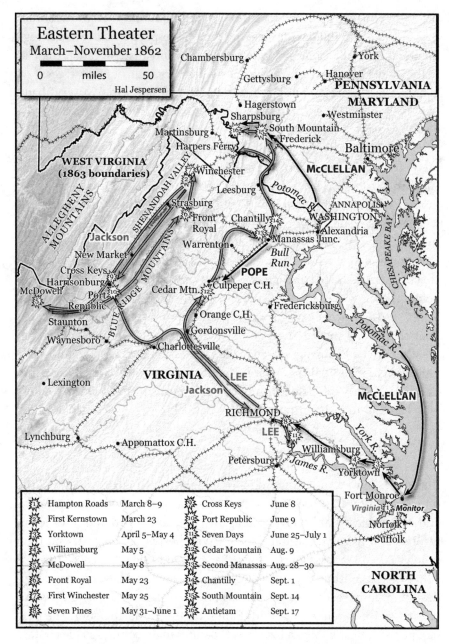

Eastern Theater
March–November 1862

0   miles   50

Hal Jespersen

Hampton Roads	March 8–9	Cross Keys	June 8
First Kernstown	March 23	Port Republic	June 9
Yorktown	April 5–May 4	Seven Days	June 25–July 1
Williamsburg	May 5	Cedar Mountain	Aug. 9
McDowell	May 8	Second Manassas	Aug. 28–30
Front Royal	May 23	Chantilly	Sept. 1
First Winchester	May 25	South Mountain	Sept. 14
Seven Pines	May 31–June 1	Antietam	Sept. 17

night of March 14 and through the next day. That night, a thunderstorm came up, dropping nearly another inch of precipitation. It was "such a rain as you never saw," George Barnard wrote, "it seemed as if the windows of heaven were open, and it actually poured down, and the water is some places was knee deep in the road besides fording creeks where it was waist deep."[21] Rain and mud made sleeping difficult, especially since many regiments lacked tents. Some soldiers stood in the rain all night rather than lay in the mud. Others tried to construct shelters from surrounding trees.[22] Lt. George North Jr. of the 20th New York, writing from "Camp Misery," had a new shelter tent but hated it. "It is very pleasant to wake up in a cold bath every morning," he noted sarcastically.[23]

On March 17, the first of McClellan's troops filed onto transports for the two-day voyage to Fort Monroe, a process that continued into April. Close to four hundred vessels of every shape and size eventually delivered more than 121,000 fighting men to the Peninsula. Back in Alexandria, the weather was fickle. At first it was pleasant. Afternoon highs temperatures rose into the fifties and even reached 62 degrees on March 28. Warm sunshine delighted the first regiments shipping south. Then an unexpected storm dumped an inch and a half of snow on March 29 and into March 30 before the snow turned to rain. The next day, the high rose to 62 degrees. Washington weather stayed warm until another brief and unexpected bout of cold and snow arrived on April 7, the last snow of the long winter. Weather on the Peninsula seemed better. Skies were fair, and highs usually registered in the middle to upper forties through the end of April, then into the fifties afterward, aside from a cooler spell near midmonth. Soldiers who had endured the bitter winter near Washington welcomed spring.[24]

But McClellan was not satisfied. Action in the Shenandoah Valley and the official reaction to those events threw his plans into new disarray. At the end of February, Banks advanced against Jackson as ordered. McClellan wanted him to drive the Rebels from Winchester, garrison it, and then swing back to Manassas. From there Banks could shield the capital as Lincoln insisted. With vastly superior numbers, the initial advance went well despite muddy roads. On March 6, Brig. Gen. James Shields's division, moving south to rendezvous with Banks, occupied Martinsburg. The next day, just as Johnston began his retreat, Banks's main column made contact with Jackson's command.[25] The two armies sparred for the next five days, during which a "savagely cold storm" struck on March 10.[26] Jackson finally ordered a retreat up the Valley on the night of March 11, with temperatures probably around freezing.[27]

The next day dawned clear and cold as Banks took the town. His pursuit was minimal, as he had accomplished his mission of taking Winchester. Jackson's men leisurely hiked down the Valley Pike to Rude's Hill, a natural fortress, burning strategic bridges as they went. Lt. Sandie Pendleton of Jackson's staff described how strong winds aided in the quick destruction of three particular railroad bridges on March 16. On that same day, McClellan also decided that Banks's mission was complete, ordering him to leave enough troops to check Jackson and get on to Manassas. The weather grew warm and sunny, almost reaching 50 degrees, before it worsened again. Rain fell late on March 18, snow the next day, and it rained again on the foggy twentieth.[28]

The next day, Jackson learned that his pursuers had withdrawn. Despite more snow, he turned back toward Winchester the next day. It was sunny, with temperatures rising to an afternoon high of 52 degrees in Washington. That afternoon, his cavalry encountered what they thought to be a few Federal regiments at Kernstown, four miles south of Winchester. Jackson attacked. The Union force actually was Shields's entire division, and it drove the outnumbered Confederates from a muddy battlefield in disarray. Temperatures fell back into the upper thirties during the night as Jackson's sullen little army fell back again to Rude's Hill. Kernstown was a Union victory tactically, but operationally the front began to unravel for the Federals. McClellan ordered Banks to return to the Valley and eliminate the threat Jackson posed, even though it would leave Washington uncovered. McClellan arranged to leave a token force to protect the capital while spinning the numbers. His army rivals, Stanton, and Lincoln all saw through the general's sleight of hand. Already worried about western Virginia, the president had just created the new Mountain Department in western Virginia for Republican favorite John C. Frémont, and had sent the former presidential candidate 10,000 of McClellan's men. On April 4, as McClellan left the city, Lincoln halted McDowell's 30,000-man corps and held it to protect Washington, detaching both McDowell and Banks from the Army of the Potomac. McClellan suddenly had 40,000 fewer troops thanks to Jackson and Lincoln.[29]

~

On the Peninsula, weather conditions grew ominous as McClellan packed to leave Washington. On March 26, Maj. Gen. John Wool at Fort Monroe

reported deep mud that precluded troop movements. During the cool afternoon of March 29, a "pelting rain" began that evolved into "torrents"
through the night and into the next morning. At Fort Monroe, the resident
army weather observer recorded three-quarters of an inch of rain on March
30. Camped in a plowed field, Sergeant Brewster described the great quantities of red mud the rain produced. These were red-clay Ultisols, though of
a different consistency. Nearly all of the Confederacy's Ultisols belonged to
the Udult suborder. Along the coast, however, the suborder Aquult domi-
nates. Sandy Aquults are found in wet areas near sea level, where the water
table is near the surface. They are even more prone to becoming "bottomless" mud. Any significant rain quickly turned Aquult Ultisol roads and
fields into quagmires while flooding the Peninsula's many streams. Worse,
those morasses would teem with mosquitoes carrying malaria.[30]

On the night of April 2, McClellan arrived and made last preparations.
That evening, "a tremendous Thunder shower" struck. Undeterred, on
April 4, 55,000 Federal soldiers took up the march to Richmond on two
parallel roads. The initial objective was Yorktown, on the northern side of
the Peninsula along the York River. From there and at fortified forward positions such as Big Bethel, Confederate major general John Magruder had
warded off the troops at Fort Monroe all winter with about 13,000 men. Recently stymied by Johnston's works at Manassas and Centreville, McClellan
did not intend a repeat performance. His plan was to quickly swing around
Magruder's southern flank and into the enemy's rear. While the southern
column nearer the James warded off any movement from Richmond, the
other would reduce the works at Yorktown.[31]

Bad weather mitigated against speed from the first steps. As historians Judkin Browning and Timothy Silver observe, "McClellan launched his
offensive at the worst possible moment in the worst possible location."[32]
The morning low was 50 degrees, barely rising to an afternoon high of 54
degrees. Rain had left the narrow roads already in poor shape, and almost
immediately the advance began to stretch out and bog down. That afternoon it again began to "rain like guns." The next day was worse. "Many
awful mud holes" filled the road, according to Brewster. "Before this it had
been raining, almost ever since we started, and now it grew dark and thun-
dered and lightened and the rain poured in torrents, but we struggled along
through the mud which was of the consistency of thick molasses on a hard
floor, and awful slippery."[33]

Covered in mud, McClellan seemed to be everywhere.[34] The weather worried him. He wrote that "the roads are infamous & I have had great difficulty in moving." Still, by the rainy evening of April 6, Union cavalry was outside Yorktown. There it first caught sight of the Warwick Line, stretching across the wet, gray horizon behind a rising river and marshy ground. McClellan's intelligence, collected on the fly after he abandoned Urbanna as an objective, had told him nothing about its existence. Nor did the general's maps show the true course of the Warwick River, which ran directly across his line of march through thick woods. Behind the dirty river, impressed enslaved laborers had constructed fourteen miles of engineered works across the Peninsula, from the James to the York. Imposing river batteries as well as the *Virginia* on the James anchored its flanks and kept the Federal navy from landing men in the rear.[35] In effect, as historian Richard Miller pithily describes it, McClellan faced a fortified "isthmus."[36]

Sunday, April 6—the first day of battle at Shiloh in Tennessee—was clear and even lovely on the Peninsula, aside from yet another brief storm. Fair conditions and light winds allowed Thaddeus Lowe to go aloft in his hot-air balloon to get a better look at the Confederate works. He reported that they were strong. On the ground, the mud remained deep. "We have no baggage tonight," McClellan wrote his wife, "our wagons being detained by the bad roads."[37] Unexpectedly facing Magruder's works and fooled by the amateur actor's stagecraft—sights and sounds designed to inflate his numbers in Federal minds—McClellan stopped. Assaulting such works would be madness. Instead, he would bring up his heavy artillery and lay siege to Yorktown. Only after his big guns had pounded the Warwick Line into dust and wood chips would he advance. It was the safe decision. But that evening brought a new shock: Lincoln's decision to keep McDowell at Washington. Thanks to the same faulty intelligence, McClellan believed that the Confederates outnumbered him. Dismayed, he immediately began working to get the corps back. Lincoln replied that McClellan already had 100,000 men. The country, he asserted, wanted action.[38]

Haste was in short supply at the front, however, due to the real necessities of siege operations coupled with the continuing rain. McClellan's men needed the next ten days simply to prepare to begin the siege. As historian Earl Hess points out, they had to improve the roads enough to shift men, heavy guns, and wagons of supplies forward. The big guns necessitated relatively flat roads, which in turn meant hand grading. The army also took over a local sawmill to produce lumber for shoring defenses. Quartermasters created supply depots. Engineers laid out batteries and connecting trenches. Toiling largely at night, sometimes under sniper fire, McClellan's infantry began working axes, picks, and shovels on April 17, building the batteries. At the same time, the Confederates labored to strengthen and extend their works, which were far less complete than the Union commander believed. In part, that meant constructing dams that could flood the Warwick River to a width of fifty feet while rendering existing fords useless. Richmond sent reinforcements as well. Arriving on April 14 ahead of his army, Johnston inspected the works. Returning to the capital, he warned Davis and Lee that they were inadequate for a long siege.[39]

All of this labor-intensive work would have been hard in normal conditions. Instead, it took place in rainy weather that produced acres of red mud and ruined country lanes. "The weather has varied between rain and sunshine," Mat Richards wrote, "in the proportion of about two hours of sunshine to twenty two of rain."[40] While that was an exaggeration, it was atypically rainy. At Fort Monroe, the official observer had recorded seven days of rain in April 1861, totaling 5.5 inches. In contrast, it rained fourteen out of thirty days in April 1862. Although the monthly accumulation actually was lower in 1862—4.3 inches—the frequency of the rain made for perpetual mud and hard digging. April 1862 was notably cooler as well, with an average high of 55 degrees (as opposed to 60 degrees) and a daily mean temperature of 52 degrees (as opposed to 57 degrees). Afternoon high temperatures rose into the sixties on April 14 and on into the seventies on the seventeenth before a cooling trend, beginning on April 20, reduced highs into the fifties (and twice into the upper forties) for the rest of the month.

It was stormy too. On April 7, just as the work began, a major coastal storm blew up around noon with such intensity that transports off Fort Monroe were unable to unload troops, while others closer to Washington could not begin the trip south. High temperatures fell into the forties for five days as the winds continued. It was no better for the men after landing. Lt. Col. Harry Purviance complained on April 9 that his 85th Pennsylvania could not get to the front due to the roads. Cpl. Joseph B. Laughton of the 38th New York described mud to his knees.[41] Inside the Warwick Line, soaked Confederates tried to stay warm while knee deep in water in their trenches. Few had tents, and they slept beneath what Pvt. Tally Simpson called "little houses made of blankets."[42]

Federals further complained about their tents. More had received shelter halves, a process that continued throughout the campaign, but others resorted to brush arbors in vain attempts to stay dry. Most everything either leaked or gave way to sheer volume; the army was always wet. Lt. Oliver Wendell Holmes Jr. of the 20th Massachusetts complained that the mud at his regiment's camp was knee deep and his men were soaked. "No tents," he continued, "no trunks—no nothing—it has rained like the devil last night all day and tonight and you may guess what the mud is in clayey soil where it was a real annoyance before. Marching will have to be slow, for the roads have constantly to be made or mended for artillery."[43] That meant more corduroying. De Trobriand described such roads as "a sort of rough floor, formed by small sticks resting on sleepers, and covered over with a light layer of leaves."[44]

Some men bore up with the weather and labor required. Lt. George Barnard defended his commander, hoping that "the boobies who have been snarling at McClellan all winter will see by and by that he knows more about war, than newspaper editors and country senators." Barnard saved his hatred for the administration.[45] Others were less content. "Rain and mud have outgeneraled the Army of the Potomac the last week," Purviance wrote.[46]

The muddy, heavy work took until the end of the month, due to what McClellan's chief of artillery called "the peculiarities of the soil and by the continuance of heavy rains during the greater part of the operations."[47] In Hampton Roads, the officers of the newly arrived ironclad USS *Galena* recorded frequent gales, rain, fog, and a thunderstorm on April 26. Finally, on April 30—the fourth rainy day out of five—McClellan's first siege battery opened up on the Warwick Line. The Confederates returned fire, but their inferior weapons were no match for 100-pounder and 200-pounder rifled Parrotts. Combined with his existing concerns about the fortifications and Yankee reinforcements, this Federal barrage was enough to convince Johnston that the time had come again to ignore Davis's wishes and retreat to Richmond. May opened the next day cloudy but warmer, with a high of 60 degrees at Fort Monroe. Seemingly, the rain had passed. Concerns about his supply train delayed Johnston's start until the warm, still night of May 3. Confederate artillerymen opened up in order to cover the retreat and then fled, abandoning almost eighty smoothbore guns. An eerie quiet fell. The next morning, observers in the balloon reported the Warwick Line abandoned. Pickets confirmed the news; moving into the works, a few men died when they tripped buried land mines. Surprised but delighted, McClellan telegraphed Washington to announce his premature triumph. His soldiers were less enthused. Their labor and exposure had merely allowed the Rebels to run to another redoubt.[48] Worse, they again discovered that their enemies had been "living in luxury" in wooden huts.[49]

From Yorktown, the Confederates marched all day on May 4 along two roads that intersected just east of the old colonial capital of Williamsburg. There they found a wet, reddish wasteland and heavy roads that slowed their columns to a crawl. Major Wainwright described the soil around the town as "underlain by a bed of shell marl which again lies in a subsoil of heavy clay; the soil above the marl is a very light sand, and in places not over a foot or two thick. The immense rains we have had all this spring . . . have converted it into the consistency of soft mortar."[50] Roads were equally bad. "The highways . . . were saturated by the spring rains," Confederate general James Longstreet remembered, "cut into deep ruts by the haul of heavy trains, and puddled by the tramp of infantry and cavalry. The wood and fallow lands were bogs, with occasional quicksands adding severest labor to the usual toils of battle."[51] As the 8th Virginia's Pvt. Randolph Shotwell happily observed, Confederate feet and wheels left the churned roads full of "ruts, holes, and muck" for the Federal divisions leading the pursuit.[52]

The day was lovely at first, but clouds began to gather late in the afternoon. Before dark drizzle began. After midnight, hard showers drenched and chilled the men. Rainfall stretched into the new day.[53] By the morning of May 5, Johnston faced the possibility that his train could bog down entirely on the one narrow road westward. Accordingly, he sent Longstreet and about a fourth of the entire command to hold off the Yankees while the rest dragged the train to safety. With the vehicles moving so slowly, Longstreet decided to fight. Magruder had partially constructed a fallback line at Williamsburg, running four miles between two creeks and anchored by a large earthen redoubt named for himself. Open fields of fire and abatis of felled timber lay in the approaches to the works, which were filling up with both rainwater and Confederate defenders. The ditch in front, nine feet deep, effectively formed a moat. Lacking enough men to use the entire line, Longstreet concentrated on defending Fort Magruder.

At about 7 A.M., the sky was gloomy with thick gray clouds. Joseph Hooker's mud-covered men moved against a stiff west wind toward the fort. The rain picked up again, falling so hard that Hooker's gunners could not properly situate their guns or sight them effectively. Already soaked, the infantry slogged across sodden fields and picked their way through wet abatis as townspeople watched from beneath umbrellas. Heintzelman,

Hooker's corps commander, later lamented that the elements had been arrayed against them. Hooker himself might have added incompetence to the list. He expected help from his right in the shape of Bull Sumner's column on the other road from Yorktown, led by Brig. Gen. William F. "Baldy" Smith's brigade, but Sumner had stopped a mile back and would not move.

Sensing a shift in momentum, Longstreet launched a counterattack. Some Federals ran for the rear. Heintzelman ordered drummers to beat a cheerful roll, but the drums were too soaked to make noise. Reinforcements moving up the road sank to their knees in the mire. Only a Confederate ammunition shortage—the wagons were stuck in the rear, up to their axles in mud—and the midafternoon arrival of Brig. Gen. Philip Kearney's muddy brigade prevented a rout. Together, Hooker and Kearney drove the Confederates back into the abatis as the rain again intensified. Roughly at the same time, Brig. Gen. Winfield Scott Hancock's brigade artillery opened up on the Confederate left after a two-mile scramble through the dripping woods. Longstreet sent Brig. Gen. Jubal Early's reserve brigade to deal with Hancock. Early ineffectively attacked through a thick forest, his poorly trained men slipping and falling in the muck. Hancock counterattacked with bayonets and held the flank.[54]

The Battle of Williamsburg ended in stalemate, murky darkness, and rain. During the long, wet night, Longstreet withdrew. It was not easy, as both his artillery and wagons were axle deep in mud. Soldiers tugged at them with ropes but finally abandoned five guns, other vehicles, and many horses. Animals on both sides drowned or else died of their futile exertions to escape the mud.[55] Shotwell described the night march as horrendous: "roads literally knee-deep in soft mud and slush—and with artillery, wagons, ambulances and footmen all jumbled together in the narrow roads. . . . The clay and sand of the roads was now worked into a liquid mortar, which overspread the entire surface, hiding the deep holes cut by heavy gunwheels, until man or beast discovered them by stumbling therein."[56]

May 6 broke fair before clouds again darkened and brought more rain in the afternoon. Maj. Gen. D. H. Hill, commanding the Confederate rear guard, described an army on the brink of collapse:

> Thousands of soldiers had sought shelter from the storm of the night before in barns and outhouses, and it was with the utmost difficulty they could be driven out. Cold, tired, hungry, and jaded, many seemed indifferent alike to life or capture. The roads were in truly horrible con-

dition. Horses with difficulty could wade through the mud and slush, and to footmen the task seemed almost impossible. The straggling was enormous. . . . The Yankee cavalry followed slowly in our rear, picking up stragglers, who had too little life and energy to keep up. . . . Six miles from Williamsburg we encountered a swamp of the most formidable character here many wagons and ambulances were found abandoned and had to be destroyed by the rear guard.[57]

Confederates deserted by the thousands that night. Charles Brewster described how wounded and abandoned Confederates "lay all night in the mud, with no covering, and rainy and bitter cold it was horrible to hear their groans they fairly made night hideous."[58]

At Williamsburg, after a night of "indescribable misery and horror," the Federal army was in little better shape. Having slept in the mud without fires—the rain extinguished campfires—McClellan's soldiers were rain soaked, chilled, and hungry. The Federals did not mount a pursuit until evening, except for token cavalry and ineffective fire from gunboats.[59] McClellan blamed the "infamous" state of the roads and the rain. "No signs of stopping," he wrote, "roads awful."[60] Conditions in the rear were dreadful. "The roads, and the fields by this time were worked up into mud," Sergeant Brewster wrote, "knee deep and it would start my long boots partly off, at every step." His regiment moved "through such horrible mud, that you cannot by any possible means get any idea of it." He noted abandoned wagons, "many of them stuck in the mud up to the bottoms of them and of dead mules and horses there is no end, and the stench is horrible."[61]

Finally, the weather cleared. The next week was fair and warm, with high temperatures rising into the seventies; May 11 reached 80 degrees at Fort Monroe. Both armies used the drying roads to make headway toward Richmond, although heat made for hard and increasingly dusty marching. That was especially true for the withdrawing Confederates, whose teams were so worn down that many men carried their belongings on their backs. Not surprisingly, they left a trail of abandoned equipment and effects in their wake. As for the roads, the degree of damage that McClellan's army faced behind Johnston's command was severe. Knee-deep mud dried into powder, a sort of instant mud that only required water. Some of McClellan's men blamed him for their failure to catch the Rebels, others defended him, but the general cited bad roads and poor maps.[62]

Not everyone in the Army of the Potomac was up to the renewed march. Labor at Yorktown and the rigors of Williamsburg added greatly to the sick detail. Charles Tripler—whose bad relationship with McClellan was reaching the breaking point—did little to hide his disgust. The troops had marched to Williamsburg in a "drenching rain" and "with nothing in their haversacks. They had no shelter from the rain, and nothing to eat. The roads were shocking." Not surprisingly, the surgeon continued, "a large number of men were thrown on my hands—some of them sick, most of them tired and exhausted." Overwhelmed by numbers, Tripler, with help from the US Sanitary Commission, sent shiploads of sick or injured men to Washington, and put others into hospitals in Williamsburg.[63]

Heat exhaustion took a further toll. Sgt. George A. Mitchell of the 5th New York Zouaves wrote his parents that "as many as 40 of our Regiment, dropped down in the road from the effects of the sun." He was among them. "I felt it coming over me, and I staggered to a fence and kept myself up, until the dizziness passed away, when I went in the woods and laid down for about 2 hours. At the same time the dizziness came over me, there was a blindness also and I could not see anything for about 5 or 10 minutes."[64]

On the York River, Brig. Gen. William B. Franklin's division landed, moved up the Peninsula to West Point, but failed to interdict the retreating gray columns. At Norfolk, pressed by the navy and Wool moving his forces against the city (a result of President Lincoln's brief personal foray ashore), the Confederates blew up the *Virginia* and headed for Suffolk on a hot, dusty road. By scorching May 13, McClellan was at Cumberland Landing on the Pamunkey River, a tributary of the York. There the army halted, as rain returned on the evening of May 14. Precipitation continued off and on through the next two weeks, leaving the roads miry again. Once the rain passed and the roads dried, the army aimed for the rain-swollen Chickahominy River, which flowed east of Richmond and then southeast to the James. Johnston had crossed the Chickahominy on May 16 after learning that the James was open to the enemy. His army was only seven miles from the capital. Johnston hoped to lure McClellan away from the protection of his gunboats and then strike. McClellan, however, was in no hurry. He planned to wait for McDowell's corps, which, according to reports, was on the way.[65]

Union cavalry reached the Chickahominy on rainy May 20. As the rest of the army slowly closed up, McClellan called for McDowell. Four days later, he learned that Lincoln had decided to send McDowell into the Shenandoah Valley instead, where Federal plans to tame Stonewall Jackson (described in the next chapter) had failed miserably. McClellan was apoplectic. Making matters worse, afternoon squalls and thunderstorms hit Union camps and river shipping on May 22. Drizzle followed on the afternoon of May 23, and rain fell sporadically on four of the next six days. A total of nearly five inches of precipitation fell at Fort Monroe. Once again, soldiers encountered mud in abundance.[66] On May 24, Wainwright described "a steady, hard rain all day, turning the whole country into a sea of mud and rendering the roads almost impassable." The next day brought "another heavy rain; and a very cold one too. . . . The water comes down most tropically, in sheets instead of detached drops as it does farther north."[67]

During this period, McClellan wrote constantly about rain, the poor state of the roads, and his own deteriorating health. "I have been troubled by the old Mexican complaint," he wrote his wife, referring to malaria, "brought on I suppose by exposure to the wet."[68] He was not alone in blaming the elements for the widespread illnesses that struck the army in May and would worsen in June.[69] As historian Kathryn Shively Meier explains, soldiers were more likely to blame the rain for their sickness than any other factor. Such exposure affected men in several negative ways. Soldiers believed that constant wetness contributed greatly to the diseases that infamously ran rampant on the Peninsula, especially malarial fevers, typhoid fever, rheumatism, diarrhea, dysentery, and what they simply called "Chickahominy fever" or "the Virginia Quickstep." And in a way it did. Contaminated drinking water was the leading cause of diarrhea, while mosquitoes that flourished in swamps widened by flooding carried malaria. According to mid-nineteenth century medical knowledge, however, swamps contained deadly vapors, or "miasmas," that produced malaria. As historian Andrew Bell observes, Confederates expected miasmatic swamps to become allies. Acclimation and quinine did help the Confederates somewhat, but both armies suffered from the nonaligned insect powers.

Rain, meanwhile, precluded restful sleep and thus lowered resistance to disease. Muddy shoes and clothing became heavy dead weights, exhausting marching men. Calories burned from the extra labor were not easily replaced, with supply wagons stuck in the mud miles away. Constant exposure depressed morale. Some soldiers found ways to minimize their exposure, especially in rainy, muddy weather, but often that required straggling to find a dry place to sleep or a warm civilian meal. But both armies frowned on straggling more than they feared the power of disease to winnow their forces. Officers did their best to keep men in the ranks. The war allowed no rest. Coupled with an inadequate military health-care system, including insufficient supplies of quinine, men sickened and died in droves, weakening the Army of the Potomac's actual effectiveness.[70]

As May drew to a close, McClellan put his men to work constructing bridges across the Chickahominy. He planned to lead his army across the morass and bring his artillery within range of Richmond. Weather and erroneous reports of Confederate activity to the north altered those intentions. Late on May 26, mist and light sprinkles began to fall. The next morning, torrential showers left river bottoms swampy. Two inches of rain fell at Fort Monroe that day alone, by far the heaviest daily precipitation total of the month so far. Advancing in the mud through flooded, snake-infested streams and a steady morning downpour heavy enough to snuff out cooking fires, elements of Brig. Gen. Fitz John Porter's new corps slogged fourteen slow miles before overwhelming an isolated Confederate brigade at Hanover Court House, north of Richmond. As historian Stephen Sears maintains, the battle delayed the completion of McClellan's advance across the Chickahominy. Brig. Gen. Erasmus Keyes's sickly IV Corps was isolated west of the rising river, near a crossroads called Seven Pines, about a mile southeast of the Fair Oaks station on the railroad that ran from Richmond to West Point on the York. Heintzelman's III Corps was set to follow Keyes but moved slowly through the muck. Sensing an opportunity, Johnston decided to destroy the IV Corps. He issued orders to attack on May 31 along three parallel roads. Farthest south, Longstreet would open the battle.[71]

By then, however, rains had returned to the Peninsula in new force. May 30 began with clouds and morning fog. Near 5 P.M., IV Corps skirmishers moved forward under an artillery barrage until a thunderstorm broke with such force that it halted the advance. The attackers scurried back though an ankle-deep flash flood to their shelter tents.[72] It was, wrote Capt. Newton Curtis of New York, "the worst storm and heaviest fall of rain during that time. . . . [F]lashes of lightning were almost continuous, and the thunder was appalling."[73] Another Union soldier called it "the most terrific thunderstorm it had ever been my lot to witness."[74] It roared on throughout the night, rain penetrating tents while lightning lit the sky. A man in the 44th New York died from a lighting strike. High water flooded Federal camps; pickets often stood knee deep in water.

More crucially, the fearsome storm raised water levels in the Chicka-hominy and other streams so rapidly that the onrushing muddy torrents began to wash away Federal bridges, leaving only two intact at dawn. Sur-rounding marshlands now stretched a mile. According to Col. Wesley Brainerd, whose engineers tried to erect a bridge during the storm, flood-waters up to a foot in depth extended for a half mile from the submerged bank. Watching the water rise near his own camp, Johnston deduced that the Chickahominy, too, had to be out of its banks. Brig. Gen. William Pen-dleton, commanding Confederate artillery, assured him that it would take twenty-four hours for the high waters to fall back, thus trapping any ene-mies on the west side of the river. McClellan's army was cut in two, save any bridges that survived, and the trapped, isolated corps could receive lit-tle or help from the other side. Victory was in Johnston's grasp.[75]

Dawn on the thirty-first was cloudy and foggy, with occasional drizzle. Lt. Edgar Newcomb measured 30 inches of floodwater at his regimental camp, while Capt. Joseph Kirkland of the 102nd Pennsylvania remembered up to two feet of water on his front. At the other end of the Peninsula, the weather observer at Fort Monroe recorded 2.25 inches of rain, about a third of the month's entire total. "The unfinished rifle pits in front were filled," Cpl. Luther Dickey of the 85th Pennsylvania wrote, "and every depression in the roads and elsewhere had become tiny lakes."[76]

For the Confederates, the view was no better. "The storms had flooded the flat lands," Longstreet remembered, "and the waters as they fell seemed weary of the battle of the elements, and inclined to have a good rest on the soft bed of sand which let them gently down to the substratum of clay."[77] Events quickly proved that the storm was less of a boon than Johnston ex-pected. Soldiers were exhausted from lack of sleep. One of his division commanders slept late and got his men moving even later. Boggy roads impeded artillery and marching men. Flooded roads caused halts. The sur-rounding countryside in some cases was knee deep with water and hip deep in swampier expanses. Some columns—including Longstreet's—took the wrong roads. At one point, Longstreet halted to build a bridge over a fordable creek.

It thus took until the hot early afternoon—it was 80 degrees at 2 P.M. on the *Galena*—for the Confederates to untangle their lines and attack. They promptly encountered felled trees and partially built earthworks sur-rounded by natural moats. Piecemeal assaults failed. About a mile north at Fair Oaks, in what essentially became a separate battle, Bull Sumner used a rickety bridge to cross a division and turn back the Confederate attack there. Again, swollen streams and deep mud impeded both armies. Some artillery never made it to the field due to the deep mire. Because of flooding and confusion at headquarters, Johnston never got half of his army into action. He himself fell late in the afternoon, seriously wounded by shrapnel.[78]

Years later, Johnston expressed regrets that he had not waited another day before attacking. While he largely meant to reference reinforcements that might have joined him, the weather of June 1 was better. Afternoon temperatures remained in the eighties on the *Galena*, reaching a scorching 88 degrees at 3 P.M. Skies cleared, and floodwaters receded.[79] Randolph Shotwell remembered that "the occasional bursts of sunshine alternating with dripping showers, added to the ghostliness of the numerous corpses lying about as we moved toward the forest."[80]

The Confederate command situation was equally murky. Johnston's second in command, Maj. Gen. Gustavus Smith, floundered before launching a renewed attack in the morning. It failed, and the battle was over by noon. Two hours later, a worried President Davis ordered Smith to turn over command of the army to General Lee.[81] Lee's first action was to pull back to Richmond. The Federals followed gingerly, with McClellan again citing weather and ground conditions as the chief delaying factors. It rained still more after midnight on June 2, and the battlefield stank with the wet and decomposing dead. "I only wait for the river to fall," the Union commander confidently wrote Stanton on June 2, "to cross with the rest of the force & make a general attack." Later that day, he assured his wife that "the Chickahominy is now falling & I hope we can complete the bridges tomorrow. I can do nothing until that is accomplished."

But the Peninsula's fierce spring was not done either. That day was hot (89 degrees at noon on the *Galena*), but at night more clouds rolled in. June 4 brought rain all day and into the night. Two days later, John Babcock, McClellan's scout and a close associate of Allen Pinkerton, wrote that the Chickahominy bridges were unsafe to cross due to nine inches of rain over the previous six days. Babcock said nothing about whether that flooding hampered his scouting, but one wonders how much his report blinded McClellan. Five days of periodic rain and winds from the north followed, beginning on June 6. At Fort Monroe, two inches fell in total, bringing new flooding. The days were warm too, with highs in the seventies and eighties until the tenth.

The rain wrecked the Union advance. Three days later, McClellan wrote

Stanton that "the Chickahominy River has risen so far as to flood the entire bottoms to the depth of three & four feet. I am pushing forward the bridges in spite of this and the men are working night and day up to their waists in water to complete them. The whole face of the country is a perfect bog entirely impassable for artillery or even cavalry except directly in the narrow roads which renders any general movement either of this or the rebel army utterly out of the question at present until we have more favorable weather."[82]

On the wet, chilly morning of June 10, McClellan wrote his wife again that "it is raining hard & has been for several hours!" Hoping to find God's will in it, he added, "it is quite certain that there has not been for years & years such a season—it does not come by chance." Rain still prevented movement, he continued, "the Chickahominy is so swollen & the valley so covered with water that I cannot establish safe communication over it—then again the ground is so muddy that we cannot use our artillery—the guns sink up to their axle trees." He sounded a similar note to Stanton, admitting: "I am completely checked by the weather. The roads and fields are literally impassable for Artillery, almost so for Infantry. The Chickahominy is in a dreadful state. . . . I shall attack as soon as the weather & ground permit, but there will be a delay—the extent of which no one can foresee, for the season is altogether abnormal."[83]

While historians largely have either ignored the weather at this stage, or else damned McClellan for excuse-making, some men agreed with him.[84] The morale of others reached low ebb. The conviction that the southern environment was malevolent deepened.[85] Corporal Dickey narrated a scene "where Jupiter Pluvius seemed to be the only reigning sovereign." The downpour of June 4 drove men to high ground as camps flooded. The next morning, they found that "every gully, brooklet or stream of any kind was overflowing, while the rain continued without abatement, the men frequently marching in water ankle deep, and in fording streams the water would occasionally reach the waists of the shorter men."[86]

June 11 dawned cloudy but stayed dry and grew warm, with a late-afternoon high of 74 degrees. McClellan hoped that the rain was over. While it did rain four more times in June, it was light except for "a terrible storm" on the twenty-fourth. Steamy heat now became the main weather story. Temperatures reached 92 degrees on June 14 and 95 degrees the next day. While readings fell back into the seventies and then low eighties from June 16 through June 22, heat and humidity characterized the rest of the month.[87] McClellan planned to use the drier weather to reconstruct bridges lost to "flood & fire," but he cautioned Stanton that it would take a good month to complete. Told that McDowell's force would be sent after all, he advised Stanton to route them by water, for the roads were still a mess. He reiterated the bad state of the roads on June 15, following heavy afternoon rains. "This will retard our operations somewhat," he warned the secretary, "as a little rain causes the ground in this section to become soft and boggy rendering it impossible to move Artillery except directly in the travelled roads. . . . [I]t is absolutely necessary that we should have some few days of dry weather to make the ground firm enough to sustain our horses & guns."[88]

Desperate to save his capital, Lee had no time to hope for dry weather. He had opposed Johnston's retreat to Richmond. Now in command, he was determined to give up no more ground. His first step was to send Jackson reinforcements. The more success Jackson had in the Valley, the more it would divert Union troops from McClellan. Lee then proposed using some of his men to defend Richmond while leading the rest on an offensive strike. Holding Richmond that way meant constructing new earthworks east of the capital. Working in the same heat, mud, and dust, Confederates griped about how the "King of Spades" made them do slaves' labor. Lee reorganized his army, ridding himself of men such as Gustavus Smith. But where to attack? After midnight on June 12—the first dry day following the rains—Brig. Gen. J. E. B. Stuart led his cavalry north from the city. Stuart and his men rode completely around the Federal army, arriving back in Richmond from the south on the sixteenth. They brought with them crucial information. Porter's flank was in the air, open to attack, and did not extend far enough north to block Confederate reinforcements. Even better, the York River Railroad—the spine of the Federal supply line—was vulnerable. A successful attack would turn McClellan's flank and sever his communications. But now Lee needed reinforcements. He called for Jackson, who for the last month had defied both the enemy and the weather in the Shenandoah.[89]

Chapter 7

Hopeless, Starless Night

Virginia, Spring–Summer 1862

After Kernstown, Maj. Gen. Stonewall Jackson's defeated army trudged back to Rude's Hill. Banks's hesitance gave the Confederates nearly three weeks to rest, refit, and acquire new recruits and conscripts. Jackson received promises of help too, as Johnston left Maj. Gen. Richard Ewell's division behind as he headed southeast to Yorktown. Both sides endured the colder mountain version of the same rainy weather that began soaking the Peninsula. While April began pleasantly, with highs into the sixties, it rained on the fifth. Snow fell two days later, enough to turn the ground white. Rain, sometimes mixed with snow and sleet, followed over the next three days, positing a heavy storm system across Virginia to the Atlantic. Three inches lay near Winchester on April 10 as temperatures retreated into the thirties. Ice covered the trees and broke many branches, blocking roads. Higher temperatures afterward meant rising water and deepening mud.[1]

As elsewhere, that mud figured heavily in soldier accounts. In contrast to the Potomac valley, most of the soils in the Shenandoah and surrounding mountains were brown Inceptisols of the Udepts suborder, typically found in humid mountain forests. The Inceptisol band runs south, like a flattened letter "S," from lower New England and southern New York, through the Appalachians, to the Georgia–North Carolina border. Ultisols only appeared in the central Valley. The difference was obvious to men who had spent time that winter trying to navigate churned red clay. Inceptisols tend to be less "bottomless," although the amount of rain destined to fall in the Shenandoah that spring would make some of that difference moot. This was soil that seemed more "normal" to most Federals than to most Confederates.[2]

It rained again on hot April 15, part of a pattern that never reached the

Federal capital. The next day, on muddy roads, Banks struck. Reinforced with the division Lincoln had stripped from McClellan, Banks moved in force against Rude's Hill. Jackson retreated to a formidable position at Swift Run Gap, east of Harrisonburg. Although warm—the high temperature in Washington on April 17 was 82 degrees—thunderstorms, rain, and mud made the retreat difficult. Wagons and guns mired down, forcing men to extricate them by hand. The Confederates finally arrived at the gap on rainy April 19. Over the next week and a half, both sides dealt with a spotty pattern of clear, warm weather, with temperatures sometimes in the sixties, alternating with cooler weather and rain. Precipitation fell six times between the nineteenth and the end of the month, mostly during hard storms, as on the coast. Higher elevations were colder. Sleet fell on April 21, hail the next day, and heavy snow covered the ground on the twenty-fourth before the precipitation transitioned to rain. The earth grew soft and treacherous for wheeled vehicles, with men wading it to their ankles. Making matters worse, the Confederates had no tents, which Jackson had sent into storage. The same bad roads meant that Federal tents often were days behind in mud-bound trains. Union soldiers thus built shelters out of fence rails covered with rubber blankets or straw, while Confederates—forbidden to tear down fences—slept in the woods or in barns.[3]

While enduring such weather, two reports changed Jackson's plans. On April 19, he learned that Major General Frémont's newly created army was concentrating in western Virginia for a march into the Valley. Frémont targeted Staunton before turning south toward East Tennessee. Brig. Gen. Robert Milroy's brigade was already in motion. Two days later, Jackson received a letter from Lee that placed McDowell at Fredericksburg and moving south, apparently in preparation for an overland march to Richmond. Banks advanced to Harrisonburg, complaining that it had rained five of the last six days and he could only cross waterways at bridges. He guessed that Jackson was headed east to join Johnston. Lee was adamant, however, that Stonewall needed to stay put and strike the enemy somehow. As a consequence, Lincoln might well tie down Banks and McDowell away from the Richmond front.[4]

At first, Jackson was unsure what to do about three Union forces arcing and pressing across his perimeter, each alone comparable in size to his own force. At the end of April, he made his decision. On April 30—the same day that McClellan opened his bombardment at Yorktown—Jackson marched south. It was slow going. A storm the previous night had left the road, in

John Apperson's words, "almost impassable. . . . [T]he ground is thoroughly saturated with water and the condition of the roads indescribable." The next day, men lost their shoes in the muck.[5] Lt. McHenry Howard of the Confederate 1st Maryland described "a quagmire . . . between the foot of the mountain and the river. . . . The dirt road was almost impassable for guns, caissons, wagons, and even light ambulances, and if they tried to get on better by turning off into the woods, . . . the ground there was found to be as soft. Wheels sank to their hubs, and deeper, and although the men lent their hands and shoulders, it seemed impossible sometimes to extricate them."[6] The roads were so bad that Jackson and his staff dismounted at times to push bogged-down wagons and guns.[7]

May 2 brought "a furious thunderstorm" and an apparent tornado to Banks's army at Harrisonburg. "Tents were blown over, trees uprooted, teams landed in unaccountable places, and the sutlers' wagons were blown in into the stream," according to Lt. Col. Benjamin Cook of the 12th Massachusetts.[8] The Confederates experienced only sun, temperatures in the sixties, and a road so bad that Jackson joined one of his regiments in helping corduroy it. In some cases, men lifted up wagons and carried them by hand. Slowly and painfully, the column feinted south toward Harrisonburg, worrying Banks enough to make him retreat to New Market. Jackson then turned east to the edge of the Valley. The next day, as lovely and backbreaking as the one before it, his army climbed up into the Blue Ridge. Seemingly, he was fulfilling Banks's confident prediction at the same moment that Johnston was abandoning Yorktown.[9] Artilleryman George Neese described "the muddiest and worst road that I ever saw or dreamed of." The preceding supply train had succeeded "in knocking the bottom out. . . . At some points the mud was too deep in the road to venture in, and we cut saplings and brush away with our pocket knives to make a sort of roadway around the bottomless mud holes." They also built "bridges" out of cordwood, yet still spent much of the day prying out vehicles and animals. "It may seem incredible," Neese wrote, "but twice to-day I helped to pry out with fence rails a horse that was in mud up to its shoulders. . . . [I]t is the deepest and softest and blackest mud I ever saw."[10]

To the tired and dirty men's consternation, they reached the Virginia Central Railroad only to promptly reverse course right back into the Valley toward Staunton. Jackson was going after Frémont, not Banks, using his soldiers' legs and backs to fool the enemy. Some thought of Romney. It rained on the afternoon of May 5—the same day as the Battle of Williamsburg—as the southern army rested in Staunton. Skies cleared up the next day. At dawn on the seventh, Jackson's army headed west into the Shenandoah Mountains. Historian James I. Robertson describes the area where the Confederates operated as "a miniature Switzerland." Warm temperatures probably reached into the low seventies. Dust and heavy rain that night made for a difficult climb. Ahead of them, Loring's old command, now under Brig. Gen. Edward "Allegheny" Johnson, drove in Milroy's outposts east of the village of McDowell. The next morning, Jackson and Johnson attacked. During the fighting, a fresh Federal brigade arrived, commanded by Brig. Gen. Robert C. Schenck, who assumed overall command. The Federals lined up behind a rain-swollen river and dared Jackson to attack through high water. The stalemate shifted when Milroy attacked late in the day, hoping to spoil what he thought was Jackson's attempt to plant artillery on a hilltop. The assault failed.[11]

During the night, the Federals retreated. Jackson followed slowly. The weather turned hot, reaching 86 degrees in Georgetown on May 10, although one assumes that it was cooler in the mountains. The Federals augmented the heat by setting forest fires in their rear. Jackson pursued two days before turning back, satisfied that he had kept Frémont out of the Valley. After resting on the Sabbath, Jackson headed back into the Shenandoah and called for Ewell, who was at Swift Run Gap. He hoped to unite with the division at Harrisonburg and attack Banks before Richmond could transfer Ewell to the Peninsula. Banks was weaker now, having complied with orders to send some brigades to McClellan. Those Federals endured both rain and 70-degree temperatures that felled some with sunstroke. With what he had left, Banks dug in at Strasburg, south of Winchester.

The diminished Federal force seemed ripe for the picking, but getting to it was frustratingly slow. Periodic showers ruined the road and soaked Jackson's column as it descended from the mountains. Streams became water obstacles. Mud grew deep, dried into thick dust, and reverted to mud with the next storm. Still lacking shelter, men slept in the rain or else stole away to farmers' outbuildings. Wet, hungry, worn down, and in some cases angry about Congress's extension of their enlistments, the Confederates grumbled; a few grew mutinous. Finally, Jackson and Ewell met on hot May 18, agreeing to crush Banks's remaining force while they could. As Jackson rode away from the meeting, yet another hard shower soaked his party.[12]

Before dawn, Jackson put his column into motion. The day grew clear, but the effects of the recent rain lingered. The Confederates bridged the swollen North River, using planks and wagons driven into the waterway. The next day, well to the southeast, McClellan reached the Chickahominy in the rain and added to the pressure for action in the Valley. Under cloudy skies, Jackson drove his men to Harrisonburg, while Ewell's separate column entered the Luray Valley. Rain that night gave way to another clear, warm day (74 degrees in Georgetown) and more dusty roads. Jackson reached New Market and then turned east to Ewell's camps. United at last under Jackson, the Confederates rolled north along the South Fork of the Shenandoah. Front Royal's small garrison guarded the junction of the Shenandoah River's two branches as well as the bridges and trestle of the east–west Manassas Gap Railroad.[13]

On May 22, Jackson sent his cavalry around Front Royal to cut the telegraph and block any escape to the north, then flanked the garrison with his infantry by climbing through the hills to the south. Temperatures again reached into the eighties, causing men to fall out with heat prostration. At 2 P.M., Jackson attacked after a march of more than twenty sweltering miles, intent on seizing the two bridges across the river's forks before the Federals could burn them. Without these spans, the Confederates would find themselves marooned at the edge of the storm-filled waterways. Desperate to stymie him, the retreating garrison piled hay on the bridges and set it alight, but the wood beneath was too soaked with rain to burn. Jackson took the town and most of the Union troops, thus placing himself between Banks at Strasburg and McDowell.[14]

That night grew cool and rainy. Denied fire and shelter, Confederates spooned each other and tried to sleep. When Jackson learned that Banks was retreating to Winchester, he wasted no time, sending Ewell there on a parallel road while leading his own force cross-country to the turnpike at Middletown, in Banks's rear. Rain continued sporadically, with occasional morning hail and rapidly cooling temperatures. In Georgetown, the afternoon high was 60 degrees, 23 degrees cooler than the day before and 8 degrees cooler than the morning. The rough road that connected the two thoroughfares became muddy. Arriving on the heights above Middletown, Jackson saw that most of Banks's troops already had passed, but their train had not. Confederate artillery opened a devastating fire on it before Jackson turned down the pike after Banks, his men often slowing down to plunder abandoned wagons. Both columns trudged on through the cold darkness until the Federals reached Winchester at about 2 A.M.

Dawn, May 25, arrived with temperatures in the low to middle fifties, heavy dew, and a thick morning fog that Jackson used to hide his advancing brigades. An artillery fight opened the day. Then the infantry advanced carefully through the dim morning until they all but stumbled into fog-shrouded Union lines. When the initial assault stalled, Jackson dispatched reinforcements that broke the position and drove the enemy through Winchester's streets. Jackson ached to destroy the Federals on the road, but his own exhausted units were almost as unorganized. What was left of Banks's command—half of his men were dead or captured—kept going until they crossed the Potomac, even though the river was running four to five feet high at the ford. Numbers of horses and mules drowned. Washington greeted the news of this rout with shock. Historians differ on the reasons why—was it fear or a sense of opportunity—but Lincoln promptly issued orders halting McDowell's advance to the Peninsula. Instead, his corps would head for the Shenandoah.[15]

Tired Confederates lingered at Winchester until May 27, when new orders came directing Jackson to demonstrate against Harpers Ferry. The more he could threaten Washington or Maryland, the more likely he would deny McClellan reinforcements. The next day, the army marched for Charlestown and drove away its defenders. Jackson approached Harpers Ferry on May 30 and unleashed artillery. There, he learned of new dangers. Hoping to bag his army, Lincoln had ordered Frémont to Harrisonburg and half of McDowell's corps into the Luray Valley from the east. As historian Robert Tanner illustratively describes it, Frémont's army would become the anvil and McDowell's contingent the hammer. Even though Frémont promptly disregarded orders and instead marched for Strasburg—lining up a more difficult pincer movement—Jackson was in trouble. He ordered his army to flee back to Winchester.[16]

The capricious weather changed again. May 30 began with dark clouds and humid warmth that reached 85 degrees in Georgetown. Rain started falling sporadically, but with force, before noon, bringing cooler temperatures. A weather system rolled out of the mountains, proceeded east to Washington and Fredericksburg, and then inundated the Chickahominy at Seven Pines. In the Valley that afternoon, thunderstorms rumbled. As the Confederates started south, gradually becoming soaked, Jackson and his staff rode to Charlestown and boarded a one-car train for Winchester. That dark night, as rain came down in sheets and his army staggered in, additional dispatches convinced Jackson that holding the town was untenable. Front Royal had fallen that morning to Shields's division, just returning to the Valley. Hoping to hurry him along, McDowell had ordered Shields to travel with a minimum of baggage and to utilize the new shelter tents. With Front Royal lost, Jackson had one escape avenue left, the Valley Pike, but he had to cover rapidly the thirty miles to Strasburg to escape the Federal pincers.[17]

Skies remained cloudy and threatening the next day, and streams were running high. By afternoon, the Confederate column stretched out for fifteen miles in 70-degree heat, with the train in the lead and a growing legion of stragglers at the tail end. Rain returned at about 3 P.M. At nightfall, the troops reached Strasburg; the Federal trap had failed to spring. Beset with rain and muddy roads, Frémont had moved too slowly. Shields had stopped as well to wait for reinforcements. Meanwhile, Jackson's "foot cavalry" marched over thirty miles on a rare rainless day. That night, as if to protect their rear, rain returned with a vengeance, ushering in both the month of June and what historian James Robertson has called the rainiest week of the campaign. Robert K. Krick suggests that the spring of 1862 was perhaps the rainiest in the second half of Virginia's nineteenth century.[18] Soldiers expressed amazement at the volume of water falling on them.

During another timely morning lull in the rain, Ewell moved out early to shove Frémont's lead regiments away from the road. The rest of Jackson's escaping column resumed its drive south. Federal movements were not as prompt. Shields got another tardy start and reached Strasburg only once the Rebels were gone. The pincers closed without catching the prey. Jackson's men kept moving all day and through the night, despite temperatures reaching into the upper seventies and mud to the top of their shoes. Heavy evening thunderstorms and hail assailed them. By the warm morning of June 2, they were worn out. Straggling grew common. Officers and men alike begged for food from civilians.[19]

Mercurial weather continued. In Georgetown, it was 84 degrees. In the Valley, the day was "uncommonly hot," according to brigade commander Richard Taylor, "the sun like fire, and water scarce along the road." Late in the day, "heavy clouds gathered, and the intense heat was broken by a regular downpour."[20] Wheels and marching feet churned the turnpike into deep muck. The result, according to James Robertson, was "gridlock."[21] From New Market, Franklin Riley wrote that his comrades "had to lock arms to steady each other or fall in the mud. . . . . [W]e slip and slide a mile or two, then form line of battle across the road." It rained most of the night. The next day resembled the previous one, with morning heat—92 degrees in

Georgetown meant the hottest day of the year so far—and frequent showers. The column reached Rude's Hill, where Jackson hoped to rest his men. But the weather did not cooperate. Around 3 P.M., "the clouds opened and it rained so hard that our camp nearly floated away."[22] Staff officer Jedediah Hotchkiss observed: "The Gen. was almost afloat at night from the heavy rainfall. . . . We spent a very unpleasant night; it rained very hard and flooded our tents." The rain continued heavily into June 4, while temperatures dropped noticeably.[23] Pvt. William McClendon of the 15th Alabama, barefoot, described the road as "as batter which exposed the sharp edges of the rocks so that it was impossible for a bare-footed man to travel far."[24]

As Robertson explains, Jackson escaped the trap "with the help of speed and heavy rains."[25] Conditions for the pursuing Federals were sometimes worse. Many crossed swollen creeks and negotiated roads already whipped into slush by their quarry. Burned bridges played a role as well; Frémont's pursuit stopped for a day when high water washed away the bridge over the North Fork. The swollen South Fork and other destroyed bridges kept Frémont separated from Shields, whose column strung out for twenty miles.[26] "During the whole of this time . . . the rain poured down in torrents," Shields reported, "so that the Shenandoah overflowed its banks, and the mountain streams became rivers. It became impossible to move forward; the wagons sank in the mud to the axles."[27]

Then the rain stopped. The June 5 high was 71 degrees in Washington. Roads remained treacherously muddy in the Valley, however, and water levels remained remarkably high in its streams. According to Hotchkiss, locals described the rapidly running North River as "higher than it had been in 25 years."[28] Shields's column advanced to near New Market but halted at the South Fork, where "the bridge is gone and the river very high."[29] Jackson continued south through Harrisonburg toward Port Republic, where the North River and South River joined to form the South Fork of the Shenandoah. Near Harrisonburg, the Confederates used a hastily built ferry to move the sick, the wounded, and the train across the North River.

That day and the next remained sunny and dry; June 8 hit 82 degrees. Waterways remained high, however, neutralizing many fords and keeping the Federal forces separated. Along with geography and the exhausted state of Jackson's men—they had marched over a hundred miles in bad conditions since leaving Harpers Ferry—high water became a key factor in the general's decision to stand and fight at Port Republic. He controlled the last bridge over the wide North River as well as the bluffs and fords across the narrower South River. Shields and Frémont needed the bridge and fords to consolidate their forces. Jackson sent Ewell up the Harrisonburg road toward Cross Keys and kept his own command near Port Republic.[30]

June 8 dawned "bright, warm, calm and peaceful," according to Henry Kyd Douglas.[31] It was 63 degrees in Georgetown, rising to 72 degrees by afternoon. Union cavalry under Shields shattered the quiet as they stormed into town, intending to seize the bridge. Before Confederate artillery drove off these raiders, they seized three members of Jackson's staff and nearly bagged the general too. As the horse soldiers withdrew, Frémont moved against Ewell, who had deployed behind a creek. After an artillery fight, the Federals advanced against Ewell's flank with precision, only to encounter an aggressive Confederate defense. After hours of uncoordinated assaults, Frémont withdrew to high ground and the protection of his own guns.[32]

Little more than "a rambling skirmish," according to historian Robert Tanner, the Battle of Cross Keys left Frémont on his heels. But why had Shields not moved in concert? That evening, Jackson drafted a bold, desperate plan to utilize Federal caution. He would destroy Shields's smaller force the next day, somewhere on the still-muddy road between the North River and the Blue Ridge, while Ewell renewed the fight with Frémont. If successful, Jackson would cross both of the flooded rivers in town and then hit Frémont as well. Jackson spent much of the night supervising the construction of a new bridge over the South River, which remained too high to ford easily. That evening the rain returned; Douglas blamed it on the artillery fire at Cross Keys. The new day began with fog and rain. Temperatures dropped into the fifties. Jackson struck, but nothing went according to his audacious plan. Shields's men were too tough to fold. Federal artillery tore gaping holes in the advancing Confederate line before the infantry counterattacked. Jackson abandoned any hope of defeating Frémont that day and called on Ewell for help, telling him to burn the bridges in town after his men passed through. Meanwhile, the adversaries surged back and forth in the mud until the Federals began withdrawing under pressure around 10:30 A.M. Returning to Port Republic after a brief pursuit, Jackson saw Frémont's troops in the hills above town, stymied by the still-flooded South River. Safe for the moment, he withdrew into the Blue Ridge as "a cold rain" fell. Isolated but satisfied that the Rebels were in retreat, Frémont fell back to Middletown and camped with Banks. Rain continued the next day until the retreating column neared Front Royal. The Valley again belonged to Stonewall Jackson.[33]

Long studied by scholars and soldiers, the Valley Campaign remains a tactical model. Outmanned three-to-one, Jackson used stealth, sweat, and daring to immobilize three distinct Union forces and drive the Federals from the Shenandoah. In a few short weeks, his army marched 350 miles and won five battles. It took another two years for the Union army to make another serious incursion into the Confederacy's chief breadbasket. Elsewhere, Confederate morale rebounded. Washington also denied McDowell's corps to McClellan. Disliked by many of his men at the beginning of the campaign, Jackson's exploits won over most of his troops and welded them into an elite fighting force.

Judging the Valley Campaign out of environmental context, however, risks turning it into an object lesson with a false moral. As Frémont vainly insisted, rain and flood favored the Confederates. It was perhaps the rainiest spring in a quarter of a century, if not quite the worst spring in the entire history of the Valley, as Frémont complained. While much has been made of how Jackson utilized the mountains and passes of the Valley, he relied just as often on rain-swollen rivers to divide enemy forces. The heavy rains of the final week made his last triumphs possible. At the soldier's level, hail, rain, and mud invariably created extra toil. Bad weather and poor winter supply combined to create what historian Kathryn Shively Meier calls a "logistical breakdown" in Frémont's command that left his men hungry, ill clad, and mutinous. Shocked by their condition, Brig. Gen. Carl Schurz lectured Lincoln for relying on Frémont. Jackson's soldiers, meanwhile, built roads, carried wagons down mountains on their shoulders, and got sick even in the absence of the coast's miasmatic swamps. They would not recover easily.[34]

Jackson's first impulse was to request reinforcements and renew the campaign, going perhaps as far north as Pennsylvania. A dispatch from Lee changed his mind. On a cool June 16, Jackson received orders to come to Richmond, using as much stealth as possible. Two days later, his exhausted army moved out behind a screen of planted rumors and headed for the Virginia Central Railroad. He crossed the Blue Ridge and used the railroad to shuttle his infantry forward to Gordonsville, while the cavalry, supply train, and part of the artillery utilized the road network. From there, the army theoretically could head for Washington, Fredericksburg, or the Confederate capital.[35] Improving weather aided the movement even as the transition in topography brought the Confederates back to the realm of red clay. The result, Pvt. Edward Moore of the Rockbridge Artillery recalled, was being "choked, day after day, by the red dust of the Piedmont region."[36]

While his army marched through red-dust clouds for their capital, Jackson raced ahead. He met with Lee and his other lieutenants on the hot and humid afternoon of June 23. Temperatures were in the mideighties, and storm clouds gathered ominously. As Lee explained his plans, the still-critical role of the recent rains became obvious. Although the roads finally were drying out, the Chickahominy remained high and the surrounding land wet and swampy. On McClellan's right flank, Porter's V Corps remained isolated north of the river near Mechanicsville. It became Lee's primary target. He wanted Jackson to loop his troops into Porter's rear and launch a surprise attack. Aside from a diversion to the south, the rest of the army would pitch in en echelon. Confederate numbers, about 60,000 men, would give Lee a two-to-one edge over the isolated Federals. If successful, his army would drive Porter east, and McClellan would have to pull out of his Richmond line and move northeast to protect his York River supply route. Once out in the open, Lee could attack him as well. The Confederate generals set June 26 for the attack. As if to underscore the importance of the river, a gathering storm brought rain for the first time in a week. Two inches fell in the Federal camps that night, while water levels rose in the Chickahominy and other creeks and streams.[37]

The next two days remained warm and humid as Confederate troops shifted into position. Some roads remained in bad shape, with the ground often miry. Despite massive outbreaks of dysentery, chronic diarrhea, and "Chickahominy fever," McClellan's army was active as well. On the cooler morning of June 25, with highs only reaching into the low seventies that day, McClellan sent two III Corps divisions forward to seize high ground at Oak Grove, about two miles distant, where he planned to place siege guns. The battle raged all day, but the Federals only gained about a half mile. That evening, Porter reported that Confederate reinforcements had arrived on his front, supposedly including Jackson, and seemed to be angling for the rear of V Corps. Beauregard was said to be on the scene as well with much of his western army, giving Lee some 200,000 men as opposed to the 92,000 he actually had. Although he vastly inflated the numbers, McClellan correctly deduced Jackson's pending role in an angry message to Secretary Stanton. He blamed Washington's refusal to meet his troop needs for any impending calamity before Richmond. Still expecting the main attack from the west, McClellan ordered his army to throw up works in the soft earth and prepare to fight on the defense. The initiative had shifted.

Skies remained clear as the new day began. Temperatures rose back into the eighties, with high humidity. Jackson was supposed to attack after 8 A.M., but his exhaustion and that of his men were so great that his units never got in position. He later blamed mud, high water, and damaged bridges. Chomping at the bit, Maj. Gen. A. P. Hill disregarded Lee's orders to wait for Jackson's assault. In midafternoon, he attacked a well-entrenched Federal position at Beaver Dam Creek. The assault failed miserably but still shook McClellan enough that he ordered Porter to fall back several miles to a stronger position at Boatswain's Swamp. Later that night, McClellan learned that Jackson had not been involved in the day's fighting, leading him to worry that his vital railroad supply line north was compromised. Rejecting any thought of fighting for it, McClellan asked Porter to hold off the enemy north of the Chickahominy while he shifted the rest of the army south to the James and the protection of the navy's gunboats. Porter would then follow. Although the Federal commander asserted that he was only changing his base, historians correctly assert that abandoning the railroad meant he was giving up any thoughts of a siege, for his heavy guns had to travel by rail. Yet as historian Ethan Rafuse adds, that was the best of several bad options available to Little Mac at this time.[38]

The following day, June 27, was sultry, with only a slight wind. Lee again tried to crush Porter's corps before it could get across the swollen river. Once again, Jackson had the key role. Once again, friction undermined Confederate plans. Porter had shifted his lines during the night into an east–west configuration north of the Chickahominy that surprised Lee. With Jackson's contingent still stumbling in a daze toward the Cold Harbor crossroads—and finally arriving at the wrong Cold Harbor—A. P. Hill's men again bore the brunt of the bloody initial assaults against Boatswain's Swamp. The field became sunbaked and sweltering that afternoon; Col. William Oates remembered even after the war how the heat of the day plus frequent firing finally made his regiment's rifles too hot to handle. Alabamian William McClendon described being drenched in sweat despite fighting in his shirtsleeves. It was nearly dark that summer's day before Brig. Gen. John Bell Hood's Texas Brigade finally broke the Federal line and forced Porter to retreat. Yet with help from Federals south of the river, inky darkness, and rain so light that McClendon thought it was dew, Porter escaped, burning the bridges behind him. Cold, wet, and spent, the Confederates collapsed on the wet field and slept. Lee took enormous casualties at the Battle of Gaines Mill; James McPherson notes that he lost twice as many men then as the Confederates had on both days at bloody Shiloh.[39]

The weather remained hot, with daily highs reaching well into the eighties and only occasional rain after dark. A race to the south began on hot, dusty roads and through dank, wet swamps. Continuing to blame Washington, McClellan tried to move his men, guns, and wagons through largely fordable White Oak Swamp to the safety of the James.[40] Lee understood his opponent's goal and pushed his troops just as hard, determined to catch McClellan's army on narrow dry corridors before the Federals reached the relative safety of the James. Confusion, overcomplication, bad maps, destroyed bridges, roadblocks, and questionable leadership all stymied him at every turn. Meanwhile, evening rain continued periodically to create muddy roads. It rained hard, for example, during the night of June 28. At Savage's Station the following day, Major General Magruder attacked the Federal rear guard alone after Jackson again failed to arrive on time—his men were back at the Chickahominy building a bridge. The day was hot enough for sunstroke to fell soldiers. That night a vicious thunderstorm hammered the armies from midnight until dawn, raising water levels and turning road dust into mud. The following day brought Lee further discouragement as his complicated attack plan south of the swamp unraveled in confusion. Marching beneath such a hot sun was hellish for men on both sides. Some drank from roadside puddles, seeking relief. Once again, Jackson failed to do his part, falling asleep under a tree at one point, but so too did some of his comrades. But McClellan, too, reached the end of his rope. He spent much of the day on the *Galena* instead of at the front. His subordinates brought the army through and arrayed its units on a slight elevation above the river called Malvern Hill. On July 1, Lee launched repeated but uncoordinated assaults up its slopes on what the *Richmond Whig* called the hottest day of the season.[41] According to D. H. Hill, what followed was "not war—it was murder."[42]

After midnight, with the dead and wounded piled in heaps along Malvern Hill, McClellan ordered a retreat eight miles east to Harrison's Landing, the farthest point of naval control on the James River. Despite the day's tactical victory and several subordinates' fervent pleas to stay and fight, the commanding general insisted that the army fall back to the safety of the gunboats until rested and reinforced; only then could it absorb the next attack. To his wife, he confessed to mental exhaustion. Yet the decision itself was not illogical on its face. As Ethan Rafuse correctly maintains, the march across the Peninsula to the James left massive Confederate casualties. Harrison's Landing was a superior position to anything near the York River. Surrounded by creeks, a swamp, and the river itself, the birthplace of Pres. William Henry Harrison provided strong ground. Lee could not cut McClellan's communications or drive the Federals away, while the James provided a promising avenue straight into Richmond.[43]

There were two major problems with the "change of base," however. The more practical issue was weather, which rarely seemed to be on McClellan's side. If the defining weather story of the Peninsula Campaign was torrential rain and mud, the Seven Days' Battles were about heat. These were vicious engagements fought in a hot physical environment shaped by prior precipitation. The dead at Malvern Hill immediately began to decompose.

No sooner had the fighting ceased than heavy sheets of rain and strong winds returned, as if on cue, for the next twenty-four hours. Both physically and psychologically, the deluge that began during the retreat had a devastating effect on Federal morale. While few Union officers wrote much about weather in their battle reports, descriptions of the soppy horrors of the morning after Malvern Hill and the subsequent march to Harrison's Landing are ubiquitous. Officer after officer felt compelled to draw posterity's attention to the "drenching" and "heavy" rain that continued all day, the soaked and muddy uniforms of battle-weary and hungry men, the rising water, and the terrible state of the roads that, in some places, left men knee deep in mud. The rain continued cruelly as they reached their camps and bivouacked. *Look what we had to march through*, these officers collectively protested.[44] Brig. Gen. Daniel Butterfield spoke for many when he complained of "mud and rain which it is impossible to describe."[45] So deep was the mud that Thomas Hyde saw "a mule go all under, except his ears. . . . He was not a very large mule, and he certainly was not a playful one after he was dragged out."[46]

By and large, Union writers described a hellish but orderly retreat.[47] The Confederates saw it differently. With his usual caustic wit, D. H. Hill wrote: "They retreated in the night, leaving their dead unburied, their wounded on the ground, three pieces of artillery abandoned and thousands of superior rifles thrown away. None of their previous retreats exhibited such unmistakable signs of rout and demoralization. . . . Arms, accouterments, knapsacks, overcoats, and clothing of every description were wildly strewn on the road-side, in the woods, and in the field. Numerous wagons and ambulances were found stuck in the mud, typical of Yankee progress in war."[48] Historian Stephen Sears essentially concurs with Hill. "Something about this downpour seemed the last straw," he writes, "seemed to wash away the bonds that had held the army together during the week of fighting, and what began as a stampede ended as a rout."[49] Historian Zachery Fry notes that the Army of the Potomac left behind half of its wheeled vehicles and two-thirds of its tents. Much of its reported discipline seems to have been wishful thinking.[50]

In contrast, worn-out Confederates soldiers still at Malvern Hill spoke little about the weather. Some slept on the field, exhausted and unconcerned with the rain. In many cases, they sheltered beneath new Federal blankets, rubber blankets, and tents, all captured on the Peninsula.[51] The next morning arrived with fog and a cold, heavy sunrise shower. Lt. Col. W. W. Blackford of Jeb Stuart's staff remembered how the elements combined with the rain to make "the scenes on the battlefield, if possible, more ghastly."[52] Longstreet recalled "a wide sweep of heavy clouds that covered the dead. . . . [T]he heavy clouds began to let down a pelting rain that became more severe and delayed all movements."[53] As Longstreet alluded, continuing rain and churned roads—augmented by felled trees and wrecked bridges—prevented any real pursuit until the rain stopped on July 3. Lee surveyed Harrison's Landing and pronounced it all but impregnable.[54]

While he was safe from the Confederates, McClellan faced a second threat in his rear. A good percentage of the northern people and most Republicans were done with him. Lincoln could not ignore public opinion with fall elections in the offing. Already on June 26, the same day that Lee attacked at Mechanicsville, he had created the new Army of Virginia out of Union forces in the Shenandoah. To command it, the president chose successful western general John Pope, a loyal Republican, friend, and advocate of punitive war-making—all things that McClellan was not. Lincoln first envisioned the new army assisting McClellan by causing enough trouble east of the Blue Ridge and north of Richmond to make Lee send precious regiments after it. The Seven Days altered his thinking. Lincoln's concerns brought him to Harrison's Landing on July 8 in the hopes of persuading

McClellan to renew the offensive. On board the *Galena*, it was a blistering 99 degrees at 3 P.M.[55] McClellan handed the president a letter that urged Lincoln to hold the line on conciliation instead of calling for a harsher, more punitive war against southern armies and civilians, a war that would include emancipation. The irony, as historian James Oakes points out, was that thanks to Congress's law prohibiting army commanders from returning self-emancipating slaves, McClellan's army had liberated more "contrabands" than any other Federal force. During their meeting, Lincoln said nothing in response, but he soon disappointed McClellan's hopes. Later in July, the president moved steadily toward broadening the conflict into a war against slavery. As historian Glenn David Brasher establishes, McClellan's failure to take Richmond cleared the way politically for the Second Confiscation Act and the Emancipation Proclamation.[56]

Lincoln also moved more directly against McClellan at this time. Unwilling to support him but also wary of firing him with elections pending, the president launched a complicated flank attack. On July 11, he appointed Henry Halleck general in chief of the army. While Lincoln waited for Halleck to arrive from the West, Major General Pope functioned as his advisor. Historian John Hennessy believes that Pope must have pressed Lincoln with the same plan he had urged on members of Congress and the cabinet, which centered on uniting the two Federal armies in Virginia north of Richmond under his command. Halleck arrived in late July with permission to fire McClellan if necessary. Rejecting the general's new plan to cross the James and seize Petersburg, Halleck advised him to either move straight up to Richmond or give up. In response, McClellan demanded 30,000 reinforcements.[57]

While commanders and the commander in chief sparred for control of the war effort, McClellan's men and laboring freedmen endured six weeks of brutal midsummer weather on the Peninsula. At Fort Monroe, the average daily high in July was 82 degrees, with highs reaching into the nineties during the second week of the month. It was even hotter near Harrison's Landing. Although recordkeeping on the *Galena* was hit and miss, the average high on that ship was 84 degrees, including readings above 90 degrees on eight days between July 7 and July 17, including a measurement of 100 degrees on the tenth; a surgeon claimed a reading of 102 degrees that day. August was even hotter, with an average afternoon high of nearly 89 degrees at Fort Monroe. The first half of August brought 90-degree readings, with daily highs of 95 degrees August 8–11. Bugler Oliver Norton of the

83rd Pennsylvania claimed that temperatures reached 109 degrees on the eighth. While that probably was an exaggeration—it was "only" 98 degrees on the *Galena*—it did reach 105 degrees there on the tenth.[58] One soldier wrote home that the four temperature readings at his camp were "'hot, hotter, hot as hell, [and] hotter than hell.'"[59]

Men coped as best they could. On July 10, Lt. George Barnard admitted to his mother that he had slept outside in the nude, preferring insect bites to the steamy night air.[60] Thomas Galway, too, admitted, "we take off all our clothing to escape it, and the flies swarm all over us."[61] Lt. George Sanford of the 1st US Cavalry described August 15 as "the hottest day I ever remember in my life."[62] At least it was drier. After the post–Malvern Hill deluge, it rained only on July 11, through the night of July 16 and into the next day, heavily on July 26 and July 27, and as a persistent drizzle at the end of the month. Eight days of thunderstorms and three days of showers to begin August made that month wetter. In part, the Federals coped through the continued issue of shelter tents, which proceeded apace until they were the army's standard shelter.[63]

Penned into cramped Harrison's Landing by mosquito-rich swamps and snake-infested waterways, enough flies often covered the men to remind one writer of the plagues of biblical Egypt. The soldiers lacked good water, sweated in the heat and humidity, and grew sick with malaria, scurvy, and fevers. Historian Zachery Fry notes that McClellan lost as many men to disease at the landing as Grant would lose two years later during the Overland Campaign. Historians Judkin Browning and Timothy Silver estimate that July 1862 was the Army of the Potomac's sickest month of the war, with 20 percent of its men down with disease. Diarrhea (the "Virginia Quickstep"), malaria, and typhoid struck Federal camps hard.[64]

By the end of the July, Major General Keyes, an anti-McClellan Republican, was so worried about the climate and the army that he began pressing colleagues in Washington and even the president to pull the troops off the Peninsula. If nothing else, he said, use the army's health an excuse for withdrawal. Whether or not such concerns were genuine or face saving, others realized that the brutal climate offered a plausible way out of the dilemma. Halleck had heard enough. He ordered Little Mac on July 30 to send his sick and wounded to Washington. Four days later, he directed him to start moving the entire army in stages back to the capital. Realizing that Pope would command the united force, and still insisting that he could take Richmond if reinforced, McClellan protested vehemently. Halleck refused to waver. In language reminiscent of Keyes's letters, the general in chief wrote: "To keep your army in its present position until it could be so re-enforced would almost destroy it in that climate. The months of August and September are almost fatal to whites who live on that part of James River. . . . This delay might not only be fatal to the health of your army, but in the meantime General Pope's forces would be exposed to the heavy blows of the enemy without the slightest of assistance from you."[65]

Halleck was not being disingenuous. In Mississippi, he had made essentially the same decision; he feared southern summers. But McClellan was unconvinced—and bitter. He evaded his orders until mid-August before ordering his men to march back to Fort Monroe. In 80-plus-degree weather, it was a brutal trek. Lt. Janvrin Graves of the 5th New Hampshire described dust and great thirst. "What little [water] we had," he added, "was gathered from the prints of the feet of mules that had gone along."[66] So ended the Peninsula Campaign, born in torrential rain, dying in choking dust.

Chapter 8

Most Awful Dry

Virginia, July–November 1862

Maj. Gen. John Pope spread out his new army into a defensive posture along the Rapidan and Rappahannock Rivers and waited for McClellan. Once united, the combined force was to descend on the Richmond from the north. In the meantime, Pope inaugurated a motivational campaign designed to stir up some fight in jaded men repeatedly bested by Stonewall Jackson. On July 14, he issued clumsy general orders—preapproved in content by Stanton and Lincoln—that essentially accused his men and officers of cowardice. Eastern troops were too concerned with protecting the rear and lines of retreat, he said. "Let us study the probable lines of retreat of our opponents, and leave our own to take care of themselves. Let us look before us, and not behind. Success and glory are in the advance, disaster and shame lurk in the rear."[1]

A few days later, Pope made his western "hard war" tactics official policy. His army was to live off the land, only paying Unionists for provisions with postwar vouchers. In order to squelch guerrilla depredations, he made local civilians responsible for their actions to the extent of burning their homes or demanding their labor. Any man arrested near a guerrilla action who refused to take an oath of allegiance to the Union would lose his home. Those who took the oath and broke it would be executed and their property seized. As historian John Hennessy notes, officers recognized this as a slap both at them and at McClellan. For the rank and file, the most obvious immediate result was a "summer rampage" of foraging. Pope had inadvertently issued a license to steal.[2]

Unfortunately for all concerned, there was not always a lot to take. Virginia farm production in 1862 suffered significantly. Too much rain in the spring, followed by a devastating drought in midsummer, slashed yields. North of Richmond, plantation son Benny Fleet complained in July, "there was no wheat hardly, we won't cut any more." A month later, his father lamented, "our corn . . . is the worst crop I have ever seen grow on that land." Heavy rain and drought reduced Virginia's wheat crop to less than a third of its usual yield.[3]

Sad laments like the Fleets could be heard across the Confederacy. Poor crops were unexpected. In 1861, Confederate fields produced bumper yields. Only cotton and sugarcane had declined, due to farmers' decision to plant grains instead and because of localized insect infestations. Heavy rain straddling August and September further injured cotton in the Louisiana, Mississippi, and Texas fields and delayed its picking and the Louisiana cane harvest for nearly a month, until late in September. Yet, in the end, many observers still thought that the Confederacy had produced too much cotton and not enough food. Early in 1862, politicians and editors urged farmers to shun cotton and plant corn and other eatables. Most did, though not easily. They lacked enough labor, with so many men in the army and more going in as conscripts. Horses, mules, and farm implements commonly imported from the North were in short supply. Farmers also faced myriad other problems that included everything from lost territory, escaping slaves, and cold soldiers burning fence rails to an outbreak of hog cholera and an epidemic of equine glanders spread by army horses and mules.[4]

Trumping everything else, however, was the weather. First came the rain. In Augusta, Georgia, one editor complained in March that 1862 was remarkably wet, which he feared would lead to drought at harvest time. In Mississippi and South Carolina, incessant rain held up corn planting. South of New Orleans, rain delayed planting until May. It was worse in upcountry Louisiana, South Carolina, and Georgia, where rain and cold stunted sprouting corn and flooded fields well into June. Mildew, blight, and fungal rust also struck wet Georgia wheat fields. East-central Alabama produced a record wheat crop, but cotton—which germinates poorly in wet soil—struggled. In Arkansas and Texas, wheat was productive, but farms lacked enough laborers to bring it in. In North Carolina and Kentucky, wheat looked healthy, but rain delayed corn planting into May, a bad situation that extended on north to Indiana. In Mecklenburg County, North Carolina, a third of the county's annual average rainfall had occurred already, saturating soil that was both uncultivated and too cold to incubate seeds.[5]

Drought followed in June and July. The southern corn crop came in badly almost everywhere, with the exception of southern Georgia and northern Florida, parts of South Carolina, the bottoms along the Mississippi River, and occupied Middle Tennessee. Wheat suffered to such a degree that the *Montgomery Advertiser* deemed it a failure. Too much rain, then too little, ravaged the cotton states. In North Georgia, the combined effects of heavy rain, fungal wheat rust, insects, and finally drought beginning in late May produced a wheat crop only a sixth of the previous year's yields. To the southwest in Georgia, a Columbus editor lamented drought, noting the bad effect on local corn, as well as caterpillars ruining local cotton. In LaGrange, Georgia, wheat suffered, oats proved a total failure, and farmers by late June feared for their corn. In Selma, Alabama, another correspondent noted that drought came at the worst possible moment, just as local corn was about to tassel. He feared famine. Eventually, the drought extended as far west as Texas. Soldiers' wives there wrote letters complaining of dry wells and dead crops. The situation was no better in the Upper South. North Carolina suffered generally, as did East Tennessee. Along the Kentucky-Tennessee border, rust destroyed the winter-wheat crop, and dry weather killed spring wheat. Oats and tobacco largely failed too, although corn did better. In Virginia, the situation was so bad that the Confederate War Department banned sales of Virginia flour beyond the commonwealth. Maryland suffered drought-related corn failure. Inflation and distress followed to the degree that some Confederates began to fear famine.[6]

With a few local exceptions, such as localized drought north of the Ohio River and insect-troubled wheat in Iowa and Maryland, the North produced average or better yields in every category. To be sure, rainy weather in the Midwest caused apprehension early in June. But by late July, the *New York Herald* reported average to better production all across the Union, with record wheat crops in Illinois, Minnesota, and Pennsylvania as well as massive corn production in Ohio. In September, the *Cincinnati Commercial Tribune* summarized an *American Agriculturalist* report that indicated higher-than-average production across the loyal states in apples, corn, potatoes, spring and winter wheat, and rye, plus average yields in other categories. "A careful examination and comparison of the many hundred reports from all across the country," the editors concluded, "indicate that, taken as a whole, the present year has been unusually favorable to our great agricultural interests."[7]

Confederate farmers could only dream about such news. The meticulous diary of one upcountry South Carolina planter offers insight into the trepidation that the unusual weather produced during that baffling year. In

1862, David Golightly Harris was a thirty-eight-year-old planter who owned over five hundred acres of land and ten slaves near Spartanburg. A vocal Confederate patriot, he had done his best to avoid military service. In January, Harris expressed amazement at the relatively mild winter, which "so far has been very warm and dry. The roads," he added, "has been as good this winter as they usually are in the summer." He had no ice for his ice-house, for there had been none to cut. At the end of the month, he shook his head in wonder that "there certainly has never [been] such a warm winter as this has been so far. It has been warm almost all the time, and most of the time it has been cloudy and but little rain."

But with a new month, the weather changed drastically. Heavy and near-constant rain began falling in the upcountry just as it had on soldiers across the war-torn Confederacy. "Such weather never has been seen at this season of the year," Harris wrote on February 8. Sunshine was so rare that it merited notice on the twentieth. In March, rain and some of the coldest temperatures of the winter interrupted spring plowing. Frost late in the month threatened his peach crop. Harris and his slaves only began planting corn on April 12, despite still-soggy fields, in hopes of getting the seeds in the ground before more downpours. "Last year I began planting on the 27th of March," he wrote in his journal. "It has been many years since I began planting so late." Subsequent entries through April continued the same theme: "Rain, rain, forever. It seems that we will never have a time to work any more." By the end of the month, his exasperation was evident. "Such [a] miserable wet Spring so far," he complained on April 27. "The like was never seen before. Not one third of my crop is planted, and the land is getting so foul, that I think we will have to break it up again or plant in the weeds."[8]

As summer approached, weather conditions again shifted. His scourge weeks earlier, rain was now too infrequent. "I have just been over my wheat crop," Harris wrote on May 16, "and am satisfied that I will not make more than one fourth (1/4) of a crop." Almost a month later, he added that "the wheat is worse than I thought it would be. I will save but little, and that little will not be worth much." On July 1, Harris described drought. "The weather is very dry," he complained. "We have had no rain in a long time, and now need it very much." By August, he had to admit, "my crop has never been good, and is now loosing faster than it ever has before. . . . Still very dry, O, how dry, everything in the vegetable land is wilting burning up for the want of rain. I am loosing corn faster than I have ever made it. I made but little wheat, but little oats, now if I miss a corn crop, it will be a desperate bad chance for us." Near the end of the month, Harris grimly tallied his losses. "I thought that I would make 250 or 300 bushels" of wheat, "but lo! It came out 25 bushels, and very poor at that." And the drought continued. In September, he wrote: "Still dry. The weather has been most awful dry for a long time, and still continues so." On a dusty October 4, Harris recorded that he was "sowing wheat all the week as hard as we can jerk it. The weather is still as dry as it can be."[9]

Often farmers themselves, soldiers immediately recognized drought. When the 27th Indiana crossed the Blue Ridge on July 7, the high was 95 degrees in Washington, the hottest day of the month. At Culpeper, Edmund Brown observed that "the soil everywhere is of a dark reddish color, as if a brick-yard might have at some period embraced it all."[10] Chaplain Henry Pyne of the 1st New Jersey Cavalry explained that "the hot sun of July was scorching the plains which spread from the foot of the Bull Run mountains into the Northern Neck, parching the scanty grass of the early summer, splitting the earth till it was a network of dusty gaping crevices, and transforming the turbid mountain streams into sluggish currents, creeping through the deep beds of sweltering mud." When thunderstorms struck, "cut up" roads became "deep receptacles of stagnant water and immeasurable mire."[11] A Georgian wrote in late July that "the weather is fine, but the crops are very backward in this part of the State."[12]

While modern historians generally know nothing about it, the Confederate drought of 1862 was one of the major events of the Civil War. Left with too little food, the Davis administration and Congress faced hard choices about whether to prioritize feeding civilians or soldiers. In choosing the latter, Richmond enacted policies that alienated the Confederacy's common citizenry. Historians have long recognized the role that taxation in kind, impressment, and inflation played in creating the notion of a "rich man's war and poor man's fight," but their discussions almost always fail to recognize the weather-borne origins of those policies.[13]

~~~

While heat and drought deepened, Pope's turn toward "hard war" enraged Confederates. Lee condemned him as a "miscreant" and his men as criminals. He threatened to hang one Union officer for every Virginia civilian executed. Such outbursts did little to alter the dire conundrum that placed

Lee's army and Richmond between two powerful Federal forces that not only threatened the capital individually but also would outnumber him greatly if combined. Banks's occupation of Culpeper Court House on July 12 finally forced his hand. Lee ordered Jackson to take his men north to face Pope while he awaited McClellan's next move.[14]

On the Peninsula, weather conditions remained hot and sometimes stormy. On July 14, with the high reaching 88 degrees in Georgetown, Jackson and his staff led the way north through steamy Richmond. About sundown, a massive storm came up and drove the general indoors.[15] More storms followed the next three of four afternoons, although temperatures usually were cooler due to cloud cover. When Jackson's two divisions stepped into Gordonsville on July 19, highs only reached the midseventies. By chance, a Federal cavalry raid against the Virginia Central Railroad that day alerted Pope to the Rebel presence. Over the next hot and dry week, his forces poked and prodded the Confederates until the Union general knew that he faced a sizable portion of Lee's army. Sending A. P. Hill's Light Division plus an additional brigade as reinforcements, Lee wanted Pope "suppressed" quickly, and Jackson was eager to give it a try.[16]

A new sign suddenly rose in the night sky. From near Richmond, B. W. Jones of the 3rd Virginia described "a large comet . . . visible now in the northwestern sky, and is getting nearer and plainer to view every evening. Its shape is much like that of a Turkish cimeter. What it may portend," he added, "if anything, no one, perhaps, knows."[17] If the comet was an omen of anything, it was a heatwave. On hot and stormy August 6—two days after Halleck finally told McClellan to leave the Peninsula—Pope ordered a concentration at Culpeper before marching against the railroad and Jackson's flank. "The weather was still very oppressive," Edmund Brown of Indiana remembered. "The dust rose up into our faces in blinding suffocating sheets. Part of this march was made at night," he added, to escape the worst heat of the day.[18]

Jackson responded by ordering a quick strike against Banks. The march that followed was brutal. Temperatures reached the nineties and kept climbing. "The straggling was deplorable," Lt. J. F. J. Caldwell of the 1st South Carolina wrote, "although hardly anything else was to be expected in such heat as we had."[19] On August 8, as Jackson approached Cedar (or Slaughter) Mountain south of Culpeper, the 7 A.M. "low" was 80 degrees. The high at 2 P.M. that day was 96 degrees. Red road dust covered parched, heat-stricken soldiers. Straggling became endemic. Confederates died in the road of sunstroke. The march only covered eight miles thanks to the heat and Jackson's confusing orders. Historian John Hennessy observes that the eighth was "surely one of the worst days of marching any of Jackson's troops ever did."[20]

But the next day was even worse: 84 degrees at 7 A.M. and 98 degrees at 2 P.M. Around noon, Ewell's Division made contact with Banks's drawn-up Federal forces and opened an artillery duel that continued throughout the day, despite a brief shower that changed nothing. Around 5 P.M., Banks attacked, hitting the confused Confederate flank and steadily rolling it back until Jackson counterattacked and drove away the exhausted and outnumbered Federals at about 7 P.M. Just as worn out by the heat and effort, the Confederate pursuit quickly ended. While it is common to describe any battle as "hellish," Cedar Mountain came closest in actuality. Robert K. Krick calls August 9 the hottest day of battle anywhere in Virginia during the entire war.[21] "The air was as hot as a bake oven," according to Brown, "The sun beat mercilessly into our faces. Our small cloth caps, with narrow visers, were poor protection for our heads and eyes, while, with our heavy, regulation dress coats tightly buttoned, our bodies seemed to be a furnace of fire. . . . As we passed along in the intense heat we saw many . . . lying on the ground, frothing at the mouth, rolling their eyeballs and writing in painful contortions."[22]

Brutal heat and drought conditions shaped the battle in many ways. Both sides saw the dust clouds of their marching enemies before making contact. The artillery duel felled gunners by the score, while prone Confederates lay in open fields without a hint of shade. Soldiers fainted while marching into action. Others convulsed from sunstroke, straggled, or stole away to search for water. Krick maintains that the maddening heat also contributed to soldiers in the 5th Connecticut murdering prisoners.[23]

The day after the battle, August 10, was nearly as scorching, 94 degrees at 2 P.M. "It was a hot sunny day," Wyman White of the 2nd US Sharpshooters wrote in his diary, "and my tongue would stick to the roof of my mouth and the thought of water was torture."[24] A heavy afternoon thunderstorm created mud, which thirsty men lapped up.[25] Others turned to the odious task of burying the decomposing dead. "It was a miserable day," according to Henry Kyd Douglas, "and one of a deal of unpleasant work for me."[26] More of Pope's tired and wet divisions arrived that evening. After another stifling day of hasty burials, aided by a truce, Jackson quietly retreated to Gordonsville. The wounded remained, "packed in miserably ventilated buildings during the burning August weather," according to Chaplain Pyne.[27]

The Battle of Cedar Mountain was a Pyrrhic victory tactically, but Lee greeted its report with enthusiasm. Finally convinced that McClellan was withdrawing, he began shifting most of the army to Gordonsville, leaving a mere two divisions and a brigade of cavalry to cover the capital. The general arrived on August 15 and met with Longstreet and Jackson. As John Hennessy explains, Lee saw that Pope had placed himself into a "V" created by the Rapidan and Rappahannock Rivers. Attacking the Union left while cavalry destroyed the Rappahannock bridges to the rear could cut of a Federal retreat. With his horse soldiers coming on slowly, however, Lee had to wait. The Confederates paused and recovered, enjoying dry weather and much cooler temperatures. Autumnal afternoons only registered temperatures in the middle to upper seventies.[28]

Once in the field, timetables and several moving parts slowed the Confederate advance even more. By cool August 18, the army still was south of the river. More confusion left a vital ford uncovered just as a Federal cavalry column splashed across. Its commander ended up with captured copies of Lee's orders. Pope hastily ordered a retreat through Culpeper and across the Rappahannock. The forced retrograde produced hardship and bitterness.[29] By day, according to Edmund Brown, "the dust was again very bad, and we also suffered much for water."[30] The Union army cleared the river before midnight on August 19 and slipped from the trap. Lee followed closely. Maj. Rufus Dawes of the 6th Wisconsin remembered tracking the Confederates the next day by following their soaring dust clouds. Temperatures rose back into the mideighties.[31]

Lee reached the Rappahannock on August 20 and began shifting troops to his left. As John Hennessy memorably puts it, the army "sidled northward like a family of crabs" through August 24, looking for a less defended river crossing.[32] Morning fog and daily thunderstorms impeded the river probing and frequent counterbattery firing. For men without tents, the rain made the brief campaign miserable. For others, it was deadly. Pvt. Joseph Kaufman of the 10th Virginia reported seven Georgians struck by lightning, one of whom was killed, after midnight.

August 22 brought the heaviest weather of all during the "crab walk," decisively affecting two operations. Well after midmorning, Stuart led 1,500 troopers across the river and around Pope's right. He intended to cut the Federals' supply line, the Orange and Alexandria Railroad. Lee hoped this would distract Pope long enough so he could start pushing his own infantry across the river. Arriving in Warrenton late in the afternoon, wet from the day's rain, Stuart approached a strategic bridge that crossed Cedar Run near Catlett's Station.[33] "All was going on as well as we could wish," staff officer Blackford recalled, "when a violent clap of thunder and a furious wind announced the coming of a storm; then came a deluge of rain; it seemed not to come in drops but in streams, as if it were poured from buckets, and it was driven almost horizontally with such stinging force that it was impossible to keep a horse's head to the blast."[34]

Slowed by the storm and utter darkness, Stuart found the station lightly guarded; most of the Federals were under cover. Closing within a hundred yards, the Confederates charged. A "terrific thunder storm was raging," Sgt. B. J. Haden of the 1st Virginia Cavalry later wrote, "and the rain falling in torrents, and the darkness so intense that the whitest horse could not be seen immediately in front of you, except by the lightning which was almost incessant."[35] Most of the terrified garrison bolted, but Stuart's troopers found the bridge too soaked to burn. Axes failed as well since the river rose quickly, endangering the axmen in the water. Stuart retreated to Warrenton, his men laden with plunder—including Pope's dress coat—but leaving the wet bridge intact.[36] "Raiding with General Stuart is poor fun and a hard business," Cpl. George Neese complained, adding, "this morning our battery, guns, horses, and men, looks as if the whole business had passed through a shower of yellow mud last night."[37]

Farther south, the deluge played havoc with infantry crossing the river. Late in the day, during a thunderstorm, Jackson ordered a worried Ewell to send three brigades across at Sulphur Springs. The 13th Georgia and two artillery batteries waded across. A mile away, Early's Brigade crossed deeper water by using an abandoned dam as a narrow footpath. It was dark before the last man touched the northern bank. By then, rising water had submerged the dam by at least a foot. Heavy rain fell all night. The river was six feet above normal by midnight, and the fords in the vicinity were flooded beyond use. Early's and the other detachment were marooned. The next morning brought both more rain. With the river still so high that the Confederates were otherwise blocked, Pope consolidated his army and started for Sulphur Springs, intending to destroy the isolated Confederates. Worried about just such a response, Jackson had his men build a bridge on the foundations of one burned by the Federals.[38] "He set the example in his own person," Douglas remembered, "until he was completely drenched by the falling rain and covered with mud from head to foot."[39]

Tensely, the Confederates across the river waited behind a swollen tributary. Luckily for them, Milroy's brigade approached hesitantly and stopped when it encountered Early's artillery. During the night, Early finally withdrew. As Hennessy concludes, the episode was a turning point. The full day required to extricate the Confederates had allowed Pope to block Lee on the opposite bank. On August 24, pressed for time, Lee changed his tactics. He ordered Jackson to flank Pope on the Federal right, drive into the Union rear near Manassas, and force the enemy to follow. Longstreet's unofficial corps would remain in place, aggressively demonstrating to keep Pope occupied. Once Pope shifted north to meet the new threat, Lee would follow. It was a risky plan that not only divided the Confederate army but also would place a Union army and the Bull Run Mountains between the divided halves, with only a single mountain gap offering a connection. But the four-day rains had left little recourse.[40]

Before dawn, Jackson's men took to the road. The day became warm and humid, with an afternoon high of 78 degrees in Georgetown. The rain had ended, at least, but the drought returned. The Confederates marched hard without respite. By nightfall, they had reached the Manassas Gap Railroad at Salem, well north of the Federals' right flank. Pope knew that Jackson was in the field but incorrectly concluded that he was returning to the Shenandoah. Temperatures soared into the upper eighties the next day as Stonewall's sweaty column marched steadily up the railroad and through Thoroughfare Gap to Gainesville. Once there, Jackson left the railroad and headed south to cut the Orange and Alexandria at Bristoe Station. In two days, his column had covered an astounding fifty-six miles in sultry conditions. Still unsatisfied, he ordered Brig. Gen. Isaac Trimble to make a night march to Manassas Gap, at the junction of the two railroads, and seize its warehouses and railcars packed with Federal stores. The next day, with highs over 90 degrees, brought not only massive plundering and feasting but also skirmishing when Federal troops from Washington encountered the raiders. Alerted, Pope shifted most of his army toward Manassas and Gainesville in three rapidly moving columns, hoping to find and crush the outnumbered Confederates before Lee and Longstreet could arrive. He vainly expected help from McClellan. Late in the afternoon, Ewell repulsed Joe Hooker's division and fell back with a warning that Pope had arrived.

After considering retreat or maneuver, Jackson offered battle near the old Bull Run battlefield, hoping that Lee's reinforcements would arrive before McClellan's.[41]

The night that followed was dark, cloudy, and punctuated by light rain around midnight.[42] August 28 dawned "a fine day," according to Jed Hotchkiss.[43] Morning clouds blocked the sun, and temperatures fell notably; the afternoon high was 80 degrees. Weather historian David Ludlum suggests that a low-pressure trough, moving quickly to the east, caused this change. Pope's men hurried through dust clouds to encircle and destroy Jackson's corps. The problem was that conflicting cavalry reports seemed to place Jackson everywhere at once. At the end of the day, near Groveton east of Manassas, Jackson clumsily struck a Federal division as it marched unawares up the Warrenton Turnpike. Both sides inflicted serious casualties, but Confederate miscues allowed the Federals to get away in the darkness. That night, Pope issued orders to consolidate his army at Groveton and attack Jackson before he could retreat.

Rain fell in Washington that night. The next day, August 29, arrived with temperatures rising close to 90 degrees. The stench of the dead from the previous day's fighting was strong. There was no breeze; William McClendon of the 15th Alabama remembered campfire smoke rising straight up. All day, Pope launched repeated but uncoordinated attacks against Jackson's position, made strong by woods and the cuts and fills of an unfinished railroad. That night, a shower fell on the wounded and dead. Still convinced that Jackson had to fall back, Pope repeated his tactics the next hot afternoon. So intent was he on breaking the Confederate line that he barely noticed Longstreet's dust-covered men approaching his exposed left flank. They slammed the Federals there back to Henry House Hill.[44] Night fell, "a furious rain-storm" began, and temperatures dipped into the midsixties. Polk admitted defeat and sent orders for a retreat to Centreville through the cold, rainy night.[45]

Morning saw "incessant rain" continue, according to Douglas, who added, "the heavens weep over every bloody battlefield."[46] A few miles away, Pope's Federals suffered through "the melancholy rain . . . that comes after battle."[47] Despite conditions that Longstreet recalled as "nasty and soggy," burying the rapidly decomposing dead in the rain occupied many exhausted Confederates.[48] Others took the road again as Lee ordered Jackson on another march around Pope's right. The column trudged ten miles over muddy roads before halting. Pope missed it entirely until Stuart's cavalry pushed close enough to Federal lines that he sensed an attack. The Union commander sent two brigades back to Fairfax to look to his line of retreat and informed Halleck that the correct move was now to pull the army back to Washington.

Jackson's men marched hard to cut off that retreat. Pope shifted more troops to block him. They collided north of Chantilly at Ox Hill. At 5 P.M., with black storm clouds gathering, a Federal corps attacked.[49] As Longstreet described it, "the rain and thunder-storm burst with great violence upon the combatants, the high wind beating the storm in the faces of the Confederates."[50] New Jersey cavalryman Henry Pyne remembered that "a tremendous thunderstorm burst above our heads, its reverberating peals drowning the report of the carbines, and its dense obscurity veiling the combatants."[51] Lightning struck trees on the battlefield "in our very midst," according to Brig. Gen. Alpheus Williams, who added that the tenor of the fighting rose and fell in direct opposition to the strength of the storm.[52] Weapons misfired in the rain; the captain of the 1st South Carolina Rifles reported that two-thirds of his regiment's arms were useless. New Englander Rufus Mead Jr. likened the noise to the voice of God. Unable to see or hear their foe in the thunder, artillery, and evening gloom, many confused men backed away and sought shelter. Others kept firing despite their inability to hear commands. J. F. J. Caldwell of the 1st South Carolina remembered that prone men in the reserve line nearly drowned.[53]

Night finally brought an end to both the storm and the battle. Exhausted men lay down on the soaked earth and slept in sopping uniforms. They arose to what Edward Moore of the Rockbridge Artillery called a "beautiful" morning, "the sun having just risen in a clear sky above the mists overhanging and marking the course of the Potomac a mile to the east."[54]

Ox Hill, John Hennessy concludes, placed a "bloody exclamation point" at the end of the Second Manassas Campaign. But almost immediately, a new campaign began. In a few short weeks, Lee had shifted the front from his besieged capital to his enemy's. Jackson once again resembled the general who had dominated the Shenandoah, while Pope had failed miserably and panic ruled in Washington. Terrified of losing the capital, and well aware that Pope had lost the confidence of his men, Lincoln and Halleck turned to McClellan on a hot September 1. McClellan took charge of the capital's defenses and, at Lincoln's urging, asked his subordinates to rescue Pope. Nearly an inch of rain fell that evening, drenching defeated soldiers in muddy fields. The next morning, clear and much cooler, found Lincoln and Halleck at McClellan's doorstep. Demoralization in the Army of Virginia and Pope's own demeanor were so bad that, despite Lincoln's reservations and the cabinet's disgust, Halleck asked McClellan to assume command when the beaten troops entered the city. The two armies would unite in Washington's defense. Shaking off his post-Peninsula lethargy, McClellan rode from his headquarters to the front like Achilles leaving his tent, basking in cheers.[55]

Lee could neither wait on the enemy to recover nor attack Washington's formidable defenses. In contrast, going north promised great rewards. Logistically, shifting the front to Maryland's untouched farms would provide a respite at home and better eating for his men. Burning bridges and otherwise disrupting rail traffic at Harrisburg, Pennsylvania, would cleave Union transportation between East and West. But Lee envisioned greater rewards still. The liberation of Maryland's Confederates might well expand the Confederacy while forcing Lincoln to flee Washington. That could deal a body blow to the Republicans in the looming 1862 midterm elections. That could end the war.[56]

Augmented by reinforcements but missing stragglers, Lee began moving north on September 3. The next day, his first elements crossed the Potomac. Western Marylanders were predominantly Unionists and hardly welcoming, but Confederates looked happily on their fruit trees and cornfields. By September 7, most of the army was in Unionist Frederick, Maryland, northwest of Washington. Frederick stood astride the east–west National Road, while the Baltimore and Ohio Railroad ran by to the south. Temperatures had risen steadily back into the eighties during the march, but the nights were cool and dewy enough to require blankets. Skies were dry, other than a rainstorm during the night of the fourth.[57] "The weather was as pleasant as could be desired," William McClendon of the 15th Alabama wrote. "The sun shone out beautifully in the day-time, sending forth his rays of warmth; just right to make us feel good. The nights were dark, except for the light of the stars, which shone with all their brilliance and glory from a clear blue star-lit September sky."[58] The one negative was the dust. It was hard to see "three rods distant," according to Confederate George Neese.[59]

McClellan, technically still only in command of the Washington defenses, on September 5 ordered his combined, reinforced, and reorganized forces to pursue Lee. The enhanced Army of the Potomac marched north along three separate but equally dusty paths, arcing carefully to protect Washington and Baltimore. Despite the heat, dust, and sunstroke, morale rebounded. Little Mac's expressed intention was to find Lee and force him back across the Potomac. Biographer Ethan Rafuse adds that McClellan's true goal was to meet the emergency and buy himself breathing room before rebuilding his army again. Only then could he launch a more decisive campaign into Virginia.

On September 10, after reports placed Lee at Frederick, McClellan called for additional reinforcements and went after him. Gentle showers overnight calmed the dust without doing any damage to roads. A storm at dusk on September 12 likewise did no damage. The Federal march to Frederick was otherwise dry and relatively pleasant. Locals greeted the soldiers as deliverers. Of more concern to McClellan were a bewildering series of reports suggesting that Lee had divided his army and was moving elements in different directions: northwest toward Pennsylvania, west along the National Road, and southwest toward Harpers Ferry. Hopeful that the Confederates were in retreat, McClellan promised the president to push on to Frederick.[60]

On September 13, when McClellan arrived in Frederick, the weather was almost ideal for campaigning—clear and 77 degrees in Washington. Around noon, a soldier found a copy of Lee's confidential Special Order 191. The fabled "Lost Orders"—the second set of Lee's orders lost that summer—confirmed and detailed Lee's divided troop movements. Three columns, under Jackson's overall command, had moved in separate directions toward the Potomac and Harpers Ferry, still occupied despite McClellan's warnings to Halleck and a potential threat in the Confederate rear. Lee expected the garrison to flee but reassessed his tactics on the fly when it did not. The balance of the Confederate army advanced west on the National Road, via the gap over South Mountain, to wait for Jackson three days hence. McClellan was exuberant; he could destroy outnumbered elements of Lee's army in turn. Yet he also reacted carefully, rightfully concerned about conflicting reports from the field. His army would move out, but only the next morning. The bulk would march toward Turner's Gap, over South Mountain, and on to Boonsboro. Two divisions under Franklin would make for Crampton's Gap and then turn southwest in an attempt to defeat Jackson.[61]

September 14 was sunny and cool after a chilly night—61 degrees in Georgetown at 7 A.M. and 75 degrees at 2 P.M. No doubt it was even cooler in the Blue Ridge Mountains. Yet the day felt brutally hot to marching men on uneven ground. Making it worse was what Longstreet called the "impalpable powder" of the road, rising in "clouds of dust from under our feet," as his Confederates returned hastily to South Mountain as reinforcements.[62] Aware of the lost orders thanks to a secessionist citizen and surprised by how quickly McClellan had brought up his army, Lee knew that he had to hold him off until Jackson returned. Before noon, the lead Union brigades met the Confederates on the heights at Turner's Gap and nearby Fox's Gap. Lee still held the vital passes as the sun fell—but barely. The night was dark and felt cool as temperatures dipped toward sixty. Rufus Dawes remembered shivering at Turner's Gap. Franklin, meanwhile, had moved hesitantly but still held Crampton's Gap by evening. Lee ordered the two passes abandoned and called for a concentration near Sharpsburg, north and east of the Potomac. He would fight with his back to the river, unwilling to quit the campaign.[63]

September 15 was much warmer, with the temperature in Georgetown reaching 84 degrees. A dense early morning fog shrouded Harpers Ferry. McClellan's main force crossed over South Mountain and marched toward Sharpsburg, but Franklin stopped short of Harpers Ferry. He reported that the garrison there had fallen and that he needed reinforcements. Arriving east of Sharpsburg late in the day, McClellan was wary. Rolling terrain prevented him from getting a good view of Lee's thin numbers a mile away. An immediate attack seemed foolish. Historian Stephen Sears suggests that McClellan also might have believed that Jackson already had returned. It rained during the night, but without much effect. Both generals largely spent the sixteenth aligning their forces. The high that day only reached 74 degrees, while heavy morning fog again, coupled with the lay of the ground and poor intelligence, kept McClellan from getting a good sense of the enemy's intentions until midmorning, frustrating his hopes of attacking. Lee considered a march to Hagerstown but, in the end, secured his position between Antietam Creek to the east and the town and the Potomac River to the west.[64]

In the meantime, Jackson had taken control of Harpers Ferry and paroled its surrendered defenders. Hotchkiss described the general and his men as being "dirty as the ground itself and . . . nearly the same color."[65] After an overnight march, most of them arrived at Sharpsburg before noon, minus A. P. Hill's division, still at Harpers Ferry. That night, Lee completed his line of battle, with Jackson on the left and Longstreet on the right. McClellan positioned his army in an arc and ordered Hooker to attack and overwhelm the Confederate left at daybreak. On the Federal left, Maj. Gen. Ambrose Burnside's corps would pitch in at the opportune moment. Lee's initial response would determine whether Hooker's attack or Burnside's became the main assault.

The battle that followed the next morning, the bloodiest single day of the war, devolved into three overlapping fights, rolling from north to south. Dawn was gray and misty as attacking Federals went into position on their army's right, but temperatures soon rose into the midseventies on what soldiers described as a clear and lovely late-summer day. While Hill's men complained of dust as they marched hard from Harpers Ferry, soldiers generally mentioned few such irritations except the acrid smell of farmers' damp manure and their own sweat. The weather provided optimal conditions for mass killing after daybreak. The friction of war, McClellan's incorrect estimates of Confederate strength, and his inability to coordinate his attacks allowed Lee to shift his men to where they were most needed. Burnside's tardy crossing of Antietam Creek further undermined the Federal effort. Generations of scholars have debated Burnside's decision to cross the Antietam on a single bridge, rather than look for fords, without realizing that the creek was lower than usual and potentially fordable due to the drought. Night finally fell on a horrific stalemate. Temperatures lingered around 70 degrees in Georgetown overnight. At about 9 P.M., light rain began to fall.[66]

September 18 was an official Confederate Day of Thanksgiving. Ministers pointed to God's blessings on the new nation, including weather and harvests that prevented famine. At Sharpsburg, the sun rose on ghastly horror. Temperatures climbed into the eighties; swollen casualties turned black in the heat. Lee expected McClellan to renew the battle, but despite having 30,000 fresh men, he did not. Little followed except a truce to exchange the dead and wounded. That night, in a driving thunderstorm, Lee's army abandoned Maryland and crossed the knee-deep Potomac. By morning, all of the Confederates were across, shrouded by a heavy fog. He soon abandoned any hopes of returning and kept moving into the Shenandoah until halting the army north of Winchester. Other than sending troops to reoccupy Harpers Ferry, McClellan held tight. He was proud of his army and their victory, convinced that he had saved the North. He also knew that the men needed rest and refitting. In one narrow sense, Lincoln agreed. Five days after the battle, he released the Preliminary Emancipation Proclamation, having kept his vow to hold it until his armies had won a victory. Yet the proclamation also was a strong repudiation of McClellan's Harrison's Landing letter and soft-war proclivities. And McClellan recognized it as such.[67]

McClellan's decision not to pursue Lee further frustrated Lincoln to the breaking point. After two weeks of inactivity by the army, the president traveled to Sharpsburg, arriving on cloudy October 1 and staying four days. Lincoln counseled movement south before winter weather made Virginia roads useless. McClellan replied with familiar reasons to wait: His men were tired and sick; he needed new troops and supplies; the army required reorganization. Many soldiers privately agreed. Major Wainwright noted a general lack of clothing, blankets, and shoes. Regiments without tents were not uncommon. Lincoln was not sympathetic, however, and left camp in a foul mood. Once back in Washington, he peppered McClellan's headquarters with advice to cross the river into the Shenandoah. Stuart's successfully destructive "second ride around McClellan," lasting from October 10 until October 12, soured the atmosphere even more and initiated snippy finger pointing. W. W. Blackford of Stuart's staff partially credited their success on the gray, misty weather, which hid the riders from Federal signal stations, tamped down tell-tale dust, and kept farmers in their barns instead of in their fields. But Lincoln was uninterested in weather-related excuses. He all but ordered McClellan to take the army back to Virginia, privately admitting that only the upcoming elections prevented him from firing McClellan immediately.[68]

For the men in the Army of the Potomac, unaware of this drama, the month after Antietam brought a welcome rest. The area around the battlefield was physically lovely, if dry and dusty from drought. Exact temperature readings for the period come from Washington, unfortunately, and must be used with caution. As the army's provost marshal, Brig. Gen. Marsena Patrick, noted, conditions were harsher in western Maryland than farther east toward the capital. But, clearly, the rest of September remained largely dry with only occasional showers, highs that with exceptions hovered in the seventies, and morning lows that ranged from 68 degrees on the ninth down to 50 degrees on the twenty-seventh. October was a bit rainier, with misty precipitation on the second, heavy nighttime rain on October 12 and October 17, more rain on the twentieth, and a long rainy spell between October 23 and 27. The first ten days in October were actually hotter and more humid; seven of the ten reached the eighties, with two hitting 88 degrees. Two distinct cooling trends after that reduced temperatures again. October 12, at 56 degrees, brought a cloudy period, with highs in the sixties and lows in the fifties. Six days later, lows fell to the forties. Rufus Mead woke up to three-eighths of an inch of ice on October 21, writing three days later that frost on the ground looked like snow.[69]

Federal recollections confirm the impression that Sharpsburg and vicinity was chilly after dark. McClellan wrote, "we are so near the mountains that it is quite cold at night."[70] Wainwright's main complaints involved dust, but on October 23 (high 54 degrees), he complained that "the weather today is really cold, and very uncomfortable. The high winds make our outdoor fires almost of no good, blowing the smoke in your face on whichever side you get."[71] Edmund Brown lamented that "winds, which at the first were fresh and bracing, were becoming cutting and hard to bear."[72]

Men increasingly complained of the cold, sometimes citing a lack of overcoats or blankets. Sgt. Dayton Flint of the 15th New Jersey wrote home asking for mittens, but his tent was his main concern. Some regiments, especially newly mustered ones, had no shelters. Others had left theirs on the Peninsula or lost them at Second Bull Run. Sgt. John Hartwell of the 121st New York described sleeping under a shelter made of cornstalks.[73] Most of the army, however, now used shelter tents. Indeed, some regiments moved into them for the first time along the Antietam, as the transition from larger tents continued. They remained unpopular. Provost Marshal Patrick observed that "shelter tents are worth very little for protection, & they are getting very weak. . . . I am sending everywhere for Tents, but do not get them."[74] Brigadier General Williams likewise damned them as "a mere sieve" and blamed them for sickness in the new regiments.[75]

In Virginia, Lee's Confederates likewise experienced autumn and the growing shadow of winter. In September, they described fine days, cool nights, and dusty but firm roads. Sandie Pendleton described early October at Jackson's Bunker Hill camp as "hot as midsummer," adding that the winds were as dusty "as ever a wind that blew over the desert of Sahara."[76] He hoped for rain. So did Pvt. John Apperson of the 1st Virginia, who wrote that drought since the first of August had left the land "parched" and the dust in his camp "shoe mouth deep." Marching feet and teams pulling wagons kept dust in the air constantly, stinging eyes and mouths.[77] Sent to draw maps of the spring's battles, Hotchkiss similarly was struck by the effects of the continuing drought in the Shenandoah. While the corn crop at Cross Keys seemed promising, the ground was so dry and hard there and elsewhere that only with difficulty were farmers seeding winter wheat. When October turned cooler and wetter, soldiers reacted favorably at first but soon complained of hard nights and frosty, foggy mornings. Many lacked tents.[78]

Meanwhile, the official pressure on McClellan to move south continued. Finally, on stormy October 22, he wrote Halleck that he would start. The weather gods promptly decided once again to torment Little Mac and his men. On October 24, rain set in; a massive weather system was crossing the Confederacy. On October 26 (as described in the next chapters), Federals west of the Appalachians awoke to snow stretching from Kentucky south to northern Mississippi and west to the Indian Territory. In Virginia, rain peppered the Army of the Potomac as it began crossing its namesake river, with winds out of the southwest. Hotchkiss labeled it a nor'easter. That night the Federal army slept in mud.

The next day was cold and windy enough to blow down tents, but at least the rain stopped. At the end of the month, Federal soldiers welcomed the return of Indian summer, despite a heavy rain on Halloween night that left more red mud. The warm weather only lasted until the night of November 2. Dark clouds, wind, and cold returned in force the next morning. In Washington, highs dropped from 71 degrees on the second down to 53 degrees the next day. McClellan, nonetheless, felt cheered by what he deemed perfect marching conditions in early November. But the political damage was done. In Washington, his slow pace of advance was the last straw. The midterm elections, damaging as they were to Republicans, cleared the way to make a change. And in the end it was Lee, not McClellan, who made better use of the weather and firmer roads, shifting his army in stages over the Blue Ridge to the piedmont town of Culpepper Court House. From there, he hoped to stymie McClellan's advance south.[79]

In the field, "bleak November" continued.[80] November 6, according to Mason Tyler, was "the coldest day we had yet experienced."[81] The Washington high only reached 45 degrees, and the mercury dropped into the thirties overnight. It was colder still in the Valley; Capt. Newton Curtis of the 16th New York wrote that "ice covers the still waters."[82] That night, snow began falling as far north as New York, as far west as Chicago, and as far south as Greensboro, Alabama, near the Mississippi border, which received a light dusting. Snow covered the ground in Richmond, and up to ten inches fell north of the city. In Kentucky and Tennessee, rain fell on November 6 before changing to snow the next day. In northern Virginia, snow fell steadily throughout November 7 as temperatures remained in the thirties. Major Wainwright complained that he "found the water in my tent coated with ice," while Rufus Mead described ice an inch thick.[83] Confederates suffered too. Near Culpeper, barefoot Randolph Shotwell remembered "a heavy snow-storm. . . . I stood sentry this night with only a pair of well-worn stockings upon my feet, and a thin half-cotton blanket wrapped around me in lieu of overcoat and under-clothing, while large drops of sleet scored my face, and the earth was covered with snow!"[84]

The snowfall, two to three inches deep at the front, ruined roads, bogged down trains, and stopped McClellan's advancing army in its tracks at Warrenton. In Richmond, J. B. Jones expected the snow to "produce a cessation of hostilities" and perhaps even a negotiated peace. Scenes of barefoot soldiers marching in snow provoked the War Department to order impressment of footwear, coats, and blankets from the city's merchants.[85] A dramatic change in the seasons of war was coming, to be sure, but one that brought more fighting, not less. That snowy November day, Lincoln fired McClellan and replaced him with Ambrose Burnside. Flurries continued the next day as cold men stamped their feet and absorbed the shocking news.[86]

Chapter 9

Drought Almost Unprecedented

The West, May–October 1862

Braxton Bragg inherited daunting problems when he took command of the Confederate Department of the Mississippi at Tupelo on June 20. His army was poorly supplied, hungry, and sick. Bad morale reached new depths after Shiloh and the retreat into Mississippi. Soldiers told and retold stories about Bragg's alleged cruelty and penchant for military executions. He judged many of his officers as wanting. Above all, there was the operational problem of what to do next now that Halleck's Federals held Corinth. Outnumbered over two to one, Bragg lacked the manpower and transportation to retake the city directly. But if not that, what?[1]

At that moment, Halleck provided an answer. The Confederates had an unusual ally that summer: the mosquito. The Union commander feared pressing deeper into the malarial South until autumn ended the fever season. Then there was the weather. The drought that bedeviled Pope and Lee back east not only began earlier west of the Appalachians but also grew worse, leaving little to forage. Shackled to a single railroad northward, Halleck dispersed his men to safeguard his supply line from guerrillas and handed off Vicksburg to the navy. There would be no rest for Buell, however. Just a few days before Bragg replaced Beauregard, Halleck ordered Buell to march east across northern Alabama along the Memphis and Charleston Railroad. His target was Chattanooga. Maj. Gen. Ormsby Mitchel's Federal force near Huntsville would join him along the way, and they would take the city. From there, Lincoln's cherished project of liberating East Tennessee could become a reality—even Atlanta might be within reach.[2]

Buell, however, was skeptical. The drought concerned him. By early June, northern Alabama was foraged out thanks to Mitchel's command. Buell's column would require constant resupply, but, again thanks to the drought, water levels in the recently flooded Cumberland and Tennessee Rivers were falling dangerously low. Even Halleck admitted that Buell could not expect waterborne supplies past Florence, Alabama, in the northwestern corner of the state. He would have to depend on Memphis and the railroad. Unfortunately, Confederate horsemen could harass that single line with impunity. Buell understood that he would have to divert parts of his command to defend it. For all those reasons, he advocated marching to Chattanooga by way of Nashville instead, which Halleck rejected. Buell reluctantly issued orders for the Army of the Ohio to march on June 10. His first objectives were Florence and Decatur, Alabama. From there, he could draw rail-borne supplies by railroad from Louisville via Nashville.[3]

Once in motion, Buell's two lead divisions elongated. The weather grew stifling, with daytime highs in the triple digits, according to one soldier. Troops thus marched before sunup and halted during midday heat. While that saved lives, it also slowed progress. So, too, did burdened draft animals. Red-clay road dust rose into the air as thick, suffocating clouds. Straggling grew common. Rations soon became scarce, as river transports could not get past Eastport, Mississippi, due to shallow water. Federal quartermasters and commissary officers thus had to offload supplies there and cart them to Iuka, where they would be loaded onto railcars. At Tuscumbia, workmen unloaded those same supplies and ferried them across the Tennessee to Decatur for reloading and reshipping by rail. All that took time and created shortages at the front. The railroad itself lacked enough locomotives, while road and bridges required repair and protection. All of Buell's concerns, in short, came true.[4]

Like McClellan, Buell was a soft-war advocate who opposed visiting hostilities upon civilians. Nevertheless, hungry soldiers ignored his injunctions against foraging but found little due to the drought. Capt. F. W. Keil of the 35th Ohio described corn near Florence as "rather puny in appearance."[5] Mitchel's men also dealt with drought-induced shortages. "The crop of peaches proved to be nearly a failure in the vicinity where we expected to feast very heavily on them," Pvt. Ormond Hupp of the 5th Indiana Battery wrote, "but the weather was too dry and but few came to maturity."[6]

At the beginning of July, just as the Seven Days flamed in Virginia, Buell was at Huntsville. To the east, the van of his army dug in within thirty miles of Chattanooga at Battle Creek, Tennessee, and Stevenson, Alabama. Four other divisions were on the way. Conditions were brutal. Keil remembered marching "only . . . from four to ten o'clock a. m., when the regiment went into camp."[7] Chaplain John J. Hight of the 58th Indiana, meanwhile, described marching into Huntsville "on one of the hottest days we had ever experienced." Officers had ordered the men to put their blouses back on for a better appearance before entering town. Hight wrote: "Before we were through the business part of the city, men began to fall out by the dozens and hunt for a shade. They were utterly exhausted. Some of them came a few hours later to the Regiment . . . but many others were turned into the hospital and not a few never were with the regiment again."[8]

In the meantime, Washington grew unhappy with Buell's slow progress. Lincoln needed good news to calm the political waters after McClellan failed to take Richmond. Instead, the methodical Buell used July and the first part of August to carefully array his six divisions. His final main line against Chattanooga stretched over sixty miles, from McMinnville, Tennessee, south to Battle Creek. Anxious to fight, men spent most of their time repairing and protecting the vital logistical network. That was no small task given the poor condition of the rails as well as ever-present Confederate guerrillas and cavalry. Col. Nathan Bedford Forrest's and Col. John Hunt Morgan's men did particular damage to the track, bridges, and warehoused supplies. Federal cavalry responded ineffectively. More and more of Buell's men found themselves in small garrisons built from scratch along the railroads and major arteries, spending hot days laboring on the railroad and hunting for food. Morale plummeted in the heat of a harsh Alabama summer.[9]

On July 10, Bragg reported to Richmond. "A long and disastrous drought," he concluded, "threatening destruction to the grain crop, continues here, and renders any move impracticable for want of water." Two days later, he amplified on his reluctance to move against Corinth, writing that "a drought almost unprecedented has left the country, naturally dry, without water sufficient for the inhabitants. The enemy in their strongly-fortified positions, garnished with heavy artillery, rely entirely on wells, as we do here."[10]

Bragg believed that Buell's exposed flank offered a better alternative. Other factors pointed to a more daring option. From East Tennessee, outnumbered Confederate commander Maj. Gen. Edmund Kirby Smith issued anxious requests for help against Buell. Influential Confederates in

Richmond insisted that a strike north not only could regain Tennessee but also liberate restless Kentuckians. Colonel Morgan insisted that white Kentuckians only wanted the appearance of a friendly army to overthrow an increasingly hostile occupation. Bragg paid attention to the "Kentucky bloc" and their "Kentucky dream." On July 21, he informed Richmond that he was moving his army to Chattanooga to relieve Kirby Smith and block Buell. That no easy task. With the most direct rail routes blocked by the enemy, Bragg shuttled his infantry south to Mobile by rail, crossed the wide bay on ferries, and then entrained his men to Chattanooga via Atlanta, a total distance of 776 miles. Cavalry and artillery traveled more slowly overland.[11]

For the men packed in the railcars, the journey was marvelous. Cheering crowds supplied them with food, water, and whiskey. Lt. William P. Rogers of the 13th Tennessee saw "beautiful corn, as far as the eye could see" as his train moved south from Tupelo; drought had not yet ravaged eastern Mississippi. Farther south in the piney woods, however, he described "the poorest country in the world" and "very small crops growing." From Atlanta to Chattanooga on the night of July 31, rain fell, the only rain Rogers noted on the entire trip.[12]

Six days after they left Tupelo, the first elements of infantry disembarked in Chattanooga. It was one of the most monumental troop movements of the war. Bragg met with Kirby Smith, and they agreed that the latter would capture Cumberland Gap before the combined armies turned to fight Buell; Kentucky would follow. Kirby Smith marched out of Knoxville on hot August 13, his numbers augmented with crack troops from Bragg's army, including Brig. Gen. Patrick Cleburne's brigade. As they moved north, the road became drier, hotter, and devoid of crops. The column reached Barbourville, Kentucky, on August 18. Once there, he changed his mind about seizing the gap, if he had ever intended to honor his agreement with Bragg at all. No one in the Confederacy felt the potential glory of liberating Kentucky more than Kirby Smith. He exaggerated his difficulties in communications to Bragg, describing the region around the gap as devoid of supplies while soldiers privately reported feasting. Kirby Smith bypassed the gap, with its garrison of about 6,500 men, and struck north on August 24, marching straight for Lexington. The path through the Cumberland Mountains was rugged and increasingly devoid of fresh water.

August 29 was hot as Kirby Smith's parched Army of East Tennessee cleared the mountains and approached the Bluegrass town of Richmond.

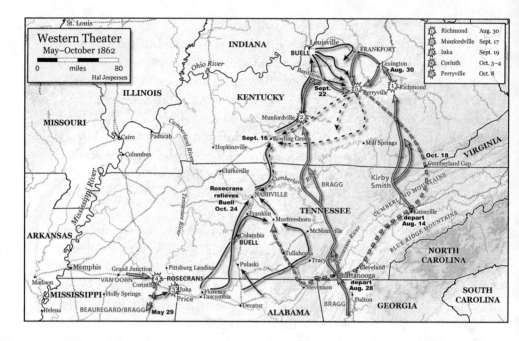

While no record of Richmond temperatures survives, it was 85 degrees in Louisville. Spearheaded by Cleburne's men, the next morning Kirby Smith attacked a hastily gathered, poorly trained Federal force of relatively equal numbers south of town, commanded by Maj. Gen. Bull Nelson. The battle ended with the Federals driven into town and Nelson wounded. The day itself was debilitating for a running fight; the 2 P.M. high reached 87 degrees.[13] Dehydrated men went in to battle with empty canteens and drank from puddles or wagon ruts. Capt. John W. Lavender of the 4th Arkansas wrote: "We had no water until 2 P.M. . . . [M]y mouth and tongue was so dry and I was so overcome with heat that I could hardly speak." He was about to faint when a woman brought him a pitcher of water.[14]

Fought concurrently with the Second Battle of Manassas, the Battle of Richmond was the most lopsided Confederate victory of the war. Entire Federal brigades ceased to exist afterward. Kirby Smith's men captured thousands of prisoners, the enemy's artillery, several thousand rifles, uniforms, wagons, and assorted other stores. The Federal survivors fell back in disarray toward Lexington, drenched by a rare shower that night. Although wounded, Nelson kept going until he reached Cincinnati. Newly appointed departmental commander Maj. Gen. Horatio Wright met what was left of Nelson's army in Lexington on August 31 and concluded that they could not hold that city. Casting about for a willing officer who would organize a retreat, he turned to Capt. Charles C. Gilbert, who had fought at Pea Ridge before joining Nelson's staff. Wright gave him the spurious rank of "Acting Major General" and ordered him to take command of the Richmond survivors as well as reinforcements. Wary of Kirby Smith, he told Gilbert to fall back through Frankfort, the state capital, in order to screen Louisville.[15]

Burning what his men could not carry, Gilbert led the column west. "Clouds of dust rose from the roads to the westward leading to Versailles and Frankfort," Lt. Albion Tourgée of the raw 105th Ohio wrote, "on which our wagon-trains were already in motion. To the south and southeastward were other dust-clouds, showing the course of the main body of the enemy."[16] For the rest of their lives, the soldiers remembered the "Hell March." Highs rose from 83 degrees on September 3 toward the nineties. No clouds blocked the hot sun. Yellowish-brown Alfisol road dust, once part of the substratum but now on the surface since the brown topsoil was long gone, was ankle deep. It formed thick, suffocating clouds; Tourgée could not see his dust-covered comrades more than a few steps away. At night, floating dust shrouded the stars. Water was scarce too. Soldiers died of heatstroke or else filled ambulances. Men threw away their equipment along the road. Stragglers were many; some were captured. About the only people who welcomed the Federals were the enslaved, who offered water or their strong backs and shoulders in exchange for a place in the column. Thankful soldiers turned away their pursuing slaveowners at gunpoint.[17]

Gilbert's desiccated command arrived in Louisville on hot September 5. Wright was pleased, gave Gilbert command of Louisville, and ordered him to organize the new regiments pouring into the city. The Old Northwest had panicked after Kirby Smith took Lexington on the second. State governors pushed new and untrained regiments into Louisville as well as Cincinnati in hopes of keeping the Confederates south of the Ohio River. Once in Louisville, the new recruits spent most of their time marching in the streets. With the average high temperature that month at 81 degrees, some died of heatstroke. The worst day was September 16, when Brig. Gen. James Jackson ordered an unfortunate grand review through downtown amid 86-degree temperatures.[18] Tourgée thought it was hotter, and wrote, "the paved streets were glistening hot beneath the feet yet unhealed after the 'hell-march'; the unpaved ones ankle-deep with dust. As usual, there were numerous delays, and then a killing pace to make up for them." The inevitable result "was a dozen or two of sunstrokes and a score or two of breakdowns. The ambulances were full before the reviewing-stand was reached and the march back to camp one of the sorriest sights an unsympathetic populace ever beheld."[19] Comrade-in-arms Pvt. Joshua Ayre observed, "quite a number are reported dead out of an Indiana regiment that was with us while others are not expected to live."[20]

As September lengthened, nights and mornings became cooler, with highs largely in the sixties. Yet rain fell only on September 17, September 27, and September 29, for a total of about half an inch. Bad water led to numbers of men hospitalized with diarrhea. Apprehension grew as the city waited for Kirby Smith. But he was not coming. Expecting to be greeted by eager recruits, most of the roadside cheers came from women and children. The commonwealth's most eager secessionists already had enlisted a year earlier. Historian Earl Hess estimates that perhaps only 4,000 men eventually joined his ranks. Others first demanded arms, a functioning Confederate state government, and the presence of Breckinridge's "Orphans"—in short, a guarantee that the Confederate occupation would be permanent. Disappointed, and concerned about the activity north of the Ohio, Kirby Smith established garrisons up to the falling river and begged Bragg to come join him.[21]

Bragg reached the same conclusion. His troops began marching north from Chattanooga on August 26, aiming generally for Lexington, where he expected to link up with Kirby Smith and then fight Buell. Lacking enough supplies and transportation, Bragg also intended to live off the land. To hold Mississippi and protect his western flank from U. S. Grant as well as Pope's old army—now under Brig. Gen. William S. Rosecrans's command—he looked to Maj. Gen. Earl Van Dorn and Maj. Gen. Sterling Price. They had marched to Mississippi after Pea Ridge—unwillingly in Price's case. Bragg asked them to check Grant and Rosecrans, then strike north into western Tennessee.[22]

Meanwhile, Bragg charted a course that bypassed well-defended Nashville. The weather was "intensely hot and sultry," according to Adj. William L. Trask of Austin's Louisiana Sharpshooters. "No rain had fallen in this neighborhood for two months, and everything is parched by the sun." The army's first challenge was surmounting the Cumberland Plateau. Heat and steep climbs led to rampant straggling. Water was scarce, stagnant, and dangerous. Soldiers discovering good water off the road sold cups of it to comrades. Men and animals suffered, sometimes collapsed, and occasionally died. "There was no water and we suffered for it," Trask wrote, "haven't seen a drop of water since leaving the foot of the Ridge."[23]

With stragglers and foragers trailing, the army marched to Sparta, Tennessee, and rested there for three days. Reports of drought-ravaged fields and bone-dry watercourses along Bragg's planned path so discouraged him that he changed course toward the usually fruitful valleys of the Barren and Green Rivers.[24] Aide Stoddard Johnson affirmed that the "difficulty in fording the Cumberland, . . . together with the scarcity of water, forage, and subsistence, were prevailing reasons for not longer considering the propriety of assuming that line of march."[25]

Bragg encountered little opposition during the first days of his campaign, simply because Buell's army was retreating away from him. Alarmed by Kirby Smith's swift strike and then Bragg's obvious preparations, Buell misinterpreted the movements and hastily pulled back on August 20. He assumed that Nashville was the Confederates' goal—as Bragg hoped he would—and ordered his lieutenants to find a strong place to fight a defensive battle there while amassing supplies west of the mountains. The Union general insisted that his army could not fight in the barren, drought-plagued Cumberlands. In August 1862, only 2.6 inches of rain fell in Louisville and a little over 3 inches in Clarksville, Tennessee.[26] Buell supporters later pointed to drought in his defense. Even before the war, they maintained, the region barely had been self-sufficient for food production. "Bad" 1862 crop yields in northern Alabama created "scarcity" and inflation, while water was "very destitute." Commissaries "in a season of drought" wrestled with shortages of corn, wheat, and forage. The army's chief commissary maintained that he "found in all the farms and plantations but a few bushels of old corn, and that not more than sufficient to feed the families and negroes living on the farms."[27]

Buell concluded that he had no choice but to keep moving. Despite pleas from subordinates such as Maj. Gen. George Thomas, the Federals retreated to Middle Tennessee. On September 5, the army concentrated in nearby Murfreesboro.[28] The retreat was "dusty and tiresome," according to Lt. Col. Wilbur Hinman of the 65th Ohio. Days were hot, roads were dusty, and water was scarce. Most Federals were without tents, having been ordered to leave them behind. Some had no blankets. Hinman described huts made from "boards, rails, and bushes." Drizzle on August 24 only slickened mountain roads. It rained again, more substantially, at the end of month. "The night set in rainy and cool," he wrote. "As long as the weather was fine, it was all very fair to live without tents, . . . but a storm very quickly took all poetry out of such a life." The next day "toward noon there was a drenching storm, after which the sun took a hand in the game, and beat down fiercely upon us with blistering effect."[29]

The retreat further opened the breach between soldiers and their commander. Drought and half rations led to foraging. Ordered to respect property rights, the men plundered with growing impunity. Planters paid a heavier price in this, but all residents suffered. Soldiers happily catalogued a list of food taken from civilians: apples, corn, pawpaws, peaches, potatoes, and livestock. Officers increasingly looked the other way or even encouraged such behavior, arguing that starving out secessionists would hasten the end of the war.[30] Before long, foraging escalated into vandalism, looting, and a complete breakdown of discipline.[31]

Buell did not tarry in Nashville. Reasonably sure that a strong garrison could hold the city, he decided to retreat all the way to his base at Louisville. As historian Earl Hess notes, the supply line back from Nashville to Louisville was the longest thus far in the war, and one quite vulnerable due to its many bridges and three major tunnels. Buell's goal became simply to get to Louisville before Bragg did. Soon, both armies were racing north toward the Ohio River on parallel paths. Bragg was ahead on the more direct course as he approached the Kentucky state line. Buell marched his men harder, from before dawn to occasionally as late as midnight, trying to make up for lost time. Soldiers complained about 90-degree heat, massive clouds of blinding road dust blown into faces by stiff winds, the pace, and increasingly skimpy rations.

Most of all, they noted a growing lack of potable water due to the drought. Historian Christopher Phillips asserts that, in 1862, the southern Kentucky Bluegrass endured the worst drought in memory. Waterways dried up, trees died, and even songbirds fled the scene. Only 2.76 inches of rain fell in Louisville in September, with most of that (1.97 inches) during an eight-hour period on the eleventh. Soldier accounts confirm a similar paucity. Drummer William Bircher of the 2nd Minnesota noted road dust four inches thick, adding that roadside streams and wells along their route had all run dry. Wilbur Hinman complained that the only water available in Kentucky was the rainwater found in scum-covered, stinking limestone basins. It smelled and tasted so bad, he noted, that even the mules refused it. Minnesotan Jeremiah Donahower agreed, adding that the ponds were thick with mud and manure. He drank water from them anyway and used it to mix army-issued flour for bread. Capt. S. F. Horrall of the 42nd Indiana admitted this he and his comrades drank from ponds in which the Confederates had left dead mules to foul them. Men were willing to drink such water because they had no alternatives. Springs were rare, wells were often reserved for officers, and watercourses were dry. Many men grew sick from the heat, bad water, and green corn. Diarrhea and dehydration were rampant.[32]

On rainy September 12, with highs in the sixties, the Confederates entered Glasgow, Kentucky, to a rapturous reception. While they relished the attention as well as the opportunity to wash, eat, and "nurse . . . lame feet," they found it hard to forget their march. Pvt. Willie Bryant of the 3rd Florida looked back down the 200 miles he had hiked and confessed, "we have suffered on this march those only can know who have experienced it, it is impossible to describe it . . . many a poor fellow has been killed by it and is buried by the road side, and I am only surprised there are not more, thousands have been left sick at houses and hospitals established along the road, and by the side of the road to make their way *somewhere* the best they could." He blamed "scarcity of water, dusty roads, heat and hunger. . . . O! it has been inhuman!"[33]

Bragg was only two days ahead of Buell, although he expected the Federals to stop at Bowling Green. He sent a brigade under Brig. Gen. James Chalmers to Cave City, on the Louisville and Nashville Railroad. Chalmers decided to attack the small Federal garrison at Munfordville that protected a mammoth railroad bridge across the Green River. With him rode a detachment of Kirby Smith's cavalry that Chalmers had encountered. When the well-entrenched garrison proved more than a match for the reinforced brigade, Bragg led his entire army on a forced march to Munfordville, through the night and into a hot day under a broiling sun. While the brief siege was bloodless and ended in a surrender on September 18, the detour cost the Confederates time and allowed Buell to come closer. Bragg considered stopping to fight the Federal army there but instead marched north and east to Bardstown. Many disappointed southerners had assumed that Louisville was their goal.[34]

The march's new phase undermined morale. Days remained hot, but nights grew cool enough to disturb men without blankets. Potable water grew even scarcer; there was no rain between September 17 and September 27. Capt. James Iredell Hall of the 9th Tennessee remembered that the "only water accessible was pond water and that was warm and . . . so muddy that we could not wash our faces in it."[35] Pvt. W. E. Mathews of the 33rd Alabama wrote that his comrades "obtained water under deep lime-sinks, some of these being partly full of water, and Federals had utilized some of the partly filled sinks as a place to butcher cattle and dumped offal into them, making the water unfit to drink."[36] More diarrhea followed.[37]

Bragg's army arrived in Bardstown on September 22, after what Col. Marcellus Mundy of the 23rd Kentucky called "the most terrible march that soldiers ever did make in this country."[38] In nearby Louisville, it was 84 degrees. Over the next several days, the general dealt with insubordination, confusion, and disappointment. Kirby Smith refused to come to Bardstown, and few Kentuckians came forward to fight. Kentucky secessionists had overstated their support in the commonwealth. This surprised and disappointed Bragg and his men. The general's mood darkened to the point of considering a retreat to Tennessee. Instead, convinced by local leaders that it was fear of Union reprisals that held back would-be Confederates, Bragg decided to go to Lexington to meet with Kirby Smith and then move against Frankfort. There they would formally install Kentucky's rump Confederate governor and implement conscription.[39]

The final disappointment for Bragg at this moment was the failure of his hoped-for western support. For soldiers stationed in scrubby and underpopulated northeastern Mississippi during the summer of 1862, weather conditions were similar to what Buell's and Bragg's armies faced. Pvt. Maurice Marcoot of the Federal 15th Missouri wrote in June that "the weather at the time was sultry, so much that many of our boys sickened and died."[40] Sgt. William Ruyle of the Confederate 5th Missouri agreed. His comrades dug wells, built brush "harbors" for shelter, and got sick. "During this time," he concluded, "the weather was very hot and health still bad."[41]

Price and Van Dorn wasted August arguing. On September 11, prodded by Bragg, Price moved his Army of the West—no more than a division in size—north from around Tupelo. With Halleck now in Washington, Grant

held de facto Federal department command in northern Mississippi. Price
hoped to either threaten Grant's communications or else retake Corinth
if the Federals pulled out. His march coincided with an unexpected spell
of stormy weather. Muddy roads mired down the column's train. The following day was hot and cloudy, with temperatures reportedly around 90
degrees. Reaching Iuka, Price stopped at the railroad—amid yet another
afternoon rain—to wait for Van Dorn. The Yankees had abandoned the
town without much fighting, and the Confederates feasted on abandoned
enemy stores. As it turned out, Van Dorn was four days' march away at
Holly Springs, expending most of his energies trying to take control of
Price's command. The two generals agreed to rendezvous at Rienzi, which
required the Missourian to pull back to the west.[42]

Price's halt and Van Dorn's inaction shifted the initiative to Grant. Having lost three divisions to Buell, he had shortened his lines.[43] The effort
brought illness and exhaustion. Marcoot wrote of his brigade's march to
Corinth on September 7: "The day was hot and water was such a scarcity enroute that when we reached our camp in the evening we were almost wild with thirst. Ere long numerous impromptu wells, two feet deep,
which rapidly filled with swamp water, were provided." The results were
predictable. "Our thirst was relieved," he continued, "but the evil results of
drinking the vile stuff harassed many of us for some days after."[44] Reports
of Price's sudden activity changed the situation. Grant ordered more troops
to Corinth. Alexander Dowling described the 11th Iowa's subsequent march
as tough. On September 14, "several of the men became overheated, for it
was a dreadfully hot day and the roads were dusty. . . . It was one of the
hardest marches I have ever been on." An overnight storm did little to relive Corinth's precarious water situation. "On account of the dry weather
all summer," Downing explained, "the springs no longer furnish the branch
with running water, and we are compelled to go for our drinking water
from a stagnant pool."[45]

Sensing an opportunity but misunderstanding Price's intentions, Grant
decided to attack Price before he could be reinforced. Iuka was roughly
twenty miles away. The plan he drew up, in the estimation of one biographer, was "too clever."[46] On September 16, he divided his larger force
and launched a complicated pincer movement. Rosecrans moved with two
divisions plus cavalry south to Rienzi. There he would turn east to Iuka.
Meanwhile, Maj. Gen. Edward O. C. Ord and three divisions moved along
the Memphis and Charleston Railroad; Grant rode with Ord. Rain poured

on September 17 and into the cool next morning, leaving the roads muddy and slow. On the following night, Ord's column reached Iuka. Skirmishing began. Rosecrans had yet to arrive, however, delayed by the longer distance, terrain, and muddy roads. The next afternoon, September 19, Price began his planned retreat. Late in the day, his Confederates ran smack into Rosecrans's approaching column on the same road. The recent rain had tamped down any dust, making for splendid marching but offering no advance warning of enemy troop movements. Vicious fighting raged for two hours until nightfall and just beyond into an unseasonably cold darkness.[47]

Fooled by poor communications and "acoustic shadow," Grant knew nothing of the battle until the next day. Ord, under orders not to go into action until he heard the sounds of battle, likewise did nothing. Updated the next morning, Grant planned a counterattack but found Price gone. Ord marched in to Iuka, while Rosecrans mounted an ineffective pursuit that worsened his relationship with Grant. Northern Mississippi remained in flux, but Bragg could count on little help or relief. Rain and mud had played their roles, and Iuka grew rife with the stench of decomposition.[48]

On September 25, six days after the Battle of Iuka, Buell's dehydrated and exhausted army staggered into Louisville. The sky was cloudless and the high 73 degrees. The 15th Ohio's Alexis Cope marveled at how much the drought-ravaged Ohio River had fallen, "so low that it was only navigable for small boats."[49] Some Hoosiers deserted by wading home. While his men cleaned out cornfields, Buell worked to absorb the city's raw recruits and the reinforcements from Grant into a reorganized Army of the Ohio. It did not go smoothly. His veterans detested the new recruits as hesitant and effeminate cowards. Then, on September 29, subordinate Brig. Gen. Jefferson C. Davis murdered Bull Nelson for derisive comments made about Hoosiers in the Battle of Richmond. Desperate for a loyal man, Buell gave a corps to Charles Gilbert. That appointment created consternation among other officers. The army commander also fended off Washington, as Lincoln had decided to fire Buell and replace him with Thomas. Only Thomas's reluctance and Halleck's second thoughts left Buell in place.

On October 1—the same day that Bragg arrived in Lexington—Buell moved most of his 57,000-man force toward the 16,800 Confederates at Bardstown. Three Federal corps marched to the southeast on three roads to maximize available water and forage. Two divisions under Brig. Gen. Joshua Sill, meanwhile, feinted toward Frankfort, hoping to pin Kirby Smith in place while confusing Bragg.[50] Conditions on the march soon proved sadly familiar to Buell's veterans and taxed the new soldiers to their limits. The high temperature rose to 86 degrees. Hot, worn out, and thirsty, the "fresh fish" threw away newly issued equipment and sometimes passed out along the roads. Others slipped away to forage for corn and fruit; many had not eaten breakfast. For every Federal such as the literary Lieutenant Tourgée, who later remembered basking in the colorful fall leaves, ripe corn, and bucolic farm scenes, there were more who simply complained of heat and stifling dust that rose high beyond the treetops. Light showers began during the afternoon of October 2 and lasted sporadically into the next morning, but 0.16 of an inch of rain did little more than briefly hold down the dust. Another shower on the morning of October 4 (0.19 of an inch) produced similar results. Men drank from stagnant ponds and puddles. Drummer Bircher described his comrades using a spoon and dirty handkerchiefs to filter roadside water.[51]

Elements of Buell's center II Corps took Bardstown with little fighting on October 4. To the north, Sill approached the capital that same gray, rainy morning. Panic and confusion ensued, marring Gov. Richard Hawes's inaugural speech and the festivities that followed. The Confederates fled in haste, embarrassing the newly installed government. Thoroughly convinced by erroneous reports from Kirby Smith that Sill represented most of Buell's army, Bragg ordered senior subordinate Maj. Gen. Leonidas Polk to march north and hit the Union flank. Polk refused. Feeling pressure from the northwest, he instead withdrew southeast toward Danville. Heat and dust plagued the retreat, except when occasional storms left the road slick. Water was scarce the entire way. Soon, the Confederate column strung out. Stragglers wandered off, some never to return.[52]

Events also were coming to a head in Mississippi. After the Battle of Iuka, Rosecrans occupied Corinth with his army of 23,000 troops. Ord and 12,000 men took up a position to the northwest at Bolivar, Tennessee. Grant was at Jackson, as much of the remainder of his army took up garrison duty in area towns. Meanwhile, Price and Van Dorn concentrated at Ripley, Mississippi. The weather was hot, with occasional showers. Pvt.

Ephraim Anderson described a hard evening rain during a march to Ripley on September 28 that left roads muddy and men soaked. The next day was steamy. Headstrong as ever, Van Dorn led the combined army from town on the morning of September 30. He moved first toward Bolivar before turning southeast for a quick march to Corinth. The days were hot and the road dusty, with little water to be found. Rain on the morning of October 2 barely settled the dust. Van Dorn approached the railroad city from the northwest on the hot morning of October 3, trusting reports that its defenses there were weak. Rosecrans held three concentric lines of entrenchments, redoubts, and batteries.[53]

At about 10 A.M., Van Dorn launched his assault against the Union works. The morning was cool, but as the day lengthened, it became blistering hot. Col. John Sanborn of the 4th Minnesota reported that "the heat during the engagement of my command was most intense, said to be 108° in the shade, and more men were carried off the field on litters from the effects of sun-stroke than from wounds."[54] Others cited heat exhaustion and delirium. Three earthquake tremors added to the developing drama. After hours of determined fighting, the Confederates breached the outermost ring of rifle pits and drove their defenders into the stronger, inner works, overall advancing about two miles. As night fell, Rosecrans pulled his men back into the more compact innermost line. Sweaty and exhausted combatants collapsed. The colonel of the 7th Illinois reported that his men had nothing to drink all day except a barrel of vinegar.[55] Only a cooler night brought relief. According to Van Dorn's biographer, "the hot day, the hard fighting, the lack of supplies, and Van Dorn's poor tactical planning had taken their toll."[56]

Van Dorn dismissed his subordinates' notions of a night attack and bivouacked. He later reported: "My troops were not veterans. . . . They were greatly exhausted by heat, by thirst, and by the fatigue which excess of valor created."[57] The next day brought what Col. John Stevenson, whose brigade was marching to reinforce Rosecrans, called "a very oppressive sun," although fewer reports of October 4 mention the deleterious effects of heat.[58] Van Dorn pounded the defenders with artillery and launched a mismanaged frontal assault. One brigade briefly penetrated the strong defenses on the Federal right, while toward the center the Confederates had short-lived success against the innermost line and briefly entered town before being repulsed. Union reinforcements stemmed both breaches, however, and Federal artillery raked the field. In the ironic words of one Union soldier, the Confederate attack melted like thawing snow. Van Dorn escaped to Holly Springs, but his army and his career as its commander were in shambles.[59]

Battered but undefeated, Rosecrans's men abandoned the tiring pursuit and returned to Corinth. The weather remained hot and occasionally rainy until October 23, when temperatures unexpectedly dropped. The night grew so cold that water froze "¼ inch in thickness." Two days later, two inches of snow fell, a once-in-fifty-years event there, according to modern meteorologists. Although warmth returned at the end of the month, and the snowy mud turned back into dust, a new season had arrived.[60]

In Kentucky on October 7, most of Polk's retreating troops passed through the small market town of Perryville. Not remarkable at the moment, Perryville had three critical features. In addition to various springs, pools of stagnant water remained in the bed of the Chaplin River, which bisected the town. Perryville also stood at the hub of the three roads Buell was using to drive south. Finally, steep rolling hills west of town offered cover to a defending force. By that evening, Polk had grown alarmed at increasing Federal pressure from the west. Back-and-forth cavalry fighting had occurred much of the day in that direction. After a series of murky and poorly explained dispatches that did credit to no one, Bragg agreed that Polk should stop and defeat the pursuing force before resuming his march northward. No Confederates grasped that there was a Union corps on the road or that the other two corps were about to arrive from the northwest and southwest. Indeed, one Confederate division continued moving north while the rest of the army backtracked to Perryville. They bivouacked along the dry riverbed except for a brigade of Arkansans that took up positions west of town in the hills along the pike. A lone regiment took up a lonelier position at the far western point of the line on a rolling eminence called Peters Hill. Behind them in a valley were springs of precious water.[61]

For the Federals approaching Perryville, the final days of the march were excruciating. Afternoon temperatures recorded by the Smithsonian observer in Danville rose from 75 degrees on October 5 to 85 degrees the next day and 90 degrees on the seventh. The landscape grew rolling and rocky, while the turnpikes south and east of Bardstown produced "suffocating" white limestone dust.[62] Columns marched with empty canteens, only to find nothing along the way except scattered scummy ponds. Rations ran out, which led to formal property seizures and extracurricular foraging. Gilbert's corps, in particular, fell apart. His imperious and profane ways, and notably his pattern of reserving precious water reserves for officers, led to repeated incidents of near mutiny. One angry Hoosier bayoneted Gilbert's horse.[63]

"Our marching was very severe on us," Cpl. George Morris of the 81st Indiana later wrote, "we suffered a great deal for water. The enemy drank up all the streams and wells on each side of the road. Some of the men went three and four miles to get water." October 7 was worse. "We were thankful for any kind of water we could get," Morris wrote, "although some of it was not fit for animals to drink."[64] Capt. Levi Ross of the 86th Illinois described water that was "almost nauseating, . . . blue and thick from the slime of frogs and hogs."[65]

Gilbert's corps staggered toward Peters Hill from the west and settled into camp. The night was beautiful and cloudless, with a 9 P.M. temperature of 75 degrees in Danville. A full moon bathed the ground with light, yet the men had no water. Before daylight on October 8, they went forward to seize the springs, discovered by scouts earlier in the tense night. The Confederates contested them. While the morning was relatively cool, with a temperature of 72 degrees, the day grew increasingly hot even as the fighting around Peters Hill became a hellish vortex. Regiments stirred up enormous clouds of dust. Finally grasping that he had underestimated the numbers of enemy troops, Polk broke off combat late in the morning and fell back into a defensive line. This angered Bragg, who arrived unexpectedly not long afterward to discover a silent field. Finding Polk's dispositions faulty as well—the Confederate right was completely in the air—Bragg shifted troops from his stronger left in order to launch an afternoon attack against what he believed to be the Union forces' vulnerable left flank. Instead, when the assault finally went off at about 2 P.M.—the temperature was then 90 degrees—it squarely hit Buell's I Corps. Commanded by Maj. Gen. Alexander McDowell McCook, it was just taking a position on the northern side of the field. Fighting spread south across McCook's front to the banks of Doctor's Creek, all but dry from the drought except for scattered pools and puddles that had attracted thirsty Federals. The two forces battled into the evening. The Confederates steadily forced back McCook's line through the bloody afternoon but with nightfall could not break it.[66]

Rampant confusion marked the Battle of Perryville. Injured in a fall the previous evening while chastising foragers and tricked by acoustic shadow, Buell spent most of the day relaxing on his cot. An equally confused Gilbert squandered an opportunity to take the town and get into the Confederate rear after his corps repelled a feeble assault. On the right, Maj. Gen. Thomas Crittenden's II Corps wasted the day sparring with cavalry. Mc-Cook's men did the lion's share of the fighting until late in the day, when Buell and Gilbert reluctantly sent him a few fresh regiments after reports trickled into headquarters. The Confederate command situation was no better. Soldiers remained desperate for water and searched the countryside for it. Some shoved aside the dead to drink from the bloody pools in the bed of Doctor's Creek.[67]

A full moon exposed the horrors of the day. Only then did Bragg finally realize that Buell's army was at Perryville rather than farther north. He was woefully outnumbered. Bragg abandoned the field during the night and retreated, first to Harrodsburg and then to his supply depot fifteen miles beyond. Buell pursued tentatively. The roads remained dusty, but the weather turned cooler on October 10, with a high of only 66 degrees that day and 58 degrees the next. Rain stretched through the night; a half inch fell in Danville. Scattered rain fell again on the night of October 12–13. Both rain events resulted in mud that slowed marching feet and wheels. The nights grew colder as well, with temperatures falling into the fifties on October 10 and remaining there.[68] "I have endured exposure to nearly all weather now," Willie Bryant of the 3rd Florida wrote, "heat, cold, rain, hunger, thirst, fatigue to prostration, without being really sick, rheumatism or colds, and am to-day, a cold misty fall day, and after marching thro' rain and mud all yesterday, and sleeping on the ground last night with a single wet blanket over me, the better for the service."[69]

Wounded in the fighting, Ohioan Joshua Ayre wrote, "it has been wet and cold for the last 36 hours, but take it all together I think myself lucky."[70] He was not. The first frost appeared on the night of October 14, the day that Ayre died of gangrene. His death resembled the tragic fates of so many of Perryville's more than 1,800 wounded. Within twenty-four hours of the battle, most structures around the town had become primitive hospitals, including barns and sheds. Buell had left most of his medical supplies in Louisville to save time, so doctors could do little. Many of the wounded lay outside waiting for treatment; some for days.[71] "Lying on the ground," Wilbur Hinman wrote, "with no shelter from the fierce heat of the sun by day or the dews of the night, were some three hundred rebel wounded.

. . . [M]any of them were in the most horrible condition that the mind can conceive." Overwhelmed, Hinman and his comrades brought them water. "There was nothing else we could do."[72] There was still little water to be had, and much of it was polluted. Typhoid flared up, as did sepsis, because surgeons only infrequently washed their hands due to this lack of clean water. Drought had increased the sufferings of the wounded.[73]

By the time of that first frost, however, the Confederate army was gone. Despite a tardy junction with Kirby Smith and his command, Bragg concluded on dark, misty October 13 that he had neither the supplies nor the numbers to hold Kentucky. In part due to the drought, the stores he had anticipated at Camp Breckinridge were so meager that he could only feed his troops for four days. Already angry at Kentucky for its cold shoulder and worried about spending the winter in such a barren and unfriendly place, he ordered a retreat to Cumberland Gap and Tennessee. The Confederate armies slipped past Buell's forces and trudged south into the mountains on two separate roads. Conditions grew cool with elevation and the passing of the season. In Danville, high temperatures rose back into the low seventies after the midmonth rainy spell but again fell into the sixties on October 20. Mornings were frosty. Fog and mist became common. All along the way, the Confederates left behind wounded and dying men. Sullen and exhausted, they passed through Cumberland Gap on the eighteenth and entrained in Morristown for Knoxville.[74]

On October 25, just as it had in northern Mississippi, the weather changed. From a 2 P.M. high of 75 degrees in Danville the day before, the high fell to a mere 40 degrees. That afternoon it began to snow. John Lavender remembered that "the snow fell to the Depth of 12 inches, was not Extremely cold but very Disagreeable for [men] in our condition."[75] From Knoxville, Sgt. Archie Livingston wrote his mother that "many, many soldiers" endured the snow without "shoes & blankets, and only clothed by a shirt & pr pants of thin material and even unprotected by a tent or tent Fly. I can tell you dear Mother that many soldiers suffer more than our *wealthy and comfortable families know or can realize*."[76]

The same weather affected Buell's army. It had saved the commonwealth for the Union at Perryville, but Bragg had escaped. Only faint praise accompanied the increasing pressure coming from Washington. Lincoln wanted Buell to follow the Rebels into East Tennessee before winter made the roads impassable. The general pursued only halfheartedly and soon halted. The mountains were too barren for operations, he argued, especially with winter near. Instead, Buell decided to go to Nashville before confronting the Confederates. Lincoln was incredulous. How could Bragg's army operate in the hills but not Buell's? On October 24, Halleck fired Buell and created the new Department of the Cumberland for Rosecrans. Grant received the new Department of the Tennessee, which stretched down the Mississippi almost to New Orleans.[77]

It took time for the new orders to reach the strung-out army in south-central Kentucky along the road to Nashville. The new pattern of warm days and colder nights had persisted along the way.[78] Then, on the night of October 24, the same major weather system that brought two inches of snow to northern Mississippi—and soon would pour heavy rain on McClellan's advance on the Potomac—rolled into Kentucky. At 7 A.M. the next morning, the temperature reading was only 46 degrees as skies turned dark.[79] Near Columbia, Tennessee, Crittenden's men went into camp that night after trudging twenty-five miles in cold rain and afternoon snow that had produced ankle-deep "slush." Temperatures that night fell into the thirties. "Our limbs shook and our teeth chattered with the cold," Hinman wrote. Lacking tents and in many cases overcoats and blankets, the men built shelters of "rails and boughs." By morning, "the snow lay fully eight inches deep, and the cold wind swept keenly across the fields."[80] The soldiers of the 58th Indiana, lacking tents and blankets, covered up in hay. The next morning, with "the scene resembling very much a populous country cemetery, . . . a resurrection and a transformation of scenery" occurred "when our soldiers began to wake up and crawl out from under their covering of snow."[81]

Fifty miles to the north, Gilbert's corps halted for the night. "Sunday morning we had five inches of snow," Chaplain William Haigh wrote, "and the weather [was] severely cold. The men tried to make themselves comfortable by building sheds of rails and straw, but we were almost suffocated with the smoke of the camp fires."[82] Farther east, it rained before turning to snow. The 86th Indiana awakened during the night to the sound of tree limbs cracking under the weight. Several men were injured. Nearby, Pvt. L. A. Simmons and the 84th Illinois built shelters of "brush and our single blankets. . . . [B]efore 10 o'clock, a snow-storm set in, and by daylight, at least a foot of snow had fallen." The next day, the Illinoisans marched "in snow, water, slush and mud. . . . We talked of Valley Forge and old revolutionary times. . . . [W]e noticed . . . bloodstained footprints in the snow—blood from the sore and lacerated, and almost frozen feet of the soldiers."[83]

Heat, deep dust, and drought shaped the Kentucky Campaign from first to last. The Battle of Perryville began over water. Then, on October 26, men woke up in snow to learn that they had a new commanding officer. Rosecrans decided to continue Buell's plans and marched toward Nashville. The armies that fought in the dust of Perryville now headed toward a new rendezvous. Few had any illusions. "The season was pressing sharply upon winter," aide William Bickham wrote, "and winter in Tennessee means cold, and snow, and rain, and boundless mud; and these mean hospitals thronged with suffering soldiers, and valleys crowded with the bodies of the dead."[84]

Chapter 10

A Fruitless Winter Campaign

Fredericksburg, November 1862–January 1863

Ten days of Indian summer followed the first snow of the season in northern Virginia. Capt. Robert McAllister from New Jersey compared November 11 to a summer's day. Nights remained cool and sometimes frosty, however, and the warmth soon passed. Daytime highs after November 21 settled into the forties for two weeks, while morning lows fell below freezing on the twenty-fourth and twenty-fifth. Precipitation grew frequent. A smattering fell on November 12, with steadier rains beginning on November 16 occurring off and on for six days. Rain and snow fell on the night of the twenty-eighth. Jed Hotchkiss returned to Lieutenant General Jackson's camps high in the Blue Ridge to find his comrades on the move for Fredericksburg amid light morning snow.[1]

During this unsettled weather period, the Fredericksburg Campaign began. As historian Francis O'Reilly explains, Lee's narrowed hopes rested on preventing a follow-up Union victory after Antietam. Dragging the war through the winter might deepen northern war-weariness and help anti-administration Peace Democrats. For exactly the same reasons, Lincoln needed a battlefield victory—and soon. Recent Democratic gains at the polls, coupled with growing anger over emancipation and talk of a draft, threatened his party's control of the war.

With the Orange and Alexandria Railroad blocked by Lee at Culpepper Court House, McClellan had started concentrating his command at Warrenton, preparatory to a new turning movement over the wide Rappahannock River at Fredericksburg. That operational plan continued with only some modification after Major General Burnside took command of the Army of the Potomac. Federal cavalry, moving out late because of the snow and rain, assured Burnside that the road east to Fredericksburg and beyond remained open. Pressed for action, the general told Secretary of War Stanton that, like McClellan, he planned to feint toward Lee at Culpepper and then race around the enemy's right flank. Using pontoon bridges to cross the river—the bridges at Fredericksburg were in ruins—he would then descend upon Richmond.[2]

No one in Washington liked the plan. Lincoln and Halleck wanted Burnside to attack down the Orange and Alexandria and smash Lieutenant General Longstreet's corps near Culpepper before Jackson could arrive from the Blue Ridge. Debate followed. While he waited, Burnside reorganized his army into three "grand divisions." Finally, on warm November 14, Lincoln hesitantly supported Burnside. The high in Washington that day was 60 degrees, and winter seemed far away. The next day, Burnside put his troops in motion toward the Rappahannock. Lee assumed the obvious and pulled back toward Culpepper. The Army of the Potomac turned southeast and marched hard for Fredericksburg.[3]

Cold rain peppered the Union troops as they waded through depressingly familiar Virginia mud. Streams and creeks overflowed. Roads were treacherous, with thick mud and deep potholes that swallowed up horses and mules. Everything the men wore or carried became soaked. Still, the first elements arrived at Falmouth—across the river opposite Fredericksburg—on the rainy afternoon of November 17.[4] Pvt. John Haley of the 17th Maine described "mud nearly ankle deep. . . . [R]oad phenomenally bad and growing worse."[5] Pvt. Wyman White of the 2nd US Sharpshooters said the mud was "half knee deep" and compared it to "soft soap."[6]

Yet just as Burnside hoped, his bold march caught Lee flatfooted in the mud. Rumors ran through the army that they would reach Richmond in a few days. There was only one problem: the pontoon bridges were not waiting at Falmouth, having not left Washington until November 19. Rain and mud would now slow their passage. Nor could the army receive supplies except overland by wagon, as the Richmond, Fredericksburg, and Potomac Railroad required repairs and the reconstruction of the wharves at Aquia Creek on the Potomac. His swift movement halted, Burnside grew hesitant. Bull Sumner, commanding the Right Grand Division, urged Burnside to let him cross the Rappahannock anyway. A subordinate had watched a cow wade across the river; men could do the same. Burnside refused. Continuing rain was raising the water level, he said, and Sumner might be trapped on the other side. Hooker, who proposed crossing his Center Grand Division at a different point, received a similar response.[7]

And so the Union army, in camps from Falmouth north to Stafford

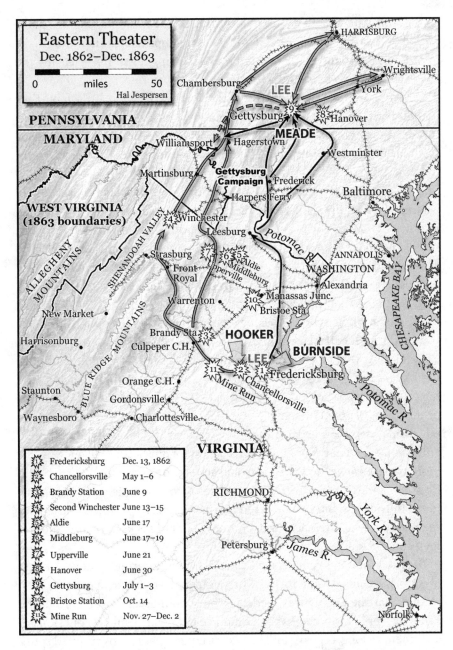

Eastern Theater
Dec. 1862–Dec. 1863

| 0 | miles | 50 |
| Hal Jespersen | | |

HARRISBURG

Wrightsville

Chambersburg

LEE

York

PENNSYLVANIA

Gettysburg 9

8 Hanover

MARYLAND

Williamsport • Hagerstown

MEADE

Westminster

Martinsburg •

Gettysburg Campaign • Frederick

Harpers Ferry

Baltimore

WEST VIRGINIA
(1863 boundaries)

4 Winchester

Leesburg

Potomac R.

ANNAPOLIS

ALLEGHENY MOUNTAINS

SHENANDOAH VALLEY

Strasburg

7 6 5 Aldie

Middleburg

Upperville

WASHINGTON

Front Royal

Warrenton •

10 Manassas Junc.

CHESAPEAKE BAY

New Market •

Bristoe Sta.

Alexandria

Harrisonburg •

Brandy Sta. 3

Culpeper C.H. •

HOOKER

LEE

BURNSIDE

Staunton •

Orange C.H. •

11 2 1 Fredericksburg

Gordonsville •

Mine Run

Chancellorsville

BLUE RIDGE MOUNTAINS

Waynesboro •

• Charlottesville

VIRGINIA

RICHMOND •

1	Fredericksburg	Dec. 13, 1862
2	Chancellorsville	May 1–6
3	Brandy Station	June 9
4	Second Winchester	June 13–15
5	Aldie	June 17
6	Middleburg	June 17–19
7	Upperville	June 21
8	Hanover	June 30
9	Gettysburg	July 1–3
10	Bristoe Station	Oct. 14
11	Mine Run	Nov. 27–Dec. 2

Petersburg •

James R.

York R.

Potomac R.

Norfolk •

Court House, waited for the bridges. Cool, damp, and muddy conditions precluded comfort. "When it rains," Chaplain Frank Morse of the new 37th Massachusetts explained to his wife, "it make a deep mud. The wheels sink into the mud and then into the dry sand underneath. There is no bottom to the soil as in New England. In a short time the army wagons will make a mud hole of such depth that it will become impassable. Then they make another road around it." That often meant cutting down trees, leaving the road to Aquia Creek littered with stumps.[8]

The northerners celebrated Thanksgiving with what little food they could obtain. Skimpy rations and rampant illness depressed morale, but it helped to get out of the weather and warm up in front of a fire. Lessons from the previous winter on the Potomac also came into play. Mostly without sanction, soldiers began to build winter shelters. While some still relied on canvas alone, log-tent hybrids promptly popped up like mushrooms.[9] Maj. Charles Wainwright wrote that "most of us have got up small stoves in our tents. Many of the men have 'logged up,' so as to raise their shelter tents, and make a close hut."[10] Regiments such as the 2nd Rhode Island surrounded their camps with cedars to provide an added windbreak. New recruits copied the veterans, although many of the new men lacked tents and had to use their ponchos as roofs.[11]

While no single style of housing emerged, the range of options had narrowed through experience. John Haley noticed two competing designs. "The New Yorkers built up by digging down: they dug a hole and built their shelter over it. We dug a place, built a stockade of the earth and pine logs, and put our shelters on top of *that*." His comrades added chimneys until "it was claimed by some that our chimneys are all wrong side up. To our dismay, we soon learned that they were right. Our houses soon filled with smoke, and our eyes almost washed out of our heads."[12] Even within a more narrow range, however, personal adaptation continued. Adj. Charles Brewster's mess in the 10th Massachusetts, for example, dug a fireplace into a hillside and pitched their tent against it. Heating likewise varied but seemed to rely on fireplaces and chimneys built of sticks or barrels. No one mentioned California or Crimean ovens.[13]

Bad weather and Federal snafus provided Lee a second chance. Unsure of what Burnside was up to, he at first equivocated despite a growing conviction that the enemy was Fredericksburg bound. Lee assumed that the Federals would cross the Rappahannock quickly and sent two divisions to stall them as long as possible. The rest of Longstreet's corps sprinted south for the North Anna River, where Lee would make a stand. He also called for Jackson's corps to come south before winter weather turned the roads into morasses and strike Burnside's communications. Jackson was on the move on November 21 despite cold weather, occasional snow, and an urgent lack of shoes. Lee was halfway to the North Anna when he learned that Burnside was still at Falmouth. Again improvising, he redirected Longstreet to the high ground overlooking Fredericksburg and told Jackson to hurry to the area. He welcomed the rain, hoping it would delay Burnside's train.[14]

As with the Federals across the river, rain slowed the Confederate investment of the heights and left men miserable. Chew's Virginia Battery arrived on November 20. "It had been raining all day," Lt. E. H. Moorman wrote, "and all hands were soaking wet and it was so cold the men could hardly take harness off the horses. The greatest trouble was to get a fire started, but we finally succeeded and managed to do a little cooking." He asked plaintively, "Oh My Country! My Country! how can you repay me for this night's suffering."[15]

By November 23, Longstreet's corps was on the wet west bank, outnumbered three to one. The men did their best to cope with the weather. Lt. Col. William Stewart of the 61st Virginia boasted of the "stick and clay chimney with a barrel stack" attached to his tent.[16] He was lucky; many of Longstreet's units lacked tents and, in some cases, blankets. The men also needed shoes, leading to a short-lived experiment to protect their feet with moccasins crafted from fresh cattle hides. Diarrhea and upper respiratory ailments were ubiquitous.[17]

The local civilian population mostly fled. Women and children clogged the roads leading out of town, sometimes abandoning wagons and property that formed additional bottlenecks. Some found shelter in roadside structures, but others resorted to the same brush arbors favored by the soldiers. Others crafted makeshift tents out of blankets and quilts.[18] "I never saw such a pitiful procession than they made," Robert Stiles of the Richmond Howitzers remembered, "trudging through the deep snow. . . . I saw little children tugging along with their doll babies,—some bigger than they were,—but holding their feet up carefully above the snow and women so old and feable that they could carry nothing and could barely hobble themselves."[19]

November ended on a "tolerably mild" note, according to Lt. Edgar Newcomb of the 19th Massachusetts, with a high of 48 degrees after a morning low of 32 degrees. The first day of December was warmer still, with an afternoon high of 53 degrees and heavy clouds. Jackson's brigades began arriving, after failing to cut Burnside's communications, and deployed south of Longstreet's corps. The next week brought cold wind and rapidly declining winter temperatures. Snow covered the ground on December 3. More rain and snow fell the next day from Washington to the Rappahannock. The fifth brought plummeting temperatures that remained in the thirties all day, as a coastal depression skirted northward up the Eastern Seaboard. Midafternoon rain changed into five fresh inches of snow, with occasional hail. On December 7, the 7 A.M. low was 16 degrees and the afternoon high was 26 degrees. The ground froze to a depth of two inches. Ice remained in Alexandria as late as December 8, and hard morning freezes lasted through the eleventh. Churned-up road mud froze solid, as did the Rappahannock below Fredericksburg, icing in Federal gunboats. These same days notably brought similar snowstorms to the battle fronts in Middle Tennessee and northern Arkansas (discussed in later chapters) and point to a massive weather event across the middle of the country to the Atlantic coast.

Such weather brought sheer physical misery. Colonel de Trobriand described how the snow weighed down pine boughs over his camp, put out fires, and covered sentries until they looked like "plaster statues half confounded with the tree trunks. One would have said that Death, not satisfied with the bloody part reserved to him, wished to bury us all under the same winding-sheet."[20] Other soldiers routinely described frostbite and their constant search for food, wood, and warmth. Capt. George Barnard wrote home for a buffalo robe, adding that he had gone to the surgeon to beg him for a blanket to cover a dying man; when the doctor refused, Barnard stole his. Soldiers scrambled to construct huts. Men in shelter tents added chimneys or built large fires next to them, filling tents and camps with acrid smoke. Morale declined as disgust with Washington grew. Soldiers damned their officers, Congress, and the press.[21]

It was especially bad for those Federals caught in the open. The repaired Richmond, Fredericksburg, and Potomac first delivered supplies to Falmouth on November 23, and the first pontoon bridges arrived two days later. Yet with Longstreet digging in across the river, Burnside spent additional days searching for a better place to cross. The rain and bad roads deeply worried his lieutenants. On rainy and snowy December 5, Burnside roused his army for a crossing twelve miles downriver at a place called Skinker's Neck. The army was in motion before the general learned that the Confederates had blocked the site. That night, that men bivouacked by the snowy road before turning back to their old camps the following morning.[22] Back in camp, Brewster wrote: "The roads are awful. . . . [W]e passed lots of mud holes filled with dead mules and horses. . . . Water in a tin cup beside me freezes almost solid in a few moments. . . . I am so cold I cannot write more now."[23]

At least the Confederates were equally miserable. Brig. Gen. William Pendleton ached for the "poor fellows in camp. There are still a few unprovided with shoes, more with inadequate clothing, and all without tents. They manage to eke out some kind of shelter, wither with oil cloths or a blanket over poles, or brushwood covered with leaves."[24] Pvt. Richard Waldrop of Jackson's 21st Virginia brought a stray dog inside his tent to keep warm.[25]

But Virginia's weather moderated. As historian Robert Krick asserts, lingering stories of wounded men freezing to death on a frigid Fredericksburg battlefield involve more legend than fact. Daytime highs rose steadily after December 9, reaching 56 degrees on the thirteenth and almost 70 degrees on the fifteenth. Nights were cold to be sure, with 7 A.M. temperatures well below freezing until December 13. Yet Krick is correct to conclude that the Battle of Fredericksburg took place in a sort of "Indian-summer."[26] The men themselves noticed the welcome change in their letters and diaries, if not always in accounts after the war. On December 10, Pvt. J. P. Coburn of the 141st Pennsylvania wrote his father that "the weather is warm and pleasant today & the snow which has lain for several days is fast disappearing."[27]

The armies shook themselves from cold slumbers and returned to war. After Skinker's Neck, Burnside cast about for other alternatives but found none. If the president wanted a campaign that winter, the army would have to cross at Fredericksburg. On warmer December 9, Burnside informed his generals. He asserted that Lee was spread thin and would never expect such a bold assault. A quick strike, he claimed, would divide the two enemy corps. Sumner's Right Grand Division would go through town, while Maj. Gen. William B. Franklin's Left would cross downriver. Hooker's Center would wait in reserve. Only Sumner offered support. In response, Burnside hesitated, called another meeting for the next day, dug in his heels, and demanded their loyalty. He hurried to get the army ready. Soldiers received ammunition, three days' rations, and in some cases tents and blankets. Union engineers prepared to lay the pontoon bridges at 3 A.M., building two on the north end of the town, a third downriver, and two others south of Fredericksburg for Franklin. With loud cooperation from the navy as well as diversions, Burnside tried to convince Lee that he was actually about to cross elsewhere.[28] "We have a fine day for our preparations," Major Wainwright wrote, "not so cold, as it has been."[29]

After nightfall, temperatures fell into the twenties. The night was "cold and raw" as well as foggy, according to Col. Wesley Brainerd of the 50th New York Engineers.[30] Long caravans of pontoon boats, wagons, and troops snaked through the cold darkness toward the riverbank. Once the moon set, around 1 A.M., the engineers began moving equipment down to the water's edge. On the heights, 147 Federal artillery pieces unlimbered. Heavy fog off the Rappahannock shrouded the bridge builders as they began constructing the five spans. But around 4:30 A.M., Confederate pickets heard activity. At five o'clock, two signal guns alerted Fredericksburg's defenders. Brig. Gen. William Barksdale's Mississippi brigade and a contingent of Floridians waited in their riverside entrenchments, their orders to contest any crossing while Lee concentrated the rest of his army. Ten minutes later, Barksdale's men opened a devastating fire on the bridge builders. Federal artillery responded with explosive force, targeting enemy muzzle fire in the darkness until the sun rose, then blasting the riverfront. Fredericksburg's remaining civilians fled or hid in basements and outbuildings.

In Washington, it was 24 degrees.[31] Randolph Shotwell of the 8th Virginia remembered the morning's "frosty chill."[32] Smoke, mixed with the fog and mist off the river, enveloped Fredericksburg and strained Union gunners' ability to locate targets. As the morning passed and the stalemate deepened, the Federals pushed more guns to the river. Around ten o'clock, the fog finally lifted, although enough acrid gunsmoke remained to shroud the scene. The town's defenders broke up into small cadres, making it harder for enemy artillery to neutralize them, and took cover in cellars during barrages. Through a combination of courage and coercion, most of the bridge builders persevered despite their dwindling numbers. A mile downriver, the engineers at Stafford Heights had more luck, and, facing only light resistance, their two bridges were in place before noon. Burnside frustrated Franklin, however, holding him in place until the other spans were ready. To accomplish that, he ordered the entire city shelled. Solid shot and exploding shells devastated Fredericksburg to a degree unprecedented so far during the war, yet the artillery still failed to silence the defenders. Around 2:30 P.M., Burnside agreed to the engineers' plea to ferry infantry across the Rappahannock, although he deemed it a suicidal mission. By then the day had grown warm, with a high in Washington of 50 degrees. Elements of three regiments crossed the river in rowboats under the heaviest artillery fire of the day. As historian Francis O'Reilly notes, it was the first time in history that American troops seized a beachhead under fire. Deployed as skirmishers and under orders to take no prisoners, the Federals savagely fought their way into town with rifles and bayonets. When night began to fall—sunset came before five o'clock—both sides returned to aiming at muzzle flashes. Finally, around 7:00 P.M., the last of Barksdale's survivors escaped under orders toward the main line on the heights west of town.[33]

The temperature fell below freezing mark and stood at 28 degrees the following morning. Brig. Gen. Joseph Kershaw, commanding a South Carolina brigade, reported that one of his men died of the cold. Franklin's Left Grand Division finally crossed the river at the lower bridges. In the frosty daylight of December 12, Fredericksburg was a gap-toothed, smoldering ruin. Mist and fog lingered into afternoon, frustrating Confederate artillery as they tried to contest the various Union crossings. Most of the rest of the Army of the Potomac rumbled down thawing roads and streamed over fog-covered bridges to the west bank. Ignoring Franklin and others who pressed to lead the main attack against Jackson's fog-shrouded works on Prospect Hill south of town, Burnside dallied for hours before issuing opaque orders that seemed to call for Franklin and Sumner to storm both flanks of Lee's position and force him to retreat. On the heights above town, the Confederates prepared to receive these assaults, with emotions running the gamut from dread to—in Stonewall Jackson's case—glee. Lee was confident. Using natural features, including an old sunken road on Marye's Heights, his Confederates wielded picks and shovels to add gun pits, improve other positions, and chop down trees to create a killing zone.[34]

The warming trend, meanwhile, continued during the day, with an afternoon high of almost 57 degrees. Frozen soil melted into ankle-deep mud. The night grew frosty, however, with temperatures again falling back toward freezing. During that cold night, the Army of the Potomac slipped its traces. For reasons still debated, the night degenerated into an angry bacchanalia of drunken vandalism and vengeful destruction that shocked staid observers in both armies. With exceptions, officers looked the other way or even participated in the riot. Brig. Gen. Marsena Patrick, the army's chief provost, confined himself to protecting the bridges and seizing stolen property. As O'Reilly observes, Fredericksburg became the first American city sacked since Washington in 1814. Furious Confederates around their fires ached to exact revenge.[35]

Saturday, December 13, dawned with warmer temperatures just above freezing and low, overcast skies pierced by a red sun. A thick, misty fog mixed with lingering gunsmoke effectively hid both armies from each other until well after 9 A.M. Longstreet remembered that, at daybreak, the farthest he could see in the soup was about sixty-five yards. Pvt. John Apperson of the 1st Virginia, brigaded in Longstreet's corps, described better vision up to several hundred yards but still could not see the enemy. For the Confederates behind their makeshift barricades, however, there could be no doubt of what was about to happen, given the audible sounds of shouting officers, marching feet, and rumbling batteries.[36] Longstreet opined that the fog amplified the sounds of the Union army as it moved into position so that he could hear enemy officers in "almost startling clearness. . . . [S]o distinctly were the voices of the officers brought to us that they seemed quite near at hand."[37] Across the field, Federals felt equally blinded and relied on memories of what they had last seen of the Confederates to guide their assaults.[38]

The fog lifted around ten o'clock. The Army of the Potomac, newly arrayed in line of battle with unfurled flags, presented a breathtaking sight. Private Shotwell likened the scene to a curtain rising on stage as the fog rolled away. Yet the actors' roles remained sketchy. Burnside was still finalizing orders just before daybreak. The result was confusion. Sumner's grand division was to move through town and assault Longstreet on the heights. Burnside's orders to Franklin were tardy, vague, contrary to previous discussions, and open to question. Hindsight suggests that he wanted the Left Grand Division to launch a heavy assault. Followed by Sumner's attack, the two wings of the Union army would roll up Lee's flanks and force him out of his works and away from the river. Instead, Franklin interpreted his assignment narrowly as a limited diversion. Why he did so remains open to debate. Jackson's position looked more formidable than Longstreet's, although it contained serious flaws. Franklin despaired of his troops receiving adequate support, as the hill and water topography south of town essentially divided the planned Federal effort into two separate battles. Historian George Rable suggests that the general simply had lost faith in Burnside, while Francis O'Reilly adds that Franklin was convinced that his commander had slighted him with favoritism to others.[39]

Whatever the reasons, Franklin refused to ask for clarification and did as little as possible. His initial attacking force consisted of a single division commanded by Maj. Gen. George Meade, with a second division under Brig. Gen. John Gibbon in reserve. Meade's men were still forming as the fog lifted. Confederate artillery, initially consisting of only two isolated guns, opened fire. As the fighting developed, several batteries on Prospect Hill caught Meade out in the open and stopped his division short of the railroad running south of town. An hour-long artillery duel followed. The day turned warm, with the afternoon temperature rising again to 56 degrees. Meade moved forward across sodden ground around 1 P.M., with effective support from his own artillery. One of his brigades penetrated a gap in the Confederate line, but Jackson's reserves prevented collapse. Gibbon's supporting assault, launched at 1:30 P.M., accomplished little. Franklin sent no reinforcements, and Brig. Gen. David Birney refused to help. A Confederate counterattack drove Meade and Gibbon back until it reached the murderous range of Federal canister fire and musketry. Watching his men at this moment, an admiring Lee made the famous comment that went something like, "It is well this is so terrible! We should grow too fond of it!" Terrible it was. Shattered by sheets of soft lead, the surviving Confederates withdrew. Hot artillery fire set wet broom sage afire, burning some of the wounded and dead between the lines. Despite repeated pleas from Burnside to renew the attack, Franklin had seen enough. He lied to his commanding officer, claiming that he already had committed all of his men and could do no more.[40]

By that time, Sumner's massive assault needed all the help it would not get. Assuming that Franklin was doing his part, Burnside launched the next phase of his attack around noon. Brig. Gen. William H. French's division went forward from town with orders to seize the heights. That involved moving through scattered properties on the western edge of town and over saturated, muddy, open country pockmarked with a few additional buildings and fences. A partially drained millrace protected by an embankment crossed the ground about a third of the way to the foot of Marye's Heights. It was five feet deep and fifteen feet wide, big enough to require using three footbridges to cross it, but these were not intact. Federal skirmishers drove pickets back from the millrace, but troops bunched up at the funnel points, creating targets for Confederate artillery. Once French's surviving men made it past the millrace, they found the enemy behind hastily barricaded natural features, including the sunken road and a stone wall along the base of the heights. Confederate musketry from the sunken road as well as canister fire broke up what was left of the assault and mangled most of the attackers.

Undeterred, Burnside had Sumner feed in reinforcements. When those brigades failed, he stubbornly ordered more sent in. Always the story was the same—powerful Confederate fire destroyed courageous brigades before they reached the muddy slopes of Marye's Heights. By three o'clock, Longstreet had turned back four Union divisions, and his men stood four deep at the stone wall. Undeterred, physically and mentally exhausted, and worried that he might be compared to McClellan at Antietam, Burnside refused to quit. He sent new orders to Franklin while calling for Hooker's reserve troops to take their turn. Four more divisions suffered the same fate as Sumner's. By dusk, the open ground and slope were covered with dead men, the wailing wounded, and healthier soldiers pinned down by relentless Confederate fire. Hooker profanely told Burnside that more attacks were madness, but the latter remained adamant. As the sun set a little before 5 P.M., Hooker sent one last division, brigade by brigade, against the Confederates. The last of the fourteen separate attacks failed. Burnside wanted to try again, but his commanders and nightfall finally combined to stymie him.[41]

For the Army of the Potomac, the day was unmitigated disaster, with casualties nearly three times as large as its foe's losses. The dark night, lit by a waning gibbous moon, brought confirmation of this. Federals crisscrossed the soggy field searching for the wounded and dead. Ambulances rumbled. Looted homes and businesses became gory hospitals. Contrary to legend, wounded Federals did not freeze to death that night on the field— that was impossible, as the temperature hovered around 40 degrees. Yet it was cold enough. Unable to build fires, Maj. Rufus Dawes remembered men trying to stay warm by spooning each other atop oilcloths. The soldiers of Pvt. William McClendon's 15th Alabama did likewise. But no one froze.[42]

Burnside refused to admit defeat, volunteering to personally lead a renewed attack in the morning. He wired the president that he would renew the fight in a few hours. To the west, Lee met with his generals. The next day dawned chilly at 40 degrees, with a stiff wind that made it feel colder. Fog enveloped the horrific battlefield. Confederate sharpshooters pinned down Federals in the cold muck. Fresh Union brigades began moving into position in town, while survivors of the previous day's fighting rested, looted, or fretted. The morning warmed up quickly. By afternoon, it was 63 degrees in overcast Washington, the warmest day of December so far. But at midmorning, Burnside's generals, spearheaded by Sumner, finally convinced him to cancel his suicidal planned attack. Disappointed, Lee vainly tried to bait his adversary. Instead, brief afternoon truces allowed men to collect their comrades. Soldiers began building fires, eating, drinking, and strengthening their lines. Then, at about 6:15 P.M., the night sky seemed slowly to catch fire.[43] "There was a very fine display of the Northern Lights to be seen in the heavens for over an hour," Oliver Coolidge of the 24th Massachusetts wrote, "the heavens were filled with long streaks of pale yellow light then all blended together and turned to a blood red & formed a complete fan shaped form and moved from NE to SW the sight was splendid some of our boys pretended to see the future destinys of our Army in the sign in the heavens." Confederates interpreted the rare aurora borealis as symbolic of their apparent victory and future hopes.[44]

The day that followed became the warmest of the month, registering 56 degrees at 7 A.M. and rising to over 68 degrees at 2 P.M. Morning fog again obscured the battlefield, where dead and dying men still lay. Aside from local bursts of gunfire and the constant train of ambulances crossing the Rappahannock, the armies stared at each other all day. The Union commander and his generals debated what to do next. The more the Confederates fortified, the more Burnside's lieutenants wanted no part of another assault. Around dark, a nearly despondent Burnside gave in and ordered a withdrawal. While the Confederates did little to harass the retreat, the weather cruelly taunted both armies. Temperatures fell 20 degrees overnight as howling rain moved in from the south. Loud enough to cover the sounds of retreat, heavy showers doused the withdrawal, which began at around 3 A.M., turning the roads into quagmires as winds shifted to the northwest.[45]

Once across the river, the surviving Federals trudged to their shebangs or just lay down in the mud to sleep. The next morning, Lee realized that Burnside was gone. Disappointed, he moved his army into Fredericksburg.

Along the way, men collected discarded shelter tents, blankets, and overcoats that would help keep them warm and dry during the winter. The dreary day remained cool, with the high rising only to 43 degrees.[46]

~

As December passed by, northern Virginia weather remained mercurial. The Federal withdrawal coincided with a cold front and downturn in temperatures that lasted until just before Christmas. Six straight mornings began with below-freezing readings, with the winter solstice the coldest day by far: 20 degrees that afternoon. The constant refreezing and rethawing of the ground became treacherous. Ice formed on the Potomac and the Rappahannock, threatening supply lines. The northern lights returned during the early morning of December 19, the only cloudy day of the cold snap. A warm front finally arrived with dark, heavy skies on December 23, bringing a more moderate phase. Christmas Day saw an unseasonable high of 51 degrees and muddy fields clear of snow. Despite a general lack of traditional feasting as well as heavy cloud cover, soldiers praised the holiday's warmth. The next day, temperatures made it all the way to sixty, and daytime highs remained comfortably warm until New Year's Eve.[47]

Hopes for a quiet winter, the contrary signs of a renewed offensive, widespread sickness attributed in part to exposure, and constant rumors all led soldiers to spend a great deal of time debating the issue of shelter. Should they wait? Build snug lodgings now? Construct temporary expedients? Reflecting the chaos at Federal headquarters, no one was quite sure what to do next, except to move beyond tents when possible. While some units received their first shelter tents, most Federals found them inadequate during the cold snap. In some cases, they added wood-and-mud chimneys and fireplaces to them. Others began building hybrid canvas-log quarters of various sizes or repaired and improved existing prebattle shanties. Evidence suggests that most still relied on familiar designs from the previous winter, with chinked log walls, roofs made from tents or ponchos, and attached chimneys. Fireplaces provided heat. Despite Charles Tripler's entreaties the previous winter, many men again dug basements.[48] Demand for firewood and logs for lodgings soon denuded the riverbanks. According to John Haley, the 17th Maine was reduced to "driving down some stakes and then weaving brush between them."[49] Others unearthed stumps.

A scarcity of tools created problems as well. When sharpshooter Wyman White discovered that no one in his company had an axe, he stole one.[50]

Confederates were equally uncertain and busy. There seems to have been even greater variety in architecture in their camps than in those across the river. Some men decided to ride out the weather under canvas. They snuggled under blankets or, in the case of the 2nd Georgia, used cut-up church carpets. Others, such as Pvt. Franklin Riley of the 16th Mississippi, saw little reason to do much more than add a chimney to tents, sometimes erected over a dug-out hole.[51]

Using captured Federal shelter tents, taken up in abundance from the battlefield, men in the 12th North Carolina constructed log-canvas hybrids on the Federal model, complete with fireplaces.[52] Ham Chamberlayne wrote about Jackson's men at Moss Neck "grotesquely settled in huts of wood & canvas in various proportions and of every (ugly & curious) kind."[53] Lt. J. F. J. Caldwell of the 1st South Carolina left another detailed description of postbattle housing in Jackson's command. Having largely lived in tents, his South Carolinian comrades "were extremely unskillful in fitting together the logs that comprised our houses, and in constructing, for houses or tents, chimneys that would draw or throw out heat." At first, many of them simply stuck to what they knew, though often with a twist. "Many of the men," he wrote, "burrowed into the ground under the airy covering of dilapidated Yankee flies, brought from the battlefields of the last campaigns." Others built Confederate versions of canvas-log shebangs. "But the common house was a log hut, daubed with mud. They were too close, as a rule, and damp." Chimneys and fireplaces provided heat. Officers pitched tents and added "a chimney at one side of the door, and hung up an oil cloth or other thick cloth for a door."[54]

Shotwell described another common variant, writing that his comrades "made shift to do without cabins by weatherboarding their tents—i. e.— covering them outside with a layer of pine poles upon which was spread [a] covering of leaves, brush and dirt. Thus weatherboarded the tent serves to shelter from the roughest of the blasts, but does not serve to shut out the cold."[55] Cpl. Berry Benson of the 1st South Carolina and a friend built a simple shelter with two tent flies, "one end closed by bushes wattled together, the other with an oil-cloth. Such, with a floor of poles laid close together and raised a foot or so off the ground, was our house during the winter of 1862–63."[56] Many of his comrades, however, erected more elaborate structures they called "Merrimacs" for their alleged resemblance to the ironclad:

> Two heavy forks of trees were posted in the ground, and across the forks was laid a stout horizontal pole. Leaning against this pole were set other poles or fence rails, the lower ends resting on the ground. The roof . . . was covered first with leaves, then with earth on top of the leaves. One end was generally closed by bushes wattled together or poles driven in the ground; the front being sometimes left open, sometimes closed by an old blanket or oil-cloth. To give more room, some of the men set such a structure or tent over a square hole in the ground, from two to four feet deep. Some of the officers' quarters, perhaps most of them, were made so.[57]

In Washington, skies were clear on the chilly morning of January 1, 1863, as the Emancipation Proclamation went into effect and changed the war. As historian Andrew Lang argues, widespread perceptions of the southern climate helped shape, in part, Lincoln's careful phrasing about specifically enlisting African American soldiers "to garrison forts, positions, stations, and other places." White Union volunteers chafed at occupation duties in garrisons, finding such mundane service beneath them. Along with their officers, including generals such as Halleck and Grant, they assumed that African Americans were better suited for garrison duty and labor details due to their alleged racial acclimation to tropical climates, which made such work dangerous for white men.

Summer was a long way away at Fredericksburg, but soldiers expressed hope that the worst of winter was behind them. The weather raised soldiers' expectations.[58] Despite cold nights, the first half of January 1863 continued relatively mild if, as Lt. Col. Benjamin Cook of the 12th Massachusetts put it, "changeable."[59] Afternoon temperatures rose daily into the fifties (56 degrees on January 5) before declining again. Rain fell in Fredericksburg on January 3, the night of the fourth, and again on the sixth. January 7 then turned cold, with highs only in the low thirties and snow flurries. Water froze in tents. A new warm front brought wet weather and higher temperatures, although it rained heavily on dreary January 10, lasting through the night. Chaplain Frank Morse wrote home that he feared the Virginia mud more than the Rebel army. Instead, the weather turned fair yet again. Afternoon highs worked their way back up to 50 degrees on January 11, fell back into the forties, and then hit a remarkable 68 degrees on the rainy fifteenth. A strong wind from the southwest blew down tents on the Confederate side of the river.[60]

"We have been blessed so far this winter in regard to weather," Surgeon Spencer Welch wrote on January 11.[61] It did seem a miracle. Noting that his men were leaving their tents open and keeping fires down until night, Charles Wainwright wrote that "the natives say it is unusual to have such weather at this time; last year we were up to our eyes in mud at this time." But, he added, the south wind might soon bring rain, "which will quickly change the aspect of the country if it comes, and probably knock in the head the movement which is evidently in contemplation, for we have just received orders to be ready to start tomorrow morning."[62]

Encouraged by mild weather, the opposing commanders remained committed to winter operations. Confederate cavalry stayed active against Burnside's supply line. On the spring-like day after Christmas, Jeb Stuart launched a raid that brought in badly needed supplies while painfully embarrassing Union horsemen. Nonetheless, Lee necessarily remained tethered to a reactive defense. The next major move had to be Burnside's. The Union commander did not operate in a military vacuum. Defeat at Fredericksburg had stunned Washington and induced waves of anger and defeatism across the North. Democrats sought to use the debacle to roll back Republican policies while bringing a halt to the fighting generally. The price of gold rose while the value of Union greenbacks plummeted. Emancipation and a looming military draft kept the populace further agitated. Fredericksburg widened a growing divide within the Republican Party as well, one that nearly resulted in the Radical Republicans shoving more moderate William Henry Seward out of the cabinet in hopes of controlling Lincoln. The Joint Congressional Committee on the Conduct of the War, dominated by Radical Republicans, blamed the Democrat Franklin for the Fredericksburg defeat. Within the Army of the Potomac's officer corps, constant finger pointing emerged—at the War Department, at Halleck, or most cannibalistically at each other. Everyone's most frequent target was Burnside. While not entirely unsympathetic, common soldiers teetered on the edge of losing faith in a general they increasingly viewed as incompetent and weak. Disloyal officers schemed against him while advancing themselves or attempting to engineer a return of McClellan. Halleck and

Stanton demanded action. Others bombarded the army commander with advice, which included not wasting the unusually good weather. Worst of all, Burnside had lost much faith in himself.[63]

For all of these reasons, Burnside had to renew the campaign—and soon. He decided to recross the river seven miles south of town, near the mouth of Muddy Creek and almost opposite the mansion owned by the new Confederate secretary of war, James A. Seddon. Stung by all of the obvious disloyalty around him, Burnside revealed specifics only to a few, notably Halleck. He used much of December's improving weather in amassing supplies, obtaining new pontoons, and keeping his men busy corduroying red-clay roads. He reorganized his command structure too, promoting Meade to lead a corps. By the end of the year, Burnside was nearly ready to move. On chilly December 30, however, President Lincoln derailed his plans, curtly informing the general not to renew the fighting without White House approval. Shocked, Burnside left for Washington, arriving on January 1, 1863, and met twice with the president. Lincoln admitted that he had opened his door to some of the general's disgruntled subordinates, who had convinced him that the army was demoralized and that the proposed plan was doomed. Burnside was shocked; none of them knew his plans. Lincoln refused to accept the general's resignation, but he also refused to identify the informants or allow the army commander to fire them.

Frustrated and embarrassed, Burnside returned to Falmouth. Only after Lee sent a division to North Carolina to block a Federal incursion—false rumors also indicated that he had sent men to Tennessee to help Bragg— did Lincoln stage an about-face. By then, the planned crossing was an open secret, and Lee fortified accordingly. Burnside scrambled for an alternative, conducting much of the reconnaissance himself. He concluded that the best he could do was to push his army across the Rappahannock at two fords upriver, several miles west of Fredericksburg. The new campaign would begin on January 17. While the unreliable Sumner demonstrated in town, Franklin would cross at U.S. Ford and Hooker at Banks Ford. Burnside's critics predictably opposed him. The White House finally provided only reluctant acquiescence, carefully couched to protect the administration in the event of another failure. It was a bad state of affairs that promptly got worse for the Federals. Lee shifted troops upriver, forcing Burnside to delay again. Learning that Confederates were at U.S. Ford but not at the other one, he ordered both Franklin and Hooker to Banks Ford, with the movement to begin on January 20. If it worked, the army would cross the river above and below the ford, then drive into Lee's left.[64]

It was too late, although no one in 1863 knew it. Across the North, people marveled at the mild winter. "The weather in the Northern States has been mild and salubrious beyond any other within our recollection," wrote the editors of the *Scientific American*. "The Hudson river is open nearly to Albany, and steamers are now running as freely on it as during the month of November. West of the Hudson there is no snow, and the rivers and creeks have not yet been bound in icy fetters. The Mississippi is open from Quincy in Illinois, and the weather in the West has also been unusually warm."[65]

As if to torment Burnside, the winter deteriorated almost as soon as the Army of the Potomac moved out. The general's indecision, the back-biting officers, and Lincoln's clumsy wavering had combined to squander the good weather. During the windy and showery night of January 15–16, temperatures began falling, from an afternoon high of 68 degrees on the fifteenth to only 44 degrees the next day. They kept plummeting afterward, to 30 degrees on January 17 and 22 degrees the next day, with a frigid morning low of 13 degrees and freezing rain in Fredericksburg. Skies in Washington on January 19 ominously turned "snowlike," but in Fredericksburg, the most notable weather effect that day was a stiff wind from the northeast.[66]

The next morning, officers read Burnside's orders for the march. "The auspicious moment seems to have arrived," he had written, "to strike a great and mortal blow in the rebellion."[67] Yet the army began crawling toward Banks Ford only at midday. Once again, Burnside continuously issued orders up to the last moment, wasting much of the morning. Sumner's demonstration commenced early enough, but Hooker's grand division did not hit the road until about 11 A.M. Franklin's first units, facing the longer march, stepped off about an hour later. Temperatures rose above freezing, from 29 degrees at 7 A.M. to a 2 P.M. high of 36 degrees. Skies were low and gray. As the temperature inched up, hard roads became deep and sticky, and these became clogged with too many soldiers and trains.[68] But Burnside still expressed confidence. He told Baldy Smith that "with good weather we were 48 hours ahead of them."[69]

In retrospect, Burnside could not have chosen a worse time to march. Falling barometers and northeastern winds presaged disaster. Using records from around the continent, historian Harold Winters concludes that the high-altitude jet stream, which for weeks had blocked major storm systems from entering Virginia, was shifting to the east. Behind it was a massive high-pressure system, an invisible fortress of arctic cold stretching across North America. David Ludlum believes that the center of the high probably was across upper New York and lower New England. High-pressure systems developing that far north in winter open a back door to storm systems developing in the Gulf of Mexico or along the South American coast. That seems to be what happened in mid-January 1863. As Burnside's men prepared to march, a slow-moving low-pressure system carried warm air from the Gulf of Mexico up the coast into the Carolinas. The next day, as the Army of the Potomac marched to the Rappahannock fords, barometers plummeted and skies grew dark.[70]

Burnside's grumbling soldiers watched the afternoon sky and began to fear rain or snow. The first precipitation began to fall around nightfall—sundown came at 4:55 P.M.—although soldier memoirists disagreed as the exact moment. Closer to the river, Hooker halted within two miles of Banks Ford, with the rest of his grand division strung back toward the army's rear areas. Franklin was even farther to the east and rear. Soldiers were pitching their tents when evening fog along the river dissolved into rain. Strong winds from the northeast blew the rainfall, soaking uniforms and equipment while upending tents.[71] "It was a cold and driving storm," Rufus Dawes remembered, "which aided by the gale penetrated the clothing and cut the faces of the men as they staggered along. It was with the greatest difficulty that the artillery and wagon trains were dragged through the deep mud. The storm raged and howled, and the rain poured in torrents during the night."[72]

After midnight, the steady rain metamorphosed into a roaring, violent storm.[73] Cpl. William Myers of the 106th Pennsylvania wrote home that "it rained as if the world was coming to an end."[74] The army's movement already seemed a failure. "The rain is likely to close the whole affair," Major Wainwright wrote, "and send us wading homewards through the mud tomorrow, for it is falling very steady; a regular northeaster."[75] Across the river, the Confederates huddled under shelter. "Our tents flap and flutter in the air like so many sails in a storm," the 1st Virginia's John Apperson wrote, "and the rain batters against the tent in a manner not pleasing to the ear."[76]

"It was a wild night," Private White of the 2nd US Sharpshooters concluded. He had abandoned his regiment for the relative comfort of a quartermaster's tent. The next morning, January 21, he tried to return, only to find the campsite deserted and the muddy plain littered with "their tents, their equipment, and in many cases their rifles and ammunition, everything laying on the wet ground. It struck me that they must have deserted, and I afterwards found that to be the case. Hundreds of men, being entirely discouraged, broke to the rear and started toward the North and home."[77]

In Georgetown, C. B. Mackee laconically wrote, "1.25 rain last night & windy." Sunrise brought little change. Although temperatures continued to rise to a Washington high of 42 degrees that afternoon, heavy rain pounded the armies all day, measuring two additional inches.[78] The high Rappahannock roared, creeks went out of their banks, and standing water occupied every low spot. The north bank of the river dissolved into a deep gooey mass of red mud.[79] "At daylight every thing [seemed] one sea of mud," Benjamin Cook wrote.[80] Despite the developing morass, gale-force winds, and torrential rains that ceased only for brief moments, Burnside was determined to continue and, as Dawes heard a disgusted comrade put it, "'wade on to glory.'" Bitter soldiers returned to the march that morning. The underbrush and pine thickets along the roads were so thick that trying to go across country was impossible. Trapped in the churned-up roadways, Burnside's men sank in mud that rose above their shoes at first but grew deeper as the day progressed, reaching knees by afternoon. Wringing-wet uniforms and cold rain chilled soldiers. Captain McAllister wrote that he had never seen so much straggling.[81]

When pontoons, wagons, and caissons sank in the mud, teamsters double-teamed and triple-teamed them. Sgt. George A. Mitchell of the 5th New York described twenty-eight mules pulling a pontoon boat, unsuccessfully, and twenty-two mules hitched to a single caisson. Animals died by the hundreds that day, thrashing pitifully in the muck. Soldiers by the dozens attached ropes and, by companies, dragged vehicles until the men themselves collapsed into the red mud with exhaustion. A soldier trying to corduroy the road sank so deep that his comrades had to dig him out. Some regiments kept slogging and hauling until midafternoon, when Hooker's men reached a particularly treacherous ravine—promptly renamed "Profanity Gulch"—that sucked in everything with wheels. Creeks rose to flood stage front and rear, trapping regiments. Vehicles and dying horses and mules sank beyond extrication.[82] Officer George Sanford of the 1st US Cavalry opined that the pontoon train "could no more be moved than the pyramids of Egypt."[83]

Throughout the day, Burnside had been in the saddle, desperate to overcome the unexpected storm with sheer will. Mud covered him by nightfall. That evening, with the rain still showing no sign of letting up, he admitted that he no longer had the jump on Lee. Formations remained mired down at Falmouth, with a strung-out army in between. Just bringing up the rest of his men and the majority of his pontoons would eat up the next day. Before midnight, with the rain continuing, he broke the bad news to Washington.[84] "I moved the greater portion of the command, with a view to crossing above," he wrote Halleck, "but, owing to the severe storm which began after that the enemy has discovered our design. The roads are almost impassable, and the small streams are very much swollen. I shall try to run any unnecessary risks. It is most likely that we will have to change the plan."[85]

It kept raining. "The morning dawned upon as woe-begone a set of men as could be well imagined," wrote the 15th New Jersey's chaplain.[86] But the wind blew from the north, signaling that the center of the system had passed. Temperatures held steady, with a morning low of 38 degrees and an afternoon high of 43 degrees. Additional rain grew lighter until it stopped that evening, roughly forty-eight hours after it began. Rations ran out. Some Federals only received a shot of whiskey, and promptly started slugging each other. Despite the desperate efforts of soldiers and whip-wielding teamsters, the Army of the Potomac was stuck in the mud.[87]

Worse still, the Confederates now were on the scene. Lee raced back to Fredericksburg from Richmond when he learned of the Federal movement, only to find Jackson refusing to accept Longstreet's authority or correct appraisal of Burnside's plans. Lee immediately allowed Longstreet to put troops at the upriver fords as he wanted. Two divisions began moving on January 21. The same weather conditions that terrible day created misery aplenty, but as Francis O'Reilly notes, macadamized and planked roads allowed the Confederates to move much farther than the Federals—fifteen miles that day as opposed to Burnside's four. By night, Confederates held Banks Ford. Early the next morning, their artillery shelled the opposite bank. While the gunfire produced few casualties, vocal taunts and ridicule took the last wind out of Union morale. A group of Confederates found paint and wrote "Burnside stuck in the mud" across a barn roof. That insult, more than any other, seared into memories to be recounted in the years that followed. It was too much for Joe Hooker, possibly drunk, who openly excoriated Burnside. The Army of the Potomac seemed on the verge of mutiny.[88]

Burnside gave up. "The elements were against us," he later complained.[89] Faced with hellish weather and open opposition, he decided to order a withdrawal back to Falmouth. Yet he tarried for hours, hoping to first meet with Halleck and have the general in chief take responsibility for the retreat. When Halleck refused, Burnside issued the orders on his own and left for headquarters. Regiments began chopping down trees to corduroy the miry roadways and to free wagons and artillery pieces. On January 23, with skies clearing after morning fog and high temperatures rising to 50 degrees, the two grand divisions began retracing their soggy steps to Falmouth. The sun came out about noon, a welcome stranger.[90]

While the rain had stopped, the march back to Falmouth was excruciating. "Our Division was detailed to assist a regular Battery back to camp," Elisha Hunt Rhodes wrote. "The mud was so deep that sixteen horses could not pull one gun. The companies of men would take hold of a rope . . . and pull the gun out of the mire."[91] Writers noted ten or even twenty horses to a single gun. "In squads of two and three," Benjamin Cook remembered, "Burnside's unfortunate army splashed, swam, and floundered in the endeavor to regain its old camping-grounds."[92] John Haley agreed. "It was a weary way," he wrote, "the mud ankle deep, and progress slow, but most of us reached camp by sunset. Our feet are encased in the soil of Virginia despite the most frantic efforts to shake it off. The quantity of soil that has changed places in the last twenty-four hours would furnish a subject for geologic speculation."[93]

The roads were riddled as well with dead animals. A reporter counted "seventy-five dead horses . . . in the short space of three miles, between the ford and Beriah Church. Dead horses are so abundant that a man today was endeavoring to contract for horses manes and tails."[94] Brig. Gen. Alpheus Williams wrote home that "one can't go a mile without drowning mules in mud-holes. It is solemnly true that we lost mules in the middle of the road, sinking out of sight in mud-holes. A few bubbles of air, a stirring of the watery mud, indicated the last expiring efforts of many a poor long-ears."[95] Dayton Flint similarly wrote his father about the "destruction of horse flesh. . . . To give you an idea of it, within a distance of one mile from the river on one road alone there were 52 dead horses and mules. Our way back to camp was clearly marked by their bodies. In one place I counted ten horses but twenty yards apart."[96]

The brief campaign was over, in de Trobriand's words, "leaving no traces of our 'mud march' except extinguished fires, fallen trees, and dead animals lying by the side of the buried road."[97] The Federals assumed their misery would continue. "Tonight it looks like more rain," Williams wrote home. "If it comes, the Lord help us, for I don't exactly see how we can help ourselves." As far as he was concerned, any further attempt to fight a winter campaign would bring only disaster. Desertion was at epidemic levels. Exposure, hardship, failure, and Burnside had "greatly destroyed the spirits of the men." Malaise extended to the highest echelons. Franklin later wrote: "I came to the conclusion that Burnside was fast losing his mind. So I looked upon the rain which stopped his second attempt to cross the river as almost a Providential interference in our behalf."[98]

Chapter 11

Misery

The Mississippi River Valley, September 1862–March 1863

When Maj. Gen. Earl Van Dorn crossed the Mississippi after the Battle of Pea Ridge, he left the Trans-Mississippi theater nearly devoid of Confederate troops. Federal forces saw an opportunity. Maj. Gen. Samuel Curtis's victorious army hurried south into central Arkansas and failed to take Little Rock only because the overland supply line from Missouri again came up short. Previous foraging and summer drought made it impossible for his army to live off the land. Curtis diverted to the Mississippi and the promise of easier logistics, capturing Helena on July 12, 1862. At about the same time, a Union column from Kansas commanded by Col. William Weer marched for the Indian Territory, intent on ending Confederate resistance and reclaiming lost homes and farms for Loyalists. After a small victory at Locust Grove on July 3, Confederate Cherokee resistance crumpled. Weer made it as far as the Arkansas border before drought, summer heat, a stunted corn crop, and lack of forage stopped him short. Drought-stricken prairie grass was so dry that his enemies set it ablaze to stop his progress. Low on food and desperate for water, local creeks having dried up, Weer's officers mutinied at midmonth and took their men back to Kansas.[1]

Confederate authorities expected that drought would continue blocking access through the arid Indian Territory. They knew, however, that they had to do more than rely on the weather. General Beauregard, the closest thing the Confederacy had to an overall commander west of the Mississippi, was still in command at Corinth when he ordered former Arkansas congressman Thomas L. Hindman back to the state. As commander of the new Trans-Mississippi District, Major General Hindman acted decisively. He declared martial law, unilaterally assumed the powers of a military governor, commandeered food and supplies, and instituted conscription. He recruited disillusioned Missourians, especially former State Guardsmen, for a new army, and authorized partisan-ranger bands that expanded an ugly guerrilla war across southern Missouri. By mid-August, Hindman had amassed 20,000 recruits in Arkansas, while bushwhackers set Missouri on fire. President Davis soon appointed his old friend Lt. Gen. Theophilus Holmes as commander of the new Trans-Mississippi Department as a way to curb Hindman's authoritarian ways and calm local civilian leaders. Instead, Holmes ignored the complaints and gave Hindman command of the District of Arkansas, which included Missouri and the Indian Territory.[2]

With Holmes watching his back, Hindman was free to go to war that autumn on his terms. Yet he still had to consider the weather. Faced with the same geographic and climatic realities as his predecessors, he had to move soon, before winter trapped him on the Arkansas River or marooned his army in the barren Boston Mountains. Early in September, just as Bragg moved into Kentucky and Lee crossed the Potomac into Maryland, Hindman led about 6,000 men north to Pea Ridge. It rained hard as the column approached Missouri. The district commander had every intention of driving on to Springfield until Holmes tugged at his reins and called him back for consultation.

While Hindman made his way back to Little Rock, the commander of the Union District of Missouri fretted. Vastly inflating Confederate numbers, Brig. Gen. John M. Schofield poured troops into Springfield and called on the abolitionist doctor-turned-general James Blunt for reinforcements from Kansas. The weather remained hot, water scarce, the roads dusty and parched; forced marches to Springfield wore men out. Washington grew alarmed. On September 19, the same day as the Battle of Iuka and two days after Antietam, Halleck created a new Department of the Missouri. Appointed to command the department, Curtis promptly reorganized Schofield's and Blunt's men into the new Army of the Frontier under Schofield's command.[3]

Drought continued unabated across Arkansas, especially south of the White River. The two contesting armies began a confusing new dance up and down the convergence of northwestern Arkansas, southwestern Missouri, and the Indian Territory, one that would last well into 1863. The Confederates won a skirmish at Newtonia, Missouri, on September 30. Schofield and Blunt sent more men toward the town despite rain and muddy roads that bogged down their artillery. Hindman's army, still minus its absent commander, retreated into Arkansas past Pea Ridge. Schofield wanted to maintain his pursuit, but Curtis knew the country too well, warning his subordinate not to march too far into the barren Ozarks with winter imminent. As if to underscore Curtis's concerns, heavy precipitation followed on October 3 and October 4, then more torrentially on October 8, October 9, and into the morning of the following day. A hard wind blew from the east. Streams and creeks swelled. Wheeled vehicles sank into road muck. The rain and mud made it tough going, especially for inexperienced soldiers.

When the rain finally ended, significantly colder temperatures set in. Near Springfield on October 11, Lt. Benjamin McIntyre of the 19th Iowa noted the first morning frost of the season. Ahead of the Federals near Yellville, Arkansas, Capt. Eathan Allen Pinnell of the Confederate 8th Missouri described frost that persisted over the next week.[4] More rain in mid-October washed out the Wire Road in Missouri and sank Federal wagon trains in the mud. As historian William Shea notes, the end of the drought in October also ended Schofield's hopes of driving quickly and easily into Arkansas. His muddy army reached Pea Ridge and halted three days to wait for supplies. The war and the drought had left nothing to eat around the old battlefield.

On October 20, Schofield divided his army. Blunt's men, reorganized as the Kansas Division, went after a Confederate column under Col. Douglas Cooper that was moving northward through the Indian Territory toward Kansas. Two days later, Blunt attacked Cooper just west of the Arkansas–Indian Territory border and drove the enemy into headlong retreat. Meanwhile, Schofield and the rest of the Army of the Frontier, styled the 1st and 2nd Missouri Divisions, resumed moving south. Temperatures dropped almost simultaneously. Rejoining his army at Huntsville, Arkansas, Hindman took one look at the barren hinterlands surrounding him and ordered another retreat. The Confederates, sick with typhoid and other fevers that soldiers blamed on the weather, fell back into the Boston Mountains. They stopped at Brashears, topographically the strongest defensive point in the area. Schofield could not follow Hindman that far south and still feed his men and animals. He halted near Bentonville.

As if to add an exclamation point, the same massive snow system that blanketed armies to the east dropped two to three inches of snow overnight on October 24 and 25.[5] "This has been the severest storm I ever saw in Oct.," Pinnell wrote in his diary, "it would have done credit to January." Observing sick men in the snow with nothing but a blanket for warmth, he added, "our condition is wretched to a degree which I never expected to see."[6] Pvt. J. D. Barnes of the 20th Iowa added that "the oldest inhabitants had never known the like before, and as a natural result they attributed it to the presence of the Yankee army being in the vicinity."[7]

While the rank and file dug out, Curtis and Schofield discussed what to do. Both agreed that Blunt should cross into the Indian Territory to assist tribal allies in creating pro-Union governments. Curtis initially did not approve of Schofield's intent to winter in northwestern Arkansas, however, since he did not expect Hindman to renew his offensive. Instead, Curtis wanted to detach elements of the Army of the Frontier for service at Vicksburg, as both Washington and Major General Grant requested. Then Hindman, reinforced but running out of food, changed his mind and struck north for Fayetteville, hoping both to exploit its road system and to better feed his men. Delayed by the recent snow, the Confederates marched on cool October 27. The next day, Federal cavalry stopped them decisively at the White River. Hindman had to accept reality. He retreated all the way to the Arkansas River, where he could feed his men over the winter. Schofield followed to Fayetteville and closed active operations himself. Destroying anything of value to the enemy, he headed back to Springfield on November 4. His men marched in a haze of fire and smoke, leaving behind them what historian William Shea calls a "logistical desert" that hopefully would blunt Confederate campaigning. For soldiers who had been on the move for weeks, this withdrawal was the hardest yet.[8] One Iowan wrote that "the dust was two or three inches deep and wind enough to raise it up in quantities and shower it down on us." Two days later, he described "ice on Salat Creek to day for the first time this winter. We have crossed this stream 15 times today."[9]

Schofield's exhausted men assumed that they were going into winter quarters. As Shea points out, they already had marched five hundred miles back and forth through rough country, and winter was near. Over the next several days, however, Washington's demands, generals' whims, and ill-timed rumors dashed their hopes. Curtis had no intention of letting the Missouri Divisions winter in Missouri if they could be useful at Vicksburg. False rumors of a Confederate advance convinced the department commander momentarily to divert the divisions to points south of Springfield. When this alarm passed, Curtis ordered the divisions into motion toward the east and service on the Mississippi. It all came as a rude shock to the tired soldiers.[10] Chester Barney recollected "constructing 'winter quarters,' and after a laborious day spent in carrying stores and building chimneys in our tents—working in the rain to accomplish the work—[we] were ordered the same night to prepare to march on the following morning." Learning that Hindman had sent cavalry under Brig. Gen. John S. Marmaduke north on what actually was a foraging expedition, Blunt, meanwhile, assumed the worst and prepared to fight Hindman's entire army. Rain returned on November 16. Curtis ordered the Missouri Divisions to reverse course and support Blunt, although their instructions confusingly contained an added admonition not to move until the rain stopped or if specific orders arrived to do so.[11]

Such orders arrived in the rainy evening of the sixteenth. The next morning, the Missouri Divisions took to the road to rescue Blunt in what Barney called "a drenching rain—the roads being in the worst possible condition." They pressed on, "splashing through mud and wading innumerable small creeks, now much swollen from the rain, which fell faster as night approached." They stopped well after dark when they came "upon the wagon train of the first brigade, which we found stuck fast in the mud and blocking our way. And still the rain continued, with no probability of the wagons being immediately extricated." The men gathered wheat stacks to lie upon and fell asleep.[12] Lt. Benjamin McIntyre of the 19th Iowa described "Egyptian darkness" that night. "I can truly say that I never saw a night or was in such a storm," he wrote.[13] A comrade agreed. "It commenced raining soon after we started," he wrote, "and we were soon wet to the skins night coming on it was the darkest night ever saw . . . lunging through mud water and rain completely blinded and bewildered striving to follow those who were before us." Men fell out all night, while wagons and a battery of artillery mired down.[14] The next day was little better.

Late on November 18, near the Wire Road, new information arrived. There had been no Confederate invasion.[15] Worn out, the wet, dirty, and grumpy men of the Missouri Divisions sagged into camp in the vicinity of the Wilson's Creek battlefield. While the rain largely stopped, temperatures varied considerably, from freezing conditions on November 20, to Indian summer's brief warmth around the twenty-third, to another cold spell with a raw wind and snow flurries beginning two days later. Despite extensive refitting that included new overcoats, morale sank after the useless march. Occasional foraging expeditions did little to help. Along the border with the Indian Territory, the situation in Blunt's more abolitionist Kansas Division was similar, although somewhat cheerier thanks to visible signs of local Unionism and the collapse of slavery.[16]

Federals in general looked forward hopefully to a quiet winter. But the fighting season in 1862 was not yet over. In Arkansas, Hindman's Confederates had endured the same harsh weather and hard marching. If anything, conditions for them were worse. Illness was rampant. Food was in short supply due, in part, to the drought-ravaged low levels of the Arkansas River. Uniforms had come apart but were only replaced late in November. Many men lacked weapons or shoes. Few had proper shelter. Despite such limitations, Hindman yearned to act. When he learned that Schofield had fallen back from Fayetteville, he edged back to Fort Smith. Marmaduke's foraging expedition further raised hopes. On November 24, Hindman learned of the Missouri Divisions' march east to Helena and Vicksburg, without the vital additional information that Curtis had turned back to support Blunt. From Cane Hill, roughly located between Fort Smith and Fayetteville, Marmaduke proposed an attack on Blunt's presumably isolated command. Confederate plans fell through almost immediately. That same day, Blunt received intelligence that Marmaduke was isolated himself at Cane Hill, thirty miles away, and immediately decided to attack. He telegraphed Curtis, who ordered the Missouri Divisions to the Kansans' support. Brig. Gen. Herron would command the two divisions in place of an ill Schofield; Blunt would assume overall command. Four days later, on November 28, Blunt's column approached Cane Hill, hit the Confederates there by surprise, and drove them away.[17]

Blunt halted there, daring Hindman to attack. As William Shea notes, the Federals at Cane Hill were over a hundred miles from the Missouri Divisions that evening but only thirty-five miles from Hindman's army. Hindman was no fool. Gathering arms and ammunition as quickly as possible, he led his army across the Arkansas River on December 1 and marched for Cane Hill, despite Holmes's worries. He expected to be in position to attack Blunt by December 6. The early days were cloudy but warm, good for a quick movement. But on the fourth, a weather disaster struck. At the foot of the Boston Mountains, temperatures dropped and rain fell in torrents. Overnight, the rain turned to snow, just as it had eastward to Virginia. The next day saw the Confederates climbing into the mountains in a driving rain that soaked roads and swelled three dozen creeks. "Shoes disintegrated," Shea writes, "ammunition was soaked, wagons were swept downstream, and equipment was lost." When they went into camp that night, many soldiers were also without food, their wagons miles behind. Temperatures fell into the twenties, and a lunar eclipse brought pitch darkness. Such weather put Hindman a day behind schedule.[18]

The next day, December 6, saw the Confederates doggedly advancing despite bad roads, driving back Federal skirmishers. Blunt expressed confidence. Weather had not slowed down Herron, who marched six hours after receiving his orders. In what Shea calls "an epic of human endurance," the Missouri Divisions marched a remarkable thirty miles on the sixth despite the same rain and cold that beset the Confederates. It had snowed south of Wilson Creek on the night of December 3. Twenty-degree mornings and 40-degree days followed on the fourth and the fifth. Roads alternated between frozen and slushy, with shoes disintegrating. On December 6, as the divisions approached Fayetteville, the morning temperature was 18 degrees. Yet Blunt expected the Missouri Divisions' cavalry to join him before nightfall, with the balance to follow. Resting that evening in the same room where Price and Van Dorn had slept the night before Pea Ridge, Hindman was shocked to learn that Herron was so close. The price of his slow, cold, muddy ascent now confronted him. Yet he refused to retreat, having come so far. Desperately, Hindman adjusted his plans. He would intercept Herron a few miles away at a crossroads called Prairie Grove, defeat him, and then turn on Blunt at Cane Hill.[19]

Dan Thomas of the 34th Arkansas described the morning of December 7 as "one of the most beautiful days you ever saw, . . . clear cold & frosty. Sunrise was beautiful to behold the Suns rays shined through the tree tops with uncommon refulgence."[20] Riding out before sunup, Marmaduke's job was to keep the two Federal contingents apart. He attacked Union cavalry near the Prairie Grove junction, pursued it until reaching Herron's main line, and fell back to the safety of Hindman's army on the Prairie Grove ridge. After a two-hour artillery fight, Herron assaulted the Confederate position. The attack faltered, and a counterattack failed due to the strength of Federal artillery. Herron charged again, but the results were the same. Running out of reserves, he faced disaster until about 2:30 P.M., when Blunt's division arrived and assailed Hindman's left. A Confederate counterattack ended in a bloody hail of shell and canister as dusk closed in.[21]

That night, the Confederates quietly retreated from the field, leaving their wounded with guns to fend off the voracious hogs that roamed the area. In some cases, it was in vain. The night was cold and frosty, and men slept without fire or shelter. The next morning, the two commanding generals agreed to a brief truce to tend to the dead and wounded. Oddly enough, they also agreed jointly to name the battle "Prairie Grove." Much to Blunt's consternation, Hindman also used the truce to continue his withdrawal.

The Confederates retraced their steps all the way to the Arkansas River. Shocked by the bedraggled condition of the army and especially its supply problems, Holmes ordered Hindman to retreat to Little Rock.

Blunt evacuated his wounded and, to facilitate forging, spread out his army across northwestern Arkansas. Milder weather at midmonth, with daytime highs in the seventies, brightened the otherwise gory and blasted battlefield. Rain fell on December 13 and 14, December 20, and finally on Christmas Day.[22] After the holiday, the Federals launched a quick strike over the Boston Mountains to the Arkansas River, intending only to harry Hindman away. Blunt and Herron followed separate and deeply muddy roads south, skirmished their way to Van Buren, and bombarded the town. Hindman ordered Fort Smith evacuated and burned precious Confederate supplies there. The Army of the Frontier occupied Van Buren until December 30, then marched back north, leaving warehouses and Confederate river transports burning.[23]

The theater's back-and-forth activity levied an increasing toll on the soldiers. In an effort to force Blunt out of Arkansas, Hindman sent Marmaduke's cavalry into the Federal rear on December 31. Blunt's army began returning northward on January 2, 1863. More heavy rain and bad roads slowed both forces. Marmaduke struck for Springfield, unsuccessfully attacking its defenses on January 8. Blunt's column, meanwhile, arrived in Fayetteville to find Schofield waiting, having recovered and resuming command. His orders, calling for a formal review and then for regiments to cut their transportation in half, resulted in "murmurs of discontent," according to Barney, "from the fact that the rainy season had set in, rendering the roads exceedingly disagreeable for marching, and by being deprived of a large portion of our wagons the men would be under the necessity of carrying their knapsacks, instead of having them hauled."[24]

Toting their belongings on their backs, the Missouri Divisions fell back. It was not easy. The men reached Huntsville on January 10 and halted for twelve days. Winter soon again blasted the men of both armies. Rain and four inches of afternoon and evening snow followed on the fourteenth. Snow the next day covered the ground as far north as Rolla. It was cold too; Sgt. Maj. John Bonnell of the 19th Iowa reported a thermometer reading of below zero. By then, the men, according to Barney, suffered "under more than ordinary complication of all the discomforts and ills incident to a winter campaign." Bad roads limited rations. Orders and countermanding orders "all day exposed [the troops] to the rain without shelter, without wagons loaded and ready to move." Angry at their commander, they abandoned Schofield's "tender-footed policy" against foraging from locals and pillaged at will until the general relocated their camps outside of Huntsville. On January 19, heavy rain, snow, and sleet left the roads so deep that Schofield delayed their march. Only on January 22, after one last sleet storm, were the roads passable enough to march for Bentonville. Even then, Barney added, "our starving mules proved unable to draw the wagons through the mud." Soldiers spent the next day trying to pull the vehicles from the sucking muck. The Federals reached Pea Ridge in the rain on January 25, bivouacked in Missouri on the "quite cold" and rainy following day, and reached camps south of Springfield on warmer January 30.[25] The army rode out the rest of the winter there, enduring one more snowfall of six to seven inches on February 3–4. Much more cold weather followed, however. Benjamin McIntyre wrote that he "met an old puke this morning who told me they seldom had as cold weather as at present." The soldiers coped with rain and more cold either in tents or commandeered civilian houses.[26]

Hindman's Confederate army, meanwhile, retreated back to Little Rock. That march was hellish for men without shoes, proper clothing, tents, and often even blankets, all the while suffering in the same winter conditions their foes endured. Rain delayed baggage trains and food supplies. The massive storm at midmonth "made the roads impossible for trains," according to Eathan Pinnell. "We moved camp about one hundred yds, to evade the mud, but to little purpose. We have pitched our tent, floored it with pine boughs, eaten our breakfast, made a good fire, and if we had our blankets, would be prepared to spend the night comfortably." Instead, ten inches of snow fell over the next twenty-four hours. "The condition of the men in camp is to a degree of wretchedness beyond any descriptive powers," he continued. "The sick lying in old leaky tents on wet blankets. The well shivering around their fires in their wet clothes, and many of them without shoes, poor fellows your lots are hard ones." On January 16, they marched "three miles through mud knee deep, covered with ten inches of snow," to board a steamer that would take them to the capital. Temperatures, according to Pinnell, "would do credit to the latitude of Greenland."[27] Holmes reported that half of the troops deserted along the way.[28]

On January 19, Pinnell's 8th Missouri Infantry pitched tents at the Little Rock Arsenal. He had had enough of war. "It is raining," he wrote, "snow melting and very muddy, which makes our quarters anything but comfortable, it being anything but possible to get from the fires to the building with dry feet. We have to sit, stand lie, or walk about with cold wet feet. It is not in the powers of an innocent and passionate pen to describe the suffering of this command for the last week. We marched through mud until our mules commenced dying and our teams could go no further we then took the loads from our wagons and continued our march and halted not until we reached our place of destination." Enduring more snow (on February 5), frequent rain, and constant mud—all of which he recorded meticulously—Pinnell and his comrades remained in and around Little Rock until late February, then moved to near Pine Bluff.[29]

A successful river-borne Federal raid on Arkansas Post on cold January 10 and 11—an unexpected digression from the campaign for Vicksburg as described below—cost the Confederacy another 4,800 men and the last fort below Little Rock. Sgt. William Eddington of the 97th Illinois recorded thirty-six hours of rain followed by eight inches of snow. His comrades cut down trees and built bonfires to stay warm, then found themselves ankle deep in thawed mud. The prisoners made their way by water to Memphis in the same rain and snowstorm. Arkansas Post was the final blow for Hindman, who requested a transfer away from Holmes—whom he blamed—and back to the Army of Tennessee. Davis approved the transfer and replaced Holmes with Lieutenant General Kirby Smith, killing two problematic birds with one stone.[30]

Prairie Grove and Arkansas Post, according to William Shea, "effectively knocked Confederate Arkansas out of the war." North of the Arkansas River, only guerrillas, occasional cavalry raids, and local violence continued after January 1863.[31] The Confederacy permanently lost this territorial expanse for a host of reasons. Unionism was strong there. The army never had enough men, competent officers, or equipment to control the region. Confederate soldiers endured the Boston Mountains and the Ozark Plateau with too few shoes, blankets, and tents. Many got sick, and some deserted. But the drought followed by a harsh winter played significant roles as well. Delay at Prairie Grove was pivotal. Just as during the Pea Ridge Campaign, the better-equipped and better-led Federals more effectively marched through terrible winter conditions to accomplish their goals. Tents, shoes, and determined generals counted for much in the harsh Trans-Mississippi.

East of the Mississippi, the opening scenes of another campaign began as winter approached. Raised to departmental command, Grant organized an overland operation against Vicksburg. At the beginning of November 1862, he began massing troops at Grand Junction, southeast of Memphis. Using the Mississippi Central Railroad as his supply line, Grant targeted Holly Springs, Grenada, and Jackson, Mississippi. At Jackson, the Mississippi Central intersected the east–west Southern Railroad of Mississippi. Grant assumed that cutting off Vicksburg's main supply line would compel the Confederates, commanded since Van Dorn's demotion by Lt. Gen. John C. Pemberton, to abandon the city. If not, Grant would head west along the railroad and strike the city's eastern defenses. As historians William Shea and Terence Winschel note, this plan was risky. The Mississippi Central's many bridges were vulnerable. Moreover, Pemberton anticipated Grant's moves. His men and impressed slaves worked overtime to build up Vicksburg's earthworks.[32]

Grant's campaign began with cool but dry weather. The remarkable Smithsonian weather observer in the area was Robert McCary, a formerly enslaved barber living in the deepest heart of a slave society. He recorded two days of rain in Natchez that month—November 12 and November 18—and an average high of 64 degrees. Soldiers marching to Grand Junction complained of dusty roads, northwest winds, and cold sleeping at night. The rains turned the dust to mud. Frost appeared on the eighteenth. The Federals were hungry too. As Grant's two columns moved south, they reentered desolated northern Mississippi. Foraging evolved into plundering and vandalism. New regiments, politicized by policies such as the Second Confiscation Act and the Preliminary Emancipation Proclamation, were especially prone to thievery.

Cavalry from Curtis's command, commanded by Brig. Gen. Alvin P. Hovey, launched a supporting raid into the Confederate rear near the end of November. Hovey targeted Grenada, but bad weather intervened. Storms on windy December 1 brought deep mud. Cold rain continued intermittently across the state until the fifth. Presumably, this was the same warm front that brought the rain and snow to Prairie Grove. The weather turned cold after that. Mud retarded Federal progress, Confederate retreat, and the arrival of reinforcements in gray. Hovey's exhausted raiders, sick of the muddy roads, turned back to Arkansas with little accomplished other than some railroad track destroyed and five hundred slaves liberated. But while the raid's obvious results were meager, the incursion frightened Pemberton. He pulled his main defensive line back some sixty miles to wet, muddy Granada, leaving Grant an open road south.[33]

Grant's overland plan soon came apart. Some of the difficulties were self-inflicted. His decision to reopen trade with the North brought in a swarm of cotton traders and other sharpers eager to deal with less-than-patriotic Confederates and freelancing soldiers. Grant's ham-fisted responses, focusing primarily on the Jews among the newcomers, brought down well-deserved wrath on his head. Politics played another major role. For the same reasons that Lincoln held on to McClellan and jettisoned Buell—votes—he now authorized former Illinois Democratic congressman John A. McClernand to raise a new army and lead it down the Mississippi to Vicksburg. In the Midwest, the failure to reopen the Mississippi had

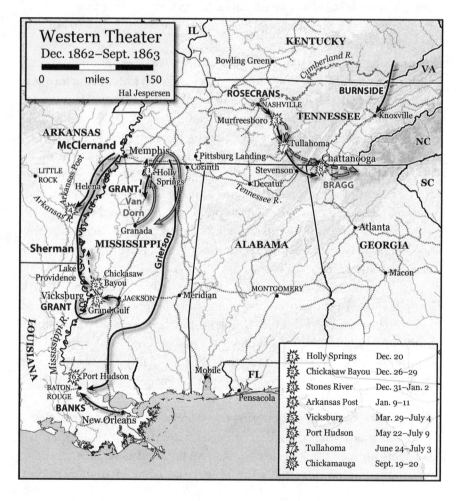

	Holly Springs	Dec. 20
	Chickasaw Bayou	Dec. 26–29
	Stones River	Dec. 31–Jan. 2
	Arkansas Post	Jan. 9–11
	Vicksburg	Mar. 29–July 4
	Port Hudson	May 22–July 9
	Tullahoma	June 24–July 3
	Chickamauga	Sept. 19–20

emerged as a political liability for Republicans and threatened their majorities in Illinois and Indiana. Grant reacted badly. He had disliked McClernand since Fort Donelson, and now this new army was siphoning off regiments he needed. In Washington, Halleck hopped on board the anti-McClernand bandwagon, resentful of being left out of the loop. The two West Pointers united against the political general despite their own ugly rivalry. With Halleck's tacit approval, Grant used his powers as department commander to assert command authority both over McClernand's regiments and any river-borne assault against Vicksburg. He then hastily ordered Maj. Gen. William Tecumseh Sherman to lead a force of some 33,000 men, taken from both the Army of the Tennessee and Curtis's Arkansas forces, down the river on transports. Grant told him to move up the Yazoo River to Haynes' Bluff, fifteen miles north of Vicksburg, march inland, and take the city before McClernand could. Grant would distract the enemy at Grenada.[34] As historian Michael Ballard puts it, Grant "changed a slow, methodical advance into North Mississippi into a race for Vicksburg, a race between himself and McClernand."[35]

Aided by dry weather and good roads, Grant marched to Oxford, where he received orders from Halleck allowing him to use McClernand's new army as a corps.[36] Aside from rain on December 2 and December 4, and a bit more on the fifteenth, the weather was warm, dry, and inviting. December 20, however, brought disaster to Grant. At dawn, Van Dorn, now commanding a 2,500-man cavalry division, appeared out of the thin frosty air at Holly Springs. His horsemen easily captured the garrison and supply depot; confiscated horses and mules; loaded up on supplies, including new guns and ammunition; and torched what his men could not carry off. With the weather colder but the roads still solid, they rode on as far as Bolivar, Tennessee, before turning back. At roughly the same time, cavalry from Bragg's army under Brig. Gen. Nathan Bedford Forrest arrived in West Tennessee. Forrest mangled Federal communications and wrecked sections of the Mobile and Ohio Railroad. The news stunned Grant. Not only had Van Dorn destroyed his supply base but Forrest's rampage also had ensured that replacing what was lost would be difficult.

Grant saw no alternative but to retreat. His twin columns wearily turned back toward the north, their rations cut to the bone.[37] Pvt. Alexander Downing described dusty roads, anger, and wanton retributive destruction. "We pulled down vacant houses to build bunks and windbreaks," he wrote on December 21, "to protect us from the cold wind." More foraging and vandalism followed. "Holly Springs has certainly paid dear for burning our supplies," he wrote on Christmas Day. Afterward, cold, heavy rain fell in torrents, dogging the army as it plodded through the deep muck back toward Grand Junction and LaGrange, Tennessee. As Downing added bitterly, their extra clothing was stored at La Grange, out of reach until the end of the march.[38]

The same rain system tormented the Federals in Tennessee, including those pursuing Forrest after the "charge 'em both ways" defeat at Parker's Cross Roads on December 31. Lt. Col. Zephaniah Spaulding, commanding the 27th Ohio, wrote that "the rain fell in torrents, drenching the command to the skin." Three Ohio regiments pursued Forrest to the Tennessee River. "The road, naturally one of the worst ever traveled, had been rendered impassable by the rain, which kept up all day," Spaulding wrote. At the river, they watched Forrest and his men escape as numerous Buckeyes "sunk to the waists in mud-holes." Col. Edward F. Noyes of the 39th Ohio added that "the rain fell in torrents. The road was covered by jagged rocks, whose crevices were filled with mud. The men in stepping from rock to rock frequently slipped and fell, bruising them severely. Returning at night in the darkness the men could not keep their footing, but fell every few rods."[39]

Holly Springs did not stop Sherman, however. His expeditionary force—half of Grant's army—embarked at Helena on the same warm day as Van Dorn's raid. As Shea and Winschel point out, Sherman heard about the attack before he left but had no notion that Grant would retreat. Two days behind schedule, he rushed ahead impulsively. Weather north of Vicksburg was favorable: clear, generally cool, and pleasant. On December 23, Sherman landed at Milliken's Bend and sent a brigade to wreck the railroads, then moved on down the river. On Christmas Day, his waterborne force arrived at DeSoto's Point, a swift-moving hairpin turn in the Mississippi north of Vicksburg. When Sherman learned that Pemberton had mined the Yazoo River at Chickasaw Bayou, below Haynes' Bluff, he and Rear Adm. David Porter sought an alternative. They chose Walnut Hills, landed there the next day, and beheld their mistake.[40]

Black, clayey Aquert Vertisols dominate the lower Mississippi Valley, especially the essentially flat west bank opposite Vicksburg. Annual flooding, sand, and silt created low-lying natural levees around the river's seemingly innumerable meandering loops and lakes. This was America's ground zero for slave-based plantation agriculture. Sherman described the rich black soil in the floodplain as "terrible for heavy trains of wagons" when wet. The eastern bank is quite different. Udalf Alfilsols generally dominate inland from the eastern bank inland, but as geographer Warren Grabau explains, the high, craggy bluffs that shelter Vicksburg are more complicated geologically. Limestone and shale at the river's edge give way to a thin, higher layer of red clay and gravel. On top of that is a robust layer of "loess," a fertile, yellowish-brown, sand-and-clay loam. Melting Ice Age glaciers at the end of the Pleistocene Epoch bulldozed tons of silty loess sediment into countless fingers of northern streams. As those streams ran and dried up over time, massive mounds of fine loess were left behind. Winds picked up the lightest silt and carried it into the Mississippi River valley.

By 1863, a narrow, variegated band of loess covered the east bank of the river from Baton Rouge north to the Ohio. The loess bluffs at Vicksburg are markedly deep and ten to fifteen miles wide. Loess is easily erodible and easy to dig until one reaches the clay beneath. Rain, loess, and recent deforestation were responsible for the steep-faced high bluffs, sharp edges, deep gullies, and mazes of cane-choked ravines that bedeviled Sherman's men as they looked up from the muddy, wooded bayou bottom. A two-tiered natural fortress, two hundred feet above the river and linked south to Vicksburg by graded roads, awaited their attacks. Worse, only a levee and a sandbar offered reasonably solid ground for leaving the river.[41] The Confederate position, according to Sherman, was "as difficult as it could possibly be from nature and art."[42]

Worse yet, despite hard rain on December 27, the Confederates had fortified above the bluffs. Sherman worried both about the "non-arrival" of Brig. Gen. A. J. Smith's division and what the rain would do to his two solid approaches. With support from the gunboats, his men skirmished their way to the base of the hills on December 28—with additional help from a heavy early morning fog—but a massive assault the next afternoon failed miserably. Heavy rain and collapsing temperatures that night, starting around sundown, punished soldiers who had left coats, blankets, rain gear, and tents behind. A recorded 2.45 inches of rain fell between December 26 and December 28.

Thrashing about for a response, Sherman decided to move to Haynes' Bluff, when Porter assured the general that he could get past the mines with what historians Shea and Winschel call "the world's first minesweeper."

Porter could not brush aside the worsening post-Christmas weather, however. Heavy fog welcomed the new year. Sailors could barely see beyond ten paces, and the gunboats were paralyzed. Torrential rain turned roads into goo. Sherman fretted that one more heavy rain would result in mud so deep that he could not escape with his guns and ammunition. Porter confided to Washington that he believed the rain had closed off Vicksburg from the north and ruined Sherman's hopes. The constant sounds of troop trains arriving in Vicksburg further unnerved the attackers. Sherman had had enough. Through another heavy all-day rain on January 2, 1863, his force steamed back to Milliken's Bend, where he found McClernand. McClernand argued that rain would make it impossible to move troops anywhere in the vicinity. Porter agreed. McClernand took command of Sherman's force, renamed it the Army of the Mississippi, and launched the assault on Arkansas Post that broke Confederate resistance in Arkansas. He would have gone farther had Grant not recalled them.[43]

On January 20—the same day that the Mud March began in Virginia—the *Natchez Daily Courier* reported an earlier "terrible storm of rain and wind, . . . almost a hurricane from the east," that struck on the night of the seventeenth and again on the night of the eighteenth. "We have not the exact measure," the editor continued, "but should judge that 9 or 10 inches of rain have fallen within the past ten days."[44] Over the next several days, Grant's army left their camps near Memphis and returned to Vicksburg's environs by water. They spread out along the west bank of the Mississippi, from above DeSoto's Point north to Lake Providence near the Arkansas line. The necessity of having enough solid ground to hold an army amid a rising river and flooded banks compelled this spread-out configuration. Grant remained determined to find a way to take the city, but an amphibious attack seemed doomed to failure. Yet for political and morale reasons, he did not believe that he could retreat and start over from Memphis. He thus settled on a plan to take his army down the Louisiana side of the river, cross the Mississippi with the navy's assistance, and get at Vicksburg from the east.

Unfortunately, the weather refused to cooperate. Simply put, remarkable Mississippi delta flooding left Grant's army stuck in the mud. At the best of times, the banks of the river were low and often swampy, subject to annual spring floods. Massive rain well beyond the norm during the first three months of 1863 submerged the land and roads around Vicksburg except for the levees and spots of high ground, where the soldiers pitched their tents. It rained on nine out of twenty-eight days in February. On February 1, the river smashed through a cut levee at Helena and flooded much of the town, including a slave refugee camp. Another long rainy spell occurred between February 12 and February 17. March was almost as bad, with rain on eight days and a hailstorm on March 8. The Mississippi rose in some places to levels not seen since 1815. Cold, gray skies and frequent fog added to the men's misery while limiting knowledge of enemy activity. The Federals wintered under white canvas, largely Sibley tents. Unable to find enough dry land to dig wells or latrines, they drank from the river and befouled it with their waste. Fevers and especially diarrhea followed. Hundreds of men died and were interred underfoot in the same random islands of dry land.[45] Shea and Winschel call it "an archipelago of misery."[46]

Trapped in such an environment, soldiers in both armies struggled to stay warm and dry. After the fighting at Chickasaw Bayou, the 40th Alabama went into camp in what Maj. Elbert Willett described as "low and black soil, very slippery in wet weather." They remained at this site through most of January. "Most of the time was cold and rainy weather very disagreeable for soldiering. . . . It rained almost incessantly, and the camp and roads became very muddy indeed." Rain and mud made any movement difficult.[47] To the east, along what was left of Pemberton's quickly diminishing Granada line, rain and mud caused suffering as well. On January 15, Maj. Walter Rorer of the 20th Mississippi, attached to Maj. Gen. William Loring's Confederate division, wrote his cousin that "after a long *spell* of cold, rain, and gloom, the sun is once more shining and all seems pleasant and cheerful again. I am sure while the rainy and gloomy weather lasted that more than half our soldiers thought the Southern Confederacy was not worth fighting for."[48] The 5th Missouri's William Ruyle described a sad Christmas. Then in early January, his regiment began building "cabins out of pine poles. . . . Our mess built a cabin 10 feet square," he continued, "made boards and covered it stable fashion, with a comb to it. Most of the boys built theirs sheep-house fashion, that is without any comb, all the water to run off one side. We built a chimney with mud jams and made ourselves comfortable generally, for a season."[49]

Facing such conditions, and anticipating spring flooding as a matter of course, Grant knew that he could not march his men south along the river until April at the earliest. Yet he was under tremendous pressure from Washington and the press to do something. Dealing with cotton traders and enlisting African American troops in the wake of the Emancipation Proclamation took some time. Given command over Union forces in Arkansas, Grant began calling for the troops Curtis tried to supply before Prairie Grove. Finally, he initiated various expedients utilizing the region's maze of rivers, streams, lakes, and bayous, hoping to bypass the guns of Vicksburg and take his men south to drier, higher land. As historian Lisa Brady points out, midcentury Americans firmly believed that it was possible to control and civilize nature. With Island No. 10 as the shining example, Grant hoped for good results; if nothing else, he would keep his men busy.

The highest-priority effort—President Lincoln's pet project—involved digging out the aborted Federal canal from the previous year across DeSoto's Point. Grant sent 4,000 of Sherman's men and 2,000 newly emancipated men there to work on it with picks and shovels, all in full sight of the Confederate defenses. The plan was to clear out a channel six feet deep and sixty feet wide. Had they been successful, transports could have moved down the Mississippi while avoiding Vicksburg's defenses. But constant rain and wet terrain doomed their efforts. Although the workforce kept at their labors until late March, they never finished the canal. At the same time, Grant gave corps commander Maj. Gen. James B. McPherson the thankless assignment of finding and creating a usable water route from Lake Providence to the Red River. Two rivers and two bayous linked the lake and the Red, but dank earth and cypress forests blocked navigation. Despite near-constant rain, McPherson's men breached the levee between the lake and the Mississippi on foggy February 2. While that raised the water level in the lake, it was not high enough to negate the many snags.[50]

A third expedient, developed as the canal project lurched toward failure, involved blowing up the levee at Yazoo Pass. In theory, this would allow troops to travel safely by water to Haynes' Bluff via a series of lakes, streams, and rivers. "Sticky, slimy clay," as Grant called it, impeded transportation, especially in regards to hauling coal for the navy's boilers. The explosive destruction of the dam in early February created a manmade freshwater tsunami that devastated farms and plantations down the Yazoo. Once the rain stopped and the flooding subsided, on February 24, a flotilla of gunboats and one of McClernand's brigades on transports steamed hesitantly through the breached levee into an old channel of the Mississippi.

They made slow but steady progress until March 11, when they confronted an earth-and-sand fort at the conjunction of two tributaries. Loring, recently arrived from the Granada line and far from Stonewall Jackson, commanded this stronghold, dubbed Fort Pemberton. In a series of actions that lasted until March 16, his garrison blocked the Union expedition and sealed off the Yazoo Pass route.

Grant tried yet again. Porter led an army-navy expedition into Steele's Bayou and Black Bayou, hoping that the higher waters in the Yazoo would allow ships to pass through to the rear of Fort Pemberton or else to Haynes' Bluff. Water travel was imperative, for according to Sherman, all the surrounding land remained flooded. It seemed to be working until March 19, when Confederates confronted the ironclads and cut down cypress trees fore and aft. Trapped, Porter sent word to Sherman, who sent a brigade to drive off the Confederates and remove the obstacles so that Porter would not have to blow up his gunboats.[51]

In the end, Grant's sideshows came to nothing due to the local terrain and seemingly endless rain. As March began, spring came surprisingly early. Plantation daughter Kate Stone noted unusually warm weather, observing that "the fruit trees are in full bloom now and our young orchard makes quite a show." Yet with rare exception, the rain continued unabated. "Storms and rain for two days," Stone wrote on March 24. "There has been almost constant rain since Christmas. The oldest inhabitants say they never saw such persistent rains. It might be the rainy season of the tropics. Some think the cannonading at Vicksburg brings on the rains." She and her family waited for dry roads so that they could flee to Texas.[52]

Grant contemplated escape too. "At last the waters began to recede," he wrote, "the roads crossing the peninsula behind the levees of the bayous were emerging from the waters; the troops were all concentrated from distant points at Milliken's Bend preparatory to a final move which was to crown the long, tedious and discouraging labors with success."[53] On March 29, he ordered McClernand down the lone road on the west side of the Mississippi. It was wet and deep, and the river was rising as it always did in March, but Grant's patience was at an end. The second phase of the Vicksburg Campaign began.[54]

Chapter 12

Dreary

Tennessee, October 1862–April 1863

Braxton Bragg's army retreated from Kentucky to Morristown, Tennessee, arriving on October 21. After Perryville, the men were worn out, hungry, angry, and sick. At Morristown, they boarded railroad cars that took them to snowy Knoxville. An apparent temperature inversion there made conditions worse, trapping smoke within the city. Drawing new clothing, they rode on to Bridgeport, Alabama, where they ferried across the Tennessee River and crawled onto trains that carried them to Tullahoma, Tennessee. From there they marched to Murfreesboro, thirty miles west of Union-occupied Nashville. There they rendezvoused with Maj. Gen. John C. Breckinridge's Kentuckians. In the meantime, Polk, Kirby Smith, and Bragg detoured to Richmond, all hoping to drag President Davis into command politics. Davis stuck with Bragg despite his growing unpopularity and, on October 24, melded Kirby Smith's army into Bragg's, creating the Army of Tennessee.

Bragg decided to let the Yankees come to him so he could fight a defensive battle. Reports that Rosecrans had replaced Buell did nothing to alter his intentions. Perhaps they should have. Murfreesboro was a key position, situated along the vital Nashville and Chattanooga Railroad. But as historians Peter Cozzens and Thomas Connelly both point out, it was a weak spot to await battle. There was less food and forage than expected, with lines of communication extending over a hundred miles back to Chattanooga. Bragg arrayed his army in a position that could be flanked with relative ease. The president's decision to send one of Bragg's divisions to Vicksburg made things worse. The weather was tough as well. After snow on November 7, temperatures grew warmer, with highs in the sixties on the tenth and the eleventh and again, with one exception, from the fourteenth through the nineteenth. Rain accompanied the warmth, however, leaving about two inches of total precipitation in Clarksville. After that, temperatures turned cold again. Daytime highs fell into fifties, and morning lows hovered around freezing. Thunderstorms on November 27 caused minor flooding. More rain preceded sleet on December 2, and heavy snow on the night of December 4 lasted throughout most of the next day, accumulating to a depth of three inches. The same system produced snow in Arkansas and Virginia. After the winter storm, temperatures dropped again. Cold, heavy rain fell on December 15, hard enough to extinguish fires.[1] Soldiers suffered through it all. A Texas Ranger wrote home that "the army is fearfully deficient in blankets and shoes." He hoped that Bragg would attack so that at least he and his comrades could capture Federal supplies.[2]

~~~

In early December, Bragg shifted his battalions across a fifty-mile front to block the approaches from Nashville and ordered his men to build winter quarters. Log cabins and tents with attached chimneys rose almost immediately. Thirty miles away in Nashville, Rosecrans's army—for the moment called the XIV Army Corps—endured the same bad weather. McCook's corps had arrived in the capital on snowy November 7. The balance of the army trickled in over several days, marching in rain, cold, wind-borne dust, and occasional snow. Water remained scarce. Rain on November 18 helped relive the situation somewhat, but the effects of the drought continued to plague the army. Low water in the Cumberland River hindered resupply, while the low Tennessee River prevented Federal gunboats from denying supplies to Bragg.[3]

Rosecrans's decision to rest, refit, and reorganize his force instead of going immediately after Bragg won favor among his tired soldiers. So did new rain gear. The War Department finally began equipping the western armies in piecemeal fashion with equipment comrades back east had been using for months. The soldier-historians of the 86th Indiana remembered chilly December 6 as a red-letter day for "its first supply of ponchos, or rubber blankets, after which time the men were somewhat better protected from wind and rain when doing guard and picket duty, or milking the farmers' cows."[4] Not all innovations were welcome, however. Just as in Virginia, soldiers in the Department of the Cumberland balked at the transition to shelter tents.[5] Cpl. George Morris of the 81st Indiana described aversion to the flimsy "dog tents," writing that "they were condemned by both officers and men, and considered a grand humbug—something gotten up to kill the men by exposure. They were issued to all our companies, some of the men taking them and others refusing them."[6] Only logistical problems prevented more outrage, as some regiments did not receive the tents until spring.[7]

As December began, however, any sort of shelter grew more welcome. Temperatures turned much colder. The same cold front that hit Hindman's Confederates before Prairie Grove produced in Clarksville a low of 9 degrees at 7 A.M. on December 7, which rose to a "high" of 27 degrees at 2 P.M. Soldiers struggled to stay warm. Sgt. Jay Caldwell Butler of the 101st Ohio wrote home that day about how he and his tent mate "manage to keep pretty warm as we have three woolen and two rubber blankets between us. This, I believe, is called the sunny south," he added, "but I believe that so many northerners have congregated together here that their cold, frigid sentiments have chilled the balmy atmosphere to freezing point as, the other morning upon rising, I found the water frozen quite thick in our tent."[8] George Morris, meanwhile, related how "some of the boys had old camp kettles hung in their tents, which they would fill with live coals, warming up their tents very well—sometimes it made them too warm."[9] Rations remained in short supply as well. Col. John Beatty of the 3rd Ohio longed for "two weeks of rainfall . . . to make the Cumberland navigable, and thus ensure to us abundant supplies."[10]

Clear skies and warmer days followed until two inches of rain fell on December 15. Highs reached into the forties on December 8, into the fifties on December 10, and peaked at 70 degrees on December 13. After that, highs generally remained in the fifties or sixties, with the exception of 35 degrees on the seventeenth.[11] "We have splendid weather here all the time," Charles Dunham wrote on December 23 from north of Nashville. "Just about summer weather as our Ingin summers are in Ill. till now, it is raining at a two forty rate."[12] Rosecrans's soldiers experienced a sad Christmas season, largely spurned by Nashville's white population, but cloudy Christmas Eve (65 degrees) and the holiday itself (64 degrees) were unusually warm.[13]

The unseasonably warm Christmas night at Rosecrans's headquarters was anything but festive, however. The general's relative inactivity frustrated Washington after the 1862 elections and the debacle at Fredericksburg. Across the North, morale plummeted. Resurgent antiwar Democrats and frustrated Radical Republicans increasingly condemned the Lincoln administration. The approach of the Emancipation Proclamation's effective date on New Year's Day 1863 heightened anxieties among Lincoln's critics. The beleaguered president grew desperate for good news. Having just fired Buell, he and Halleck twice discussed dismissing Rosecrans too. The general could tarry no longer. The army had enough rations, intelligence had established Bragg's numerical inferiority, and much of the Confederate cavalry was away. The Cumberland was rising to normal depths, and the Rebels had gone into winter quarters.

By candlelight on Christmas night, Rosecrans unveiled plans he had developed with George Thomas. These were based on the erroneous information that Bragg's line lay along Stewart's Creek, ten miles from Murfreesboro. McCook's Right Wing would march south toward the town of Triune, due west of Murfreesboro. Scouts erroneously placed Hardee's Confederates there. Commanding the Center after Charles Gilbert's post-Perryville fall from grace, Thomas would move along McCook's right and then turn east to follow and support him. The Left Wing under Thomas Crittenden would drive to the southeast toward Murfreesboro through Lavergne. Crittenden's job was to keep Bragg busy while the rest of the Federal army drove Hardee from Triune and shoved the Confederate left across Stewart's Creek. Orders radiated from headquarters instructing the men to rise before dawn and begin marching at first light.[14]

December 26 "dawned drearily," William Sumner Dodge wrote. "Thick volumes of mist hugged the valleys and dense masses of black clouds over hung the heavens."[15] It was 60 degrees at Clarksville at 7 A.M. and presumably close to that in Nashville. Around 9 A.M., morning drizzle turned into heavy rain, preventing temperatures from rising.[16] "Rain was pouring down in streams which gathered into volumes in the gullies," Rosecrans's aide William Bickham added, "and made foaming yellow torrents of the little brooks that lately stole around the hills."[17] Mud soon began slowing down the drenched Union columns. A division of McCook's wing and Federal cavalry encountered limited resistance, further delaying progress.

In Murfreesboro, Bragg and his Confederates had spent a pleasant and restful Christmas season, other than a few executions. Officers attended balls while the rank and file ate and drank their fill. Signs of a Federal advance had grown ominous, and yet when the collision of horsemen finally came on the afternoon of the twenty-sixth, it surprised the Confederates. That night, temperatures fell steadily, dropping into the upper forties by morning, with a stiff breeze blew out of the northwest. Officers ordered their men not to build fires and give away their positions. Federals across the muddy, churned-up ground using the new shelter tents crawled between rubber and woolen blankets, by which they stayed tolerably warm and dry. Others, left awaiting the wagons carrying their Sibley tents, suffered.[18] According to Pvt. Ira Owens, the 74th Ohio in Thomas's Center column "had neither shelter tents nor gum blankets, consequently we were exposed to all the rain, which continued nearly all night, so that we had to sit up nearly the whole time."[19]

Both commanding generals also struggled with the fog of war. Looking for his Right Wing, Rosecrans and his staff got lost in the dark. Bragg struggled to make sense of incomplete and tardy reports coming in from his cavalry. Only at 9:30 P.M. did he realize that Rosecrans's entire army was on the move. Around midnight, he dispatched orders for a concentration of the Army of Tennessee at Murfreesboro. It would be up to his mounted arm to hold off the Federals long enough to effect this move. As the sun rose on December 27, Rosecrans discovered an additional foe in the weather.[20] It was colder than the previous morning, 48 degrees at 7 A.M. The day began "more dreary than the previous morning," according to Bickham, as "the clouds which had broken up at noon yesterday had again massed heavily, and a dense pall of mist shrouded the horizon. Shaking his head with an air of disappointment, the Chief said ominously, 'Not much progress today, I fear.'"[21]

McCook's column, nonetheless, set out in the thick fog, "deep mud," and "glare of slush" that "was dissolving the turnpike." He expected the fog to lift soon, but as the men trudged on in soaked, heavy uniforms, it hugged the ground. "The fog was so dense," Bickham continued, "that it was impossible to distinguish objects a hundred and fifty yards distant. Movement was therefore greatly retarded." Two miles up the road, with the mud ankle deep, the column ran into Confederate skirmishers. The fog by then "was so dense that it was impossible to distinguish friend from foe." Shaken, McCook halted until 1 P.M., when the fog finally lifted. He pursued the Confederates through Triune until the weather rallied again for the Confederates. "It had now begun to rain," wrote Bickham, "and thick fog again obscured the country." Sleet fell, and then hail, with a wind so hard that it blew the hail horizontally across the road. "The ground was also very heavy and movement was seriously retarded," Bickham added. "General McCook therefore determined to halt."[22] Rosecrans informed Washington that the weather had slowed the advance and allowed Hardee to get away. They were already a day behind schedule.

Conditions had been no better elsewhere that Saturday. Thomas's column slogged through heavy rain, muddy dirt roads, and deep fields to Stewartsboro, where his wet and hungry men camped in Crittenden's rear. The Left Wing had started late, around 9 A.M., also delayed by the fog. It was so thick that Wilbur Hinman insisted that he could not see farther than ten yards. Some units stood in place nearly until noon, waiting for the traffic jam ahead to clear. Once conditions somewhat improved in the afternoon, the column moved down the firmer Murfreesboro Pike through Lavergne to seize the vital bridge across Stewart's Creek. Cornfields along the road proved muddy and treacherous as the troops swung into line of battle near the bridge. The Confederates tried to destroy the span, but it was too wet to burn.[23]

"The night promised to be only murkier and gloomier than the wearisome day had been," Charles Francis wrote. "Just as we received orders to stack arms, . . . the sky cleared just above the western horizon, and for the space of half-a-minute the sun reappeared in indescribably great glory—then vanished. This was instantly taken as a good omen, and the drooping spirits of the soldiers rose at once, and the army gave a tremendous shout that rent the air."[24] Crittenden's troops saw the sun too. L. A. Simmons of the 84th Illinois wrote that "just before sunset the dense clouds broke away in the West, and a double rainbow, very bright and beautiful, spanned the sky in out front. A few centuries ago, this might have been considered a glorious omen." Instead, the rainbow was "beheld for a few minutes, and speedily forgotten."[25]

Confederate cavalry continued to provide Bragg with poor information about Federal movements that night, but the general could see well enough that Murfreesboro was the target. More importantly, his horse soldiers had bought time to allow the rest of the army to concentrate west of town along both banks of Stones River. The river worried Lieutenant General Hardee, who asserted that more rain might well flood it and bisect the army.[26] Meanwhile, the men experienced the same hard conditions as their pursuers. Pvt. William Trask of Hardee's escort related that "the day had been terrible, the march tiresome, tedious and troublesome. Wagons and artillery had moved in the softened clay and the roads were strewn with camp equipage, thrown off to lighten them. I was covered with mud, cold and hungry, my feet nearly frozen and my shoes full of water."[27]

Sunday, December 28, brought early fog but then a welcome bright sky and frost, with a 7 A.M. temperature of 31 degrees. "Providence smiled that morning," Bickham wrote, "for the mist was swept away by a strong western breeze, and the sun broke through the clouds, shining with genial luster."[28] By afternoon, temperatures were in the midfifties. Bragg took advantage of the clearing weather to deploy in line of battle along the river. Rosecrans did not attack on that Sabbath, aside from a reconnaissance that seemed to confirm the enemy's lines. His devout Roman Catholicism was a factor, but so was his army's exhaustion. Two days of cold rain and mud had left his men spent. They welcomed the chance to dry out their clothing and blankets. The ground remained wet and soft through the day, however, which made for more uncomfortable sleeping that cold night as temperatures fell back into the upper thirties.[29]

Rosecrans finalized plans to launch an attack on the Stewart's Creek positions at dawn on December 29. Morning arrived with clear skies and more frost. Crittenden's Left Wing moved forward in line of battle, the mud almost knee deep in some spots, only to discover the Confederates were gone. Crittenden pressed on down the Nashville Turnpike until late afternoon, when he reached Stones River and found a line of troops in gray on the far bank. Clouds began to gather with a noticeable rise in temperature; an unexpected warm front was moving in from the north bringing more rain. At sunset, Rosecrans ordered Crittenden to cross the river and take Murfreesboro. Before events convinced Crittenden to countermand the order, one brigade crossed the cold, waist-deep, fifty-foot-wide waterway. That night, rain returned as temperatures hovered around 50 degrees. Soldiers slept in the mud, ankle deep in plowed fields. Confederates pulled down fences for small fires, but their Federal foes were forbidden to do so. It was a miserable night.[30]

While Bragg and his lieutenants extended their lines and prepared for the attack they expected the next morning, Rosecrans struggled vainly to get the rest of his army into position. Around midnight, he ordered the slow-moving McCook to bring his wing up at dawn. The ugly new day, December 30, arrived with dark skies and thick morning fog that obscured the rolling ground dotted with cedar forests. Noontime gusts out of the northwest chased away the fog but also blew down tree branches. Rain fell all day, sometimes as drizzle, but often in driving torrents. It was colder too, 40 degrees at 2 P.M. Soaked men shivered in deep mud or lay on wet blankets in line of battle. Some constructed makeshift shelters of blankets and rifles bayoneted into the muck. McCook moved up slowly against resistance from Confederate skirmishers. By nightfall, Rosecrans's army was in position along Stones River. Overnight, temperatures fell below freezing, and the earth grew hard. There were no fires.[31] "The eve of battle was dreary," Bickham wrote. "It had rained nearly all day, and the atmosphere was humid. A blustering wind swept coldly from the North, whistling dismally through the forests."[32]

That bleak night, Bragg made the signal decision to take the initiative and attack first. He accepted a plan from Lieutenant General Polk that essentially was a mirror image of the afternoon assault at Perryville. Led by Hardee's troops, the Confederates would slam McCook's Federal right. Wheeling like a gate, they then would roll up the enemy back past the Nashville Turnpike and the Nashville and Chattanooga Railroad to the river. Bragg thus would cut off Rosecrans from his main lines to Nashville. As the wind blew hard from the northeast and the rain kept falling, Confederate units shifted into jump-off positions. Maj. Gen. Pat Cleburne sifted his division from the right to the left, wading the cold river. At his headquarters, Rosecrans unwittingly assisted Bragg by putting a quite similar plan into motion, despite Thomas's misgivings. Confident that Crittenden's assault from the Federal left would find success in the morning, McCook and his subordinates exhibited what historian Peter Cozzens calls "an air of indifference." With the exception of men such as Brig. Gen. Philip Sheridan, they ignored the sounds of enemy troops in the wet woods.[33]

The rain stopped before dawn. The morning of December 31 was surprisingly bright and frosty, with temperatures around freezing. At around 6:20 A.M., Bragg launched a devastating surprise attack on the Union right. Striking the weaker end of Rosecrans's line, waves of wet and chilled Confederates hammered it back three miles toward the turnpike and the railroad like, to use the well-worn analogy, a jackknife folding back into its handle. Sheridan's tenacious division near the rocky and wooden center of the re-fusing line slowed down the increasingly weary attackers, while Rosecrans masterfully hurried reinforcements from his idle left to a new line along the pike. The Federals finally stemmed the nearly continuous assault near dark, as the exhausted Confederate reserves failed to reach the turnpike. Bragg claimed victory: Rosecrans had no choice but to retreat toward Nashville, he concluded. Some of Union commander's generals wanted to do just that, but Rosecrans, supported by Thomas and others, decided instead to stay and fight.[34]

Clear skies and cold temperatures marked this first day of the Battle of Stones River, or Murfreesboro as the Confederates called it. At Clarksville, the daytime high reached 38 degrees, enough for frosty soil to melt into mud. That night, temperatures fell sharply into the twenties. The sky remained clear, with a bright moon during the first part of the night. Comrades searched for wounded men. For the soldiers and especially the wounded, the freezing night was agonizing and long remembered. Some built fires in violation of orders. Alexis Cope described how men in the 15th Ohio built fires only to have Rosecrans himself order them extinguished.[35] L. A. Simmons of the 84th Illinois remembered "that long, chilly comfortless night" and wondered, "who can describe the horrible sufferings of the thousands who were lying wounded on the field. . . . [W]e were so situated that a fire could not be allowed, and lying in the frozen ground, with few blankets to cover us, we could only chill, shiver, and ache with cold."[36] In such circumstances, some men showed remarkable kindness. Federal brigade commander William B. Hazen wrote that "a Rebel came over to our position, wrapped in a blanket, which he gave me. It was stiff and glazed with blood and long use, but it proved the most comfortable blanket I ever saw."[37]

The next morning, the first of 1863, was a "bright and beautiful beginning for another year," according to the chaplain of the 58th Indiana. "The sun rose in majestic splendor, shedding its light upon all around."[38] The 7 A.M. low was 22 degrees. The day proved to be somewhat warmer, as temperatures rose into the low forties. The chill morning found the Federal army still in position. January 1, the same day that Lincoln's Emancipation Proclamation took effect, saw relatively little action other than probes and repositioning. Rosecrans extended his left to the east, across Stones River, to high ground beyond. Many of his troops dug in. Rosecrans's moves thoroughly mystified Bragg, who awoke expecting to the find the battlefield in his possession and the Yankees in retreat. As the day passed and the enemy remained in position, he wavered. Confederate morale began to slip as Federal confidence rose.[39]

That night, temperatures remained above freezing, in part due to another shower. The following morning dawned with temperatures around 40 degrees. A gray morning sky gave way to more sun, while temperatures rose to nearly 60 degrees in the afternoon. The field remained muddy. Desperate to secure his victory, Bragg decided to launch a heavy late-afternoon assault against Rosecrans's new position across the river. He chose Breckinridge's relatively fresh division to carry out this attack. Relations between Bragg and Breckinridge already were bad, as the Kentuckian blamed the general for his failure to recover his home state, while Bragg put the onus on Kentuckians. Once the former vice president saw the Federal line for himself—high ground strengthened by over fifty guns arrayed hub to hub— he protested that the attack would be suicidal. Bragg remained adamant. Breckinridge launched the assault at 4 P.M., an hour before nightfall, despite new rain and sleet. The Confederates drove Union defenders through the slush and across the river, but they surged too far. The massed guns on the hill shredded the Rebel advance as it drew near. A Union counterattack then retook the lost ground. Adding insult to injury, rain fell throughout the night as a new cyclonic system moved in from the west. Federal pioneers dug rifle pits, threw up abatis and barricades, and waited for a renewed assault in the morning.[40]

"Saturday morning dawned inauspiciously," Bickham wrote. "The rain fell in torrents. The field of battle was a morass. The camps were wretched muck of mud and slop. Military operations upon an important scale were impracticable."[41] Despite official reports that all of the Federal wounded were under canvas, Simmons estimated that nine-tenths of the wounded at division hospitals lay out of doors.[42] After sporadic fighting that rainy and windy day, Bragg reluctantly ordered a retreat to Tullahoma, thirty-six miles to the southeast on the road to Chattanooga. Not only were Federal reinforcements on the way with supplies but also the continuing rain was raising Stones River into a deep torrent, which could cut his army in two, just as Hardee had warned. Plus, his men were worn out, although perhaps not to the degree that some of his nervous subordinates claimed. "Our forces had been in line of battle for five days and nights," Bragg later reported, "with but little rest, having no reserves; their baggage and tents had been loaded and the wagons were 4 miles off; their provisions, if cooked at all, were imperfectly prepared, with scanty means; the weather had been severe from cold and constant rains, and we had no change of clothing, and in many cases we could not have fires."[43]

Leaving a third of his army behind as casualties, Bragg withdrew in the rain that dark, cheerless night. A local businessman insisted that the rain was not as cold as one would expect in January, but the mud was deep, up to nine inches in places according to Squire Bush. Clear skies the next day did little to repair the muddy road, increasingly chewed up by feet, hooves, and wheels. It rained again on January 5 and January 6, drenching the retreating Confederates as they tried to sleep on wet ground without fires. Many fell sick. Conditions turned cold, with the afternoon high declining from 52 degrees in Clarksville on January 5 to only 33 degrees two days later. Bragg split his army in two, leaving Polk at Shelbyville along the Duck River while the rest of the army continued to a nearly deserted Tullahoma, situated at the foot of the Cumberland Plateau. Bush noted hard rain the night of the ninth.[44] "Like Perryville and Shiloh," William Trask wrote, "we had gained another bloody victory, only to run away from it."[45]

The fighting at Stones River was a misery for everyone involved. Rain, mud, and cold temperatures made for wretched campaigning. Fog and mud delayed Rosecrans's advance significantly, while rain and sleet tactically affected the fighting on January 2. Both commanders acknowledged that winter conditions had drained ability and morale. Col. William P. Chandler, commanding the 35th Illinois, could have been praising both armies when he wrote of his regiment, "the officers and men deserve great credit for their patience and endurance, being exposed to drenching rain, cold and hunger, without fire nearly all the time, for a week."[46]

Rosecrans's army held the field, but it had lost a comparable number of casualties to Bragg's and had relatively little to show for it. As historian Earl Hess succinctly points out, Rosecrans "had lost 433 men for each mile he advanced."[47] The larger operational situation had not changed. Nor did the victory outshine Union failures elsewhere or undermine the northern peace movement. Worse yet for Lincoln, Rosecrans did not press Bragg afterward. Convinced that his army was too battered to follow, the Union commander took the town but advanced no farther, content to bury the dead and try to restore his army. It was Buell all over again as far as Washington was concerned.[48]

Indeed, to the consternation of his president, Rosecrans outdid his predecessor by beginning to construct an immense supply base along the Nashville Turnpike and the railroad north of Murfreesboro, preparatory to any pursuit of Bragg. In time, Fortress Rosecrans's two hundred acres of earthworks and warehouses would compose the largest base of operations during the war. Bad weather did much to both make it possible to begin and then to delay construction, as heavy rain and occasional snow raised the Cumberland high enough for supply transports finally to get through. "It was unusually rainy, even for the winter season," William Sumner Dodge wrote, "and lurid skies, humid atmosphere, deep mud, miserable tents, and inexperience in the new condition of life, all conspired to produce sickness and death, and convert the camp into one giant field-hospital"[49] Charles Dunham wrote that "the people say they cant recollect when they had so much at a time."[50]

Dodge and Dunham were right about the weather being "unusually rainy." At Clarksville, some form of precipitation fell on eighteen of January's thirty-one days. Nearly ten inches of snow fell on the sixteenth alone, but most precipitation came in the form of cold rain, with almost nine inches of rain and melted snow measured during the month. By way of comparison, just a little over five inches of rain and melted snow accumulated on sixteen days during the previous January. Skies were dark as well; twenty of thirty-one days earned a score of nine or ten on a scale of ten that measured cloudiness, while only six merited a zero for cloudless skies. The average daytime high was 46 degrees, but two days of 67-degree temperatures (January 12 and January 13) skewed that mean significantly. Eleven January days never exceeded freezing, with highs of 27 degrees on January 15 and 16 degrees on January 16, the day of the big snow.[51]

The snowstorm of mid-January elicited particular notice. In the Harpeth River valley, Pvt. James Birney Shaw of the 10th Indiana described it. "About 9 o'clock at night," he wrote, "it turned very cold and by morning it was down to zero. The blankets of the men were frozen fast to the ground, and many were torn and rendered useless." The column, which had been chasing raiders under Forrest's command, gave up its pursuit and headed back to Nashville "in snow that was shoe top deep, and the thermometer at zero." The march was "probably the most severe of any during our term of service."[52]

February brought only relative relief. Three more inches of snow fell on the fifth, just as it did in the Trans-Mississippi. It actually rained more often than in January, on fifteen of twenty-eight days, but only for a total of accumulation (including snow melt) of well over six inches. Eight inches of rain and accumulated snow fell during February 1862, by comparison, during and after the fighting at Forts Henry and Donelson. February 1863 was incredibly dreary, however. Twenty-one of twenty-eight days merited a cloudiness measurement of nine or ten, with every day between February

8 and February 26 dark. The mean daytime high again was 46 degrees, but the month saw two notable cold snaps, when highs did not reach freezing, between February 2 and February 6, and February 22–23. It was 9 degrees on the morning of the sixth. There were warm days too, including two (February 11 and February 19) that saw afternoon highs above 60 degrees.[53]

In short, the first two months of winter in Tennessee were often cold, wet more often than not, and almost always dark and dreary. Midwesterners sometimes compared Middle Tennessee weather to that back home, but the rain drew special attention. Low-lying campsites and streams regularly flooded. Roads constantly washed out, exhausting men and animals. Chaplain William Haigh of the 36th Illinois described flooded tents and added that Stones River sounded "like the rumbling of the [railroad] cars."[54] Morale sank, buoyed only by the knowledge that more rain meant a higher Cumberland River, which meant more to eat.

The long winter wore on, with only rumors of raids and occasional expeditions to break the tedium. Construction details cut down trees, cleared land, blew up rocky outcroppings, constructed earthworks, burned existing buildings to clear fields of fire, and erected other buildings for military use. Soldiers and former slaves worked long days until Fortress Rosecrans was ready for occupation in March. The men got sick with malaria, pneumonia, and diarrhea. Measles and scorbutic taint, a maddening itch thought related to dietary deficiencies, also appeared. While affected members of the rank and file went to hospitals, officers occasionally headed home on furlough. Some never returned. Most of the soldiers relied on canvas for shelter, but some did create hybrids on the eastern model.[55]

Conditions were no better in the Confederates camps. "We encamped in a low, muddy place," Col. James Cooper of the 20th Tennessee wrote in January, "very distant from wood, and the weather was bitter cold. . . . On the whole it was as disagreeable a month as I passed the whole time I was in the army."[56] Two months later, Pvt. Francis Nicks of the 3rd Florida wrote: "It has been very cold and wet. . . . [T]his is the worst country I ever saw in my life. It rains all the time and when it ain't raining it is snowing."[57] The Confederates, too, largely remained under canvas, with brick or stick chimneys. Men lacking tents built shelters from cedar boughs.[58]

Gradually, winter evolved into spring. Good weather on February 25 encouraged one observer to express hope that "General *Mud*, who has been the arbiter of the destiny of the two armies, will soon have to resign his throne."[59] Those hopes proved premature. Rain continued, with a long wet spell between March 3 and March 10 and another between the eighteenth and twenty-eighth. The monthly aggregate totaled five inches. Skies generally remained dreary as well, with twenty-one of the month's thirty-one days registering a cloudiness score of nine or ten. Conditions were especially hard in the field. Reports of a Confederate advance on Murfreesboro during the rainy periods notably forced men out into the muck. The Duck River rose so high on March 8 that the pontoon bridge spanning it washed away, forcing Federal and Confederate cavalry to skirmish from the opposite banks.[60]

The only real difference was temperature. The average high rose to 53 degrees during March, but the second half of the month was notably warmer. Five days, beginning with March 14, made it into the seventies, while four additional days registered in the sixties.[61] Roads began to improve. April brought better conditions still. Spring was coming. Farmers began planting corn. It rained twelve days that month, but precipitation in Clarksville measured only a little over three inches, compared to over eight inches during April 1862, the drenching month of Shiloh. Sunny days outnumbered cloudy ones, and temperatures reached a mean daily high of 66 degrees, with twelve days above 70 degrees, including an 85-degree reading on the eighteenth.[62]

As spring pressed on, Rosecrans amassed supplies and developed a plan for a summer campaign that would drive Bragg from Tennessee. He had no way of knowing that more bad weather would derail his grand scheme from its outset.

Chapter 13

Nature Conspired against Us

Chancellorsville, January–May 1863

In upcountry South Carolina, planter David Golightly Harris came home in February 1863 from brief militia service hoping to sow oats and break his land for corn. Like many farmers that spring, he was hopeful and apprehensive by turns. Inflation and simple supply and demand promised profit for farmers far from the front if the season was good but money spent on food if not. He yearned to get to work, but cold temperatures, frequent rain, and sleet in March thwarted him. He only began breaking his cornfield on March 27, writing, "it is too late for me to begin, but I am scared yet. The weather has been so wet that we could not plow much." The end of "cold and wet" March brought "FROST & ICE. . . . The Spring is quite late." Harris and his slaves began plowing in early April but found the soil "tough, owing to the many rains we have had lately." A late frost on the fourth threatened his fruit. "Spring time is coming very slow," he complained. Four days later, more frost threatened his neighbors' crops. "Those who have planted corn will have to do it all over again," he observed, "or I am no prophet."[1]

Harris was not alone. People fretted everywhere. The editors of the *New England Farmer* pronounced April "a little backward" due to cold temperatures and stormy weather that hurt blossoms and delayed spring grain planting.[2] Georgia editors worried about spring planting when April arrived with indications of a hard freeze.[3] In central Georgia, Molie Evans wrote to her soldier-husband, "I saw your wheat yesterday it don't look so well . . . on account of bad weather some people is very sceard their wheat will be killed I gess all that is jointed is killed we had frost and ice both this week!"[4]

Back in South Carolina, frost kept coming until mid-April. Rain accompanied warmer weather, again halting Harris's plows. A false spring gave way to more cold and rain. His fields stayed wet for weeks. "The Spring is late," Harris lamented on April 26, "but at least has set in earnest. Our wheat-crops are very promising." May brought warm weather but rain returned, again preventing plowing. Then temperatures fell. Within days, the weather was too dry again, and his fields grew hard. The frustrated farmer started plowing corn on May 17, but the weather stayed cool. "This is not growing weather," Harris wrote. A few days later, he complained that cool nights kept his cane crop from flourishing; even his silkworms were sluggish. By mid-June, Harris worried about a second bad year in a row due to the unusual spring weather. "Such a summer as this certainly was never seen. There has not been one hot day yet & but very few warm days. I fear the crops will be bad."[5]

Farther south, there was more hope. Near Jacksonville, Florida, plantation mistress Octavia Bryant reported abundant rain, a healthy cotton crop, and thriving corn. Early in May, wheat seemed fine south of Atlanta, although corn caused some concern. Good reports from East Tennessee and Mississippi spoke of thriving corn and wheat. Then, as May drew to a close, fear of another drought resumed. Skies remained clear and blue, the ground began to dry out, and the atmosphere became dusty. When rain returned, it was with a vengeance. In Macon, a weather observer recorded 7.1 inches on May 21, a record in the city. Across Georgia, torrential rain threatened to ruin the winter-wheat harvest. One observer noted drought developing north of a line from Augusta to Macon. Except in North Georgia, corn was poor.[6]

In Virginia, the future hung in the balance. On the coast, New Englander Aaron K. Blake saw "splendid weather" but added that "all the people say it is very backward here."[7] In early June, J. B. Jones noted good reports from down south but lamented that dry weather nearly had killed his garden.[8] The *Alexandria Gazette* agreed that "rain is again much wanted."[9]

Ambrose Burnside left for Washington on January 23, right after the Mud March, only to get lost in an ironic fog on the way to the train station. The general left his ambulance when a pile of dead mules blocked the road, and he waded through ankle-deep mud until his party found the road again. He arrived near sunup, went straight to the White House, and handed Lincoln an ultimatum. Burnside wanted four generals, including Joe Hooker, driven from the army and four more, including William Franklin, relieved from duty. Otherwise, he would resign himself. The meeting was testy. The next morning, the president told General in Chief Halleck and Secretary of War Stanton that he would replace Burnside with Hooker, in part to placate Radical Republicans. Hooker had told the press that the nation needed a dictator—but Lincoln was willing to risk such sentiments for a victory. Major Generals Sumner and Franklin had to go too. Burnside seemed relieved to no longer be in charge of the Army of the Potomac.[10]

January 25 was warm, the fourth of five days to reach the fifties, but the mud in camp was so deep that officers canceled drill. The next day was even warmer, reaching 59 degrees, but the air was foggy and the sky cloudy. A new weather front was approaching. As if to place an exclamation mark on Hooker's ascent to command, snow began falling in the Shenandoah Valley on January 26 and spread east. Rain turned to snow in northern Virginia the following evening, with wintry precipitation extending south beyond Richmond. More snow the next day, with winds from the southwest and mixed with sleet, left six inches accumulation in Washington and a foot along the Rappahannock.[11]

The armies viewed the snow differently. Lee's men were hungry and sick. Scurvy, due to nutritional deficiencies, and sanitation-based typhoid were common. Ill-fed horses could not pull. Yet morale was good. The snow halted labor on field works and brought hope of a quiet winter. Considering the Mud March as well as the snow, Jed Hotchkiss concluded that "surely the Lord is on our side."[12] Confederates celebrated like children, organizing elaborate snowball fights. "Most of these fellow had never seen snow before," Pvt. Westwood Todd of the 12th Virginia wrote, "and were perfectly delighted at the sight."[13] Lee wrote that, with the weather making roads difficult for artillery movement, he hoped to finally put his men into winter quarters.[14]

Very few Federals wrote anything about having fun. The Army of the Potomac remained demoralized. The change in command initially provided only mixed results. The politicians, newspaper editors, and other civilians who had demanded winter battles were still in place. All came in for their share of the blame as the bluecoats sulked in their tents. But so did the weather. No one could deny that Burnside had been unlucky in the Mud March. Defeat, disillusion, boredom, insufficient supplies, and cold took their toll as the snow fell and eventually melted into more mud. For most, belief in the overall cause, each other, and God remained strong. But it would require competent leadership, rest, and resupply to fan their hopes into optimism.[15]

That task was now Joe Hooker's after he took command on January 26. The next evening, as he attended meetings in the capital, rain turned to snow at Falmouth, with high winds and temperatures that sank into the thirties. Reviving temperatures on the twenty-ninth brought a thaw but also new depths of red-clay mud. Hooker immediately went to work on multiple fronts. He jettisoned Burnside's grand divisions, fired and replaced upper-level commanders, appointed a chief of staff, and tried to deal directly with Lincoln while bypassing Halleck. He reorganized his artillery and cavalry, and created an effective intelligence service. The general also focused on morale. At the end of Burnside's tenure, desertions in his army had reached two hundred a day. Hooker rotated men home on furlough, mandated more and better rations, and confronted corrupt commissary officers. He prioritized better medical care. New shelter tents led to a second wave of hut construction, not to mention occasionally corduroyed campgrounds. Division and corps insignia, ostensibly to better identify stragglers, had the happy added effect of boosting esprit de corps. So too did allowing regiments to inscribe battle honors on their banners.[16]

Yet there was nothing Hooker could do about the nasty weather. Starting with the vicious late-January storm that created the Mud March, the winter of 1863 became remarkably wet. Some form of precipitation fell thirty-four of fifty-nine days (58 percent) in February and March. Soldiers knew it was unusual. "We have snow and rain here about every other day," Capt. Robert McAllister of the 11th New Jersey wrote home late in March.[17] The inevitable result was deeper mud. "But O such a mud!" Chaplain Frank Morse of the 37th Massachusetts exclaimed on January 31. "The ground freezes nights so that it is quite hard in the morning. But by the middle of the day, all is mud again. It is mud, mud, mud wherever you go and the very worst kind of mud at that. . . . I hear the sentinels feet go splash, splash, as he walks his beat in front of my tent. There has been a mud puddle in the middle of my tent since yesterday."[18]

Snow fell seven times that February, starting with a smattering on the night of the third. Two to three inches plus sleet followed on February 5 and lasted into the next day. This was part of a wider system moving up from the south, much like the Mud March storm. More snow fell on the eleventh. At Falmouth, Maj. Charles Wainwright measured half a foot on

February 17, but that was nothing compared to a blizzard that started six days later. Screaming northwest gales that night left deep snow on Washington's Birthday. One Confederate, Lt. E. H. Moorman, woke up under eight inches of it as Federal cannons announced the holiday. Another measured ten inches to a foot by midday. Jed Hotchkiss counted fifteen inches, while Pvt. John Southard of the 49th New York told his sister there was two feet of snow in his camp. A Philadelphia correspondent simply called it the dreariest Washington's Birthday he could remember. Lee lamented to his wife that snow was up to his knees and his men had to dig out headquarters' horses. It was the hardest snowstorm any of them had seen in the war.[19]

And that was only the half of it. Rain fell regularly. All told, only ten of February's twenty-eight days were dry. "Just the weather to keep Hooker mud-bound," the *Charleston Mercury*'s Richmond correspondent quipped.[20] Precipitation started lightly during the evening of February 1. Between the fifth and the seventh, Confederate camps flooded, and roads again became all but useless. More rain and wind followed late on February 11, lasted two days, then fell again on the fifteenth. It caught many soldiers in the open, as Lee had ordered two divisions to Richmond to meet a rising Federal threat south of the James River. Off and on from February 18 through February 21, rain (sometimes mixed with snow) deluged camps and produced knee-deep muck. More fell at February's end, damaging railroad bridges south to Richmond.[21]

A month after Burnside's ouster, Hooker's army remained stuck in the red mud. At least it was warmer and above freezing, most of the time. Temperatures rollercoastered throughout the month. From an afternoon high of 52 degrees on the first day of February, highs fell into the twenties on the third, bringing great distress to the men in the field. Near Alexandria, ice formed in the Potomac. But the same front that brought rain and snow on February 5 heralded spring-like highs that steadily rose every day to a peak of 60 degrees on the tenth. Wainwright wrote home hopefully that day about singing bluebirds that seemed to promise an early spring. Afternoon highs remained well above freezing during the rest of the month, often in the forties and even fifties. The only exceptions were during the blizzard, when it was 26 degrees on February 22 and 32 degrees the next day. Nights often were bitter, however. Eight mornings registered below freezing; February 4 hit 10 degrees. The combination of frequent precipitation and inconstant temperatures produced cycles of deep mud and frozen earth.[22]

And the winter dragged on. Defying folk wisdom, March came in with a lion of a north wind and a driving rainstorm mixed with hail and went out with "a heavy storm of rain, snow, and sleet."[23] Ice-choked rivers extended across the North. In Washington, rain, snow, or hail fell eleven days that month. As was usual, soldiers at Fredericksburg or in the Shenandoah Valley recorded more precipitation than C. B. Mackee observed in Washington, noting sixteen days with some precipitation. The majority of these storms moved up from the Gulf. Light snow, accompanied by strong winds, fell along the Rappahannock on the night of March 10, while additional squalls appeared on the thirteenth. A stronger snowstorm, with northeast winds and sleet, followed on the afternoon of March 19 and lasted two days. Mississippian Franklin Riley measured nearly a foot of snow at this time.[24]

In Richmond, J. B. Jones described how snow, especially at the spring equinox, shut down food shipments into the capital and set the stage for the notorious Richmond Bread Riot of April 2. That day, perhaps 3,000 hungry women plundered city stores for food they could not afford. President Davis, the city police, and militia troops finally dispersed the looters. At the time, observers attributed the riot to immorality, Union instigation, speculation, or greed. More recently, historians have seen it as the result of coldhearted inattention and callous government policies that especially injured the suffering wives of soldiers. Politicized women demanded their due and forced the Confederate government to respond. Yet there were more fundamental, if slighted, causes at work, including an influx of refugees into Richmond, an interrupted transportation system, and the needs of the army. Most basic of all, however, was weather. Over the long term, the poor harvests of 1862 had come home to roost, while the immediate catalyst—as Jones recognized—was a snowstorm that cut off the city from farms.[25]

Frequent rain continued as well. "I wish I was a frog," Lt. Ham Chamberlayne wrote on March 5, "we would all be merrier that way."[26] That same day, the Daily Richmond Examiner noted ice in the capital's gutters. It rained at Fredericksburg on March 2, sporadically from the night of March 5 through March 8, and again after the snow of March 10. Another rainy spell began on the twenty-sixth and lasted until the end of the month. Sleet and hail fell with thunder on March 15. All told, there was some type of precipitation along the Rappahannock on seventeen of thirty-one days that month. Frost was common as well, despite somewhat warmer temperatures that remained above freezing save for five nights. Ten days, in contrast, saw afternoon highs in the fifties. The first days of spring brought appropriate weather, and March 25 hit a remarkable 70 degrees as a wet warm front moved through.[27] Overall, the weather, as Wainwright wrote, was "as changeable as is possible even in March."[28]

The inevitable results were flooded rivers and deep, almost fathomless mud. No sooner did roads start to dry out than more precipitation arrived. Pvt. Wilbur Fisk of the 2nd Vermont judged the mire to be better than what he had seen a year earlier, but few agreed.[29] All soldiers could do was endure. In between drilling, fortifying, and constructing corduroy roads in knee-deep mud, men tried to stay warm and dry. Mud led to canceled drill, inspections, and church services and delayed troop movements to a staggering crawl. On bad days, soldiers huddled in their shelters, smoky with green pinewood fires. Leaky tents flooded. Union sutlers made money selling boots and other gear, but wood remained the greatest need. Regiments sometimes moved their camps and rebuilt shelters in the rain and snow if firewood ran out. Soldiers lined their shelters with pine boughs for insulation, denuded local forests, and then dug up the stumps and roots for fuel.[30] "We are still enjoying life in our new camp," Cpl. J. P. Coburn of the 141st Pennsylvania wrote on March 25, "which has ceased to be 'in the woods' & as it has not been christened to my knowledge, I call it 'Stump O' for want of a better name."[31]

The continuing bad weather and its effects, coupled with the stalemate along the Rappahannock and the monotony in camp, invariably affected morale. The precise effects varied from soldier to soldier. Some expressed satisfaction in their warm huts and maintained that they preferred winter camping to summer marching. Hoosier Edmund Brown suggested that morale varied with the weather, being better on warm, sunny days. But while the warmth of victory and snug shanties helped counterbalance the elements, even the Confederates' continuing snowball battles could only do so much to keep spirits up as winter continued. Impassable roads delayed supplies well into March. The Washington's Birthday blizzard forced Lee to institute short rations for a time. Union division commander Brig. Gen. James Wadsworth turned to oxen when his mules could no longer pull wagons through muddy roads, despite corduroying. Many soldiers on both sides still lacked shoes and winter clothing. Disease, including pneumonia, reached staggering proportions. Desertions continued.[32] Noting that most everything was in short supply, historian Ernest Furgurson writes, "for plain surviving, that winter was the hardest time they ever faced."[33]

Malaise affected even the highest ranks. Lee wrote his daughter on February 6: "I am so cross now that I am not worth seeing anywhere. Here you will have to take me with the three stools—the snow, the rain, and the mud. The storm of the last twenty-four hours has added to our stock of all, and we are now in a floating condition. . . . Our horses and mules suffer the most. . . . The roads are wretched, almost impassable." On February 23, he added that a "young French officer, full of vivacity, and ardent for service with me," had arrived. "I think the appearance of things will cool him. If they do not, the night will, for he brought no blankets."[34]

The situation across the river was not much better in terms of supply and worse regarding morale until Hooker's reforms began to take hold.[35] Some found solace in black humor. Rufus Dawes described a night march in rain that grew difficult as his 6th Wisconsin comrades "plunged and staggered" through bottomless mud "with great difficulty and serious loss of temper. Suddenly some wag shouted out . . . 'Four fathom.' Instantly, from some other part of the column came out in drawling intonation, 'Four and a half.' Then another shouted: 'Quarter less twain,' but when the squeaking voice of orator Jones sang out 'No bottom,' the regiment raised a universal shout, and waded into camp without further complaint."[36]

"The month of March passes by leaving us still in the mud," Col. Wesley Brainerd concluded.[37] Clear skies and rising temperatures initially promised a better April. An approaching warm front raised the afternoon high to 68 degrees in Washington on April 2. The north wind blew with gale force, hard enough to start drying out roads and even rip roofs off Federal huts. But winter had one more cruel blow up its sleeve. The last snowstorm of the season, and one of the fiercest, began around dark on April 4. It dumped a foot of snow overnight in Washington. By Easter noon, six inches lay at the front and eight inches in the Shenandoah. Soldiers described the vicious wind as much as the snow.[38] "The weather has been more disagreeable since the beginning of April than at any previous time this winter," Confederate surgeon Spencer Welch wrote that snowy holiday. "The wind has blown almost incessantly and furiously at times. To-day is one of the windiest and most disagreeable that I ever saw. It is awful." His only solace was that "such weather as this will delay 'Fighting Joe' Hooker's movements for some time, and it is so much the better for us."[39]

Increasingly anxious about opposition on the home front, Lincoln accepted Hooker's invitation to visit Falmouth, hoping to jar the army into motion. With a party including his wife and son Tad, the president left Washington on April 4, just as the snowstorm hit. High winds and choppy water made for a rough voyage and delayed his arrival until Easter, just as the snow tapered off. Over the next five days, the weather cleared. Afternoon temperatures rose to 66 degrees on cloudy April 10. Strong north winds, however, created a noticeable chill. Nights were cold but above freezing, and patches of snow remained in shadows. For several days, the Lincolns watched the army pass in review over windy and muddy parade grounds, the resentful men sometimes without overcoats. The president visited hospitals and even took his son to Fredericksburg, granting the boy's wish to see some actual Rebels. In between, Lincoln urged Hooker to act decisively. The destruction of Lee's army had to be his primary objective, Lincoln asserted, while not repeating the bloody frontal assaults of the previous December. He sounded the same themes once back in Washington. Hooker agreed. On balmy April 11, with the afternoon high reaching 72 degrees, he sent his chief of staff to the White House with his plans. Two days hence, Hooker would send nearly all of his cavalry into Lee's rear and take the rest of the army upriver to cross the Rappahannock. Forced to retreat, Lee would find the road to Richmond blocked and his railroad supply line cut. His only alternative would be to fall back to the southwest. The road to Richmond would open wide. Lincoln sent his immediate approval.[40] "My plans are perfect," Hooker reportedly boasted, "and when I start to carry them out, may God have mercy on General Lee, for I will have none."[41]

On April 13, Maj. Gen. George Stoneman rode out of Falmouth with nearly 10,000 troopers, four batteries, and over a brigade of infantry specifically tasked with seizing the Rappahannock fords. It was the largest cavalry force assembled so far in the war. The rest of the army stripped down their camps, cooked eight days' rations, and prepared to march. The morning was overcast but warm, and the afternoon high reached 54 degrees. Observers described a lovely day with little dust thanks to a shower the previous evening. Unencumbered by precipitation, dust, or mud, the horse soldiers covered twenty-four miles. The next day, with a high reaching 62 degrees, Stoneman identified four fords for crossing but hesitated to push across despite light opposition. Transferring supplies from wagons to mules also burned daylight.

By nightfall, only one brigade was south of the river as clouds began filling the skies. After midnight, yet another ill-timed nor'easter arrived to torment the seemingly cursed Union army. A smaller sibling of the Mud March tempest, the new storm unleashed twenty-four hours of torrential rain that soaked men, raised the river as much as seven feet, and lique-fied red-clay roads. Stoneman barely retrieved his advanced brigade before floodwaters and Confederate cavalry could cut it off. Even then, several troopers drowned. At Falmouth, camps flooded. Hooker had assured Lin-coln that the campaign would continue despite the weather when word came that Stoneman was mired north of the river. The reports discouraged Hooker and frustrated Lincoln. The soldiers wondered if fate simply was against them.

The rain halted early on April 16, a day that soon became spring-like. Several observers reflected on peach blossoms and plant life while not-ing rapidly drying roads.[42] Blue skies did nothing to cure Lincoln's anxiety, however. Facing another crushing failure a la Burnside, the president gath-ered up Stanton and Halleck and hurried to the front on the nineteenth. Hooker explained that he had altered his plans based on recent events and fresh intelligence. Instead of forcing Lee to retreat, he could crush him in a vice as long as Federal troops in southeastern Virginia occupied Long-street's detached element. Without them, Lee only had about 60,000 men compared to Hooker's 134,000 troops. To confuse his opponent, Hooker would send two divisions to the Mud March crossings at Banks Ford and U.S. Ford while two corps—about 40,000 men—crossed the river at Fred-ericksburg. A flanking column of three corps would move farther upriver to Kelly's Ford. With Stoneman crossing ahead of them, the big flanking column would hurry over the Rappahannock and Rapidan Rivers using pontoons, race through a tangled new-growth forest called the Wilderness, link up with the forces at the lower fords, and strike Lee hard from the west with 70,000 men. Hooker's last two corps, held close by in reserve, would fight where needed.[43]

All the Union commander needed to destroy the Army of Northern Vir-ginia, he told his superiors, was for the favorable weather to continue. It did not. Heavy rain began after dark on April 19 and persisted. The Potomac overflowed up into the new state of West Virginia, where Confederate cavalry was harassing the Baltimore and Ohio Railroad and resident Unionists. Hooker wrote Lincoln on April 21, blaming the rain for his continued delay. That day was promising, cool but dry with a high of 52 degrees. The next day was warmer, with temperatures rising to 64 degrees. But rain returned that night, extending into April 24. Chamberlayne thought this new storm the hardest of the winter yet. Noting unnamed anti-McClellan officers who had not fought on the Peninsula a year earlier, Major Wainwright defended his old commander against those who complained about the rain—it had been worse on the Peninsula, he huffed. Still, the storm left close to an inch of rain in Washington, while at Falmouth, the wind blew hard enough to knock down trees.[44]

Hooker rightly receives praise for his work in rebuilding the Army of the Potomac and its morale following the Mud March. Adding weather to the calculations makes his achievement seem even more impressive. From January 26, when Hooker took command, through the end of April, rain or snow fell on fifty-two of ninety-five days, a remarkable 55 percent of the time. The general's many celebrated reforms took place in the context of an exceedingly rainy winter and early spring that truly averaged precipitation every other day. Red Virginia mud was a constant during the army's rebirth.[45] But across the Rappahannock, Lee's outnumbered Confederates had endured the same conditions with fewer supplies, worse shelter, and less support. Nevertheless, they, too, were ready to fight.

Hooker's sweeping turning movement swirled counterclockwise in the sprinkling rain of warm April 27. As the high approached 72 degrees, the three corps in the flanking column—their arrangement determined by the positions of their winter camps—moved quickly toward the upriver fords. The troops crossed the Rappahannock the next day, a slightly cooler one that warmed only to 62 degrees. That night, a thunderstorm hit the area, giving way to a cold, all-night rain out of the northeast that continued on as mist in the morning. More began falling a little before noon. This again muddied the roads and made transportation tedious, especially for artillery and supply trains. At one juncture, the 64th New York resorted to picking up mired hospital wagons by hand and carrying them to drier spots. The Signal Corps blamed the rain, leaks, and an ill-timed lightning strike for the failure of their telegraph line, strung all the way to U.S. Ford. Pea-soup fog enveloped the Rappahannock valley from Fredericksburg west to the fords, severely limiting visibility. Yet Hooker's men pushed on. Hidden by the fog, the flanking troops waded the coursing Rapidan, with water up to their waists, and marched into the Wilderness. Stoneman's cavalry crossed and headed south. Maj. Gen. John Sedgwick, meanwhile, led the Fredericksburg wing back across the Rappahannock and into the city over newly constructed and fog-shrouded pontoon bridges. Although the fog initially interfered, Sedgwick stirred up enough commotion to hold Lee in place. A thunderstorm at about 4:30 P.M. lasted about an hour.

Fog and mist returned the next morning, but April 30 turned into a warm, cloudy day with a high of 64 degrees, hot enough to weary rookie troops. By that evening, the upriver corps were concentrated nine miles west of Fredericksburg at Chancellorsville, the grandly named crossroads hamlet where the Chancellor family's brick home stood. Arriving there late in the day, Hooker sent for a reserve corps, issued a congratulatory order to his men, and prepared to hammer Lee's army into Sedgwick's anvil. The weather had not derailed the Federal campaign.[46]

Both armies went into the next day's fighting still wet to the skin in clammy, rain-soaked uniforms. The night was foggy as well. Hooker's bold moves initially confused Lee, who expected the main effort at Fredericksburg. Only scattered elements of cavalry were in position to contest the river crossings. As the situation developed, Lee divided his army. While a division plus another brigade would hold the Fredericksburg defensive line, the rest of his army shifted eastward and began digging in near the edge of the Wilderness. Hooker enjoyed a two-to-one advantage to the west and over a four-to-one advantage at Fredericksburg.

Hooker's advance continued the next day, May 1. Thick, early morning fog gave way to a bright sky and a high of 74 degrees in Georgetown. Around noon, the advances of the two armies collided two miles east of Chancellorsville. Given the weight of arms, Federal victory seemed assured. Whatever the reason why—and historians still offer many criticisms, defenses, and conjectures about Hooker's inner failings—around 2 P.M. he ordered his dismayed generals to stop and fall back into a defensive posture near the woods surrounding the house. The men spent the balance of daylight hours digging and throwing up abatis. Defending Hooker, Stephen Sears maintains that this was all according to plan. Lee was not yet out of his works in Fredericksburg, Hooker wanted the Confederates to do the attacking, and he wanted his best brigades on the receiving end of those assaults.

Lee refused to comply. As temperatures that night dropped into the fifties, Lee, Jackson, and Jeb Stuart sat around a small fire and hatched their
greatest gamble of the war.[47] The next morning, while Lee held the line
with about 15,000 men, Jackson swung south through early morning fog
and turned east through the Wilderness with his corps of 30,000 troops.
According to Stuart, Hooker's right flank was in the air two miles west of
Chancellorsville, ripe for a blindside attack. The day was hot, and on a narrow road in a tangled forest, men fell out of line or fainted. The weather
helped in another manner.[48] Surgeon J. F. J. Caldwell of the 1st South Carolina remembered that "the roads were . . . just wet enough to be easy on the
feet and free from dust."[49] The column produced no tell-tale dust clouds.

The fatiguing march ended up taking longer than anticipated due to
contact with the enemy, which forced Jackson to divert farther south.
Hooker misinterpreted the firefight as evidence of Lee retreating and did
little in response. Maj. Gen. Oliver O. Howard's XI Corps, largely the remnant of Frémont's old Valley corps and damned as the worst in the army,
was unprepared. Jackson's men emerged from the woods at about 5:15 P.M.,
after a twelve-mile march, and slammed Howard back two miles toward
the Chancellor house. The fighting continued after dark, under a bright full
moon as a thunderstorm raged in the western sky. Seeking out Hooker's defensive line, Jackson fell to friendly fire. The bright moonlight behind the
corps commander and his aides all but blinded the unfortunate regiment
involved. Later that night, as the fighting finally died down, a brief shower
fell on the wounded and dead to end the anxious day.[50]

Too many accounts of Chancellorsville all but end with Jackson's
wounds. The battle, however, was far from over. Sunday, May 3, began with
heavy dew and fog along the river. After 8:30 A.M., the day quickly turned
sunny and hot, reaching an unforgiving 80 degrees beneath a cloudless sky.
It was the hottest day of 1863 so far in northern Virginia—and the bloodiest. All through the Sabbath, parched and exhausted men battled furiously on two fronts. To the east, Sedgwick's men stormed Marye's Heights
and surged three miles into Lee's rear before Confederate reinforcements
stopped them. To the west, Hooker abandoned the open high ground at
Hazel Grove, surrendering the field's prime spot for artillery, in order to
eliminate a salient in his line. He waited for Sedgwick to strike Lee. The
result, according to historian Ernest Furgurson, was Confederate artillery's most effective day of the war. Aided by the guns at Hazel Grove, Stuart—temporarily commanding Jackson's corps—and Lee sent in wave after

brutal wave of morning assaults against Hooker's works. They hammered the Federals away from Chancellorsville and northward into a southward-facing, horseshoe-shaped reserve line. Hooker remained passive, especially after a severe midmorning concussion caused by a Confederate cannonball smashing into the Chancellor's porch. As the day continued, men sometimes stopped killing long enough to try to rescue wounded friends and foes from raging brushfires in the Wilderness. Many, nonetheless, burned to death. It was the second-bloodiest day of the Civil War.

The next day was nearly as hot, with the high reaching 76 degrees in Georgetown and 79 degrees in Alexandria. While Hooker again sat inertly behind his fieldworks, despite a two-to-one advantage in men and a fresh corps, Lee peeled off another division and joined his reinforced right wing to destroy Sedgwick. His attack failed, with the Federals holding their ground at the end of the day as another thunderstorm flared up. But that night, worried about Lee's numbers and confused by Hooker's conflicting messages, Sedgwick withdrew back across the Rappahannock under the cover of a deep fog. Hooker decided on retreat as well. His first priority, he reasoned, was protecting Washington. There also was the matter of Longstreet's divisions, rumored to be nearby despite good intelligence to the contrary. Ignoring a majority of his corps commanders, Hooker sat still again the next day. Morning fog hid his artillery as crews began to shift their guns. Desperate to keep the initiative, Lee ordered Fredericksburg reoccupied and sent the rest of his right wing back toward Chancellorsville, hoping to attack Hooker again before nightfall despite the Federal fortifications. The high again reached 76 degrees.[51]

As the afternoon began, however, the weather turned. Sgt. Rice Bull of the 123rd New York was a Confederate prisoner when "about noon thunder heads began to form in the west and south and before one in the afternoon we heard the sound of thunder." The storm began around three o'clock—although soldiers estimates of the time varied anywhere from two until five—and lasted two hours. No one debated its severity. "The thunder and lightning were terrific," Bull continued, "and the rain came in sheets." The battleground flooded. "Where most of the wounded lay," he explained, "it was from four to six inches deep. The condition of most of the wounded was deplorable. More than half had no tent covering, so had to take the full force of the storm." Two wounded men drowned in rainwater pouring off a cabin roof into their faces.[52] Capt. A. W. Bartlett of the 12th New Hampshire, meanwhile, described something like a tornado, "an aerial volcano from which came not only a deluge of water, but fish, toads, frogs, and snakes, that are not supposed to have their habitations above."[53]

The thunderstorm announced a dramatic change. In Washington, temperatures fell from the upper seventies into the forties overnight, with the wind shifting to the northwest.[54] Lee's hoped-for attack bogged down in the newly developed mud. Covered by darkness and cold rain, the Army of the Potomac began to retreat toward U.S. Ford. Hooker's artillery crossed at about 7:30 P.M.; the general himself had gone over at about seven o'clock. After that, his timetable fell apart. The mud was too deep. Wheeled traffic backed up a mile back from the ford. Even with double teaming, artillery captains abandoned caissons and other vehicles. Worse still, not only was the Rappahannock running fast due to the heavy storm but also, by 5 P.M., it was six feet or more above morning levels. This cut off Hooker from his army. He tried to direct troop movements using signalmen, but, in the end, individual corps commanders moved to the river without much coordination.[55]

"The ford as well as its approaches were perfectly useless," Colonel Brainerd wrote, "and our bridges were threatened with destruction."[56] Rushing water particularly endangered the uppermost of three pontoon bridges, while the ends of all three were submerged. According to Wainwright, Major General Meade praised Providence when he heard that one of the bridges was swept away, as he assumed that Hooker would have to stand and fight after all. Dismantling the weakest bridge and using pieces of it, Brainerd's men shored up the other two. As the rain continued to pour and the north wind howled, cold and soaked troops crossed in utter darkness. Some men erected shelter tents once they got across, but most collapsed and slept in the mud.[57]

Dawn found temperatures in the midforties and brigades still jammed up at the crossings. Rain continued into the early afternoon as the soaked army began trudging to camp, sometimes wading through knee-deep mud. The retreating Federals left behind so many of their belongings that Confederate brigadier general Robert Rodes boasted that his entire division reequipped itself with haversacks, oilcloths, and shelter tents. Around 5 P.M., another storm came on with rain and hail. The river remained high; Lt. N. D. Preston of the 10th New York Cavalry watched one man drown.[58] Slowly, the Federals sloshed and struggled back to Falmouth. On the Confederate side of the river, prisoner Rice Bull lamented, "it seemed that all nature had conspired against us."[59]

Lee had wanted to attack U.S. Ford that rainy morning until he learned that the enemy was gone. The general was furious; Hooker had escaped. Reluctantly, he ordered his men back to their camps. The casualties at Chancellorsville were staggering; Lee had lost over 13,000 men and Hooker over 17,000. In Washington, Lincoln expressed deep concerns about the northern reaction, then set out for Aquia Creek to meet with Hooker. Panic developed in Washington as rumors spread that Lee was on his way. Rain returned in the evening, with a slow drizzle falling in the capital all day May 7 and again until early afternoon on the still-chilly eighth. At the front, Hooker's men continued to stumble through the mud to reach their old camps.[60] Capt. Mason Tyler of the 37th Massachusetts wrote, "my diary says, mud almost as bad as that in the 'mud march.'"[61]

Once back in their camps, soldiers in both armies went to work repairing their shelters. Horses needed attention too; Stoneman reported that many were suffering from "mud fever," an infectious skin ailment. A welcome change in the weather arrived on May 9. Summer essentially arrived over a month early as far west as the Mississippi, bringing hot days, warm nights, and little precipitation. Adding to the unusual weather, May 28 saw a forgotten hurricane strike northwest Florida near Apalachicola—still the only recorded hurricane in history to make landfall in the United States during the month of May. Its modern discoverers retroactively named it "Hurricane Amanda" for the US Navy bark it wrecked. In Virginia, days were humid and oppressive, including May 12, the day of Stonewall Jackson's massive funeral in Richmond. Seven days reached into the eighties that month, and temperatures soared to 90 degrees on May 22 and 92 degrees the next day. Rain only fell on the afternoons of May 13 and May 14. The first week in June saw this trend continue. Highs reached the eighties, and rain was brief and scattered, with a light sprinkling during the evening of June 2, a shower on the third, and an afternoon thundershower on the sixth. The countryside turned green, with blankets of wildflowers covering untrodden fields. Local men hoed corn. Yet to the farmers in the ranks, there were clear signs that a renewed drought was beginning as a new campaign beckoned.[62]

Chapter 14

Unsurpassed in Inclemency

Gettysburg, May–August 1863

After Chancellorsville, the armies in Virginia found themselves right back where they had been for six months. Hooker minimized his failures and blamed the XI Corps, Sedgwick, and Stoneman. He launched a major overhaul of the army's command structure while promising future triumphs. The corps commanders meanwhile targeted Hooker and each other. Lincoln informally sounded out Maj. Gen. John Reynolds of I Corps about taking command. He turned down the opportunity, citing his fears of Washington's interference. Many of the rank and file wanted a change too. Some clamored for McClellan, a notion that left Radical Republicans horror stricken. In the meantime, Federal soldiers headed for home as two-year enlistments ran out. After Chancellorsville, Hooker lost about 20 percent of his army in this manner, not counting his 12-percent battlefield casualties.[1]

Across the river, Lee could not suppress his soaring confidence despite the death of Jackson and the additional loss of a dozen brigade commanders. With God's obvious help, his men had done the impossible. Now that Longstreet and his troops back with the army, Lee advocated doing it again. Called to Richmond in mid-May to discuss the Federal noose tightening in the West, the general responded with bold plans for a second invasion of the North that would safeguard Virginia while forcing Grant away from Vicksburg. Privately, Lee hoped that shoving the Federal army across the Susquehanna River also would force Lincoln to abandon Washington. More fundamentally, the drought of 1862 and the late planting of crops in 1863 had left Lee's men and horses running out of sustenance. In order to feed his army, the general had to go elsewhere. At a second conference on May 26—just as Grant settled down for the siege of Vicksburg—Davis yielded. Lee planned to go through the Shenandoah Valley to the Potomac and beyond. Hooker would have to abandon war-blighted Fredericksburg and follow.

Federal pickets and scouts caught on quickly, yet Hooker hesitated. On May 27, he began to shift his men, but only in anticipation of an enemy attack from Fredericksburg. Lee misjudged his foe as well. The Confederate commander stayed in place until he learned that Union forces in southeastern Virginia were not moving on Richmond as feared. The next day, June 3, two-thirds of the Army of Northern Virginia quietly decamped for Culpeper Court House, moving slowly in case Hooker tried to pounce on Richmond. Lt. Gen. A. P. Hill's newly organized Third Corps remained behind as a rear guard. Spotty rain left roads sticky but passable. These surfaces quickly dried into powdery dust as the army advanced. Temperatures measured in the mideighties. Confederates groaned about marching in such heat, the worst many of them had endured thus far in the war, according to historian Robert Wynstra. One Alabamian complained that a third of his brigade fell out on the road.

Two more days passed before Hooker deduced Lee's intentions. He sent Sedgwick across the Rappahannock to feel the enemy while asking Washington for permission to attack the tail of the Confederate column. The White House smelled a trap and refused; Lincoln told Hooker to head off Lee.[2] Hooker then ordered his cavalry to attack Stuart's horsemen at the column's head. Scouts reported the Rebel cavalry near Brandy Station on the Orange and Alexandria Railroad, where Stuart screened the two infantry corps at Culpeper. Brig. Gen. Alfred Pleasonton's column of Union horse soldiers moved out on June 6 through fatiguing heat (86 degrees) and afternoon thunderstorms that bothered Lee's columns as well. The next day saw clearing skies and cooler temperatures, with Washington's afternoon high only reaching 70 degrees. June 8 was even cooler, with lows dropping into the fifties overnight and only rising to 66 degrees during the day. Such weather was perfect not only for the grand review Stuart staged for Lee at Brandy Station that day but also for Pleasonton's closing columns. That night, temperatures fell into the upper fifties. The next morning, the Federals waded the foggy Rappahannock and shocked Stuart. For the rest of the long, hot day—the afternoon high reached 82 degrees—the two forces fought the largest cavalry battle of the war in a choking dome of road dust and smoke so thick that it obscured the colors of uniforms.[3] Stuart's Confederates survived, but the Federals' good showing signified the end of Confederate cavalry dominance in the East. But Pleasonton accomplished little else. Based on what scant intelligence his cavalry provided, Hooker pressed again for permission to attack Hill. If Lee kept moving north, he even proposed seizing Richmond before sending men back north to deal with the Rebel army. Lincoln blanched, suspecting that Hooker wanted no part of Lee again. Destroying the Army of Northern Virginia was his goal, the president reminded the general, not Richmond.

Hooker finally shifted toward Culpeper. Still uncertain of Lee's intentions, he aimed to stay between the Confederates and Washington. He also divided his army into two wings: One would fall back quickly up the Orange and Alexandria Railroad toward Manassas, while the other would hold ground as the army shifted its base from Aquia Creek. As historian Edwin Coddington maintains, those plans surrendered the initiative to Lee, who on beastly hot June 15 finally called for Hill to come on. Lt. Gen. Richard Ewell's reorganized Second Corps was at Winchester, albeit weakened by hundreds of men who had fallen out amid the 90-degree heat. Maj. Gen. Robert Rodes's division was across the Potomac, and Confederate cavalry was already in Pennsylvania, sweeping up a bounty of supplies, kidnapping African Americans, and otherwise raising hell. Longstreet's First Corps was moving north toward Ewell while guarding the gaps for Hill. Lee's army thus was stretched out like a rattlesnake, with its rattles still at Fredericksburg but its fangs in the Union.[4] "The animal must be very slim somewhere," Lincoln observed to Hooker. "Could you not break him?"[5]

The weather grew hotter and drier. June 15 was the first of four straight days to reach into the nineties in Washington. Aside from a refreshing shower during the afternoon of the eleventh, the only substantial precipitation until the end of the month came with thunder, lightning, and heavy downpours all night on June 13 and again on June 18 and June 19. Nearly an inch of rain fell each evening, making roads slick enough to slow progress before drying out. At the headquarters of Hooker's Signal Corps, lighting struck a tree on the eighteenth and stunned several men. High in the Blue Ridge, that same storm brought hail and sleet. Capt. A. W. Bartlett of the 12th New Hampshire remembered a temperature drop of 26 degrees, which left wet men suffering for the coats and blankets they had thrown away. Rain late on June 19 left mud to the ankles. Lt. Thomas Galwey observed how rain had eroded graves containing First Bull Run casualties.

Thunderstorms aside, the main story during this stage of the campaign was heat and dust. Lee's march into the Valley carried the army into a different universe of soil. Parallel streams of grayish-brown Alfisols and browner

Inceptsols stretched to the southwest from New York and Pennsylvania into Virginia like the colors of a runny oil painting, with small islands of red clay added for variety. There was enough dust to encompass both armies like a turtle's shell, but Union troops had it worse. Their forced marches took them north along the Orange and Alexandria railroad through Virginia's hotter and parched piedmont—with its now-familiar red clay—east of the mountains. Federal accounts invariably describe baked rutted roads, barren fields, and dangerous heat, especially as temperatures between June 15 and June 18 surpassed 90 degrees.[6] Marsena Patrick complained, "it is killing for men to march in this weather."[7]

June 15, with its afternoon high of 92 degrees and few shade trees along the march route, was the deadliest day of all. A. W. Bartlett remembered dust so deep and thick that men covered their faces with their handkerchiefs and wet them until they ran out of water. Many collapsed; the ambulances were full. Sgt. John Hartwell of the 121st New York wrote, "hundreds fell Sun Struck some died . . . was extremely hot & dust so thick many times we could not see 2 rods."[8] Pvt. Wilbur Fisk of the 2nd Vermont would have agreed. "All day long," he wrote, "we tugged our weary knapsacks in the broiling sun, and many fell out to fall out no more. . . . The dry dirt seemed to be particularly adapted to draw the rays of the sun, and the blistering heat of the road reflected, seemed like the breath from a furnace, seven times heated. The road was lined with stragglers, and many fell dead in their tracks. Our corps alone lost forty-six men from sunstroke. Some say that other corps lost upwards of a hundred each."[9] John Haley of the 17th Maine described the road dust as "scalding. . . . The soil of Virginia was sucked into our throats, sniffed into our nostrils, and flew into our eyes and ears until our most intimate friends would not have recognized us. On no other march have we suffered so with thirst and heat. . . . [M]en fell by the roadside to die from sunstroke." They marched until nearly midnight.[10]

The next day, Ewell broke Federal resistance at Winchester. One Union survivor described massive straggling during their retreat due to "the excessive heat of the day."[11] June 17 was no better, with the afternoon high reaching 94 degrees.[12] Col. Robert McAlister of the 11th New Jersey complained of "roads more dusty than I had ever witnessed"[13] Rufus Dawes of the 6th Wisconsin compared the sun to a "furnace" and added: "Many a poor fellow marched his last day yesterday. Several men fell dead on the road."[14] Lt. Charles Brewster claimed that a division in VI Corps lost thirty men to sunstroke; ten died. Occasionally, onlookers pitied the trudging

Yankees. Judging the temperature as "100 ½ degrees," one described how "a woman marched in the ranks, carrying the accoutrements of an exhausted soldier."[15]

Charles Wainwright, meanwhile, described an "intensely hot" and dusty day that brought the Federal I Corps to the old Chantilly battleground. "The air was very hot and close out on the open; for these two miles it was intolerable—absolutely difficult to breathe. . . . I felt as I should suffocate while there. The sides of the road were lined with men, who had dropped from exhaustion. There must have been near a thousand of them, many of whom had fainted entirely away." On June 19, he and others first noticed drought. "The country is very dry," the major wrote. "The crops, were there any, would be suffering from the drought on this sandy soil."[16]

In contrast, Jed Hotchkiss described the Shenandoah as green and thriving. "We found the grass, clover, and timothy, perfectly luxuriant," he wrote in his journal on June 11, "a great change from the bare fields of Fredericksburg."[17] Yet while there was less evidence of drought west of the Blue Ridge at that stage, the Confederates still sweltered. A growing lack of water due to the absence of springs along mountain roads was agonizing. Trying to catch up with Ewell, Longstreet's and Hill's troops marched hard. Fainting men fell out in droves. Sgt. Randolph Shotwell wrote extensively of the agonies of marching on June 17:

> Dead or alive? I am sure I hardly know which! If not dead we soon shall be, if there is not a change of some sort. Flesh and blood cannot sustain such heat and fatigue as we have undergone this day. It is terrible! All along the roadside since 9 o 'clock this morning I have seen men dropping, gasping, dying,—or already dead! Think of it! Most of our men are just out of winter-quarters, where they were well screened from the Sun; and now under the combined effect of heat, fatigue, thirst, and intolerable dust they wilt and drop, like wax-figures in a fiery furnace! The dust is almost suffocating! Pulverized by sixty thousand pairs of feet of men, and nearly as many of horses and cattle, it forms a fine impalpable powder, sufficiently light to fill the air like smoke; and penetrate the eyes, ears, nostrils, hair, and skin, until its power of annoyance is unbearable! Then, when one's clothing is utterly saturated with perspiration mixing with the dust in a grimy paste; and above all, weighs the heavy musket, the muffling blankets, gripping waist band and belt (upon which hang the heavy cartridge and cap boxes) and the chafing

canteen straps—is it strange that one sees hundreds of men gasping for breath, and lolling out their tongues like madmen? Is it any wonder that coup de soleil is of hourly occurrence! Some of the men say that fully two dozen men were killed today by sun stroke. I saw that number "down" but whether they recovered subsequently I cannot say.[18]

Only as men climbed higher into the mountains did conditions change. "Gracious! What a contrast!" Shotwell wrote on June 18, as his regiment passed through a gap in the Blue Ridge. "This evening we are positively shivering around our camp-fires, with hail and sleet falling upon us, the ground white with snow. . . . Some of the hail-stones were as large as hickory nuts."[19]

On June 19, Lt. Charles Blackford described more men dead from sunstroke along the road. Two days later, Federal Rufus Dawes noted, "One of our men in company 'I' has become a lunatic from the effect of the heat."[20] By then, however, the heatwave finally broke. The high temperature that afternoon only reached 81 degrees, and it rained hard that night. The next nine days were notably cooler, with a high of 70 degrees on rainy June 20, an ever cooler high of 61 degrees on the cloudy summer solstice, and highs in the seventies after that. Overnight lows generally remained in the sixties. It grew significantly wetter as well. Rain on the afternoon of June 19 and again on the twentieth raised the Potomac and its local tributaries to the degree that the Confederate advance stalled for two days. Afternoon drizzle on June 22 grew hard after dark. Hill's corps marched through hard rain in Hagerstown on the twenty-fourth. More rain two days later mired roads north of the Potomac. Rain and wind from the northeast that day also annoyed Maj. Gen. Jubal Early's division of Ewell's corps as it rousted the local militia out of a lovely Pennsylvania college town called Gettysburg. Another hard rain followed the next day, leaving some of Early's men knee deep in mud and hundreds straggling. Drizzle returned on June 28 and June 29, then rained from darkened skies into the night, sometimes hard, the next day.[21]

Dawes found the rain unusual. "I don't think I ever before saw at this time of year such a long continued, misty, drizzling storm as we have been marching through since we crossed the Potomac."[22] He was right, but only to a point. At Pennsylvania College in Gettysburg, the Rev. Dr. Michael Jacobs was both a professor and a minister. He also was the Smithsonian's longtime local-weather observer as well as an affiliate of Philadelphia's

Franklin Institute. In his cramped hand, he recorded 2.71 inches of rain in June 1863, with over half of that (1.43 inches) falling from the twenty-fifth through the end of the month. By way of comparison, between June 25 and June 30, rain fell three times in 1861 (total 0.179 inches), once in 1862 (0.176 inches), and five times in 1863. The last week of June 1863 was rainier than it had been recently, but not to a significant degree. Still, the roads south from Jacobs's office were already wet and muddy after days of rain as the opposing armies approached him for an unexpected rendezvous.[23]

As the weather evolved, so did the campaign. From June 17 and into relatively chilly June 21, the cavalry engaged in a running fight from Aldie to Middleburg to Upperville in northern Virginia as the Confederates screened their army's march. Ewell was north of the river scouring the region for supplies, Longstreet was moving toward the Potomac, and Hill had just arrived in the Valley. Divisions of both Hill's and Longstreet's corps began crossing the Potomac on the twenty-fourth. Evidence of Ewell's continuing movement north, screened by Stuart until his three cavalry brigades rode off on a still-controversial raid, demanded a reaction. Only on drizzly June 25, after he realized that all of Lee's army was in Maryland and panic-stricken Pennsylvania, did Hooker give orders to cross the river and give chase. By the evening of the twenty-seventh, his entire army was north of the Potomac, camped east of the passes through South Mountain. The heart of Lee's command, however, was almost fifty miles farther away in Chambersburg, at the northern end of the macadamized road network that ran back into the Shenandoah. Elements of Ewell's corps stretched even farther to the northeast, toward the Susquehanna River and Harrisburg. Everywhere the Confederates went, they gobbled up food, horses, and other supplies from the previously untroubled countryside. They also kidnapped hundreds more African Americans, intending to reenslave any former bondspeople among them.

What Hooker would have done about Lee remains open to question. On June 27, he went to Harpers Ferry, hoping to absorb its garrison into his army. When Halleck expressed his unwillingness to abandon that position, Hooker submitted his resignation, which the president accepted.[24] Lincoln and Halleck's choice to replace him was one of Hooker's most vocal opponents, corps commander George Meade. By turns aristocratic and disagreeable, he took command of the Army of the Potomac at Frederick, Maryland, on drizzly June 28. Halleck ordered him to lead the army toward the Susquehanna while covering Washington and Baltimore. Meade issued orders to concentrate near Frederick and move to the Pennsylvania border the next day. For good measure, he also called away the Harpers Ferry garrison that had cost Hooker his army. Bone-tired men again took to the road on rainy June 29. Despite traffic jams and confusion, most made twenty miles that day and camped just south of the state line. Reports placed Longstreet and Hill at Chambersburg, moving toward Gettysburg, while Ewell's twin columns were astride the Pennsylvania Railroad at Carlisle and near the vital railroad bridge across the Susquehanna at York. Meade shifted two corps to his left to reinforce the two already at Emmitsburg under Reynolds. During the rainy day, he made plans to keep moving after Lee while preparing a stout—and later controversial—entrenched line in the rear. Historians continue to debate which his first priority was, but Meade ordered his army toward Gettysburg while giving the aggressive Reynolds discretion to initiate battle.[25] Rain left some roads "almost impassable" for the army, as divisional commander Maj. Gen. David Birney of the III Corps complained.[26]

Lee learned that the Federals had crossed the Potomac on June 28. He gave up any designs on Harrisburg and ordered a concentration at Cashtown, east of one of South Mountain's vital passes and eight miles west of Gettysburg. Geography constrained Confederate options; holding the passes was crucial if Lee wanted to get home with the immense trains of foraged and badly needed stores, which stretched out over fourteen miles long, and the herds of livestock that perhaps numbered up to 50,000 head of cattle, 35,000 sheep, and 20,000 horses and mules. By the rainy night of June 30, the Army of Northern Virginia's concentration nearly was complete. Hill and Longstreet were on the scene, and Ewell was a day's march to the north. Tired men slept on soggy ground around Gettysburg.[27]

Lee was adamant that no fighting take place until the army was reunited. Combat began anyway. According to Professor Jacobs—who continued to take his routine weather observations throughout the three-day battle—

July 1 dawned warm and cloudy, with a temperature of 72 degrees and a slight breeze from the south. That morning, Maj. Gen. Henry Heth's division of Hill's corps encountered Brig. Gen. John Buford's two cavalry brigades, which had dismounted northwest of Gettysburg. Buford's horse soldiers bought valuable time for Reynolds, whose infantry began to arrive midmorning. About noon, the ill-fated XI Corps arrived and went into line on the right of a developing arc in order to check Ewell's approaching corps. The temperature rose only slightly, to 76 degrees, while the afternoon sky largely cleared. Nevertheless, exertion and wool uniforms made the day feel hot. Hill and Ewell fed men into the unexpected battle until Lee arrived and unleashed them completely. The Confederates broke the Federal line and hammered it south through the streets of Gettysburg and onto the high ground beyond. Lee asked Ewell to keep pushing until he surmounted Cemetery Hill, the northernmost point of the fishhook-shaped high ground south of Gettysburg. Ewell demurred. That night, clouds returned, but temperatures remained steady. The rest of Meade's army arrived and went into line all along the rugged heights, from Culp's Hill at the fishhook's northeastern barb to formidable Little Round Top at its southern eye. Out to the west, Lee ignored Longstreet's pleas to back away to another position like Fredericksburg and made plans to attack the Federal flanks.[28]

July 2 was much hotter, starting out at 74 degrees at 7 A.M. and reaching 81 degrees at 2 P.M. A soft southern wind offered little relief. While dawn and dusk were cloudy, midday brought a near cloudless sky.[29] Some men found the weather pleasant, but others complained that the day was "scorching."[30] In such temperatures, the armies fought until well after dark. On the Union left, Longstreet launched a late-afternoon attack that carried his men through the bizarre, rocky moonscape of Devil's Den to the eastern slope of Little Round Top. His soldiers fought doggedly and, while coming close, were unable to turn the position. Heat, a lack of water, and fatigue all played roles in blunting Confederate success, at least as far as they were concerned. Lt. Col. L. H. Scruggs of the 4th Alabama complained that his men marched twenty-four miles to reach the battlefield and were already worn down when they went into action. He blamed fatigue and the steep topography for their failure to secure Little Round Top. Many of Col. William Oates's Alabamians fainted from exhaustion, heat, and thirst during the ascent of Big Round Top; he halted and let them lie down several minutes before advancing. Oates also sent men back to a well a hundred yards in the rear to fill canteens. To his dismay, the general attack began before the water bearers returned; those men became disoriented and were captured. Years later, Oates wondered if an extra five minutes and full canteens would have resulted in victory. Instead, the Confederate assault failed as Col. Joshua Chamberlain led his now-legendary bayonet charge down the hill against the Alabamians. The heat in the close woods and the day's exertions drained Oates to the degree that he turned over regimental command to a subordinate at the foot of Little Round Top. A mile north, an equally desperate attack through a peach orchard and wheat field produced similar, bloody results. As night fell, Ewell tardily launched attacks on Cemetery Hill and Culp's Hill that achieved little. As a bright moon rose in the sky, 18,000 fresh casualties lay on the field, nearly doubling the battle's total losses to that point.[31]

And there were thousands more to come. Convinced that Meade's line almost had broken, Lee again ignored Longstreet and renewed the battle on July 3. Noting increased Federal strength on the flanks, Lee concluded that the Union center had to be weakened if the flanks were reinforced. First light brought unfinished business elsewhere, as the Federals on Culp's Hill began fighting to regain its slope. The day was already warm, as overnight temperatures had dipped no lower than 73 degrees. Under another cloudy sky, the renewed contest for the hill began, stretching into the afternoon. By 2 P.M., with the Culp's Hill fighting ended and Longstreet's massed artillery pounding the Federal center in anticipation of the final assault, the temperature was 87 degrees, the hottest day of July in Gettysburg. Gathering clouds and a slight breeze signaled a summer thunderstorm on the horizon as Longstreet's mile-wide line of battle, the 14,000-man strong Pickett-Pettigrew Charge, prepared to advance from the east. Ordered to remain in the open for hours rather than rest in the shade of Seminary Ridge's trees to the rear, some of Pickett's men already were so prostrated by the heat that they could neither stand up nor march forward. Others collapsed from sunstroke once in line. Some shammed heat prostration, leading to moments of anger and confusion as to who was shirking and who was actually sick. Weather historian David Ludlum theorizes that it probably was 90 degrees when the Confederates marched in parade-ground order over a mile of open ground toward Cemetery Ridge. Union artillery and then rifle fire ripped great holes in the Confederate line as it drew near. Some of the attackers crossed the Emmitsburg Road, and a few hundred even penetrated the Federal line before reserves sealed the breach. The assault failed. In the mile between the two armies, thousands of dead and wounded littered the baked earth.[32]

~~~

Historians often describe the three days of Gettysburg as hot, but average afternoon highs only reached July norms on the third. If anything, the first two days of the battle were cool for the month. David Ludlum believes that a Bermuda high prevailed over the entire eastern half of the nation during the battle, creating "stagnant conditions typical of summertime." Yet conditions already were evolving. Analyzing Jacobs's data, Ludlum identifies "the transformation during the battle period of a modified polar air mass into one having tropical characteristics."[33] The next phase began when the thunderstorm that had threatened all day finally hit before midnight. Soldiers described wet uniforms, waterlogged rifle pits, and flooded tents as they caught glimpses of the carnage on the field through flashes of lightning.[34]

That stormy night, Lee prepared his retreat, hoping to find a place north of the Potomac where Meade might do the attacking. Two possible routes beckoned, both of which involved steep climbs and descents. Going back the way they came involved utilizing the macadamized Chambersburg Pike, first west to Cashtown Pass, then south through Maryland to the Potomac at Williamsport. A more direct route ran though Fairfield, around Jack's Mountain, across South Mountain at steep and narrow Monterey Pass, and then on to Williamsport via Hagerstown. This was shorter by twenty miles but contained long sections of dirt roads. In south-central Pennsylvania, that meant crossing not only parallel bands of Alfisols and Inceptisols but also a thin finger of "bottomless" red clay Ultisols pointing north from the Potomac and through Gettysburg's Adams County right up to where it poked Devil's Den and the Round Tops. Lee chose to use both. Brig. Gen. John Imboden's cavalry would shepherd the army's longer train, seized supplies, five batteries of artillery, and all the wounded who could be moved over the longer route. Preceded by a second long train that left before daylight on the Fourth of July, the infantry and most of the artillery would take the Fairfield Road the next night. Additional cavalry would screen both columns. The next day involved anxious preparations. With his own army battered and bloodied, not to mention stuck in the mud as well, Meade spent the day feeding and resting his men. The day's heat combined with the stench of 7,000 dead men and 3,000 dead animals, human and animal waste, sweat, and lingering gunsmoke to produce a toxic atmosphere.[35]

Weather impeded Lee more than Meade did. July 4 was cooler, with highs reaching only 76 degrees before falling back to 69 degrees at 9 P.M. The wind shifted to the west and southwest. The barometer dropped. Dreary dawn brought brief but heavy showers beginning at around 6 A.M., then a thunderstorm after noon. Another thunderstorm with torrential rain blew up at 2:30 P.M. local time and lasted until four o'clock. It rained yet again after dark, starting at about 10:30 P.M. and persisting through the night, blocking out the full moon and producing an inky black sky. Professor Jacobs measured 1.39 inches of precipitation at the end of the day.[36]

The cycles of rain on the fourth made life difficult in the Federal camps, leaving tents awash and wounded men occasionally in danger of drowning in swollen creeks. Exhausted soldiers could not rest. Emergency troops approaching Gettysburg encountered knee-deep mud and creeks flooded to the degree that some of those men nearly drowned too. But the weather exponentially compounded the misery for the Confederates. Imboden and his train, seventeen miles long, rolled out in the afternoon rain. Longstreet's and then Hill's corps stole away in the dark, with Ewell's train already gone and leading the way. The Second Corps took up the rear at 2 A.M.[37] The roads were a "universal quagmire," according to J. F. J. Caldwell. Rain fell rapidly, with occasional flashes of lightning.[38] On the Cashtown route with the long train, it was hard going. Lee had told Imboden to avoid Chambersburg itself and keep moving whatever the obstacles, but the roads were worse than the commanding general had anticipated. The narrow Fairfield route was even tougher. Lee considered returning to Gettysburg, the only thing stopping him being that Imboden already had left.[39]

"We started off in the rain," musician Julius Lineback of the 26th North Carolina wrote from Imboden's column, "and travelled until 9 or 10 o'clock, a motley procession of wagons, ambulances, wounded men on foot, straggling soldiers and band boys, splashing along in the mud, weary, sad and discouraged."[40] The night was full of misery. Artilleryman George Neese remembered: "The road was muddy and slippery, the night dark; rainy, dreary, and dismal. The train moved very slowly, with halts and starts all night. Every time an ambulance wheel struck a rock I heard the pitiful groans of the wounded."[41] Most wagons had no covers, and rain beat in their faces of the wounded. Along the way, exhausted men got lost or fell back into the muck. Horses refused to pull; some died in the road. When the roads jammed up, teamsters steered into surrounding fields only to bog down in mud and the crushed remnants of crops.[42]

Out on the Fairfield Road, Pvt. Westwood Todd of the 12th Virginia described a column barely holding together as a fighting force. "The heavy rain which continued throughout that night of inky darkness, and the passage of army trains and artillery made the roads almost impassable for foot soldiers," he wrote. "We were up to our knees in mud and water all night. It was impossible to preserve the company organization in such darkness and difficult marching. The men would halloo out the names of their companies in order to keep together."[43]

Reports of Lee's retreat came in to Federal headquarters in the early morning hours of July 5. They did nothing to change Meade's plans. He decided to harass the enemy with cavalry while force-marching the bulk of his army south on the longer but better-constructed route east of the mountains. The Harpers Ferry garrison, having reached Frederick, would hold the South Mountain passes. At Middletown, Maryland, seven miles west of Frederick, he planned to turn west through the gaps and hit Lee's exposed flank. Frederick offered the added advantage of railroads and turnpikes that made it an excellent supply base for an ill-supplied army marching without trains. Meade was confident that he could take the time to rest his men first, as he had the better road and the rising Potomac would prevent Lee's escape. Unconvinced, Washington began to badger him to pursue and beat the Confederates north of the river.

Late on the rainy morning of July 5, Meade issued orders. Sedgwick's fresh corps would trail Lee to find out whether he was fleeing or looking for another place to fight. The rest of the Army of the Potomac would head south in three columns. These would rendezvous at Middletown in two days and, reunited, fight Lee somewhere in Maryland. But the fog of war already had intervened. A detachment of Federal cavalry had attacked Ewell's supply train overnight at Monterey Pass. Brig. Gen. Judson Kirkpatrick, commanding that force, erroneously boasted that he had struck and largely destroyed Lee's main train. When Sedgwick's corps caught up with the rear guard west of Fairfield on the fifth, more skirmishing followed. Both Sedgwick and Brig. Gen. Gouverneur Warren, Meade's chief engineer and acting chief of staff, misread the situation. Warren told his boss that Lee's main column had stopped and was fortifying. Although he feared fighting at the mountain gaps, Meade did not hesitate. He recalled his other moving parts and redirected his army toward Fairfield, while ordering Sedgwick to find out for sure the enemy's size and intentions. It was only midday on July 6 that Sedgwick admitted that Lee was still in full retreat. By then, Meade wanted no part of the muddy, churned-up route the Confederates had used. The next day, he restarted the originally planned concentration east of the mountains. Thirty hours, largely rainy, were lost.[44]

Lee's mud-splattered army approached the Potomac in fits and starts. Both columns stretched out to thirty miles in length. Aggressive Union cavalry menaced the Confederates all the way to the river. The retreat was thoroughly miserable, "about as cheerful as a tomb," according to Cpl. George Neese.[45] "What sorry specimums of humanity we 'rebels' must have appeared," Sgt. William White wrote, "standing in that muddy road with our 'Confederate grey' drenched to our very skins, our slouched hats drawn down over our faces, and our forms trembling and shaking with cold."[46] Aside from a brief lull at midmorning, rain had continued into the fifth. The skies were dark, complementing a morning low of 69 degrees and an afternoon high that increased only three degrees. Near Greencastle, local citizens attacked a lost segment of the train with axes, disabling wagons, while small contingents of cavalry made brief forays against it. Late in the afternoon, a thunderstorm struck as Confederates struggled up into the mountains and tried to rest without fires. July 6 was rainy but at least warmer, with a high of 76 degrees at 2 P.M. Back in Gettysburg, the clouds parted and bright sky reappeared toward evening. Farther south, however, Confederates reported more rain into the wee hours of the seventh. The wind shifted from south to north overnight, alerting observers to another approaching storm.

The routes remained exceedingly bad. Mud in the Fairfield Road was at least a foot deep. In some spots, soldiers waded in water and mud to their knees. Dead horses, wounded men, abandoned wagons, and strewn equipment clogged their path.[47] Lineback described roads "deep with a gritty mud that wore the feet of our barefooted boys badly and getting into the shoes of those who possessed such articles, was almost as bad for them."[48] Lt. J. E. Green of the 53rd North Carolina wrote in his diary that the artillery "cut up" the roads so badly that day that the infantry finally "left the road and marched through fields, and those fields were sone in wheat which was then almost ripe, & was finely ruined by being tramped down."[49]

Despite rain, mud, and Federal horsemen, the first wagons of Imboden's train pulled into dreary Williamsport during the evening on July 6. The process continued throughout the night until the town was all but gridlocked with 5,000 wagons and ambulances. Soldiers found oceans of deep, sandy, yellowish-brown Inceptisol mud there. Also, at thirteen feet, the Potomac ran dangerously high and was full of debris. To Imboden's delight, a Confederate ordnance train was waiting across the river with more ammunition. Yet the situation remained dire. Federal horsemen on the fourth had destroyed the pontoon bridge four miles downriver at Falling Waters. All that remained was the Williamsport ferry, connected to Virginia by a single cable—and Imboden nearly lost that. Rallying wounded men and teamsters, however, he fought off Federal cavalry until help arrived.[50]

The next day, similar to the previous one in temperatures, saw the rest of the army begin arriving in Williamsport. The town now stank with tons of wet livestock manure and thousands of diarrheic men. There was the smell of death too. Over a thousand sheep and 700 cattle drowned in a failed river crossing on July 7; their carcasses snagged in the river or washed ashore as far downriver as Harpers Ferry. Buzzing green flies swarmed everywhere. Williamsport was an ecological death trap, yet there was little chance to escape it. Lee found the Potomac out of its banks. The bad weather did not let up either, as rain fell periodically all day and continued heavily into the night before finally stopping.[51] The river continued to rise until it reached "near-record height."[52] "It is an open question when we shall cross to 'Ole Virginny Shore,'" Randolph Shotwell wrote.[53]

Barricaded by the flooded Potomac and running out of food and forage, Lee had no choice but to prepare to fight with the river at his back. On July 11, engineers laid out an extensive nine-mile-long line that ran along high ground from a dam near the river to a creek near Hagerstown. It covered the road into Williamsport as well as the ford at Falling Waters, four miles distant. A waist-high creek and flooded lowlands with knee-deep mud stretched out in front of the works. Observers and later historians judged the position as strong as the Confederate works at Fredericksburg. A welcome change in the weather facilitated construction. On July 8, the rain diminished into drizzle and ceased entirely after 2 P.M. Dark skies cleared on the ninth, while only light rain returned the next day. Clear skies and warmer temperatures dried out men and earth into July 11. In Gettysburg, Jacobs recorded successive highs of 72 degrees, 81 degrees, 79 degrees, and 84 degrees, along with winds from the north or west and a rising barometer.[54]

~~~

Meade's "multi-pronged race to the Potomac River" began in earnest on July 7, the third day of sustained rain.[55] Despite the better-constructed pikes on his route, the Federals' path south toward Frederick took them through the rare northern band of sticky, bottomless red clay. Pvt. John Haley compared the mud to lard. When wagons and artillery stalled in the roads, infantry took to the boggy red fields, which promptly sucked at their feet and legs. Despite horrendous mud, flooded creeks, steady rain, and an evening thunderstorm, Meade's corps commanders drove their men furiously. Elements of the XI Corps marched over thirty miles straight into Middletown, and by midnight, the army straddled the Maryland mountains. Meade was delighted. He was a day ahead of schedule, and his supply trains were arriving with desperately needed shoes, uniforms, and food. The forced march came at a steep price, however. Like a runner sprinting at the beginning of a marathon, the first day of the pursuit exhausted the Army of the Potomac. Men collapsed in muddy bivouacs along the road and rolled up in wet blankets. Many now were shoeless thanks to the mud.[56] "We rose sick, tired, played out, and crosser than a dozen she-bears," John Haley remembered. "Our clothes and blankets were wet and heavy and we had no chance to dry them. Such depression swept over me that I suffered a collapse of nearly all my powers so that it was almost impossible to proceed when the column was set in motion at six o'clock."[57]

Some soldiers encountered heavy fog on the mountain slopes, but all endured rain falling so hard that they could not light fires. "It has done nothing but pour since we left Gettysburg," New York artilleryman Lt. George Breck groaned. "It rained pitchforks. The only way we could see to picket and feed our horses was by feeling."[58] Drizzle and rain continued into the afternoon before the sun came out, creating more knee-deep red mud on the road to Frederick. Professor Jacobs recorded 1.3 inches of rain in Gettysburg that day. One officer described rusting swords and rifles. Between the armies, cavalry sparred for the gaps. At Boonsboro on the National Road, Buford's artillery fought off Stuart. Six inches of wheat-field mud retarded the guns' recoil to the degree that all but one of the gun carriages suffered broken axles. The muddy struggle south continued, especially for those brigades that had not yet crossed the mountains. Artillery horses could no longer pull. While specific numbers are unavailable, historian Kent Masterson Brown indicates that, from the beginning of the campaign through July 9, the Army of the Potomac ruined 15,000 horses. Two corps marched without artillery due to a lack of healthy horses.

Meade made his headquarters at Turner's Gap and arrayed his army in a north–south line west of the mountains, from near Sharpsburg up to Boonsboro, or roughly along the dividing line between the firmer Alfisol belt to the front and the bottomless Ultisol in the rear. As the weather turned dry and hot, he advanced carefully. A cavalry victory on July 10 allowed him to push troops up to within two miles of Lee's works while making contact with the river. Federal troops probed the enemy line the next day as the sky again began to darken. Convinced that Lee planned to stand and fight, Meade knew there was much to do before launching an assault so as not to replicate Fredericksburg. All of the army was not yet up, as I Corps was still negotiating South Mountain, and Halleck insisted that Meade hold off until he maximized his numbers with those soldiers. Men and horses desperately needed rest and food. Unreliable emergency troops and nine-month volunteers, already worn out, required integration into the army. It took a day to replace worn-out uniforms and especially shoes; rain, mud, and jagged macadamized roads had left much of his army barefoot.[59]

July 12 was hot, with an afternoon high of 84 degrees in Gettysburg. Dark clouds had gathered overnight, and around 3 A.M. a violent thunderstorm announced the beginning of a new rainy period that would bring another half inch of rain to Gettysburg over the next two days. Morning fog was thick and, combined with rain, disrupted Federal signal corpsmen. In Maryland, the armies shifted their positions despite deep mud that adhered to shoes and wheels. When Ewell abandoned Hagerstown under pressure and fell back to the Potomac, Meade occupied the town. Lee expected an all-out attack on his left any moment, but it did not come.

By nightfall, Meade's army stretched south along the Hagerstown Pike to beyond the National Road, with Antietam Creek to its back. Lee's waited in a parallel line just to the west. Meade wrote Washington that he would attack the Confederates on the morrow, but he soon developed second thoughts. The ghosts of Fredericksburg again haunted the army that dark,

rainy night. Meade called another council of war. A majority of corps commanders vehemently opposed an assault; Lee's works seemed formidable.
Meade flinched. But the next day, after riding to the front in the continuing
rain, he resolved to attack anyway. He ordered a reconnaissance in force
all along the line for 7 A.M. on July 14; an assault would follow. Men in the
ranks assumed that the rain was responsible for the delay.[60] Major Wainwright wrote that the rain had left "the fallow fields in such a state that it
was difficult even to walk about them. To have kept the batteries supplied
with ammunition or to have charged in line over them would have been
impossible."[61]

While Meade wavered, Lee was busy. He was willing to fight another
Sharpsburg, but Meade's refusal to attack frustrated him. Williamsport, too,
had become a stinking and potentially lethal menace. And the Potomac
threatened to rise again with the recent rains. All day on July 12, three ferries ran wagons across the river. "Most of the horses had to be *swum over*,"
Pvt. Edward Moore of the Rockbridge Artillery remembered, "as there was
little room in the ferry-boats for them. The river was so high that this was
very dangerous, and only expert swimmers dared to undertake it. . . . I saw
numbers swept down by the current and landed hundreds of yards below,
many on the side from which they had started."[62]

Near-constant rain and frequent storms marked the next day. Near
Frederick, a landslide stopped a train full of Federal reinforcements. At
Falling Waters, Lee's engineers completed rebuilding the pontoon bridge
using lumber stripped from Williamsport homes and buildings. At Williamsport itself, the river was fordable, but at a depth of four feet, it was
still deep enough so that smaller horses had to swim. And runoff from
the latest rains was flooding it again. Lee saw God's hand in the brief window of opportunity and took it. That night, with temperatures falling into
the upper sixties along with occasional thunder and lightning, the infantry
began crossing back to Virginia as bands played to cover the noise. Ewell's
corps forded at Williamsport, while the rest of the army took the bridge.
The night was pitch black; a few torches did little to help visibility. The
fast-moving river reached up to soldiers' armpits or even their faces as they
crossed, their weapons and cartridges held up over their heads. Rain kept
falling, sometimes in sheets. On the banks, soldiers found mud in depths
that reached from the ankles to the knees; it sucked off thousands of shoes.
In an environment where men simply had trouble standing up, straggling
grew ubiquitous.[63] Describing the "dense night and yellow mud," Val Giles

of the 4th Texas remembered a comrade who complained, "Hell is not a half mile from here."[64]

Longstreet wrote of the terrible night:

At the ends of the bridge were green willow poles to prevent the wheels cutting through the mud, but the soil underneath was wet and soggy under the long season of rain, and before night rain again began to fall. The night that followed was one seldom experienced even in the life of a soldier. The rain fell in showers, sometimes in blinding sheets, during the entire night; the wagons cut deep in the mud during the early hours, and began to "stall" going down the hill, and one or two of the batteries were "stalled" before they reached the bridge. The best standing points were ankle deep in mud, and the roads half-way to the knee, puddling and getting worse. We could only keep three or four torches alight, and those were dimmed at times when heavy rains came. Then, to crown our troubles, a load of the wounded came down, missed the end of the bridge, and plunged the wagon into a raging torrent. . . . The ground under the poles became so puddled before daylight that they would bend under the wheels and feet of the animals until they could bend no further, and then would occasionally slip to one side far enough to spring up and catch a horse's foot and throw him broadside in the puddled mud.[65]

Yet by noon on July 14, everyone was across except the two-division rear guard and assorted stragglers. Federal cavalry surprised them at Falling Waters. The Confederates lost upwards of seven hundred prisoners before the balance escaped and cut the ropes securing the bridge. The rest of the army, safe in Virginia, lurched toward Bunker Hill along roads equally bad as those left behind. The day turned hot, reaching 84 degrees in Washington.[66]

Precisely 3.24 inches of rain fell in Gettysburg during the ten-day period stretching from the end of the battle to Lee's escape across the Potomac, almost more than the normal mean for the entire month. Now in the Valley, the Confederates marched through Martinsburg to Bunker Hill and Darkesville on the pike to typhoid-ridden Winchester, where they rested for five days. Meade's disappointed men waited north of the river. Lincoln was crestfallen at Lee's escape from an apparent trap. A message from Halleck was so incendiary that Meade tried to resign. On July 17, while Lincoln flayed the army commander in a cabinet meeting, the Federals finally crossed the Potomac. As always, Meade wanted to remain between the Confederates and the capital. Pushed by the government, he hurried up the Loudoun Valley, seizing the nearest passes, including Manassas Gap, on July 23. Lee had no choice but to fall back to Culpepper, where the campaign began.

The Army of the Potomac lost almost 15,000 more veterans and nine-month recruits during the pursuit. Others headed to New York City to confront draft rioters. The ugly anti-Republican and white-on-black riot of July 13 through July 16 saw mob violence, bacchanalian looting, racial lynching, and literal class warfare, all taking place in an environmental pressure cooker. As historian Adrian Cook points out, hot and humid weather on the thirteenth first drove people out of doors. Once the rioting started, little information initially got through to Washington because of storm-damaged telegraph wires. Rising temperatures, humidity, and rain heavy enough to snuff out house fires shaped "Draft Week," the worst riots in American history. The city's Smithsonian weather observer recorded an incredible 3.68 inches of precipitation along with shifting winds. New York that week was stormy in every sense of the word.[67]

Washington, meanwhile, discouraged any fresh campaign against Lee. Meade took his army back to the Rappahannock and halted. The weather was noticeably hotter. During the second half of July, Washington recorded only two days with afternoon highs below 80 degrees. Six days topped 85 degrees. Periods of rain continued as well. Thunderstorms and occasional showers blowing up from the south between July 15 and July 18 deposited nearly an additional inch of rain. Lee's men recorded more rain on the twenty-third, followed by a round of strong evening rainstorms between July 25 and July 30 that left another inch of rain and associated mud. The Rapidan grew too high to cross with artillery without getting the gunpowder wet. In between the rains, it was hot and dry enough for marching men to fall out again with heat exhaustion.[68]

Weather seemed out of joint everywhere that summer. The editors of a New York journal observed that, "after a long drouth, the Northern and Eastern States were visited by heavy and continuous showers during the latter half of July and the first part of August. The rainfall was most extraordinary in amount, equaling fourteen inches in some localities."[69] The editors of the *American Agriculturalist* struggled to make sense of reports from around the country: "The season . . . has been remarkable for the variety of weather in different parts of the country, and even in localities but a few miles apart. Within the boundaries of a single State there was an abundance of rain all through the Spring and Summer, while at points but little distant, a parching drouth dried up the grass, and kept back the corn and the grain crops."[70]

To the south, too much rain became the newest danger. Historian Paul Gates notes that "extraordinarily heavy and long-continued rains in Georgia" that summer "held back the corn and spoiled much of the promising wheat crop."[71] Things were little better in Virginia, where drought and heavy rain combined with the other frictions of wartime to reduce crops, drive up prices, and increase distrust between the government and citizens.[72] People began to go hungry, especially in the cities. J. B. Jones lamented on July 29: "Still raining! The great fear is that crops will be ruined, and famine, which we have long been verging upon, will be complete. Is Providence frowning upon us for our sins, or upon our cause?" On hot August 2, warm, fair weather failed to dispel "the pall of death over our affairs." Only a victory or European intervention could shake the "gloom," Jones thought. Food helped, however. On August 9, he described his encouraging garden, writing, "my potatoes have, so far, failed; but as they are still green they may produce a crop later in the season. The lima beans, trailed on the fence, promise an abundant crop; and the cabbages and peppers look well."[73]

Lee's army rested near Culpeper. At the beginning of August, concerned by aggressive Federal probes across the Rapidan, the general fell back beyond the Rappahannock. Confederates complained of close, suffocating heat during this time. So did their Federal pursuers, soaked in sweat. Summer highs remained brutal. From August 1 through August 12, afternoon highs reached into the nineties every day. On three occasions—August 4, August 10, and August 11—they topped 100 degrees, hitting 104 degrees on the tenth. It was so hot at midmonth, Mississippian Franklin Riley observed, that dogs refused to chase cats. Others judged it the hottest stretch they had known in Virginia. Shade was useless. With rare exceptions, 90-degree weather continued until the twenty-sixth, when rain and

70-degree weather hinted of autumn. To that point, August had been dry aside from six thunderstorms.[74] The thunderstorms largely were local in character and not reflected in records penned near Washington. They also were deadly. Lt. Col. Benjamin Cook of the 12th Massachusetts described men killed by lightning, as did Lt. Col. William Stewart of the 61st Virginia, who related how lighting struck an oak tree, ran through a musket leaned against it, and killed a reclining Virginian in his "fly tent"; it also "fearfully shocked one or two others."[75] Presumably, the "fly tent" was a Federal shelter tent. J. F. J. Caldwell noted that "from ten to twenty thousand" Rebels had captured "small 'Yankee' flies" during their northern excursion. "The camps were everywhere white with them, and with them only."[76]

Heat and dry weather produced stifling dust clouds.[77] "Marching on a dusty day is difficult," Franklin Riley wrote. "Our nostrils and our throats become feverish. Dust fills our eyes, our ears, our shoes, irritating our skin. Grit grates between our teeth. We have argued the subject at length. Which is worse, mud or dust? Mud (rain) possibly worse, but dust is a close second."[78] Sunstroke and straggling ensued.[79] "The last day's march was the hottest I ever experienced," Pvt. John Worsham wrote on August 1. "More than half the men, overcome by the heat, fell out of ranks on the march. Every tree we came to along the road side had a squad of men, officers as well as men, under its shade."[80] Conditions were stifling in camp too. Federals erected their tents with the bottom two to three feet off the ground to improve air circulation. Pvt. Richard Waldrop of the 21st Virginia wrote that to beat the heat, "a good many of us discard pants while in camp."[81] On August 11, with the high at 101 degrees, a Union soldier described comrades wearing "nearly a Georgia costume, a Hat, drawers and shirt."[82]

Weather enveloped the Gettysburg Campaign. Killing heat and rain made the march into Pennsylvania taxing. Mud still lay on the ground on July 1. The first three days of July provided almost perfect weather for battle. Torrential rain afterward left a mixed legacy. Rain trapped the Confederates at the Potomac for up to a week, but at the same time it dumped tons of water along Meade's line of pursuit. Better roads meant little when jams sent men traipsing into farmers' bottomless red-clay fields. Dealing with mud as well as time and distance slowed the Federal pursuit considerably and wore men to a frazzle.

Many historians agree with Lincoln that Meade's caution allowed Lee to "escape." Others defend the Union commander, noting Lincoln's unrealistic hopes and the army's exhaustion. Hardly anyone—the president, official Washington, the Union citizenry—fully appreciated the significance of the victory or the depth of its costs until months later, perhaps when Lincoln himself journeyed to Gettysburg and stood by the mud of the new national cemetery to eulogize the dead. Few grasp it fully even today. The veterans of the Army of the Potomac better understood how heat, rain, dust, and mud shaped the war's most celebrated campaign.[83] Their enemies—wet, muddy, often shoeless—knew it too. William Pendleton wrote home, "we have been exposed to a continuance of weather almost unsurpassed in inclemency again and again, marching day and night through a drenching rain and mud interminable."[84] Farther west, along the Mississippi River, other soldiers were learning similar lessons about the power of weather in shaping the war.

Chapter 15

Heat and Drought

Vicksburg and Port Hudson, March–August 1863

Violent thunderstorms lashed the Army of the Tennessee on the night of March 28, 1863. The next day, with temperatures near freezing, rain, and a sharp wind blowing from the north, U. S. Grant opened the final phase of the Vicksburg Campaign. He ordered John McClernand's corps to New Carthage, a town tucked into one of the Mississippi's meandering loops. Grant's plan, conceived two months earlier but checked by the winter's near-constant rain, high water, and deep mud, involved marching his entire army down the Louisiana side of the river through its deep black soil. David Porter's gunboats would run past the batteries at Vicksburg. The army and navy would rendezvous, Porter would ferry the troops across, and the army would move inland.

The demarcation between phases was not as sharply drawn as some texts allow. Some troops spent two muddy weeks in early April on yet another failed canal project, trying to create a safe channel for transports. Washington prodded Grant to send McClernand farther south in order to cooperate with Nathaniel Banks in Louisiana. And Grant wrestled with his own doubts. Of his lieutenants, ironically only McClernand supported his plan. Porter warned that high water and fast spring currents would prevent poorly powered gunboats from returning north if the general changed his mind. Grant wavered, went up the Yazoo River with Porter and Tecumseh Sherman to reconnoiter the city's northern approaches, and then stuck to his plan.[1]

By then, McClernand was in motion to the south on what historians William Shea and Terence Winschel deem "the most difficult advance of the war."[2] March 31 was a "fair day" after rain, sleet, and frost. The river was falling at last, but roads atop narrow levees remained boggy enough to require frequent corduroying and sometimes pontoons to span gaps.[3] While greening foliage reflected the arrival of spring, deep mud, buzzing insects, snakes, and snipers added to the Federals' vexations. There was little to eat. The weather at least remained dry and warm. Late on April 3—Good Friday—the head of McClernand's column arrived at New Carthage, only to find the village mostly underwater due to a breached levee. The next day, a tornado struck Vicksburg, killing a reported eleven soldiers. High water, the foreboding swamps, and pesky Confederate resistance stymied the strung-out Federal advance for two more weeks. While McClernand searched for a way past the roadblock, rain fell between April 11 and April 14, and the river began rising again.[4] "On this march, it rained about half the time," Sgt. William Eddington of the 97th Illinois complained, "and everywhere was water, mud, and slush."[5]

Delayed by McClernand, James McPherson's corps only got moving from Lake Providence toward Milliken's Bend on April 16. That signal day was momentous for another reason. Ten days earlier, Grant had asked Porter to run the batteries. It took time to assemble the transports required by the army to cross the river afterward. More worrisome were orders from Washington directing Porter to take his fleet south into the lower Mississippi so that his foster brother, Rear Adm. David Farragut, could return his ships to saltwater. Porter then was to support Banks's campaign against the Confederate river stronghold at Port Hudson, Louisiana, 240 miles downriver from Vicksburg.

To help Grant, Porter had to move soon, but rain on April 13 and April 14 held him up. Finally, at 9:15 P.M. on the calm, moonless night of the sixteenth, seven ironclads, three army transports, a ram, and a tug raised steam and started south. The little fleet hugged the Louisiana shore. Porter's flagship, the USS *Benton,* took the lead. A light breeze blew over the river from the east. Lashed to the vessels were barges filled with coal for the ships and supplies for Grant. The city's batteries began firing, tardily and slowly at first but then more rapidly as men rushed to their guns from an unfortunately timed ball. Burning cotton bales and barrels of tar on shore lit up the dark riverbank and blinded sailors with refractive smoke and pyrotechnics. Once under fire, the fleet veered to the Mississippi side, hoping that depressed Confederate guns would be unable to hit targets at a steeper angle. Confused and tied to the unwieldly barges, Porter's vessels lurched in and out of formation while returning fire. He lost only two vessels and a barge. On the clear morning of April 17, McClernand's men first saw an ominous flaming wreck coming downriver, but the rest of the

Union fleet soon followed in triumph. Grant was so pleased that he and Porter arranged for a second successful running through heavy rain on the night of the twenty-second. The message was clear. The Union navy, not Confederate shore batteries, controlled the Mississippi.[6]

At his headquarters in Jackson, John Pemberton reacted with confusion, in part due to a series of diversions also launched by Grant. McClernand's mud-delayed slog, as well as the Union commander's own growing doubts, nonetheless erased any hopes of quickly crossing the river before the Confederates could react. Porter reported that the enemy were building earthworks near the most likely landing site at Grand Gulf, adding that heavy clouds of dust gave away the arrival of more troops there as well. Grant ordered his men to move on to a plantation settlement called Hard Times, opposite the mouth of the Big Black River and three miles above Grand Gulf. Despite flooding as deep as ten feet, a wide expanse of dry land and a good steamboat landing could be found there.[7]

Steamy heat and road dust marked the move to Hard Times for those unlucky enough to miss river transportation. McClernand arrived there on April 21, with McPherson behind and Sherman still in the rear. It rained hard that night and periodically through the next trying day, bogging down wagons in blue-black mud. Charles A. Dana, Stanton's eyes at the front, warned the secretary of war that, while the roads were serviceable, any more storms would leave the army in bad straits.[8] The next day, instead, brought clearing afternoon skies and warmth, although the road remained "muddy beyond description. We had seen deeper mud in Mississippi last fall," Jenkin Jones wrote, "but none so hard as this to travel; the soil being of a bluish clay, was made into wax, the wheels clogging so as to hide all traces of spoke or fellow."[9]

In the most famous of Grant's diversions, Col. Benjamin Grierson had led 1,700 horsemen deep into Mississippi, starting on that clear morning following the running of the Vicksburg batteries. Sherman's more recent diversion up the Yazoo planted additional doubts in Pemberton's mind, enough to stop him from sending further reinforcements to Grand Gulf. McClernand wanted to cross then and there, but the navy first had to silence the guns on the eastern riverbank. On the clear, cool morning of April 29, Porter tried this and failed. Nearly six hours of fighting resulted in little more than horribly mangled casualties that tuned Grant's weak stomach. The general then shifted his focus farther south to Bruinsburg. According to a "contraband," the firm riverbank there lay at the end of a good road to Port Gibson, and the cavalry usually stationed there were off after Grierson.

While McClernand again shifted south, Porter ran the Grand Gulf batteries. Starting the next morning, the navy shuttled McClernand's corps and a division of McPherson's across to Mississippi. Temperatures grew hot on the crowded rivercraft. Once ashore, sweating Federals hastened inland and secured the beachhead on a commanding line of east–west bluffs. Like the area north of Vicksburg, ruggedly steep ridges, deep ravines, scattered small farms, and tangles of green undergrowth defined these sparsely populated environs.[10] As historian Lisa Brady observes, "Grant traded one troublesome landscape for another."[11] By midmorning on May 1, Grant had 22,000 men across the river in what geographer Warren Grabau calls "the greatest amphibious operation in American history up to that time."[12] Grant himself later wrote that he "felt a degree of relief scarcely ever equaled since. . . . I was on dry ground on the same side of the river as the enemy. All the campaigns, labors, hardships, and exposures, from the month of December previous to this time, that had been made and endured, were for the accomplishment of this one object."[13]

Once the army was across the Mississippi, Porter left to link up with Banks. McClernand kept his men moving through the night on the main road toward Port Gibson. Before dawn, the advance encountered Brig. Gen. John Bowen's Confederates—Sterling Price's old division with additional troops—in a steep labyrinth of ridges, tangled canebreaks, and forests west of the town. Despite heat and numerous cases of heatstroke, the Federals shoved the outgunned Confederates back until they gave way. Reinforced from Vicksburg and Grand Gulf, the defenders made another stand in the hot afternoon, only to be outflanked. They retreated again. Joining them this time was a smaller force fighting a separate battle on the Bruinsburg Road. Port Gibson lay in Federal hands by morning; the Grand Gulf garrison fled a day later. (It was this news that so upset Jefferson Davis that he proposed sending part of Lee's army west.) Grant decided to push ahead with his entire force rather than send some units to reinforce Banks, as Washington wanted. Unwilling to head directly to Vicksburg's imposing entrenchments through unfavorable topography, however, he elected to wait for Sherman, unite his army, and move northeast toward the railroad that connected Vicksburg to Jackson, forty miles to the east. Somewhere between the river and Jackson, Grant would cut the railroad, secure his rear, and then turn back to the west.[14]

While the bulk of the army waited, daytime weather was warm and "pleasant." Despite a hard rain overnight on May 4, the roads began to dry out. But temperatures rose well beyond local norms as an apparent warm front pushed through Mississippi to Virginia. On hot May 7, Grant cut his communications and resumed his advance, although Sherman still was crossing the river. The three corps moved on separate roads, slowly enough that Sherman could catch up, and dispersed so that foragers could gather adequate supplies. Jenkin Jones described sultry temperatures and solid but dusty roads.[15]

The Confederates fanned out, hoping to block the various Union approaches. Only on May 12 did Pemberton lead his army across the Big Black River, also ordering Brig. Gen. John Gregg, commanding a brigade in Jackson, to harry Grant's flank or rear. On that stifling day, Gregg attacked McPherson's larger column head on as it crossed a creek south of Raymond. Drought had dried up area streams. Less than a foot of water ran in the deep bed of this creek—now essentially a trench as deep as a man's height—while clouds of road dust enveloped it. Grabau believes that an "inversion layer" covered the field that day, trapping smoke and dust close to the ground. Normally, air temperatures cool as they rise from the earth. When a warmer layer of air develops at altitude during periods of high pressure, however, it functions much like a stopper in a bottle, trapping airborne pollutants beneath it. Dust and smoke, resembling "great impenetrable balls of dirty cotton" in the dark, windless sky, prevented both commanders from seeing the field and led to Gregg's assault. The weight of the Federal column prevailed, and the Confederates retreated to Jackson.[16]

Misled by McPherson's smog-confused and exaggerated reports of enemy strength ahead, as well as his own underestimation of Pemberton's numbers, Grant decided to follow Gregg to Jackson. His intention was to wreck the railroad there and block Joe Johnston's rumored reinforcements before himself turning back to strike Vicksburg. On hot and sunny May 13, as storm clouds gathered and Confederates in Vicksburg mourned Stonewall Jackson, General Johnston arrived in the state capital. Before dawn, as rain fell hard, he decided that it could not be held. Confederate troops fled north toward Canton—and right out of the campaign—through torrential rain. The sky remained cloudy and showery after daylight. The Federals slowly advanced through now-swollen creeks and up muddy Alfisol roads that gave way to Inceptisols along the Pearl River. Grant remembered water as deep as a foot in the road.[17] Sgt. Osborn Oldroyd of the 29th Ohio described "a wet and muddy time" as his regiment pushed guns and wagons. "What a sight! Ambulances creeping along at the side of the track—artillery toiling in the deep ruts while the Generals with their aids and orderlies splashed mud and water in every direction in passing."[18]

Soaked and muddy as they were, Federal troops bloodied the Confederate rear guard and took Jackson.[19] For two bright days, Sherman's men wreaked havoc, wrecking railroads, cutting communications, and burning factories and warehouses. The balance of the army waited to the west in a seven-mile-long line anchored at Raymond. Captured orders indicated that Pemberton was moving east to join forces with Johnston. The Confederates, in fact, were on the move, but not as Grant expected. Aware of the fall of Jackson and concerned about the state of the roads, Pemberton's target was the Federals' largely abandoned supply line. Washed-out bridges and flooded creeks slowed his approach, and his army camped that night well west of Raymond.

Early the next morning, May 16, Grant hurried out his troops. Confronted by the enemy's surprise appearance as well as conflicting orders from Johnston, Pemberton retreated. The sheer speed of Grant's oncoming movement, however, forced Pemberton to halt and deploy his troops in line of battle. Champion Hill, rising 140 feet above the surrounding plain, dominated the northern end of that line. Its steep eastern face as well as surrounding ravines, sunken roads, and thick forests made it ideal for defense. Grant attacked before noon and drove away the outnumbered defenders as the day grew excruciatingly hot. Bowen's violent counterattack regained the crest for a time, but a lack of ammunition or timely help doomed its defense. The Confederates retreated and broke. Had McClernand not lagged, Grant fumed, he would have bagged the entire Rebel army.[20]

Pemberton's defeated army reached the Big Black that night and filed into old log-and-cotton-bale works covered with dirt along its low but steep eastern bank. A shallow bayou to the north, filled with felled timber, and swampy ground to the south anchored the position. A moat offered further protection. Hoping that William Loring's cut-off division might still arrive to help, Pemberton decided to fight. It was a fateful decision. With McClernand in the lead, Grant followed hard the next morning. Sabbath weather was hot, and there was little to drink on the way except water coved in green scum. Reaching the bridgehead, a single brigade, using a hidden and unguarded approach, hit a brigade of East Tennessee conscripts. Demoralized Confederates raced across two bridges to the opposite bank. When these bridges gridlocked, men jumped into the deep and swiftly flowing river below. Some drowned. Others set the bridges afire and fled to Vicksburg, a defeated mob. Pemberton lost nearly 2,000 men, eighteen guns, and scores of arms in the action. Hours later, covered in dust, the survivors entered a city shaken by the news. Pemberton called in outlying units to bolster the city's formidable eight miles of works. He also issued orders to bring inside the lines anything that could be eaten.

Grant's engineers threw up new bridges over the Big Black. The next morning, warm and windy May 18, the army moved up to the imposing works as the Confederates used its massive dust clouds to track its progress. It was a moment of pride for Grant. As James M. McPherson notes, in less than three weeks, the general had marched his army 180 miles, fought and won five battles, and driven Pemberton's army into their works. For Sherman, it was sublime; he finally gained the ground his men had fought and bled for during the previous December. His doubts about Grant's plans evaporated. But there was still much to do. Hoping to take advantage of Confederate demoralization—which he overestimated—Grant ordered Sherman's fresher corps to assault the works. Beneath a blistering afternoon sun, Sherman attacked at 2 P.M. on May 19 after an artillery barrage from river and land. The attack failed miserably, leaving wounded and pinned-down Federals desperate for cover and shade in the arid, open field. While Grant vainly scouted for a weak spot over the next three days, the afternoons remained hot and dusty, while nights were cool and damp.[21] Urged on by his subordinates, still worried about Johnston arriving in his rear, and wary of a long siege, Grant threw his entire force against the works at 10 A.M. on the twenty-second. Aside from a brief breakthrough on McClernand's front, that attack failed as well. The Army of the Tennessee suffered over 3,000 casualties, many due to sunstroke. Grant unfairly blamed McClernand's reports for continuing the assaults well past any hope of success.

Grant afterward inexplicably refused to ask for a truce to bury the dead and rescue the wounded. These casualties thus lay between the lines and under an unforgiving sun for three days, until the stench became unbearable. Only clouds and a brief shower on May 23 brought any relief, settling the dust and moistening the lips of the abandoned wounded. The dead turned black, swelled, and burst with noxious bodily gases, attracting flies that produced maggots by the millions. For soldiers on both sides, but especially the Confederates—the dead were clumped in front of their works—

the sickening smell became unbearable. Pemberton begged Grant "in the name of humanity" to retrieve his wounded (if any survived) and bury his stinking dead. The Union commander finally agreed to a brief truce.[22]

On the same day, May 25, Grant settled down to a siege that eventually lasted six weeks. West Point–trained engineers on both sides used the truce to scout the ground between the two armies. After daybreak on the twenty-sixth, Federal pioneers, detailed soldiers, and African American "contra-bands" began digging no less than thirteen zigzag approaches, or "saps," toward the enemy works. These saps needed to be deep enough to hide men from enemy fire and wide enough to allow a column to pass four abreast, which meant a lot of digging in the hot sun. The soft, silty loess made the work easier, and like the nearby ravines, the trenches generally held up without reinforcement. Sharpshooters and Confederate artillery caused more difficulties. Under fire during daylight, sappers labored behind im-provised stockades and often large sap rollers, a sort-of mobile cylindrical entrenchment woven of bamboo, cane, and vines and stuffed with dirt or cotton. Such medieval vehicles provided protection from small-arms fire. For a time, Maj. Gen. John A. Logan's men also utilized a railroad flatcar, piled high with cotton bales and rolled on wooden wheels. Confederates in the trenches finally set the vehicle afire with improvised incendiary bullets. Behind the lines, other Federals constructed artillery positions and a maze of interior trenches. Farther east, seven of Sherman's divisions kept watch for any sign of Johnston. Halleck stripped Memphis and other commands to provide Grant reinforcements. Reestablished communications with Por-ter's fleet and newly constructed roads soon meant a steady supply of food for the besieging forces.

The outnumbered Confederates in their "ditches," in contrast, messed on increasingly meager rations, endured sun and rain without adequate shelter, and tried to strengthen their own lines. They also did their best to keep their heads down. Sharpshooting ran up a terrible body count. The defenders lost roughly five times as many men as the besiegers, mostly to head wounds and bullets to the upper body. Counting Porter's gunboats as well as fieldpieces, Grant also had double the artillery and many more pow-erful rifled pieces. Federal gunners slowly and steadily pummeled the Con-federate works into powder. As Warren Grabau notes, bullets and shrapnel more easily penetrate loess than other soils. Cotton bales reinforced with wood within entrenchments stopped bullets better but could catch fire. Every day through June, the city's defenders watched helplessly as the saps drew nearer, praying in vain for Johnston and relief. When Logan's sap reached a prominent redan, former miners among the Union troops sank a deep mine underneath the Confederate works. On June 25, they blew it up, creating a giant crater. After vicious fighting, the Confederates held. The Federal exploded a second mine on July 1 with similar results.[23]

Inside Vicksburg, civilians, too, endured the bombardment. Some died. Food dwindled, and the prices for what was left rose exorbitantly. Although often exaggerated, Vicksburg's famished civilians did sometimes eat mule meat, horsemeat, and, toward the end, cats, dogs, frogs, and rats. At night or during heavy daytime shelling, residents hid in dank caves dug into the soft loess hills by well-paid workmen and enslaved laborers, where they worried about explosions that might bury them alive. Rain, though infrequent, created flooding and mudslides. Fading hopes and the constant strain of the bombardment wore them down quickly.[24]

On May 22, as Grant's men fruitlessly assailed Pemberton's works, the other great summer siege of the Federal campaign for the Mississippi began in Louisiana. Major General Banks had expected a corps of reinforcements from Grant before moving down the Red River from Alexandria. The entrenched high bluffs of Port Hudson, on the east bank of the Mississippi twenty-five miles north of Baton Rouge, represented the other Confederate bottleneck on the river. With terrain similar to Vicksburg's, it was another natural Gibraltar augmented by months of engineering and artillery. When Banks learned that no help was coming—Grant had marched to Jackson— he floundered. He considered heading for Grand Gulf, expecting to link up with Grant, but then had second thoughts about moving so far away from New Orleans. He decided to take Port Hudson after all, encouraged by reports that it was lightly defended.

Banks called for help and moved against the enemy on May 14, the same day that Grant took Jackson. Starting in the wee hours of May 22, his Army of the Gulf crossed the Mississippi on Farragut's transports in afternoon rain. Port Hudson was a mere dozen miles away. Johnston had reduced its garrison to about 6,000 defenders, and its northern perimeter was devoid of fortifications. With his reinforcements, Banks had over a four-to-one manpower advantage over the garrison forces. But his cautious approach gave them just enough time to throw up a new line of works and fell trees in his way. Banks then methodically encircled the town, with his flanks on the river. On sizzling hot May 27, under a beautiful sky, he launched a poorly coordinated attack from the north and east, marked by the courage of his soldiers—including the first major assault of the war involving African American troops—and the incompetence and insubordination of his subordinates. Unable to storm the position, Banks dug in, called for more men, and began shelling. Worried about the summer heat and its negative effects, he hoped that a Confederate surrender would soon follow.[25]

At both Vicksburg and Port Hudson, engineers and sappers did all they could to accomplish their tasks and stay alive, but the weather was out of their hands. From the very beginning, the hot sun took a toll on exposed men who already had been marching and fighting in Mississippi heat for weeks. They now labored in an exposed, blasted landscape eerily reminiscent of a deadly, giant ant farm. On May 26—the day Grant opened his siege—Confederate quartermaster Samuel Swan observed that "the endurance of our men is taxed to the uppermost, they having to lie under a boiling sun all day motionless."[26] Not surprisingly, the siege has gone down in history as "abnormally hot and dry," according to Warren Grabau.[27] Just how hot it was is open to question, however, since historians lack precise measurements. On average, summer afternoon highs in Vicksburg reach around 90 degrees and occasionally top the 100-degree mark. Yet a close reading of available evidence suggests that every day at Vicksburg was not broiling. The almost complete lack of real numbers, coupled with the biases of observers, limit what one can know for certain. So do soldier disagreements about the definition of "hot." Wisconsin's Jenkin Jones, for example, described May 30 as "warm and dull," while the Ohioans Osborn Oldroyd and Edward Schweitzer settled on "hot."[28] On the USS *Black Hawk*, the afternoon was "sultry."[29] In contrast, southerner Swan described it as a "pleasant" day, adding that there was "a good breeze" and "cumulus clouds which afford . . . shade . . . to the men lying in the trenches."[30]

It was the near-constant lack of rain, however, not any heat, that became the major weather factor. May was unusually dry. Before the siege, precipitation fell only three times: on the night of May 4, ten days later during the fighting for Jackson, and finally as a brief shower on May 23. When the siege began on May 26, in other words, it had not rained substantially for almost two weeks. Showers then commenced during the afternoon of May 29.[31] These were "hot" showers, according to Schweitzer, but described as "gentle" by Jones.[32] Capt. Gabriel Killgore of the 17th Louisiana reported "occasional hard showers" in his sector and complained that "the trenches are muddy and everything disagreeable."[33] These showers were too limited to have much effect, however, and proved to be the last rain for twelve days.

The lack of rain dramatically affected both civilians and soldiers. Grabau estimates that Grant's army at the beginning of the siege needed at least 81,240 gallons of water per day to survive. That meant the massive logistical task of moving an average of 338 wagons per day, each loaded down with barrels of Mississippi or Yazoo River water. Reinforcements as well as the ongoing lack of rain dramatically increased those needs as the siege progressed. While Vicksburg's unappetizing diet is the stuff of legends, potable water was the bigger issue on the Confederate side as well. Grabau notes that the city and its wider environs not only lacked abundant springs before the war but also sat atop a water table too deep to be reached with contemporary wells. Worse still, local creeks tended to dry up in hot weather. Antebellum Vicksburg was entirely dependent upon the river and rainwater caught in cisterns. With the river occupied, carrying a bucket of water involved a dangerous two-mile round trip.[34]

Thus, the cisterns assumed vital importance. Dora Richards Miller and her husband controlled two of them in town. A young elite woman and a secret Unionist, she lived in the cellar of the shelled-out ruins of a rented house, evicted from a safer cave by the landowner. "The weather has been dry a long time," she wrote on June 7, "and we hear of others dipping up the water from ditches and mud-holes. This place has two large underground cisterns of good cool water, and every night in my subterranean dressing-room a tub of cold water is the nerve-calmer that sends me to sleep in spite of the roar." While one remained undisturbed for family use, soldiers commandeered the other.[35] Yet the cisterns could not provide nearly enough water. As Grabau points out, the city's water system was designed for a population of 5,000 people. During the siege, some 35,000 thirsty souls depended upon it, although many Confederates shied away from the water's smell and potential ill effects.[36] Instead, they relied upon water "hauled at night from the Mississippi River, . . . which being covered in bundles with blankets makes very good drinking."[37]

As the siege progressed, the water situation steadily grew worse. Skies generally remained clear and bright; no precipitation fell. Temperatures varied from pleasantly warm to uncomfortably hot. Jones labeled May 31 as "very warm."[38] The night that followed was windy, which became a factor when Federal artillery fire turned the predawn hours of June 1 into what Swan called a "night of terrors" in the besieged city. "The wind was blowing quite a stiff breeze and the shells were falling thick and fast," he explained, "when a fire broke out on the south side of Washington street and burnt down a whole square of the business part of town."[39] Jones went on to describe the following day as "oppressive."[40] June 3—when Lee's army began what would become the march to Gettysburg—was "more comfortable," in Schweitzer's words. The change in the weather, Swan added, was heaven sent. "Continual duty in the trenches during the very hot weather and the poor food is telling on them slowly," he wrote of his comrades.[41]

While a little rain wet Jackson on June 4, none fell at Vicksburg. The long weekend that followed not only brought incessant artillery fire but also consistent heat, calm air aside from occasional breezes from the south or west, and dry-as-a-bone conditions.[42] Like many, Swan linked the heat to sickness and noted dysentery in Confederate ranks on the sixth. Grant was ill too, although his critics blamed alcohol. The next day, Swan lamented the condition of "the poor mules and artillery horses" that had "cropped the grass bare and the hills are naked and desolate. The stock is starving by degrees and much of it will die in a few more days."[43]

Fifteen miles upriver, action occurred on hot June 7 at Grant's former supply base at Milliken's Bend. Desperate to help Pemberton but rebuffed by Generals Lee and Bragg, President Davis had turned to the Trans-Mississippi forces. Eager to help his patron but also low on manpower, Lieutenant General Kirby Smith directed his commands in Arkansas and Louisiana to attack Federal garrisons on the west side of the river. But it took weeks for Lt. Gen. Theophilus Holmes to get moving against the Federal river post and supply base at Helena, Arkansas. That left Maj. Gen. Richard Taylor in Louisiana to bear the load of any relief missions. In theory, a successful campaign against Lake Providence, Milliken's Bend, and Young's Point in Grant's rear could force him to weaken his hold on Vicksburg, as had happened with Holly Springs the previous year. What Kirby Smith did not suspect was that Grant already had shifted his communications to the east bank. Little remained on the Louisiana side except hospitals and camps of instruction for newly mustered regiments of US Colored Troops. Taylor knew better but followed orders anyway. At dawn on June 7, with the skies clear, one of his divisions stormed the Federal position along the town levees. Initially successful, the Confederates retreated at midmorning under bombardment from Federal gunboats. Along with their wounded, the Confederates carried away black prisoners with the intention of returning them to slavery. Other African Americans died in battlefield atrocities. In time, Milliken's Bend became a rallying cry, but in the short run, it did nothing to help Pemberton.[44]

Back in Vicksburg on June 8, Samuel Swan observed that "scarcely a sprinkle of rain has fallen since the siege commenced."[45] Grant's chief engineer reported that intense heat prevented midday labor in the saps. But conditions were about to change. Daybreak on June 10 was cloudy and rainy. On the *Black Hawk*, the deck officer noted "weather overcast with rain squalls" through the morning and heavy rain in the afternoon. A thunderstorm roared through the early evening. Rain extended east to Jackson. In Vicksburg, fieldworks flooded and sharpshooters searched for cover.[46] Jones wrote: "The dusty valley was converted into a bed of a wild rushing stream. . . . Got thoroughly drenched and slept in wet blankets and on the wet ground."[47]

The following day began with clouds and cooler temperatures. The rain had settled the dust. To the east, Johnston pushed two divisions up to the Big Black but refused to let them cross. As the storm system passed, the skies cleared, and the days once again grew hot.[48] "The hospitals begin to be filled up," Swan recorded in his diary, "showing how much exposure, fatigue, hot weather, and short rations and wounds are diminishing our effective force."[49] Historian Lindsey Rae Privette confirms this observation, noting a 57-percent increase in Federal diarrhea cases from May to June. Others succumbed to sunstroke and occasionally insanity.[50]

"The weather was exceedingly warm," Capt. Chester Barney of the 20th Iowa wrote. "We suffered very much while in the pits from a want of water, which it was impossible to procure during the day. Each man filled his canteen therefore previous to entering the pit, but the water after being exposed to the hot rays of the sun a few hours became too hot for use."[51] But conditions again changed. Rain fell after sundown on June 13, during the later afternoon of torrid June 15, and the next day.[52] "The weather is very pleasant," Swan wrote on the eighteenth, "the nights cool and the atmosphere seems to be pure and beautiful. Great care has been taken to remove all dead animals and throw them into the river. Water is regularly hauled for the men at the trenches from the river, and, so far, not much sickness has affected the army." The Confederate quartermaster sounded a more ominous note about Federal artillery, writing that "they are beginning to interfere with the water haulers and are making the lower part of the town very warm."[53] Not everyone found the weather pleasant, however. Oldroyd wrote on the eighteenth that "a few sunstrokes have occurred, but without proving fatal so far. One poor fellow even dropped at midnight when I presume the surgeon's diagnosis must have been—moonstruck."[54]

In Virginia, the heatwave ended on June 19 as cooler temperatures and rain set in. But in Mississippi, it grew hot again as Federal sappers and gunners drew near the Confederate works. Charles Dana reported a high of 95 degrees that day, adding that the shelling was fouling nearby springs. Sunday, June 21, brought midday clouds and somewhat cooler temperatures.[55] The next day, Pemberton turned five hundred slaves into the Federal lines, unwilling to feed them any longer. Grant picked out the strongest and sent the rest back to bondage. A rainstorm blew up the next afternoon, and skies remained cloudy on delightfully cool June 24. Evening brought gentle showers. The next day was much the same.[56] "The weather is hot," Oldroyd admitted. "Some of the rebel prisoners have said that we could not stand this heat, but I guess the Yanks can stand it if they can, and if it should actually get too hot, we will cool their country off. The nights are pleasant enough and we are thankful for the comfort of the sleep which they allow us."[57]

Despite breezes from the south, June 26 was "hot and disagreeable" according to Schweitzer.[58] The next day was little better. That night, a fine misting rain descended in the darkness.[59] On the twenty-eighth, under pressure from Richmond, Johnston decided to move his small army—recently reinforced by a division—up to the Big Black and Sherman's lines. They marched on July 1. Heat and dust, not to mention reluctance, made it tough going. Straggling reached epidemic proportions. Sgt. Johnny Green of the Confederate 9th Kentucky complained that "the sand was shoe mouth deep & so hot that it actually blistered our feet. More than half the regiment fell by the wayside that day."[60]

July began with another miniheatwave. On the second, Dana wrote Secretary of War Stanton, "thermometer at noon above 100 degrees."[61] Soldiers on both sides understood that the siege was nearly over. Whenever possible, they saved their strength. At several points, the Federal saps approached the outer Confederate works so closely that men from the two armies held conversations. Miners also dug underground toward the defenders' works despite foul air and excruciating heat. At headquarters, Grant prepared to launch another assault on July 6. One suspects that it would have carried easily. Pemberton's men were exhausted. Confederate rations were down to only some peas and rice and an inadequate single cup of water per day. Dysentery, diarrhea, and malaria were rampant. Morale hit rock bottom as men concluded that they had waited in vain for Johnston. If Pemberton could not feed them, one group wrote to their general, he should surrender them. Pemberton himself seemed lost. On hot July 1, he broached a breakout option to his subordinates. Led by Bowen, they told him no. There were no more draft animals to pull wagons and guns—many had died and the men had eaten the rest—and the soldiers themselves were too emaciated and dehydrated to carry their supplies.

Pemberton agreed to discuss surrender. He chose the Fourth of July, hoping that he might find Grant in a better mood to offer lenient terms. The third of July was hot. Pemberton ordered his men to raise white flags and then sent out a note to Grant asking for a truce and negotiations. An eerie hush fell over the numb city. Resident Mary Ann Loughborough described the sudden silence as unnerving after six weeks of almost constant gunfire. Grant responded to the request with the "unconditional surrender" spirit of Fort Donelson. Pemberton initially reacted with anger, but Bowen arranged an informal afternoon meeting. Thanks to careful manipulations, both commanding generals thought that the other had requested the meeting. Bowen succeeded in getting permission for some of the generals' subordinates to meet while the commanding officers sat under a shade tree and chatted about old times in Mexico. According to the final agreement, the Union army would take Vicksburg the next morning. Grant, who was not sure that he could feed up to 30,000 prisoners over the long haul, agreed to parole the captured garrison, issue the men rations, and let them go away to eat off their countrymen. Sick men could leave later under the same terms. With any luck, Grant thought, most of them would desert and go home. The agreement only ran into snags when Confederates unsuccessfully began demanding to take their slaves with them in defiance of the Emancipation Proclamation. Several hundred others actually chose life in

Union prisons rather than a return to the Confederate army.[62]

July 4 was another typical Vicksburg day: hot, clear, and dry. The Confederates abandoned their works, and the victorious Federals entered the city. The sights and smells of the place shocked them, not the least the weakened condition of their opponents, the desperate appearances of the city's women, the magnitude of destruction, the caves, and the overwhelming stench. Grant watched the Stars and Stripes go up at the courthouse, met with Admiral Porter at the river, and sent word of victory off to Washington. The news electrified the Union. Coupled with Lee's retreat from Gettysburg, the war's end somehow seemed in sight. Down South, many came to the same conclusions, but with entirely different emotions. Confederate desertion rates spiked. Well might Grant look back as he did at the end of his life and see Vicksburg as the turning point.[63]

And yet there was still marching and killing to be done along the river over the next month before the fall of Vicksburg could bear its full fruits. To the north, Holmes finally had cobbled together a force of almost 8,000 men from across Arkansas, hoping to cut Grant's supply line at Helena. Confederate columns marched hopefully on June 22. Unfortunately for them, central Arkansas was at the center of a developing rain system. Heavy precipitation between June 24 and June 28 east of Little Rock made for a black, sticky mess while flooding creeks and washing away bridges. The anticipated five-day forced march to Helena turned into an exhausting eleven-day slog. Unaware of the surrender at Vicksburg, Holmes vainly attacked Helena's high ground and deceptively formidable works at dawn on July 4. After a brief breakthrough, well-placed Federal artillery smashed the assault to bits. A final Federal infantry charge sent the survivors reeling back to the west in confusion.[64]

Grant worried more about Johnston than Holmes. The ink was barely dry on the surrender when he sent Sherman to the east with an overwhelming thirteen divisions, about two-thirds of the entire Army of the Tennessee. Never eager to attack anyway, Johnston retreated. In 90-degree heat and smothering dust clouds, Johnston's Confederates trudged back to Jackson and its earthworks, poisoning wells and waterways with slaughtered animals as they passed. Sherman's thirsty and dusty men followed slowly, avoiding the heat of the day when possible but also pillaging with

angry vengeance in retaliation for the poisoned water. Sgt. William Eddington swore that it was over 100 degrees in the shade, while the road dust was
four inches deep before marching feet stirred it up into suffocating clouds.
Comrades drank from scum-covered puddles along the way. Some fell in-
sensible by the roadside. A storm on the night of July 7 left the following
morning refreshingly cool before the sweltering heat returned.

Sherman arrived near Jackson on July 10. Unwilling to attack well-built
works needlessly, he arranged his units in an arc, anchored at both ends
by the Pearl River, and waited for his artillery, ammunition train, and reinforcements to come up for a siege. When a cavalry raid against the Federal
train failed, Johnston literally burned his bridges behind him and abandoned the capital on the evening of the sixteenth, leaving behind massive
stores of arms and ammunition. Heavy thunderstorms followed the next
day, signaling an ironic change in the weather over the next two weeks that
brought seven more days of rain between July 18 and August 1. Deep mud
and flooded roads slowed down Johnston's army, as did intense heat and
humidity when the sun came out. His discouraged men walked forty miles
before halting.[65]

Sherman decided not to pursue the Confederates other than with a
token column due to the "intense heat, dust, and fatigue of the men." He
assured a colonel that "heat and drought are doing more execution than
bullets" to Johnston's command, although he had no real proof of the assertion. Grant, nonetheless, passed along that supposition to Washington
as fact, writing Halleck, "Sherman says most of [Johnston's] army must
perish from heat, lack of water, and general discouragement."[66] Over the
next week, Sherman's men methodically burned and otherwise destroyed
what they had left intact during the first occupation of Jackson in May.
They then turned back to Vicksburg in the by-now-familiar extreme heat
and parching dust, alleviated only by a thunderstorm on July 22 that also
flooded the Big Black crossings. Because of the heat, Grant allowed Sherman to take his time. Still it was a hard march. Soldiers drank from pools
of scum-covered water in bayous. In their after-action reports, regimental
colonels regularly mentioned the heat and lack of water encountered as
serious foes.[67] Sherman issued orders sending his corps into camps east of
Vicksburg stretching to the Big Black, adding, "the probabilities are, that
we will rest through the heat of the summer in these camps."[68]

By then, all but the sick Confederates were gone, marching east through
the same dust, heat, and rain toward parole camps in Alabama. Thousands

deserted along the way. The weather remained stiflingly hot but became increasingly rainy. A storm with hail on the night of July 7 gave way to 90-degree heat the next day. It rained again on the ninth and on the night of the twelfth, with storms lasting into the following day. The July 22 storm that flooded the Big Black continued into the next day as well, followed by a series of afternoon storms at month's end. The storm on July 27 was accompanied by winds strong enough to blow down shelters.[69]

At Port Hudson, meanwhile, the garrison had held out for days after the fall of Vicksburg. Temperatures rose into the midnineties, hot enough to fell marching men with sunstroke. Infrequent rain allowed the development of ankle-deep dust. Five years later, Capt. Orton Clark of the 116th New York remembered the heat as "suffocating," adding, "it really seemed that the air was directly from the burning fiery furnace mentioned by the Prophet Daniel."[70] Likewise, Pvt. Henry T. Johns of the 49th Massachusetts—about to win the Medal of Honor—wrote retrospectively of the thick dust, "the trees and bushes are covered with it, and in the sunlight look like smouldering fires." Johns and his comrades tried to cope with the heat by dressing lightly. "A straw hat, a shirt, a pair of breeches and of shoes (sometimes stockings) complete our wardrobe," he described. "Some tried to dispense with the use of shoes, but the ground was too much like fire to allow them to continue that kind of economy."[71]

Banks was less patient and less skilled than Grant. Three weeks into his siege, he demanded that the Confederates surrender immediately. When they did not, Banks launched an assault on June 14. Morning fog gave way to sultry heat and a clear sky that day. Marked by poor preparation, mediocre leadership, and even mutiny in some regiments, the attack failed. One soldier described with horror what the "intense heat" had done to wounded and slain men left for four days without shelter, to the degree that rotting bodies fell apart when moved.

Banks then returned to the spade. Soldiers and freedmen dug, sweated, and in many cases fell victim to sunstroke, despite confining most labor to nighttime. Water grew scarce as wells dried up, creeks rans dry, and the river dropped so much than its banks turned fetid. Banks's assistant adjutant general wrote that the hard soil soon resembled a bake oven. Infrequent but hard showers produced humidity to the consistency of steam. News arrived on July 7 that Vicksburg had surrendered. Disheartened, the defenders of Port Hudson gave up two days later. As historians William Shea and Terence Winschel observe, battle, heatstroke, and disease by then had whittled Banks's 30,000-man army down to about 8,000 effectives. Like their counterparts at Vicksburg, the Confederates of Port Hudson received paroles and began walking to Alabama amid rain and mud.[72]

Grant and Banks, albeit often working at cross-purposes, had nonetheless cut the Confederacy in two at last. "The Father of Waters," Lincoln rejoiced in August, "again goes unvexed to the sea." Yet, as far as the White House was concerned, there were still vexations aplenty to deal with in Tennessee, not the least of which were William Rosecrans, Braxton Bragg, and the year's mercurial weather.[73]

Chapter 16

A Specimen of the Four Seasons

Tennessee, May–October 1863

After Stones River, William Rosecrans held Murfreesboro for months, into the spring of 1863. Troops and hired freedmen built a massive base and drilled while waiting for better roads. The general's inactivity, calls for more supplies, and general testiness irked superiors. Grant's advance into Mississippi, coupled with Hooker's defeat at Chancellorsville, brought Washington's frustrations to a boil. When Braxton Bragg shipped off Breckinridge's Kentuckians to reinforce Johnston in Mississippi, Lincoln wrote Rosecrans, hoping that the general would move against the Army of Tennessee to prevent further transfers. He did not. On June 2, General in Chief Halleck ordered the newly renamed Army of the Cumberland out against Bragg, threatening to transfer part of the command to Grant if Rosecrans resisted.[1]

Even then, it took three weeks more before Rosecrans finally took the field. His campaign plan, however, was ingenious. Tullahoma, Tennessee, was a hard place to defend. A complicated regional road network offered numerous approaches and flanking opportunities. Bragg had to monitor a front seventy miles wide with too few troops. Its only defensive attribute was the southeastern arc of a range of rugged hills and ravines known as the Highland Rim, which separate Murfreesboro from Tullahoma. Rosecrans required control of at least one of a few critical gaps. While the Nashville and Chattanooga Railroad ran through Wartrace in a straight line, the other major connectors diverged first to nearby communities, as if they wanted to avoid Tullahoma as long as possible. One ran south to Shelbyville before turning southeast. Leonidas Polk's corps held strong works there, blocking that approach. To the northeast, William J. Hardee's corps controlled the railroad as well as the three critical gaps that fed into the main highway to Chattanooga. Bragg's cavalry safeguarded his flanks. Outnumbered, poorly informed by his cavalry, running low on food and transportation, consumed with internal dissention, and sick, the Confederate commander never considered taking the offensive. Yet as historian Thomas Connelly maintains, he never decided how or where to fight a defensive battle either.[2]

Federal planning took full advantage of both the topography and the confusion. Through the spring, various feints kept Bragg addled. Rosecrans's final plan involved massive misdirection. Most of his cavalry, as well as his Reserve Corps, would demonstrate against Polk at Shelbyville, but the main effort involved seizing the more lightly defended gaps and racing to Manchester. The army would travel light to accelerate the movement. With luck, the bluecoats would turn Hardee's right and seize the railroad bridge over the Elk River in the Army of Tennessee's rear. Bragg then would have to abandon his works and either give up East Tennessee or risk annihilation.[3]

While Rosecrans could dupe Bragg, however, he could not control weather. May 1863 was lovely. In Clarksville, the closest Smithsonian station, the mean monthly high temperature was 73 degrees, and the mean morning low was 57 degrees, quite similar to the previous May. Sixteen of the month's days reached highs in the seventies. With two isolated exceptions on May 13 and May 23, rain came in two distinct spells, the first from May 2 through May 7, and the other at the end of the month. The latter period is associated with "Hurricane Amanda," which moved across Tennessee as a tropical storm.[4] On the twenty-first, Col. John Beatty of the 3rd Ohio summed up May when he wrote, "the days now give us a specimen of the four seasons. At sunrise it is pretty fair winter for this latitude. An hour after, good spring; at noon, mid-summer; at sunset, fall."[5]

Precipitation returned on June 2 and settled in for six of the next nine days, extending the longer rainy spell that began on May 28. Nearly an inch and a half of rain fell in Clarksville during the first eleven days of June, with well over half of that (0.95 inches) on the tenth. Muddy roads followed. Within the Highland Rim in the Central Basin, dominant Alfisols at the center give way to "bottomless" red clay at the edges, with isolated tracts of Inceptisols and Mollisols adding to the variety. Temperatures remained seasonable, with a mean of almost 70 degrees. With three exceptions, morning lows remained above 60 degrees. Once the rain passed, however, days grew hot, reaching 81 degrees on the fifteenth.[6] As elsewhere, rain and cooler temperatures came at exactly the wrong time for local wheat farmers. Pvt.

Charles Dunham of the 129th Illinois wrote from Gallatin on June 21: "The wether is pretty good now but thare has been so much bad that it may spoilt pretty much all the wheat thare is. . . . A number of sitisens told me that it had grone in the shock that it was not fit for anything."[7]

On warm June 23, with a high of nearly 80 degrees again, the feint against Polk began. Elements of Thomas Crittenden's corps, meanwhile, moved well to the east on the McMinnville Road, aiming to turn south and open the turnpike to Manchester. The rest of the army began sliding toward the gaps to support Crittenden. That night, rain began pelting the shelter tents. As many soldiers later noted, it was a sound they would hear almost constantly over the next two weeks. With winds from the west or occasionally the southwest, a massive rain system stalled over southeastern Tennessee from the wee hours of June 24 through July 7, bringing an incredible 7.58 inches of rain. Modern records confirm that Rosecrans launched his campaign during one of the wettest periods in the Tullahoma area's recorded history.[8]

At first, the rain was only a nuisance. The morning of June 24 brought gray skies and periodic drizzle. Late in the morning, mounted Federals armed with Spencer repeaters seized Hoover's Gap. Despite a tardy but vigorous afternoon counterattack in heavy rain, they still held it at nightfall. The rest of Thomas's corps began arriving. A few miles to the west, Liberty Gap fell to Alexander McCook's corps despite worsening field conditions. As night approached, rain fell steadily and grew heavy between about 3 A.M. and morning. Columns of Federal troops approached the breakthroughs while the roads from Murfreesboro devolved into yellowish mire. These grew so bad that regiments began sending back their baggage.[9] "Everything was dripping wet," Lt. Albion Tourgée of the 105th Ohio wrote. "The men held their guns beneath their arms under their shining ponchos. The water ran off the muzzles. Hat brims were turned down; the cloaks of the horsemen dripped as they splashed back and forth in the muddy road which lay between two yellow torrents. . . . [D]arkness fell suddenly, and . . . we lay upon our arms in the dripping wood, with the dead and wounded friends and foes about us."[10]

The next two days brought additional drenching rains and confusion. Bragg remained transfixed at Shelbyville well into June 26. He drew up plans to strike Rosecrans at Liberty Gap, convinced by scattered reports that the main Union thrust would be there. News that evening from Manchester shocked him. Confederate attempts to regain the gaps had failed, and Hardee had pulled back his division protecting the Manchester Pike. Before midnight, with his flanks caving in, Bragg ordered a retreat across the flooded Duck River to his Tullahoma works.[11]

Thus it was the weather, not the Confederates, that offered Rosecrans his biggest problem. At Clarksville, 2.57 inches of rain fell on June 25, the rainiest day of the campaign. By nightfall, the army was nearly immobile. Another 1.18 inches fell on the twenty-sixth, mostly as periodic showers, which turned mountain roads and creeks into rivers of mud. Feet sank and shoes disappeared from them. Wet and mud-splattered infantry—men who had been immobile for months—pulled stalled vehicles up sharp inclines. Traffic backed up. Soldiers stood for hours in rain and muck.

The rain let up on June 27, bringing only about 0.32 of an inch to Clarksville. That morning, Federals occupied Manchester and flanked Bragg's line on the Duck River. At Shelbyville, on the other end of the Confederate position, Federal cavalry struck the rearguard troops, who discovered that their guns were so wet that few would fire. Fleeing the field, many Confederates drowned crossing the flooded river. Still other columns bore down on the railroad. Yet due to the terrible roads, the overall advance was slow. Traffic congested with every breakdown. Federals pushed and dragged wagons and artillery over slick hills. Confederates crossed the Duck River with the enemy only a few miles at their backs. So deep was the mud that it took all day on June 28 for Bragg's army to stumble into Tullahoma, while another 2.2 inches fell from hard showers, the second-worst rain day of the campaign. Short periods of scorching sun and humidity mixed in with the precipitation; the high was 80 degrees after three days in the seventies. After dark, a thunderstorm struck troops still on the roads.[12]

For the men of both armies, the campaign was horrendous. Chaplain William Haigh of the 36th Illinois remembered that the rain fell hard enough to penetrate his rubber poncho. "The water varied from ankle to waist deep," he continued, "with mud in proportion. Men pronounced it the hardest they had ever seen."[13] George Morris estimated that the mud was always at least six inches deep and sometimes up to his knees. Shoes disintegrated. Soaked and covered in mud, men collapsed. At night, they slept on fence rails when they could, hoping to stay out of the mud.[14] As Michael Bradley relates, a Confederate joked "that the town's name was derived from the Latin word tulla, meaning mud, and the Greek word homa, meaning more mud."[15]

June 29 was wet again, bringing 0.4 of an inch of additional rain. Temperatures were cooler, with the high reaching 71 degrees. In Tullahoma, Bragg faced doom. Not only did Rosecrans possess several options for cutting the Confederates off from Chattanooga, but also his own men could no longer ford the swollen Elk River. Worse yet, Federal troops already held one of the three nearby bridges, and the other two were poorly guarded by the Confederates. Only the weather forestalled disaster. All along Rosecrans's routes, wagons and artillery sank to their hubs. Mules collapsed.[16] The soil, Albion Tourgée quipped, had become "a mixture of quicksand and glue."[17]

When Bragg learned that the Federals were advancing against him from Manchester—mud had so delayed Crittenden that Rosecrans turned to Thomas—his first reaction was to stand and fight. Polk disagreed vehemently, unwilling to trust their escape route to Maj. Gen. Joe Wheeler's uncertain cavalry. Hardee wavered with each new shred of information but confided to Polk that Bragg was in no shape to command. Uncertain of what to do and poorly served by his senior officers, Bragg froze. It was dry at daybreak—Thomas noted hopefully that the roads were drying—but the rain soon returned, with over another half inch falling during the day. It was hotter as well, with a high of 84 degrees. In Tullahoma, new reports of Federal cavalry in the rear arrived, coupled with conflicting but decisive information about Rosecrans's advance. Bragg worried about how long the roads behind him would allow transit. That evening, in mud up to the men's knees, the Army of Tennessee slogged eight miles to the Elk River. The Confederates crossed through the night and next morning at the two bridges, then set them alight around noon on July 1. At the Elk, they finally caught a bit luck: The rain held off until late afternoon, allowing the spans to burn. On the second—a rare dry day with temperatures still in the mid-eighties—the army retreated on to the Cumberland Mountains. Bragg had decided to give up the entire region and head for his base at Chattanooga. The exhausted army climbed over the mountains on rainy July 3, crossed the Tennessee River on the Fourth of July, and regrouped in the wet shade of Chattanooga's heights. The rain kept coming through July 7, bringing an additional half inch.[18]

Rosecrans followed as far as the Elk River and halted. The new heat of July 2, combined with the physical exertion deep roads required, had caused rampant straggling. More rain the next day, including a thunderstorm, raised the river back to flood stage, which complicated fording even for mounted men and made the crossing of artillery impossible. Even after the Elk began to drop, men could only cross through the strong, stormy current while hanging on to a cable secured to trees and stretched from bank to bank. Once across, the army faced imposing mountains in heavy rain, with rations dissolving in the men's haversacks. Rosecrans halted. He again would use the railroad system to amass men and supplies before tackling the seemingly barren mountains as well as Bragg. The Army of the Cumberland was back to where it had started almost a year before under Buell.[19]

Rosecrans's accomplishment was remarkable nonetheless. At the price of fewer than six hundred casualties, he had defied some of the worst weather of the war, maneuvered the Confederates to the Georgia border, and regained Middle Tennessee for the Union. Bragg's army lived to fight another day, but Michael Bradley is right to conclude that Rosecrans hardly could have accomplished more. Just as Curtis, Grant, and Thomas had demonstrated earlier, a well-equipped and well-led army could maneuver and fight despite terrible weather conditions, albeit slowly and with much suffering and loss. Unfortunately for Rosecrans, Grant's triumph at Vicksburg, coupled with Meade's victory in Pennsylvania, made his own campaign look unimpressive in Washington. Unwilling as always to acknowledge logistics and the role of bad weather, the administration badgered Rosecrans to finish off Bragg's army and occupy Chattanooga. The general became so fed up that he offered his resignation. Lincoln refused it, but the damage was done.[20]

Yet if Washington refused to acknowledge the importance of the Tullahoma Campaign—and if scholars continue to do so today—Rosecrans's men were proud of the accomplishment. During and after the war, they stressed how rain had deprived them of complete triumph.[21] Col. B. F. Scribner put it succinctly when he wrote that "like Napoleon," Rosecrans only had been "'stopped by the elements.'"[22]

For the next six weeks, the armies recovered from the campaign and prepared for the next. Midsummer weather was typically hot. The lack of hard data from anywhere closer than Clarksville limits what can be said for sure about the Chattanooga front, but one at least can extrapolate. The mean high temperature in Clarksville from July 5 through the end of the month was a fairly typical 79 degrees. Eleven days rose above 80 degrees, with two distinct periods of heat, July 5 through the tenth (with the exception of July

7) and from the twenty-third to the end of the month. August, unsurprisingly, was much hotter. From August 1 through August 15, the mean high was 84 degrees, with every day registering in the eighties and five reaching at least 85 degrees.[23] In a normal year, Chattanooga in the afternoon is only about 2 degrees cooler than Clarksville, although 1863 variations may have been wider. Lt. Jeremiah Donahower of the 2nd Minnesota, for example, praised August 8 as perfect, "with a clear sky and bright shining sun but [it] did not bring with it the extreme heat and debilitating effect usual to days in the month of August in this Southland. . . . The temperature did not go above 75."[24] At Clarksville, in contrast, the high reached 83 degrees, with cloudy skies.

The same caveats are necessary when it comes to precipitation. On average, Clarksville is slightly rainier than Chattanooga in June. The months of July and August are rainier in Chattanooga by over half an inch. Once the historic rainy period ended on July 7, the rest of that month saw eight additional rainy days, though with total accumulation of only 1.4 inches. The first half of August was drier if often cloudy, with only 0.84 of an inch of rain in total.[25] At Hillsboro, a thunderstorm on the afternoon of August 13 struck with "appalling violence," according to Wilber Hinman, "accompanied by a high wind which made rude havoc with the camp. A tree was blown down and the top fell on several tents of the Sixty-fourth, injuring a number of men, four of them severely."[26] There was mud as well, but as the armies moved into the Appalachians, mountain Inceptisols provided a somewhat more solid foundation.[27]

In a line of camps along the base of the Cumberlands, Rosecrans's Federals coped with the heat and occasional storms. Bountiful fruits and berries supplemented government rations. Men slept without tents, which had been lost or abandoned during the campaign. Lt. L. A. Simmons, for example, described his regiment building brush arbors for shade. Sgt. Jay Butler constructed a shanty using part of a roof from an abandoned house and a barn door.[28]

Inside dusty Chattanooga, the Confederates waited. "A sense of aimlessness" characterized the Army of Tennessee, according to historian Thomas Connelly. Heat, skimpy rations, boredom, and defeat affected morale. Hundreds deserted, and many more fell ill. Disillusionment with Bragg festered. Sick and in the throes of his own torpor, the general planned to wait for Rosecrans to make the first move and then respond with force. Topography contributed to his decision. Steep, drought-ravaged mountains and ridges that provided little subsistence even in good years, as well as the meandering Tennessee River, formed Chattanooga's castle walls. High ground commanded the roads leading into the city. The result was "a maze of mountain barriers." Yet holing up in Chattanooga offered hazards as well. Bragg's front was a hundred miles long, and his troop numbers were shrinking. He placed his cavalry poorly, leaving obvious weak points west of the city uncovered. Promises of reinforcement and a proposed concentration with Johnston's Mississippi army proved fleeting. Rosecrans could approach the city with superior numbers from various directions, some unguarded. Chattanooga was as much a trap as fortress.[29]

Rosecrans began to spring that trap on August 15. Buoyed by intelligence that underestimated Bragg's numbers, the Union commander again relied upon deception. He ordered loud demonstrations of artillery and cavalry north of the city, hoping to shift Bragg's gaze there. The approach of a corps of Ambrose Burnside's new Army of the Ohio from Kentucky through the Cumberlands augmented that deception. Halleck wanted Burnside to take Knoxville and then assist Rosecrans. Outnumbered Confederates in East Tennessee fell back toward Chattanooga as Burnside drew nearer. With the Confederates peering north, Rosecrans's army advanced to the southeast through the Cumberlands, unseen by any Confederate scout. The men marched on a sixty-mile-wide front, aiming toward points on the twisting river south and west of the city. The first days were hot and dusty. Around noon on the sixteenth, showers and a powerful thunderstorm west of the city once again doused soldiers on the road. Jeremiah Donahower described a half hour of high winds and two hours of lightning and heavy rain. One comrade died and others fell wounded when a bolt blew up a battery's ammunition chest. As poor roads began to worsen, the trains mired and progress slowed.[30] "The remark was common," L. A. Simmons remembered, "that 'it always rains when Gen. Rosecrans starts on a campaign.'"[31]

But that was the last of the rain this time. Drought soon set in. For the next two weeks, the army slogged over the mountains and into the Tennessee River valley. The weather was blistering hot as well as dry. George Morris swore that a thermometer reached 100 degrees on August 17. In the dry mountains, men who had experienced a once-in-a-lifetime deluge now had difficulty finding enough water to avoid dehydration. Across the summit, conditions changed. Soldiers noted more humidity, less dust, and better roads. The intense heat finally broke all across the South on August 27, as the Army of the Cumberland cozied up to the banks of the big river. Two days later, the first elements crossed the Tennessee. More followed over the next week, across five bridges or rowing flatboats, until most everyone except the rear guards were across.[32]

To their amazement, they crossed without opposition. In a repeat of the Tullahoma disaster, Bragg and his lieutenants ignored accurate reports and remained fixated on the northern horizon. On August 30, Bragg ordered Maj. Gen. Simon Buckner's little East Tennessee command join him in anticipation of Burnside and Rosecrans linking up north of Chattanooga. Two days later, elements of Burnside's cavalry rode into occupied Knoxville to great applause. Only the day after that, September 2, did Bragg finally realize that Rosecrans was crossing the Tennessee to the south, not the north. The shocking news again paralyzed the high command for days.[33]

The only saving grace was reinforcements. Two divisions from Johnston arrived first. James Longstreet, with two of his three divisions, was on the way from Virginia. But what to do with them? Rosecrans made that decision for Bragg. After midnight on September 3, he issued orders intended to push his army over the mountains and into the Confederate rear, cutting the Western and Atlantic Railroad. By necessity, given the terrain and forage, his corps marched separately. Crittenden's hewed closest to Chattanooga along the Georgia-Tennessee border. McCook swung south into Alabama before turning east. Thomas's corps made for the gaps in between. September 5, the day the movement began, was hot and humid, setting the pattern for those to follow. Federals toiled through daunting, drought-ravaged terrain without enough water.[34]

Bragg wavered until the fifth, when by chance he found a detailed account of Rosecrans's campaign plan in a captured edition of the Copperhead *Chicago Times*. The next morning, his left turned, he issued orders to abandon Chattanooga and move south toward Rome, Georgia. Along the way, he intended to strike part of Rosecrans's separated army. Yet Bragg continued to second guess his reports and himself. Only after sundown on September 7 did the Army of Tennessee begin leaving the city. Once on the road, the slow-moving Confederates endured the same drought.[35] Pvt. W. E. Mathews of the 33rd Alabama remembered "a street in dust half way up to our knees. We appeared to be a low line of dusty creatures without feet."[36]

Federals occupied Chattanooga the next day after reports reached Rosecrans of dust clouds south of the city. Faux deserters sent into Federal lines reinforced the picture of collapse. Jubilant at what seemed to be Bragg's full retreat—perhaps all the way to Atlanta—Rosecrans ordered a pursuit. Thomas disagreed, preferring to first concentrate and resupply. The army was too separated, he counseled, and there were rumors of Confederate reinforcement. Rosecrans was undeterred. His methodical caution gave way to the thrill of the chase. But Bragg was not running. He already had sent troops into a mountain cul-de-sac called McLemore's Cove. He wanted them to strike the lead division of Thomas's corps as it approached the town of La Fayette. Confusion and poor corps leadership threw away a grand opportunity to wreck part of the Federal army there. Rosecrans halted his pursuit and ordered a concentration at Lee and Gordon's Mills, south of Chattanooga on the road to La Fayette. The army began to draw together in heat and dust as its commander sought help from Burnside and even Grant. Bragg tried to hurt the Federals before that concentration took place, but his plans came to naught on hot and dusty September 13 when Polk failed him. He would try one last time to destroy a piece of the Army of the Cumberland before Rosecrans escaped the mountains. Longstreet was due to arrive at any moment. Bragg's plan was to move north, wedge his army between the enemy and Chattanooga eight miles distant, and attack at Lee and Gordon's Mills and along Chickamauga Creek. The Army of Tennessee moved north.[37]

At that moment, the draining heat of the campaign ended, and in startling fashion. In August, a late drought had stunted midwestern crops. Then on August 30, a devastating early frost struck as far north as Minnesota—with ice 1/8 of an inch thick—south into Kentucky, east into Ohio, and as far west as Kansas. After a survey of 126 correspondents across the Old Northwest, the editors of the *Chicago Daily Post* concluded that the frost "'ran in streaks.'" Ground zero was a "Frost Belt" that "embraced an area about two degrees in width," running from the Mississippi River "eastward into Indiana," on a line with Chicago to the north and Springfield to the south. Within that belt, frost killed half the crops in the field and destroyed experimental sorghum fields planted as a substitute for Louisiana sugarcane. In particular, the frost devastated farms in the Wabash Valley of Indiana. In east-central Illinois, a correspondent reported that half the corn crop was ruined, as were most fruits. Local attempts to produce two others southern staples—cotton and tobacco—came to naught once drought combined with the frost. North of the "Frost Belt," in northern Illinois, Wisconsin, and Minnesota, about a quarter of the total crop was ruined. Similar "streaks" ran through Michigan, with the eastern counties especially hurt. Oats suffered to the degree that prices rose dramatically. The Department of Agriculture estimated that frost destroyed 40 percent of crops in Indiana and 30 percent in Illinois, Michigan, and Minnesota.[38]

Incredibly, the August 30 frost disaster was only a precursor. After two more weeks of drought from the Great Plains south into Georgia, a massive cold front barreled across the parched North toward the Confederacy and the Atlantic in mid-September. A smattering of rain heralded dramatic drops in temperature and what one observer called "a hard black" frost. Black frosts—sometimes called killing frosts—occur when a dry atmosphere lacks sufficient moisture to produce familiar icy frost on surfaces. Instead, the water inside leaves and stems freezes, killing the plant while darkening it. Black frosts are ruinous to agriculture. One can track this particular black frost using Smithsonian data as well as newspaper accounts. In Wisconsin, it wrecked what was left of the corn crop. In northeastern Missouri, highs fell from 89 degrees on September 16 to 56 degrees the next day. In the Illinois "Frost Belt," black frost finished off any unharvested crops that survived the previous disaster. Near Saint Louis, the high on the sixteenth was 82 degrees, with "a few drops of rain." The next day's high was 58 degrees. Outside of Louisville, heavy frosts destroyed three-quarters of the local tobacco crop; tobacco prices soared overnight. Corn and potatoes suffered too. Damage extended south into Middle Tennessee, where a correspondent wrote that everything still in the field was ruined. In eastern Kentucky, a plague of grasshoppers added to the devastation.[39]

In the North, the effects of late-summer drought and the twin frosts became evident in October, when the Department of Agriculture compiled returns from around the Union. As compared to 1862, the summer had produced better yields in wheat and oats but not in barley and rye, while fall harvests of buckwheat, corn, and potatoes were worse across the board. Corn threatened to come up short during the coming winter as well. Even with those decreased numbers, northern crop production in 1863 remained robust enough to feed the populace and the army while allowing the export of millions of bushels of grain to foreign markets. The drought-ravaged Confederacy told a different story. Confederate food output actually increased over drought-ravaged 1862, as farmers had turned from cotton to food. Yet they still could not produce enough. A host of war-related factors hurt southern food supplies, including army demands, depredations, abandoned lands, occupation, self-emancipating slaves, and too many conscripted small farmers. The late-summer drought followed by frost provided the final coup de grace. Urban Confederates increasingly found empty shelves and began going hungry. Soldiers would soon suffer as well.[40]

In East Tennessee, the August 30 frost simply brought a welcome end to the worst of the heatwave, but it was the massive mid-September front that played a major role in the battle to come. It arrived in the region on the night of September 17, just as the two armies prepared for battle. As elsewhere, a few sprinkles fell during the night, the first rain since August 16. A howling north wind and falling temperatures followed. Soldiers lacking blankets huddled for warmth. September 18 opened with gray skies. A wailing wind screamed like a ghost through the morning, raising quantities of thick road dust into the hazy air. Marching feet and rolling wheels circulated even more. Temperatures grew cold. While exact readings for the battlefield do not exist, they almost certainly fell into the fifties, if not the upper forties, given both the general pattern and the closest records from Clarksville, where the afternoon high dropped from 80 degrees on the seventeenth to only 54 degrees the next day. The Confederates converged on the creek and formed a north–south line east of the La Fayette Road. The first of Longstreet's contingent, under Maj. Gen. John Bell Hood, arrived and deployed as well. Alerted by the dust clouds the Confederates and the north winds threw into the air, Rosecrans hurried the rest of his forces into position. Scattered fighting began to the south, where the armies converged.[41]

Temperatures kept dropping that night, into the forties, accompanied by a cold north wind. Confederates who had waded the creek now shivered in wet uniforms.[42] Tourgée remembered "a cold wind blew from the north" and that "the firelight shone on the rubber ponchos the men wore to shield them from the chill night wind."[43] Other units marched through the chilly darkness, sometimes stopping to build fires that alerted the enemy. "We moved about a quarter of a mile per hour through the whole night," Judson Bishop of the 2nd Minnesota remembered, "halting every few rods just long enough to get stiff and cold."[44]

By all accounts, the morning of the nineteenth was lovely if frosty and dotted with mist and smoke.[45] Col. James Cooper of the 20th Tennessee thought that "the world never seemed half so attractive before, now that there was a good chance of leaving it soon."[46] Shortly after dawn, Confederate cavalry ran in to a Federal regiment west of the creek. The fighting quickly escalated into a full-scale battle along the La Fayette Road, shaped by the narrow byway, thick forests, scattered small farms, and smoke. Bragg shifted divisions to his right and launched one after another piecemeal against Rosecrans's lengthened left. He hoped to turn the Union flank and shove the enemy into McClemore's Cove. The Federals refused to play along. While comrades to the north held, Union divisions counterattacked to the south. Fighting continued after sundown, as Bragg launched one last attempt against Rosecrans's left. When the shooting stopped around 9 P.M., 13,000–16,000 casualties lay strewn across the fields in bloody heaps.[47]

Night brought horrors all its own. While the cold autumn sky was clear and dotted with stars around a slender crescent moon, the smoke-filled forests were dark and ominous. Overnight temperatures plunged to levels colder than those of the previous night. Toward morning, frost developed.[48] The historians of the 86th Indiana remembered "pinching cold," while Pvt. James Birney Shaw of the 10th Indiana noted how "water froze in our canteens," implying temperatures in the low thirties.[49] Water was otherwise scarce for Federals due to their position—the Confederates held the creek—as well as the month-long drought, which had left small streambeds dry. Soldiers carrying canteens had to walk two or three miles in the dark to fill them. As usual, the wounded suffered most of all, in part due to the cold and a lack of sufficient blankets at overcrowded field hospitals. To try to compensate, attendants placed the wounded close together and built fires at their feet. All across the dark battlefield, others shrieked in pain. Scattered picket fire discouraged their relief, but some men went out anyway to find friends and comrades. Others tore down fence rails and built fires. But where officers allowed none, the men shivered, spooned each other, or huddled under blankets. Historian Peter Cozzens asserts that the Confederates especially suffered due to the predominance of homespun cotton clothing among them instead of wool.[50]

While the soldiers suffered, the generals planned. Sick and dazed by exhaustion, Bragg reorganized his army overnight. He combined his divisions into two wings, Polk in command on the right and Longstreet on the left. At first light, Polk would attack en echelon, hoping to complete the work of the previous day by slamming the Yankees back into the cove. Longstreet would launch his assault after Polk began. Confusion inevitably followed, augmented by sloppy planning and a paucity of written follow-up orders. No one seemed to understand their assigned tasks or make much of an effort to clarify them. Alighting from his train only that night, Longstreet had not even seen the ground, much less most of the men he was about to command. Across the field, an equally worn-out Rosecrans realized that enemy reinforcements now left his army outnumbered. He held an odd council of war, which included Major General McCook singing an old ballad at Rosecrans's request, and concluded to fight on the defense while protecting his escape routes north. At critical points, men began constructing field works. Lines contracted.[51]

September 20, destined to be another of the war's bloody Sabbaths, dawned with cold, frosted turf. Surgeon J. B. Clifton of the 16th Georgia observed ice in a bucket. Stiff soldiers rose from their hard, fitful sleep and built fires to make coffee. The sky was bright and red, but within an hour, "a dense fog or vapor," as L. A. Simmons called it, developed in the Chickamauga Creek bottomland and "obscured the blazes of the thousand fires."[52] Thick fog and smoke remained suspended over low-lying ground until about 8 A.M., leaving dry dust where the frost had been. The field also was almost unbearably silent—to such a degree that it induced anxiety. Contrary to orders, Polk attacked at about 9:30 A.M. While many soldier-authors later assumed that the bishop had waited for the fog to dissipate, the real reasons lay more in Bragg's vague orders plus D. H. Hill's and Polk's cavalier attitudes. When the Confederates finally advanced, they stormed newly established log barricades without adequate reserves to support them from the rear. Despite repeated assaults, the Federal left held. Bragg's plan had failed.[53]

But there was still Longstreet. Through the morning, as the weather warmed, the newly arrived lieutenant general arranged his units to deliver a crushing blow against a vulnerable point in the Union line. If successful, this powerful thrust would turn the Federal right while seizing control of the field's major roads. An hour before noon, Longstreet requested Bragg's permission to try it, not knowing that the general had just ordered an all-out attack. After some confusion, Longstreet struck at about 11:30 A.M. His lead division encountered no initial resistance. Reacting to the earlier threat to his left as well as the result of poor staff work, Rosecrans had ordered a brigade to move into a nonexistent hole in his line, in so doing creating a real gap a quarter-mile wide. Longstreet drove straight into that opening. Panic spread, and the Federal right collapsed. Two corps, their commanders, and Rosecrans fled for Chattanooga, leaving behind a veritable arsenal of abandoned equipment. Dust cloaked the retreating corps like a shroud. Others joined a spirited rear-guard action that Major General Thomas assembled on Horseshoe Ridge at the north end of the field. Flushed with success, Longstreet hardly seemed to know what to do next, while Bragg failed to grasp the situation and denied him support. Indeed, Bragg, near physical collapse and seething at Polk for his failures, soon left the field himself. The timely arrival of Rosecrans's reserve division helped Thomas defend the high ground until the rest of the Army of the Cumberland was safely away on roads Bragg neglected to block.[54]

That night, the battlefield again turned cold. Thomas led his men back into Chattanooga, leaving to the Confederates a cold and blasted landscape.[55] "It was one of the most beautiful moon light nights I ever beheld," Johnny Green of the Confederate 9th Kentucky remarked.[56]

The Federal campaign ended in bloody shambles and left bodies strewn aplenty. Almost in spite of their leaders, the Army of Tennessee had won a major victory at last. But almost immediately, its fruits began slipping away. Disgusted with Bragg, Longstreet never reported that the Federals had fled. When a cold morning heralded the last official day of summer, Bragg ordered probes against an enemy that everyone else knew was already gone. Coupled with the disarray that always followed battle, as well as a lack of wagons and horses, he mounted no pursuit for two days. Seductive reports seemed to indicate that Rosecrans would keep retreating beyond Chattanooga. When the Confederates finally moved out on September 23 after another frosty night, it was to cut off a nonexistent retreat across the Tennessee. Only at midday could Bragg accept the reality that Rosecrans remained, just as at Stones River, locked and loaded behind the city's extensive rifle pits and earthworks. Even then, he spent the next week expecting the Federals to make a run for the north. When Bragg finally settled down for a siege on September 29, he did not expect it to last long, as Rosecrans's army allegedly only had food enough for another week. The general arrayed his outnumbered army as best he could on Lookout Mountain and Missionary Ridge but lacked the numbers to extend his lines to the river. Shelling the Federals proved futile. Bragg tried to use his cavalry to cut off enemy troops from their base. That too accomplished little. In mid-October, with the enemy still in Chattanooga, his generals debated sending infantry to cut off Rosecrans's most direct supply line as well as Longstreet's scheme to shift the army south to Rome, Georgia, and against the base at Bridgeport, Alabama. Bragg wanted no part of that either. As historian Earl Hess observes, the Confederate commander's operational thinking increasingly became defensive. He simply waited for Rosecrans's army to starve.[57]

And so nothing much happened. The Army of Tennessee sat in place while its leader and his nearly mutinous generals spent the rest of September and half of October fighting each other for control. Bragg's decision to purge Lieutenant General Polk as well as Major General Hindman instigated a vigorous countereffort that became a campaign to convince Richmond to fire Bragg. Longstreet wrote to Lee, pleading for him to come and take command, while at Chattanooga most of the generals looked to Longstreet or General Johnston as preferred replacements. Twelve generals eventually signed an anti-Bragg petition, and Major General Forrest threatened to murder Bragg before submitting his resignation. President Davis defused the situation by sending Forrest to Mississippi; then he went west himself. In the end, Davis not only sustained Bragg fully but also helped him conduct his purges. The sad doings dragged into November as Bragg isolated himself. In the meantime, the rank and file complained about the breakup of familiar brigades and divisions while growing weary from short rations. Over two thousand men deserted.[58]

Inside Chattanooga, the besieged Army of the Cumberland exhibited less overt dissention, but the loss of faith in Rosecrans was equally obvious. When news of Chickamauga and the retreat reached the capital, Halleck went into motion. He ordered Meade and Grant to send troops to help Rosecrans. Joe Hooker was soon on the way via railroad with a second chance and two corps from Virginia. Eleven days later, he arrived in Bridgeport. Rosecrans hoped the fresh troops would reopen Chattanooga's supply line. Sherman, meanwhile, took to the road with four divisions from Mississippi.[59]

For the rest of September and most of October, there was little to do in Chattanooga but wait and survive. Harsh weather did little to improve glum moods in either army. The cold on the eve of Chickamauga had signaled the onset of a quite different season. On average, Chattanooga's October temperatures run just a degree cooler than those in Clarksville, where over half the month saw highs only reach into the fifties or below. The twenty-third was the coldest day in Clarksville, with an afternoon high of only 36 degrees. Four days that month never got out of the forties. Two distinct cold spells occurred, one between October 3 and October 8 and the other from October 22 through October 27. Nights were cold, with temperatures for nine falling into the thirties. Morning frost was common except on warm mornings, when heavy dew took its place.[60]

Perhaps more crucially, October was rainy. Fifteen days registered some sort of precipitation, for a monthly total of just over six inches in Clarksville, twice the modern average there or in slightly rainier Chattanooga. September ended with heavy rain and October began with a terrific storm, accompanied by winds hard enough to blow down tents. Longstreet aide Charles Blackford wrote home that the storm's rain was hard enough to drown campfires and wash away the firewood. Precipitation also raised the Tennessee's levels and deposited from a foot to eighteen inches of water in the Federal works; soldiers had to open up their entrenchments to drain them. The period between October 12 and October 23 brought rain every day save two. This watery onslaught also raised the river, soaked troops, and ruined roads. Rain at the end of the month did likewise.[61]

As October wore on and the dust turned to mud, men wearied of it quickly. Blackford wrote at midmonth: "There is a tradition . . . that there has been a time in the past when it wasn't raining, but saving and excepting one or two days I have seen nothing to make me give credence to such a belief. It has rained almost incessantly and the ground is knee-deep in mud and slush and the air so dark and dank that it may be cut with a knife."[62] Fog rose almost daily as well. Forward observers and Federal commanders along the river worried about a literal "fog of war" along no-man's land. "We frequently had the most dense fogs one could conceive of," Confederate Johnny Green wrote. "They would originate at the Tennessee river & then come rolling along the valley & up the mountainside like a moving mountain & it seemed to approach as fast as a man could walk; when you reached us you could not even see a horse twenty feet away; indeed you could not tell at that distance that there was any object there."[63] Many assumed that the "pestilential" fog brought widespread illness with it.[64]

Miserable soldiers in both armies coped with the wet, dismal siege as best they could, but it was not easy. Inside Chattanooga, there were too few coats and blankets. Shoes and uniforms wore out in the rain and the muck. Even when Federals still had tents, Chattanooga's hilly geography caused problems.[65] The 36th Illinois, for example, camped at two sites. The first, according to Chaplain Haigh, "had its disadvantages, for in heavy rains the water poured in streams down the hillside, and was with great difficulty kept out of tents." But the new campground nearer the river was worse. It was "very low and flat there," so "there was not only no opportunity for drainage, but it was at night and morning enveloped in thick fog, and justified the strong expression of Major [George D.] Sherman as we took possession of our new quarters, 'there, Gentlemen, is where you can get your ague in solid chunks.'"[66] Federals began building what L. A. Simmons called "shanties of every conceivable description."[67]

Confederates faced similar difficulties. Blackford complained, "I have no bed and water runs through my tent, as the ditch only gathers [the rain] so it can creep through my floor of dark mould, which is literally spongy with moisture, and my poor oilcloth does not keep they dampness off me."[68] They were at least newly supplied with quantities of "small tent flies, gum cloths, and blankets" gathered up at Chickamauga, "where they were thrown away by the fleeing Yankees."[69] Others built shanties of scrap wood.

Food was an even more crucial issue. Both sides complained of hunger. Confederates subsisted on parched corn, meat scraps, and the occasional rat. Having neither the men nor the will to close off Chattanooga from the west, Bragg allowed trickles of supplies to come in to the city from the railhead at Bridgeport over the mountains by wagon train. As October progressed, however, the rain, terrain, bad roads, and Confederates combined to threaten even those shipments. A cavalry raid on rainy October 1 not only intercepted food and ammunition but also seized the wagons as well. A week later, Confederate infantry in Lookout Valley shut off one of the two remaining routes. The single road remaining became deep with mud as the midmonth downpours ensued. The end result was something akin to starvation for the Federals. When rations grew lean enough, Billy Yank ate everything from the butchers' offal to stray dogs, even cracker crumbs plucked from the mud beneath supply wagons.[70]

The army's animals suffered more than men. Simmons wrote that the beasts became "completely worn out, and hundreds of mules had died all along the road to Stevenson [Alabama]. It is said that enough were killed

on the circuitous route . . . to have made a single line of carcasses tough-
ing each other from Chattanooga to Stevenson, but we think this estimate
quite too large."[71] Inside the city, horses died in droves. Facing a lack of forage, headquarters simply decided to let their artillery horses starve rather
than feed them the forage needed for supply transport.[72]

~

Heavy rain returned on October 22 and continued the next day. Chattanooga once again lay in the path of a massive midwestern weather system
that pushed on into Virginia and south to the Gulf of Mexico. Between October 22 and October 25, it dumped snow from the Rockies east to Illinois
and Indiana and brought rain as far south as South Carolina and heavy gales
to the Gulf Coast. Temperatures in Tennessee hit their lowest points of the
month, reaching 37 degrees in Clarksville on the twenty-third and falling
to 33 degrees overnight.[73]

Near dark, a small party of riders arrived in dank Chattanooga on the
one road from Stevenson. Mud covered their trousers and boots, and rain
had soaked them to the skin. Arriving at headquarters, they stood or sat
awkwardly near a fire in their wet uniforms until one of U. S. Grant's aides
suggested that dry clothing and something to eat might be in order.

It was an oddly stiff meeting, given the stakes and the circumstances.
Six days earlier, Halleck intercepted Grant and his family in Indianapolis as Grant traveled to Louisville per orders. In Grant's rail car, Halleck
gave him command of the vast new Military District of the Mississippi,
which essentially encompassed his Vicksburg army, Burnside's new command, and the Army of the Cumberland. Given a choice of commanders
in Chattanooga, Grant agreed with Halleck's wishes to replace Old Rosy
with Thomas. He disliked both men but detested Rosecrans more. A telegram, designed to ease Halleck's frantic fears of the army retreating from
Chattanooga, enjoined Thomas to hold out at all costs. Thomas's reply was
quick: "I will hold the town till we starve." Two days later, Grant met awkwardly with both Rosecrans and his old friend Hooker in Stevenson, then
rode on to Bridgeport. According to Grant, Rosecrans "made some excellent suggestions as to what should be done. My only wonder was that he
had not carried them out." Grant crossed the mountains. "There had been
much rain," he remembered, "and the roads were almost impassable from
mud, knee-deep in places, and from washouts on the mountainsides. . . .

The roads were strewn with the débris of broken wagons and the carcasses of thousands of starved horses and mules."[74]

Now, Thomas and Grant met face to face in Chattanooga. That night after supper, the generals and their staffs discussed a bold plan to open up a better supply line from Bridgeport. The Tennessee River made two hairpin loops just past Chattanooga. The smaller one near the city, Moccasin Point, poked south toward Longstreet's Confederates and Lookout Mountain. The larger one twisted first north and then south around Raccoon Mountain. Maj. Gen. Baldy Smith suggested a plan that involved bridging the river at Brown's Ferry on the western side of Moccasin Point. From the ferry, a road led south and then west to Kelley's Ferry at the western base of the larger loop. Federal transports could safely unload supplies at Kelley's Ferry for a relatively short overland trip, while the currents past that spot were too strong for the steamboats at the army's disposal. Grant first wanted to see it for himself. Hurting from a serious fall, he telegrammed Washington asking that Sherman be given command of the Army of the Tennessee, then limped to bed.[75]

Chattanooga remained cold, but at least the rain had stopped. On the chilly morning of October 24, with temperatures in the thirties, Grant, Thomas, and Smith rode out to survey the key positions of the Brown's Ferry plan. The skies were gray and the roads mushy, with a mist in the air. Grant liked what he saw and approved the operation. He told Hooker to leave a division to guard the railroad at Bridgeport, cross the Tennessee River with everything else he had, and move up through Lookout Valley toward Brown's Ferry. From Chattanooga, under cover of darkness, Brig. Gen. William B. Hazen's brigade would float nine miles down the river to Brown's Ferry in pontoon boats, seize the high ground, and wait for a second brigade to row across in support. If all went well, Hooker would meet them there, and the supply line would be open.[76]

The plan was risky from the start, and later complications made it hairier still. Hooker had his doubts and moved gingerly, as if Stonewall Jackson might again hit his unprotected flank. Grant started without him. Then Bragg received reports of Hooker's activity. He ordered Longstreet to send troops into Lookout Valley to see what was happening. But the Federals caught a bit of luck, thanks to the Army of Tennessee's ongoing command cancer. Longstreet, still feuding with Bragg, did nothing to comply. Indeed, for reasons that remain unclear, most of the Confederate brigade stationed near Brown's Ferry pulled out on October 25, leaving a mere two regiments behind. The unit's commander, Brig. Gen. Evander Law, came close to divining Grant's plans, but no one paid any attention to his calls for more troops.[77]

Law's worst fears came to pass. Around 3 A.M. on October 27, Hazen's brigade embarked. Not only was the night pitch black after moonset but fog also rolled in over the river valley, together hiding the attackers like a cloak. No Confederates on Lookout Mountain saw them pass. At around 4:30 A.M., the Federals waded ashore in the fog and, after a few wild volleys, took the position in a few minutes. They threw up breastworks as fast as they could and waited for reinforcement. A small regimental counterattack collapsed quickly in the foggy darkness as Federal skirmishers and Confederates fired blindly in the fog at less than twenty feet away from each other. As the sun rose, the fog remained thick. Law arrayed the rest of his brigade to block the road out of the ferry to Lookout Mountain and sent a plea for help to Longstreet. A second Federal brigade crossed the river at 7 A.M. Both waited for Hooker, still a day away.[78]

Longstreet did nothing. Late on October 27, Bragg found out about the attack. His understandable confusion and Longstreet's insubordination dragged on through the next misty day. Temperatures rose to 60 degrees as a testy meeting full of angry recrimination took place atop windy Lookout Mountain. Bragg ordered Longstreet to retake the ferry in force. Instead, the lieutenant general decided to hit Hooker's rear. Hooker himself had arrived at Brown's Ferry around 3:45 P.M. on the twenty-eighth, but most of his column stretched back down the road. He acted just as he had at Chancellorsville on the first day, as if there was no threat from the enemy. His divisions camped haphazardly at points along the road with little thought of defense. In Hooker's slack dispositions, Longstreet saw an opportunity. He launched a night attack against a division at Wauhatchie Station, on the Nashville and Chattanooga Railroad. At midnight, two Confederate divisions, including Law's brigade, struck. After the initial surprise, the outnumbered Federals held on tenaciously, firing at rifle flashes in the darkness. Hooker tried to send help but botched his dispositions. Law held the high ground against the Federal assaults, then withdrew before dawn.[79]

Over the next several days, Bragg and Longstreet blamed each other for the loss of the valley. Bragg decided to get rid of the insubordinate general too, using a suggestion Davis had made. On November 3, he sent Longstreet into East Tennessee to drive Burnside out of Knoxville. General Lee wanted his men back with the Army of Northern Virginia anyway, and Davis's promise to restore the brigades Bragg had loaned out earlier would mostly compensate. The numbers would look better, of course, if Grant sent part of his army to help Burnside. Longstreet thought the decision was madness, but within forty-eight hours, his ill-supplied men were on the move away from Bragg.[80]

Grant, meanwhile, came close to firing Hooker, but the supply line from Bridgeport to Brown's Ferry—soon nicknamed the "Cracker Line"—was open for business. In a real sense, the siege of Chattanooga was over. Still, Sherman remained two weeks' march away. Hungry men and weak animals in the city also needed to regain their strength. Frustrated with the delay and urged by Washington to do something to help Burnside, Grant ordered Thomas to attack Missionary Ridge on November 7 and drive on toward Knoxville. Baldy Smith and Thomas talked him out of this, but their hesitance left a bad taste.[81] Grant concluded that "nothing was left to be done" but to wait restlessly for his favorite lieutenant to arrive while encouraging Burnside to "hold on."[82]

Chapter 17

The Hardest Spell of Weather

East Tennessee, Winter 1863–1864

While the campaign to break out of Chattanooga hung fire, better weather arrived. The first half of November 1863 in East Tennessee was much drier than soppy October. Rain fell in Middle Tennessee only four times, to a little over half an inch, but still enough to raise the river. Temperatures were unsettled. The month started out with a brief heatwave that reached 77 degrees in Clarksville on the second.[1] In Chattanooga, Chaplain John J. Hight of the 58th Indiana wrote: "[I] wore my hat during preaching. . . . The heat of the sun required it today."[2] Colder temperatures arrived along with rain on November 5, but four days of Indian summer returned at midmonth. Fog partially obscured Lookout Mountain until the cold returned.[3] Bragg's Confederates—especially those high on the mountain—lacked tents and sometimes blankets. Col. John Moore later complained that his men were "exposed to a cold north wind, the ground being sometimes covered with snow." Despite the threat of enemy artillery, he established his headquarters in Robert Cravens's house on the northern edge of the mountain. Escaping the wind, and not any "reckless display of courage," convinced him to chance "Yankee shells" there.[4]

For Longstreet's Confederates, higher elevations made East Tennessee weather even tougher to bear. The rain early in November overlapped their railroad ride to the staging area at Sweetwater, halfway between Chattanooga and Knoxville. Cavalry and artillery followed under their horse power. Delays caused by underpowered locomotives and overuse—Bragg's reinforcements came south on the return runs—slowed the transfer. Men sometimes had to walk along slick roadbeds. Lt. Col. Charles Blackford of Longstreet's staff headed a letter home "Camp in the mud, east Tennessee," and wrote that "the mud is terrible; and the constant rain made it worse. We stalled every half-mile."[5] Then the weather turned cold. Surgeon J. B.

Clifton of the 16th Georgia described "heavy frost, and plenty of ice on the water" on November 9. "This evening it began to snow," he added, "but did not last long." The next day was cold but clear.[6] Delayed by poor transportation and a paucity of rations, the task force of 12,000 soldiers did not get moving again until the cold and rainy evening of November 13. Frequent showers followed, and a severe thunderstorm the next night shook tents loose and swayed trees. Shoes, wheels, and doubled-teamed hooves sank into the mud.

Bad weather affected Burnside too. His mission was to hold Knoxville. He had placed two divisions at the Tennessee River to contest any crossing, but with Longstreet's approach, he abandoned his supplies and withdrew as fast as possible, hoping to widen the gap between Longstreet and Bragg. November 15 saw men on both sides wading deep mud while dragging wagons and guns over slick mountain ridges. Mud and terrain slowed the Army of the Ohio's retreat considerably but prevented Longstreet from getting between the Federal column and Knoxville, which would have compelled Burnside to fight away from the formidable earthworks there. Mud-covered soldiers went into line that night without fires as temperatures fell into the thirties. Thick fog settled over the Federal line. The next day was cool and rainy, with highs reaching perhaps the midforties. Using dif-

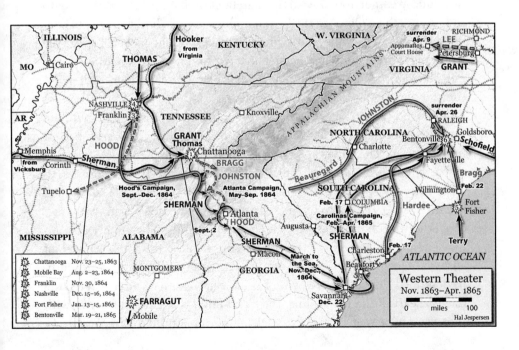

ferent roads, both armies moved as fast as they could through glue-like road muck for the crossroads at Campbell's Station, southwest of Knoxville. Burnside got there first and held on as repeated Confederate attacks failed to dislodge him. Evening brought drizzle that further reduced the roads to something like a river. Through the night and the next day, the Federals splashed and slipped into Knoxville's imposing fortifications. Longstreet's two unappetizing choices now were either a siege—for which his army was unprepared—or an assault that was likely doomed to fail.[7]

Grant had ordered Sherman and two corps to Chattanooga on September 23. The columns moved slowly across northern Mississippi, past Corinth and Iuka, and into northern Alabama. Until late October, Washington burdened them with the additional task of repairing their railroad supply line behind them as they went. The march took Sherman's men high into the same mountains that had worn out the Army of the Cumberland earlier in the season. As historian Peter Cozzens points out, their list of complaints was strikingly similar—exhaustion, bad roads, little food or forage, dying horses and mules, and wrecked wagons—as Sherman refused to abandon his train.[8] Weather, too, slowed the march. Lt. Col. Aden Cavins of the 97th Indiana wrote on October 18: "[L]ast night it rained all night except about one-half hour . . . [while] our regiment [was] standing picket. I spent the whole night in encouraging the men to make fires to keep them warm." The rain ended before the column reached Iuka, but it grew colder, with night-time lows in the thirties. Cavins complained on the twenty-fifth: "I cannot keep warm of nights, by wearing all my clothes, overcoat and all, but I am getting hardened to it. Ice froze over in a bucket and over half an inch thick in a wash pan. The winds are damp and fierce."[9]

November brought no respite. East of Florence, the 6th Wisconsin Battery's Pvt. Jenkin Jones reported heavy rain on November 5: "The rain fell in torrents. . . . The clay, which in dry weather made good roads, was soon converted into bottomless mud." They remained muddy as his column crossed into Tennessee. On the eighth, temperatures dropped. "Froze half an inch of ice on water," Jones wrote from Fayetteville. On the eleventh, he described "horses covered with frost."[10] Sherman soon after entered the rugged heart of the mountains. Dark and rainy November 14 began with "not a star to be seen or ray of daylight. . . . Commenced to rain very heavy

. . . and it continued until noon, with loud peals of thunder and vivid light-ning. The road ran along the summit for about five miles which was very muddy and hard to travel."[11]

Sherman woke up in Bridgeport on November 14 and took a boat to meet Grant and Thomas. Grant assigned him a crucial role in the battle set to commence on November 21: striking Bragg's right at Missionary Ridge. As the generals met, Sherman's men trudged to the Tennessee. The weather was sunny and pleasant at first, if cold at night. Starting on the seventeenth, his brigades began crossing a pontoon bridge over the South Chickamauga River, hoping to catch Bragg unawares.[12] Heavy river fog the next day helped the deception work. Chaplain Hight called it "one of the heaviest fogs I ever saw. It was so thick at ten a. m. that an object could not be seen a few yards off." Even when the fog lifted that afternoon, "a hazy atmosphere of Indian summer prevented us from seeing objects very dis-tinctly."[13]

Rain held off until chilly November 20, returning in volume that evening as the first of Sherman's brigades marched into Chattanooga. With the remaining troops queued up across the river, traffic backed up from the bridge. Grant postponed his attack. More rain fell all day on the twenty-first, flooding tents and entrenchments. Grant delayed again. The combi-nation of bad weather and Sherman's tardiness reached its climax on warm, lovely, and dry November 22, when the swollen Tennessee River began to batter away the pontoon bridge. Progress again halted.[14]

Bragg misread Grant, however. On the rainy twenty-first, with a high temperature of probably around 50 degrees, Bragg first learned that Sher-man was approaching. Lacking enough cavalry—he had sent if off piece-meal for strikes against Federal communications—he jumped to the con-clusion that the column was moving against Longstreet instead of his own right. On the following night, he ordered Maj. Gen. Patrick Cleburne and two divisions away from Missionary Ridge to bolster Longstreet. The next morning, November 23, was cloudy and gray, with temperatures in the upper thirties and every indication of more rain. During the day, the ther-mometer moved into the fifties as Federal observers saw Cleburne's troops leave. Grant guessed their destination and once again put his own plans on hold. Instead, he sent a large reconnaissance in force against the Con-federate outpost on steep Orchard Knob, 2,000 yards from his lines and near the base of Missionary Ridge. His men moved with parade-ground precision across open, soggy ground beneath a dark sky. Achieving surprise, the Federals overachieved and easily took the height. Encouraged by Thomas, Grant decided to keep it. Bragg reacted by shifting troops from his weakened left to Missionary Ridge while calling back Cleburne. Half of the ridge's defenders held rifle pits at its base, while the rest went into line on the natural crest.[15]

The following morning, according to Lt. Jeremiah Donahower of the 2nd Minnesota, was "sunless and dismal. . . . [O]ver Look Out Mountain hung a dense bank of mist."[16] Afternoon highs reached perhaps 60 degrees, despite a steady drizzle that continued all day with brief interruptions. The steep, craggy, and heavily wooded mountain was to be the scene of the day's fighting. While Grant had focused on breaking Bragg's line at Missionary Ridge, Thomas had campaigned for an effort against Lookout Mountain on the Confederate left. After the capture of Orchard Knob shifted the tactical front—and with some of Sherman's men yet to arrive—Grant ordered Hooker to demonstrate against enemy positions at the mountain with his three divisions and seize the heights if possible. Hooker eagerly reinterpreted those orders into a full-scale assault against the troops on the bench, which if successful would force the Confederates on the summit to flee.

The attack at first faltered as Hooker's lead division encountered flooded Lookout Creek and had to cross on a single, hastily constructed footbridge. Shrouded by fog and rain—but supported by overwhelming Federal artillery—his wet easterners attacked at about 9:30 A.M. With relative ease, they shoved their way through the stretched and weak Confederate defensive line to the mountain's base. One division drove the defenders up the slopes to the Cravens house, on the shelf on the mountain's northern side. The rest followed. That afternoon, the fog grew thicker as temperatures fell; a massive cold front had arrived from the west. Around the house, visibility dropped to no more than a few steps. Firing wildly into the fog, the Federal advance stumbled to a stop, allowing the Confederates to form a new line. The fighting went on until night, with scattered gunfire continuing until midnight.[17]

Throughout the day, "a dense cloud enveloped the side of the mountain," Lt. L. A. Simmons wrote, "and though the summit was in full view above the cloud, the furiously contending forces upon the Northern slope were entirely hidden."[18] The mountaintop, Brigadier General Hazen agreed, was "above the clouds, as poetically described, for there were great banks of fog below."[19] Occasionally, open spaces appeared, allowing soldiers below to see men and flags. For them, the battle was largely an aural experience.[20]

On Lookout Mountain, the Confederates slipped away during the night; Bragg sent them to Missionary Ridge. While Lieutenant General Hardee counseled retreat, lest the army be trapped by rain-swollen and rising waters, Bragg decided to hold Missionary Ridge. A hard rain, meanwhile, dissolved the soon-to-be legendary fogbank, fully exposing the mountain. Temperatures dropped into the thirties. Federal soldiers shivered in wet, frost-laden blankets. Many slept without fires, their positions too close to the enemy. Others decided they had no choice but to have them if they wanted to survive cold approaching 30 degrees.[21] It was an eerie night as well. In addition to the wailing and moans of the wounded, a bright full moon broke into view after midnight. Then, just as the Confederates began quietly evacuating, a total lunar eclipse plunged the city into blackness. Historian Peter Cozzens maintains that the daytime defeat, the sights of the dead, and the night sky's dark omen sank Lookout Mountains' defeated Johnny Rebs into "a strange ennui."[22]

But all was not rosy for the Union cause. Sherman was stuck. During the Lookout Mountain fight, he had moved ahead on what he thought was Missionary Ridge only to find himself on an entirely separate eminence. In between lay a wide ravine and formidable Confederate fortifications at steep Tunnel Hill. That cold night, Grant readjusted his plans. Sherman still would strike the crushing blow from the north, while Hooker would move on Bragg's left at Rossville Gap and Thomas would advance to the base of Missionary Ridge.[23] Morning brought chillier temperatures than the previous day—perhaps 30 degrees at daybreak—but the same soggy ground; at least the rain held off. Indeed, the skies seemed remarkably bright. Yet little went right for Grant at first. Sherman's repeated assaults failed to make headway at Tunnel Hill. Hooker remained south of swollen Chattanooga Creek and its burned bridges for hours. When he finally got across, he met stiff resistance. Late in the afternoon, with afternoon temperatures dropping back toward the thirties, Grant sent Thomas against the rifle pits to the east, hoping that this would help Sherman. Taking these positions easily, Thomas's men kept going up the incline, without orders or much unit cohesion, at least in part to escape the killing zone created by enemy fire. The Confederates' foolish placement of guns and works on the natural crest made their fire increasingly ineffective. In an hour, the Army of the Cumberland breached Bragg's line. The Federals then drove the broken Army of Tennessee to the east toward Chickamauga Station. Only Grant's own shock, Peter Cozzens concludes, saved thousands of Confederates from capture. The night turned bitterly cold, with frost and temperatures probably bottoming in the upper twenties.[24]

The next day, November 26, was the first national Thanksgiving Day, as proclaimed by Lincoln. In Virginia (as discussed in chapter eighteen) George Meade opened his Mine Run Campaign, an operation shaped by rain and extreme cold. Those same factors affected operations in Tennessee. Heavy fog returned to the Tennessee River valley as Bragg's army staggered toward Dalton, Georgia, on the vital Western and Atlantic Railroad. In Chattanooga, thick fog made everything beyond ten yards invisible. A bright moon that night looked down on cold men and mud, with the mercury probably in the upper thirties.

The Federal pursuit on November 27 ended when Hooker failed to dislodge Cleburne at Ringgold Gap. Worried about supplies and still anxious about supporting Burnside, Grant broke it off.[25] The Confederates staggered into Dalton that night in a cold drizzle, blaming Bragg and Jeff Davis for their shame. They had left behind a third of their artillery, a trail of debris, and thousands of prisoners, deserters, and stragglers.[26] Cpl. William Bevens of the 1st Arkansas pronounced it "the coldest night our thinly clad men had ever experienced."[27] In Clarksville the next day, it was 28 degrees at 2 P.M. Chattanooga's temperatures should have been similar, and indicate the passage of a massive arctic cold front. The following days brought rain and sleet, with highs in the upper twenties or low thirties and overnight lows in the teens. They also saw Bragg's resignation from command of the Army of Tennessee.[28]

In the years that followed, Confederate veterans struggled to explain what had happened on Missionary Ridge. While Bragg was everyone's favorite scapegoat—and still is—Pvt. P. D. Stephenson of the 13th Arkansas also blamed the weather. The army had spent the "'sickly season'" in the "swampy bottom of the Chickamauga River, . . . which heavy rains convert into a vast morass or quagmire. . . . Rains came on us, making sickness worse, making roads impassable, cutting off supplies of every kind from us, and reducing us by November 25 and 26 to an army of half-sick (even those fit for duty), half-starved, half-clothed men, our ranks thinned by the thousands under medical cure." They had no shelter except "booths or tree branches and a few little fly tents" erected in "a lake of mud fifty or sixty feet or more wide." Near their camp, someone had erected a sign reading "'Mule underneath here.' A mule had actually sunk out of sight in the mud at that spot. . . . [T]he wonder is that there was any fight left in us."[29] That final assessment was true. Bad weather shaped everything that happened in the fight for Chattanooga.

~~~

In the days that followed Missionary Ridge, the Knoxville Campaign played out in weather that was even worse. Having failed to cut off Burnside's retreat, Longstreet's Confederates followed the Army of the Ohio on November 17. The next morning, dense fog blanketed the front north of a bend in the Tennessee River. Longstreet brought up skirmishers, intending to shove aside a pesky Federal cavalry screen. When the little contingent refused to budge, he poured in more men until the position broke late in the afternoon.[30] The following day, Longstreet moved up to Burnside's works north and west of the city. The so-called "siege" of Knoxville began. In truth, Longstreet lacked enough men to starve out the city and its defenders. Indeed, he also was running out of supplies and managed to get entrenchments prepared only through the lucky capture of enemy picks and shovels. Burnside, reasonably well supplied with food enough for a week or perhaps two, also had an open supply line to friendly farmers south of the city. He countered Confederate moves with more digging, rationing, and killing any horses and mules he did not need. Over the next few days, Union entrenchments assumed an even more a formidable quality, complete with augmented forts, redoubts, extensive trenches, telegraph wire strung as impediments, and water hazards created by flooding already swollen waterways. Cold temperatures and rain made labor in Knoxville's flooded defenses a miserable ordeal. The Confederates, out in the open, resorted to digging out burrows in their works for shelter. Civilians, too, abandoned life above ground and moved into cellars or ravines to escape Confederate shelling.[31]

Longstreet felt increasing pressure to act or to leave. His men were hungry and barefoot. Bragg sent frantic messages asking him to hurry back before Grant attacked. Yet there was no obvious course of action; Longstreet had no idea what to do. He first planned an assault on the night of November 22, intending to strike newly named and strengthened Fort Sanders on the Federal line's northwestern corner. It stood on high ground above sloping land to the front and behind a wide, deep manmade ditch and felled timber, but it rested dangerously in a vulnerable salient. He soon had second thoughts and cast about for alternatives. None emerged. Longstreet returned to the idea of striking Fort Sanders on the twenty-fifth but again delayed when hopeful word came that Bragg was sending reinforcements. Grant's attack on Missionary Ridge that day assured that those men would never arrive. In the meantime, Burnside's men and freedpeople kept digging and fortifying. Longstreet finally issued orders for an attack on November 28. While the ditch concerned him, an optical illusion convinced him that it was no more than three feet deep. Three brigades under Maj. Gen. Lafayette McLaws would charge Fort Sanders at dawn.[32]

The weather refused to cooperate. The night of November 27, as elsewhere in East Tennessee, turned extremely cold, with high wind and drizzle. Heavy rain followed around sunup. Seven Federal cavalrymen drowned when an ice-covered rope foundered their ferry. Longstreet delayed until 2 P.M. and relented again when McLaws objected.[33] The Confederate commander blamed the weather, which was "so heavy and murky as to hide the fort from view of our artillery, so operations were put off until the 29th."[34] That night, McLaws pushed skirmishers up to the fort while his artillery repositioned. But as rumors began to arrive that Bragg had lost Chattanooga, a command crisis ensued. McLaws argued for canceling the attack entirely and returning to Virginia. Longstreet declared that such a course would be disgraceful.[35]

The next morning was frigid and damp. Concerned about the ground and the felled trees, McLaws attacked with only two brigades, keeping the others in reserve. He arrayed his men in the predawn darkness north and west of the fort. They shivered in the bitter cold without fires. Thick fog formed along the river. Skies were heavy and gray. What followed was disaster. Confederate artillery opened up around 6 A.M. The infantry went forward about twenty minutes later, led by skirmishers through uneven terrain, tangled abatis, and spider webs of low-strung telegraph wire. Fifty yards from the fort, Federal gunfire opened up. The attackers hit the ditch only to discover to their horror that it was from four to six feet deep and eight to twelve feet wide. Above them, the nearly sheer face of the fort rose another twelve feet, covered in ice due to buckets of water poured down it. The Confederates had no scaling ladders. The assault largely died there in the ditch, although a few Confederates made it to the top of the parapet by standing on comrades' shoulders. Flanking fire from small arms and artillery raked them, while Federal artillerymen directly above them dropped shells with flaming short fuses into the ditch. The attack was over in forty minutes. The defenders took hundreds of prisoners, but the ditch also was filled with corpses and inches of blood. Burnside offered a ceasefire. While the Confederates built fires to warm the wounded, the Federals went into no-man's land to return broken men and captured blankets. Officers from the old army gave coats and hats to former comrades now in gray.

As the survivors fell back, an ill-timed dispatch from Davis arrived informing Longstreet that Bragg was in retreat and that he needed to rejoin him. Giving no thought to a renewed assault, Longstreet made plans to retreat to Chattanooga. When later dispatches told him that such a course was impossible—the Yankees were in the way and held the railroad—he decided instead to hold his ground, in hopes of drawing the enemy away from Bragg, before returning to Virginia. The brittle siege would continue. The evening following the assault brought 24-degree temperatures, according to historian Earl Hess. It was 16 degrees at 7 A.M. the next morning, and the temperature never rose above freezing that sunny day.[36]

Longstreet was right to assume that, with Bragg in retreat, his old friend Grant would act quickly to rescue Burnside. As soon as he broke off his pursuit, Grant ordered out a relief column. On rainy November 28, he sent Sherman with most of his command. Worn down and battle weary, Sherman's men found the forced march agonizing and unwelcome. To save time, many regiments left their shelter tents behind. Sparse rations grew tighter.[37] Recent rains had ruined the roads. Chaplain Haigh of the 36th Illinois complained of ankle-deep mud, while Cpl. Edward Schweitzer of the 30th Ohio judged it knee deep.[38] "The roads were muddy," the historians of the 86th Indiana remembered. "The regiment went splashing along through the mud like so many wild horses, wading streams knee-deep and deeper. . . . [T]he men were wet to their trunks by plunging into mud holes and wading streams."[39]

It was frightfully cold as well. Haigh recalled conditions "so cold that ice, one and three-quarters thick, stood in the sun all day."[40] While daytime temperatures rose steadily into the forties and then the fifties starting on December 2, nights remained cold. Warm daylight hours and sweaty exertion, not to mention wet uniforms from crossing flooded waterways, produced constant dampness that made those chilly nights more difficult. Even men with tents slept cold, with pine boughs or fence rails to keep them off the frozen earth.[41] Lt. Col. Wilbur Hinman of the 65th Ohio later called the effort "the most disagreeable, comfortless, and altogether wretched campaign of [the brigade's] entire army service. The men thought they had been in 'hard times' before, but no previous [or] subsequent experiences were so bountifully productive of bodily misery and discomforts as that midwinter excursion into the wilds of East Tennessee."[42]

Worst of all, it seemed to be for nothing. During the night of December 4, Longstreet left the Knoxville area and moved away to the north. Cold and rainy weather mired down his transportation and then froze the roads into jagged hazards that cut into bloody feet. Men ignored orders and built fires of fence rails. Thankfully, the rain stopped, and bright skies appeared. Shivering and staggering, the column collapsed at Rogersville. Burnside launched a short pursuit but stopped at Strawberry Plains, assuming that Longstreet would keep going. He did not. While his men did want to stay on the move until they were back with Lee, Longstreet decided to hold out in East Tennessee if he could be supplied by railroad from Virginia. Richmond approved and gave him departmental command on December 10. His men looked ahead with foreboding to a long winter in the mountains.[43]

Sherman learned on December 5 that Longstreet was in retreat. He entered Knoxville the next day, annoyed that the men he had come to save clearly had been eating better than his own troops. But the march was worth it. All but a sliver of Tennessee was now in Federal hands, much to Lincoln's delight. Leaving two unhappy divisions to bolster Burnside, Sherman took the muddy road back to Chattanooga with the balance, arriving at midmonth after a round trip of 250 miles. His proud men boasted that they had defeated both the Confederates and the East Tennessee mud.[44]

For Grant and Sherman, December 1863 brought a frustrating conclusion to a year of unparalleled success. They wanted to keep pressing the Confederates. Both first assumed that Longstreet would keep moving into Virginia on his own, so they looked elsewhere. Prior to leaving Mississippi, both had advocated a campaign against Mobile, one of the Confederacy's last windows to the world. Grant persisted, while Sherman called for a thrust from Chattanooga through largely untouched Alabama to the manufacturing citadel at Selma or else returning to Vicksburg for a march across Mississippi. Quickly shifting his army to New Orleans for a drive to Mobile and on into Alabama, Grant maintained, would help exhaust the enemy's remaining resources while keeping his men busy. This route made more sense, he believed, than going into the barren mountains of North Georgia.

Washington hesitated, while Longstreet remained in East Tennessee.

The War Department had approved a plan to send Banks's army through Louisiana into Texas, in part to secure cotton for northern mills but also to counter French imperial expansion in Mexico. Halleck also worried about the enemy stirring in Arkansas and a possible Confederate counteroffensive up the Mississippi. Grant also had to deal with a looming manpower shortage, as Union three-year enlistments drew to a close. New legislation aimed at keeping men in the field authorized month-long furloughs home, among other inducements, for those who would reenlist for the war as "veteran volunteers." Ultimately, about 58 percent of soldiers did so. Either way, Grant's numbers would decline over the winter despite the additions of conscripts and substitutes. The general adjusted accordingly. He left Chattanooga and moved his headquarters to Nashville, leaving Thomas in the southeastern Tennessee city. Sherman arrayed his men in northern Alabama from Stevenson through Decatur and back up into Tennessee.[45]

The weather of December 1863 justified the decision to stop. The month was wetter than usual. Almost 4.8 inches of rain fell in Clarksville, as opposed to the modern mean average of about 4.3 inches. Chattanooga sees typically 5.3 inches during the month, so one can hypothesize that perhaps 6 inches fell that December. Most of the precipitation appeared during two distinct periods, from December 4 through December 18 and after a cold, windy, and altogether dreary Christmas Day through December 28. It was cold, too, with an average morning low of 36 degrees in Clarksville and a mean 2 P.M. high of 46 degrees. Little was average that winter, however, as temperatures actually fluctuated greatly. Twelve mornings began at freezing or below, with the nineteenth and twentieth in the teens. Highs trended downward, from the fifties in the month's first week down into the twenties on December 18 and December 19 before rebounding at the solstice.[46]

In and around Chattanooga, Sherman's and Thomas's men shivered under canvas at first. Soldiers planning to "veteranize" and go home saw no reason to build more substantial huts, relying instead on big fires until available firewood turned to ash. Drummer William Bircher of the 2nd Minnesota and his comrades stripped earthworks of floors and supports to burn. Food was in short supply too. The single railroad proved painfully inadequate to properly feed men and animals in Chattanooga and Knoxville. Bircher's regiment went on half rations on December 22. In January 1864, some soldiers would either bank their tents with earth, construct shanties, or build cabins. The 15th Illinois, for example, camping near Woodville,

Alabama, constructed cabins built from the logs of a nearby beech forest. Their structures included fireplaces, tents attached to the doorway for
cooking and washing, and doors made of foraged boards. Flooring and furniture came from a white-oak tree and a borrowed crosscut saw. They also
built a rude church for their chaplain, who also used it as a school for local
African American children.[47]

In contrast, the Confederates at Dalton, Georgia, prepared for winter
by building cabins as soon as possible—the standard southern practice. It
took about a week of industry. Officers relied on enslaved labor, at least
in part, but the rank and file largely built their own shelters. Officers also
sometimes provided their men incentives, as when the staff of the 40th Alabama offered a gallon of brandy to the company that built the best cabins.
While some men chose the Federal model and utilized a canvas roof, the
practice of providing a froe to each regiment encouraged most to construct
them from pine boards. As for the cabins, some soldiers split oak timbers
to build their shelters, while others left the logs intact. Captured shelter
tents served as doors.[48] "In our winter quarters," Lt. R. M. Collins of the
15th Texas Cavalry later wrote, "there was as great a variety of architecture
as there was to be found in any city or town in the country." These ranged
from the "tidy" to the "filthy as a pig pen" built from "odds and ends that
[the builder] can pick up here and there."[49] The artillerymen of Lumsden's
Alabama Battery built their cabins seven feet in indoor height to pole rafters, with a twelve-foot-by-fourteen-foot leveled floor plan. Built of logs,
they also boasted stick-and-mud chimneys, board roofs, bunks, benches,
and a blanket for a door. "Soldiers were fixed to defy the coldest days of
winter and sleep in comfort on the coldest nights," Sgt. James Maxwell explained. "A good fat bed-fellow was a luxury not to be despised and on coldest nights, 'spooning' was the prevailing fashion with covering well tucked
under. When one wanted to turn over, it was necessary for the other to do
the same. Some times they would do so by word of command as if at drill
with 'one time and two motions.'"[50]

With their shelters built, but lacking enough blankets or shoes, the Confederates remained indoors as much as possible, only emerging for drill,
parade, and the hunt for wood. Pickets, as usual, suffered the most. All
endured short rations, notably including a dearth of edible meat. Tough
beef shipped in brine proved unappetizing, even when supplemented with
cornmeal, sweet potatoes or peanuts, and occasionally whiskey when there
was nothing else to supply.[51]

Conditions were most brutal near Knoxville. Longstreet stopped a renewed Federal cavalry pursuit at Bean's Station, northeast of the city, on cold December 14. Thirty-six hours of hard rain prior to the battle, historian Earl Hess notes, slowed Longstreet's muddy approach to a crawl. His soaked and mud-splattered men suffered immensely without tents and enough shoes. Many fell out before the fighting began. Hard-pressed during the day, the Federal horsemen fell back during the night to Blaine's Cross Roads, an entrenched position Longstreet wanted nothing to do with.[52] "And now the weather grew very heavy," the general recollected, "and the roads, already bad, became soft and impracticable for trains and artillery. . . . As winter had broken upon us in good earnest, it seemed necessary for us to give up the game of war for the time, seek some good place for shelter, and repair railroads and bridges, to open our way back to Richmond."[53]

Blaine's Cross Roads became the northern edge of Federal-occupied East Tennessee, while the Confederates fell back across the flooded Holston River to Russellville and Morristown on the East Tennessee and Virginia Railroad. Longstreet flirted with various plans but, in the end, decided to ride out the winter where he was. Conditions were exceedingly harsh. A soldier wrote: "The weather is so cold that water freezes ten minutes after nightfall. . . . [T]he icicles that fringe the mill-races are as thick as a man's body."[54] Food, uniforms, blankets, bedding, and especially shoes were in great demand. Men wrote of bloody footprints in the snow and referenced Valley Forge.[55] They tried to deal with a dire shortage of shoes by wearing camp-made moccasins, as many of Sherman's Federals had done on the way to Knoxville. "They were better than nothing for a time," Sgt. W. R. Houghton of the 2nd Georgia remembered, "but when near the fire they shrank amazingly, and when wet by the rains, they became too large."[56] Longstreet later admitted, "we were not quite happy, tattered blankets, garments, and shoes (the latter going—many gone) opened ways, on all sides, for piercing winter blasts."[57]

The Federals across the Holston had it little better. "No one recalls those long, long weeks without a shiver," Hinman wrote. "The weather was exceedingly inclement. For a week it rained a good part of the time, with freezing nights, the mercury dropping lower and lower as the winter advanced—that is to say, such would have been the case had the soldiers been supplied with thermometers. But they didn't need them. Blue noses, tingling toes, shaking limbs, and chattering teeth were an excellent substitute to indicate low temperatures."[58] The historians of the 86th Indiana added:

"It was often so cold that when attempting to write letters or make entries in our diaries the ink would freeze in the pens. It would often be necessary to heat the pen and write as rapidly as possible until it cooled off."[59]

Frequent breakdowns in transportation and supply created shortages in nearly everything. With rations reduced and firewood dwindling, men spent their days scouring the camp's environs for something to eat and burn. Lacking axes, soldiers used their bayonets to cut wood. Soldiers of the 86th Indiana crossed the swollen and frigid Holston in boats in order to forage for corn on the other side, until ice formed in the river. Salt was in short supply. Uniforms rife with lice withered into rags without available replacements. Half of the Federals lacked overcoats, and even more needed socks. The garrison also had too few tents. Some built shelters from brush. Others slept at night with only a poncho or dried leaves on the ground, with a single blanket above and a comrade beside them to keep them warm.[60] Large fires kept a man warm enough until "the fire would burn low and the cold would begin to assert. Then he would awaken with benumbed and aching toes, stirring up the fire he would 'thaw out' his pedal appendages and return to his couch of leaves, straw on the cold ground, [and] curl up 'spoon' fashion with his bunkmate for another brief nap."[61]

And then it got worse. "The outstanding weather event of the Civil War period in the North," weather historian David Ludlum concludes, "occurred at the very close of the year 1863, when an arctic air mass of record extreme intensity created severe storm conditions over much of the upper Midwest and dashed into the Lower Lakes region and the Ohio Valley with a spectacular temperature plunge." While Ludlum calls it "the Great Arctic Outbreak," midwesterners referred to it for the rest of their lives as "the Cold New Year's Day." It brought untold misery at the beginning of 1864. People and animals froze to death, trains became marooned in windblown snowdrifts up to fifteen feet high, and steamboats were trapped in ice. Small wonder people were still talking about it as late as the Great Depression as the coldest day of their lives. It also was the coldest day of the Civil War.[62]

In mid-December, some observers claimed to see it coming. Noting the early absence of brook trout and of observing muskrats double walling their burrows, the *St. Paul Press* warned Minnesotans of "a winter of unusual severity," perhaps the worst since 1857.[63] The *Portland Transcript* in Maine likewise cited muskrats. The rodents seemed remarkably prescient come December 28, when the first of two massive low-pressure systems—one following the path of the other—moved from the southern Great Plains toward the Great Lakes. Both dumped snow along their northwestern arcs. Between the two storms, a mighty blast of arctic air elbowed its way in from western Canada. Temperatures plummeted. Chicago's highs, for example, fell from 29 degrees on snowy December 28 to 10 degrees by the end of the year. That was only the preamble, however. On January 1, 1864, the 7 A.M. low was -25 degrees, with winds from the northwest, and temperatures rose to a "high" of -16 degrees at 2 P.M. Below-zero temperatures continued until January 9, when the high rose to 10 degrees. In the meantime, more snow fell on the fourth. Newspapers reported that numerous travelers nearly froze to death around Chicago, while two children of a soldier died when their drunken mother left them unattended.[64]

With local variations, the same frigid pattern repeated across the interior of the divided nation. On January 1 and the next day, Milwaukee saw daytime temperature readings of -20 degrees, with lows down to -38 degrees. The city newspaper reported several cases of near death due to exposure, as well as a disruption of rail travel. Someone at Fort Snelling recorded an incredibly -50 degrees on the morning of the second. North of Cairo, Illinois, the Mississippi River froze over in below-zero weather; ice floated down to Saint Louis and beyond. Cattle and hogs froze to death in pens. Railroads travelers suffered frostbite. The *Indianapolis Journal* reported -20 degrees in the city at daybreak on January 1. Confederates imprisoned at Camp Morton swore that several comrades and guards froze to death.[65]

Near Cincinnati, meanwhile, a high of 44 degrees on December 31 was followed by one of -7 degrees on January 1. The surgeon at Newport Barracks, Kentucky, wrote, "this was the greatest change of temperature in so short a time, of which I have any record, and is probably unparalleled in this latitude."[66] At the prisoner of war camp on Johnson's Island, Henry Kyd Douglas noted below-zero temperatures, collapsing as low as -28 degrees. The year 1864 came in with the death of a comrade, while the next day saw the thermometer fall "so far below Zero, that it can't be counted." It was "just the place," he joked, "to convert visitors to the theological belief of the Norwegian that hell has torments of cold instead of heat."[67]

Frigid arctic air also penetrated deep into the trans-Appalachian South—only the lack of snow cover from the passing storms mitigated temperatures in many areas. In Tyler, Texas, Kate Stone wrote that "the New Year came wailing in, borne on the wings of a freezing norther." Several inches of snow fell, "frozen hard" in the cold weather and "howling" wind.[68] The *Houston Tri-Weekly Telegraph* reported the Colorado River frozen over south of Austin, while a reader near Dallas noted that the ground was frozen to a depth of up to eight inches, almost certainly ruining the winter-wheat crop.[69] The 3rd Texas Cavalry was trying to ferry arms across the Mississippi when the "blizzard swooped down upon us." According to Lt. S. B. Barron, "by the time we reached a camp two miles beyond, icicles were hanging from our horses, and everything we possessed that was damp was freezing. The cold continued to increase, next morning everything was frozen stiff, and it would have been possible to skate on the ponds near the camps."[70] At Monroe, Louisiana, Lt. Col. A. W. Hyatt did describe comrades "sliding" on frozen ponds.[71] In Ouachita County, Arkansas, Capt. Eathan Pinnell of the Confederate 8th Missouri Cavalry wrote that "the oldest citizens here say this is the hardest spell of weather they have ever known, and many of them have been here for forty years."[72] Newspapers reported Federal soldiers frozen to death in Tennessee at Island No. 10 and Fort Pillow.[73]

The Cold New Year's was no better at the East Tennessee front, where the weather first grew ominous on December 30. After a clear morning, rain fell overnight north of Knoxville and continued throughout New Year's Eve. Temperatures fell abruptly in Clarksville—and presumably from Chattanooga up to Knoxville—from the low forties in the morning down to 10 degrees at 9 P.M.[74] At Blaine's Cross Roads, Chaplain Haigh wrote, the rain "turned into a storm, the wind blowing so hard it seemed as if everything would go to pieces."[75] Morning brought a 7 A.M. low of -8 degrees to Clarksville, rising to 1.5 degrees that afternoon before reverting to zero that night. It almost certainly was much worse closer to the mountainous front. In Chattanooga, Pvt. James Shaw claimed that the morning temperature was -18 degrees. That night, Capt. F. W. Keil of the 35th Ohio recorded temperatures in the city ranging from -6 degrees to -10 degrees, enough to freeze ponds at the base of Missionary Ridge so thickly that soldiers crossed them on foot. Federal cavalryman Eastham Tarrant swore that the morning reading on January 1 was an unlikely -29 degrees. By the end of the cold spell, six inches of snow lay on the ground in Knoxville.[76]

Near Chattanooga, "good fires in our snug little shanties" and enough blankets proved sufficient for lucky soldiers who had them, according to L. A. Simmons. Life was harder for those still in tents, who had to rely on big fires when they could find enough wood. Pickets and cavalry vedettes risked their lives just walking out on duty. On the night of January 1, guards changed every half hour to keep the men alive.[77] West of Chattanooga, the camp rumor was that nine furloughed men had frozen to death on a train between the city and Knoxville. Jenkin Jones described a hellish march to Huntsville, Tennessee, that commenced on January 7. "The roads are frozen and very rough," he explained, "the weather extremely cold, the air damp and filled with frozen mists, covering our clothes with ice and sleet." That night, an inch of snow fell. In Huntsville on the morning of January 9, locals told Jones that it was "the coldest day known for years. Animals and wagons covered with ice," he added. Sunshine later that day melted the icy roads into deep muck. The next day, his battery began erecting shelters, as other regiments under Sherman now did.[78]

As usual, conditions were worse around Knoxville. In the field inspecting his supply line, Grant described temperatures around zero and a frozen, jagged path to the city, littered with dead animals and broken wagons. He immediately gave up any thought of attacking Longstreet that winter. Temperatures on January 10 fell to the point that ice floated in the Holston River.[79] Longstreet complained of two weeks of temperatures well below zero, with the frigid cold leaving "rough angles of frozen mud as firm and sharp as so many freshly-quarried rocks, and the poorly protected feet of our soldiers sometimes left bloody marks along the roads."[80] In such harsh conditions, his men struggled to build solid winter shelters.

The Federals at Blaine's Cross Roads already lacked sufficient clothing and forage for their animals. They fell prey to pneumonia, rheumatism, and fevers. Lieutenant Colonel Hinman noted several cases of frostbite, including damage to the victims' "faces, hands, and feet."[81] The chaplain of the Federal 1st Kentucky Cavalry reported six pickets frozen to death, although he admitted that he had not actually seen the bodies. Pickets from both armies joined together to build fires.[82] Swirling winds often made standing by those blazes intolerable, and even then only one side of the body warmed while the other froze. Some men never recovered from such exposure, Haigh added, noting a lieutenant who died once he got home from the shock of the Cold New Year's.[83]

Bitter cold lasted almost into the middle of January. After that, temperatures rose, reaching the thirties on the eleventh, 41 degrees the next day, 57 degrees on the twenty-second, 65 degrees the following day, and an incredibly unseasonable 72 degrees on January 27—a shift of 80 degrees in twenty-seven days. As for precipitation, an additional half inch of snow fell on January 7, extending deep into Georgia, the first snow to fall on Sherman's men while in Alabama. Nearly an inch of rain total followed between the seventh and the end of the month. The area north of Knoxville saw greater extremes. Heavy rain and then six inches of snow fell on the eighteenth.[84] The 86th Indiana, on a foraging expedition, woke up in surprise to be "like so many logs rolled together and buried in the snow." Confederate John Evans experienced a similar scene, adding that stories of men sleeping warmly under snow proved to be true. Warmer temperatures after that brought slick roads and deep mud, which sank boots and horses' hooves.[85] At Dalton, one Confederate soldier lamented the "great oceans of mud [that] surround us."[86]

"Oceans" of mud and the coldest days of the war closed active operations in the West until spring. Elsewhere, however, commanders continued defying the gods of winter.

Chapter 18

At the North Pole

Virginia, Fall 1863–Winter 1864

On August 26, 1863, the Confederacy's long, hot summer broke in Virginia. High temperatures fell into the pleasant midseventies during the day and down to the upper fifties before dawn. Skies were fair and dry, with only a bit of rain on the twenty-ninth. Pleasant weather continued into September, although 80-degree temperatures briefly returned between September 6 and September 9, part of the same heatwave that extended down to Chattanooga in the West. But even then, nights remained cool. On the twelfth, a violent storm starting in the afternoon brought winds fierce enough to uproot trees and drop a half inch of rain before dawn. One falling tree so frightened Virginian George Neese that he went to a prayer meeting that night.

Neese had more to worry about than trees. Buoyed by fair weather, a season of military parry and thrust began west of Fredericksburg once Meade became aware that Longstreet and his divisions had gone to Tennessee. On September 13, Federal cavalry and infantry shoved their way across the newly rain-swollen Rappahannock and Hazel Rivers and occupied Culpeper Court House. Unwilling to launch a frontal assault against Lee's formidable positions behind the Rapidan, however, Meade stalled. Lacking enough men to drive on to Richmond either, he decided to winter in place. The armies camped warily, with frequent skirmishing and occasional blowups at the front.[1]

Autumn arrived officially on the equinox. Soon thereafter, the massive mid-September cold front (discussed in chapter 16) arrived. Once it had devastated midwestern agriculture and chilled the wounded at Chickamauga, it pressed on to affect the East. There, the temperature collapse happened more gradually, over three days instead of two. A separate tropical storm in the Atlantic, starting south of Florida and cutting across the eastern Carolinas on September 18, added a dramatic twist to the weather as it made its way up the coast. In Annapolis, September 17 was the hottest day of the month, with a 2 P.M. reading of 82 degrees. Three days later, it was 60 degrees the Maryland capital. September 16 was likewise the hottest day of the month in New York City, with a reading of 84.7 degrees, but on the nineteenth, highs only made it up to 57.5 degrees. The *Augusta Constitutionalist* reported frost south of Atlanta. Farmers there feared for their pea and potato crops, while in the city itself, people lit fires and dug out winter clothing.[2]

In Virginia, an afternoon high of 80 degrees at Fort Monroe on September 18 gave way to a high of 67 degrees the next day and 62 degrees the day after that. Five subsequent September mornings saw temperature drop into the forties. Frost appeared in the Shenandoah on September 20 and on the Rappahannock three days later, marking the equinox with ice. Nights grew uncomfortable, especially for pickets. Some blamed the weather for a reoccurrence of camp diarrhea. Fog and gray skies shrouded the final days of the month. September was relatively dry at least, with just 1.7 inches of rain in Alexandria and a tad more in Georgetown. Most of this fell during a single twenty-four-hour period, from September 18 into the morning of the next day as the tropical storm passed nearby. That torrential rainfall, accompanied by gales from the east, capped off a gray period of mist and occasional showers that shadowed Meade's lunge to the river.[3]

Soldiers huddled under canvas. The 6th Wisconsin's Lt. Col. Rufus Dawes described "a broad line of glistening white tents" near Culpeper stretching four miles in either direction "as far as I can see to the east and the west." That "great white line," he added, "is the strength of the North in the cause of justice, freedom, and humanity."[4] But his enemies had a "white line" of their own. Confederates, too, slept under captured Federal canvas, invariably called "Yankee flies." Pvt. Franklin Riley of the 16th Mississippi considered them "a commentary on the war. Close by must be 10–20,000 of them, mostly white, all (almost all) captured from the enemy. From the beginning of the war the Yankees have been our commissary."[5]

At the tactical and operational level, the second half of September brought relative inaction. "A Capital day for Campaigning," Federal provost marshal Marsena Patrick groused on September 22, "but we have been lying Still and doing just nothing."[6] The first week of October brought little change. Pleasant conditions persisted, with highs fluctuating between 60 degrees and 71 degrees. A warm front swirling from the east brought an inch and a half of rain on October 2 and into the next morning. Streams rose, and dusty roads grew miry. Morning lows wavered from 63 degrees on October 2 to 43 degrees on October 6, part of a wider cooling trend across the Southeast. Soldiers turned to improving their shelters. Some men in blue "stockaded" their tents with scrounged lumber and equipped them with camp stoves bought from sutlers.[7] At Bristoe Station on the Orange and Alexandria Railroad, the 2nd Rhode Island began constructing winter quarters on October 7. Elisha Hunt Rhodes boasted of his eighteen-foot-by-ten-foot "hotel," built with boards and equipped with a window, door, and desk foraged from a nearby village. "It now looks as if we were to stay here during the winter and guard the railroad."[8]

Rhodes spoke much too soon. Lee was not willing to surrender the Rappahannock without a fight. On rainy October 8, as temperatures fell into the low fifties, the Confederate commander launched a counterstroke. The bulk of his army headed west across the railroad and then swung north, around rainy Cedar Mountain, for the Army of the Potomac's right flank. Meade had no choice but to fall back across the Rappahannock all the way to the safety of Centreville and Manassas. His men sullenly abandoned their new winter accommodations—and camp stoves—and took to the road. Federal sharpshooter Wyman White described with horror coming upon the skeleton of a Union soldier, still in uniform; he assumed it was one of the June sunstroke victims. With lows dipping into the midforties, Confederates tore down fences for firewood. On frosty October 12, they reoccupied Culpeper. Lee extended the pursuit until the gray and foggy fourteenth, when A. P. Hill's corps stumbled into a Federal corps at Bristoe Station and sustained heavy casualties.

Over the next several days, Lee's soldiers busied themselves tearing up the railroad south of Bristoe Station before falling back to a line stretching from Culpeper to Rappahannock Station. Even if Meade regained the ground later, he now would have to rebuild his supply line, while Lee shortened his. Daytime temperatures during the brief campaign hovered in the sixties. Alexandria saw rain only on October 13 and October 14 (0.4 of an inch total), while in Georgetown nearly a half inch fell on the afternoon of the sixteenth. Soldiers under Lee and Meade described additional showers on October 8, October 9, and October 15, then an all-day torrential rain on the sixteenth. Coupled with similar conditions at Chattanooga, it is easy to envision a wider system extending across the Appalachians into central Virginia.[9]

Disappointed once, the men in both armies hoped that Meade's retreat truly marked the end of active operations for the year. The roads were now in bad shape, and winter was coming. Chaplain Frank Morse of the 37th Massachusetts noted how his flock interpreted the sight of wild geese flying south as a harbinger of a long, desolate winter.[10] Soldiers began thinking again of housing. Storms and cold weather arrived on October 18. Sheets of rain followed the next morning, just as men began to fall in. Rain over the next two days raised water levels in local streams and delayed fording when Union troops shifted positions. Sharp cold winds arrived from the west on the twenty-third, part of the same massive midwestern system that soaked Grant as he arrived in Chattanooga. The rain in Virginia lasted two additional days and was cold too. Hardly able to hold his pen, Chaplain Morse compared Virginia to Greenland. Neese poetically depicted the winds as winter killing autumn. Ice appeared in creeks and streams.[11]

Men again began erecting cabins, afraid of freezing to death yet concerned that their efforts might be wasted. Pvt. John Casler's mess "hesitated . . . fearing that we would have to move again, and leave them. But as regiment after regiment continued to build and the officers were having permanent quarters put up, we concluded that we would build also." At length, they "put up a nice log shanty, covered with clapboards[,] went to an old barn nearby and got some planks for a floor and bunks, built a stick chimney, and were prepared to live in high style."[12] Federals acted similarly, with preference toward their log-canvas hybrids. Soldiers installed stoves when they could. Lieutenant Colonel Dawes described the "log crib" he and another man built, "eight feet long, four feet wide, and two deep, and packed . . . full of dry leaves, which makes us a warm and comfortable bed."[13] Even snug cabins could prove to be cold. "Every time someone opens the blanket that serves as a door," Rhodes wrote, "I imagine myself at the North Pole."[14]

The first week of November brought little change. The general trend involved cold mornings, averaging in the forties, and warm afternoons. On November 3 and November 5, afternoon highs topped 70 degrees. Then on the seventh, Meade dashed the hopes of soldiers on both sides. Although he really wanted to fall back to Washington and ride out the winter there, Lincoln again demanded action. At midmorning that day, two corps forced their way across the Rappahannock at Rappahannock Station and Kelly's Ford. After ugly night fighting, Lee's shattered line retreated to the Rapidan in heavy fog. Not only were the gains of his recent advance lost, so were the tidy new cabins. Casler winced that he first heard the long roll as his mates were testing their fireplace for the first time. As if to add insult to injury, the weather then turned colder. Fording the icy Rapidan was excruciating. An inch of snow fell on November 9. It melted quickly; the Georgetown high was 46 degrees—but the Blue Ridge remained white. A howling wind from the west and below-freezing morning lows followed.[15]

Some Federals, to their delight, discovered excellent shelter. Capt. George Barnard described "splendid log cabins with nice large fire places," adding, "it is quite pleasant to find ready made houses all ready waiting for us at the end of our march."[16] Others had more work to do. Ever hopeful, soldiers on both sides quickly began new construction projects—without orders. Meade knew that going into winter quarters would cost him his command. Chaplain Alanson Haines agreed that "the state of feeling in the country was such that it would not suffer the idea of the army going into winter quarters before a general engagement had taken place."[17] The Federals built anyway. Staff officer Thomas Hyde remembered how men "built ourselves houses, or fixed up tents comfortably with rough chimneys and fireplaces and board floors, and settled down to the routine of winter quarters, as we supposed."[18]

Over the next two weeks, autumn weather remained mercurial. Indian-summer temperatures rose to 72 degrees on November 12. A thunderstorm hit on the evening of the fourteenth. As to the west at Chattanooga, warm spells were fleeting. On rainy and frosty November 15, the afternoon high was 53 degrees, with rain, sharp wind, and mud bad enough to cancel preaching in some regiments. Soldiers huddled around their fires that night. The fickle temperatures rebounded, climbing back to 72 degrees on the twentieth, but soldiers observed with concern a distinct halo around the moon, an often accurate harbinger of bad winter weather. Sure enough, rain returned on dark November 21 as a system moved west from Tennessee. With it came deep mud and highs in the fifties. It rained between November 23 and November 25—the same dreary days as the battles for Chattanooga—and most heavily on the twenty-fourth, canceling Jefferson Davis's planned review of the Army of Northern Virginia. Falling temperatures pointed to snow. That day also brought a rare and frightening portent. On Lookout Mountain that night, soldiers peered at the lunar eclipse with foreboding. Across the mountains in Virginia, an unnerving "blood rain" fell. Descriptions of blood rain range back to Homer. British officials and the media attributed red rain in 2016 and 2017 to airborne dust from the Sahara. Scientists investigating a similar occurrence in India linked it to the airborne spores of a particular form of algae.[19] Whatever the cause in 1863, it was a chilling sight. The Mississippian Riley wrote, "we had a strange experience: rain, red, as if it were blood. If I believed in omens, I would be frightened."[20]

~~~

The blood rain was a portent of sorts. November 26, Thanksgiving Day, was also the second coldest day of the month, reaching only 44 degrees in Georgetown. Hyde likened it a winter back in Maine. Instead of feasting, however, Meade's army left camp before daylight and moved through the ghastly Wilderness to the foggy Rapidan. Unwilling to swing west, sever his communications, and risk the mud, Meade had wanted to head east to Fredericksburg. But Lincoln wanted no part of that place again. The compromise was to cross the rivers to the southeast in three columns, turn west, and surprise Lee's extreme right along Mine Run, on the western edge of the Wilderness. Scouts reported that the lower fords were unguarded and the roads open. But heavy rain and mud delayed the operation two days. By nightfall, with temperatures in the midthirties, Meade's skirmishers were across the rain-swollen Rapidan, although not as far as he hoped. The lead corps had dawdled, gotten lost, and floundered in thawing roads. A lack of pontoons further delayed bridging the flooded Rapidan. So did steep, wet banks.[21]

Chaplain Henry Pyne of the 1st New Jersey Cavalry remembered that "the frost penetrated through all the blankets which the men could venture to remove from their horses; and around blazing fires of fence rails, without any Thanksgiving dinner, and but a poor pretence of supper, officers and men lay down to catch what sleep they could."[22] Sharpshooter White claimed that pickets in a nearby regiment froze to death during the night. Confederates rushing over frozen roads to confront the enemy and counterattack encountered the same conditions. One of Lee's aides described icicles in men's facial hair, while another soldier recounted numb extremities and frostbite. As historian Adam Petty points out, frozen roads at least allowed a swifter move than the mud the Federals had waded during the day.[23]

November 27 began with a Georgetown temperature of 28 degrees, the coldest morning of the month. To the west, Bragg's army was falling back into Dalton, Georgia. Along the Rapidan, the ground remained frozen and so frosty that it seemed to have snowed in spots. Farmers began killing hogs. A day behind schedule, Meade ached to make up for lost time but discovered Lee and his army now blocking the way. More slowdowns, strung-out columns, poor orientation, and skirmishing consumed the morning and early afternoon. Elements of the armies stumbled into an intense battle late in the cold day at Payne's Farm. That night, Lee's Confederates pulled back to high ground behind Mine Run and hastily began constructing works.

Thawing, frosty earth and 40-degree temperatures turned roads into deep morasses. More rain added to the misery. Beginning as mist and heavy fog after sunup, it soon fell in torrents until about 2 P.M. Federal artillery bogged down heading to the front, while the rain obscured observations of Lee's lines. Federals already in the valley lay on the marshy ground, waiting to attack thoroughly demoralizing Rebel works reminiscent of Fredericksburg's. Surprised by Lee's strength, Meade probed all day but found no weak spots in the defenses. The armies slept that night in mud and without fires when within sight of the enemy. Men awoke the next morning—the day of the Fort Sanders assault at Knoxville—covered with frost and wet from a final shower. A cold north wind blew. Temperatures stayed in the forties. Meade again grasped for a possible place to strike, under enormous pressure from Washington. But action came with labor. Although the roads somewhat improved as the dry day progressed, they remained deep enough to require improvement and prevented a planned assault on the Confederate right. The sky remained dark and cloudy until late afternoon, when the sun at last peeped through. But temperatures dropped that night, down through the thirties. Few slept well.[24]

That night, Meade drew up plans to attack both of Lee's flanks the next morning. Many of his men considered it suicidal. As historians Martin Graham and George Skoch later observed, "the wait through this cold, seemingly endless night was perhaps the most difficult of the war for these Union troops."[25] November 30 dawned clear, with a morning low of 27 degrees in Georgetown, eventually rising only to 30 degrees. A strong wind blew at Mine Run, while the waterway, flooded out of its banks, held a thin layer of ice. On the Federal right, men would have to wade that frozen water before tackling Lee's works. Anticipating the attack, many Union soldiers pinned their names to their jackets and waited to charge to their doom. They did not. Meade canceled the attack when Maj. Gen. Gouveneur Warren refused to advance. Lee's men had stayed busy improving their works, the II Corps commander realized, and he judged them too strong to break.[26]

What followed was what Pvt. John Haley called "the coldest night we have known in Virginia."[27] It was much worse away from the campfires. Sgt. Luther Furst observed that pickets had "to be carried in on stretchers."[28] Provost Marshal Patrick reported, "it is said that more were frozen last night. . . . [O]ur pickets suffered intensely and the wounded suffered still more." He reported stories of men so frozen that comrades carried them out of the works.[29] "The night was bitter cold," Chaplain Haines wrote, "ice freezing nearly an inch thick, and it was reported some men actually froze to death on the picket line."[30] Others dismissed such reports. A doctor told Charles Wainwright that the rumors were false, although too many of the men had frozen hands and feet.[31]

But there was nothing fictional about the cold. December 1 opened with a morning low of 21 degrees in Georgetown and 16 degrees closer to Richmond. At Mine Run, water froze in canteens. Temperatures rose to 40 degrees by afternoon but fell back to freezing after dark. Looking again at Lee's works, Meade gave up. That night, as a stiff wind came up from the south, his army marched back across the Rapidan. Meade would not risk another Mud March.[32] "The marching for a time was very tedious," Haines remembered, "the column halting every few steps, so that we could not get exercise enough to keep warm."[33] At other times, some retreating Federals double-quicked simply for the warmth of increased blood flow.[34] A few just gave up. Chaplain Pyne described stragglers "fagged out with sleeplessness and numb with cold" who "seemed utterly careless of the danger of capture by the enemy. . . . Some could not even be beaten into motion, one man, especially, muttering that he might as well freeze to death and starve in Belle Isle as anywhere else, and throwing himself stubbornly on the ground."[35]

Meade's mournful retreat dragged on through the next morning, which began with a temperature of 34 degrees and frost. The frozen road and its jagged ruts impeded progress; Wyman White worried about breaking a leg in deep wagon ruts. The same conditions affected the Confederates. Hoping to capture the momentum, Lee spent the night massing troops to his right, hoping to hit the Federal left at daybreak. The Confederate attack ground to a halt when skirmishers found the Federals gone.[36] Rain and mud followed by freezing cold and hard roads brought the Mine Run Campaign to a frustrating conclusion.

Meade's men began repairing and improving their huts, with activity peaking during the month's second week. They again did so without any official direction from anyone above company officers. As Chaplain Haines remembered, "for fear of public opinion, no order to do so was given to the troops."[37] Yet the men built.

Most of the cabins they constructed were the now-standard log-walled, canvas-roofed hybrid shebangs, three to five logs high, with a door, fireplace, stick-and-mud chimneys, and elevated bunks. The closest thing to a standard size was eight feet by ten feet, although many were larger or smaller. Red Virginia clay filled in the spaces between logs. Among the variations were board floors, brick or stone chimneys, and indoor plastering using the local mud. Officers obtained camp stoves and scrounged windows, doors, and furniture from neighboring homes. Most camps boasted regular rows of cabins and cleared streets. Some soldiers also spent a great deal of time crafting homemade furniture. Soldiers built stables for horses when they had them, although a lack of canvas sometimes left their mounts exposed to the elements. The need for so much wood soon exhausted local forests so that, by January 1864, soldiers found themselves walking up to four miles for firewood.[38] Nonetheless, historian Daniel Sutherland asserts that the Army of the Potomac was in better shape now when it came to housing than the previous winter at Falmouth, comparing the camps to "a Yankee village."[39] The Confederates also settled into camp. Well equipped with "Yankee flies," most of them copied Federal architectural styles. One variation, however, involved height. Sgt. Berry Benson of the 1st South Carolina lived in a sizable cabin "about 12 feet square" but described others as "the oddest little structures, which could hardly be entered on all fours. A passerby could tiptoe and spit down the chimney."[40]

December temperatures rose and fell as if by whim, but the general trend was more in keeping with the season than the war's two previous Decembers. The first few days were warm, with a high of 61 degrees on the fourth. Nights stayed cold and frosty, with lows down into the thirties. A thin layer of ice again covered Mine Run. Temperatures fell over the next three days, accompanied by a hard freeze and showers on the sixth. Nights became tough to bear, with morning lows of 20 degrees on windy December 7 and a hard frost and morning low of 18 degrees on December 8. Canteens burst open with expanding ice. Another surge of frenzied hut construction followed. Too cold to sleep—temperatures were just below freezing—Sgt. John Hartwell wrote home on the ninth that the ground was frozen six inches deep.

As the middle of the month approached, precipitation returned. Sprinkles on December 11 evolved into a hard rain, with winds from the south. The next day not only cleared off but also produced a remarkable high of 72 degrees. December 14 brought the strongest winds yet, more rain, and knee-deep mud. Maj. Howard Smith of the 1st New York Dragoons worried that the elements were ready to launch a separate winter campaign. Highs dipped into the thirties on the nineteenth as the wind shifted to the northwest. Cold weather stretched through the holiday season, with snow beginning on December 23 and lasting through Christmas. More than one soldier called the following few days colder than any endured the previous winter. The morning low in Georgetown was 19 degrees on Christmas Eve, 22 degrees Christmas morning, and 15 degrees on December 26. The Potomac nearly froze over at Alexandria. It actually may have been colder to the south, as Benny Fleet recorded a low of 15 degrees on Christmas Eve morning. Dreary rain and muddy fields followed the holiday, as a warm front from the west ended the month. New Years' Eve was rainy but relatively warm, with a 2 P.M. high of 46 degrees.[41]

Exposure and cold, coupled with other discontents, produced the inevitable morale problems of winter quarters. Daniel Sutherland observes that desertion, "an alarming increase in drunkenness and general lawlessness," and at least one murder gripped the Army of the Potomac. Local citizens became the victims of vandalism, robbery, and sexual assault. Some soldiers blamed substitutes and conscripts, but there was enough guilt to go around.[42]

～❦

Then came the Cold New Year's. While David Ludlum depicts the event as a trans-Appalachian phenomenon, the northeastern states endured bitter cold as well. An observer in Boston, for example, reported a high of 10 degrees on January 2, 1864, with wind from the north. Ice closed the port of Providence, Rhode Island. Strong winds blew through New York City from the north to such a degree that gales disrupted traffic in the harbor. Temperatures fell there from a high of 45 degrees on foggy January 1 to 10 degrees at midnight. Buffalo endured its heaviest snowstorm since 1844, and temperatures fell from 42 degrees at midnight on December 31 to -9 degrees on January 2. At least four people froze to death in Philadelphia as temperatures fell to 8 degrees. Snow delayed rail traffic into both Philadelphia and Baltimore from the north, while ice in the Susquehanna River blocked ferry traffic.[43]

Farther down the coast, bad weather reigned too. Sgt. John Bell of the 85th Pennsylvania, stationed at Hilton Head, South Carolina, noted that "New Year's Day was cold and windy and for a time during the afternoon was very disagreeable." His officers canceled most duties. The next day brought a morning low of 22 degrees and an afternoon high of 39 degrees.[44] The Cold New Year penetrated even Florida, where Capt. Winston Stephens of the 2nd Florida Cavalry wrote his wife from near Jacksonville: "On Saturday morning [January 2] we had ice about two inches thick. . . . [T]his is the coldest spell I have felt since the Spring of 1852."[45]

Wedged in between the Northeast and the south Atlantic, the soldiers of the eastern theater suffered as much. "New Years day, 1864, will long be remembered as 'The cold New Years,'" wrote Col. Wesley Brainerd. "Never before or since in my recollection did such an intense and stinging cold day fall upon us."[46] The first day of 1864 brought a steady drop in temperatures, from 45 degrees at 7 A.M. in Georgetown to 12 degrees that night. Mud froze solid enough to bear up wagons. The night was exceedingly windy. To the southwest, snow fell. The next morning was calmer but absolutely frigid, with a low at 7 A.M. of 6 degrees, rising to 20 degrees by afternoon before sinking back to 6 degrees after dark. For men under canvas, January 2 was the day to remember. Archibald Henderson wrote home for his ice skates.[47]

The next day was clear and a bit warmer: 21 degrees at daybreak but rising to 31 degrees by afternoon. Chaplains, nonetheless, canceled services due to the cold. Those rising temperatures signaled another dramatic January weather shift. Around 9 A.M. on the fourth, snow began falling, turning to rain after dark. Four inches accumulated in Washington; less fell at the front. Temperatures dropped into the midtwenties. Dawes of the 6th Wisconsin related how some reenlisted comrades started for home, only to freeze so badly on that train that one was hospitalized in Alexandria. In that same city, the editor of the local newspaper noted that the Potomac was frozen from bank to bank for the first time in years. Three to four more inches of snow arrived in camp—and as far south as Richmond—on the night of January 7. Some of it fell on ice frozen five inches thick. The morning low in Georgetown that day was 16 degrees. Elisha Hunt Rhodes maintained that a rare thermometer in camp rose only to 8 degrees.

And the cold got worse. Overnight, temperatures fell from 22 degrees at 9 P.M. to 12 degrees the next morning. On the night of January 9, Rev. C. B. Mackee recorded a 9 P.M. temperature of -6 degrees; his thermometer rose to only 10 degrees the following morning. As elsewhere, temperatures remained bitterly cold until the middle of the month, keeping the ground frozen and covered with snow. A warming trend brought welcome highs in the forties, plus thaws of deep mud so extensive that one soldier longed for the good old days at Falmouth. January 24 reached 62 degrees and January 28, a summer-like 72 degrees. Farmers began plowing. The month remained mostly dry, other than rain on the eighteenth and after dark on the thirtieth.[48]

"We are not sorry that it stormed," Pennsylvanian James Coburn wrote his parents, "for I believe one more week of fine weather would have instituted a winter campaign."[49] Instead, the camps along the Rappahannock and Rapidan were scenes of orange-red desolation. "Such a sea of mud round Brandy Station was enough to engulf the most hardy," Meade staffer Theodore Lyman wrote home. "There is no platform to get on, nothing but the driest spot in the mud. . . . The whole country, besides the mud, is now ornamented with stumps, dead horses and mules, deserted camps, and thousands upon thousands of crows."[50]

As luck so often had it, a new turn in the weather coincided negatively with the plans of Federal generals. Southeast of Richmond, Maj. Gen. Benjamin Butler's Army of the James at Fort Monroe made ready to advance up the Peninsula. Reports that Lee had sent thousands of troops to join an ongoing siege at New Berne, North Carolina, encouraged Butler to strike. In order to divert Richmond's defenders, or force Lee to recall his men, the Union general asked for a demonstration along the Rapidan front. With Meade in Washington, General in Chief Halleck ordered acting army commander John Sedgwick to assist Butler. Sedgwick wanted no part of it. The reports of enemy troop departures were erroneous, he insisted, and the roads were a muddy mess. Secretary of War Stanton and Halleck ordered him to comply anyway. On February 6, II Corps marched to Morton's Ford but without its commander, for Warren was ill.[51] Not only did the Confederates occupy quite strong positions but also the "boisterous, rainy, stormy cold weather" persisted.[52] That meant mud in abundance. Lyman wrote home, "to Morton's Ford is some ten miles, but you might as well call it fifty, such is the state of the roads. Mud, varying from fetlocks to knees, then holes, runs, ditches and rocks—such was the road."[53]

As the advance brigade of II Corps arrived at the ford, thick fog and mist shrouded the river. Despite orders not to cross, skirmishers at first, then a full brigade, waded through the icy water to the south bank. The Federals made surprisingly good progress initially despite uneven terrain, mud, showers, and effective Confederate artillery fire. Two more brigades as well as Federal guns were across by early afternoon. Sedgwick was ready to put in even more men until Warren arrived and saw a disaster developing. Lee was piling in reinforcements, and the Union advance had ground to a stop. A Confederate counterattack at dusk raised the pressure on those across the Rapidan. Once the sun went down, Warren pulled back. Temperatures fell to 42 degrees, cold for men who had twice waded a relatively deep river. The Federals remained in the vicinity through cold February 7, then returned to their camps as temperatures plummeted. For a week after the Morton's Ford affair, morning lows came in at the freezing mark or below. Meanwhile, a war of words commenced. Partly blaming the mud, Sedgwick complained that the only result of the operation was to show Lee the weakest point in his line. The remark nearly cost the major general his corps. As it was, Butler never got close to Richmond.[54]

The second half of February brought less activity, inclement temperatures, and little precipitation. Valentine's Day was spring-like and breezy, with a high of 53 degrees, but a bitter arctic blast followed, reminiscent of winter in Vermont, according to Wilbur Fisk. Between two and three inches of new snow and colder temperatures followed late on February 15. The snow melted, but Provost Marshal Patrick observed on the night of the sixteenth that a thermometer read 12 degrees. Morning lows through February 19 were absolutely bone-chilling, slipping to 6 degrees, with a fierce northwest wind. Canteens and ink bottles inside shanties froze solid. The Potomac froze over. In Richmond, J. B. Jones found the water in his bedroom's washbasin frozen. Benny Fleet recorded a morning low of 2 degrees on the eighteenth—the lowest reading at his plantation since 1857—and went skating with his brother.

But the weather slowly warmed up again. Temperatures rose daily through February 23, when the afternoon high was 66 degrees. The main

beneficiary was the road system, which dried out to the degree that soldiers once again began complaining of dust and worrying about action.
Lamenting their winter loads, some men also threw away overcoats and
spare clothing. They soon had second thoughts. February 29 brought rain
mixed with snow. Confederate John Apperson thanked God for it, as rain
would slow down the enemy, who were once again in the field. In Washington, Brig. Gen. Judson Kilpatrick had persuaded Lincoln to allow him to
launch a raid on Richmond to free Federal prisoners. Lincoln liked the idea
and ordered Meade to support it with a sizable diversion. The army commander ordered Sedgwick's VI Corps to advance toward Madison Court
House while cavalry under Brig. Gen. George Custer rode toward Charlottesville. Custer's men burned mills and carried away joyous slaves, despite getting lost in a storm on the night of the twenty-ninth. As for VI
Corps, the roads were dry and even dusty at first, but miserable March 1
was rainy, and they soon turned to familiar red muck. By the time Sedgwick's corps arrived at its destination, rain was turning to snow, with hail
and sleet mixed in. The Federals retreated the next day.

Kilpatrick's force of 4,000 troopers and artillery composed the main
show, however. Little went right. The raiders reached the Richmond defenses on chilly and rainy March 1, with temperatures barely above freezing; a light sheet of new snow covered the ground come morning. The
city's extensive earthworks gave Kilpatrick pause. Ultimately, the raid accomplished little except igniting a controversy. After Federal colonel Ulric
Dahlgren fell, Confederates discovered—or at least claimed to discover—
dispatches on his person that called for the murders of Davis and his cabinet as well as the fiery destruction of Richmond. Meade disavowed any
knowledge of the plan, but the Confederacy raged with reports of Yankee
barbarity.[55]

On March 2, the day Dahlgren died, Congress confirmed Ulysses Grant's
promotion to the rank of lieutenant general. Grant had come a long way
in three years from clerking in his father's store. Lincoln ordered him to
Washington for his commission as well as to take command of the entire
US Army; Halleck was redesignated as army chief of staff. The new general
in chief headed east with his son on March 4. Five days later, Grant stood
in the White House as the president presented him with both his third star

and his added responsibilities. The day was pleasant. After the cold, rain, and snow of the first, March had been more temperate and much liked by soldiers in the field, despite some frosty mornings. At the front, creeks ran at near capacity, and camp streets flooded. Grant went down to Brandy Station to meet with Meade. He found a much put-upon major general. Meade had been under fire since Gettysburg, but complaints from his enemies within the Army of the Potomac as well as pro-Hooker elements in Congress peaked that month. Grant's sudden ascension to command undermined the anti-Meade campaign, but the army commander still expected the worst. He offered to step aside, but Grant left him in command. Before leaving for Nashville to meet with Sherman and plan the western campaigns, Grant made his first critical decision as general in chief. Realizing that he needed to be close to Washington, yet wary of getting caught up in the capital's intrigues, he concluded to make his headquarters in the field with the Army of the Potomac.[56]

Weather conditions fluctuated in Virginia during Grant's absence. "We are now having real March weather, at least as to changeableness," Wainwright wrote on the thirteenth, "no two successive days being alike."[57] Temperatures ranged from the sixties on fair and windy March 12 and March 13 before dropping back into the thirties by March 16. Trees began to bud. As roads dried, soldiers began to anticipate earlier-than-usual campaigning. Winter was not done, however. On March 15, snow fell in the Federal camps. After a lovely but cold morning, with a 7 A.M. temperature of 30 degrees, a nor'easter brought heavy snow to the Rapidan late on the seventeenth.[58] Fisk wrote, "more snow has fallen here within the last six hours than we have had before this winter and still it comes. The prospect this evening is that it will snow all night—and, for all of any signs that are apparent now, it may keep on snowing forever."[59]

The next three days were windy, increasingly cloudy, and pleasantly warm, with afternoon high in the fifties. Men caught their breath. Then what historian Daniel Sutherland calls "a monster snowstorm" arrived from the north early in the afternoon of March 22. Snow persisted until after midnight.[60] On the Rapidan, from ten to fifteen inches had accumulated in camps by the next morning. That same day, as men in both armies frolicked and threw snowballs, Grant returned to Washington. Warmer weather and clear skies brought a rapid melt, but conditions remained capricious. On Good Friday, March 25, the lieutenant general arrived in muddy Culpeper amid heavy rain. The army reacted with misgivings, in part out of loyalty to Meade but also because Grant seemed so unspectacular at first view. Some were wary of any new suggestion that the western armies (and their commanders) were superior to easterners. They also disliked Meade's new reorganization—approved by Grant—that consolidated and rearranged units while working in a slew of untrusted new recruits and draftees. But the foul weather did not help either. Easter Sunday, while warm with an eventual high of 58 degrees, was so rainy and muddy that many Confederate ministers canceled services. The weather did not deter North Carolina governor Zebulon Vance, however, who spoke to Tar Heel troops as well as Lee, Ewell, and Hill. In the Shenandoah, five more inches of snow fell, but only a smattering affected the main armies. The Monday after Easter was delightful, with a high of 64 degrees, but the month ended with rain and cooler days.[61]

At the end of the month, the Army of the Potomac had to march in review for Grant through rain and mud. "There was no enthusiasm," Wainwright wrote, "and as the rain increased, we were quickly dismissed without passing in review."[62] There was little excitement across the river either. "Rain/wind—about the same type [of] weather we had last year," Franklin Riley wrote. "And, as was true then, so long as it rains we are relatively immune from attack. 'The more it rains, the more we rest.' The Rapidan is too high to cross. Ground is thawing; thus, except where they have been corduroyed, the roads are impassable. . . . Rain now for a week, snow, then rain, transforming the roads and countryside into a swamp."[63] Grant's juggernaut remained in check in Virginia thanks to the mud. Elsewhere, in Mississippi and across the big river, however, the new general in chief's plan to win the war already was in motion.

Chapter 19

Distant Thunder

The Mississippi River Valley, Winter–Spring 1864

Mercurial weather marked the winter of 1863–64, with conditions ranging from the coldest days of the war to periods reminiscent of spring. Military operations were equally spasmodic. Days of bloody campaigning periodically broke up the boreal monotony of winter in camp. In Virginia, Lee and Meade held fast after Mine Run and Morton's Ford, waiting for spring's solid roads. In the West, brutal cold, snow, and mud largely shut down operations from East Tennessee down into northern Alabama. Grant's ascent to command toward winter's official end, however, brought marching and fighting elsewhere. As an army commander, Grant had never shied away from winter operations. Stymied in East Tennessee and constrained by the administration from taking Mobile, he oversaw three other significant, if often forgotten, late winter–early spring campaigns near the Mississippi River. All were components of his strategic vision. Inhospitable weather at times challenged all three and decisively shaped the last.[1]

The first campaign predated Grant's final promotion and influenced his strategic thinking once he arrived in Virginia. Heartily sick of icy East Tennessee and Appalachian Alabama, Sherman received Grant's permission early in January 1864 to return to Vicksburg. There he would strip the garrisons along the Mississippi and from as far away as Corinth, then use these forces to mop up the Confederates who remained east of the river. The most serious threat consisted of two divisions shielding the vital rail junction at Meridian, near the Alabama border, under Lieutenant General Polk. Sherman had wanted to march to Meridian back in July, after Vicksburg fell, but heat and exhaustion had forced him to relent. He quietly continued to lay plans, however, until called to Tennessee. After Chattanooga, Grant folded the Meridian raid into his wider Mobile operational planning. When Halleck squelched that, Grant let Sherman return west before the then–general in chief could block that too, instructing him to wreck the region's railroads and exhaust its food and forage. Still expecting to drive on Atlanta that spring before pushing on to Mobile or perhaps Savannah, Grant wanted the Confederate base along his right neutralized.

As the plan gelled in January, Sherman would lead the main column, while about 7,000 cavalryman under Brig. Gen. William Sooy Smith rode from Memphis to take on Major General Forrest's pesky horsemen. Grant liked Smith, but Sherman wondered if the former division commander was up to the task. Additional feints from East Tennessee toward Dalton and from the navy at Mobile Bay would prevent reinforcement from Polk. Smith and Sherman would rendezvous in Meridian and then move into Alabama, at least as far as Demopolis if not industrial Selma.[2] Sherman's four divisions, roughly 25,000 men, moved out on February 3. Abandoning his supply line entirely, he planned to live off the countryside, just as Grant had done the previous spring. Two columns marched eastward along the general route of the Southern Railroad, maximizing available forage. The trek to Meridian turned out to be easy. The men ate well off the land, and the days were pleasant. Although exact measurements are lacking, February in central Mississippi generally sees highs around 60 degrees and overnight lows around 40 degrees. No evidence suggests any great deviation in 1864. Nights were cold enough to require fires, but soldiers easily slept on the dry ground without the tents they had left behind. Drying roads and warming temperatures made for easy marching and plentiful foraging. When difficulties did arise, Sherman's pioneers quickly repaired destroyed bridges and improved swampy roads.

In increasing numbers, enslaved people abandoned fields to follow the blue columns, while the Federals burned down slaveowners' homes. No Confederate opposition appeared until Sherman crossed the Big Black River. Even then, frequent skirmishing did little to slow down the Yankees, although it worried Sherman enough to unite his columns. There was no real reason to fear. Polk's Confederates were retreating in a hurry. Fooled entirely by the naval feint at Mobile, Polk insisted that the port city, not Meridian, was Sherman's true target. Consequently, he shooed half of his outnumbered army south and led the rest toward Alabama, intending to hit Sherman's rear when the Federals turned south.[3] For Confederates and especially Mississippians, the retreat was demoralizing. Maj. W. A. Rorer of the 20th Mississippi wrote: "It has been my misfortune to witness many night marches, but I think this one was one of the worst I have ever known, the night was cold and dark. . . . In the course of the night, the army became one mass of stragglers."[4]

Sherman reached Jackson late on February 5. The Federals destroyed everything the enemy had repaired since the last fiery visit, then pushed on into a largely untouched territory of pines, poor soil, and rolling hills. Fire and crowbars wrecked the infrastructure. The weather was warm enough to cause sweat as the men engaged in their destructive activity. Despite rough roads pitted with mud holes, Sherman reached Meridian without serious incident on Valentine's Day. There he remained six days, waiting for Smith's cavalry while wreaking havoc on the railroads, burning storehouses and abandoned homes, and taking or destroying livestock and other supplies. Rain arrived with the Federals. Meridian typically is a tad colder at night than Jackson in February, with an average overnight low of 39 degrees. Normally, it also sees a bit over five inches of precipitation, all of which seemed to arrive at once in 1864. Heavy clouds shrouded February 14. Sprinkles in the morning gave way to a hard rain as the first Federals entered town. While soldiers pillaged civilian blankets and found shelter, men still on the road suffered under their ponchos. Heavy rain continued until noon the next day, leaving streets of mud and swollen streams that at least annoyed foragers and railroad wreckers. February 16 was sunnier, but that night temperatures fell below freezing for the first time on the expedition. Frost-covered ground turned hard. On the eighteenth, winter returned in force.[5] That night, Sherman abandoned his plans to drive on into Alabama. He would return to Vicksburg, taking a different path in order to maximize the physical devastation to the region.

There is no evidence that the worsening weather directly affected Sherman's decision, but it did play a key role in shaping the real deciding factor. Sooy Smith fulfilled Sherman's doubts thoroughly. He started his column ten days late, unwilling to leave until the last of his three brigades recovered from a hard ride through floodwaters and Tennessee mud. The cavalry moved well enough until the Valentine's Day rainstorm. Swollen waterways slowed Smith down, but so did his chronic rheumatoid arthritis—he blamed the weather—and his reluctance to face Forrest. Nor did he rein in his men's zeal to dally, pillage, and burn. On February 18, the cavalry was only at Okolona, not even halfway to Meridian. Snow began falling; Smith wanted to turn back. More snow fell overnight on February 19 into February 20. The general, now quite ill, again called for a retreat; surely, Sherman was on the way back to Vicksburg by now, he argued. After midnight, the column turned back toward Memphis. Pursued closely by Forrest, the Federals fought a running rearguard action before the Confederates let up. Smith arrived in Memphis on February 26. Late the next day, a snowstorm followed. He reported to his superiors that his horses were ruined.[6]

In Meridian, unseasonably cold conditions lingered. On the night of February 18, Sgt. Charles Snedeker of the 124th Illinois recoded "ice . . . 3/8 of an inch in thickness." The following day was cold with light snow. The Federals burned their "She-Bangs" and other unoccupied buildings and left.[7] "Meridian," Sherman later reported, "no longer exists."[8] They headed west in two columns; escaping slaves and white Unionists followed. The retrograde ran to the north of the earlier route, through farm country largely devoid of military targets. The weather soon turned warm and sunny. Aside from swamps and occasional Confederate cavalry strikes, the confident Federals moved steadily, foraging and burning as they passed. At Canton on February 27, Sherman ordered his subordinates to wreck the Southern Railroad and left for Vicksburg to contact Major General Banks and Rear Admiral Porter, who were completing preparations for a presumably similar quick strike up the Red River. His troops spent three days wrecking Canton despite more rain.[9]

Because of that precipitation and freezing temperatures, "the final few days of the expedition," in historian Buck Foster's words, "proved to be the worst."[10] Men and horses dragged wagons and guns through the familiar mud of Mississippi. The lead units crossed the Big Black on March 3. Many soldiers thereafter prepared to head north for their veteran furloughs. Up to 7,000 escaped slaves also settled into camps near Vicksburg. As for weather, March briefly turned warm.[11] In Demopolis, Confederate W. A. Rorer worried "that the weather will be so warm that wheat crop will be so much advanced a cold spell in March or April will ruin it. Our independence depends upon our grain crops as much or more than anything else."[12]

The closest student of the campaign judges its results favorably. The Federals came away with massive amounts of food and numbers of animals. They also left an ugly scar of destruction that offered a glimpse of what Sherman would accomplish later in the year. Planters complained that the loss of their slaves inhibited planting, cutting into the Confederate food supply. Yet Sherman could have done even more had Smith joined him.

Forrest reaped the acclaim for keeping the Federal forces apart, but Smith himself was largely responsible for his failure to reach Meridian and Sherman's consequent inability to chase Polk into Alabama. Without the flooding of late January and subsequent bad weather, Smith might well have accomplished his mission. As it was, flooding and snow indirectly preserved the Alabama frontier.[13]

Despite Grant's fixation on Mobile, Halleck was determined to send a Federal force up the Red River toward Shreveport and on into East Texas. Since May 1863, Shreveport had been headquarters to Lieutenant General Kirby Smith's Army of the Trans-Mississippi, the largest Confederate presence west of the river. It boasted industries and a small naval presence that included gunboats and submarines. The real aims of the planned campaign, however, were economic and political. New England's slacking textile mills needed cotton. Almost since the beginning of the war, Union military and political leaders—including Butler and McClellan—had advocated a cotton-gathering expedition into the Red River valley. By mid-1863, such hopes rested upon Banks, the former Massachusetts politician with close ties to New England's textile barons. Reported bumper crops in the region meant that "tens of thousands of cotton bales" sat awaiting capture and transit. Humming mills in the spring would mean happier Republicans come fall.[14]

Despite his popularity back home—and his presidential hopes—Banks struggled. His political administration of Louisiana was troubled. Factional infighting threatened Lincoln's hopes for wartime reconstruction.[15] Port Hudson seemed anticlimactic after the fall of Vicksburg. Ordered to send troops to occupy Houston and the Texas Hill Country in response to French activity in Mexico, a poorly planned amphibious campaign in early September failed miserably at Sabine Pass, on the Texas-Louisiana border. Banks's subsequent two-pronged expedition toward Texas in October was just as disappointing. A cold overland march toward the Sabine through the Bayou Teche region ended while still in Louisiana when food and forage became hard to find.[16]

The accompanying coastal campaign, the Rio Grande Expedition, careened closer to disaster. On the way to the Texas coast in navy transports, Union troops endured rain, gale force winds out of the north, and heavy

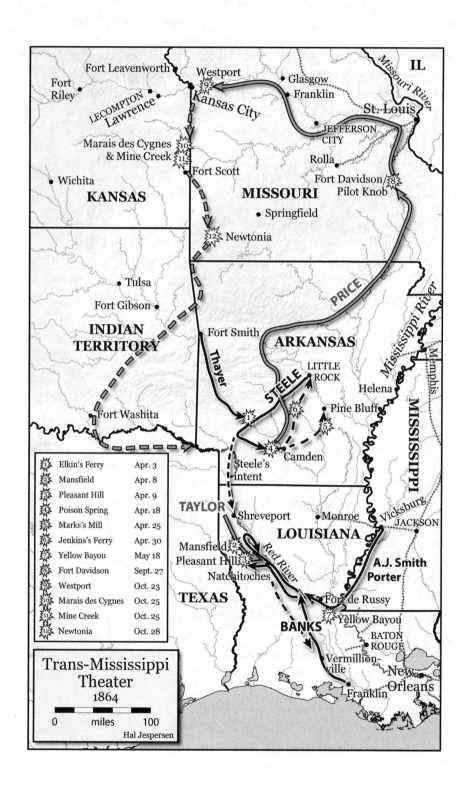

Trans-Mississippi
Theater
1864

	Elkin's Ferry	Apr. 3
2	Mansfield	Apr. 8
3	Pleasant Hill	Apr. 9
4	Poison Spring	Apr. 18
5	Marks's Mill	Apr. 25
6	Jenkins's Ferry	Apr. 30
7	Yellow Bayou	May 18
8	Fort Davidson	Sept. 27
9	Westport	Oct. 23
10	Marais des Cygnes	Oct. 25
11	Mine Creek	Oct. 25
12	Newtonia	Oct. 28

0   miles   100

Hal Jespersen

swells in the Gulf of Mexico from October 26 through November 1. This was the same massive midwestern weather system that shaped Grant's early days in Chattanooga and brought frigidity to Virginia. Out in the Gulf, twenty-four gunboats and troopships made only begrudging progress against the howling wind. Seasickness was endemic. On October 30, the fleet passed Aransas Pass near Corpus Christi. Lt. Benjamin McIntyre of the 19th Iowa, on the floundering troopship *Gen. Banks,* wrote: "Since midnight the storm has increased and at daylight we seemed at the mercy of the waves. . . . Col. Murray very reluctantly consented that the mules and battery might be thrown overboard which was done, with many other things." McIntyre further described "swells . . . like mountains. . . . [O]ur splintered and all but wrecked little craft staggers like a drunken man."[17] By morning, the *Gen. Banks* was taking on water. Ominously, according to a comrade, "two Sharks crossed our bows, and the sailors at once predicted a death on board, during the night sometime one of the 15th Maine died."[18]

Aside from the unfortunate Mainer, the soldiers debarked on the largely unpopulated barrier islands and sang hymns of thanksgiving. Banks occupied the sandy islands up and down the Texas Gulf coast and also sent troops up the mouth of the Rio Grande. They settled into garrison duty that, for some, lasted until August 1864. Good weather at least helped morale. Aside from stiff winds that blew sand in the men's faces, as well as a brief cold snap at the end of November, conditions were delightful. Pvt. J. Irvine Dungan of the 19th Iowa exulted, "here, even in mid-winter, everything is in bloom, and the weather warm and pleasant."[19] The Cold New Year's, however, brought "the coldest day of the Season."[20]

Militarily, the expedition accomplished next to nothing, despite Banks's spread-eagle rhetoric about the Stars and Stripes flying over Texas sand and his contacts with Mexican generals. Halleck was unimpressed; Banks needed to get up the Red River, preferably in cooperation with Sherman and Maj. Gen. Frederick Steele's Union troops in Arkansas. But Lincoln urged the general to hold elections in occupied Louisiana, an Augean task that pulled Banks back to New Orleans. Politics consumed much of his time into March.[21] He did not forget the general in chief, however. In late January 1864, Banks began planning his campaign with Halleck. It was ambitious. Veteran troops from Vicksburg, nearly all of Porter's Mississippi River Squadron, and five of Banks's divisions would rendezvous at Alexandria, in central Louisiana, from where they would move northwest to Shreveport. Porter's fleet would provide support, supplies, and firepower.

Another 10,000 Federals in Arkansas under Steele would move on Shreveport from the north. Kirby Smith would have no choice but to fight or flee to Texas.

But Banks promptly encountered friction in the rear. After Sherman returned from Meridian, he met the New Englander in New Orleans. Unwilling to serve under him—Sherman wanted to lead the campaign himself—he only agreed to lend 10,000 men if they served under his friend Admiral Porter. Sherman further stipulated that his men could go no farther than Shreveport and that he wanted them back by mid-April—Atlanta beckoned. Privately, Sherman warned Porter not to trust Banks, who he thought would abandon the navy if anything went awry. Steele refused do much, either, beyond sending out cavalry until Grant, by now general in chief of the US Army, ordered him to march with his full force.[22]

By then, Banks and Porter were on the move. A "warm, humid spring" came to Louisiana as the Red River Campaign began. March typically is warm there, with mean average highs in Baton Rouge of 70 degrees, overnight lows of 51 degrees, and relative humidity well over 50 percent during the day, rising to 85 percent near dawn. Shreveport is only slightly cooler but more humid at noon.[23] Sherman's contingent, commanded in the field by Brig. Gen. A. J. Smith, embarked on transports and left Vicksburg on March 10, steaming south. Late the next evening, Smith rendezvoused with Porter at the mouth of the Red.[24] On board the USS Carondelet, deck officers described conditions over the next days as "warm and pleasant" and the nights as "cool."[25]

After Smith's men disembarked, Porter took most of his fleet, 104 vessels, up the Red, clearing log obstructions as they went. The plan was to meet again at Fort De Russy, the iron-casemated, earthen-walled key to Kirby Smith's defenses on the lower river.[26] Strong on its river front, the landward rear was weak. As Smith's men moved forward, a Confederate division fled north, abandoning the fort's defenders. On March 14, as cloudy skies cleared, Federal troops attacked De Russy's vulnerable rear while Porter pounded it from the river. The garrison surrendered.[27]

Kirby Smith issued orders to abandon Alexandria. Porter took the town the next day. The officers of the USS Carondelet and the USS Choctaw recorded cooler conditions and described March 16 as "cold," with a strong wind from the northwest. Dense river fog rose on the seventeenth as warmer temperatures returned. Rain fell after midnight on the twentieth.[28] While waiting for Banks, sailors gathered thousands of cotton bales under naval prize law and sent them downstream to market. While he anticipated a bonanza—as commander, he would profit from every bale sold—Porter also worried. He had expected to find the Red River rising with the spring thaws to the north. Instead, it was falling, something that had not happened in March in nearly a decade. Making matters worse, Confederate engineers upriver blew up a dam and diverted much of the river into low-lying fields near Grand Ecore and Natchitoches. Getting his deeper-draft gunboats upriver, or back down it, was starting to look chancy.[29]

Scattered Confederate opposition and heavy rain delayed Banks's concentration, and the inauguration of a Republican governor kept him in New Orleans until March 5. Additional troops, stripped from the Texas islands, arrived. Initially using the railroad to send men west, Banks planned to march northwest along Bayou Teche. Heavy rain on March 8 and March 9 sank his hopes. Infantry, artillery, and the train bogged down in peaty, black clay along the swampy waterway. Banks had no choice but to stop. Rain and mud cost him five days, until the sky and soil grew dry.[30] Dust then filled the air. A reporter described "a pillar of cloud by day, hiding us from ourselves, if not from the enemy."[31] Light rain on the nineteenth did little to help. Straggling grew common. Banks's cavalry finally entered Alexandria the next day. Rain returned that night, while heavier torrents and hail fell just to the north. The weather, while difficult for marching, brought benefits. To the north, Union horsemen overwhelmed Confederates who had pulled in their vedettes during the storm.[32] Pvt. James K. Ewer of the 3rd Massachusetts Cavalry memorialized the affair as his regiment's "Mud March," writing that "the mud was something fearful. In some places it was up to the horses' girths."[33]

The next day was colder. A persistent drizzle grew harder during the late afternoon; snow flurries fell in southwestern Arkansas. While the next two days brought sunshine, rain returned on the morning of March 24 and continued through the night, accompanied in the afternoon by a thunderstorm and stiff winds. Banks finally arrived in Alexandria by riverboat, accompanied by reporters and speculators. His infantry marched in the following day. The weather cleared. Once in Alexandria, the general dealt with outraged planters and cotton buyers and, under directions from Washington, called local elections. To add to his woes, new orders arrived. Grant had sided with Sherman. Now Banks suddenly needed to move quickly so he could return A. J. Smith's troops by mid-April. Already a week late, he had to advance right away and hope that snags were few.[34]

That was not to be. Porter faced a dilemma. The river was rising as the floodplain emptied back into the Red, but it was still low. As if to emphasize this, the powerful ironclad USS *Eastport* ran aground twice. Yet Porter would not leave it, fearing the Confederate fleet in Shreveport. Cautious of low water and snipers, he took four days to inch his flotilla north to Grand Ecore, located on bluffs four miles from Natchitoches. Cavalry followed on March 26, and the infantry the next day, as gale force winds blew up from the south. Heavy rain overnight reduced the road to soup. Banks himself tarried until the Alexandria elections were over on April 1, then followed by steamer. Before he left, he telegraphed Washington, confidently assuring Halleck and Lincoln that he would take Shreveport by April 10 and then pursue the enemy into Texas.[35]

Banks's tone worried administration officials, but initial reports seemed to bear up his boasts. Encountering little opposition other than humidity, a hot sun on March 29 that felled many soldiers, and roads six inches deep in mud or dust (which produced a massive dust cloud), the Federals took Natchitoches easily. Banks then made plans for the final push to Shreveport. They were seriously flawed. He relied on a local Unionist river pilot to guide him, never guessing that the man's real goal was to steer the Yankees away from his cotton. Since the pilot's property lay on the better river road, he persuaded Banks to take a longer and rougher route to the west, far from the support of the navy's guns. Pressed for time, the general left on April 6 without adequate reconnaissance—despite Porter's pleadings—and with a long train. Using only the one road, his column stretched for miles.

Worse yet, the long string of pleasant days ended.[36] April 6 "was a dark and stormy night," James Ewer dramatically wrote. "The men could barely see their horses' heads." Heavy rain the next day turned the local red clay into slippery goo.[37] A reporter described the wet road as nothing more than "a broad, deep, red-colored ditch."[38] Still, Banks could have succeeded had Kirby Smith had his way. Entranced by Steele to the north, the Confederate commander had decided to let Banks exhaust himself against Shreveport's concentric works. But Maj. Gen. Dick Taylor demurred vigorously. He wanted to fight in the open—and farther south. As the Confederates drew in what forces they could, Taylor was determined to stand and fight between Shreveport and Natchitoches.[39]

Capt. Eathan Allen Pinnell of the Confederate 8th Missouri was one of Taylor's reinforcements. He described rain and mud all along the way from Arkansas. Hail fell on March 21. The next day, the Missourians marched through "ten times more mud. . . . [T]he last eight miles was principally of a sticky soil which made it excessively fatiguing." At 9 A.M. on March 24—the same day that Banks steamed into Alexandria—"it commenced raining and continued until we went into camp, which made the road most outrageously muddy. For about three hours we marched through the rain and arrived in camp wet and weary. I never endured a more fatiguing day's march than this has been." A thunderstorm approached from the south-west that evening. The next day saw the Missourians in Shreveport. Day-time temperatures were pleasant until the end of the month, and rain fell only once more in March. The nights, however, were "disagreeably cold." On April 4, a localized weather cell struck during the night with rain and strong winds.[40]

At Pleasant Hill, sixty miles southeast of Shreveport, cavalry from the two armies collided on April 7. Ignoring his commander, Taylor fell back seventeen miles to Mansfield and chose the most propitious ground in Banks's muddy red path, Sabine Cross Roads, where he arrayed his army of about 9,000 men. He would hit Banks with artillery as the Federals emerged from woods, hopefully draw the enemy troops closer, and then fold in their flanks upon them. The next day, April 8, was a Confederate day of prayer; devout Kirby Smith had ordered Taylor not to fight. The rain passed, leaving deep red mud but warmer temperatures. Taylor welcomed arriving reinforcements and waited to disobey his chief. Just after noon, Banks's cavalry appeared. Four hours passed as the long Federal column drew up and the lead division cautiously went into line. Around 4 P.M., Taylor's left charged, probably due to garbled instructions. He then ordered in his right, which crushed the Federal defenders. The Confederates smashed a second Federal division before encountering a third that held its ground until dark.[41]

"It was a terribly cold night," New Yorker Orton Clark remembered, "and with nothing to keep us warm, we shivered, gnawed our scanty sup-ply of hard tack, and listened to the sounds of Jollity and mirth" coming from the Confederate line.[42] Taylor had stopped the enemy in his tracks, but the killing was not over. Banks pulled his men back to Pleasant Hill to reunite with A. J. Smith's veterans at the tail of the long column. Anxious to get away, these soldiers threw away equipment and abandoned wagons and nineteen guns, many mired down in the muddy road. Taylor again dis-regarded Kirby Smith's hesitancy and, with more reinforcements now on hand, launched a pursuit the next morning. He hoped to shove Banks back to Natchitoches. The day was exceptionally lovely. Exhaustion and sixteen miles delayed Taylor's all-out attack until 4:30 P.M. The Federal left and center again caved in during the battle that followed, but the right held long enough for Smith's Vicksburg veterans to launch a successful counterattack. At nightfall, both armies backed away. Banks decided to retreat instead of pushing on to Shreveport or marching to the river to link up with Porter. The decision left Smith close to mutiny. The news angered other officers and men as well. They still wanted to fight, but Banks was done.[43]

The news also surprised Porter, who had steamed north out of Grand Ecore on rainy April 7 with a stripped-down attack squadron of eight gunboats and at least twenty army transports. Low water and snags delayed his progress. He entered a manmade channel studded with batteries called Tones Bayou. The Confederates had lowered the water level there by diverting the river into a parallel waterway. On April 10, the admiral discovered that the Confederates had blocked the bayou as well by sinking a massive steamer across its width, a sandbar quickly forming around it. It was here that Porter learned about the battle at Mansfield and Banks's retreat. Unwilling to wait for the enemy to appear in force and blast his bottled-up ships to pieces, Porter fled. Harassed by musketry and artillery fire, the squadron retreated as fast as the river allowed, reaching Grand Ecore on the fifteenth, the first truly hot day of the campaign. Banks was already there. Both turned back toward Alexandria. Often under fire, Porter lost three vessels on the way south, including the *Eastport*. The army burned Grand Ecore and marched away on warm April 21. Anxious that Taylor might cut him off, Banks drove his men hard, although not hard enough to prevent extensive looting. Men fell out by the dozens. Two days later, with temperatures growing hot and fatiguing, Banks broke through Taylor's blocking force. His dirty, ragged, and exhausted army reached Alexandria and began constructing fortifications despite enjoying a five-to-one preponderance in manpower.[44] Grant and Stanton were ready to fire Banks, but Lincoln refused, lest he lose votes in New England. Instead, the chief of staff created a new military division and gave it to Maj. Gen. Edward R. S. Canby. Banks now became Canby's subordinate.

Porter had more immediate issues to face. With the river running six feet below normal depth, he could not get his boats over the falls at Alexandria. A former logging engineer suggested building a temporary wooden dam south of the falls in order to raise the water level. Soldiers, many of them African American, worked on the dam for a week. On May 9, loaded down with cotton, the gunboats passed one by one over the falls. Once the army broke down the dam, Porter's riverboats steamed for the Mississippi, happily escaping the Red River on May 15. The army left Alexandria burning on stifling May 13. Banks reached Simmesport on the eighteenth and found Canby waiting. Banks went on to New Orleans, and Canby took charge of the army in the field.[45]

The campaign was over. Bad weather played only a limited role. Rain and bad roads delayed Banks's march to Alexandria and gave the Confederates a week to gather additional troops. Dust and mud annoyed the combatants. Naval officers presumably grew bored with their daily notations of "pleasant" days and cool nights until the falling river alarmed them. Mud delayed the march to Sabine Cross Roads, but the road used was bad even in good weather. No accounts cite mud as a major factor at Mansfield, despite rain that continued into the day of battle.[46]

An old army friend of Grant's, Frederick Steele first gained attention at Wilson's Creek, where he commanded the rear guard. During the Vicksburg Campaign, he led a division under Sherman. After Vicksburg fell, Grant gave him command of the Department of Arkansas, with instructions to seize Little Rock and crush Maj. Gen. Sterling Price's remaining Confederates. Little had changed geopolitically in the state since Prairie Grove. Leaving Helena at the head of 12,000 men in August 1863, Steele maneuvered Price out of Little Rock and drove him into the southwest. The Missourian's superior, Lt. Gen. Theophilus Holmes, received most of the blame. When Holmes resigned in February 1864, Price took command of what was left of Confederate Arkansas, still dreaming of reclaiming Missouri. In Little Rock, Steele, like Banks, found himself dealing with a political mess. Lincoln wanted a Union government elected by March 1864. The general expected Rebels to disrupt the balloting but had to watch many of his men leave on furlough.[47]

For all those reasons, Steele avoided cooperating with Banks in what he thought an unnecessary and poorly conceived operation. Banks wanted him to march on Shreveport through southwestern Arkansas, driving Price before him as he went. In early February, Steele countered that the roads were bad, could not bear artillery or trains, and were likely to "be impracticable for several months to come." He was not exaggerating. In Arkadelphia, mean average monthly rainfall today is four inches in February and more than five inches through May. Ongoing mud was a real possibility. It would be better, Steele suggested, either to move independently up the Ouachita River toward Texas—and away from Banks—or else follow the Ouachita southeast to Monroe in northeastern Louisiana. From there, he could march due west to Shreveport, sometimes using the bed of an unfinished railroad. Banks was open to the idea but then lost contact with Steele for a month. Steele did manage to write to Halleck during this interim, promising to drive the Confederates out of Arkansas in the spring once he had enough "cavalry horses and means of transportation. Owing to the severity of the weather and a want of long forage," he continued, "our loss in animals has been very heavy." Washington could not expect results until he was better supplied and the roads dried out. All he would promise Banks was a cavalry demonstration.[48]

Grant ordered Steele to cooperate with Banks. Stung by his harshness, Steele issued marching orders on March 17, two days after Porter arrived in Alexandria. He would unite his spread-out VII Corps and head south. Brig. Gen. John Thayer would bring most of his Frontier Division from Fort Smith to a rendezvous at Arkadelphia. Five thousand strong, the Frontier Division was a fascinating conglomeration of midwesterners, local white Unionists, African Americans, and Native Americans from Kansas. Both commanders struggled for supplies. Not only was the local railroad network incomplete and unreliable but also, like the Red River, the Arkansas was late rising. Low water, snags, and snipers bottled up half of Steele's supplies. Lacking any alterative except further delay, he decided to live off the land. The problem, as the general knew, was that southern Arkansas already had been scoured by the Confederates. His men would have to forage extensively "'without bringing starvation upon the people.'"[49]

Weather not only shaped Steele's preparations but also determined his line of march. The shortest route to Shreveport ran south via Camden, through low country prone to deep mud in spring. The path along the Ouachita via Pine Bluff promised better supply from Little Rock but also exposed the capital to Price. That left the route Banks had suggested, the Old Military Road through the Confederate state capital at Washington. It gave the Rebels no operational advantage; Steele might even break up the enemy government along the way. But it also was the longest path.[50]

Thayer left Fort Smith on March 21, just as Banks's troops and Porter's fleet met in Alexandria. On a longer and steeper path, Thayer almost immediately bogged down in mud created by a rain system north of the Oua-chita Mountains. A Kansas officer wrote: "The weather was rainy, cold and disagreeable, the roads soft and spongy. Numerous mud-holes were found by the enterprising teamsters, and the wagons, sticking fast in them, made our progress slow and difficult. . . . Many places in the road had to be 'cor-duroyed' to render them passable. The country became mountainous and stony, which, with the mud-holes, used up the mules pretty fast."[51]

Steele marched from Little Rock two days later, slowly and in two col-umns. Soldiers who had spent the winter in garrison were not ready for a forced march, he reasoned. The first morning was clear, but on the evening of March 24, torrential precipitation moved up from Louisiana to the Ar-kansas River. It soaked the road before them, especially in the bottomland. The next day, the train savaged this soggy roadbed. Steele halted so that his engineers—white veterans and African American recruits—could cor-duroy near the banks.[52] "Upon leaving the bottom," Chief Engineer Junius Wheeler wrote, "we were met with long and steep hills of a sticky red clay, which clung to the wheels with great tenacity, and to overcome it the an-imals were forced to exert their utmost strength. So exhausted were the mules that they were unable to make but a short march."[53]

On March 26, the Federals brushed past Confederate cavalry and marched on to the Ouachita River at Rockport. Wheeler reported that a nearby ford was no deeper than thirty inches but was rising quickly due to the recent rain. Steele could have crossed right away. Instead, he halted so that Wheeler could lay down a pontoon bridge over the fordable river, just in case. The rest of the army sat idly until the morning of the twenty-seventh, already hungry on half rations. Steele wrote to Sherman that his famished horses were so worn down that half of his cavalry was dis-mounted. Draft animals suffered too. Finding the region gleaned, the Fed-erals now had to bring in forage from as far as forty miles away. Steele's col-umn arrived in Arkadelphia on March 29. Thayer, also slowed by his train, mud, and mountains, still was not there.[54]

Afternoon showers fell across central Arkansas on March 31. Steele waited a day and then left without Thayer. That meant moving into Confederate-held territory with only half his corps while extending his al-ready precarious supply line to the snapping point. Steele believed that he had no choice; his men were eating out Arkadelphia rapidly. Unwilling to turn back and risk Grant's ire, his only hope was to seize enemy stockpiles in Washington. Cavalry sparred frequently as the distance between the armies narrowed. Confederate horsemen had orders to slow Steele down. They did so effectively, often forcing the infantry to deploy into line of battle. The Union column stumbled to the banks of the Little Missouri River only to find Brig. Gen. John Marmaduke's Confederate cavalry arrayed on the opposite bank. Scouts found an alternate ford, and the Federals crossed the river under fire. Finally hearing from Thayer—he was three or four days back—Steele halted. Price's men dug in at Prairie D'Ane, northeast of Washington, and hoped to hold off the Federals long enough for Kirby Smith to send reinforcements.[55]

Then the weather changed. The same system bringing rain and mud to Mansfield and Pleasant Hill spilled north into Arkansas. Engineer Wheeler had fretted about just such an event for days. "I regarded the Little Missouri River at that time to be a more serious obstacle than the enemy," he wrote. Normally placid, after heavy rain, "the color of its water, rapid current, sudden turns and bends and driftwood and snags make it a copy of its namesake, only differing in size." Worse still, the bottomland was low, flat, and "alluvial, . . . generally of a very dark color, in many places resting on a mushy, sticky, yellow clay, which would squeeze out of crevices and holes wherever any pressure was brought to bear near it." The ford was a disaster waiting to happen. And it did. Late on April 7—the day of the Battle of Mansfield—the rains came, leaving "a sea of mud" and a swiftly coursing river. Wheeler lamented that "all the work of the day before was undone; corduroying and bridges were all afloat, the whole bottom was nearly under water, and the Little Missouri was no longer fordable, having risen 3 feet." The road demanded repair even before his men could erect a 140-foot bridge, constructed with doubled pontoons and strengthened with cables running tree to tree.[56]

The engineers completed their work just as Thayer arrived on the evening of the ninth, with a train of empty wagons. He was shocked to find no supplies waiting for him; Steele's men had consumed them. Steele sent his empty wagons toward Little Rock with orders to transport enough food and supplies to Camden for another month. Steele would punch Price at Prairie D'Ane, force the Confederates back on their heels, veer east, and fall back on Camden. In theory, the supplies and the army would meet inside the town's abandoned works. With a supply line back to Little Rock, the Federal column then could continue on to Louisiana.[57]

While the wagons rolled north, Steele attacked Price that steamy afternoon. Masked by gunsmoke pressed to the earth by a temperature inversion, Federal troops drove the enemy over the rolling prairie and into their works but could do no more. The night that followed was "cold and clear," according to Musician A. F. Sperry of the 33rd Iowa, who also remembered shivering men. The next day was "beautiful," sunny, and largely quiet other than chirping birds and a Federal cavalry demonstration in the afternoon. The dust cloud the horsemen generated convinced Price that enemy reinforcements had arrived. He abandoned his works that night and retreated. Steele sent his men forward the next morning only to find the earthworks largely empty.

While his cavalry poked at Price, Steele turned for Camden. The Confederates pursued, nevertheless, sometimes shelling the retreating Federals. Bad roads and "a whole series of swamps" forced the engineers to corduroy washed-out segments.[58] An officer from Kansas described a "swamp . . . about two miles wide, and corduroyed with logs all the way. The advance passed over during the day, and worked up the mud into a kind of porridge, which covered the logs from six to twenty inches deep. Six mules went down in one hole and were drowned in the mud." The night of April 14, according to Sperry, was "too cold to let us sleep any."[59]

The Federals occupied Camden around noon on April 15. They found there rumors of Banks's retreat, but the expected supplies from Little Rock were nowhere to be seen. Determined to hold his position until he heard definitively from Louisiana, Steele sent out foragers with nearly two hundred wagons to secure a reported cache of food. The train bounced back toward Prairie D'Ane. Foragers brought in 5,000 bushels of corn and other foodstuffs. On the eighteenth, as it returned to Camden, Marmaduke's horsemen ambushed the column at Poison Spring. Seizing the wagons, corn, and four guns, the Confederates murdered dozens of prisoners, nearly all from the 1st Kansas (Colored). Confederate Choctaws scalped and otherwise desecrated the bodies.[60]

The Poison Spring Massacre, coupled with the loss of supplies and 20 percent of his rolling stock, added to Steele's woes. On April 19, the corps only had three days of rations left and one day of forage. Thankfully, a train arrived from Little Rock via Pine Bluff the next day with enough half rations for ten days more. Steele, nonetheless, faced bleak operational alternatives. In Louisiana, Banks scapegoated him. By courier, the general claimed victories that Steele doubted. His initial reaction to these questionable reports was to wait for supplies before moving south. Then, on April 21, another dispatch from Banks arrived dated the fifteenth, the same day that Steele entered Camden. The New Englander again clamed victories and told Steele that he could still take Shreveport; remarkably, what he did not state was that he had begun his retreat south. Lacking that last bit of information, Steele expressed his willingness to cooperate still but carefully listed the many reasons why doing so would be difficult. Chief among them were his dire supply situation and reports that Kirby Smith was moving north from Shreveport with three divisions. By April 21, one of these three columns, led by Brig. Gen. James Fagan, was halfway to Little Rock, moving to cut off any Federal retreat. The other two were converging on Camden. Steele did not trust Banks any more than Sherman did and had no idea what to do next.[61]

Kirby Smith and his subordinates ultimately made the decision for him. On April 23, the empty supply train headed back to Pine Bluff. Along with teamsters and escorts, an assortment of sutlers, cotton buyers, and perhaps 300 black refugees marched with it. Soldiers pressed the African Americans into service to repair roads. At dawn on April 25, as skies cleared, Fagan's and Brig. Gen. Jo Shelby's cavalry attacked the column near Marks' Mills. After a morning of vicious fighting, some of it hand to hand, most of the Federal infantry guarding the train surrendered, while the cavalry retreated to Camden. Once again, Confederate soldiers murdered captured African Americans, about 150 teamsters and civilians whom the Federals had freed in Camden through the Emancipation Proclamation. Local whites scooped up the survivors and took them to Texas for sale.[62]

When news of the debacle reached Camden, Steele knew his army, in Michael Forsyth's words, was "vulnerable to annihilation."[63] On the afternoon of April 26, the Federals burned anything the Confederates could use, including wagons and hardtack, and left town at night with only the food they could carry. Engineers pulled up the bridge over the Ouachita behind them. Kirby Smith drove his two divisions and Price's army hard to Camden in pursuit. Anxious to destroy the enemy column and reclaim Little Rock, the Confederates pressed on until they stalled at the Ouachita; Kirby Smith had forgotten to bring his pontoon train. The next morning, pioneers threw up a narrow bridge made up of logs and scrap wood. The troops had to cross in single file, ten feet apart, over the rickety span. Kirby Smith still hoped to drive Steele into Fagan's waiting bayonets, but he had no idea how to inform Fagan, who by then had moved to the Military Road looking for food and forage. Communication issues and haste stymied the

Confederate commander again when he sent a quarter of his cavalry to the Indian Territory to block a nonexistent Federal campaign.[64]

Moving as fast as possible, throwing away knapsacks and spare clothing, the Federals pressed northward. After a few hours of sleep, the column continued its march on April 28 as dark clouds gathered in the western sky. The men bivouacked near Princeton and cleaned out the town. They were only a few miles from Fagan, but, unaware of the situation, he had just left the town and was moving west, away from the Federals.[65] "Only the weather could slow Steele now," Forsyth notes.[66] As the retreating column moved north on April 29 into the "Saline Bottom," rain began to fall hard. Afternoon downpours worsened a five-mile-wide belt of swampy land that lay along that river in Steele's path, raising the Saline itself into a roaring torrent. Wheeler judged the situation worse than the quagmire faced at the Little Missouri. Reaching Jenkins' Ferry around 2 P.M., cavalry found the river there impossible to ford. The engineers would have to erect a bridge before anyone could cross. Meanwhile, the infantry closed up through the morass. Using fence rails and felled trees, they constructed works anchored by a creek, the swamp, and heavy timber. Any attack would have to roll down into muddy bottomland through a funnel a quarter of a mile wide.[67] According to A. F. Sperry, "during the greater part of the night it rained heavily. . . . [T]here was no place to lie down; and if there had been, the rain was too cold a covering."[68]

Wheeler's pioneers toiled in that rain and knee-deep mud to erect the pontoon bridge by nightfall. The labor exhausted them, yet the cavalry and half the train was across by midnight. Many wagons remained stuck in the mud. By morning, most of the artillery was over as well, although there, too, the wet clay claimed prizes. Another consolation was that the same rain and mud had slowed down Kirby Smith's pursuing Confederates. Already exhausted by forced marching, they now had to slop through rain and deep mud most of the night to reach the Federal position. At some points, the combination of floodwaters and mire was waist deep. A brief stop around midnight left soldiers soaked from reclining on flooded ground. Many fell out. Worse, the flooded Saline cut off Fagan's division completely, precluding a Confederate concentration.[69] Confederate surgeon Junius Bragg wrote that the "sounds of distant thunder fell upon the ear, which, as it came nearer, swelled into a roar. In the darkness one could see nothing. Then a flash of lightning would come and reveal a long line of bayonets, stretching away down the road and out into the darkness." It was so dark, Bragg continued, that a horseman ran him down. It was Kirby Smith.[70]

"The morning of April 30, 1864, was a gloomy one for our little army," the Iowan Sperry wrote, "and the exceedingly unpleasant weather was but an unimportant item among so much else that was disagreeable." Hungry and exhausted, the Federals felt surrounded in the chill fog.[71] In front of them lay a shallow moat, "one continuous sea of mud and mire," according to Surgeon Charles Lothrop of the 1st Iowa Cavalry.[72] Rain and fog continued without intermission. Kirby Smith sent his cavalry forward to feel the enemy position. They failed to fully recognize it, reporting back that only a rear guard was present. Without adequately assessing the position further, the lieutenant general rushed in a division at around 8 A.M., expecting to smash the outnumbered Federals against the river. The troops surged into the funnel of open land regiment by regiment, due to the narrow field. Shoes sank into mud and floodwaters two feet deep. Concentrated Federal fire from the front and wooded flanks shredded the Confederates' repeated assaults, even as they neared the barricades in the vortex of rain, standing water, fog, smoke, fire, and lead.[73]

Men on both sides described chaos. Pvt. Joseph Blessington of the 16th Texas wrote that because of the "dense fog and the dense clouds of smoke which hung in the thick woods, many times, opposing lines could only be discovered by the flash of their muskets. . . . [E]ven the elements were terribly convulsed. They seemed to groan with the heavy burden of storms which had been gathered from the hemispheres, to pour upon the heads of God's erring children the vial of wrath, as an admonition to both armies to stay their bloody hands."[74] Sperry remembered that "the battle had not long continued before a dense cloud of powder-smoke settled so closely down, that at a few feet distant, nothing was distinguishable. It seemed now almost impossible to fire other than at random. The rebels did, indeed, mostly fire too high or too low." The Federals realized that, in their lower position at the base of the slope, they could "stoop down and look under the smoke sufficiently to discover the precise position of the rebel masses; and then a horizontal fire at the level of the breast, could not fail to hit its mark, unless a tree stood in its way."[75]

Jenkins' Ferry also saw retaliation. After Poison Spring, soldiers of the 2nd Kansas (Colored), encouraged by their colonel, swore an oath to take no more prisoners. Finding two Rebel guns mired deep in the mud, they shouted "Remember Poison Springs!," took the guns, and bayoneted most of the gunners, including those trying to surrender. Just after noon, with the rain finally stopping, a third assault on the Federal left only lengthened the casualty list.[76] "The ground being too soft to ride," Surgeon Bragg wrote, "the officers dismounted and took their places on foot" beside their "cold, wet and hungry" men.[77]

Once the shooting stopped, the Federal line mounted a brief, spoiling pursuit, then pulled back to the river. The angry men of the 2nd Kansas continued killing and mutilating wounded Rebels. Across the field, Confederates did the same with wounded black men. By 2 P.M., Steele's column, minus the worst of his wounded, was across the Saline, and the pontoon bridge was removed. Danger remained, however. Steele worried about the Confederate division (Fagan's) that had been in his path. His own men and draft animals were famished and worn. Most had nothing at all to eat. Now they had to trudge through more deep mud if they were to make the last fifty miles to Little Rock.[78] And the north bank of the Saline was in worse shape than the south. "Crossing the river," Sperry wrote, "we found ourselves in a slough, which was in places waist-deep; and in which we waded, rather than walked, for some three miles. Teams stuck, and had to be abandoned." One abandoned wagon, its lone mule dying in the mud "with his last drowning kick," contained "a half-dozen negro babies, of assorted sizes." Sperry did not see it himself but reported that one exhausted mother threw away her child "as a soldier would his knapsack."[79]

That night, Federal cavalry reported that the road ahead was too steep and muddy for the train and artillery to negotiate. Steele ordered his essential transportation and artillery double teamed. The rest of the train burned in the darkness. Animals too weak to work were abandoned. By 1 A.M., the corps was in motion through seemingly bottomless swampland. Later in the day, Steele detoured his wounded to Pine Bluff, while the rest of the column stumbled and waded toward the capital.[80] The march was excruciating. Yet although he could not realize it, Steele's road home was clear. Low on supplies, Kirby Smith could not pursue with the swollen Saline in his front and his pontoons miles of incompetence away. He denied Fagan's request to try to swim his cavalry across the river. His men, too, were exhausted. Late on May 1, meanwhile, with skies clearing, Federal cavalry reached Little Rock with an urgent request for provisions. The next day, Steele's retreating column met a relief train from the capital, carrying 30,000 rations. That night, men filled their bellies with such delight that they could all but ignore the arrival of a cold front. Little Rock appeared in the distance late in the morning of the third.[81]

The Camden Expedition was over, with colder weather marking the transition. At both the tactical and operational levels, it was a dismal Federal failure that bookended Banks's defeat in Louisiana. The low Arkansas River and Steele's decision to march without adequate provisions doomed it from the start. In trying to reach Louisiana, he nearly starved his corps into collapse and achieved nothing while losing nearly 3,000 men, 70 percent of his rolling stock, 2,500 mules, and nine guns. Hindsight suggests that at least in regards to weather, Steele had been right to drag his feet. The combination of Arkansas geography, typical spring weather bringing heavy rains, and deep clay mud shaped the campaign just as Steele warned Banks it would.

The Confederates had more to show for their efforts, having held on to their threatened territory. Except at Jenkins' Ferry, weather conditions had favored them. Yet just as Taylor pleaded, Kirby Smith would have better served his cause by pursing Banks instead of Steele. His fantasy of liberating Arkansas, just like his chimera of rescuing Kentucky two years earlier, was beyond his grasp, ending at a flooded river without pontoons. Price already had enough men to help the Arkansas mud swallow Steele's expedition. Michael Forsyth rightly adds that a more vigorous effort against Banks might well have kept XIX Corps in the Trans-Mississippi West instead of its eventual destination in Virginia. Worst of all, violence and racial atrocity marred the expedition, as it did elsewhere across the war zone in early 1864. On sunny February 20, Confederates killed African American Federal prisoners after the battle at Olustee, Florida. And the most infamous of all the war's atrocities, the Fort Pillow Massacre in western Tennessee, occurred on April 12, just six days before Poison Springs. There was more such cruelty ahead on spring's stormy horizon.[82]

Chapter 20

Festering in the Sun

Virginia, April–June 1864

While Grant kept watch on events in the Mississippi River valley, the wider war was now his immediate concern. At muddy Culpeper, he began developing a grand strategy for winning it before the November elections. He based his plans on forward movement and concentrated effort. Countering the Confederates' ability to *concentrate in space* against piecemeal campaigns, Grant wanted to assail the enemy at several points simultaneously. *Concentration in time* would prevent them from shifting men from quiet fronts to hot ones, as they had done effectively in the past.

According to plan, Sherman would drive on Atlanta and destroy Joe Johnston's Army of Tennessee. Banks, once back from the Red River, would move on Mobile, that long-desired target in the Grant playbook. Given full latitude, the general in chief also would have outdone McClellan in the East. Back in January, he had suggested that Halleck send much of Meade's Army of the Potomac to North Carolina. There it could wreck Lee's supply railroads and force the Confederates to come after the Federals. Halleck dissuaded him; Lincoln would never allow that army to uncover the capital and give Lee a chance to scoot north again. Obliged to continue to attack Lee and Richmond overland, Grant decided to swing Meade downriver and well to the east—through the Wilderness and past Mine Run—to turn Lee's right while maintaining the Federal supply line. He envisioned a complementary operation toward Richmond from southeastern Virginia, endorsing Butler's scheme to move up the James to Bermuda Hundred and City Point. Butler could use the railroads there to drive on Petersburg and the capital, creating a potent diversion. Finally, Grant planned to send smaller forces from West Virginia against Lee's western supply line in the Shenandoah. As clumsily modified by area commander Maj. Gen. Franz Sigel, that operation eventually involved marching up the Shenandoah while two raiding parties moved into Southwest Virginia, wrecked the Virginia and Tennessee Railroad, and destroyed the region's vital saltworks. Overwhelmed at every turn, the Confederacy would implode.[1]

The plan looked good on paper, but out in the elements, unsettled weather stymied Grant. He needed dry roads to concentrate additional troops in Virginia—notably Major General Burnside's IX Corps—but rain, snow, and deep mud at Culpeper continued. Clouds and light rain on April 1 gave way to northwestern gales and heavy torrents that turned into snow before dawn. Rev. C. B. Mackee reported nearly an inch accumulation, while in Richmond, J. B. Jones complained of "several inches."[2] The snow stopped, but rain kept coming for days. Melting snow and slush created more mud and swollen waterways. Flooding washed away bridges up to Washington, blockading supply and mail trains. Hail fell on chilly April 5. Rain continued out of the northwest until the next day, when temperatures rose into the upper fifties. After a false spring that greeted the Confederates' Fast Day, rain returned with gusto, along with highs in the sixties, from April 9 into April 12. The ground could hold no more. Water flooded camps, wrecked roads, and washed away more bridges, again stopping the armies' trains. Back in camp, Howard Smith of the 1st New York Dragoons quipped that his regiment's shanties had become boats that only awaited iron cladding.[3]

The one good result of the rain, according to Charles Wainwright, was that it "insures our remaining at peace for at least one week more."[4] Peace lasted longer than that. April's showers and downpours returned in cycles. The roads around Culpeper only began to dry out around April 13; the Washington high that afternoon reached 60 degrees. Soldiers on both sides expected a movement, but another round of precipitation two days later undid any progress. A wet cold snap followed, with rain, snow in the Blue Ridge, and frost in Richmond. Bull Run flooded as did the Potomac at Long Bridge. Nights grew cold, with lows in the forties.

Spring only arrived for good in April's fourth week. Cherry trees blossomed in Richmond, but J. B. Jones lamented that frost and rain had all but killed his garden. He was not alone in worrying about food. The editor of the *Lynchburg Republican* reported that the dry winter had left the winter-wheat crop in dire shape. There would be little in the way of oats, he added, as farmers could not obtain seed. At the front, peach trees blossomed, blackberry bushes grew leaves, and other trees began to bud. The high temperature on April 23 soared to 78 degrees. Men put out fires and ventilated their cabins by knocking out the mud chinking. The winter finally seemed over, even if it rained one last time, during the night of the twenty-fourth.[5]

Veterans, nonetheless, looked back on April—and ahead to May—with trepidation. "The spring is more backward and colder than it was at this time last year," Wainwright observed, "much as it was in 1862. I trust we are not going to have a whole summer of rain as we had then."[6] But Grant was optimistic. "By the 17th of April," he later wrote, "spring had so far advanced as to justify me in fixing a date for the great move." In truth, wet weather forced him to "fix" several additional dates: April 27, April 30, May 2, and finally May 5, at Sherman's request. Orders went out for an advance in Virginia on May 4 and into Georgia the next day.[7] The bustle alerted Lee, who arrayed his army. Among his men along the Rapidan were Longstreet's two divisions, which had just escaped the snows of East Tennessee.[8]

May Day was beautiful, by all accounts, with an afternoon high of 63 degrees. The next day was similar.[9] At about 6 P.M., however, Lt. N. D. Preston of the 10th New York Cavalry saw a frightening sight in the southwestern sky. "Something was moving toward the camps," he wrote, "hiding from view the entire landscape in its passage. It was an awful spectacle. Men viewed the approaching curtain with blanched cheeks and palsied tongues. Presently its near approach revealed its true character. It was a cloud of dust—Virginia real estate on the rampage." Saturated with dust, either a tornado or a sudden microburst approached with fury.[10]

Sgt. William White of the Richmond Howitzers described chaos:

> Angry west winds came sweeping from the mountains with a hurricane-like sound, whirling our camp furniture through the giddy mazes of a tempest dance: our tent-flies flew away on the bosom of the breeze and the tree-tops came crashing to the earth; then came the rain and hail, driving full into our faces, and then the cry of fire! What an indescribable turmoil now! Fence-rails, tree-tops, skillets, tin-pans, tents and tarpaulins whirling around in a dance of maudlin merriment, and the fierce red flames licking out their forky tongues in spiteful glee.[11]

Cooler conditions followed the freak storm. The afternoon high fell 9 degrees in a day, to 59 degrees on May 3. Winds held enough dust aloft to alert Confederates along the river. That night, with temperatures hovering

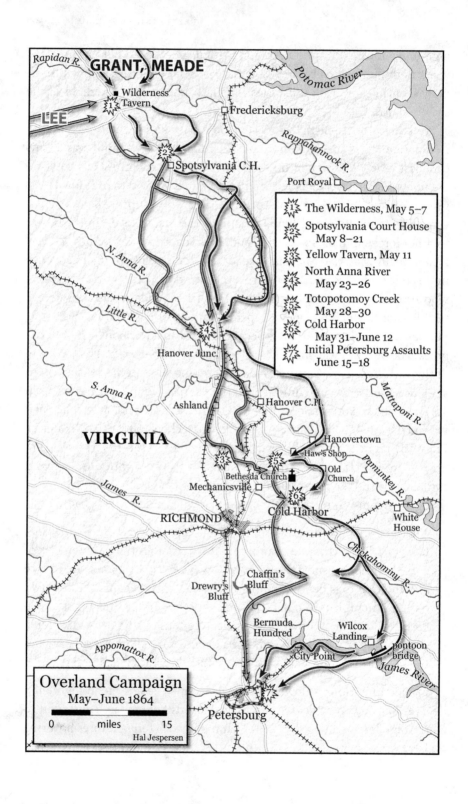

Rapidan R.

GRANT, MEADE

Potomac River

■ Wilderness
Tavern

☆1☆

□ Fredericksburg

LEE

Rappahannock R.

☆2☆

□ Spotsylvania C.H.

Port Royal □

	The Wilderness, May 5–7
☆1☆	
☆2☆	Spotsylvania Court House May 8–21
☆3☆	Yellow Tavern, May 11
☆4☆	North Anna River May 23–26
☆5☆	Totopotomoy Creek May 28–30
☆6☆	Cold Harbor May 31–June 12
☆7☆	Initial Petersburg Assaults June 15–18

N. Anna R.

Little R.

☆4☆

Hanover Junc.

S. Anna R.

Ashland □

□ Hanover C.H.

Mattaponi R.

VIRGINIA

□ Hanovertown

☆3☆

☆5☆ Haw's Shop □

Bethesda Church ■

□ Old Church

Pamunkey R.

Mechanicsville □

☆6☆

James R.

RICHMOND

Cold Harbor

Chickahominy R.

White
House

Chaffin's
Bluff

Drewry's
Bluff

Bermuda
Hundred

Wilcox
Landing □

Appomattox R.

City Point

pontoon
bridge

James River

☆7☆

Overland Campaign
May–June 1864

0   miles   15

Hal Jespersen

Petersburg

around 50 degrees, Federal columns "moved on through the interminable forest and endless night," as Pvt. John Haley remembered. "The winds tossed the leafless branches of the trees, seeming to moan and shudder."[12]

May 4 was beautiful, with clear skies, solid roads, a brisk morning low of 49 degrees, and afternoon highs nearing 67 degrees at a temporary Federal weather station near Warrenton, known as the "Rendezvous Station." "A sun as bright as the 'sun of Austerlitz' shone down upon the scene," Col. Horace Porter wrote confidently, thinking of Napoleon's crushing defeat of his enemies in 1805. "Its light brought out in vivid colors the beauties of the landscape which lay before us, and its rays were reflected with dazzling brilliance from the brass field-pieces and the white covers of the wagons as they rolled lazily along in the distance."[13]

Flashes of sun-reflecting bayonets and a growing dust cloud made it obvious that the Army of the Potomac, followed by Burnside's independent corps, again was coming across the Rapidan. Facing no opposition at the fords, they bore east into the foreboding Wilderness. Despite Meade's intention to move quickly, he halted in the afternoon to let his trains catch up. He assumed that Lee either would stand at Mine Run or fall back to his North Anna defenses. That night, clouds rolled in. Some Federals expected the precipitation that always seemed to greet their forward movements. In the darkness, Lee sent two corps east to block the enemy in the Wilderness long enough for Longstreet's divisions—twenty miles away—to come up and smash the Federal flank. It could be Chancellorsville all over again.[14]

Early the next morning, Ewell's corps approached from the west on the Orange Turnpike through thick morning fog. It was 52 degrees at Warrenton that morning, but the dreaded Confederate rain for once had not come. Ewell ran into the V Corps as it moved southeast. Skirmishing escalated. Outnumbered, the Confederates backed off and threw up fieldworks. The unexpected attack worked like a charm operationally. With Grant's enthusiastic assent, Meade halted and turned west to damage the Confederates. The fighting escalated into essentially two full-scale battles, one involving Ewell's corps, and the other fought by A. P. Hill's corps three miles to the south on the Orange Plank Road. Meade finally realized that Lee had launched a major assault down the Wilderness's narrow lanes and through its tangled vines, briars, and dense new-growth thickets of pine and oak.

Dense terrain, limited sightlines, and thick smoke undermined the Federals' numerical superiority, negated the strength of their artillery, and confused everyone. Lines of battle fell apart. Regiments and couriers got lost. Lee faced the same factors while losing ease of movement. Wounded men burned alive—or committed suicide first—when gunfire ignited windwhipped infernos in the undergrowth. The afternoon temperature rose to 75 degrees, but in the suffocating woods, soldiers remembered stifling heat. Attacks and counterattacks flared until night. With temperatures in the high fifties, the Federals still held the two intersections they needed to continue south. Grant was optimistic that a counterattack at dawn, involving Burnside as well as Meade's army, could crush Hill's corps and roll up Lee's right. II Corps would hold off Longstreet if he arrived. Lacking confidence in Burnside, Meade and his subordinates expected the worst.[15]

The morning of May 6 was again clear, dry, and pleasant, with temperatures in the upper fifties. As the Federals prepared to strike, Ewell launched an unexpected assault that set John Sedgwick's corps back on its heels. To his left, Gouverneur Warren refused to attack with his V Corps until Sedgwick got moving forward. In stark contrast, Winfield Scott Hancock's II Corps roared out of its positions and broke most of Hill's corps. The Federals drove the Confederates for almost a mile, right through Lee's field headquarters. Lee himself attempted to lead a counterattack until his adoring men refused to let him risk his life. While the "Go Back, General Lee" incident went down in lore, what really stopped Hancock was the timely appearance of Longstreet's corps, coupled with the tardy arrival of Burnside. Longstreet's veterans drove Hancock away, and a subsequent flank attack nearly broke the Federal line entirely. The counterattack only faltered when Longstreet fell, seriously wounded by friendly fire. Another stalemate ensued in the smoky thickets of the Wilderness. By midday, haze and dust were so thick that George Neese described the sun as a red ball he barely could see in the sky. It was hot too. During the afternoon, temperatures climbed to 91 degrees as a week-long heatwave began. More fires broke out, with a west wind pushing flames up to the Union barricades and setting them alight. At the end of the day, Maj. Gen. John B. Gordon's flanking attack on the Federal right drove the blue line back a mile.[16]

The night of May 6 was close, with a 9 P.M. temperature of 73 degrees at Warrenton. It felt hotter to wool-clad men who had fought all day in the Wilderness. "It was a night of sweltering heat," Capt. Mason Tyler of the

37th Massachusetts recollected. "No rain had fallen for several days, and the many wheels and feet of horses and men pounded the dry soil into impalpable dust, which rose hundreds of feet in the air." Heat, dust, and continuing forest fires made it hard to sleep. So did the screams of wounded men burning to death.[17] At Federal headquarters, steamy conditions added to the tension. Grant refused to quit, famously snapping at one brigadier who had the temerity to try to explain Lee's genius. Yet both the carnage and Lee's stubbornness shocked the general in chief. He spent the next day weighing his options. Dispatches arrived: Sherman had attacked Johnston in Georgia, and Butler held City Point. Temperatures spiked to a broiling 89 degrees in Washington. Smoke, ashen dust, and a morning fog lingered over the Wilderness like a death shroud. Finally, unwilling to waste more lives in the thick vegetation—and dissatisfied with Meade and his corps commanders—Grant took the reins. He issued orders to pull out of line that night, swing around Lee's right, and move south ten miles to the junction at Spotsylvania Court House. If Grant gained that crossroads, Lee would have to come out and fight superior numbers in more-open space. He also would be unable to send help south against Butler. Expecting to retreat, the Federals cheered when they realized that Grant was leading them south, through warm darkness thick with a dust that Meade aide Theodore Lyman likened to flour.[18]

Fog rolled in the next morning, mixed with the dust and lingering smoke. The heatwave dragged on as the fighting shifted south. Lee deduced Grant's intentions and ordered Stuart's cavalry and Maj. Gen. Richard Anderson—who had replaced Longstreet in corps command—to get to Spotsylvania first. Anderson's infantry hacked a path through a Wilderness on fire. It was an exhausting trek, made worse by the flames. They made better time than Meade, however, whose worn-out columns jammed up in the gloomy dark. The next day, May 8, was blistering hot, with a high of 95 degrees. All day, weary and mismanaged Federal cavalry and infantry failed to block the Confederates. Worse, when Meade and cavalry commander Maj. Gen. Phil Sheridan blamed each other, Grant played favorites, ordering Meade to give in to Sheridan's wishes to mass his troopers and go after Stuart. At that moment, Grant became the de facto commander of the Army of the Potomac. Meanwhile, Lee's army trudged into Spotsylvania Court House. On the ninth—85 degrees with thick haze—his men constructed an imposing semicircle of works defined by a salient in the center, which someone christened the "Mule Shoe" for its shape, that followed the modest rolling ground. It was the weakest part of the line, leading Lee to concentrate his artillery there. The Federals dug in as well, forming a wider arc north of the Confederate position. Thick red dust filled the stifling sky.[19]

Grant believed that Lee was shifting to attack Burnside, coming in from the northeast. Late in the day on hot and humid May 10—the high reached 93 degrees at the Rendezvous Station—he attacked the Confederate works from their western base toward the Mule Shoe. The intended general assault came off piecemeal. Lee sent a division against the western attackers' right flank on the Po River. The fighting that blistering afternoon was poorly coordinated, vicious, and marked by a raging brush fire on the Union right. The only Federal bright spot came when twelve handpicked VI Corps regiments commanded by Col. Emory Upton briefly penetrated the far left end of Mule Shoe using innovative tactics and strict fire control. Without his promised support, however, Upton had to fall back. Yet his limited success encouraged Grant to try it again, but with two corps next time.[20]

As Grant finalized his plans, staff officer Porter noted "a threatening sky" that "was not propitious for the movement, but in this entertainment there was to be 'no postponement on account of the weather,' and the preparations went on regardless of the lowering clouds and falling rain."[21]

Aside from spotty thunderstorms on the ninth, no rain had fallen since the first of the month. Stifling heat in the woods, solid roads, and dense dust clouds shaped the early days of the campaign. That changed on the afternoon of May 11, as a strong front moved in from Georgia—Sherman's army was at Resaca—and other points west. Temperatures climbed to 84 degrees before the sky grew cloudy. Around 4 P.M., the first in a series of devastating thundershowers broke out across eastern Virginia.[22]

The rain's first military effects were felt to the south. Two days earlier, Sheridan and a massive force of 12,000 troopers rode away to the southeast at dawn. Freed from screening, picketing, and Meade's ire, Sheridan ached to take on Jeb Stuart and end Confederate cavalry domination in Virginia. With less than half his strength—he left four brigades with Lee—Stuart pursued. The Confederates struck the rear of Sheridan's column twice but could not slow it down. At about 8 P.M., a thunderstorm soaked George Custer's troopers as they hit Lee's supply line at Beaver Dam Station on the Virginia Central Railroad. They burned the station as well as 1.5 million badly needed rations. The next day brought more heat, choking road dust, and sporadic confrontations. Leaving a brigade to pursue Sheridan, Stuart raced east in order to cut of the enemy before they reached Richmond. Outnumbered three-to-one, he expected help from the city's garrison. Sheridan pulled up late in the day just across the South Anna River.[23]

May 11 dawned with clear skies and a hot wind. At the South Anna, Stuart's pursuing brigade hit Sheridan's rear guard and fought for hours. Sheridan's main column moved on. At a derelict crossroads inn called Yellow Tavern, just two miles from the Richmond defenses, fresher Federals encountered Stuart's troopers. Holding the high ground, Stuart hoped to hold the bluecoats off long enough to receive reinforcement and then launch a flanking counterattack. But help never arrived. In Richmond, Gen. Braxton Bragg (now President Davis's chief military advisor) refused to send him the closest men—a few thousand raw militiamen in the nearby trenches— and instead looked to Petersburg for support. The sky began to turn dark with a massive storm developing.[24] Three distinct weather systems collided over the capital at that time. "They came in heaviest volume from the southeast in parallel lines," Jones observed, "like lines of battle swooping over the city. There were at the same time shorter and fuller lines from the southwest, and others from the north. The meeting of these was followed by tremendous clashes of lightning and thunder; and between the pauses of the artillery of the elements of above, the thunder of artillery on earth could be distinctly heard."[25]

What Jones heard was the Battle of Yellow Tavern. "Just as the battle began," Pvt. R. H. Peck of the 2nd Virginia Cavalry remembered, "the cloud reached us and a dreadful storm followed. The lightning and cannonading were so terrific that sometimes we couldn't tell the flash of one for the other. . . . We fought nearly the whole time in a down-pour of rain."[26] Stuart went down with a bullet to the gut. Wet Confederates soon broke in all directions. A gust of wind blew down the steeple of St. John's Episcopal Church in the capital. Stuart died the next evening in Richmond, one of many to fall in the sheets of rain and its resulting red mud at Yellow Tavern. Sheridan slipped off to the east, impeded by darkness, rain, and mud. After more fighting the next day—in a blinding thunderstorm at the swampy, waist-deep banks of the swollen Chickahominy—he linked up the Union navy on the James. The rain continued, with tornadoes touching down through the night.[27]

~~~

Back at Spotsylvania on May 11, a mix of drizzle and steady showers followed the same line of late-afternoon thunderstorms. Rain continued through the night. Rifle pits and ditches flooded. Fields grew slippery and soggy. Temperatures fell into the upper fifties after dark, leaving wet men shaking and chilled. The negative effect on Federal morale was palpable.[28] Capt. Mason Tyler remembered how the storm complex "soaked the earth and drenched the foliage of the forest and enveloped the scene with a thick covering of mist and fog, which added much to the gloom and distress of the occasion."[29] It also retarded Grant's preparations. II Corps regiments moved out at 2 A.M. and struggled for hours to reach their positions. "The wind sobbed dearly over the meadows and through the trees," John Haley remembered, "rain fell steadily, and the night was so dark men had to almost feel their way."[30]

The storm negatively affected the Confederates as well. It was Lee's turn to make a dangerously wrong assumption. Convinced by the Federals' activity that they were retreating, he ordered his artillery out of the soggy salient so that it would be ready to move. The infantry relaxed and crawled into shelters. Around midnight, pickets reported alarming indications that the enemy actually was massing across from the salient. Maj. Gen. Edward Johnson's men occupied the front of this weak point; he begged for artillery, but it came too late. Concerned with mist, thick fog, and dark leaden clouds, Hancock delayed his advance a half hour, hoping for better light. At 4:45 A.M., with temperatures around 60 degrees and the wind gusty, he attacked. Sweeping up the slope and out of dense fog—also over sleeping or shocked Confederate pickets—the attackers did not stop to fire. Massed lines bypassed scattered musketry and leaped over the parapets. The defenders reacted with confusion. Some fought, others fled, and still more surrendered. Within minutes, Hancock controlled the forward point of the Mule Shoe, as defined by "angles" on the east and west. Lee's line had broken.[31]

Hancock and his amazed men hardly could believe their luck, so much so that they stopped advancing. While the Federals took prisoners or milled about, Confederate reserves launched the first of five counterattacks, this one running north through trees and fog into the sloppy Mule Shoe. Lee himself tried to lead it, only to be dissuaded once more by shouts of "Lee to the rear!" The reserves shocked Hancock's men and drove them back to the works. Both sides packed more and more men into the melee. To the west, VI Corps struck the line about 6 A.M., without punching through. To the east, Burnside made little headway. At the western end, thereafter known as the "Bloody Angle," the intense, chaotic stalemate became brutal, a Jenkins' Ferry writ large. And it kept raining. Mist cycled back and forth into steady rain all day and into the evening. Trenches and low places filled with dead men and water that turned red with blood. Wet powder refused to ignite. Struggling to keep their footing in the muck, soldiers thrust their bayonets or swung their weapons like prehistoric clubs. Gun crews pushed their pieces to the log barricades and fired canister indiscriminately, shattering wood and flesh. Men churned the mud knee deep in places.

Grant's entire force was now engaged. To the west, Warren's V Corps assault at Laurel Hill—thrown together to help IV Corps—melted in the face of formidable works and Confederate fire. At the Mule Shoe, Lee's engineers and survivors created a new line of works in the rear, across the base of the salient. The fighting went on well into the moonless, drizzling night. Hours after midnight, the survivors in mud-covered gray finally fell back to the new line, minus 4,000 prisoners and another 4,000 dead. Johnson's venerable Stonewall Brigade ceased to exist. Grant lost over 6,000 casualties. The dead from both armies lay half buried in the mud; their comrades' shoes had pounded them into the mire.[32]

"The battle near the 'angle' was probably the most desperate engagement in the history of modern warfare," Porter later wrote with forgivable hyperbole, "and presented features that were absolutely appalling. It was chiefly a savage hand-to-hand fight across the breastworks. Rank after rank was riddled by shot and shell and bayonet-thrusts, and finally sank, a mass of torn and mutilated corpses." Artillery pounded the breastworks and their defenders into pieces. Porter remembered "wild cheers, savage yells, and the frantic shrieks" that rose "above the sighing of the wind and the pattering of the rain. . . . Even the darkness of night and the pitiless storm failed to stop the fierce contest."[33] Modern historians agree. Gordon Rhea observes that "the Civil War had seen its share of horrors. . . . They paled, however, when measured against the slaughter along the short stretch of earthworks where the salient's western tip bent south."[34]

Grant spun the day as a success. His men had taken thousands of prisoners, he said, captured nearly thirty guns, and caused irreparable damage to the enemy. Yet both the stalemate on the stinking field and the rain dragged on another four days, turning roads into impassable channels of mud. Reverend Mackee recorded 1.19 inches of rain through this period, while temperatures in Washington rose into the seventies. At desolate Spotsylvania, exhaustion, burying the dead, delayed shock, and horror claimed most of May 13. The Confederates also strengthened their works while Grant probed, eager to strike before the enemy recovered. Torrential and cold rain fell that night. Deep fog shrouded the field. Grant's plan to shift two corps overnight and hit Lee on the fourteenth came to nothing amid heavy showers, thunderstorms, and the waist-deep Ni River.[35] "It was pitch dark," Lt. George Barnard wrote his father, "raining like fury and the mud knee deep. . . . The suffering of the men is almost indescribable, this lasted till the morning, the men falling over at every step as our road took us by the woods filled with uncared for wounded, howling for help as they heard us groping along while I saw men in the ranks so utterly wretched that they threw themselves in the middle of the road wallowing in the mud under the horses' feet howling and crying like madmen. I never knew such a horrible night."[36]

"Every thing in confusion on account of the mud," Brig. Gen. Marsena Patrick wrote, "which was as deep as I ever Saw in Virginia—The 5' and 6' Corps and all Artillery, Ambulance & Head Quarters Trains were stalled, & all the roads blocked up."[37] Wainwright described a "most extraordinary" overnight march. "They say the men got lost in the wood on every side, and that mud was ankle deep the whole way." The next day brought rain, with brief moments of hot sun. "The whole country is a sea of mud."[38] That night, Lee moved east to counter Grant. Rain fell steadily from east to west, with nearly an inch at Warrenton. Showers and fog marked the next afternoon. Neither army could do much except probe.[39] Grant finally admitted that he could do nothing "until we can have twenty-four hours of dry weather."[40]

~~◦

The precipitation stopped at Spotsylvania at about 8 A.M. on May 17. It had rained the great part of six days and into a seventh. Although the roads remained sloppy, sunny skies mixed with clouds encompassed the front.

Temperatures rose to 76 degrees before settling into the midsixties after dark. Here was the better weather Grant needed. Adding to his upbeat mood, good news arrived from other fronts. Sherman had forced Johnston out of Dalton. Butler had seized the outer works at Drewry's Bluff on the James River, cut communications south of Richmond, and now threatened the capital. In Southwest Virginia, Brig. Gen. George Crook's and Brig. Gen. William Averell's raiders reported serious damage to the railroad. Assuming that Lee's army was near its breaking point, Grant decided to press his apparent advantages—including good weather—and attack in force. He ordered Hancock and Horatio Wright to overwhelm Lee at dawn. Soldiers stumbled through dense fog and the moonscape of the salient. They discovered their enemies waiting for them behind their most formidable defenses yet. Confederate artillery decimated the assault waves.[41]

The failed attack was only the beginning of disappointments and depression that day. Mud-splattered couriers with bad news rode into camp. A small Confederate force hastily assembled by Major General Breckinridge had blunted Sigel's slow advance up the Shenandoah on a spongy field just south of New Market. That battle took place in cycles of sunshine and showers that gave way after noon to steady rain and finally a thunderstorm. The sticky ground at New Market grew so muddy that part of it later became known as the Field of Lost Shoes for the number of men and boys who lost theirs in a wheat field's ankle-deep muck. In heavy rain, Breckinridge broke Sigel's line. Only swelling rivers allowed the Federals to escape unpursued.

More reports arrived from farther west. Banks had failed in Louisiana and was in retreat. The twin Federal columns out of West Virginia were too, after defeating a small Confederate force at Cloyd's Mountain but doing no long-term damage to the railroad or saltworks.[42] Just south of Richmond, Confederates under Gen. P. G. T. Beauregard emerged from thick fog rising off the James at dawn on May 16 and attacked Butler's army at Drewry's Bluff. "It is difficult, for one who was not in it," Surgeon James Emmerton of the 23rd Massachusetts later wrote, "to form a fair idea of the density of that fog. Even before the action became general a column of the enemy, almost within stone's throw, was only detected by a momentary lift of the fog, showing their massed feet on the opposite slope." Conversely, the dense river fog allowed many Federal soldiers to escape.[43] Beauregard forced Butler back into narrow and triangular Bermuda Hundred, formed by the James and Appomattox Rivers, and constructed works across its five-mile long neck. Richmond was safe from the south. Coupled with Sheridan's hollow cavalry raid, all of Grant's complementary operations in Virginia suddenly were dismal failures. Lee's flanks and rear were safe, and now reinforcements were heading to him.[44]

Faced with such "discouraging" reports as well as his own stalemate, the general in chief decided that he would not to fight it out on the Spotsylvania line all summer, after all. He issued orders to II Corps "for a movement by the left flank on toward Richmond, to commence on the night of the 19th." Grant did not want to shift the same entrenched fighting to the south. Presumably, Lee would fall back on the North Anna River at Hanover Junction, astride the Virginia Central Railroad. Grant hoped that the sight of a single corps, seemingly unsupported, would tempt Lee out into the open so that he then could swoop down with the rest of the Army of the Potomac.[45]

May 19 opened with "beautiful spring time," according to Chaplain Alanson Haines of the 15th New Jersey.[46] Afternoon temperatures reached 68 degrees as II Corps made ready while the rest of the army wheeled into a new line running from north to south. Lee interrupted Grant's preparations with a strong reconnaissance in force against the north end of the new line just as a thunderstorm began to rumble and rain. At best, Ewell's II Corps attack might seize the road to Fredericksburg and block the Federals' supply line. Shocked, Grant dispatched Porter, who in turn sent in a division of heavy artillerymen recently pulled from northern forts and converted to infantry. At great loss, the "heavies" held their ground in the rain.[47] But the attack troubled Grant enough that he delayed his turning movement. The next day, May 20, was clear and lovely but hotter at 78 degrees, signaling the end of the cooler temperatures that had accompanied the rainy stretch and the true beginning of mounting summer heat. Soldiers searched for shade. The night, Hancock moved out in another dank fog, eventually halting the next afternoon. The new day was much hotter, hitting 87 degrees and bringing on yet another thunderstorm.

Heat and dust affected the Confederates as well. Instead of taking the Federal bait, Lee pushed his army south toward the North Anna—exactly where Grant had hoped he would not go. Rejecting Meade's advice, Grant decided to match Lee's march. Defeats elsewhere and his own stalemate in Virginia were turning northern public opinion against Grant and Lincoln. The general in chief needed to win a battle. Despite their growing exhaustion, both armies drove south, the Federals in some disarray. It was hot the next day—86 degrees at 2 P.M.—but at least skies were clear and the sandy roads largely firm. Lee won the race to the river.

On May 23 (78 degrees), Meade's sweating, dust-covered V Corps reached the waist-deep North Anna at Jericho's Mills. Just before 6 P.M., A. P. Hill's furious attack failed to prevent Warren establishing a position south of the river. When Hancock's corps secured a second crossing, they effectively pierced Lee's line. Unwilling to surrender the nearby railroad, however, Lee had his engineers and soldiers work all night to construct a remarkable line of entrenchments. Shaped like an inverted V, with its point on the North Anna at Ox Ford, the mother of all salients protected Hanover Junction while using the works and the river to divide Federal forces. Grant's men, ordered that day to chase Lee across the river, discovered the massive wedge with chagrin. Six miles and the salient separated the two wings; Grant likened his force to two separate armies. In the middle, Burnside's attempt to force Ox Ford failed miserably during a violent late-afternoon thunderstorm. Nearby, lightning killed two troopers in the 10th New York Cavalry and stunned several more, as well as their mounts. Rain continued until almost dawn, raising the river and slowing any bridge building.[48]

May 25 was hot again—the high was 83 degrees—and quiet. Grant had no intention of attacking that line. The army would have to sidle south again; the only question was how. That night, as thunderstorms struck, his generals debated whether to support Meade and flank to the east—as usual—or abandon the supply line a la Vicksburg and spin west toward Lee's railroad. Grant launched the new flanking movement to his left on the twenty-sixth, led by Sheridan's horse soldiers and the army's trains. It was 72 degrees at Warrenton. Rain started before sunup and continued off and on all day, drizzling and storming between moments of sun. Trenches flooded. At one point, lightning killed a pioneer in the unlucky 10th New York Cavalry and blinded the man's horse. The North Anna continued to rise. That night, Grant's infantry crossed it as a hailstorm struck nearby.

The next day was hotter, around 80 degrees. Conditions were brutal for tired men lacking adequate water. Scores fell out; some died. At Haw's Shop, opposing cavalry struggling to find their enemies' positions fought a long but ultimately inconclusive battle. By the early morning of May 29, the Federal army was across the Pamunkey River and deploying cautiously. Lee again had followed in a parallel, southerly line, this time back to Atlee's Station, only nine miles from Richmond—Seven Days country. Helped by much cooler weather—the high that day was only 70 degrees—the Confederates dug in on slightly higher ground behind low swamps and Totopotomoy Creek, which ran from near Richmond into the Pamunkey. On warmer May 30 (84 degrees at 2 P.M.), Lee allowed Lt. Gen. Jubal Early—commanding the corps of a sick Ewell—to attack Warren's corps near Bethesda Church. The assault, launched late in the day and mismanaged, failed with heavy casualties, but it at least demonstrated that the Army of Northern Virginia was not beaten. Grant decided to try to flank Lee's works yet again, initially using Baldy Smith's XVIII Corps, just transferred from Bermuda Hundred. High temperatures hit 90 degrees as both armies shifted to the southeast. The vital, five-pointed crossroads at Cold Harbor, north of the Chickahominy and along the shortest Federal path to the James, lay ahead. Sheridan seized it that evening.[49]

June began with a high of 90 degrees that was "oppressive," according to Mason Tyler, who added that "the soil, pulverized and kicked into the air by thousands of feet of horse and men who for hours were marching by us, made the atmosphere in the rear of the column almost suffocating."[50] Confederate infantry failed to drive Sheridan away. They then dug in as Wright and Smith approached. The subsequent Federal attack that evening, with temperatures around 80 degrees, almost penetrated the incomplete Confederate earthworks. Encouraged, Grant sent Hancock to Cold Harbor to join the other corps and strike again at dawn.[51]

The June 2 attack never materialized. The long march left Hancock's men exhausted, lost, and strung out. The new day's heat stifled them. Powdery, whitish dust penetrated every exposed orifice. And Smith's men were out of ammunition. Massive dust clouds alerted the Confederates to the arrivals of these new troops. Fires in nearby pine woods added to the haze and heat. Lyman likened "Cool Arbor" to the Sahara. Still convinced that Lee's army was about to implode, and lacking other viable options, Grant decided to once again throw in all he had. Meade delayed the assault twice before Grant called it off altogether that evening, citing both the extreme heat that day—90 degrees in the afternoon—and the worn-out state of the attack troops. He decided to let the men rest before they hit the line en masse at dawn. Lee, meanwhile, shifted reserves south. His concave line stretched for six miles down to the Chickahominy. Grant never went down to see the position for himself, while Meade left the details to others. Rain returned to the front, with storms late in the afternoon and drizzle that night. Some who had thirsted in the dust all day welcomed the rain, even though it reduced some of the works to mud. All of them suspected what was about to happen.[52]

The drizzle ended before dawn, but fog hugged the ground as the assault forces moved into position. Promptly at 4:30 A.M., Hancock's artillery opened up. The guns pounded the Confederate works for ten minutes while obscuring the field even more with smoke. Three corps—Hancock's, Smith's, and Wright's—surged forward and almost immediately separated into independent entities. The other two Federal corps to the north did nothing at all. At the southern end of the line, Federal attackers briefly broke through a weakened sector where a Confederate colonel had pulled his men out of the flooded works so that they could sleep dry. This success came to nothing, however, as a fierce counterattack soon retook the position. The balance of Hancock's attackers either died, fell wounded, or took cover in the shrouded no-man's land between the opposing works. To their right, Wright held back once he saw the ugly fix Hancock was in. Smith's troops never reached the Rebel works. The final two corps got moving at 7 A.M. but accomplished nothing. Meade pressed on here and there but gave up just after noon.[53]

The bloody day had been hot, reaching 81 degrees by afternoon. Periodic showers soaked the dead, the suffering wounded, and others pinned down by constant gunfire. Their miseries had only begun. Through that day and on through June 4—a cooler, rainier day with a high of 64 degrees—neither Grant (as at Vicksburg) nor Lee would ask for a truce to allow men to retrieve the wounded from between the lines. Scattered firefights continued along the front. Rain fell through the night and transitioned into a mist the next morning. When Grant finally sent a message about a truce to Lee on the fifth—the high rose to 76 degrees that day—they clashed over protocol. Nothing happened during muggy June 6 as temperatures climbed to 90 degrees. Rain fell that night. Only late on the seventh did the two generals reach an agreement. By then, it was meaningless; most of the wounded had died of their agonies in the open ground, tortured by sun and rain.[54]

Colonel Porter wrote that no one who did not experience Cold Harbor could ever understand how the fallen suffered. "The bodies of the dead were festering in the sun," he wrote, "while the wounded were dying a torturing death from starvation, thirst, and loss of blood. In some places the stench became sickening. . . . They were subjected to broiling heat by day and the chilling winds and fogs at night."[55] As historian Mark Grimsley succinctly declares, "it was a sorry episode in both . . . [Grant's and Lee's] careers."[56]

~~~

Grant later admitted that Cold Harbor left his men unwilling to charge fieldworks. The rivers and swampy topography east of Richmond undermined any hopes for maneuver. Accordingly, he fell back on a backup plan. Just as at Vicksburg, he now planned to cut off the enemy's supply lines and either make them come out and fight or starve them out.

That would take time. For the moment, Grant looked to other fields for progress. Back on May 25, he had ordered Maj. Gen. David Hunter, now commanding Sigel's old army, to destroy the transportation junction and supply depot at Lynchburg and backtrack down the Virginia Central Railroad. Hunter's men were to live off the land and destroy the surplus, to the degree that they starved out the Valley. Historian Lisa Brady dates the beginning of the destruction of the Shenandoah's agricultural resources, known as "The Burning," to these orders. Now, on June 7, Grant sent Sheridan out to join Hunter. Once the two had accomplished their wrecking missions, Grant would disengage, swing his army quickly around Lee's right yet again, cross the James, and aim for the railroad hub at Petersburg. But his subordinates failed him again. Sheridan only got as far as Trevilian Station east of Charlottesville before encountering Lee's cavalry, falling back after two days of fighting. Hunter stopped long enough in Lexington to burn down the Virginia Military Institute and headed for Lynchburg. Desperate to save his supply line, Lee sent Early by rail on June 10 to stop Hunter. After brief fighting on June 17–18, Hunter not only retreated but also fled into the West Virginia mountains, leaving the Valley wide open.[57]

By then, Grant was across the James. For once, the weather cooperated. With the exception of hot and showery June 9, it was ideal for marching, with highs in the seventies. Even the rain helped lay down the dust. Ever the loyal McClellanite, Charles Wainwright groused that Grant had it easy when it came to weather. June 12 was "perfect," with a high of 74 degrees. That night, the army pulled out of line at Cold Harbor and headed south once again. Smith's corps boarded transports for Petersburg while the other corps marched to the Chickahominy and crossed on pontoon bridges.[58] "Although there was moonlight," Porter remembered, "the dust rose in such dense clouds that it was difficult to see more than a short distance, and the march was exceedingly tedious and uncomfortable."[59] The next morning, ferries shuttled troops across the wide James near Wilcox Landing to establish a beachhead on the south bank. Engineers then began building what would be the longest military pontoon bridge in American history. The rest of the army trudged in, worn down and dusty. On the chilly night of June 14—temperatures fell into the upper fifties—and into the next, significantly hotter day (81 degrees), the army crossed the river.[60]

Porter remembered a glorious fifteenth. "The bright sun shining through a clear sky upon the scene," he wrote, "cast its sheen upon the water, was reflected from the burnished gun-barrels and glittering cannon, and brought out with increased brilliance the gay colors of the waving banners."[61] Other memories were less enthusiastic. "The yellow clay hardened by the sun and ground to powder by the tramp of a great army, rose up in thick, black columns and settled upon us," Lt. James Clark of the 115th New York wrote, "filling our eyes and causing our eye-balls to roll with pain. The rays of the sun beat upon us with scorching power; our lips cracked open for want of water, and the perspiration rolled from our bodies in a continuous stream."[62]

Grant pushed Hancock toward Petersburg, hoping that Smith already occupied the town. Reports came in that Lee was shifting troops south to bolster the tiny garrison there. Once again, the Army of the Potomac did not meet Grant's high expectations. After nearly two months of constant campaigning, thousands of soldiers were worn out, or worse. As historian Carol Reardon points out, many combat stressors exhausted the army during the Overland Campaign. Difficult weather was one of them, the wider environment was another, and the constant campaigning amplified them all. Grant demanded endurance to the breaking point and beyond.[63] And so, Smith's men, supported by Butler, fell out in droves from sunstroke on June 14. An afternoon thundershower only added to the oppressive humidity. Smith took some imposing but lightly held fortifications that evening and then halted. His hesitancy and fears of Lee arriving with reinforcements, combined with Beauregard's obstinacy and a handful of reinforcements from Drewry's Bluff, saved Petersburg when at its weakest.

Grant kept punching, however. Soldiers described exhaustion, heat in the lower eighties, and massive clouds of dust.[64] Provost Marshal Patrick called June 16 "the most oppressive [day] of the Season, so far."[65] Thomas McParlin, the medical director of the Army of the Potomac, reported "many cases of heat apoplexy."[66] Lyman, perhaps reflecting the view at Meade's headquarters, described Burnside's column as "used up."[67] Even Grant and his staff felt the effects of the hot weather. Porter noted that "the general and most of the staff had ordered thin, dark-blue flannel blouses to be sent to them to take the place of the heavy uniform coats which they had been wearing. The summer clothing arrived, and was now tried on." For the first time, Grant's celebrated private's uniform with general's straps appeared— simply as a way to beat the heat. That night, Lyman found the general in chief wearing nothing but a shirt and his underwear.[68]

In the end, Grant's effort to take Petersburg foundered. Although Butler managed to creep up to the Richmond and Petersburg Railroad, Meade's evening assault on hot and dusty June 16 failed. He blamed the condition of his men, although his corps commanders behaved poorly: Hancock and Smith were ill, and Smith remained tentative. The soldiers remembered Cold Harbor and wanted no part of Lee's works, however thinly manned. Grant generally remained aloof at his headquarters. The next day, June 17, was the hottest yet at 91 degrees. Confederate counterattacks drove off Butler and retook the railroad. To the south, Burnside made some progress but received no support. Beauregard pulled back into his last line of defense. Meade's final attacks on steamy June 18 (88 degrees) were similarly barren. As the Federals seized abandoned fieldworks, Lee arrived in force.[69] Grant recognized that his men were dead tired and let them rest. The Confederates followed suit. The weather remained hot, with highs in the eighties.

On June 21, Lincoln arrived unannounced by steamer, accompanied by his son Tad. He spent two days reviewing troops. Porter joked that the president's black suit made him look like an undertaker—but not for long.[70] "By the time he reached the troops," he added, "he was completely covered in dust, and the black color of his clothes had changed to Confederate gray."[71] The three-day idyll ended on the twenty-second, when Grant began his campaign against Richmond's supply lines. Coupled with Hunter's failure at Lynchburg, the main armies in Virginia began to settle into a siege. Lee once again seemed to have bested an opponent, and northern public opinion turned against Grant. Lincoln's political opposition depicted him as a butcher who had murdered over 55,000 northern boys in Virginia for nothing. The president himself began to wonder if he stood a chance of reelection come autumn.[72]

Chapter 21

This God-Forsaken Country

Virginia, June–December 1864

On June 23, the editor of the Unionist *Alexandria Gazette* stepped away from war reports to discuss the weather. "A great drought prevails," he observed, "the gardens and pastures suffer much." Within days, the *Richmond Sentinel* described drought creeping across the state. It soon became apparent that, unlike the two previous Confederate droughts, the damage in 1864 was largely confined to the Old Dominion, Missouri, and points north. Noting rain during the last days of July, the editor of the *Richmond Whig* expressed relief that oats and wheat had been harvested before the drought took hold. In mid-August, however, the *Danville Register*'s editor lamented that it had not rained appreciably in his town since the first week in June. Corn and garden vegetables were dying in the fields. The *Richmond Examiner,* citing a reader who had kept a weather diary for forty years, reported that August 1864 and its upper-nineties and one-hundred-degree temperatures made it the hottest August since 1838.[1] Soldiers agreed. "I have seen droughts and dust," Capt. Robert McAllister wrote from Petersburg, "but the equal of this I have never seen. How Virginians are going to live for the want of crops is more than I can tell. There must be not war but famine in the state. The growing crops are burnt by the drought and the fields laid waste by war."[2]

The North burned up too. The Department of Agriculture's report for April and May predicted a winter-wheat crop 30 percent below average, a bad yield after a harsh winter and drought. By mid-June, drought extended from western Pennsylvania across the Midwest. Farmers plowed under failing wheat and planted corn. Fruit yields were below average as well in the Midwest, while the cold had ruined grapes everywhere. Oats, sorghum, and forage crops at least thrived. The department blamed the war more than the weather, pointing to the absence of male labor and the army's insatiable demands. By August, however, as the drought continued, anti-Lincoln observers saw an opening. Drought-ravaged spring wheat and other grains, potatoes, and pasture grasses were in trouble. An article in the *New York World*—reprinted hopefully in the South—worried about the effect the drought would have on inflation and trade with Europe. The Department of Agriculture admitted that "widely-extended and severe drought has given rise to serious apprehension about a failure of the fall crops" but tried to mollify citizens. Recent rain brought hope. Wheat had done better than feared, with the total crop only perhaps 14 percent smaller than the previous bumper year. Corn seemed stable. Tobacco, vegetables, and hay were thriving. Machines had replaced absent men in the harvest. There was no disaster.[3]

In September, Horace Greeley's pro-Lincoln *New York Daily Tribune* trumpeted those rosy conclusions. While wheat and corn had come in below par in New York, the midwestern yield had been fine, if not at record levels. "The Rebel leaders, North and South," Greeley wrote, "have all summer long cherished hopes of embarrassment to military operations, directly and indirectly, from the predicted failure of wheat, and corn, and oats. In that, as in other calculations, they are to be disappointed. . . . There is to be no want among the people, no famine prices, no exorbitant demands upon the Treasury to sustain the armies in the field."[4]

The government's final report, issued in November, demonstrated better overall yields in most states. Marginal declines occurred only in New Hampshire, New York, Pennsylvania, Wisconsin, West Virginia, and especially Ohio, where wheat suffered grievously. Farmers had produced over 55 million fewer bushels of corn than in two previous years, yet 1864 still was better than frostbitten 1863, with an uptick of almost 79 million bushels. Wheat yields were down over 2 million bushels from 1862, yet in 1864 the Union states still produced nearly 161 million bushels. Farmers produced about four million fewer potatoes in 1864, but again the real drop off came between 1862 and 1863. Buckwheat yields equaled 1862 figures.[5]

The commonly taught notion that northern farm production increased during the war is demonstrably false. Mechanization never fully countered the droughts and early frosts of 1863, the drought of the summer of 1864, and a tightened labor market as sons and farmhands went into uniform. Northern crop output declined after 1862 because of weather and the constant pull of the army. Yet it did not suffer to the degree that agriculture stumbled in the war-torn Confederacy. When voters headed to the polls, the Department of Agriculture could proclaim that the Lincoln government was withstanding not only the rebellion but also the elements themselves.

~~~

Down south in Virginia, the men of both armies tried to catch their breath in the humid air and airborne dust clouds south of Richmond. Forest fires added to the air's contamination. They yearned for water and shade, especially those in the rifle pits. Some fell to sniper fire while seeking water. While men did die of sunstroke on June 24, the following three days came in for special condemnation, as soldier after soldier noted readings above 100 degrees. Many again stripped down to their shirts and drawers. A smattering of thunder and rain on the twenty-seventh barely affected the dust. South Carolina surgeon Spencer Welch hoped that the weather would soon be too hot for fighting.[6] Lt. Oliver Wendell Holmes of the 20th Massachusetts thought that the armies had reached their limit, writing: "I think there is a kind of heroism in the endurance . . . of men—I tell you many a man has gone crazy since this campaign begun from the terrible pressure on mind and body."[7]

July was even worse. In Georgetown, Rev. C. B. Mackee recorded afternoon temperatures at 90 degrees or above on sixteen of the month's thirty-one days. That most intense "dog days" heat came in three waves, from July 6 through July 13, from July 17 through July 20 (excepting July 18), and from July 27 through the end of the month. July 8 and July 31 reached 98 degrees.[8] Occasional reports from the front depicted higher temperatures still. At Petersburg, Capt. Elisha Hunt Rhodes surely had access to a broken thermometer when he claimed a high of 124 degrees in Petersburg on July 2. But at Deep Bottom on the James River, a soldier in the 1st Connecticut Artillery may well have seen a reading of "104 in the shade" on the seventh.[9] That same day, Theodore Lyman came across Brig. Gen. Francis Barlow in the latter's tent, listening to a band concert "in his shirt and drawers." Barlow promptly invited the staff officer to "take off my trousers and make myself at home."[10] By the end of the month, sunstroke was common. Pvt. John Haley of the 17th Maine suggested on July 6 that it was "hot as blazes, and this is no idle phrase. The sun must be several million miles nearer the earth than when it went down last night." The end result, he added, was that the army had lost its "vim" and "pugnacity."[11]

The drought-stricken front was also remarkably dry, with only brief

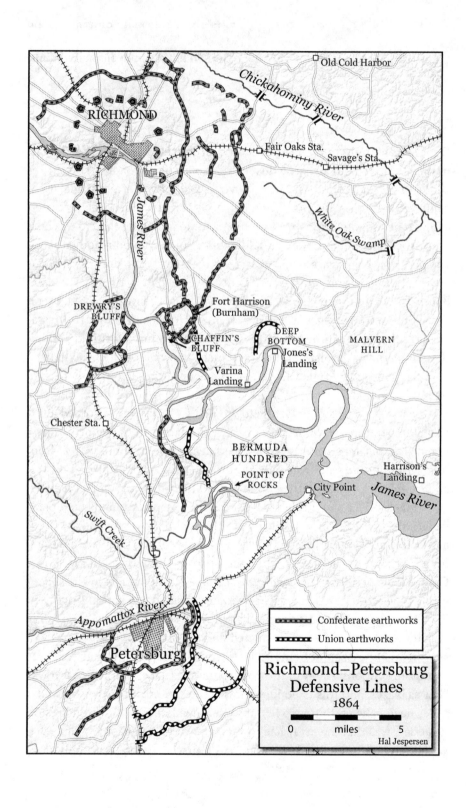

Old Cold Harbor

Chickahominy River

RICHMOND

Fair Oaks Sta.

Savage's Sta.

James River

White Oak Swamp

DREWRY'S
BLUFF

Fort Harrison
(Burnham)

CHAFFIN'S
BLUFF

DEEP
BOTTOM

MALVERN
HILL

Jones's
Landing

Varina
Landing

Chester Sta.

BERMUDA
HUNDRED

Harrison's
Landing

POINT OF
ROCKS

City Point

James River

Swift Creek

Appomattox River

Petersburg

Confederate earthworks
Union earthworks

Richmond–Petersburg
Defensive Lines
1864

0   miles   5

Hal Jespersen

showers on July 4, July 7, July 12, and July 18. Soldiers described hazy air filled with fine particles of dust akin to flour, only smaller. Searching for metaphors, a few likened the scene to an imagined Sahara. Finally, a hard, welcome, all-day rain arrived on sultry July 19, flooding trenches knee high. It persisted as sprinkles and then became an afternoon thunderstorm the next day. More rain fell overnight on cooler July 24–25, with a cold wind from the northeast. Trenches flooded again. Final thundershowers fell on the twenty-seventh and the evening of the thirty-first.

For sweaty soldiers, that sweltering July meant digging entrenchments in increasingly denuded fields and shooting across the lines. Dust not only covered them but also got into their food, their water, their mouths, and their eyes. Grant admitted to Meade that heat and dust kept him from going up to the front regularly, since dust clouds hid the enemy. Men built brush arbors for shade or jury-rigged tents from a blanket and inverted, bayoneted muskets. Most had to carry water to the parched front from new wells in the rear, as the closest streams had run dry.[12]

While the armies dug in, Grant faced thorny issues. The military stalemate in Virginia threatened to drag on past the fall elections. He had to make hard decisions about what to do with Meade and his often-lackluster corps commanders. The cancerous Army of the James required action too, but Lincoln's political needs temporarily shielded Butler. Above all, there was the growing dilemma in the Shenandoah Valley. Hunter's poor performance, capped off by his foolish retreat into the mountains, had created an opening for the Confederates. On July 4, Grant learned to his dismay that Lee had sent Early north down the Valley toward the Potomac and to threaten Washington.[13]

Like their comrades in Petersburg, Early's men grappled with what he later called "the great drought during the summer of 1864."[14] Aside from a shower on June 24, the Shenandoah was arid, and the Lower Valley saw drought. On July 5, they reached Harpers Ferry. The next day, 15,000 men began crossing the Potomac near Sharpsburg. Under pressure from the White House, Grant dispatched a division from VI Corps to Washington, a city he had all but stripped of troops previously. On the night of July 8, the only rain of the campaign fell as the Confederates crossed the Catoctin Mountains.[15] "It poured down rain that night," wrote Sgt. Maj. John

Young of the 4th North Carolina, "and nearly all of us got soaked through & through."[16]

The next day brought sun, heat, and dust. Temperatures rose to 92 degrees. At midmorning, Early encountered a smaller force of Federals holding the bluffs above the Monocacy River a few miles from Frederick on the main road to Washington. From Baltimore, Maj. Gen. Lew Wallace brought a small force of cavalry and emergency troops, supplemented by some of Grant's men. He hoped to stall Early long enough for the rest of VI Corps to arrive. Early sent cavalry and infantry against Wallace's left flank—the one held by the VI Corps men—and slowly forced it to give way. The Federals fought hard but that evening retreated toward Baltimore.[17]

But Early was not bound for Baltimore. The road to Washington, forty miles away, was now wide open, although Wallace had cost the Virginian a vital day. Then began what historian Benjamin Franklin Cooling aptly calls "a race against time—and the temperature."[18] Oven-like heat and dust characterized a long hot July 10 as the Confederates staggered toward Lincoln's capital. In thick road dust and the heat of midday—the high again reached 92 degrees—men fell out as the column skirted to the north.[19] John Worsham wrote that his division looked "almost like skirmishers, and all the men did not get up until night."[20] It was worse in the rear. "I have never seen so much dust," Pvt. John Apperson wrote. "At times it was impossible to see more than 30 or 60 yards ahead. No prospect for rain. The earth is baked like a brick."[21] That night, Young wrote, "we are nearly broke down."[22] It was still 82 degrees at 9 P.M. "The heat during the night had been very oppressive," Early remembered, "and but little rest was obtained."[23]

Along with the exertions of the march, heat and its related lack of sleep took another grim toll the next day. Early pushed on hard, only to multiply his numbers of stragglers and cases of sunstroke and heat exhaustion. His dust-shrouded column stretched out. Around 11 A.M., opposing skirmishers opened fire. Two hours later, with temperatures reaching 90 degrees, Federal artillery opened up from Fort Stevens, the northern link in Washington's formidable system of forts. Early by then had perhaps 3,500 men in good-enough physical condition to fight, and another 6,500 wilting in the heat. They were enough to seize undermanned works, he thought hopefully, until clouds of dust rose to the south. Faded-blue coats revealed veterans as the rest of VI Corps as well as elements of XIX Corps began arriving. After Monocacy, Grant had ordered the balance of both corps to the capital by water transport, with Maj. Gen. Horatio Wright in command.

The next day, July 12, temperatures again rose to 90 degrees. Skirmishing and battery fire continued. Around two, an unexpected rainstorm doused Brig. Gen. Emory Upton's debarking Federals at that docks but did not reach Georgetown. The Lincolns followed these troops to the front. When a brigade emerged from the defenses in line of battle at 5 P.M., Early gave in to reality; the reinforced position was too strong for his diminished army. The Confederates fell back that stuffy night, recrossed the Potomac near Leesburg on July 14 (high, 88 degrees), and returned to the Shenandoah. The Federals mounted a bungled pursuit. The next days remained hot until a cooler spell, from July 21 through July 25, brought some relief. Temperatures then soared again, reaching 98 degrees on July 29 and July 31. No rain fell after July 12 aside from scattered thunderstorms until just after midnight on the twenty-fifth.[24]

Early had embarrassed the Federal government, taken a shot at Lincoln himself in the Fort Stevens ramparts, and returned with desperately needed horses, livestock, food, and $220,000 in ransom money gleaned from the city fathers of Maryland towns. The price of gold skyrocketed. Democrats pronounced the Lincoln reelection campaign dead. Exacerbating matters, Confederate cavalry remained active in Maryland through July, most infamously torching Chambersburg, Pennsylvania, on the thirtieth after its leaders could not fork over a ransom. In the capital, Army Chief of Staff Halleck and Secretary of War Stanton turned against Grant and Meade. Yet Early could have hurt Lincoln's reelection campaign much more had he taken Washington, if only for a few hours. Because of the intense heat and dust, however, he had arrived a day too late—and that made all the difference.[25]

Grant reacted to the raid with frustration. He told Halleck that Hunter needed to pursue the Confederates vigorously with "veterans, militiamen, men on horseback, and everything that can be got to follow [them] to eat out Virginia clear and clean as far as they go, so that crows flying over it for the balance of this season will have to carry their provender with them."[26] Grant's main problem remained on his immediate front, however. Worried that Lee might send troops south to Georgia or that Halleck and Stanton might interfere in his plans, Grant needed to act. One option was to flank Lee to the west and cut his rail connections. The Confederates then would have to emerge from their trenches to stop him. That required more men and time, however, and the general in chief was pressed for both. At this point Burnside offered an alternative. Pennsylvania miners in his corps had proposed digging a mine over five hundred feet to a point underneath a Confederate redoubt in a salient, packing it with powder, and blowing it sky high. Not only would the explosions kill many a Reb, but it also would open a door into Lee's works. Grant was open to the idea; he had used mines at Vicksburg. Once II Corps operations against Lee's left fizzled out at Deep Bottom on July 27 and July 28—afternoon highs in the low nineties led soldiers to faint on the march—Grant gave the okay.[27]

The Confederates soon were alert to Federal mining and sank counter-mines of their own. Noting that it was "sprinkling some," Sgt. James Albright wrote in his diary on July 20 that the Confederates "are tunneling & Grant is also, and some *mines* may be *sprung* any day, & many souls blown into eternity."[28] Rain on the twenty-fifth slowed work and flooded some countershafts. The Federals finally exploded their mine early on the morning of July 30. Twenty feet underneath the Confederate redoubt, 8,000 pounds of gunpowder exploded at about 4:45 A.M., killing nearly three hundred South Carolinians. For perhaps fifteen minutes, survivors stood stunned from the blast, which created a massive crater 170 feet long, 60 feet wide, and 30 feet deep. The Federal assault, however, went awry. The lead brigade charged into the crater rather than around it as planned. The balance of the division followed into the cavity, trailed by an African American division. The Confederates recovered their wits and bombarded the trapped attackers. Brig. Gen. William Mahone's furious Confederates then gathered around the lip of the crater and fired into it, murdering black soldiers trying to surrender. Meade and Grant blamed Burnside, who left the army two weeks later.[29] This assault "was the saddest affair I have witnessed in the war," Grant later reported.[30]

Soldiers described heat as part of the horror. Temperatures reached 97 degrees that day. Lt. James Clark of the 115th New York wrote: "The sun pours down its scorching rays, and many are sun-struck and carried in wild delirium from the pits. All are exhausted and sink down almost helpless from the strain. 'Water! water! water!' groan the wounded. 'Water! water!' fiercely gasp all the men. Oh heavens! what a thirst!" Survivors drank from a "dirty pool," but the wounded in the open suffered. "Sergeant G— is over come with heat, and is crazy. His eyes glare fitfully, and his eye-balls roll painfully in their sockets. 'We'll fight 'em till we die, won't we boys?' he said, and then swooned away."[31] Across the lines, Lt. Col. William H. Stewart of the 61st Virginia remembered that "the extreme heat of that July sun had already caused putrefaction to set in and the bodies in our front and rear, and especially the blood soaked earth in the trenches, exhaled such a nauseating smell that I was forced to abandon my supper."[32]

The next day was again hot, with the high reaching 98 degrees in Washington.[33] Massive dust clouds, in Clark's words, "swept over the country like a tornado. The day was the warmest of the season, being at the heighth of the great drouth." As his unit returned to camp, "many were overcome with the heat, until the sides of the road were covered with soldiers suffering with sun-stroke. Some dropped down dead in the ranks, while others fell out and died by the road side. The division lost more men that day, killed by the sun, the want of water, and by hard marching, than it did in the terrible battle of the day before."[34]

That same day, Grant met with Lincoln at Fort Monroe. Both faced a crisis of will. Northern civilian morale collapsed in hot July 1864 in the face of continuing stalemates in Virginia and Georgia. People longed for peace, something Democrats promised in their campaigns. Only emancipation, these politicians proclaimed, stood in the way of peaceful reunion. Even Horace Greeley encouraged peace talks, going to Canada with Lincoln's personal secretary to meet with representatives from Richmond. Those discussions and others failed. Confederate agents and a motley crew of fifth columnists, meanwhile, plotted paper insurrections. Both Stanton and Halleck were ready to sacrifice Grant and call off the Petersburg Campaign, if necessary. Grant and Lincoln both desperately needed victories. The meeting between commander in chief and his general in chief thus largely turned on how to best defend the capital and destroy Early's corps, which again had moved north into Maryland. Federals in the area had pursued the Confederates as far as Frederick, leaving hundreds of sun-stricken men along the road.

Lincoln and Grant rejected each other's suggestions for the general to lead a combined Federal force against Early, including Meade and apparent Democratic presidential standard-bearer George McClellan. They settled reluctantly on Phil Sheridan, who took command of the new Army of the Shenandoah at Harpers Ferry on August 7. His assignments were to smash

Early's forces, which had fallen back to Winchester, and end the Valley's ability to feed Lee's army. Sheridan moved south three days later through blistering heat, forcing Early out of Winchester and up the Valley. Dozens of Federals again fell out as Sheridan refused to halt at midday; some died. Worried about his supply line, however, he retreated through Winchester on August 14. His men complained about the scarcity of water until thunderstorms began and persisted through the twenty-second.[35] But Grant needed more. He told Sheridan, "give the enemy no rest. Do all the damage to railroads and crops you can. Carry off stock of all descriptions, and negroes, so as to prevent further planting. If the war is to last another year, we want the Shenandoah Valley to remain a barren waste."[36] As historian Lisa Brady writes, Grant wanted Sheridan to transform the region "from a civilized, improved landscape into a virtual wilderness."[37]

~

August brought little new to Virginia's weather. At least eleven afternoons reached into the nineties that month, and five days reached or exceeded 95 degrees: August 1 and every day between August 10 and August 13. The *Richmond Examiner* cited hotter temperatures still, with temperatures ranging from 94 degrees to 101 degrees between August 7 and August 14. The month was more humid as well. Rain came as brief showers on August 2, localized sprinkles the next afternoon, and another brief shower on the ninth. Then the evening of the thirteenth brought an abrupt change: The "great drought" finally broke. With wind from the southeast, a wave of thunderstorms pounded Petersburg for a week. Trenches on August 15 and August 16 filled with two or three feet of rushing water. Capt. A. W. Bartlett of the 12th New Hampshire claimed that up to seventeen men drowned in the works. Reverend Mackee recorded exactly 2.58 inches of rain total between August 13 and August 25. Mud was everywhere as earthworks washed away and roads became unusable. J. B. Jones rejoiced that the rain had saved his turnips and tomatoes, given that the drought had killed everything else in his garden, but soldiers were less charitable.[38] "Everything by extremes here in this God-forsaken country," Bartlett complained.[39]

Confederate gunner James Albright wrote hopefully on August 28 that the weather "was beginning to feel like Fall."[40] The apparent arrival of autumn directly affected operations. Determined to keep Lee from sending reinforcements to Early, Grant sent Hancock's exhausted II Corps to Deep Bottom to stage a surprise assault on the Confederate left. As their transports arrived late in the afternoon of August 13, the first of the thunderstorms struck. Poor planning and delays ruined any surprise, and II Corps skirmished in rain, lightning, and mud. Lee pulled men from the west to bolster the imperiled position, even going there himself. Warren's V Corps then moved west on the eighteenth to seize and tear up the Petersburg Railroad at Globe Tavern, three miles south of Petersburg. Warren accomplished his mission and dug in. The Confederates desperately hit the muddy entrenchments of V Corps but failed to retake the northern link of their supply line. A massive counterattack bloodied Hancock at Reams Station on hot August 25 but again failed to dislodge Warren. The Federals extended their main works to the site, incorporating it into their main lines and forcing Lee to respond in kind, thus forcing a rerouting of southern supplies via a roundabout thirty-mile wagon route.[41]

Far from Petersburg, other significant matters came to a head. Chicago weather on the whole had been unseasonably cool that August, with highs in the seventies predominate during the second half of the month. On cool and cloudy August 30, the high only reached 68 degrees. That day, Democrats meeting in the city approved an antiwar party platform that attacked the Lincoln administration as tyrannical and called for an immediate armistice followed by peace negotiations. In part, the platform reflected the continuing stalemates in Virginia and Georgia. The following sunny day, delegates nominated George B. McClellan for the presidency.[42]

At Petersburg, stalemate dragged on as autumn drew near. Until the end of September, the front largely was quiet aside from artillery firing, the pop and zing of snipers' bullets, and Federal celebrations following the fall of Atlanta (see chapter 22). Only September 2, September 21, and September 29 reached 80 degrees, while five days failed to reach into the seventies. Mornings were even cooler, with half the month's days starting out in the fifties. Frequent clouds and rain often accompanied the cooler temperatures. A thunderstorm on September 5, according to John Haley, left up to a foot of water in nearby trenches and ruined food. Drizzle occurred on September 6, September 11, and September 12. Showers returned on September 21 and September 22, and hard rain fell the next two days, as it did at the end of the month. In Georgetown, where rain events were fewer, Rev-

erend Mackee recorded 1.93 inches of rain. Federal engineers actively corduroyed supply roads, while men worked to shore up rain-damaged works
and make better shelters.[43]

The Shenandoah was cooler, rainier, and more active militarily. Sheridan began probing south toward Winchester. Two weeks of skirmishing
followed, frequently punctuated by rain and mud. On the afternoon of
September 3, elements of each army fought sharply in a rain-soaked collision near Berryville. A north wind brought more rain the next three days,
flooding tents in Sheridan's command. Rained returned on the ninth, while
thunder and lightning erupted the next morning. Storms that night and
the next day blew down or flooded tents. More rain arrived on September
14 as a Confederate division prepared to leave the Valley for Petersburg.[44]

By then, both Grant and Lincoln were frustrated with the developing
draw in the lower Shenandoah. On September 17, as Grant left for New
Jersey and a brief reunion with his family, Early aggressively moved northward to cut the Baltimore and Ohio Railroad at Martinsburg. Not only did
he fail to reach his target, but the movement also left his outnumbered
army spread out. Sheridan reacted quickly and marched toward Winchester. After overnight rain, September 19 was a bright day, with temperatures probably in the seventies. That day, the two armies fought stubbornly
between Winchester and Opequon Creek. Using his almost four-to-one
advantage in men, Sheridan shoved Early back, withstood a strong counterattack, and turned the Confederate left. Resistance collapsed, and Early
retreated up the Valley. Sheridan pursued vigorously. Three days later, he
smashed Early again at Fisher's Hill. They fell back almost to Staunton.[45]

Republicans and dissident War Democrats throughout the North,
united since June in their support of Lincoln's reelection, breathed a collective sigh of relief. Grant wanted Sheridan to continue on to Charlottesville and wreck the James River Canal. Instead, Sheridan stopped at Harrisonburg and fell back, returning to the destruction that Grant initiated in
late August. With deliberate intention over the next few weeks, Sheridan's
men carried away all the foodstuffs and livestock they could, killed any
surplus livestock, dismantled fences, looted homes, burned crops, freed
enslaved laborers, and as much as they could demolished the Valley's agricultural infrastructure of barns, mills, and tools. As historian Edward Ayers
points out, most of the destruction took place near roads, as Federals were
afraid to push too far into the guerrilla-laden bush. "The Burning" was not
all-encompassing, but it was brutal enough. The only real resistance came

from the sky in the form of rain, which fell on September 23 and September 24 and again at the end of the month and continued into October 4 before the Valley turned cold.[46] Sheridan reported to Grant the destruction of over 2,000 barns and seventy mills along with the confiscation of 4,000 cattle, 3,000 sheep, and an unreported number of horses.[47]

Grant wanted to keep Lee from sending troops into the Valley before Sheridan could complete this destruction and finish off Early. At best, the Federals might even capture Richmond or Petersburg. Once again, he decided to attack at two places. On hazy September 29, Butler's two corps approached Lee's works north of the James at Chaffin's Bluff and New Market Heights. They seized Fort Harrison, the largest fortification in the Confederate line north of the James. Confederate counterattacks failed to dislodge them, and the fort became a critical link in extended Federal works. The same day, Meade moved west toward the South Side Railroad, Lee's only other supply line to the west and south. With any luck, Lee would have pulled men from this portion of his defenses to reinforce Chaffin's Bluff. Unfortunately for Meade, it began to rain again, heavily enough to bog down his advance and sometimes stop the fighting. Men, wagons, and caissons stuck in the Virginia clay both there and at Fort Harrison. Heavy downpours, stiff winds, and straggling characterized October 1 as the fighting continued. By the time the weather cleared off on the second, the South Side Railroad was safe, although Wright had pushed forward his works near the Petersburg line.[48] A soldier in the 1st Connecticut Artillery commented that "'the roads were muddy, regular Virginia mud, deep and nasty; it sticks to you like a brother.'"[49]

Rain at the end of September marked the beginning of significantly cooler weather. September 29 and September 30 reached 80 degrees, but 1864 would not see such temperatures again. The high on October 1 was 56 degrees, the rest of the week made it into the seventies, and after that only the fifteenth saw an afternoon reading above 70 degrees.[50] As A. W. Bartlett wrote, "after it rained, it cleared off cold for the season."[51] Highs in the sixties and even in the fifties became the norm. Soldiers saw the first frosts on October 9 and October 10. Morning temperatures fell into the midthirties. Nights were colder, with frost and a low of 36 degrees at the end of the month. At Petersburg, rain fell on the night of October 12, again with snow on October 22, on October 27 and into the next day, and on the thirtieth.[52]

The men in the Shenandoah faced colder conditions and active campaigning. "The Burning" continued into October. The same weather patterns that chilled men at Petersburg swept through the Valley with additional precipitation. A hard nighttime shower came on October 7 and then hail the following night. On dark October 9, scattered snowflakes flew on a west wind. The next morning brought thick frost. Winter was coming. Most everyone in blue, Sheridan included, believed that the campaign was over. Early was whipped. Another retrograde followed, with VI Corps going all the way north to Front Royal. Sheridan was ready to return to Petersburg via Washington with all of his forces until Grant and Halleck advised him to keep XIX Corps in the Valley for the time being to strike the local railroads still supplying Richmond. Some men began constructing huts and fireplaces. Local civilian refugees took to the windy roads, many fleeing slavery and others the destruction.[53]

But Early was not beaten yet. He received reinforcements. Confederate cavalry searched for places for the enhanced army to strike a counterblow until their forward movement was blunted on frosty October 9. Eager to redeem the Valley, Early marched north on the twelfth, a chilly day that only reached 52 degrees in Georgetown. His troops collided with Federal cavalry the next rainy day, creating enough alarm to force Sheridan to recall VI Corps. Sheridan relaxed, however, when he learned that Early had fallen back to Fisher's Hill. On October 14, most of the Federal army camped under canvas on the ridges between Middletown and the steep banks and twisting bed of nearby Cedar Creek. Sheridan left for Washington to meet with Stanton and Halleck.

To the south from Fisher's Hill, Early scouted the Federal front. On October 18, he adopted Maj. Gen. John B. Gordon's plan to send the Georgian's division around the wide open Federal left that night and strike it by surprise the next morning, followed by a general assault from south. It was a hard night march for Gordon's column along narrow roads between the North Fork of the Shenandoah River and the north face of Massanutten Mountain. The moon was nearly full, at least, but at times the attackers had to march single file. A welcome fog shielded the shivering Confederates—it was 43 degrees at 7 A.M.—and dampened sound as they forded the cold river. Early's other two columns went into position to the south of the Federal camps.[54]

The surprise from the fog worked. The attack went off at 5 A.M., when Confederates charged and drove shocked Federals out of their warm tents.

The fog, increasingly mixed with gunsmoke, obscured the field enough to confuse both sides and partially derail Early's attack. Some Federal units responded well in the din and chaos, slowing down the Confederate advance long enough to stage a fighting retreat to high ground a mile away. Sheridan charged in from Winchester, where he had spent the night while returning from the capital, and recognized a fatal Confederate blunder. Exhausted, cold, and hungry Johnny Rebs had stopped to forage the Union camps. Early was trying to reorganize them for a new assault, a halfhearted effort that went forward at about 1 P.M., to little effect. Sheridan massed his men and counterattacked around 4 P.M., with his infantry in the middle while cavalry on the flanks raced toward the Confederate rear. The men in gray stood stiffly at first, but when Early's left caved in, his army fled in confusion. Leaving behind twenty-four captured guns and a host of supply wagons, they kept going until they reached Fisher's Hill. Overnight temperatures fell into the forties.[55]

Cedar Creek ended as the final disaster for the Confederate cause in the Shenandoah, and the effective end of the campaign. Early blamed his men, but the rest of the Confederacy blamed Early. Often lost in the debate was the role the morning fog played in first hiding his assault, then confusing and dividing the attackers. Early afterward led his army back up the Valley, where it remained until mid-November, when the first divisions returned to Petersburg. Sheridan, the hero of the hour, was content to let him go. His own dramatic ride from Winchester, later immortalized in verse, gave Republicans an additional victory to cheer as the November elections approached.[56]

Sheridan's men rested at Cedar Creek through November, until most of them also returned, by divisions and corps, to the Army of the Potomac. The weather turned colder. Most afternoon highs that month landed in the fifties, followed by nearly as many days in the forties. Five mornings began below freezing: November 6, November 15, and November 23–25; seven others registered in the thirties. As for precipitation, soldiers recorded twelve days of rain during the month, as well as snow mixed with rain on November 5, November 13, November 19, and briefly once more on November 22.[57] Election day, November 8, was relatively warm, if foggy, for Union soldiers after three days of rain. Sleet and snow fell on the twenty-fourth.

At the end of the year, Early, a single division, and some cavalry wintered at Staunton. Sheridan, XIX Corps, and two divisions of cavalry hun-

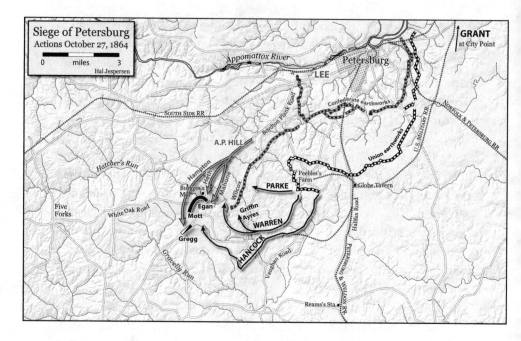

Siege of Petersburg
Actions October 27, 1864

0   miles   3
Hal Jespersen

kered down at Winchester. Both groups endured a worsening winter. Federals again favored their hybrid quarters, although some preferred tents augmented by fireplaces and chimneys. Many waited impatiently for their overcoats, stored months before in Washington.[58] The Confederates were more poorly supplied, often lacking coats, shoes, and the blankets they had lost at Cedar Creek. "There is not a tent in this brigade but the officers,'" conscript John Armfield complained, "except what the soldiers captured from the Yanks, but we have stretched up some blankets for a tent and keep a fire at the mouth of it and manage to sleep pretty comfortable."[59]

November finally brought an end to activity on the Richmond-Petersburg front, too, but not before Grant made one more stab at Lee's communications. Rain near the end of October coincided with his last campaign of the year. On October 27, eight days after Cedar Creek, Grant launched another twin movement. While the Army of the James carried out a diversion north of the James, elements of three corps headed west to seize the South Side Railroad and cut the Boydton Plan Road. "The morning was dark and gloomy," Horace Porter remembered, "a heavy rain was falling, the roads were muddy and obstructed, and tangled thickets, deep woods, and swampy streams confronted the troops at all points." Drenched Confederates rushed to the road and firmly blunted the attack.[60] That night, temperatures fell into the upper fifties. Pvt. John Haley remembered "a most dismal and comfortless night. Rain fell continually, and we were soon drenched and shivering with cold."[61] "These operations closed for the winter the series of battles in front of Petersburg and Richmond," Colonel Porter wrote, "cold weather and the condition of the roads rendering further important movements impracticable."[62]

While the western armies marched all across the map in November and December, the easterners settled down for the winter. The next three months saw sharpshooting, skirmishing, and misery enough, but no major action. The heavy showers of October halted briefly on November 1 but soon returned on a northwest wind. Rifle pits and trenches flooded; Haley likened them to pig sties. The morning low on November 6 in Washington was 32 degrees. A warm front carried morning fog, 60-degree highs, rain, and occasional sleet over the three of the next four days. Deep red Virginia mud lay thick on election day. Lincoln sat in the White House and watched it rain as he waited alone. The results of his reelection came in late, slowed by storms and downed wires.

On the night of November 10, a south wind brought a much drier cold front that stalled over the eastern part of Virginia for a week. Highs fell into the forties, while morning lows dipped toward freezing. Rain returned out of the northeast on the night of the eighteenth and lasted, with few breaks, until cold November 22, when torrential rains and waist-deep mud in a few Federal works gave way to snow and freezing temperatures. By morning, it was 23 degrees in Georgetown. Deep mud froze at the front, covered by snow. J. B. Jones measured three inches of snow in Richmond as well as an inch of ice on the cold but clear morning of November 24. But then temperatures once again rose, up to remarkable highs of 70 degrees on the month's final two days. Soldiers dried out their soaked clothing and belongings, sometimes by simply crawling on top of the works and basking.[63]

This unusual warmth continued into the first week of December. Pvt. Wilbur Fisk wrote, "The weather—a topic that all sensible people can fall back upon when others fail—has been very pleasant and Indian summer–like for the past week."[64] Soldiers at Petersburg still complained of cool mornings, gusty winds, and airborne dust. On the seventh, rain fell at Petersburg, ending the latest dry spell. The high temperature was 58 degrees that day.

Then the bottom fell out, quite possibly related to the winter's negative NAO reading. A massive arctic cold system swept out of the northern Midwest on December 6, bringing colder temperatures and snow to the Great Lakes. In Chicago, the morning low was 0 degrees at 7 A.M. on December 8 and only 4 degrees a few hours later. Similar readings occurred across the region. The system moved south and east and hit the Atlantic coast the following day, with temperature collapses also as far south as Mississippi and South Carolina. This notably created havoc for troops in Tennessee (as shown in chapter 23). In Virginia, the morning low on the ninth was 19 degrees. That night it began to snow and sleet to the depth of two to four inches, depending upon the locale.[65] Ham Chamberlayne described the worst weather days since Romney. Charles Wainwright was in the field with V Corps when the winter precipitation started "soon after dark, followed by a fine rain and cold. This morning everything was sheeted with ice; each spray of the trees and blade of grass was completely coated."[66]

December largely stayed cold. Conditions remained especially frigid through the thirteenth, with morning lows around freezing. The snow began to melt on the eleventh, however, leaving a layer of mud a foot deep, but it froze again into ice as a bitingly cold north wind, strong enough to blow down tents, slowly shifted to the southeast. Freezing rain fell on the morning of December 14. A warm front brought dark skies, rain, and higher temperatures on the eighteenth, with the high rising to 51 degrees the next day.[67] J. B. Jones called it "the darkest and most dismal day that ever dawned upon the earth except one."[68]

Highs fell back into the thirties and stayed there through Christmas. It rained on the night of December 20, stretching into the winter solstice and flooding the trenches yet again. The weather was worse in the Shenandoah, with sleet, hail, and snow. As historian J. Tracy Power notes, the cold Christmas season produced depression. Confederate desertions increased. A brief warming spell from Christmas Day through the twenty-eighth, with fog and mist that Marsena Patrick likened to Scotland, did little to help spirits. More bad weather arrived in the form of rain before dawn on December 28. Snow fell on New Year's Eve.[69]

Cold and wet weather, as well as the cessation of active hostilities, led as usual to a frenzy of shelter construction after the December 7 storm.

Despite fears of impermanence, quarters went up "like mushrooms on a damp night," according to Oliver Norton, now of the 8th USCT.[70] Occupying the outer rim of the trenches, Federals had more access to timber and built hybrid log structures, with tents for roofs and wooden floors. Thinly clad, often shoeless, and sometimes without blankets, Confederates still preferred log cabins, but a lack of axes and especially nails that winter created problems. John Armfield's mess built their cabin using an axe they purchased with their own money. Virginia artilleryman B. W. Jones had access to wood but no nails or planking. His cabin had slab-covered sides, a slab roof with logs added to hold the wood down, and a dirt floor. It was not as neat as his first wartime cabin, he admitted, but he was more comfortable than men still living in tents. There were many troops under captured Federal canvas that winter. Some soldiers simply dug into the earth and erected a captured shelter half over the hole. Confederates in more denuded areas had trouble building fires, much less shanties. The end result was a winter of ragged shelter.[71] "Elaborate or beautiful they are not," Jones wrote a friend. "Original, unique, grotesque they are." And so, 1864 came to an end in war-torn Virginia.[72]

Chapter 22

Appeal against the Thunderstorm

Georgia, February–September 1864

In South Carolina, David Golightly Harris looked to 1864 with trepidation. New legislation sent him back to the army, although he had hired a substitute just two months earlier. As cold January gave way to cool but dry February, Harris was desperate to get his farm in shape before he left. His enslaved workforce worked his disappointing winter wheat and barley while breaking cornfields and planting potatoes. On February 15, rain fell as they sowed oats. Harris remained optimistic until a sudden freeze the next day cost him nearly a week in the fields. March arrived with ample rain. His hopes for a good crop after two bad years seemed to be coming true until disaster struck on March 17. A cold snap not only froze his land again but also nearly killed his fruit crop. The same thing happened to farmers as far east as the Atlantic coast, west into Alabama and Mississippi, and south to Florida. Rain, snow, and sleet followed on March 20, when Harris took a train into Columbia; the train shuddered to a stop in a snowbank. "This is a remarkable snow-storm for the season," he wrote. "*Snow. Snow.* At home the snow was about nine inches deep, and much of it was on the ground when I got home."[1]

Snow and rain ruined Harris's mood. He was not alone. The editor of the *Macon Telegraph* wondered if the cold and its injury to the local peach crop was God's judgment on a sinful nation. The *Charleston Mercury* reported that the cold winter had harmed crops all the way to Texas, while the *Augusta Daily Constitutionalist* noted the dire shape of winter wheat in southwest Georgia. For the third summer in a row, farmers like Harris got their crops in late. "The Spring is backward," he lamented on April 3. His fields stayed so wet that his enslaved field hands did no plowing between March 19 and April 11. When they tried on April 12, rain sent them indoors early. "It looks as if starvation was on us," Harris worried. "And right now just in the nick of time I must leave to go to the army." Desperately, he sent his plowmen out in the mud. "I will leave on record," he wrote four days later, "that [it] is certainly a very cold, backward Spring. The woods are as barren now as they were on new years day. Scarcely a sign of vegetation only on the earliest trees on the creeks. FROST, FROST, yesterday & this morning. There is but [little] improvement in the wheat. It looks very bad. I have not seen a single stalk of corn up."[2]

In mid-April, Harris left for his regiment, placing his farm in the hands of his wife, Emily. Although she bemoaned her own inexperience and inability, she did a remarkable job of keeping the farm going despite her acute loneliness, a fault-finding husband, tax collectors, poachers, increasingly recalcitrant slaves, sick children, and the continuing unusual weather. Frequent rain in May and June forced her to replant her corn even as her stores of it ran out. Others did the same as far west as central Mississippi. Harris's wheat and oats suffered from too much rain. Although both rebounded somewhat in July, the yield across the region was discouraging, with the *Macon Telegraph* pronouncing the local crop a failure. Reports of drought in Missouri, to the north in Virginia, and on into the Union also began to appear. An added problem for Harris was her inability to hire enough additional labor to cut her wheat before rain ruined it. She ended up with less than half of her husband's usual crop, while her cotton fared so badly that she turned to prayer. At least she wrote nothing about the cotton army-worm infestation that had ravaged fields in Louisiana in July and August. On the Harris place, however, the latter month was hot enough to kill livestock. Emily Harris was afraid to send her mules into the field.[3]

It was hot everywhere in the middle of August. On the twentieth, the editor of the *Macon Telegraph* opined that "it appears as if his Satanic Majesty had opened the gates of—well! and was driving out the hot air to Macon."[4] Reprinting an essay in the London-based *Fraser's Magazine,* the *Charleston Mercury* blamed the heat on the Gulf Stream, which it maintained was carrying Mexican heat as far north as Newfoundland.[5] That warmth spared her mules, but Harris continued to struggle. Two cows died after gorging in her cane field. As she mourned the loss of milk, news arrived that the Yankees had taken Atlanta. "The prospect for Peace is not so bright as it has been," she wrote sadly, "or as we thought it was." There was nothing left to do but butcher the dead cows, skin off the grease for soap, and feed the meat to the hogs.[6]

Like millions in 1864, Emily Harris's hopes and fears rose and fell with the weather and the progress of the armies. By the end of June, she had reason to hope. Grant's grand plan to end the war seemingly was in shambles. Banks's failures meant that Mobile remained safe. In Virginia, Union hopes wilted with the wheat. Let down by subordinates, stymied by Lee, and too often the victim of his own blunt aggressiveness, the hero of Vicksburg became "Butcher Grant" in the northern mind. His forces, worn out physically and mentally, dug in at Petersburg.

In Georgia, the Confederates had lost more territory than in Virginia, yet even there a tenacious Army of Tennessee at Atlanta and another summer siege threatened to upend Grant's strategic plan entirely. Just as in Virginia, extreme weather would play a central role in the campaign until it reached a climax in September, about the time Harris's cows died.

The brutal cold and frequent precipitation that made the East Tennessee–Northwest Georgia front so miserable in January 1864 continued into the winter. Early February was cool and rainy. In Clarksville, Tennessee— again, the closest Smithsonian observation site to Chattanooga—afternoon highs fluctuated in the forties and fifties. As before, one can extrapolate using Stewart's records as well as regional averages. Februarys in Chattanooga are about 2 degrees warmer than Clarksville on average, although soldier recollections in 1864 suggest colder temperatures and more precipitation. Heavy rain began on Valentine's Day. Near Knoxville, floodwaters drenched low-lying fields. Temperatures grew bitterly cold after that, just as in Virginia, suggesting an active arctic weather system that stretched south to Atlanta. At Clarksville, highs fell from 45 degrees on February 15 to only 19 degrees the next afternoon and 15 degrees that night. In Macon, young LeRoy "Loy" Gresham noted a similar trend. It had been 56 degrees on Valentine's Day but only reached 24 degrees on February 17.

Soldiers at the front described frozen ground and canceled drills. Cpl. Edward Schweitzer of the 30th Ohio watched full canteens burst as the water within froze into ice. Daytime temperatures thankfully moderated beginning on February 19 as warmth rolled south and east. With the exception of some snow on the twenty-first, the month passed pleasantly enough, with highs of 73 degrees in Clarksville on February 23 and 67 degrees four days later. Thirty-degree weather and heavy precipitation then returned and lasted until March 4. Spotty rain continued thereafter into

March 15. Temperatures collapsed; it was 25 degrees in Clarksville on the fifteenth. Longstreet's Confederates saw flurries on March 16, a day before heavy snow on the Virginia front.[7]

Just as in the East, a massive snowstorm accompanied the spring equinox. When it ended the next day, eight inches lay in Huntsville, nearly a foot had accumulated inside Chattanooga, and eighteen inches rested at the base of Lookout Mountain. In the city, citizens told Schweitzer that they had never seen a late-season snow so deep. The storm pushed into Georgia, bringing sleet on March 22. North of Knoxville, Longstreet's men staged another epic snowball battle. Temperatures rising into the fifties soon melted the snow, but rain on March 24—and snow at Longstreet's camps—deepened the mud. Easter Sunday, March 27, was lovely across much of the Southeast, but again Longstreet's men complained of snow, sleet, gales, and mud as they began leaving Tennessee. On the Union side, Capt. Alexis Cope watched helplessly as his recruits grew sick and never got past the hospital in Murfreesboro. Veterans returning from furlough received a rude welcome of rain.[8]

Sherman met with Grant in Nashville on March 21 and took command of the Military Division of the Mississippi. His assignment was to drive on Atlanta and destroy Joe Johnston's Army of Tennessee. He arrived in Chattanooga early on rainy March 28. Sherman envisioned a campaign of maneuver through an Appalachian Ridge and Valley landscape of thick forests, steep mountains, narrow valleys, and red-clay soils that historian Richard McMurry aptly compares to a washboard. From Chattanooga, Maj. Gen. George Thomas's Army of the Cumberland, accompanied by the smaller Army of the Ohio, commanded by Maj. Gen. John Schofield after Burnside's transfer east, would hold Johnston at Dalton. At the same time, Maj. Gen. James B. McPherson would lead Grant and Sherman's old Army of the Tennessee into Johnston's rear. Sherman expected that McPherson's force would include both A. J. Smith's corps, despite the recent disaster in Louisiana, and two additional XVII Corps divisions held up in Illinois. He hoped in vain. Nevertheless, he still expected Johnston to retreat and to be unable to send any help to Lee. Sherman reorganized his 110,000-man army group at the corps level, amassed supplies, secured control of the railroads, and tried to counter threats to Federal communications. He also scaled back his rolling stock, convinced that the combination of railroad transport on the Western and Atlantic and foraged local food and fodder would feed his army, just as during the Meridian dry run.

At Dalton, Johnston learned of Longstreet's return to Virginia, vainly asked for reinforcements, and waited in his extensive works with a total force of 64,000 men. Misjudging Sherman completely, he strengthened his right as blocking the likely Federal line of advance. Both armies also coped with what historian Albert Castel judged an especially wet April. At Clarksville, only 3.57 inches fell in total—less than the local monthly average of 4.11 inches—but the frequency of precipitation precluded any effective drying out. At the front, it rained sixteen days out of thirty in April. Quantities of red mud followed and persisted. Federals began paring their baggage, packing away what they could not carry south.[9]

May began pleasantly. In Clarksville, the high reached 68 degrees on May 4. In Chattanooga, the average temperature in May is just over half a degree warmer, which suggests a reasonable approximation. But as the Federals shifted into their final positions near Confederate-occupied Rocky Face Ridge through May 7, afternoon highs rose dramatically, reaching 80 degrees on the fifth. The heat affected the Confederates, including four divisions Lt. Gen. Leonidas Polk hurried to Georgia as Sherman's plans became obvious. Johnston still was unaware of Snake Creek Gap, however, leaving it completely undefended. On dusty May 8, as temperatures reached 79 degrees, Thomas and Schofield demonstrated while McPherson marched unopposed into the gap. Reaching its end the next day—it was again 79 degrees at 2 P.M.—he cautiously pushed a single division toward the railhead, then called it back. Fearful of the odds and worried about his flank, he had fumbled the chance to establish a firm presence in Johnston's weak rear.[10]

Annoyed but comforted that the "foliage and absence of dust" would not allow Johnston to see his movements, Sherman shifted his army west across the Confederate front toward Resaca. Johnston reacted slowly, not abandoning the front until May 12. While the armies sidled south, the weather changed again. Heavy rain and thunderstorms, beginning on the night of May 9 and lasting the next two days, soaked men and bogged down Sherman's wagons. Presumably, this same weather front continued tracking toward Spotsylvania. At 9 P.M. on the tenth, a heavy storm flooded portions of Snake Creek Gap. The rains blew off the next day but left behind clouds, wind, and a Clarksville high of only 54 degrees. Cpl. George Morris of the 81st Indiana likened the day to one in November. The wind, at least, help dry the roads. By May 13, Cope complained of large airborne dust clouds in occupied Dalton. At Resaca, the Army of Tennessee—now including many of Polk's 20,000 men—dug in behind works just west of town and the railroad. Johnston arrayed his men from the east–west flowing Oostanaula River north to the looping Connasauga River. The line was so flawed topographically that Sherman assumed that his opponent would fall back. Instead, Johnston offered battle. The Federals deployed and attacked repeatedly but ineffectively over two days, wasting chances to cut off Johnston from the south. The weather was mostly clear and warm, but rain returned on the fifteenth.[11]

After midnight, the Confederates fell back, alarmed that Sherman had bridged the Oostanaula. The geography changed as they trudged south of that river. Gone were the rugged valleys of Appalachia, replaced by the rolling hills of Georgia's piedmont. The red-clay soil remained, however. Johnston marched on to Adairsville, where he discovered much too late that his maps were useless—the valley was too wide to defend. Sherman pursued, wrongly assuming that Johnston was racing for the far bank of the Etowah River. Afternoon highs hovered around 70 degrees. Clouds gathered on the sixteenth, followed by fog, rain, and mud the next day. That night, the Confederates slipped away in the rain and thick fog.[12]

Using the regional road network, Johnston now hoped to divide Sherman's force and conquer an isolated segment. Two dusty roads led from Adairsville south to Cassville: one directly to the southeast, and the other south through Kingston. Expecting Sherman to use both, Johnston waited at Cassville. After the fog blew off on the morning of hot and humid May 19—the day reached 79 degrees in Clarksville—he told his enthusiastic men that the retreating had ended and victory was in their grasp. He was wrong. Lt. Gen. John Bell Hood, leading a Confederate corps since the winter, called off his flanking attack on the direct route when he saw Federal cavalry on his flank and assumed the worst. Johnston then fell into a defensive line south of town and resumed retreating during the night, this time into the Allatoona Mountains. Sherman stopped south of the Etowah to rest his men, many of whom had succumbed to the heat on the nineteenth.[13]

The next three days grew hotter, with morning fog and afternoon temperatures rising to 86 degrees in Clarksville on May 23. Soldiers complained of heat, choking dust, and not enough water. Corporal Schweitzer at least noted a good regional wheat crop. Federal supply wagons arrived that day and returned north with the wounded and sick. The wagons suddenly became important because Sherman decided to temporarily abandon his railroad and drive on Dallas, fifteen miles from the Western and Atlantic and in Johnston's rear. Not only would the Rebels have to abandon Allatoona but also, Sherman hoped, would keep retreating to Atlanta. Johnston, however, used his interior lines to meet the threat. It was slow going for both armies. The country they traversed was underpopulated, with poor roads, thick forests, steep grades, and high humidity.[14]

The Atlanta Campaign entered a new phase on May 24 in a dark, bloody place Federal soldiers soon would call the "Hell Hole." A storm system moved into northwestern Georgia as the armies marched toward Dallas. "From the beginning of the campaign," Sgt. Rice Bull of the 123rd New York remembered, "we had fine weather. There had been little rain and no extreme heat; while it was dry and dusty it had been easy traveling. . . . On May 25 the weather changed, and I find recorded in my diary that for twenty-one days it stormed every day." Bull remembered storms invariably arising while he was out in the open, either on the march or in breastworks. Trains bogged down, drenched men dragged them out of the mud, and soldiers tried to sleep on flooded ground. Memory plays tricks, of course. It did not rain a few of those days—indeed, the end of May was largely dry—and Bull was a day off as to when the storms began. But he was right on target in describing the campaign's muddy new tenor.[15]

In Clarksville, the high on May 24 was 20 degrees cooler than the previous day, down to a humid 66 degrees. The sky at the front was cloudy. Heavy showers began in the afternoon. At about 8 P.M., a violent thunderstorm opened up, lasting well into the next morning. Torrential rain put out fires and soaked men without tents or sometimes even ponchos. Roads and earthworks devolved into mud. Soldiers remembered the night sky as black and gloomy. By midday on May 25, Johnston's muddy army was dug in on a line from near Dallas northeast to the crossroads at New Hope Church. As Richard McMurry observes, the men's skill in building fieldworks had increased exponentially through May until it reached near perfection in the Hell Hole.

At about 4 P.M., Joe Hooker's XX Corps charged in a narrow column of brigades at New Hope Church. Just as the assault began, a thunderstorm erupted. The Confederates shattered the attack, inflicting three-to-one casualties. The next day, Johnston slid his army to the right to Pickett's Mill. Two Federal divisions advanced, one going down into a hot, steep ravine and then up the opposite slope. These men discovered a Confederate division waiting behind new works. Federal officer Ambrose Bierce damned the resulting engagement as murder. As dark night approached, another storm rained on the dead and dying. Alexis Cope described thunder as louder than artillery. Men, animals, and wagons slipped down steep inclines.[16]

Sherman's gambit failed: Johnston blocked his road south, his men grew hungry in a barren region, and rain made the roads too muddy to rely on wagons. His only choice was to return to the railroad. That decision resulted in another fight at Dallas on May 28. The next days were dusty; rain only fell on the twenty-ninth. And it was hot; in Clarksville, the high hit 82 degrees on May 31. Exposed in their works, soldiers remembered the heat and their thirst.[17] "The days were exceedingly warm," Maj. Gen. Alpheus Williams wrote, "and the air filled with the noisome odors of the dead, man and beast."[18] Sherman described "one universal skirmish extending over a vast surface."[19]

Between June 3 and June 6, Sherman's army group returned to the railroad at Acworth, about twenty-five miles from Atlanta. While his engineers toiled to bridge the Etowah, he rested his men. On June 11, Johnston fell back to the east toward Marietta. There the Confederates constructed a long series of earthworks anchored by three imposing mountains. The "Lost Mountain Line" ran from that mountain on the left, northeast to Pine Mountain, and then southeast to Brushy Mountain. This new position blocked both the railroad and Sherman's highway south.

During this pause in combat, rain fell incessantly, beginning on June 2 with showers during the morning, thunder and hail before noon, and torrential rain during the afternoon. The hail ruined shelters, while the lightning killed men. The next day saw heavy afternoon rain, mud up to waist deep in spots, flooded creeks, and entrenchments filled with water. It rained gently all day on June 4 and harder on the fifth, when the Confederates pulled back to their new line. The next days were hot, humid, and cloudy, with occasional thunder and brief showers on June 6. In Clarksville, the high both days was 80 degrees, probably a good approximation of that at the front, given that mean June temperatures in Atlanta run just more than half a degree cooler. Rain fell steadily again on hot June 7 and lasted periodically until June 10, with hard showers, storms, humidity, and highs generally in the seventies except for June 9, when it reached 82 degrees in Clarksville. Oceans of rain soaked soldiers to their skin, ruined roads, bogged down trains in mire, and flooded entrenchments. Lucky men huddled beneath shelter, while the rest were miserable, often unable to sleep in the deep clay mud. Many got sick from exposure. The only good thing about the weather, according to Confederate private William Trask, was that it was too rainy for the two sides to kill each other.[20]

Few soldiers failed to comment on the rain. Capt. S. F. Horrall of the 42nd Indiana remembered how enemy fire kept his regiment pinned down in their "ditch" as it "gathered water, from ankle to knee-deep, according to the rainfall, and those of the men not on picket duty were kept busy bailing out the water. . . . [M]en slept sitting, standing, kneeling, and every way except lying down."[21] Rice Bull wrote on June 4 that "the Army was simply floundering in the mud, and there was scarcely a time when our clothing was dry."[22] The Confederates bore the brunt of it, however, as they were more often on the move. Capt. John Lavender of the 4th Arkansas described knee-deep mud and waist-deep creeks and compared his comrades to cattle. "The Darkness being so Dence," he wrote, "made all Desperate men swearing, cursing the Confederacy, the united States and all that was in it."[23] On June 9 at Kennesaw Mountain, Lt. Col. W. A. Rorer of the 20th Mississippi wrote, "our marches have all been made at night, and many times in rain and mud." The mud was "half leg deep and numbers of . . . [the soldiers] are [bare]footed, the mud being so adhesive as to pull a shoe to pieces."[24]

Sherman pushed his men through the rain, urging McPherson and Schofield on June 5 to ignore the weather and keep moving. The Federals' turn to suffer fully finally came on the tenth, when Sherman began moving toward Pine Mountain, a salient in an otherwise solid line of works. As forward units skirmished, the rain continued almost without letup, creating veritable swamps that bogged down the Federal advance through June 13. Maj. Gen. William B. Hazen complained that the roads were so deep that his division's artillery could barely move. Creeks flooded, and supply trains foundered. Horses, mules, wagons, and guns in both armies sank. Men who relied on wagons for their tents huddled beneath makeshift shelters constructed from ponchos, if they had them. Sgt. Walter Clark of the 63rd Georgia claimed that his wet uniform absorbed red-clay mud until it ran up the inside seams of his pants like a stripe. Temperatures grew cooler too. In Clarksville, morning lows fell to 56 degrees on the thirteenth, the coldest morning of the month. Aside from skirmishing, the war in Georgia came to a stop.[25] "Eleven days rain!" Samuel French exclaimed. "If it keeps on, there will be a story told like unto that in the Bible, only it will read 'It rained forty days and it rained forty nights, And the ark rested on the Kennesaw heights!'"[26]

The night of June 13 was dry if cold; Trask likened it to a January day. The break in the fighting continued on cloudy June 14. Although the ground remained soggy, the end of the rain helped morale. Confederate leadership took advantage of the lull to ride to Pine Mountain and decide whether to hold it. Sherman—also reconnoitering near Pine Mountain because the rain had stopped—ordered his artillery to clear away the gray-clad company on the summit. One projectile killed Lieutenant General Polk. Afterward, Johnston ordered the mountain abandoned.

The next three days remained clear. In Clarksville, highs rose from 70 degrees on June 13 to a steamy 81 degrees on June 17. On the sixteenth, Federal troops seized high ground on the Confederate left. That night, William Hardee's corps fell back to high ground near Mud Creek, briefly creating the "Second Kennesaw Line." It, too, was flawed and easily enfiladed. During the night of the seventeenth, rain fell periodically and hard, continuing into the following afternoon, flooding new rifle pits and waterways, before dispersing into a fine mist. That wet night, Johnston pulled his entire force back to a new line—the "Third Kennesaw Line"—that curved around the big mountain. Mud made the roads almost useless. It kept raining across Georgia all day on June 19, through the evening of June 20, and all day June 21. Sherman's Federals slogged through the morass to Kennesaw Mountain. Aside from rugged Dalton, the Confederates built their strongest line of the campaign at Kennesaw, but it was not immune to weather.[27] Lt. R. M. Collins of the 15th Texas Cavalry wrote, "on some parts of our line the men were in water up to their arm-pits."[28]

"The weather throughout most of June was beastly in the extreme," wrote the historians of the 86th Indiana. "With this extreme heat and with every creek, swamp, and lagoon full of water, and the decaying vegetable matter washed into swamps and ponds, it is a wonder that the Union forces did not die all in a heap." One might say the same thing about their opponents.[29]

$\sim$

"During our operations about Kenesaw," Sherman reported, "the weather was villainously bad, the rain fell almost continually for three weeks, rendering our narrow wooded roads mere gullies, so that a general movement would have been impossible."[30] He admitted that he had moved slowly due to "an uninterrupted rain from June 2 to about the 22nd, and the peculiar sub-mountainous character of the country from the Etowah to the Chattahoochee."[31]

But that was in the past. The rain finally ended on June 22, with clear skies and 81-degree heat. Roads began to dry. Hot summer weather would be the theme of the campaign's next phase, just as in drought-stricken Virginia. Sherman immediately capitalized on the change, sending Schofield's army and Hooker's corps forward. They encountered one of Hood's divisions at Kolb's Farm, south of Marietta, and struck it hard. That night, the moon shone so brightly in a clear sky that Schofield ordered his men to carry their guns barrel down or wrapped in blankets or coats so that the Confederates would not see the light reflected in their movements behind the lines.

While a Federal victory, Kolb's Farm—and the recent weather—left Sherman with a dilemma. The roads remained wet and boggy enough to preclude marching for days. Yet if he sat tight, Johnston might send troops to strike the Western and Atlantic or even to reinforce Lee at Petersburg. The only other option, he concluded, was to attack the Army of Tennessee's works head on and hope they were thin enough to punch through. On June 26, Sherman ordered demonstrations to mislead the Confederates. One involved dispatching a division to Olley's Creek, which that unit crossed without opposition. The next morning, after an artillery barrage, Sherman hit Johnston with divisions from all three armies. Thomas's central attack, aimed at a salient, failed miserably. Kennesaw Mountain became another Cold Harbor, complete with the horrible aftermath. At least one division commander, Maj. Gen. Jefferson C. Davis, partially blamed the heat for his exhausted men's failure to overwhelm the enemy works. Some troops lay pinned down for five days, without water or shade, while temperatures rose into the mideighties. Only on June 29 did the sides arranged a truce so that they could bury the bloated and stinking dead. Readings hit 90 degrees the next day. In their works, the Federals cut brush and small tree limbs to create rude arbors over their trenches.[32]

Sherman went back to flanking maneuvers. Finally, exploiting the accidental breakthrough on Olley's Creek, Schofield's and McPherson's armies crossed there and headed for the Chattahoochee River, the last water barrier to Atlanta. Johnston responded by abandoning his Kennesaw line on the night of July 2 and marching his army to new works centered at Smyrna. The Army of the Cumberland pursued, the men skirmishing and sometimes stopping to catch their breath in the heat. On the Fourth of July, elements of the Army of the Tennessee flanked Johnston's left, forcing another retreat. The Confederates fell back into another prepared line of strong fortifications, anchored at both ends by the rain-swollen Chattahoochee. Unwilling to launch another direct assault, Sherman decided to cross north of Johnston's works once the swollen river fell. Johnston expected his opponent to try to flank him again but assumed it would be once again to his left, where he massed his forces. He guessed wrong. One of Schofield's brigades finally crossed the Chattahoochee on July 8 in a large dust cloud, followed by cavalry at a second ford the next morning. Armed with repeating rifles, the Federal horsemen swept aside all resistance. As Sherman's army secured the crossings, Johnston retreated to the south bank of Peachtree Creek, just three miles from the center of Atlanta. Large dust clouds gave him away. Panic erupted in the city as thousands fled the oncoming armies. Surrendering the Chattahoochee cost Johnston dearly. On July 17, encouraged by Bragg's reports from the front, President Davis fired the general and replaced him with Hood, elevated provisionally to full general. While this drama occupied the Confederates, Sherman shifted toward Roswell.[33]

The weather remained warm and dry. Rain fell only in scattered local thunderstorms during six July evenings, notably on the twelfth and every night from the fourteenth through the sixteenth. Dr. George Cooper, the Army of the Cumberland's medical director, reported that, from late June through mid-August, "the heat was at no time oppressive, nor did the thermometer show over 90° in the shade on the hottest days."[34] But it was hot enough. The combination of heat and dust led to sunstroke, especially on July 1 and July 6 among Sherman's shifting troops.[35] Jesse Dozier of the 26th Illinois wrote: "There were several days, the heat was the greatest I ever experienced. In marching the men would two thirds, fall out of the ranks and get in the shade. There were several men sunstroke in marching from Marietta to the river."[36]

Sherman formulated his plans. Both Grant and Halleck warned that stalemate in Virginia meant that Lee actually could send reinforcements to Georgia now. Their advice was to cut Atlanta's railroads to the east and south and hunker down. For him to suffer defeat at this juncture could mean losing the war. Sherman, often remembered for his anxiety, calmed his superiors. Expecting nothing offensively from Johnston, he would keep swinging his army from the north to the east in order to cut the Georgia Railroad to Augusta while pressuring the Confederates in the city. On hot and dusty July 18, the same day that Hood assumed command, McPherson cut the Georgia Railroad near Decatur. Only the Macon and Western Railroad now connected Atlanta to the rest of the Confederacy.[37]

Once he learned of the change in Confederate command, Sherman expected Hood to attack and ordered Thomas to send a corps to bolster the left. He was right about Hood's intentions but guessed wrong as to where they would lead. Confederate scouts reported that a gap had formed between Thomas's left and Schofield's right near Peachtree Creek. Hood determined to drive into the opening and then roll to the west, hitting a vulnerable Army of the Cumberland as it crossed the creek. If the Confederates could drive Thomas into the triangle formed by the creek and the Chattahoochee, they might well maul his command. But nothing went as planned. July 20 was fiercely hot; the best evidence suggests that the afternoon high was around 90 degrees. Worried about McPherson to the east, Hood ordered his units to shift in that direction. The attack began three hours late, long into the afternoon. One Confederate corps briefly managed to breach the Federal lines, but Thomas's men stood fast. Heat helped the Union defense. The colonel of the 22th Mississippi reported men all but fainting from the heat as they approached the enemy works. The commander of the 33rd Mississippi added that the heat was so intense that his men had trouble loading and firing their weapons.[38] "The day had been hot," Rice Bull remembered, "and we were as wet [with sweat] as though we had been in the water."[39]

But Hood was not done. While Thomas stopped to lick his wounds, McPherson kept pushing east of Atlanta, tearing up tracks and fighting a series of small but ugly skirmishes. On the evening of July 21, a light shower barely settled the dust. Hood decided to pull his army back into the city's extensive fortifications and then hit McPherson's exposed southern flank. His exhausted men began moving that humid night—more slowly than Hood anticipated—and trudged on into the foggy morning over difficult, brushy ground. None were aware that McPherson had strengthened his left with an additional corps. Temperatures were perhaps around 80 degrees, and sunstroke claimed more men. Just after noon, Hardee launched the assault. Again, the Confederates briefly penetrated the enemy line only to be driven back. Weather again played a role. Brig. Gen. Mark Lowrey, commanding a Confederate brigade, reported that many of his men fell out during their advance due to the effects of heat. McPherson died during this action, known as the Battle of Atlanta, but Hood failed to break Sherman's tightening grip on the city.[40]

The next days brought little change. Other than clouds on July 23 and rain on the night of July 26, conditions remained sunny and hot, with afternoon highs probably around 80 degrees. Dust was everywhere until the rain of the twenty-sixth briefly created mud in the trenches. At headquarters, Sherman decided to shift the Army of the Tennessee from his left to his right, toward the Macon and Western Railroad down the city's west side. Cavalry rode out to hit the rail line farther south. Hood responded by sending his old corps, now commanded by Lt. Gen. Stephen D. Lee, to block the advance. On cloudy July 27, Lee launched a series of unsuccessful attacks near Ezra Church.[41] "It was a terribly hot July afternoon," Alabama artilleryman Sgt. James Maxwell later wrote, "and the men with jackets, blankets, haversacks and all else possible strewn on the ground were panting like dogs, and so wet with sweat as if just out [of] a river, when they threw themselves down in the shade of the trees on the edge of the field after the firing ceased."[42]

July ended with humid 80-degree heat, straggling, and heat exhaustion. Some sought shade instead of staying in line, weakening Confederate resistance. A thunderstorm hit during the evening of the thirty-first.[43] "It rained very hard," Corporal Schweitzer wrote, "the water overflowed camp washing away our beds that we had made of leaves the lightning wounded several men."[44]

⌇

"The month of August," Pvt. Edmund Brown of the 27th Indiana wrote, "was not as hot as July had been. Some days the sun blazed upon us without mercy, but others were more tolerable, and the nights were comfortable."[45] Until its last days, August remained a month of middling summer heat. To the south in Macon on August 7, Loy Gresham wrote: "Mercury 82° at 9 A.M. The thermometer has not been above 90° this season certain, and I have not seen it over 89°."[46]

Sherman's siege works arced around the northern half of the city. Hood extended his on the west side, shielding the Atlanta and West Point Railroad's connection to the Macon and Western at East Point. Neither commander had the manpower to extend his lines more or the desire to launch direct assaults. Aside from sending cavalry into the enemy rear, there was little else to be done. The resulting stalemate pleased no one. With Grant stuck at Petersburg, Democrats ready to meet in convention, and warnings that his men would be out of food by mid-September, Sherman knew that he needed to break the deadlock. His initial reaction was to bombard Atlanta into submission. While causing some destruction and more terror, the shelling did nothing to drive out Hood. Inside the city, citizens endured the same heat, dust, vermin, and stench as the surrounding soldiers.[47]

The weather in the earthworks was often hot but not broiling. Local and isolated showers, usually not enough to produce mud, fell in Atlanta thirteen times in August, most heavily between August 18 and August 21. That system—one that may have extended into Virginia—flooded trenches with several inches of water and produced a rainbow on the twentieth.[48]

Sherman broke the military stalemate on the night of August 25. Sending XX Corps on muddy roads to hold the Western and Atlantic bridge over the Chattahoochee, he abandoned his works to the north and east and rotated his army group counterclockwise toward East Point to the south and beyond to the railroad at Fairburn. On hot August 26, with temperatures probably in the low to middle eighties, the Federals marched all day and dug in. Many fell by the wayside due to the heat and still air. Hood, poorly informed by his cavalry and thoroughly baffled, did nothing. That night, as it rained again, Sherman left two corps to protect his rear and sent the Army of the Tennessee and the Army of the Cumberland's IV Corps toward the railroad. Cloud cover cloaked their movement. The troops reached the railroad on clear and hotter August 28, with afternoon highs probably near 80 degrees, and began wrecking it at two points. After morning fog, the twenty-ninth was hot but did not stop the Federals from continuing their destructive work.

Hood and his lieutenants thought that Sherman was merely extending his line. Then on August 30, the Army of the Tennessee—now commanded by Maj. Gen. Oliver Otis Howard—moved on toward Jonesboro, southeast of Atlanta. Only cavalry blocked them at first. At 6 P.M., Hood learned that a sizable enemy force was south of the city. He ordered two corps under Hardee to race there and drive them back. But that took time. Hardee attacked about 3 P.M. on the thirty-first. Again, he let Hood down. Poorly managed, Jonesboro was a Confederate disaster, with the attackers suffering ten-to-one casualties. Many Johnny Rebs simply gave up. The day ended with Sherman's men wedged between the sections of a divided Army of Tennessee. On the afternoon of September 1, with temperatures probably in the upper seventies, Sherman attacked, with little success.[49]

By then, Hood had decided that the only way to save his army was to abandon Atlanta. His men still inside the city burned or blew up everything that might be of value to the Union war effort and evacuated during the night of September 1–2. The army reunited at Lovejoy's Station, south of Jonesboro, that hot and cloudy afternoon. Large dust clouds again gave away their movement. Federal cavalry entered the city before noon on the second. It soon began raining. Showers started falling at about 3 P.M. on the third, dragged into the next day, and retuned on the fifth. Sherman's grimy men rejoiced at the fall of Atlanta. So did people across the North, especially Republicans. Coupled with the successful recent naval battle on hot and humid August 5 that shut down Mobile Bay, an end to the war seemed in sight. The Democrats, in contrast, had made the unintentional mistake of approving their antiwar platform just as the Battle of Jonesboro erupted. Candidate McClellan immediately found himself in a ticklish position. Just as the platform reflected the military stalemate, McClellan's warlike acceptance letter acknowledged the fall of Atlanta and the renewed hope throughout the North.[50]

In the excitement surrounding the fall of Atlanta, it is easy to forget that the Army of Tennessee remained a serious threat. Sherman himself entered the city on cloudy September 7, having already ordered the complete evacuation of its civilians. His stated goals for this were to control the railroads and ensure the safety of his garrison, but in truth, he wanted to break Georgia's will to continue the war.[51] Refusing the city government's request to delay the depopulation of Atlanta, Sherman replied, "you might as well appeal against the thunder-storm as against these terrible hardships of war."[52] Perhaps 1,700 remaining residents refugeed through Confederate lines between September 12 and September 21. The weather was hot, with daytime temperatures in the seventies and eighties, and largely dry. Just as the last refugees left Atlanta, autumn and cooler temperatures arrived with the equinox. A new season in Georgia's war was in the offing.[53]

Chapter 23

Yankee Weather

The Trans-Mississippi and the West, September–December 1864

In the autumn of 1864, three armies flashed across the map of the western Confederacy like jagged cracks across a sheet of ice. With Atlanta, Mobile Bay, and the Shenandoah Valley in Federal hands, Confederate leaders initiated two desperate campaigns in September, hoping to reclaim territory and derail the Republicans at the polls. Both began as invasions but evolved into long raids. Once Lincoln and his party survived the elections, Sherman launched the third march, designed to shorten the war by taking devastation to the citizens of the Confederacy.

The first campaign originated in Louisiana. Gen. Edmund Kirby Smith longed for a way to undermine Lincoln and help the antiwar Peace Democrats to power across the North. Maj. Gen. Sterling Price offered an answer. Two Confederate cavalry raids led by Brig. Gen. Jo Shelby, one into Missouri a year earlier and a second through Arkansas that May, convinced Price that Federal occupation in both states was tenuous. Disparate garrisons of militia or untested recruits concentrated on countering the ongoing ugliness of a brutal guerrilla war. Little more than a rail line or string of telegraph wire connected them to one another. In theory, they would be no match for seasoned troops. As early as May, after the failures of Steele and Banks, Kirby Smith had contemplated marching into Missouri. In August, with Confederate fortunes on the brink, he acted. Price would take nearly all of the Department of Arkansas's cavalry, storm into Missouri, and seize either Saint Louis or the state capital at Jefferson City. Secessionist guerrillas and other Missourians hungry for liberation surely would rise up to join them. Infantry would follow from both Louisiana and the Indian Territory. If successful, this effort would redeem Arkansas and Missouri, ensure Lincoln's electoral defeat, and lead to the Confederacy entering peace talks with the victorious Copperheads. Orders from Richmond quickly derailed the second part of the military plan. Anxious for a diversion to save Atlanta, the War Department ordered Kirby Smith to send all of his infantry across the Mississippi. The general sent Price north anyway, hoping that he could still seize Saint Louis, embarrass Washington, gather recruits and supplies, and install the peripatetic Confederate state government with cavalry alone.[1]

On hot and dusty August 28, a week behind schedule due to logistical failures, Price left Camden, Arkansas, with 4,000 cavalry and headed northeast into the drought-stricken Mississippi Valley. Skirting occupied Little Rock, the column picked up reinforcements and rendezvoused with Shelby on September 13 in northeastern Arkansas. There, Price created the Army of Missouri out of the 12,000 men at his disposal. It was an undisciplined, ragged, sick, and sometimes shoeless force. A third of the men were unarmed, and a thousand were on foot. Under orders from Kirby Smith, who did not fully trust him, Price organized it into three divisions commanded by seemingly more-dependable veterans of the Camden Campaign: Brigadier Generals Shelby, Marmaduke, and Fagan. Another veteran of that campaign, Major General Steele, proved as reluctant to act as he had during the spring. With three times as many men, he nevertheless let the Confederates pass by while he safeguarded Little Rock and the Arkansas River. Worse yet, Steele commandeered one of Maj. Gen. A. J. Smith's three Federal divisions, on transports at Cairo to rejoin Sherman at last following the Red River debacle, to help him accomplish this static goal.[2]

Missouri and Virginia still bore the brunt of the 1864 summer drought in the South. Exact temperature measurements are lacking, but again one can extrapolate. George P. Ray operated the closest Smithsonian station in Canton, Missouri, located on the Mississippi north of Mark Twain's Hannibal. Canton temperatures in September generally are almost 2 degrees cooler than those in the southeastern Missouri town of Farmington, Price's first major goal. Ray recorded highs in the upper seventies through the end August. A sudden heatwave welcomed September, with Canton highs of 97 degrees, 101 degrees, and 103 degrees the first three days of that month. Afternoon and evening rain on the fourth brought two cooler days that did not reach 70 degrees, but the heat rebounded, reaching 90 degrees on September 9 and 97 degrees on September 11. It was dry as well, with only 0.34 of an inch of rain falling at Canton in the second half of August and 1.55 inches of rain on three days for the month of September.[3] And it was humid; Sgt. Maj. William Forse Scott of the 4th Iowa Cavalry described the hot spell as "sultry almost beyond endurance."[4]

September 18 was cooler in Canton thanks to rain. Temperatures reached 62 degrees at 2 P.M., 18 degrees cooler than the previous day. On the eighteenth, Confederates captured a small Federal garrison and executed two prisoners who previously had served in gray. As historian Mark Lause notes, the twin killings inaugurated the brutality that accompanied the entire campaign. Two days later, the prosecession Missourians reentered their home state as temperatures rose back into the eighties. A tenth of an inch of rain failed to settle the morning's dust. Beginning on hot and windy September 22 (90 degrees in Canton), the invaders passed through Farmington, where they looted, terrorized, and conscripted. Rain fell on the afternoon of the twenty-third, with a thunderstorm that night.

No one in Saint Louis understood what was happening. Department of the Missouri commander William Rosecrans—in semiexile since Chattanooga—had no idea how many men his Iuka foe led but underestimated the threat. His deputy was Brig. Gen. Thomas Ewing Jr., Sherman's foster brother and brother-in-law as well as the officer notorious for depopulating four Missouri counties after the Lawrence Massacre. Ewing borrowed a few hundred men from A. J. Smith and headed to the front, traveling by train south to Pilot Knob. Smith was to follow with two brigades but halted when he learned that Shelby was at Farmington. Ewing continued on to Fort Davidson, a large earthen hexagon that defended Pilot Knob and a nearby railroad terminus. Ignoring advice from Shelby, who thought it a needless diversion from taking Saint Louis, Price ordered Fort Davidson taken. His Confederates attacked outlying troops on the foggy, rainy, and cool morning of September 27—it was 64 degrees in Canton—and drove them into the defenses. Ewing refused to surrender. An ill-advised afternoon assault failed. That night, Ewing and about 1,400 men slipped away after igniting a long fuse to the fort's powder magazine. The resulting explosion left a massive crater, buried many of the 800 Confederates who had died during the fighting that day, and was heard twenty miles distant. The damp atmosphere, wind, and terrain, however, created an acoustic shadow so intense that Price, in a nearby town, never heard the blast. Angry Confederates took out their frustrations on the prisoners they swept up over the next days. At Centralia on September 27, bushwhackers led by Quantrill veteran "Bloody Bill" Anderson killed, scalped, and mutilated twenty-three captured Federals.[5]

When Price crossed into Missouri, the state's southernmost rivers were too low to offer much hindrance. Brig. Gen. John McNeill warned Rosecrans on September 26 that "the Osage can be crossed at this stage everywhere; it is merely a succession of pools. The Gasconade is almost a dry river and can be waded from its mouth to its source. No attention need to be paid to fords on either stream."[6] But on the twenty-seventh, the drought began to break at last. Rainy weather, cooler temperatures, and atrocities marked the week, with rain falling all the way south to Georgia. From September 27 through October 6, Ray measured a whopping 6.37 inches of rain as well as highs in the fifties. That much precipitation began to reverse the effects of the summer drought and affected operations on both sides.[7] Price's army, slowed down by a 500-wagon train, entered Saint Louis County on rainy October 1, all but destroyed the rail center at Pacific, rounded up blacks and potential conscripts, and skirmished with militia. His troops were forty-five miles from Saint Louis. Pillaging, destruction, rape, and murder marked the night. Price probably had a two-to-one advantage over Rosecrans, hunkered down inside the city's earthworks, but the Missourian concluded that *he* was outnumbered two to one. Worse, there was no support from Kirby Smith, and the Missouri River now was high enough to block a movement north to capture the river port. On the rainy night of October 2, Price turned west toward Jefferson City, remaining south of the swollen Missouri.[8]

Gobbling up isolated militia garrisons and committing new atrocities, the Confederates rolled west. They crossed the rising Gasconade and turned toward the state capital on October 4 while nearly another inch of rain fell. What eventually stopped Price and saved Jefferson City's tiny garrison was the nine-day rain event. On cool October 6, the first sunny day of the new month, Price discovered that the Osage was too deep to cross except at fords. He probed for a weak spot, but a nasty firefight at the most promising ford stopped him. Blocked by high water and again convinced that he was outnumbered, Price turned away. The invasion at that moment devolved into a massive cavalry raid. Price at least hoped to gather men and supplies in his home state before ripping into Kansas. Many factors shaped that end, but heavy rain and a watery moat around Jefferson City were crucial.[9]

The Army of Missouri headed west along the Missouri River. The region was the most pro-Confederate in the state, yet Price's men continued foraging and pillaging. Soon the weather turned cold; on October 8, the high in Canton was 54 degrees. Frost appeared. Officers noted their men's exhaustion, illness, and poor morale. At the same time, two larger Federal forces gathered to stop them. In Kansas, Maj. Gen. Samuel Curtis concentrated his scattered cavalry as well as militia into the Army of the Border, which he sent under Maj. Gen. James Blunt toward Missouri. To the east, Federals troops coalesced at Jefferson City under Maj. Gen. Alfred Pleasonton, the Federal commander at Brandy Station sent west after Gettysburg. Pleasonton, however, refused to move until fully reinforced by A. J. Smith and Rosecrans's infantry as well as an additional division from Arkansas.[10]

October 14 was the last warm afternoon of the month, with the high in Canton reaching 75 degrees. After that, highs stayed in the fifties or even the forties. Rain fell on the night of the nineteenth. The new day brought temperatures in the forties as well as a nagging mist. Ignoring Rosecrans's caution, Pleasonton surged ahead despite a smattering of snow. A strong northwest wind blew up as the Confederates tried to escape the developing trap by storming Blunt's defenses at the Little Blue River and driving the Federals through Independence. Afraid to lose Kansas City, Curtis began building works and placing artillery along the Big Blue River, which flowed into the Missouri east of the city. That night was cold enough for water to freeze in canteens. The next day remained frosty, with a Canton high of 54 degrees and gentle breezes from the west. Many Federals wore their overcoats all day as the Confederates fought to cross the river. Shelby finally pierced Curtis's line and forced him to fall back to Westport, south of the city. The Confederates killed many of the Kansans taken prisoner, particularly any African Americans. But while Price got his long train across the Big Blue, Pleasonton arrived in force and attacked the rear guard, retaking Independence after nightfall.[11]

Price waffled about how to respond until Shelby convinced him to retreat to the south, lest they be crushed between a blue-clad hammer and anvil. Across the lines, equal confusion reigned. Curtis's subordinates debated mutiny before persuading him to stand and fight, not retreat across the border. October 23 brought clear skies and a 7 A.M. Canton temperature of 45 degrees. The high would reach 64 degrees that afternoon, making it the warmest day in the second half of October. Desperate to save his train—now the only tangible success of the campaign—Price sent Shelby's division and most of Fagan's to attack the Federals at Westport. But Blunt had moved out already to attack the Confederates. These forces collided south of town around seven o'clock. After hours of desperate back-and-forth fighting, disaster appeared in the Confederate rear in the form of Pleasonton's cavalry, which attacked the remainder of Price's army. Marmaduke's division collapsed around noon; the massive train only escaped due to Federal confusion. To the north, Curtis and Blunt's counterattack drove the Confederates straight into Pleasonton's ranks. Between 2 and 2:30 P.M., the two Federal armies met. The outnumbered Confederates largely broke and fled, although Fagan's men fought long enough in the rear to save their comrades. A deliberately set prairie fire further covered the retreat. The Battle of Westport ended in a decisive Union victory. Temperatures collapsed that night; in Canton, it was 31 degrees the next morning.[12]

All that was left to Price was escape. His worn-out men—those who had not surrendered in droves or fallen in action—were aided by Rosecrans (who recalled Smith) and the Kansas militia (which went home). Price swerved into Kansas with his train and 3,000 head of cattle. Mist evolved into thunderstorms that night, allowing Federal cavalry to approach without being heard. Before dawn on October 25, with temperatures probably in the upper forties and skies rapidly clearing, Pleasonton hit Price's rear guard at the Marais des Cygnes River. A massive cavalry fight followed, as Confederates protected their train as it crossed jammed-up and muddy Mine Creek. Shelby organized a new defensive line that slowly gave ground all day before the Federals broke off. Price ordered his empty wagons burned and escaped after midnight. His column crossed back into Missouri and headed for Arkansas. Immense clouds of dust gave them away. Much to Curtis's astonishment, Pleasonton headed into Kansas to rest his men. After a nasty fight at Newtonia on October 28, Blunt called off his pursuit too. Only Curtis refused to yield.[13]

The weather turned wetter and colder, with morning lows frequently below freezing and accompanied by rain, sleet, or snow. Price's raiders staggered into the Ozarks. "Weather horrible," staff officer William McPheeters wrote on November 2, "cold and rainy. [The] army rested today and luxuriated in the mud and rain." The next day, he added: "The rain of yesterday turned into snow last night. The army remained stationary today. Indeed in the state of the command, stock, and weather it would have been almost impossible to have moved. A miserable, cold, snowy, muddy disagreeable day it has been."[14] The Federals endured the same harsh conditions, not to mention empty bellies after their trains mired in the rear. Maj. Chapman Charlot of Curtis's staff complained, "movements greatly retarded by the rain and the almost impassable condition of the roads."[15] William Forse Scott remembered that "very little corn could be found, the snow covered the grass and for two or three days [the horses] could eat only twigs and such dry grass as was tall enough to rise above the snow."[16] Lt. Henry Fike, marching east with Smith's corps, measured "fourteen or fifteen inches" of snow on the fourth.[17]

Pneumonia spread through Confederate ranks. Morale plummeted. At Fayetteville on rainy November 2, Fagan's men refused to fight. With only a remnant of his army remaining, Price fled into the Indian Territory. Horses died of exhaustion, and starving Confederates ate their flesh. Rain fell overnight on November 7 after the column crossed the Arkansas River into the Choctaw Nation. It continued the next day before briefly turning to snow. Showers and thunderstorms followed. As Curtis ordered a ceremonial firing of thirty-four guns—it was Election Day—wind tore down trees and torrents of rain fell. He now gave up, too, and turned for Kansas. On November 10, with draft animals dying by the hundreds, Price's army broke up. With only 3,500 men accompanying him, he veered into Texas before returning to Arkansas. A blue norther greeted them. Price's survivors had ridden nearly 1,500 miles but had accomplished little other than depriving Sherman of two divisions and wrecking railroads that were soon repaired.[18] "Beginning in torrid heat and ending in snow and zero cold," the invasion was a failure.[19]

On rainy September 25, with Price storming back into Missouri, Jefferson Davis arrived at the Georgia front. He planned to meet with General Hood, review troops, and deal somehow with the Army of Tennessee's cancerous command situation. Three days later, the president decided to remove Lieutenant General Hardee, leave Hood in command, and approve the Texan's proposed strike northward against Sherman's supply line. Hood had advocated such a movement since the fall of Atlanta, but its final form showed Davis's fingerprints. If Sherman followed him, minus any troops left to hold Atlanta, Hood would choose where to fight. If Sherman instead turned away for the Gulf or even for the Atlantic, Hood would follow. A few days later, hoping to deflect criticism, Davis created a western command for General Beauregard, who would serve as Hood's superior but with little real power over the army.[20]

On the night of September 29, the Army of Tennessee sidestepped Atlanta and began trudging north toward the Western and Atlantic Railroad. The weather was quite different now, with clouds and rain predominating for a week, just as in Missouri. On October 2, elements of Hood's army struck Sherman's supply line northwest of the city and began tearing up track. Thunderstorms brought rain in the afternoon, which lasted through the night. Worried about Hood's intentions, Sherman sent troops after him as daytime showers turned into another all-night rain. Soldiers reluctantly crawled out of their dry tents to mount the pursuit. The fourth brought morning rain and slippery roads. Sherman left a corps to hold Atlanta and went after Hood himself with the balance of his army group, just as Davis hoped. From the heights of Kennesaw Mountain, the Union commander saw indications of battle to the north, where a Confederate division had struck the Federal garrison at Allatoona Pass unsuccessfully. Clouds soon closed in, blocking his view. Afternoon rain continued into the night and fell heavily into the early afternoon of October 6. Back in Atlanta, rising waters carried away a bridge over the Chattahoochee.[21]

Both the weather and Hood proved to be changeable. As in Missouri, conditions became not only drier but also cooler on October 7. Soldiers built fires that night. Frost appeared the next morning. Hood abandoned the railroad, as well as any previous plan, and swerved west toward New Hope Church and Alabama. He aimed to strike the railroad again, this time north of the Etowah. If Sherman came after him, he would pull him north toward the Tennessee River. That night, pursuing Federals pulled out their overcoats as a strong wind blew from the northwest. On October 13, with conditions still cool and frosty at night, Hood held Dalton and had damaged the railroad extensively between Tunnel Hill and Resaca. Sherman was coming after him hard, with his forward elements already at Resaca. Historian Thomas Connelly argues that Hood was in a splendid position to stop and fight as Davis originally wanted. Instead, on chilly October 16, he decided to move west into Alabama toward the Tennessee River and change the course of the war by invading Tennessee and perhaps even Kentucky. As if to encourage him, the weather grew warm and pleasant. Four days later, the Army of Tennessee was in Gadsden. Cool, frosty, and dry conditions held through the month, aside from rain and mud on October

27, as Hood moved deeper into Alabama.[22] Hoosier George Morris remembered how "the sun broke through the clouds, and one of the most beautiful rainbows spread itself over us, and appeared to be right close to us. We sincerely hoped that it was a harbinger of peace and happiness. It was a glorious sight to see the troops, with banners and flags marching under it."[23]

Sherman let Hood go at this point, breaking off his pursuit on October 28 just inside the Alabama border. About 25,000 Federals already were scattered across Tennessee in various garrisons. Sherman sent Schofield's Army of the Ohio—which temporarily included IV Corps of the Army of the Cumberland—to Tennessee to bolster them. The various units, ultimately numbering about 60,000 soldiers, came under the command of George Thomas at Nashville.

Thomas had enough men to deal with Hood, Sherman concluded. He turned back toward Atlanta. For weeks, he had lobbied Grant and Washington hard with an alternative plan. "I propose we break up the road from Chattanooga and strike out with wagons for Milledgeville Millen and Savannah," Sherman wrote on October 9. "Until we can repopulate Georgia it is useless to occupy it, but utter destruction of its roads, houses, and people will cripple their military resources. . . . I can make the march and make Georgia howl." Grant and Lincoln had reservations but gave their approval on dark and rainy November 2. Sherman would march to the sea, cut the Confederacy in half once again, and move north into Lee's rear.[24]

The armies that had contended at Atlanta began moving away from each other. The rain that tortured Price's retreat at the beginning on November extended eastward beyond northern Alabama and Middle Tennessee, where it became what historian Wiley Sword later called "a meteorological catastrophe" for Hood.[25] Alabama artilleryman Maxwell recalled "white loblolly mud . . . axle deep" as the army passed through a small belt of Udalf Alfisols in northeastern Alabama that was surrounded by the region's dominant red clay.[26] The Confederates "suffered a great deal from cold," Sgt. Archie Livingston of the 3rd Florida wrote on October 29, "so freezing & cold that it did [seem] to me—I could not stand it. Amid all this some of the Army of Tenn were barefoot. Hundreds were indifferently clad, and without good blankets."[27]

A day earlier, Hood's army had reached the Tennessee River at Decatur,

Alabama. Expecting to rendezvous with Forrest's cavalry, it instead found a tenacious garrison. Hood improvised westward to Tuscumbia, opposite Florence on the far bank. His engineers used the trestles of a destroyed railroad bridge to speed bridge construction. Unfortunately, it began raining on the night of November 1 and, with two breaks, continued for the next ten days. At Clarksville to the north, the Smithsonian weather observer measured 3.57 inches of rain during the period as well as afternoon high temperatures that rose from the fifties to the sixties before reverting. On sunny November 13, Hood's army began crossing the Tennessee, a process that took another rainy week to complete. Snow flurries, the first of the season, fell on the morning of the twenty-first, with more the next day. Altogether, 3.2 inches of precipitation fell at Clarksville while Hood crossed the river, with two-thirds of it on November 18. Nearly 7 inches total fell on Hood's army as it waited to cross the Tennessee.[28]

His hungry, ill-clad, and soaked soldiers suffered greatly. "Winter was now setting in with its severest vigor," Pvt. Thomas Head of the 16th Tennessee wrote on cold November 13, "and many of the men were barefooted and destitute of many other articles of clothing."[29] The crossing itself was excruciating. Sergeant Maxwell remembered "moving on to the bridge after dark" on November 20 "and occupying several hours in crossing, moving a few paces in the bridge, then halting and standing shivering in a drizzling rain, until again a few paces could be gained. Then at the north bank, getting our teams up the steep banks through mud axle deep, by doubling teams and all hands at the wheels."[30] Musician Walter Clark of the 63rd Georgia described "a driving snowstorm in a bitterly cold wind. . . . [M]y face became so thoroughly chilled that the snow that fell on it failed to melt."[31] North of the river the next day, Maj. Gen. Samuel French saw mud "four to twenty inches deep" as well as snow and endured a cold wind. More snow and cold temperatures the next day—the high was 21 degrees in Clarksville—froze the earth "so hard that it bore the wagons." The thaw that followed the next afternoon, with a high of 33 degrees, then turned the soil to goo as his corps reached Columbia. Columns left the roads searching for drier ground in forests and fields. Rain on the twenty-sixth made more mud.[32]

The Federals, meanwhile, used their control of the regional railroad network to shift troops ahead of Hood. While Thomas exercised overall command in Nashville, Schofield oversaw the troops massing at the most advanced position to the south. Pulaski, Tennessee, was seventy-five miles from the state capital. Schofield's force there included the Army of the Cumberland's IV Corps as well as part of his own Army of the Ohio. His orders were to delay Hood until Thomas could concentrate his command, which would include A. J. Smith's corps when it finally arrived from Missouri.[33] As the Federals waited, they endured the same cold rain and cool temperatures as their foes. George Morris described taking refuge from the rain in a cave on November 1, then slogging twelve miles through mud and rain the next day. By the fourth, "the roads were so bad that it gave them more work getting the wagons along. The rain continued all day and we moved slowly." A "perfect hurricane" followed on the sixth, and rain followed them to Pulaski.[34] Once there, soldiers discovered rising waterways. At Columbia, more rain flooded the Duck River, destroyed a bridge, and temporarily cut off supplies from Nashville. Rain on November 20 gave way to snow the next morning.[35] It did not stick, according to Pvt. Jenkin Jones of the 6th Wisconsin Battery, because "the wind blew it all away. Kept getting colder and colder." Jones crawled into his tent with "an iron skillet filled with coals" and "prepared for a severe night." That night, Clarksville temperatures fell from 24.8 degrees at 9 P.M. to 17 degrees the next morning. "We slept tolerably warm with the exception of feet," he reported. "Ground is all hard. Water froze four inches thick." A brief warming spell gave way to more rain and mud. "Boys skating on ponds, like old times," the artilleryman noted on the twenty-fourth.

Hood's army had been moving north toward them for a week. On that same November 24—the Indian-summer high was 51 degrees—Schofield realized that he had erred in relying on bad weather to slow down the Confederates. When Hood arrived in force at Columbia on rainy if warm November 27, the Union general abandoned his new works, fell back across the flooded Duck River, and burned the bridges. Thomas sent orders for Schofield to retreat to a point north of Franklin on the Harpeth River. Hood resorted to flanking maneuvers. His engineers erected a pontoon bridge east of Columbia. On warm November 29—the afternoon high was 69 degrees—two Confederate corps slipped past Schofield and marched up the Nashville Pike to Spring Hill, thus dividing the retreating Federal force in two between Columbia and Spring Hill.

What followed that warm night remains one of the great mysteries of the war. Somehow, Schofield marched infantry and his train right by the Confederates at Spring Hill and pushed on to Franklin. Participants and historians have argued all manner of blame, from Hood for his vague orders and overconfidence, to the incompetence of corps commanders Maj. Gen. Frank Cheatham and Lt. Gen. Alexander Stewart (and in Cheatham's case alleged drunkenness), to a probably mythical wild party involving officers and local women, to divine intervention. But there were more-basic factors involved. Sunset clearly came at about 4:30 P.M. that late November day, providing Schofield with the cover of darkness.[36] And, as Capt. Alexis Cope of the 15th Ohio remembered, there was "a mist covering the low ground between us and the enemy."[37]

Whatever the cause, Hood was furious. The next day, he learned that Schofield was renovating old works on the southern edge of Franklin, his back to the rain-swollen Harpeth River. The Federals had no pontoons and needed to buy time to repair the town's bridges—one destroyed by the swift flood—and get the train across. That afternoon, Hood arrived south of Franklin. It was tragically beautiful, sunny and clear after a week of gloom and rain, with a high around 61 degrees. Hood ignored pleas to flank the town and instead ordered a direct assault over two miles of mostly open ground. Subordinates such as Major General Cleburne deemed it suicide, but the Texan insisted that here was the best chance to wreck Schofield's army before it could escape to Nashville. A similar assault by troops he commanded had succeeded at Gaines' Mill in 1862. But in the end, Cleburne was right. Hood lost up to 6,000 men, including Cleburne and five other generals, while failing to pierce the Federal lines for more than a few moments. At some points on the battlefield, dead Johnny Rebs lay seven deep. That night, the bridges were repaired and Schofield escaped toward Nashville.[38]

Rain returned on December 2, as if the skies wept. In Nashville, heavy rain and ankle-deep mud made labor difficult for Union soldiers constructing entrenchments in anticipation of a Confederate attack. At least it was still warm, about 71 degrees on the first and 65 degrees the next afternoon. December 3, however, ushered in four days of cooler weather, with highs in the fifties and even 44 degrees on December 4. Nighttime lows reached the upper thirties. The mud was terrible for marching, yet to the south, Hood decided to go on to Nashville, arriving on the third. The Confederates began constructing works at Nashville the next day; Hood hoped that Thomas might come out to strike his positions. As historian Richard McMurry notes, the five miles of entrenchments were too extensive for the roughly 25,000 soldiers Hood had left. Nor did he possess enough ammunition for a siege.

Skirmishing and artillery firing followed, but for the moment, both generals were content to be patient. Thomas wanted to marshal all his available forces before assailing the Army of Tennessee. A. J. Smith's divisions had just arrived, but Thomas worried that he did not have enough cavalry to deal with Forrest. Administration officials were less sanguine. Lincoln and Stanton in Washington as well as Grant at Petersburg all fumed at the general's cautious inaction. Lincoln compared Thomas to Rosecrans and McClellan. Grant wanted him to act as well. The two men had had an uneasy relationship since that wet 1863 night in Chattanooga. Now the general in chief castigated him for not going out to fight an inferior force, fretting that Hood might slip north to the Ohio River if Thomas did not act soon. Thomas, in response, argued that gunboats on the Cumberland River were enough to keep Hood south of it. On December 6, Grant ordered Thomas to fight. When the general still did not, Grant began planning to fire him.[39]

At that point, bad weather intervened. The same massive arctic system that struck Virginia with icy fury dipped through the Midwest to hit Middle Tennessee as well. Nashville and the two warring armies were squarely in its path. At 7 A.M. on cloudy and showery December 7, the temperature west of the city in Clarksville was 63 degrees, with rain and winds from the southwest. By 2 P.M., the mercury had dropped to 37 degrees, a 26-degree decrease. Temperatures collapsed over the next five days as the massive arctic air mass behind the front settled into the Cumberland Valley, with winds from the west. Afternoon highs December 8–12 were 25 degrees, 21 degrees, 24 degrees, 16 degrees, and 22 degrees respectively. Nights were worse. Over those same five days, morning lows were 19 degrees, 18.6 degrees, 18.8 degrees, 8.2 degrees, and an incredible 3 degrees on the twelfth. Local civilians described them as the coldest days in recent memory. Along with bone-chilling cold came more precipitation on December 9, starting as rain out of the southeast before becoming freezing rain, sleet, and finally snow mixed with sleet. By nightfall, three inches of snow covered a sheet of ice two inches thick, with frozen ground beneath it all. Neither army could move. The sun disappeared until the twelfth.[40]

Conditions on the line were excruciating. Icy ground and below-freezing temperatures made it next to impossible to move even on foot from place to place without slipping and falling. Artillery and supply wagons were immobilized. Skirmishing and picket firing all but ended. Gloveless and coatless, Forrest's cavalry tore up railroad tracks on December 9 and December

10, but only with difficulty. Sleep was impossible. A hasty issue of Federal overcoats benefited some men, but most Confederates had no coats at all, and 3,500 of them reportedly were barefoot. Soldiers tried to build substantial quarters, but most Federals—dug in farther from nearby woods in a moonscape of entrenchments—could not locate enough material to create more than chimneys and fireplaces. They huddled in their tents near camp stoves or around big fires, often built contrary to orders. Tentless Confederates, meanwhile, dug holes big enough for a mess to sleep around a fire, sometimes under carpets taken from area homes. On December 10, Hood contracted part of his lines simply so his men could cut wood to burn. Available firewood, nonetheless, started to run out on the thirteenth; the armies had denuded the front for perhaps five miles and stripped properties of fence rails. Luckily, that was the first day that temperatures rose, reaching 40 degrees at 2 P.M. and near 50 degrees after dark. Deep mud returned too as snow and ice melted. By then, pickets had grown so desperate to avoid a freezing death that they not only built fires in defiance of their officers but also concluded a truce so they all could go out and search for wood.[41]

Years later, the 65th Ohio's Lt. Col. Wilbur Hinman wrote that "the authorities at Washington, who continued to clamor day and night for an advance, should have sent fifty thousand pair of skates, which alone would have made it possible to execute their orders."[42] Hinman correctly pointed out that the administration—and Grant—refused to accept the cold and ice as excuses for Thomas's seeming inaction. The general in chief usually paid no heed to weather, whatever the consequences for his men. On December 13, he ordered Maj. Gen. John A. Logan to Nashville. If Thomas still had not moved when Logan arrived, he was to assume command. The next day, Grant himself left for Nashville. He got as far as Washington when he learned that Thomas had struck at last.[43]

A break in the weather allowed Thomas to attack Hood. December 14 saw temperatures rise into the forties, with the wind shifting to the north. As the ice melted, a dense fog developed, blocking the vision of the opposing armies. Extensive mud and slop deepened beneath. The next day was much warmer, with a morning low of 46 degrees and a remarkable afternoon high of 60 degrees. Thick fog again shielded Federal preparations. Once it began to lift after 7 A.M., Thomas sent out two divisions from his left as a diversion and dispatched his cavalry to sweep Hood's left. Federal infantry under Smith and Schofield then struck the Confederate left hard after noon, while IV Corps assaulted the Confederate right. Historian James McPherson memorably compares Thomas to a boxer, leading with a left jab and then swinging a powerful roundhouse punch with his right. Smashed in on their left and with most of their strongest positions overrun, the Confederates retreated. Under a full moon, they hastily dug a more compact line a mile to the south. Temperatures remained in the upper fifties overnight, facilitating their labor. The next morning began at 59 degrees. Thomas repeated his plan, striking the Confederates' right first, then launching Schofield to deliver a hammer blow on their left. Dark clouds arrived in the afternoon with a smattering of rain. Toward dark, Hood's left collapsed. His army retreated south through the night.[44]

Over the next two weeks, Hood's mangled, ragged, and hungry army staggered back to Alabama and the safety of the Tennessee River, pursued hard by Federal cavalry and often afraid to rest. Skirmishing in the rear was a daily occurrence. As if to add more pain to Confederate wounds, the weather turned bad again during the retreat, in a manner reminiscent of the miserable conditions in the days before the Battle of Stones River two years earlier. Once again, a wider midwestern system trending south and east was the culprit. In Middle Tennessee, the rain of December 16 inaugurated a six-day deluge out of the northwest that brought nearly three inches of rain and a half inch of snow to Middle Tennessee. Local waterways rose, initially delaying a Federal bridge over the Harpeth. Fields around Spring Hill flooded. Mud mixed with road dust grew so deep that at times men and wagons could hardly move through it. Soldiers blue and gray lost shoes, and rocks sliced open their exposed feet. The commander of the 2nd US Colored Brigade estimated that half of his men needed new shoes before they reached Murfreesboro due to the ankle-deep mud. At night, tents flooded. Both armies were soaked and unable to dry out.

Daytime temperatures at least stayed unusually warm in Clarksville through December 17 before falling to 37 degrees on December 19—the day Hood's army crossed the Duck River and burned the bridges. It was 34 degrees on the twentieth, 30.5 degrees on the snowy and dark winter solstice, and 16.5 degrees on the twenty-second. Rain froze on trees along the road. That night, the mercury fell to 10.5 degrees. The high was 28 degrees on frosty December 23, when Thomas finally got infantry across the Duck. A brief warming trend created new obstacles of mud, as did rain on Christmas. By then, Confederate unit cohesion had all but fallen apart. The high was 37 degrees on December 28, the day that Hood's men—only half of those who had crossed the Tennessee River at Florence—recrossed the Tennessee and brought an end to the campaign.[45]

Halleck pushed Thomas to continue on and catch Hood. Thomas replied on December 21: "We cannot control the elements. . . . [P]ursuing an enemy through an exhausted country, over mud roads, completely sogged with heavy rains, is no child's play."[46] His men agreed. In their official reports, officers emotionally reminded the brass how their men had suffered. George Cooper, Thomas's medical director, maintained that "probably in no part of the war have the men suffered more from inclement weather than in the month of December, 1864." He continued, "the result of this weather and the hard marching was . . . severe infections of the pulmonary viscera, rheumatism, and diarrheas, which served to fill the hospitals in this vicinity to their utmost capacity."[47] After the war, veterans likened conditions during their pursuit of Hood to those at Valley Forge, and asserted that the remnant Army of Tennessee only escaped them because of the heavy rain, deep mud, and swollen streams.

But the Confederates hardly felt lucky. "The morale of the army was shattered if not destroyed," Walter Clark later wrote. "If the soliloquy of a gaunt Tennessean as he rose from a fall in the mud on the retreat fairly represented the sentiment of his comrades, it was badly shattered. He is reported to have said: 'Ain't we in a —— of a fix, a one-eyed president, a one-legged general, and a one-horse Confederacy.'"[48]

When Sherman sent Schofield and IV Corps off to Tennessee to defend it against Hood, he reorganized the troops retained in Georgia. The remaining two Cumberland corps, including Hooker's old command, became the Army of Georgia, under the direct command of Maj. Gen. Henry Slocum. Major General Howard maintained command of the Army of the Tennessee, consolidating its three corps into two. With Maj. Gen. Judson Kirkpatrick's division of cavalry, Sherman now commanded about 62,000 hardened veterans after he culled his larger army group of both sick men and bad officers. With those four corps and the cavalry division, he prepared to march toward Savannah via the state capital at Milledgeville.[49]

The Federal return to Atlanta was leisurely and devastatingly destructive. Cassville went up in flames on November 5. Rome suffered the same fate five days later. The weather remained cool. On wet November 9, Sherman issued marching orders in Kingston for the coming campaign.[50] He instructed his men to "forage liberally on the country," seizing horses, mules, and wagons from the rich, "who are usually hostile." Their commanders received the power to take in "able-bodied" African Americans as pioneers, providing resources were available to feed them. They also were to "destroy mills, houses, cotton-gins, &c." in areas where enemy guerrillas appeared and "enforce a devastation more or less relentless according to the measure of such hostility."[51] This was the Meridian Campaign writ large.

While there were no bushwhackers operating in Atlanta, that city felt Federal hostility first. As early as November 11, fires broke out within its limits. On the fourteenth—a "cool and pleasant" day, according to Iowan Alexander Downing—Sherman's men set fire to what was left of Atlanta.[52] The next morning was cool, clear, and dry, with solid roads. Warm temperatures and clouds appeared in the afternoon. As the city continued to blaze, Sherman left for Savannah, 285 miles away. The men marched at an easy pace for 1864 veterans, usually covering an average of twelve miles a day. They often stopped to destroy railroads tracks and buildings while foragers gathered food. The two wings of the army soon diverged, successfully confusing the Confederates as to their ultimate destination. Howard's army initially went south to Lovejoy Station and Jonesboro, as if Macon was its goal. On November 22, the only serious action of the march took place at Griswoldville, east of Macon, when Howard swept aside a sad assortment of old men and boys in the local militia. Slocum's wing bore more easterly toward Augusta before turning south toward Milledgeville, which it occupied on November 23. His men encountered little resistance. As autumn passed, the two corps in each wing also spread out, maximizing food gathering and increasing the levels of vandalism directed against a largely female civilian population.[53]

From the first day out of Atlanta, good weather was Sherman's greatest ally. "'This is the perfection of campaigning,'" Sherman reportedly told aide Henry Hitchcock on November 18, "'such weather and such roads as this.'"[54] As participants chronicled and historians such as Lisa Brady and Ted Steinberg have reaffirmed, weather conditions were ideal for the March to the Sea. Afternoon highs reached into the fifties and sixties during the rest of November, if records on the South Carolina coast are any guide. Exact readings from middle Georgia are lacking, but in general, temperatures at Beaufort and Hilton Head—both sites of diligent army weather observers—are 4.5 degrees warmer than Milledgeville's. If that held true in 1864, then highs along the march reached into the sixties between November 15 and November 19 and again after November 26.[55]

Moreover, rain fell only during one stretch of November. Mist and fog on the night of the eighteenth lasted through the wet and dreary morning of the twenty-first as the two armies struggled through hilly piedmont terrain, which became slippery red-clay mud mixed with sand. The inevitable bogged-down trains, artillery, and driven herds of cattle followed. Hitchcock described gooey ruts up to two feet in depth, while soldiers splashed through mud to their ankles. The rain also heralded a brief forty-eight-hour cold snap out of the northwest, between the morning of the Battle of Griswoldville on November 22 and the morning of November 24. This was the leading edge of the same system that brought misery to Hood's Confederates at Florence. Highs in middle Georgia dipped close to freezing, snow flurries blew about on the night of the twenty-second and the following day, and the morning low on the twenty-third—the day that Milledgeville surrendered—most likely was around 20 degrees. To the south in Macon, LeRoy Gresham recorded 17 degrees at 8 A.M. and a high of 34 degrees two days later. Soldiers noted optimistically that frozen soil at least eliminated the mud problem. Sgt. Rice Bull of the 123rd New York explained that his comrades did not mind being cold as long as they were dry. Marching kept them warm during the day, while big fires did the same at night.

The cold snap ended soon enough. Rising daytime temperatures entered the seventies at month's end, along with enough rain on November 29 to require corduroying. As Lisa Brady points out, however, it was the region's rivers, wet banks, and swamps that provided the majority of work for Sherman's growing cadres of African American pioneers, men who sought freedom though reshaping the environment that they had worked differently while enslaved.[56]

The foggy beginning of December saw Federal columns more than halfway to the coast, and the day warm enough for men to seek shade under the region's pines. Slocum was near Louisville, and Howard approached Millen. Beaufort and Savannah temperatures are routinely the same on average and provide good estimates of conditions during the second half of the march. One can assume that the month's first week saw 70-degree readings. As highs slipped back into the upper sixties, Federal infantry kept moving, eating up great quantities of food while wrecking railroads and burning cotton, barns, mills, public buildings, and homes. The sight of a handful of emaciated Federal escapees from Andersonville Prison in Milledgeville erased any sympathy for Georgians. Little now slowed Sherman's troops other than occasional skirmishing and the sandy gray Aquod Spodosols of the Georgia coast. Drizzle, beginning on the night of December 6 and lasting through most of December 7, left the roads bad enough to require corduroying, especially when the ground was already swampy. Hitchcock expressed amazement at the odd soil, crusty on top but a veritable quicksand below. Trailing behind the soldiers were numbers of African Americans seeking freedom and protection. On the eighth—the hottest day of the month, with an afternoon high of 80 degrees—corps commander Jefferson C. Davis infamously pulled up his pontoon bridge over Ebenezer Creek, abandoning hundreds of these refugees. Many drowned trying to swim the rain-chilled river, while others fell prey to Confederate guerrillas.

A northeast wind and five days of cooler temperatures followed. Highs fell into the forties as Sherman's men reached Hardee's entrenchments and 13,000 Confederate troops outside Savannah. The city's swamps limited solid access and made its defenses stronger. Hardee's engineers also had flooded area rice fields. Blocked by the Rebels and nature from the Atlantic and the Federal navy offshore, Sherman sent troops to seize Fort McAllister, an earthen fortification overlooking the Ogeechee River and access to the sea. Temperatures continued to slide; the morning low in Macon on December 12 was 17 degrees at 9:45 A.M., rising perhaps to 38 degrees in the afternoon. The next day was warmer when the fort fell, and temperatures rose into the seventies on the fifteenth. The navy begin to resupply Sherman, as the swampy rice-producing lowlands west of Savannah had not filled Federal bellies as well as the cornfields of middle Georgia. Hardee refused to surrender, but on December 20, he led his men into South Carolina. The next day began with a thunderstorm and remained showery as Sherman accepted Savannah's surrender.[57]

Sherman's men now rested after their long march. Their letters home were exuberant, full of pride and accounts of how well they had eaten off a Georgia countryside that had recovered from drought in 1864. Temperatures fluctuated. On December 22, Loy Gresham recorded a reading of 29 degrees in Macon, while in Savannah, Frederick Sherwood of the 50th Illinois recorded an inch of ice that night. The ground again froze, a harsh reality for men under canvas. But the mercury rose into the fifties and then sixties starting on Christmas Eve, with that festive evening brightened by massive campfires. Highs hit 72 degrees for a grand review on the twenty-seventh before declining again. Rain, meanwhile, set in on Christmas Day, lasting into the afternoon on December 28 before falling again on the morning of New Year's Eve. That night, Sgt. Jesse Bean of the 4th Minnesota measured a half inch of ice in the woods. Federals hopeful of a long occupation began building huts out of scrounged boards or at least attached fireplaces and chimneys to their tents.[58]

Lincoln and Grant had worried about Sherman's scheme at its genesis, but his veterans had triumphed. As Lisa Brady maintains, Sherman wrecked middle Georgia's "physical, economic, and cultural landscapes" and reduced residents' "improvements" and "civilization" back to a state of nature. He had proven that the Confederacy could do nothing to stop him.[59] It would be a mistake, however, to assume that it could have been easy to march across Georgia under any circumstances. Sherman knew that. "The weather through our march was perfect," he reported, "only two days of rain from Atlanta to the outskirts of Savannah; the roads in fine order."[60] Ted Steinburg was right to conclude that "but for the weather, . . . Sherman's march could have gone down as one of the most insane misadventures in the annals of military history."[61] Instead, in David Ludlum's words, "Yankee weather" prevailed.[62]

Chapter 24

Tears of Rain

The War Ends, December 1864–May 1865

By Christmas 1864, the Confederacy was imploding. Missouri, northern Arkansas, and the Indian Territory remained firmly in Federal hands. Thomas has defended Nashville and was driving Hood's Confederates from the state. Sherman's cocky veterans rested in Savannah after crossing Georgia with ill intent. Stalemate continued in Virginia, although only until the weather cleared enough to permit more campaigning against Lee's supply lines.

While Grant waited impatiently for the winter mud to dry, he commissioned yet another auxiliary campaign designed to shorten the war. The target this time was Fort Fisher, a massive earthen structure standing at the mouth of the Cape Fear River near the city of Wilmington, North Carolina, the Confederacy's last open doorway to the rest of the world. Trusted David Porter would supply the military transports for the attacking troops as well as the warships to pound the fort. Competent Maj. Gen. Godfrey Weitzel, one of Butler's corps commanders, would lead an expeditionary force of two divisions to take Fort Fisher. It would be Fort Henry again, only writ large. Unfortunately, the operation quickly went off the rails. Butler pulled rank and demanded to lead the troops himself. He then came up with the odd notion of exploding a steamer near the fort in order to soften up its defenses. Porter liked the idea, as did Lincoln. Grant did not, but he had little choice than to allow Butler extra time to pack the USS *Louisiana* with black powder.

On December 10, just as the fleet prepared to sail, the same massive winter storm out of the Midwest that paralyzed Nashville and Petersburg struck Hampton Roads. The ships could not leave until the fourteenth. Butler's transports arrived off Fort Fisher as afternoon temperatures rose into the seventies. Porter's warships turned up on December 19 after taking on coal and water. As luck would have it, a ferocious nor'easter drove the transports back to Beaufort, North Carolina. Grant complained that "three days of fine weather were squandered."[1] The nor'easter lasted through the twenty-second, giving Braxton Bragg time to send a division of reinforcements to the garrison. As the storm finally abated, Porter exploded the *Louisiana*. It did no harm to the fort, nor did a massive naval bombardment the next day. On a warm Christmas morning, supported by yet another bombardment, a Federal division landed, captured a battery, but concluded that Fort Fisher could be taken. Despite Porter's entreaties and direct orders from Grant, Butler quit, recalling the troops. He not only worried about Confederate reinforcements but feared the arrival of another storm.[2] Edson J. Harkness later declared that he was "surprised, for everything appeared propitious. . . . Little or no surf was breaking on the beach. Nothing indicated bad weather."[3] But a new storm that night dumped nearly an inch of rain and disrupted the withdrawal enough that Butler left a brigade behind. Those men endured torrential rain and sleet on the misty beach until dawn on December 27. The expedition had accomplished nothing except giving Grant the final excuse he needed to fire Butler and replace him with Maj. Gen. Edward E. O. Ord.[4]

Two weeks later, Grant and Ord sent the expedition back to Fort Fisher, this time under Maj. Gen. Alfred Terry. Heavy gales delayed the rendezvous with Porter at Beaufort until cloudy January 8, 1865. Winter weather, largely out of the northwest, remained stormy enough to delay Terry's arrival four days.[5] Even then, as Harkness remembered, "the waves . . . swept the shores so heavily, and night was so near, that Porter postponed disembarkment."[6] The next day brought better winds and skies, with a high of 58 degrees. With good weather at last, Terry landed without incident. Two days later, under effective covering fire from Federal gunboats, he forced the surrender of Fort Fisher. Drizzle fell the following day as a party of Federal soldiers accidentally exploded the captured stronghold's powder magazine, senselessly killing another two hundred men. In the end, raw coastal winter weather, coupled with Butler's questionable leadership, briefly delayed—but not prevent—the fall of the Confederacy's last connection to the Old World.[7]

Four days after the fall of Fort Fisher, Sherman issued orders for a march into South Carolina, the cradle of secession. As with the March to the Sea, he first had to convince his superiors. Grant worried about the roads and wanted to move the western army group to Petersburg by water. Sherman countered that it would take longer to collect transports than it would for him to march to Virginia. Grant finally agreed.[8] Sherman shuttled O. O. Howard's Right Wing—XVII Corps and three divisions from the XV Corps—to Beaufort, South Carolina, by water. This wing would flank and drive away the vastly outnumbered Confederates who waited behind earthworks and flooded fields north of Savannah. After that, XIV Corps and XX Corps, composing the Left Wing under Henry Slocum, would cross the Savannah River and move through rice fields on the so-called Union Causeway. Sherman expected to reach central North Carolina in two months, where he would join not only Terry but also John Schofield's command, newly returned from Tennessee.[9]

Sherman's conviction that he could move quickly through the Carolinas was based in part upon his unrealistic hope that the surprisingly good weather he had enjoyed in Georgia would continue. After a cold and wet start to the new year, with a 7 A.M. reading of 25 degrees up the coast in Hilton Head, conditions along the Georgia coastline had been pleasant enough. Weather historian David Ludlum observes that January 1865 was the coldest month of the war in the region, with an average temperatures almost 6 degrees lower than usual. Even then, afternoon highs generally rose into the fifties, while nightly temperatures stayed above freezing.

Rain, however, was to become the crucial factor in the Carolinas Campaign. Nearly 4 inches fell that month at Hilton Head, almost 4.8 inches at Beaufort, and even more appeared inland. Sherman had been lucky in Georgia but now would pay for that good fortune in South Carolina. For many years after, locals spoke of the high water of January 1865 as the "Sherman Flood."

Rain first appeared on January 5 and January 6 and returned as storms on January 9 and January 10. A doctor in Hilton Head recorded a half inch on the tenth, while flooding developed from Augusta north to Camden. The storms also produced wind and waves that impeded the Right Wing's water transport and stopped the Left Wing in its muddy tracks south of the river.[10] "We were to have started by January 10," Sgt. Rice Bull wrote, "but a great storm struck us, and for three days the rain continued and was heavy. All the vicinity of Savannah was afloat. The river rose rapidly and overflowed its banks. The currents was so rapid that the pontoon bridge connecting the city with the South Carolina side was in danger of breaking. Before we could cross, the bridge had to be strengthened; it was not safe until January 16."[11]

Three dry days passed before the first regiments of Slocum's wing could move across the Savannah River. "The heavy rains of January," Sherman reported, "had swelled the river, broken the pontoon bridge, and overflowed the whole 'bottom,' so that the causeway was four feet under water, and Gen. Slocum was compelled to look higher up for a passage over the Savannah River. He moved up to Sister's Ferry, but even there the river, with its overflowing bottoms, was near three miles wide."[12] On the eve of the march, soldiers noted warming temperatures and gathering clouds. At midnight on January 19, it began to rain heavily. More showers around noon slowed the advance until the next day.[13] "We were pretty well drenched when we halted," Bull wrote. His brigade stopped until January 24, waiting for the rest of the Left Wing to move up through the deepening mud. "It rained almost constantly," he continued. "The river rose rapidly and overflowed its banks with the low country back of the river submerged in many places."[14]

Rain and unseasonable warmth continued through windy January 23, followed by colder days that saw highs briefly revert to the forties and fifties. Both wings encountered roads through bottomless mud, swampy quicksand, and low rice fields that required frequent corduroying and repair. At times, troops could only progress by filing along dikes and the flooded causeway. XX Corps commander Alpheus Williams noted that, at one point, his corduroy logs began to float. At another juncture, he found forty wagons bogged down and the mules nearly drowned in mud. Draft horses and mules floundered and died everywhere, requiring men to stop and drag them out. Soldiers endured wind, soaked uniforms, wood too wet to burn, and beds on inundated earth.[15] The mud itself changed, from the red clay that predominated in Georgia and South Carolina to the sandy Spodosols that ring Savannah like a citadel's wall.

Writing home on January 23, Major General Williams wrote, "I fear . . . we have a terrible job before us." He was prophetic.[16] The balance of January remained dry, cold enough in the mornings to produce thin layers of ice up to a half inch thick here and there on standing water, but warm during the afternoons. Slocum could not get all of his corps across the swollen, flooded river until the beginning of February. And that was just the start of troubles. As historian Joseph Glatthaar observes, it rained half of the days between January 27 and March 10, the entire period that XX Corps spent in South Carolina. At nearby Hilton Head, the army's weather observer measured 3.95 total inches in January and an additional 1.40 inches by February 15, as Sherman's men approached the state capital. His counterpart at Beaufort measured even more, 4.76 inches in January, far above normal. North in Camden, a Confederate observer recorded a whopping 10.70 inches of rain during January. Temperatures generally reached the fifties and sixties, other than a cold snap between February 6 and February 11 that brought a bit of snow on the ninth. The air temperature was not especially cold except during a few mornings, but it was lower than normal. More importantly, it felt cold to wet soldiers encased in mud.[17]

What Sherman called "the real march" opened on February 1, when his four corps began moving north against Maj. Gen. Joe Wheeler's cavalry and a division of Confederate infantry at the Salkehatchee River. A Federal division drove them away. A week after that, cavalry clashed at Aiken, with Wheeler securing a minor victory. Aside from these fights, Sherman's real enemies during the first half of February were the terrain and the mud, with their potency augmented by Wheeler's pioneers, who burned bridges and felled trees across roads. At some points, swamps were waist deep. Sherman's soldiers and African American pioneers responded with veteran skills and usually kept the columns moving, if not as quickly as their commander had hoped. His chief engineer later reported that his men had corduroyed four hundred miles of roads and reworked roads twice that length.[18] "So well organized were our pioneer battalions," Sherman wrote, "and so strong and intelligent our men, that obstructions seemed only to quicken their progress. Felled trees were removed and bridges rebuilt by the heads of columns before the rear could close up."[19]

It was not that simple, of course. Corduroying through lowlands, sticky clay, and rainy swamps was time consuming, exhausting, and frustrating when a few hours of traffic meant additional labor to repair the corduroy and manhandle animals and wagons that got stuck anyway. Heavy rain and swift currents also created headaches for the soldiers charged with constructing pontoon bridges over wide, flooded waterways. And pontoons were useless through the low country's swamps and flooded rice fields. Swamps meant wading through numbingly cold and dank water, often to the knees and sometimes up to the shoulders. Water, mud, and hard use ruined uniforms and shoes.[20] Yet the men had kept moving, much to the amazement of a Confederate high command that had relied upon weather and terrain, rather than almost nonexistant manpower, to stop them.

Lt. Gen. William J. Hardee had expected the Union march to stall at the flooded Salkahatchee. Gen. Joseph Johnston also was impressed by enemy progress. According to Jacob Cox, Johnston told him after the war, "when I learned that Sherman not only had started, but was marching through those very swamps, at the rate of thirteen miles a day, making corduroy roads every foot of the way, I made up my mind that there had been no such army since the days of Julius Caesar."[21] Four years of dealing with red clay in all kinds of weather had proven an effective teacher.

As in Georgia, Sherman's men also foraged extensively, looted, and destroyed much of South Carolina's infrastructure. They saw little they liked, either in the land, the farms, or the people. Indeed, destruction grew to new heights as his soldiers encountered whites, especially of the planter class, in the state they blamed for starting the war.[22] "The whole army was burning with the insatiable desire to wreck vengeance on South Carolina," Drummer William Bircher wrote. "Marched twenty miles and destroyed all the houses, barns, and fences on our route."[23] They burned towns, too, a dozen in the lower half of the state. That destruction culminated with the burning of the biggest political target of all, Columbia, on February 17. Much has been written since that day about who started the fires, with authors alternately fingering fleeing Confederates, freed Union prisoners of war, the recently enslaved, or drunken soldiers. Some Federals certainly acted out their malice that evening in a manner reminiscent of the sack of Fredericksburg, even as others tried to quell the blaze. All of the groups mentioned probably were involved to some degree, although no one ever took responsibility.[24]

What is not in dispute is the role that the weather played. February 17 was sunny and warm, with the wind howling from the southwest and west and pushing the fires to the east. Surgeon James Gaskill described a "terrific" wind that blew up during that afternoon. "The leaves took fire, which it was impossible to arrest & our Div. was driven to seek refuge in an open field. The air became laden with smoke sand & flying leaves. Several men were overpowered and fainted as if from suffocation. The sun was scarcely visible. Early in the day the rebs before leaving set fire to some cotton & buildings containing stores. The gale spread the fire & the city was soon enveloped in smoke & flame. Most of the city—in fact nearly the entire business part, was consumed." The next morning, a third of Columbia lay in ruins, "a smouldering wreck."[25]

While Sherman's westerners waded through South Carolina's dank high water, the eastern armies spent the first weeks of 1865 trying to stay warm and dry in the muddy or else frozen works at Petersburg. David Ludlum points out that the winter of 1864–65 was the coldest of Virginia's four wartime winters, with January and February 1865 averages at Fort Monroe below normal. January opened with frigid temperatures of 29 degrees at Georgetown during the afternoon of New Year's Day and 18 degrees the next morning. Soldiers faced sharp winds and frozen ground. Two inches of snow fell late on the third, extending north and west into the Shenandoah. January 6 actually would be the warmest day of the month until the thirty-first. The sixth also brought the execution of a deserter, more rain, and thawing mud. "A more lonely or disagreeable day I never saw," New York artilleryman Pvt. Alexander Rose wrote, "and to night I feel sad and everything looks gloomy."[26]

More gloom was in the forecast. January 8 started out at 16 degrees. North of Richmond, farmers brushed aside snow to their shoe tops and cut ice up to three inches thick from local waterways. Clouds and rain briefly returned to the frozen Valley on January 9 and to Petersburg the next wet day. Union provost marshal Marsena Patrick complained about deep mud on the tenth, while Confederate James Albright complained of high water and flooded trenches. Lt. George Cary of the 1st Maine assured his brother that locals could not remember a worse winter. In the Shenandoah, Pvt. William Wilson of the 12th Virginia Cavalry described thunder, swollen rivers, and snow to his belly. Snow continued in the mountains through January 17, but at Petersburg and Richmond, a bright if frosty snap began on January 11, lasting six days until flurries fell on the seventeenth. Highs fluctuated in the thirties and forties during that stretch.[27]

But January 19 was "a miserably cold day," according to Pvt. John Haley, "overcast and gloomy. The very air seemed laden with sadness and uneasiness, as cheerless as a graveyard."[28] In Richmond, J. B. Jones agreed. The nineteenth—Robert E. Lee's birthday—was alive with rumors that the Confederate Senate had made him general of all the Confederate armies. The weather was cold—29 degrees at 2 P.M.—and ominous. Jones wrote, "the day has grown dark and cold, indicating snow, and a dismal gloom rests upon the faces of the increasing party of croakers." After a brief clearing on January 20, with a morning low of 15 degrees, the twenty-first was a "dark, cold, sleety day, with rain. Troopers from the army," Jones reported, "have icicles hanging from their hats and caps, and their clothes covered with frost, and dripping." Precipitation doused campfires. Sleet and rain, extending west into the mountains, continued on January 22, "another day of sleet and gloom. The pavements are almost impassable from the enamel of ice; icicles hang from the houses, and the trees are bent down with the weight of frost. . . . It rained very fast all day yesterday, and I apprehended the railroad bridges have been destroyed in many places." The cold rain lasted, which, along with the appearance of Union peace commissioner Francis Preston Blair, worried the diehard Jones. "This weather, bad news, etc. etc.," he wrote, "predispose both the people and the army for *peace*—while the papers are filled with the acts of leniency of Sherman at Savannah, and his forbearance to interfere with the slaves."[29]

At last, the rain and sleet stopped on January 24, but what Brig. Gen. Robert McAllister called "a real northern winter" followed.[30] Temperatures fell steadily to a bone-chilling 9 degrees on the morning of the twenty-eighth, rising to 21 degrees in Georgetown that afternoon. The day was so cold that Jones walked around Richmond searching for a thermometer. In a telling commentary on both Confederate supply and meteorology, he could not find one. Flurries continued, having begun the previous day. Temperatures started to rise, up to 42 degrees at the end of the month, with clear blue skies. In Washington, not far from the frozen Potomac, the House of Representatives passed the Thirteenth Amendment, ending slavery in the United States, and sent it to the states for ratification. That same bright day, Confederate commissioners, including Vice Pres. Alexander Stephens, arrived at Grant's headquarters, requesting a meeting with Lincoln and Secretary of State Seward in the aftermath of Blair's trip to Richmond. Lincoln and Seward met with the Confederates on the steamer *River Queen* on cloudy February 3, without reaching any resolution. Rain and snow fell briefly, but to no account.[31]

Expecting this summit to fail, Grant prepared to resume operations on the Richmond-Petersburg line. Only the absence of Phil Sheridan's command and "the fact that the winter had been one of heavy rains, and the roads were impassable for artillery and teams," had held him back so far. "It was necessary to wait until they had dried sufficiently to enable us to move the wagon-trains and artillery necessary to the efficiency of an army operating in the enemy's country."[32] He decided to launch another limited operation against Lee's supply line. While II Corps and V Corps held back the Confederate infantry, Federal cavalry would hit the Boydton Plank Road and destroy enemy supply trains. The Federals moved out on February 5, a clear and cold day with a Georgetown high of 38 degrees. That afternoon, the Confederates struck back near Hatcher's Run. Temperatures fell overnight down to 23 degrees at daybreak. Cold rain and then sleet began to fall. The two warring forces—cold and soaked to the skin—attacked and counterattacked as the weather worsened. By nightfall, cold and wet Federals held a section of the road. Snow and freezing rain continued to fall overnight. Uniforms and blankets froze. Unable to build fires until daylight, soldiers erected brush arbors. Four inches of snow lay on the ground at sunrise, and icicles hung from tree limbs. That afternoon, V Corps took Dabney's Mill as freezing rain and sleet pounded the battlefield.[33]

In the face of some of the war's most miserable fighting, Grant extended his lines to Hatcher's Run and temporarily interdicted Lee's supply line, but the Union forces could not hold the road. He decided to wait for spring, Sheridan, and Sherman after all. Artillery and sniping again replaced movement and pitched battles. Bitter morning lows of 6 degrees on both February 13 and February 14—the coldest of the winter—seemed to confirm his decision. Rain and sleet struck Petersburg on the fifteenth. Temperatures rose into the forties that afternoon, inaugurating a new cycle of daytime thaw and nightly refreezing that persisted until the twenty-fourth, when the afternoon high rose to 60 degrees and stayed near that mark for the rest of the month. Rain fell every day during that period save one.[34]

To the south, Sherman kept moving and soon entered hillier terrain. Although the rain halted and highs rose back into the fifties on February 19, the "Sherman Flood" persisted. Pvt. William Westervelt of the 17th New York Zouaves described how a hundred men dragged wagons out of "heavy" roads and up steep hills, "where the wet clay was about as slippery as grease. . . . [W]oe to the unlucky man who lost his footing and fell. He was apt to be trampled by all the men who were behind him, or run over by the wagon." They found the Wateree River "swollen by the most recent rains, and the current was running like a millrace."[35]

Under Sherman's direction, details pulled teams and wagons up the steep clay back and onto a new corduroy road. Engineers erected a pontoon bridge only to see it washed away by the rapid current and driftwood. Yet the weather remained relatively pleasant until rain returned near dark on February 23, lasting with occasional halts into March 4. Soldiers again spent their days getting wheeled vehicles through muck that varied from six inches to six feet deep. It was bad at the front of the column, but even worse in the rear. After dark, men slept on wet ground or else sat up through the night. Poorly fed on coffee, parched corn, and peas, their clay-stained uniforms and shoes disintegrating from constant wetness, soldiers found the push exhausting.[36] "We marched twelve miles," Drummer Bircher wrote on March 1. "The roads were filled with broken fencerails for the entire length of our march, some lying lengthwise, others crosswise, and others with their ends sticking from two to four feet." That evening, his column left the road and took off overland into the steepest hills they had encountered in the state. "If we never knew before what South Carolina mud was like, we knew it then. It was not only knee-deep, but so sticky that when we set one foot down we could scarcely pull the other out." On March 4, with "at least twelve inches of mud underfoot," his 2nd Minnesota entered North Carolina.[37]

Miles to the north, it was raining in Washington. Drizzle beginning on chilly March 3—the high only reached 44 degrees—turned into a steady, soaking rain that night. It was still coming down hard in the morning, when the 7 A.M. temperature was 42 degrees. A gale blew as thousands of people walked down flooded streets and sidewalks toward the squishy, rain-saturated lawn east of the Capitol. Reporter Noah Brooks later claimed that he had never seen Washington muddier. The showers continued until about 11 A.M., soaking those who waited in the chill air, mud, and standing water. After noon, dignitaries who had been inside the Capitol walked out to the temporary platform at the East Portico, escaping the embarrassment of new Vice Pres. Andrew Johnson's alcohol-fueled ramblings. Cheers cut through the gloom as the president appeared.[38] Michael Shiner, formerly enslaved and for many years a painter at the Washington Navy Yard, wrote in his journal, "before he Came out . . . the wind blew and it rained with out inter mission and as soon as Mr Lincoln came out the wind ceasis blowing an the rain ceased raining and the Sun Came out and it was near as clear as it could be and calm and at the mean time there was a Star comet made its apperence South west rite over the Capitol and it Shined just as bright as it could be."[39] With that dramatic backdrop, Lincoln read a second-inaugural speech full of Old Testament judgment and collective blame until its closing hopes for peace and reconciliation. Many, including the president himself, viewed both the weather and the rare sight of Venus at midday as powerfully positive omens. Later, Brooks wondered if they had got it wrong. Lincoln, "illumined by the deceptive brilliance of a March sunburst," he observed, "was already standing in the shadow of death."[40]

~~~

"Dear me," Dexter Horton wondered, "when will we see daylight again?"[41] The rain finally stopped for three days as the rest of Sherman's army began crossing the border into North Carolina. His soldiers judged the country poor and sandy, the people beneath contempt. Orders went out quickly to dial back the destruction, as the state contained many antisecessionists and fed-up Confederates who longed for peace. "The roads were very bad," Jesse Bean commented. "We had bid adieu to S. Carolina leaving our marks of revenge behind us to show the Generations to come."[42] Four more days of heavy rain, beginning on March 7, required more corduroying and bridge building. At night, men stood around fires rather than lie down in the muck. At points, the land was too wet to even park the trains. One officer called this the hardest march of the entire war. Welcome sunshine and dry weather appeared as the army stopped at Fayetteville. High temperatures remained in the fifties until cloudy March 15, when the high crossed the 70-degree mark. Some of the soldiers engaged in wrecking the Fayetteville Arsenal while the rest again headed out. Another high-pressure system approached as they took to the road for Goldsboro, bringing a thunderstorm late in the afternoon of the fifteenth and heavy rain the next day.[43]

"Our greatest enemy in this campaign was rain," Rice Bull noted that day. But this was about to change abruptly.[44] Not long after becoming general in chief, Lee had placed General Johnston in command in South Carolina, with the assignment of stopping Sherman before he joined up with Schofield and reached Petersburg. Johnston commanded about 20,000 men across the state, including Hardee's troops; the garrison at Charleston; Lt. Gen. Wade Hampton's brigade, dispatched home from Virginia; and what was left of the Army of Tennessee. Divided at first between Augusta and Charleston, they fell back into North Carolina once Sherman's route clarified. As the Federals drew closer to Raleigh, Johnston struck back. He sent two divisions under Hardee up against two Left Wing divisions plus Kilpatrick's cavalry at Averasborough. On rainy March 15, the Union cavalry ran into Hardee's infantry. Wind, dark skies, and rain marked the next day as well, when Sherman directed a series of Federal attacks that drove the Confederates away after dark.[45]

The hard rain continued through the night, delaying Johnston's concentration as troops and wagons jammed up at narrow bridges. Rain the next day mired down both armies. Mules and wagons sank in the sandy roads.[46] Frederick Sherwood described the day as "very unpleasant the Roads to be corduroy again," but adding with some pride, "Gen Sherman makes good roads bad & bad roads good he goes whare many dare not go."[47] The rain stopped that night, and soldiers commented on how fair March 18 was. Rain had left the lowland near the Black River flooded, however, and the roads in a horrible state.[48] Sergeant Bull called the crossing here "the worst we had met for depth of water it was up to my cartridge box and many of the shorter men had to remove their belts to keep their cartridges dry."[49]

March 19 was warm and lovely, with blue skies and temperatures probably in the sixties. As Slocum pushed his Left Wing up the road to Bentonville, he encountered enemy troops. Confident that he faced only cavalry and artillery, he sent two divisions forward, only to discover Confederate infantry hidden in the nearby woods. With help from Hampton, Johnston had created the perfect trap but lacked enough men on the scene to spring it effectively. Slocum put his lead divisions into a defensive line and waited for the rest of his strung-out corps to come up. As the Federals began to arrive, however, so too did Confederate reinforcements, delayed by bad roads. Around 3 P.M., Johnston attacked and nearly caved in Slocum's left. Panicked Federals ran. Repeated frontal and flanking assaults followed but could not dislodge Slocum completely, as other divisions came into line. The sun went down on a bloody scene. Sherman arrived with the Right Wing that night, after a forced march, while the Confederates entrenched. Only scattered fighting took place the next day, another warm and dry one. Rain returned on the morning of the twenty-first, beginning as drizzle before turning into showers and then a steady downpour. Parts of the saturated battlefield flooded several inches deep. A two-brigade Federal reconnaissance in force drove into Johnston's rear and nearly cut off his line of retreat before Sherman prematurely called it back. Despite three-to-one odds, he decided to let the Rebels go. They fell back toward Raleigh that night, burning their bridge behind them. Instead of following, Sherman turned east for Goldsboro and Schofield. Rain and mud had shaped the Battle of Bentonville, easily the largest fight during Sherman's twin marches, by denying Johnston's outnumbered army the chance to maul part of Slocum's left. Flooding delayed both armies arriving on the field, but Johnston paid the larger price.[50]

The weather grew fair again afterward. Sunshine dried out the roads. On March 24—only a few days behind his boast—Sherman's columns began arriving in Goldsboro. "We had finished a sixty-six day march that covered five hundred miles," Rice Bull wrote from there. "It was the rains and the floods, and the swamps and the rivers, and the roads that counted big."[51]

In Virginia, Grant waited impatiently for dry weather, solid roads, and Sheridan's cavalry. All three were taking their sweet time. Sheridan finally routed what was left on Early's army in rain, sleet, and fog near Waynesboro on March 2. His muddy men occupied Charlottesville the next rainy day and waited for their bogged-down train. On the sixth, using captured mules as well as 2,000 freedmen to move supplies, the Federals headed for Lynchburg, moving slowly to destroy Virginia Central Railroad track, mills, supplies, and sections of the James River Canal. When rain-swollen rivers blocked him, Sheridan veered east toward the old Federal supply base at White House. His mud-spattered horsemen arrived there on March 19, while Sherman fought to the south at Bentonville. Sheridan joined Grant on rainy March 27.[52]

At Petersburg, the armies rode out the month. March 1865 was not especially cold, with below-freezing temperatures developing only on the frosty mornings of March 5 through March 7 and again throughout the night of March 10–11. In contrast, eight that month days reached highs into the sixties, with five more reaching the seventies. A heavy wind on the twenty-third was strong enough to uproot trees, leading to two deaths, and to stir up a massive dust storm. But rain and mud remained the real weather story. Sporadic precipitation lasted into March 10, when rain, hail, and a bit of snow that night spoiled the last Confederate day of prayer. Rain and wet snow fell overnight on windy March 15–16, leaving a rainbow across the sky even as Confederates digested the news that their government had agreed to recruit African American soldiers. It rained four more times that month.[53] "The last three days of March were the stormiest known in the memory of the oldest inhabitant," Cpl. Herbert Beecher of the 1st Connecticut Artillery claimed.[54]

On March 24, Grant met with Lincoln at the front. The Union general in chief planned to attack the Confederates five days hence, but his counterpart beat him to it. Lee had watched Sherman draw near with foreboding, but he needed to get Grant to contract his lines before escaping toward the west and uniting with Johnston. Before dawn on March 25, cleverly preceded by infiltrators, Maj. Gen. John B. Gordon's corps stormed Fort Stedman, which lay between City Point and Petersburg. The Confederates took the stronghold and three nearby batteries before a counterattack drove them back, less 5,000 men captured. Two days later, Sherman arrived at Grant's headquarters, and both generals met with Rear Admiral Porter and the president. Sensing the end, Lincoln advised his commanders to deal leniently with their defeated foes.[55]

The projected Federal movement began as planned on March 29. Using his two-to-one advantage, Grant targeted the extended Confederate right. Once Sheridan had swept past the Confederate flank to destroy supply lines, two corps would follow. As always, Grant gave the weather no heed. In the short run, it cost him. Torrential rain and knee-deep mud played

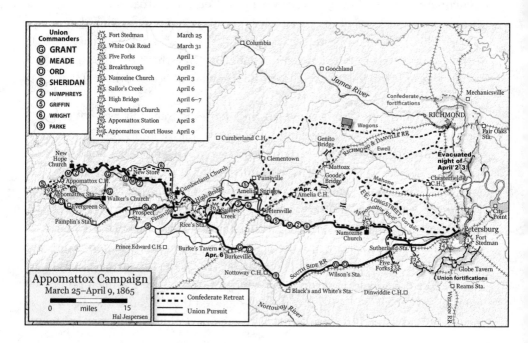

havoc with the movement. Troops had to stop and corduroy the roads they used. Still more pulled artillery, ambulances, and sunken wagons by hand as horses and mules sank or gave out. Ammunition was soon in short supply due to the mud. Unwilling to fall back, Grant ordered Sheridan to take his cavalry as well as V Corps and smash the Confederate right. Lee in the meantime had sent Maj. Gen. George Pickett and five brigades of infantry to join the cavalry already there and hold the line. The rain ended before noon on March 31, but the ground remained deep and waterways flooded as the Confederates fought with Warren's corps at White Oak Road. Pickett fell back to the vital road junction at Five Forks.[56]

After morning fog, April 1 was a beautiful day, sunny and windy, although the recent downpours left plenty of mud. In Georgetown, the high rose to 61 degrees. At Five Forks, Sheridan and Warren smashed Pickett's lines and captured half of his men while sending the other half fleeing in confusion. That dark and cloudy night, Sheridan fired Warren, allegedly for being sluggish, while Grant made plans to finish the job with an all-out assault. After more morning fog, April 2 was another lovely day. At several points, VI Corps punched through Lee's defenses, pursuing retreating troops until the Federals lost momentum. With this, the siege of Petersburg effectively ended. The Confederates fell back to an inner line that starry night, then began to flee to the west. Davis and his government abandoned their capital of four years for Danville, near the North Carolina border. Chaos reigned in Richmond, where fires eventually consumed more real estate than in Atlanta or Columbia. On the following day, April 3, Federal units occupied both Petersburg and Richmond while Sheridan raced south and west to cut off Lee, clashing with a portion of his rear guard at Namozine Church. African American troops symbolically were among the first to enter the fallen capital. Lincoln was not far behind, to be greeted with joy by the city's black population. "On to Richmond" had taken four years and tens of thousands of lives, but it finally had happened.[57]

Showers began after dark that night, dampening the fires and deepening the mud in the occupied cities. Events began to happen quickly, as rain and mud dogged both the hunted and the hunters. Confederate columns stumbled west toward a rendezvous at Amelia Court House, jettisoning equipment as they went. Lee encountered high water at the Appomattox River, which flooded the ground around one of the bridges he had planned to use. On the only two remaining spans—one built for trains—the Army of Northern Virginia filed westward. The next day, April 4, opened with drizzle before the sun broke through. The Confederates tramped over wet, ruined roads into Amelia only to discover that promised rations were not there. They gleaned the area for something to eat, losing more valuable time while waiting for the last of the army to arrive. It rained hard that night, drenching both armies and wrecking the roads still more.

On still-cloudy April 5, Lee learned that Sheridan was moving into position from the south, along the South Side Railroad, to cut him off from Danville and Johnston in North Carolina. With his dwindling ranks, Lee turned north and then west toward Farmville and resupply. Grant and Sheridan guessed his intentions. The next day was warm and wet, with an afternoon high in Georgetown of 72 degrees. Showers returned during the wee hours, dousing the desperate Confederates, and continued into the morning. The men staggering over deep, wet earth, Lee's dog-tired army separated into fragments as it approached the relative safety of the Appomattox River where it looped back to the southwest at Farmville. The soggy ground was in rough shape for marching. In the muddy bottomland of swollen Sailor's Creek east of town, pursuing Federals attacked the army's rear during the afternoon. Three distinct fights followed, lasting until dark. For the Confederates, it was a disaster. Federals captured 20 percent of Lee's remaining men, including eight generals, and seized most of his train.[58]

What was left of the Army of Northern Virginia pushed on, with Sheridan's horsemen at their heels. While crossing the South Side Railroad's High Bridge over the Appomattox, the Confederates held of the enemy but failed to destroy the span. Unable to halt long in Farmville with the river thus breached, Lee's hungry men wolfed down a few rations and kept moving. More supplies waited about thirty miles west at Appomattox Station. Grant kept pressing, confident that Sheridan, using a shorter road, could reach Appomattox Station before Lee. On showery April 7, Grant sent Lee a message asking for his surrender, the first in a series of notes over the next day and a half. While this back and forth continued, so did the fighting, as pursuer and quarry clashed at Cumberland Church. The weather tuned colder, and frost appeared. On the fair but cooler afternoon of April 8, with a high in the midfifties, Federal cavalry attacked the Confederates at Appomattox Station. That night, Brigadier General Custer's cavalry captured the supply trains waiting there as well as several guns, seized the high ground, and blocked the road. Lee fell back three miles to Appomattox Court House, now hemmed in front and rear. He still refused to capitulate, but he let Grant know that he was open to discussions. He also ordered a final attempt at escape at sunrise. If that failed, Lee decided, he would ask for an armistice.[59]

The next morning, Palm Sunday, was foggy. Gordon's corps and some cavalry advanced until they encountered Federal infantry waiting in strength. The assault fizzled. Lee asked for a truce, which he received when the message caught up with Grant two hours later as he met with Sheridan miles away. By then, the fog had lifted, but skies remained overcast with occasional showers. Grant turned back. The two generals in chief met at 1:30 P.M. in Wilmer McLean's house in town. Grant famously was splattered with mud from the recent rains and boggy roads, while Lee had changed into a clean uniform before the meeting. They spent a few minutes discussing first the weather, then the war with Mexico. Finally, Lee turned to the matter at hand. Reading Grant's proposed terms, he asked if his men could keep their privately owned horses and mules. Grant agreed, noting that they would soon need them for spring planting. Lee signed the agreement and rode away. Grant left over an hour later, stopping to order a stop to a celebratory gun salute. Three days later, the Army of Northern Virginia formally surrendered. Not every Confederate in Virginia sought a parole that day—this process went on at many places into May—but their war essentially was over. It rained hard during the surrender and periodically over the next five days, just as it had done throughout the Appomattox Campaign. Lee's men began walking home in rain and mud, some of it deep.[60]

Lincoln returned to Washington on Palm Sunday. A telegram arrived later announcing Lee's capitulation. Rain that night and drizzle throughout the next day did little to dampen the celebratory mood in the capital. Cannons boomed, bells rang, and wet flags seemed to be flapping everywhere. Tired from his journey, an otherwise happy Lincoln delivered a speech to a throng at the White House on the misty night of April 11. He again stressed his themes of binding up the nation's wounds. His message fell flat on the ears of damp people standing in wet grass who wanted to bask in triumph as well as on those Radicals who looked forward to retribution. Many wandered away, looking to find a dry place. The next day was hot, reaching 78 degrees after the previous day's high of 58 degrees, and brought more showers that turned into heavy rain at dusk.

April 13 was dry and cooler. Good Friday dawned chilly at 47 degrees—Lincoln lit a fire in his office's fireplace—but it became beautiful and bright, nearly reaching 70 degrees in the afternoon. The sunshine reflected the president's buoyant mood. Lincoln held meetings and went to the War Department, vainly hoping for news from Sherman, then returned to the White House to meet with Grant and the cabinet. The general stayed behind long enough to wiggle his way out of the president's invitation to join him at Ford's Theatre that night; Mary Lincoln and Julia Grant wanted no part of each other after an ugly moment during their husbands' meeting at City Point. The Lincolns then took a carriage ride. As the vehicle bounced through the streets, the temperature began to drop into the midfifties. Dark clouds gathered, followed by spotty showers and strong gusts of wind. The Lincolns arrived late at Ford's as a dense fog enveloped the wet city. During the third act of *Our American Cousin,* actor and Confederate sympathizer John Wilkes Booth shot the president in the back of the head, leapt from the presidential box, and escaped into the dank fog and darkness. Lincoln died the next morning. Outside, the wind seemed to moan. Drizzle turned the streets to mud.[61] A silent, weeping crowd quickly gathered in what Noah Brooks later called "tears of rain."[62]

The Civil War did not end that gray, rainy week with Lee's surrender and the death of Lincoln. Instead, it petered out slowly, like a storm dissolving into drizzle. In North Carolina, Sherman's men had enjoyed warm and lovely weather until April 7. Then on rainy April 10, they went after Johnston. Once again, the Federals waded through mud and dragged out mired wagons. The effort ended quickly when news of Lee's surrender arrived the next day. Union troops took Raleigh on the thirteenth, with rain falling all day. Hot and sunny April 14 saw the weather clear as Johnston contacted Sherman about a truce. Four days later, after a nighttime shower, Johnston surrendered. Sherman's terms were so generous that Washington officials ordered the generals to meet again to sign a more rigorous capitulation on the basis of Grant's terms with Lee. The weather stayed warm and dry as the generals did so on the twenty-sixth.[63] "We remained in camp until April 27," William Bircher wrote from North Carolina. "The weather had been warm at times, and hot at others, but, take it as a whole, it had been what would be called June weather in Minnesota."[64]

But still the war dragged on. After two ferocious battles, Mobile fell on April 12. Lt. Gen. Dick Taylor surrendered Confederate forces in Alabama on May 4. Lieutenant General Forrest waited five days before he capitulated. The next day, at the conclusion of a raid across Alabama and Georgia, elements of Maj. Gen. James Wilson's cavalry captured Jefferson Davis near Irwinville, Georgia, as he attempted to escape to Texas. Two days after that, the last battle of the war occurred at Palmito Ranch, Texas. Ironically, it was a Confederate victory. On May 23 and May 24, Grant's and Sherman's armies marched down Pennsylvania Avenue in a grand review before many of the men turned for home. Two days later, General Kirby Smith surrendered. The last Confederates to give up were the crew of the CSS *Shenandoah*, who sailed their ship into Liverpool on the dark night of November 6 and escaped into the city.

David Harris had slipped away from his unit in March 1865. He began sowing oats, although later than he wanted due to yet another wet March. Rain in April kept him from planting corn until the thirteenth. The first Federal soldiers arrived in town on May 1, and although they did not remain long, they were precursors of new things to come. Unseasonably cold weather gave way to warmth, but Harris had little hope. On May 15, he wrote: "I certainly have never seen a poorer prospect for a crop. *Wheat is poor, late, thin, low and ugly. Oats are only a little better.*" The earth itself was unresponsive, "cold, hard, & dry." A storm on May 26 did more damage. "'Misfortune never comes alone,'" he quoted, "& famine follows war. I have read of the time that tried mens souls," he added, "I think this is the time that tries mens souls, pockets and his bowels at the same time. The Lord only knows what is to be the fate of our unlucky country. I must fear the worst is yet to come." Among the "worst" was a proclamation freeing local slaves. Harris fumed when he discovered the first of his former bondsmen up and gone. White farmers resisted emancipation, increasingly with violence as the rest of 1865 passed. As the following years made clear, the war for Confederate independence might have been over, but the bloody struggle for black equality or else white supremacy—what some scholars call the next chapter in a "long Civil War"—was only beginning. "Everything is quiet," Harris wrote on Christmas Day, "though no one knows what to do."[65]

Conclusion

At the end of May 1862, Col. Wesley Brainerd wrestled with God. He had left a pregnant wife and a business a year before to help save the Union. Alongside his 50th New York Engineers, he had since slogged up the Peninsula for two months "covered from head to toe in mud." They also had braved a blistering sun, suffocating dust, snake-infested swamps, flooded creeks and rivers, the legendary miasmas of the Virginia Tidewater, and the muskets of the Confederate army. At Chickahominy Creek, he and his men had waded into bottomland flooded up to a foot deep and erected a bridge in the rain, the river around them "rising rapidly and running like a mill race." While the Battle of Seven Pines was not a defeat, the Confederates got away nonetheless. Brainerd struggled to understand why. "Was the sudden rising of the stream a direct interposition of the *Almighty?*" he wondered. "I think it was. *He* did not design to have the war end until his own good time."[1]

Brainerd was not alone in looking for the hand of Providence in the weather. The Bible taught as much, and even Abraham Lincoln tried to grasp the Almighty's purposes in the dank morning clouds and sudden sunshine of his second inauguration. Not everyone thought that way, of course. The soldiers sampled for this volume spoke much less about Providence and weather that one might expect. Brainerd was an exception. Even Confederate ministers were reluctant to point to drought as a sign of God's wrath. A survey of their sermons reveals greater obsessions with defending slavery and countering the sins of speculation and excessive theater going.[2]

Today, of course, we are much more likely to ascribe weather like that of the Peninsula Campaign to science: to climate, warm and cold fronts, the jet stream, tropical depressions, the El Niño–Southern Oscillation, and the murky workings of the North Atlantic Oscillation. Even a postmodern mind, however, cannot fully escape the gist of Brainerd's plaintive question. What effect did weather really have on the Civil War? If we continue to think of capital-W "Weather" as a third combatant, the first answer is that it defied expectations. Going into the war, as Mark Fiege explains, Weather seemed to favor the Confederacy. The roads were already bad, rain was abundant, and wet red clay accurately promised immense problems for invading armies that had to bring men and supplies overland into an unfamiliar environment.

Yet over and over, Weather defied expectations and favored the Union cause and—perhaps even more—emancipation. To be sure, it was an untrustworthy ally. Brainerd was right to see Weather wrecking George McClellan's campaign on the Peninsula, yet that failure led directly to the Emancipation Proclamation. "Normal" conditions on the Peninsula in the spring of 1862 would have boosted McClellan's chances of taking Richmond, and while that in itself would not have ended the war immediately, one can envision a reassembled United States in 1863 in which slavery remained legal. Stonewall Jackson's 1862 campaign in the Shenandoah Valley, Ambrose Burnside's Mud March, George Meade's pursuit of the Army of Northern Virginia to the flooded Potomac after Gettysburg, and the barbaric mud at the Mule Shoe salient at Spotsylvania likewise present examples of Weather's temporary alliances with Robert E. Lee. Yet in the end, as demonstrated from Cheat Mountain and Romney to Nashville and Bentonville, Weather usually had a better, if strained, relationship with the boys in blue.[3] It also dragged out the war until—as Lincoln concluded—it occasioned the end of American slavery.

Part of the uneasy alliance between Billy Yank and Weather derived from the North's better industrial base. Better and more uniforms, overcoats, shoes, shelter tents, and rubber ponchos gave Federals an edge in the field when the rain poured or the snow flew. The Confederacy had to gin up new factories to produce some of those items, rely on battlefield captures for more—including all those seas of captured white "flies"—or otherwise do without, as when disease and southern animal deaths led to a dearth of shoe leather. Few of the war's images are more suggestive than the raw moccasins of James Longstreet's desperate soldiers during the Cold New Year in East Tennessee. Setting aside the tired question of whether the war was the last traditional war or the first modern conflict—it was neither if one looks beyond America—the Union army was more modern than its enemy, including in its dealings with climate and weather. Confederates reflected what Fiege calls "an older military ecology."[4]

Food was part of that hand-to-mouth ecology. The populous North could produce more of it and had the industrial means to get it and everything else to its armies when local supply problems did not intrude, as they did during Don Carlos Buell's march across Alabama. Northern agriculture was never an invincible "king" or immune to Weather's vagaries—wartime production peaked in 1862 before the heat and killing frosts of 1863 and drought in 1864—but neither did it suffer the full brunt of Weather's wartime assault on the Confederacy. Heavy ENSO-related spring rains, followed by the all-but-forgotten summer droughts and food shortages in 1862 and 1863—and again in Virginia in 1864—were without question Weather's cruelest betrayals of the Confederacy. Hunger weakened soldiers and undermined government, nationalism, and morale. A "rich man's war, poor man's fight" mentality ate at the Confederacy's innards.[5]

Individuals reflected traditional-modern differences as well. While historians often have depicted Lincoln as an untutored military genius whose vision exceeded his petty generals until Ulysses Grant arrived, he never really understood logistics or the realities of moving armies in bad weather. Time and again, as with Buell in Kentucky, McClellan in Virginia, William Rosecrans in Tennessee, and Meade in Pennsylvania, Lincoln became the worst kind of armchair general. He expected the impossible, willed his armies to overcome deep mud or snow, and turned against generals who fell short or worried about their men. While his lack of military experience and constant political necessity spurred much of his intolerance, so did his wider attitudes. Lincoln, Fiege observes, represented a wider nineteenth-century Whiggish mindset that saw nature as something to be overcome, tamed, and used for man's benefit, like a wild horse broken to ride. After Gettysburg, the president "exhibited the modern machine age mentality, but his army was not a machine—it was a collection of organisms, of biological bodies, that quite simply got tired."[6]

The old trope of "Lincoln finds a general" thus takes on new meaning. In Grant, Lincoln finally found a kindred spirit, if one more skilled in logistical reality. Unlike McClellan or Joe Johnston, Grant routinely ignored Weather's threats to his plans and armies and, as in the Wilderness, asked his subordinates what they were going to do to overcome and tame it. Then he launched repeated frontal assaults to defeat Weather right along with the Rebels. That second front cost him many more lives, but in the end, Grant won that war too.[7]

But he did not win it without his privates, noncommissioned officers, and junior officers. Some recent historians have taken a "dark turn" in Civil War studies that delineates the ugliness of the conflict along with its triumphs. Henry Kyd Douglas, who described a battlefield at night as "gruesome" and "horrid," surely would approve.[8] One can hardly imagine a darker experience than suffering for years in the rain, mud, snow, sleet, and heat of summer with little to eat, soaked or frozen ground for a bed, and disease coursing through camp. Soldiers drowned in floods, died of heat exhaustion, collapsed in mud, froze to death, burned alive when dry forests caught fire, fell prey to environmental diseases, were struck by fateful lightning, and lost their minds. They did not survive Weather's assaults. Those who did, as Kathryn Shively Meier demonstrates, often developed individual practices of "self-care" that ran counter to military discipline. But soldiers also adapted as armies. The evolution of winter housing provides a notable example of troops doing their best to hold Weather at bay. They pooled their labor, erected substantial shelters whenever they could, and experimented with different styles, modifications, and hybrid designs. Southern forests paid the price, but a majority of men fought off winter. Adaptions and experience extended to campaigning as well. Some of the men who barely made it back from Mill Springs in 1861 ended up fighting at Nashville in 1864 or trudging successfully through the Carolinas in 1865 on corduroyed roads. Weather had been their drill instructor.[9]

Back in 1861, according to one private, William Loring had boomed, "'until they are able to sleep in winter amidst the snow and ice without tents, they are not soldiers!'"[10] In the howling storm of the Civil War, the survivors had become soldiers indeed.

Then at the end of 1865, out in the Pacific west of Peru, water temperatures once again began ticking upward with shifting currents. Another El Niño, the strongest since 1844–45, was rising to meet Reconstruction.[11]

Notes

ABBREVIATIONS

ADAH   Alabama Department of Archives and History, Montgomery

AU   Special Collections, Auburn University, Auburn, Ala.

CWC   Civil War Collection: Confederate and Federal, 1861–1865

CWCDJ   Civil War Correspondence, Diaries, and Journals Collection

CWDC   Civil War Document Collection

CWMC   Civil War Miscellaneous Collection, U.S. Army Military History Institute, Carlisle, Pa.

CWTI   *Civil War Times Illustrated* Collection

Duke   David M. Rubenstein Rare Book & Manuscript Library, Duke University, Durham, N.C.

Emory   Manuscript, Archives, and Rare Book Library, Emory University

HCWRTC   Harrisburg Civil War Round Table Collection, U.S. Army Military History Institute, Carlisle, Pa.

LC   Library of Congress, Washington, D.C.

Mead Diary   Rufus Mead Jr. Diary, Rufus Mead Jr. Papers

MHS   Massachusetts Historical Society, Boston

MMC   Miscellaneous Manuscript Collection

MnHS   Minnesota Historical Society, Saint Paul

NARA   National Archives and Records Administration, Washington, D.C.

NARA-CP   National Archives and Records Administration, Archives II, College Park, Md.

NCDAH   North Carolina Department of Archives and History, Raleigh

ND   Manuscripts of the American Civil War. Department of Special Collections, Hesburgh Libraries, University of Notre Dame, South Bend, Ind.

NRCS Soils   NRCS Soils, *Map of Soil Orders of the United States,* http://hydro_bm.esri.com/Soils/soilOrderMap1Beta.htm, accessed May 1, 2017

NYHS/CWPSD   New-York Historical Society, Civil War Primary Source Documents Collection, through EBSCO Information Services Database, accessed July 20, 2017

OHS   Ohio Historical Society, Columbus

OR   US War Department. *The War of the Rebellion: A Compilation of the Official Records of the Union and Confederate Armies.* 129 vols. Washington, D.C.: 1880–1901 (all citations to ser. 1)

ORN   US Navy Department. *Official Records of the Union and Confederate Navies in the War of the Rebellion.* 30 vols. Washington, D.C.: Government Printing Office, 1894–1927 (all citations to ser. 1)

RG 24.2.2   Logs, Records of the Bureau of Naval Personnel

RG 27.5.7   Records of the Division of Station Facilities and Meteorological Observations and Its Predecessors, Microfilm T907

SHC-UNC   Southern Historical Collection, University of North Carolina, Chapel Hill

SHSM-R   State Historical Society of Missouri–Rolla

TSLA   Tennessee State Library and Archives, Nashville

USAMHI   US Army Military History Institute, Carlisle, Pa.

UT-CAH   Center for American History, University of Texas–Austin

INTRODUCTION

1. See, for example, Tucker and Russell, *Natural Enemy,* 1–6.

2. Fiege, *Republic of Nature,* 209, 210; Fiege, "Gettysburg," 95.

3. Shalit, *Psychology of Combat,* 5. I am grateful to Kathryn Shively for this reference.

4. Two welcome recent works are Stith, *Extreme Civil War;* and Taylor, *Embattled Freedom.*

5. Twain, *English as She Is Taught,* 16.

6. "What Is the Difference between Weather and Climate?," accessed Nov. 18, 2018.

7. Greensboro, Ala., Apr. 1861, Reel 2, RG 27.5.7, NARA-CP. All temperatures in the book are given in Fahrenheit.

8. Thomas, "Weathering the Storm," 87.

9. Powers, *War and the Weather;* Dyrenforth and Newton, "Can We Make It Rain?," 385–404; Fleming, *Fixing the Sky,* 61–64. Powers's pseudoclimatology still crops up as gospel in Civil War circles and on the internet; it even appeared as fact in a recent history of the war.

10. *Annual Report of the Board of Regents of the Smithsonian Institution,* 35–36; Krick, *Civil War Weather,* see esp. 1–6, 80; Darter, "List of Climatological Records," vii–xiv; Ludlum, *Early American Winters,* 121; Rohland, *Changes in the Air,* 105–6; Thomas, "Weathering the Storm," 89–91, 96–98.

11. Mergen, *Weather Matters,* 7–29; Rohland, *Changes in the Air,* 105–6.

12. Wiley, *Life of Billy Yank,* 55–58, 76–77, 127; Wiley, *Life of Johnny Reb,* 59–67, 74–75, 79, 244–45; Daryl Black, email to author, Aug. 24, 2011.

13. Freeman, "An Address," 10–11.

14. Winters, *Battling the Elements,* see esp. 1–4, 33–44 (quotation, 1).

15. Krick, *Civil War Weather.*

16. Kirby, "American Civil War: An Environmental View," accessed Oct. 25, 2018.

17. Brady, *War upon the Land*; Browning and Silver, "Nature and Human Nature," 388–415; Drake, *The Blue, the Gray, and the Green*; Fiege, "Gettysburg"; Fiege, *Republic of Nature*; Meier, *Nature's Civil War*; Morris, "A More Southern Environmental History," esp. 582, 595; Nelson, *Ruin Nation*; Sharrer, *Kind of Fate*; Smith, *Smell of Battle*; Steinberg, *Down to Earth*; Tucker, "Impact of Warfare on the Natural World," 27–28. I discuss the McClellan myth in Noe, "'I Am Completely Checked by the Weather.'"

18. Davis, *Late Victorian Holocausts*, esp., 6, 13, 279.

19. For more in-depth discussion, see Diaz and Kiladis, "Atmospheric Teleconnections"; Enfield, "Overview of El Niño/Southern Oscillation"; Grove and Adamson, *El Niño*, vii, 1–11, 107–27, 125; Fagan, *Floods, Famines, and Emperors*, 3–63.

20. Grove and Adamson, *El Niño*, 19–97; Fagan, *Floods, Famines, and Emperors*, xi–xiii, 3–44, 89–218, 269–90.

21. Herweijer, Seager, and Cook, "North American Droughts," 160–62, 164, 165 (quotation, 165).

22. Flores, "Bison Ecology," 479–82; Hämäläinen, *Comanche Empire*; Davis, *Late Victorian Holocausts*, 271; Grove and Adamson, *El Niño*, 147. Adamson described "unambiguous" El Niño events in 1844–45 (very strong), 1849–50 (moderate), 1851–52 (weak), 1853–54 (weak), and 1856–57 (moderate).

23. Davis, *Late Victorian Holocausts*, 12–15, 17–18, 213–38; Grove and Adamson, *El Niño*, 96–97, 147; Mergen, *Weather Matters*, 23–25, 40–41; Keller, "MU Expert Studies Civil War Weather," accessed June 21, 2014; "Science of Backward Weather Forecasting," accessed June 21, 2014.

24. Cook, D'Arrigo, and Mann, "Well-Verified Winter," accessed Nov. 15, 2018; Cornes et al., "Estimates of the North Atlantic Oscillation," 28–48; Fagan, *Floods, Famines, and Emperors*, 65–85; "North Atlantic Oscillation (NAO)," accessed Nov. 15, 2018; "North Atlantic Oscillation (NAO) Index," accessed Nov. 15, 2018. I am grateful to Cary Mock for first stressing the importance of the NAO.

25. Gates, *Agriculture and the Civil War*, 16, 29, 34–40, 85–90, 113–16.

26. Fiege, "Gettysburg"; Fiege, *Republic of Nature*, 199–227; Robinson, *Bitter Fruits of Bondage*, see esp. 121, 126–30, 307n30. Leading internalist accounts that all but ignore weather include McCurry, *Confederate Reckoning*, and Williams, *People's History of the Civil War*.

27. Gates, *Agriculture and the Civil War*, 148, 153, 177–78, 183–84 (quotation, 148).

28. Readers should note that I have quoted sources verbatim, bad spelling and all, but sometimes have changed the capitalization of the first word of a quotation to better fit the larger sentence.

29. Thomas, "Weathering the Storm," 91–93 (quotations, 91, 93).

30. I am grateful to George Rable and Kathryn Shively for their thoughts. See also Tucker and Russell, *Natural Enemy*, 1; Fiege, *Republic of Nature*, 203; and Noe, "Jigsaw Puzzles," 236–43.

CHAPTER 1

1. Crawford, *Genesis of the Civil War*, 426–27, 430 (quotations, 426–27).

2. Charleston, S.C., Apr. 1861, Reel 464, RG 27.5.7, NARA-CP; Crawford, *Genesis of the Civil War*, 432–44; Doubleday, *Reminiscences*, 155; *OR*, 1(1):21, 31, 40; Goodheart, *1861*, 149, 150, 167; Swanberg, *First Blood*, 309, 312.

3. *OR*, 1(1):41; Krick, *Civil War Weather*, 21.

4. Charleston, S.C., Apr. 1861, Reel 464, RG 27.5.7, NARA-CP; Elliott, *Bloodless Victory*, 6, 10; Crawford, *Genesis of the Civil War*, 439–41; Doubleday, *Reminiscences*, 162–63, 175; *OR*, 1(1):12, 24; Goodheart, *1861*, 173, 174–76, 184; Smith, *Smell of Battle*, 34–38; Swanberg, *First Blood*, 312–13. Smithsonian observers Dr. Joseph Johnson and Dr. John L. Dawson recorded highs of 74 degrees on April 13, 70 degrees on April 14, and 74 degrees again on April 15. Readings dropped to a high of only 57 degrees by April 17.

5. Greensboro, Ala., Apr. 1861, Reel 2, RG 27.5.7, NARA-CP; Chicago, Ill., Apr. 1861, Reel 116, ibid.; Tower Grove, Mo., Apr. 1861, Reel 290, ibid.; Natchez, Miss., Apr. 1861, Reel 2, ibid.; New York City, Apr. 1861, Reel 360, ibid.; Gettysburg, Pa., Apr. 1861, Reel 445, ibid.

6. Kimble, *Our American Weather*, 75–79; David M. Ludlum, *American Weather Book*, 68–71 (quotation, 68).

7. Richmond, Va., Apr. 1861, Reel 527, RG 27.5.7, NARA-CP; Chicago, Ill., Apr. 1861, Reel 116, ibid.; *Alexandria (Va.) Gazette*, Apr. 17, 1861; Jones, *Rebel War Clerk's Diary*, 1:15–16 (quotation, 16). See also Krick, *Civil War Weather*, 21, 23.

8. Fleet and Fuller, *Green Mount*, 51–54. See also *Alexandria (Va.) Gazette*, Apr. 19, 1861; Baird, *Journals of Amanda Virginia Edmonds*, 46 (hereafter Baird, *Journals of Edmonds*); Leech, *Reveille in Washington*, 53–54.

9. Krick, *Civil War Weather*, 21; Roper, *Repairing the "March of Mars,"* 18, 75–84 (quotations, 80, 81, 83).

10. "Diary of Horatio Nelson Taft," Apr. 16, 1861, accessed May 12, 2014. See also Russell, *My Diary North and South*, 64–68.

11. Russell, *My Diary North and South*, 65, 70.

12. "Diary of Horatio Nelson Taft," Apr. 15–30, 1861 (quotations, Apr. 15, 16), accessed May 12, 2014. Rain started in New York City on April 13, with more than three inches falling on April 17 before clearing out for the arrival of the Fort Sumter garrison. See also Georgetown, D.C., Apr. 1861, Reel 81, RG 27.5.7, NARA-CP; New York City, Apr. 1861, Reel 360, ibid.; *Charleston Mercury*, Apr. 25, 1861; *St. Louis Daily Missouri Republican*, Apr. 27, 1861; Krick, *Civil War Weather*, 23; McPherson, *Battle Cry of Freedom*, 284–86; and White, *Abraham Lincoln and Treason*, 3–4, 11–27.

13. Adams, *Living Hell*, 13–27, 38, 45; Wiley, *Life of Billy Yank*, 17–44; Wiley, *Life of Johnny Reb*, 15–27, 244–45. For historians' debates over "what they fought for," see Noe, *Reluctant Rebels*, 3–7.

14. Meier, *Nature's Civil War*, 45–47, 51–52.

15. Baechler et al., "Guide to Determining Climate Regions," 2–4. See also Fiege, *Republic of Nature*, 201–2; and Ludlum, *American Weather Book*, 70. For a map to the climate zones, see "IECC Climate Zone Map," accessed Nov. 5, 2019.

16. *Augusta (Ga.) Chronicle*, June 1, 1861.

17. *Augusta (Ga.) Chronicle*, Apr. 13, 26, 1861; *Daily Columbus (Ga.) Enquirer*, Apr. 11, 1861; *Charleston Mercury*, Apr. 11, 18, 27, May 25, 1861; *New-Orleans Price-Current and Commercial Intelligencer*, Apr. 10, 1861; *New Orleans Daily True Delta*, Apr. 25, 26, 1861; *Dallas Weekly Herald*, May 8, 1861.

18. *Dallas Weekly Herald*, May 22, 1861.

19. Anderson, *Brokenburn*, ix, 14, 15, 18, 21 (quotations, 15, 18). See also *St. Louis Daily Missouri Republican*, May 10, 1861.

20. *Baton Rouge Daily Advocate*, May 14, 16, 21, 1861.

21. *Alexandria (Va.) Gazette*, May 20, 1861.

22. *Charleston Mercury*, May 14, 1861.

23. *Augusta (Ga.) Chronicle*, June 1, 1861. See also *Charleston Mercury*, June 6, 1861.

24. *Augusta (Ga.) Chronicle*, May 21, 23, June 2, 4, 5, 9, 20, 25, 1861. See also *Augusta (Ga.) Daily Constitutionalist*, June 11, 1861; *Charleston Mercury*, May 7, 25, June 24, 1861; *Macon (Ga.) Daily Telegraph*, June 22, July 1, 4, 6, 8, 1861; and *New Orleans Daily True Delta*, June 5, 1861.

25. *Charleston Mercury*, May 30, 1861. See also *Augusta (Ga.) Chronicle*, June 9, 22, 1861.

26. *Augusta (Ga.) Chronicle*, June 1, 1861.

27. *Augusta (Ga.) Daily Constitutionalist*, June 19, 1861. For sermons, see De Veaux, *Fast-Day Sermon*, 5; Mitchell, *Sermon*, 19–20.

28. Reprinted in the *Augusta (Ga.) Daily Constitutionalist*, June 23, 1861.

29. Baechler et al., "Guide to Determining Climate Regions," 2–3; Watson, *Life in the Confederate Army*, 4, 127, 138, 141–54, 163 (quotations, 127, 142, 143, 144, 163). See also *New Orleans Daily True Delta*, May 19, 1861; and Hearn, *Capture of New Orleans*, 29–30. Others noted unusually heavy rain in Louisiana that spring. To the north in Madison Parish, Kate Stone wrote on May 23: "How pleasant to have smooth, dry ground underfoot again after so many months of mud. It has been such a long, muddy winter and spring. No one knows what mud is until he lives on a buckshot place and travels buckshot roads." See Anderson, *Brokenburn*, 14.

30. *New Orleans Daily True Delta*, May 7, 9, 11, 1861.

31. Baechler et al., "Guide to Determining Climate Regions," 2–3. Used extensively in today's building and energy industries, heating-degree days reflect how much artificial heating modern buildings require.

32. *Arkansas State Gazette* (Little Rock), Apr. 27, June 15, 1861. See also *St. Louis Daily Missouri Republican*, Apr. 13, 16, 18, 23, 26, 1861.

33. *St. Louis Daily Missouri Republican*, June 3, 4, 7, 8, 1861. For Kansas, see *St. Louis Sunday Morning Republican*, June 9, 1861.

34. *Charleston Mercury*, May 11, 1861. See also *Macon (Ga.) Daily Telegraph*, May 7, 25, 1861; and *New Orleans Daily True Delta*, Apr. 27, 1861.

35. Sutherland, *Reminiscences of a Private*, 11, 17. See also *St. Louis Daily Missouri Republican*, June 1, 1861.

36. Robertson, *Letters of General Robert McAllister*, 31 (hereafter Robertson, *Letters of McAllister*).

37. *St. Louis Daily Missouri Republican*, June 6, 1861. See also *St. Louis Daily Missouri Democrat*, June 7, 1861.

38. Baechler et al., "Guide to Determining Climate Regions," 2–4; Norton, *Army Letters*, 9; Luther C. Furst Diary, 2–5 (quotation, 5), HCWRTC, USAMHI; Steinberg, *Down to Earth*, 90.

39. Furst Diary, 3–4 (quotation, 4), HCWRTC, USAMHI; Graves, *Bedford Light Artillery*, 11.

40. Woodbury, *First Rhode Island*, 60, 62. See also *OR*, 2:715–16.

41. Dobbins, *Grandfather's Journal*, 16–20 (quotations, 16, 19).

42. Drake, *Life of General Robert Hatton*, 360 (hereafter Drake, *Life of Hatton*).

43. Turner, *Reminiscence of Lieutenant John Newton Lyle*, 43 (hereafter Turner, *Reminiscence of Lyle*).

44. Lesser, *Rebels at the Gate*, 52–53, 61–65; Rafuse, *McClellan's War*, 103–6. Rafuse maintains that while McClellan remained in Cincinnati, he still maintained control of operations.

45. *Alexandria (Va.) Gazette*, May 10, 1861 (quotation); Horn and McGuire, "Climate of West Virginia," 422–39.

46. *OR*, 2:64–74 (quotation, 67); *Richmond Whig*, July 12, 1861; Lesser, *Rebels at the Gate*, 64–73; McPherson, *Battle Cry of Freedom*, 299–300; Rafuse, *McClellan's War*, 103–6.

47. *Charleston Mercury*, June 11, 1861; Lesser, *Rebels at the Gate*, 83–87; Zinn, *Battle of Rich Mountain*, 1–5.

48. *OR*, 2:198–201, 205, 236–39, 242–43; *Richmond Whig*, July 9, 1861; Beatty, *Citizen-Solider*, 13, 19; Sears, *Papers of George B. McClellan*, 41, 43, 46 (hereafter Sears, *Papers of McClellan*); Zinn, *Battle of Rich Mountain*, 1–5.

49. Zinn, *Battle of Rich Mountain*, 1–5.

50. Zinn, *Battle of Rich Mountain*, 5.

51. *OR*, 2:202–4, 206–7, 210, 215–17, 220–21, 247–48, 251; Lesser, *Rebels at the Gate*, 87–94, 98–104; Rafuse, *McClellan's War*, 110–17; Zinn, *Battle of Rich Mountain*, 5–32.

52. *OR*, 2:220, 222.

53. *OR*, 2:222–23; Lesser, *Rebels at the Gate*, 109–27; Rafuse, *McClellan's War*, 110–17; Zinn, *Battle of Rich Mountain*, 32–33.

54. *OR*, 2:78–102; *Carolina Observer* (Fayetteville, N.C.), June 10, 1861; *Richmond Whig*, June 18, 1861; Blackford et al., *Letters from Lee's Army*, 15; Casler, *Four Years in the Stonewall Brigade*, 16; Fort Monroe, Va., June 1861, Reel 522, RG 27.5.7, NARA-CP; White, "Diary of the War," 95–100; Cobb, Hicks, and Holt, *Big Bethel*, esp. 22–23, 49, 81, 144, 205.

55. *OR*, 2:80.

56. *OR*, 2:85.

57. Crockett, "Climate of Virginia," 398–401, 411, 413, 416; Fort Monroe, Va., June 1861, Reel 522, RG 27.5.7, NARA-CP; *Augusta (Ga.) Daily Constitutionalist*, June 25, 1861; *Charleston Mercury*, June 25, 1861.

58. Guelzo, *Fateful Lightning*, 154; McPherson, *Battle Cry of Freedom*, 333–37 (quotation, 334); Noe, "Heat of Battle," 54–62, 76.

59. McPherson, *Battle Cry of Freedom*, 335–36, 339–40.

60. Goodheart, *1861*, 350–51, 366–70; Chesnut, *Diary from Dixie*, 79; Jones, *Rebel War Clerk's Diary*, 1:56; Roper, *Repairing the "March of Mars,"* 103.

61. Crockett, "Climate of Virginia," 418; *Charleston Mercury*, July 2, 1861; *Richmond Whig*, July 2, 1861; Kimble, *Our American Weather*, 147.

62. Everson and Simpson, *"Far, Far from Home,"* 21, 24; *New Orleans Daily True Delta*, June 29, 1861.

63. "Diary of Horatio Nelson Taft," July 1–7, 1861, accessed May 12, 2014; Quint, *Second Massachusetts*, 33. See also Howard, *Recollections*, 30; McPherson, *Battle Cry of Freedom*, 335–36, 339.

64. Kimble, *Our American Weather*, 146–48, 150–71; Georgetown, D.C., July 1861, Reel 81, RG 27.5.7, NARA-CP; New York City, July 1861, Reel 360, RG 27.5.7, NARA-CP; Krick, *Civil War Weather*; 30; McPherson, *Battle Cry of Freedom*, 339.

65. *Richmond Whig*, July 9, 1861.

66. Robertson, *Letters of McAllister*, 39. See also *Augusta (Ga.) Chronicle*, July 6, 1861; and Curtis, *First Bull Run to Chancellorsville*, 33.

67. Baird, *Journals of Edmonds*, 52.

68. Roper, *Repairing the "March of Mars,"* 103–8 (quotations, 106, 107, 108).

69. *OR*, 2:303–5, 308, 318–19, 338–34; *Augusta (Ga.) Daily Chronicle*, July 10, 1861; *Charleston Courier*, July 10, 1861; *Macon (Ga.) Daily Telegraph*, July 3, 10, 1861; *New Orleans Daily True Delta*, July 9, 1861; McPherson, *Battle Cry of Freedom*, 340.

70. *OR*, 2:305, 339, 452; Kimble, *Our American Weather*, 146–47, 150–71; Georgetown, D.C., July 1861, Reel 81, RG 27.5.7, NARA-CP; Woodbury, *First Rhode Island*, 76–83; Davis, *Battle at Bull Run*, 93, 97, 108, 152; Rhodes, *All for the Union*, 24; Woshner, *India-Rubber*, 101, 121–22.

71. William B. Westervelt, "Lights and Shadows of Army Life, as Seen by a Private Soldier," 2, Box 121, CWMC, USAMHI. This is an incomplete typescript of Westervelt's 1886 book by the same title (published in Marlboro, N.Y., by C. H. Cochran).

72. Georgetown, D.C., July 1861, Reel 81, RG 27.5.7, NARA-CP; Davis, *Battle at Bull Run*, 152, 154; Rhodes, *All for the Union*, 26.

73. Everson and Simpson, *"Far, Far from Home,"* 29, 31.

74. Howard, *Recollections*, 30, 33. See also Bartlett, *Military Record of Louisiana*, 38; Blackford, *War Years*, 23; Casler, *Four Years in the Stonewall Brigade*, 16; Turner, *Reminiscence of Lyle*, 79.

75. Long, *Civil War Day by Day*, 97.

76. *OR*, 2:318.

77. Douglas, *I Rode with Stonewall*, 9; Casler, *Four Years in the Stonewall Brigade*, 25.

78. *OR*, 2:319, 333, 413; Georgetown, D.C., July 1861, Reel 81, RG 27.5.7, NARA-CP; Woodbury, *First Rhode Island*, 92. For woolen uniforms, see McClendon, *Recollections*, 28.

79. Fry [Tyler], *"Wooden Nutmegs" at Bull Run*, 66.

80. Howard, *Recollections*, 35. See also Blackford, *Letters from Lee's Army*, 30; Blackford, *War Years*, 33; Early, *War Memoirs*, 20; Peck, *Reminiscences*, 5.

81. Turner, *Reminiscence of Lyle*, 84.

82. Smith, *Smell of Battle*, 50–51.

83. Howard, *Recollections*, 35.

84. Sutherland, *Reminiscences of a Private*, 37.

85. Johnston, *Narrative of Military Operations*, 42.

86. *OR*, 2:344.

87. *OR*, 2:573.

88. *OR*, 2:334; McPherson, *Battle Cry of Freedom*, 340–47.

89. Woodbury, *First Rhode Island*, 109–10.

90. Rhodes, *All for the Union*, 30.

91. Francis, *Narrative of a Private Soldier*, 12.

92. *OR*, 2:504, 519, 529 (quotation, 504). Peck, *Reminiscences*, 6; Blackford et al., *Letters from Lee's Army*, 34, 36. William C. Davis agreed with Beauregard. See *Battle at Bull Run*, 244.

93. Howard, *Recollections*, 43. See also Casler, *Four Years in the Stonewall Brigade*, 32; and Roper, *Repairing the "March of Mars,"* 117.

94. Turner, *Reminiscence of Lyle*, 92.

95. Turner, *Reminiscence of Lyle*, 104. See also Everson and Simpson, *"Far, Far from Home,"* 39–40; Howard, *Recollections*, 45–46; and *Richmond Whig*, Aug. 9, 1861.

96. Oates, *War between the Union and the Confederacy*, 76.

97. Dobbins, *Grandfather's Journal*, 33; Everson and Simpson, *"Far, Far from Home,"* 37; Bartlett, *Military Record of Louisiana*, 54; Kimble, *Our American Weather*, 172.

98. Georgetown, D.C., Aug. 1861, Reel 81, RG 27.5.7, NARA-CP; Dobbins, *Grandfather's Journal*, 34; Everson and Simpson, *"Far, Far from Home,"* 37–38.

99. Armstrong, *"Good Hand of Our God,"* 4; Vedder, *"Offer unto God Thanksgiving,"* 5.

100. Everson and Simpson, *"Far, Far from Home,"* 61–63.

101. Blight, *When This Cruel War Is Over*, 27, 30; Cook, *Twelfth Massachusetts*, 25–28; Furst Diary, 11–12, HCWRTC, USAMHI; Rhodes, *All for the Union*, 41; "Diary of Horatio Nelson Taft," Aug. 5, 1861, accessed May 12, 2014.

102. Edwin Birley to Brother, Aug. 10, 1861, Washington, D.C., Edwin Birley Collection: Correspondence, NYHS/CWPSD. See also Mead Diary, vol. 1, Aug. 28–30, 1861, LC.

103. Robertson, *Letters of McAllister*, 67, 69.

104. Georgetown, D.C., July 1861, Reel 81, RG 27.5.7, NARA-CP.

105. Rafuse, *McClellan's War*, 118–19, 130–33; Guelzo, *Fateful Lightning*, 156–57; Westervelt, "Lights and Shadows of Army Life," CWMC, USAMHI.

CHAPTER 2

1. McPherson, *Battle Cry of Freedom*, 290–91; McQuigg, "Climate of Missouri," 725; Parrish, *Turbulent Partnership*, 4–8, 15–17; Piston and Hatcher, *Wilson's Creek*, 24–30.

2. Tower Grove, Mo., May 1861, Reel 290, RG 27.5.7, NARA-CP; *Daily Louisville (Ky.) Democrat*, June 11, 1861; *St. Louis Daily Missouri Republican*, May 17, 1861; Knox, *Camp-Fire and Cotton-Field*,

28–50; McPherson, *Battle Cry of Freedom*, 290–92; Parrish, *Turbulent Partnership*, 17–32; Piston and Hatcher, *Wilson's Creek*, 30–47, 80–81.

3. Tower Grove, Mo., June 1861, Reel 290, RG 27.5.7, NARA-CP; Davis, *Late Victorian Holocausts*, 12–15, 17–18, 213–38; Mergen, *Weather Matters*, 23–25, 40–41; Keller, "MU Expert Studies Civil War Weather," accessed June 21, 2014; "Science of Backward Weather Forecasting," accessed June 21, 2014; McQuigg, "Climate of Missouri," 725–26, 740; *St. Louis Daily Missouri Democrat*, June 14, 30, 1861; *St. Louis Daily Missouri Republican*, June 10–27, 1861; Piston and Hatcher, *Wilson's Creek*, 57, 69, 72, 76–79; Matson, *Life of Matson*, 60.

4. Tower Grove, Mo., July 1861, Reel 290, RG 27.5.7, NARA-CP; *St. Louis Daily Missouri Republican*, July 2, 6, 1861; Matson, *Life Experiences*, 60–61 (quotation, 61); Piston and Hatcher, *Wilson's Creek*, 103–5.

5. Piston and Hatcher, *Wilson's Creek*, 74–75; *OR*, 3:18; Knox, *Camp-Fire and Cotton-Field*, 61–62; Lane, "Recollections of a Volunteer," 8–9, accessed July 20, 2014; William G. Piston, email to author, Sept. 16, 2018.

6. Quoted in Piston and Hatcher, *Wilson's Creek*, 104–5.

7. *OR*, 3:44–45; Piston and Hatcher, *Wilson's Creek*, 125–28; Matson, *Life Experiences*, 60–61.

8. Matson, *Life Experiences*, 61.

9. Wilkie, *Pen and Powder*, 250–51.

10. *OR*, 3:44–45; Piston and Hatcher, *Wilson's Creek*, 128–32.

11. Piston and Hatcher, *Wilson's Creek*, 104–5, 110, 114, 121.

12. Piston and Hatcher, *Wilson's Creek*, 123; Watson, *Life in the Confederate Army*, 182–83, 186.

13. Piston and Hatcher, *Wilson's Creek*, 132–38 (quotation, 134); Knox, *Camp-Fire and Cotton-Field*, 63.

14. Tower Grove, Mo., July–Aug. 1861, Reel 290, RG 27.5.7, NARA-CP; *Richmond Whig*, Aug. 9, 1861; *St. Louis Daily Missouri Democrat*, July 29, Aug. 5–10, 1861; *St. Louis Daily Missouri Republican*, July 29, 30, 31, Aug. 6–10, 1861; "Science of Backward Weather Forecasting," accessed June 21, 2014.

15. Sanford, *Fighting Rebels and Redskins*, 128.

16. *OR*, 3:47; *St. Louis Daily Missouri Republican*, July 19, 20, 22, 23, 1861; Piston and Hatcher, *Wilson's Creek*, 139; McQuigg, "Climate of Missouri," 727.

17. Knox, *Camp-Fire and Cotton-Field*, 63–64, 65–67. See also Matson, *Life Experiences*, 63.

18. Lane, "Recollections of a Volunteer," 12, accessed July 20, 2014. See also *OR*, 3:47–52; and Watson, *Life in the Confederate Army*, 206.

19. Lane, "Recollections of a Volunteer," 11–13, accessed July 20, 2014; *OR*, 3:99; Piston and Hatcher, *Wilson's Creek*, 138–59; McQuigg, "Climate of Missouri," 727.

20. *OR*, 3:99, 104, 127; *Augusta (Ga.) Chronicle*, Aug. 28, 1861; Piston and Hatcher, *Wilson's Creek*, 148, 151–63.

21. Watson, *Life in the Confederate Army*, 211–12. See also Cater, *As It Was*, 87; Piston and Hatcher, *Wilson's Creek*, 162–63.

22. Cater, *As It Was*, 89.

23. *OR*, 3:58, 59–60, 65–66; Piston and Hatcher, *Wilson's Creek*, 164–78, 181–88.

24. Lane, "Recollections of a Volunteer," 14, accessed July 20, 2014.

25. *OR*, 3:60–62, 66–67; Piston and Hatcher, *Wilson's Creek*, 192–257; Ross, "Outdoor Sound Propagation," 1; Watson, *Life in the Confederate Army*, 219.

26. Watson, *Life in the Confederate Army*, 219. See also Piston and Hatcher, *Wilson's Creek*, 257–61.

27. *OR*, 3:62–63, 67–69; Piston and Hatcher, *Wilson's Creek*, 261–86.

28. Watson, *Life in the Confederate Army*, 229.

29. Phillips, *Rivers Ran Backward*, 141; Piston and Hatcher, *Wilson's Creek*, 304–28; *St. Louis Daily Missouri Republican*, Aug. 20, 22, 23, Sept. 3–15, 1861.

30. Anderson, *Memoirs*, 53–66 (quotations, 53, 61, 66). See also *OR*, 3:190–91; and *St. Louis Daily Missouri Republican*, Sept. 22, 1861.

31. Lesser, *Rebels at the Gate*, 127–29, 134–37, 173–79; McPherson, *Battle Cry of Freedom*, 301–2; Noe, *Southwest Virginia's Railroad*, 112–13; Williams, *West Virginia*, 58–59, 64–65, 75–78; Williams, *Hayes of the 23rd*, 76–81; Zinn, *Lee's Cheat Mountain Campaign*, 2–4, 12, 14.

32. Williams, *West Virginia*, 59–61; Zinn, *Lee's Cheat Mountain Campaign*, 2, 5–7, 45, 64, 72–76.

33. Horn and McGuire, "Climate of West Virginia," 422–39; *St. Louis Daily Missouri Republican*, July 18, 1861; Lesser, *Rebels at the Gate*, 140; Zinn, *Lee's Cheat Mountain Campaign*, 91; Kevin Law, email to author, July 22, 2014.

34. RWW to Father, July 23, 1861, Monterey, Va., Richard Woolfolk Waldrop Papers, SHC-UNC.

35. Worsham, *One of Jackson's Foot Cavalry*, 14–15 (quotation, 14); Zinn, *Lee's Cheat Mountain Campaign*, 6.

36. Worsham, *One of Jackson's Foot Cavalry*, 15–16 (quotation, 15). See also Lesser, *Rebels at the Gate*, 142–45, 164–66; and Zinn, *Lee's Cheat Mountain Campaign*, 67–69, 76–81.

37. Lee, *Recollections and Letters*, 40, 55. See also Zinn, *Lee's Cheat Mountain Campaign*, 91.

38. Worsham, *One of Jackson's Foot Cavalry*, 15; Head, *Sixteenth Regiment, Tennessee Volunteers*, 23–30 (quotations, 26, 27, 28; hereafter Head, Sixteenth Tennessee).

39. Drake, *Life of Hatton*, 368–69, 373. See also Bishop, *Civil War Generals of Tennessee*, 22–23; Lesser, *Rebels at the Gate*, 170; Zinn, *Lee's Cheat Mountain Campaign*, 117.

40. Horn and McGuire, "Climate of West Virginia," 423.

41. Drake, *Life of Hatton*, 369–73 (quotations, 369–70, 373). See also Zinn, *Lee's Cheat Mountain Campaign*, 93.

42. Zinn, *Lee's Cheat Mountain Campaign*, 60.

43. Drake, *Life of Hatton*, 363–78 (quotations, 375–76, 376–77).

44. Beatty, *Citizen-Solider*, 57–60. See also Zinn, *Lee's Cheat Mountain Campaign*, 93.

45. Drake, *Life of Hatton*, 377–78.

46. Williams, *Diary and Letters of Rutherford Birchard Hayes*, 2:80.

47. Member of the Bar, *Cheat Mountain*, 61.

48. Chamberlayne, *Ham Chamberlayne*, 33.

49. Lee, *Recollections and Letters*, 41–42, 43.

50. Worsham, *One of Jackson's Foot Cavalry*, 16–17; Drake, *Life of Hatton*, 376; Lee, *Recollections and Letters*, 41–44; Member of the Bar, *Cheat Mountain*, 62; Zinn, *Lee's Cheat Mountain Campaign*, 95, 96; *Charleston Mercury*, Sept. 14, 1861. See also *Augusta (Ga.) Chronicle*, Sept. 7, 1861.

51. Chamberlayne, *Ham Chamberlayne*, 35, 37. See also Lesser, *Rebels at the Gate*, 183.

52. Lee, *Recollections and Letters*, 44.

53. Lesser, *Rebels at the Gate*, 185–91; Zinn, *Lee's Cheat Mountain Campaign*, 100, 112–15.

54. Member of the Bar, *Cheat Mountain*, 63.

55. Head, *Sixteenth Tennessee*, 30–31; Zinn, *Lee's Cheat Mountain Campaign*. 128–35.

56. Member of the Bar, *Cheat Mountain*, 76–77, 85–87 (quotation, 76).

57. Member of the Bar, *Cheat Mountain*, 68–71; Head, *Sixteenth Tennessee*, 42. See also Lesser, *Rebels at the Gate*, 193–94; and Zinn, *Lee's Cheat Mountain Campaign*, 126–40, 176.

58. *OR*, 5:184–85, 186–87, 191–92 (quotations, 191); Zinn, *Lee's Cheat Mountain Campaign*, 140–78; Worsham, *One of Jackson's Foot Cavalry*, 17–19.

59. *OR*, 5:185–86; Toney, *Privations of a Private*, 15; *Augusta (Ga.) Chronicle*, Nov. 2, 1861.

60. Clark, *Under the Stars and Bars*, 30.

61. *OR*, 5:123–27, 128–65, 814–15, 842–45, 850; Beatty, *Citizen-Solider*, 69–70; Williams, *Diary and Letters of Rutherford Birchard Hayes*, 2:87–91; Lowry, *September Blood*, esp. 73–121; Noe, *Southwest Virginia's Railroad*, 113; Zinn, *Lee's Cheat Mountain Campaign*, 202–3.

62. Williams, *Diary and Letters of Rutherford Birchard Hayes*, 2:99–100.

63. Ludlum, *Early American Hurricanes*, 127; Partagas and Diaz, "Reconstruction of Historical Tropical Cyclone Frequency," 35–37, accessed Oct. 14, 2018; Toney, *Privations of a Private*, 16; Williams, *Diary and Letters of Rutherford Birchard Hayes*, 2:70; Zinn, *Lee's Cheat Mountain Campaign*, 196–203; Kevin Law, email to author, July 22, 2014.

64. Head, *Sixteenth Tennessee*, 52. See also R. W. Waldrop to Mother, Sept. 23, 1861, Valley Mountain, Waldrop Papers, SHC-UNC; Beatty, *Citizen-Solider*, 70; *Richmond Whig*, Oct. 4, 1861.

65. Lee, *Recollections and Letters*, 49.

66. Head, *Sixteenth Tennessee*, 52–53.

67. Williams, *Diary and Letters of Rutherford Birchard Hayes*, 2:102–3.

68. Beatty, *Citizen-Solider*, 70.

69. Quoted in Lesser, *Rebels at the Gate*, 225.

70. Williams, *Diary and Letters of Rutherford Birchard Hayes*, 2:106–8 (quotation, 106). See also *Augusta (Ga.) Daily Constitutionalist*, Oct. 22, 1861; *St. Louis Daily Missouri Democrat*, Oct. 11, 1861; and Lesser, *Rebels at the Gate*, 214–15.

71. *Augusta (Ga.) Daily Constitutionalist*, Oct. 8, 1861; Zinn, *Lee's Cheat Mountain Campaign*, 203.

72. Lee, *Recollections and Letters*, 50.

73. Head, *Sixteenth Tennessee*, 53–54.

74. R. W. Waldrop to Mother, Oct. 26, 1861, Greenbrier River, Waldrop Papers, SHC-UNC. See also *Richmond Whig*, Nov. 1, 1861.

75. Lesser, *Rebels at the Gate*, 203–5, 215–17 (quotation, 203); Zinn, *Lee's Cheat Mountain Campaign*, 203.

76. Worsham, *One of Jackson's Foot Cavalry*, 17; Lesser, *Rebels at the Gate*, 197.

77. Lee, *Recollections and Letters*, 44, 46–47.

78. Krick, *Civil War Weather*, 43.

79. *OR*, 5:389, 390, 396–97, 1003–4, 1041; Robertson, *Stonewall Jackson*, 287–88, 293, 294–96; Tanner, *Stonewall in the Valley*, 60–68.

80. Robertson, *Stonewall Jackson*, 297–301 (quotation, 297).

81. Henry Kyd Douglas to unknown, [Jan. 1862], Henry Kyd Douglas Papers, 1861–1949, Duke.

82. *New Orleans Daily True Delta*, Nov. 21, 1861.

83. *Alexandria (Va.) Local News*, Dec. 6, 1861; *Daily Columbus (Ga.) Enquirer*, Dec. 4, 1861; Chamberlayne, *Ham Chamberlayne*, 52–58; Clark, *Under the Stars and Bars*, 38; Neese, *Three Years in the Confederate Horse Artillery*, 8–12; Roper, *Repairing the "March of Mars,"* 155–76; Toney, *Privations of a Private*, 17; Worsham, *One of Jackson's Foot Cavalry*, 22.

84. Roper, *Repairing the "March of Mars,"* 175.

85. Richard Woolfolk Waldrop to Mother, Dec. 29, 1861, Winchester, Va., Waldrop Papers, SHC-UNC.

86. *OR*, 5:392, 1018; Clark, *Under the Stars and Bars*, 43. For similar accounts, see *Alexandria (Va.) Local News*, Jan. 1, 2, 1862; *Augusta (Ga.) Chronicle*, Dec. 31, 1861; Baylor, *Bull Run to Bull Run*, 31; Casler, *Four Years in the Stonewall Brigade*, 62; Drake, *Life of Hatton*, 397; Neese, *Three Years in the Confederate Horse Artillery*, 12; Krick, *Civil War Weather*, 43; Robertson, *Stonewall Jackson*, 295; and Tanner, *Stonewall in the Valley*, 69–71.

87. *OR*, 5:390–91; Baylor, *Bull Run to Bull Run*, 31; Casler, *Four Years in the Stonewall Brigade*, 62; Clark, *Under the Stars and Bars*, 43, 44–45; Drake, *Life of Hatton*, 399; McComb, "Tennesseans in the Mountain Campaign," 211; Neese, *Three Years in the Confederate Horse Artillery*, 12–13; Worsham, *One of Jackson's Foot Cavalry*, 25; Roper, *Repairing the "March of Mars,"* 179–80; Toney, *Privations of a Private*, 19–20; Turner, *Reminiscence of Lyle*, 139, 140; Richard Woolfolk Waldrop to Father, Jan. 12, 1862,

Unger's Store, Va., Waldrop Papers, SHC-UNC; Krick, *Civil War Weather*, 43; Robertson, *Stonewall Jackson*, 304–9; Tanner, *Stonewall in the Valley*, 69–71; Krick, *Civil War Weather*, 43.

88. OR, 5:392; Casler, *Four Years in the Stonewall Brigade*, 62–63; Neese, *Three Years in the Confederate Horse Artillery*, 17–18; Worsham, *One of Jackson's Foot Cavalry*, 26; Turner, *Reminiscence of Lyle*, 142; Toney, *Privations of a Private*, 21, 24–25; Richard Woolfolk Waldrop to Father, Jan. 12, 1862, Unger's Store, Va., Waldrop Papers, SHC-UNC; Krick, *Civil War Weather*, 43; Robertson, *Stonewall Jackson*, 309–11; Tanner, *Stonewall in the Valley*, 74–76.

89. OR, 5:392, 1046; Baylor, *Bull Run to Bull Run*, 31; Clark, *Under the Stars and Bars*, 46. See also Neese, *Three Years in the Confederate Horse Artillery*, 19; Roper, *Repairing the "March of Mars,"* 181–82; Turner, *Reminiscence of Lyle*, 137, 142–43; and Tanner, *Stonewall in the Valley*, 74–79.

90. Worsham, *One of Jackson's Foot Cavalry*, 26.

91. OR, 5:393; Roper, *Repairing the "March of Mars,"* 181–85 (quotation, 181). See also Galwey, *Valiant Hours*, 17; Neese, *Three Years in the Confederate Horse Artillery*, 20; Worsham, *One of Jackson's Foot Cavalry*, 27, 28; Toney, *Privations of a Private*, 24–25; Krick, *Civil War Weather*, 43; Robertson, *Stonewall Jackson*, 311–13; and Tanner, *Stonewall in the Valley*, 79.

92. Henry Kyd Douglas to My Dear Perversity, Jan. 26, 1862, Winchester, Va., Douglas Papers, Duke; OR, 5:393, 1033, 1034, 1039, 1042, 1046–47; Richard Woolfolk Waldrop to Sister, Jan. 22, 1862, Romney, Waldrop Papers, SHC-UNC; Waldrop to Father, Jan. 28, Feb. 1, 1862, Romney, ibid.; Waldrop to Father, Feb. 7, 1862, Winchester, ibid. See also Chamberlayne, *Ham Chamberlayne*, 58, 63, 66, 70; Drake, *Life of Hatton*, 403; Edward Hitchcock McDonald Reminiscences, 21–31, 32–33, SHC-UNC; Neese, *Three Years in the Confederate Horse Artillery*, 20; Roper, *Repairing the "March of Mars,"* 188–211; Robertson, *Stonewall Jackson*, 312–13, 315–21; and Tanner, *Stonewall in the Valley*, 79–88.

93. Worsham, *One of Jackson's Foot Cavalry*, 29.

94. Quaife, *From the Cannon's Mouth*, 52–53; Robertson, *Stonewall Jackson*, 313–14; Tanner, *Stonewall in the Valley*, 86–93; OR, 5:394, 1039, 1041; Turner, *Reminiscence of Lyle*, 137–38.

CHAPTER 3

1. "Diary of Horatio Nelson Taft," Aug. 21, 1861, accessed May 12, 2014.

2. Kimble, *Our American Weather*, 196, 214–16, 218; Krick, *Civil War Weather*, 36; *Augusta (Ga.) Chronicle*, Aug. 27, 1861; *Augusta (Ga.) Daily Constitutionalist*, Aug. 29, Sept. 7, 1861; *Charleston Courier*, Sept. 24, 1861; *Daily Columbus (Ga.) Enquirer*, Aug. 30, Oct. 10, 1861; *St. Louis Daily Missouri Republican*, Aug. 30, 1861; Baird, *Journals of Edmonds*, 58; Blackford et al., *Letters from Lee's Army*, 42; Blight, *When This Cruel War Is Over*, 36, 48, 51; Dobbins, *Grandfather's Journal*, 37–42; McClendon, *Recollections*, 32; Oates, *War between the Union and the Confederacy*, 79; Roper, *Repairing the "March of Mars,"* 138–41; Ludlum, *American Weather Book*, 186–87; Crockett, "Climate of Virginia," 415.

3. Krick, *Civil War Weather*, 36; Richmond, Va., Sept. 1861, Reel 527, RG 27.5.7, NARA-CP; *Augusta (Ga.) Daily Constitutionalist*, Sept. 12, 1861; *Daily Louisville (Ky.) Democrat*, Sept. 27, 1861; *Hannibal (Mo.) Messenger*, Oct. 4, 1861; *St. Louis Daily Missouri Republican*, Oct. 2, 1861; Baird, *Journals of Edmonds*, 58; Blackford et al., *Letters from Lee's Army*, 42; Blight, *When This Cruel War Is Over*, 36, 48, 51; Dobbins, *Grandfather's Journal*, 37–42; de Trobriand, *Four Years in the Army of the Potomac*, 95–97; Howe, *Touched with Fire*, 9; McClendon, *Recollections*, 32; Mead Diary, vol. 1, Sept. 3–30, 1861, LC; Oates, *War between the Union and the Confederacy*, 79; Roper, *Repairing the "March of Mars,"* 138–41. Soldier records from the front that autumn actually are more closely aligned with the records of Smithsonian observer Charles Meriwether near Richmond.

4. "Diary of Horatio Nelson Taft," Sept. 27, 1861, accessed May 12, 2014; Winkle, *Lincoln's Citadel*, 208–9.

5. Member of Company C, *Twenty-Seventh Indiana*, 48.

6. *St. Louis Daily Missouri Republican*, Oct. 12, 1861; Ludlum, *American Weather Book*, 228–30; Kimble, *Our American Weather*, 225–27.

7. Richmond, Va., Oct. 1861, Reel 527, RG 27.5.7, NARA-CP; Krick, *Civil War Weather*, 38; "Diary of Horatio Nelson Taft," Oct. 3–8, 1861, accessed May 12, 2014; Ludlum, *American Weather Book*, 230.

8. Blackford et al., *Letters from Lee's Army*, 46. See also *Charleston Mercury*, Oct. 18, 1861.

9. Quaife, *From the Cannon's Mouth*, 18.

10. R. Mead Jr. to Friends and Home, Oct. 11, 1861, Darnestown, Md., Rufus Mead Jr. Papers, LC; Mead Diary, vol. 1, Oct. 7–11, 1861, ibid.

11. *Richmond Whig*, Oct. 11, 1861. See also Georgetown, D.C., Oct. 1861, Reel 81, RG 27.5.7, NARA-CP; Richmond, Va., Oct. 1861, Reel 527, ibid.; Krick, *Civil War Weather*, 38; "Diary of Horatio Nelson Taft," Oct. 3–8, 1861, accessed May 12, 2014; Ludlum, *American Weather Book*, 230.

12. Oates, *War between the Union and the Confederacy*, 80. See also Mead Diary, vol. 1, Oct. 12–15, 1861, LC; Krick, *Civil War Weather*, 38; Krick, *Civil War Weather*, 38; *Alexandria (Va.) Local News*, Oct. 9, 14, 1861.

13. Lee, *Memoir of William Nelson Pendleton*, 160–63 (quotations, 160, 163) (hereafter Lee, *Memoir of Pendleton*); Ballard, *Ball's Bluff*, 3. Several newspapers reprinted a July plea for blankets from the *Iredell (N.C.) Express*. See, for example, *Augusta (Ga.) Chronicle*, July 17, 1861; and *New Orleans Daily True Delta*, July 16, 1861. For spooning, see, for example, George M. Barnard to Inman, Oct. 14, 1861, Camp Barnes, George Middleton Barnard Papers, CWCDJ, MHS.

14. Robertson, *Letters of McAllister*, 85.

15. Blackford et al., *Letters from Lee's Army*, 49.

16. Curtis, *First Bull Run to Chancellorsville*, 74–75.

17. Weymouth, *Memorial Sketch of Lieut. Edgar M. Newcomb*, 28 (hereafter, Weymouth, *Sketch of Newcomb*).

18. Rhodes, *All for the Union*, 44; Policastro, "Crimean Oven," 10–11.

19. *OR*, 5:891, 896–97, 934, 941 (quotations, 896, 934); Symonds, *Joseph E. Johnston*, 132–33.

20. *OR*, 5:84, 9, 664; Rafuse, *McClellan's War*, 135, 146, 159–61.

21. Krick, *Civil War Weather*, 38; Ballard, *Ball's Bluff*, 3–12; Rafuse, *McClellan's War*, 139–40.

22. *OR*, 5:290–99; Ballard, *Ball's Bluff*, 13–39; Rafuse, *McClellan's War*, 140–41; Winkle, *Lincoln's Citadel*, 210–12.

23. *OR*, 5:300–302; Blackford et al., *Letters from Lee's Army*, 49. See also Krick, *Civil War Weather*, 38; McPherson, *Battle Cry of Freedom*, 362–63; Rafuse, *McClellan's War*, 140–41; Robertson, *Letters of McAllister*, 87; Member of Company C, *Twenty-Seventh Indiana*, 59–61; and Quaife, *From the Cannon's Mouth*, 23.

24. Hamilton, *Papers of Randolph Abbott Shotwell*, 1:121, 122 (hereafter Hamilton, *Papers of Shotwell*).

25. Hamilton, *Papers of Shotwell*, 1:122–24 (quotation, 122); Ballard, *Ball's Bluff*, 37–39. See also Quaife, *From the Cannon's Mouth*, 23; *OR*, 5:325.

26. Blackford et al., *Letters from Lee's Army*, 50.

27. Member of Company C, *Twenty-Seventh Indiana*, 61. See also *OR*, 5:334; Krick, *Civil War Weather*, 38.

28. Member of Company C, *Twenty-Seventh Indiana*, 61.

29. *Times* (London), Nov. 5, 1861, quoted in *Charleston Mercury*, Dec. 3, 1861.

30. Krick, *Civil War Weather*, 38; George M. Barnard to Inman, Oct. 23, 1861, Camp Barnes, Barnard Papers, CWCDJ, MHS; Mead Diary, vol. 1, Oct. 21–31, 1861, LC; "Diary of Horatio Nelson Taft," Oct. 24, 1861, accessed May 12, 2014; *Alexandria (Va.) Local News*, Oct. 25, 1861.

31. Everson and Simpson, *"Far, Far from Home,"* 81. See also Fleet and Fuller, *Green Mount,* 83; George M. Barnard to Inman, Oct. 26, 1861, Camp Barnes, Barnard Papers, CWCDJ, MHS.

32. *American Agriculturalist,* Nov. 1, 1861. For drought, see *Street & Smith's New York Weekly,* Jan. 30, 1862.

33. "Diary of Horatio Nelson Taft," Nov. 2, 1861, accessed May 12, 2014; *Alexandria (Va.) Local News,* Nov. 4, 1861; *Charleston Mercury,* Nov. 11, 1861; *Richmond Whig,* Nov. 12, 1861; Chenoweth, "New Compilation of North Atlantic Tropical Cyclones," 8681–82; Long, *Civil War Day by Day,* 132; Ludlum, *Early American Hurricanes,* 101–2; Cary Mock, email to author, Nov. 2, 2019.

34. De Trobriand, *Four Years in the Army of the Potomac,* 115–16; Krick, *Civil War Weather,* 40; "Diary of Horatio Nelson Taft," Oct. 30–31, 1861, accessed May 12, 2014; *Alexandria (Va.) Local News,* Oct. 28, 29, 1861; *Charleston Mercury,* Oct. 28, 29, 1861; Quaife, *From the Cannon's Mouth,* 29; Warfield, *Confederate Soldier's Memoirs,* 75.

35. Malles, *Bridge Building in Wartime,* 44.

36. Sears, *Papers of McClellan,* 123.

37. Warfield, *Confederate Soldier's Memoirs,* 75.

38. Ludlum, *American Weather Book,* 244; Krick, *Civil War Weather,* 40; "Diary of Horatio Nelson Taft," Nov. 6, 1861, accessed May 12, 2014; Dobbins, *Grandfather's Journal,* 48–49; Everson and Simpson, *"Far, Far from Home,"* 86–87; Fleet and Fuller, *Green Mount,* 85; Roper, *Repairing the "March of Mars,"* 151–54.

39. Quaife, *From the Cannon's Mouth,* 24–25, 29.

40. Kimble, *Our American Weather,* 225; George M. Barnard to Inman, Nov. 9, 1861, Camp Barnes, Barnard Papers, CWCDJ, MHS; Norton, *Army Letters,* 32–33; "Diary of Horatio Nelson Taft," Nov. 10–16, 1861, accessed May 12, 2014; *Alexandria (Va.) Local News,* Nov. 12, 1861.

41. Tucker, *God in the War,* 6; *Alexandria (Va.) Local News,* Nov. 16, 1861.

42. Quaife, *From the Cannon's Mouth,* 35. See also George M. Barnard to Inman, Nov. 18, 1861, Camp Barnes, Barnard Papers, CWCDJ, MHS.

43. Francis, *Narrative of a Private Soldier,* 13. See also Blight, *When This Cruel War Is Over,* 56, 60, 63; "Diary of Horatio Nelson Taft," Nov. 20, 24, 1861, accessed May 12, 2014; and Krick, *Civil War Weather,* 40, 42.

44. Dickey, *Eighty-Fifth Regiment Pennsylvania Volunteer Infantry,* 15–16 (hereafter Dickey, *Eighty-Fifth Pennsylvania*); Dobbins, *Grandfather's Journal,* 51–52; Mead Diary, vol. 1, Nov. 13–30, 1861, LC; Quaife, *From the Cannon's Mouth,* 35; Weymouth, *Sketch Newcomb,* 38; Krick, *Civil War Weather,* 40, 42.

45. Blight, *When This Cruel War Is Over,* 56, 60, 63.

46. Steinberg, *Down to Earth,* 90, 91.

47. "Ultisols," US Department of Agriculture Natural Resources Conservation Service, http://www.nrcs.usda.gov/wps/portal/nrcs/detail/soils/survey/class/?cid=nrcs142p2_053609, accessed Jan. 27, 2015. See also NRCS Soils; "Web Soil Survey," accessed Jan. 29, 2015; "Distribution Maps of Dominant Soil Orders," accessed Jan. 29, 2015; "Soil Orders Simplified," accessed Oct. 25, 2018; and Joey Shaw, email to author, Jan. 27, 2015.

48. "Distribution Maps of Dominant Soil Orders," accessed Jan. 29, 2015; NRCS Soils.

49. Brady, *War upon the Land,* 17; Dean, *Agrarian Republic,* 2–70; Fiege, *Republic of Nature,* 201–3; Levine, "'African Warfare,'" 67–68.

50. *Charleston Mercury,* Nov. 20, 1861.

51. *OR,* 5:934.

52. *OR,* 5:948–49, 951 (quotation, 948).

53. *OR,* 5:941–42 (quotation, 941); Symonds, *Joseph E. Johnston,* 132–33.

54. Hamilton, *Papers of Shotwell,* 1:131–32 (quotation, 131).

55. Johnston, *Narrative of Military Operations*, 84–85; Dobbins, *Grandfather's Journal*, 56–60; Everson and Simpson, "Far, Far from Home," 91, 93; *Daily Columbus (Ga.) Enquirer*, Jan. 1, 1862.

56. Oates, *War between the Union and the Confederacy*, 83.

57. See, for example, *Augusta (Ga.) Chronicle*, Dec. 11, 1861; Bartlett, *Military Record of Louisiana*, 66; Everson and Simpson, "Far, Far from Home," 91; and Norton, *Army Letters*, 36.

58. Lasswell, *Rags and Hope*, 52, 57. See also *Charleston Courier*, Nov. 18, 1861; Everson and Simpson, "Far, Far from Home," 91, 95, 99; Hamilton, *Papers of Shotwell*, 1:131–33; Lee, *Memoir of Pendleton*, 164–65; and Sutherland, *Reminiscences of a Private*, 51.

59. Bartlett, *Military Record of Louisiana*, 63.

60. *Hillsborough (N.C.) Recorder*, Jan. 8, 1862.

61. *Carolina Observer* (Fayetteville, N.C.), Feb. 3, 1862.

62. Rafuse, *McClellan's War*, 159–61, 66.

63. *OR*, 5:84.

64. Quaife, *From the Cannon's Mouth*, 30; Norton, *Army Letters*, 37; Nelson, *Ruin Nation*, 104, 119.

65. Mat Richards to Brother, Dec. 23, 1861, Fairfax Co., Va., M. Edgar Richards Correspondence, Box 97, CWMC, USAMHI; *Member of Company C, Twenty-Seventh Indiana*, 72–73.

66. *OR*, 5:84; [Crane], "Special Organization of the American Ambulance," 524–25; George M. Barnard to Inman, Nov. 1, 1861, Camp Barnes, Barnard Papers, CWCDJ, MHS; Rosenblatt and Rosenblatt, *Hard Marching Every Day*, 1; Billings, *Hardtack and Coffee*, 61; Blight, *When This Cruel War Is Over*, 64; *Member of Company C, Twenty-Seventh Indiana*, 72–73 (quotation, 72); Norton, *Army Letters*, 36; Policastro, "Crimean Oven," 10–11.

67. Quaife, *From the Cannon's Mouth*, 30.

68. White, *Diary of Wyman S. White*, 20. See also *Charleston Mercury*, Nov. 14, 1861.

69. *OR*, 5:84, 664–65.

70. *OR*, 5:84, 664–65. See also [Crane], "Special Organization of the American Ambulance," 525–28. Crane later utilized the California-oven system to great advantage in hospitals during the Franco-Prussian War (1870–71).

71. Quaife, *From the Cannon's Mouth*, 30, 36.

72. Weymouth, *Sketch of Newcomb*, 34; Crane, "Special Organization," 526–28.

73. Lasswell, *Rags and Hope*, 59. See also Blackford, *War Years*, 54.

74. Billings, *Hardtack and Coffee*, 74.

75. Quaife, *From the Cannon's Mouth*, 30, 36.

76. Billings, *Hardtack and Coffee*, 49, 54, 57.

77. *OR*, 5:84, 664.

78. Rosenblatt and Rosenblatt, *Hard Marching Every Day*, 2. See also Nelson, *Ruin Nation*, 120.

79. Billings, *Hardtack and Coffee*, 54–57. See also White, *Diary of Wyman S. White*, 20–24.

80. *Member of Company C, Twenty-Seventh Indiana*, 81–82.

81. Blight, *When This Cruel War Is Over*, 63, 67.

82. De Trobriand, *Four Years in the Army of the Potomac*, 125–26.

83. Quaife, *From the Cannon's Mouth*, 38–44 (quotation, 43); Krick, *Civil War Weather*, 42.

84. Nevins, *Diary of Battle*, 5. See also *Charleston Mercury*, Nov. 21, 1861.

85. Haden, *Reminiscences*, 27; Mat Richards to Brother, Dec. 23, 1861, Fairfax Co., Va., Richards Correspondence, CWMC, USAMHI.

86. Hamilton, *Papers of Shotwell*, 1:138; Sutherland, *Reminiscences of a Private*, 55.

87. Hamilton, *Papers of Shotwell*, 1:136. See also *New England Farmer*, Jan. 1, 1862, 38–39.

88. Krick, *Civil War Weather*, 42; Ludlum, *American Weather Book*, 260; Crockett, "Climate of Virginia," 415; *Carolina Observer* (Fayetteville, N.C.), Dec. 9, 1861; *Richmond Whig*, Dec. 6, 1861; Blight,

When This Cruel War Is Over, 65 (quotation, 65); Everson and Simpson, *"Far, Far from Home,"* 95, 97, 98; Dobbins, *Grandfather's Journal,* 54–60; Member of Company C, *Twenty-Seventh Indiana,* 76, 79; William H. Myers to Parents, Dec. 13, 1861, Camp Observation, in Joanne V. Fulcoly, "A Brief History of the Myers Family," William H. Myers Letters, Box 84, CWMC, USAMHI, typescript; Norton, *Army Letters,* 36–38; Quaife, *From the Cannon's Mouth,* 38–43 (quotations, 41, 43); Robertson, *Letters of McAllister,* 98, 100, 102; Weymouth, *Sketch of Newcomb,* 42; Rafuse, *McClellan's War,* 166.

89. Blight, *When This Cruel War Is Over,* 64, 65.

90. Blackford et al., *Letters from Lee's Army,* 60, 67. See also *Alexandria (Va.) Local News,* Dec. 6, 1861; and *St. Louis Daily Missouri Republican,* Dec. 20, 1861.

91. "Diary of Horatio Nelson Taft," Dec. 8–15, 1861 (quotations, Dec. 9–10), accessed May 12, 2014.

92. *Alexandria (Va.) Local News,* Dec. 12, 16, 17, 22, 23, 1861; O. S. Coolidge to unknown, Dec. 22–24, 30, 1861, Annapolis, Md., Oliver S. Coolidge Papers, 1861–1864, Duke; "Diary of Horatio Nelson Taft," Dec. 22–23, 1861, accessed May 12, 2014; Quaife, *From the Cannon's Mouth,* 44; Krick, *Civil War Weather,* 42; *American Almanac,* vol. 32, 4th ser., 2:4.

93. Lasswell, *Rags and Hope,* 58–59. See also Dobbins, *Grandfather's Journal,* 58; and Krick, *Civil War Weather,* 42.

94. Hamilton, *Papers of Shotwell,* 1:137.

95. Dobbins, *Grandfather's Journal,* 59–60; Sutherland, *Reminiscences of a Private,* 51, 55.

96. "Diary of Horatio Nelson Taft," Dec. 31, 1862, accessed May 12, 2014. See also Leech, *Reveille in Washington,* 123–24.

97. O. S. Coolidge to unknown, Dec. 30, 30–31, 1861, (two letters), Annapolis, Md., Coolidge Papers, Duke; Nevins, *Diary of Battle,* 7–8; Rafuse, *McClellan's War,* 166–77.

98. *Alexandria (Va.) Local News,* Jan. 4, 6, 1862; Baird, *Journals of Edmonds,* 65; Blight, *When This Cruel War Is Over,* 72–73, 77–78, 80; Child, *Fifth Regiment New Hampshire Volunteers,* 31–32 (hereafter Child, *Fifth New Hampshire*); Cook, *Twelfth Massachusetts,* 35, 37; de Trobriand, *Four Years in the Army of the Potomac,* 128; Dobbins, *Grandfather's Journal,* 61–63 (quotation, 62); Nevins, *Diary of Battle,* 7–8; Robertson, *Letters of McAllister,* 112, 113, 114, 117; Sparks, *Inside Lincoln's Army,* 26, 29, 31, 32, 34; Weymouth, *Sketch of Newcomb,* 43; Crockett, "Climate of Virginia," 399; Kimble, *Our American Weather,* 13–14; Krick, *Civil War Weather,* 45; Ludlum, *American Weather Book,* 2–3; Ludlum, *Early American Winters,* 122.

99. *Alexandria (Va.) Local News,* Jan. 9, 21, 25, Feb. 1, 3, 1862; *Charleston Mercury,* Jan. 16, 1862; *Richmond Whig,* Jan. 17, 1862; John C. Babcock to Jane, Feb. 10, 1862, Washington, D.C., John C. Babcock Papers, LC; Baird, *Journals of Edmonds,* 66, 67; George M. Barnard to Inman, Jan. 18, Feb. 10, 1862, Camp Barnes, Barnard Papers, CWCDJ, MHS; Barnard to Mother, Feb. 6, 1862, Camp Barnes, ibid.; Blight, *When This Cruel War Is Over,* 82, 84, 89, 89; O. S. Coolidge to unknown, Jan. 14, 15, 16, 17, 1862, Hatteras Inlet, N.C., Coolidge Papers, Duke; Mead Diary, vol. 2, Feb. 9–24, 1862, LC; Nevins, *Diary of Battle,* 11, 13, 15, 16, 18; Norton, *Army Letters,* 40; Rhodes, *All for the Union,* 52–54; Robertson, *Letters of McAllister,* 118, 120; Rosenblatt and Rosenblatt, *Hard Marching Every Day,* 6; Sparks, *Inside Lincoln's Army,* 26, 29, 31, 32, 34; "Diary of Horatio Nelson Taft," Jan. 16, 1862, accessed May 12, 2014; Crockett, "Climate of Virginia," 411, 416; Kimble, *Our American Weather,* 3–5, 24–26, 29–30; Krick, *Civil War Weather,* 45, 48; Ludlum, *American Weather Book,* 2–3, 24–27, 31–34.

100. Sparks, *Inside Lincoln's Army,* 32; Weymouth, *Sketch of Newcomb,* 46.

101. Rhodes, *All for the Union,* 52, 54 (quotation, 54).

102. M. Edward Richards to Father, Jan. 19, 1862, Fairfax Co., Va., Richards Correspondence, CWMC, USAMHI; Richards to Brother, Feb. 1, 1862, Fairfax Co., Va., ibid. See also Robertson, *Letters of McAllister,* 117; *Richmond Whig,* Jan. 24, 1862; and Rhodes, *All for the Union,* 54–56.

103. Rafuse, *McClellan's War*, 178–82; Sears, *To the Gates of Richmond*, 5–11.

104. Norton, *Army Letters*, 53, 45, 46; "Diary of Horatio Nelson Taft," Feb. 1862, accessed May 12, 2014.

CHAPTER 4

1. C.S. Const., art. IV, sec. 3; Frazier, *Blood & Treasure*, 4–22 (quotation, 5); Nelson, "Indians Make the Best Guerrillas," 101; Hall, *Sibley's New Mexico Campaign*, 3.

2. Warde, *When the Wolf Came*, 39, 42–61, 67–68. Lincoln's lack of interest in Indian affairs is a major theme of Etulain, *Lincoln and the Oregon Country*.

3. Debo, "Site of the Battle of Round Mountain," 187, 190–93; Warde, *When the Wolf Came*, 53–58, 61, 66–71. For the Lincoln administration's reply to Opothle Yahola, see *OR*, 8:25.

4. *OR*, 8:5–10, 14–21; *Clarksville (Tex.) Standard*, Nov. 16, 1861; Debo, "Site of the Battle of Round Mountain," 199–202; McBride, *Opothleyaholo and the Loyal Muskogee*, 166–70; Warde, *When the Wolf Came*, 71–80.

5. Cater, *As It Was*, 100–106 (quotation, 101). See also Dorman, *It Happened in Oklahoma*, 21–23; and Shoemaker, "Battle of Chustenahlah," 180–84.

6. *OR*, 8:12–13, 22–33; Cater, *As It Was*, 100–106; Debo, "Site of the Battle of Round Mountain," 187; Dorman, *It Happened in Oklahoma*, 21–23; McBride, *Opothleyaholo and the Loyal Muskogee*, 170–81; Shoemaker, "Battle of Chustenahlah," 180–84; Warde, *When the Wolf Came*, 80–95.

7. Alberts, *Battle of Glorieta*, 3–6; Frazier, *Blood & Treasure*, 28–32, 54–56; Hall, *Sibley's New Mexico Campaign*, 4–26.

8. *OR*, 4:5–11; Alberts, *Battle of Glorieta*, 6; Frazier, *Blood & Treasure*, 32, 34–36, 39–44, 48–72; Hall, *Sibley's New Mexico Campaign*, 26–28; Nelson, "'Difficulties and Seductions of the Desert,'" 34–48; Nelson, "Indians Make the Best Guerrillas," 100, 107–11. The closest weather observer, at Fort Craig, recorded a high of 102 degrees on June 25, with lows falling only to 75 degrees. See Fort Craig, N.Mex., June 1861, Reel 334, RG 27.5.7, NARA-CP.

9. *OR*, 4:93; Alberts, *Battle of Glorieta*, 6–11; Frazier, *Blood & Treasure*, 44–47, 73–91; Hall, *Sibley's New Mexico Campaign*, 21, 29–41, 54; Taylor, *Bloody Valverde*, 10–12; *St. Louis Daily Missouri Republican*, Nov. 11, 1861.

10. Alberts, *Battle of Glorieta*, 11; Frazier, *Blood & Treasure*, 119–29; Hall, *Sibley's New Mexico Campaign*, 42–51; Nelson, "Something in the Air"; Baechler et al., "Guide to Determining Climate Regions," 2–3; Orton, "Climate of Texas," 878, 880, 888, 891, 904, 909; "Aridisols Map," US Department of Agriculture Natural Resources Conservation Service, http://www.nrcs.usda.gov/wps/portal/nrcs/detail/soils/survey/class/?cid=nrcs142p2_053595, accessed Feb. 17, 2015; "Mollisols Map," US Department of Agriculture Natural Resources Conservation Service, http://www.nrcs.usda.gov/wps/portal/nrcs/detail/soils/survey/class/?cid=nrcs142p2_053604, accessed Feb. 17, 2015; NRCS Soils.

11. [Davidson], "Reminiscences of the Old Brigade," 59–61. See also Nelson, "Indians Make the Best Guerrillas," 112–13; Nelson, "Something in the Air"; Orton, "Climate of Texas," 880–81; and Roy R. Barkley, "Blue Norther," *Handbook of Texas Online*, June 12, 2010, https://www.tshaonline.org/handbook/online/articles/ybb01, accessed Feb. 26, 2015.

12. Hollister, *Boldly They Rode*, 13–25 (quotation, 15). See also Hall, *Sibley's New Mexico Campaign*, 61; and Lowers, "Climate of Wyoming," 961.

13. Williams, *Three Years and a Half in the Army*, 2–6 (quotation, 6).

14. Williams, *Three Years and a Half in the Army*, 8–9. See also Alberts, *Battle of Glorieta*, 13; and Hall, *Sibley's New Mexico Campaign*, 59–65, 125–27.

15. Williams, *Three Years and a Half in the Army*, 9–14 (quotations, 9, 10); *OR*, 9:636–637.

16. *OR*, 4:157, 9:636–40; Fort Craig, N.Mex., Feb. 1862, Reel 334, RG 27.5.7, NARA-CP; "Journal of Ebenezer Hanna," 1–3, 6, (Ebenezer) Hanna Papers, UT-CAH; Williams, *Three Years and a Half in the Army*, 7, 17–18; Alberts, *Battle of Glorieta*, 12–13; Frazier, *Blood & Treasure*, 146–56; Hall, *Sibley's New Mexico Campaign*, 53–56, 76–82; Houghton, "Climate of New Mexico," 803–4, 806; Nelson, "Indians Make the Best Guerrillas," 112–14; Taylor, *Bloody Valverde*, 13–40, 114; Baechler et al., "Guide to Determining Climate Regions," 2–3.

17. Alberts, *Rebels on the Rio Grande*, 51; [Davidson], "Reminiscences of the Old Brigade," 68, 85; "Journal of Ebenezer Hanna," 3, Hanna Papers, UT-CAH; Williams, *Three Years and a Half in the Army*, 7, 17–18; Alberts, *Battle of Glorieta*, 13–14; Frazier, *Blood & Treasure*, 156–78; Hall, *Sibley's New Mexico Campaign*, 82–103; Taylor, *Bloody Valverde*, 41–106.

18. [Davidson], "Reminiscences of the Old Brigade," 95.

19. Alberts, *Rebels on the Rio Grande*, 51–69; Hollister, *Boldly They Rode*, 45, 49; "Journal of Ebenezer Hanna," 3–7 (quotation, 6), Hanna Papers, UT-CAH; Alberts, *Battle of Glorieta*, 14–15; Frazier, *Blood & Treasure*, 178–87, 192–96, 198–207; Hall, *Sibley's New Mexico Campaign*, 103–23; Houghton, "Climate of New Mexico," 794, 810; Baechler et al., "Guide to Determining Climate Regions," 2–3.

20. Alberts, *Battle of Glorieta*, 20–21, 40–52; Frazier, *Blood & Treasure*, 206; Hall, *Sibley's New Mexico Campaign*, 128–34.

21. [Davidson], "Reminiscences of the Old Brigade," 86–87 (quotation, 87). See also Alberts, *Battle of Glorieta*, 52–68; Frazier, *Blood & Treasure*, 209–12; and Hall, *Sibley's New Mexico Campaign*, 134–40.

22. [Davidson], "Reminiscences of the Old Brigade," 91; Alberts, *Rebels on the Rio Grande*, 76; "Journal of Ebenezer Hanna," 11, Hanna Papers, UT-CAH; Alberts, *Battle of Glorieta*, 69–142; Frazier, *Blood & Treasure*, 212–28; Hall, *Sibley's New Mexico Campaign*, 141–60.

23. [Davidson], "Reminiscences of the Old Brigade," 91.

24. Alberts, *Battle of Glorieta*, 147, 151–64; Alberts, *Rebels on the Rio Grande*, 98, 107–14; Browning and Silver, "Weather"; Frazier, *Blood & Treasure*, 231–49, 264–66; Hall, *Sibley's New Mexico Campaign*, 180–86. I am grateful to Judkin Browning and Tim Silver for sharing the cited draft chapter from their forthcoming volume on Civil War environmental history.

25. Hollister, *Boldly They Rode*, 98.

26. Browning and Silver, "Weather," 3; Frazier, *Blood & Treasure*, 249–58, 264–66; Ingram, "California Megaflood,"accessed Nov. 5, 2019; US Geological Survey, *Overview of the ARkstorm Scenario*, 2–3, accessed Feb. 26, 2015.

27. *OR*, 4:91, 9:557, 596, 627, 673; Fort Craig, N.Mex., Apr., May 1862, Reel 334, RG 27.5.7, NARA-CP; Alberts, *Battle of Glorieta*, 147, 151–64; Alberts, *Rebels on the Rio Grande*, 98, 107–14; Browning and Silver, "Weather," 3, 8–9; Hall, *Sibley's New Mexico Campaign*, 209–26; Nelson, "Indians Make the Best Guerrillas," 114–16.

28. Alberts, *Battle of Glorieta*, 147–48; Browning and Silver, "Weather," 8–9; Frazier, *Blood & Treasure*, 264–66; Hall, *Sibley's New Mexico Campaign*, 209–26.

29. *OR*, 8:7; *Hannibal (Mo.) Messenger*, Sept. 17, 21, Oct. 17, 1861; *St. Louis Daily Missouri Democrat*, Oct. 14, 1861; *St. Louis Daily Missouri Republican*, Sept. 16–Oct. 31, 1861; Anderson, *Memoirs*, 53–66, 92, 95; Castel, *General Sterling Price*, 48–58; Watson, *Life in the Confederate Army*, 247, 254, 263.

30. Anderson, *Memoirs*, 105. See also *St. Louis Daily Missouri Republican*, Nov. 1–30, 1861; Castel, *General Sterling Price*, 58–60; and Shea, and Hess, *Pea Ridge*, 1–2.

31. *St. Louis Daily Missouri Democrat*, Nov. 27, 1861.

32. Clark, *Downing's Civil War Diary*, 20. See also *St. Louis Daily Missouri Democrat*, Dec. 2, 3, 1861; and *St. Louis Daily Missouri Republican*, Nov. 25, Dec. 3, 4, 6, 1861.

33. *OR*, 8:402.

34. *OR*, 8:695–97; Anderson, *Memoirs*, 111, 118; Castel, *General Sterling Price*, 60–61; Shea and Hess, *Pea Ridge*, 2–3.

35. *Hannibal (Mo.) Messenger*, Dec. 7, 1861; *St. Louis Daily Missouri Republican*, Dec. 22, 1865.

36. Anderson, *Memoirs*, 111–34 (quotations, 130–31, 134). See also Clark, *Downing's Civil War Diary*, 20–23; Lane, "Recollections of a Volunteer," 19, accessed July 20, 2014; and *St. Louis Daily Missouri Republican*, Dec. 5, 6, 8, 11, 14, 1861; Castel, *General Sterling Price*, 60–65.

37. Clark, *Downing's Civil War Diary*, 25–26; Shea and Hess, *Pea Ridge*, 1–2.

38. Wright, *Corporal's Story*, 21–22.

39. Shea and Hess, *Pea Ridge*, 3–10; Rafuse, *McClellan's War*, 169; William A. Ruyle Letter, SHSM-R. The Ruyle "letter" is actually a forty-one-page typescript of a memoir.

40. Shea and Hess, *Pea Ridge*, 10–12 (quotation, 10); *OR*, 8:472, 489; Bennett and Haigh, *Thirty-Sixth Regiment Illinois Volunteers*, 104 (hereafter Bennett and Haigh, *Thirty-Sixth Illinois*); "Distribution Maps of Dominant Soil Orders," accessed Jan. 29, 2015; NRCS Soils.

41. *OR*, 8:483, 499.

42. Trollope, *North America*, 2:102–7 (quotations, 103, 106–7).

43. *OR*, 8:500; Shea and Hess, *Pea Ridge*, 12–14; *St. Louis Daily Missouri Democrat*, Jan. 9, 1862; Harwood, *Pea Ridge Campaign*, 7; Bennett and Haigh, *Thirty-Sixth Illinois*, 103–8 (quotations, 103, 105, 108).

44. Shea and Hess, *Pea Ridge*, 14; *OR*, 8:540.

45. *OR*, 8:538, 540, 541.

46. Bennett and Haigh, *Thirty-Sixth Illinois*, 110.

47. *OR*, 8:547, 549. See also *St. Louis Daily Missouri Democrat*, Feb. 4, 5, 1861; and *St. Louis Daily Missouri Democrat*, Feb. 10, 1862.

48. Bennett and Haigh, *Thirty-Sixth Illinois*, 110–13 (quotations, 110); Marcoot, *Five Years in the Sunny South*, 11; Shea and Hess, *Pea Ridge*, 25–29.

49. Samuel John McDaniel Memoir, 1–2, Ser. 2, Box 34, CWTI, USAMHI. See also Harwood, *Pea Ridge Campaign*, 10–11; and *Hannibal (Mo.) Messenger*, Feb. 11, 1862.

50. Harwood, *Pea Ridge Campaign*, 11, 13–14 (quotation, 11). See also *OR*, 8:302, 562; Anderson, *Memoirs*, 144; McDaniel Memoir, 1–2, CWTI, USAMHI; Ruyle Letter, 3–5, SHSM-R; and Shea and Hess, *Pea Ridge*, 29–38.

51. Ruyle Letter, 3–5, SHSM-R. See also *OR*, 8:562; and Shea and Hess, *Pea Ridge*, 36–38.

52. *OR*, 8:562; Anderson, *Memoirs*, 144; Harwood, *Pea Ridge Campaign*, 13; Marcoot, *Five Years in the Sunny South*, 12; McDaniel Memoir, 1–2, CWTI, USAMHI; Ruyle Letter, 3–5, SHSM-R; Shea and Hess, *Pea Ridge*, 38–61.

53. Henry J. B. Cummings to Corporal and Wife, Mar. 2, 1862, Crop Hollows, Ark., Henry J. B. Cummings Papers, State Historical Society of Iowa, Des Moines; *OR*, 8:297; Ruyle Letter, 6, SHSM-R; *St. Louis Daily Missouri Democrat*, Mar. 10, 1862; *St. Louis Daily Missouri Republican*, Mar. 4, 1862; Shea and Hess, *Pea Ridge*, 55–65 (quotation, 58).

54. *OR*, 8:197; Barron, *Lone Star Defenders*, 65; Bennett and Haigh, *Thirty-Sixth Illinois*, 130; Blodgett, "Army of the Southwest," 300; Henry J. B. Cummings to Corporal and Wife, Mar. 2, 1862, Crop Hollows, Ark., Cummings Papers, State Historical Society of Iowa; Harwood, *Pea Ridge Campaign*, 14; Watson, *Life in the Confederate Army*, 283–84; Shea and Hess, *Pea Ridge*, 60, 68–78.

55. *OR*, 8:191. For more detail on the battle, see Shea and Hess, *Pea Ridge*, 81–206; Anderson, *Memoirs*, 167; and McPherson, *Battle Cry of Freedom*, 405.

56. Bennett and Haigh, *Thirty-Sixth Illinois*, 160–61; Harwood, *Pea Ridge Campaign*, 17; Shea and Hess, *Pea Ridge*, 207–22; *Hannibal (Mo.) Messenger*, Mar. 26, 1862.

57. Watson, *Life in the Confederate Army*, 304.

58. Harwood, *Pea Ridge Campaign*, 19. See also Shea and Hess, *Pea Ridge*, 223.

59. Watson, *Life in the Confederate Army*, 305.

60. McPherson, *Battle Cry of Freedom*, 405; Shea and Hess, *Pea Ridge*, 223–60.

61. McPherson, *Battle Cry of Freedom*, 405.

62. Shea and Hess, *Pea Ridge*, 261–68; *Hannibal (Mo.) Messenger*, Mar. 26,1862; Anderson, *Memoirs*, 178; Cater, *As It Was*, 122, 124–25; Ruyle Letter, 7–10, SHSM-R; Tunnard, *Southern Record*, 312, 320, 322, 324, 326; Worley, *Memoirs of Captain John W. Lavender*, 11 (hereafter Worley, *Memoirs of Lavender*); Reinhold, "Climate of Arkansas," 523.

63. Ruyle Letter, 10, SHSM-R.

64. Watson, *Life in the Confederate Army*, 326–29 (quotations, 327, 329).

65. Tunnard, *Southern Record*, 146.

CHAPTER 5

1. Harrison, *Civil War in Kentucky*, 1–12; McPherson, *Battle Cry of Freedom*, 293–96; Noe, *Perryville*, 5–7; Sanders, *Battle of Mill Springs*, 13. I discuss these events in more depth in Noe, *Perryville*, 2–7.

2. Connelly, *Army of the Heartland*, 15–20, 78–82.

3. Connelly, *Army of the Heartland*, 86–87; Harrison, *Civil War in Kentucky*, 12–19; McKnight, "Reconsidering Felix Zollicoffer," 155–64; McPherson, *Battle Cry of Freedom*, 295–97; Noe, *Perryville*, 7–10; Sanders, *Battle of Mill Springs*, 14.

4. Col. James L. Cooper Memoirs, 7, Folder 11, Box 12, Reel 5, CWC, TSLA; Cope, *Fifteenth Ohio*, 36–38; Trollope, *North America*, 2:121; Harrison, *Civil War in Kentucky*, 16–20; McKnight, "Reconsidering Felix Zollicoffer," 164–72; McPherson, *Battle Cry of Freedom*, 296–97; Noe, *Perryville*, 8–13; Sanders, *Battle of Mill Springs*, 18–28; Danville, Ky., Nov. 1861, Reel 188, RG 27.5.7, NARA-CP. Danville was home to the closest operating Smithsonian weather observer. Prof. Ormond Beatty later became a celebrated president of Centre College.

5. Danville, Ky., Nov. 1861, Reel 188, RG 27.5.7, NARA-CP; Louisville, Ky., Nov. 1861, Reel 189, ibid.; *Daily Louisville (Ky.) Democrat*, Dec. 1, 3, 1861; Anderson, "Climate of Kentucky," 128; *OR*, 7:105; 128; Bishop, *Story of a Regiment*, 29; Engle, *Don Carlos Buell*, 98–109; Noe, *Perryville*, 8–13; Sanders, *Battle of Mill Springs*, 28–29. Danville averages 3.12 inches of precipitation in November, but in 1861, the Smithsonian's observer recorded 6.636 inches of rain and an inch of snow. For Elizabethtown, south of Louisville, see Cope, *Fifteenth Ohio*, 42–46.

6. Danville, Ky., Dec. 1861, Reel 188, RG 27.5.7, NARA-CP; Connelly, *Army of the Heartland*, 86–95; Harrison, *Civil War in Kentucky*, 24–25; McKnight, "Reconsidering Felix Zollicoffer," 172–72; Sanders, *Battle of Mill Springs*, 29–33, 36–37.

7. Keil, *Thirty-Fifth Ohio*, 41.

8. Danville, Ky., Dec. 1861, Jan. 1862, Reel 188, RG 27.5.7, NARA-CP; *Daily Louisville (Ky.) Democrat*, Dec. 10, 1861; Anderson, "Climate of Kentucky," 128; *OR*, 7:105; Harrison, *Civil War in Kentucky*, 24–25; McKnight, "Reconsidering Felix Zollicoffer," 172–72; Sanders, *Battle of Mill Springs*, 29–33, 36–37.

9. Louisville, Ky., Dec. 1861, Reel 189, RG 27.5.7, NARA-CP; *OR*, 7:78; Engle, *Don Carlos Buell*, 124–25, 135, 142; Sanders, *Battle of Mill Springs*, 35–36, 37, 38; Earl J. Hess, email to author, Apr. 24, 2015.

10. J. C. Donahower, "Narrative of the Civil War," 1:189, 190, 192, Jeremiah Chester Donahower Papers, 1853–1919, M561, MnHS; "Kentucky Soils Data Viewer," accessed Apr. 29, 2015; "Inceptisols," US Department of Agriculture Natural Resources Conservation Service, http://www.nrcs.usda.gov/wps/portal/nrcs/detail/soils/survey/class/maps/?cid=nrcs142p2_053601, accessed Apr. 29, 2015.

11. Shaw, *Tenth Regiment Indiana Volunteer Infantry*, 137 (hereafter Shaw, *Tenth Indiana*). See also Bishop, *Story of a Regiment*, 34.

12. Danville, Ky., Jan. 1862, Reel 188, RG 27.5.7, NARA-CP. Normally in January, Danville and Louisville contrast only by a couple of degrees. In 1862, it turned cold in Louisville on January 2 and largely stayed that way. The highs between January 9 and January 11 were 47 degrees, 50 degrees, and 40 degrees, respectively, before a high of 19 degrees on January 13. To the southeast in Danville, however, the weather grew unseasonably warm on January 7 and hit 72 degrees on January 12 before crashing into the twenties the next day. See also Anderson, "Climate of Kentucky," 130–31; Cope, *Fifteenth Ohio*, 53–54; and Hinman, *Sherman Brigade*, 82–84. I am grateful to Josh Johnson for this analysis of the data. Johnson, email to author, Aug. 5, 2019.

13. Donahower, "Narrative of the Civil War," 1:193–94, Donahower Papers, MnHS. See also *OR*, 7:76; Hinman, *Sherman Brigade*, 82–84. Hinman, serving in the 65th Ohio, was part of a column back up the road, marching from Bardstown to Lebanon.

14. Danville, Ky., Jan. 1862, Reel 188, RG 27.5.7, NARA-CP; Louisville, Ky., Jan. 1862, Reel 189, ibid.; *OR*, 7:79; Sanders, *Battle of Mill Springs*, 38–41.

15. Donahower, "Narrative of the Civil War," 1:200, 202, 203, Donahower Papers, MnHS. See also Putnam, *Journalistic History*, 58–59.

16. Bishop, *Story of a Regiment*, 38.

17. *OR*, 7:87, 104, 108, 114; Cooper Memoirs, 11, Reel 5, CWC, TSLA; Sanders, *Battle of Mill Springs*, 53–75.

18. Keil, *Thirty-Fifth Ohio*, 37.

19. Putnam, *Journalistic History*, 59. For a similar account, see Keil, *Thirty-Fifth Ohio*, 37–38.

20. Putnam, *Journalistic History*, 75–89, 112–13; *OR*, 7:97; Bishop, *Story of a Regiment*, 39.

21. Donahower, "Narrative of the Civil War," 1:205, Donahower Papers, MnHS.

22. Bircher, *Drummer-Boy's Diary*, 13.

23. Danville, Ky., Jan. 1862, Reel 188, RG 27.5.7, NARA-CP; *OR*, 7:76, 77, 78, 81, 82–83, 85, 89, 91–92, 103, 104, 109–10, 114. See also Keil, *Thirty-Fifth Ohio*, 38; Putnam, *Journalistic History*, 59; Connelly, *Army of the Heartland*, 99; Harrison, *Civil War in Kentucky*, 27–28; and Sanders, *Battle of Mill Springs*, 88–111. Accused of drunkenness, Crittenden resigned, his career ruined.

24. Sanders, *Battle of Mill Springs*, 123–25; Hess, *Civil War in the West*, 33.

25. Donahower, "Narrative of the Civil War," 1:232, 233, 237, Donahower Papers, MnHS. See also Danville, Ky., Jan., Feb. 1862, Reel 188, RG 27.5.7, NARA-CP; Louisville, Ky., Feb. 1862, Reel 189, ibid.; Harrison, *Civil War in Kentucky*, 28; and Keil, *Thirty-Fifth Ohio*, 40.

26. Shaw, *Tenth Indiana*, 162. See also Bishop, *Story of a Regiment*, 49.

27. Bircher, *Drummer-Boy's Diary*, 29–31 (quotation, 29); Louisville, Ky., Feb. 1862, Reel 189, RG 27.5.7, NARA-CP.

28. Clarksville, Tenn., Nov. 1861–Jan. 1862, Reel 478, RG 27.5.7, NARA-CP; *Augusta (Ga.) Daily Constitutionalist*, Jan. 4, 5, 1862; Cooling, *Forts Henry and Donelson*, 38–40; Engle, *Don Carlos Buell*, 144–46. In January 1862 at Clarksville, twenty-four of thirty-one days rated a score of ten on a scale of one to ten for cloudiness, along with three nines and an eight.

29. Kirwan, *Johnny Green*, 11, 14–15; Cooling, *Forts Henry and Donelson*, 38–40.

30. Bock, "One Year at War," 185–86.

31. *New Orleans Daily True Delta*, Jan. 28, 1862.

32. Scribner, *How Soldiers Were Made*, 35; "Inceptisols," US Department of Agriculture Natural Resources Conservation Service, http://www.nrcs.usda.gov/wps/portal/nrcs/detail/soils/survey/class/maps/?cid=nrcs142p2_053601, accessed May 28, 2015; "Alfisols Map," ibid., http://www.nrcs.usda.gov/wps/portal/nrcs/detail/soils/survey/class/maps/?cid=nrcs142p2_053591, accessed May 28, 2015; NRCS Soils.

33. Trollope, *North America*, 2:110–21, 124, 126 (quotations, 124, 126, 111, 113, 126); "Inceptisols Map," US Department of Agriculture Natural Resources Conservation Service, https://www.nrcs.usda.gov/wps/portal/nrcs/detail/soils/survey/class/maps/?cid=nrcs142p2_053602, accessed May 28, 2015; NRCS Soils.

34. Cooling, *Forts Henry and Donelson*, 65–72; "Alfisols Map," US Department of Agriculture Natural Resources Conservation Service, accessed May 18, 2015; NRCS Soils.

35. Grant, *Memoirs*, 1:234. See also Cooling, *Forts Henry and Donelson*, 70–72, 81; Hughes, *Battle of Belmont*, 48, 57, 80; and McPherson, *Battle Cry of Freedom*, 394–95.

36. *OR*, 7:121–22; Grant, *Memoirs*, 1:234–35; Cooling, *Forts Henry and Donelson*, 72–80; Engle, *Don Carlos Buell*, 152–53.

37. Clarksville, Tenn., Jan., Feb. 1862, Reel 478, RG 27.5.7, NARA-CP; Connelly, *Army of the Heartland*, 107; Cooling, *Forts Henry and Donelson*, 88–100; Ludlum, *Early American Winters*, 124.

38. *OR*, 7:122–25, 128–29, 133–34, 136–43; *ORN*, 22:37–38; Clarksville, Tenn., Feb. 1862, Reel 478, RG 27.5.7, NARA-CP; Grant, *Memoirs*, 1:235–41; Cooling, *Forts Henry and Donelson*, 100–111; McPherson, *Battle Cry of Freedom*, 396–97.

39. *OR*, 7:124, 125, 130–31, 135, 153–57; *ORN*, 22:314–15.

40. Grant, *Memoirs*, 1:241–44; Cooling, *Forts Henry and Donelson*, 131; Ludlum, *Early American Winters*, 124.

41. Grant, *Memoirs*, 1:241. See also Simpson, *Grant*, 112–13.

42. Clarksville, Tenn., Feb. 1862, Reel 478, RG 27.5.7, NARA-CP; *OR*, 7:174, 189, 194, 199, 201, 206, 214, 221, 223, 224, 229, 237, 368–69; "Ultisols Map," US Department of Agriculture Natural Resources Conservation Service, http://www.nrcs.usda.gov/wps/portal/nrcs/detail/soils/survey/class/maps/?cid=nrcs142p2_053610, accessed May 28, 2015; NRCS Soils; Grant, *Memoirs*, 1:244–47; *St. Louis Daily Missouri Democrat*, Feb. 17, 1862; *St. Louis Daily Missouri Republican*, Feb. 14, 1862; Cooling, *Forts Henry and Donelson*, 122, 135, 138–48; Manarin, "Diary of Rufus J. Woolwine," 422; W. A. Rorer to Susan, Jan. 3, 1864, Canton, Miss., James M. Willcox Papers, 1831–1871, Duke; *OR*, 7:273, 283, 362, 368, 378, 379; Connelly, *Army of the Heartland*, 116–17; Ludlum, *Early American Winters*, 124–25; Ludlum, *Weather Factor*, 79–80.

43. *OR*, 7:174.

44. *OR*, 7:185. See also *St. Louis Daily Missouri Democrat*, Feb. 17, 1862.

45. Clarksville, Tenn., Feb. 1862, Reel 478, RG 27.5.7, NARA-CP; *OR*, 7:175, 188, 221, 237, 318, 613; Grant, *Memoirs*, 1:247–48; Cooling, *Forts Henry and Donelson*, 148–60, 166; Simpson, *Grant*, 112–13. Grant reported that it was 20 degrees below zero that morning, a serious overestimate. The actual temperatures recorded, as meteorologist Josh Johnson suggests, meant that rain would freeze on impact. Johnson, email to author, Aug. 5, 2019.

46. Grant, *Memoirs*, 1:245, 249. See also *OR*, 7:318.

47. Rerick, *Forty-Fourth Indiana*, 222, 35–36.

48. *OR*, 7:175, 295–96; Grant, *Memoirs*, 1:249–53, 255 (quotation, 255); Cooling, *Forts Henry and Donelson*, 160–200; McPherson, *Battle Cry of Freedom*, 399–402.

49. Clarksville, Tenn., Feb. 1862, Reel 478, RG 27.5.7, NARA-CP; *OR*, 7:266, 315, 318, 344, 356, 371.

50. Wilkie, *Pen and Powder*, 115; Matson, *Life Experiences*, 76.

51. Wilkie, *Pen and Powder*, 113.

52. Grant, *Memoirs*, 1:258; Cooling, *Forts Henry and Donelson*, 200–213; 233–38, 278.

53. Grant, *Memoirs*, 1:265–67; John W. Caldwell Diary, Mar. 14, 1862, Ser. 2, Box 30, CWTI, US-AMHI; Horrall, *Forty-Second Indiana*, 113; W. A. Rorer to Cousin Susan, Jan. 31, 1862, Russellville, Ky., Willcox Papers, Duke; Clarksville, Tenn., Feb. 1862, Reel 478, RG 27.5.7, NARA-CP; *Augusta (Ga.) Daily Constitutionalist*, Apr. 11, 1862; Connelly, *Army of the Heartland*, 136–37; Cooling, *Forts Henry and Donelson*, 232–41; McPherson, *Battle Cry of Freedom*, 403–3, 405–6.

54. Caldwell Diary, Mar. 14, 1862, CWTI, USAMHI. See also *Mobile Register*, Mar. 13, 1862.

55. Beatty, *Citizen-Soldier*, 106–9. See also Cope, *Fifteenth Ohio*, 78.

56. Levi Wagner Memoirs, 23–24, CWTI, USAMHI.

57. Grant, *Memoirs*, 1:260–65, 267–74; Cooling, *Forts Henry and Donelson*, 228–29, 247, 249–50; Engle, *Don Carlos Buell*, 176–79.

58. Clarksville, Tenn., Mar. 1862, Reel 478, RG 27.5.7, NARA-CP; Dickson, "Climate of Tennessee," 123–35; *New Orleans Daily True Delta*, Mar. 30, 1862; Clark, *Downing's Civil War Diary*, 37, 38, 40; Stillwell, "In the Ranks at Shiloh," 113; *OR*, 10(1):22–23, 29. See also "Ultisols Map," accessed May 28, 2015; and NRCS Soils.

59. Keil, *Thirty-Fifth Ohio*, 49–52 (quotations, 49, 50, 51–52).

60. Clarksville, Tenn., Feb., Mar. 1862, Reel 478, RG 27.5.7, NARA-CP; Putnam, *Journalistic History*, 66–70 (quotations, 66, 70). See also Bircher, *Drummer-Boy's Diary*, 31; Coggins, *Tennessee Tragedies*, 259–263.

61. Putnam, *Journalistic History*, 71–72 (quotation, 71). Keil, *Thirty-Fifth Ohio*, 52.

62. Keil, *Thirty-Fifth Ohio*, 52.

63. Member of the Regiment, *36th Indiana*, 95–96.

64. Clarksville, Tenn., Mar., Apr. 1862, Reel 478, RG 27.5.7, NARA-CP; Bircher, *Drummer-Boy's Diary*, 31–32; Bishop, *Story of a Regiment*, 51–52; Cope, *Fifteenth Ohio*, 94, 105; Hinman, *Sherman Brigade*, 134; Kimberly and Holloway, *Forty-First Ohio*, 20; Member of the Regiment, *36th Indiana*, 100; Putnam, *Journalistic History*, 74. Daniel, *Shiloh*, 112–15; Engle, *Don Carlos Buell*, 212–18; "Ultisols Map," accessed May 28, 2015; NRCS Soils.

65. Connolly, *Army of the Heartland*, 151–55; Daniel, *Shiloh*, 116–25.

66. Woods and Nolan, *Shiloh Diary of Edmond Enoul Livaudais*, 22, 23; *OR*, 10(1):614; Clarksville, Tenn., Apr. 1862, Reel 478, RG 27.5.7, NARA-C.

67. Connolly, *Army of the Heartland*, 155–56; Daniel, *Shiloh*, 123–25.

68. Connolly, *Army of the Heartland*, 156–57. See also Daniel, *Shiloh*, 125–30; Sutherland, *Reminiscences of a Private*, 63; Woods and Nolan, *Shiloh Diary of Edmond Enoul Livaudais*, 23; *Augusta (Ga.) Daily Constitutionalist*, Apr. 17, 1862.

69. Rerick, *Forty-Fourth Indiana*, 45. See also *OR*, 10(1):547, 567; Caldwell Diary, Apr. 6, 1862, CWTI, USAMHI.

70. Stillwell, "In the Ranks at Shiloh," 114; Cope, *Fifteenth Ohio*, 111, 124, 126, 127; Member of the Regiment, *36th Indiana*, 102; McPherson, *Battle Cry of Freedom*, 407–12; Connolly, *Army of the Heartland*, 158–73; Daniel, *Shiloh*, 131–237; Simpson, *Grant*, 130.

71. *OR*, 10(1):119, 134, 147, 159, 160, 193, 196, 205, 241, 243, 298, 335, 357, 359, 361, 367, 377, 387, 488, 506, 526, 528, 546, 562, 578, 603, 617; Kirwan, *Johnny Green*, 29; Cope, *Fifteenth Ohio*, 119; Matson, *Life Experiences*, 83; Robertson, *Battle of Shiloh*, 7; Woods and Nolan, *Shiloh Diary of Edmond Enoul Livaudais*, 31; Wright, *Corporal's Story*, 38; Connolly, *Army of the Heartland*, 173–75; Daniel, *Shiloh*, 262–95; McPherson, *Battle Cry of Freedom*, 412–13; Simpson, *Grant*, 134. Temperatures in Clarksville on April 7 were 56.6 degrees at 7 A.M. and 72.2 degrees at 2 P.M. Clarksville, Tenn., Apr. 1862, Reel 478, RG 27.5.7, NARA-CP.

72. Kirwan, *Johnny Green*, 33.

73. *OR*, 10(1):619; Kirwan, *Johnny Green*, 34; Robertson, *Battle of Shiloh*, 7; Wright, *Corporal's Story*, 47; Clarksville, Tenn., Apr. 1862, Reel 478, RG 27.5.7, NARA-CP.

74. *OR*, 10(1):160, 310, 321, 334, 388; Kimberly and Holloway, *Forty-First Ohio*, 24. See also Hinman, *Sherman Brigade*, 154.

75. Hinman, *Sherman Brigade*, 147.

76. "The Messenger: The *Civil War Monitor's* Official Newsletter," Oct. 2013, email to author; "Shiloh's 'Angel Glow' Was Lifesaver," accessed May 30, 2015.

77. Hight and Stormont, *Fifty-Eighth Regiment of Indiana Volunteer Infantry,* 57 (hereafter Hight and Stormont, *Fifty-Eighth Indiana*).

78. Bircher, *Drummer-Boy's Diary,* 32–33.

79. *OR,* 10(1):346; Daniel, *Shiloh,* 296–300, 304–9; *Augusta (Ga.) Chronicle,* Apr. 25, 1862; *Mobile Register,* Apr. 18, 1862; Bishop, *Story of a Regiment,* 53; Cope, *Fifteenth Ohio,* 140–41; Hight and Stormont, *Fifty-Eighth Indiana,* 67, 71, 72; Hinman, *Sherman Brigade,*158–59, 161; Keil, *Thirty-Fifth Ohio,* 68; Little and Maxwell, *Lumsden's Battery,* 8; Shaw, *Tenth Indiana,* 165, Wagner Memoirs, 31–32, CWTI, USAMHI; Clarksville, Tenn., Apr. 1862, Reel 478, RG 27.5.7, NARA-CP; Woods and Nolan, *Shiloh Diary of Edmond Enoul Livaudais,* 38, 41–44; Wright, *Corporal's Story,* 47.

80. Hight and Stormont, *Fifty-Eighth Indiana,* 72.

81. Anderson, *Memoirs,* 191; Barron, *Lone Star Defenders,* 80–83; *New Orleans Daily True Delta,* Mar. 25, 1862; Watson, *Life in the Confederate Army,* 345; W. E. Preston (Mathews), "The 33rd Alabama Regiment in the Civil War," ed. L. B. Williams, 19, ADAH; Brady, *War upon the Land,* 31–34; Connelly, *Army of the Heartland,* 174–76; Daniel and Bock *Island No. 10,* esp. 27, 30, 34–35, 45–46, 56, 78, 98, 122, 128, 137; Hess, *Civil War in the West,* 58; McPherson, *Battle Cry of Freedom.* 415–16.

82. *Augusta (Ga.) Daily Constitutionalist,* May 3, 1862.

83. Kimberly and Holloway, *Forty-First Ohio,* 27. See also Logbook, USS *Tyler,* Apr. 24- May 2, 1862, RG 24.2.2, NARA; Clark, *Downing's Civil War Diary,* 47–48; Connelly, *Army of the Heartland,* 176; Hess, *Civil War in the West,* 49–50; McPherson, *Battle Cry of Freedom.* 416–17. No logbook from the USS *Lexington* exists for the period, but most of the riverine logbooks I sampled for this project, such as the *Tyler's,* did not contain the detailed weather information found on oceangoing ships with standardized logbooks.

84. Logbook, USS *Tyler,* May 8–June 3, 1862, RG 24.2.2, NARA; Anderson, *Memoirs,* 200; Bennett and Haigh, *Thirty-Sixth Illinois,* 204, 207; Clark, *Downing's Civil War Diary,* 50–52; Cope, *Fifteenth Ohio,* 149–51, 162; Head, *Sixteenth Tennessee,* 70–71, 74; Connelly, *Army of the Heartland,* 176–77, 179–82.

85. Hess, *Civil War in the West,* 52–54; Noe, *Perryville,* 23–24; Ballard, *Vicksburg,* 29–63; Shea and Winschel, *Vicksburg Is the Key,* 14–32.

86. Putnam, *Journalistic History,* 99–100.

87. Anderson, *Memoirs,* 212.

88. *Charleston Mercury,* June 27, 1862; Anderson, *Memoirs,* 203, 210, 212; Barron, *Lone Star Defenders,* 104; Bennett and Haigh, *Thirty-Sixth Illinois,* 209, 215, 216; "William P. Rogers' Memorandum Book," 60–63; Cavins, *War Letters of Aden G. Cavins,* 22; Clark, *Downing's Civil War Diary,* 53–58; Cope, *Fifteenth Ohio,* 162; Donahower, "Narrative of the Civil War," 1:275, Donahower Papers, MnHS; Keil, *Thirty-Fifth Ohio,* 76–77; Marcoot, *Five Years in the Sunny South,* 14; Member of the Regiment, *36th Indiana,* 118, 121; Putnam, *Journalistic History,* 102; Rerick, *Forty-Fourth Indiana,* 267; Watson, *Life in the Confederate Army,* 381.

CHAPTER 6

1. Blight, *When This Cruel War Is Over,* 89. See also Child, *Fifth New Hampshire,* 33.

2. Everson and Simpson, "*Far, Far from Home,*" 104; 108–9 (quotation, 109).

3. Richmond, Va., Feb. 1862, Reel 527, RG 27.5.7, NARA-CP; Johnston, *Narrative of Military Operations,* 96; *OR,* 5:724, 727, 1079; Cooper, *Jefferson Davis,* 374; Rafuse, *McClellan's War,* 189–90; Symonds, *Joseph E. Johnston,* 138–39, 143.

4. Richmond, Va., Feb. 1862, Reel 527, RG 27.5.7, NARA-CP; Cooper, *Jefferson Davis,* 372–73; Davis, *Jefferson Davis,* 394.

5. Fleet and Fuller, *Green Mount,* 107.

6. Mat Richards to Sophie, Mar. 2, 1862, Camp Northumberland, M. Edgar Richards Correspond-

ence, Box 97, CWMC, USAMHI. See also Georgetown, D.C., Feb., Mar. 1862, Reel 81, RG 27.5.7, NARA-CP; Richmond, Va., Feb. 1862, Reel 527, ibid.; Krick, *Civil War Weather*, 48, 51; George M. Barnard to Inman, Mar. 4, 1862, Camp Barnes, George Middleton Barnard Papers, CWCDJ, MHS; Cook, *Twelfth Massachusetts*, 39; Dobbins, *Grandfather's Journal*, 70; Luther C. Furst Diary, 15, HCWRTC, USAMHI; Lasswell, *Rags and Hope*, 65; Rhodes, *All for the Union*, 56; and Robertson, *Letters of McAllister*, 121.

7. Gaede, *Federal Civil War Shelter Tent*, esp. 1–25; Furst Diary, 15, HCWRTC, USAMHI; Nevins, *Diary of Battle*, 21; Mat Richards to Sophie, Mar. 2, 1862, Camp Northumberland, Richards Correspondence, CWMC, USAMHI; Rhodes, *All for the Union*, 56.

8. Curtis, *First Bull Run to Chancellorsville*, 91.

9. Billings, *Hard Tack and Coffee*, 46–54. See also Gaede, *Federal Civil War Shelter Tent*, 22–25.

10. Norton, *Army Letters*, 56; Georgetown, D.C., Mar. 1862, Reel 81, RG 27.5.7, NARA-CP; Krick, *Civil War Weather*, 51.

11. Sears, *To the Gates of Richmond*, 13–14; Symonds, *Joseph E. Johnston*, 145–46; Rafuse, *McClellan's War*, 189; Tanner, *Stonewall in the Valley*, 100; *Daily Columbus (Ga.) Enquirer*, Mar. 24, 1862.

12. Taylor, *Destruction and Reconstruction*, 35.

13. Napier Bartlett wrote, "the mule was a much more hardy animal—his carcass was very rarely ever seen." *Military Record of Louisiana*, 73. See also Blackford, *War Years*, 60; Lasswell, *Rags and Hope*, 72; and Lee, *Memoir of Pendleton*, 172–73.

14. Symonds, *Joseph E. Johnston*, 146–47.

15. Rafuse, *McClellan's War*, 175–93; Sears, *To the Gates of Richmond*, 7–9, 16–17. See also Blight, *When this Cruel War Is Over*, 99–100; Child, *Fifth New Hampshire*, 44–46; Curtis, *First Bull Run to Chancellorsville*, 91; Furst Diary, 16, HCWRTC, USAMHI; Samuel L. Merrell to Children, Mar. 19, 1862, Falls Church, Va., Samuel L. Merrell Collection: Correspondence, NYHS/CWPSD; Nevins, *Diary of Battle*, 21, 25.

16. Hyde, *Following the Greek Cross*, 36.

17. Nevins, *Diary of Battle*, 23.

18. Mat Richards to Brother, Apr. 5, 1862, Manassas, Va., Richards Correspondence, CWMC, USAMHI.

19. Rafuse, *McClellan's War*, 193–97; Sears, *To the Gates of Richmond*, 16–18.

20. Davis, *Duel between the Ironclads*, 60–65, 78–79. The winner in this drama was Halleck, who gained overall command of Union forces in the West.

21. Blight, *When this Cruel War Is Over*, 101.

22. Georgetown, D.C., Mar. 1862, Reel 81, RG 27.5.7, NARA-CP; George M. Barnard to Inman, Mar. 17, 1862, Washington, Barnard Papers, CWCDJ, MHS; Child, *Fifth New Hampshire*, 46; de Trobriand, *Four Years in the Army of the Potomac*, 154–58; Hyde, *Following the Greek Cross*, 36–37; Nevins, *Diary of Battle*, 27; Norton, *Army Letters*, 59; Rhodes, *All for the Union*, 59–60; Stewart, *Pair of Blankets*, 45; Hess, *Field Armies and Fortifications*, 71; Krick, *Civil War Weather*, 49, 51; Rafuse, *McClellan's War*, 195–96; Sears, *To the Gates of Richmond*, 18–20.

23. George North Jr. to Parents, Mar. 21, 1862, Camp Misery, North Family Collection: Correspondence, NYHS/CWPSD.

24. Fort Monroe, Va., Mar., Apr. 1862, Reel 522, RG 27.5.7, NARA-CP; Georgetown, D.C., Mar., Apr. 1862, Reel 81, ibid.; Krick, *Civil War Weather*, 51, 54; de Trobriand, *Four Years in the Army of the Potomac*, 159, 163; Dickey, *Eighty-Fifth Pennsylvania*, 23; Furst Diary, 17, HCWRTC, USAMHI; Malles, *Bridge Building in Wartime*, 57–58; Samuel L. Merrell to Children, Mar. 19, 1862, Falls Church, Va., Merrell Collection, NYHS/CWPSD; Nevins, *Diary of Battle*, 28–30; Rhodes, *All for the Union*, 61; Mat Richards to Sophie, Mar. 30, 1862, Camp Northumberland, Richards Correspondence, CWMC, USAMHI; Robertson, *Letters of McAllister*, 121, 128; Rosenblatt and Rosenblatt, *Hard Marching Every Day*,

11–14; Sparks, *Inside Lincoln's Army*, 55, 59, 61–63; White, *Diary of Wyman S. White*, 46–48; Rafuse, *McClellan's War*, 196–204; Sears, *To the Gates of Richmond*, 23–35.

25. Blight, *When This Cruel War Is Over*, 107–8; "Diaries of John Waldrop . . . and William Y. Mordecai," 35–36; Dickey, *Eighty-Fifth Pennsylvania*, 27; Robertson, *Stonewall Jackson*, 326, 330; Tanner, *Stonewall in the Valley*, 101–6.

26. Quint, *Second Massachusetts*, 69. See also Robertson, *Stonewall Jackson*, 331–33.

27. Neese, *Three Years in the Confederate Horse Artillery*, 25. See also Georgetown, D.C., Feb., Mar. 1862, Reel 81, RG 27.5.7, NARA-CP; Mead Diary, vol. 2, Mar. 1, 3, 8–10, 12, 1862, LC; Krick, *Civil War Weather*, 51; and Robertson, *Stonewall Jackson*, 333–34. Winter temperatures near Winchester roughly resemble Washington's and provide a rough estimate when precipitation and cloud cover are similar. In Georgetown, it was 33 degrees.

28. Bean, "Valley Campaign," 337, 339, 341; Cook, *Twelfth Massachusetts*, 45; McDonald, *Make Me a Map of the Valley*, 6–7; Mead Diary, vol. 2, Mar. 18, 20, 22, 1862, LC; Quaife, *From the Cannon's Mouth*, 63; Roper, *Repairing the "March of Mars,"* 215–19; John Scott to Mother, Mar. 16, 1862, Washington, D.C., Margaret Scott Collection: Correspondence, NYHS/CWPSD; Worsham, *One of Jackson's Foot Cavalry*, 31; Georgetown, D.C., Feb., Mar. 1862, Reel 81, RG 27.5.7, NARA-CP; Krick, *Civil War Weather*, 49, 51; Robertson, *Stonewall Jackson*, 334–39; Tanner, *Stonewall in the Valley*, 106–9.

29. *OR*, 12(1):350; McDonald, *Make Me a Map of the Valley*, 8; Quint, *Second Massachusetts*, 73; Georgetown, D.C., Mar. 1862, Reel 81, RG 27.5.7, NARA-CP; Krick, *Civil War Weather*, 49, 51; Rafuse, *McClellan's War*, 202–7; Robertson, *Stonewall Jackson*, 339–47; Sears, *McClellan*, 170–72; Sears, *To the Gates of Richmond*, 32–34, 39; Tanner, *Stonewall in the Valley*, 118–32.

30. *OR*, 11(3):39; Fort Monroe, Va., Mar. 1862, Reel 522, RG 27.5.7, NARA-CP; Blight, *When This Cruel War Is Over*, 104; "Ultisols Map," US Department of Agriculture Natural Resources Conservation Service, http://www.nrcs.usda.gov/wps/portal/nrcs/detail/soils/ref/?cid=nrcs142p2_053610, accessed July 2, 2015; Bell, *Mosquito Soldiers*, 72–75; Joey Shaw, email to author, July 3, 2015; Meier, *Nature's Civil War*, 45.

31. Fort Monroe, Va., Apr. 1862, Reel 522, RG 27.5.7, NARA-CP; Hess, *Field Armies and Fortifications*, 71; Rafuse, *McClellan's War*, 203–4; Sears, *McClellan*, 172; Sears, *To the Gates of Richmond*, 28–31.

32. Browning and Silver, "Nature and Human Nature," esp. 409.

33. *OR*, 11(1):227, 297, 358; Blight, *When This Cruel War Is Over*, 108; de Trobriand, *Four Years in the Army of the Potomac*, 166; Browning and Silver, "Nature and Human Nature," 390.

34. Weymouth, *Sketch of Newcomb*, 54–55 (quotation, 55). See also de Trobriand, *Four Years in the Army of the Potomac*, 182.

35. Sears, *Papers of McClellan*, 236; Browning and Silver, "Nature and Human Nature," 390–92; Hess, *Field Armies and Fortifications*, 73–74; Rafuse, *McClellan's War*, 203–5; Sears, *McClellan*, 174–76; Sears, *To the Gates of Richmond*, 24–27; Brasher, *Peninsula Campaign*, 87–89, 98–99, 107–11.

36. Miller, *Harvard's Civil War*, 111.

37. Fort Monroe, Va., Apr. 1862, Reel 522, RG 27.5.7, NARA-CP; Sears, *Papers of McClellan*, 229, 230. See also Child, *Fifth New Hampshire*, 51; de Trobriand, *Four Years in the Army of the Potomac*, 168; Fleet and Fuller, *Green Mount*, 119; and Sears, *To the Gates of Richmond*, 41–43.

38. Rafuse, *McClellan's War*, 207–8; Sears, *McClellan*, 174–76, 178–79; Sears, *To the Gates of Richmond*, 173–80; Hess, *Field Armies and Fortifications*, 73–74.

39. *OR*, 11(1):275; Hess, *Field Armies and Fortifications*, 73–84; Sears, *To the Gates of Richmond*, 48–50; Symonds, *Joseph E. Johnston*, 148–49. Hess asserts that Johnston was right.

40. Mat Richards to Sophie, Apr. 21, 1862, Steamer *Spaulding*, Richards Correspondence, CWMC, USAMHI. See also *OR*, 11(1):228, 11(3):116, 124; and Browning and Silver, "Nature and Human Nature," 394–95.

41. Fort Monroe, Va., Apr. 1861, Apr. 1862, Reel 522, RG 27.5.7, NARA-CP; Blight, *When This Cruel*

War Is Over, 113, 116; Child, *Fifth New Hampshire*, 52; Dickey, *Eighty-Fifth Pennsylvania*, 30; [Joseph B. Laughton] to Mother and Father & Brothers, Apr. 14, 1862, Yorktown, Va., Joseph B. Laughton Letters, 1861–1865, Duke; Nevins, *Diary of Battle*, 32, 34; Robertson, *Letters of McAllister*, 136–37, 142.

42. Everson and Simpson, "Far, Far from Home," 117. See also Early, *War Memoirs*, 67; Lee, *Memoir of Pendleton*, 176–77; Dubbs, *Defend This Old Town*, 72.

43. Howe, *Touched with Fire*, 39. See also George M. Barnard to Inman, Apr. 10, 1862, Yorktown, Barnard Papers, CWCDJ, MHS.

44. De Trobriand, *Four Years in the Army of the Potomac*, 183.

45. George M. Barnard to Inman, Apr. 12, 1862 (quotation), Yorktown, Barnard Papers, CWCDJ, MHS; Barnard to Mother, Apr. 16, 1862, Yorktown, ibid.

46. Dickey, *Eighty-Fifth Pennsylvania*, 31.

47. *OR*, 11(1):348.

48. *OR*, 11(1):275, 342–43, 383, 602; Fort Monroe, Va., Apr., May 1862, Reel 522, RG 27.5.7, NARA-CP; Logbook, USS *Galena*, Apr. 24–May 7, 1862, RG 24.2.2, NARA; George M. Barnard to Father, May 4, 1862, Yorktown, Barnard Papers, CWCDJ, MHS; Robertson, *Letters of McAllister*, 146; Hess, *Field Armies and Fortifications*, 86–91; Sears, *To the Gates of Richmond*, 57–68; Symonds, *Joseph E. Johnston*, 152–53.

49. Miller, *Harvard's Civil War*, 119.

50. Nevins, *Diary of Battle*, 58.

51. Longstreet, *From Manassas to Appomattox*, 71. See also "Diaries of John Waldrop . . . and William Y. Mordecai," 37; Hamilton, *Papers of Shotwell*, 1:190; and Sears, *To the Gates of Richmond*, 68–69.

52. Hamilton, *Papers of Shotwell*, 1:190. See also Edwin Y. Brown, "4 and 5 May 1862 Description of the Battle of Williamsburg," 2–3 (quotation, 2), accessed Feb. 22, 2018 (page removed); Dubbs, *Defend This Old Town*, 81.

53. Dickey, *Eighty-Fifth Pennsylvania*, 36, 37; Hamilton, *Papers of Shotwell*, 1:190; Nevins, *Diary of Battle*, 47; Dubbs, *Defend This Old Town*, 88; Sears, *To the Gates of Richmond*, 70; Symonds, *Joseph E. Johnston*, 153–54.

54. *OR*, 11(1):19, 20, 23, 234–35, 275, 286, 295, 300, 424, 429, 430, 435, 451, 458, 462, 469, 470, 475, 476, 477, 481, 492, 501, 502, 508, 509, 511, 516, 520, 532, 534, 538, 539, 541, 559, 560, 595, 597, 602; Fort Monroe, Va., May 1862, Reel 522, RG 27.5.7, NARA-CP; Brown, "4 and 5 May 1862 Description of the Battle of Williamsburg," 7, 9, accessed Feb. 22, 2018 (page removed); de Trobriand, *Four Years in the Army of the Potomac*, 191; Hamilton, *Papers of Shotwell*, 1:190, 197; Hyde, *Following the Greek Cross*, 50; Johnston, *Narrative of Military Operations*, 120; Lasswell, *Rags and Hope*, 94, 95; Joseph B. Laughton to Brothers John & William, Mother & Father, May 11, 1862, Jamestown, Va., Laughton Letters, Duke; Longstreet, *From Manassas to Appomattox*, 72; Nevins, *Diary of Battle*, 49; Dubbs, *Defend This Old Town*, 88–172; Hess, *Field Armies and Fortifications*, 92–95; Sears, *Papers of McClellan*, 255–56; Sears, *To the Gates of Richmond*, 70–82.

55. *OR*, 11(1):23, 492; Brown, "4 and 5 May 1862 Description of the Battle of Williamsburg," 9, accessed Feb. 22, 2018 (page removed); Blight, *When This Cruel War Is Over*, 130; de Trobriand, *Four Years in the Army of the Potomac*, 194, 204; Hamilton, *Papers of Shotwell*, 1:197; Hyde, *Following the Greek Cross*, 50–52; Warfield, *Confederate Soldier's Memoirs*, 85.

56. Hamilton, *Papers of Shotwell*, 1:199–200.

57. *OR*, 11(1):605. See also Fort Monroe, Va., May 1862, Reel 522, RG 27.5.7, NARA-CP.

58. Blight, *When This Cruel War Is Over*, 130. See also de Trobriand, *Four Years in the Army of the Potomac*, 202; Symonds, *Joseph E. Johnston*, 155–56.

59. *OR*, 11(1):23, 497, 498, 541, 566, 572; Fort Monroe, Va., May 1862, Reel 522, RG 27.5.7, NARA-CP; Dickey, *Eighty-Fifth Pennsylvania*, 43; Furst Diary, 19–20, HCWRTC, USAMHI; Joseph B.

Laughton to Minnie, May 17, 1862, Cumberland, Va., Laughton Letters, Duke; Longstreet, *From Manassas to Appomattox,* 79; Nevins, *Diary of Battle,* 57; Weymouth, *Sketch of Newcomb,* 59.

60. Sears, *Papers of McClellan,* 255, 256.

61. Blight, *When This Cruel War Is Over,* 122–23, 130. See also *OR,* 11(3):139; Child, *Fifth New Hampshire,* 57; Malles, *Bridge Building in Wartime,* 66; Rhodes, *All for the Union,* 64; Sears, *Papers of McClellan,* 256, 257.

62. *OR,* 11(1):185, 458; Fort Monroe, Va., May, June 1862, Reel 522, RG 27.5.7, NARA-CP; Logbook, USS *Galena,* May 11, 1862, RG 24.2.2, NARA. Farther up the James, the deck officer of the *Galena* recorded only a cooler 69 degrees at 1 P.M. While *Galena* officers only recorded temperatures infrequently and at odd times, the readings that do exist for May vary wildly from 11 degrees cooler to 11 degrees warmer when compared to Fort Monroe.

63. *OR,* 11(1):185.

64. George A. Mitchell to Parents, May 12, 1862, "Somewhere in Virginia," George A. Mitchell Collection: Correspondence, NYHS/CWPSD.

65. *OR,* 11(1):24; Fort Monroe, Va., May 1862, Reel 522, RG 27.5.7, NARA-CP; Logbook, USS *Galena,* May 14–19, 1862, RG 24.2.2, NARA; Blight, *When This Cruel War Is Over,* 125, 129; Child, *Fifth New Hampshire,* 58; Curtis, *First Bull Run to Chancellorsville,* 104; de Trobriand, *Four Years in the Army of the Potomac,* 213; "Diaries of John Waldrop . . . and William Y. Mordecai," 38; Dickey, *Eighty-Fifth Pennsylvania,* 52, 53; Everson and Simpson, *"Far, Far from Home,"* 122; Fleet and Fuller, *Green Mount,* 124, 125; John B. Jenkins to Mary Benjamin, May 17, 1862, Cumberland Landing, Folder 9, Box 1, Henry C. Hoar Memorial Collection, 1861–87, Acc. 1992.46, digital projects, Swem Library, College of William and Mary, http://transcribe.swem.wm.edu/items/show/41, accessed Feb. 22, 2018 (page removed); Lasswell, *Rags and Hope,* 98; Nevins, *Diary of Battle,* 60; Westwood A. Todd Reminiscence, pt. 1, 10, SHC-UNC; Browning and Silver, "Nature and Human Nature," 392–96; Rafuse, *McClellan's War,* 211–16; Sears, *Papers of McClellan,* 257, 267, 268, 271; Sears, *To the Gates of Richmond,* 87–110; Symonds, *Joseph E. Johnston,* 158–59.

66. *OR,* 11(1):24, 661, 11(3):174, 175, 184; Fort Monroe, Va., May 1862, Reel 522, RG 27.5.7, NARA-CP; Logbook, USS *Galena,* May 20–28, 1862, RG 24.2.2, NARA; Blight, *When This Cruel War Is Over,* 134, 135, 137, 138; Dickey, *Eighty-Fifth Pennsylvania,* 54–60; Furst Diary, 23, HCWRTC, US-AMHI; Nevins, *Diary of Battle,* 68–71; Robertson, *Letters of McAllister,* 161–62; Sears, *Papers of McClellan,* 275–78; Joseph S. C. Taber Diary, 27, CWTI, USAMHI.

67. Nevins, *Diary of Battle,* 70, 71. See also Lee, *Memoir of Pendleton,* 184; Welch, *Confederate Surgeon's Letters,* 10; and Sears, *To the Gates of Richmond,* 110–17.

68. Sears, *Papers of McClellan,* 275–78 (quotation, 277). See also *OR,* 11(1):28, 11(3):193, 195.

69. Nevins, *Diary of Battle,* 69. See also George M. Barnard to Inman, Mar. 31, 1862, Gaines Mill, Va., Barnard Papers, CWCDJ, MHS; and Malles, *Bridge Building in Wartime,* 68.

70. Meier, *Nature's Civil War* 18, 20–21, 45–54, 128–31, 147–48; Bell, *Mosquito Soldiers,* 72–77; Browning and Silver, "Nature and Human Nature," 394–98, 401–2; Sears, *To the Gates of Richmond,* 163–65.

71. *OR,* 11(1):33–34, 195, 240, 680, 682, 697, 698, 700, 702, 708, 710, 712, 717, 722, 736, 744; Logbook, USS *Galena,* May 26–27, 1862, RG 24.2.2, NARA; *Augusta (Ga.) Daily Constitutionalist,* May 29, 1862; George M. Barnard to Inman, Mar. 31, 1862, Gaines Mill, Va., Barnard Papers, CWCDJ, MHS; Miller, *Harvard's Civil War,* 127; Sears, *To the Gates of Richmond,* 117–20; Symonds, *Joseph E. Johnston,* 160–63.

72. Logbook, USS *Galena,* May 30, 1862, RG 24.2.2, NARA; Dickey, *Eighty-Fifth Pennsylvania,* 63–64. See also *OR,* 11(1):873; Blight, *When This Cruel War Is Over,* 141; Fleet and Fuller, *Green Mount,* 129, 130; Miller, *Harvard's Civil War,* 126. The *Galena's* thermometer recorded 85 degrees at 6 P.M. but

only 65 degrees two hours later. With readings of 75 degrees at 2 P.M. and 70 degrees at 9 P.M. at Fort Monroe, the ship's reading is suspect.

73. Curtis, *First Bull Run to Chancellorsville*, 111.

74. Child, *Fifth New Hampshire*, 69.

75. *OR*, 11(1):38, 112, 764, 813, 937, 11(3):685; Logbook, USS *Galena*, May 31, 1862, RG 24.2.2, NARA; Child, *Fifth New Hampshire*, 69, 76, 87; Curtis, *First Bull Run to Chancellorsville*, 111; Dickey, *Eighty-Fifth Pennsylvania*, 67; Hyde, *Following the Greek Cross*, 63; Longstreet, *From Manassas to Appomattox*, 88; Norton, *Army Letters*, 82; Smith, *Battle of Seven Pines*, 18, 21, 144; Wood, *The War*, 81–82; Browning and Silver, "Nature and Human Nature," 398; Sears, *To the Gates of Richmond*, 117–21; Symonds, *Joseph E. Johnston*, 160–67.

76. Dickey, *Eighty-Fifth Pennsylvania*, 67. See also *OR*, 11(1):895; Furst Diary, 24, HCWRTC, US-AMHI; Logbook, USS *Galena*, May 31, 1862, RG 24.2.2, NARA; Fort Monroe, Va., May 1862, Reel 522, RG 27.5.7, NARA-CP; and Weymouth, *Sketch of Newcomb*, 66.

77. Longstreet, *From Manassas to Appomattox*, 91. See also Hamilton, *Papers of Shotwell*, 1:214.

78. *OR*, 11(1):41, 42, 243, 767, 778, 794, 795, 796, 802, 804, 943, 947, 958, 968, 988; Fort Monroe, Va., May 1862, Reel 522, RG 27.5.7, NARA-CP; Blight, *When This Cruel War Is Over*, 141; Dickey, *Eighty-Fifth Pennsylvania*, 67; Johnston, *Narrative of Military Operations*, 133–34, 136, 140, 142; Hamilton, *Papers of Shotwell*, 1:214; Lasswell, *Rags and Hope*, 101–3; Hess, *Field Armies and Fortifications*, 101–5; Sears, *To the Gates of Richmond*, 120–40; Symonds, *Joseph E. Johnston*, 166–72.

79. *OR*, 11(1):244; Johnston, *Narrative of Military Operations*, 142; Logbook, USS *Galena*, June 1, 1862, RG 24.2.2, NARA.

80. Hamilton, *Papers of Shotwell*, 1:216.

81. Sears, *To the Gates of Richmond*, 140–45.

82. Sears, *Papers of McClellan*, 291. See also *OR*, 11(1):46; and Logbook, USS *Galena*, June 2, 1862, RG 24.2.2, NARA.

83. Sears, *Papers of McClellan*, 291 294, 295, 297; *OR*, 11(3):223.

84. Weymouth, *Sketch of Newcomb*, 67–68. See also George M. Barnard to Mother, June 5, 1862, Gaines Mill, Va., Barnard Papers, CWCDJ, MHS; Browning and Silver, "Nature and Human Nature," 388–92; McPherson, *Battle Cry of Freedom*, 464; Rafuse, *McClellan's War*, 218–19; Sears, *McClellan*, 196–201; and Sears, *To the Gates of Richmond*, 146–50, 158–59.

85. Blight, *When This Cruel War Is Over*, 146; Hyde, *Following the Greek Cross*, 63–64.

86. Dickey, *Eighty-Fifth Pennsylvania*, 173.

87. Sears, *Papers of McClellan*, 288, 307. See also Logbook, USS *Galena*, May June 11–30, 1862, RG 24.2.2, NARA; Fort Monroe, Va., June 1862, Reel 522, RG 27.5.7, NARA-CP; "Diaries of John Waldrop . . . and William Y. Mordecai," 39–40; Dobbins, *Grandfather's Journal*, 85–88; Fleet and Fuller, *Green Mount*, 139; Richard Waldrop to Mother, June 26, 1862, Ashland, Va., Richard Woolfolk Waldrop Papers, SHC-UNC.

88. Sears, *Papers of McClellan*, 288, 300; Logbook, USS *Galena*, June 15, 1862, RG 24.2.2, NARA.

89. Lee, *Memoir of Pendleton*, 188; Sears, *To the Gates of Richmond*, 151–56, 167–74.

CHAPTER 7

1. *OR*, 12(3):63; Georgetown, D.C., Apr. 1862, Reel 81, RG 27.5.7, NARA-CP; Krick, *Civil War Weather*, 54; Bean, "Valley Campaign," 347; Cook, *Twelfth Massachusetts*, 47–48; Joseph Franklin Kaufman Diary, 4, SHC-UNC; McDonald, *Make Me a Map of the Valley*, 19–20; Mead Diary, vol. 2, Apr. 1–16, 1862, LC; Member of Company C, *Twenty-Seventh Indiana*, 117–18; Quaife, *From the Cannon's Mouth*, 67, 69; Tanner, *Stonewall in the Valley*, 136–43.

2. "Distribution Maps of Dominant Soil Orders," accessed Aug. 7, 2015.

3. *OR*, 12(3):81; Georgetown, D.C., Apr. 1862, Reel 81, RG 27.5.7, NARA-CP; Krick, *Civil War Weather*, 54; *Augusta (Ga.) Chronicle*, May 3,1862; Bean, "Valley Campaign," 351, 361; Cook, *Twelfth Massachusetts*, 48–50; Kaufman Diary, 4–7, SHC-UNC; McDonald, *Make Me a Map of the Valley*, 20–35; Mead Diary, vol. 2, Apr. 16–25, 1862, LC; Member of Company C, *Twenty-Seventh Indiana*, 118–21; Quaife, *From the Cannon's Mouth*, 69–73; Worsham, *One of Jackson's Foot Cavalry*, 37.

4. *OR*, 12(3):106; Robertson, *Stonewall Jackson*, 346–68; Tanner, *Stonewall in the Valley*, 143–61.

5. Roper, *Repairing the "March of Mars,"* 223, 224 (quotation, 223). See also Neese, *Three Years in the Confederate Horse Artillery*, 51; and Summers, *Borderland Confederate*, 11.

6. Howard, *Recollections*, 92–93. See also Cook, *Twelfth Massachusetts*, 50; McDonald, *Make Me a Map of the Valley*, 35; and Quaife, *From the Cannon's Mouth*, 72.

7. McDonald, *Make Me a Map of the Valley*, 35.

8. Cook, *Twelfth Massachusetts*, 50; Mead Diary, vol. 2, May 1–3, 1862, LC.

9. Georgetown, D.C., May 1862, Reel 81, RG 27.5.7, NARA-CP; Krick, *Civil War Weather*, 58; Cook, *Twelfth Massachusetts*, 50; Dobbins, *Grandfather's Journal*, 77–78; McDonald, *Make Me a Map of the Valley*, 35–36; Member of Company C, *Twenty-Seventh Indiana*, 122; Roper, *Repairing the "March of Mars,"* 225; Summers, *Borderland Confederate*, 11; Robertson, *Stonewall Jackson*, 368–70; Tanner, *Stonewall in the Valley*, 162–65.

10. Neese, *Three Years in the Confederate Horse Artillery*, 51–52.

11. Georgetown, D.C., May 1862, Reel 81, RG 27.5.7, NARA-CP; Krick, *Civil War Weather*, 58; McDonald, *Make Me a Map of the Valley*, 36–40; Member of Company C, *Twenty-Seventh Indiana*, 122; Thomas M. Wade Letter, Stonewall Jackson House Collection, Virginia Military Institute, Lexington; Robertson, *Stonewall Jackson*, 370–76 (quotation, 372); Tanner, *Stonewall in the Valley*, 165–74.

12. *OR*, 12(3):192; Georgetown, D.C., May 1862, Reel 81, RG 27.5.7, NARA-CP; Krick, *Civil War Weather*, 58; Cook, *Twelfth Massachusetts*, 50–51; Dobbins, *Grandfather's Journal*, 78; Kaufman Diary, 10–11, SHC-UNC; McDonald, *Make Me a Map of the Valley*, 45–46; Mead Diary, vol. 2, May 14–16, 1862, LC; Roper, *Repairing the "March of Mars,"* 233–35, 237–38; Summers, *Borderland Confederate*, 13–14; Robertson, *Stonewall Jackson*, 376–87; Tanner, *Stonewall in the Valley*, 174–98.

13. Dobbins, *Grandfather's Journal*, 79; Kaufman Diary, 12, SHC-UNC; McDonald, *Make Me a Map of the Valley*, 47–48; Robertson, *Stonewall Jackson*, 387–92; Tanner, *Stonewall in the Valley*, 198–208.

14. Georgetown, D.C., May 1862, Reel 81, RG 27.5.7, NARA-CP; Dobbins, *Grandfather's Journal*, 79; Mead Diary, vol. 2, May 22, 1862, LC; Krick, *Civil War Weather*, 58; Robertson, *Stonewall Jackson*, 392–99; Tanner, *Stonewall in the Valley*, 208–15.

15. Georgetown, D.C., May 1862, Reel 81, RG 27.5.7, NARA-CP; Krick, *Civil War Weather*, 58; Kaufman Diary, 13, SHC-UNC; McDonald, *Make Me a Map of the Valley*, 48; McClendon, *Recollections*, 53, 56; Mead Diary, vol. 2, May 23, 1862, LC; Member of Company C, *Twenty-Seventh Indiana*, 143, 155; Quaife, *From the Cannon's Mouth*. 76, 83, 85, 86; Roper, *Repairing the "March of Mars,"* 243; Robertson, *Stonewall Jackson*, 392–412; Tanner, *Stonewall in the Valley*, 208–33, 238–59.

16. Georgetown, D.C., May 1862, Reel 81, RG 27.5.7, NARA-CP; Krick, *Civil War Weather*, 58; Douglas, *I Rode with Stonewall*, 72; Robertson, *Stonewall Jackson*, 412–17; Tanner, *Stonewall in the Valley*, 263–65.

17. *OR*, 12(1):13, 634, 641, 12(3):358; Georgetown, D.C., May 1862, Reel 81, RG 27.5.7, NARA-CP; Krick, *Civil War Weather*, 58; Beirne, "Three War Letters," 292–93; Dawes, *Sixth Wisconsin*, 46; Douglas, *I Rode with Stonewall*, 72; Kaufman Diary, 14, SHC-UNC; McDonald, *Make Me a Map of the Valley*, 49; Mead Diary, vol. 2, May 30, 1862, LC; Taylor, *Destruction and Reconstruction*, 67; Robertson, *Stonewall Jackson*, 417–10; Tanner, *Stonewall in the Valley*, 265–70.

18. *OR*, 12(1):13, 649; Georgetown, D.C., May 1862, Reel 81, RG 27.5.7, NARA-CP; Krick, *Civil War*

Weather, 58; Douglas, *I Rode with Stonewall*, 72; Kaufman Diary, 14, SHC-UNC; McDonald, *Make Me a Map of the Valley*, 49; Mead Diary, vol. 2, May 31, 1862, LC; Krick, *Conquering the Valley*, 14; Robertson, *Stonewall Jackson*, 419–21; Tanner, *Stonewall in the Valley*, 270–73.

19. Georgetown, D.C., June 1862, Reel 81, RG 27.5.7, NARA-CP; Krick, *Civil War Weather*, 62; Cook, *Twelfth Massachusetts*, 53; McDonald, *Make Me a Map of the Valley*, 51; Neese, *Three Years in the Confederate Horse Artillery*, 64; Oates, *War between the Union and the Confederacy*, 101; Robertson, *Stonewall Jackson*, 421–23; Tanner, *Stonewall in the Valley*, 272–76.

20. Taylor, *Destruction and Reconstruction*, 76. See also Georgetown, D.C., June 1862, Reel 81, RG 27.5.7, NARA-CP; and Krick, *Civil War Weather*, 62.

21. Robertson, *Stonewall Jackson*, 423. See also Krick, *Conquering the Valley*, 20.

22. *OR*, 12(1):731; Georgetown, D.C., June 1862, Reel 81, RG 27.5.7, NARA-CP; Krick, *Civil War Weather*, 62; Dobbins, *Grandfather's Journal*, 82. See also Bean, "Valley Campaign," 363; Kaufman Diary, 15, SHC-UNC; McDonald, *Make Me a Map of the Valley*, 51; Mead Diary, vol. 2, June 3, 1862, LC; Robertson, *Stonewall Jackson*, 423–25; and Tanner, *Stonewall in the Valley*, 276–79.

23. *OR*, 12(3):324; McDonald, *Make Me a Map of the Valley*, 51. See also Dobbins, *Grandfather's Journal*, 82; Mead Diary, vol. 2, June 4, 1862, LC; Neese, *Three Years in the Confederate Horse Artillery*, 64; and Summers, *Borderland Confederate*, 20.

24. McClendon, *Recollections*, 60.

25. Robertson, *Stonewall Jackson*, 424, 425.

26. Nathaniel L. Parmeter Diary, 26, 27, MSS 246, Nathaniel L. Parmeter Papers, 1861–65, OHS. See also Cook, *Twelfth Massachusetts*, 53; Krick, *Conquering the Valley*, 14–15; and Robertson, *Stonewall Jackson*, 425.

27. *OR*, 12(1):686. See also ibid., 12(3):340, 358.

28. McDonald, *Make Me a Map of the Valley*, 52. See also Mead Diary, vol. 2, June 5, 1862, LC; and Krick, *Conquering the Valley*, 20.

29. Parmeter Diary, 27, Parmeter Papers, OHS. See also Cook, *Twelfth Massachusetts*, 53.

30. *OR*, 12(3):357; Georgetown, D.C., June 1862, Reel 81, RG 27.5.7, NARA-CP; Krick, *Civil War Weather*, 62; Dobbins, *Grandfather's Journal*, 82–83; McDonald, *Make Me a Map of the Valley*, 53, 55; Krick, *Conquering the Valley*, 20–21; Tanner, *Stonewall in the Valley*, 286–87.

31. Douglas, *I Rode with Stonewall*, 85.

32. Georgetown, D.C., June 1862, Reel 81, RG 27.5.7, NARA-CP; Krick, *Civil War Weather*, 62; Kaufman Diary, 15, SHC-UNC; Summers, *Borderland Confederate*, 29; Tanner, *Stonewall in the Valley*, 286–97; Robertson, *Stonewall Jackson*, 431–37.

33. *OR*, 12(1):24, 696, 699; Georgetown, D.C., June 1862, Reel 81, RG 27.5.7, NARA-CP; Cook, *Twelfth Massachusetts*, 54; Douglas, *I Rode with Stonewall*, 91; Mead Diary, vol. 2, June 10, 1862, LC; Krick, *Civil War Weather*, 62; Taylor, *Destruction and Reconstruction*, 87 (quotation); Tanner, *Stonewall in the Valley*, 296–310; Robertson, *Stonewall Jackson*, 431–45.

34. *OR*, 12(3):68, 192, 313, 324, 379–81; McPherson, *Battle Cry of Freedom*, 454–60; Meier, *Nature's Civil War*, 10, 45–47; Krick, *Conquering the Valley*, 498–503; Tanner, *Stonewall in the Valley*, 317–25; Robertson, *Stonewall Jackson*, 445–50.

35. Dobbins, *Grandfather's Journal*, 85; Robertson, *Stonewall Jackson*, 454–57; Sears, *To the Gates of Richmond*, 174–75.

36. Moore, *Story of a Cannoneer*, 86.

37. *OR*, 11(2):969; Logbook, USS *Galena*, June 23, 1862, RG 24.2.2, NARA; George M. Barnard to Inman, June 25, 1862, Richmond, Va., George Middleton Barnard Papers, CWCDJ, MHS; Kaufman Diary, 18, SHC-UNC; "Diaries of John Waldrop . . . and William Y. Mordecai," 40; Robertson, *Letters of McAllister*, 183; Sears, *Papers of McClellan*, 307; Krick, *Civil War Weather*, 60, 63; *Richmond Whig*, June

20, 1863; *Macon (Ga.) Daily Telegraph*, June 23, 26, 1862; Burton, *Extraordinary Circumstances*, 53–54; Robertson, *Stonewall Jackson*, 457–67; Sears, *To the Gates of Richmond*, 175–77, 194–95.

38. *OR*, 11(2):623, 11(3):255; Logbook, USS *Galena*, June 25, 1862, RG 24.2.2, NARA; Kaufman Diary, 18, SHC-UNC; "Diaries of John Waldrop . . . and William Y. Mordecai," 40; Dobbins, *Grandfather's Journal*, 86; Krick, *Civil War Weather*, 60, 63; Sears, *Papers of McClellan*, 308–11; Burton, *Extraordinary Circumstances*, 52, 53–54; McPherson, *Battle Cry of Freedom*, 465–67; Rafuse, *McClellan's War*, 221–25; Robertson, *Stonewall Jackson*, 467–74; Sears, *To the Gates of Richmond*, 161–63, 181–211.

39. *OR*, 11(2):322, 323; "Diaries of John Waldrop . . . and William Y. Mordecai," 40; Dobbins, *Grandfather's Journal*, 87–88; Kaufman Diary, 20, SHC-UNC; McClendon, *Recollections*, 79–81, 83; Oates, *War between the Union and the Confederacy*, 115–16; Krick, *Civil War Weather*, 60; McPherson, *Battle Cry of Freedom*, 467; Robertson, *Stonewall Jackson*, 474–84; Sears, *To the Gates of Richmond*, 217–53.

40. *OR*, 11(3):255; Logbook, USS *Galena*, June 28–29, 1862, RG 24.2.2, NARA; Sears, *Papers of McClellan*, 322–25 (quotation, 323); Dobbins, *Grandfather's Journal*, 88; Fleet and Fuller, *Green Mount*, 141; Kaufman Diary, 21, SHC-UNC.

41. *OR*, 11(2):210, 350, 464, 705, 707, 733; Logbook, USS *Galena*, June 30, July 1, 1862, RG 24.2.2, NARA; Dobbins, *Grandfather's Journal*, 88; Fleet and Fuller, *Green Mount*, 142; *Shoemaker's Battery*, 16; Krick, *Civil War Weather*, 60–61; *Richmond Whig*, July 1, 1862; McPherson, *Battle Cry of Freedom*, 468–69; Rafuse, *McClellan's War*, 225–26; Robertson, *Stonewall Jackson*, 485–91; Sears, *To the Gates of Richmond*, 252–336.

42. Hill, "McClellan's Change of Base," 394.

43. Sears, *Papers of McClellan*, 327–30, 333; Rafuse, *McClellan's War*, 229–31; Sears, *To the Gates of Richmond*, 308, 312, 336–39.

44. *OR*, 11(2):103, 124, 155, 194, 220, 236, 295, 297, 306, 383, 464, 469, 519, 530, 536, 568, 598, 619, 915, 918, 972; Logbook, USS *Galena*, July 2–3, 1862, RG 24.2.2, NARA; Blackford, *War Years*, 77; Curtis, *First Bull Run to Chancellorsville*, 142; de Trobriand, *Four Years in the Army of the Potomac*, 270; Howard, *Recollections*, 150, 153; Fry, "McClellan's Epidemic," 7–29; Sears, *To the Gates of Richmond*, 336–39.

45. *OR*, 11(2):320.

46. Hyde, *Following the Greek Cross*, 81–82.

47. For an exception, see Galwey, *Valiant Hours*, 24.

48. *OR*, 11(2):629.

49. Sears, *To the Gates of Richmond*, 338. See also Meier, *Nature's Civil War*, 138–39.

50. Fry, "McClellan's Epidemic," 11.

51. Everson and Simpson, *"Far, Far from Home,"* 136; White, "Diary of the War," 124; Worsham, *One of Jackson's Foot Cavalry*, 61, 83.

52. Blackford, *War Years*, 80. See also Westwood A. Todd Reminiscences, pt. 1, 26, SHC-UNC; and Logbook, USS *Galena*, July 3, 1862, RG 24.2.2, NARA.

53. Longstreet, *From Manassas to Appomattox*, 145–46.

54. Sears, *Papers of McClellan*, 337; John B. Evans to Molie Evans, July 5, 1862, Richmond, John B. Evans Papers, 1862–1865, Duke; Weymouth, *Sketch of Newcomb*, 73; Sears, *To the Gates of Richmond*, 338–41.

55. Sears, *Papers of McClellan*, 340; Logbook, USS *Galena*, July 8, 1862, RG 24.2.2, NARA; Hennessy, *Return to Bull Run*, 5–6, 8–9.

56. Brasher, *Peninsula Campaign*, esp. 7, 188–224; McPherson, *Battle Cry of Freedom* 499–505; Oakes, *Freedom National*, 211–13; Rafuse, *McClellan's War*, 231–37.

57. Hennessy, *Return to Bull Run*, 9–11; McPherson, *Battle Cry of Freedom* 498–506, 524–26; Rafuse, *McClellan's War*, 236–52; Sears, *To the Gates of Richmond*, 345–47, 352–55.

58. Logbook, USS *Galena*, July, Aug. 1862, RG 24.2.2, NARA; Fort Monroe, Va., July, Aug. 1862, Reel 522, RG 27.5.7, NARA-CP; George M. Barnard to Mother, July 10, 1862, Harrison's Landing, Va., Barnard Papers, CWCDJ, MHS; Child, *Fifth New Hampshire*, 96, 102; Douglas, *I Rode with Stonewall*, 114, 115; Everson and Simpson, "*Far, Far from Home*," 138–39; Kaufman Diary, 22–24, SHC-UNC; Norton, *Army Letters*, 114; Rhodes, *All for the Union*, 73, 74, 77; "Diaries of John Waldrop . . . and William Y. Mordecai," 40–41; Weymouth, *Sketch of Newcomb*, 75, 78, 79, 81–82; Brasher, *Peninsula Campaign*, 216–20; Fry, "McClellan's Epidemic," 15, 16.

59. Quoted in Fry, "McClellan's Epidemic," 15.

60. George M. Barnard to Mother, July 10, 13, 26, Aug. 1, 1862, Richmond, Va., Barnard Papers, CWCDJ, MHS; George M. Barnard to Father, June 15, Aug. 4, 9, 1862, Harrison's Landing, Va., ibid.

61. Galwey, *Valiant Hours*, 25.

62. Sanford, *Fighting Rebels and Redskins*, 168.

63. Fort Monroe, Va., July, Aug. 1862, Reel 522, RG 27.5.7, NARA-CP; Dobbins, *Grandfather's Journal*, 89–96; John B. Evans to Molie Evans, July 19, 1862, Richmond, Evans Papers, Duke; Everson and Simpson, "*Far, Far from Home*," 138–39; French, *Two Wars*, 148; Rhodes, *All for the Union*, 74.

64. Child, *Fifth New Hampshire*, 96; Isaac R. Dunkelbarger Recollections, 6, Michael Winey Collection, USAMHI; Galwey, *Valiant Hours*, 25; Rhodes, *All for the Union*, 74, 77; Sanford, *Fighting Rebels and Redskins*, 16; Weymouth, *Sketch of Newcomb*, 78; Bell, *Mosquito Soldiers*, 74–76; Browning and Silver, "Nature and Human Nature," 406–7; Fry, "McClellan's Epidemic," 7–18; Gaede, *Federal Civil War Shelter Tent*, 22–25; Meier, *Nature's Civil War*, 45; Sears, *To the Gates of Richmond*, 347–48.

65. *OR*, 11(1):83. Andrew Bell makes a similar point in *Mosquito Soldiers*, 74–76.

66. Child, *Fifth New Hampshire*, 104. See also Malles, *Bridge Building in Wartime*, 80, 82.

CHAPTER 8

1. *OR*, 12(3):473–74, 500–501; Hennessy, *Return to Bull Run*, 12–14.

2. *OR*, 12(2):50, 51, 52, 12(3):473–74, 500–501; Hennessy, *Return to Bull Run*, 14–19.

3. Fleet and Fuller, *Green Mount*, 143, 157, 163. See also Hurt, *Agriculture and the Confederacy*, 88.

4. *Augusta (Ga.) Chronicle*, Aug. 20, 26, Sept. 13, 25, 27, Oct. 25, 1861; *Augusta (Ga.) Daily Constitutionalist*, Sept. 13, 1861, Mar. 16, 1862; *Charleston Courier*, Sept. 10, Oct. 28, 1861; *Charleston Mercury*, Aug. 20, 26, Sept. 6, 9, 20, 1861; *Daily Columbus (Ga.) Enquirer*, Aug. 24, Sept. 14, 1861; *Carolina Observer* (Fayetteville, N.C.), Oct. 10, 1861; *Macon (Ga.) Daily Telegraph*, Sept. 11, 1861; *New Orleans Daily True Delta*, Aug. 27, 31, Sept. 3, 5, 12, 17, 26, 28, Oct. 3, 26, 27, 30, 1861; *St. Louis Daily Missouri Republican*, Sept. 17, 1861; Hurt, *Agriculture and the Confederacy*, 28–33, 42–50.

5. *Augusta (Ga.) Chronicle*, Apr. 10, 16, 17, 18, May 5, 26, June 5, 9, 25, 1862; *Augusta (Ga.) Daily Constitutionalist*, Mar. 16, 20, Apr. 4, 5, 25, May 8, 1862; *Charleston Mercury*, June 6, 1862; *Charleston Tri-Weekly Mercury*, June 17, 1862; *Carolina Observer* (Fayetteville, N.C.), Apr. 21, 1862; *Louisville Daily Democrat*, Apr. 25, May 4, 31, June 8, 1862; *Macon (Ga.) Daily Telegraph*, Apr. 15, 1862; *Mobile Register*, Apr. 3, May 3, 1862; *New Orleans Daily Delta*, Apr. 17, May 14, 1862; *New Orleans Daily True Delta*, Apr. 5, 20, 1862; Fiege, *Republic of Nature*, 107–14.

6. Gates, *Agriculture and the Civil War*, 86; Hurt, *Agriculture and the Confederacy*, 53–60, 63–64, 66–71, 74–75, 86–90 (quotation, 75); Steinberg, *Down to Earth*, 92–94, 96–97; *Augusta (Ga.) Chronicle*, May 19, 26, June 28, July 8, 1862; *Augusta (Ga.) Daily Constitutionalist*, May 22, June 11, Sept. 20, 1862; *Ohio Farmer* (Cleveland), Sept. 6, 1862; *Daily Columbus (Ga.) Enquirer*, June 18, Sept. 1, 1862; *Louisville Daily Democrat*, May 13, 29, 1862; *Georgia Weekly Telegraph* (Macon), June 20, July 3, 1862;

Macon (Ga.) Daily Telegraph, July 26, 1862; *Mobile Register*, July 8, 1862; *New Orleans Daily True Delta*, Aug. 2, 9, 1862; Sharrer, *Kind of Fate*, 9–18; Lasswell, *Rags and Hope*, 139.

7. *Cincinnati Commercial Tribune*, June 6, 30, Aug. 5, 7, Sept. 3, 1862 (quotation, Sept. 3); *New York Herald*, July 27, 1862.

8. Racine, *Piedmont Farmer*, 1–2, 10–11, 222–44 (quotations, 224, 225, 241–42, 244). The Georgia coast was equally gloomy. See Myers, *Children of Pride*, 196–97.

9. Racine, *Piedmont Farmer*, 244–65 (quotations, 246, 252, 255, 256, 257, 259, 261).

10. Member of Company C, *Twenty-Seventh Indiana*, 185, 188, 190. See also Quint, *Second Massachusetts*, 98–99; Sparks, *Inside Lincoln's Army*, 102, 104, 106; Georgetown, D.C., July 1862, Reel 81, RG 27.5.7, NARA-CP; and Krick, *Civil War Weather*, 65.

11. Pyne, *Ride to War*, 41, 45. See also Cook, *Twelfth Massachusetts*, 58; Sparks, *Inside Lincoln's Army*, 107; and Krick, *Civil War Weather*, 65.

12. *Daily Columbus (Ga.) Enquirer*, Aug. 5, 1862.

13. See Robinson, *Bitter Fruits of Bondage*, esp. 121, 126–30, 307n30; McCurry, *Confederate Reckoning*, 206; and Williams, *People's History of the Civil War*, 93–95, 171, 183, 203–4.

14. Hennessy, *Return to Bull Run*, 21–24 (quotation, 21).

15. Blackford et al., *Letters from Lee's Army*, 85; Douglas, *I Rode with Stonewall*, 120; Joseph Franklin Kaufman Diary, 20–22, SHC-UNC; Georgetown, D.C., July 1862, Reel 81, RG 27.5.7, NARA-CP; Krick, *Civil War Weather*, 65.

16. McDonald, *Make Me a Map of the Valley*, 61–63 (quotations, 62); Hennessy, *Return to Bull Run*, 23–26 (quotation, 26); Robertson, *Stonewall Jackson*, 514–15, 518–21.

17. Jones, *Under the Stars and Bars*, 51.

18. Member of Company C, *Twenty-Seventh Indiana*, 194–95.

19. Caldwell, *Brigade of South Carolinians*, 53. See also Chamberlayne, *Ham Chamberlayne*, 90; and Howard, *Recollections*, 162, 164.

20. "Letters from Aaron P. Bates," 101; Kaufman Diary, 27, SHC-UNC; Hennessy, *Return to Bull Run*, 27–28 (quotation, 28). See also Casler, *Four Years in the Stonewall Brigade*, 103; Howard, *Recollections*, 164; D. R. Larned to Mrs. Burnside, Aug. 8, 1862, Falmouth, Va., Daniel Read Larned Papers, LC; McDonald, *Make Me a Map of the Valley*, 65–66; Georgetown, D.C., Aug. 1862, Reel 81, RG 27.5.7, NARA-CP; Krick, *Civil War Weather*, 68; and Robertson, *Stonewall Jackson*, 524–25.

21. Hennessy, *Return to Bull Run*, 28; Krick, *Civil War Weather*, 66, 68; Robertson, *Stonewall Jackson*, 526–34; White, *Diary of Wyman S. White*, 100. The definitive account of the battle is Krick, *Stonewall Jackson at Cedar Mountain*.

22. Member of Company C, *Twenty-Seventh Indiana*, 195.

23. *OR*, 12(2):154, 160, 163, 168, 211; Howard, *Recollections*, 166, 171; "Letters from Aaron P. Bates," 102, 103; McDonald, *Make Me a Map of the Valley*, 66; Member of Company C, *Twenty-Seventh Indiana*, 195; Pyne, *Ride to War*, 60; Quint, *Second Massachusetts*, 105, 306; Krick, *Stonewall Jackson at Cedar Mountain*, esp. 63, 65, 106, 126, 135, 160–61, 225, 238, 254.

24. White, *Diary of Wyman S. White*, 77.

25. Howard, *Recollections*, 174; Georgetown, D.C., Aug. 1862, Reel 81, RG 27.5.7, NARA-CP; Krick, *Civil War Weather*, 68; Krick, *Stonewall Jackson at Cedar Mountain*, 334–35, 40, 347; Robertson, *Stonewall Jackson*, 536–37.

26. Douglas, *I Rode with Stonewall*, 127.

27. *OR*, 12(2):134, 148, 160, 163, 199, 211; Pyne, *Ride to War*, 66. See also White, *Diary of Wyman S. White*, 76; Hennessy, *Return to Bull Run*, 28–30; and Robertson, *Stonewall Jackson*, 538.

28. Cook, *Twelfth Massachusetts*, 60; Welch, *Confederate Surgeon's Letters*, 18, 20; Hennessy, *Re-*

turn to Bull Run, 30–37, 42; Georgetown, D.C., Aug. 1862, Reel 81, RG 27.5.7, NARA-CP; Krick, *Civil War Weather*, 68.

29. Douglas, *I Rode with Stonewall*, 130; White, *Diary of Wyman S. White*, 79–80; Hennessy, *Return to Bull Run*, 38–51.

30. Member of Company C, *Twenty-Seventh Indiana*, 216.

31. Dawes, *Sixth Wisconsin*, 56; McClendon, *Recollections*, 97; Member of Company C, *Twenty-Seventh Indiana*, 217; Hennessy, *Return to Bull Run*, 51–59.

32. Hennessy, *Return to Bull Run*, 62.

33. Kaufman Diary, 321, SHC-UNC; Hennessy, *Return to Bull Run*, 60–70 (quotation, 62); Georgetown, D.C., Aug. 1862, Reel 81, RG 27.5.7, NARA-CP; Hennessy, *Return to Bull Run*, 66–67, 74–75; Krick, *Civil War Weather*, 66, 68.

34. Blackford, *War Years*, 104.

35. Haden, *Reminiscences*, 15.

36. OR, 12(2):553, 705; Hennessy, *Return to Bull Run*, 76–79.

37. Neese, *Three Years in the Confederate Horse Artillery*, 102.

38. OR, 12(2):13, 31, 62, 311, 383, 642, 650, 705–6; 12(3):941; Bartlett, *Military Record of Louisiana*, 113; Caldwell, *Brigade of South Carolinians*, 22; Dobbins, *Grandfather's Journal*, 98; Longstreet, *From Manassas to Appomattox*, 166; McClendon, *Recollections*, 99; "Military Reminiscences of Major Campbell Brown, 1861–1865," 89, Papers of Campbell Brown and Richard S. Ewell, Microfilm 816, TSLA; Quint, *Second Massachusetts*, 122; Welch, *Confederate Surgeon's Letters*, 22; Hennessy, *Return to Bull Run*, 70–73; Robertson, *Stonewall Jackson*, 545–46.

39. Douglas, *I Rode with Stonewall*, 130.

40. Hennessy, *Return to Bull Run*, 88–95 (quotation, 89); Robertson, *Stonewall Jackson*, 547.

41. Dobbins, *Grandfather's Journal*, 98; Haines, *Fifteenth Regiment New Jersey Volunteers*, 11 (hereafter Haines, *Fifteenth New Jersey*); Member of Company C, *Twenty-Seventh Indiana*, 217; Moore, *Story of a Cannoneer*, 105; Sparks, *Inside Lincoln's Army*, 129; Hennessy, *Return to Bull Run*, 96–137; Georgetown, D.C., Aug. 1862, Reel 81, RG 27.5.7, NARA-CP; Krick, *Civil War Weather*, 68; Robertson, *Stonewall Jackson*, 549–58.

42. OR, 12(2, supp.):844, 873, 901, 930, 935, 943, 967, 1077.

43. McDonald, *Make Me a Map of the Valley*, 73.

44. OR, 12(2):592; Georgetown, D.C., Aug. 1862, Reel 81, RG 27.5.7, NARA-CP; Bartlett, *Military Record of Louisiana*, 126; Blackford, *War Years*, 125; Hamilton, *Papers of Shotwell*, 1:299; McDonald, *Make Me a Map of the Valley*, 74, 75, 76; McClendon, *Recollections*, 108; Preston, *Tenth Regiment of Cavalry, New York*, 40 (hereafter Preston, *Tenth New York Cavalry*); Edward E. Schweitzer Diary, 1:11–12, Edward E. Schweitzer Diaries and Correspondence, Box 23, CWTI, USAMHI; Hennessy, *Return to Bull Run*, 138–438; Krick, *Civil War Weather*, 66, 68; Ludlum, *Weather Factor*, 82–83; McPherson, *Battle Cry of Freedom*, 528–32; Robertson, *Stonewall Jackson*, 559–75.

45. OR, 12(2):557–58; George M. Barnard, letter fragment, Aug. 30, 1862, George Middleton Barnard Papers, CWCDJ, MHS; Child, *Fifth New Hampshire*, 114–15 (quotation, 114). See also Galwey, *Valiant Hours*, 28; Schweitzer Diary, 1:11–12, Schweitzer Diaries and Correspondence, CWTI, USAMHI; Houghton and Houghton, *Two Boys*, 124; Longstreet, *From Manassas to Appomattox*, 190; Neese, *Three Years in the Confederate Horse Artillery*, 106; White, "Diary of the War," 127; Georgetown, D.C., Aug. 1862, Reel 81, RG 27.5.7, NARA-CP; Krick, *Civil War Weather*, 66, 68; Hennessy, *Return to Bull Run*, 435–38; and Malles, *Bridge Building in Wartime*, 84.

46. Douglas, *I Rode with Stonewall*, 142. See also Mead Diary, vol. 3, Aug. 31, 1862, LC; and Robertson, *Stonewall Jackson*, 577.

47. Pyne, *Ride to War*, 84, 85.

48. Longstreet, *From Manassas to Appomattox*, 191.

49. Cook, *Twelfth Massachusetts*, 64; McClendon, *Recollections*, 121; Hennessy, *Return to Bull Run*, 441–44; Robertson, *Stonewall Jackson*, 578–80.

50. Longstreet, *From Manassas to Appomattox*, 193.

51. Pyne, *Ride to War*, 86. For similar accounts, see Dawes, *Sixth Wisconsin*, 75; and Welch, *Confederate Surgeon's Letters*, 28.

52. Quaife, *From the Cannon's Mouth*, 110.

53. *OR*, 12(2):677, 691–92; Caldwell, *Brigade of South Carolinians*, 68; Douglas, *I Rode with Stonewall*, 144; McDonald, *Make Me a Map of the Valley*, 77; Mead Diary, vol. 3, Sept. 1, 1862, LC; Quaife, *From the Cannon's Mouth*, 110.

54. Moore, *Story of a Cannoneer*, 128. See also Quaife, *From the Cannon's Mouth*, 110; and Worsham, *One of Jackson's Foot Cavalry*, 81.

55. Hennessy, *Return to Bull Run*, 451–72; McPherson, *Battle Cry of Freedom*, 532–34; Rafuse, *McClellan's War*, 266–72; Dayton E. Flint to Father, Sept. 3, 1862, in "Civil War Letters of Dayton E. Flint," Box 40, CWMC, USAMHI; Georgetown, D.C., Sept. 1862, Reel 81, RG 27.5.7, NARA-CP; Krick, *Civil War Weather*, 71; Robertson, *Letters of McAllister*, 200; Schweitzer Diary, 1:12, Schweitzer Diaries and Correspondence, CWTI, USAMHI; Sears, *Landscape Turned Red*, 1–18; Sears, *McClellan*, 258–62; Sears, *Papers of McClellan*, 427–29 (quotation, 428). The high temperature on September 1 was only 68 degrees; the previous day's reading was 83 degrees.

56. Guelzo, *Fateful Lightning*, 169–70; Harsh, *Taken at the Flood*, 11–65; McPherson, *Battle Cry of Freedom*, 534–35; Robertson, *Stonewall Jackson*, 581–83.

57. McClendon, *Recollections*, 129; McDonald, *Make Me a Map of the Valley*, 78–79; Neese, *Three Years in the Confederate Horse Artillery*, 112; Tyler, *Recollections*, 32; Weymouth, *Sketch of Newcomb*, 85; Georgetown, D.C., Sept. 1862, Reel 81, RG 27.5.7, NARA-CP; Krick, *Civil War Weather*, 71; Harsh, *Taken at the Flood*, 66–120; McPherson, *Battle Cry of Freedom*, 535–36; Rafuse, *McClellan's War*, 274–78; Robertson, *Stonewall Jackson*, 583–91; Sears, *Landscape Turned Red*, 82–88.

58. McClendon, *Recollections*, 129. See also Dobbins, *Grandfather's Journal*, 102–3.

59. Neese, *Three Years in the Confederate Horse Artillery*, 112. See also Longstreet, *From Manassas to Appomattox*, 199–200; and McDonald, *Make Me a Map of the Valley*, 79.

60. *OR*, 19(2):224; Clark, *Iron Hearted Regiment*, 10; Cook, *Twelfth Massachusetts*, 67; McDonald, *Make Me a Map of the Valley*, 80; Schweitzer Diary, 1:13, Schweitzer Diaries and Correspondence, CWTI, USAMHI; Sparks, *Inside Lincoln's Army*, 142–43; Rafuse, *McClellan's War*, 278–81, 282–88; Sears, *Landscape Turned Red*, 76–82, 102–13; Sears, *McClellan*, 262–79.

61. Member of Company C, *Twenty-Seventh Indiana*, 228; McPherson, *Battle Cry of Freedom*, 536–38; Harsh, *Taken at the Flood*, 110–252; Rafuse, *McClellan's War*, 285–86, 288, 290–94; Sears, *Landscape Turned Red*, 89–97; Sears, *McClellan*, 279–86.

62. *OR*, 19(1):147, 895, 1051; Longstreet, *From Manassas to Appomattox*, 220. See also Dobbins, *Grandfather's Journal*, 104–5; Georgetown, D.C., Sept. 1862, Reel 81, RG 27.5.7, NARA-CP; Krick, *Civil War Weather*, 71; McDonald, *Make Me a Map of the Valley*, 81; and Sears, *Papers of McClellan*, 458.

63. Dawes, *Sixth Wisconsin*, 84; Harsh, *Taken at the Flood*, 253–97; Georgetown, D.C., Sept. 1862, Reel 81, RG 27.5.7, NARA-CP; Krick, *Civil War Weather*, 71; McPherson, *Battle Cry of Freedom*, 538; Rafuse, *McClellan's War*, 294–301; Sears, *Landscape Turned Red*, 114–49; Sears, *McClellan*, 286–91.

64. Robertson, *Letters of McAllister*, 175; Sanford, *Fighting Rebels and Redskins*, 175, 176; Rafuse, *McClellan's War*, 301–10, 312–14; Sears, *Papers of McClellan*, 465; Sears, *McClellan*, 291–303.

65. McDonald, *Make Me a Map of the Valley*, 82.

66. Caldwell, *Brigade of South Carolinians*, 75; Child, *Fifth New Hampshire*, 120; Douglas, *I Rode with Stonewall*, 169; Galwey, *Valiant Hours*, 38; Howe, *Touched with Fire*, 62–63; Longstreet, *From*

Manassas to Appomattox, 237; Quint, *Second Massachusetts*, 134; Georgetown, D.C., Sept. 1862, Reel 81, RG 27.5.7, NARA-CP; Krick, *Civil War Weather*, 71; McPherson, *Battle Cry of Freedom*, 538–45; Rafuse, *McClellan's War*, 314–28; Robertson, *Stonewall Jackson*, 607–20; Sears, *Landscape Turned Red*, 180–297; Sears, *McClellan*, 303–17; Carol Reardon, email to author, Oct. 10, 2018.

67. Dawes, *Sixth Wisconsin*, 95; Dobbins, *Grandfather's Journal*, 106; McDonald, *Make Me a Map of the Valley*, 85; Quint, *Second Massachusetts*, 141; Georgetown, D.C., Sept. 1862, Reel 81, RG 27.5.7, NARA-CP; Krick, *Civil War Weather*, 71; Harsh, *Taken at the Flood*, 251, 254; Rafuse, *McClellan's War*, 334–40; Robertson, *Stonewall Jackson*, 606–23; Sears, *McClellan*, 317–30; Sears, *Papers of McClellan*, 47. For examples of sermons, see Sinclair, *Thanksgiving*, 9–10; and Tupper, *Thanksgiving*, 8–9.

68. *OR*, 19(2):52; Blackford, *War Years*, 164, 166–67, 168, 171; Nevins, *Diary of Battle*, 107; Sears, *Papers of McClellan*, 487, 488, 490, 497–98; McPherson, *Battle Cry of Freedom*, 568–69; Rafuse, *McClellan's War*, 340–59; Sears, *McClellan*, 330–36.

69. Georgetown, D.C., Sept., Oct. 1862, Reel 81, RG 27.5.7, NARA-CP; Krick, *Civil War Weather*, 71, 73; *Alexandria (Va.) Gazette*, Oct. 1, 1862; Cook, *Twelfth Massachusetts*, 67; Luther C. Furst Diary, 28, HCWRTC, USAMHI; Frank Morse to Ellen, Sept. 24, 1862, Arlington Heights, Va., Frank C. Morse Papers, MHS; Morse to Wife, Sept. 28, 1862, Arlington Heights, Va., ibid.; Morse to Wife, Oct. 2, 1862, Berlin, Md., ibid.; Morse to Wife, Oct. 12, 1862, Downsville, Md., ibid.; Morse to Wife, Oct. 27, 1862, Williamsport, Md., ibid.; Mead Diary, vol. 3, Oct. 1–28, 1862, LC; Nevins, *Diary of Battle*, 109, 113, Quaife, *From the Cannon's Mouth*, 140; Rhodes, *All for the Union*, 82; Sanford, *Fighting Rebels and Redskins*, 183; Schweitzer Diary, 1:19, Schweitzer Diaries and Correspondence, CWTI, USAMHI; Silliker, *Rebel Yell & the Yankee Hurrah*, 41; Rhodes, *All for the Union*, 85; Tyler, *Recollections*, 50.

70. Nevins, *Diary of Battle*, 107, 108; Sears, *Papers of McClellan*, 481, 485–86 (quotations, 481, 486). See also George M. Barnard to Mother, Oct. 21, 1862, Sharpsburg, Md., Barnard Papers, CWCDJ, MHS.

71. Nevins, *Diary of Battle*, 107, 116.

72. Member of Company C, *Twenty-Seventh Indiana*, 271.

73. Britton and Reed, *To My Beloved Wife*, 27. See also George M. Barnard to Father, Oct. 19, 1862, Sharpsburg, Md., Barnard Papers, CWCDJ, MHS; Dayton E. Flint to Sister, Oct. 21, 1862, in "Civil War Letters of Dayton E. Flint," CWMC, USAMHI; Schweitzer Diary, 1:20, Schweitzer Diaries and Correspondence, CWTI, USAMHI; and Silliker, *Rebel Yell & the Yankee Hurrah*, 41.

74. Sparks, *Inside Lincoln's Army*, 157. See also Quaife, *From the Cannon's Mouth*, 140.

75. Quaife, *From the Cannon's Mouth*, 140, 141 (quotation, 140).

76. Lee, *Memoir of Pendleton*, 230. See also Baldy [Archibald Henderson] to Brother, Oct. 5, 1862, Winchester, Va., Archibald Erskine Henderson Papers, 1841–1917, Duke.

77. Roper, *Repairing the "March of Mars,"* 254, 255.

78. *Macon (Ga.) Daily Telegraph*, Oct. 21, 1862; Chamberlayne, *Ham Chamberlayne*, 122, 129; Everson and Simpson, *"Far, Far from Home,"* 146, 151, 153, 156; Galwey, *Valiant Hours*, 50–51; McClendon, *Recollections*, 166; McDonald, *Make Me a Map of the Valley*, 84–91; Nevins, *Diary of Battle*, 121; Roper, *Repairing the "March of Mars,"* 256, 257, 266–67, 270, 271, 272; Richard Woolfolk Waldrop to Charlie, Oct. 12, 1862, Richard Woolfolk Waldrop Papers, SHC-UNC; Waldrop to Mother, Oct. 26, 1862, ibid.; Waldrop to Father, Oct. 29, 1862, ibid.; Welch, *Confederate Surgeon's Letters*, 34, 35.

79. Bartlett, *Twelfth Regiment New Hampshire Volunteers*, 75 (hereafter Bartlett, *Twelfth New Hampshire*); Galwey, *Valiant Hours*, 50–51; McDonald, *Make Me a Map of the Valley*, 91–92; Neese, *Three Years in the Confederate Horse Artillery*, 132; Nevins, *Diary of Battle*, 116–17, 119–20; Quaife, *From the Cannon's Mouth*, 141; Roper, *Repairing the "March of Mars,"* 285; Sears, *Papers of McClellan*, 518, 519–20; Schweitzer Diary, 1:20, Schweitzer Diaries and Correspondence, CWTI, USAMHI; Silliker,

Rebel Yell & the Yankee Hurrah, 43–44; Sparks, *Inside Lincoln's Army,* 168; Tyler, *Recollections,* 50, 54; Richard Waldrop to Father, Oct. 29, 1862, Berryville, Va., Waldrop Papers, SHC-UNC; O'Reilly, *Fredericksburg Campaign,* 10–13.

80. Roper, *Repairing the "March of Mars,"* 285.

81. McDonald, *Make Me a Map of the Valley,* 92; Roper, *Repairing the "March of Mars,"* 287; Tyler, *Recollections,* 55–56.

82. Curtis, *First Bull Run to Chancellorsville,* 215. See also Georgetown, D.C., Nov. 1862, Reel 81, RG 27.5.7, NARA-CP; Krick, *Civil War Weather,* 77.

83. Nevins, *Diary of Battle,* 122, 126 (quotation, 122). See also Curtis, *First Bull Run to Chancellorsville,* 216; Fleet and Fuller, *Green Mount,* 180–81; Jones, *Rebel War Clerk's Diary,* 1:184, 186; Mead Diary, vol. 3, Nov. 7, 1862, LC; Roper, *Repairing the "March of Mars,"* 287; Sanford, *Fighting Rebels and Redskins,* 188; Schweitzer Diary, 1:21, Schweitzer Diaries and Correspondence,, CWTI USAMHI; Chicago, Ill., Nov. 1862, Reel 116, RG 27.5.7, NARA-CP; Georgetown, D.C., Sept., Oct. 1862, Reel 81, ibid.; Greensboro, Ala., Nov. 1862, Reel 2, ibid.; Krick, *Civil War Weather,* 77.

84. Hamilton, *Papers of Shotwell,* 1:378. For other men, see White, *Diary of Wyman S. White,* 138.

85. Bartlett, *Twelfth New Hampshire,* 35; Jones, *Rebel War Clerk's Diary,* 1:186; Robertson, *Letters of McAllister,* 216; Joseph S. C. Taber Diary, 119, CWTI, USAMHI.

86. McPherson, *Battle Cry of Freedom,* 569–71; O'Reilly, *Fredericksburg Campaign,* 1–4; Rafuse, *McClellan's War,* 360–82; Sears, *McClellan,* 336–43; Dawes, *Sixth Wisconsin,* 105; de Trobriand, *Four Years in the Army of the Potomac,* 347; Dickey, *Eighty-Fifth Pennsylvania,* 206; Haines, *Fifteenth New Jersey,* 20; Rhodes, *All for the Union,* 87; Haines, *Fifteenth New Jersey,* 20.

CHAPTER 9

1. Hattaway and Jones, *How the North Won,* 217; McWhiney, *Braxton Bragg,* 258–67; Noe, *Perryville,* 22–23; Noe, "Drought That Changed the War," 394–97.

2. Bell, *Mosquito Soldiers,* 60–61, 71; Engle, *Don Carlos Buell,* 252–53; Hess, *Banners to the Breeze,* 3–8.

3. *OR,* 10(2):280–81; Engle, *Don Carlos Buell,* 253–58; Hess, *Banners to the Breeze,* 8–9; Noe, *Perryville,* 24–26.

4. Berkeley, *In the Defense of This Flag,* 18; Cope, *Fifteenth Ohio,* 164; Keil, *Thirty-Fifth Ohio,* 76–77; Marcoot, *Five Years in the Sunny South,* 14; *Macon (Ga.) Daily Telegraph,* June 30, 1862; Engle, *Don Carlos Buell,* 258–60; Noe, *Perryville,* 42–43.

5. Keil, *Thirty-Fifth Ohio,* 77.

6. Berkeley, *In the Defense of This Flag,* 21.

7. Keil, *Thirty-Fifth Ohio,* 79, 83.

8. Hight and Stormont, *Fifty-Eighth Indiana,* 80, 81.

9. *OR,* 16(1):706; Bishop, *Story of a Regiment,* 61; Hight and Stormont, *Fifty-Eighth Indiana,* 83; Berkeley, *In the Defense of This Flag,* 23; Tarrant, *Wild Riders,* 101, 102; Engle, *Don Carlos Buell,* 260–79; Hess, *Banners to the Breeze,* 9–13; Noe, *Perryville,* 42–47.

10. *OR,* 17(2):644, 645.

11. Connelly, *Army of the Heartland,* 187–204; McWhiney, *Braxton Bragg,* 266–74; Noe, *Perryville,* 27–31. In his book, *Edmund Kirby Smith,* Joseph Parks refers to the general as "Kirby Smith" rather than "Smith." I have opted to follow his example. For the "Kentucky bloc," see Connelly and Jones, *Politics of Command.*

12. "William P. Rogers' Memorandum Book," 63–65.

13. Worley, *Memoirs of Lavender*, 20; "William P. Rogers' Memorandum Book," 67–68; Connelly, *Army of the Heartland*, 205–11; Hess, *Banners to the Breeze*, 30–34; McWhiney, *Braxton Bragg*, 267–68; Noe, *Perryville*, 31–37.

14. Worley, *Memoirs of Lavender*, 23, 26–27 (quotations, 23, 26). See also OR, 16(1):951; Louisville, Ky., Aug. 1862, Reel 189, RG 27.5.7, NARA-CP; "William P. Rogers' Memorandum Book," 68–69; Connelly, *Army of the Heartland*, 212–16; Hess, *Banners to the Breeze*, 36–43; and Noe, *Perryville*, 39–40.

15. George W. Bowers, "Memories of a Retreat," *National Tribune*, June 11, 1896, 3; "William P. Rogers' Memorandum Book," 68–69; Tourgée, *Story of a Thousand*, 80; Hess, *Banners to the Breeze*, 37–38, 42–43; Noe, *Perryville*, 83–84.

16. Tourgée, *Story of a Thousand*, 80–81; Noe, *Perryville*, 39–41, 85–86.

17. Bowers, "Memories of a Retreat"; H. M. Ford, "That Famous Retreat," *National Tribune*, July 9, 1896, 3; Morris, *Eighty-First Regiment of Indiana Volunteer Infantry*, 8 (hereafter Morris, *Eighty-First Indiana*); Tourgée, *Story of a Thousand*, 83–85, 88–92; Williams et al., *Seventy-Third Indiana*, 104, 105; Louisville, Ky., Sept. 1862, Reel 189, RG 27.5.7, NARA-CP; Connelly, *Army of the Heartland*, 216–17; Noe, *Perryville*, 84–85; *Dominant Soil Orders*, US Department of Agriculture Natural Resources Conservation Service, http://www.nrcs.usda.gov/Internet/FSE_MEDIA/stelprdb1237749.pdf, accessed Aug. 31, 2016.

18. "Civil War Diary of Joshua Ayre," 5 (hereafter "Diary of Ayre"); Tourgée, *Story of a Thousand*, 92–95; Louisville, Ky., Sept. 1862, Reel 189, RG 27.5.7, NARA-CP; Noe, *Perryville*, 85–87.

19. Tourgée, *Story of a Thousand*, 101–2.

20. "Diary of Ayre," 5–6.

21. OR, 16(2):846; "Diary of Ayre," 6–13; Louisville, Ky., Sept. 1862, Reel 189, RG 27.5.7, NARA-CP; Edmund Kirby Smith to his wife, Sept. 4, 6, 20, 1862, Edmund Kirby Smith Papers, SHC-UNC; Connelly, *Army of the Heartland*, 216–20; Hess, *Banners to the Breeze*, 44–48; Noe, *Perryville*, 40–41, 85–87.

22. Castel, *General Sterling Price*, 84–94; Hartje, *Van Dorn*, 208–10; Noe, *Perryville*, 36–37.

23. Hafendorfer, *Journal of William L. Trask*, 43, 46, 49 (hereafter Hafendorfer, *Journal of Trask*). See also Connelly, *Army of the Heartland*, 282–83; Hess, *Banners to the Breeze*, 57–58, 61–62; and Noe, *Perryville*, 63–64.

24. Noe, *Perryville*, 64–65.

25. J. Stoddard Johnson, "Bragg's Campaign in Kentucky, by a Staff Officer. No. 1—From Chattanooga to Munfordville," J. Stoddard Johnson Papers, Filson Historical Society, Louisville, Ky. William Trask notes that above Carthage, the Cumberland River was "not . . . more than a foot in depth." Hafendorfer, *Journal of Trask*, 53.

26. Louisville, Ky., Aug. 1862, Reel 189, RG 27.5.7, NARA-CP; Clarksville, Tenn., Sept. 1862, Reel 478, ibid.; Engle, *Don Carlos Buell*, 286–88; Hess, *Banners to the Breeze*, 58–61; Noe, *Perryville*, 61–62.

27. OR, 16(1):328, 475, 519, 605, 632.

28. Engle, *Don Carlos Buell*, 282–85; Hess, *Banners to the Breeze*, 59–61; Noe, *Perryville*, 47–48.

29. Hinman, *Sherman Brigade*, 252, 256, 257. See also Bircher, *Drummer-Boy's Diary*, 41, 42; and Cope, *Fifteenth Ohio*, 193, 194.

30. Keil, *Thirty-Fifth Ohio*, 90; Noe, *Perryville*, 47–54, 59–61.

31. Noe, *Southern Boy in Blue*, 89; Noe, *Perryville*, 49–50.

32. Beatty, *Citizen-Soldier*, 175; Bircher, *Drummer-Boy's Diary*, 42–43; Bishop, *Story of a Regiment*, 65–66; J. C. Donahower, "Narrative of the Civil War," 2:8–9, 13, 16, Jeremiah Chester Donahower Papers, 1853–1919, M561, MnHS; Hafendorfer, *Journal of Trask*, 60, 62; Hight and Stormont, *Fifty-Eighth Indiana*, 90; Hinman, *Sherman Brigade*, 260, 264–66; Horrall, *Forty-Second Indiana*, 138, 145; Kimberly and Holloway, *Forty-First Ohio*, 33; Scribner, *How Soldiers Were Made*, 54; Louisville, Ky.,

Sept. 1862, Reel 189, RG 27.5.7, NARA-CP; Hess, *Civil War in the West*, 92–94, 98–99; Noe, *Perryville*, 65–70, 74–75; Phillips, *Rivers Ran Backward*, 166–67, 200.

33. Blakey, Lainhart, and Stephens, *Rose Cottage Chronicles*, 148; Louisville, Ky., Sept. 1862, Reel 189, RG 27.5.7, NARA-CP.

34. Hafendorfer, *Journal of Trask*, 60; Connelly, *Army of the Heartland*, 227–32; Hess, *Banners to the Breeze*, 62–71; McWhiney, *Braxton Bragg*, 283–92; Noe, *Perryville*, 68–74.

35. James Iredell Hall Diary, 56, SHC-UNC. See also Louisville, Ky., Sept. 1862, Reel 189, RG 27.5.7, NARA-CP; and Hafendorfer, *Journal of Trask*, 63, 67.

36. W. E. Preston (Mathews), "The 33rd Alabama Regiment in the Civil War," ed. L. B. Williams, 24, ADAH. After the war, Mathews changed his name to Preston.

37. Hafendorfer, *Journal of Trask*, 68.

38. *OR*, 16(2):641.

39. Louisville, Ky., Sept. 1862, Reel 189, RG 27.5.7, NARA-CP; Connelly, *Army of the Heartland*, 232–50; Hess, *Banners to the Breeze*, 80–84; McWhiney, *Braxton Bragg*, 293–300; Noe, *Perryville*, 99–106, 124–26.

40. Marcoot, *Five Years in the Sunny South*, 14. See also *OR*, 17(1):12, 28, 40, 41; and Grant, *Memoirs*, 1:309.

41. William A. Ruyle Letter, 16, SHSM-R.

42. Ruyle Letter, 17, SHSM-R; Hess, *Banners to the Breeze*, 124–30. See also Clark, *Downing's Civil War Diary*, 68–69; Grant, *Memoirs*, 1:325–26; Castel, *General Sterling Price*, 91–99; Cozzens, *Darkest Days*, 42–54; and Hartje, *Van Dorn*, 208–12.

43. Grant, *Memoirs*, 1:335–37; Castel, *General Sterling Price*, 99–106; Cozzens, *Darkest Days*, 47–49, 53–55; Hess, *Banners to the Breeze*, 130–31.

44. Marcoot, *Five Years in the Sunny South*, 14–15.

45. Clark, *Downing's Civil War Diary*, 68–69; Grant, *Memoirs*, 1:338; Cozzens, *Darkest Days*, 53–55.

46. Simpson, *Grant*, 151.

47. *OR*, 17(1):91, 79; Clark, *Downing's Civil War Diary*, 69; Grant, *Memoirs*, 1:337–43; Ruyle Letter, 17, SHSM-R; Castel, *General Sterling Price*, 99–104; Cozzens, *Darkest Days*, 55–117; Hess, *Banners to the Breeze*, 131–40; Simpson, *Grant*, 151.

48. Grant, *Memoirs*, 1:342–43; Cozzens, *Darkest Days*, 118–48; Smith, *Smell of Battle*, 82–83.

49. Louisville, Ky., Sept. 1862, Reel 189, RG 27.5.7, NARA-CP; Cope, *Fifteenth Ohio*, 201. The Ohio continued to fall until October 17, when only sixteen inches of water ran in the canal. See *Louisville Daily Democrat*, Sept. 20, 21, 27, 28, Oct. 1, 15, 17, 1862.

50. DeRosier, *Through the South*, 24; Engle, *Don Carlos Buell*, 292–305; Hess, *Banners to the Breeze*, 80–84; Noe, *Perryville*, 89–98, 112–23.

51. Louisville, Ky., Sept. 1862, Reel 189, RG 27.5.7, NARA-CP; Bircher, *Drummer-Boy's Diary*, 45; Butler, *Letters Home*, 10; Crary, *Memoirs*, 70–71; Cope, *Fifteenth Ohio*, 204; "Diary of Ayre," 15–17; Hinman, *Sherman Brigade*, 290–91; Marshall, *Civil War Diary*, 14; Morris, *Eighty-First Indiana*, 13; Tourgée, *Story of a Thousand*, 113–14; Noe, *Perryville*, 112–20.

52. *OR*, 16(2):911; Connelly, *Army of the Heartland*, 250–59; Hess, *Banners to the Breeze*, 80–86; Noe, *Perryville*, 120–21, 124–31.

53. Anderson, *Memoirs*, 229; Clark, *Downing's Civil War Diary*, 72; Castel, *General Sterling Price*, 108–10; Cozzens, *Darkest Days*, 135–58; Hartje, *Van Dorn*, 214–21.

54. *OR*, 17(1):222. See also ibid., 276, 293, 295, 299, 367, 401; Watson, *Life in the Confederate Army*, 420; and Cozzens, *Darkest Days*, xii.

55. *OR*, 17(1):293; Castel, *General Sterling Price*, 110–13; Cozzens, *Darkest Days*, xii, 159–220; Hartje, *Van Dorn*, 221–26; Wright, *Corporal's Story*, 60.

56. Hartje, *Van Dorn*, 225.

57. *OR*, 17(1):457.

58. *OR*, 17(1):370.

59. Wright, *Corporal's Story*, 63, 66–67; Castel, *General Sterling Price*, 113–27; Cozzens, *Darkest Days*, 221–324; Hartje, *Van Dorn*, 225–46; Shea and Winschel, *Vicksburg Is the Key*, 35.

60. Jones, *Artilleryman's Diary*, 10–11 (quotation, 10). See also Clark, *Downing's Civil War Diary*, 75–79; *Houston Tri-Weekly Telegraph*, Nov. 12, 1862; Josh Johnson, email to author, Aug. 5, 2019.

61. *OR*, 16(1):1120; Bishop, *Story of a Regiment*, 71; Connelly, *Army of the Heartland*, 258–59; Hess, *Banners to the Breeze*, 84–86; Noe, *Perryville*, 131–40.

62. Barnes, Carnahan, and McCain, *Eighty-Sixth Regiment, Indiana Volunteer Infantry*, 56 (hereafter Barnes, Carnahan, and McCain, *Eighty-Sixth Indiana*); "Diary of Ayre," 17–18; Hinman, *Sherman Brigade*, 292; Danville, Ky., Oct. 1862, Reel 188, RG 27.5.7, NARA-CP.

63. Bennett and Haigh, *Thirty-Sixth Illinois*, 243–45; Butler, *Letters Home*, 12; Hinman, *Sherman Brigade*, 291; Berkeley, *In the Defense of This Flag*, 31; Tourgée, *Story of a Thousand*, 115; Noe, *Perryville*, 117, 119–23.

64. Morris, *Eighty-First Indiana*, 14, 15.

65. "Life of L. A. Ross," 45–46, Levi Adolphus Ross Papers, Abraham Lincoln Presidential Library and Museum, Springfield, Ill.

66. *OR*, 16(1):237, 239, 356, 1037; Barnes, Carnahan, and McCain, *Eighty-Sixth Indiana*, 62; Berkeley, *In the Defense of this Flag*, 32; Crary, *Memoirs*, 74; Dodge, *Waif of the War*, 34, 41; Donahower, "Narrative of the Civil War," 2:34, Donahower Papers, MnHS; Morris, *Eighty-First Indiana*, 15; Danville, Ky., Oct. 1862, Reel 188, RG 27.5.7, NARA-CP; Hess, *Banners to the Breeze*, 86–105; McWhiney, *Braxton Bragg*, 311–19; Noe, *Perryville*, 140–305.

67. Barnes, Carnahan, and McCain, *Eighty-Sixth Indiana*, 65; Horrall, *Forty-Second Indiana*, 150; Morris, *Eighty-First Indiana*, 17; Danville, Ky., Oct. 1862, Reel 188, RG 27.5.7, NARA-CP; Connelly, *Army of the Heartland*, 259–65; Engle, *Don Carlos Buell*, 306–11; McWhiney, *Braxton Bragg*, 319–20; Noe, *Perryville*, 277–98, 306–15.

68. *OR*, 16(2):602; Barnes, Carnahan, and McCain, *Eighty-Sixth Indiana*, 65; Beatty, *Citizen-Soldier*, 182; Bennett and Haigh, *Thirty-Sixth Illinois*, 292; Bircher, *Drummer-Boy's Diary*, 46; Cope, *Fifteenth Ohio*, 207, 208; Hafendorfer, *Journal of Trask*, 83–86; Hinman, *Sherman Brigade*, 297, 304; Horrall, *Forty-Second Indiana*, 162; Morris, *Eighty-First Indiana*, 17; Williams et al., *Seventy-Third Indiana*, 110; Simmons, *84th Reg't Ill. Vols.*, 16 (hereafter Simmons, *84th Ill.*); Danville, Ky., Oct. 1862, Reel 188, RG 27.5.7, NARA-CP; Connelly, *Army of the Heartland*, 266–74, 279–80; Hess, *Banners to the Breeze*, 106–10; McWhiney, *Braxton Bragg*, 320–25.

69. Blakey, Lainhart, and Stephens, *Rose Cottage Chronicles*, 158; Danville, Ky., Oct. 1862, Reel 188, RG 27.5.7, NARA-CP.

70. "Diary of Ayre," 21.

71. "Diary of Ayre," 22; Noe, *Perryville*, 308–11, 325–26, 347–52.

72. Hinman, *Sherman Brigade*, 296.

73. Noe, *Perryville*, 347–52.

74. Danville, Ky., Oct. 1862, Reel 188, RG 27.5.7, NARA-CP; Hafendorfer, *Journal of Trask*, 84–86, 91; Hess, *Banners to the Breeze*, 110–20; Hess, *Braxton Bragg*, 78; Noe, *Perryville*, 327–30, 334–39.

75. Worley, *Memoirs of Lavender*, 33. See also Little and Marshall, *Lumsden's Battery*, 13.

76. Coski, "'I Am for Anything for Success,'" 76 (hereafter Coski, "Letters of Livingston").

77. Noe, *Perryville*, 342–43; Shea and Winschel, *Vicksburg Is the Key*, 35.

78. Bennett and Haigh, *Thirty-Sixth Illinois*, 300–1; Donahower, "Narrative of the Civil War," 2:40, Donahower Papers, MnHS; Hinman, *Sherman Brigade*, 304.

79. Danville, Ky., Oct. 1862, Reel 188, RG 27.5.7, NARA-CP.

80. Hinman, *Sherman Brigade*, 306–7, 310.

81. Hight and Stormont, *Fifty-Eighth Indiana*, 105.

82. Bennett and Haigh, *Thirty-Sixth Illinois*, 301.

83. Simmons, *84th Ill.*, 18–19. See also Barnes, Carnahan, and McCain, *Eighty-Sixth Indiana*, 74; and Kimberly and Holloway, *Forty-First Ohio*, 36.

84. W. D. B. [Bickham], *Rosecrans' Campaign*, 12. See also Bennett and Haigh, *Thirty-Sixth Illinois*, 303.

CHAPTER 10

1. Georgetown, D.C., Nov. 1862, Reel 81, RG 27.5.7, NARA-CP; George M. Barnard to Mother, Nov. 13, 16, 1862, Warrenton, Va., George Middleton Barnard Papers, CWCDJ, MHS; Bartlett, *Twelfth New Hampshire*, 35; Aaron K. Blake to Sister, Nov. 26, 30, 1862, Fairfax Seminary, Va., Aaron K. Blake Correspondence, Box 10, CWMC, USAMHI; Dickey, *Eighty-Fifth Pennsylvania*, 206; Early, *War Memoirs*, 165; Fleet and Fuller, *Green Mount*, 181, 184; McDonald, *Make Me a Map of the Valley*, 93–96; Frank Morse to Wife, Nov. 13, 1862, New Baltimore, Va., Frank C. Morse Papers, MHS; Morse to Wife, Nov. 20, 24, 1862, Stafford Court House, Va., ibid.; Robertson, *Letters of McAllister*, 218, 220, 223–24, 226–27, 228–32; Roper, *Repairing the "March of Mars,"* 301, 303; White, *Diary of Wyman S. White*, 109–10; Krick, *Civil War Weather*, 77.

2. O'Reilly, *Fredericksburg Campaign*, 11–22; Rable, *Fredericksburg*, 42–57.

3. O'Reilly, *Fredericksburg Campaign*, 22–27; Rable, *Fredericksburg*, 58–73; Howe, *Touched with Fire*, 71–73; Nevins, *Diary of Battle*, 127–29; Silliker, *Rebel Yell & the Yankee Hurrah*, 52.

4. *OR*, 21:551; George M. Barnard to Father, Nov. 20, 1862, Fredericksburg, Barnard Papers, CWCDJ, MHS; Britton and Reid, *To My Beloved Wife*, 29–30; Child, *Fifth New Hampshire*, 147; J. P. Coburn to Parents, Nov. 24, 1862, Fredericksburg, Va., James Parley Coburn Papers, USAMHI; Cook, *Twelfth Massachusetts*, 78–79; Curtis, *First Bull Run to Chancellorsville*, 219; Dawes, *Sixth Wisconsin*, 106; Malles, *Bridge Building in Wartime*, 94–96; Rhodes, *All for the Union*, 87–89; Robertson, *Letters of McAllister*, 224, 228, 230; Silliker, *Rebel Yell & the Yankee Hurrah*, 52; *Alexandria (Va.) Gazette*, Nov. 22, 1862; *Daily Richmond Enquirer*, Nov. 20, 1862.

5. Silliker, *Rebel Yell & the Yankee Hurrah*, 52.

6. White, *Diary of Wyman S. White*, 109.

7. O'Reilly, *Fredericksburg Campaign*, 27, 30–33, 45–49; Rable, *Fredericksburg*, 63–71, 80–83, 87–90; *OR*, 21:150, 789; George M. Barnard to Father, Nov. 20, 1862, Fredericksburg, Barnard Papers, CWCDJ, MHS; Bartlett, *Twelfth New Hampshire*, 35; Robertson, *Letters of McAllister*, 232.

8. Frank Morse to Wife, Nov. 26, 1862, Stafford Court House, Va., Morse Papers, MHS.

9. Bartlett, *Twelfth New Hampshire*, 36–37; Cook, *Twelfth Massachusetts*, 79; Hall, *Personal Experience*, 3, 5; Frank Morse to Wife, Nov. 27, 1862, Stafford Court House, Va., Morse Papers, MHS; Silliker, *Rebel Yell & the Yankee Hurrah*, 54; Rable, *Fredericksburg*, 81, 102–7.

10. Nevins, *Diary of Battle*, 130–31. See also Weymouth, *Sketch of Newcomb*, 97; Rable, *Fredericksburg*, 100.

11. Rhodes, *All for the Union*, 88–89; Tyler, *Recollections*, 60; Rable, *Fredericksburg*, 101.

12. Silliker, *Rebel Yell & the Yankee Hurrah*, 53. The 17th Maine was brigaded with three New York regiments—the 1st, 37th, and 101st. See also Rable, *Fredericksburg*, 101.

13. Blight, *When This Cruel War Is Over*, 190; Britton and Reid, *To My Beloved Wife*, 33; J. P. Coburn to Parents, Dec. 7, 1862, Fredericksburg, Va., Coburn Papers, USAMHI; Weymouth, *Sketch of Newcomb*, 99.

14. *OR*, 21:1027, 1035; *Charleston Mercury*, Nov. 17, 1862; O'Reilly, *Fredericksburg Campaign*, 37.

15. *Shoemaker's Battery*, 24.

16. Stewart, *Pair of Blankets*, 71; O'Reilly, *Fredericksburg Campaign*, 27.

17. Rable, *Fredericksburg*, 91–93.

18. O'Reilly, *Fredericksburg Campaign*, 45; Rable, *Fredericksburg*, 84–86.

19. Stiles, *Four Years under Marse Robert*, 128.

20. De Trobriand, *Four Years in the Army of the Potomac*, 361.

21. *OR*, 21:61; Weymouth, *Sketch of Newcomb*, 98, 99. See also Georgetown, D.C., Nov., Dec. 1862, Reel 81, RG 27.5.7, NARA-CP; *Alexandria (Va.) Gazette*, Dec. 6, 8, 1862; George M. Barnard to Father, Dec. 6, 1862, Fredericksburg, Barnard Papers, CWCDJ, MHS; Barnard to Mother, Dec. 6, 8, 1862, Fredericksburg, ibid.; Blackford et al., *Letters from Lee's Army*, 135, 141; Britton and Reid, *To My Beloved Wife*, 34; Cook, *Twelfth Massachusetts*, 79; Curtis, *First Bull Run to Chancellorsville*, 219–20; de Trobriand, *Four Years in the Army of the Potomac*, 361–62; Everson and Simpson, "*Far, Far from Home*," 164; Luther C. Furst Diary, 30, HCWRTC, USAMHI; Jones, *Rebel War Clerk's Diary*, 1:203; McDonald, *Make Me a Map of the Valley*, 97–98; Nevins, *Diary of Battle*, 133; Norton, *Army Letters*, 127–28; Preston, *Tenth New York Cavalry*, 52; Rhodes, *All for the Union*, 89; Mat Richards to Sophie, Dec. 7, 1862, Belle Plain, Va., M. Edgar Richards Correspondence, Box 97, CWMC, USAMHI; Robertson, *Letters of McAllister*, 236, 237; Sparks, *Inside Lincoln's Army*, 185, 186; Stiles, *Four Years under Marse Robert*, 127–28; Tyler, *Recollections*, 61, 62; Richard Waldrop to Mother, Dec. 6, 1862, Guinea's Depot, Richard Woolfolk Waldrop Papers, SHC-UNC; Warfield, *Confederate Soldier's Memoirs*, 137; Welch, *Confederate Surgeon's Letters*, 36; Krick, *Civil War Weather*, 77, 80; Ludlum, *Early American Winters*, 126–27; O'Reilly, *Fredericksburg Campaign*, 38–43; and Robertson, *Stonewall Jackson*, 647.

22. *OR*, 21:812–13; O'Reilly, *Fredericksburg Campaign*, 43–53.

23. Blight, *When This Cruel War Is Over*, 194, 195. See also Haines, *Fifteenth New Jersey*, 22; Mat Richards to Sophie, Dec. 7, 1862, Belle Plain, Va., Richards Correspondence, CWMC, USAMHI.

24. Lee, *Memoir of Pendleton*, 237. See also Hamilton, *Papers of Shotwell*, 1:392; Robertson, *Stonewall Jackson*, 649; Roper, *Repairing the "March of Mars*," 317–20; and White, "Diary of the War," 143.

25. Richard Waldrop to Mother, Dec. 6, 8, 1862, Guinea's Depot, Waldrop Papers, SHC-UNC.

26. Krick, *Civil War Weather*, 6, 78, 80 (quotation, 6).

27. J. P. Coburn to Dad, Dec. 10, 1862, Fredericksburg, Va., Coburn Papers, USAMHI. See also Furst Diary, 30, HCWRTC, USAMHI.

28. *OR*, 21:371; O'Reilly, *Fredericksburg Campaign*, 52–56; Rable, *Fredericksburg*, 148–55; Georgetown, D.C., Dec. 1862, Reel 81, RG 27.5.7, NARA-CP; Krick, *Civil War Weather*, 80.

29. Nevins, *Diary of Battle*, 135.

30. Georgetown, D.C., Dec. 1862, Reel 81, RG 27.5.7, NARA-CP; Malles, *Bridge Building in Wartime*, 109–10 (quotation, 109); Sparks, *Inside Lincoln's Army*, 187; *Macon (Ga.) Daily Telegraph*, Jan. 2, 1863.

31. O'Reilly, *Fredericksburg Campaign*, 57–66; Rable, *Fredericksburg*, 158–61; Georgetown, D.C., Dec. 1862, Reel 81, RG 27.5.7, NARA-CP; Krick, *Civil War Weather*, 80; Westwood A. Todd Reminiscence, pt. 1, 74, SHC-UNC.

32. Hamilton, *Papers of Shotwell*, 1:397.

33. Georgetown, D.C., Dec. 1862, Reel 81, RG 27.5.7, NARA-CP; Blackford et al., *Letters from Lee's Army*, 143; Blackford, *War Years*, 189; Dawes, *Sixth Wisconsin*, 109; Silliker, *Rebel Yell & the Yankee Hurrah*, 55; O'Reilly, *Fredericksburg Campaign*, 57–99; Rable, *Fredericksburg*, 156–58, 161–70; Krick, *Civil War Weather*, 80.

34. O'Reilly, *Fredericksburg Campaign*, 99–118; Rable, *Fredericksburg*, 170–76, 190; Krick, *Civil War Weather*, 80; Georgetown, D.C., Dec. 1862, Reel 81, RG 27.5.7, NARA-CP; *OR*, 21:588; Bartlett,

Twelfth New Hampshire, 40; Blackford, *War Years*, 192; Hamilton, *Papers of Shotwell*, 1:409–10; D. R. Larned, "Pencil Notes of Battle of Fredericksburg, Dec. 11–15, 1862," Daniel Read Larned Papers, LC.

35. O'Reilly, *Fredericksburg Campaign*, 118–26; Rable, *Fredericksburg*, 164–65, 177–84; *OR*, 21:240; Bartlett, *Twelfth New Hampshire*, 40, 41–42; Blackford et al., *Letters from Lee's Army*, 143–44; Silliker, *Rebel Yell & the Yankee Hurrah*, 57.

36. Blackford et al., *Letters from Lee's Army*, 145; Caldwell, *Brigade of South Carolinians*, 41; Dawes, *Sixth Wisconsin*, 110; Early, *War Memoirs*, 171–72; Galwey, *Valiant Hours*, 59; Hall, *Personal Experience*, 6; Hamilton, *Papers of Shotwell*, 1:410–11; Longstreet, *From Manassas to Appomattox*, 306; McClendon, *Recollections*, 159; Nevins, *Diary of Battle*, 144; Warfield, *Confederate Soldier's Memoirs*, 138; Roper, *Repairing the "March of Mars*," 324; Georgetown, D.C., Dec. 1862, Reel 81, RG 27.5.7, NARA-CP; Krick, *Civil War Weather*, 80; O'Reilly, *Fredericksburg Campaign*, 127–28; Rable, *Fredericksburg*, 190, 195.

37. Longstreet, *From Manassas to Appomattox*, 306.

38. Dawes, *Sixth Wisconsin*, 110; Early, *War Memoirs*, 172; Furst Diary, 31, HCWRTC, USAMHI; Galwey, *Valiant Hours*, 59.

39. Dawes, *Sixth Wisconsin*, 110; Early, *War Memoirs*, 172; Galwey, *Valiant Hours*, 59; Hamilton, *Papers of Shotwell*, 1:411; Longstreet, *From Manassas to Appomattox*, 307; O'Reilly, *Fredericksburg Campaign*, 131–38; Rable, *Fredericksburg*, 190–96, 219.

40. Bartlett, *Twelfth New Hampshire*, 42; O'Reilly, *Fredericksburg Campaign*, 127–245, 355–63, 422–29; Rable, *Fredericksburg*, 196–217, 245–54.

41. *OR*, 21:420, 437; O'Reilly, *Fredericksburg Campaign*, 246–355, 363–422; Rable, *Fredericksburg*, 218–44, 255–67; Robertson, *Stonewall Jackson*, 651–62.

42. Krick, *Civil War Weather*, 6, 78, 80; Georgetown, D.C., Dec. 1862, Reel 81, RG 27.5.7, NARA-CP; George M. Barnard to Father, Dec. 16, 1862, Falmouth, Barnard Papers, CWCDJ, MHS; Dawes, *Sixth Wisconsin*, 111; McClendon, *Recollections*, 162; Oates, *War between the Union and the Confederacy*, 168; Sanford, *Fighting Rebels and Redskins*, 193; Silliker, *Rebel Yell & the Yankee Hurrah*, 59, 61.

43. Oliver Coolidge to unknown, Dec. 14, 1862, Falmouth, Va., Oliver S. Coolidge Papers, 1861–1864, Duke; Nevins, *Diary of Battle*, 145; Wood, *The War*, 110; O'Reilly, *Fredericksburg Campaign*, 430–43; Rable, *Fredericksburg*, 267–79.

44. Oliver Coolidge to unknown, Dec. 14, 1862, Falmouth, Va., Coolidge Papers, Duke. See also O'Reilly, *Fredericksburg Campaign*, 441; and Rable, *Fredericksburg*, 279.

45. Georgetown, D.C., Dec. 1862, Reel 81, RG 27.5.7, NARA-CP; Krick, *Civil War Weather*, 80; *Alexandria (Va.) Gazette*, Dec. 16, 1862; O'Reilly, *Fredericksburg Campaign*, 443–54; Rable, *Fredericksburg*, 279–84; *OR*, 21:385, 555, 557; Blackford, *War Years*, 194; Britton and Reid, *To My Beloved Wife*, 35; Oliver Coolidge to unknown, Dec. 15, 1862, Falmouth, Va., Coolidge Papers, Duke; Dawes, *Sixth Wisconsin*, 113; Hall, *Personal Experience*, 7; Nevins, *Diary of Battle*, 146; Oates, *War between the Union and the Confederacy*, 171; Shoemaker's Battery, 26; White, *Diary of Wyman S. White*, 152.

46. Georgetown, D.C., Dec. 1862, Reel 81, RG 27.5.7, NARA-CP; *OR*, 21:417; *Alexandria (Va.) Gazette*, Dec. 18, 1862; Bartlett, *Twelfth New Hampshire*, 49, 51; Briggs, *Civil War Surgeon*, 82; Britton and Reid, *To My Beloved Wife*, 35; Dawes, *Sixth Wisconsin*, 113; Dobbins, *Grandfather's Journal*, 113; A. F. H [Archibald Henderson] to Brother, Dec. 20, 1862, Fredericksburg, Va., Archibald Erskine Henderson Papers, 1841–1917, Duke; Nevins, *Diary of Battle*, 146; Oates, *War between the Union and the Confederacy*, 171; Sparks, *Inside Lincoln's Army*, 193; Tyler, *Recollections*, 67; Krick, *Civil War Weather*, 80; O'Reilly, *Fredericksburg Campaign*, 447–56; Rable, *Fredericksburg*, 282–87.

47. Georgetown, D.C., Dec. 1862, Reel 81, RG 27.5.7, NARA-CP; Krick, *Civil War Weather*, 80; *OR*, 21:868, 884, 890; *Augusta (Ga.) Daily Constitutionalist*, Jan. 3, 1863; Britton and Reid, *To My Beloved Wife*, 38; OSC to unknown, Dec. 27, 1862, Falmouth, Va., Coolidge Papers, Duke; Dobbins, *Grandfather's Journal*, 112–17; Douglas, *I Rode with Stonewall*, 208; Everson and Simpson, *"Far, Far from Home*,"

168; Dayton E. Flint to Sister, Dec. 28, 1862, White Oak Church, Va., in "Civil War Letters of Dayton E. Flint," Box 40, CWMC, USAMHI; Jones, *Rebel War Clerk's Diary*, 1:219–20; Jones, *Under the Stars and Bars*, 64, 66; Baldy [Archibald Henderson] to Brother, Dec. 18, 1862, Fredericksburg, Va., Henderson Papers, Duke; Frank Morse to Ellen, Dec. 23, 27, 1862, White Oak Church, Va., Morse Papers, MHS; Robertson, *Letters of McAllister*, 243; Roper, *Repairing the "March of Mars,"* 334, 335; Silliker, *Rebel Yell & the Yankee Hurrah*, 64; Welch, *Confederate Surgeon's Letters*, 39; O'Reilly, *Fredericksburg Campaign*, 462–64; Rable, *Fredericksburg*, 363–70.

48. *OR*, 21:957–59; *Alexandria (Va.) Gazette*, Dec. 29, 1862; George M. Barnard to Father, Dec. 18, 1862, Falmouth, Barnard Papers, CWCDJ, MHS; Barnard to Mother, Dec. 24, 1862, Falmouth, ibid.; A. K. Blake to Aunt Adda, Jan. 16, 1863, Falmouth, Va., Blake Correspondence, CWMC, USAMHI; Britton and Reid, *To My Beloved Wife*, 38; Dawes, *Sixth Wisconsin*, 115, 116; Dobbins, *Grandfather's Journal*, 112–17; Dayton E. Flint to Sister, Dec. 28, 1862, White Oak Church, Va., in "Civil War Letters of Dayton E. Flint," CWMC, USAMHI; Furst Diary, 33, HCWRTC, USAMHI; Galwey, *Valiant Hours*, 67–68; Hall, *Personal Experience*, 7–8; Norton, *Army Letters*, 127–28, 131; Robertson, *Letters of McAllister*, 243, 254, 256; Tyler, *Recollections*, 69; White, *Diary of Wyman S. White*, 117; Rable, *Fredericksburg*, 354–57.

49. Silliker, *Rebel Yell & the Yankee Hurrah*, 62. See also George M. Barnard to Father, Dec. 21, 1862, Falmouth, Barnard Papers, CWCDJ, MHS; and Rable, *Fredericksburg*, 356.

50. White, *Diary of Wyman S. White*, 117–18. See also *Charleston Mercury*, Jan. 24, 1863.

51. Blackford, *War Years*, 200; Dobbins, *Grandfather's Journal*, 120; Houghton and Houghton, *Two Boys*, 71; Jones, *Under the Stars and Bars*, 68; "Diaries of John Waldrop . . . and William Y. Mordecai," 45; Rable, *Fredericksburg*, 363.

52. Baldy [Archibald] Henderson to Brother, Jan. 4, 1863, Fredericksburg, Va., Henderson Papers, Duke. See also John B. Evans to Wife, Jan. 18, 1863, Fredericksburg, Va., John B. Evans Papers, 1862–1865, Duke; and Welch, *Confederate Surgeon's Letters*, 41.

53. Chamberlayne, *Ham Chamberlayne*, 153–54.

54. Caldwell, *Brigade of South Carolinians*, 104–5.

55. Hamilton, *Papers of Shotwell*, 1:442.

56. Benson, *Berry Benson's Civil War Book*, 34.

57. Benson, *Berry Benson's Civil War Book*, 34.

58. Georgetown, D.C., Jan. 1863, Reel 81, RG 27.5.7, NARA-CP; Lang, *In the Wake of War*, 129–44; Rable, *Fredericksburg*, 371–72.

59. Cook, *Twelfth Massachusetts*, 86.

60. Georgetown, D.C., Jan. 1863, Reel 81, RG 27.5.7, NARA-CP; Krick, *Civil War Weather*, 83; *Alexandria (Va.) Gazette*, Jan. 12, 1863; Baird, *Journals of Edmonds*, 130, 131; George M. Barnard to Father, Jan. 6, 1863, Falmouth, Barnard Papers, CWCDJ, MHS; Blackford et al., *Letters from Lee's Army*, 157, 158; Blight, *When This Cruel War Is Over*, 205, 208; A. K. Blake to Mother, Jan. 4, 1863, Falmouth, Va., Blake Correspondence, CWMC, USAMHI; Child, *Fifth New Hampshire*, 170–71; Cook, *Twelfth Massachusetts*, 86; Dobbins, *Grandfather's Journal*, 119–20; John B. Evans to Father & Mother, Jan. 11, 1863, Richmond, Va., Evans Papers, Duke; McDonald, *Make Me a Map of the Valley*, 105–8; Frank Morse to Nellie, Jan. 2, 1863, Brandy Station, Va., Morse Papers, MHS; Morse to Nellie, Jan. 4, 1863, White Oak Station, Va., ibid.; Morse to Nellie, Jan. 10, 1863, Fredericksburg, Va., ibid.; Mead Diary, vol. 3, Jan. 1–12, 1863, LC; Nevins, *Diary of Battle*, 155, 156, 157; Robertson, *Letters of McAllister*, 252, 254, 255; Roper, *Repairing the "March of Mars,"* 336, 338, 340, 341, 343, 344; Sparks, *Inside Lincoln's Army*, 200; Richard Waldrop to Father, Jan. 11, 1863, "In Camp," Waldrop Papers, SHC-UNC; Welch, *Confederate Surgeon's Letters*, 41.

61. Welch, *Confederate Surgeon's Letters*, 41; O'Reilly, *Fredericksburg Campaign*, 462–64.

62. Nevins, *Diary of Battle,* 157. See also Caldwell, *Brigade of South Carolinians,* 106.

63. *OR,* 21:916; O'Reilly, *Fredericksburg Campaign,* 460–62, 464–67, 469–73; Rable, *Fredericksburg,* 323–37, 343–53, 373–83, 389–94, 402–3.

64. O'Reilly, *Fredericksburg Campaign,* 460–76; Rable, *Fredericksburg,* 409–12.

65. *Scientific American,* Jan. 17, 1863, 35.

66. Krick, *Civil War Weather,* 83; Ludlum, *Early American Winters,* 127–28; *Charleston Mercury,* Jan. 19, 1863; A. K. Blake to Aunt Adda, Jan. 16, 1863, Falmouth, Va., Blake Correspondence, CWMC, USAMHI; Blake to Sister, Jan. 19, 1863, Falmouth, Va., ibid.; J. P. Coburn to Folks at Home, Jan. 18, 1863, Camp Pitcher, Coburn Papers, USAMHI; Cook, *Twelfth Massachusetts,* 86; de Trobriand, *Four Years in the Army of the Potomac,* 406; Dobbins, *Grandfather's Journal,* 121–22; McDonald, *Make Me a Map of the Valley,* 109–10; Nevins, *Diary of Battle,* 157, 158; Robertson, *Letters of McAllister,* 258, 259; Roper, *Repairing the "March of Mars,"* 344, 346; Sparks, *Inside Lincoln's Army,* 202, 203.

67. *OR,* 21:127.

68. O'Reilly, *Fredericksburg Campaign,* 476–78; Rable, *Fredericksburg,* 412–13; Krick, *Civil War Weather,* 83; Cook, *Twelfth Massachusetts,* 86; de Trobriand, *Four Years in the Army of the Potomac,* 407; Dayton E. Flint to Father, Jan. 27, 1862, White Oak Church, Va., in "Civil War Letters of Dayton E. Flint," CWMC, USAMHI; Haines, *Fifteenth New Jersey,* 38; McDonald, *Make Me a Map of the Valley,* 110; Rhodes, *All for the Union,* 97.

69. US Congress, *Report of the Joint Committee,* 723, quoted in O'Reilly, *Fredericksburg Campaign,* 477.

70. Winters, *Battling the Elements,* 35–39; Ludlum, *Early American Winters,* 127–28; Ludlum, *Weather Factor,* 87–88; Robertson, *Letters of McAllister,* 260; O'Reilly, *Fredericksburg Campaign,* 483; *OR,* 21:756.

71. *OR,* 21:69; Cook, *Twelfth Massachusetts,* 86; de Trobriand, *Four Years in the Army of the Potomac,* 407; Haines, *Fifteenth New Jersey,* 38; Hall, *Personal Experience,* 8; Nevins, *Diary of Battle,* 158; Silliker, *Rebel Yell & the Yankee Hurrah,* 67; White, *Diary of Wyman S. White,* 120–21; O'Reilly, *Fredericksburg Campaign,* 478; Rable, *Fredericksburg,* 413. It did snow in the Shenandoah Valley. See "Augusta County: Diary of Alansa Rounds Sterrett (1860–1913)," Jan. 20–23, 1863, Valley Personal Papers, *Valley of the Shadow,* http://valley.lib.virginia.edu/papers/AD9001, accessed July 10, 2019.

72. Dawes, *Sixth Wisconsin,* 116.

73. *OR,* 21:753–55, 990; Aaron K. Blake to Sister, Jan. 19, 1863, Falmouth, Va., Blake Correspondence, CWMC, USAMHI; de Trobriand, *Four Years in the Army of the Potomac,* 407; Haines, *Fifteenth New Jersey,* 38; Sam to Sister, Jan. 28, 1863, White Oak Church, Va., David E. Cronin Papers: Correspondence, NYHS/CWPSD; Silliker, *Rebel Yell & the Yankee Hurrah,* 67; White, *Diary of Wyman S. White,* 120–21; O'Reilly, *Fredericksburg Campaign,* 478; Rable, *Fredericksburg,* 412–13.

74. William H. Myers to Parents, Jan. 24, 1863, Falmouth, Va., in Joanne V. Fulcoly, "A Brief History of the Myers Family," William H. Myers Letters, Box 84, CWMC, USAMHI, typescript.

75. Nevins, *Diary of Battle,* 158.

76. Roper, *Repairing the "March of Mars,"* 346. See also Lee, *Memoir of Pendleton,* 232; and McDonald, *Make Me a Map of the Valley,* 110.

77. White, *Diary of Wyman S. White,* 121–22 (quotation, 122).

78. Krick, *Civil War Weather,* 83; Ludlum, *Weather Factor,* 88.

79. Dawes, *Sixth Wisconsin,* 116–17; Dobbins, *Grandfather's Journal,* 122; Dayton E. Flint to Father, Jan. 27, 1862, White Oak Church, Va., in "Civil War Letters of Dayton E. Flint," CWMC, USAMHI; McDonald, *Make Me a Map of the Valley,* 110; Roper, *Repairing the "March of Mars,"* 347; Rable, *Fredericksburg,* 413.

80. Cook, *Twelfth Massachusetts,* 86.

81. Dawes, *Sixth Wisconsin*, 116. See also McDonald, *Make Me a Map of the Valley*, 110.

82. *OR*, 21:69, 1000; E. DeLoss Burton to Jennie Burton, Jan. 28, 1863, Aquia Creek, Va., Edmond Family Collection: Correspondence, NYHS/CWPSD; Dawes, *Sixth Wisconsin*, 116–17; de Trobriand, *Four Years in the Army of the Potomac*, 408–9; Dayton E. Flint to Father, Jan. 27, 1862, White Oak Church, Va., in "Civil War Letters of Dayton E. Flint," CWMC, USAMHI; Haines, *Fifteenth New Jersey*, 38–39; Hall, *Personal Experience*, 8–9; George A. Mitchell to Parents, Jan. 25, 1863, Henry House, Va., George A. Mitchell Collection: Correspondence, NYHS/CWPSD; Quaife, *From the Cannon's Mouth*, 157–58; William H. Peacock to Sarah, Jan. 28, 1863, Falmouth, Va., William H. Peacock Correspondence, Box 89, CWMC, USAMHI; Rhodes, *All for the Union*, 97; Sam to Sister, Jan. 28, 1863, White Oak Church, Va., Cronin Papers: Correspondence, NYHS/CWPSD; John B. Southard to Albertine S. Southard, Jan. 26, 1863, Fredericksburg, Va., Southard Family Collection: Correspondence, ibid.; White, *Diary of Wyman S. White*, 122–23; O'Reilly, *Fredericksburg Campaign*, 478–82; Rable, *Fredericksburg*, 413–18.

83. Sanford, *Fighting Rebels and Redskins*, 193–94.

84. O'Reilly, *Fredericksburg Campaign*, 482; Rable, *Fredericksburg*, 415–18.

85. *OR*, 21:752.

86. Haines, *Fifteenth New Jersey*, 39.

87. Krick, *Civil War Weather*, 83; Winters, *Battling the Elements*, 38; Cook, *Twelfth Massachusetts*, 86–87; Haines, *Fifteenth New Jersey*, 39–40; McDonald, *Make Me a Map of the Valley*, 110; Quaife, *From the Cannon's Mouth*, 158–60; Roper, *Repairing the "March of Mars,"* 347; Silliker, *Rebel Yell & the Yankee Hurrah*, 70; White, *Diary of Wyman S. White*, 123.

88. O'Reilly, *Fredericksburg Campaign*, 483–86; O'Reilly, *Fredericksburg*, 1111; Cook, *Twelfth Massachusetts*, 86–87; Dayton E. Flint to Father, Jan. 27, 1862, White Oak Church, Va., in "Civil War Letters of Dayton E. Flint," CWMC, USAMHI; Haines, *Fifteenth New Jersey*, 39–40; Rhodes, *All for the Union*, 97; White, *Diary of Wyman S. White*, 123.

89. *OR*, 21:69.

90. Krick, *Civil War Weather*, 83; Winters, *Battling the Elements*, 38; O'Reilly, *Fredericksburg Campaign*, 488–89; *OR*, 21:69; de Trobriand, *Four Years in the Army of the Potomac*, 409; Dobbins, *Grandfather's Journal*, 123; McDonald, *Make Me a Map of the Valley*, 110; William H. Myers to Parents, Jan. 24, 1863, Falmouth, Va., in Fulcoly, "Brief History," Myers Letters, CWMC, USAMHI; Robertson, *Letters of McAllister*, 261–62; Roper, *Repairing the "March of Mars,"* 348; Sparks, *Inside Lincoln's Army*, 206.

91. Rhodes, *All for the Union*, 97. See also Hall, *Personal Experience*, 9.

92. Cook, *Twelfth Massachusetts*, 87. See also White, *Diary of Wyman S. White*, 124; and *Alexandria (Va.) Gazette*, Jan. 26, 28, 1863.

93. Silliker, *Rebel Yell & the Yankee Hurrah*, 70.

94. Reprinted in *Alexandria (Va.) Gazette*, Jan. 29, 1863.

95. Quaife, *From the Cannon's Mouth*, 159. See also Rhodes, *All for the Union*, 97.

96. Dayton E. Flint to Father, Jan. 27, 1862, White Oak Church, Va., in "Civil War Letters of Dayton E. Flint," CWMC, USAMHI.

97. De Trobriand, *Four Years in the Army of the Potomac*, 409.

98. *OR*, 21:1009.

CHAPTER 11

1. *OR*, 13:487, 859, 860, 890; Shea, *Fields of Blood*, 1–5; Heath, "First Federal Invasion of the Indian Territory," 409–19.

2. *OR*, 13:859, 928; Banasik, *Serving with Honor*, 1, 4, 5; Shea, *Fields of Blood*, 1–12.

3. Banasik, *Serving with Honor*, 10, 11, 12; Barney, *Recollections*, 37, 43; Tilley, *Federals on the Frontier*, 7, 10, 12, 15, 17; Vaught, "Diary of an Unknown Soldier," 61, 62; Shea, *Fields of Blood*, 12–26.

4. *OR*, 13:334, 721, 724, 770; David B. Arthur Diary, Oct. 11, 1862, accessed Oct. 19, 2016; Banasik, *Serving with Honor*, 14–18; Barney, *Recollections*, 56–62; John H. Bonnell Diary 9, 10, 16, Box 11, CWDC, USAMHI (transcript); Leake, "Campaign of the Army of the Frontier," 276–77; Tilley, *Federals on the Frontier*, 23–26; Vaught, "Diary of an Unknown Soldier," 66; Watson, *Life in the Confederate Army*, 247; Shea, *Fields of Blood*, 26–28.

5. Bonnell Diary, 11, 15, CWDC, USAMHI; Leake, "Campaign of the Army of the Frontier," 278; Tilley, *Federals on the Frontier*, 37–38; Shea, *Fields of Blood*, 28–49.

6. Banasik, *Serving with Honor*, 21.

7. Barnes, *What I Saw You Do*, 11.

8. *OR*, 22(1):34; Barney, *Recollections*, 83–84; Shea, *Fields of Blood*, 45–65 (quotation, 63).

9. Vaught, "Diary of an Unknown Soldier," 74.

10. Tilley, *Federals on the Frontier*, 45, 47, 48; Shea, *Fields of Blood*, 49–67.

11. *OR*, 13:794–96; Leake, "Campaign of the Army of the Frontier," 280; Shea, *Fields of Blood*, 67–71.

12. Barney, *Recollections*, 102–5 (quotations, 102–3). See also Leake, "Campaign of the Army of the Frontier," 280; and Shea, *Fields of Blood*, 66–67.

13. Tilley, *Federals on the Frontier*, 48. The soldier refers to Exodus 10:21.

14. Vaught, "Diary of an Unknown Soldier," 79. See also Leake, "Campaign of the Army of the Frontier," 280.

15. Arthur Diary, Nov. 17–18, 1862, accessed Oct. 19, 2016; Bonnell Diary, 20, CWDC, USAMHI; Vaught, "Diary of an Unknown Soldier," 79; Shea, *Fields of Blood*, 71–73.

16. Arthur Diary, Nov. 19–28, 1862, accessed Oct. 19, 2016; Bonnell Diary, 20, 22, CWDC, USAMHI; Vaught, "Diary of an Unknown Soldier," 79–80; Shea, *Fields of Blood*, 73–78.

17. Banasik, *Serving with Honor*, 24–29 (quotation, 27); Shea, *Fields of Blood*, 79–124.

18. Shea, *Fields of Blood*, 124–35 (quotation, 128).

19. Bonnell Diary, 22–23, CWDC, USAMHI; Monnett, "Yankee Cavalryman," 291; Shea, *Fields of Blood*, 108–30.

20. Dan Thomas to Sallie R. Thomas, Dec. 18, 1862, Camp Mazzard, Ark., Prairie Grove Battlefield State Park, Prairie Grove, Ark.

21. Barney, *Recollections*, 138; Monnett, "A Yankee Cavalryman," 293; Shea, *Fields of Blood*, 135–240.

22. Arthur Diary, Dec. 12, 13, 14, 1862, accessed Oct. 19, 2016; Barnes, *What I Saw You Do*, 19; Bonnell Diary, 24–27, CWDC, USAMHI; Leake, "Campaign of the Army of the Frontier," 287; Shea, *Fields of Blood*, 240–67.

23. *OR*, 22(1):167; Arthur Diary, Dec. 27, 1862, accessed Oct. 19, 2016; Tilley, *Federals on the Frontier*, 90; Shea, *Fields of Blood*, 269–82.

24. Barney, *Recollections*, 161. See also *OR*, 22(1):194–205.

25. Barney, *Recollections*, 161–64. See also *OR*, 22(1):191, 194–205. For specific weather data, see also Arthur Diary, Jan. 13–30, 1863, accessed Oct. 19, 2016; Bonnell Diary, 30–36, CWDC, USAMHI; Matson, *Life Experiences*, 117; and Tilley, *Federals on the Frontier*, 92, 99–106.

26. Tilley, *Federals on the Frontier*, 107–31 (quotation, 109). See also Arthur Diary, Feb. 1–28, 1863, accessed Oct. 19, 2016; and Bonnell Diary, 36–47, CWDC, USAMHI.

27. Banasik, *Serving with Honor*, 42–48 (quotations, 47).

28. *OR*, 22(1):796; 53:867; Shea, *Fields of Blood*, 283.

29. Banasik, *Serving with Honor*, 49–57 (quotation, 49).

30. Shea, *Fields of Blood*, 283–85; Collins, *Chapters*, 67, 74–77; Eddington, "Civil War Memoirs," accessed Oct. 21, 2016; Logbook, USS *Black Hawk*, Jan. 9–12, 1863, RG 24.2.2, NARA.

31. Shea, *Fields of Blood*, 284–87 (quotation, 284).

32. Grant, *Memoirs*, 1:350–52; Ballard, *Vicksburg*, 78–82; Shea and Winschel, *Vicksburg Is the Key*, 35–38.

33. *OR*, 17(1):530–32, 539; Natchez, Miss., Nov. 1862, Reel 277, RG 27.5.7, NARA-CP; Cavins, *War Letters of Aden G. Cavins*, 27; Clark, *Downing's Civil War Diary*, 80–86; Jones, *Artilleryman's Diary*, 12–17; William A. Ruyle Letter, 25, SHSM-R; [Willet], *Company B*, 13; Ballard, *Vicksburg*, 82–92, 102–4; Davis, *Black Experience in Natchez*, 61–62; Grice, "History of Weather Observations, Natchez," 9–10; Hess, *Civil War in the West*, 114–16; Shea and Winschel, *Vicksburg Is the Key*, 38–39.

34. Ballard, *Vicksburg*, 80–81, 83–84, 101–3, 104–7; Hess, *Civil War in the West*, 116–18; Shea and Winschel, *Vicksburg Is the Key*, 39–43.

35. Ballard, *Vicksburg*, 101.

36. *OR*, 17(2):374, 387, 779; Clark, *Downing's Civil War Diary*, 87.

37. Barron, *Lone Star Defenders*, 134; Jones, *Artilleryman's Diary*, 20–22; Ballard, *Vicksburg*, 108–11, 112–13, 121–28; Hess, *Civil War in the West*, 121; Shea and Winschel, *Vicksburg Is the Key*, 43–45.

38. *OR*, 17(1):560, 17(2):498; Clark, *Downing's Civil War Diary*, 88–91. For the weather, see also Cavins, *War Letters of Aden G. Cavins*, 28, 29.

39. *OR*, 17(1):571–78 (quotations, 572, 574, 576).

40. Shea and Winschel, *Vicksburg Is the Key*, 46–48; Logbook, USS *Black Hawk*, Dec. 8–23, 1862, RG 24.2.2, NARA.

41. Grabau, *Ninety-Eight Days*, 18–25; Brady, *War upon the Land*, 39; "Geologic Activity," accessed Nov. 14, 2016; "Alfilsols Map," US Department of Agriculture Natural Resources Conservation Service, https://www.nrcs.usda.gov/wps/portal/nrcs/detail/soils/survey/class/maps/?cid=nrcs142p2_053591, accessed Nov. 14, 2016; "Vertisols Map," ibid., https://www.nrcs.usda.gov/wps/portal/nrcs/detail/soils/survey/class/maps/?cid=nrcs142p2_053612, accessed Nov. 14, 2016; *OR*, 17(1):606, 613, 17(2):862 (quotation, 17[2]:862).

42. *OR*, 17(1):606. See also Brady, *War upon the Land*, 42.

43. *OR*, 17(1):607, 609, 614, 626, 631, 17(2):529, 585, 811, 878, 886, 887 (quotation, 17[2]:878); Logbook, USS *Black Hawk*, Dec. 25, 1862 Jan. 2, 1863, RG 24.2.2, NARA; [Willet], *Company B*, 15–19; Shea and Winschel, *Vicksburg Is the Key*, 46–55 (quotation, 54); Ballard, *Vicksburg*, 111–12, 129–55; Ludlum, *Early American Winters*, 130.

44. *Natchez Daily Courier*, Jan. 20, 1863.

45. Logbook, USS *Black Hawk*, Jan. 1–Feb. 17, 1863, RG 24.2.2, NARA; *Augusta (Ga.) Daily Constitutionalist*, Feb. 11, 1863; *Augusta (Ga.) Chronicle*, Mar. 10, 1863; Cavins, *War Letters of Aden G. Cavins*, 33, 35, 36; Clark, *Downing's Civil War Diary*, 94–107; Grant, *Memoirs*, 1:370, 381–82; Schweitzer Diary, 1:26–37, Schweitzer Diaries and Correspondence, CWTI, USAMHI; Wright, *Corporal's Story*, 70–71; Ballard, *Vicksburg*, 160–61; Fiege, "Gettysburg," 96; Manning, *Troubled Refuge*, 123; Shea and Winschel, *Vicksburg Is the Key*, 60–62; Steinberg, *Down to Earth*, 96–97.

46. Shea and Winschel, *Vicksburg Is the Key*, 60.

47. [Willet], *Company B*, 27–28.

48. W. A. Rorer to Cousin Susan, Jan. 15, 1863, "Camp," James M. Willcox Papers, 1831–1871, Duke.

49. Ruyle Letter, 26, SHSM-R.

50. *OR*, 24(1):15–16, 117–21, 24(3):13; Clark, *Downing's Civil War Diary*, 97, 100–107; Grant, *Memoirs*, 1:372, 374–76; Ballard, *Vicksburg*, 156–60, 164–74; Brady, *War upon the Land*, 42–43; Hess, *Civil War in the West*, 134–36, 140–44; Shea and Winschel, *Vicksburg Is the Key*, 60–68.

51. *OR*, 24(1):436, 24(3):36 (quotation, 24[3]:36); W. A. Rorer to Cousin Susan, Feb. 22, 1863, Grenada, Miss., Willcox Papers, Duke; Schweitzer Diary, 1:31–34, Schweitzer Diaries and Correspondence, CWTI, USAMHI; Anderson, *Brokenburn*, 184; Ballard, *Vicksburg*, 174–90; Brady, *War upon the Land*, 42–48; Shea and Winschel, *Vicksburg Is the Key*, 68–75.

52. Anderson, *Brokenburn*, 169, 172, 177, 184.

53. Grant, *Memoirs*, 1:384.

54. *OR*, 24(1):408–9, 448; Grabau, *Ninety-Eight Days*, 52–54; Shea and Winschel, *Vicksburg Is the Key*, 90.

CHAPTER 12

1. *Civil War Diary of First Sergeant Squire Helm Bush*, 2 (hereafter *Civil War Diary of Bush*); Barnes, Carnahan, and McCain, *Eighty-Sixth Indiana*, 91; Bircher, *Drummer-Boy's Diary*, 50; Bishop, *Story of a Regiment*, 77; Blakey, Lainhart, and Stephens, *Rose Cottage Chronicles*, 170; Cope, *Fifteenth Ohio*, 224, 225; J. C. Donahower, "Narrative of the Civil War," 2:46, 47, Jeremiah Chester Donahower Papers, 1853–1919, M561, MnHS; Hinman, *Sherman Brigade*, 320–21; Kimberly and Holloway, *Forty-First Ohio*, 37; Morris, *Eighty-First Indiana*, 25; "William P. Rogers' Memorandum Book," 73–76; W. E. Preston (Mathews), "The 33rd Alabama Regiment in the Civil War," ed. L. B. Williams, 30, ADAH; Clarksville, Tenn., Nov., Dec., 1862, Reel 478, RG 27.5.7, NARA-CP; *Louisville Daily Democrat*, Nov. 14, 1862; Connelly, *Autumn of Glory*, 13–29; Cozzens, *No Better Place to Die*, 1–2, 7–11, 29; Hess, *Banners to the Breeze*, 185–86; Hess, *Braxton Bragg*, 93, 95–96, 101–6; McDonough, *Stones River*, 3, 37; McWhiney, *Braxton Bragg*, 322–34, 337–38, 341–45; Noe, *Perryville*, 327–30, 334–39.

2. *Houston Tri-Weekly Telegraph*, Dec. 8, 1862. See also Blakey, Lainhart, and Stephens, *Rose Cottage Chronicles*, 178.

3. Barnes, Carnahan, and McCain, *Eighty-Sixth Indiana*, 77, 80, 81, 83–84, 90, 92; Bircher, *Drummer-Boy's Diary*, 49–50; Cope, *Fifteenth Ohio*, 219–20, 221, 224; DeRosier, *Through the South*, 32, 35, 36, 38–39, 47, 49; Donahower, "Narrative of the Civil War," 2:46, 47, Donahower Papers, MnHS; Clarksville, Tenn., Dec. 1862, Reel 478, RG 27.5.7, NARA-CP Cozzens, *No Better Place to Die*, 18, 31, 35, 40–42; Hess, *Banners to the Breeze*, 187; McDonough, *Stones River*, 33, 36–37.

4. Barnes, Carnahan, and McCain, *Eighty-Sixth Indiana*, 92–93. See also *OR*, 20(2):59, 180; Francis, *Narrative of a Private Soldier*, 93; and Phillips, *Rivers Ran Backward*, 221.

5. Cope, *Fifteenth Ohio*, 225. See also Hinman, *Sherman Brigade*, 386.

6. Morris, *Eighty-First Indiana*, 23–24.

7. Barnes, Carnahan, and McCain, *Eighty-Sixth Indiana*, 137; Bennett and Haigh, *Thirty-Sixth Illinois*, 429; Bircher, *Drummer-Boy's Diary*, 63; Marcoot, *Five Years in the Sunny South*, 28; Simmons, *84th Ill.*, 49.

8. Butler, *Letters Home*, 41. See also Clarksville, Tenn., Dec. 1862, Reel 478, RG 27.5.7, NARA-CP; and *Mobile Register*, Dec. 16, 1862.

9. Morris, *Eighty-First Indiana*, 22.

10. Beatty, *Citizen-Soldier*, 191.

11. Clarksville, Tenn., Dec. 1862, Reel 478, RG 27.5.7, NARA-CP.

12. DeRosier, *Through the South*, 50.

13. *Civil War Diary of Bush*, 3; Clarksville, Tenn., Dec. 1862, Reel 478, RG 27.5.7, NARA-CP; Cozzens, *No Better Place to Die*, 43–45; McDonough, *Stones River*, 57–63.

14. *Nashville Daily Union*, Dec. 25, 28, 1862; Cozzens, *No Better Place to Die*, 14–15, 18–19, 26–28, 44–47; Hess, *Banners to the Breeze*, 178–84; McDonough, *Stones River*, 64–66.

15. Dodge, *Waif of the War*, 56.

16. Col. James L. Cooper Memoirs, 21, Reel 5, Folder 11, Box 12, CWC, TSLA; Clarksville, Tenn., Dec. 1862, Reel 478, RG 27.5.7, NARA-CP; Hinman, *Sherman Brigade*, 334.

17. W. D. B., *Rosecrans' Campaign*, 147. See also Hess, *Banners to the Breeze*, 187–88.

18. *OR*, 20(1):218, 262, 269, 291, 532; Dodge, *Waif of the War*, 58–59; Francis, *Narrative of a Private Soldier*, 94–95; Hight and Stormont, *Fifty-Eighth Indiana*, 109–10; Hinman, *Sherman Brigade*, 335, 356; Owens, *Greene County*, 30; W. D. B., *Rosecrans' Campaign*, 156; Clarksville, Tenn., Dec. 1862, Reel 478, RG 27.5.7, NARA-CP; Connelly, *Autumn of Glory*, 44–45; Cozzens, *No Better Place to Die*, 42–44, 47–52; Hess, *Banners to the Breeze*, 185, 187–88; McDonough, *Stones River*, 50–57; McWhiney, *Braxton Bragg*, 344–48.

19. Owens, *Greene County*, 30.

20. Connelly, *Autumn of Glory*, 45–46; Cozzens, *No Better Place to Die*, 52–56; Hess, *Banners to the Breeze*, 188–90.

21. W. D. B., *Rosecrans' Campaign*, 164. See also Dodge, *Waif of the War*, 60.

22. W. D. B., *Rosecrans' Campaign*, 164, 166, 167. See also *OR*, 20(1):252, 253, 302, 319, 328, 339, 843, 897, 901, 20(2):245, 246; Clarksville, Tenn., Dec. 1862, Reel 478, RG 27.5.7, NARA-CP; Hight and Stormont, *Fifty-Eighth Indiana*, 111; and Cozzens, *No Better Place to Die*, 56–59.

23. *OR*, 20(1):183, 190, 218, 274, 277, 279, 319; Hess, *Banners to the Breeze*, 190.

24. Francis, *Narrative of a Private Soldier*, 95. See also Dodge, *Waif of the War*, 60.

25. Simmons, *84th Ill.*, 26.

26. Connelly, *Autumn of Glory*, 46; Cozzens, *No Better Place to Die*, 59–61; Hess, *Banners to the Breeze*, 191–92.

27. Hafendorfer, *Journal of Trask*, 92–93.

28. W. D. B., *Rosecrans' Campaign*, 172–73. See also *OR*, 20(1):762; and Clarksville, Tenn., Dec. 1862, Reel 478, RG 27.5.7, NARA-CP.

29. Bennett and Haigh, *Thirty-Sixth Illinois*, 322; *Civil War Diary of Bush*, 3; Francis, *Narrative of a Private Soldier*, 96; Hight and Stormont, *Fifty-Eighth Indiana*, 112; Hinman, *Sherman Brigade*, 337; Owens, *Greene County*, 31; W. D. B., *Rosecrans' Campaign*, 172–73; Clarksville, Tenn., Dec. 1862, Reel 478, RG 27.5.7, NARA-CP; Cozzens, *No Better Place to Die*, 60–63; Hess, *Banners to the Breeze*, 192.

30. *OR*, 20(2):254; Bennett and Haigh, *Thirty-Sixth Illinois*, 327; *Civil War Diary of Bush*, 3; Cope, *Fifteenth Ohio*, 232; Francis, *Narrative of a Private Soldier*, 102–3; Hinman, *Sherman Brigade*, 337, 338; W. D. B., *Rosecrans' Campaign*, 174; Worley, *Memoirs of Lavender*, 37; Clarksville, Tenn., Dec. 1862, Reel 478, RG 27.5.7, NARA-CP; Cozzens, *No Better Place to Die*, 64–70; Hess, *Banners to the Breeze*, 192–93.

31. *OR*, 20(1):407; Bircher, *Drummer-Boy's Diary*, 50; Cope, *Fifteenth Ohio*, 232–33; Dodge, *Waif of the War*, 63; Owens, *Greene County*, 32; W. D. B., *Rosecrans' Campaign* 181–82, 185, 196; Worley, *Memoirs of Lavender*, 38; Connelly, *Autumn of Glory*, 47–52; Cozzens, *No Better Place to Die*, 70–73; Hess, *Banners to the Breeze*, 192–93.

32. W. D. B., *Rosecrans' Campaign*, 203.

33. *OR*, 20(1):407; *Augusta (Ga.) Daily Constitutionalist*, Jan. 8, 1863; Cozzens, *No Better Place to Die*, 73–80 (quotation, 78); Hess, *Banners to the Breeze*, 194–96; Hess, *Braxton Bragg*, 106–7; McWhiney, *Braxton Bragg*, 348–50. I am grateful to Chris Kolakowski for stressing Cleburne's shift across the river.

34. *OR*, 20(1):689; Cope, *Fifteenth Ohio*, 234; Connelly, *Autumn of Glory*, 52–61; Cozzens, *No Better Place to Die*, 81–174; Hess, *Banners to the Breeze*, 197–215, 217–18; Hess, *Braxton Bragg*, 106–7; McDonough, *Stones River*, 81–152; McWhiney, *Braxton Bragg*, 344–62.

35. *OR*, 20(1):778; Cope, *Fifteenth Ohio*, 234; Eby, *Observations*, 76; Hinman, *Sherman Brigade*, 361–62; Hess, *Banners to the Breeze*, 216–18; McDonough, *Stones River*, 152–65.

36. Simmons, *84th Ill.*, 33.

37. Hazen, *Narrative*, 83. See also Cozzens, *No Better Place to Die*, 167–70.

38. Clarksville, Tenn., Dec. 1862, Jan. 1863, Reel 478, RG 27.5.7, NARA-CP; Hight and Stormont, *Fifty-Eighth Indiana*, 120; Spence, *Diary*, 60; Hess, *Banners to the Breeze*, 215.

39. Beatty, *Citizen-Soldier*, 205; Bircher, *Drummer-Boy's Diary*, 52; *Civil War Diary of Bush*, 4; Clarksville, Tenn., Jan. 1863, Reel 478, RG 27.5.7, NARA-CP; Connelly, *Autumn of Glory*, 61–62; Cozzens, *No Better Place to Die*, 171–76; Hess, *Banners to the Breeze*, 218–19; McDonough, *Stones River*, 166–68; McWhiney, *Braxton Bragg*, 365–66.

40. *OR*, 20(1):244, 248, 250, 289, 407; Bircher, *Drummer-Boy's Diary*, 53; Clarksville, Tenn., Jan. 1863, Reel 478, RG 27.5.7, NARA-CP; Spence, *Diary*, 61; Hess, *Braxton Bragg*, 99–100; Connelly, *Autumn of Glory*, 62–60; Cozzens, *No Better Place to Die*, 177–205; Hess, *Banners to the Breeze*, 219–25; Ludlum, *Early American Winters*, 132; McDonough, *Stones River*, 169–203; McWhiney, *Braxton Bragg*, 366–70.

41. W. D. B., *Rosecrans' Campaign*, 319.

42. Simmons, *84th Ill.*, 36; Preston (Mathews), "33rd Alabama," 34, ADAH; Connelly, *Autumn of Glory*, 66–68; Cozzens, *No Better Place to Die*, 196–202; Hess, *Banners to the Breeze*, 225–27; McWhiney, *Braxton Bragg*, 370–73.

43. *OR*, 20(1):668–69. See also Hess, *Braxton Bragg*, 99–102.

44. *OR*, 20(1):220, 221, 265, 271, 277, 336, 472, 486, 515, 539, 583, 778, 881; Bennett and Haigh, *Thirty-Sixth Illinois*, 371, 374, 375; Bircher, *Drummer-Boy's Diary*, 53–54; Blakey, Lainhart, and Stephens, *Rose Cottage Chronicles*, 188; *Civil War Diary of Bush*, 4–5; Clay, "On the Right," 589; Cope, *Fifteenth Ohio*, 244; Dodge, *Waif of the War*, 73; Hafendorfer, *Journal of Trask*, 100; Hight and Stormont, *Fifty-Eighth Indiana*, 125, 126; Hinman, *Sherman Brigade*, 356; Scribner, *How Soldiers Were Made*, 87; Simmons, *84th Ill.*, 36; Spence, *Diary*, 63; Sutherland, *Reminiscences of a Private*, 121; W. D. B., *Rosecrans' Campaign*, 322; Preston (Mathews), "33rd Alabama," 34, ADAH; Connelly, *Autumn of Glory*, 66–68; Cozzens, *No Better Place to Die*, 196–202; Hess, *Banners to the Breeze*, 225–27; McWhiney, *Braxton Bragg*, 370–73.

45. Hafendorfer, *Journal of Trask*, 97.

46. *OR*, 20(1):294. See also ibid., 385, 386, 403, 736, 894, 904.

47. Hess, *Banners to the Breeze*, 299.

48. *OR*, 20(1):221, 490; Cozzens, *No Better Place to Die*, 204–7; Hess, *Banners to the Breeze*, 230–31.

49. Dodge, *Waif of the War*, 75. See also Barnes, Carnahan, and McCain, *Eighty-Sixth Indiana*, 129; Bennett and Haigh, *Thirty-Sixth Illinois*, 411; "Fortress Rosecrans," accessed Oct. 11, 2016; Jones, "Building Fortress Rosecrans," accessed Oct. 11, 2016.

50. DeRosier, *Through the South*, 52.

51. Clarksville, Tenn., Jan. 1862, Jan. 1863, Reel 478, RG 27.5.7, NARA-CP; *Augusta (Ga.) Daily Constitutionalist*, Jan. 18, 1863.

52. Shaw, *Tenth Indiana*, 198.

53. Clarksville, Tenn., Feb. 1862, Feb. 1863, Reel 478, RG 27.5.7, NARA-CP.

54. Bennett and Haigh, *Thirty-Sixth Illinois*, 410. See also ibid., 411; Beatty, *Citizen-Soldier*, 213, 214, 216; Bircher, *Drummer-Boy's Diary*, 58–59; Cope, *Fifteenth Ohio*, 260, 261, 264, 265; DeRosier, *Through the South*, 52, 54; Donahower, "Narrative of the Civil War," 2:54, Donahower Papers, MnHS; Hinman, *Sherman Brigade*, 368; Marcoot, *Five Years in the Sunny South*, 26; Morris, *Eighty-First Indiana*, 38; Simmons, *84th Ill.*, 43; Spence, *Diary*, 71.

55. H Bishop, *Story of a Regiment*, 81; Dodge, *Waif of the War*, 77; Donahower, "Narrative of the Civil War," 2:59, Donahower Papers, MnHS; Spence, *Diary*, 72, 73, 74; Hinman, *Sherman Brigade*, 371; Simmons, *84th Ill.*, 40; Woodward, *Outlines of the Chief Camp Diseases*, 57–73; Jones, "Building Fortress Rosecrans," accessed Oct. 11, 2016.

56. Cooper Memoirs, 27, Reel 5, CWC, TSLA.

57. Francis R. Nicks to Mike, Mar. 9, 1863, Tullahoma, Tenn., "Lincoln Letters," *Florida Memory*, accessed May 14, 2013.

58. *Civil War Diary of Bush*, 5, 6, 7; Cooper Memoirs, 28, reel 5, CWC, TSLA; "William P. Rogers' Memorandum Book," 79–80; Francis R. Nicks to Mike, Mar. 9, 1863, accessed May 14, 2013.

59. *Mobile Register*, Mar. 4, 1863.

60. Clarksville, Tenn., Mar. 1863, Reel 478, RG 27.5.7, NARA-CP; Barron, *Lone Star Defenders*, 151; Beatty, *Citizen-Soldier*, 228, 229, 234; Bennett and Haigh, *Thirty-Sixth Illinois*, 417; Bircher, *Drummer-Boy's Diary*, 59–61; Cope, *Fifteenth Ohio*, 265, 267, 271, 272, 273; Morris, *Eighty-First Indiana*, 41–43.

61. Clarksville, Tenn., Mar. 1863, Reel 478, RG 27.5.7, NARA-CP.

62. Clarksville, Tenn., Apr. 1862, Apr. 1863, Reel 478, RG 27.5.7, NARA-CP; Beatty, *Citizen-Soldier*, 229; Bircher, *Drummer-Boy's Diary*, 61–63; Cope, *Fifteenth Ohio*, 271, 273; DeRosier, *Through the South*, 63, 64; Morris, *Eighty-First Indiana*, 43.

CHAPTER 13

1. Racine, *Piedmont Farmer*, 276–86 (quotations, 283, 284, 285, 286). See also Hurt, *Agriculture and the Confederacy*, 125–27, 165–68.

2. *New England Farmer*, June 1, 1863.

3. *Alexandria (Va.) Gazette*, Apr. 29, 1863; *Augusta (Ga.) Daily Constitutionalist*, Mar. 24, Apr. 8, 19, 1863; *Macon (Ga.) Daily Telegraph*, Apr. 2, 3, 1863; *Richmond Whig*, Apr. 24, 1863.

4. Molie to John, Apr. 4, 1863, John B. Evans Papers, 1862–1865, Duke.

5. Racine, *Piedmont Farmer*, 286–96 (quotations, 289, 296).

6. Blakey, Lainhart, and Stephens, *Rose Cottage Chronicles*, 232, 239; Myers, *Children of Pride*, 373, 374; *Augusta (Ga.) Chronicle*, May 8, 23, June 13, 30, 1863; *Augusta (Ga.) Daily Constitutionalist*, May 9, 15, 23, 24, 26, 29, June 11, 1863; *Macon (Ga.) Daily Telegraph*, May 23, 29, 30, June 1, 4, 15, 1863; *Mobile Register*, May 30, 1863; *Natchez Daily Courier*, May 9, 1863.

7. A. K. Blake to Father, May 23, 1863, Portsmouth, Va., Aaron K. Blake Correspondence, Box 10, CWMC, USAMHI. See also *Baltimore Sun*, June 15, 30, 1863.

8. Jones, *Rebel War Clerk's Diary*, 1:340–41.

9. *Alexandria (Va.) Gazette*, June 10, 1863.

10. *OR*, 21:69; D. R. Larned to Mrs. Burnside, Jan. 28, 1863, Daniel Read Larned Papers, LC; O'Reilly, *Fredericksburg Campaign*, 489–92; Rable, *Fredericksburg*, 421–23; McPherson, *Battle Cry of Freedom*, 584–85.

11. *Charleston Mercury*, Feb. 2, 1863; Baird, *Journals of Edmonds*, 131; J. P. Coburn to Father, Jan. 28, 1863, Old Place, James Parley Coburn Papers, USAMHI; Dawes, *Sixth Wisconsin*, 33; Dobbins, *Grandfather's Journal*, 123; J. B. Evans to Wife, Jan. 29, 1863, Richmond, Va., Evans Papers, Duke; Jones, *Rebel War Clerk's Diary*, 1:248; Mead Diary, vol. 3, Jan. 27–29, 1863, LC; William H. Peacock to Sarah, Jan. 28, 1863, Falmouth, Va., William H. Peacock Correspondence, Box 89, CWMC, USAMHI; Preston, *Tenth New York Cavalry*, 60; Roper, *Repairing the "March of Mars,"* 351; Sparks, *Inside Lincoln's Army*, 209; Summers, *Borderland Confederate*, 43; Richard Waldrop to Father, Jan. 29, 1863, Port Royal, Richard Woolfolk Waldrop Papers, SHC-UNC; "Diaries of John Waldrop . . . and William Y. Mordecai," 46; White, "Diary of the War," 155; Krick, *Civil War Weather*, 83.

12. McDonald, *Make Me a Map of the Valley*, 111. See also Fiege, *Republic of Nature*, 207.

13. Westwood A. Todd Reminiscence, pt. 1, 81, SHC-UNC. See also John B. Evans, Fredericksburg, Va., to Wife, Jan. 31, 1863, John B. Evans Papers 1862–1865, Duke; O'Reilly, *Fredericksburg Campaign*, 497–98. See also Benson, *Berry Benson's Civil War Book*, 34; Caldwell, *Brigade of South Carolinians*,

107; J. B. Evans to Wife, Jan. 29, 1863, Fredericksburg, Va., Evans Papers, Duke; Evans to Wife, Jan. 31, 1863, Fredericksburg, Va., ibid.; Moore, *Story of a Cannoneer*, 166; Oates, *War between the Union and the Confederacy*, 174; Stewart, *Pair of Blankets*, 78; Stiles, *Four Years under Marse Robert*, 157–58; Richard Waldrop to Father, Jan. 29, 1863, Port Royal, Waldrop Papers, SHC-UNC; and Warfield, *Confederate Soldiers' Memoirs*, 139–40.

14. *OR*, 21:1108.

15. E. DeLoss Burton to Jennie Burton, Jan. 28, 1863, Aquia Creek, Va., Edmond Family Collection: Correspondence, NYHS/CWPSD; Frank Morse to Nellie, Jan. 27, 1863, Fredericksburg, Va., Frank C. Morse Papers, MHS; Rable, *Fredericksburg*, 423–26, 434–35; O'Reilly, *Fredericksburg Campaign*, 494–97; McPherson, *Battle Cry of Freedom*, 584. For a Federal snowball fight, see White, *Diary of Wyman S. White*, 130–31.

16. Furgurson, *Chancellorsville*, 11, 29–35, 56; Sears, *Chancellorsville*, 60–64, 67–80; Krick, *Civil War Weather*, 83; Caldwell, *Brigade of South Carolinians*, 106; Sam to Sister, Jan. 28, 1863, White Oak Church, Va., David E. Cronin Papers: Correspondence, NYHS/CWPSD; E. DeLoss Burton to Jennie Burton, Jan. 28, 1863, Aquia Creek, Va., Edmond Family Collection: Correspondence, ibid.; Haines, *Fifteenth New Jersey*, 41–42; Frank Morse to Ellen, Jan. 31, 1863, Fredericksburg, Va., Morse Papers, MHS; Morse to Wife, Feb. 5, 1863, Fredericksburg, Va., ibid.

17. Robertson, *Letters of McAllister*, 275. See also Blight, *When This Cruel War Is Over*, 218; and Mead Diary, vol. 3, Feb. 2–27, 1863, LC.

18. Frank Morse to Ellen, Jan. 31, 1863, Fredericksburg, Va., Morse Papers, MHS.

19. *OR*, 25(1):8, 39, 25(2):96, 643; Alexandria, Va., Feb. 1863, Reel 518, RG 27.5.7, NARA-CP; *Alexandria (Va.) Gazette*, Feb. 26, 1863; Baird, *Journals of Edmonds*, 131, 133, 134; Blackford et al., *Letters from Lee's Army*, 167; A. K. Blake to Sister, Feb. 6, 1863, Falmouth, Va., Blake Correspondence, CWMC, USAMHI; Blight, *When This Cruel War Is Over*, 213, 215; Chamberlayne, *Ham Chamberlayne*, 150; Britton and Reed, *To My Beloved Wife*, 42–53; J. P. Coburn to Father, Jan. 28, Feb. 22, 1863, Old Place, Coburn Papers, USAMHI; Dobbins, *Grandfather's Journal*, 123–27; J. B. Evans to Wife, Jan. 29, 1863, Richmond, Va., Evans Papers, Duke; Everson and Simpson, "*Far, Far from Home*," 186, 189, 195; Fleet and Fuller, *Green Mount*, 200–1; Dayton E. Flint to Sister, Feb. 1, 1862, White Oak Church, Va., in "Civil War Letters of Dayton E. Flint," Box 40, CWMC, USAMHI; Flint to Sisters, Feb. 23, 1863, White Oak Church, ibid.; Hamilton, *Papers of Shotwell*, 1:446–48; Baldy [Archibald] Henderson to Brother, Feb. 19, 27, 1863, Guinea's Station, Va., Archibald Erskine Henderson Papers, 1841–1917, Duke; Howard, *Recollections*, 196; Jones, *Rebel War Clerk's Diary*, 1:248, 255, 258, 262, 267; Lee, *Recollections and Letters*, 92–93; Malles, *Bridge Building in Wartime*, 130; McDonald, *Make Me a Map of the Valley*, 112–16; Mead Diary, vol. 3, Feb. 17, 1863, LC; William H. Myers to Parents, Feb. 15, 1863, Falmouth, Va., William H. Myers Letters, Box 84, CWMC, USAMHI; Nevins, *Diary of Battle*, 164, 165, 166–67, 168–69; William H. Peacock to Sarah, Jan. 28, 1863, Falmouth, Va., Peacock Correspondence, CWMC, USAMHI; Preston, *Tenth New York Cavalry*, 60, 61; Robertson, *Letters of McAllister*, 265–67; Roper, *Repairing the "March of Mars,"* 351; *Shoemaker's Battery*, 27; Silliker, *Rebel Yell & the Yankee Hurrah*, 71–72; John B. Southard to Sister, Mar. 1, 1863, "Camp," Southard Family Collection, NYHS/CWPSD; Sparks, *Inside Lincoln's Army*, 209; Summers, *Borderland Confederate*, 43; Richard Waldrop to Father, Jan. 29, 1863, Port Royal, Waldrop Papers, SHC-UNC; "Diaries of John Waldrop . . . and William Y. Mordecai," 46; Warfield, *Confederate Soldier's Memoirs*, 142; White, "Diary of the War," 155, 163, 164; Krick, *Civil War Weather*, 83, 88.

20. *Charleston Mercury*, Feb. 11, 1863.

21. *Charleston Mercury*, Feb. 11, 1863. See also Alexandria, Va., Feb. 1863, Reel 518, RG 27.5.7, NARA-CP; and John B. Southard to Sister, Mar. 1, 1863, "Camp," Southard Family Collection, NYHS/CWPSD.

22. *Charleston Mercury*, Feb. 11, 1863. See also *Alexandria (Va.) Gazette*, Feb. 4, 1863; *Carolina Observer* (Fayetteville, N.C.), Feb. 9, 1863; and Frank Morse to Ellen, Feb. 26, 1863, Fredericksburg, Va., Morse Papers, MHS.

23. Nevins, *Diary of Battle*, 175. See also Alexandria, Va., Mar. 1863, Reel 518, RG 27.5.7, NARA-CP; *American Agriculturalist*, Apr. 1, 1863; Robertson, *Letters of McAllister*, 270; *Shoemaker's Battery*, 29; John B. Southard to Sister, Mar. 1, 1863, "Camp," Southard Family Collection, NYHS/CWPSD; Welch, *Confederate Surgeon's Letters*, 46; *Working Farmer & United States Journal*, Apr. 1, 1863.

24. Krick, *Civil War Weather*, 91; Alexandria, Va., Mar. 1863, Reel 518, RG 27.5.7, NARA-CP; *American Agriculturalist*, Apr. 1, 1863; *Southern Illustrated News*, Apr. 4, 1863; Britton and Reed, *To My Beloved Wife*, 54–63; Chamberlayne, *Ham Chamberlayne*, 164; Oliver S. Coolidge to unknown, Mar. 8, 1863, Newport News, Va., Oliver S. Coolidge Papers, 1861–1864, Duke; Cook, *Twelfth Massachusetts*, 92; Dobbins, *Grandfather's Journal*, 128–31; Douglas, *I Rode with Stonewall*, 216. 217; Everson and Simpson, *"Far, Far from Home,"* 202–6; Fleet and Fuller, *Green Mount*, 209, 211, 215; Luther C. Furst Diary, 34, 35, HCWRTC, USAMHI; Hamilton, *Papers of Shotwell*, 1:453, 456–67, 458, 459; Jones, *Rebel War Clerk's Diary*, 1:267, 271, 274, 277–79; Lee, *Memoir of Pendleton*, 252; McDonald, *Make Me a Map of the Valley*, 117–24; R. Mead to Folks at Home, Mar. 12, 1863, Stafford Court House, Va., Rufus Mead Jr. Papers, LC; Mead Diary, vol. 3, Mar. 1–31, 1863, ibid.; Neese, *Three Years in the Confederate Horse Artillery*, 152–53; Peck, *Reminiscences*, 21; Robertson, *Letters of McAllister*, 275; *Shoemaker's Battery*, 28, 29; Summers, *Borderland Confederate*, 50, 51; White, "Diary of the War," 165.

25. Jones, *Rebel War Clerk's Diary*, 1:267, 271, 274, 277–79; Fiege, *Republic of Nature*, 208; Hurt, *Agriculture and the Confederacy*, 127–30; McCurry, *Confederate Reckoning*, 178–80, 184–98.

26. Chamberlayne, *Ham Chamberlayne*, 159.

27. Krick, *Civil War Weather*, 91; *Daily Richmond Examiner*, Mar. 6, 1863; Baird, *Journals of Edmonds*, 135, 136; Aaron K. Blake to Sister, Mar. 15, 1863, Suffolk, Va., Blake Correspondence, CWMC, USAMHI; Britton and Reed, *To My Beloved Wife*, 54–63; Jim Coburn to Folks at Home, Mar. 25, 1863, Potomac Creek, Va., Coburn Papers, USAMHI; Cook, *Twelfth Massachusetts*, 92; Dobbins, *Grandfather's Journal*, 128–31; Baldy [Archibald] Henderson to Brother, Mar. 13, 25, 1863, Guinea Station, Va., Henderson Papers, Duke; Jones, *Rebel War Clerk's Diary*, 1:267, 271, 274, 277–79; Lee, *Memoir of Pendleton*, 252; Malles, *Bridge Building in Wartime*, 132; McDonald, *Make Me a Map of the Valley*, 117–24; R. Mead to Folks at Home, Mar. 15, 1863, Stafford Court House, Va., Mead Papers, LC; Frank Morse to Wife, Mar. 6, 13, 1863, Fredericksburg, Va., Morse Papers, MHS; Nevins, *Diary of Battle*, 175; Peck, *Reminiscences*, 21–23; White, "Diary of the War," 166. The five freezing nights were March 4, 5 (19 degrees at 7 A.M.), 12, 13, and 15.

28. Nevins, *Diary of Battle*, 171.

29. George M. Barnard to Father, Mar. 28, 31, 1863, Falmouth, George Middleton Barnard Papers, CWCDJ, MHS; Blight, *When This Cruel War Is Over*, 218; Rosenblatt and Rosenblatt, *Hard Marching Every Day*, 57.

30. Baird, *Journals of Edmonds*, 135; A. K. Blake to Sister, Feb. 6, 1863, Falmouth, Va., Blake Correspondence, CWMC, USAMHI; Britton and Reed, *To My Beloved Wife*, 43, 50, 51, 53; Jim Coburn to Folks at Home, Mar. 5, 13, 1863, Camp Pitcher, Coburn Papers, USAMHI; John B. Evans to Molie Evans, Feb. 23, 1863, Fredericksburg, Va., Evans Papers, Duke; Dayton E. Flint to Sisters, Feb. 15, 1862, White Oak Church, Va., in "Civil War Letters of Dayton E. Flint," CWMC, USAMHI; Everson and Simpson, *"Far, Far from Home,"* 189, 195; Haines, *Fifteenth New Jersey*, 45; Malles, *Bridge Building in Wartime*, 130; William H. Myers to parents, Feb. 15, 1863, Falmouth, Va., Myers Letters, CWMC, USAMHI; Nevins, *Diary of Battle*, 165, 168; Rhodes, *All for the Union*, 100; Silliker, *Rebel Yell & the Yankee Hurrah*, 73; Todd Reminiscence, pt. 1, 85, 88, SHC-UNC; Warfield, *Confederate Soldier's Memoirs*, 142; Sears, *Chancellorsville*, 75–76.

31. Jim Coburn to Folks at Home, Mar. 25, 1863, "Stump O," Coburn Papers, USAMHI.

32. Benson, *Berry Benson's Civil War Book*, 36; Blackford et al., *Letters from Lee's Army*, 165–66; Caldwell, *Brigade of South Carolinians*, 107; Dawes, *Sixth Wisconsin*, 129; Everson and Simpson, *"Far, Far from Home,"* 177–82, 197–98; Dayton E. Flint to Father, Mar. 3, 1863, White Oak Church, Va., in "Civil War Letters of Dayton E. Flint," CWMC, USAMHI; Lee, *Recollections and Letters*, 93; Malles, *Bridge Building in Wartime*, 132; Member of Company C, *Twenty-Seventh Indiana*, 294. Robertson, *Letters of McAllister*, 277; Stewart, *Pair of Blankets*, 78; Todd Reminiscence, pt. 1, 81–82, SHC-UNC; Tyler, *Recollections*, 76; Welch, *Confederate Surgeon's Letters*, 42; Furgurson, *Chancellorsville*, 36–39.

33. Furgurson, *Chancellorsville*, 10.

34. Lee, *Recollections and Letters*, 92.

35. Furgurson, *Chancellorsville*, 11.

36. Dawes, *Sixth Wisconsin*, 122.

37. Malles, *Bridge Building in Wartime*, 135.

38. *Alexandria (Va.) Gazette*, Apr. 6, 1863; Britton and Reed, *To My Beloved Wife*, 63, 65–66; Dobbins, *Grandfather's Journal*, 132; Everson and Simpson, *"Far, Far from Home,"* 206–8; Furst Diary, 35, HCWRTC, USAMHI; Henry A. Genet to Revi, Apr. 5, 1863, Falmouth, Va., Henry A. Genet Collection: Letter, 1863, NYHS/CWPSD; McDonald, *Make Me a Map of the Valley*, 125–26; Mead Diary, vol. 3, Apr. 4–6, 1863, LC; Neese, *Three Years in the Confederate Horse Artillery*, 153; Nevins, *Diary of Battle*, 176; Norton, *Army Letters*, 146; Rosenblatt and Rosenblatt, *Hard Marching Every Day*, 60–61; "Diaries of John Waldrop . . . and William Y. Mordecai," 47; Krick, *Civil War Weather*, 94.

39. Welch, *Confederate Surgeon's Letters*, 46–47. For similar conclusions, see Everson and Simpson, *"Far, Far from Home,"* 208; and Nevins, *Diary of Battle*, 176.

40. George M. Barnard to Father, Apr. 6, 12, 1863, Falmouth, Barnard Papers, CWCDJ, MHS; Britton and Reed, *To My Beloved Wife*, 66; Chamberlayne, *Ham Chamberlayne*, 168; Jim Coburn to Ones at Home, Mar. 25, 1863, Potomac Creek, Va., Coburn Papers, USAMHI; Dobbins, *Grandfather's Journal*, 132–33; Everson and Simpson, *"Far, Far from Home,"* 212; McDonald, *Make Me a Map of the Valley*, 127; Norton, *Army Letters*, 148; Robertson, *Letters of McAllister*, 282; Sparks, *Inside Lincoln's Army*, 230, 231; Furgurson, *Chancellorsville*, 59–64; Sears, *Chancellorsville*, 114–20; Krick, *Civil War Weather*, 94.

41. Quoted in Sears, *Chancellorsville*, 120.

42. Furgurson, *Chancellorsville*, 64–66; Sears, *Chancellorsville*, 120–29; Krick, *Civil War Weather*, 94; *OR*, 25(1):89, 214, 1068, 1081; Britton and Reed, *To My Beloved Wife*, 67, 68; Jim Coburn to Ones at Home, Apr. 16, 1863, "Old Camp," Coburn Papers, USAMHI; Coburn to Ones at Home, Apr. 17, 1863, Camp Sickles, Va., ibid.; de Trobriand, *Four Years in the Army of the Potomac*, 428; Dobbins, *Grandfather's Journal*, 133–34; Haines, *Fifteenth New Jersey*, 47; Baldy [Archibald] Henderson to Brother, Apr. 18, 1863, Fredericksburg, Va., Henderson Papers, Duke; Jones, *Rebel War Clerk's Diary*, 1:295–96; McDonald, *Make Me a Map of the Valley*, 128, 130. 131, 133; R. Mead to Folks at Home, A[pr.] 20, 1863, Stafford County House, Va., Mead Papers, LC; Neese, *Three Years in the Confederate Horse Artillery*, 154–55; Nevins, *Diary of Battle*, 181, 182; William H. Peacock to Sarah, Apr. 17, 1863, Falmouth, Va., Peacock Correspondence, CWMC, USAMHI; Preston, *Tenth New York Cavalry*, 68; Racine, "Unspoiled Heart," 4, 5; Roper, *Repairing the "March of Mars,"* 412, 415, 416; Rosenblatt and Rosenblatt, *Hard Marching Every Day*, 66; *Shoemaker's Battery*, 31.

43. Furgurson, *Chancellorsville*, 66–68, 88; Sears, *Chancellorsville*, 128–32.

44. *OR*, 25(2):236–37, 242; Bauer, *Soldiering*, 35, 38; Baylor, *Bull Run to Bull Run*, 136; Britton and Reed, *To My Beloved Wife*, 72–73, 78, 80; Chamberlayne, *Ham Chamberlayne*, 162, 170; Dobbins, *Grandfather's Journal*, 134–35; J. B. Evans to Wife, Apr. 27, 1863, "Camp," Evans Papers, Duke; Everson and Simpson, *"Far, Far from Home,"* 219, 220; Haines, *Fifteenth New Jersey*, 48; A. E. Henderson to

Brother, Apr. 28, 1863, Fredericksburg, Va., Henderson Papers, Duke; Edward Hitchcock McDonald Reminiscences, 79, SHC-UNC; McDonald, *Make Me a Map of the Valley*, 134–35; Mead Diary, vol. 3, Apr. 15–30, 1863, LC; Neese, *Three Years in the Confederate Horse Artillery*, 155–57; Nevins, *Diary of Battle*, 183–84; Preston, *Tenth New York Cavalry*, 68; Quaife, *From the Cannon's Mouth*, 176, 180; Racine, "Unspoiled Heart," 5–6; Robertson, *Letters of McAllister*, 288; Roper, *Repairing the "March of Mars,"* 419, 420; Rosenblatt and Rosenblatt, *Hard Marching Every Day*, 73; Sanford, *Fighting Rebels and Redskins*, 197–98; Sparks, *Inside Lincoln's Army*, 236; Summers, *Borderland Confederate*, 58; Krick, *Civil War Weather*, 94.

45. *OR*, 25(1):195.

46. Furgurson, *Chancellorsville*, 87–100, 105–13; Sears, *Chancellorsville*, 136–81; Krick, *Civil War Weather*, 94; *OR*, 25(1):197, 218, 229, 258, 266, 286, 297, 340, 486, 521, 546, 748, 755, 809, 865, 1059, 1078, 25(2):294, 316, Bartlett, *Twelfth New Hampshire*, 65–67; Bauer, *Soldiering*, 38; Blight, *When This Cruel War Is Over*, 220, 221; Chamberlayne, *Ham Chamberlayne*, 171; Cook, *Twelfth Massachusetts*, 92; Douglas, *I Rode with Stonewall*, 218; Early, *War Memoirs*, 193; Everson and Simpson, "Far, Far from Home," 222; McDonald, *Make Me a Map of the Valley*, 135–36; Neese, *Three Years in the Confederate Horse Artillery*, 158, 160; Nevins, *Diary of Battle*, 185; Pyne, *Ride to War*, 111; Racine, "Unspoiled Heart," 8; Sanford, *Fighting Rebels and Redskins*, 198; Stiles, *Four Years under Marse Robert*, 166; White, "Diary of the War," 166, 167.

47. Furgurson, *Chancellorsville*; 114–43; Krick, *Civil War Weather*, 98; Alexandria, Va., June 1862, Reel 518, RG 27.5.7, NARA-CP; Lively, *Calamity at Chancellorsville*, 21; Robertson, *Stonewall Jackson*, 704, 709–15; Sears, *Chancellorsville*, 181–235; Bartlett, *Twelfth New Hampshire*, 68; Britton and Reed, *To My Beloved Wife*, 81; Child, *Fifth New Hampshire*, 175, 176; J. P. Coburn to Folks at Home, May 1, 1863, Rappahannock, Va., Coburn Papers, USAMHI; Dobbins, *Grandfather's Journal*, 136; Douglas, *I Rode with Stonewall*, 220; French, *Two Wars*, 166; Malles, *Bridge Building in Wartime*, 141; McDonald, *Make Me a Map of the Valley*, 137; Nevins, *Diary of Battle*, 190; Quaife, *From the Cannon's Mouth*, 185; Quint, *Second Massachusetts*, 160; Stiles, *Four Years under Marse Robert*, 168.

48. Furgurson, *Chancellorsville*, 87–100, 105–13; Lively, *Calamity at Chancellorsville*, 33; Robertson, *Stonewall Jackson*, 715–20; Sears, *Chancellorsville*, 136–81; Krick, *Civil War Weather*, 94; Caldwell, *Brigade of South Carolinians*, 112; Dobbins, *Grandfather's Journal*, 136; Quaife, *From the Cannon's Mouth*, 188.

49. Caldwell, *Brigade of South Carolinians*, 112.

50. Furgurson, *Chancellorsville*, 144–216; Olson, "Fatal Full Moon," 24–29; Robertson, *Stonewall Jackson*, 718–36; Sears, *Chancellorsville*, 235–307; Caldwell, *Brigade of South Carolinians*, 112; McDonald, *Make Me a Map of the Valley*, 139; Silliker, *Rebel Yell & the Yankee Hurrah*, 80.

51. Furgurson, *Chancellorsville*, 216–322; Krick, *Civil War Weather*, 95, 98; Sears, *Chancellorsville*, 307–427; *OR*, 25(1):247, 251, 802, 25(2):402; Bauer, *Soldiering*, 53–54, 67, 74; Dawes, *Sixth Wisconsin*, 138; Dobbins, *Grandfather's Journal*, 137; Malles, *Bridge Building in Wartime*, 142; McDonald, *Make Me a Map of the Valley*, 140; Member of Company C, *Twenty-Seventh Indiana*, 329; Quaife, *From the Cannon's Mouth*, 199, 200; Rhodes, *All for the Union*, 112.

52. Bauer, *Soldiering*, 74–75. See also *OR*, 25(1):204; Mead Diary, vol. 3, May 5, 1863, LC; and Nevins, *Diary of Battle*, 200. For a similar scene, see White, "Diary of the War," 178–79.

53. Bartlett, *Twelfth New Hampshire*, 91–92.

54. Bauer, *Soldiering*, 75–76; Krick, *Civil War Weather*, 98; Alexandria, Va., May 1863, Reel 518, RG 27.5.7, NARA-CP.

55. Furgurson, *Chancellorsville*, 312–17; Sears, *Chancellorsville*, 428–30; *OR*, 25(1):260, 266, 268, 279, 283, 369, 488, 498, 741, 831, 872, 912, 989; George M. Barnard to Father, May 8, 1863, Falmouth, Barnard Papers, CWCDJ, MHS; Silliker, *Rebel Yell & the Yankee Hurrah*, 85.

56. Malles, *Bridge Building in Wartime*, 144.

57. *OR*, 25(1):204; Bartlett, *Twelfth New Hampshire*, 92–93; Britton and Reed, *To My Beloved Wife*, 82; Haines, *Fifteenth New Jersey*, 59; Malles, *Bridge Building in Wartime*, 144–45; McDonald, *Make Me a Map of the Valley*, 141; Moore, *Story of a Cannoneer*, 177; Nevins, *Diary of Battle*, 200; Quint, *Second Massachusetts*, 171; Silliker, *Rebel Yell & the Yankee Hurrah*, 85; Sparks, *Inside Lincoln's Army*, 242; Furgurson, *Chancellorsville*, 312–17; Sears, *Chancellorsville*, 428–30.

58. *OR*, 25(1):280, 301, 534, 536, 692, 757, 945, 957, 989; Britton and Reed, *To My Beloved Wife*, 83; Child, *Fifth New Hampshire*, 177; Dobbins, *Grandfather's Journal*, 138; Hyde, *Following the Greek Cross*, 135; McDonald, *Make Me a Map of the Valley*, 141; Member of Company C, *Twenty-Seventh Indiana*, 347; Nevins, *Diary of Battle*, 201; William H. Peacock to Sarah, May 6, 1863, Falmouth, Va., Peacock Correspondence, CWMC, USAMHI; Preston, *Tenth New York Cavalry*, 73; White, *Diary of Wyman S. White*, 148; Furgurson, *Chancellorsville*, 315–17.

59. Bauer, *Soldiering*, 77.

60. Furgurson, *Chancellorsville*, 317–22; Krick, *Civil War Weather*, 98; Lively, *Calamity at Chancellorsville*, 107; Sears, *Chancellorsville*, 426; Dobbins, *Grandfather's Journal*, 138; Isaac R. Dunkelbarger Recollections, 13, Michael Winey Collection, USAMHI; John B. Evans to Wife, May 8, 1863, Fredericksburg, Evans Papers, Duke; Everson and Simpson, *"Far, Far from Home,"* 230; McDonald, *Make Me a Map of the Valley*, 141; Silliker, *Rebel Yell & the Yankee Hurrah*, 86.

61. Tyler, *Recollections*, 91.

62. *OR*, 25(2):474; George M. Barnard to Father, May. 20, 1863, Barnard Papers, CWCDJ, MHS; Blight, *When This Cruel War Is Over*, 228, 229; Britton and Reed, *To My Beloved Wife*, 84–97; Carter, *Yorktown to Santiago*, 76; Child, *Fifth New Hampshire*, 177, 193; J. P. Coburn to Folks at Home, May 8, 16, 22, 1863, Camp Sickles, Va., Coburn Papers, USAMHI; Cook, *Twelfth Massachusetts*, 95; Dobbins, *Grandfather's Journal*, 139–43; Douglas, *I Rode with Stonewall*, 229; Fleet and Fuller, *Green Mount*, 230; Dayton E. Flint to Sister, May 10, 1863, Rappahannock, in "Civil War Letters of Dayton E. Flint," CWMC, USAMHI; Flint to Sisters, May 25, 1863, White Oak Church, Va., ibid.; Furst Diary, 37–38, HCWRTC, USAMHI; Galwey, *Valiant Hours*, 86–87; J. E. Green Diary, 5–7, P.C. 694, NCDAH; Haines, *Fifteenth New Jersey*, 69; Hyde, *Following the Greek Cross*, 135; Jones, *Rebel War Clerk's Diary*, 1:340; Jones, *Under the Stars and Bars*, 110; McDonald, *Make Me a Map of the Valley*, 142–46, 148, 149; Mead Diary, vol. 3, May 6–31, 1863, LC; Member of Company C, *Twenty-Seventh Indiana*, 305; Frank Morse to Wife, May 18, 1863, Morse Papers, MHS; Morse to Ellen, Mar. 21, 1863, Fredericksburg, Va., ibid.; Morse to Ellen, May 25, 1863, Fredericksburg, Va., ibid.; Neese, *Three Years in the Confederate Horse Artillery*, 165; Nevins, *Diary of Battle*, 206, 208, 211; John Richardson Porter Diary 2, May 21, 24, 27, 31, June 2, 3, 4, 1863, John Richardson Porter Letter Book and Diaries, 1859–1868, Duke; Quaife, *From the Cannon's Mouth*, 206; Quint, *Second Massachusetts*, 174, 175; Racine, *"Unspoiled Heart,"* 36, 38; Robertson, *Letters of McAllister*, 315–16; Roper, *Repairing the "March of Mars,"* 440, 441, 446, 447, 448, 451, 456; Rosenblatt and Rosenblatt, *Hard Marching Every Day*, 89–90, 93; Stewart, *Pair of Blankets*, 90; Summers, *Borderland Confederate*, 71; Tyler, *Recollections*, 93; White, "Diary of the War," 181, 183; White, *Diary of Wyman S. White*, 150; Chenoweth and Mock, "Hurricane 'Amanda,'" 1735–42; Furgurson, *Chancellorsville*, 343–45; Gates, *Agriculture and the Civil War*, 86; Krick, *Civil War Weather*, 95–96, 97, 98, 99, 101; Lively, *Calamity at Chancellorsville*, 129.

CHAPTER 14

1. Furgurson, *Chancellorsville*, 330–43; Sears, *Chancellorsville*, 431–49; Coddington, *Gettysburg Campaign*, 26–46.

2. Brown, *Retreat from Gettysburg*, 12–17; Coddington, *Gettysburg Campaign*, 3–25, 47–54; Guelzo,

Gettysburg, 32–35, 46–51; Wynstra, *At the Forefront,* 17–18, 19; McDonald, *Make Me a Map of the Valley,* 148, 149; Neese, *Three Years in the Confederate Horse Artillery,* 165; Quint, *Second Massachusetts,* 175; Roper, Repairing the "March of Mars," 456; White, "Diary of the War," 183.

3. Blackford, *War Years,* 213, 214; Haines, *Fifteenth New Jersey,* 69; McDonald, *Make Me a Map of the Valley,* 149; Neese, *Three Years in the Confederate Horse Artillery,* 169; Quint, *Second Massachusetts,* 175; Coddington, *Gettysburg Campaign,* 53–67; Guelzo, *Gettysburg,* 51–57.

4. Coddington, *Gettysburg Campaign,* 66–74, 86–92; Guelzo, *Gettysburg,* 57–66; Wynstra, *At the Forefront,* 19–70.

5. *OR,* 27(1):39; Wynstra, *At the Forefront,* 54.

6. Coddington, *Gettysburg Campaign,* 74–75; Guelzo, *Gettysburg,* 67–68; Krick, *Civil War Weather,* 101; Wynstra, *At the Forefront,* 69–70; Bartlett, *Twelfth New Hampshire,* 115; Britton and Reed, *To My Beloved Wife,* 100–103; Caldwell, *Brigade of South Carolinians,* 131; Child, *Fifth New Hampshire,* 202–3; Dobbins, *Grandfather's Journal,* 144–45; Luther C. Furst Diary, 39, HCWRTC, USAMHI; Galwey, *Valiant Hours,* 90, 91; J. E. Green Diary, 12, P.C. 694, NCDAH; Hamilton, *Papers of Shotwell,* 1:479; Malles, *Bridge Building in Wartime,* 156, 157, 158; Mead Diary, vol. 3, June 18, 1863, LC; Member of Company C, *Twenty-Seventh Indiana,* 355, 356, 357, 358; Neese, *Three Years in the Confederate Horse Artillery,* 181, 182; Nevins, *Diary of Battle,* 222; John Richardson Porter Diary 2, June 17, 19, 1863, John Richardson Porter Letter Book and Diaries, 1859–1868, Duke; Preston, *Tenth New York Cavalry,* 99; Racine, "Unspoiled Heart," 39–40; Rhodes, *All for the Union,* 113; Robertson, *Letters of McAllister,* 323, 324; Roper, Repairing the "March of Mars," 462; Rosenblatt and Rosenblatt, *Hard Marching Every Day,* 104–6; Silliker, *Rebel Yell & the Yankee Hurrah,* 90, 93; Sparks, *Inside Lincoln's Army,* 259, 260, 261; Stewart, *Pair of Blankets,* 91–92; Tyler, *Recollections,* 94; White, "Diary of the War," 192–93; "Distribution Maps of Dominant Soil Orders," accessed Mar. 2, 2017.

7. Sparks, *Inside Lincoln's Army,* 259.

8. Britton and Reed, *To My Beloved Wife,* 102; Bartlett, *Twelfth New Hampshire,* 114. See also de Trobriand, *Four Years in the Army of the Potomac,* 476; Quaife, *From the Cannon's Mouth,* 212.

9. Rosenblatt and Rosenblatt, *Hard Marching Every Day,* 105–6.

10. Silliker, *Rebel Yell & the Yankee Hurrah,* 91, 92. See also *OR,* 27(1):530; and Coddington, *Gettysburg Campaign,* 76–77.

11. *OR,* 27(2):99.

12. Silliker, *Rebel Yell & the Yankee Hurrah,* 92.

13. Robertson, *Letters of McAllister,* 324.

14. Dawes, *Sixth Wisconsin,* 153.

15. Cook, *Twelfth Massachusetts,* 97. See also Blight, *When This Cruel War Is Over,* 236.

16. Nevins, *Diary of Battle,* 221. For drought, see also Bartlett, *Twelfth New Hampshire,* 114; Rosenblatt and Rosenblatt, *Hard Marching Every Day,* 107–8, 109; and Silliker, *Rebel Yell & the Yankee Hurrah,* 90.

17. McDonald, *Make Me a Map of the Valley,* 150.

18. Hamilton, *Papers of Shotwell,* 1:478–79.

19. Hamilton, *Papers of Shotwell,* 1:479. See also Rosenblatt and Rosenblatt, *Hard Marching Every Day,* 107.

20. Dawes, *Sixth Wisconsin,* 155. See also Blackford et al., *Letters from Lee's Army,* 177.

21. Gettysburg, Pa., June 1863, Reel 445, RG 27.5.7, NARA-CP; *OR,* 27(1):304, 27(2):613; Baird, *Journals of Edmonds,* 154; George M. Barnard to Father, June 23, 1863, Aldie, George Middleton Barnard Papers, CWCDJ, MHS; Bartlett, *Twelfth New Hampshire,* 116–18; Blackford et al., *Letters from Lee's Army,* 183; Blight, *When This Cruel War Is Over,* 236, 237; Britton and Reed, *To My Beloved Wife,* 103–6; Caldwell, *Brigade of South Carolinians,* 132; Child, *Fifth New Hampshire,* 203; J. B. Clifton Diary,

1–2, P.C. 589, NCDAH; Cook, *Twelfth Massachusetts*, 98; Dawes, *Sixth Wisconsin*, 156, 157; de Trobri-and, *Four Years in the Army of the Potomac*, 478; Dobbins, *Grandfather's Journal*, 146–47; Everson and Simpson, "*Far, Far from Home*," 248–49; Fremantle, *Three Months in the Southern States*, 221, 223, 235; Furst Diary, 39, HCWRTC, USAMHI; Green Diary, 12, 16, NCDAH; Howard, *Recollections*, 207–8, 209; Lee, *Memoir of Pendleton*, 280; Julius A. Lineback, "The 26th Regimental Band: Being a History of the Military Band Attached to the 26th Regiment, No. Ca. Troops, Pettigrew's Brigade, Heth's Division, Hill's Corps, Army of Northern Virginia. 1862–1865," 110, Julius A. Lineback Papers, SHC-UNC; Malles, *Bridge Building in Wartime*, 168; McDonald, *Make Me a Map of the Valley*, 154–56; Mead Diary, vol. 3, June 20–27, 1863, LC; Member of Company C, *Twenty-Seventh Indiana*, 359, 361; Neese, *Three Years in the Confederate Horse Artillery*, 181, 185; Nevins, *Diary of Battle*, 222, 224, 225; Quaife, *From the Cannon's Mouth*, 223; Quint, *Second Massachusetts*, 177, 178; Porter Diary 2, June 25, 26, 30, 1863, Porter Letter Book and Diaries, Duke; Racine, "*Unspoiled Heart*," 42, 45; Rhodes, *All for the Union*, 113; Robertson, *Letters of McAllister*, 327; Roper, *Repairing the "March of Mars*," 477, 483; Rosenblatt and Rosenblatt, *Hard Marching Every Day*, 107–8, 109; Silliker, *Rebel Yell & the Yankee Hurrah*, 96, 97; Sparks, *Inside Lincoln's Army*, 264, 266; Welch, *Confederate Surgeon's Letters*, 55–56; White, "Diary of the War," 195; White, *Diary of Wyman S. White*, 159; Guelzo, *Gettysburg*, 67–68, 107–8; Krick, *Civil War Weather*, 101; Wynstra, *At the Forefront*, 92, 104–259.

22. Dawes, *Sixth Wisconsin*, 157.

23. Gettysburg, Pa., June 1861, June 1862, June 1863, Reel 445, RG 27.5.7, NARA-CP; Ludlum, *Weather Factor*, 90–91.

24. Alexander, "'Slave Hunt,'" 82–89; Brown, *Retreat from Gettysburg*, 17, 20, 25–36; Coddington, *Gettysburg Campaign*, 79–80, 103–79; Guelzo, *Gettysburg*, 68–85; Krick, *Civil War Weather*, 101; Racine, "*Unspoiled Heart*," 45.

25. Coddington, *Gettysburg Campaign*, 209–41; Guelzo, *Gettysburg*, 85–92, 115–19.

26. *OR*, 27(1):482, 742 (quotation, 482).

27. Brown, *Retreat from Gettysburg*, 20–22, 23, 28, 34; Coddington, *Gettysburg Campaign*, 180–208; Fiege, "Gettysburg," 102; Fiege, *Republic of Nature*, 215; Guelzo, *Gettysburg*, 92–114.

28. Coddington, *Gettysburg Campaign*, 260–384; Guelzo, *Gettysburg*, 119–231; Gettysburg, Pa., July 1863, Reel 445, RG 27.5.7, NARA-CP; Dawes, *Sixth Wisconsin*, 178; McDonald, *Make Me a Map of the Valley*, 157.

29. Gettysburg, Pa., July 1863, Reel 445, RG 27.5.7, NARA-CP.

30. Preston, *Tenth New York Cavalry*, 107. See also Malles, *Bridge Building in Wartime*, 162; McDonald, *Make Me a Map of the Valley*, 157.

31. *OR*, 27(2):391, 393; Oates, *War between the Union and the Confederacy*, 206, 211, 212; Coddington, *Gettysburg Campaign*, 385–469; Guelzo, *Gettysburg*, 235–363.

32. Mead Diary, vol. 4, July 3, 1863, LC; Coddington, *Gettysburg Campaign*, 493–534; Guelzo, *Gettysburg*, 405–30; Gettysburg, Pa., July 1863, Reel 445, RG 27.5.7, NARA-CP; Hess, *Pickett's Charge*, 168; Ludlum, *Weather Factor*, 92; Reardon, *Pickett's Charge*, 18–19; Rollins, *Pickett's Charge*, 215.

33. Ludlum, *Weather Factor*, 91; Dailey, "Climate of Pennsylvania," 331.

34. Tyler, *Recollections*, 109. See also *OR*, 27(1):393, 743; and Mead Diary, vol. 4, July 4, 1863, LC.

35. Brown, *Retreat from Gettysburg*, 42–43, 78–86, 93–94, 108, 117–18, 140, 164–65; Coddington, *Gettysburg Campaign*, 536–41; Guelzo, *Gettysburg*, 450–54; Smith, *Smell of Battle*, 75–83; Wittenberg, Petruzzi, and Nugent, *One Continuous Fight*, 5, 29; Gettysburg, Pa., July 1863, Reel 445, RG 27.5.7, NARA-CP; *OR*, 27(1):225; Caldwell, *Brigade of South Carolinians*, 144; Isaac R. Dunkelbarger Recollections, 16, Michael Winey Collection, USAMHI; Fremantle, *Three Months in the Southern States*, 274, 276; Haines, *Fifteenth New Jersey*, 95; Hamilton, *Papers of Shotwell*, 2:30; Hyde, *Following the Greek Cross*, 159; Lineback, "26th Regimental Band," 125, Lineback Papers, SHC-UNC; McDonald, *Make*

Me a Map of the Valley, 159; Roper, *Repairing the "March of Mars,"* 487; White, "Diary of the War," 210; Fiege, *Republic of Nature,* 220; Daryl Black, email to author, Apr. 17, 2017.

36. Gettysburg, Pa., July 1863, Reel 445, RG 27.5.7, NARA-CP; *OR,* 27(1):225. I use Jacobs's times. But note that in a forthcoming book, Eric Wittenberg suggests that Jacobs's totals may have been too low. See chapter 13 of "Analysis of George Gordon Meade's Command," 20.

37. *OR,* 27(1):801, 27(2):246; George M. Barnard to Father, July 4, 1863, Gettysburg, Barnard Papers, CWCDJ, MHS; Bartlett, *Twelfth New Hampshire,* 136; Caldwell, *Brigade of South Carolinians,* 144; Haines, *Fifteenth New Jersey,* 95; Roper, *Repairing the "March of Mars,"* 487–88; Silliker, *Rebel Yell & the Yankee Hurrah,* 107; Brown, *Retreat from Gettysburg,* 78–79; Guelzo, *Gettysburg,* 435; Wittenberg, Petruzzi, and Nugent, *One Continuous Fight,* 6, 27, 30.

38. Caldwell, *Brigade of South Carolinians,* 144. See also Brown, *Retreat from Gettysburg,* 128.

39. Brown, *Retreat from Gettysburg,* 121–28; Coddington, *Gettysburg Campaign,* 536–37, 539–44, 810n27; Wittenberg, Petruzzi, and Nugent, *One Continuous Fight,* 6, 11; *OR,* 27(2):436.

40. Lineback, "26th Regimental Band," 126, Lineback Papers, SHC-UNC.

41. Neese, *Three Years in the Confederate Horse Artillery,* 190.

42. Clifton Diary, 4, NCDAH; Brown, *Retreat from Gettysburg,* 150–54, 157; Wittenberg, Petruzzi, and Nugent, *One Continuous Fight,* 7, 40–43.

43. Westwood A. Todd Reminiscence, pt. 1, 135, SHC-UNC.

44. Brown, *Retreat from Gettysburg,* 167, 188, 190–92, 212–14, 258–62; Coddington, *Gettysburg Campaign,* 539, 544–50, 556; Guelzo, *Gettysburg,* 434–36, 438; Wittenberg, "Analysis of George Gordon Meade's Command," 30; Wittenberg, Petruzzi, and Nugent, *One Continuous Fight,* 36, 43–47, 50–74, 81–90, 149–50; *OR,* 27(1):79; Bartlett, *Twelfth New Hampshire,* 136–37; Rhodes, *All for the Union,* 117; Tyler, *Recollections,* 110.

45. Neese, *Three Years in the Confederate Horse Artillery,* 191. Wittenberg, Petruzzi, and Nugent, *One Continuous Fight,* discusses in great detail the more than twenty engagements and skirmishes that took place during the retreat.

46. White, "Diary of the War," 211.

47. White, *Diary of Wyman S. White,* 174. See also Gettysburg, Pa., July 1863, Reel 445, RG 27.5.7, NARA-CP; *OR,* 27(2):558; Bartlett, *Military Record of Louisiana,* 194; Child, *Fifth New Hampshire,* 206; Fremantle, *Three Months in the Southern States,* 276, 279, 280; Howard, *Recollections,* 213; Lineback, "26th Regimental Band," 129, Lineback Papers, SHC-UNC; Malles, *Bridge Building in Wartime,* 165; McDonald, *Make Me a Map of the Valley,* 159; Edward Hitchcock McDonald Reminiscences, 88, SHC-UNC; Oates, *War between the Union and the Confederacy,* 239; Brown, *Retreat from Gettysburg,* 160–61, 180, 190; Ludlum, *Weather Factor,* 93; and Wittenberg, Petruzzi, and Nugent, *One Continuous Fight,* 11, 13, 16–20.

48. Lineback, "26th Regimental Band," 128, Lineback Papers, SHC-UNC. See also "Distribution Maps of Dominant Soil Orders," accessed Mar. 2, 2017.

49. Green Diary, 22, NCDAH.

50. Howard, *Recollections,* 213; Lineback, "26th Regimental Band," 129, Lineback Papers, SHC-UNC; Brown, *Retreat from Gettysburg,* 88–92, 162, 167–69, 170, 194–96, 211, 234–55, 280–81; Coddington, *Gettysburg Campaign,* 550–55, 565–66; Wittenberg, Petruzzi, and Nugent, *One Continuous Fight,* 24–26, 92–95, 123–41, 160–62.

51. Blackford et al., *Letters from Lee's Army,* 189; Clifton Diary, 5, NCDAH; Longstreet, *From Manassas to Appomattox,* 428; McDonald, *Make Me a Map of the Valley,* 159; Brown, *Retreat from Gettysburg,* 42, 284–85, 297.

52. Ludlum, *Weather Factor,* 93.

53. Hamilton, *Papers of Shotwell,* 2:34.

54. Gettysburg, Pa., July 1863, Reel 445, RG 27.5.7, NARA-CP; Howard, *Recollections*, 215; Lineback, "26th Regimental Band," 131, Lineback Papers, SHC-UNC; McDonald, *Make Me a Map of the Valley*, 159–60; Mead Diary, vol. 4, July 8, 1863, LC; Neese, *Three Years in the Confederate Horse Artillery*, 196, 198; Hamilton, *Papers of Shotwell*, 2:36–37; Brown, *Retreat from Gettysburg*, 287, 293–95, 309–12; Coddington, *Gettysburg Campaign*, 565–66; Guelzo, *Gettysburg*, 436–37; Wittenberg, Petruzzi, and Nugent, *One Continuous Fight*, 188, 207, 240.

55. Wittenberg, Petruzzi, and Nugent, *One Continuous Fight*, 151.

56. Brown, *Retreat from Gettysburg*, 266; Coddington, *Gettysburg Campaign*, 555–56; Wittenberg, Petruzzi, and Nugent, *One Continuous Fight*, 143–52, 164; OR, 27(1):736, 27(2):243; Blight, *When This Cruel War Is Over*, 242; Britton and Reed, *To My Beloved Wife*, 107; Dawes, *Sixth Wisconsin*, 185; Haines, *Fifteenth New Jersey*, 99; Malles, *Bridge Building in Wartime*, 165; Mead Diary, vol. 4, July 7, 1863, LC; Preston, *Tenth New York Cavalry*, 130; Silliker, *Rebel Yell & the Yankee Hurrah*, 109; Sparks, *Inside Lincoln's Army*, 269; "Distribution Maps of Dominant Soil Orders," accessed Mar. 2, 2017.

57. Silliker, *Rebel Yell & the Yankee Hurrah*, 109–10.

58. George Breck to Ellen, July 8, 1863, Middleton, Md., Battery L, 1st New York Light Artillery, Vertical Files, Gettysburg National Military Park Library, Gettysburg, Pa.

59. Brown, *Retreat from Gettysburg*, 288–90; Coddington, *Gettysburg Campaign*, 556–65; Guelzo, *Gettysburg*, 437–38; Ludlum, *Weather Factor*, 93; Wittenberg, Petruzzi, and Nugent, *One Continuous Fight*, 169–78, 188–97, 201, 206–34, 238–39, 242, 245–46; OR, 27(1):296, 27(3):652; Bartlett, *Military Record of Louisiana*, 137; Britton and Reed, *To My Beloved Wife*, 108; Child, *Fifth New Hampshire*, 209; Dawes, *Sixth Wisconsin*, 185; Furst Diary, 42, HCWRTC, USAMHI; Haines, *Fifteenth New Jersey*, 99; Malles, *Bridge Building in Wartime*, 165; Nevins, *Diary of Battle*, 259; Preston, *Tenth New York Cavalry*, 130; Racine, "Unspoiled Heart," 53; Sparks, *Inside Lincoln's Army*, 269; White, *Diary of Wyman S. White*, 175.

60. Gettysburg, Pa., July 1863, Reel 445, RG 27.5.7, NARA-CP; OR, 27(1):214, 27(2):243, 27(3):657; Blight, *When This Cruel War Is Over*, 244; Britton and Reed, *To My Beloved Wife*, 117; Child, *Fifth New Hampshire*, 209; de Trobriand, *Four Years in the Army of the Potomac*, 520–21; Galwey, *Valiant Hours*, 125; McDonald, *Make Me a Map of the Valley*, 160; Mead Diary, vol. 4, July 12–13, 1863, LC; Silliker, *Rebel Yell & the Yankee Hurrah*, 111; Howard M. Smith Diary and Letters, 80, MMC, LC; Brown, *Retreat from Gettysburg*, 319, 326–28; Coddington, *Gettysburg Campaign*, 569–70; Guelzo, *Gettysburg*, 439–40; Wittenberg, Petruzzi, and Nugent, *One Continuous Fight*, 248, 252–53, 258–60, 262.

61. Nevins, *Diary of Battle*, 264.

62. Moore, *Story of a Cannoneer*, 200. See also Guelzo, *Gettysburg*, 438–39; and Wittenberg, Petruzzi, and Nugent, *One Continuous Fight*, 264–65.

63. Gettysburg, Pa., July 1863, Reel 445, RG 27.5.7, NARA-CP; OR, 27(2):310, 323, 558, 640; Blackford et al., *Letters from Lee's Army*, 192; Caldwell, *Brigade of South Carolinians*, 148–49; Child, *Fifth New Hampshire*, 209; Galwey, *Valiant Hours*, 127; Lasswell, *Rags and Hope*, 189; Lee, *Memoir of Pendleton*, 295–96; Lee, *Recollections and Letters*, 101; Lineback, "26th Regimental Band," 133–35, Lineback Papers, SHC-UNC; Longstreet, *From Manassas to Appomattox*, 429; McDonald Reminiscences, 89; SHC-UNC; Neese, *Three Years in the Confederate Horse Artillery*, 198; *Shoemaker's Battery*, 49; Smith Diary and Letters, 80, MMC, LC; Stewart, *Pair of Blankets*, 113; White, "Diary of the War," 215; Brown, *Retreat from Gettysburg*, 321–23–25, 328–43; Guelzo, *Gettysburg*, 438–39; Wittenberg, Petruzzi, and Nugent, *One Continuous Fight*, 242, 271–79.

64. Lasswell, *Rags and Hope*, 189.

65. Longstreet, *From Manassas to Appomattox*, 429–30. See also OR, 27(2):361.

66. Brown, *Retreat from Gettysburg*, 343–52; Coddington, *Gettysburg Campaign*, 569–72; Krick, *Civil War Weather*, 104; Guelzo, *Gettysburg*, 440; Wittenberg, Petruzzi, and Nugent, *One Continuous*

Fight, 282–95; *OR*, 27(1):991; Gettysburg, Pa., July 1863, Reel 445, RG 27.5.7, NARA-CP; Clifton Diary, 6, NCDAH; Smith Diary and Letters, 81–82, MMC, LC; Sparks, *Inside Lincoln's Army*, 272; "Diaries of John Waldrop . . . and William Y. Mordecai," 47.

67. New York City, July 1863, Reel 360, RG 27.5.7, NARA-CP; Brown, *Retreat from Gettysburg*, 356–83, 388–89; Cook's *Armies of the Streets*, 62–63, 67, 93–94, 97; Wittenberg, Petruzzi, and Nugent, *One Continuous Fight*, 299–302; 322–24, 345–48.

68. Krick, *Civil War Weather*, 102, 104; Bartlett, *Twelfth New Hampshire*, 140; Blackford et al., *Letters from Lee's Army*, 194, 197; Britton and Reed, *To My Beloved Wife*, 113; Child, *Fifth New Hampshire*, 209–10, 233–34; Clifton Diary, 8, NCDAH; Cook, *Twelfth Massachusetts*, 108; Furst Diary, 44, HCWRTC, USAMHI; Galwey, *Valiant Hours*, 128, 129; Green Diary, 31–33, NCDAH; Howard, *Recollections*, 220; Lineback, "26th Regimental Band," 137, 138, Lineback Papers, SHC-UNC; McDonald, *Make Me a Map of the Valley*, 162–63; Mead Diary, vol. 4, July18–30, 1863, LC; Frank Morse to Ellen, July 21, 1863, Frank C. Morse Papers, MHS; Nevins, *Diary of Battle*, 264; Norton, *Army Letters*, 166; Preston, *Tenth New York Cavalry*, 136, 138; Quaife, *From the Cannon's Mouth*, 231, 237–38, 241, 243, 245; Racine, "Unspoiled Heart," 57; Mat Richards to Annie, Aug. 30, 1863, M. Edgar Richards Correspondence, Box 97, CWMC, USAMHI; *Shoemaker's Battery*, 50; Smith Diary and Letters, 80–81, MMC, LC; Sparks, *Inside Lincoln's Army*, 273; "Diaries of John Waldrop . . . and William Y. Mordecai," 48; Warfield, *Confederate Soldier's Memoirs*, 152; White, *Diary of Wyman S. White*, 184.

69. *Working Farmer & United States Journal*, Sept. 1, 1863.

70. *American Agriculturalist*, Sept. 1, 1863.

71. Gates, *Agriculture and the Civil War*, 86.

72. Hurt, *Agriculture and the Confederacy*, 132–39, 143–62.

73. Jones, *Rebel War Clerk's Diary*, 1:390, 2:4, 9. See also Fleet and Fuller, *Green Mount*, 254.

74. Alexandria, Va., July, Aug. 1863, Reel 518, RG 27.5.7, NARA-CP; Blight, *When This Cruel War Is Over*, 252, Clifton Diary, 9–10, NCDAH; Dobbins, *Grandfather's Journal*, 155–57; McDonald, *Make Me a Map of the Valley*, 164–73; R. W. Waldrop to Father, Aug. 11, 1863, Orange Court House, Waldrop Papers, SHC-UNC; Everson and Simpson, "Far, Far from Home," 268, 273; Furst Diary, 44–46, HCWRTC, USAMHI; Green Diary, 36–39, NCDAH; Howard, *Recollections*, 221, 222; Dayton E. Flint to Sister, Aug. 16, 1863, "Civil War Letters of Dayton E. Flint," Box 40, CWMC, USAMHI; Malles, *Bridge Building in Wartime*, 175; Mead Diary, vol. 4, Aug. 1–30, 1863, LC; Nevins, *Diary of Battle*, 271, 273, 276; Norton, *Army Letters*, 173, 174, 179; William H. Peacock to Sarah, Aug. 20, 1863, Beverly Ford, Va., William H. Peacock Correspondence, Box 89, CWMC, USAMHI; Quaife, *From the Cannon's Mouth*, 248, 252; Rosenblatt and Rosenblatt, *Hard Marching Every Day*, 125, 130, 132; Sparks, *Inside Lincoln's Army*, 284; Stewart, *Pair of Blankets*, 118; Worsham, *One of Jackson's Foot Cavalry*, 110–11; Sutherland, *Seasons of War*, 268–69. Robert Krick draws readings from Alexandria, as Mackee's records for the month are missing. See *Civil War Weather*, 2, 106, 173n51, 173n57. The storms occurred on August 4, 6, 7, 15, and 16. Toward the end of the month, a thunderstorm struck on August 24, followed by rain on August 25 and 29.

75. Cook, *Twelfth Massachusetts*, 108; Stewart, *Pair of Blankets*, 118. See also Howard, *Recollections*, 221.

76. Caldwell, *Brigade of South Carolinians*, 158.

77. Dawes, *Sixth Wisconsin*, 193, 195; White, "Diary of the War," 220; White, *Diary of Wyman S. White*, 185; Worsham, *One of Jackson's Foot Cavalry*, 110–11.

78. Dobbins, *Grandfather's Journal*, 155.

79. Blight, *When This Cruel War Is Over*, 252; Dawes, *Sixth Wisconsin*, 195.

80. Worsham, *One of Jackson's Foot Cavalry*, 110.

81. R. W. Waldrop to Father, Aug. 11, 1863, Orange Court House, Waldrop Papers, SHC-UNC. See also Rosenblatt and Rosenblatt, *Hard Marching Every Day*, 130.

82. William Hamilton to Boyd Hamilton, Aug. 11, 1863, quoted in Sutherland, *Seasons of War*, 273. The assertion that Civil War soldiers were too modest to even fully unbutton their jackets, fostered by generations of reenactors, clearly needs reevaluation.

83. See, for example, Coddington, *Gettysburg Campaign*, 572–77; Fiege, "Gettysburg," 104; Fiege, *Republic of Nature*, 223; Guelzo, *Gettysburg*, 461–65; Wittenberg, Petruzzi, and Nugent, *One Continuous Fight*, 329–44; and *OR*, 27(2):247, 249, 256, 261.

84. Lee, *Memoir of Pendleton*, 297. See also Wittenberg, Petruzzi, and Nugent, *One Continuous Fight*, 296.

CHAPTER 15

1. Grant, *Memoirs*, 1:380–82, 384–85, 388; Jones, *Artilleryman's Diary*, 42; Ballard, *Vicksburg*, 192–95; Grabau, *Ninety-Eight Days*, 60–66, 82–83; Shea and Winschel, *Vicksburg Is the Key*, 90–91, 95–96; Simpson, *Grant*, 171; Maynard, "Vicksburg Diary," 40.

2. Shea and Winschel, *Vicksburg Is the Key*, 91.

3. Jones, *Artilleryman's Diary*, 42. See also Maynard, "Vicksburg Diary," 40; Edward E. Schweitzer Diary, 1:34, Edward E. Schweitzer Diaries and Correspondence, Box 23, CWTI, USAMHI; and Ballard, *Vicksburg*, 194.

4. Ballard, *Vicksburg*, 194–98; Grabau, *Ninety-Eight Days*, 62–66; Shea and Winschel, *Vicksburg Is the Key*, 91–92; *OR*, 24(1):75; *Augusta (Ga.) Chronicle*, Apr. 8, 1863; Clark, *Downing's Civil War Diary*, 107–10; Eddington, "Civil War Memoirs," accessed Oct. 21, 2016; Grant, *Memoirs*, 1:382, 384, 388–89, 392–93; Jones, *Artilleryman's Diary*, 43–46; Maynard, "Vicksburg Diary," 41–43; Schweitzer Diary, 1:35, Schweitzer Diaries and Correspondence, CWTI, USAMHI.

5. Eddington, "Civil War Memoirs," accessed Oct. 21, 2016. See also *OR*, 24(1):33.

6. Ballard, *Vicksburg*, 198–203, Grabau, *Ninety-Eight Days*, 74–77, 86; Shea and Winschel, *Vicksburg Is the Key*, 95–101, 187; Logbook, USS *Benton*, Apr. 21–22, 1863, RG 24.2.2, NARA; Grant, *Memoirs*, 1:386–87, 392–93; Maynard, "Vicksburg Diary," 44; Wilkie, *Pen and Powder*, 313.

7. *OR*, 24(1):80, 127, 24(3):211; Logbook, USS *Benton*, Apr. 13–17, 1863, RG 24.2.2, NARA; Anderson, *Memoirs*, 290; Grant, *Memoirs*, 1:394–95; Jones, *Artilleryman's Diary*, 48–49; Maynard, "Vicksburg Diary," 43, 44; Ballard, *Vicksburg*, 203–13, 214–16; Grabau, *Ninety-Eight Days*, 81–88; Shea and Winschel, *Vicksburg Is the Key*, 91–93, 94–95, 101–2.

8. *OR*, 24(1):80–81, 642, 717, 721, 762, 769, 775; Logbook, USS *Benton*, Apr. 22–27, 1863, RG 24.2.2, NARA; Jones, *Artilleryman's Diary*, 49–50; Grant, *Memoirs*, 1:394–95; Clark, *Downing's Civil War Diary*, 111; Maynard, "Vicksburg Diary," 44; Schweitzer Diary, 1:35–36, Schweitzer Diaries and Correspondence, CWTI, USAMHI; Ballard, *Vicksburg*, 213–17; Grabau, *Ninety-Eight Days*, 88–98.

9. Jones, *Artilleryman's Diary*, 49, 50. See also Logbook, USS *Benton*, Apr. 28, 1863, RG 24.2.2, NARA; and Maynard, "Vicksburg Diary," 45.

10. *OR*, 24(1):634, 24(2):243; Grant, *Memoirs*, 1:394–401; Jones, *Artilleryman's Diary*, 51; Logbook, USS *Benton*, Apr. 29, 1863, RG 24.2.2, NARA; Maynard, "Vicksburg Diary," 45; Ballard, *Vicksburg*, 211–13, 217–21; Grabau, *Ninety-Eight Days*, 104–49; Simpson, *Grant*, 191; Shea and Winschel, *Vicksburg Is the Key*, 93, 101–9.

11. Brady, *War upon the Land*, 53.

12. Grabau, *Ninety-Eight Days*, 148–49.

13. Grant, *Memoirs*, 1:400–401.

14. *OR*, 24(1):593; Grant, *Memoirs*, 1:401–12; Osborn, "Tennessean at the Siege of Vicksburg," 354 (hereafter Osborn, "Tennessean at Vicksburg"); Ballard, *Vicksburg*, 224–50; Grabau, *Ninety-Eight Days*, 154–78. 195–200, 267–68; Shea and Winschel, *Vicksburg Is the Key*, 106–19, 187.

15. Ballard, *Vicksburg*, 250–71; Grabau, *Ninety-Eight Days*, 179–84, 200–22; Shea and Winschel,

Vicksburg Is the Key, 119–21, 127–28; *OR*, 24(1):85, 707; Clark, *Downing's Civil War Diary*, 112–14, Jones, *Artilleryman's Diary*, 54; Oldroyd, *Soldier's Story*, 8; Schweitzer Diary, 1:37, Schweitzer Diaries and Correspondence, CWTI, USAMHI.

16. Ballard, *Vicksburg*, 271–75; Grabau, *Ninety-Eight Days*, 222–38 (quotation, 229); Shea and Winschel, *Vicksburg Is the Key*, 121–24; Jones, *Artilleryman's Diary*, 55–56; Maynard, "Vicksburg Diary," 46. Similar inversion layers today are often responsible for smoggy days in cities.

17. *OR*, 24(1):50, 638, 24(2):125, 314; Eddington, "Civil War Memoirs," accessed Oct. 21, 2016; Fremantle, *Three Months in the Southern States*, 99; Grant, *Memoirs*, 1:417–23; Jones, *Artilleryman's Diary*, 56, 56; Maynard, "Vicksburg Diary," 46; Oldroyd, *Soldier's Story*, 20–21; William A. Ruyle Letter, 30, SHSM-R; Ballard, *Vicksburg*, 275–81; Grabau, *Ninety-Eight Days*, 239–50; Shea and Winschel, *Vicksburg Is the Key*, 125–26.

18. Oldroyd, *Soldier's Story*, 20.

19. Grabau, *Ninety-Eight Days*, 250–68; Shea and Winschel, *Vicksburg Is the Key*, 125–26; "Distribution Maps of Dominant Soil Orders," accessed May 1, 2017; NRCS Soils.

20. *OR*, 24(1):262, 596, 24(2):63, 64; Clark, *Downing's Civil War Diary*, 115; Grant, *Memoirs*, 1:424–36; Ruyle Letter, 30–32, SHSM-R; Schweitzer Diary, 1:39, Schweitzer Diaries and Correspondence, CWTI, USAMHI; Ballard, *Vicksburg*, 282–310; Grabau, *Ninety-Eight Days*, 257–313; Shea and Winschel, *Vicksburg Is the Key*, 127–37; Smith, *Champion Hill*, esp. 109–329.

21. *OR*, 24(1):731, 24(2):387; Grant, *Memoirs*, 1:440–44; Maynard, "Vicksburg Diary," 47; [Miller], "Woman's Diary," 770–71; Ballard, *Vicksburg*, 312–32; Grabau, *Ninety-Eight Days*, 319–20, 326–34, 340–70; McPherson, *Battle Cry of Freedom*, 631; Shea and Winschel, *Vicksburg Is the Key*, 138–47.

22. *OR*, 24(1):276–77; Grant, *Memoirs*, 1:444–45; Ballard, *Vicksburg*, 332–51; Grabau, *Ninety-Eight Days*, 370—82; Shea and Winschel, *Vicksburg Is the Key*, 147–52; Simpson, *Grant*, 203; Smith, *Smell of Battle*, 83; Jones, *Artilleryman's Diary*, 62–63; Maynard, "Vicksburg Diary," 48; Oldroyd, *Soldier's Story*, 32–37; Schweitzer Diary, 1:40, Schweitzer Diaries and Correspondence, CWTI, USAMHI.

23. Ballard, *Vicksburg*, 360–84; Grabau, *Ninety-Eight Days*, 408–46; Hess, *Civil War in the West*, 152–54; Shea and Winschel, *Vicksburg Is the Key*, 153–60; Grant, *Memoirs*, 1:446–64.

24. Ballard, *Vicksburg*, 384–88, 390–92; Shea and Winschel, *Vicksburg Is the Key*, 161–62; Smith, *Smell of Battle*, 86–112; [Loughborough], *Cave Life in Vicksburg*, 55–143; [Miller], "Woman's Diary," 767–75.

25. Hewitt, *Port Hudson*, 1–5, 122–72; Shea and Winschel, *Vicksburg Is the Key*, 187–98; *OR*, 26(1):111; "Fortification and Siege of Port Hudson," 323; Irwin, *Nineteenth Army Corps*, 169.

26. Osborn, "Tennessean at Vicksburg," 360.

27. Grabau, *Ninety-Eight Days*, 443.

28. Jones, *Artilleryman's Diary*, 65; Schweitzer Diary, 1:41, Schweitzer Diaries and Correspondence, CWTI, USAMHI; Oldroyd, *Soldier's Story*, 39.

29. Logbook, USS *Black Hawk*, May 30, 1863, RG 24.2.2, NARA.

30. Osborn, "Tennessean at Vicksburg," 362.

31. Osborn, "Tennessean at Vicksburg," 360. See also *OR*, 24(1):90; Charles Henry Snedeker Diary, May 26–29, 1863, RG 844, AU; and Sanders, "Climate of Mississippi," 221, 222.

32. Schweitzer Diary, 1:41, Schweitzer Diaries and Correspondence, CWTI, USAMHI. See also Logbook, USS *Black Hawk*, May 26–29, 1863, RG 24.2.2, NARA; and Jones, *Artilleryman's Diary*, 65. Osborn Oldroyd describes evening rain on May 30, but no other source mentions this. *Soldier's Story*, 39.

33. Maynard, "Vicksburg Diary," 49.

34. Grabau, *Ninety-Eight Days*, 442–44; W. A. Rorer to unknown, June 13, 1863, Madison County, Miss., James M. Willcox Papers, 1831–1871, Duke. See also Privette, "If the Water Were Good."

35. [Miller], "Woman's Diary," 772.

36. Grabau, *Ninety-Eight Days*, 445–46; Privette, "If the Water Were Good."

37. Osborn, "Tennessean at Vicksburg," 362.

38. Jones, *Artilleryman's Diary*, 66. See also Snedeker Diary, June 1–14, 1863, AU.

39. Osborn, "Tennessean at Vicksburg," 362.

40. Jones, *Artilleryman's Diary*, 67. See also Logbook, USS *Black Hawk*, June 1–3, 1863, RG 24.2.2, NARA; and Schweitzer Diary, 1:41, Schweitzer Diaries and Correspondence, CWTI, USAMHI.

41. Osborn, "Tennessean at Vicksburg," 363.

42. Jones, *Artilleryman's Diary*, 67. See also Logbook, USS *Black Hawk*, June 6–9, 1863, RG 24.2.2, NARA; *Richmond Whig*, June 9, 1863; *Civil War Diary of Bush*, 23; Maynard, "Vicksburg Diary," 49–50; Oldroyd, *Soldier's Story*, 44; and Schweitzer Diary, 1:41–42, Schweitzer Diaries and Correspondence, CWTI, USAMHI.

43. Osborn, "Tennessean at Vicksburg," 364, 365. See also Simpson, *Grant*, 206.

44. Ballard, *Vicksburg*, 391; Barnickel, *Milliken's Bend*, esp. xi–xv, 83–148; Grabau, *Ninety-Eight Days*, 383–412; Shea and Winschel, *Vicksburg Is the Key*, 162–65; Logbook, USS *Choctaw*, June 6–7, 1863, RG 24.2.2, NARA.

45. Osborn, "Tennessean at Vicksburg," 364, 365.

46. OR, 24(2):183, 185, 408, 693–94; Logbook, USS *Black Hawk*, June 10, 1863, RG 24.2.2, NARA; Logbook, USS *Choctaw*, June 10, 1863, ibid.; *Civil War Diary of Bush*, 16; Clark, *Downing's Civil War Diary*, 121; Maynard, "Vicksburg Diary," 50; Osborn, "Tennessean at Vicksburg," 366; Schweitzer Diary, 1:42, Schweitzer Diaries and Correspondence, CWTI, USAMHI; Snedeker Diary, June 10, 1863, AU; [Willet], *Company B*, 37.

47. Jones, *Artilleryman's Diary*, 69.

48. Jones, *Artilleryman's Diary*, 69. See also Logbook, USS *Choctaw*, June 11, 1863, RG 24.2.2, NARA.

49. Osborn, "Tennessean at Vicksburg," 366. See also Logbook, USS *Black Hawk*, June 11, 1863, RG 24.2.2, NARA; and Ballard, *Vicksburg*, 394–95.

50. Privette, "If the Water Were Good." Noting that off-duty Federals could escape to higher ground and shade, Privette suspects that the situation among Confederates was worse.

51. Barney, *Recollections*, 169–90 (quotation, 190).

52. OR, 24(1):101; Logbook, USS *Black Hawk*, June 12–18, 1863, RG 24.2.2, NARA; *Civil War Diary of Bush*, 16; Clark, *Downing's Civil War Diary*, 122; Grant, *Memoirs*, 1:457; Maynard, "Vicksburg Diary," 50; Oldroyd, *Soldier's Story*, 54–55; Schweitzer Diary, 1:42, Schweitzer Diaries and Correspondence, CWTI, USAMH; Snedeker Diary, June 11–15, 1863, AU; [Willet], *Company B*, 37. It was at this juncture that Grant finally fired McClernand.

53. Osborn, "Tennessean at Vicksburg," 367.

54. Oldroyd, *Soldier's Story*, 56.

55. OR, 24(1):104; Logbook, USS *Black Hawk*, June 19–21, 1863, RG 24.2.2, NARA; Clark, *Downing's Civil War Diary*, 123; Jones, *Artilleryman's Diary*, 71, 72; Maynard, "Vicksburg Diary," 50, 51; Osborn, "Tennessean at Vicksburg," 367–68; Tilley, *Federals on the Frontier*, 168.

56. OR, 24(2):291; Logbook, USS *Black Hawk*, June 23–25, 1863, RG 24.2.2, NARA; *Civil War Diary of Bush*, 16; Jones, *Artilleryman's Diary*, 72; Maynard, "Vicksburg Diary," 51; Schweitzer Diary, 1:43, Schweitzer Diaries and Correspondence, CWTI, USAMH; Snedeker Diary, June 24, 1863, AU; Tilley, *Federals on the Frontier*, 170; Smith, *Smell of Battle*, 95.

57. Oldroyd, *Soldier's Story*, 64.

58. Schweitzer Diary, 1:43, Schweitzer Diaries and Correspondence, CWTI, USAMH. See also Logbook, USS *Black Hawk*, June 26, 1863, RG 24.2.2, NARA.

59. Schweitzer Diary, 1:43, Schweitzer Diaries and Correspondence, CWTI, USAMH.

60. Kirwan, *Johnny Green*, 79–80. See also Ballard, *Vicksburg*, 404–5; Grabau, *Ninety-Eight Days*, 472–76; and *Civil War Diary of Bush*, 17.

61. *OR*, 24(1):114.

62. Ballard, *Vicksburg*, 397–403; Grabau, *Ninety-Eight Days*, 492–93, 502–3; Shea and Winschel, *Vicksburg Is the Key*, 170–78; *OR*, 24(1):112, 281–83, 24(2):190, 192; Grant, *Memoirs*, 1:462–71, 476–77; Logbook, USS *Black Hawk*, July 1–3, 1863, RG 24.2.2, NARA; Kirwan, *Johnny Green*, 79–80; [Loughborough], *Cave Life in Vicksburg*, 137; Schweitzer Diary, 2:1, Schweitzer Diaries and Correspondence, CWTI, USAMH.

63. Ballard, *Vicksburg*, 398–403; Grabau, *Ninety-Eight Days*, 492–503; Phillips, *Diehard Rebels*, 118–21; Shea and Winschel, *Vicksburg Is the Key*, 177–79; Grant, *Memoirs*, 1:472–75; Logbook, USS *Black Hawk*, July 4, 1863, RG 24.2.2, NARA.

64. Grabau, *Ninety-Eight Days*, 477–91; Shea and Winschel, *Vicksburg Is the Key*, 165–67.

65. *OR*, 24(2):521, 534, 560, 590, 594, 599, 602, 609, 634, 24(3):475, 482; *Civil War Diary of Bush*, 17–19; Eddington, "Civil War Memoirs," accessed Oct. 21, 2016; French, *Two Wars*, 182; Kirwan, *Johnny Green*, 80; Maynard, "Vicksburg Diary," 52; Osborn, "Tennessean at Vicksburg," 373; Schweitzer Diary, 2:1–4, Schweitzer Diaries and Correspondence, CWTI, USAMH; Ballard, *Vicksburg*, 404–10; Grabau, *Ninety-Eight Days*, 505–6; Privette, "If the Water Were Good"; Shea and Winschel, *Vicksburg Is the Key*, 179–85.

66. *OR*, 24(2):528, 532, 24(3):529. See also *OR*, 24(3):482, 522, 531, 539; and *Richmond Whig*, July 10, 1863.

67. *OR*, 24(2):537, 557, 571, 576, 587, 613, 623, 634, 637, 24(3):522, 536; Barney, *Recollections*, 215; Clark, *Downing's Civil War Diary*, 128–32; Kirwan, *Johnny Green*, 82–84; Shea and Winschel, *Vicksburg Is the Key*, 185–86.

68. *OR*, 24(3):543.

69. *OR*, 24(3):529; Clark, *Downing's Civil War Diary*, 127–28; Bruce Hoadley to Cousin Em, July 30, 1863, Black River Bridge, Robert Bruce Hoadley Papers, 1861–1866, Duke; Jones, *Artilleryman's Diary*, 79–83; Maynard, "Vicksburg Diary," 52; Ruyle Letter, 33, SHSM-R; Tilley ed., *Federals on the Frontier*, 183, 186, 194; Grabau, *Ninety-Eight Days*, 503–4.

70. Clark, *One Hundred and Sixteenth Regiment of New York State Volunteers*, 113 (hereafter Clark, *116th New York*).

71. Johns, *Forty-Ninth Massachusetts*, 288–89. See also *OR*, 26(1):128, 140.

72. H. F. Morse to Sis, June 12, 18, 22, 1863, Port Hudson, La., Frank C. Morse Papers, MHS. See also Hewitt, *Port Hudson*, 168–79; Shea and Winschel, *Vicksburg Is the Key*, 198–204; Carter, "Fourth Wisconsin," 84–87; "Fortification and Siege of Port Hudson," 329, 333, 334–35, 341; Irwin, *Nineteenth Army Corps*, 196–97, 210, 217–18; Johns, *Forty-Ninth Massachusetts*, 323; and Stevens, *Fiftieth Regiment of Infantry Massachusetts Volunteer Militia*, 151, 162, 191.

73. Basler, *Collected Works of Abraham Lincoln*, 6:409.

CHAPTER 16

1. Hess, *Knoxville Campaign*, 5; Cozzens, *This Terrible Sound*, 14, 15–17.

2. Connelly, *Autumn of Glory*, 112–26; Cozzens, *This Terrible Sound*, 17–18; Hess, *Braxton Bragg*, 113–38, 144–45.

3. Cist, *Army of the Cumberland*, 155–57; Bradley, *Tullahoma*, 52–53; Cozzens, *This Terrible Sound*, 17.

4. Clarksville, Tenn., May 1862, May 1863, Reel 478, RG 27.5.7, NARA-CP; Bircher, *Drummer-Boy's*

Diary, 63–65; Cope, *Fifteenth Ohio*, 277; DeRosier, *Through the South*, 70; Fremantle, *Three Months in the Southern States*, 144, 147; Morris, *Eighty-First Indiana*, 46. Bircher remembered receiving shelter halves in early May, adding credence to Rosecrans's frequent complaints that his army received short shrift from the War Department.

5. Beatty, *Citizen-Soldier*, 271.

6. Clarksville, Tenn., June 1863, Reel 478, RG 27.5.7, NARA-CP; US Environmental Protection Agency, "Summary Table: Characteristics of Ecoregions of Tennessee," accessed Aug. 16, 2017; Fremantle, *Three Months in the Southern States*, 155. See also Chenoweth and Mock, "Hurricane 'Amanda,'" 1735–42. It did not rain on June 4, 6, and 8.

7. DeRosier, *Through the South*, 74.

8. Clarksville, Tenn., June, July 1863, Reel 478, RG 27.5.7, NARA-CP; Bishop, *Story of a Regiment*, 88; J. C. Donahower, "Narrative of the Civil War," 2:75, Jeremiah Chester Donahower Papers, 1853–1919, M561, MnHS; Bradley, *Tullahoma*, 51–53, 94; Cozzens, *This Terrible Sound*, 18; Dickson, "Climate of Tennessee," 371. Michael Bradley describes it as a once-in-five-hundred-years rain event. Meteorologist Josh Johnson cautions that official records for Tullahoma only go back to 1893, making it impossible to know how rare the rain event actually was. Those records, however, do confirm that it was greatly out of the ordinary. Record monthly rainfalls since 1893 are 5.68 inches in June 1999 and 8.25 inches in July 1936. Johnson, email to author, Aug. 5, 2019.

9. Clarksville, Tenn., June 1863, Reel 478, RG 27.5.7, NARA-CP; US Environmental Protection Agency, "Summary Table: Characteristics of Ecoregions of Tennessee," accessed Aug. 16, 2017; *OR*, 23(1):442, 475, 498, 523, 529, 530, 567, 588, 602, 603, 611, 613; Beatty, *Citizen-Soldier*, 285; Bennett and Haigh, *Thirty-Sixth Illinois*, 436–37; Bishop, *Story of a Regiment*, 88; Cope, *Fifteenth Ohio*, 286; Dodge, *Waif of the War*, 81; Donahower, "Narrative of the Civil War," 2:75, Donahower Papers, MnHS; Hinman, *Sherman Brigade*, 391–92; Horrall, *Forty-Second Indiana*, 186; Keil, *Thirty-Fifth Ohio*, 114; Marshall, *Civil War Diary*, 26; Morris, *Eighty-First Indiana*, 48; Owens, *Greene County*, 40; Scribner, *How Soldiers Were Made*, 122; Williams et al., *Seventy-Third Indiana*, 166, 174; W. E. Preston (Mathews), "The 33rd Alabama Regiment in the Civil War," ed. L. B. Williams, 39, ADAH; Bradley, *Tullahoma*, 53–67, 71–73; Connelly, *Autumn of Glory*, 126–27; Cozzens, *This Terrible Sound*, 14–15, 18–19.

10. Tourgée, *Story of a Thousand*, 201, 203.

11. *OR*, 23(1):481, 524, 567; Cist, *Army of the Cumberland*, 158; Bradley, *Tullahoma*, 67–75; Connelly, *Autumn of Glory*, 127–29; Cozzens, *This Terrible Sound*, 18–19.

12. Clarksville, Tenn., June 1863, Reel 478, RG 27.5.7, NARA-CP; *OR*, 23(1):406, 499, 500, 501, 504, 590, 597; Beatty, *Citizen-Soldier*, 286; Bircher, *Drummer-Boy's Diary*, 65; Cist, *Army of the Cumberland*, 161; Cope, *Fifteenth Ohio*, 286, 293; Hazen, *Narrative*, 99; Hight and Stormont, *Fifty-Eighth Indiana*, 147, 148; Hinman, *Sherman Brigade*, 392; Owens, *Greene County*, 51; Williams et al., *Seventy-Third Indiana*, 166; Simmons, *84th Ill.*, 58–59; Preston (Mathews), "33rd Alabama," 39, ADAH; Bradley, *Tullahoma*, 75.

13. Bennett and Haigh, *Thirty-Sixth Illinois*, 437.

14. Bradley, *Tullahoma*, 80–81; Connelly, *Autumn of Glory*, 128–29; Clarksville, Tenn., June 1863, Reel 478, RG 27.5.7, NARA-CP; *OR*, 23(1):540, 591; Bennett and Haigh, *Thirty-Sixth Illinois*, 437; Cist, *Army of the Cumberland*, 164; Cope, *Fifteenth Ohio*, 294; Morris, *Eighty-First Indiana*, 50; Hinman, *Sherman Brigade*, 394; Marcoot, *Five Years in the Sunny South*, 30; Williams et al., *Seventy-Third Indiana*, 166–67; Simmons, *84th Ill.*, 59; Stormont, *Fifty-Eighth Indiana*, 149; Bradley, *Tullahoma*, 76–80.

15. Bradley, *Tullahoma*, 81.

16. Clarksville, Tenn., June, July 1863, Reel 478, RG 27.5.7, NARA-CP; *OR*, 23(1):456; Bennett and Haigh, *Thirty-Sixth Illinois*, 438; Cope, *Fifteenth Ohio*, 294; Dodge, *Waif of the War*, 85; Simmons, *84th Ill.*, 59; Connelly, *Autumn of Glory*, 129–34; Cozzens, *This Terrible Sound*, 19–20.

17. Tourgée, *Story of a Thousand*, 203. See also Scribner, *How Soldiers Were Made*, 123.

18. *OR*, 23(1):402, 522, 531, 23(2):437; Clarksville, Tenn., June, July 1863, Reel 478, RG 27.5.7, NARA-CP; Cist, *Army of the Cumberland*, 164–65; Simmons, *84th Ill.*, 60–62; Sutherland, *Reminiscences of a Private*, 127; Bradley, *Tullahoma*, 81–89; Connelly, *Autumn of Glory*, 129–34; Cozzens, *This Terrible Sound*, 19–20; Hess, *Braxton Bragg*, 146–49.

19. *OR*, 23(1):408, 435, 436, 478, 531, 541; Bennett and Haigh, *Thirty-Sixth Illinois*, 438–39; Bircher, *Drummer-Boy's Diary*, 66; Bishop, *Story of a Regiment*, 88–89; Cist, *Army of the Cumberland*, 167; Cope, *Fifteenth Ohio*, 294–95; Dodge, *Waif of the War*, 85; Marshall, *Civil War Diary*, 26; Morris, *Eighty-First Indiana*, 50; Williams et al., *Seventy-Third Indiana*, 167; Shaw, *Tenth Indiana*, 211; Simmons, *84th Ill.*, 59–61; Cozzens, *This Terrible Sound*, 21–27.

20. Bradley, *Tullahoma*, 91–94; Cozzens, *This Terrible Sound*, 21–23.

21. See, for example, *OR*, 23(1):433, 436, 468, 473, 477, 482, 538, 546, 549; Beatty, *Citizen-Soldier*, 295; Cist, *Army of the Cumberland*, 168–71; Fisher, *Staff Officer's Story*, 70–71; Marcoot, *Five Years in the Sunny South*, 30; Scribner, *How Soldiers Were Made*, 123; Tourgée, *Story of a Thousand*, 201–3; and Cozzens, *This Terrible Sound*, 21.

22. Scribner, *How Soldiers Were Made*, 123.

23. Clarksville, Tenn., July, Aug. 1863, Reel 478, RG 27.5.7, NARA-CP; *Macon (Ga.) Telegraph*, Aug. 13, 1863; Bennett and Haigh, *Thirty-Sixth Illinois*, 443; Bircher, *Drummer-Boy's Diary*, 66; Butler, *Letters Home*, 83; Dickson, "Climate of Tennessee," 375.

24. Donahower, "Narrative of the Civil War," 2:81, Donahower Papers, MnHS; Clarksville, Tenn., Aug. 1863, Reel 478, RG 27.5.7, NARA-CP; Dickson, "Climate of Tennessee," 375.

25. Clarksville, Tenn., July, Aug. 1863, Reel 478, RG 27.5.7, NARA-CP; Beatty, *Citizen-Soldier*, 294; DeRosier, *Through the South*, 76–79; Dickson, "Climate of Tennessee," 371, 375.

26. Hinman, *Sherman Brigade*, 400.

27. US Environmental Protection Agency, "Summary Table: Characteristics of Ecoregions of Tennessee," accessed Aug. 16, 2017; Josh Johnson, email to author, Aug. 5, 2019.

28. Butler, *Letters Home*, 81–82; DeRosier, *Through the South*, 76, 77; Donahower, "Narrative of the Civil War," 2:86, Donahower Papers, MnHS; Simmons, *84th Ill.*, 62–63.

29. Connelly, *Autumn of Glory*, 137–50, 162–65 (quotations, 139, 145). See also Cozzens, *This Terrible Sound*, 27–29; Hess, *Braxton Bragg*, 151–52; and *Macon (Ga.) Telegraph*, Aug. 13, 1863.

30. Cozzens, *This Terrible Sound*, 31–34, 37; Hess, *Knoxville Campaign*, 9–12; Beatty, *Citizen-Soldier*, 319; Cope, *Fifteenth Ohio*, 298; Donahower, "Narrative of the Civil War," 2:86–87, Donahower Papers, MnHS; Hight and Stormont, *Fifty-Eighth Indiana*, 167; Hinman, *Sherman Brigade*, 405–6; Kimberly and Holloway, *Forty-First Ohio*, 46; Williams et al., *Seventy-Third Indiana*, 169.

31. Simmons, *84th Ill.*, 69–70.

32. Bircher, *Drummer-Boy's Diary*, 69–72; Cope, *Fifteenth Ohio*, 299, 300, 302; Morris, *Eighty-First Indiana*, 53; Cozzens, *This Terrible Sound*, 39–40.

33. Connelly, *Autumn of Glory*, 158–63, 166–70; Cozzens, *This Terrible Sound*, 39–40, 47–50; Hess, *Knoxville Campaign*, 11–16.

34. Cozzens, *This Terrible Sound*, 46–47, 50–53; Collins, *Chapters*, 144; Bircher, *Drummer-Boy's Diary*, 71–74; Hinman, *Sherman Brigade*, 412.

35. Sutherland, *Reminiscences of a Private*, 133. See also Bircher, *Drummer-Boy's Diary*, 73; Connelly, *Autumn of Glory*, 170–74; and Cozzens, *This Terrible Sound*, 53–57.

36. Preston (Mathews), "33rd Alabama," 41, ADAH.

37. Connelly, *Autumn of Glory*, 175–85; Cozzens, *This Terrible Sound*, 53, 59–97; Hess, *Braxton Bragg*, 154–60; McPherson, *Battle Cry of Freedom*, 670–72; *OR*, 30(1):702; Butler, *Letters Home*, 86.

38. *Chicago Daily Post*, quoted in *New York Evening Journal*, Sept. 17, 1863, and *New York Herald*,

Sept. 26, 1863. See also *Augusta (Ga.) Constitutionalist,* Sept. 12, 1863; *Cleveland Plain Dealer,* Sept. 17, 1863; *Louisville Daily Democrat,* Sept. 26, 1863; *Nashville Journal,* Sept. 18, 1863; *New York Evening Post,* Sept. 21, 1863; *Prairie Farmer,* Aug. 22, 1863; *Richmond Whig and Public Advertiser,* Oct. 2, 1863; Cozzens, *This Terrible Sound,* 569n63; Gates, *Agriculture and the Civil War,* 146–49, 153; and Tucker, *Chickamauga,* 411–12n2.

39. *Chicago Tribune,* quoted in *New York Daily Tribune,* Sept. 29, 1863; New Harmony, Ind., Sept. 1863, Reel 140, RG 27.5.7, NARA-CP; Springdale, Ky., Sept. 1863, Reel 193, ibid.; Upper Alton, Ill., Sept. 1863, Reel 132, ibid.; Wyaconda Prairie [indexed as Canton], Mo., Sept. 1863, Reel 280, ibid.; *Cleveland Plain Dealer,* Sept. 30, 1863; *Louisville Daily Democrat,* Sept. 23, Oct. 1, 1863; *New England Farmer,* Dec. 1, 1863; *New York Daily Tribune,* Oct. 12, 1863; Cozzens, *This Terrible Sound,* 569n63; Tucker, *Chickamauga,* 411–12n2.

40. *New York World,* Oct. 26, 1863; *New York Herald,* Oct. 27, 1863; Gates, *Agriculture and the Civil War,* 109–15, 118–19; Hurt, *Agriculture and the Confederacy,* 142–90.

41. Connelly, *Autumn of Glory,* 185–200; Cozzens, *This Terrible Sound,* 97–104; Tucker, *Chickamauga,* 188–90; *Macon (Ga.) Telegraph,* Sept. 23, 1863; Bircher, *Drummer-Boy's Diary,* 73, 74; Bishop, *Story of a Regiment,* 95–97; Collins, *Chapters,* 150; Cope, *Fifteenth Ohio,* 308; Doan, *Reminiscences,* 3; Hight and Stormont, *Fifty-Eighth Indiana,* 180; Simmons, *84th Ill.,* 84–85; Clarksville, Tenn., Sept. 1863, Reel 478, RG 27.5.7, NARA-CP.

42. *OR,* 30(2):182, 185.

43. Tourgée, *Story of a Thousand,* 217. See also Clarksville, Tenn., Sept. 1863, Reel 478, RG 27.5.7, NARA-CP; and *OR,* 30(1):878, 923.

44. Bishop, *Story of a Regiment,* 97.

45. Simmons, *84th Ill.,* 88. See also Cope, *Fifteenth Ohio,* 309; and Tourgée, *Story of a Thousand,* 222.

46. Col. James L. Cooper Memoirs, 34, Reel 5, Folder 11, Box 12, CWC, TSLA.

47. Connelly, *Autumn of Glory,* 200–207; Cozzens, *This Terrible Sound,* 104–279.

48. Bennett and Haigh, *Thirty-Sixth Illinois,* 459; Collins, *Chapters,* 151; Hight and Stormont, *Fifty-Eighth Indiana,* 186; Kirwan, *Johnny Green,* 93; Longstreet, *From Manassas to Appomattox,* 438; Simmons, *84th Ill.,* 93; Connelly, *Autumn of Glory,* 207; Cozzens, *This Terrible Sound,* 280–81.

49. Barnes, Carnahan, and McCain, *Eighty-Sixth Indiana,* 186; Shaw, *Tenth Indiana,* 230.

50. *OR,* 30(1):224, 261, 495, 592, 597, 663, 714, 30(2):490; Bennett and Haigh, *Thirty-Sixth Illinois,* 459; Hight and Stormont, *Fifty-Eighth Indiana,* 186; Kirwan, *Johnny Green,* 93; Shaw, *Tenth Indiana,* 230, 237; Simmons, *84th Ill.,* 93; Connelly, *Autumn of Glory,* 207; Cozzens, *This Terrible Sound,* 280–81, 283–91.

51. Connelly, *Autumn of Glory,* 207–21; Cozzens, *This Terrible Sound,* 292–304; Hess, *Braxton Bragg,* 162–64.

52. Simmons, *84th Ill.,* 99. See also *OR,* 30(1):57–58, 329; Bishop, *Story of a Regiment,* 104; J. B. Clifton Diary, 14, P.C. 589, NCDAH; Donahower, "Narrative of the Civil War," 2:124, Donahower Papers, MnHS.

53. *OR,* 30(1):329, 955, 967; Bennett and Haigh, *Thirty-Sixth Illinois,* 462; Bishop, *Story of a Regiment,* 104; Collins, *Chapters,* 154; Donahower, "Narrative of the Civil War," 2:124, Donahower Papers, MnHS; John H. Freeman Diaries and Memoirs, 60, Reel 18, Box C26, CWC, TSLA; Hinman, *Sherman Brigade,* 426; Levi Wagner Memoirs, 78, CWTI, USAMHI; Connelly, *Autumn of Glory,* 221–22; Cozzens, *This Terrible Sound,* 304–56; Hess, *Braxton Bragg,* 163–67.

54. Connelly, *Autumn of Glory,* 222–30; Cozzens, *This Terrible Sound,* 356–509; *OR,* 30(1):507, 862; Bennett and Haigh, *Thirty-Sixth Illinois,* 477; Hinman, *Sherman Brigade,* 441; Longstreet, *From Manassas to Appomattox,* 450.

55. Freeman Diaries and Memoirs, 61, CWC, TSLA; Keil, *Thirty-Fifth Ohio*, 142; Kirwan, *Johnny Green*, 99.

56. Kirwan, *Johnny Green*, 99.

57. Connelly, *Autumn of Glory*, 230–34; Cozzens, *Shipwreck of Their Hopes*, 31–38; Cozzens, *This Terrible Sound*, 510–36; Hess, *Braxton Bragg*, 165–68; Barnes, Carnahan, and McCain, *Eighty-Sixth Indiana*, 212; Cist, *Army of the Cumberland*, 230–31; Simmons, *84th Ill.*, 103.

58. Connelly, *Autumn of Glory*, 234–53; Cozzens, *Shipwreck of Their Hopes*, 23–31. Hess, *Braxton Bragg*, 169–90.

59. Cozzens, *Shipwreck of Their Hopes*, 1–3, 18; Grant, *Memoirs*, 1:494–96.

60. Clarksville, Tenn., Oct. 1863, Reel 478, RG 27.5.7, NARA-CP; Dickson, "Climate of Tennessee," 375; Cope, *Fifteenth Ohio*, 337; Hight and Stormont, *Fifty-Eighth Indiana*, 201, 202; 199, 205; McClendon, *Recollections*, 193; Quint, *Second Massachusetts*, 197; Cozzens, *Shipwreck of Their Hopes*, 11–14.

61. Clarksville, Tenn., Oct. 1863, Reel 478, RG 27.5.7, NARA-CP; *OR*, 30(4):9, 12, 13, 15, 16, 38, 339, 340, 343, 369, 396, 416, 422; Barnes, Carnahan, and McCain, *Eighty-Sixth Indiana*, 215, 217, 221; Bennett and Haigh, *Thirty-Sixth Illinois*, 492; Bircher, *Drummer-Boy's Diary*, 8; Clifton Diary, 15–17, NCDAH; Cope, *Fifteenth Ohio*, 337; Hight and Stormont, *Fifty-Eighth Indiana*, 201, 202; Manarin, "Diary of Rufus J. Woolwine," 432; Marcoot, *Five Years in the Sunny South*, 39; Mead Diary, vol. 4, Oct. 7–24, 1863, LC; Morris, *Eighty-First Indiana*, 67; Quint, *Second Massachusetts*, 195, 197; Simmons, *84th Ill.*, 117; Tourgée, *Story of a Thousand*, 260, 261; Dickson, "Climate of Tennessee," 375; Cozzens, *Shipwreck of Their Hopes*, 20–21.

62. Blackford et al., *Letters from Lee's Army*, 220.

63. Kirwan, *Johnny Green*, 104. See also *OR*, 30(4):107, 132, 216, 285, 315, 335, 442.

64. Blackford et al., *Letters from Lee's Army*, 210, 213 (quotation, 210).

65. Barnes, Carnahan, and McCain, *Eighty-Sixth Indiana*, 214; Donahower, "Narrative of the Civil War," 2:166, Donahower Papers, MnHS; Morris, *Eighty-First Indiana*, 67; McClendon, *Recollections*, 193; Cozzens, *Shipwreck of Their Hopes*, 8–9, 30.

66. Bennett and Haigh, *Thirty-Sixth Illinois*, 500–501.

67. Simmons, *84th Ill.*, 117. See also Cope, *Fifteenth Ohio*, 335.

68. Blackford et al., *Letters from Lee's Army*, 220. See also Blakey, Lainhart, and Stephens, *Rose Cottage Chronicles*, 277.

69. McClendon, *Recollections*, 193.

70. Bennett and Haigh, *Thirty-Sixth Illinois*, 498, 499; Bircher, *Drummer-Boy's Diary*, 80; Cist, *Army of the Cumberland*, 231–32; Cozzens, *Shipwreck of Their Hopes*, 11–21, 29–31.

71. Simmons, *84th Ill.*, 122.

72. Cist, *Army of the Cumberland*, 232; Dodge, *Waif of the War*, 101; Cozzens, *Shipwreck of Their Hopes*, 9–11, 21–22.

73. Cozzens, *Shipwreck of Their Hopes*, 1–7; Tucker, *Chickamauga*, 411–12n2; New Harmony, Ind., Oct. 1863, Reel 140, RG 27.5.7, NARA-CP; Springdale, Ky., Oct. 1863, Reel 193, ibid.; Upper Alton, Ill., Oct. 1863, Reel 132, ibid.; Annapolis, Md., Sept. 1863, Reel 212, ibid.; New York City, Sept. 1863, Reel 360, ibid.; Wyaconda Prairie [indexed as Canton], Mo., Oct. 1863, Reel 280, ibid.; Hilton Head, S.C., Sept. 1863, Reel 467, ibid.; Fort Monroe, Va., Sept. 1863, Reel 522, ibid.; Banasik, *Serving with Honor*, 115; Barney, *Recollections*, 243–44; Clifton Diary, 17, NCDAH; Dickey, *Eighty-Fifth Pennsylvania*, 288, 289; D. R. Larned to Mrs. Burnside, Oct. 31, 1863, Knoxville, Tenn., Daniel Read Larned Papers, LC; Porter, *Campaigning with Grant*, 1–5; Tilley, *Federals on the Frontier*, 239.

74. Grant, *Memoirs*, 1:496–99 (quotations, 497, 498). See also Cozzens, *Shipwreck of Their Hopes*, 43–45.

75. Cozzens, *Shipwreck of Their Hopes*, 45–47, 51–55; Grant, *Memoirs*, 1:499–500, 506.

76. Blakey, Lainhart, and Stephens, *Rose Cottage Chronicles*, 277; Clifton Diary, 17–18, NCDAH; Cope, *Fifteenth Ohio*, 365; Grant, *Memoirs*, 1:504–5; Hight and Stormont, *Fifty-Eighth Indiana*, 205, 206; [Willet], *Company B*, 44; Cozzens, *Shipwreck of Their Hopes*, 48–57.

77. Connelly, *Autumn of Glory*, 254–57; Cozzens, *Shipwreck of Their Hopes*, 52–59.

78. Charles Banks, "Missionary Ridge," *National Tribune*, May 12, 1892; Bennett and Haigh, *Thirty-Sixth Illinois*, 507; Grant, *Memoirs*, 1:505; Kimberly and Holloway, *Forty-First Ohio*, 60; Morgan, "Brown's Ferry," 345, 347; Connelly, *Autumn of Glory*, 257–61; Cozzens, *Shipwreck of Their Hopes*, 59–70.

79. *OR*, 31(1):123; Clarksville, Tenn., Oct. 1863, Reel 478, RG 27.5.7, NARA-CP; Grant, *Memoirs*, 1:508–9; Connelly, *Autumn of Glory*, 259–61; Cozzens, *Shipwreck of Their Hopes*, 70–101; Hess, *Braxton Bragg*, 190–92.

80. Connelly, *Autumn of Glory*, 262–67; Cozzens, *Shipwreck of Their Hopes*, 101–5; Hess, *Braxton Bragg*, 191–94.

81. Cozzens, *Shipwreck of Their Hopes*, 105–8, 111–12; Grant, *Memoirs*, 1:506–7, 511–16.

82. Grant, *Memoirs*, 1:516.

CHAPTER 17

1. Clarksville, Tenn., Nov. 1863, Reel 478, RG 27.5.7, NARA-CP; Bircher, *Drummer-Boy's Diary*, 81; J. B. Clifton Diary, 18, P.C. 589, NCDAH; Mead Diary, vol. 4, Nov. 1–15, 1863, LC; Cozzens, *Shipwreck of Their Hopes*, 110. Rain fell on November 3, 5, 6, and 14.

2. Hight and Stormont, *Fifty-Eighth Indiana*, 206.

3. Clarksville, Tenn., Nov. 1863, Reel 478, RG 27.5.7, NARA-CP; Beatty, *Citizen-Soldier*, 353; *OR*, 31(2):59, 564; Barnes, Carnahan, and McCain, *Eighty-Sixth Indiana*, 225; Clifton Diary, 19, NCDAH; Hight and Stormont, *Fifty-Eighth Indiana*, 210; [Willet], *Company B*, 44–45.

4. Moore, "Battle of Lookout Mountain," 426–27. See also W. E. Preston (Mathews), "The 33rd Alabama Regiment in the Civil War," ed. L. B. Williams, 92, ADAH.

5. Blackford et al., *Letters from Lee's Army*, 227; Hess, *Knoxville Campaign*, 32–35.

6. Clifton Diary, 19, NCDAH.

7. Clifton Diary, 19–20, NCDAH. See also *OR*, 31(1):403; Longstreet, *From Manassas to Appomattox*, 491–92; Manarin, "Diary of Rufus J. Woolwine," 433; Mead Diary, vol. 4, Nov. 16, 18, 1863, LC; Tarrant, *Wild Riders*, 242–45; and Hess, *Knoxville Campaign*, 37–76.

8. *OR*, 31(1):370, 387, 388; Cozzens, *Shipwreck of Their Hopes*, 2, 47, 103, 108–10, 122.

9. Cavins, *War Letters of Aden G. Cavins*, 66, 68. See also Clarksville, Tenn., Oct., Nov. 1863, Reel 478, RG 27.5.7, NARA-CP.

10. Jones, *Artilleryman's Diary*, 120–25. See also Raum, "With the Western Army: Sherman's March to Chattanooga," *National Tribune*, Apr. 3, 1902, 1–2; Edward E. Schweitzer Diary, 2:17–19, Edward E. Schweitzer Diaries and Correspondence, Box 23, CWTI, USAMHI; Cozzens, *Shipwreck of Their Hopes*, 110.

11. Jones, *Artilleryman's Diary*, 125–27. See also Schweitzer Diary, 2:19, Schweitzer Diaries and Correspondence, CWTI, USAMHI; and Cozzens, *Shipwreck of Their Hopes*, 110.

12. Grant, *Memoirs*, 1:520, 522–23; Raum, "With the Western Army: Sherman's March to Chattanooga," *National Tribune*, Apr. 2, 1902, 2; Cozzens, *Shipwreck of Their Hopes*, 110, 112–16, 120–21.

13. Hight and Stormont, *Fifty-Eighth Indiana*, 211. See also Bircher, *Drummer-Boy's Diary*, 83.

14. *OR*, 31(2):40, 63; Beatty, *Citizen-Soldier*, 356; Bircher, *Drummer-Boy's Diary*, 83; Grant, *Memoirs*, 1:523–25, 2:1; Jones, *Artilleryman's Diary*, 127–31, 133–35; Morris, *Eighty-First Indiana*, 70; Schweitzer

Diary, 2:19–21, Schweitzer Diaries and Correspondence, CWTI, USAMHI; Cozzens, *Shipwreck of Their Hopes*, 120–24.

15. *OR*, 31(2):398; Connelly, *Autumn of Glory*, 268–67; Cozzens, *Shipwreck of Their Hopes*, 124–42; Clarksville, Tenn., Nov. 1863, Reel 478, RG 27.5.7, NARA-CP; Dickson, "Climate of Tennessee," 375; Bircher, *Drummer-Boy's Diary*, 84; J. C. Donahower, "Narrative of the Civil War," 2:199, Jeremiah Chester Donahower Papers, 1853–1919, M561, MnHS; Jones, *Artilleryman's Diary*, 136; Tourgée, *Story of a Thousand*, 275.

16. Donahower, "Narrative of the Civil War," 2:201, 205, Donahower Papers, MnHS. See also *OR*, 31(2):110, 156, 175.

17. *OR*, 31(2):175; Connelly, *Autumn of Glory*, 272–73; Cozzens, *Shipwreck of Their Hopes*, 161–88; Ludlum, *Early American Winters*, 132–33; Ludlum, *Weather Factor*, 94–96; Clarksville, Tenn., Nov. 1863, Reel 478, RG 27.5.7, NARA-CP; Barnes, Carnahan, and McCain, *Eighty-Sixth Indiana*, 239; Dodge, *Waif of the War*, 110, 112; Donahower, "Narrative of the Civil War," 2:205, 205, Donahower Papers, MnHS; Grant, *Memoirs*, 2:5–11; Hazen, *Narrative*, 172; Hight and Stormont, *Fifty-Eighth Indiana*, 215; Jones, *Artilleryman's Diary*, 139; Keil, *Thirty-Fifth Ohio*, 167; William Rickards, "Above the Clouds," *National Tribune*, Jan. 1, 1885; Simmons, *84th Ill.*, 130; [Willet], *Company B*, 47.

18. Simmons, *84th Ill.*, 131.

19. Hazen, *Narrative*, 172.

20. Barnes, Carnahan, and McCain, *Eighty-Sixth Indiana*, 240; Keil, *Thirty-Fifth Ohio*, 167; Tourgée, *Story of a Thousand*, 276.

21. Barnes, Carnahan, and McCain, *Eighty-Sixth Indiana*, 242; Connelly, *Autumn of Glory*, 273–74; Cozzens, *Shipwreck of Their Hopes*, 186–98; Hess, *Braxton Bragg*, 200–201; Clarksville, Tenn., Nov. 1863, Reel 478, RG 27.5.7, NARA-CP; Dickson, "Climate of Tennessee," 375; Collins, *Chapters*, 176; Jones, *Artilleryman's Diary*, 141; Simmons, *84th Ill.*, 132.

22. Cozzens, *Shipwreck of Their Hopes*, 196–98 (quotation, 198); Jones, *Artilleryman's Diary*, 141; Willoughby, "Eclipse of Moon at Missionary Ridge," 590.

23. Grant, *Memoirs*, 2:12–14; Cozzens, *Shipwreck of Their Hopes*, 198–204.

24. Clarksville, Tenn., Nov. 1863, Reel 478, RG 27.5.7, NARA-CP; Collins, *Chapters*, 177; Cope, *Fifteenth Ohio*, 385; Grant, *Memoirs*, 2:15–16; Rickards, "Above the Clouds"; Connelly, *Autumn of Glory*, 275–76; Cozzens, *Shipwreck of Their Hopes*, 204–360.

25. Clarksville, Tenn., Nov. 1863, Reel 478, RG 27.5.7, NARA-CP; Dickson, "Climate of Tennessee," 375; Collins, *Chapters*, 188–89; Dodge, *Waif of the War*, 117; Donahower, "Narrative of the Civil War," 2:239, 251 (quotation, 239), Donahower Papers, MnHS; Jones, *Artilleryman's Diary*, 142; Kirwan, *Johnny Green*, 113; Schweitzer Diary, 2:23, 3:23, Schweitzer Diaries and Correspondence, CWTI, USAMHI; Simmons, *84th Ill.*, 136; Toney, *Privations of a Private*, 50, 56–57; Connelly, *Autumn of Glory*, 276–78; Cozzens, *Shipwreck of Their Hopes*, 362–85.

26. Connelly, *Autumn of Glory*, 277; Cozzens, *Shipwreck of Their Hopes*, 394–98; Grant, *Memoirs*, 2:25–26.

27. Sutherland, *Reminiscences of a Private*, 145.

28. *OR*, 31(2):48, 157, 351; Clarksville, Tenn., Nov. 1863, Reel 478, RG 27.5.7, NARA-CP; Dickson, "Climate of Tennessee," 375; Bircher, *Drummer-Boy's Diary*, 86; Jones, *Artilleryman's Diary*, 145–46; [Willet], *Company B*, 51; Connelly, *Autumn of Glory*, 277–78; Cozzens, *Shipwreck of Their Hopes*, 395–98; Hess, *Braxton Bragg*, 202–4, 212–13.

29. Stephenson, "Missionary Ridge," 540–51. See also Hess, *Braxton Bragg*, 201–13.

30. Tarrant, *Wild Riders*, 247; Hess, *Knoxville Campaign*, 77–94.

31. Clifton Diary, 21, NCDAH; Mead Diary, vol. 4, Nov. 21, 24, 1863, LC; Tarrant, *Wild Riders*, 258; Hess, *Knoxville Campaign*, 94–111, 119–23.

32. Hess, *Knoxville Campaign*, 111–15, 118–19, 125–40, 142.

33. *OR*, 31(1):437, 490, 491; Barnes, Carnahan, and McCain, *Eighty-Sixth Indiana*, 283; Clifton Diary, 21NCDAH; Mead Diary, vol. 4, Nov. 28, 1863, LC; Hess, *Knoxville Campaign*, 140–41.

34. Longstreet, *From Manassas to Appomattox*, 503.

35. Hess, *Knoxville Campaign*, 141–47.

36. *OR*, 31(1):70, 298, 308, 319, 344, 486, 490, 31(2):72, 374; Clifton Diary, 21, NCDAH; Longstreet, *From Manassas to Appomattox*, 505; Mead Diary, vol. 4, Nov. 29, 1863, LC; Hess, *Knoxville Campaign*, 147–75, 177–78.

37. Cozzens, *Shipwreck of Their Hopes*, 386–87; Hess, *Knoxville Campaign*, 179–89; *OR*, 31(2):71; Barnes, Carnahan, and McCain, *Eighty-Sixth Indiana*, 292; Grant, *Memoirs*, 2:24–32; Hight and Stormont, *Fifty-Eighth Indiana*, 228.

38. Barnes, Carnahan, and McCain, *Eighty-Sixth Indiana*, 285; Bennett and Haigh, *Thirty-Sixth Illinois*, 538; Hinman, *Sherman Brigade*, 464, 466; Schweitzer Diary, 3:23, Schweitzer Diaries and Correspondence, CWTI, USAMHI.

39. Barnes, Carnahan, and McCain, *Eighty-Sixth Indiana*, 285.

40. Bennett and Haigh, *Thirty-Sixth Illinois*, 538. See also *OR*, 31(1):262, 263, 31(2):433; Hight and Stormont, *Fifty-Eighth Indiana*, 230; and Hinman, *Sherman Brigade*, 464.

41. Clarksville, Tenn., Nov., Dec. 1863, Reel 478, RG 27.5.7, NARA-CP; Barnes, Carnahan, and McCain, *Eighty-Sixth Indiana*, 285–86, 292, 302, 304, 306; Bennett and Haigh, *Thirty-Sixth Illinois*, 545 Cavins, *War Letters of Aden G. Cavins*, 72–74; Hinman, *Sherman Brigade*, 464; Schweitzer Diary, 3:24, Schweitzer Diaries and Correspondence, CWTI, USAMHI.

42. Hinman, *Sherman Brigade*, 464, 465.

43. *Macon (Ga.) Telegraph*, Jan. 27, 1864; Hess, *Knoxville Campaign*, 191–94.

44. *OR*, 31(1):339, 31(3):317, 365, 391, 448; Cozzens, *Shipwreck of Their Hopes*, 386–88; Hess, *Knoxville Campaign*, 195–200.

45. Grant, *Memoirs*, 2:32–33, 37–39, 42–43; Hattaway and Jones, *How the North Won*, 473–76, 479–80; McPherson, *Battle Cry of Freedom*, 719–20.

46. Clarksville, Tenn., Dec. 1863, Reel 478, RG 27.5.7, NARA-CP; Dickson, "Climate of Tennessee," 375; Barnes, Carnahan, and McCain, *Eighty-Sixth Indiana*, 299, 301, 302, 304, 307; Bennett and Haigh, *Thirty-Sixth Illinois*, 545; Bircher, *Drummer-Boy's Diary*, 87–88, 91–94; Cavins, *War Letters of Aden G. Cavins*, 72–74; Cope, *Fifteenth Ohio*, 402, 403; Jones, *Artilleryman's Diary*, 149, 151–53, 155–59; Schweitzer Diary, 3:27–30, Schweitzer Diaries and Correspondence, CWTI, USAMHI; Shaw, *Tenth Indiana*, 278.

47. *OR*, 31(1):329, 31(2):355; Bircher, *Drummer-Boy's Diary*, 91, 92, 93, 94; Butler, *Letters Home*, 97; Cavins, *War Letters of Aden G. Cavins*, 70, 72, 74; Jones, *Artilleryman's Diary*, 151–59; Schweitzer Diary, 3:29–30, Schweitzer Diaries and Correspondence, CWTI, USAMHI; Shaw, *Tenth Indiana*, 278; *Military History and Reminiscences of the Thirteenth Regiment Illinois Volunteer Infantry*, 404–7; Tourgée, *Story of a Thousand*, 293; Willison, *Reminiscences*, 83.

48. Collins, *Chapters*, 192–93; Coski, "Letters of Livingston," 79; Johnston, *Narrative of Military Operations*, 279; Kirwan, *Johnny Green*, 117–18; Little and Maxwell, *Lumsden's Battery*, 30; [Willet], *Company B*, 53; Preston (Mathews), "33rd Alabama," 49, ADAH.

49. Collins, *Chapters*, 192, 193.

50. Little and Maxwell, *Lumsden's Battery*, 30–31.

51. Collins, *Chapters*, 193; Coski, "Letters of Livingston," 79; Johnston, *Narrative of Military Operations*, 279; Kirwan, *Johnny Green*, 118–19; [Willet], *Company B*, 53.

52. *OR*, 31(1):480, 533; *Macon (Ga.) Telegraph*, Jan. 27, 1864; Longstreet, *From Manassas to Appomattox*, 512–14; Hess, *Knoxville Campaign*, 200–3, 207–20.

53. Longstreet, *From Manassas to Appomattox*, 515.

54. *Richmond Whig*, Jan. 5, 1864.

55. Longstreet, *From Manassas to Appomattox*, 520–22; McClendon, *Recollections*, 199; Hess, *Knoxville Campaign*, 218–20, 224–30, 232; *Macon (Ga.) Telegraph*, Jan. 27, 1864; Mead Diary, vol. 4, Dec. 1–31, 1863, LC; *Richmond Whig*, Jan. 5, 1864.

56. Houghton and Houghton, *Two Boys*, 67. For the Federals, see Kimberly and Holloway, *Forty-First Ohio*, 75.

57. Longstreet, *From Manassas to Appomattox*, 521.

58. Hinman, *Sherman Brigade*, 466.

59. Barnes, Carnahan, and McCain, *Eighty-Sixth Indiana*, 307.

60. *OR*, 31(1):349; Barnes, Carnahan, and McCain, *Eighty-Sixth Indiana*, 298, 301, 302, 304, 306, 307; Cope, *Fifteenth Ohio*, 399, 402; Hinman, *Sherman Brigade*, 466; Marcoot, *Five Years in the Sunny South*, 43–44; Hess, *Knoxville Campaign*, 227–28. Wilbur Hinman particularly sang the praises of the regiment's ponchos. See *Sherman Brigade*, 503–4.

61. Barnes, Carnahan, and McCain, *Eighty-Sixth Indiana*, 307.

62. Ludlum, *Early American Winters*, 133; *Columbus (Ga.) Daily Enquirer*, Jan. 24, 1864; *Fairmont (Ind.) News*, Jan. 12, 1922; *Indianapolis News*, Jan. 12, 1918; *Macon (Ga.) Telegraph*, Jan. 21, 1864; *Milwaukee Daily Sentinel*, Jan. 4, 5, 6, 1864; *Richmond (Ind.) News*, Dec. 29, 1933; *National Intelligencer* (Washington, D.C.), Jan. 5, 1864; *Working Farmer & United States Journal*, Feb. 1, 1864; Barnes, Carnahan, and McCain, *Eighty-Sixth Indiana*, 308; Clark, *Downing's Civil War Diary*, 160; Cope, *Fifteenth Ohio*, 403; Holliday, *Indianapolis and the Civil War*, 584–85; *Military History and Reminiscences of the Thirteenth Regiment Illinois Volunteer Infantry*, 403–4; Hubert, *Fiftieth Regiment, Illinois Volunteer Infantry*, 249; Scott and Angel, *Thirteenth Regiment Tennessee Volunteer Cavalry U.S.A.*, 123; Shaw, *Tenth Indiana*, 278; Willison, *Reminiscences*, 83; Starr, *Union Cavalry*, 351.

63. *Saint Paul Press*, cited in *Farmers' Oracle*, Dec. 11, 1863.

64. Chicago, Ill., Dec. 1863, Jan. 1864, Reel 116, RG 27.5.7, NARA-CP; *Philadelphia Inquirer*, Jan. 4, 1864; *National Intelligencer* (Washington, D.C.), Jan. 5, 1864; *Portland (Maine) Transcript*, Jan. 16, 1864; Bohnak, *So Cold a Sky*, 113–14.

65. Laborville, Mo., Dec. 1863, Jan. 1864, Reel 285, RG 27.5.7, NARA-CP; New Harmony, Ind., Dec. 1863, Jan. 1864, Reel 140, ibid.; Springdale, Ky., Dec. 1863, Jan. 1864, Reel 193, ibid.; Topwer Grove, Mo., Dec. 1863, Jan. 1864, Reel 290, ibid.; Upper Alton, Ill., Dec. 1863, Jan. 1864, Reel 132, ibid.; Wyaconda Prairie [indexed as Canton], Mo., Dec. 1863, Jan. 1864, Reel 280, ibid.; *Columbus (Ga.) Daily Enquirer*, Jan. 24, 1864; *Macon (Ga.) Telegraph*, Jan. 21, 1864; *Milwaukee Daily Sentinel*, Jan. 6, 1864; *Moore's Rural New-Yorker*, Jan. 9, 1864; *Philadelphia Inquirer*, Jan. 4, 1864; *National Intelligencer* (Washington, D.C.), Jan. 5, 1864; *Working Farmer & United States Journal*, Feb. 1, 1864; Berkeley, *In the Defense of This Flag*, 75–76.

66. Newport Barracks, Ky., Dec. 1863, Jan. 1864, Reel 191, RG 27.5.7, NARA-CP; Holloway, "Treatment of Prisoners at Camp Morton," 761.

67. Henry Kyd Douglas to Miss Tippie, Dec. 17, 1863, Johnsons Island, Ohio, Henry Kyd Douglas Papers, 1861–1949, Duke; Douglas to My Dear Friend, Dec. 31, 1862 (quotation), "Hospital Room," ibid.; Douglas, *I Rode with Stonewall*, 260–61 (quotation, 260).

68. Anderson, *Brokenburn*, 271, 272.

69. *Houston Tri-Weekly Telegraph*, Jan. 18, 1864.

70. Barron, *Lone State Defenders*, 174, 175.

71. A. W. Hyatt Journal, in Bartlett, *Military Record of Louisiana*, 12.

72. Banasik, *Serving with Honor*, 130, 131.

73. *Columbus (Ga.) Daily Enquirer*, Jan. 24, 1864; *Macon (Ga.) Telegraph*, Jan. 2, 4, 5, 1864; *Phila-*

delphia Inquirer, Jan. 7, 1864; Banasik, *Serving with Honor*, 132–35; Myers, *Children of Pride*, 418, 423, 426, 430, 431; Ludlum, *Early American Winters*, 133.

74. Clarksville, Tenn., Dec. 1863, Reel 478, RG 27.5.7, NARA-CP; Dickson, "Climate of Tennessee," 375; Cope, *Fifteenth Ohio*, 403; Marshall, *Civil War Diary*, 46–47; Marcoot, *Five Years in the Sunny South*, 45; Mead Diary, vol. 4, Dec. 30–31, 1863, LC; Tarrant, *Wild Riders*, 280; Ludlum, *Early American Winters*, 133.

75. Bennett and Haigh, *Thirty-Sixth Illinois*, 646.

76. Clarksville, Tenn., Dec. 1863, Reel 478, RG 27.5.7, NARA-CP; Dickson, "Climate of Tennessee," 375; Ludlum, *Early American Winters*, 133; Bircher, *Drummer-Boy's Diary*, 95; Hubert, *Fiftieth Regiment, Illinois Volunteer Infantry*, 248–50; Jones, *Artilleryman's Diary*, 159; Keil, *Thirty-Fifth Ohio*, 176; Shaw, *Tenth Indiana*, 278; Tarrant, *Wild Riders*, 280.

77. Simmons, *84th Ill.*, 144. See also Bircher, *Drummer-Boy's Diary*, 95; Cope, *Fifteenth Ohio*, 403; Keil, *Thirty-Fifth Ohio*, 176; Morris, *Eighty-First Indiana*, 72; Puntenney, *Thirty-Seventh Regiment Indiana Infantry*, 67; Shaw, *Tenth Indiana*, 278; Tourgée, *Story of a Thousand*, 290, 293; and [Willet], *Company B*, 52–54.

78. Jones, *Artilleryman's Diary*, 161–64 (quotations, 161, 163). See also Schweitzer Diary, 4:1–2, Schweitzer Diaries and Correspondence, CWTI, USAMHI.

79. *OR*, 32(2):71; Cope, *Fifteenth Ohio*, 411; Grant, *Memoirs*, 2:34–35; Manarin, "Diary of Rufus J. Woolwine," 433; Simpson, *Grant*, 248.

80. Longstreet, *From Manassas to Appomattox*, 526. See also *OR*, 32(2):60; and Blackford et al., *Letters from Lee's Army*, 234.

81. Hinman, *Sherman Brigade*, 467. See also *OR*, 32(1):33, 32(2):194; and Barnes, Carnahan, and McCain, *Eighty-Sixth Indiana*, 308–9.

82. Tarrant, *Wild Riders*, 281.

83. Bennett and Haigh, *Thirty-Sixth Illinois*, 546, 550 (quotation, 546).

84. Clarksville, Tenn., Dec. 1863, Reel 478, RG 27.5.7, NARA-CP; Dickson, "Climate of Tennessee," 375; Clifton Diary, 27, NCDAH; Hight and Stormont, *Fifty-Eighth Indiana*, 241, 242; Jones, *Artilleryman's Diary*, 164–71; Manarin, "Diary of Rufus J. Woolwine," 433–34; Marshall, *Civil War Diary*, 46; Morris, *Eighty-First Indiana*, 72–73; Schweitzer Diary, 4:3–7, Schweitzer Diaries and Correspondence, CWTI, USAMHI; Simmons, *84th Ill.*, 146–47; Tarrant, *Wild Riders*, 283–84; [Willet], *Company B*, 54–60.

85. Barnes, Carnahan, and McCain, *Eighty-Sixth Indiana*, 311–15 (quotation, 313). See also *OR*, 31(3):45; John B. Evans to Wife, Jan. 24, 1864, Russellville, Tenn., John B. Evans Papers, 1862–1865, Duke; Hight and Stormont, *Fifty-Eighth Indiana*, 241–42; and Longstreet, *From Manassas to Appomattox*, 529.

86. *Macon (Ga.) Telegraph*, Jan. 18, 20, 1864 (quotation, Jan. 18).

CHAPTER 18

1. *OR*, 29(1):129; Alexandria, Va., Aug., Sept. 1863, Reel 518, RG 27.5.7, NARA-CP; G. M. Barnard to Father, Aug. 30, 1863, Beverly Ford, Va., George Middleton Barnard Papers, CWCDJ, MHS; *Augusta (Ga.) Constitutionalist*, Sept. 12, 1863; Krick, *Civil War Weather*, 106, 108; Sutherland, *Seasons of War*, 277–87.

2. Annapolis, Md., Sept. 1863, Reel 212, RG 27.5.7, NARA-CP; Hilton Head, S.C., Sept. 1863, Reel 467, ibid.; New York City, Sept. 1863, Reel 360, ibid.; *Augusta (Ga.) Constitutionalist*, Sept. 24, 1863.

3. Alexandria, Va., Aug., Sept. 1863, Reel 518, RG 27.5.7, NARA-CP; Fort Monroe, Va., Sept. 1863, Reel 522, ibid.; Krick, *Civil War Weather*, 106, 108; Blight, *When This Cruel War Is Over*, 258; Britton

and Reed, *To My Beloved Wife*, 123; Dawes, *Sixth Wisconsin*, 204, 205, 210; Dobbins, *Grandfather's Journal*, 160–62; Fleet and Fuller, *Green Mount*, 265, 270; J. E. Green Diary, 39, 42–43, P.C. 694, NCDAH; Haines, *Fifteenth New Jersey*, 109; Jones, *Under the Stars and Bars*, 136; Malles, *Bridge Building in Wartime*, 176, 178; McDonald, *Make Me a Map of the Valley*, 174–77; Neese, *Three Years in the Confederate Horse Artillery*, 207, 213; Nevins, *Diary of Battle*, 284; Norton, *Army Letters*, 180; Preston, *Tenth New York Cavalry*, 140; Quaife, *From the Cannon's Mouth*, 256, 257, 258; Quint, *Second Massachusetts*, 190, 191, 192; Rhodes, *All for the Union*, 122, 124, 125; Rosenblatt and Rosenblatt, *Hard Marching Every Day*, 153–54; Sparks, *Inside Lincoln's Army*, 285, 289, 291; *Macon (Ga.) Telegraph*, Oct. 8, 1863; Partagas and Diaz, "Reconstruction of Historical Tropical Cyclone Frequency," 48, 50, accessed Oct. 14, 2018.

4. Dawes, *Sixth Wisconsin*, 204.

5. Dobbins, *Grandfather's Journal*, 162.

6. Sparks, *Inside Lincoln's Army*, 289.

7. Blight, *When This Cruel War Is Over*, 259; Britton and Reed, *To My Beloved Wife*, 133; Dobbins, *Grandfather's Journal*, 163; Green Diary, 39, 44, NCDAH; Baldy Henderson to Brother, Oct. 2, 1863, Germanna Ford, Va., Archibald Erskine Henderson Papers, 1841–1917, Duke; Malles, *Bridge Building in Wartime*, 179; McDonald, *Make Me a Map of the Valley*, 178; Neese, *Three Years in the Confederate Horse Artillery*, 215; Nevins, *Diary of Battle*, 284; Rhodes, *All for the Union*, 125, 127; *Shoemaker's Battery*, 58–59; Silliker, *Rebel Yell & the Yankee Hurrah*, 121, 124; Sparks, *Inside Lincoln's Army*, 242; Sutherland, *Seasons of War*, 280–81.

8. Rhodes, *All for the Union*, 127.

9. *OR*, 29(1):448; Graham and Skoch, *Mine Run*, 1–2, 4, 5–7; Sutherland, *Seasons of War*, 289–99; Alexandria, Va., Aug., Oct., 1863, Reel 518, RG 27.5.7, NARA-CP; Krick, *Civil War Weather*, 110; Britton and Reed, *To My Beloved Wife*, 136, 137, 139; Caldwell, *Brigade of South Carolinians*, 161–62; Dawes, *Sixth Wisconsin*, 213, 214; Dobbins, *Grandfather's Journal*, 164–66; Galwey, *Valiant Hours*, 150, 159, 161, 162; Green Diary, 45, 46, 47, NCDAH; Malles, *Bridge Building in Wartime*, 180; Neese, *Three Years in the Confederate Horse Artillery*, 225–26, 228; Nevins, *Diary of Battle*, 288, 289, 291, 292; Rhodes, *All for the Union*, 128; Robertson, *Letters of McAllister*, 343; Silliker, *Rebel Yell & the Yankee Hurrah*, 124; White, *Diary of Wyman S. White*, 196; White, "Diary of the War," 225.

10. Frank Morse to Ellen, Oct. 29, 1863, Warrenton, Va., Frank C. Morse Papers, MHS.

11. *OR*, 29(1):397; Britton and Reed, *To My Beloved Wife*, 141, 145–49; Cook, *Twelfth Massachusetts*, 110; Dawes, *Sixth Wisconsin*, 214, 215, 217; Dobbins, *Grandfather's Journal*, 165–66; Galwey, *Valiant Hours*, 163; Green Diary, 47, 48, NCDAH; Haines, *Fifteenth New Jersey*, 115; McDonald, *Make Me a Map of the Valley*, 179–80; Frank Morse to Ellen, Oct. 19, 1863, Gainesville, Va., Morse Papers, MHS; Morse to Ellen, Oct. 24, 1863, Warrenton, Va., ibid.; Frank C. Neese, *Three Years in the Confederate Horse Artillery*, 229, 231; Nevins, *Diary of Battle*, 295; Rhodes, *All for the Union*, 128–29; Robertson, *Letters of McAllister*, 349; Silliker, *Rebel Yell & the Yankee Hurrah*, 124; Sparks, *Inside Lincoln's Army*, 300; Welch, *Confederate Surgeon's Letters*, 81; White, "Diary of the War," 229; *Charleston Mercury*, Oct. 23, 1863. Only some of the rain described by soldiers, however, can be found in Washington-area records, again suggesting spotty local cells.

12. Casler, *Four Years in the Stonewall Brigade*, 195.

13. Dawes, *Sixth Wisconsin*, 223; Luther C. Furst Diary, 48, HCWRTC, USAMHI. See also Frank Morse to Ellen, Oct. 24, 1863, Warrenton, Va., Morse Papers, MHS; White, "Diary of the War," 230; and Rhodes, *All for the Union*, 130.

14. Rhodes, *All for the Union*, 129.

15. *OR*, 29(1):11; Graham and Skoch, *Mine Run*, 4–5, 7–38; Krick, *Civil War Weather*, 112; Long, *Civil War Day by Day*, 431; Sutherland, *Seasons of War*, 299–304; Krick, *Civil War Weather*, 112; Britton and Reed, *To My Beloved Wife*, 149–51, 153, 156; Casler, *Four Years in the Stonewall Brigade*, 195–96;

J. P. Coburn to Parents, Nov. 13, 1863, Brandy Station, James Parley Coburn Papers, USAMHI; Dobbins, *Grandfather's Journal*, 167–68; Furst Diary, 50, HCWRTC, USAMHI; Galwey, *Valiant Hours*, 163; Green Diary, 49, NCDAH; McDonald, *Make Me a Map of the Valley*, 180–82; Frank Morse to Ellen, Nov. 5, 6, 1863, Warrenton, Va., Morse Papers, MHS; Morse to Ellen, Nov. 8, 1863, ibid.; Nevins, *Diary of Battle*, 301; Norton, *Army Letters*, 188, 190; Rosenblatt and Rosenblatt, *Hard Marching Every Day*, 157; Sparks, *Inside Lincoln's Army*, 303; White, "Diary of the War," 230; *Charleston Mercury*, Nov. 11, 1863; *Macon (Ga.) Telegraph*, Nov. 13, 1863.

16. G. M. Barnard, to Inman, Dec. 8, 1863, "Headquarters," Barnard Papers, CWCDJ, MHS.

17. Haines, *Fifteenth New Jersey*, 117.

18. Hyde, *Following the Greek Cross*, 173. See also Frank Morse to Ellen, Nov. 17, 1863, Stone House, Va., Morse Papers, MHS; and Graham and Skoch, *Mine Run*, 38–39.

19. Krick, *Civil War Weather*, 112; Britton and Reed, *To My Beloved Wife*, 156, 158; Dobbins, *Grandfather's Journal*, 168–69; Furst Diary, 50, 51, HCWRTC, USAMHI; Galwey, *Valiant Hours*, 165; Green Diary, 52, NCDAH; Baldy Henderson to Brother, Nov. 21, 1863, Morton's Ford, Va., Henderson Papers, Duke; Jones, *Rebel War Clerk's Diary*, 2:102, 105; McDonald, *Make Me a Map of the Valley*, 182–84; Frank Morse to Ellen, Nov. 15, 1863, Stone House, Va., Morse Papers, MHS; Neese, *Three Years in the Confederate Horse Artillery*, 238; Preston, *Tenth New York Cavalry*, 152; Racine, "Unspoiled Heart," 82; Rhodes, *All for the Union*, 132, 133; Mat Richards to Annie, Nov. 21, 1863, Kelly's Ford, Va., M. Edgar Richards Correspondence, Box 97, CWMC, USAMHI; Robertson, *Letters of McAllister*, 362; Rosenblatt and Rosenblatt, *Hard Marching Every Day*, 163; *Shoemaker's Battery*, 61; *Charleston Mercury*, Nov. 18, 1863; *Sunday Daily Star* (London), Oct. 17, 2017; *Guardian* (London), July 19, 2016; Bast et al., "European Species," 1–3, accessed Oct. 29, 2017.

20. Dobbins, *Grandfather's Journal*, 169.

21. *OR*, 29(2):409; Krick, *Civil War Weather*, 112; Agassiz, *Meade's Headquarters*, 52; G. M. Barnard to Father, Dec. 1, 1863, "Camp in the Field," Barnard Papers, CWCDJ, MHS; Blackford, *War Years*, 243; Haines, *Fifteenth New Jersey*, 118; Hyde, *Following the Greek Cross*, 173–74; McDonald, *Make Me a Map of the Valley*, 185; Graham and Skoch, *Mine Run*, 38–48; Hattaway and Jones, *How the North Won*, 476–77; Petty, "Wilderness, Weather, and Waging War," 9, 13–18.

22. Pyne, *Ride to War*, 163.

23. White, *Diary of Wyman S. White*, 204; Petty, "Wilderness, Weather, and Waging War," 17–18.

24. *OR*, 29(1):16, 696, 711, 725, 753, 765, 795, 796, 829, 836, 888, 889, 890, 893, 29(2):481, 492; Krick, *Civil War Weather*, 111, 112; Agassiz, *Meade's Headquarters*, 54, 56; G. M. Barnard to Father, Nov. 28, 1863, The Wilderness, Va., Barnard Papers, CWCDJ, MHS; Barnard to Father, Aug. 30, 1863, Beverly Ford, Va., ibid.; Britton and Reed, *To My Beloved Wife*, 165–66; Dawes, *Sixth Wisconsin*, 224–25; Fleet and Fuller, *Green Mount*, 284; Furst Diary, 52, HCWRTC, USAMHI; Green Diary, 54, NCDAH; Haines, *Fifteenth New Jersey*, 118; Howard, *Recollections*, 243; McDonald, *Make Me a Map of the Valley*, 185–86; Neese, *Three Years in the Confederate Horse Artillery*, 241; Preston, *Tenth New York Cavalry*, 152; Rhodes, *All for the Union*, 134; Sparks, *Inside Lincoln's Army*, 315, 316; Westwood A. Todd Reminiscence, pt. 1, 161, SHC-UNC; Tyler, *Recollections*, 126, 127; White, "Diary of the War," 233–34; Worsham, *One of Jackson's Foot Cavalry*, 117; Graham and Skoch, *Mine Run*, 48–74; Long, *Civil War Day by Day*, 438–40; Petty, "Wilderness, Weather, and Waging War," 18–26.

25. Graham and Skoch, *Mine Run*, 74.

26. Krick, *Civil War Weather*, 111, 112; Britton and Reed, *To My Beloved Wife*, 166; Galwey, *Valiant Hours*, 175, 176; Neese, *Three Years in the Confederate Horse Artillery*, 242; Silliker, *Rebel Yell & the Yankee Hurrah*, 130; Graham and Skoch, *Mine Run*, 74–80; Hattaway and Jones, *How the North Won*, 477–78; Long, *Civil War Day by Day*, 449; Petty, "Wilderness, Weather, and Waging War," 26–29.

27. Silliker, *Rebel Yell & the Yankee Hurrah*, 132.

28. Furst Diary, 53, HCWRTC, USAMHI.

29. Sparks, *Inside Lincoln's Army*, 316, 318 (quotation, 316). See also G. M. Barnard to Father, Dec. 1, 1863, "Camp in the Field," Barnard Papers, CWCDJ, MHS.

30. Haines, *Fifteenth New Jersey*, 120.

31. Nevins, *Diary of Battle*, 305. Robert Krick considers reports of men frozen to death to be "mythical." See *Civil War Weather*, 113.

32. Krick, *Civil War Weather*, 114; Agassiz, *Meade's Headquarters*, 58, 59; Dobbins, *Grandfather's Journal*, 171; Fleet and Fuller, *Green Mount*, 284; Furst Diary, 53, HCWRTC, USAMHI; Haines, *Fifteenth New Jersey*, 120–22; Jones, *Rebel War Clerk's Diary*, 2:110; McDonald, *Make Me a Map of the Valley*, 186; Preston, *Tenth New York Cavalry*, 154; Rhodes, *All for the Union*, 135; Petty, "Wilderness, Weather, and Waging War," 29.

33. Haines, *Fifteenth New Jersey*, 120. See also Agassiz, *Meade's Headquarters*, 58; and Furst Diary, 53, HCWRTC, USAMHI.

34. Tyler, *Recollections*, 129.

35. Pyne, *Ride to War*, 171.

36. "Diary of John Waldrop . . . and William Y. Mordecai," 49; McDonald, *Make Me a Map of the Valley*, 187; White, *Diary of Wyman S. White*, 205; Petty, "Wilderness, Weather, and Waging War," 30.

37. Haines, *Fifteenth New Jersey*, 122. See also Krick, *Civil War Weather*, 114; Frank Morse to Mother and Sister, Dec. 6, 1863, Stone House, Va., Morse Papers, MHS; and William H. Peacock to Sarah, Dec. 8, 1863, Rappahannock Station, Va., William H. Peacock Correspondence. Box 89, CWMC, USAMHI.

38. Blight, *When This Cruel War Is Over*, 269; Britton and Reed, *To My Beloved Wife*, 168, 169, 171, 173, 174; J. P. Coburn to Parents, Dec. 9, 1863, Brandy Station, Coburn Papers, USAMHI; Dawes, *Sixth Wisconsin*, 229–30; Haines, *Fifteenth New Jersey*, 122; Malles, *Bridge Building in Wartime*, 189; McDonald, *Make Me a Map of the Valley*, 187; Frank Morse to Ellen, Dec. 5, 8, 10, 11, 1863, Stone House, Va., Morse Papers, MHS; William H. Peacock to Sarah, Dec. 8, 1863, Rappahannock Station, Va., Peacock Correspondence, CWMC, USAMHI; Pyne, *Ride to War*, 173–74; Racine, "Unspoiled Heart," 88, 97–98; Rhodes, *All for the Union*, 135; Tyler, *Recollections*, 132; White, *Diary of Wyman S. White*, 207.

39. Sutherland, *Seasons of War*, 328.

40. Benson, *Berry Benson's Civil War Book*, 55.

41. Krick, *Civil War Weather*, 114; Baylor, *Bull Run to Bull Run*, 184, 185; Blight, *When This Cruel War Is Over*, 269, 271–72; Britton and Reed, *To My Beloved Wife*, 168–71, 173–75, 177; Cook, *Twelfth Massachusetts*, 122; Dawes, *Sixth Wisconsin*, 228, 232; "Diaries of John Waldrop . . . and William Y. Mordecai," 49; Dobbins, *Grandfather's Journal*, 171–74; Fleet and Fuller, *Green Mount*, 292; Green Diary, 56–59, NCDAH; Edward Hitchcock McDonald Reminiscences, 95, 97, SHC-UNC; Jones, *Rebel War Clerk's Diary*, 2:111, 112, 114, 116, 117, 119, 122; McDonald, *Make Me a Map of the Valley*, 186–91; Frank Morse to Ellen, Dec. 11, 1863, Stone House, Va., Morse Papers, MHS; Morse, to Nellie, Dec. 17, 29, 31, 1863, Brandy Station, Va., ibid.; Neese, *Three Years in the Confederate Horse Artillery*, 243–45; Nevins, *Diary of Battle*, 307–8, 309, 310; William H. Peacock to Sarah, Dec. 23, 1863, Rappahannock Station, Va., Peacock Correspondence, CWMC, USAMHI; Racine, "Unspoiled Heart," 88, 89, 91; Rosenblatt and Rosenblatt, *Hard Marching Every Day*, 172, 175, 181; Howard M. Smith Diary and Letters, 94–100, MMC, LC; Sparks, *Inside Lincoln's Army*, 322, 324, 327; Tyler, *Recollections*, 130; White, "Diary of the War," 237, 238; *Alexandria (Va.) Gazette*, Dec. 28, 1863.

42. Sutherland, *Seasons of War*, 308–14.

43. Annapolis, Md., Jan. 1864, Reel 212, RG 27.5.7, NARA-CP; New York City, Dec. 1863, Jan. 1864, Reel 361, ibid.; *Baltimore Sun*, Jan. 4, 6, 1864; *New-York Daily Herald*, Jan. 4, 1864; *Philadelphia Inquirer*, Jan. 4, 1864; *Portland (Maine) Transcript*, Jan. 16, 1984; *National Intelligencer* (Washington, D.C.), Jan. 5, 1864; *Working Farmer & United States Journal*, Feb. 1, 1864.

44. Dickey, *Eighty-Fifth Pennsylvania*, 304, 305. See also Beaufort, S.C., Jan., 1864, Reel 464, RG 27.5.7, NARA-CP; and Hilton Head, S.C., Jan., 1864, Reel 467, ibid.

45. Blakely, Lainhart, and Stephens, *Rose Cottage Chronicles*, 301.

46. Malles, *Bridge Building in Wartime*, 183.

47. Krick, *Civil War Weather*, 116; Baird, *Journals of Edmonds*, 178; Britton and Reed, *To My Beloved Wife*, 177; Fleet and Fuller, *Green Mount*, 297; Green Diary, 60, NCDAH; Baldy Henderson to Brother, Jan. 2, 1864, Petersburg, Va., Henderson Papers, Duke; Jones, *Rebel War Clerk's Diary*, 2:122–23; McDonald, *Make Me a Map of the Valley*, 191; Neese, *Three Years in the Confederate Horse Artillery*, 248; Racine, "Unspoiled Heart," 92; Rhodes, *All for the Union*, 137; Robertson, *Letters of McAllister*, 377, 378, 379; Smith Diary and Letters, 100, MMC, LC; Welch, *Confederate Surgeon's Letters*, 85–86; White, *Diary of Wyman S. White*, 211.

48. *OR*, 33:347; Krick, *Civil War Weather*, 116; Agassiz, *Meade's Headquarters*, 64–65; Baird, *Journals of Edmonds*, 183; Blight, *When This Cruel War Is Over*, 274; Britton and Reed, *To My Beloved Wife*, 183–84, 186–93; J. P. Coburn to Parents, Jan. 12, 1864, Brandy Station, Coburn Papers, USAMHI; Coburn to unknown, Jan. 19, 1864, Camp Bullock, Va., ibid.; Coburn to Parents, Jan. 22, 1864, Camp Bullock, Va., ibid.; Coburn to Parents, Jan. 31, 1864, Camp Bullock, Va., ibid.; Dawes, *Sixth Wisconsin*, 236; "Diaries of John Waldrop . . . and William Y. Mordecai," 50; Dobbins, *Grandfather's Journal*, 176–79; Fleet and Fuller, *Green Mount*, 299, 305, 306; Green Diary, 61–63, NCDAH; Baldy Henderson to Brother, Jan. 23, 1864, Camp Godwin, Henderson Papers, Duke; Jones, *Rebel War Clerk's Diary*, 2:125–27, 131–39; McDonald, *Make Me a Map of the Valley*, 191–93; Frank Morse to Nellie, Jan. 4, 7, 11, 15, 1864, Brandy Station, Va., Morse Papers, MHS; William H. Peacock to Brother, Jan. 21, 1864, Rappahannock Station, Va., Peacock Correspondence, CWMC, USAMHI; Peacock to Sarah, Jan. 31, 1864, Rappahannock Station, Va., ibid.; Rhodes, *All for the Union*, 138; Robertson, *Letters of McAllister*, 380, 385–86, 388; Roper, *Repairing the "March of Mars,"* 490, 491, 493, 495; Smith Diary and Letters, 100–106, MMC, LC; Sparks, *Inside Lincoln's Army*, 329; Welch, *Confederate Surgeon's Letters*, 87, 88; *Alexandria (Va.) Gazette*, Jan. 7, 1864; *Charleston Mercury*, Jan. 9, 1864; *Richmond Whig*, Jan. 9, 1984.

49. J. P. Coburn to Parents, Jan. 31, 1864, Camp Bullock, Va., Coburn Papers, USAMHI.

50. Agassiz, *Meade's Headquarters*, 64, 65.

51. Graham and Skoch, *Mine Run*, 85–88, 90–92; Sutherland, *Seasons of War*, 326–27.

52. Britton and Reed, *To My Beloved Wife*, 197.

53. Agassiz, *Meade's Headquarters*, 69.

54. *OR*, 33:126; Graham and Skoch, *Mine Run*, 88–90, 92–96; Krick, *Civil War Weather*, 118; Sutherland, *Seasons of War*, 326–28; Agassiz, *Meade's Headquarters*, 70, 71; Britton and Reed, *To My Beloved Wife*, 198; Smith Diary and Letters, 108–9, MMC, LC.

55. *OR*, 33:185, 189; Britton and Reed, *To My Beloved Wife*, 199–202; J. P. Coburn to Parents, Feb. 14, 19, 1864, Camp Bullock, Va., Coburn Papers, USAMHI; Coburn to Parents, Mar. 3, 1864, Camp Bullock, Va., ibid.; Cook, *Twelfth Massachusetts*, 124; "Diary of John Waldrop . . . and William Y. Mordecai," 50; Dobbins, *Grandfather's Journal*, 180–83; Fleet and Fuller, *Green Mount*, 308; Green Diary, 66–67, 68, 69, NCDAH; Haines, *Fifteenth New Jersey*, 126, 128–31; Jones, *Under the Stars and Bars*, 153; Jones, *Rebel War Clerk's Diary*, 2:148–53, 162, 163, 156, 160–61; McDonald, *Make Me a Map of the Valley*, 196; Pyne, *Ride to War*, 178–80; Robertson, *Letters of McAllister*, 394–97; Roper, *Repairing the "March of Mars,"* 509, 510, 511, 512, 513, 519, 521, 523; Rosenblatt and Rosenblatt, *Hard Marching Every Day*, 191–92, 195–98; Silliker, *Rebel Yell & the Yankee Hurrah*, 137; Smith Diary and Letters, 110–11, MMC, LC; Sparks, *Inside Lincoln's Army*, 336, 337, 338, 342; Tyler, *Recollections*, 136; Graham and Skoch, *Mine Run*, 95–96; Krick, *Civil War Weather*, 117–19; Sutherland, *Seasons of War*, 335–36; Wittenberg, *Like a Meteor*, 224–47.

56. Aaron K. Blake to Sister, Mar. 3, 1864, Portsmouth, Va., Aaron K. Blake Correspondence, Box 10, CWMC, USAMHI; Britton and Reed, *To My Beloved Wife*, 203–4, 205; "Diary of John Waldrop . . .

and William Y. Mordecai," 51; Dobbins, *Grandfather's Journal*, 183; Grant, *Memoirs*, 2:44–48; Green Diary, 69, 70, NCDAH; Jones, *Rebel War Clerk's Diary*, 2:165–68, 169; McDonald, *Make Me a Map of the Valley*, 196; Nevins, *Diary of Battle*, 327; Roper, *Repairing the "March of Mars,"* 531, 532, 533; Graham and Skoch, *Mine Run*, 96–97; Krick, *Civil War Weather*, 120; Sutherland, *Seasons of War*, 342–43.

57. Nevins, *Diary of Battle*, 329–30.

58. Krick, *Civil War Weather*, 120; Benson, *Berry Benson's Civil War Book*, 58; Nevins, *Diary of Battle*, 329; Smith Diary and Letters, 113, MMC, LC.

59. Rosenblatt and Rosenblatt, *Hard Marching Every Day*, 201.

60. Sutherland, *Seasons of War*, 342. See also Krick, *Civil War Weather*, 120; Britton and Reed, *To My Beloved Wife*, 205, 208–9; Dobbins, *Grandfather's Journal*, 184–85; Green Diary, 69–71, NCDAH; Jones, *Rebel War Clerk's Diary*, 2:170–75; McDonald, *Make Me a Map of the Valley*, 196–97; Neese, *Three Years in the Confederate Horse Artillery*, 253; Nevins, *Diary of Battle*, 329, 332; Roper, *Repairing the "March of Mars,"* 539, 540; Rosenblatt and Rosenblatt, *Hard Marching Every Day*, 203–5; *Shoemaker's Battery*, 69; Toney, *Privations of a Private*, 61; "Diaries of John Waldrop . . . and William Y. Mordecai," 51; and White, *Diary of Wyman S. White*, 224, 225.

61. Baird, *Journals of Edmonds*, 190; Britton and Reed, *To My Beloved Wife*, 210–11; Jim Coburn to Parents, Mar. 23, 1864, Camp Bullock, Va., Coburn Papers, USAMHI; Dobbins, *Grandfather's Journal*, 185; Dayton E. Flint to Father, Mar. 28, 1864, White Oak Church, in "Civil War Letters of Dayton E. Flint," Box 40, CWMC, USAMHI; Grant, *Memoirs*, 2:50, 52; Green Diary, 72, NCDAH; Jones, *Rebel War Clerk's Diary*, 2:175–78; McDonald, *Make Me a Map of the Valley* 197–98; Neese, *Three Years in the Confederate Horse Artillery*, 253; Robertson, *Letters of McAllister*, 403; Roper, *Repairing the "March of Mars,"* 540; Smith Diary and Letters, 114, MMC, LC; "Diaries of John Waldrop . . . and William Y. Mordecai," 51; Graham and Skoch, *Mine Run*, 96–98; Krick, *Civil War Weather*, 120; Sutherland, *Seasons of War*, 342–46.

62. Nevins, *Diary of Battle*, 338.

63. Dobbins, *Grandfather's Journal*, 186.

CHAPTER 19

1. Simpson, *Grant*, 266–88.

2. *OR*, 32(1):173–75; Grant, *Memoirs*, 2:33–35, 39–41; Foster, *Sherman's Mississippi Campaign*, 14–26, 30–32, 124–27; Simpson, *Grant*, 249–50.

3. *OR*, 32(1):175; Clark, *Downing's Civil War Diary*, 165, 166; Grant, *Memoirs*, 2; Benjamin Hieronymous Diaries, Feb. 3–6, 1864, SC 694, Abraham Lincoln Presidential Library, Springfield, Ill.; Scott, *Thirty-Second Iowa*, 122; Charles Henry Snedeker Diary, Feb. 1–5, 1864, RG 844, AU; William B. Westervelt, "Lights and Shadows of Army Life, as Seen by a Private Soldier," 42, Box 121, CWMC, USAMHI; Foster, *Sherman's Mississippi Campaign*, xi, 42, 44, 53–85, 102; Sanders, "Climate of Mississippi," 222.

4. W. A. Rorer to Cousin Susan, Feb. 24, 1864, Demopolis, Ala., James M. Willcox Papers, 1831–1871, Duke.

5. *OR*, 32(1):175–76; 217, 244, 246; Clark, *Downing's Civil War Diary*, 167, 168; Hieronymous Diaries, Feb. 8–18, 1864, Lincoln Presidential Library; Snedeker Diary, Feb. 6–18, 1864, AU; Westervelt, "Lights and Shadows of Army Life," 40–42, CWMC, USAMHI; Foster, *Sherman's Mississippi Campaign*, 85–90, 96–124.

6. *OR*, 32(1):251–60; 273, 278, 285, 32(2):392; Barron, *Lone Star Defenders*, 178–79; Foster, *Sherman's Mississippi Campaign*, 122–49; Sanders, "Climate of Mississippi," 222.

7. Snedeker Diary, Feb. 19–20, 1864 (quotation, Feb. 19), AU. See also *OR*, 32(1):217.

8. *OR*, 32(1):176.

9. *OR*, 32(1):176–77; Clark, *Downing's Civil War Diary*, 168, 170; Hieronymous Diaries, Feb. 18–26, 1864, Lincoln Presidential Library; Scott, *Thirty-Second Iowa*, 126; Snedeker Diary, Feb. 20–29, 1864, AU; Foster, *Sherman's Mississippi Campaign*, 149–64.

10. Foster, *Sherman's Mississippi Campaign*, 164.

11. *OR*, 32(1):219, 220; Clark, *Downing's Civil War Diary*, 171, 174–75; Hieronymous Diaries, Feb. 26–Mar, 2, 1864, Lincoln Presidential Library; W. A. Rorer to Cousin Susan, Mar. 4, 1864, Demopolis, Ala., Willcox Papers, Duke; Snedeker Diary, Mar. 1–31, 1864, AU; Westervelt, "Lights and Shadows of Army Life," 42, CWMC, USAMHI; Foster, *Sherman's Mississippi Campaign*, 164–67.

12. W. A. Rorer to Cousin Susan, Mar. 4, 1864, Demopolis, Ala., Willcox Papers, Duke.

13. *OR*, 32(1):175; Foster, *Sherman's Mississippi Campaign*, 146–49, 164–75.

14. Joiner, *Howling Wilderness*, 1–15, 21–26; Joiner, *One Damn Blunder*, 1–7, 15 (quotation, 4).

15. Cox, *Lincoln and Black Freedom*, 46–97.

16. *OR*, 26(1):322; Eddington, "Civil War Memoirs," accessed Feb. 23, 2018; A. W. Hyatt Journal, in Bartlett, *Military Record of Louisiana*, 11; Tilley, *Federals on the Frontier*, 208–27; Joiner, *Howling Wilderness*, 12–15; Joiner, *One Damn Blunder*, 8–9.

17. Tilley, *Federals on the Frontier*, 242–46 (quotations, 242, 243). See also *OR*, 26(1):397; and Barney, *Recollections*, 243–45.

18. Dungan, *Nineteenth Regiment, Iowa Volunteer Infantry*, 116.

19. Dungan, *Nineteenth Regiment, Iowa Volunteer Infantry*, 117–20, 123. See also Tilley, *Federals on the Frontier*, 252–81; and Orton, "Climate of Texas," 904, 907, 910.

20. Tilley, *Federals on the Frontier*, 283–99 (quotation, 283). See also Ludlum, *Early American Winters*, 133.

21. *OR*, 26(1):396–405, 807, 834–35; Cox, *Lincoln and Black Freedom*, 68–73; Joiner, *Howling Wilderness*, 14–15; Joiner, *One Damn Blunder*, 9–10.

22. Joiner, *Howling Wilderness*, 48–58; Joiner, *One Damn Blunder*, 17–29, 35–43.

23. Banasik, *Serving with Honor*, 139–45; Joiner, *Howling Wilderness*, xvii. See also Sanders, "Climate of Louisiana," 699, 700.

24. Joiner, *One Damn Blunder*, 45.

25. Logbook, USS *Carondelet*, Mar. 11–15, 1864 (quotation, Mar. 11), RG 24.2.2, NARA. For similar records, see Logbook, USS *Chocktaw*, Mar. 10–14, 1864, ibid.; Logbook, USS *Neosho*, Mar. 10–14, 1864, ibid.; and Logbook, USS *Mound City*, Mar. 10–14, 1864, ibid. For this study, I examined the logs of nine additional navy vessels: the *Cincinnati, Cricket, Forest Rose, Lafayette, Louisville, Mound City, Neosho, Osage*, and *Ozark*. None included temperature measurements.

26. Joiner, *Howling Wilderness*, xvii; Joiner, *One Damn Blunder*, 20–22, 47.

27. Joiner, *Howling Wilderness*, 58–61, 65–67; Joiner, *One Damn Blunder*, 47–52; Logbook, USS *Chocktaw*, Mar. 14, 1864, RG 24.2.2, NARA; Logbook, USS *Neosho*, Mar. 14, 1864, ibid.; Logbook, USS *Mound City*, Mar. 14, 1864, ibid.

28. Logbook, USS *Carondelet*, Mar. 15–18, 1864, RG 24.2.2, NARA; Logbook, USS *Chocktaw*, Mar. 15–20, 1864, ibid.

29. Joiner, *Howling Wilderness*, 25, 62–65, 67–68; Joiner, *One Damn Blunder*, 59–62, 64–68; Forsyth, *Camden Expedition*, 72.

30. "Vertisols," US Department of Agriculture Natural Resources Conservation Service, https://www.nrcs.usda.gov/wps/portal/nrcs/detail/soils/survey/class/maps/?cid=nrcs142p2_053611, accessed Feb. 13, 2018; "Vertisols Map," https://www.nrcs.usda.gov/wps/portal/nrcs/detail/soils/survey/class/maps/?cid=nrcs142p2_053612, accessed Feb. 13, 2018; *OR*, 34(1):177, 34(2):548; Banasik, *Serving with Honor*, 146–48; Ewer, *Third Massachusetts Cavalry*, 133, 136–36; Logbook, USS *Carondelet*, Mar. 17–20, 1864, RG 24.2.2, NARA; Joiner, *Howling Wilderness*, 68–69; Joiner, *One Damn Blunder*, 53–58.

31. *New York Times*, Apr. 15, 1864, quoted in Andrews, *North Reports*, 500.

32. *OR*, 34(1):324, 326, 334, 335, 34(2):690; Clark, *116th New York*, 146; Pellett, *114th Regiment, New York State Volunteers*, 174–75 (hereafter, Pellett, *114th New York*); Pitcock and Gurley, *I Acted from Principle*, 127; Joiner, *Howling Wilderness*, 63–64; Joiner, *One Damn Blunder*, 54.

33. Ewer, *Third Massachusetts Cavalry*, 138.

34. Logbook, USS *Carondelet*, Mar. 20–25, 1864, RG 24.2.2, NARA; Logbook, USS *Chocktaw*, Mar. 20–24, 1864, ibid.; Clark, *116th New York*, 146; Pellett, *114th New York*, 178; Pitcock and Gurley, *I Acted from Principle*, 128, 129; Joiner, *Howling Wilderness*, 68–69; Joiner, *One Damn Blunder*, 58–60, 68–70.

35. *OR*, 34(1):249; Logbook, USS *Carondelet*, Mar. 25–28, 1864, RG 24.2.2, NARA; Clark, *116th New York*, 149; Joiner, *Howling Wilderness*, 30, 69–72; Joiner, *One Damn Blunder*, 64–66.

36. Logbook, USS *Carondelet*, Mar. 25–Apr. 7, 1864, RG 24.2.2, NARA; Clark, *116th New York*, 150; Pellett, *114th New York*, 188–89; Joiner, *Howling Wilderness*, 30, 72–85; Joiner, *One Damn Blunder*, 68–68, 75–82.

37. Ewer, *Third Massachusetts Cavalry*, 138. See also *OR*, 34(1):199, 257, 345, 365, 436; and Logbook, USS *Carondelet*, Apr. 6–7, 1864, RG 24.2.2, NARA.

38. Andrews, *North Reports*, 506.

39. Joiner, *One Damn Blunder*, 20–29, 33–35, 52–59, 62–64.

40. Banasik, *Serving with Honor*, 146–49. See also A. W. Hyatt Journal, in Bartlett, *Military Record of Louisiana*, 13; and Pitcock and Gurley, *I Acted from Principle*, 127–34.

41. *OR*, 34(1):452; Logbook, USS *Carondelet*, Mar., Apr. 7–8, 1864, RG 24.2.2, NARA; Banasik, *Serving with Honor*, 150, 152; Pitcock and Gurley, *I Acted from Principle*, 134–40; Scott, *Thirty-Second Iowa*, 136; Joiner, *Howling Wilderness*, 87–99; Joiner, *One Damn Blunder*, 82–91, 93–104.

42. Clark, *116th New York*, 157–58.

43. *OR*, 34(1):452, 458; Logbook, USS *Carondelet*, Apr. 8–9, 1864, RG 24.2.2, NARA; Clark, *116th New York*, 160; Pellett, *114th New York*, 215; [Blessington], *Campaigns of Walker's Texas Division*, 200; Joiner, *Howling Wilderness*, 99–108; Joiner, *One Damn Blunder*, 103–4, 107–20.

44. Logbook, USS *Carondelet*, Apr. 10–25, 1864, RG 24.2.2, NARA; Logbook, USS *Mound City*, Apr. 10–25, 1864, ibid.; Logbook, USS *Neosho*, Apr. 10–25, 1864, ibid.; Clark, *116th New York*, 167, 173; Pellett, *114th New York*, 223, 229; Joiner, *Howling Wilderness*, 21, 33–35, 41, 131–57; Joiner, *One Damn Blunder*, 137–57, 161–62.

45. Clark, *116th New York*, 178; Joiner, *Howling Wilderness*, 157–61; Joiner, *One Damn Blunder*, 159–75.

46. Joiner, *Howling Wilderness*, 177–85; Joiner, *One Damn Blunder*, 173–75.

47. Forsyth, *Camden Expedition*, 33, 38–43, 66–69.

48. *OR*, 34(2):246–47, 305, 415, 423, 491 (quotations, 246, 423); Forsyth, *Camden Expedition*, 66–69; Joiner, *Howling Wilderness*, 55; Reinhold, "Climate of Arkansas," 523. A survey of ship logs in the National Archives again revealed only vague indications of calm, bright, cloudy, or rainy days. See, for example, Logbook, USS *Fawn*, March–May, 1864, RG 24.2.2, NARA.

49. Forsyth, *Camden Expedition*, 71–73, 90 (quotation, 73).

50. Forsyth, *Camden Expedition*, 73; Joiner, *Howling Wilderness*, 110–12.

51. White, "Bluecoat's Account," 83. See also Crawford, *Kansas in the Sixties*, 109.

52. *OR*, 34(1):672–73; Logbook, USS *Fawn*, Mar. 24, 25, 1864, RG 24.2.2, NARA; Pitcock and Gurley, *I Acted from Principle*, 128, 129; Sperry, *33rd Iowa*, 60; Forsyth, *Camden Expedition*, 73–74.

53. *OR*, 34(1):672–73.

54. *OR*, 34(1):673; Sperry, *33rd Iowa*, 64–66; Forsyth, *Camden Expedition*, 74–82.

55. *OR*, 34(1):674–75 (quotation, 674); Sperry, *33rd Iowa*, 66–68; Forsyth, *Camden Expedition*, 82–85; Joiner, *Howling Wilderness*, 112–16.

56. *OR,* 34(1):67; Logbook, USS *Fawn,* Mar. 31–Apr. 8, 1864, RG 24.2.2, NARA.

57. Forsyth, *Camden Expedition,* 89–91; Joiner, *Howling Wilderness,* 116–17.

58. Sperry, *33rd Iowa,* 63–78 (quotations, 70, 71, 74). See also White, "Bluecoat's Account," 85; Forsyth, *Camden Expedition,* 91–100; and Joiner, *Howling Wilderness,* 117, 119–20.

59. Sperry, *33rd Iowa,* 75–78 (quotations, 75). See also Forsyth, *Camden Expedition,* 100–1.

60. Crawford, *Kansas in the Sixties,* 116–17; Lothrop, *First Regiment Iowa Cavalry,* 177–79; Sperry, *33rd Iowa,* 80–81; Forsyth, *Camden Expedition,* 100–103, 106–17; Joiner, *Howling Wilderness,* 120–21; Urwin, "'We Cannot Treat Negroes,'" 132–42.

61. Pitcock and Gurley, *I Acted from Principle,* 146; Forsyth, *Camden Expedition,* 103, 109, 117–25; Joiner, *Howling Wilderness,* 118–19, 122–23.

62. Sperry, *33rd Iowa,* 84–85; USS *Fawn,* Apr. 20–25, 1864, RG 24.2.2, NARA; Forsyth, *Camden Expedition,* 103, 109, 125–37; Joiner, *Howling Wilderness,* 118–19; Urwin, "'We Cannot Treat Negroes,'" 138–39, 142–43.

63. Forsyth, *Camden Expedition,* 139.

64. Bragg, "Chasing Steele," 9; Forsyth, *Camden Expedition,* 139–44; Joiner, *Howling Wilderness,* 123–24.

65. Bragg, "Chasing Steele," 10; Pitcock and Gurley, *I Acted from Principle,* 148–49; Sperry, *33rd Iowa,* 86–89; Forsyth, *Camden Expedition,* 144–49.

66. Forsyth, *Camden Expedition,* 149.

67. *OR,* 34(1):556, 677, 757; Cathey, "Extracts," 104; Crawford, *Kansas in the Sixties,* 118–19; Pitcock and Gurley, *I Acted from Principle,* 149–51; White, "Bluecoat's Account," 87; Forsyth, *Camden Expedition,* 149–51, 154–55; Joiner, *Howling Wilderness,* 125–26.

68. Sperry, *33rd Iowa,* 88–89.

69. *OR,* 34(1):481, 677–78, 697, 782, 799–800, 813, 815; Crawford, *Kansas in the Sixties,* 118–19; Forsyth, *Camden Expedition,* 150–51, 153–55, 170; Lothrop, *First Regiment Iowa Cavalry,* 166 .

70. Bragg, "Chasing Steele," 10.

71. Cathey, "Extracts," 105; Sperry, *33rd Iowa,* 90.

72. Lothrop, *First Regiment Iowa Cavalry,* 166. See also *OR,* 34(1):741; and Cathey, "Extracts," 104.

73. *OR,* 34(1):799–800, 813, 815; Bragg, "Chasing Steele," 10; Forsyth, *Camden Expedition,* 154–64; Joiner, *Howling Wilderness,* 126.

74. [Blessington], *Campaigns of Walker's Texas Division,* 250–51.

75. Sperry, *33rd Iowa,* 91.

76. *OR,* 34(1):813, 818; Crawford, *Kansas in the Sixties,* 117, 123–25; Forsyth, *Camden Expedition,* 164–71; Joiner, *Howling Wilderness,* 126; Urwin, "'We Cannot Treat Negroes,'" 143–44.

77. Bragg, "Chasing Steele," 11.

78. Sperry, *33rd Iowa,* 94–95; Forsyth, *Camden Expedition,* 170–71, 173, 178; Urwin, "'We Cannot Treat Negroes,'" 144–46.

79. Sperry, *33rd Iowa,* 94.

80. *OR,* 34(1):557, 670, 727; Forsyth, *Camden Expedition,* 173–74.

81. Lothrop, *First Regiment Iowa Cavalry,* 166–67; Sperry, *33rd Iowa,* 96–98; Forsyth, *Camden Expedition,* 170–71, 173–78.

82. Forsyth, *Camden Expedition,* 178–85; Joiner, *Howling Wilderness,* 127, 129. The Olustee Campaign generally involved clear weather, except for a hard rain on the night of February 10–11. See Nulty, *Confederate Florida,* 78, 99, 124. There is little discussion of weather conditions before or during the Fort Pillow affair, but the ground was wet from recent rain. See Cimprich, *Fort Pillow;* Ward, *River Run Red;* and Wills, *River Was Dyed with Blood.*

CHAPTER 20

1. Grant, *Memoirs*, 2:51–62; Grimsley, *And Keep Moving On*, 2–12; Noe, *Southwest Virginia's Railroad*, 130–31; Rhea, *Wilderness*, 46–57.

2. Grant, *Memoirs*, 2:65; Jones, *Rebel War Clerk's Diary*, 2:179. See also Krick, *Civil War Weather*, 122; Rhea, *Wilderness*, 6–7, 20, 48; and Simpson, *Grant*, 289.

3. Baird, *Journals of Edmonds*, 191; Britton and Reed, *To My Beloved Wife*, 213–14; Cook, *Twelfth Massachusetts*, 126; Dawes, *Sixth Wisconsin*, 243; "Diaries of John Waldrop . . . and William Y. Mordecai," 51; Dobbins, *Grandfather's Journal*, 186–88; J. E. Green Diary, 73–74, P.C. 694, NCDAH; Jones, *Rebel War Clerk's Diary*, 2:179, 181, 182, 183–84, 185; McDonald, *Make Me a Map of the Valley*, 198–99; Frank Morse to Nellie, Apr. 5, 1864, Brandy Station, Va., Frank C. Morse Papers, MHS; Neese, *Three Years in the Confederate Horse Artillery*, 253; Nevins, *Diary of Battle*, 339–40; Rhodes, *All for the Union*, 141; Robertson, *Letters of McAllister*, 405, 406; Howard M. Smith Diary and Letters, 115–16, MMC, LC; Krick, *Civil War Weather*, 122.

4. Nevins, *Diary of Battle*, 340. See also Rosenblatt and Rosenblatt, *Hard Marching Every Day*, 205.

5. Agassiz, *Meade's Headquarters*, 82–83; James W. Albright Diary, 1–4, SHC-UNC; George Barnard to Father, Apr. 25, 27, 1864, "Headquarters, 1st Div., 5th Corps," George Middleton Barnard Papers, CWCDJ, MHS; Blight, *When This Cruel War Is Over*, 284, 289; Britton and Reed, *To My Beloved Wife*, 215, 218–20; J. B. Clifton Diary 33, P.C. 589, NCDAH; Green Diary, 74–76, NCDAH; Jones, *Rebel War Clerk's Diary*, 2:185–89, 191–92; McDonald, *Make Me a Map of the Valley*, 199–200; Nevins, *Diary of Battle*, 342–43; Rhodes, *All for the Union*, 142, 143; Robertson, *Letters of McAllister*, 408, 410; Rosenblatt and Rosenblatt, *Hard Marching Every Day*, 208; Smith Diary and Letters, 117–20, MMC, LC; Richard Waldrop to Mother, Apr. 15, 1864, Pisgah Church, Richard Woolfolk Waldrop Papers, SHC-UNC; Waldrop to Sister, Apr. 25, 1864, Pisgah, ibid.; Rhea, *Wilderness*, 48; Simpson, *Grant*, 284–85; *Augusta (Ga.) Daily Constitutionalist*, Apr. 12, 1864.

6. Nevins, *Diary of Battle*, 342.

7. Grant, *Memoirs*, 2:65–66 (quotation, 65). See also Rhea, *Wilderness*, 32–35; and Simpson, *Grant*, 289.

8. Grimsley, *And Keep Moving On*, 24; McMurry, *Atlanta*, 52; Rhea, *Wilderness*, 20–29.

9. Britton and Reed, *To My Beloved Wife*, 221; Clifton Diary, 34, NCDAH; Dobbins, *Grandfather's Journal*, 190; Green Diary, 77, NCDAH; Benjamin Wesley Justice to Wife, May 4, 1864, Orange County, Va., Benjamin Wesley Justice Papers, Emory; McDonald, *Make Me a Map of the Valley*, 200; Frank Morse to Nellie, Apr. 27, 28, 30, 1864, Brandy Station, Va., Morse Papers, MHS; Rhodes, *All for the Union*, 143; Krick, *Civil War Weather*, 122, 129.

10. Preston, *Tenth New York Cavalry*, 169–70. See also Britton and Reed, *To My Beloved Wife*, 221; Clifton Diary, 34, NCDAH; Dobbins, *Grandfather's Journal*, 190; Galwey, *Valiant Hours*, 197, 201; Green Diary, 77, NCDAH; Benjamin Wesley Justice to Wife, May 4, 1864, Orange County, Va., Justice Papers, Emory; McDonald, *Make Me a Map of the Valley*, 200; Neese, *Three Years in the Confederate Horse Artillery*, 258; Rhodes, *All for the Union*, 143; White, "Diary of the War," 240; and Krick, *Civil War Weather*, 122, 129.

11. White, "Diary of the War," 240.

12. Silliker, *Rebel Yell & the Yankee Hurrah*, 141. See also Britton and Reed, *To My Beloved Wife*, 221; Clifton Diary, 34, NCDAH; Howard, *Recollections*, 268; McDonald, *Make Me a Map of the Valley*, 200; Nevins, *Diary of Battle*, 347; Preston, *Tenth New York Cavalry*, 170; Charles E. Wood Diary, May 2–3, 1864, Charles E. Wood Diary and Correspondence, Box 125, CWMC, USAMHI; Krick, *Civil War Weather*, 129; and Rhea, *Wilderness*, 60–64.

13. Porter, *Campaigning with Grant*, 42. See also Britton and Reed, *To My Beloved Wife*, 221; Galwey, *Valiant Hours*, 195; Howe, *Touched with Fire*, 103; McDonald, *Make Me a Map of the Valley*, 201;

Nevins, *Diary of Battle*, 349; Rosenblatt and Rosenblatt, *Hard Marching Every Day*, 215; "Diaries of John Waldrop . . . and William Y. Mordecai," 5; Welch, *Confederate Surgeon's Letters*, 91; and Krick, *Civil War Weather*, 125.

14. Grimsley, *And Keep Moving On*, 24–30; Rhea, *Wilderness*, 64–93, 118–19; Simpson, *Grant*, 292–93; Krick, *Civil War Weather*, 129.

15. McDonald, *Make Me a Map of the Valley*, 201; Grimsley, *And Keep Moving On*, 30–47; Rhea, *Wilderness*, 93–282; Simpson, *Grant*, 293–96; Krick, *Civil War Weather*, 125, 129; Petty, "Reconsidering the Wilderness's Role in the Battle," 413–38.

16. Dobbins, *Grandfather's Journal*, 191; Grant, *Memoirs*, 2:113–14; McDonald, *Make Me a Map of the Valley*, 202; Neese, *Three Years in the Confederate Horse Artillery*, 261; Porter, *Campaigning with Grant*, 62; Sparks, *Inside Lincoln's Army*, 368; Grimsley, *And Keep Moving On*, 47–58; Rhea, *Wilderness*, 283–430; Simpson, *Grant*, 297–99; Krick, *Civil War Weather*, 129.

17. Tyler, *Recollections*, 163; Krick, *Civil War Weather*, 125.

18. Agassiz, *Meade's Headquarters*, 102; Dobbins, *Grandfather's Journal*, 191; Galwey, *Valiant Hours*, 201; Grant, *Memoirs*, 2:118–21; McDonald, *Make Me a Map of the Valley*, 202; Porter, *Campaigning with Grant*, 74, 80, 82; Grimsley, *And Keep Moving On*, 58–61; Rhea, *Spotsylvania*, 7–17; Rhea, *Wilderness*, 430–52; Simpson, *Grant*, 299–303; Krick, *Civil War Weather*, 129.

19. Agassiz, *Meade's Headquarters*, 104, 107; Britton and Reed, *To My Beloved Wife*, 226; J. P. Coburn to unknown, May 8, 1864, James Parley Coburn Papers, USAMHI; Galwey, *Valiant Hours*, 202; Grant, *Memoirs*, 2:114–15, 119–27; Malles, *Bridge Building in Wartime*, 214, 215; McDonald, *Make Me a Map of the Valley*, 202; Nevins, *Diary of Battle*, 355; Grimsley, *And Keep Moving On*, 61–73; Krick, *Civil War Weather*, 125; Rhea, *Spotsylvania*, 7, 17–122; Simpson, *Grant*, 301–5.

20. Britton and Reed, *To My Beloved Wife*, 226; Dobbins, *Grandfather's Journal*, 192; Grant, *Memoirs*, 2:127–32; Malles, *Bridge Building in Wartime*, 216; McDonald, *Make Me a Map of the Valley*, 203; Sparks, *Inside Lincoln's Army*, 371; "Diaries of John Waldrop . . . and William Y. Mordecai," 51; Grimsley, *And Keep Moving On*, 73–84; Krick, *Civil War Weather*, 125; Rhea, *Spotsylvania*, 122–88, 212–23; Simpson, *Grant*, 305–7.

21. Porter, *Campaigning with Grant*, 100, 101.

22. Krick, *Civil War Weather*, 129.

23. Foster, *Reminiscences*, 67–70; Preston, *Tenth New York Cavalry*, 175; Grimsley, *And Keep Moving On*, 110–13; Rhea, *Spotsylvania*, 189–97.

24. Grimsley, *And Keep Moving On*, 113–17; Krick, *Civil War Weather*, 125; Rhea, *Spotsylvania*, 197–206.

25. Jones, *Rebel War Clerk's Diary*, 2:207. Krick, *Civil War Weather*.

26. Peck, *Reminiscences*, 46–47. See also Preston, *Tenth New York Cavalry*, 181.

27. Carter, *Yorktown to Santiago*, 111; Isaac R. Dunkelbarger Recollections, 21, Winey Collection, USAMHI; Foster, *Reminiscences*, 74–77; Peck, *Reminiscences*, 47–48; Grimsley, *And Keep Moving On*, 116–18; Rhea, *Spotsylvania*, 206–12; Rhea, *To the North Anna*, 41–59.

28. OR, 36(1):297, 334, 358; Benson, *Berry Benson's Civil War Book*, 70; Blight, *When This Cruel War Is Over*, 292; Britton and Reed, *To My Beloved Wife*, 227; Caldwell, *Brigade of South Carolinians*, 188; Cook, *Twelfth Massachusetts*, 131; Dobbins, *Grandfather's Journal*, 192; Douglas, *I Rode with Stonewall*, 282; Haines, *Fifteenth New Jersey*, 172; Benjamin Wesley Justice to Wife, May 11, 1864, Justice Papers, Emory; D. R. Larned to Sister, May 13, 1864, "in the Woods," Daniel Read Larned Papers, LC; Neese, *Three Years in the Confederate Horse Artillery*, 266; Toney, *Privations of a Private*, 71; Henry P. Turner Diary, May 11, 1864, Box 116, CWMC, USAMHI; "Diaries of John Waldrop . . . and William Y. Mordecai," 52; Grimsley, *And Keep Moving On*, 83–84; Krick, *Civil War Weather*, 125, 129; Rhea, *Spotsylvania*, 221–25, 228–31.

29. Tyler, *Recollections*, 170. Robert Krick notes that rain was lighter to the north in Warrenton, suggesting a strong local cell over Spotsylvania. *Civil War Weather*, 124.

30. Silliker, *Rebel Yell & the Yankee Hurrah*, 154. See also McDonald, *Make Me a Map of the Valley*, 203.

31. OR, 36(1):335, 358, 1044, 1078–79; Casler, *Four Years in the Stonewall Brigade*, 212; Grant, *Memoirs*, 2:136–37; Benjamin Wesley Justice to Wife, May 16, 1864, Spotsylvania Court House, Va., Justice Papers, Emory; McDonald, *Make Me a Map of the Valley*, 203; Page, "Captured Guns," 535; Porter, *Campaigning with Grant*, 101–6; Stiles, *Four Years under Marse Robert*, 261; Toney, *Privations of a Private*, 71; Tyler, *Recollections*, 182; Worsham, *One of Jackson's Foot Cavalry*, 134; Grimsley, *And Keep Moving On*, 84–86; Hess, *Trench Warfare*, 45–48, 59–73; Krick, *Civil War Weather*, 125, 129; Rhea, *Spotsylvania*, 225–46; Simpson, *Grant*, 310–11.

32. OR, 36(1):230, 412, 491, 500, 620; Britton and Reed, *To My Beloved Wife*, 227; Caldwell, *Brigade of South Carolinians*, 188–95; Clifton Diary, 35, NCDAH; Dobbins, *Grandfather's Journal*, 194; Grant, *Memoirs*, 2:137–38; Hyde, *Following the Greek Cross*, 200–201; McDonald, *Make Me a Map of the Valley*, 204; Neese, *Three Years in the Confederate Horse Artillery*, 268, 269; Page, "Captured Guns," 536; Porter, *Campaigning with Grant*, 106–10; Rhodes, *All for the Union*, 151–52; Sparks, *Inside Lincoln's Army*, 372; Tyler, *Recollections*, 195; Grimsley, *And Keep Moving On*, 86–91; Rhea, *Spotsylvania*, 246–307.

33. Porter, *Campaigning with Grant*, 110–11.

34. Rhea, *Spotsylvania*, 291–92.

35. OR, 36(1):5, 69, 70, 298, 525, 543, 549, 570, 984, 1092; Benson, *Berry Benson's Civil War Book*, 77; Blight, *When This Cruel War Is Over*, 296; Dawes, *Sixth Wisconsin*, 269–70; Dobbins, *Grandfather's Journal*, 194; Green Diary, 82, NCDAH; Benjamin Wesley Justice to Wife, May 14, 1864, Spotsylvania Court House, Va., Justice Papers, Emory; Malles, *Bridge Building in Wartime*, 219; McDonald, *Make Me a Map of the Valley*, 204; Neese, *Three Years in the Confederate Horse Artillery*, 271; Sparks, *Inside Lincoln's Army*, 373; Turner Diary, May 13, 1864, CWMC, USAMHI; Tyler, *Recollections*, 203–4; Grimsley, *And Keep Moving On*, 90–91; Krick, *Civil War Weather*, 129; Rhea, *Spotsylvania*, 308–11; Rhea, *To the North Anna*, 21–33, 65–87.

36. George Barnard, to Father, May 14, 1864, "Headquarters, 1st Div., 5th Corps," Barnard Papers, CWCDJ, MHS.

37. Sparks, *Inside Lincoln's Army*, 373.

38. Nevins, *Diary of Battle*, 369, 370, 372. See also Graves, *Bedford Light Artillery*, 45.

39. Britton and Reed, *To My Beloved Wife*, 229; Caldwell, *Brigade of South Carolinians*, 201; Clifton Diary, 35, NCDAH; Dobbins, *Grandfather's Journal*, 194–95; Galwey, *Valiant Hours*, 214; Green Diary, 83, NCDAH; Thomas L. McCarty Diary, May 15, 1864, (Thomas L.) McCarty Papers, UT-CAH; McDonald, *Make Me a Map of the Valley*, 204–5; Ethel Lowerre Phelps, ed., "A Chaplain's Life in the Civil War: The Diary of Winthrop Henry Phelps," 1, Winthrop Henry Phelps Papers, LC; Porter, *Campaigning with Grant*, 119–20; Sparks, *Inside Lincoln's Army*, 373; Turner Diary, May 15–16, 1864, CWMC, USAMHI; Tyler, *Recollections*, 204; Krick, *Civil War Weather*, 124; Rhea, *To the North Anna*, 87–125.

40. OR, 36(2):810. See also OR, 36(1):5.

41. OR, 36(1):72, 36(2):840; Britton and Reed, *To My Beloved Wife*, 229; J. P. Coburn to Ones at Home, May 17, 1864, Wilderness, Va., Coburn Papers, USAMHI; Dobbins, *Grandfather's Journal*, 196; Galwey, *Valiant Hours*, 216; Grant, *Memoirs*, 2:140–41; Green Diary, 83, NCDAH; Jones, *Rebel War Clerk's Diary*, 2:213, 214; McCarty Diary, May 18, 1864, McCarty Papers, UT-CAH; Porter, *Campaigning with Grant*, 123–24; Roper, *Repairing the "March of Mars,"* 545; Richard Waldrop to Father, May 17, 1864, Waldrop Papers, SHC-UNC; Grimsley, *And Keep Moving On*, 91–92; Krick, *Civil War Weather*, 129; Rhea, *To the North Anna*, 126–53.

42. Bruce, "Battle of New Market," 553–54; Farrar, *Twenty-Second Pennsylvania Cavalry*, 221–23; Grant, *Memoirs*, 2:142; Lincoln, *Thirty-Fourth Mass.*, 280, 282–83; Lynch, *Diary*, 58–60; Manarin, "Diary of Rufus J. Woolwine," 436; Davis, *Battle of New Market*, 33, 50, 57, 69, 70, 74, 77, 80, 81, 86, 97, 99, 123, 135–38, 163; Grimsley, *And Keep Moving On*, 91–110; Noe, *Southwest Virginia's Railroad*, 131–33; Rhea, *To the North Anna*, 126–27.

43. Beecher, *First Light Battery*, 2:440–44; Emmerton, *Twenty-Third Regiment Mass. Vol. Infantry*, 185–86 (quotation, 185). See also Bartlett, *Twelfth New Hampshire*, 175–82; Clark, *Iron Hearted Regiment*, 116–17; Derby, *Bearing Arms in the Twenty-Seventh Massachusetts*, 271; Jones, *Under the Stars and Bars*, 188; Kreutzer, *Notes and Observations*, 191–92; and Smith Diary and Letters, 123, MMC, LC.

44. Bartlett, *Twelfth New Hampshire*, 175–82; Clark, *Iron Hearted Regiment*, 116–17; Derby, *Bearing Arms in the Twenty-Seventh Massachusetts*, 271; Grimsley, *And Keep Moving On*, 118–29; Rhea, *To the North Anna*, 126–27, 153–55; Robertson, *Back Door to Richmond*, 144, 145, 149, 166, 178, 182, 213, 220.

45. Grant, *Memoirs*, 2:142. See also Porter, *Campaigning with Grant*, 125; Grimsley, *And Keep Moving On*, 129–31; Krick, *Civil War Weather*, 129; and Rhea, *To the North Anna*, 155–63.

46. Haines, *Fifteenth New Jersey*, 187.

47. Blackford et al., *Letters from Lee's Army*, 245; Britton and Reed, *To My Beloved Wife*, 230; McCarty Diary, May 19, 1864, McCarty Papers, UT-CAH; Porter, *Campaigning with Grant*, 128; Robertson, *Letters of McAllister*, 424; Grimsley, *And Keep Moving On*, 131–34; Krick, *Civil War Weather*, 129; Rhea, *To the North Anna*, 164–88.

48. *OR*, 36(1):389, 432, 464, 465; Agassiz, *Meade's Headquarters*, 129; Britton and Reed, *To My Beloved Wife*, 232; Clifton Diary, 36, 37, NCDAH; Dobbins, *Grandfather's Journal*, 196; Galwey, *Valiant Hours*, 219, 223, 225; Grant, *Memoirs*, 2:146–52; Haines, *Fifteenth New Jersey*, 188; Benjamin Wesley Justice to Wife, May 20, 25, 1864, Spotsylvania Court House, Va., Justice Papers, Emory; Malles, *Bridge Building in Wartime*, 223, 226; Nevins, *Diary of Battle*, 379–80; Porter, *Campaigning with Grant*, 135; Preston, *Tenth New York Cavalry*, 186; Pyne, *Ride to War*, 208; Rosenblatt and Rosenblatt, *Hard Marching Every Day*, 222; Wood Diary, May 20, 1864, Wood Diary and Correspondence, CWMC, US-AMHI; Grimsley, *And Keep Moving On*, 134–35, 136–46; Krick, *Civil War Weather*, 129; Rhea, *To the North Anna*, 188–98, 212–354.

49. *OR*, 36(1):311, 390, 688, 750; Bartlett, *Twelfth New Hampshire*, 200; Blackford et al., *Letters from Lee's Army*, 248; Britton and Reed, *To My Beloved Wife*, 233; Dawes, *Sixth Wisconsin*, 277–78; "Diaries of John Waldrop . . . and William Y. Mordecai," 52; "Diary of Creed T. Davis," 12; Green Diary, 86, NCDAH; Haines, *Fifteenth New Jersey*, 195; Neese, *Three Years in the Confederate Horse Artillery*, 276, 278; Phelps, "Chaplain's Life," 5, Phelps Papers, LC; Porter, *Campaigning with Grant*, 151; Preston, *Tenth New York Cavalry*, 188–89; Pyne, *Ride to War*, 207–14; Roper, *Repairing the "March of Mars,"* 549; Smith Diary and Letters, 125, MMC, LC; Sparks, *Inside Lincoln's Army*, 377, 378; Grimsley, *And Keep Moving On*, 146–60, 196–200; Krick, *Civil War Weather*, 123, 129; Rhea, *Cold Harbor*, 27–194.

50. Tyler, *Recollections*, 210.

51. Galwey, *Valiant Hours*, 229; Pyne, *Ride to War*, 215; Grimsley, *And Keep Moving On*, 200–207; Krick, *Civil War Weather*, 132; Rhea, *Cold Harbor*, 195–270.

52. *OR*, 36(1):87, 245, 344; Agassiz, *Meade's Headquarters*, 140. See also Bartlett, *Twelfth New Hampshire*, 202; Blight, *When This Cruel War Is Over*, 311; Cook, *Twelfth Massachusetts*, 134; Dobbins, *Grandfather's Journal*, 198; George M. Edgar to Colonel Johnston, July 24, 1902, Richmond, Ky., George Mathews Edgar Papers, SHC-UNC; Green Diary, 88, NCDAH; Haines, *Fifteenth New Jersey*, 206; McDonald, *Make Me a Map of the Valley*, 209; Neese, *Three Years in the Confederate Horse Artillery*, 279; Preston, *Tenth New York Cavalry*, 194; Pyne, *Ride to War*, 222; Rhodes, *All for the Union*, 158; Silliker, *Rebel Yell & the Yankee Hurrah*, 165; and Rhea, *Cold Harbor*, 271–317.

53. Agassiz, *Meade's Headquarters*, 143; George M. Edgar to Colonel Johnston, July 24, 1902, Rich-

mond, Ky., Edgar Papers, SHC-UNC; J. K. Thompson to George M. Edgar, July 22, 1902, Charleston, W.Va., ibid.; Grimsley, *And Keep Moving On*, 207–19; Krick, *Civil War Weather*, 132; Rhea, *Cold Harbor*, 270–395; Simpson, *Grant*, 326–31.

54. *OR*, 36(1):368; Bartlett, *Twelfth New Hampshire*, 214; Britton and Reed, *To My Beloved Wife*, 237; Clifton Diary, 39, NCDAH; "Diary of Creed T. Davis," 13, 14; Dobbins, *Grandfather's Journal*, 198; Grant, *Memoirs*, 2:169–71; Green Diary, 89, NCDAH; Hamilton, *Papers of Shotwell*, 2:90; McCarty Diary, June 3, 1864, McCarty Papers, UT-CAH; McDonald, *Make Me a Map of the Valley*, 209–10; Neese, *Three Years in the Confederate Horse Artillery*, 281; Sparks, *Inside Lincoln's Army*, 380; White, "Diary of the War," 257; Wood Diary, June 4, 1864, Wood Diary and Correspondence, CWMC, US-AMHI; Krick, *Civil War Weather*, 132. In Baltimore, Republicans and dissident prowar Democrats met in convention on June 7 as the National Union Party. They unanimously renominated Lincoln for the presidency. Coupled with the grinding campaign continuing in Georgia, Cold Harbor ensured that Lincoln had a tough fight ahead.

55. Porter, *Campaigning with Grant*, 184.

56. Grimsley, *And Keep Moving On*, 220.

57. Grant, *Memoirs*, 2:172–77; Brady, *War upon the Land*, 78–79; Grimsley, *And Keep Moving On*, 222–23; McPherson, *Battle Cry of Freedom*, 735–39.

58. Britton and Reed, *To My Beloved Wife*, 238; "Diary of Creed T. Davis," 14; Grant, *Memoirs*, 2:177–81; Haines, *Fifteenth New Jersey*, 214; McCarty Diary, June 12, 1864, McCarty Papers, UT-CAH; McDonald, *Make Me a Map of the Valley*, 210; Neese, *Three Years in the Confederate Horse Artillery*, 288; Nevins, *Diary of Battle*, 413; Smith Diary and Letters, 126–27, MMC, LC; Sparks, *Inside Lincoln's Army*, 381, 382; "Diaries of John Waldrop . . . and William Y. Mordecai," 53; Krick, *Civil War Weather*, 132.

59. Porter, *Campaigning with Grant*, 195.

60. Grant, *Memoirs*, 2:185; McCarty Diary, June 14, 15, 1864, McCarty Papers, UT-CAH; Roper, *Repairing the "March of Mars,"* 554; White, "Diary of the War," 262; Simpson, *Grant*, 331–37.

61. Porter, *Campaigning with Grant*, 197.

62. Clark, *Iron Hearted Regiment*, 135. See also Frank Morse to Nellie, June 15, 1864, Charles City Court House, Va., Morse Papers, MHS.

63. Reardon, *With a Sword in One Hand*, 104–21.

64. Beecher, *First Light Battery*, 2:484; J. P. Coburn to Parents, June 17, 1864, Petersburg, Va., Coburn Papers, USAMHI; Dobbins, *Grandfather's Journal*, 200; Grant, *Memoirs*, 2:185–89; Sparks, *Inside Lincoln's Army*, 384, 385; Stiles, *Four Years under Marse Robert*, 309; Tyler, *Recollections*, 218.

65. Sparks, *Inside Lincoln's Army*, 384.

66. *OR*, 36(1):253.

67. Agassiz, *Meade's Headquarters*, 164.

68. Agassiz, *Meade's Headquarters*, 166; Porter, *Campaigning with Grant*, 203; Simpson, *Grant*, 337–38.

69. Albright Diary, 21, SHC-UNC; Bartlett, *Twelfth New Hampshire*, 220; Britton and Reed, *To My Beloved Wife*, 240, 241; Caldwell, *Brigade of South Carolinians*, 213; J. P. Coburn to Parents, June 17, 1864, Petersburg, Va., Coburn Papers, USAMHI; Haines, *Fifteenth New Jersey*, 218; Nevins, *Diary of Battle*, 422; Smith Diary and Letters, 127, MMC, LC; McPherson, *Battle Cry of Freedom*, 740–42; Simpson, *Grant*, 337–41.

70. Albright Diary, 21–23, SHC-UNC; Bartlett, *Twelfth New Hampshire*, 220; Britton and Reed, *To My Beloved Wife*, 241; Caldwell, *Brigade of South Carolinians*, 215; Dobbins, *Grandfather's Journal*, 200; Grant, *Memoirs*, 2:190–91; Haines, *Fifteenth New Jersey*, 219; McCarty Diary, June 22, 23, 1864, McCarty Papers, UT-CAH; Frank Morse to Nellie, June 23, 1864, Morse Papers, MHS; Porter, *Campaigning with Grant*, 218; Rosenblatt and Rosenblatt, *Hard Marching Every Day*, 229; Tyler, *Recollections*, 229; Simpson, *Grant*, 341–43.

71. Porter, *Campaigning with Grant*, 218.

72. Grant, *Memoirs*, 2:190–91, 194–96; Grimsley, *And Keep Moving On*, 223–24; Simpson, *Grant*, 341–45.

CHAPTER 21

1. *Alexandria (Va.) Gazette*, June 23, 1864. See also ibid., June 30, 1864; *Richmond Examiner*, Aug. 17, 1864; *Richmond Sentinel*, July 5, 1864; *Richmond Whig*, July 27, 1864; *Richmond Whig and Public Advertiser*, Aug. 15, 1864; and D. V. Gilkerson to Brother, June 6, 1864, Letters of the Gilkerson Family, 1862–1864, *Valley of the Shadow*, http://valley.lib.virginia.edu/papers/A1104, accessed July 10, 2019.

2. Robertson, *Letters of McAllister*, 462.

3. *Charleston Mercury*, Aug. 9, 1864; *Cincinnati Daily Commercial*, Sept. 5, 15, 1864; *New York Evangelist*, Sept. 1, 1864; *North American and United States Gazette* (Philadelphia), Sept. 13, 1864; *OR*, 41(4):827.

4. *New York Daily Tribune*, Sept. 13, 1864. See also the *Cincinnati Daily Commercial*, Sept. 5, 1864; and *Philadelphia Inquirer*, Sept. 15, 1864.

5. *New York Daily Tribune*, Nov. 8, 1864. See also *Saint Paul Pioneer & Democrat*, Nov. 18, 1864.

6. *OR*, 40(1):494, 622, 635, 637; Agassiz, *Meade's Headquarters*, 178–79; James W. Albright Diary, 24–27, SHC-UNC; George Barnard to Father, June 24, 1864, "Headquarters, 1st Div., 5th Corps," George Middleton Barnard Papers, CWCDJ, MHS; Bartlett, *Twelfth New Hampshire*, 221; Britton and Reed, *To My Beloved Wife*, 244–45; Child, *Fifth New Hampshire*, 263, 264; J. B. Clifton Diary, 40, P.C. 589, NCDAH; J. P. Coburn to Parents, June 26, 1864, Petersburg, Va., James Parley Coburn Papers, USAMHI; John Willis Council Diary, 6, P.C. 1169.1, NCDAH; Dawes, *Sixth Wisconsin*, 292; "Diary of Creed T. Davis," 14; Dobbins, *Grandfather's Journal*, 201; Benjamin Wesley Justice to Wife, June 27, 1864, Petersburg, Va., Benjamin Wesley Justice Papers, Emory; Thomas L. McCarty Diary, June 26–30, 1864, (Thomas L.) McCarty Papers, UT-CAH; Frank Morse to Nellie, June 26, 1864, Frank C. Morse Papers, MHS; Nevins, *Diary of Battle*, 429, 430; Rhodes, *All for the Union*, 166; James A. Reynolds Diary, June 26–30, 1864, Bound Vol. 15, Richmond National Battlefield Park, Richmond, Va.; Robertson, *Letters of McAllister*, 454, 455; Silliker, *Rebel Yell & the Yankee Hurrah*, 176–77; Sparks, *Inside Lincoln's Army*, 388; "Gilbert Thompson Journal, 1857–1901," June 26, 1864, Gilbert Thompson Papers, Manuscript/Mixed Material, LC, https://www.loc.gov/item/mm81095752/, accessed Nov. 27, 2018; Tyler, *Recollections*, 233; Krick, *Civil War Weather*, 132; A. Wilson Greene, email to author, Nov. 21, 2018. Franklin Riley claimed readings of 100 degrees in the shade on June 25 and 105 degrees the next day. Gilbert Thompson wrote that it reached 106 degrees on June 26. Mason Tyler, meanwhile, claimed readings of 102 degrees for three days running. Charles Wainwright mentioned 101 degrees in the shade on June 25.

7. Howe, *Touched with Fire*, 149–50. "Orcus," originally the name of a Roman deity, was another term for hell.

8. Krick, *Civil War Weather*, 134; *OR*, 40(1):31, 33, 37; Sanford, *Fighting Rebels and Redskins*, 251; Howard M. Smith Diary and Letters, 131–32, MMC, LC.

9. Rhodes, *All for the Union*, 166; Beecher, *First Light Battery*, 2:511 (quotation, 511).

10. Agassiz, *Meade's Headquarters*, 186.

11. Silliker, *Rebel Yell & the Yankee Hurrah*, 178, 179.

12. *OR*, 40(1):35, 36, 37, 40(3):35, 335, 336, 444, 446; Albright Diary, 27–38, SHC-UNC; Agassiz, *Meade's Headquarters*, 184, 186, 189, 193, 194; *Augusta (Ga.) Daily Constitutionalist*, July 31, 1864; Bartlett, *Twelfth New Hampshire*, 222–23; Britton and Reed, *To My Beloved Wife*, 246, 254; Caldwell, *Brigade of South Carolinians*, 221–22; Child, *Fifth New Hampshire*, 264–73; Clark, *Iron Hearted Regiment*, 141, 143, 144; Clifton Diary, 4, 43, NCDAH; J. P. Coburn to Parents, July 11, 22, 1864, Petersburg, Va.,

Coburn Papers, USAMHI; O. D. Cooke to My Dear Col., July 20, 1864, Petersburg, William J. Clarke Papers, SHC-UNC; Council Diary, 8, NCDAH; Dickey, *Eighty-Fifth Pennsylvania*, 347–49; Dobbins, *Grandfather's Journal*, 202–6; John B. Evans to Companion, July 13, 21, 1864, Petersburg, Va., John B. Evans Papers, 1862–1865, Duke; Haines, *Fifteenth New Jersey*, 221–23; Jones, *Rebel War Clerk's Diary*, 2:241–58; Nevins, *Diary of Battle*, 431, 434, 436, 438, 439; Rhodes, *All for the Union*, 161, 166–69; Robertson, *Letters of McAllister*, 456–65; Rosenblatt and Rosenblatt, *Hard Marching Every Day*, 232–34; Silliker, *Rebel Yell & the Yankee Hurrah*, 178–79, 182, 184–85, 187; Smith Diary and Letters, 133, MMC, LC; Sparks, *Inside Lincoln's Army*, 391, 392, 397; Tyler, *Recollections*, 236; White, "Diary of the War," 275; Power, *Lee's Miserables*, 121.

13. Simpson, *Grant*, 346–55.

14. Early, *War Memoirs*, 459.

15. McDonald, *Make Me a Map of the Valley*, 211–14; Cooling, *Monocacy*, 1, 11–12, 85–87; Simpson, *Grant*, 355–57; Vandiver, *Jubal's Raid*, 31, 32, 54, 55, 56, 59–104.

16. John G. Young Diary, 38, John G. Young Papers, P.C. 1076, NCDAH.

17. McDonald, *Make Me a Map of the Valley*, 215; Worsham, *One of Jackson's Foot Cavalry*, 151; Cooling, *Monocacy*, 85–165; Krick, *Civil War Weather*, 134; Vandiver, *Jubal's Raid*, 109–21, 149, 150, 151.

18. Cooling, *Monocacy*, 180.

19. McDonald, *Make Me a Map of the Valley*, 215; Cooling, *Monocacy*, 163–65, 180–84; Krick, *Civil War Weather*, 134; Vandiver, *Jubal's Raid*, 122–53.

20. Worsham, *One of Jackson's Foot Cavalry*, 156.

21. Roper, *Repairing the "March of Mars,"* 569.

22. Young Diary, 39, Young Papers, NCDAH.

23. Early, *War Memoirs*, 389.

24. Britton and Reed, *To My Beloved Wife*, 259–61; Early, *War Memoirs*, 389, 391; J. E. Green Diary, 97–99, P.C. 694, NCDAH; Haines, *Fifteenth New Jersey*, 230, 232, 236–37; McDonald, *Make Me a Map of the Valley*, 215–19; William W. Old Diary, July 11, 1864, MMC, LC; Rhodes, *All for the Union*, 169; Roper, *Repairing the "March of Mars,"* 572, 577–79; "Augusta County: Diary of Alansa Rounds Sterrett (1860–1913)," July 16, 1863, Valley Personal Papers, *Valley of the Shadow*, http://valley.lib.virginia.edu/papers/AD9001, accessed July 10, 2019; Tyler, *Recollections*, 252, 254; Young Diary, 40, Young Papers, NCDAH; Cooling, *Monocacy*, 184–200; Krick, *Civil War Weather*, 134; McPherson, *Battle Cry of Freedom*, 757–58; Vandiver, *Jubal's Raid*, 153–73.

25. Cooling, *Monocacy*, 200–225; Simpson, *Grant*, 360–61; Vandiver, *Jubal's Raid*, 173–74.

26. *OR*, 37(2):301.

27. *OR*, 40(1):136, 321, 622, 40(3):474, 476, 789, 801, 806; Grant, *Memoirs*, 2:198–201; Krick, *Civil War Weather*, 134; Levin, *Remembering the Battle of the Crater*, 10–14; McPherson, *Battle Cry of Freedom*, 758–59; Simpson, *Grant*, 364–67.

28. Albright Diary, 34, SHC-UNC.

29. Grant, *Memoirs*, 2:201–4; Stewart, *Pair of Blankets*, 152; Krick, *Civil War Weather*, 134; Levin, *Remembering the Battle of the Crater*, 15–32; McPherson, *Battle Cry of Freedom*, 759–60; Simpson, *Grant*, 364–67.

30. *OR*, 40(1):17.

31. Clark, *Iron Hearted Regiment*, 145, 154. Clark incorrectly dates the assault. See also *OR*, 40(1):64, 165, 291, 324, 362, 529, 548, 551, 555, 556, 618.

32. Stewart, *Pair of Blankets*, 162.

33. Krick, *Civil War Weather*, 134.

34. Clark, *Iron Hearted Regiment*, 156–57. See also Blackford, *War Years*, 261.

35. Britton and Reed, *To My Beloved Wife*, 267–68, 270, 272–74; Buffum, *Memorial of the Great*

Rebellion, 92–95; Grant, *Memoirs,* 2:204–9, 213–14; Green Diary, 99, 103; NCDAH; Haines, *Fifteenth New Jersey,* 251–52; Lee, *Memoir of Pendleton,* 363; McDonald, *Make Me a Map of the Valley,* 219–24; Rhodes, *All for the Union,* 176–77; Roper, *Repairing the "March of Mars,"* 582, 584–86, 589, 591; Rosenblatt and Rosenblatt, *Hard Marching Every Day,* 246–47; Tyler, *Recollections,* 258, 260, 267; Walker, *Vermont Brigade,* 47–48; Hattaway and Jones, *How the North Won,* 615–16; McPherson, *Battle Cry of Freedom,* 760–73; Simpson, *Grant,* 367–69; Wert, *Winchester to Cedar Creek,* 15–16, 25–26, 31–38.

36. *OR,* 43(1):917.

37. Brady, *War upon the Land,* 80.

38. Krick, *Civil War Weather,* 137; *OR,* 42(1):308, 568, 694, 42(2):419, 434; Albright Diary, 39–47, SHC-UNC; Bartlett, *Twelfth New Hampshire,* 226–28; Beecher, *First Light Battery,* 2:550, 553, 553; Dawes, *Sixth Wisconsin,* 303; de Trobriand, *Four Years in the Army of the Potomac,* 628–29; Dickey, *Eighty-Fifth Pennsylvania,* 347–51, 353–56, 384; Dobbins, *Grandfather's Journal,* 206–10; Green Diary, 99, 103; NCDAH; Jones, *Rebel War Clerk's Diary,* 2:258–75; Nevins, *Diary of Battle,* 451; Preston, *Tenth New York Cavalry,* 224–26, 228; Pyne, *Ride to War,* 240–41; *Richmond Examiner,* Aug. 17, 1864; Welch, *Confederate Surgeon's Letters,* 103; White, "Diary of the War," 277, 278.

39. Bartlett, *Twelfth New Hampshire,* 228.

40. Albright Diary, 46, SHC-UNC.

41. *OR,* 42(1):191, 504, 505, 550, 926; Beecher, *First Light Battery,* 2:550, 553; de Trobriand, *Four Years in the Army of the Potomac,* 628–29, 634; Grant, *Memoirs,* 2:209, 211–12; White, "Diary of the War," 268, 277, 278; Hattaway and Jones, *How the North Won,* 616–17; Simpson, *Grant,* 367–72. A. Wilson Greene has pointed out to me that "Weldon Railroad" was slang. Greene, email to author, Nov. 21, 2018.

42. Chicago, Ill., Aug. 1864, Reel 116, RG 27.5.7, NARA-CP.

43. *OR,* 42(1):164, 180; Albright Diary, 48–57, SHC-UNC; Dickey, *Eighty-Fifth Pennsylvania,* 385–86; Dobbins, *Grandfather's Journal,* 211–15; Fleet and Fuller, *Green Mount,* 337, 341; Rosenblatt and Rosenblatt, *Hard Marching Every Day,* 254; Silliker, *Rebel Yell & the Yankee Hurrah,* 197, 200, 201; Sparks, *Inside Lincoln's Army,* 429, 432; Krick, *Civil War Weather,* 139. Temperatures on September 6, 8, 12, 14, and 25 failed to reach into the seventies.

44. *OR,* 43(1):1026, 43(2):34; Britton and Reed, *To My Beloved Wife,* 282–83, 287; "Diary of Creed T. Davis," 22–23; Garnett, "Diary," 4; Grant, *Memoirs,* 2:214–16; McDonald, *Make Me a Map of the Valley,* 226–28; Ethel Lowerre Phelps, ed., "A Chaplain's Life in the Civil War: The Diary of Winthrop Henry Phelps," 36–37, Winthrop Henry Phelps Papers, LC; Rhodes, *All for the Union,* 180–82; Smith Diary and Letters, 141–44, MMC, LC; Young Diary, 55, 57–59, Young Papers, NCDAH; Wert, *Winchester to Cedar Creek,* 38–45.

45. Ayers, *Thin Light of Freedom,* 236; Simpson, *Grant,* 379–80; Wert, *Winchester to Cedar Creek,* 47–134.

46. Baker, "Diary and Reminiscences," 114; Britton and Reed, *To My Beloved Wife,* 291–92, 294; "Diary of Creed T. Davis," 24–25; Grant, *Memoirs,* 2:216–18; Haines, *Fifteenth New Jersey,* 269; McDonald, *Make Me a Map of the Valley,* 228–34; Neese, *Three Years in the Confederate Horse Artillery,* 314, 315, 316; Rosenblatt and Rosenblatt, *Hard Marching Every Day,* 254; Ayers, *Thin Light of Freedom,* 236–41, 248–49; Brady, *War upon the Land,* 82–90; Simpson, *Grant,* 378–79; Wert, *Winchester to Cedar Creek,* 157–61.

47. *OR,* 43(1):30.

48. *OR,* 42(1):546, 550, 556, 558, 571, 620, 621, 662, 683, 43(1):6; Albright Diary, 57, SHC-UNC; Beecher, *First Light Battery,* 2:579–81; de Trobriand, *Four Years in the Army of the Potomac,* 651; Dobbins, *Grandfather's Journal,* 215; Grant, *Memoirs,* 2:218–19; Jones, *Rebel War Clerk's Diary,* 2:297–98; Nevins, *Diary of Battle,* 469; Preston, *Tenth New York Cavalry,* 228–29.

49. Beecher, *First Light Battery*, 2:582.

50. Krick, *Civil War Weather*, 139, 141. See also Phelps, "Chaplain's Life," 43, Phelps Papers, LC.

51. Bartlett, *Twelfth New Hampshire*, 242.

52. *OR*, 42(1):703, 716, 718; Agassiz, *Meade's Headquarters*, 261; Albright Diary, 57–63, SHC-UNC; Bartlett, *Twelfth New Hampshire*, 243, 243, Beecher, *First Light Battery*, 2:601, 606, 607; J. P. Coburn to Parents, Oct. 16, 1864, Petersburg, Va., Coburn Papers, USAMHI; Council Diary, 1, NCDAH; Dobbins, *Grandfather's Journal*, 215–18; Fleet and Fuller, *Green Mount*, 342, 343; Jones, *Rebel War Clerk's Diary*, 2:297–304, 307, 309–19; Alexander Grant Rose III Diary, 49–52, Box 100, CWMC, USAMHI; Krick, *Civil War Weather*, 139, 141.

53. *OR*, 43(2):313, 894; Britton and Reed, *To My Beloved Wife*, 295; "Diary of Creed T. Davis," 25–26; Garnett, "Diary," 12; McDonald, *Make Me a Map of the Valley*, 234–37; Neese, *Three Years in the Confederate Horse Artillery*, 322, 328; Rhodes, *All for the Union*, 191, 192; Rosenblatt and Rosenblatt, *Hard Marching Every Day*, 260; Sanford, *Fighting Rebels and Redskins*, 301–2; Tyler, *Recollections*, 295; Richard Waldrop to Mother, Oct. 2, 1864, Mt. Sidney, Richard Woolfolk Waldrop Papers, SHC-UNC.

54. Wert, *Winchester to Cedar Creek*, 168–76.

55. Early, *War Memoirs*, 444–45; Haines, *Fifteenth New Jersey*, 275; McDonald, *Make Me a Map of the Valley*, 239; Wert, *Winchester to Cedar Creek*, 177–238.

56. Wert, *Winchester to Cedar Creek*, 246–51.

57. Krick, *Civil War Weather*, 143.

58. John J. Armfield to Wife, Nov. 15, 24, 26, 1864, New Market, Va., John J. Armfield Papers, P.C. 286, NCDAH; Baker, "Diary and Reminiscences," 114; Britton and Reed, *To My Beloved Wife*, 305–11, 315; George A. Cary to Mother, Oct. 10, 18, 1864, "Camp," Cary Family Papers, 1856–1920, SpC MS 85, Special Collections, University of Maine, Orono; "Diaries of John Waldrop . . . and William Y. Mordecai," 55, 56; "Diary of Creed T. Davis," 26–28; John B. Evans to Wife, Nov. 15, 1864, New Market, Va., Evans Papers, Duke; Haines, *Fifteenth New Jersey*, 283; A. E. Henderson to Brother, Oct. 30, 1864, New Market, Va., Archibald Erskine Henderson Papers, 1841–1917, Duke; Hyde, *Following the Greek Cross*, 236; McDonald, *Make Me a Map of the Valley*, 242–46; Rhodes, *All for the Union*, 192, 195, 196–97; Rosenblatt and Rosenblatt, *Hard Marching Every Day*, 260, 270, 273, 276, 280, 284; Smith Diary and Letters, 151–55, MMC, LC; Tyler, *Recollections*, 294, 295, 298, 306, 307, 309.

59. John J. Armfield to Wife, Nov. 26, 1864, New Market, Va., Armfield Papers, NCDAH.

60. *OR*, 42(1):437, 439, 735, 796, 808; Porter, *Campaigning with Grant*, 309. See also Armstrong, *Nuggets of Experience*, 74; Chamberlayne, *Ham Chamberlayne*, 288; Rose Diary, 52, CWMC, USAMHI; Grant, *Memoirs*, 2:225; Stewart, *Pair of Blankets*, 184; Wert, *Winchester to Cedar Creek*, 160–68.

61. Silliker, *Rebel Yell & the Yankee Hurrah*, 214. See also Krick, *Civil War Weather*, 141.

62. Porter, *Campaigning with Grant*, 313.

63. Krick, *Civil War Weather*, 143; Agassiz, *Meade's Headquarters*, 273, 276, 277, 278; Albright Diary, 66–70, SHC-UNC; Bartlett, *Twelfth New Hampshire*, 252; Beecher, *First Light Battery*, 2:625, 626, 628; Brooks, *Washington in Lincoln's Time*, 216–18; "Diary of Creed T. Davis," 28–30; Dobbins, *Grandfather's Journal*, 219–21; Jones, *Rebel War Clerk's Diary*, 2:320–43; McCarty Diary, 16–19, McCarty Papers, UT-CAH; Nevins, *Diary of Battle*, 481; Preston, *Tenth New York Cavalry*, 236; Robertson, *Letters of McAllister*, 533, 543, 544; Rose Diary, 53–56, CWMC, USAMHI; Silliker, *Rebel Yell & the Yankee Hurrah*, 216–17, 220–21; Welch, *Confederate Surgeon's Letters*, 114; White, "Diary of the War," 296; James M. Willet to Wife, Nov. 20, 1864, Petersburg, Va., James M. Willet Collection: Correspondence, NYHS/CWPSD.

64. Rosenblatt and Rosenblatt, *Hard Marching Every Day*, 284. See also Norton, *Army Letters*, 244.

65. Chicago, Ill., Dec. 1864, Reel 116, RG 27.5.7, NARA-CP; Newport Barracks, Ky., Dec. 1864, Reel 190, ibid.; Springdale, Ky., Dec. 1864, Reel 193, ibid.; Annapolis, Md., Dec. 1864, Reel 212, ibid.; Natchez, Miss., Dec. 1864, Reel 277, ibid.; Wyaconda Prairie (Canton), Mo., Dec. 1864, Reel 280, ibid.; New York City, Dec. 1864, Reel 360, ibid.; Gettysburg, Pa., Dec. 1864, Reel 445, ibid.; Beau-

fort, S.C., Dec. 1864, Reel 464, ibid.; Krick, *Civil War Weather*, 146; Agassiz, *Meade's Headquarters*, 288; Albright Diary, 70–72, SHC-UNC; Beecher, *First Light Battery*, 2:630–32; Britton and Reed, *To My Beloved Wife*, 320–21; Caldwell, *Brigade of South Carolinians*, 244; George E. Cary to Sister Sue, Dec. 1, 1864, "Camp," Cary Family Papers, University of Maine; Council Diary, 11, NCDAH; "Diary of Creed T. Davis," 30; Dobbins, *Grandfather's Journal*, 223; Haines, *Fifteenth New Jersey*, 290; Jones, *Rebel War Clerk's Diary*, 2:343–50; McDonald, *Make Me a Map of the Valley*, 246; Norton, *Army Letters*, 244; Preston, *Tenth New York Cavalry*, 237; Rose Diary, 56–57, CWMC, USAMHI; Silliker, *Rebel Yell & the Yankee Hurrah*, 223–26; Sparks, *Inside Lincoln's Army*, 446, 448; A. Wilson Greene, email to author, Nov. 21, 2018.

66. Nevins, *Diary of Battle*, 489, 490–91. See also Chamberlayne, *Ham Chamberlayne*, 297; de Trobriand, *Four Years in the Army of the Potomac*, 691–94; Rhodes, *All for the Union*, 201; Robertson, *Letters of McAllister*, 552–56; Silliker, *Rebel Yell & the Yankee Hurrah*, 225–26.

67. Krick, *Civil War Weather*, 146; Agassiz, *Meade's Headquarters*, 296–97, 300; Britton and Reed, *To My Beloved Wife*, 321–22; George E. Cary to Sister Fannie, Dec. 18, 1864, Fredericksburg, Cary Family Papers, University of Maine; "Diary of Creed T. Davis," 31; Dobbins, *Grandfather's Journal*, 224; Jones, *Rebel War Clerk's Diary*, 2:351–56; McDonald, *Make Me a Map of the Valley*, 247–48; Rhodes, *All for the Union*, 201; Rose Diary, 57, CWMC, USAMHI; Silliker, *Rebel Yell & the Yankee Hurrah*, 227–28; Sparks *Inside Lincoln's Army*, 449.

68. Jones, *Rebel War Clerk's Diary*, 2:357.

69. Krick, *Civil War Weather*, 146; Albright Diary, 73–76, SHC-UNC; John J. Armfield to Wife, Dec. 22, 25, 1864, Petersburg, Va., Armfield Papers, NCDAH; Bartlett, *Twelfth New Hampshire*, 255; Britton and Reed, *To My Beloved Wife*, 322–24; George E. Cary to Little Sis, n.d., [1864], "Camp," Cary Family Papers, University of Maine; Chamberlayne, *Ham Chamberlayne*, 307; "Diaries of John Waldrop . . . and William Y. Mordecai," 56; "Diary of Creed T. Davis," 31–32; Fleet and Fuller, *Green Mount*, 350; Haines, *Fifteenth New Jersey*, 291; Jones, *Rebel War Clerk's Diary*, 2:359–70; Lee, *Memoir of Pendleton*, 381; McDonald, *Make Me a Map of the Valley*, 248–50; Rhodes, *All for the Union*, 202–3; Robertson, *Letters of McAllister*, 560; Rose Diary, 58–59, CWMC, USAMHI; Silliker, *Rebel Yell & the Yankee Hurrah*, 229–30; Sparks, *Inside Lincoln's Army*, 453; Killian Van Rensselaer to Nina, Dec. 26, 1864, Petersburg, Va., Killian Van Rensselaer Papers: Letters and Military Records, NYHS/CWPSD; Power, *Lee's Miserables*, 223–34.

70. Norton, *Army Letters*, 240.

71. Agassiz, *Meade's Headquarters*, 291; J. Armfield to Wife, Dec. 22, 31, 1864, Petersburg, Va., Armfield Papers, NCDAH; Beecher, *First Light Battery*, 2:628; Britton and Reed, *To My Beloved Wife*, 319–20; George E. Cary to Mother, Nov. 18, 1864, "Camp," Cary Family Papers, University of Maine; Chamberlayne, *Ham Chamberlayne*, 295; "Diary of Creed T. Davis," 319; Dobbins, *Grandfather's Journal*, 219, 221, 225–26; John B. Evans to Wife, Dec. 2, 1864, Richmond, Evans Papers, Duke; Fleet and Fuller, *Green Mount*, 347; Haines, *Fifteenth New Jersey*, 290; Jones, *Under the Stars and Bars*, 222–23; John A. E. Henderson to Brother, Nov. 21, Dec. 31, 1864, Petersburg, Va., Henderson Papers, Duke; Norton, *Army Letters*, 240, 243; Rhodes, *All for the Union*, 200, 203; Robertson, *Letters of McAllister*, 551; Rosenblatt and Rosenblatt, *Hard Marching Every Day*, 284–85; Silliker, *Rebel Yell & the Yankee Hurrah*, 217, 221, 223; Power, *Lee's Miserables*, 219–26.

72. Jones, *Under the Stars and Bars*, 222.

CHAPTER 22

1. Racine, *Piedmont Farmer*, 316–25 (quotation, 325). For similar conditions elsewhere, see *Augusta (Ga.) Daily Constitutionalist*, May 7, 14, 1864; *Charleston Mercury*, Mar. 18, Apr. 2, 1864; *Houston Daily Telegraph*, Mar. 9, 1864; *Macon (Ga.) Telegraph*, Mar. 17, 26, 1864; and *Richmond Sentinel*, Mar.

29, Apr. 1, 14, 1864. For a more favorable assessment of peaches and wheat, see *Charleston Mercury*, Apr. 25, 1864; and *Richmond Whig*, Apr. 20, 1864.

2. Racine, *Piedmont Farmer*, 325–29 (quotations, 326, 328). See also *Augusta (Ga.) Daily Constitutionalist*, Apr. 16, 1864; *Charleston Mercury*, Apr. 16, 1864; Dunaway, *Sermon*, 7; and *Macon (Ga.) Telegraph*, Apr. 28, 1864.

3. Racine, *Piedmont Farmer*, 329–40. See also John B. Evans to Companion, July 21, 1864, Petersburg, Va., John B. Evans Papers, 1862–1865, Duke.

4. *Macon (Ga.) Telegraph*, Apr. 20, 1864.

5. *Charleston Mercury*, Aug. 26, 1864.

6. Racine, *Piedmont Farmer*, 340–41 (quotation, 341). See also *Augusta (Ga.) Daily Constitutionalist*, Apr. 7, May 14, June 24, 30, 1864; *Columbus (Ga.) Daily Enquirer*, June 21, 1864; *New Orleans Daily True-Delta*, Mar. 26, Apr. 14, June 21, 23, July 13, Aug. 11, 1864; and *Macon (Ga.) Telegraph*, Mar. 26, Apr. 14, June 21, 23, July 13, Aug. 11, 1864.

7. Clarksville, Tenn., Feb., Mar. 1864, Reel 478, RG 27.5.7, NARA-CP; Barnes, Carnahan, and McCain, *Eighty-Sixth Indiana*, 320–23, 325; Berkeley, *In the Defense of This Flag*, 83; J. B. Clifton Diary, 28–30, P.C. 589, NCDAH; DeRosier, *Through the South*, 107–9; Gresham Diaries, Feb. 1–Mar. 17, 1864, accessed Nov. 7, 2018; Hight and Stormont, *Fifty-Eighth Indiana*, 264; Jones, *Artilleryman's Diary*, 180–88; Lee, *Memoir of Pendleton*, 315; Myers, *Children of Pride*, 438, 439; Marshall, *Civil War Diary*, 50–51; Edward E. Schweitzer Diary, 4:8–13, Edward E. Schweitzer Diaries and Correspondence, Box 23, CWTI, USAMHI; Frederick Sherwood Journal, Mar. 7–20, 1864, Box 2, Earl M. Hess Collection, USAMHI; Castel, *Decision in the West*, 67–68; Dickson, "Climate of Tennessee," 375; McMurry, *Atlanta*, 15–16.

8. Bennett and Haigh, *Thirty-Sixth Illinois*, 567, 569; Butler, *Letters Home*, 106; Clifton Diary, 31, NCDAH; Collins, *Chapters*, 200–201; Cope, *Fifteenth Ohio*, 417–18; Coski, "Letters of Livingston," 80; DeRosier, *Through the South*, 110, 111; Graves, *Bedford Light Artillery*, 41; Gresham Diaries, Mar. 17–31, 1864, accessed Nov. 7, 2018; Jones, *Artilleryman's Diary*, 188; Longstreet, *From Manassas to Appomattox*, 546; Marshall, *Civil War Diary*, 51; Morris, *Eighty-First Indiana*, 81; Quint, *Second Massachusetts*, 218; Schweitzer Diary, 4:18, Schweitzer Diaries and Correspondence, CWTI, USAMHI; Sherwood Journal, Mar. 20–23, 1864, Hess Collection, USAMHI.

9. Clarksville, Tenn., Apr. 1864, Reel 478, RG 27.5.7, NARA-CP; Barnes, Carnahan, and McCain, *Eighty-Sixth Indiana*, 327; Bircher, *Drummer-Boy's Diary*, 112–13; Cooke, "Letters," 417–22; DeRosier, *Through the South*, 113–15; Hight and Stormont, *Fifty-Eighth Indiana*, 278, 284; Jones, *Artilleryman's Diary*, 193–204; Member of Company C, *Twenty-Seventh Indiana*, 464; Morris, *Eighty-First Indiana*, 81–82; Quint, *Second Massachusetts*, 218, 223; Schweitzer Diary, 4:20–21, Schweitzer Diaries and Correspondence, CWTI, USAMH; Sherwood Journal, Apr. 1–27, 1864, Hess Collection, USAMHI; Castel, *Decision in the West*, 116–18; Dickson, "Climate of Tennessee," 375. Rain fell during March 31–April 1, the night of April 3 into April 4, the morning of April 8, the afternoon of April 9, overnight on April 11–12, on April 17 and into the next day, overnight on April 23–24, on the night of April 26–27, and as localized showers on April 28 and 30. In most cases—April 15 and 16 were exceptions—rain systems in Tennessee and North Georgia corresponded to similar reports from Virginia. Macon was drier, with intermittent rainfall between April 7 and 9, on April 18, and on April 24. See Gresham Diaries, Apr. 1864, accessed Nov. 7, 2018.

10. *OR*, 38(2):115, 38(3):351; Clarksville, Tenn., May 1864, Reel 478, RG 27.5.7, NARA-CP; Black, "Marching with Sherman," 311–12; Cope, *Fifteenth Ohio*, 425, 426; Jones, *Artilleryman's Diary*, 205–6; Member of Company C, *Twenty-Seventh Indiana*, 464–65; Owens, *Greene County*, 58; Quaife, *From the Cannon's Mouth*, 304; Sherwood Journal, May 1–9, 1864, Hess Collection, USAMHI; Castel, *Decision in the West*, 79–154; McMurry, *Atlanta*, 26–67; Dickson, "Climate of Tennessee," 375.

11. *OR*, 38(1):520, 848, 850, 38(2):148, 38(3):351, 398, 497, 38(4):120; Clarksville, Tenn., May 1864, Reel 478, RG 27.5.7, NARA-CP; Bennett and Haigh, *Thirty-Sixth Illinois*, 579; Bircher, *Drummer-Boy's Diary*, 113–14; Black, "Marching with Sherman," 312–13; Cooke, "Letters," 69–70; Cope, *Fifteenth Ohio*, 432; French, *Two Wars*, 193; Member of Company C, *Twenty-Seventh Indiana*, 481; Morris, *Eighty-First Indiana*, 87; Quaife, *From the Cannon's Mouth*, 307–8; Sherwood Journal, May 9–15, 1864, Hess Collection, USAMHI; Sutherland, *Reminiscences of a Private*, 159; Wright, *Corporal's Story*, 96; Castel, *Decision in the West*, 154–86; McMurry, *Atlanta*, 67–74.

12. Clarksville, Tenn., May 1864, Reel 478, RG 27.5.7, NARA-CP; Bircher, *Drummer-Boy's Diary*, 114; Black, "Marching with Sherman," 313; Cope, *Fifteenth Ohio*, 442; Gresham Diaries, May 17, 1864, accessed Nov. 7, 2018; Hinman, *Sherman Brigade*, 527; Little and Maxwell, *Lumsden's Battery*, 37; Hafendorfer, *Journal of Trask*, 144; Sherwood Journal, May 16–17, 1864, Hess Collection, USAMHI; Castel, *Decision in the West*, 186–96; McMurry, *Atlanta*, 74–76.

13. Clarksville, Tenn., May 1864, Reel 478, RG 27.5.7, NARA-CP; Bircher, *Drummer-Boy's Diary*, 114–15; Black, "Marching with Sherman," 313; Cope, *Fifteenth Ohio*, 443, 446; J. C. Donahower, "Narrative of the Civil War," 3:53, Jeremiah Chester Donahower Papers, 1853–1919, M561, MnHS; Member of Company C, *Twenty-Seventh Indiana*, 484; Castel, *Decision in the West*, 196–211, 213–17; McMurry, *Atlanta*, 75–84.

14. *OR*, 38(1):861, 986, 38(4):274; Clarksville, Tenn., May 1864, Reel 478, RG 27.5.7, NARA-CP; Bircher, *Drummer-Boy's Diary*, 115; Bishop, *Story of a Regiment*, 148; Black, "Marching with Sherman," 313–14; Cavins, *War Letters of Aden G. Cavins*, 80; DeRosier, *Through the South*, 123; Donahower, "Narrative of the Civil War," 3:62, Donahower Papers, MnHS; Hazen, *Narrative*, 253; Morris, *Eighty-First Indiana*, 95; Owens, *Greene County*, 62; Schweitzer Diary, 4:25, Schweitzer Diaries and Correspondence, CWTI, USAMHI; Sherwood Journal, May 22, 1864, Hess Collection, USAMHI; Castel, *Decision in the West*, 217–19; McMurry, *Atlanta*, 84–88.

15. Bauer, *Soldiering*, 121–22.

16. *OR*, 38(1):318, 333, 391, 418, 660, 668, 861, 866, 38(2):24, 30, 124, 150, 167, 171, 180, 264, 382, 396, 438, 38(3):153, 352, 705, 986, 990; Clarksville, Tenn., May 1864, Reel 478, RG 27.5.7, NARA-CP; Barnes, Carnahan, and McCain, *Eighty-Sixth Indiana*, 359; Bauer, *Soldiering*, 117; Bennett and Haigh, *Thirty-Sixth Illinois*, 593; Bierce, "Crime at Pickett's Mill," 37–45; Bircher, *Drummer-Boy's Diary*, 116; Black, "Marching with Sherman," 314; Cope, *Fifteenth Ohio*, 448; Hazen, *Narrative*, 254; Hight and Stormont, *Fifty-Eighth Indiana*, 306; Marshall, *Civil War Diary*, 69, 70; Member of Company C, *Twenty-Seventh Indiana*, 484; Morris, *Eighty-First Indiana*, 95–96; Quaife, *From the Cannon's Mouth*, 312; Schweitzer Diary, 4:24–25, Schweitzer Diaries and Correspondence, CWTI, USAMHI; Sherwood Journal, May 24–27, 1864, Hess Collection, USAMHI; Tarrant, *Wild Riders*, 334; Castel, *Decision in the West*, 219–41; McMurry, *Atlanta*, 88–94.

17. Bircher, *Drummer-Boy's Diary*, 116–17; Black, "Marching with Sherman," 314–15; Cope, *Fifteenth Ohio*, 450; Hafendorfer, *Journal of Trask*, 155; Morris, *Eighty-First Indiana*, 98; Padgett, "With Sherman," pt. 1, 292; Sherwood Journal, May 28–30, 1864, Hess Collection, USAMHI; [Willet], *Company B*, 66; Castel, *Decision in the West*, 241–52; McMurry, *Atlanta*, 91–92.

18. Quaife, *From the Cannon's Mouth*, 315.

19. *OR*, 38(4):385.

20. *OR*, 38(1):242, 304, 318, 333, 468, 594, 863, 868, 869, 875, 38(2):126, 172, 225, 265, 294, 310, 384, 410, 512; Clarksville, Tenn., June 1864, Reel 478, RG 27.5.7, NARA-CP; Bauer, *Soldiering*, 122–24; Bircher, *Drummer-Boy's Diary*, 116–18; Black, "Marching with Sherman," 315–16; Cooke, "Letters," 80, 81; Cope, *Fifteenth Ohio*, 478–82; Donahower, "Narrative of the Civil War," 3:71, Donahower Papers, MnHS; Gresham Diaries, June 1–10, 1864, accessed Nov. 7, 2018; Hafendorfer, *Journal of Trask*, 155–57; French, *Two Wars*, 201; Hight and Stormont, *Fifty-Eighth Indiana*, 315; Horrall, *Forty-Second Indi-*

ana, 221–22; Marshall, *Civil War Diary*, 75, 77; Member of Company C, *Twenty-Seventh Indiana*, 503; Morris, *Eighty-First Indiana*, 99–100, 102; Owens, *Greene County*, 64, 66; Padgett, "With Sherman," pt. 1, 292–93, 295; Quaife, *From the Cannon's Mouth*, 315; Schweitzer Diary, 4:27–29, Schweitzer Diaries and Correspondence, CWTI, USAMHI; Sherwood Journal, June 1–10, 1864, Hess Collection, USAMHI; Worley, *Memoirs of Lavender*, 92; Castel, *Decision in the West*, 252–60; McMurry, *Atlanta*, 94–102; Carter, "Climate of Georgia." 78; Dickson, "Climate of Tennessee," 375.

21. Horrall, *Forty-Second Indiana*, 221–22.

22. Bauer, *Soldiering*, 122–24 (quotation, 122–23).

23. Worley, *Memoirs of Lavender*, 92. See also French, *Two Wars*, 201.

24. W. A. Rorer to unknown, June 9, 1864, Kennesaw Mountain, James M. Willcox Papers, 1831–1871, Duke.

25. *OR*, 38(1):148, 178, 267, 304, 370, 648, 38(2):126, 38(3):707, 38(4):414; Clarksville, Tenn., June 1864, Reel 478, RG 27.5.7, NARA-CP; Barnes, Carnahan, and McCain, *Eighty-Sixth Indiana*, 376; Bauer, *Soldiering*, 124, 125; Bennett and Haigh, *Thirty-Sixth Illinois*, 603; Bircher, *Drummer-Boy's Diary*, 118–19; Black, "Marching with Sherman," 316–17; Butler, *Letters Home*, 124; Dodge, *Waif of the War*, 147; Cavins, *War Letters of Aden G. Cavins*, 82; Clark, *Downing's Civil War Diary*, 195–96; Clark, *Under the Stars and Bars*, 107–8; Cooke, "Letters," 84, 85; Cope, *Fifteenth Ohio*, 483; Donahower, "Narrative of the Civil War," 3:81, Donahower Papers, MnHS; French, *Two Wars*, 202; Gresham Diaries, June 11–14, 1864, accessed Nov. 7, 2018; Hazen, *Narrative*, 262–63; Hafendorfer, *Journal of Trask*, 157–58; Keil. *Fifty-Fifth Ohio*, 192; Marshall, *Civil War Diary*, 82, 83; Member of Company C, *Twenty-Seventh Indiana*, 504; Morris, *Eighty-First Indiana*, 102; Owens, *Greene County*, 66; Padgett, "With Sherman," pt. 1, 296; Quaife, *From the Cannon's Mouth*, 317, 320; Quint, *Second Massachusetts*, 237; Schweitzer Diary, 4:29–30, Schweitzer Diaries and Correspondence, CWTI, USAMHI; Sherwood Journal, June 10–14, 1864, Hess Collection, USAMHI; [Willet], *Company B*, 6; Carter, "Climate of Georgia," 78; Dickson, "Climate of Tennessee," 375.

26. French, *Two Wars*, 202.

27. *OR*, 38(1):304, 370, 366, 460, 496, 597, 669, 776, 786, 885, 38(2):99, 100, 131, 132, 150, 159, 173, 229, 358, 385, 398, 418, 443, 467, 518, 569, 850, 38(3):347, 431, 984, 38(4):508, 511, 519, 544, 775, 783; Clarksville, Tenn., June 1864, Reel 478, RG 27.5.7, NARA-CP; Barnes, Carnahan, and McCain, *Eighty-Sixth Indiana*, 382–84; Barron, *Lone Star Defenders*, 195–97; Bircher, *Drummer-Boy's Diary*, 119; Black, "Marching with Sherman," 317–18; Clark, *Downing's Civil War Diary*, 197–200; Clark, *Under the Stars and Bars*, 117, 125–26; Collins, *Chapters*, 218–20; Cope, *Fifteenth Ohio*, 489; Dodge, *Waif of the War*, 153; Donahower, "Narrative of the Civil War," 3:86, 96, 103, 104, 106, 114, Donahower Papers, MnHS; French, *Two Wars*, 202; Gresham Diaries, June 14–21, 1864, accessed Nov. 7, 2018; Hight and Stormont, *Fifty-Eighth Indiana*, 320, 327; Hinman, *Sherman Brigade*, 540–41; Johnston, *Narrative of Military Operations*, 339; Hafendorfer, *Journal of Trask*, 158–59, 160; Kirwan, *Johnny Green*, 136–37, 148; Little and Maxwell, *Lumsden's Battery*, 41; Marshall, *Civil War Diary*, 91, 92; Morris, *Eighty-First Indiana*, 106; Quint, *Second Massachusetts*, 237–38; Schweitzer Diary, 4:31, Schweitzer Diaries and Correspondence, CWTI, USAMHI; Scribner, *How Soldiers Were Made*, 262–63; Sherwood Journal, June 14–23, 1864, Hess Collection, USAMHI; [Willet], *Company B*, 69–70; Wright, *Corporal's Story*, 111–12; *Augusta (Ga.) Daily Constitutionalist* June 21, 1864; Castel, *Decision in the West*, 260–90; McMurry, *Atlanta*, 102–4; Carter, "Climate of Georgia," 78; Dickson, "Climate of Tennessee," 375. In Clarksville, the June 13 low was 61 degrees, but clearly the Pine Mountain line felt colder to men in soaked uniforms.

28. Collins, *Chapters*, 220.

29. Barnes, Carnahan, and McCain, *Eighty-Sixth Indiana*, 386.

30. *OR*, 38(1):68.

31. *OR*, 38(5):123.

32. *OR*, 38(1):632, 704, 885, 890, 38(4):572, 581, 38(5):14; Clarksville, Tenn., June 1864, Reel 478, RG 27.5.7, NARA-CP; Barnes, Carnahan, and McCain, *Eighty-Sixth Indiana*, 398; Bircher, *Drummer-Boy's Diary*, 120; Black, "Marching with Sherman," 318–19; Cavins, *War Letters of Aden G. Cavins*, 84–85; Cope, *Fifteenth Ohio*, 514; DeRosier, *Through the South*, 127; Donahower, "Narrative of the Civil War," 3:126, Donahower Papers, MnHS; French, *Two Wars*, 205; Kirwan, *Johnny Green*, 148; Padgett, "With Sherman," pt. 1, 297; Schweitzer Diary, 4:31–34, Schweitzer Diaries and Correspondence, CWTI, USAMHI; Castel, *Decision in the West*, 290–322, 323–24; McMurry, *Atlanta*, 104–9; Carter, "Climate of Georgia," 78; Dickson, "Climate of Tennessee," 375.

33. *OR*, 38(1):225, 431, 38(5):94, 87; Castel, *Decision in the West*, 322–23, 324–58, 360–65; McMurry, *Atlanta*, 109–11, 113–20, 129–40.

34. *OR*, 38(1):178.

35. *OR*, 38(1):281, 334, 347, 351, 365–66, 431, 650, 671, 890, 892–97, 899, 900, 38(2):402, 412, 571, 663, 38(3):287, 38(5):65, 92; Clarksville, Tenn., July 1864, Reel 478, RG 27.5.7, NARA-CP; *Atlanta Daily Intelligencer*, July 2, 1864; Barnes, Carnahan, and McCain, *Eighty-Sixth Indiana*, 408, 410; Bauer, *Soldiering*, 138, 139, 143–44; Bennett and Haigh, *Thirty-Sixth Illinois*, 612; Black, "Marching with Sherman," 319–22; Cavins, *War Letters of Aden G. Cavins*, 87–88; Cope, *Fifteenth Ohio*, 516, 520, 521; DeRosier, *Through the South*, 127, 129, 130; Othniel Gooding to Lucy, July 10, 1864, Chattahoochee River, Ga., Othniel Gooding Papers, c.00275, University Archives and Historical Collections, Michigan State University, East Lansing; Hinman, *Sherman Brigade*, 607; Hafendorfer, *Journal of Trask*, 164–66; Marshall, *Civil War Diary*, 111, 112; Member of Company C, *Twenty-Seventh Indiana*, 514, 517; Padgett, "With Sherman," pt. 1, 298, 300; Quaife, *From the Cannon's Mouth*, 322, 323, 329; Schweitzer Diary, 4:34–38, Schweitzer Diaries and Correspondence, CWTI, USAMHI; Simmons, *84th Ill.*, 185; [Willet], *Company B*, 72, 74. Rain fell on July 2, 10, and 12 and on every night during July 14–16.

36. Black, "Marching with Sherman," 322.

37. *OR*, 38(5):178; McMurry, *Atlanta*, 140–42, 147; Castel, *Decision in the West*, 358–60.

38. *OR*, 38(2):100, 38(1):887, 889; Clarksville, Tenn., July 1864, Reel 478, RG 27.5.7, NARA-CP; Bauer, *Soldiering*, 150; Black, "Marching with Sherman," 323; Schweitzer Diary, 4:39, Schweitzer Diaries and Correspondence, CWTI, USAMHI; McMurry, *Atlanta*, 142–52; Castel, *Decision in the West*, 360–83; Carter, "Climate of Georgia," 78; Dickson, "Climate of Tennessee," 375.

39. Bauer, *Soldiering*, 150.

40. *OR*, 38(1):551, 38(3):426, 454, 492, 732; Clarksville, Tenn., July 1864, Reel 478, RG 27.5.7, NARA-CP; Black, "Marching with Sherman," 323; Marshall, *Civil War Diary*, 114; Morris, *Eighty-First Indiana*, 121; Schweitzer Diary, 4:40, Schweitzer Diaries and Correspondence, CWTI, USAMHI; McMurry, *Atlanta*, 152–55; Castel, *Decision in the West*, 383–414; Carter, "Climate of Georgia," 78; Dickson, "Climate of Tennessee," 375.

41. *OR*, 38(1):909, 911; Bauer, *Soldiering*, 154; Black, "Marching with Sherman," 323, 324; Morris, *Eighty-First Indiana*, 122; Padgett, "With Sherman," pt. 1, 298, Schweitzer Diary, 4:41, Schweitzer Diaries and Correspondence, CWTI, USAMHI; Worley, *Memoirs of Lavender*, 97; McMurry, *Atlanta*, 155–59; Castel, *Decision in the West*, 414–36.

42. Little and Maxwell, *Lumsden's Battery*, 48.

43. *OR*, 38(1):650, 38(3):785, 800, 942, 38(5):308; Clarksville, Tenn., July 1864, Reel 478, RG 27.5.7, NARA-CP; Barnes, Carnahan, and McCain, *Eighty-Sixth Indiana*, 427, 435; Bauer, *Soldiering*, 157; Black, "Marching with Sherman," 325; Butler, *Letters Home*, 141; DeRosier, *Through the South*, 134; Morris, *Eighty-First Indiana*, 123; Owens, *Greene County*, 80; Padgett, "With Sherman," pt. 1, 304; Schweitzer Diary, 4:41, 43, Schweitzer Diaries and Correspondence, CWTI, USAMHI; Carter, "Climate of Georgia," 78; Dickson, "Climate of Tennessee," 375.

44. Schweitzer Diary, 4:43, Schweitzer Diaries and Correspondence, CWTI, USAMHI.

45. Member of Company C, *Twenty-Seventh Indiana,* 531.

46. Gresham Diaries, Aug. 7, 1864, accessed Nov. 7, 2018.

47. *OR,* 38(5):354, 413, 415, 552; McMurry, *Atlanta,* 159–69; Castel, *Decision in the West,* 436–80; Venet, *Changing Wind,* 160.

48. *OR,* 38(1):178, 321, 672–73, 713, 762, 914, 916, 917, 919–27, 929–31, 38(2):633, 636, 645, 682, 733, 825, 38(5):422, 425, 623; Clarksville, Tenn., Aug. 1864, Reel 478, RG 27.5.7, NARA-CP; Black, "Marching with Sherman," 325–38; Cope, *Fifteenth Ohio,* 541, 549, 550; DeRosier, *Through the South,* 136–37, 139, 141–42; Gresham Diaries, Aug. 1864, accessed Nov. 7, 2018; Owens, *Greene County,* 81–84; Padgett, "With Sherman," pt. 1, 305, 306, 307, 309; Schweitzer Diary, 4:44–50, Schweitzer Diaries and Correspondence, CWTI, USAMHI; [Willet], *Company B,* 77–81; Carter, "Climate of Georgia," 78; Dickson, "Climate of Tennessee," 375. Rain fell on the nights of August 2 and 3, overnight August 6–7, around 3 P.M. on August 8, swiftly on August 10, the night of August 11–12, at dusk on August 16, and on August 25 and 26.

49. *OR,* 38(1):512, 926, 935, 38(2):863, 38(3):107; Clarksville, Tenn., Aug. 1864, Reel 478, RG 27.5.7, NARA-CP; Black, "Marching with Sherman," 328; Cope, *Fifteenth Ohio,* 550; Kirwan, *Johnny Green,* 152; Owens, *Greene County,* 84; Padgett, "With Sherman," pt. 1, 309; Schweitzer Diary, 4:50, Schweitzer Diaries and Correspondence, CWTI, USAMHI; McMurry, *Atlanta,* 164, 169–73 Castel, *Decision in the West,* 480–508; Carter, "Climate of Georgia," 78; Dickson, "Climate of Tennessee," 375.

50. *OR,* 38(1):167, 429, 933, 935, 936, 38(3):526, 38(5):770; Clarksville, Tenn., Sept. 1864, Reel 478, RG 27.5.7, NARA-CP; Black, "Marching with Sherman," 329–30; DeRosier, *Through the South,* 144; Schweitzer Diary, 4:51–52, Schweitzer Diaries and Correspondence, CWTI, USAMHI; Williams et al., *Seventy-Third Indiana,* 182; Friend, *West Wind,* 161; McMurry, *Atlanta,* 173–80; Carter, "Climate of Georgia," 78; Dickson, "Climate of Tennessee," 375.

51. Castel, *Decision in the West,* 527–29, 533–42, 548–49.

52. *OR,* 39(2):419.

53. Clarksville, Tenn., Sept. 1864, Reel 478, RG 27.5.7, NARA-CP; Clark, *Downing's Civil War Diary,* 218; Cope, *Fifteenth Ohio,* 564; DeRosier, *Through the South,* 145, 147, 148, 153; Hight and Stormont, *Fifty-Eighth Indiana,* 371, 373; Morris, *Eighty-First Indiana,* 128, 129; Quaife, *From the Cannon's Mouth,* 343; Schweitzer Diary, 4:52–57, Schweitzer Diaries and Correspondence, CWTI, USAMHI; Padgett, "With Sherman," pt. 1, 313, 314; Carter, "Climate of Georgia," 78; Dickson, "Climate of Tennessee," 375. The exceptions were September 5, 18, 21, and 23. September 30 was hot.

CHAPTER 23

1. Castel, *General Sterling Price,* 196–203; Lause, *Price's Lost Campaign,* 1–15.

2. Pitcock and Gurley, *I Acted from Principle,* 212–13, 214–15; Castel, *General Sterling Price,* 203–7; Lause, *Price's Lost Campaign,* 15–29.

3. Pitcock and Gurley, *I Acted from Principle,* 212–13, 214–15, 219; Wyaconda Prairie (Canton), Mo., Aug., Sept. 1864, Reel 280, RG 27.5.7, NARA-CP; McQuigg, "Climate of Missouri," 732. It rained on September 4, 6, and 7.

4. Scott, "Last Fight for Missouri," 301.

5. *OR,* 41(1):447, 41(3):954, 978; Wyaconda Prairie (Canton), Mo., Sept. 1864, Reel 280, RG 27.5.7, NARA-CP; McQuigg, "Climate of Missouri," 732; Henry C. Fike Diaries, Sept. 18–27, 1864, C2215, State Historical Society of Missouri, Columbia; Pitcock and Gurley, *I Acted from Principle,* 221, 224; Castel, *General Sterling Price,* 208–21; Lause, *Price's Lost Campaign,* 29–62, 68, 97.

6. *OR,* 41(3):386.

7. *OR*, 41(1):462; Wyaconda Prairie (Canton), Mo., Sept., Oct. 1864, Reel 280, RG 27.5.7, NARA-CP; McQuigg, "Climate of Missouri," 732; Fike Diaries, Sept. 27–Oct. 6, 1864, State Historical Society of Missouri; Pitcock and Gurley, *I Acted from Principle*, 225–27; Castel, *General Sterling Price*, 222.

8. Wyaconda Prairie (Canton), Mo., Oct. 1864, Reel 280, RG 27.5.7, NARA-CP; McQuigg, "Climate of Missouri," 732; Lause, *Price's Lost Campaign*, 80–91, 101–43.

9. *OR*, 41(1):368–69, 462; Wyaconda Prairie (Canton), Mo., Oct. 1864, Reel 280, RG 27.5.7, NARA-CP; McQuigg, "Climate of Missouri," 732; Pitcock and Gurley, *I Acted from Principle*, 226, 227; Castel, *General Sterling Price*, 222–25; Lause, *Price's Lost Campaign*, 144–75.

10. Wyaconda Prairie (Canton), Mo., Oct. 1864, Reel 280, RG 27.5.7, NARA-CP; McQuigg, "Climate of Missouri," 732; Fike Diaries, Oct. 8–9, 1864, State Historical Society of Missouri; Castel, *General Sterling Price*, 225–29; Lause, *Collapse of Price's Raid*, 1–65.

11. Wyaconda Prairie (Canton), Mo., Oct. 1864, Reel 280, RG 27.5.7, NARA-CP; McQuigg, "Climate of Missouri," 732; Fike Diaries, Oct. 19–21, 1864, State Historical Society of Missouri; [Hinton], *Rebel Invasion*, 166; "Samuel J. Reader's Autobiography," 26, 29, accessed July 6, 2018; Castel, *General Sterling Price*, 229–32; Lause, *Collapse of Price's Raid*, 65–101.

12. Wyaconda Prairie (Canton), Mo., Oct. 1864, Reel 280, RG 27.5.7, NARA-CP; McQuigg, "Climate of Missouri," 732; Castel, *General Sterling Price*, 232–37; Lause, *Collapse of Price's Raid*, 101–39.

13. *OR*, 41(1):319, 351, 390, 493, 494, 515, 518, 527, 556, 580, 599, 601; Wyaconda Prairie (Canton), Mo., Oct. 1864, Reel 280, RG 27.5.7, NARA-CP; McQuigg, "Climate of Missouri," 732; Fike Diaries, Oct. 25–Nov. 4, 1864, State Historical Society of Missouri; [Hinton], *Rebel Invasion*, 190, 198–200, 273, 283, 295; Pitcock and Gurley, *I Acted from Principle*, 236–37, 240; "Samuel J. Reader's Autobiography," 290, 291, 293, 295, accessed July 6, 2018; Scott, "Last Fight for Missouri," 323; Castel, *General Sterling Price*, 237–46; Lause, *Collapse of Price's Raid*, 143–79.

14. Pitcock and Gurley, *I Acted from Principle*, 239–40.

15. *OR*, 41(1):529. See also ibid., 514, 515, 518, 529, 546, 647, 41(4):418, 421.

16. Scott, "Last Fight for Missouri," 327.

17. Fike Diaries, Nov. 4, 1864, State Historical Society of Missouri.

18. *OR*, 41(1):515, 530, 661; Wyaconda Prairie (Canton), Mo., Oct., Nov. 1864, Reel 280, RG 27.5.7, NARA-CP; McQuigg, "Climate of Missouri," 732; [Hinton], *Rebel Invasion*, 292–93, 304; Pitcock and Gurley, *I Acted from Principle*, 241–50; Scott, "Last Fight for Missouri," 327; Castel, *General Sterling Price*, 246–55; Lause, *Collapse of Price's Raid*, 179–94.

19. Scott, "Last Fight for Missouri," 292.

20. Connelly, *Autumn of Glory*, 470–79.

21. *OR*, 45(1):580, 733; Barnes, Carnahan, and McCain, *Eighty-Sixth Indiana*, 448–49; Clark, *Downing's Civil War Diary*, 218–19; Cope, *Fifteenth Ohio*, 568; DeRosier, *Through the South*, 153; French, *Two Wars*, 248–49, 285; Hight and Stormont, *Fifty-Eighth Indiana*, 376; Jones, *Artilleryman's Diary*, 254, 256; Morris, *Eighty-First Indiana*, 130; Owens, *Greene County*, 92–93; Padgett, "With Sherman," pt. 1, 319; Quaife, *From the Cannon's Mouth*, 344; Edward E. Schweitzer Diary, 4:58–59, Edward E. Schweitzer Diaries and Correspondence, Box 23, CWTI, USAMHI; Frederick Sherwood Journal, Oct. 1–7, 1864, Box 2, Earl M. Hess Collection, USAMHI; Castel, *Decision in the West*, 548–53; Connelly, *Autumn of Glory*, 480.

22. Charles Brown to father, Mother & Etta, Oct. 20, 1864, Chattanooga, Tenn., Charles S. Brown Papers, 1864–1865, Duke; Cater, *As It Was*, 195; Clark, *Under the Stars and Bars*, 153; Clark, *Downing's Civil War Diary*, 222; Cope, *Fifteenth Ohio*, 584; Coski, "Letters of Livingston," 82, 83; DeRosier, *Through the South*, 155, 156, 159; French, *Two Wars*, 288–89; Jones, *Artilleryman's Diary*, 260, 262–65; Morris, *Eighty-First Indiana*, 133; Owens, *Greene County*, 93; Padgett, "With Sherman," pt. 1, 319;

Quaife, *From the Cannon's Mouth*, 345, 346; Schweitzer Diary, 4:59–63, Schweitzer Diaries and Correspondence, CWTI, USAMHI; Sherwood Journal, Oct. 6–31, 1864, Hess Collection, USAMHI; Connelly, *Autumn of Glory*, 480–83.

23. Morris, *Eighty-First Indiana*, 133.

24. *OR*, 39(3):162. See also Grant, *Memoirs*, 2:230–40; and McPherson, *Battle Cry of Freedom*, 808.

25. Sword, *Embrace an Angry Wind*, 257.

26. Little and Maxwell, *Lumsden's Battery*, 52.

27. Coski, "Letters of Livingston," 83.

28. *OR*, 45(1):357, 582, 583, 585, 735, 1216; Clarksville, Tenn., Nov. 1864, Reel 478, RG 27.5.7, NARA-CP; French, *Two Wars*, 288–89; Elliot, *Doctor Quintard*, 179; McDonough and Connelly, *Five Tragic Hours*, 16–18; Sword, *Embrace an Angry Wind*, 64–74.

29. Head, *Sixteenth Tennessee*, 147.

30. Little and Maxwell, *Lumsden's Battery*, 53.

31. Clark, *Under the Stars and Bars*, 154. See also Cater, *As It Was*, 196; McDonough, *Nashville*, 33, 44, 45; and McDonough and Connelly, *Five Tragic Hours*, 31, 35.

32. French, *Two Wars*, 290. See also *OR*, 45(1):112, 143, 146, 392, 402, 586, 652, 657, 730, 736; Clarksville, Tenn., Nov. 1864, Reel 478, RG 27.5.7, NARA-CP; Col. James L. Cooper Memoirs, 49, Reel 5, Folder 11, Box 12, CWC, TSLA; McDonough and Connelly, *Five Tragic Hours*, 31; and McMurry, *John Bell Hood*, 169.

33. McDonough and Connelly, *Five Tragic Hours*, 19–22, 27–28; Sword, *Embrace an Angry Wind*, 69–86.

34. Morris, *Eighty-First Indiana*, 135–38 (quotation, 136). See also Clark, *Downing's Civil War Diary*, 225; Hinman, *Sherman Brigade*, 633; and Jones, *Artilleryman's Diary*, 266–74.

35. Cope, *Fifteenth Ohio*, 590–92.

36. Connelly, *Autumn of Glory*, 494–502; McDonough and Connelly, *Five Tragic Hours*, 28–59; McMurry, *John Bell Hood*, 170–74; Sword, *Embrace an Angry Wind*, 86–155. See also Barnes, Carnahan, and McCain, *Eighty-Sixth Indiana*, 472; and Bennett and Haigh, *Thirty-Sixth Illinois*, 629. On this same day, the Sand Creek Massacre occurred in eastern Colorado Territory. After a long march through snow, deep at times, troops commanded by Col. John Chivington of Glorieta Pass fame killed scores of peaceful Arapahoe and Cheyenne people in the mistaken belief that they were Confederate sympathizers. See Kelman, *Misplaced Massacre*.

37. Cope, *Fifteenth Ohio*, 605.

38. Clarksville, Tenn., Nov. 1864, Reel 478, RG 27.5.7, NARA-CP; McDonough, *Nashville*, 80; McDonough and Connelly, *Five Tragic Hours*, 60–168; McMurry, *John Bell Hood*, 174–76; Sword, *Embrace an Angry Wind*, 157–257.

39. Clarksville, Tenn., Dec. 1864, Reel 478, RG 27.5.7, NARA-CP; Barnes, Carnahan, and McCain, *Eighty-Sixth Indiana*, 480; Jones, *Artilleryman's Diary*, 279–82; Logbook, USS *Neosho*, Dec. 2–6, 1864, RG 24.2.2, NARA; McMurry, *John Bell Hood*, 174–76; Simpson, "Failure to Communicate," 105–11; Sword, *Embrace an Angry Wind*, 272–99.

40. Clarksville, Tenn., Dec. 1864, Reel 478, RG 27.5.7, NARA-CP; Barnes, Carnahan, and McCain, *Eighty-Sixth Indiana*, 4482–84; Cope, *Fifteenth Ohio*, 635–37; Jones, *Artilleryman's Diary*, 284–86; Hinman, *Sherman Brigade*, 678; Logbook, USS *Neosho*, Dec. 7–13, 1864, RG 24.2.2, NARA; McDonough, *Nashville*, 153–55; Sword, *Embrace an Angry Wind*, 290–306.

41. *OR*, 45(1):127, 153–54, 359–60, 361, 561, 747, 45(2):103, 114, 115, 117, 130, 132, 143, 145, 152, 155, 685; Barnes, Carnahan, and McCain, *Eighty-Sixth Indiana*, 482–84; Cater, *As It Was*, 201; Clark, *Under the Stars and Bars*, 154–55, 156; F. H. Cline to Wife, Dec. 12, 1864, Nashville, Tenn., Daisy J. Cline Papers, Missouri History Museum, St. Louis; Cope, *Fifteenth Ohio*, 635–41; Elliot, *Doctor Quin-*

tard, 193; Hinman, *Sherman Brigade,* 678; Martin Lewis Hursh Diary, 61–62, SC 808, Indiana Historical Society, Indianapolis; Jones, *Artilleryman's Diary,* 284–87; Morris, *Eighty-First Indiana,* 145; McDonough, *Nashville,* 155–257; Sword, *Embrace an Angry Wind,* 302–5.

42. Hinman, *Sherman Brigade,* 678.

43. Simpson, "Failure to Communicate," 109–19.

44. *OR,* 45(1):215, 435; Clarksville, Tenn., Dec. 1864, Reel 478, RG 27.5.7, NARA-CP; Barnes, Carnahan, and McCain, *Eighty-Sixth Indiana,* 487; Cope, *Fifteenth Ohio,* 637; Jones, *Artilleryman's Diary,* 286; Logbook, USS *Neosho,* Dec. 14–17, 1864, RG 24.2.2, NARA; Morris, *Eighty-First Indiana,* 146; Simmons, *84th Ill.,* 226; McDonough, *Nashville,* 153–256; McPherson, *Battle Cry of Freedom,* 813; Sword, *Embrace an Angry Wind,* 306–403.

45. *OR,* 45(1):42, 111, 135, 143, 152, 158, 160, 161, 162, 163, 167, 171, 173, 182, 291, 292, 315, 317, 360, 362, 392, 506, 513, 515, 518, 521, 544, 554, 566, 655, 661, 728, 732, 735, 736, 741, 750, 45(2):265, 298, 299, 442; Chicago, Ill., Dec. 1864, Reel 116, RG 27.5.7, NARA-CP; Newport Barracks, Ky., Dec. 1864, Reel 190, ibid.; Wyaconda Prairie (Canton), Mo., Dec. 1864, Reel 280, ibid.; Clarksville, Tenn., Dec. 1864, Reel 478, ibid.; Barnes, Carnahan, and McCain, *Eighty-Sixth Indiana,* 508–15; Barron, *Lone Star Defenders,* 252, 267; Bennett and Haigh, *Thirty-Sixth Illinois,* 694–702; Cater, *As It Was,* 203–4; Clark, *Under the Stars and Bars,* 154–62; Cooper Memoirs, 53, 58, 59, CWC, TSLA; Cope, *Fifteenth Ohio,* 662–72; Elliot, *Doctor Quintard,* 203–6, 208; Hinman, *Sherman Brigade,* 684–85; Hursh Diary, 63–66, Indiana Historical Society; Jones, *Artilleryman's Diary,* 288–94; Little and Maxwell, *Lumsden's Battery,* 57–62; Morris, *Eighty-First Indiana,* 138–48; Sutherland, *Reminiscences of a Private,* 219; Krick, *Civil War Weather,* 143; McPherson, *Battle Cry of Freedom,* 813–15; Sword, *Embrace an Angry Wind,* 404–22.

46. *OR,* 45(2):295–96.

47. *OR,* 45(1):111. See also Barnes, Carnahan, and McCain, *Eighty-Sixth Indiana,* 510; Bennett and Haigh, *Thirty-Sixth Illinois,* 693–95.

48. Clark, *Under the Stars and Bars,* 155.

49. Glatthaar, *March to the Sea,* 17–38, 100–101; McPherson, *Battle Cry of Freedom,* 808.

50. Clark, *Downing's Civil War Diary,* 227–28; Timothy Pendegrast Diary, 4–5, William Wirt Pendegrast Family Papers, M38, MnHS; Hébert, *Long Civil War,* 141–66.

51. *OR,* 39(3):713–14.

52. Clark, *Downing's Civil War Diary,* 228–29. See also Black, "Marching with Sherman," 454; Schweitzer Diary, 4:66, Schweitzer Diaries and Correspondence, CWTI, USAMHI; and Tourgée, *Story of a Thousand,* 334.

53. Clark, *Downing's Civil War Diary,* 228–29. See also Pendegrast Diary, 5–6, Pendegrast Family Papers, MnHS; Tourgée, *Story of a Thousand,* 334; Glatthaar, *March to the Sea,* 7–9, 101–12, 156–65; and Kennett, *Marching through Georgia,* 241–307.

54. Hitchcock, *Marching with Sherman,* 68.

55. Beaufort, S.C., Nov. 1864, Reel 464, RG 27.5.7, NARA-CP; Hilton Head, S.C., Nov. 1864, Reel 467, ibid.; Brady, *War upon the Land,* 99–104; Steinberg, *Down to Earth,* 91–92; Carter, "Climate of Georgia," 78; Landers, "Climate of South Carolina," 360.

56. *OR,* 44:66, 82, 120, 132, 134, 136, 164, 190, 214, 215, 217, 223, 232, 243, 253, 270–71, 291, 313, 316, 322, 334, 339, 345, 500, 509, 520, 828; Beaufort, S.C., Nov. 1864, Reel 464, RG 27.5.7, NARA-CP; Hilton Head, S.C., Nov. 1864, Reel 467, ibid.; Bauer, *Soldiering,* 173, 186; Bircher, *Drummer-Boy's Diary,* 141–44; Bishop, *Story of a Regiment,* 160, 168; Black, "Marching with Sherman," 455–56; Clark, *Downing's Civil War Diary,* 229–32; Cox, *March to Sea,* 42; Gresham Diaries, Nov. 1864, accessed Nov. 7, 2018; Hazen, *Narrative,* 315; Hight and Stormont, *Fifty-Eighth Indiana,* 420–21; Hitchcock, *Marching with Sherman,* 67–68, 73, 76, 80–81, 83, 90, 99, 111, 116; Rufus Mead Jr. to Folks at Home, Dec. 28, 1864, Savannah, Ga., Rufus Mead Jr. Papers, LC; Mead Diary, vol. 5, Nov. 19–22, 1864, ibid.; Owens,

Greene County, 10; Padgett, "With Sherman," pt. 2, 56, 58–59, 61; Pendegrast Diary, 9, 11, 12, 13–19, 22, Pendegrast Family Papers, MnHS; Quint, *Second Massachusetts,* 250; Schweitzer Diary, 4:66–69, Schweitzer Diaries and Correspondence, CWTI, USAMHI; Sherwood Journal, Nov. 23–29, 1864, Hess Collection, USAMHI; Tourgée, *Story of a Thousand,* 336, 338; William B. Westervelt, "Lights and Shadows of Army Life, as Seen by a Private Soldier," 61, Box 121, CWMC, USAMHI; Brady, *War upon the Land,* 98–104; Kennett, *Marching through Georgia,* 253–54; Steinberg, *Down to Earth,* 91–92; Carter, "Climate of Georgia," 78; Landers, "Climate of South Carolina," 360.

57. *OR,* 44:88, 232, 257, 275, 292, 309, 318, 651, 653; Beaufort, S.C., Dec. 1864, Reel 464, RG 27.5.7, NARA-CP; Bauer, *Soldiering,* 194, Bircher, *Drummer-Boy's Diary,* 145, 148, 151–53; Black, "Marching with Sherman," 457–58; Clark, *Downing's Civil War Diary,* 233–39; Gresham Diaries, Dec. 1–20, 1864, accessed Nov. 7, 2018; Hazen, *Narrative,* 331; Hitchcock, *Marching with Sherman,* 120, 152–53, 156; Rufus Mead Jr. to Folks at Home, Dec. 28, 1864, Savannah, Ga., Mead Papers, LC; Mead Diary, vol. 5, Dec. 7, 1864, ibid.; Owens, *Greene County,* 102–3, 105; Pendegrast Diary, 24, 27–29, 31–32, 35–37, Pendegrast Family Papers, MnHS; Quint, *Second Massachusetts,* 251; Schweitzer Diary, 4:70–73, Schweitzer Diaries and Correspondence, CWTI, USAMHI; Sherwood Journal, Dec. 1–21, 1864, Hess Collection, USAMHI; Tourgée, *Story of a Thousand,* 339–42; Westervelt, "Lights and Shadow of Army Life," 63, CWMC, USAMHI; Carter, "Climate of Georgia," 78; Landers, "Climate of South Carolina," 360; Brady, *War upon the Land,* 101–5; Glatthaar, *March to the Sea,* 10, 64, 103–4, 119–55; McPherson, *Battle Cry of Freedom,* 809–13.

58. *OR,* 44:828; Beaufort, S.C., Dec., 1864, Reel 464, RG 27.5.7, NARA-CP; Jesse S. Bean Diary, Dec. 26–31, 1864, SHC-UNC; Bircher, *Drummer-Boy's Diary,* 153–59; Black, "Marching with Sherman," 459; Charles Brown to Mother & Etta and "Any Other Man," Dec. 16, 1864, Savannah, Ga., Brown Papers, Duke; Clark, *Downing's Civil War Diary,* 239–42; Hitchcock, *Marching with Sherman,* 201; Bruce Hoadley to Cousin Em, Dec. 18, 31, 1864, Savannah, Robert Bruce Hoadley Papers, 1861–1866, Duke; Padgett, "With Sherman," pt. 2, 56, 58; Schweitzer Diary, 4:73–74, Schweitzer Diaries and Correspondence, CWTI, USAMHI; Sherwood Journal, Dec. 22–31, 1864, Hess Collection, USAMHI; "Spodosols Map," https://www.nrcs.usda.gov/wps/portal/nrcs/detail/soils/survey/class/maps/?cid= nrcs142p2_053608, accessed July 20, 2018.

59. Brady, *War upon the Land,* 93.

60. *OR,* 44:792.

61. Steinberg, *Down to Earth,* 92.

62. Ludlum, *Weather Factor,* 96.

CHAPTER 24

1. Grant, *Memoirs,* 2:267.

2. Beaufort, S.C., Dec. 1864, Reel 464, RG 27.5.7, NARA-CP; Grant, *Memoirs,* 2:263–66; Gragg, *Confederate Goliath,* 48–105.

3. Harkness, "Expedition against Fort Fisher," 162.

4. *OR,* 42(1):964, 994, 995, 1005, 42(3):1049, 1076, 1085–86, 1302, 46(2):3–4; Beaufort, S.C., Dec. 1864, Reel 464, RG 27.5.7, NARA-CP; Grant, *Memoirs,* 2:266–67.

5. *OR,* 46(1):396, 433; Gragg, *Confederate Goliath,* 102–11.

6. Harkness, "Expedition against Fort Fisher," 165.

7. *OR,* 46(2):5, 18, 69, 79, 90, 93, 122, 123, 126; Beaufort, S.C., Jan. 1865, Reel 464, RG 27.5.7, NARA-CP; Gragg, *Confederate Goliath,* 111–236.

8. Grant, *Memoirs,* 2:271, 272.

9. *OR,* 47(1):17–19, 22; Brady, *War upon the Land,* 108.

10. Beaufort, S.C., Jan. 1865, Reel 464, RG 27.5.7, NARA-CP; Hilton Head, S.C., Jan. 1865, Reel 467, ibid.; Jesse S. Bean Diary, Jan. 2–16, 1864, SHC-UNC; Bircher, *Drummer-Boy's Diary*, 159–60; Black, "Marching with Sherman," 459–60; Clark, *Downing's Civil War Diary*, 243–47; Hazen, *Narrative*, 336; Timothy Pendegrast Diary, 38–39, William Wirt Pendegrast Family Papers, M38, MnHS; Quint, *Second Massachusetts*, 256; Edward E. Schweitzer Diary, 5:1–3, Edward E. Schweitzer Diaries and Correspondence, Box 23, CWTI, USAMHI; Glatthaar, *March to the Sea*, 11–12, 109; Ludlum, *Early American Winters*, 134; Cary Mock, email to author, May 3, 2018.

11. Bauer, *Soldiering*, 202.

12. *OR*, 47(1):17.

13. *OR*, 47(1):193, 315, 336, 426, 495, 498, 523–24, 565, 580, 619, 642, 47(2):95, 100, 115, 118, 136; Black, "Marching with Sherman," 461; Frederick Sherwood Journal, Jan. 5–18, 1865, Box 2, Earl M. Hess Collection, USAMHI.

14. Bauer, *Soldiering*, 203–4.

15. *OR*, 47(1):608; Bauer, *Soldiering*, 203–11; Bean Diary, Jan. 19–Feb. 12, 1865, SHC-UNC; Bircher, *Drummer-Boy's Diary*, 162–65; Black, "Marching with Sherman," 461–65; Clark, *Downing's Civil War Diary*, 246–53; Eaton, "Diary of an Officer in Sherman's Army," 241–44; James R. M. Gaskill Memoranda, Jan. 22–23, 1865, Chicago History Museum, Chicago, Ill.; Hight and Stormont, *Fifty-Eighth Indiana*, 459–61, 465–71; Hitchcock, *Marching with Sherman*, 216; Owens, *Greene County*, 107–8; Padgett, "With Sherman," pt. 2, 59, 65–71; Quaife, *From the Cannon's Mouth*, 367–73; Quint, *Second Massachusetts*, 259–62; Schweitzer Diary, 5:2–7, Schweitzer Diaries and Correspondence, CWTI, USAMHI; Sherwood Journal, Jan. 5–21, 1865, Hess Collection, USAMHI.

16. Quaife, *From the Cannon's Mouth*, 373.

17. *OR*, 47(1):187, 195, 224, 316, 347, 566, 582, 683, 692, 720, 731, 47(2):290; Hilton Head, S.C., Jan., Feb. 1865, Reel 467, RG 27.5.7, NARA-CP; Bauer, *Soldiering*, 204–11; Bean Diary, Jan. 27–Feb. 12, 1865, SHC-UNC; Bircher, *Drummer-Boy's Diary*, 162–65; Black, "Marching with Sherman," 461–65; Clark, *Downing's Civil War Diary*, 249–53; Eaton, "Diary of an Officer in Sherman's Army," 241–44; Gaskill Memoranda, Jan. 27, 29–31, 1865, Chicago History Museum; Hitchcock, *Marching with Sherman*, 216, 220, 229, 233; Hight and Stormont, *Fifty-Eighth Indiana*, 466, 467, 471; Padgett, "With Sherman," pt. 2, 68–71; Quint, *Second Massachusetts*, 260–62; Schweitzer Diary, 5:3–7, Schweitzer Diaries and Correspondence, CWTI, USAMHI; Sherwood Journal, Jan. 28–31, 1865, Hess Collection, USAMHI; William B. Westervelt, "Lights and Shadows of Army Life, as Seen by a Private Soldier," 64, Box 121, CWMC, USAMHI; Glatthaar, *March to the Sea*, 108–18; Ludlum, *Early American Winters*, 134; Cary Mock, email to author, May 3, 2018.

18. *OR*, 47(1):187, 224, 347, 377, 620, 682, 683, 692, 720, 731, 734, 768, 47(2):290, 319, 329, 336, 1118; Hitchcock, *Marching with Sherman*, 236, 239–40, 245, 247, 256, 260; Brady, *War upon the Land*, 114–19; Glatthaar, *March to the Sea*, 109–14.

19. *OR*, 47(1):19.

20. Glatthaar, *March to the Sea*, 109–15. See also Bauer, *Soldiering*, 207–11; Bircher, *Drummer-Boy's Diary*, 164; Clark, *Downing's Civil War Diary*, 251; Eaton, "Diary of an Officer in Sherman's Army," 243; Padgett, "With Sherman," pt. 2, 70.

21. Cox, *Military Reminiscences*, 531–32. The quotation, appears variously in other sources. See, for example, McPherson, *Battle Cry of Freedom*, 828.

22. Brady, *War upon the Land*, 108–15; Glatthaar, *March to the Sea*, 67–69, 79–80, 119–55.

23. Bircher, *Drummer-Boy's Diary*, 164.

24. Bauer, *Soldiering*, 211; Bean Diary, Feb. 16–17, 1865, SHC-UNC; Bircher, *Drummer-Boy's Diary*, 165; Bishop, *Story of a Regiment*, 172; Black, "Marching with Sherman," 464–65; Eaton, "Diary of an Officer in Sherman's Army," 244; Brady, *War upon the Land*, 118–19; Glatthaar, *March to the Sea*,

142–46; Lucas, *Sherman and the Burning of Columbia*; McPherson, *Battle Cry of Freedom*, 829; Nelson, *Ruin Nation*, 11, 44–59.

25. Gaskill Memoranda, Feb. 17–18, 1865, Chicago History Museum. See also Hilton Head, S.C., Jan., Feb. 1865, Reel 467, RG 27.5.7, NARA-CP; Eaton, "Diary of an Officer in Sherman's Army," 244; McPherson, *Battle Cry of Freedom*, 829; and Simms, *City Laid Waste*, 65.

26. Alexander Grant Rose III Diary, 59, Box 100, CWMC, USAMHI. See also James W. Albright Diary, 79, SHC-UNC; Britton and Reed, *To My Beloved Wife*, 326–27; Caldwell, *Brigade of South Carolinians*, 253–55; George E. Cary to Sister Susan, Jan. 7, 1865, Petersburg, Cary Family Papers, 1856–1920, SpC MS 85, Special Collections, University of Maine, Orono; "Diary of Creed T. Davis," 32; Dobbins, *Grandfather's Journal*, 227–28; Fleet and Fuller, *Green Mount*, 297; Jones, *Rebel War Clerk's Diary*, 2:371–79; McDonald, *Make Me a Map of the Valley*, 251–52; Rhodes, *All for the Union*, 205, 206; Sparks, *Inside Lincoln's Army*, 455, 456; Summers, *Borderland Confederate*, 86; Krick, *Civil War Weather*, 149; and Ludlum, *Early American Winters*, 136–37.

27. Krick, *Civil War Weather*, 149; Albright Diary, 79–81, SHC-UNC; Britton and Reed, *To My Beloved Wife*, 327; George E. Cary to Brother Herbert, Jan. 10, 1865, Petersburg, Cary Family Papers, University of Maine; Cary to Sister Sue, Jan. 13, 1865, Petersburg, ibid.; "Diaries of John Waldrop . . . and William Y. Mordecai," 56; Dobbins, *Grandfather's Journal*, 228–29; Douglas, *I Rode with Stonewall*, 322; Fleet and Fuller, *Green Mount*, 299; Jones, *Rebel War Clerk's Diary*, 2:379–91; McDonald, *Make Me a Map of the Valley*, 252–53; Robertson, *Letters of McAllister*, 562–63; Rose Diary, 59, CWMC, US-AMHI; Silliker, *Rebel Yell & the Yankee Hurrah*, 235, 239; Sparks, *Inside Lincoln's Army*, 457, 460; A. Wilson Greene, email to author, Nov. 21, 2018.

28. Silliker, *Rebel Yell & the Yankee Hurrah*, 237.

29. Jones, *Rebel War Clerk's Diary*, 2:391–95. See also Albright Diary, 82, SHC-UNC; Bartlett, *Twelfth New Hampshire*, 260; Dobbins, *Grandfather's Journal*, 229–30; McDonald, *Make Me a Map of the Valley*, 254; Robertson, *Letters of McAllister*, 568; Silliker, *Rebel Yell & the Yankee Hurrah*, 238; Krick, *Civil War Weather*, 149.

30. Robertson, *Letters of McAllister*, 570.

31. Jones, *Rebel War Clerk's Diary*, 2:395–408. See also Albright Diary, 82–84, SHC-UNC; Dobbins, *Grandfather's Journal*, 230–31; Fleet and Fuller, *Green Mount*, 305–6; Grant, *Memoirs*, 2:287–90; McDonald, *Make Me a Map of the Valley*, 254–55; Robertson, *Letters of McAllister*, 569–72; Sparks, *Inside Lincoln's Army*, 465; Tyler, *Recollections*, 324; and Krick, *Civil War Weather*, 149.

32. Grant, *Memoirs*, 2:293.

33. *OR*, 46(1):89, 223, 248, 259, 267, 290, 291, 46(2):479; Albright Diary, 85–86, SHC-UNC; Britton and Reed, *To My Beloved Wife*, 331–32; Caldwell, *Brigade of South Carolinians*, 261; Dobbins, *Grandfather's Journal*, 231; Jones, *Rebel War Clerk's Diary*, 2:409–12; Preston, *Tenth New York Cavalry*, 241–42; Rhodes, *All for the Union*, 212; Robertson, *Letters of McAllister*, 572; Roper, *Repairing the "March of Mars*," 359–60; Rose Diary, 61, CWMC, USAMHI; Sparks, *Inside Lincoln's Army*, 468; Stewart, *Pair of Blankets*, 191–92; Tyler, *Recollections*, 327–28; Westwood A. Todd Reminiscences, pt. 2, 281, SHC-UNC; Krick, *Civil War Weather*, 152.

34. Robertson, *Letters of McAllister*, 578. See also Albright Diary, 86–90, SHC-UNC; Britton and Reed, *To My Beloved Wife*, 332; George E. Cary to Mother, Feb. 15, 1865, Petersburg, Cary Family Papers, University of Maine; Cary to Sister Susan, Feb. 19, 1865, Petersburg, ibid.; Cary to Mother, Feb. 23, 1865, "Camp," ibid.; Cary to Sister Susan, Feb. 26, 1865, Petersburg, ibid.; Dobbins, *Grandfather's Journal*, 232–34; Fleet and Fuller, *Green Mount*, 308; Jones, *Under the Stars and Bars*, 231; Jones, *Rebel War Clerk's Diary*, 2:414–35; Norton, *Army Letters*, 253; Preston, *Tenth New York Cavalry*, 245; Rhodes, *All for the Union*, 213–15; Robertson, *Letters of McAllister*, 585–91; Rose Diary, 61–62, CWMC, US-AMHI; Silliker, *Rebel Yell & the Yankee Hurrah*, 245–46; Sparks, *Inside Lincoln's Army*, 470–73; Tyler,

Recollections, 329, 331; Krick, *Civil War Weather,* 152; and Simpson, *Grant,* 407–9. It did not rain on February 27.

35. Westervelt, "Lights and Shadows of Army Life," 64, 65, CWMC, USAMH. See also Bircher, *Drummer-Boy's Diary,* 166.

36. *OR,* 46(2):693, 47(1):122, 200, 231, 409, 427, 440, 446, 532, 566, 583, 594, 622, 632, 633, 686, 688, 689, 722, 732, 783, 904, 47(2):541, 554, 565, 599, 619; Hilton Head, S.C., Jan., Feb. 1865, Reel 467, RG 27.5.7, NARA-CP; Bauer, *Soldiering,* 212–16, 217, 219; Bean Diary, Feb. 17–28, 1865, SHC-UNC; Bircher, *Drummer-Boy's Diary,* 166–70; Bishop, *Story of a Regiment,* 172–74; Black, "Marching with Sherman," 465–66; Charles Brown to Folks, n.d., [1865], Goldsboro, N.C., Charles S. Brown Papers, 1864–1865, Duke; Clark, *Downing's Civil War Diary,* 256–59; Eaton, "Diary of an Officer in Sherman's Army," 244–47; Gaskill Memoranda, Feb. 19–28, 1865, Chicago History Museum; Hazen, *Narrative,* 356–57, 358–59, 362–63; Hight and Stormont, *Fifty-Eighth Indiana,* 438–90; Johnston, *Narrative of Military Operations,* 377; Owens, *Greene County,* 112–13; Padgett, "With Sherman," pt. 2, 71–73; Quint, *Second Massachusetts,* 262–65; Schweitzer Diary, 5:9–10, Schweitzer Diaries and Correspondence, CWTI, USAMHI; Sherwood Journal, Feb. 17–27, 1865, Hess Collection, USAMHI; Westervelt, "Lights and Shadows of Army Life," 65, CWMC, USAMH; Cary Mock, email to author, May 3, 2018; Glatthaar, *March to the Sea,* 12, 108.

37. Bircher, *Drummer-Boy's Diary,* 168–69, 170.

38. Krick, *Civil War Weather,* 154; Brooks, *Washington in Lincoln's Time,* 235–41; Allen and Krowl, "Here Comes the Sun," accessed Aug. 10, 2018.

39. "Diary of Michael Shiner Relating to the Washington Navy Yard," accessed Aug. 10, 2018. See also Brooks, *Washington in Lincoln's Time,* 239.

40. Brooks, *Washington in Lincoln's Time,* 239, 241. The "comet" probably was Venus. See Olson, *Celestial Sleuth,* 215–17.

41. Eaton, "Diary of an Officer in Sherman's Army," 247.

42. Bean Diary, Mar. 8, 1865, SHC-UNC. See also Black, "Marching with Sherman," 466–67; Eaton, "Diary of an Officer in Sherman's Army," 247; Quaife, *From the Cannon's Mouth,* 374; Glatthaar, *March to the Sea,* 146.

43. *OR,* 47(1):203, 231–32, 282, 329, 333, 340, 341, 348, 356, 364, 445, 532, 574, 585, 595, 623, 633, 634, 664, 669, 670, 678, 690, 723, 747, 748, 752, 807, 904, 47(2):729, 735, 738, 741, 751, 754, 757, 763, 822, 861; Bauer, *Soldiering,* 219–23; Bean Diary, Mar. 8–10, 12, 15–16, 1865, SHC-UNC; Bircher, *Drummer-Boy's Diary,* 171–75; Black, "Marching with Sherman," 467; Clark, *Downing's Civil War Diary,* 260, 262; Eaton, "Diary of an Officer in Sherman's Army," 249; Hight and Stormont, *Fifty-Eighth Indiana,* 500; Hazen, *Narrative,* 364, 365; Benjamin F. Hunter Memoir, Mar. 15, 1865, Box 15, CWTI, USAMHI; Padgett, "With Sherman," pt. 2, 74; Quaife, *From the Cannon's Mouth,* 373–74; Quint, *Second Massachusetts,* 265–67; Schweitzer Diary, 5:10, 17, Schweitzer Diaries and Correspondence, CWTI, USAMHI; Sherwood Journal, Mar. 6–16, 1865, Hess Collection, USAMHI; Hughes, *Bentonville,* 4–14.

44. Bauer, *Soldiering,* 225.

45. *OR,* 47(1):907; Glatthaar, *March to the Sea,* 167–69; Hughes, *Bentonville,* 14; McPherson, *Battle Cry of Freedom,* 828–29, 830. For the weather, see Bauer, *Soldiering,* 225–27; Bean Diary, Mar. 15–16, 1865, SHC-UNC; Bircher, *Drummer-Boy's Diary,* 175; Black, "Marching with Sherman," 467; Clark, *Downing's Civil War Diary,* 262; Eaton, "Diary of an Officer in Sherman's Army," 249; Hunter Memoir, Mar. 15, 1865, CWTI, USAMHI; Schweitzer Diary, 5:12, Schweitzer Diaries and Correspondence, CWTI, USAMHI; Sherwood Journal, Mar. 15–16, 1865, Hess Collection, USAMHI.

46. Bauer, *Soldiering,* 227; Bishop, *Story of a Regiment,* 175; Eaton, "Diary of an Officer in Sherman's Army," 249; Sherwood Journal, Mar. 17, 1865, Hess Collection, USAMHI; Hughes, *Bentonville,* 14–16.

47. Sherwood Journal, Mar. 17, 1865, Hess Collection, USAMHI.

48. Bauer, *Soldiering,* 229–30; Quint, *Second Massachusetts,* 271; Sherwood Journal, Mar. 18, 1865, Hess Collection, USAMHI; Hughes, *Bentonville,* 16–33.

49. Bauer, *Soldiering,* 230.

50. *OR,* 47(1):596, 694, 1131; Hilton Head, S.C., Jan., Mar. 1865, Reel 467, RG 27.5.7, NARA-CP; Bircher, *Drummer-Boy's Diary,* 175; Eaton, "Diary of an Officer in Sherman's Army," 250; Schweitzer Diary, 5:12–14, Schweitzer Diaries and Correspondence, CWTI, USAMHI; Sherwood Journal, Mar. 19–21, 1865, Hess Collection, USAMHI; Westervelt, "Lights and Shadows of Army Life," 68, CWMC, USAMH; Krick, *Civil War Weather,* 154; Glatthaar, *March to the Sea,* 169–72; Hughes, *Bentonville,* 33–211.

51. Bauer, *Soldiering,* 235.

52. *OR,* 46(1):476, 477, 478, 480, 495, 498, 46(2):918, 919; Grant, *Memoirs,* 2:293–95; McDonald, *Make Me a Map of the Valley,* 258–61.

53. Agassiz, *Meade's Headquarters,* 304, 307, 309–10, 321; Albright Diary, 90–98, SHC-UNC; Britton and Reed, *To My Beloved Wife,* 335–36, 229–41, 345; Caldwell, *Brigade of South Carolinians,* 267, 270; George E. Cary to Pastor, Mar. 17, 1865, Petersburg, Cary Family Papers, University of Maine; Cary to Mother, Mar. 24, 1865, Petersburg, ibid.; Cary to Sister Sue, Mar. 29, 1865, Petersburg, ibid.; Chamberlayne, *Ham Chamberlayne,* 313; Child, *Fifth New Hampshire,* 293–94; John Willis Council Diary, 12–16, P.C. 1169.1, NCDAH; Dobbins, *Grandfather's Journal,* 235–38; Jones, *Rebel War Clerk's Diary,* 2:436–63; McDonald, *Make Me a Map of the Valley,* 262–63; Nevins, *Diary of Battle,* 499, 501, 507, 510; Rhodes, *All for the Union,* 217–19, 221, 223–34; Robertson, *Letters of McAllister,* 592, 594; Alexander Grant Rose III Diary, 63–65, Box 100, CWMC, USAMHI; Silliker, *Rebel Yell & the Yankee Hurrah,* 246, 249, 252, 255; Krick, *Civil War Weather,* 154; A. Wilson Greene, email to author, Nov. 21, 2018. Seventy-degree temperatures appeared on March 14, 16, 20, 21, and 29. It rained on March 21, 27, and 29, thereafter continuing sporadically into March 31.

54. Beecher, *First Light Battery,* 2:655.

55. Grant, *Memoirs,* 2:296–99; McPherson, *Battle Cry of Freedom,* 845; Simpson, *Grant,* 413–19.

56. *OR,* 46(1):53, 136, 264, 484, 489, 627, 653, 676, 698, 702, 710, 718, 803, 827, 843, 846, 878, 892, 1102, 1192, 46(3):281, 282, 325, 334, 393; Britton and Reed, *To My Beloved Wife,* 345; de Trobriand, *Four Years in the Army of the Potomac,* 715; Grant, *Memoirs,* 2:300–305; Rhodes, *All for the Union,* 223–34; Rose Diary, 65, CWMC, USAMHI; McPherson, *Battle Cry of Freedom,* 845; Simpson, *Grant,* 419–22; A. Wilson Greene, email to author, Nov. 21, 2018.

57. Albright Diary, 99, SHC-UNC; Britton and Reed, *To My Beloved Wife,* 346; Caldwell, *Brigade of South Carolinians,* 287; Grant, *Memoirs,* 2:305–23; Graves, *Bedford Light Artillery,* 57; Howard, *Recollections,* 361; Jones, *Rebel War Clerk's Diary,* 2:464–65; McDonald, *Make Me a Map of the Valley,* 264; Preston, *Tenth New York Cavalry,* 247; Rose Diary, 66, CWMC, USAMHI; Warfield, *Confederate Soldier's Memoirs,* 203; Krick, *Civil War Weather,* 156; McPherson, *Battle Cry of Freedom,* 845–46; Simpson, *Grant,* 422–25; A. Wilson Greene, email to author, Nov. 21, 2018.

58. *OR,* 46(1):631; Albright Diary, 100–101, SHC-UNC; Grant, *Memoirs,* 2:322–33; Graves, *Bedford Light Artillery,* 59–60; Howard, *Recollections,* 370, 377; Jones, *Rebel War Clerk's Diary,* 2:470–71; McDonald, *Make Me a Map of the Valley,* 265; Rose Diary, 67–69, CWMC, USAMHI; Silliker, *Rebel Yell & the Yankee Hurrah,* 259; Talcott, "Petersburg to Appomattox," 67–68; Warfield, *Confederate Soldier's Memoirs,* 204; Krick, *Civil War Weather,* 156; McPherson, *Battle Cry of Freedom,* 846–48; Simpson, *Grant,* 426–27; Varon, *Appomattox,* 7–17.

59. *OR,* 46(1):1233, 1239; Albright Diary, 101, SHC-UNC; Grant, *Memoirs,* 2:333–40; John Richardson Porter Diary 6, Apr. 7, 1865, John Richardson Porter Letter Book and Diaries, 1859–1869, Duke; Krick, *Civil War Weather,* 156; Varon, *Appomattox,* 17–49.

60. Albright Diary, 101, SHC-UNC; Britton and Reed, *To My Beloved Wife*, 349; Caldwell, *Brigade of South Carolinians*, 308; Douglas, *I Rode with Stonewall*, 333; Grant, *Memoirs*, 2:340–49; Nevins, *Diary of Battle*, 522; Rose Diary, 71–74, CWMC, USAMHI; Silliker, *Rebel Yell & the Yankee Hurrah*, 265; Janney, "We Were Not Paroled," 192–219; Krick, *Civil War Weather*, 156; Ludlum, *Weather Factor*, 98–99; Varon, *Appomattox*, 49–78.

61. Brooks, *Washington in Lincoln's Time*, 250–60; Krick, *Civil War Weather*, 156; Oates, *With Malice toward None*, 458–71; Thomas, *Abraham Lincoln*, 513–21.

62. Brooks, *Washington in Lincoln's Time*, 260.

63. *OR*, 47(1):210, 699, 725, 936, 937; Bean Diary, Apr. 2, 10, 14, 15, 21, 1865, SHC-UNC; Bircher, *Drummer-Boy's Diary*, 175, 180, 182–84; Black, "Marching with Sherman," 470–73; Clark, *Downing's Civil War Diary*, 265–70; Collins, *Chapters*, 289, 297; Eaton, "Diary of an Officer in Sherman's Army," 251–52; R. B. Hoadley to Cousin Em, Apr. 8, 1865, Goldsboro, N.C., Robert Bruce Hoadley Papers, 1861–1866, Duke; Padgett, "With Sherman," pt. 2, 77; Quaife, *From the Cannon's Mouth*, 381–82; Quint, *Second Massachusetts*, 277; Schweitzer Diary, 5:15–18, Schweitzer Diaries and Correspondence, CWTI, USAMHI.

64. Bircher, *Drummer-Boy's Diary*, 184.

65. Racine, *Piedmont Farmer*, 368–400 (quotations, 369, 374–75, 377, 400). For a "long Civil War," see Downs, *After Appomattox*; Earle and Burke, *Bleeding Kansas, Bleeding Missouri*; Emberton, *Beyond Redemption*; Grimsley, "Wars for the American South"; and Marrs, *Nineteenth-Century American Literature*.

CONCLUSION

1. Malles, *Bridge Building in Wartime*, 58–82 (quotations, 66, 67–68, 71).

2. Not long ago, a minister asked me about the issue of providential intervention, albeit with the caveat that he knew that professional historians were reluctant to discuss such things.

3. Brasher, *Peninsula Campaign*, 188–224; Fiege, *Republic of Nature*, 203.

4. Fiege, *Republic of Nature*, 224, 225.

5. Fiege, *Republic of Nature*, 221–25. For hunger in the Confederacy, see also Joan E. Cashin's argument in *War Stuff*, 54–62, 78–81.

6. Fiege, *Republic of Nature*, 156–98, 222–23 (quotation, 223). See also Stoker, *Grand Design*.

7. Williams, *Lincoln Finds a General*; Reardon, *With a Sword in One Hand*, 104–21.

8. Douglas, *I Rode with Stonewall*, 109.

9. Sternhell, "Revisionism Reinvented?"; Meier, *Nature's Civil War*; Wills, *Inglorious Passages*, esp. 93–115.

10. Worsham, *One of Jackson's Foot Cavalry*, 14.

11. Grove and Adamson, *El Niño*, 147. Grove and Adamson describe two El Niños during the Reconstruction era, one in 1865–66 ("strong") and the other in 1868–69 ("strong"), as well as a "very strong" one in 1877–78.

Works Consulted

PRIMARY SOURCES

Archival Sources

Abraham Lincoln Presidential Library and Museum, Springfield, Ill.
> Benjamin Hieronymous Diaries, SC 694
> Levi Adolphus Ross Papers

Alabama Department of Archives and History, Montgomery
> W. E. Preston (Mathews). "The 33rd Alabama Regiment in the Civil War,"
> edited by L. B. Williams

Auburn University, Special Collections, Auburn, Ala.
> Charles Henry Snedeker Diary, RG 844

Chicago History Museum, Chicago, Ill.
> James R. M. Gaskill Memoranda

Duke University, David M. Rubenstein Rare Book & Manuscript Library, Durham,
N.C.
> Charles S. Brown Papers, 1864–1865
> Oliver S. Coolidge Papers, 1861–1864
> Henry Kyd Douglas Papers, 1861–1949
> John B. Evans Papers, 1862–1865
> Archibald Erskine Henderson Papers, 1841–1917
> Robert Bruce Hoadley Papers, 1861–1866
> Joseph B. Laughton Letters, 1861–1865
> Mary Margaret McNeill Papers, 1861–1870
> John Richardson Porter Letter Book and Diaries, 1859–1868
> James M. Willcox Papers, 1831–1871

Emory University Manuscript, Archives, and Rare Book Library
> Benjamin Wesley Justice Papers

Gettysburg National Military Park Library, Gettysburg, Pa.
> Vertical Files

Indiana Historical Society, Indianapolis
    Martin Lewis Hursh Diary, SC 808
Library of Congress, Washington, D.C.
    John C. Babcock Papers
    Miscellaneous Manuscript Collection
        William W. Old Diary
        Howard M. Smith Diary and Letters
    Daniel Read Larned Papers
    Rufus Mead Jr. Papers
    Winthrop Henry Phelps Papers
Massachusetts Historical Society, Boston
    Civil War Correspondence, Diaries, and Journals Collection
        George Middleton Barnard Papers
    Lyman Family Papers
    Frank C. Morse Papers
Michigan State University, University Archives and Historical Collections, East Lansing
    Othniel Gooding Papers c.00275
Minnesota Historical Society, Saint Paul
    Donahower, Jeremiah Chester, Papers, 1853–1919, M561
    Pendegrast, William Wirt, Family Papers, M38
Missouri History Museum, Saint Louis
    Daisy J. Cline Papers
National Archives and Records Administration, Washington, D.C.
    RG 24.2.2, Records of the Bureau of Naval Personnel, Logs
        USS *Benton*
        USS *Black Hawk*
        USS *Carondelet*
        USS *Cincinnati*
        USS *Cricket*
        USS *Fawn*
        USS *Forest Rose*
        USS *Galena*
        USS *Lafayette*
        USS *Louisville*
        USS *Mound City*
        USS *Neosho*
        USS *Osage*
        USS *Ozark*
        USS *Tyler*
National Archives and Records Administration, Archives II, College Park, Md.

RG 27.5.7, Records of the Weather Bureau, Records of the Division of Station Facilities and Meteorological Observations and Practices. Microfilm T907

New-York Historical Society, Civil War Primary Source Documents Collection, New York (through EBSCO Information Services Database. https://www.ebscohost.com/archives/featured-archives/civil-war-primary-source-documents; accessed July 20, 2017)

    Edwin Birley Collection: Correspondence

    David E. Cronin Papers: Correspondence

    Edmond Family Collection: Correspondence

    Henry A. Genet Collection: Letter, 1863

    Samuel L. Merrell Collection: Correspondence

    George A. Mitchell Collection: Correspondence

    North Family Collection: Correspondence

    Margaret Scott Collection: Correspondence

    Southard Family Correspondence: Correspondence

    Killian Van Rensselaer Papers: Letters and Military Records

    James M. Willet Collection: Correspondence

North Carolina Department of Archives and History, Raleigh

    John J. Armfield Papers, P.C. 286

    J. B. Clifton Diary, P.C. 589

    John Willis Council Diary, P.C. 1169.1

    J. E. Green Diary, P.C. 694

    John G. Young Papers, P.C. 1076

Ohio Historical Society, Columbus.

    Nathaniel L. Parmeter Papers, 1861–1865: Diary, MSS 246.

Prairie Grove Battlefield State Park, Prairie Grove, Ark.

    Dan B. Thomas Letter

Richmond National Battlefield Park, Richmond, Va.

    James A. Reynolds Diary, Bound Vol. 15

State Historical Society of Iowa, Des Moines

    Henry J. B. Cummings Papers

State Historical Society of Missouri, Columbia

    Henry C. Fike Diaries, C2215

State Historical Society of Missouri–Rolla

    William A. Ruyle Letter

Tennessee State Library and Archives, Nashville

    Papers of Campbell Brown and Richard S. Ewell. Microfilm 816

    Civil War Collection: Confederate and Federal, 1861–1865. Microfilm

        Col. James L. Cooper Memoirs, Folder 11, Box 12, Reel 5

        John H. Freeman Diaries and Memoirs, Box C26, Reel 18

US Army Military History Institute, Carlisle, Pa.
    Civil War Document Collection
        John H. Bonnell Diary, Box 11 (transcript)
    Civil War Miscellaneous Collection
        Aaron K. Blake Correspondence, Box 10
        "Civil War Letters of Dayton E. Flint," Box 40
        William H. Myers Letters, Box 84
        William H. Peacock Correspondence, Box 89
        M. Edgar Richards Correspondence, Box 97
        Alexander Grant Rose III Diary, Box 100
        Henry P. Turner Diary, Box 116
        William B. Westervelt, "Lights and Shadows of Army Life, as Seen by a
            Private Soldier," Box 121 (incomplete typed transcript)
        Charles E. Wood Diary and Correspondence, Box 125
    Civil War Times Illustrated Collection
        John W. Caldwell Diary, Ser. 2, Box 30
        Benjamin F. Hunter Memoir, Box 15
        Samuel John McDaniel Memoir, Ser. 2, Box 34
        Edward E. Schweitzer Diaries and Correspondence, Box 23
        Joseph S. C. Taber Diary
        Levi Wagner Memoirs
    James Parley Coburn Papers
    Harrisburg Civil War Round Table Collection
        Luther C. Furst Diary
    Earl M. Hess Collection
        Frederick Sherwood Journal, Box 2
    Michael Winey Collection
        Isaac R. Dunkelbarger Recollections
University of Maine, Special Collections, Orono
    Cary Family Papers, 1856–1920, SpC MS 85
University of North Carolina, Southern Historical Collection, Chapel Hill
    James W. Albright Diary, 01008-z
    Jesse S. Bean Diary, 03605-z
    William J. Clarke Papers, 00153
    George Mathews Edgar Papers, 03633
    James Iredell Hall Diary, 302
    Joseph Franklin Kaufman Diary, 03110-z
    Julius A. Lineback Papers, 04547
    Edward Hitchcock McDonald Reminiscences, 2131
    Edmund Kirby Smith Papers, 404
    Westwood A. Todd Reminiscence, 722-z

Richard Woolfolk Waldrop Papers, 2268-z
University of Texas–Austin, Center for American History
   (Ebenezer) Hanna Papers
   (Thomas L.) McCarty Papers
Virginia Military Institute, Lexington
   Stonewall Jackson House Collection

Published Works

Agassiz, George R., ed. *Meade's Headquarters, 1863–1865: Letters of Colonel Theodore Lyman from the Wilderness to Appomattox.* Boston: Atlantic Monthly, 1922.

Alberts, Don E., ed. *Rebels on the Rio Grande: The Civil War Journal of A. B. Peticolas.* Albuquerque: University of New Mexico Press, 1984.

The American Almanac and Repository of Useful Knowledge for the Year 1861. Vol. 32, 4th. ser., vol. 2. Boston: Crosby, Nichols, Lee, 1861.

Anderson, Ephraim McD. *Memoirs: Historical and Personal; Including the Campaigns of the First Missouri Confederate Brigade.* St. Louis: Times Printing, 1868.

Anderson, John Q., ed., *Brokenburn: The Journal of Kate Stone, 1861–1868* (Baton Rouge: Louisiana State University Press, 1955.

Annual Report of the Board of Regents of the Smithsonian Institution, Showing the Operations, Expenditures, and Condition of the Institution for the Year 1861. Washington, D.C.: Government Printing Office, 1861.

Armstrong, George D. *"The Good Hand of Our God Upon Us": A Thanksgiving Sermon Preached on Occasion of the Victory of Manassas, July 21st, 1861, in the Presbyterian Church, Norfolk, Va.* Norfolk: J. D. Ghiselin Jr., 1861.

Armstrong, Nelson. *Nuggets of Experience: Narratives of the Sixties and Other Days, with Graphic Depictions of Thrilling Personal Adventures.* San Bernardino, Calif.: Times-Mirror, 1906.

Baird, Nancy Chappelear, ed. *Journals of Amanda Virginia Edmonds: Lass of the Mosby Confederacy, 1857–1867.* Stephens City, VA: Commercial, 1984.

Baker, I. Norval. "Diary and Reminiscences of I. Norval Baker." *Winchester-Frederick County Historical Society Papers* 3 (n. d.): 96–128.

Banasik, Michael E., ed. *Serving with Honor: The Diary of Captain Eathan Allen Pinnell, Eighth Missouri Infantry (Confederate).* Unwritten Chapters of the Civil War West of the River, vol. 3. Iowa City: Camp Pope Bookshop, 1999.

Barnes, James A., James R. Carnahan, and Thomas H. B. McCain. *The Eighty-Sixth Regiment, Indiana Volunteer Infantry. A Narrative of Its Service in the Civil War of 1861–1865.* Crawfordsville, Ind.: Journal, 1895.

Barnes, J. D. *What I Saw You Do: A Brief History of the Battles, Marches, and Sieges of the Twentieth Iowa Volunteer Infantry, during Their Three Years' of Active Service in the War of the Rebellion.* Port Byron, Ill.: Owen & Hall, 1896.

Barney, C. [Chester]. *Recollections of Field Service with the Twentieth Iowa Infantry Volunteers; or, What I Saw in the Army, Embracing Accounts of Marches, Battles, Sieges, and Skirmishes, in Missouri, Arkansas, Mississippi, Louisiana, Alabama, Florida, Texas, and along the Northern Border of Mexico.* Davenport, Iowa: Self-published, 1865.

Barron, S. B. *The Lone Star Defenders: A Chronicle of the Third Texas Cavalry, Ross' Brigade.* New York: Neale, 1908.

Bartlett, A. W. *History of the Twelfth Regiment New Hampshire Volunteers in the War of the Rebellion.* Concord, N.H.: Ira C. Evans, 1897.

Bartlett, Napier. *Military Record of Louisiana, including Biographical and Historical Papers Relating to the Military Organizations of the State.* New Orleans: L Graham, 1875. Reprint, Baton Rouge: Louisiana State University Press, 1964.

Basler, Roy C., ed. *The Collected Works of Abraham Lincoln.* 9 vols. New Brunswick, N.J.: Rutgers University Press, 1952–53.

Bauer, K. Jack, ed. *Soldiering: The Civil War Diary of Rice C. Bull, 123rd New York Volunteer Infantry.* San Rafael, Calif.: Presidio, 1977.

Baylor, George. *Bull Run to Bull Run; or, Four Years in the Army of Northern Virginia. Containing a Detailed Account of the Career and Adventures of the Baylor Light Horse, Company B, Twelfth Virginia Cavalry, C.S.A., with Leaves from My Scrapbook.* Richmond: B. F. Johnson, 1900. Reprint, Washington, D.C.: Zenger, 1983.

Bean, W. G., ed. "The Valley Campaign of 1862 as Revealed in the Letters of Sandie Pendleton." *Virginia Magazine of History and Biography* 78 (1970): 326–64.

Beatty, John. *The Citizen-Solider; or, Memoirs of a Volunteer.* Cincinnati: Wilstach, Baldwin, 1879.

Beecher, Herbert W. *History of the First Light Battery Connecticut Volunteers, 1861–1865.* 2 vols. New York: D. T. De La Mare, n.d.

Beirne, Rosamond Randall, ed. "Three War Letters." *Maryland Historical Magazine* 40 (December 1945): 287–94.

Bennett, L. G., and William M. Haigh. *History of the Thirty-Sixth Regiment Illinois Volunteers, during the War of the Rebellion.* Aurora, Ill.: Knickerbocker & Hodder, 1876.

Benson, Susan Williams, ed. *Berry Benson's Civil War Book: Memoirs of a Confederate Scout and Sharpshooter.* Foreword by Herman Hattaway. Athens: University of Georgia Press, 1992.

Berkeley, John Lee, comp. and ed. *In the Defense of This Flag: The Civil War Diary of Pvt. Ormond Hupp, 5th Indiana Light Artillery.* Bradenton, Fla.: McGuinn & McGuire, 1994.

Bierce, Ambrose Birce. "The Crime at Pickett's Mill: A Plain Account of a Bad Half Hour with Jo. Johnston." In *Ambrose Bierce, a Sole Survivor: Bits of Autobiogra-*

phy, edited by S. T. Joshi and David E. Schultz, 37–45. Knoxville: University of Tennessee Press, 1998.

Billings, John D. *Hardtack and Coffee.* Boston: G. M. Smith, 1887. Reprint, Old Saybrook, Conn.: Konecky & Konecky, n.d.

Bircher, William. *A Drummer-Boy's Diary: Comprising Four Years of Service with the Second Regiment Minnesota Veteran Volunteers, 1861 to 1865.* St. Paul: St. Paul Book and Stationery, 1889.

Bishop, Judson W. *The Story of a Regiment: Being a Narrative of the Second Regiment, Minnesota Veteran Volunteer Infantry, in the Civil War of 1861–1865.* St. Paul: N.p., 1890.

Black, Wilfred W., ed. "Marching with Sherman through Georgia and the Carolinas: Civil War Diary of Jesse L. Dozier." *Georgia Historical Quarterly* 52 (1968): 308–36, 451–79.

Blackford, Susan Leigh, Charles Minor Blackford, and Charles Minor Blackford III, eds. *Letters from Lee's Army, or, Memoirs of Life in and out of the Army in Virginia during the War between the States.* New York: Charles Scribner's Sons, 1947.

Blackford, W. W. *War Years with Jeb Stuart.* New York: Charles Scribner's Sons, 1945.

Blakey, Arch Frederic, Ann Smith Lainhart, and Winston Bryant Stephens Jr., eds. *Rose Cottage Chronicles: Civil War Letters of the Bryant-Stephens Families of North Florida.* Gainesville: University Press of Florida, 1998.

[Blessington, Joseph P.] *The Campaigns of Walker's Texas Division.* New York: Lange, Little, 1875.

Blight, David W., ed. *When This Cruel War Is Over: The Civil War Letters of Charles Henry Brewster.* Amherst: University of Massachusetts Press, 1992.

Blodgett, Edward A. "The Army of the Southwest and the Battle of Pea Ridge." In *Military Essays and Recollections: Papers Read before the Commandery of the State of Illinois, Military Order of the Loyal League of the United States,* 2:289–312. Chicago: A. C. McClurg, 1894.

Bock, H. Riley. "One Year at War: Letters of Capt. Geo. W. Dawson, C.S.A." *Missouri Historical Review* 71 (1979): 165–97.

Bragg, Dr. J. N. "Chasing Steele through Jenkins Ferry." *Ouachita County Historical Quarterly* (Spring 1998): 9–12.

Briggs, Wattes DeBlois, ed. *Civil War Surgeon in a Colored Regiment* (Berkley, Calif.: By the author, 1960.

Britton, Ann Hartwell, and Thomas J. Reed. *To My Beloved Wife and Boy at Home: The Letters and Diaries of Orderly Sergeant John F. L. Hartwell.* Madison, N.J.: Fairleigh Dickinson University Press, 1997.

Brooks, Noah. *Washington in Lincoln's Time.* New York: Century, 1895.

Bruce, D. H. "Battle of New Market, Va." *Confederate Veteran* 15 (December 1907): 553–54.

Buffum, Francis H. *A Memorial of the Great Rebellion: Being a History of the Fourteenth Regiment New-Hampshire Volunteers, Covering Its Three Years of Service, with Original Sketches of Army Life, 1862–1865.* Boston: Franklin, 1882.

Butler, Jay Caldwell. *Letters Home: Jay Caldwell Butler, Captain, 101st Ohio Volunteer Infantry.* Arranged by Watson Hubbard Butler. N. p., 1930.

Caldwell, J. F. J. *The History of a Brigade of South Carolinians First Known as "Gregg's" and Subsequently as "McGowan's Brigade."* Philadelphia: King & Baird, 1866. Reprint, Dayton, Ohio: Morningside, 1984.

Carter, George W. "The Fourth Wisconsin at Port Hudson." In *War Papers Read before the Commandery of the State of Wisconsin, Military Order of the Loyal Legion of the United States,* 226–40. Milwaukee: Burdick & Allen, 1903.

Carter, W. H. *From Yorktown to Santiago with the Sixth U.S. Cavalry.* Introduction by John M. Carroll. Baltimore: Lord Baltimore, 1900. Reprint, Austin, Tex.: State House, 1989.

Cashin, Joan E. *War Stuff: The Struggle for Human and Environmental Resources in the American Civil War.* Cambridge: Cambridge University Press, 2018.

Casler, John O. *Four Years in the Stonewall Brigade.* 4th ed. Dayton, Ohio: Morningside Bookshop, 1971.

Cater, Douglas John. *As It Was: Reminiscences of a Soldier in the Third Texas Cavalry and the Nineteenth Louisiana Infantry.* Introduction by T. Michael Parrish. Austin, Tex.: State House, 1990.

Cathey, Henry, ed. "Extracts from the Memoirs of William Franklin Avila." *Arkansas Historical Quarterly* 22 (Winter 1963): 99–116.

Cavins, Matilda Livingston, ed. *War Letters of Aden G. Cavins, Written to His Wife Matilda Livingston Cavins.* Evansville, Ind.: Rosenthal-Kuebler, n.d.

Chamberlayne, John Hampden. *Ham Chamberlayne—Virginian: Letters and Papers of an Artillery Officer in the War for Southern Independence, 1861–1865.* Introduction, notes, and index by C. G. Chamberlayne. Richmond: Dietz, 1932. Reprint, Wilmington, N.C.: Broadfoot, 1992.

Chesnut, Mary. *A Diary from Dixie, as Written by Mary Boykin Chesnut, Wife of James Chesnut, Jr., United States Senator from South Carolina, 1859–1861, and Afterward an Aide to Jefferson Davis and a Brigadier-General in the Confederate Army.* Edited by Isabella D. Martin and Myrta Lockett Avary. New York: D. Appleton, 1905.

Child, William. *A History of the Fifth Regiment New Hampshire Volunteers in the American Civil War, 1861–1865. In Two Parts.* Bristol, N.H.: R. W. Musgrove, 1893.

Cist, Henry M. *The Army of the Cumberland.* New York: Charles Scribner's Sons, 1882.

The Civil War Diary of First Sergeant Squire Helm Bush of Company B of the Sixth Kentucky Mounted Infantry Regiment, Volunteers, Confederate States of America. N.p., 1975.

"The Civil War Diary of Joshua Ayre." Transcribed by James Glauser. N.p., n.d.

Clark, James H. *The Iron Hearted Regiment: Being an Account of the Battles, Marches and Gallant Deeds Performed by the 115th Regiment N.Y. Vols. also a List of the Dead and Wounded; an Account of Hundreds of Brave Men Shot on a Score of Hard Fought Fields of Strife; a Complete Statement of the Harpers Ferry Surrender; Sketches of the Officers; a History of the Flags and Those Who Bore Them, Together with Touching Incidents, Thrilling Adventures, Amusing Scenes, etc. etc. etc.* Albany, N.Y.: Munsell, 1865.

Clark, Olynthus B., ed. *Downing's Civil War Diary, by Sergeant Alexander G. Downing, Company E, Eleventh Iowa Infantry, Third Brigade, "Crocker's Brigade," Sixth Division of the Seventeenth Army Corps, Army of the Tennessee, August 15, 1861–July 31, 1865.* Des Moines: Historical Department of Iowa, 1916.

Clark, Orton S. *The One Hundred and Sixteenth Regiment of New York State Volunteers: Being a Complete History of Its Organization and of Its Nearly Three Years of Active Service in the Great Rebellion.* Buffalo: Matthews & Warren, 1868.

Clark, Walter A. *Under the Stars and Bars; or, Memories of Four Years Service with the Oglethorpes, of Augusta, Georgia.* Augusta, Ga.: Chronicle Printing, 1900.

Clay, H. B. "On the Right at Murfreesboro." *Confederate Veteran* 21 (December 1913): 588–90.

Collins, R. M. *Chapters from the Unwritten History of the War between the States; or, The Incidents in the Life of a Confederate Soldier in Camp, on the March, in the Great Battles, and in Prison.* St. Louis: Nixon-Jones, 1893.

Cook, Benjamin F. *History of the Twelfth Massachusetts Volunteers (Webster Regiment).* Boston: Twelfth (Webster) Regiment Association, 1882.

Cooke, Chauncey H. "Letters of a Badger Boy in Blue: The Atlanta Campaign." *Wisconsin Magazine of History* 5 (1921): 63–98.

Cooper, William W., and Donald M. Fowler, eds. "'Your Affectionate Husband': Letters from a Catahoula Parish Confederate Soldier, September 1861–May 1862." *North Louisiana Historical Association Journal* 14 (1983): 21–40.

Cope, Alexis. *The Fifteenth Ohio Volunteers and Its Campaigns: War of 1861–5.* Columbus, Ohio: By the author, 1916.

Coski, John M., ed. "'I Am for Anything for Success': The Letters of Sergeant Archie Livingston, 3rd Florida Infantry." Transcribed by Louise Hall and Ruth Ann Coski. *North & South* 6 (April 2003): 76–86.

Cox, Jacob Dolson. *The March to Sea, Franklin, and Nashville.* New York: Charles Scribner's Sons, 1913.

———. *Military Reminiscences of the Civil War.* Vol. 2, *November 1863—June 1865.* New York: Charles Scribner's Sons, 1900.

[Crane, Edward A.] "On the Special Organization of the American Ambulance." In *History of the American Ambulance Established in Paris during the Siege of 1870–71, Together with the Details of Its Methods and Its Work,* by Thomas W. Evans, 445–574. London: Samson, Low, Marston, Low, and Searle, 1873.

Crary, A. M. *The A. M. Crary Memoirs and Memoranda.* Herington, Kans.: Herington Times, 1915.

Crawford, Samuel J. *Kansas in the Sixties.* Chicago: A. C. McClurg, 1911.

Crawford, Samuel Wylie. *The Genesis of the Civil War: The Story of Sumter, 1860–1861.* New York: Charles L. Webster, 1887.

Curtis, Newton Martin. *First Bull Run to Chancellorsville: The Story of the Sixteenth New York Infantry, Together with Personal Reminiscences.* New York: G. P. Putnam's Sons, 1906.

[Davidson, William Lott]. "Reminiscences of the Old Brigade, on the March, in the Tent, in the Field, as Witnessed by the Writers during the Rebellion." [With Charles Carroll Linn, Phil Fulcrod, et al.]. *Nesbitt Memorial Library Journal* 9 (May 1999): 51–126.

Dawes, Rufus R. *Service with the Sixth Wisconsin Volunteers.* Edited with an introduction by Alan T. Nolan. Madison: State Historical Society of Wisconsin for the Wisconsin Civil War Centennial Commission, 1962.

Derby, W. P. *Bearing Arms in the Twenty-Seventh Massachusetts Regiment of Volunteer Infantry during the Civil War.* Boston: Wright and Potter, 1883.

DeRosier, Arthur H., Jr., ed. *Through the South with a Union Soldier.* Johnson City: East Tennessee State University Research Advisory Council, 1969.

De Trobriand, Regis. *Four Years in the Army of the Potomac.* Translated by George K. Douchy. Boston: Ticknor, 1889.

De Veaux, T. L. *Fast-Day Sermon Preached in the Good Hope Church, Lowndes County, Alabama, Thursday June 13th, 1861.* Wytheville, Va.: D. A. St. Clair, 1861.

"Diaries of John Waldrop, Second Company, and William Y. Mordecai, Second Company, Combined." *Contributions to a History of the Richmond Howitzers Battalion.* Pamphlet 3. Richmond: Carlton McCarthy, 1884.

"Diary of Creed T. Davis, Private Second Company Richmond Howitzers." *Contributions to a History of the Richmond Howitzers Battalion,* Pamphlet 3. Richmond: Carlton McCarthy, 1884.

Dickey, Luther. *History of the Eighty-Fifth Regiment Pennsylvania Volunteer Infantry, 1861–1865.* New York: J. C. & W. E. Powers, 1915.

Doan, Isaac C. *Reminiscences of the Chattanooga Campaign: A Paper Read at the Reunion of Company B, Fortieth Ohio Volunteer Infantry, at Xenia, O., August 22, 1894.* Richmond, Ind.: J. M. Coe, 1894.

Dobbins, Austin C. ed. *Grandfather's Journal: Company B, Sixteenth Mississippi Infantry Volunteers, Harris's Brigade, Mahone's Division, Hill's Corps, A.N.V., May 27, 1861–July 15, 1865.* Dayton, Ohio: Morningside House, 1988.

Dodge, William Sumner. *A Waif of the War; or, The History of the Seventy-Fifth Illinois Infantry Embracing the Entire Campaigns of the Army of the Cumberland.* Chicago: Church and Goodman, 1866.

Doubleday, Abner. *Reminiscences of Forts Sumter and Moultrie in 1860–'61.* New York: Harper & Brothers, 1876.

Douglas, Henry Kyd. *I Rode with Stonewall.* Chapel Hill: University of North Carolina Press, 1940.

Drake, James Vaulx. *Life of General Robert Hatton, including His Most Important Public Speeches; Together, with Much of His Washington & Army Correspondence.* Nashville: Marshall & Bruce, 1867.

Dunaway, Thomas S. *A Sermon Delivered by Elder Thomas S. Dunaway, of Lancaster County, Virginia, before Con Baptist Church, in Connections with a Day of National Fasting, Humiliation and Prayer, April, 1864, Published by Order of the Church.* Richmond: Enquirer Book and Job Press, 1864.

Dungan, J. Irvine. *History of the Nineteenth Regiment, Iowa Volunteer Infantry.* Davenport, Iowa: Luse and Griggs, 1865.

Early, Jubal Anderson. *War Memoirs: Autobiographical Sketch and Narrative of the War between the States.* Edited with an introduction by Frank E. Vandiver. Bloomington: Indiana University Press, 1960.

Eaton, Clement, ed. "Diary of an Officer in Sherman's Army Marching through the Carolinas." *Journal of Southern History* 9 (1943): 238–54.

Eby, Henry H. *Observations of an Illinois Boy in Battle, Camp, and Prisons—1861 to 1865.* Mendota, Ill.: By the author, 1910.

Elliott, J. H. *The Bloodless Victory: A Sermon Preached in St. Michael's Church, Charleston, S.C., on the Occasion of the Taking of Fort Sumter.* Charleston: A. E. Miller, 1861.

Elliot, Sam Davis, ed. *Doctor Quintard, Chaplain C.S.A. and Second Bishop of Tennessee: The Memoir and Civil War Diary of Charles Todd Quintard.* Baton Rouge: Louisiana State University Press, 2003.

[Elliot, Stephen]. *How to Renew Our National Strength: A Sermon Preached in Christ Church, Savannah, on Friday, November 15th, 1861, Being the Day of Humiliation, Fasting, and Prayer. Appointed by the President of the Confederate States.* Savannah: John M. Cooper, 1861.

Emmerton, James A. *A Record of the Twenty-Third Regiment Mass. Vol. Infantry in the War of the Rebellion, 1861–1865, with Alphabetical Roster; Company Rolls, . . . Etc.* Boston: W. Ware, 1886.

Everson, Guy R., and Edward H. Simpson Jr., eds. *"Far, Far from Home": The Wartime Letters of Dick and Tally Simpson, Third South Carolina Volunteers.* New York: Oxford University Press, 1994.

Ewer, James K. *The Third Massachusetts Cavalry in the War for the Union.* N.p.: Historical Committee of the Regimental Association, 1903.

Farrar, Samuel Clarke. *The Twenty-Second Pennsylvania Cavalry and the Ringgold Battalion, 1861–1865.* Pittsburgh: Twenty-Second Pennsylvania Ringgold Cavalry Association, 1911.

Fisher, Horace Cecil. *A Staff Officer's Story: The Personal Experiences of Colonel Horace Newton Fisher in the Civil War.* Boston: Thomas Todd, 1960.

Fleet, Betsy, and John D. P. Fuller, eds. *Green Mount: A Virginia Plantation Family during the Civil War: Being the Journal of Benjamin Robert Fleet and Letters of His Family.* Lexington: University of Kentucky Press, 1962.

Flinn, Frank M. *Campaigning with Banks in Louisiana, '63 and '64, and with Sheridan in the Shenandoah Valley, in '64 and '65.* Lynn, Mass: Thomas P. Nichols, 1887.

"Fortification and Siege of Port Hudson—Compiled by the Association of Defenders of Port Hudson; M. J. Smith, President; James Freret, Secretary." *Southern Historical Society Papers* 14 (1886): 305–48.

Foster, Alonzo. *Reminiscences and Record of the 6th New York V. V. Cavalry.* Brooklyn, 1892.

Francis, Charles Lewis. *Narrative of a Private Soldier in the Volunteer Army of the United States, during a Portion of the Period Covered by the Great War of the Rebellion of 1861.* Brooklyn: William Jenkins, 1879.

Fremantle, Arthur James Lyon. *Three Months in the Southern States: April–June, 1863.* New York: Bradburn, 1864. Reprint, with an introduction by Gary W. Gallagher, Lincoln: University of Nebraska Press, 1991.

French, Samuel G. *Two Wars: An Autobiography.* Nashville: Confederate Veteran, 1901.

Friend, Jack. *West Wind, Flood Tide: The Battle of Mobile Bay.* Annapolis, Md.: Naval Institute Press, 2004.

Fry, Frinkle [Elnathan B. Tyler]. *"Wooden Nutmegs" at Bull Run, a Humorous Account of Some of the Exploits and Experiences of the Three Months Connecticut Brigade, and the Part They Bore in the National Stampede.* Hartford, Conn.: George L. Coburn, 1872.

Galwey, Thomas Francis. *The Valiant Hours: Narrative of "Captain Brevet," an Irish-American in the Army of the Potomac.* Edited by W. S. Nye. Harrisburg, Pa.: Stackpole, 1961.

Garnett, James M. "Diary of Captain James Garnett." *Southern Historical Society Papers* 27 (January 1899): 1–16.

Grant, U. S. *Personal Memoirs of U. S. Grant.* 2 vols. 2nd ed. New York: DeVinne, 1895.

Graves, James A. *The History of the Bedford Light Artillery.* Bedford City, Va.: Bedford Democrat, 1903.

Haden, B. J. *Reminiscences of J. E. B. Stuart's Cavalry.* Charlottesville, Va.: Progress, n.d.

Hafendorfer, Kenneth A., ed. *Civil War Journal of William L. Trask, Confederate Sailor and Soldier.* Louisville: KH Press, 2003.

Haines, Alanson A. *History of the Fifteenth Regiment New Jersey Volunteers.* New York: Jenkins & Thomas, 1883.

Hall, Henry Seymour. *Personal Experience under Generals Burnside and Hooker, in the Battles of Fredericksburg and Chancellorsville, December 11, 12, 13, and 14, 1862, and May 1, 2, 3, and 4, 1863; a Paper Prepared and Read before the Kansas Commandery of the Military Order of the Loyal Legion of the United States.* Kansas City: Franklin Hudson, 1889.

Hamilton, J. G. deRoulhac, ed. *The Papers of Randolph Abbott Shotwell.* 3 vols. Raleigh: North Carolina Historical Commission, 1929.

Harkness, Edson J. "The Expedition against Fort Fisher and Wilmington." In *Military Essays and Recollections: Papers Read before the Commandery of the State of Illinois, Military Order of the Loyal League of the United States,* 2:145–88. Chicago: A. C. McClurg, 1894.

Harwood, Nathan S. *The Pea Ridge Campaign: A Paper Read before the Nebraska Commandery of the Order of the Loyal Legion of the United States.* Omaha: Ackerman Bros. & Heintze, 1887.

Hazen, W. B. *A Narrative of Military Service.* Boston: Ticknor, 1885. Reprint, with an introduction by Richard A. Baumgartner, Huntington, W.Va.: Blue Acorn, 1993.

Head, Thomas A. *Campaigns and Battles of the Sixteenth Regiment, Tennessee Volunteers, in the War between the States, with Incidental Sketches of the Part Performed by Other Tennessee Troops in the Same War, 1861–1865.* Nashville: Cumberland Presbyterian Publishing House, 1885.

Hight, John J., and Gilbert R. Stormont. *History of the Fifty-Eighth Regiment of Indiana Volunteer Infantry.* Princeton, Ind.: Clarion, 1895.

Hill, Daniel H. "McClellan's Change of Base and Malvern Hill." In Johnson and Buel, *Battles and Leaders,* 2:383–95.

Hinman, Wilbur F. *The Story of the Sherman Brigade: The Camp, the March, the Bivouac, the Battle; and How "The Boys" Lived and Died during Four Years of Active Service.* Alliance, Ohio: By the author, 1897.

[Hinton, Richard J.] *Rebel Invasion of Missouri and Kansas, and the Campaign of the Army of the Border, against General Sterling Price, in October and November 1864.* Chicago: Church & Goodman, 1865.

Hitchcock, Henry. *Marching with Sherman: Passages from the Letters and Campaign Diaries of Henry Hitchcock, Major and Assistant Adjutant General of Volunteers, November 1864–May 1865.* Edited with an introduction by M. A. DeWolfe Howe. Introduction to the Bison Book edition by Brooks D. Simpson. Lincoln: University of Nebraska Press, 1995.

Hoke, Jacob. *The Great Invasion of 1863; or, General Lee in Pennsylvania*. Dayton, Ohio: W. J. Shuey, 1887. Reprint, New York: Thomas Yoseloff, 1959.

Hollister, Ovando James. *Boldly They Rode: A History of the First Colorado Regiment of Volunteers*. With an introduction by William McLeod Raine. Lakewood, Colo.: Golden, 1949.

Holloway, W. R. "Treatment of Prisoners at Camp Morton." *Century Magazine* 42 (1891): 757–70.

Horrall, S. F. *History of the Forty-Second Indiana Volunteer Infantry, Compiled and Written at the Request of W. M. Cockrum*. Chicago: By the author, 1892.

Houghton, W. R., and M. B. Houghton. *Two Boys in the Civil War and After*. Montgomery, Ala.: Paragon, 1912.

Howard, McHenry. *Recollections of a Maryland Confederate Soldier and Staff Officer under Johnston, Jackson, and Lee*. Introduction, corrections, and notes by James I. Robertson Jr. Dayton, Ohio: Morningside Bookshop, 1975.

Howe, Mark DeWolfe, ed. *Touched with Fire: Civil War Letters and Diary of Oliver Wendell Holmes Jr., 1861–1864*. Cambridge, Mass.: Harvard University Press, 1947.

Hubert, Charles F. *History of the Fiftieth Regiment, Illinois Volunteer Infantry in the War for the Union*. Kansas City, Mo.: Western Veteran, 1894.

Hyde, Thomas W. *Following the Greek Cross; or, Memories of the Sixth Army Corps*. Boston: Houghton Mifflin, 1894.

Irwin, Richard B. *History of the Nineteenth Army Corps*. New York: G. P. Putnam's Sons, 1893.

Johns, Henry T. *Life with the Forty-Ninth Massachusetts Volunteers*. Washington, D.C.: Ramsey and Bisbee, 1890.

Johnson, Robert Underwood, and Clarence Clough Buel, eds. *Battles and Leaders of the Civil War*. 4 vols. New York: Century, 1888.

Johnston, Joseph E. *Narrative of Military Operations, Directed, during the Late War between the States*. New York: D. Appleton, 1874.

Jones, B. W. *Under the Stars and Bars: A History of the Surry Light Artillery. Recollections of a Private Soldier in the War between the States*. Richmond: Everett Waddey, 1909.

Jones, J. B. *A Rebel War Clerk's Diary at the Confederate States Capital*. Edited with an introduction by Howard Swiggett. 2 vols. New York: Old Hickory Bookshop, 1935.

Jones, Jenkin Lloyd. *An Artilleryman's Diary*. Wisconsin History Commission Original Papers 8. Madison: Wisconsin History Commission, 1914.

Keil, F. W. *Thirty-Fifth Ohio: A Narrative of Service from August, 1861 to 1864*. Introduction by H. V. Boynton. Ft. Wayne, Ind.: Archer, Roush, 1894.

Kimberly, Robert L., and Ephraim S. Holloway. *The Forty-First Ohio Veteran Volun-

teer Infantry in the War of the Rebellion, 1861–1865. Cleveland: W. R. Smellie, 1897.

Kirwan, A. D., ed. *Johnny Green of the Orphan Brigade: The Journal of a Confederate Soldier.* Lexington: University of Kentucky Press, 1956.

Knox, Thomas W. *Camp-Fire and Cotton-Field: Southern Adventures in Time of War.* New York: Blelock, 1865.

Kreutzer, William. *Notes and Observations Made during Four Years of Service with the Ninety-Eighth N.Y. Volunteers in the War of 1861.* Philadelphia: Grant, Faires, & Roberts, 1878.

Lasswell, Mary, comp. and ed. *Rags and Hope: The Recollections of Val C. Giles, Four Years with Hood's Brigade, Fourth Texas Infantry, 1861–1865.* New York: Coward-McCann, 1961.

Leake, Joseph B. "Campaign of the Army of the Frontier." In *Military Essays and Recollections: Papers Read before the Commandery of the State of Illinois, Military Order of the Loyal Legion of the United States,* 2:269–88. Chicago: A. C. McClurg, 1894.

Lee, Robert E. *Recollections and Letters of General Robert E. Lee.* Introduction by Gamaliel Bradford. Appendix edited by Walther Taylor Thom. Garden City, N.Y.: Garden City Publishing, [1924].

Lee, Susan P., ed. *Memoir of William Nelson Pendleton, D. D.* Philadelphia: J. B. Lippincott, 1893. Reprint, Harrisonburg, Va.: Sprinkle, 1991.

"Letters from Aaron P. Bates, of 'D' Company, One Hundred and Second New York Volunteers, Regarding the Battle of Cedar Mountain, Va., August 9, 1862." In *Second Annual Report of the State Historian of the State of New York,* 101–8. Albany: Wynkoop Hallenback Crawford, 1897.

Lincoln, William S. *Life with the Thirty-Fourth Mass. Infantry in the War of the Rebellion.* Worcester: Noyes, Snow, 1879.

Little, George, and James R. Maxwell. *A History of Lumsden's Battery C.S.A.* Tuscaloosa, Ala.: R. E. Rhodes Chapter, United Daughters of the Confederacy, 1905.

Longstreet, James. *From Manassas to Appomattox: Memoirs of the Civil War in America.* Edited with an introduction by James I. Robertson. Civil War Centennial Series. Bloomington: Indiana University Press, 1960.

Lothrop, Charles H. *A History of the First Regiment Iowa Cavalry Veteran Volunteers, from Its Organization in 1861 to Its Muster Out of the United States Service in 1866.* Lyons, Iowa: Beers & Eaton, 1890.

[Loughborough, Mary Ann Webster]. *My Cave Life in Vicksburg. With Letters of Trial and Travel.* New York: D. Appleton, 1864.

Lynch, Charles H. *The Civil War Diary, 1862–1865, of Charles H. Lynch, 18th Conn. Vol's.* Hartford, Conn., 1915.

Malles, Ed, ed. *Bridge Building in Wartime: Colonel Wesley Brainerd's Memoir of the 50th New York Volunteer Engineers.* Voices of the Civil War Series. Knoxville: University of Tennessee Press, 1997.

Manarin, Louis H., ed. "The Civil War Diary of Rufus J. Woolwine." *Virginia Magazine of History and Biography* 71 (1963): 416–48.

Marcoot, Maurice. *Five Years in the Sunny South: Reminiscences of Maurice Marcoot.* N.p., 189[?].

Marshall, Joseph K. *Civil War Diary of Joseph K. Marshall, Co. E, 90th Regmt., 1st Brigade, Ohio Volunteer Infantry, Aug. 29, 1862–July 31st, 1864.* Copied by W. Louis Phillips. Columbus, Ohio, 1982.

Matson, Daniel. *Life Experiences of Daniel Matson.* N.p., 1924.

Maynard, Douglas, ed. "Vicksburg Diary: The Journal of Gabriel M. Kilgore." *Civil War History* 10 (March 1964): 33–53.

McClendon, William Augustus. *Recollections of War Times, by an Old Veteran While under Stonewall Jackson and Lieutenant General James Longstreet: How I Got In, and How I Got Out.* Montgomery, Ala.: Paragon, 1909. Reprint, San Bernardino: California Church, 1973.

McComb, William. "Tennesseans in the Mountain Campaign, 1861." *Confederate Veteran* 22 (May 1914): 210–12.

McDonald, Archie P., ed. *Make Me a Map of the Valley: The Civil War Journal of Stonewall Jackson's Topographer.* Foreword by T. Harry Williams. Dallas: Southern Methodist University Press, 1973.

A Member of Company C [Edmund B. Brown]. *The Twenty-Seventh Indiana Volunteer Infantry in the War of the Rebellion, 1861 to 1865, First Division, 12th and 20th Corps.* [Monticello, Ind.], 1899.

A Member of the Bar. *Cheat Mountain; or, Unwritten Chapter of the Late War.* Nashville: Albert B. Tavel, 1885.

A Member of the Regiment [William Grose]. *The Story of the Marches, Battles, and Incidents of the 36th Indiana Volunteer Infantry.* New Castle, Ind.: Courier, 1891.

Military History and Reminiscences of the Thirteenth Regiment Illinois Volunteer Infantry in the Civil War in the United States, 1861–1865. Chicago: Woman's Temperance Publishing Association, 1892.

[Miller, Dora Richards]. "A Woman's Diary of the Siege of Vicksburg." Introduction by George W. Cable. *Century Magazine* 30 (May–October 1885): 767–75.

Mitchell, J. C. *A Sermon Delivered in the Government Street Church on the National Fast Appointed by Jefferson Davis, President of These Confederate States, June 13, 1861.* Mobile: Farrow & Dennett, 1861.

Monnett, Howard N., ed. "A Yankee Cavalryman Views the Battle of Prairie Grove: The Splendors and Horrors of a Battlefield." *Arkansas Historical Quarterly* 21 (1962): 287–304.

Moore, Edward A. *The Story of a Cannoneer under Stonewall Jackson, in Which Is Told the Part Taken by the Rockbridge Artillery in the Army of Northern Virginia.* Introductions by Capt. Robert E. Lee Jr. and Hon. Henry St. George Tucker. New York: Neale, 1907.

Moore, John C. "Battle of Lookout Mountain." *Confederate Veteran* 6 (September 1898): 426–29.

Morgan, W. A. "Brown's Ferry." In *War Talks in Kansas: A Series of Papers Read before the Kansas Commandery of the Military Order of the Loyal Legion of the United States,* 342–50. Kansas City, Mo.: Franklin Hudson, 1906.

Morris, George W. *History of the Eighty-First Regiment of Indiana Volunteer Infantry in the Great War of the Rebellion, 1861 to 1865, Telling of Its Origin and Organization; a Description of the Material of which It Was Composed; Its Rapid and Severe Marches and Fierce Conflicts in Many Bloody Fields.* Louisville, Ky.: Franklin, 1901.

Murray, D. F. *Presidential Election, 1864: Proceedings of the National Union Convention Held in Baltimore, Md., June 7th and 8th, 1864.* New York: Baker & Godwin, 1864.

Myers, Robert Manson, ed. *The Children of Pride: Selected Letters of the Family of the Rev. Dr. Charles Colcock Jones, from the Years 1860–1868, with the Addition of Several Previously Unpublished Letters.* Abridged ed. New Haven, Conn.: Yale University Press, 1984.

Neese, George M. *Three Years in the Confederate Horse Artillery.* New York: Neale, 1911.

Nevins, Allan, ed. *A Diary of Battle: The Personal Journals of Colonel Charles S. Wainwright, 1861–1865.* New York: Harcourt, Brace, & World, 1962.

Noe, Kenneth W., ed. *A Southern Boy in Blue: The Memoir of Marcus Woodcock, 9th Kentucky Infantry (U.S.A.).* Knoxville: University of Tennessee Press, 1996.

Norton, Oliver Willcox. *Army Letters, 1861–1865. Being Extracts from Private Letters to Relatives and Friends from a Soldier in the Field during the Late Civil War, with an Appendix Retaining Copies of Some Official Documents, Papers, and Addresses of Later Date.* Chicago: O. L. Deming, 1903.

Oates, William C. *The War between the Union and the Confederacy and Its Lost Opportunities, with a History of the 15th Alabama Regiment and the Forty-Eight Battles in which It Was Engaged, being an Account of the Author's Experiences in the Greatest Conflict of Modern Times; a Justification of Secession, and Showing That the Confederacy Should Have Succeeded; a Criticism of President Davis, the Confederate Congress, and Some of the General Officers of the Confederate and Union Armies; Praise of Line Officers and Soldiers in the Ranks for Rheir Heroism and Patriotism; and including the Author's Observations and Experience as Brigadier-General in the War between the United States and Spain.* Introduction by Robert K. Krick. Dayton, Ohio: Morningside Books, 1974.

Oldroyd, Osborn H. *A Soldier's Story of the Siege of Vicksburg, from the Diary of Osborn H. Oldroyd, with Confederate Accounts from Authentic Sources, and an Introduction by Brevet Maj.-Gen. M. F. Force.* Springfield, Ill.: By the author, 1885.

Osborn, George C., ed. "A Tennessean at the Siege of Vicksburg: The Diary of Samuel Alexander Ramsey Swan, May–July 1863." *Tennessee Historical Quarterly* 14 (1955): 353–72.

Owens, Ira S. *Greene County in the War.* Xenia, Ohio: Torchlight Job Rooms, 1872.

Padgett, James A., ed. "With Sherman through Georgia and the Carolinas: Letters of a Federal Soldier, Part I." *Georgia Historical Quarterly* 32 (1948): 284–322.

———. "With Sherman through Georgia and the Carolinas: Letters of a Federal Soldier, Part II." *Georgia Historical Quarterly* 33 (1948): 49–81.

Page, R. C. M. "The Captured Guns at Spotsylvania Courthouse—Correction of General Ewell's Report." *Southern Historical Society Papers* 7 (November 1879): 535–38.

Peck, R. H. *Reminiscences of a Confederate Soldier of Co. C, 2nd Va. Cavalry.* N.p., n.d.

Pellett, Elias P. *History of the 114th Regiment, New York State Volunteers.* Norwich, N.Y.: Telegraph & Chronicle Power Press, 1866.

Pitcock, Cynthia DeHaven, and Bill J. Gurley, eds. *I Acted from Principle: The Civil War Diary of Dr. William M. McPheeters, Confederate Surgeon in the Trans-Mississippi.* Fayetteville: University of Arkansas Press, 2002.

Porter, Horace. *Campaigning with Grant.* Edited with an introduction and notes by Wayne C. Temple. New York: Bonanza, 1961.

Powers, Edward. *War and the Weather.* Rev. ed. Delavan, Wis.: E. Powers, 1890.

Preston, N. D. *History of the Tenth Regiment of Cavalry, New York State Volunteers, August, 1861, to August, 1865.* Introduction by D. McM. Gregg. New York: D. Appleton, 1892.

Puntenney, George H. *History of the Thirty-Seventh Regiment Indiana Infantry Volunteers: Its Organization, Campaigns, and Battles—Sept. '61–Oct. '64.* Rushville, Ind.: Jacksonian Book and Job Department, 1896.

Putnam, J. H. *A Journalistic History of the Thirty-First Regiment, Ohio Volunteer Infantry, with Its Lights and Shadows.* Vol. 1, *Embracing the First Year of Its Existence.* Louisville, Ky.: John P. Morton, 1862.

Pyne, Henry L. *Ride to War: The History of the First New Jersey Cavalry.* Edited with an introduction and notes by Earl Schenck Miers. New Brunswick, N.J.: Rutgers University Press, 1961.

Quaife, Milo M., ed. *From the Cannon's Mouth: The Civil War Letters of General Alpheus S. Williams.* Detroit: Wayne State University Press and the Detroit Historical Society, 1959.

Quint, Alonzo H. *The Record of the Second Massachusetts Infantry, 1861–65.* Boston: James P. Walker, 1867.

Racine, Philip N., ed. *Piedmont Farmer: The Journals of David Golightly Harris, 1855–1870.* Knoxville: University of Tennessee Press, 1990.

———. *"Unspoiled Heart": The Journal of Charles Mattocks of the 17th Maine.* Voices of the Civil War Series. Knoxville: University of Tennessee Press, 1994.

Rerick, John H. *The Forty-Fourth Indiana Volunteer Infantry: History of Its Services in the War of the Rebellion and a Personal Record of Its Members.* Lagrange, Ind.: By the author, 1880.

Rhodes, Robert Hunt, ed. *All for the Union: A History of the 2nd Rhode Island Volunteer Infantry in the War of the Great Rebellion, as Told by the Diary and Letters of Elisha Hunt Rhodes Who Enlisted as a Private in '61 and Rose to the Command of His Regiment.* Lincoln, R.I.: Andrew Mowbray, 1985.

Robertson, James I., ed. *The Civil War Letters of General Robert McAllister.* New Brunswick: New Jersey Civil War Centennial Commission by Rutgers University Press, 1965.

Robertson, Thomas Chinn. *The Battle of Shiloh from a Southern Stand-point: A Letter Written to His Mother When a Soldier Boy.* N.p., 1912.

Roper, John Herbert, ed. *Repairing the "March of Mars": The Civil War Diaries of John Samuel Apperson, Hospital Steward in the Stonewall Brigade, 1861–1865.* Transcribed by Jason Clayman, Peter Gretz, and John Herbert Roper. Macon, Ga.: Mercer University Press, 2001.

Rosenblatt, Emil, and Ruth Rosenblatt, eds. *Hard Marching Every Day: The Civil War Letters of Private Wilbur Fisk, 1861–1865.* Foreword by Reid Mitchell. Lawrence: University Press of Kansas, 1983.

Russell, William Howard. *My Diary North and South.* Edited by Eugene H. Berwanger. New York: Alfred A. Knopf, 1988.

Sanford, George B. *Fighting Rebels and Redskins: Experiences in Army Life of Colonel George B. Sanford, 1861–1892.* Edited with an introduction by E. R. Hagemann. Norman: University of Oklahoma Press, 1969.

Scott, John, comp. *Story of the Thirty-Second Iowa Infantry Volunteers.* Nevada, Iowa: By the author, 1896.

Scott, Samuel P., and Samuel P. Angel. *History of the Thirteenth Regiment Tennessee Volunteer Cavalry U.S.A.* Philadelphia: P. W. Ziegler, 1903.

Scott, William Forse. "The Last Fight for Missouri." In *Personal Recollections of the War of the Rebellion: Addresses Delivered before the Commandery of the State of New York, Military Orders of the Loyal Legion of the United States,* 3rd ser., edited by A. Noel Blakeman, 292–328. New York: G. P. Putnam's Sons, 1907.

Scribner, B. F. *How Soldiers Were Made; or, The War as I Saw It under Buell, Rosecrans, Thomas, Grant, and Sherman.* New Albany, Ind., 1887. Reprint, Huntington, W.Va.: Blue Acorn, 1995.

Sears, Stephen W., ed. *The Civil War Papers of George B. McClellan: Selected Correspondence, 1860–1865.* New York: Ticknor & Fields, 1989.

Second Annual Report of the State Historian of the State of New York. Albany: Wynkoop Hallenback Crawford, 1897.

Shaw, James Birney. *History of the Tenth Regiment Indiana Volunteer Infantry, Three Months and Three Years Organizations.* Lafayette, Ind., 1912.

Sherman, William T. *Memoirs of General William T. Sherman, by Himself.* 2 vols. in 1. Bloomington: Indiana University Press, 1957.

Shoemaker's Battery, Stuart Horse Artillery, Pelham's Battalion, afterwards Commanded by Col. R. P. Chew, Army of Northern Virginia. N.p., n.d.

Silliker, Ruth L., ed. *The Rebel Yell & the Yankee Hurrah: The Civil War Journal of a Maine Volunteer.* Introduction by Robert M. York. Camden, Maine: Down East Books, 1985.

Simmons, L. A. *The History of the 84th Reg't Ill. Vols.* Macomb, Ill.: Hampton Brothers, 1866.

Simms, William Gilmore. *A City Laid Waste: The Capture, Sack, and Destruction of the City of Columbia.* Edited with an introduction by David Aiken. Columbia: University of South Carolina Press, 2005.

Sinclair, Alexander. *A Thanksgiving Sermon Preached in the Presbyterian Church at Six-Mile Creek, Lancaster District, S.C., on Thursday, Sept. 18th, 1862.* Salisbury, N.C.: J. J. Bruner, 1862.

Smith, Gustavus W. *The Battle of Seven Pines.* New York: C. G. Crawford, 1891.

Sparks, David S., ed. *Inside Lincoln's Army: The Diary of Marsena Rudolph Patrick, Provost Marshal General, Army of the Potomac.* New York: Thomas Yoseloff, 1964.

Spence, John C. *A Diary of the Civil War.* Murfreesboro, Tenn.: Rutherford County Historical Society, 1993.

Stephenson, P. S. "Missionary Ridge." *Confederate Veteran* 21 (November 1913): 540–51.

Sperry, A. F. *History of the 33rd Iowa Infantry Volunteer Regiment, 1863–66.* Des Moines: Mills, 1866.

Stevens, William B. *History of the Fiftieth Regiment of Infantry Massachusetts Volunteer Militia in the Late War of the Rebellion.* Boston: Griffith-Stillings, 1907.

Stewart, William H. *A Pair of Blankets: War-time History in Letters to the Young People of the South.* Edited by Benjamin H. Trask. Wilmington, N.C.: Broadfoot, 1990.

Stiles, Robert. *Four Years under Marse Robert.* New York: Neale, 1903.

Stillwell, Leander. "In the Ranks at Shiloh." In *War Talks in Kansas: A Series of Papers Read before the Kansas Commandery of the Military Order of the Loyal Legion of the United States,* 109–26. Kansas City, Mo.: Franklin, Hudson, 1906.

Summers, Festus P., ed. *Borderland Confederate*. Pittsburgh: University of Pittsburgh Press, 1962.

Sutherland, Daniel, ed. *Reminiscences of a Private: William E. Bevens of the First Arkansas Infantry, C.S.A.* Fayetteville: University of Arkansas Press, 1992.

Talcott, T. M. R. "From Petersburg to Appomattox." *Southern Historical Society Papers* 32 (January 1904): 67–72.

Tarrant, E. [Eastham]. *The Wild Riders of the First Kentucky Cavalry. A History of the Regiment, in the Great War of the Rebellion, 1861–1865, Telling the Origin and Organization; a Description of the Material of Which It Was Composed; Its Rapid and Severe Marches, Hard Service, and Fierce Conflicts on Many a Bloody Field.* N.p.: Committee of the Regiment, 1894.

Taylor, Richard. *Destruction and Reconstruction: Personal Experiences of the Late War.* Edited by Richard B. Harwell. New York: Longmans, Green, 1955.

Tilley, Nannie M., ed. *Federals on the Frontier: The Diary of Benjamin F. McIntyre, 1862–1864.* Austin: University of Texas Press, 1963.

Toney, Marcus B. *The Privations of a Private: Campaigning with the First Tennessee, C.S.A., and Life Thereafter.* Introduction by Robert E. Hurst. Tuscaloosa: University of Alabama Press, 2005.

Tourgée, Albion W. *The Story of a Thousand: Being a History of the Service of the 105th Ohio Volunteer Infantry in the War for the Union from August 21, 1862 to June 6, 1865.* Buffalo: S. McGerald & Son, 1896.

Trollope, Anthony. *North America.* 2 vols. Philadelphia: J. B. Lippincott, 1863.

Tucker, Henry H. *God in the War: A Sermon Delivered before the Legislature of Georgia, in the Capitol at Milledgeville, on Friday, November 15, 1861, Being a Day Set Apart for Fasting, Humiliation and Prayer by His Excellency the President of the Confederate States.* Milledgeville, Ga.: Boughton, Nisbet & Barnes, 1861.

Tunnard, W. H. *A Southern Record: The History of the Third Regiment Louisiana Infantry.* Baton Rouge: By the author, 1866.

Tupper, H. A. *A Thanksgiving Discourse Delivered at Washington, Ga., on Thursday, September 18, 1862.* Macon, Ga.: Burke, Boykin, 1862.

Turner, Charles W., ed. *A Reminiscence of Lieutenant John Newton Lyle of the Liberty Hall Volunteers.* Roanoke: Virginia Lithography, 1987.

Twain, Mark. *English as She Is Taught.* With a biographical sketchy by Matthew Irving Lans. Boston: Mutual, 1900.

Tyler, Mason Whiting. *Recollections of the Civil War; with Many Original Diary Entries and Letters Written from the Seat of War, and with Annotated References.* Edited by William S. Tyler. New York: G. P. Putnam, 1912.

US Navy Department. *Official Records of the Union and Confederate Navies in the War of the Rebellion.* 30 vols. Washington, D.C: Government Printing Office, 1894–1927.

US War Department. *The War of the Rebellion: A Compilation of the Official Records of the Union and Confederate Armies.* 129 vols. Washington, D.C.: Government Printing Office, 1880–1901.

Vaught, Elsa, ed. "Diary of an Unknown Soldier." *Arkansas Historical Quarterly* 18 (1959): 50–89.

Vedder, C. S. *"Offer unto God Thanksgiving": A Sermon Delivered in the Summerville Presbyterian Church on Sunday, July 28, 1861.* Charleston, S.C.: Evans & Cogswell, 1861.

Venable, Charles S. "General Lee in the Wilderness Campaign." In Johnson and Buel, *Battles and Leaders,* 4:240–46.

Walker, Aldace F. *The Vermont Brigade in the Shenandoah Valley, 1864.* Burlington, Vt.: Free Press Association, 1869.

Warfield, Edgar. *A Confederate Soldier's Memoirs.* Richmond: Masonic Home, 1936.

Watson, William. *Life in the Confederate Army, being the Observations and Experiences of an Alien in the South during the American Civil War.* Introduction by Thomas W. Cutrer. Baton Rouge: Louisiana State University Press, 1995.

W. D. B. [William D. Bickham]. *Rosecrans' Campaign with the Fourteenth Army Corps; or The Army of the Cumberland: A Narrative of Personal Observation with an Appendix, Consisting of Official Reports of the Battle of Stone River.* Cincinnati: Moore, Wilstach, Keys, 1863.

Welch, Spencer Glasgow. *A Confederate Surgeon's Letters to his Wife.* New York: Neale, 1911.

Weymouth, A. B., ed. *A Memorial Sketch of Lieut. Edgar M. Newcomb, of the Nineteenth Mass. Vols.* Malden, Mass.: Alvin C. Brown, 1883.

White, Lonnie J., ed. "A Bluecoat's Account of the Camden Expedition." *Arkansas Historical Quarterly* 24 (Spring 1965): 82–89.

White, William S. "A Diary of the War; or, What I Saw of It." In *Contributions to a History of the Richmond Howitzer Battalion,* edited by Carton McCarthy, 89–286. Pamphlet 2. Richmond: Carlton McCarthy, 1883.

White, Russell C., ed. *The Civil War Diary of Wyman S. White, First Sergeant of Company F, 2nd United States Sharpshooters Regiment, 1861–1865.* Baltimore: Butternut and Blue, 1991.

Whitman, Walt. *Specimen Days & Collect.* Philadelphia: Rees, Welsh, 1882–83.

[Willet, Elbert D.]. *History of Company B (Originally Pickens Planters), 40th Alabama Regiment Confederate States Army, 1862 to 1865.* N.p.: Colonial, 1963.

"William P. Rogers' Memorandum Book." *West Tennessee Historical Society Papers* 9 (1955): 59–92.

Williams, Charles Richard, ed. *Diary and Letters of Rutherford Birchard Hayes, Nineteenth President of the United States.* 2 vols. Columbus: Ohio State Archaeological and Historical Society, 1922.

Williams, Ellen. *Three Years and a Half in the Army; or, History of the Second Colorados.* New York: Fowler & Wells, 1885.

Williams, Leander P., Job Barnard, John M. Caulfield, Ed. A. Jernegan, Wibur E. Gorsuch, and Henry C. Morgan, comps. *History of the Seventy-Third Indiana Volunteers in the War of 1861–1865.* Washington, D.C.: Carnahan, 1909.

Willison, Charles A. *Reminiscences of a Boy's Service with the 76th Ohio, in the Fifteenth Army Corps under General Sherman, during the Civil War, by That "Boy" at Three Score.* Menasha, Wis.: George Banta, n.d.

Wilkie, Franc P. *Pen and Powder.* Boston: Ticknor, 1888.

Willoughby, C. L. "Eclipse of Moon at Missionary Ridge." *Confederate Veteran* 21 (1913): 590.

Woodbury, Augustus. *A Narrative of the Campaign of the First Rhode Island Regiment in the Spring and Summer of 1861.* Providence, R.I.: Sidney S. Rider, 1862.

Wood, James H. *The War: Stonewall Jackson, His Campaigns, and Battles, the Regiment, as I Saw Them.* Cumberland, Md.: Eddy, n.d.

Woods, Earl C., and Charles E. Nolan, eds. *The Shiloh Diary of Edmond Enoul Livaudais.* Translated by Stanley J. Guerin. New Orleans: Archdiocese of New Orleans, 1992.

Woodward, Joseph Janvier, M. D. *Outlines of the Chief Camp Diseases of the United States Armies: As Observed during the Present War.* Philadelphia: Lippincott, 1863. Reprint, with an introduction by Ira M. Rukow, San Francisco: Norman, 1992.

Worley, Ted R., ed. *The War Memoirs of Captain John W. Lavender, C.S.A.* Pine Bluff, Ark.: W M. Hackett and D. R. Perdue, 1956.

Worsham, John H. *One of Jackson's Foot Cavalry.* Edited by James I. Robertson Jr. Jackson, Tenn.: McCowat-Mercer, 1964.

Wright, Charles. *A Corporal's Story: Experiences in the Ranks of Company C, 81st Ohio Vol. Infantry, during the War for the Maintenance of the Union, 1861–1864.* Introduction by W. H. Chamberlin. Philadelphia: James Beale, 1887.

Periodicals

Alexandria (Va.) Gazette
Alexandria (Va.) Local News
American Agriculturalist
Arkansas State Gazette (Little Rock)
Augusta (Ga.) Chronicle
Augusta (Ga.) Daily Constitutionalist
Baltimore Sun
Baton Rouge Daily Advocate
Carolina Observer (Fayetteville, N.C.)

Charleston Courier
Charleston Mercury
Charleston Tri-Weekly Mercury
Chattanooga Daily Rebel
Cincinnati Commercial Tribune
Clarksville (Tex.) Standard
Cleveland Plain Dealer
Columbus (Ga.) Daily Enquirer
Daily Louisville (Ky.) Democrat
Daily Richmond Enquirer
Daily Richmond Examiner
Dallas Weekly Herald
Fairmont (Ind.) News
Farmers' Oracle
Georgia Weekly Telegraph (Macon)
Guardian (London)
Hannibal (Mo.) Messenger
Hillsborough (N.C.) Recorder
Houston Daily Telegraph
Houston Tri-Weekly Telegraph
Indianapolis News
Macon (Ga.) Daily Telegraph
Macon (Ga.) Telegraph
Milwaukee Daily Sentinel
Mobile Register
Moore's Rural New-Yorker
Nashville Daily Union
Nashville Journal
Natchez Daily Courier
National Intelligencer (Washington, D.C.)
National Tribune
New England Farmer
New Orleans Daily Delta
New Orleans Daily True Delta
New-Orleans Price-Current and Commercial Intelligencer
New-York Daily Herald
New York Daily Tribune
New York Evangelist
New York Evening Journal
New York Evening Post

New York Herald
New York World
North American and United States Gazette (Philadelphia)
Ohio Farmer (Cleveland)
Philadelphia Inquirer
Portland (Maine) Transcript
Prairie Farmer
Richmond (Ind.) News
Richmond Sentinel
Richmond Whig
St. Louis Daily Missouri Democrat
St. Louis Daily Missouri Republican
St. Louis Sunday Morning Republican
Saint Paul Pioneer & Democrat
Scientific American
Southern Illustrated News
Street & Smith's New York Weekly
Sunday Daily Star (London)
Times (London)
Working Farmer & United States Journal

Electronic Sources

Arthur, David B. Diary. Manuscripts of the American Civil War. Department of Special Collections, Hesburgh Libraries, University of Notre Dame, South Bend, Ind. http://www.rarebooks.nd.edu/digital/civil_war/diaries_journals/arthur/.

Brown, Edwin Y. "4 and 5 May 1862 Description of the Battle of Williamsburg," Edwin Y. Brown Papers. Digital Projects, Swem Library, College of William and Mary. http://transcribe.swem.wm.edu/items/show/2803. Page removed.

"The Diary of Horatio Nelson Taft, 1861–1865. Volume 1, January 1, 1861–April 11, 1862." Manuscript/Mixed Material, Library of Congress. https://www.loc.gov/item/mtaft000001/.

"The Diary of Michael Shiner Relating to the History of the Washington Navy Yard, 1813–1869," transcribed and edited by John G. Sharp, 2007, 2015. Navy History and Heritage Command. https://www.history.navy.mil/research/library/online-reading-room/title-list-alphabetically/d/diary-of-michael-shiner.html.

Eddington, William R. "My Civil War Memoirs and Other Reminiscences." Transcribed by Carl, Christopher, Ron, and Mark Strohbeck. Macoupin County,

Ill., Genealogy Web. https://macoupin.illinoisgenweb.org/military/civilwar/eddingtonwilliamr.html.

"Gilbert Thompson Journal, 1857–1901." Gilbert Thompson Papers, Manuscript/Mixed Material, Library of Congress. https://www.loc.gov/item/mm81095752/.

Gresham, LeRoy Wiley. Diaries. Lewis H. Machen Family Papers, Library of Congress, Washington, D.C. https://www.loc.gov/collections/machen-family-papers/.

Jenkins, John B., to Mary Benjamin, May 17, 1862. Folder 9, Box 1, Henry C. Hoar Memorial Collection, 1861–1887, Acc. 1992.46. Digital Projects, Swem Library, College of William and Mary. http://transcribe.swem.wm.edu/items/show/41. Page removed.

Lane, Peter D. "Recollections of a Volunteer: A Memoir of the Civil War." c1865. Typescript. State Historical Society of Missouri.https://digital.shsmo.org/digital/collection/amcw/id/13181/rec/1.

Nicks, Francis R., Letter, 1863 (M88-3). "Lincoln Letters." *Florida Memory*, State Library and Archives of Florida. https://www.floridamemory.com/exhibits/lincoln/nicks/.

"Samuel J. Reader's Autobiography, Volume 3." *Kansas Memory*, Kansas Historical Society. http://www.kansasmemory.org/item/206900.

The Valley of the Shadow: Two Communities in the American Civil War. Virginia Center for Digital History, University of Virginia Library. http://valley.lib.virginia.edu/.

SECONDARY SOURCES

Published Works

Adams, Michael C. C. *Living Hell: The Dark Side of the Civil War*. Baltimore: Johns Hopkins University Press, 2014.

Alberts, Don E. *The Battle of Glorieta: Union Victory in the West*. College Station: Texas A&M University Press, 1998.

Alexander, Ted. "'A Regular Slave Hunt': The Army of Northern Virginia and Black Civilians in the Gettysburg Campaign." *North & South* 4 (September 2001): 82–89.

Anderson, O. K. "The Climate of Kentucky." In NOAA, *Climates of the States*, 1:123–35.

Andrews, J. Cutler. *The North Reports the Civil War*. Pittsburgh: University of Pittsburgh Press, 1955.

Ayers, Edward L. *The Thin Light of Freedom: The Civil War and Emancipation in the Heart of America*. New York: W. W. Norton, 2017.

Baechler, Michael C., Jennifer L. Williamson, Theresa L. Gilbride, Pamala C. Cole, Marye G. Hefty, and Pat M. Love. "Guide to Determining Climate Regions by County." Building America Best Practices Series, vol. 7.1. Washington, D.C.: US Department of Energy, 2010.

Ballard, Michael B. *Vicksburg: The Campaign That Opened the Mississippi.* Chapel Hill: University of North Carolina Press, 2004.

Ballard, Ted. *Battle of Ball's Bluff.* Washington, D.C.: Center of Military History, US Army, 2001.

Barnickel, Linda. *Milliken's Bend: A Civil War Battle in History and Memory.* Baton Rouge: Louisiana State University Press, 2013.

Beilein, Joseph M., Jr., and Matthew C. Hulbert, eds. *The Civil War Guerrilla: Unfolding the Black Flag in History, Memory, and Myth.* Lexington: University Press of Kentucky, 2015.

Bell, Andrew McIlwaine. *Mosquito Soldiers: Malaria, Yellow Fever, and the Course of the Civil War.* Baton Rouge: Louisiana State University Press, 2010.

Bernstein, Iver. *The New York City Draft Riots: Their Significance for American Society and Politics in the Age of the Civil War.* New York: Oxford University Press, 1990.

Bishop, Randy. *Civil War Generals of Tennessee.* Gretna, La.: Pelican, 2013.

Bohnak, Karl. *So Cold a Sky: Upper Michigan Weather Stories.* Negaunee, Mich.: Cold Sky, 2006.

Bostwick, Douglas W. *The Union Is Dissolved! Charleston and Fort Sumter in the Civil War.* Charleston, S.C.: History Press, 2009.

Bradley, Michael R. *Tullahoma: The 1863 Campaign for the Control of Middle Tennessee.* Shippensburg, Pa.: Burd Street, 2000.

Brady, Lisa M. *War upon the Land: Military Strategy and the Transformation of Southern Landscapes during the American Civil War.* Athens: University of Georgia Press, 2012.

Brasher, Glenn David. *The Peninsula Campaign and the Necessity of Emancipation: African Americans and the Fight for Freedom.* Chapel Hill: University of North Carolina Press, 2012.

Brown, Kent Masterson. *Retreat from Gettysburg: Lee, Logistics, and the Pennsylvania Campaign.* Chapel Hill: University of North Carolina Press, 2005.

Browning, Judkin, and Timothy Silver. "Nature and Human Nature: Environmental Influences on the Union's Failed Peninsula Campaign, 1862." *Journal of the Civil War Era* 8 (September 2018): 388–415.

Burton, Brian K. *Extraordinary Circumstances: The Seven Days Battles.* Bloomington: Indiana University Press, 2001.

Carter, Horace S. "The Climate of Georgia." In NOAA, *Climates of the States,* 1:71–89.

Castel, Albert. *Decision in the West: The Atlanta Campaign of 1864.* Lawrence: University Press of Kansas, 1992.

——. *General Sterling Price and the Civil War in the West.* Baton Rouge: Louisiana State University Press, 1968.

Chenoweth, M., and C. J. Mock. "Hurricane 'Amanda'": Rediscovery of a Forgotten U.S. Civil War Florida Hurricane." *Bulletin of the American Meteorological Society* 94 (November 2013): 1735–42.

Chenoweth, Mike. "A New Compilation of North Atlantic Tropical Cyclones, 1851–98." *Journal of Climate* 27 (December 2014): 8674–85.

Cimprich, John. *Fort Pillow, a Civil War Massacre, and Public Memory.* Baton Rouge: Louisiana State University Press, 2005.

Cobb, J. Michael, Edward B. Hicks, and Wythe Holt. *Battle of Big Bethel: Crucial Clash in Early Civil War Virginia.* El Dorado Hills, Calif.: Savas Beatie, 2013.

Coddington, Edwin B. *The Gettysburg Campaign: A Study in Command.* New York, Charles Scribner's Sons, 1968. Reprint, Dayton, Ohio: Morningside Bookshop, 1979.

Coggins, Allen R. *Tennessee Tragedies: Natural, Technological, and Societal Disasters in the Volunteer State.* Knoxville: University of Tennessee Press, 2011.

Connelly, Thomas Lawrence. *Army of the Heartland: The Army of Tennessee, 1861–1862.* Baton Rouge: Louisiana State University Press, 1967.

——. *Autumn of Glory: The Army of Tennessee, 1862–1865.* Baton Rouge: Louisiana State Press, 1971.

Connelly, Thomas L., and Archer Jones. *The Politics of Command: Factions and Ideas in Confederate Strategy.* Baton Rouge: Louisiana State University Press, 1973.

Cooling, Benjamin Franklin. *Forts Henry and Donelson: The Key to the Confederate Heartland.* Knoxville: University of Tennessee Press, 1987.

——. *Monocacy: The Battle That Saved Washington.* Shippensburg, Pa.: White Mane, 1997.

Cook, Adrian. *The Armies of the Streets: The New York City Draft Riots of 1863.* Lexington: University Press of Kentucky, 1974.

Cooper, William J., Jr. *Jefferson Davis, American.* New York: Alfred A. Knopf, 2000.

Cornes, Richard C., Philip D. Jones, Keith R. Briffa, and Timothy J. Osborn. "Estimates of the North Atlantic Oscillation Back to 1692 Using a Paris-London Westerly Index." *International Journal of Climatology* 33 (2013): 228–48.

Cox, LaWanda. *Lincoln and Black Freedom: A Study in Presidential Leadership.* Urbana: University of Illinois Press, 1985.

Cozzens, Peter. *The Darkest Days of the War: The Battles of Iuka and Corinth.* Chapel Hill: University of North Carolina Press, 1997.

——. *No Better Place to Die: The Battle of Stones River.* Urbana: University of Illinois Press, 1991.

———. *The Shipwreck of Their Hopes: The Battles for Chattanooga.* Urbana: University of Illinois Press, 1994.

———. *This Terrible Sound: The Battle of Chickamauga.* Urbana: University of Illinois Press, 1992.

Crockett, Curtis W. "The Climate of Virginia." In NOAA, *Climates of the States,* 1:398–421.

Dailey, Paul W., Jr. "The Climate of Pennsylvania." In NOAA, *Climates of the States,* 1:318–39.

Daniel, Larry J. *Shiloh: The Battle That Changed the Civil War.* New York: Simon & Schuster, 1997.

Daniel, Larry J., and Lynn N. Bock. *Island No. 10: Struggle for the Mississippi Valley.* Tuscaloosa: University of Alabama Press, 1996.

Darter, Lewis J., Jr. "List of Climatological Records in the National Archives." Washington, D.C.: National Archives, 1942.

Davis, Mike. *Late Victorian Holocausts: El Niño Famines and the Making of the Third World.* London: Verso, 2001.

Davis, Ronald L. F. *The Black Experience in Natchez, 1720–1880.* Special History Study. Natchez, Miss.: Natchez National Historic Park, 1993.

Davis, William C. *Battle at Bull Run: A History of the First Major Campaign of the Civil War.* Garden City, N.Y.: Doubleday, 1977.

———. *The Battle of New Market.* Garden City, N.Y.: Doubleday, 1975.

———. *Duel between the First Ironclads.* Garden City, N.Y.: Doubleday, 1975.

———. *Jefferson Davis: The Man and His Hour.* Baton Rouge: Louisiana State University Press, 1991.

Dean, Adam Wesley. *An Agrarian Republic: Farming, Antislavery Politics, and Nature Parks in the Civil War Era.* Chapel Hill: University of North Carolina Press, 2015.

Debo, Angie. "The Site of the Battle of Round Mountain, 1861." *Chronicles of Oklahoma* 27 (Summer 1949): 187–206.

Diaz, Henry F., and George N. Kiladis. "Atmospheric Teleconnections Associated with the Extreme Phases of the Southern Isolation." In Diaz and Markgraf, *El Niño,* 7–28.

Diaz, Henry F., and Vera Markgraf, eds. *El Niño: Historical and Paleoclimatic Aspects of the Southern Oscillation.* Cambridge: Cambridge University Press, 1992.

Dickson, Robert R. "The Climate of Tennessee." In NOAA, *Climates of the States,* 1:370–84.

Dollar, Kent T., Larry H. Whiteaker, and W. Calvin Dickinson, eds. *Border Wars: The Civil War in Tennessee and Kentucky.* Kent, Ohio: Kent State University Press, 2015.

Dorman, Robert L. *It Happened in Oklahoma.* Guilford, Conn.: TwoDot, 2006.

Downs, Gregory P. *After Appomattox: Military Occupation and the Ends of War.* Cambridge, Mass.: Harvard University Press, 2015.

Drake, Brian Allen, ed. *The Blue, the Gray, and the Green: Toward an Environmental History of the Civil War.* Athens: University of Georgia Press, 2014.

Dubbs, Carol Kettenburg. *Defend This Old Town: Williamsburg during the Civil War.* Baton Rouge: Louisiana State University Press, 2002.

Dyrenforth, Robert G., and Simon Newton. "Can We Make It Rain?" *North American Review* 53 (October 1891): 385–404.

Earle, Jonathan Halperin, and Diane Mutti Burke, eds. *Bleeding Kansas, Bleeding Missouri: The Long Civil War on the Border.* Lawrence: University Press of Kansas, 2013.

Ecelbarger, Gary L. *"We Are in for It!" The First Battle of Kernstown, March 23, 1862.* Shippensburg, Pa.: White Mane, 1997.

Emberton, Carole. *Beyond Redemption: Race, Violence, and the American South after the Civil War.* Chicago: University of Chicago Press, 2013.

Enfield, David B. "Historical and Prehistoric Overview of El Niño/Southern Oscillation." In Diaz and Markgraf, *El Niño,* 95–117.

Engle, Stephen D. *Don Carlos Buell: Most Promising of All.* Chapel Hill: University of North Carolina Press, 1999.

Etulain, Richard. *Lincoln and the Oregon Country: Politics in the Civil War Era.* Corvallis: Oregon State University Press, 2013.

Fagan, Brian. *Floods, Famines, and Emperors: El Niño and the Fate of Civilizations.* 10th anniversary ed. New York, Basic Books, 2009.

Fellman, Michael. *Inside War: The Guerrilla Conflict in Missouri during the American Civil War.* New York: Oxford University Press, 1989.

Fiege, Mark. "Gettysburg and the Organic Nature of the American Civil War." In Tucker and Russell, *Natural Enemy, Natural Ally,* 93–109.

———. *The Republic of Nature: An Environmental History of the United States.* Seattle: University of Washington Press, 2012.

Fleming, James Rodger. *Fixing the Sky: The Checkered History of Weather and Climate Control.* New York: Columbia University Press, 2010.

Flores, Dan. "Bison Ecology and Bison Diplomacy: The Southern Plains from 1800 to 1850." *Journal of American History* 78 (September 1991): 465–85.

Forsyth, Michael J. *The Camden Expedition of 1864 and the Opportunity Lost by the Confederacy to Change the Civil War.* Jefferson, N.C.: McFarland, 2003.

Foster, Buck T. *Sherman's Mississippi Campaign.* Tuscaloosa: University of Alabama Press, 2006.

Frazier, Donald S. *Blood & Treasure: Confederate Empire in the Southwest.* College Station: Texas A&M University Press, 1995.

Freeman, Douglas Southall. "An Address." *Civil War History* 1 (1955): 7–15.

Fry, Zachery A. "McClellan's Epidemic: Disease and Discord at Harrison's Landing, July–August 1862." *Civil War History* 64 (March 2018): 7–29.

Furgurson, Ernest B. *Chancellorsville 1863: The Souls of the Brave*. New York: Vintage, 1993.

Gaede, Frederick C. *The Federal Civil War Shelter Tent*. Alexandria, Va.: O'Donnell, 2001.

Gates, Paul W. *Agriculture and the Civil War*. New York: Alfred A. Knopf, 1965.

Glatthaar, Joseph T. *The March to the Sea and Beyond: Sherman's Troops in the Savannah and Carolinas Campaigns*. Baton Rouge: Louisiana State University Press, 1985.

Goodheart, Adam. *1861: The Civil War Awakening*. New York: Vintage Books, 2011.

Gordon, Stewart. "War, the Military, and the Environment: Central India, 1560–1820." In Tucker and Russell, *Natural Enemy, Natural Ally*, 42–64.

Grabau, Warren E. *Ninety-Eight Days: A Geographer's View of the Vicksburg Campaign*. Knoxville: University of Tennessee Press, 2000.

Gragg, Rod. *Confederate Goliath: The Battle of Fort Fisher*. New York: HarperCollins, 1991.

Graham, Martin F., and George F. Skoch. *Mine Run: A Campaign of Lost Opportunities, October 21 1863–May 1, 1864*. 2nd ed. Lynchburg, Va.: H. E. Howard, 1987.

Greene, A. Wilson. *The Final Battles of the Petersburg Campaign: Breaking the Backbone of the Rebellion*. Knoxville: University of Tennessee Press, 2008.

Grice, Gary K. "History of Weather Observations, Natchez, Mississippi, 1795–1985." N.p.: Midwestern Regional Climate Center, 2006.

Grimsley, Mark. *And Keep Moving On: The Virginia Campaign, May–June 1864*. Lincoln: University of Nebraska Press, 2002.

———. "Wars for the American South: The First and Second Reconstructions Considered as Insurgencies." *Civil War History* 58 (March 2012): 6–36.

Grove, Richard, and George Adamson. *El Niño in World History*. Palgrave Studies in World Environmental History. London: Palgrave Macmillan, 2018.

Guelzo, Allen C. *Fateful Lightning: A New History of the Civil War & Reconstruction*. New York: Oxford University Press, 2012.

———. *Gettysburg: The Last Invasion*. New York: Alfred A. Knopf, 2013.

Hacker, J. David. "A Census-Based Count of the Civil War Dead." *Civil War History* 57 (December 2011): 307–48.

Hall, Martin Harwick. *Sibley's New Mexico Campaign*. Austin: University of Texas Press, 1960.

Hämäläinen, Pekka. *The Comanche Empire*. New Haven, Conn.: Yale University Press, 2008.

Harrison, Lowell H. *The Civil War in Kentucky*. Lexington: University Press of Kentucky, 1975.

Harsh, Joseph L. *Taken at the Flood: Robert E. Lee and Confederate Strategy in the Maryland Campaign of 1862*. Kent, Ohio: Kent State University Press, 1999.

Hartje, Robert G. *Van Dorn: The Life and Times of a Confederate General*. Nashville: Vanderbilt University Press, 1967.

Hattaway, Herman, and Archer Jones. *How the North Won: A Military History of the Civil War*. Urbana: University of Illinois Press, 1983.

Hearn, Chester C. *The Capture of New Orleans, 1862*. Baton Rouge: Louisiana State University Press, 1995.

Heath, Gary N. "The First Federal Invasion of the Indian Territory." *Chronicles of Oklahoma* 44 (Winter 1966–67): 409–19.

Hébert, Keith S. *The Long Civil War in the North Georgia Mountains: Confederate Nationalism, Sectionalism, and White Supremacy in Bartow County, Georgia*. Knoxville: University of Tennessee Press, 2017.

Hennessy, John J. *Return to Bull Run: The Campaign and Battle of Second Manassas*. New York: Simon & Schuster, 1993.

Herweijer, Celine, Richard Seager, and Edward R. Cook. "North American Droughts of the Mid to Late Nineteenth Century: A History, Simulation, and Implication for a Mediaeval Drought." *Holocene* 16 (2006): 159–71.

Hess, Earl J. *Banners to the Breeze: The Kentucky Campaign, Corinth, and Stones River*. Lincoln: University of Nebraska Press, 2000.

———. *Braxton Bragg: The Most Hated Man in the Confederacy*. Chapel Hill: University of North Carolina Pres, 2016.

———. *The Civil War in the West: Victory and Defeat from the Appalachians to the Mississippi*. Chapel Hill: University of North Carolina Press, 2012.

———. *Field Armies and Fortifications in the Civil War: The Eastern Campaigns, 1861–1864*. Chapel Hill: University of North Carolina Press, 2005.

———. *The Knoxville Campaign: Burnside and Longstreet in East Tennessee*. Knoxville: University of Tennessee Press, 2012.

———. *Pickett's Charge: The Last Attack at Gettysburg*. Chapel Hill: University of North Carolina Press, 2001.

———. *Trench Warfare under Grant and Lee: Field Fortifications in the Overland Campaign*. Chapel Hill: University of North Carolina Press, 2007.

Hewitt, Lawrence Lee. *Port Hudson, Confederate Bastion on the Mississippi*. Baton Rouge: Louisiana State University Press, 1987.

Holliday, John H. *Indianapolis and the Civil War*. Indiana Historical Society Publications 4. Indianapolis: Edward J. Hecker, 1911.

Houghton, Frank E. "The Climate of New Mexico." In NOAA, *Climates of the States*, 2:794–810.

Horn, Victor T., and James K. McGuire. "The Climate of West Virginia." In NOAA, *Climates of the States*, 1:422–39.

Hughes, Nathaniel Cheairs, Jr. *The Battle of Belmont: Grant Strikes South*. Chapel Hill: University of North Carolina Press, 1991.

———. *Bentonville: The Final Battle of Sherman and Johnston*. Chapel Hill: University of North Carolina Press, 1996.

Hurt, R. Douglas. *Agriculture and the Confederacy: Policy, Productivity, and Power in the Civil War South*. Chapel Hill: University of North Carolina Press, 2015.

Janney, Caroline E. "We Were Not Paroled: The Surrenders of Lee's Men beyond Appomattox Court House." In *Petersburg to Appomattox: The End of the War in Virginia*, edited by Caroline E. Janney, 192–219. Chapel Hill: University of North Carolina Press, 2018.

Johnson, Ludwell H. *Red River Campaign: Politics and Cotton in the Civil War*. Baltimore: Johns Hopkins Press, 1958.

Joiner, Gary D. *One Damn Blunder from Beginning to End: The Red River Campaign of 1864*. Wilmington, Del.: Scholarly Resources, 2003.

———. *Through the Howling Wilderness: The 1864 Red River Campaign and Union Failure in the West*. Knoxville: University of Tennessee Press, 2006.

Kelman, Ari. *A Misplaced Massacre: Struggling over the Memory of Sand Creek*. Cambridge, Mass.: Harvard University Press, 2013.

Kennett, Lee B. *Marching through Georgia: The Story of Soldiers and Civilians during Sherman's Campaign*. New York: HarperCollins, 1995.

Kimble, George H. T. *Our American Weather*. New York: McGraw-Hill, 1955.

Krick, Robert K. *Civil War Weather in Virginia*. Tuscaloosa: University of Alabama Press, 2007.

———. *Conquering the Valley: Stonewall Jackson at Port Republic*. New York: William Morrow, 1996.

———. *Stonewall Jackson at Cedar Mountain*. Chapel Hill: University of North Carolina Press, 1990.

Lambert, D. Warren. *When the Ripe Pears Fell: The Battle of Richmond, Kentucky*. Richmond, Ky.: Madison County Historical Society, [1995].

Landers, H. "The Climate of South Carolina." In NOAA, *Climates of the States*, 1:353–69.

Lang, Andrew F. *In the Wake of War: Military Occupation, Emancipation, and Civil War America*. Baton Rouge: Louisiana State University Press, 2017.

Lause, Mark A. *The Collapse of Price's Raid: The Beginning of the End in Civil War Missouri*. Columbia: University of Missouri Press, 2016.

———. *Price's Lost Campaign: The 1864 Invasion of Missouri*. Columbia: University of Missouri Press, 2011.

Leech, Margaret. *Reveille in Washington, 1860–1865*. New York: Harper & Row, 1941. Reprint, New York: Carroll and Graf, 1986.

Lesser, W. Hunter. *Rebels at the Gate: Lee and McClellan on the Front Line of a Nation Divided.* Naperville, Ill.: Sourcebooks, 2004.

Levin, Kevin M. *Remembering the Battle of the Crater: War as Murder.* Lexington: University Press of Kentucky, 2012.

Levine, Roger S. "'African Warfare in All Its Ferocity': Changing Military Landscapes and Precolonial and Colonial Conflict in Southern Africa." In Tucker and Russell, *Natural Enemy, Natural Ally,* 65–92.

Lively, Mathew. *Calamity at Chancellorsville: The Wounding and Death of Confederate General Stonewall Jackson.* El Dorado Hills, Calif.: Savas Beatie, 2013.

Long, E. B. *The Civil War Day by Day: An Almanac, 1861–1865.* With Barbara Long. Introduction by Bruce Catton. Garden City, N.Y.: Doubleday, 1971.

Lowers, A. R. "The Climate of Wyoming." In NOAA, *Climates of the States,* 2:961–75.

Lowry, Terry. *September Blood: The Battle of Carnifex Ferry.* Charleston, W.Va.: Pictorial Histories, 1985.

Lucas, Marion Brunson. *Sherman and the Burning of Columbia.* College Station: Texas A&M University Press, 1976.

Ludlum, David M. *The American Weather Book.* Boston: Houghton Mifflin, 1982.

———. *Early American Hurricanes, 1492–1870.* Boston: American Meteorological Society, 1963.

———. *Early American Winters II, 1821–1870.* Boston: American Meteorological Society, 1968.

———. *The Weather Factor: An Amazing Collection of Little-Known Facts about How the Weather Has Influenced the American Scene from Colonial to Modern Times.* Boston: Houghton-Mifflin, 1984.

Manning, Chandra. *Troubled Refuge: Struggling for Freedom in the Civil War.* New York: Vintage, 2017.

Marrs, Cody. *Nineteenth-Century American Literature and the Long Civil War.* Cambridge: Cambridge University Press, 2015.

Marvel, William. *Lee's Last Retreat: The Flight to Appomattox.* Chapel Hill: University of North Carolina Press, 2002.

McBride, Lela J. *Opothleyaholo and the Loyal Muskogee: Their Flight to Kansas in the Civil War.* Jefferson, N.C.: McFarland, 2000.

McCurry, Stephanie. *Confederate Reckoning: Power and Politics in the Civil War South.* Cambridge, Mass.: Harvard University Press, 2010.

McDonough, James Lee. *Nashville: The Western Confederacy's Final Gamble.* Knoxville: University of Tennessee Press, 2004.

———. *Stones River—Bloody Winter in Tennessee.* Knoxville: University of Tennessee Press, 1980.

McDonough, James Lee, and Thomas L. Connelly. *Five Tragic Hours: The Battle of Franklin.* Knoxville: University of Tennessee Press, 1983.

McKnight, Brian D. "Reconsidering Felix Zollicoffer: The Influence of Weather and Terrain in the Rise and Fall of a Military Commander in Appalachia." In Dollar, Whiteaker, and Dickinson, *Border Wars,* 155–64.

McMurry, Richard M. *Atlanta 1864: Last Chance for the Confederacy.* Lincoln, Neb.: Bison Books, 2001.

———. *John Bell Hood and the War for Southern Independence.* Lincoln: University of Nebraska Press, 1982.

McPherson, James M. *Battle Cry of Freedom: The Civil War Era.* New York: Oxford University Press, 1988.

McQuigg, J. D. "The Climate of Missouri." In NOAA, *Climates of the States,* 2:725–42.

McWhiney, Grady. *Braxton Bragg and Confederate Defeat.* Vol. 1, *Field Command.* New York: Columbia University Press, 1969.

Meier, Kathryn Shively. *Nature's Civil War: Common Soldiers and the Environment in 1862 Virginia.* Chapel Hill: University of North Carolina Press, 2013.

Mergen, Bernard. *Weather Matters: An American Cultural History since 1900.* Lawrence: University Press of Kansas, 2008.

Miller, Richard F. *Harvard's Civil War: A History of the Twentieth Massachusetts Volunteer Infantry.* Hanover, N.H.: University Press of New England, 2005.

Morris, Christopher. "A More Southern Environmental History." *Journal of Southern History* 75 (August 2009): 581–98.

National Oceanic and Atmospheric Administration (NOAA), ed. *Climates of the States: A Practical Reference Containing Basic Climatological Data of the United States.* 2 vols. Port Washington, N.Y.: Water Information Center, 1974.

Nelson, Megan Kate. "'The Difficulties and Seductions of the Desert': Landscapes of War in 1861 New Mexico." In Drake, *The Blue, the Gray, and the Green,* 34–51.

———. "Indians Make the Best Guerrillas: Native Americans and the War for the Desert Southwest, 1861–1862." In Beilein and Hulbert, *Civil War Guerrilla,* 99–122.

———. *Ruin Nation: Destruction and the American Civil War.* Athens: University of Georgia Press, 2012.

Noe, Kenneth W. "The Drought That Changed the War." In *The* New York Times *Disunion: 106 Articles from the* New York Times *Opinionator: Modern Historians Revisit and Reconsider the Civil War from Lincoln's Election to the Emancipation Proclamation,* edited by Ted Widmer, Clay Risen, and George Kalogerakis, 394–97. (New York: Black Dog and Leventhal, 2013).

———. "Heat of Battle: Climate, Weather, and the First Battle of Manassas." *Civil War Monitor* 5 (Fall 2015): 54–62, 76.

———. "'I Am Completely Checked by the Weather': George B. McClellan, Weather and the Peninsula Campaign," In *Upon the Fields of Battle: Essays on the Military History of America's Civil War,* edited by Andrew S. Bledsoe and Andrew F. Lang, 45–70. Baton Rouge: Louisiana State University Press, 2018.

———. "Jigsaw Puzzles, Mosaics, and Civil War Battle Narratives." *Civil War History* 53 (September 2007): 236–43.

———. *Perryville: This Grand Havoc of Battle.* Lexington: University Press of Kentucky, 2001.

———. *Reluctant Rebels: The Confederates Who Joined the Army after 1861.* Chapel Hill: University of North Carolina Press, 2010.

———. *Southwest Virginia's Railroad: Modernization and the Sectional Crisis.* Urbana: University of Illinois Press, 1994.

Nulty, William H. *Confederate Florida: The Road to Olustee.* Tuscaloosa: University of Alabama Press, 1990.

Oakes, James. *Freedom National: The Destruction of Slavery in the United States, 1861–1865.* New York: Norton, 2013.

Oates, Stephen B. *With Malice toward None: The Life of Abraham Lincoln.* New York: Mentor, 1977.

Olson, Donald W. *Celestial Sleuth: Using Astronomy to Solve Mysteries in Art, History, and Literature.* New York: Springer, 2014.

———. "A Fatal Full Moon." With Laurie E. Jasinski and Russell L. Doescher. Introduction by Robert K. Krick. *Blue & Gray* 13 (May 1996): 24–29.

O'Reilly, Francis Augustín. *The Fredericksburg Campaign: Winter War on the Rappahannock.* Baton Rouge: Louisiana State University Press, 2003.

Orton, Robert. "The Climate of Texas." In NOAA, *Climates of the States,* 2:877–920.

Parks, Joseph H. *General Edmund Kirby Smith, C.S.A.* Baton Rouge: Louisiana State University Press, 1954.

Parrish, William E. *Turbulent Partnership: Missouri and the Union, 1861–1865.* Introduction by Robert L. D. Davidson. Columbia: University of Missouri Press, 1963.

Petty, Adam H. "Reconsidering the Wilderness's Role in the Battle, 4–6 May 1864." *Journal of Military History* 82 (April 2018): 413–38.

———. "Wilderness, Weather, and Waging War in the Mine Run Campaign." *Civil War History* 63 (March 2017): 7–35.

Phillips, Christopher. *The Rivers Ran Backward: The Civil War and the Remaking of the American Middle Border.* New York: Oxford University Press, 2016.

Phillips, Jason. *Diehard Rebels: The Confederates Culture of Invincibility.* Athens: University of Georgia Press, 2007.

Pierson, Michael D. *Mutiny at Fort Jackson: The Untold Story of the Fall of New Orleans*. Chapel Hill: University of North Carolina Press, 2008.

Piston, William Garrett. *Lee's Tarnished Lieutenant: James Longstreet and His Place in Southern History*. Athens: University of Georgia Press, 1987.

Piston, William Garrett, and Richard W. Hatcher III. *Wilson's Creek: The Second Battle of the Civil War and the Men Who Fought It*. Chapel Hill: University of North Carolina Press, 2000.

Policastro, Anatoly. "The Crimean Oven: On the Trail of a Civil War Mystery." Pt. 1. *Alexandria Archeology Volunteer News* 29 (Winter–Spring 2012): 10–11.

Popkins, W. A. "Imboden's Brigade at Gettysburg." *Confederate Veteran* 22 (December 1914): 552–53.

Power, J. Tracy. *Lee's Miserables: Life in the Army of Northern Virginia from the Wilderness to Appomattox*. Chapel Hill: University of North Carolina Press, 1998.

Rable, George C. *Fredericksburg! Fredericksburg!* Chapel Hill: University of North Carolina Press, 2002.

Rafuse, Ethan S. *McClellan's War: The Failure of Moderation in the Struggle for the Union*. Bloomington: Indiana University Press, 2005.

Ramsdell, Charles W. "General Robert E. Lee's Horse Supply." *American Historical Review* 35 (July 1930): 758–77.

Reardon, Carol. *Pickett's Charge in History and Memory*. Chapel Hill: University of North Carolina Press, 1997.

———. *With a Sword in One Hand & Jomini in the Other: The Problem of Military Thought in the Civil War North*. Chapel Hill: University of North Carolina Press, 2012.

Reinhold, R. O. "The Climate of Arkansas." In NOAA, *Climates of the States*, 2:522–37.

Rhea, Gordon C. *The Battle of the Wilderness, May 5–6, 1864*. Baton Rouge: Louisiana State University Press, 1994.

———. *The Battles for Spotsylvania Court House and the Road to Yellow Tavern, May 7–12, 1864*. Baton Rouge: Louisiana State University Press, 1997.

———. *Cold Harbor: Grant and Lee, May 26–June 3, 1864*. Baton Rouge: Louisiana State University Press, 2002.

———. *To the North Anna River: Grant and Lee, May 13–25, 1864*. Baton Rouge: Louisiana State University Press, 2000.

Robertson, James I. *Stonewall Jackson: The Man, the Soldier, the Legend*. New York: Macmillan, 1997.

Robertson, William Glenn. *Back Door to Richmond: The Bermuda Hundred Campaign, April–June 1864*. Newark, N.J.: University of Delaware Press, 1987.

Robinson, Armstead L. *Bitter Fruits of Bondage: The Demise of Slavery and the Col-

lapse of the Confederacy, 1861–1865. Charlottesville: University of Virginia Press, 2005.

Rohland, Eleonora. *Changes in the Air: Hurricanes in New Orleans from 1718 to the Present.* New York: Berghahn Books, 2019.

Rollins, Richard, ed. *Pickett's Charge: Eyewitness Accounts of the Battle of Gettysburg.* Mechanicsburg, Pa.: Stackpole, 2005.

Ross, Charles D. "Outdoor Sound Propagation in the U.S. Civil War." *Echoes: The Newsletter of the Acoustical Society of America* 9 (Winter 1999): 1, 4–5.

Sanders, Ralph. "The Climate of Louisiana." In NOAA, *Climates of the States,* 2:692–705.

———. "The Climate of Mississippi." In NOAA, *Climates of the States,* 1:215–28.

Sanders, Stuart W. *The Battle of Mill Springs, Kentucky.* Charleston, S.C.: History Press, 2013.

Schecter, Barnet. *The Devil's Own Work: The Civil War Draft Riots and the Fight to Reconstruct America.* New York: Walker, 2005.

Sears, Stephen W. *Chancellorsville.* Boston: Houghton Mifflin, 1996.

———. *George B. McClellan: The Young Napoleon.* New York: Ticknor & Fields, 1988.

———. *Landscape Turned Red: The Battle of Antietam.* Boston: Houghton Mifflin, 1983.

———. *To the Gates of Richmond: The Peninsula Campaign.* Boston: Houghton Mifflin, 1992. Reprint, Boston: Mariner, 2001.

Shalit, Ben. *The Psychology of Combat and Conflict.* New York: Praeger, 1988.

Sharrer, G. Terry. *A Kind of Fate: Agricultural Change in Virginia, 1861–1920.* Ames: Iowa State University Press, 2000.

Shea, William L. *Fields of Blood: The Prairie Grove Campaign.* Chapel Hill: University of North Carolina Press, 2009.

Shea, William L., and Earl J. Hess. *Pea Ridge: Civil War Campaign in the West.* Chapel Hill: University of North Carolina Press, 1992.

Shea, William L., and Terrence J. Winschel. *Vicksburg Is the Key: The Struggle for the Mississippi River.* Lincoln: University of Nebraska Press, 2003.

Shoemaker, Arthur. "The Battle of Chustenahlah." *Chronicles of Oklahoma* 38 (1960): 180–84.

Simpson, Brooks D. "A Failure to Communicate: Grant, Thomas, and the Nashville Campaign." In *The Tennessee Campaign of 1864,* edited by Stephen E. Woodworth and Charles D. Grear, 105–22. Carbondale: Southern Illinois Press, 2016.

———. *Ulysses S. Grant: Triumph over Adversity, 1822–1865.* Boston: Houghton Mifflin, 2000.

Smith, Mark M. *The Smell of Battle, the Taste of Siege: A Sensory History of the Civil War*. New York: Oxford University Press, 2015.

Smith, Timothy B. *Champion Hill: Decisive Battle for Vicksburg*. New York: Savas Beattie, 2004.

Starr, Steven Z. *The Union Cavalry in the Civil War*. Vol. 3, *The War in the West, 1861–1865*. Baton Rouge: Louisiana State University Press, 1985.

Steinberg, Ted. *Down to Earth: Nature's Role in American History*. New York: Oxford University Press, 2009.

Sternhell, Yael A. "Revisionism Reinvented? The Antiwar Turn in Civil War Scholarship." *Journal of the Civil War Era* 3 (June 2013): 239–56.

Stith, Matthew M. *Extreme Civil War: Guerrilla Warfare, Environment, and Race on the Trans-Mississippi Frontier*. Baton Rouge: Louisiana State University Press, 2016.

Stoker, Donald. *The Grand Design: Strategy and the U.S. Civil War*. New York: Oxford University Press, 2010.

Sutherland, Daniel E. *Seasons of War: The Ordeal of a Confederate Community, 1861–1865*. New York: Free Press, 1995.

Swanberg, W. A. *First Blood: The Story of Fort Sumter*. New York: Charles Scribner's Sons, 1957. Paperback reprint, 1984.

Sword, Wiley. *Embrace an Angry Wind: The Confederacy's Last Hurrah at Spring Hill, Franklin, and Nashville*. New York: HarperCollins, 1992.

Symonds, Craig L. *Joseph E. Johnston: A Civil War Biography*. New York: W. W. Norton, 1992.

Tanner, Robert G. *Stonewall in the Valley: Thomas J. "Stonewall" Jackson's Shenandoah Valley Campaign, Spring 1862*. Mechanicsburg, Pa.: Stackpole, 1996.

Taylor, Amy Murrell. *Embattled Freedom: Journeys through the Civil War's Slave Refugee Camps*. Chapel Hill: University of North Carolina Press, 2018.

Taylor, John. *Bloody Valverde: A Civil War Battle on the Rio Grande, February 21, 1862*. Albuquerque: Historical Society of New Mexico and University of New Mexico Press, 1995.

Thomas, Benjamin P. *Abraham Lincoln: A Biography*. New York: Alfred A. Knopf, 1952.

Thomas, M. Wynn. "Weathering the Storm: Whitman and the Civil War." *Walt Whitman Quarterly Review* 15 (1997): 87–109.

Tucker, Glenn. *Chickamauga: Bloody Battle in the West*. Indianapolis: Bobbs-Merrill, 1961. Reprint, Dayton, Ohio: Morningside, 1984.

Tucker, Richard P. "The Impact of Warfare on the Natural World: A Historical Survey." In Tucker and Russell, *Natural Enemy, Natural Ally*, 15–41.

Tucker, Richard P., and Edmund Russell, eds. *Natural Enemy, Natural Ally: Toward an Environmental History of War*. Corvallis: Oregon State University Press, 2004.

Urwin, Gregory J. W. "'We Cannot Treat Negroes . . . as Prisoners of War': Racial Atrocities and Reprisals in Civil War Arkansas." In *Black Flag over Dixie: Racial Atrocities and Reprisals in the Civil War*, edited by Gregory J. W. Urwin, 132–52. Carbondale: Southern Illinois University Press, 2004.

Vandiver, Frank E. *Jubal's Raid: General Early's Famous Attack on Washington in 1864*. New York: McGraw-Hill, 1960. Reprint, Westport, Conn.: Greenwood, 1974.

Varon, Elizabeth R. *Appomattox: Victory, Defeat, and Freedom at the End of the Civil War*. New York: Oxford University Press, 2014.

Venet, Wendy Hamand. *A Changing Wind: Commerce and Conflict in Civil War Atlanta*. Athens: University of Georgia Press, 2014.

Ward, Andrew. *River Run Red: The Fort Pillow Massacre in the American Civil War*. New York: Viking, 2005.

Warde, Mary Jane. *When the Wolf Came: The Civil War and the Indian Territory*. Fayetteville: University of Arkansas Press, 2013.

Wert, Jeffry D. *From Winchester to Cedar Creek: The Shenandoah Campaign of 1864*. New York: Touchstone, 1989.

White, Jonathan M. *Abraham Lincoln and Treason in the Civil War: The Trials of John Merryman*. Baton Rouge: Louisiana State University Press, 2011.

Williams, David. *A People's History of the Civil War: Struggles for the Meaning of Freedom*. New York: New Press, 2005.

Williams, John Alexander. *West Virginia: A History*. New York: W. W. Norton, 1976.

Williams, Kenneth P. *Lincoln Finds a General: A Military Study of the Civil War*. New York: Macmillan, 1949.

Williams, T. Harry. *Hayes of the 23rd: The Civil War Volunteer Officer*. New York: Knopf, 1965.

Wills, Brian Steel. *Inglorious Passages: Noncombat Deaths in the American Civil War*. Lawrence: University Press of Kansas, 2017.

———. *The River Was Dyed with Blood: Nathan Bedford Forrest and Fort Pillow*. Norman: University of Oklahoma Press, 2014.

Winkle, Kenneth J. *Lincoln's Citadel: The Civil War in Washington, DC*. New York: W. W. Norton, 2013.

Winters, Harold A. *Battling the Elements: Weather and Terrain in the Conduct of War*. With Gerald E. Galloway Jr., William J. Reynolds, and David W. Rhyne. Baltimore: Johns Hopkins University Press, 1998.

Wise, Stephen R. *Gate of Hell: Campaign for Charleston Harbor*. Columbia: University of South Carolina Press, 1994.

Wittenberg, Eric J. *Glory Enough for All: Sheridan's Second Raid and the Battle of*

Trevilian Station. Foreword by Gordon C. Rhea. Washington, D.C.: Brassey's, 2001.

———. *Like a Meteor Blazing Brightly: The Short but Controversial Life of Colonel Ulric Dahlgren.* Roseville, Minn.: Edinborough, 2009.

Wittenberg, Eric J., David Petruzzi, and Michael F. Nugent. *One Continuous Fight: The Retreat from Gettysburg and the Pursuit of Lee's Army of Northern Virginia, July 4–14, 1863.* New York: Savas Beatie, 2008.

Woshner, Mike. *India-Rubber and Gutta-Percha in the Civil War Era: An Illustrated History of Rubber & Pre-Plastic Antiques and Militaria.* Alexandria, Va.: O'Donnell, 1999.

Wynstra, Robert J. *At the Forefront of Lee's Invasion: Retribution, Plunder, and Clashing Cultures on Richard S. Ewell's Road to Gettysburg.* Kent, Ohio: Kent State University Press, 2018.

Zinn, Jack. *The Battle of Rich Mountain.* Parsons, W.Va.: McClain, 1971.

———. *R. E. Lee's Cheat Mountain Campaign.* Parsons, W.Va.: McClain, 1974.

Electronic Sources

Allen, Erin, and Michelle Krowl. "Here Comes the Sun: Seeing Omens in the Weather at Abraham Lincoln's Second Inauguration." *Library of Congress Blog,* March 4, 2015. https://blogs.loc.gov/loc/2015/03/here-comes-the-sun-seeing-omens-in-the-weather-at-abraham-lincolns-second-inauguration/.

Bast, Felix, Satej Bhushan, Aijaz A. John, Jackson Achankunju, Nadaraja Panikkar, Christina Hametner-Rieder, and Elfriede Stocker. "European Species of Subaerial Green Alga Trentepohlia annulata (Trentepohliales, Ulvophyceae) Caused Blood Rain in Kerala, India," *Phylogenetics and Evolutionary Biology* 3, no. 1 (February 2015): 1–3, https://www.researchgate.net/publication/273124757_European_Species_of_Subaerial_Green_Alga_Trentepohlia_annulata_Trentepohliales_Ulvophyceae_Caused_Blood_Rain_in_Kerala_India.

Cook, E. R., R. D. D'Arrigo, and M. E. Mann. "Well-Verified Winter North Atlantic Oscillation Index Reconstruction." 2002. IGBP PAGES/World Data Center for Paleoclimatology Data Contribution Series 2002-059. NOAA/NGDC Paleoclimatology Program. ftp://ftp.ncdc.noaa.gov/pub/data/paleo/treering/reconstructions/nao_cook2002.txt.

"Distribution Maps of Dominant Soil Orders." US Department of Agriculture Natural Resources Conservation Service. http://www.nrcs.usda.gov/wps/portal/nrcs/detail/soils/survey/class/?cid=nrcs142p2_053589.

"Fortress Rosecrans." Stones River National Battlefield. National Park Service. https://www.nps.gov/stri/learn/historyculture/foro.htm.

"Geologic Activity." Vicksburg National Military Park. National Park Service. https://www.nps.gov/vick/learn/nature/geologicactivity.htm.

"IECC Climate Zone Map." U.S. Department of Energy. https://basc.pnnl.gov/images/iecc-climate-zone-map.

Ingram, B. Lynn. "California Megaflood: Lessons from a Forgotten Catastrophe." *Scientific American,* January 1, 2013. https://www.scientificamerican.com/article/atmospheric-rivers-california-megaflood-lessons-from-forgotten-catastrophe/.

Jones, Shirley Farris. "Building Fortress Rosecrans Was 'Un-Civil.'" *Murfreesboro (Tenn.) Post.* July 15, 2007. http://www.murfreesboropost.com/building-fortress-rosecrans-was-un-civil-cms-5301.

Keller, Rudi. "MU Expert Studies Civil War Weather." *Columbia (Mo.) Daily Tribune.* July 11, 2011. https://columbiatribune.com/news/local/mu-expert-studies-civil-war-weather/article_6fe8c0e2-97bc-5f92-828f-708799996808.html.

"Kentucky Soils Data Viewer." Kentucky Geography Network. Kentucky Division of Geographic Information. http://kygeonet.ky.gov/kysoils/.

Kirby, Jack Temple. "The American Civil War: An Environmental View." *Nature Transformed: The Environment in American History.* TeacherServe. National Humanities Center. Last revised July 2001. http://nationalhumanitiescenter.org/tserve/nattrans/ntuseland/essays/amcwar.htm.

"North Atlantic Oscillation (NAO)." National Weather Service Climate Prediction Center. http://www.cpc.ncep.noaa.gov/data/teledoc/nao.shtml.

"North Atlantic Oscillation (NAO) Index." Climate Data Archive. Joint Institute for the Study of the Atmosphere and Ocean (JISAO). February 2002. http://research.jisao.washington.edu/data_sets/nao/.

NRCS Soils. *Map of Soil Orders of the United States.* https://www.nrcs.usda.gov/Internet/FSE_MEDIA/stelprdb1237749.pdf.

Partagas, J. F., and H. F. Diaz. *A Reconstruction of Historical Tropical Cyclone Frequency in the Atlantic from Documentary and Other Historical Sources: 1851–1880. Part 1, 1851–1870.* Boulder, Colo.: Climate Diagnostic Center, NOAA, 1995. HURDAT Re-Analysis Related Publications. Hurricane Research Division, Atlantic Oceanographic & Meteorological Laboratory. NOAA. http://www.aoml.noaa.gov/hrd/Landsea/Partagas/part1.htm.

"The Science of Backward Weather Forecasting." *Mizzou Weekly* 31, no. 30 (May 2010). http://mizzouweekly.missouri.edu/archive/2010/31-30/the-science-of-backward-weather-forecasting/index.php.

"Angel's Glow at the Battle of Shiloh." American Civil War Story. http://www.americancivilwarstory.com/angels-glow-shiloh.html.

"The Soil Orders Simplified." *Soils Matter, Get the Scoop!* (blog). Soil Science Society of America, Jan. 5, 2015. https://soilsmatter.wordpress.com/2015/01/05/the-soil-orders-simplified/.

US Environmental Protection Agency. *Ecoregions of Tennessee.* Last updated Oct. 29, 2015. ftp://newftp.epa.gov/EPADataCommons/ORD/Ecoregions/tn/TN-Front.pdf.

———. "Summary Table: Characteristics of Ecoregions of Tennessee." *Ecoregions of Tennessee.* Last updated Oct. 29, 2015. ftp://newftp.epa.gov/EPADataCommons/ORD/Ecoregions/tn/TNBack.pdf.

US Geological Survey. *Overview of the ARkstorm Scenario.* US Geological Survey Open-File Report 2010-1312. http://pubs.usgs.gov/of/2010/1312/.

"Web Soil Survey." US Department of Agriculture Natural Resources Conservation Service. http://websoilsurvey.sc.egov.usda.gov/App/HomePage.htm.

"What Is the Difference between Weather and Climate?" National Ocean Service, NOAA. Last updated June 25, 2018. https://oceanservice.noaa.gov/facts/weather_climate.html.

Unpublished papers

Browning, Judkin, and Tim Silver. "Weather: Winter 1862–Winter 1863." Unpublished manuscript.

Nelson, Megan Kate. "Something in the Air: The Nature of the American Civil War in the Desert Southwest, 1861–82." Paper presented to the Organization of American Historians, Providence, R.I., Apr. 8, 2016.

Privette, Lindsey Rae. "If the Water Were Good, We Would Be Happy: Contaminated Water and Dehydration during the Vicksburg Campaign." Paper presented to the Society of Civil War Historians, Pittsburgh, June 1, 2018.

Wittenberg, Eric J. "An Analysis of George Gordon Meade's Command of the Army of the Potomac." Unpublished manuscript.

Index